Using FoxPro™ 2.5 Special Edition

LISA C. SLATER
STEVEN E. ARNOTT

with Nancy Jacobsen
Joseph A. Gotthelf
and Ted Roche

FOREWORD BY DR. DAVID L. FULTON,
CREATOR OF FOXPRO AND MICROSOFT
DATABASE ARCHITECT

Using FoxPro 2.5, Special Edition

Library of Congress Catalog No.: 93-83385

ISBN: 1-56529-065-8

96 95 94 93 4 3 2 1

Interpretation of the printing code: the rightmost double-digit number is the year of the book's printing; the rightmost single-digit number, the number of the book's printing. For example, a printing code of 93-1 shows that the first printing of the book occurred in 1993.

Publisher: David P. Ewing

Associate Publisher: Rick Ranucci

Operations Manager: Sheila Cunningham

Product Development Manager: Thomas H. Bennett

Acquisitions Editor: Sherri Morningstar

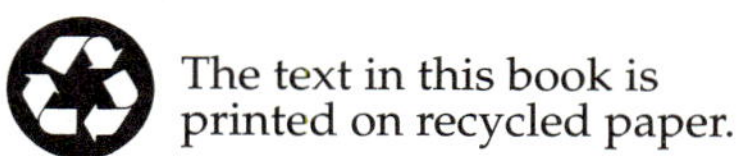

CREDITS

Title Manager
Walter R. Bruce III

Product Directors
Steven M. Schafer
Timothy S. Stanley

Production Editors
Kezia Endsley
H. Leigh Davis

Editors
William A. Barton
Barb Colter
Donald R. Eamon
J. Christopher Nelson
Andy Saff
Cheri Clark

Copy Editors
Chuck Hutchinson
Christine Prakel
Kathy Sabotin
Lori Lyons

Technical Editors
Ted Roche
John Scobey

Composed in *Cheltenham* and *MCPdigital*
by Que Corporation

Book Designer
Scott Cook

Production
Jeff Baker
Claudia Bell
Danielle Bird
Julie Brown
Jodie Cantwell
Paula Carroll
Laurie Casey
Brad Chinn
Brad Cook
Christine Cook
Brook Farling
Carla Hall-Batton
Heather Kaufman
Bob LaRoche
Jay Lesandrini
Wendy Ott
Linda Seifert
Tina Trettin
Michelle Worthington
Phil Worthington

Indexers
Joy Dean Lee
Johnna VanHoose

ABOUT THE AUTHORS

Lisa C. Slater is an independent consultant at SoftSpoken, specializing in the optimization of database-management strategy, interface design, and code for programmers working in FoxPro. She edits *FoxTalk*, a monthly journal for professional Fox programmers published by Pinnacle Publishing, and writes regularly for other publications.

Slater has been a featured speaker at Fox Developer's Conferences and numerous other Fox-related gatherings. She is the archivist for CompuServe's FoxForum, where she encounters and solves problems for a varied group of FoxPro enthusiasts on a daily basis.

Slater earned an A.B. in history and literature from Harvard University. She lives in Santa Rosa, California, and can be reached on CompuServe at 72077,2417.

Steve Arnott currently mans the helm and washes the dishes at Sea Drive of New York City. Sea Drive develops database applications for small- to medium-sized businesses, primarily in the areas of finance and manufacturing. Arnott was previously associated with Korenthal Associates, Inc., authors of PhDbase—a fuzzy search tool for FoxPro, Clipper and dBASE—and 4Print, the popular printing utility for HP LaserJets and DeskJets.

Arnott received a B.B.A. in accounting from Pace University. He can be reached on CompuServe at 70247,2614.

ABOUT THE AUTHORS

Nancy Jacobsen, who contributed substantial materials and research to Chapters 3 and 4, is a software developer, consultant, and writer. She specializes in FoxPro applications and cross-platform development. Jacobsen has been a speaker at the Microsoft Fox Developer's Conference, and has written several articles for *FoxTalk*, *Databased Advisor*, and *FoxPro Users Journal*.

Jacobsen resides in Northern California and holds an A.B. in anthropology from the University of California, Berkeley. She can be reached on CompuServe at 72230,2664.

Joe Gotthelf, who contributed substantial materials and research to Chapters 5, 6, and 7, operates August Technologies, Inc., a Philadelphia-area consulting firm providing custom software development. He also writes for *FoxTalk* and *The FoxPro Advisor*.

Gotthelf can be reached at (215) 325-9550; on CompuServe at 74017,3670; or on MCI Mail at 501-3993.

Ted Roche, who revised Chapters 21 and 22 for this edition, is a software developer and freelance writer who has worked in a variety of Xbase dialects for the past seven years. He specializes in the optimization and enhancement of large-scale FoxPro installations. He has written several articles for *FoxTalk*.

Roche received his B.A. in mathematics from Regents College. He resides in Contoocook, New Hampshire, and can be reached on CompuServe at 76400,2503.

ACKNOWLEDGMENTS

More people than we can name helped us create this book, but we would like to offer some special thanks:

to Jonathan, Joshua, and Derek Slater, Kevin Jamieson, Marcia Cooper, Larry Lynett, and Stan and Jeanne Cooper (Lisa's family) for love and patience that passes understanding

to Gladys Arnott, Nancy Arnott, and Sheila, Robert, Megan, and Matthew LaLima (Steve's family) for their constant love and support

to John Scobey and Ted Roche, our technical editors, for their keen eyes and good humor

to Walt Bruce, Leigh Davis, and Kezia Endsley, our editors at Que, for tolerating our abuse of the English language and skillfully steering this project to completion

to Jim Korenthal, Tracey Siesser, and Lew Horowitz for their patience, guidance, inspiration, and moral support

to Rich Kaiser, for his friendship and excellent taste in chianti

to the BobRed Company, for the Market Research and Product Line Development used in Omnipresent Widgets Limited

to Alan Loceff, Special Visual Consultant to the BobRedCo Product Development Team

to George Goley, whose examples showed us that anything and everything can be done in FoxPro

to Jordan Powell, Randy Brown, and Hank Fay for spurring our work on interface design principles, although they may not agree with any of our conclusions

to Peter Colclough for organizing our thoughts on the API, and Jim McKinney for helping us imagine the person who needed to read the original *Using FoxPro 2*

ACKNOWLEDGMENTS

to Bill Speights and all the readers of *Using FoxPro 2* who lent their critical eyes and their even-more critical encouragement to our continued effort

to Pat Adams for general support whenever we asked for it and specific recommendations whenever we needed them

to Glenn Hart for his belief in possibilities, which remains with us although he has left us

to the CompuServe FoxForumFolk for asking the questions we wrote this book to answer, and to all the Prodigious individuals (shepherded by Mike Rubin) who chimed in

to the BetaForum and FoxForum sysops for giving 1.61-times-maximum effort—especially Sherri Bruhn/Kennamer and Susan Graham—who have been through this before and still put up with us, Meng ("the Merciless") Phua and Morris Sim, who were new but unfazed, and Chris Pudlicki and Roger Bischoff, the original Dynamic Duo, who provided the entertainment when everyone really needed it

to Bob Fortner (on whom we blamed everything whenever possible), Steve Murch and Tod Nielsen, of Microsoft's Fox Marketing Team, for helping us understand how the wonderful product fit into the Real World

to Dr. Dave Fulton, Walt Kennamer, Janet Walker, Michael Mee, Jim Simpkins, and all of the Microsoft Fox Team for giving us a wonderful product

... and ...

to all the Betazoids for helping Microsoft Fox **make it so** <g>.

TRADEMARK ACKNOWLEDGMENTS

Que Corporation has made every effort to supply trademark information about company names, products, and services mentioned in this book. Trademarks indicated below were derived from various sources. Que Corporation cannot attest to the accuracy of this information.

dBASE is a registered trademark and dBASE IV is a trademark of Borland International, Inc.

FoxBASE, FoxBASE +, FoxBASE+/Mac, FoxGraph, FoxPro, Microsoft, MS-DOS, and Word for Windows are registered trademarks and Windows and Rushmore are trademarks of Microsoft Corporation.

IBM, PC, XT, AT, PS/2, and PC DOS are registered trademarks of International Business Machines Corporation.

Trademarks of other products mentioned in this book are held by the companies producing them.

FOREWORD

I was delighted when I heard that Lisa and Steve were updating their landmark book for Version 2.5 of FoxPro for DOS. I certainly hoped they would do so. And *Using FoxPro 2.5*, Special Edition, promises to be as essential a reference as was its predecessor.

Building on the strengths of their first book, the central focus of *Using FoxPro 2.5*, Special Edition, is on the FoxPro power tools: the Project Manager, Screen Builder, Menu Builder, and the Report and Label Writers. It is my view that learning to use the power tools is the most important step in learning to use FoxPro. *Using FoxPro 2.5*, Special Edition, does an excellent job of illustrating how the power tools work together to make it easier to develop database applications.

A welcome enhancement to this new version is the strong emphasis Lisa and Steve have put on the multi-user and multitasking features of FoxPro, an emphasis that runs through the entire volume. This material should be useful for anyone, but especially those who are just starting with multi-user programming.

It is once again a great pleasure to recommend Lisa's and Steve's book. As I noted in the foreword for *Using FoxPro 2*, it is particularly well-suited to knowledgeable end users who may have been intimidated by other database products. This is the book for you.

Dr. David L. Fulton
Database Architect
Microsoft Corporation

CONVENTIONS

The conventions used in this book have been established to help you learn to use the program quickly and easily.

- Material the user types is in `monospace typeface`.
- Menu bar selections have initial capital letters: File, Edit, Database, Record, Program, and Window.
- FoxPro commands and names of files on-disk appearing within text are in all capital letters (the BROWSE command).
- Names of fields and table aliases appearing within text have initial capital letters (the General field).
- Names of memory variables appearing within text are lowercase.
- *Italic* type is used to emphasize the authors' points or to introduce new terms.
- Screen messages, samples of program code, and push buttons appear in `monospace typeface` (the `OK` push button).

- The 2.5 icon in the margin indicates features new in Version 2.5 of FoxPro for DOS.

Because Xbase is a very English-like language, the commands and functions that make up the FoxPro dialect are usually common English words. For this reason, direct instructions you give FoxPro are capitalized in the text so that you can distinguish them from their normal English usage.

For example, "Every GET involved in one READ may be DISABLEd by using the global SHOW GETS DISABLE command." In this sentence, the words you use to give FoxPro instructions are capitalized; in one case, (DISABLEd) only the part of the word properly used in the FoxPro instructions, not the entire construct used to form the English sentence, is capitalized.

However, sections of FoxPro instructions are set off from the rest of the text by the following typeface:

```
ACTIVATE WINDOW rwindow
@ 1,1 GET m.var WHEN my_udf()
READ
RELEASE WINDOW rwindow
```

One line or an entire program may be included. When you see this typeface, you notice that different standards for capitalization are used in different sections of the book. Here, FoxPro commands and keywords are capitalized, but a few words—names of memory variables and other items created by the programmer—are not. This convention is common, but some people do the opposite, and some people capitalize no letters at all.

In this book, each author has followed his or her personal style of capitalization, giving you a fairly representative look at the conventions commonly used by Xbase programmers.

You should become comfortable with these different styles so that you can understand other people's programs wherever you see them. Sharing your work is the best way to learn! It is not important which style you pick for yourself. It is important that you adopt one convention and use it consistently so that your programs are readable and easy to maintain.

If you find one style difficult to use consistently or hard to read, try another one. FoxPro includes a tool (FoxDoc) that can standardize the capitalization in your programs for you after you write them—using any style you prefer. You learn about FoxDoc in Chapter 20.

Many features of FoxPro 2.5 were in flux while this book was being written, in the early stages of the product's release. If you have trouble duplicating the results you see in the examples, your problem may be because of your *build date* (the exact date that your copy of FoxPro was created), rather than because of anything you are doing wrong or differently.

You can find out your build date by checking the About FoxPro option on the FoxPro menu. You can also type the following in the Command window and press Enter:

```
WAIT WINDOW VERSION(1)
```

The About FoxPro option also gives you information about contacting Microsoft, to find out about updates to the product.

CONTENTS AT A GLANCE

IV FoxProgramming: Enhanced Use of the Design Tools

V Getting To Know FoxPro Commands and Functions

TABLE OF CONTENTS

II Getting Productive with FoxPro Databases

14 Organizing and Packaging Your Applications 523

IV FoxProgramming: Enhanced Use of the Design Tools

21 Using Commands and Functions To Manipulate Data 877

V Getting To Know FoxPro Commands and Functions

Introduction

Welcome to *Using FoxPro 2.5,* Special Edition. This book gives you the tools to understand your own information management needs and to fulfill them with FoxPro's powerful capabilities.

Like any database management system, or *DBMS*, FoxPro is a program that enables you to create *tables*, which are collections of similar pieces of information. Your phone book, a listing of employees in your department, and your grocery list are all tables. In a DBMS, the process of collecting and storing this information, or data, in tables is called *data input*, or *data entry*. You can sort and organize tables, even large ones, in many different ways. You can retrieve and locate individual data elements quickly and accurately.

In a relational DBMS, such as FoxPro, many tables can work together in a *database* to produce complex results or forms of *output*. Output usually is an answer to a question you pose about your data. This question, often referred to as a *query*, requires the DBMS to summarize and classify the information in your tables and to generate a representation (or report) of the answer so that you can use the information productively. In FoxPro, queries and output can take almost any form.

FoxPro is one of several DBMS software products often referred to as *Xbase* because these products evolved from the dBASE language. Almost all dBASE III and IV language constructs and programs work the same way in FoxPro as they work in dBASE. FoxPro, however, also includes many commands and features not found in any other Xbase dialect.

This book is your guide to database management in FoxPro's unique style.

What Is FoxPro?

When FoxPro was introduced in 1989, the program altered the face of MS-DOS database management. Fox Software took the interface design and flexibility of its Macintosh DBMS, FoxBASE+/Mac, and transferred these features to the PC world, without losing the speed advantage that is the hallmark of all its products. The company had already made it possible for people working on both platforms to share the same data, using FoxBASE+/Mac and FoxBASE+ for the PC. In FoxPro, Fox Software began to blur the distinctions between the ways programs looked and the ways in which people used them on the two platforms.

In FoxPro 2.0, the face was the same—but the heart had undergone some fundamental changes. FoxPro 1 brought some of the aspects of working on a Macintosh to the PC database world, proving that you can have many of the benefits of a graphical interface without the graphics. FoxPro 2 made users reassess some other assumptions and constraints in a new light:

- The traditional boundary between an *end-user* and a *programmer* became difficult to maintain, because beginners could generate useful applications without writing any lines of program code and experts became more productive by using the same techniques to develop extensive systems.
- The classic distinction between *interactive* use of the DBMS and a controlled, *programmatic* use was dispelled, because programs could be written to mimic exactly the interactive environment or even to coexist peacefully within that environment.
- The standard difference between the system's internal mechanisms and external capabilities became hard to see, because the same features with which developers created programs could be provided to end users within the programs.
- The assumed limitations of data management on personal computers were overcome, because innovative file-handling and searching techniques enabled FoxPro users to process vast amounts of information as fast or faster than on large mainframes.

In fact, no matter how accustomed you are to database management programming, FoxPro challenges some of your established theories and practices. No matter how new you are to the DBMS world, or even to computers, this program gives you access to sophisticated manipulation of your own data.

The merger of Microsoft and Fox Software, in June 1992, occurred at a crucial moment in the development of FoxPro 2.5. Many users wondered what effect the integration into a large corporation would have on the unique character of both the Fox product line and the culture of Fox Software. When FoxPro 2.5 for DOS and Windows were released in January, 1993, the new products proved to have a strong family resemblance to FoxPro 2.0. The vast resources of Microsoft are helping to market and develop FoxPro, but the Microsoft Fox team is committed to the same goals for its products as was the Fox Software personnel.

What Is New in FoxPro 2.5?

FoxPro 2.5 for DOS offers a number of new commands and functions designed to provide *cross-platform compatibility* with its sister product, FoxPro 2.5 for Windows. This release also provides the following advances:

- A new Power Tool accessory, the Transporter, supports cross-platform development of screens and reports. The Transporter also converts FoxPro 2.0 system tables for the Power Tools, providing an easy upgrade path.
- The Rushmore technology, which enables pinpointed searches using complex criteria to retrieve data sets from very large tables, has been improved still further over FoxPro 2.0, offering unmatched query speed.
- Screen input/output rates have been significantly improved, adding to users' perceptions of the product's efficiency and speed.
- The Extended version of the product supports 225 work areas (tables) open simultaneously.
- The Extended version has a new DPMI-compliant memory management scheme, enabling FoxPro Extended to run under Microsoft Windows' Enhanced Mode.
- The software is entirely multi-user. FoxPro 2.5 is not sold in a single-user version, although you can purchase the product with a limited license for use on a single computer.

How Should You Read This Book?

In keeping with the assertion that no separate classes of users exist when working with FoxPro, and because so much in FoxPro will be new to everyone, no sections of this book are specifically aimed at beginners or experts. Instead, the discussions address each subject at an entry level—no previous FoxPro knowledge is assumed. The discussion of each FoxPro tool or feature starts out with simple examples and progresses to complex ones. The examples build on one another, and most chapters require that some exercises be followed in a specific sequence. For some tools, this progression takes two consecutive chapters; others are handled in one chapter or section.

If you are new to database management, start at the beginning and work through the book at a slow pace. (Start by following the instructions in Appendix A if you have not yet installed FoxPro on your computer.) Part I gives you a good basis for mastering all the material in this book if you investigate the contents thoroughly. In Parts II, III, and IV, you may want to read about each tool until you feel out of your depth. You can return to finish these final sections at a later time. Part V introduces you to the families of commands and functions in the FoxPro language that provide the basis for the more complex examples.

If you are familiar with FoxPro and/or database management, you should still skim Part I for interface and database design hints specific to FoxPro before moving on. In Parts II, III, and IV, you progress quickly through the initial explanation of the new querying and application-building tools, spending most of your time with the tips and tricks offered as part of the discussion of each tool. Turn to Part V for a more comprehensive grasp of the enhancements to the language that you can use to design similar techniques of your own.

If you are already a FoxPro programmer, you may want to start with Part III, which concentrates on developing applications in FoxPro using the new tools. You can turn to the other chapters as the need to understand each new feature arises.

What Is Covered in This Book?

Because FoxPro has such extensive capabilities, this book maintains a fairly rapid pace through the different features available. The book is divided into five major parts and eight appendixes.

Introducing FoxPro

In Part I of this book, "Introducing FoxPro," you get an initial tour of FoxPro and database fundamentals. As you read the chapters in Part I, you work with FoxPro interactively, learning to navigate the interface and understand database management system design so you can create meaningful, related database tables and fill them with data, without programming.

Chapter 1, "Understanding FoxPro Fundamentals," tells you how to start FoxPro and takes you through the development of a simple application, from the creation of its table through a sample query and report. No programming is needed. This chapter also introduces you to some of the features of the interface, using a number of the sample applications supplied with FoxPro for practice.

Chapter 2, "Understanding the FoxPro Interface," is your complete guide to manipulating the objects and elements you see in FoxPro's rich interactive environment. You learn about editing text, managing windows, executing instructions directly as FoxPro commands, as well as through the menu-driven system, and accessing FoxPro's extensive on-line help system.

Chapter 3, "Exploring Databases and Tables," covers table structure and use. You learn how to enter new data into a table interactively and how to distinguish between different types of data. You also learn how to get output in different forms and how to set criteria for the data included in the output.

Chapter 4, "Database Management Fundamentals," takes a more comprehensive look at what a database is and does. You learn about the index files used to order data and how tables are used together in relationships. You also learn about important design considerations you should keep in mind while designing a database—including ways to make the database accessible to, and comfortable for, the people who have to use it.

Getting Productive with FoxPro Databases

After you know something about putting data into a database, Part II, “Getting Productive with FoxPro Databases,” shows you how to pull complex and organized answers out. In this part of the book, you still work interactively (without writing applications or extensive programs), but you learn that interactive use is not a limitation on the speed or sophistication with which you can search and output data in FoxPro.

Chapters 5, “Using the RQBE as the Gateway to Queries,” and 6, “Investigating Your Data with Advanced Queries,” are devoted to FoxPro’s *RQBE* (Relational Query By Example), which can be used to create queries from multiple tables without programming.

Chapter 7, “Querying with SQL and Searching with Rushmore,” builds on what you learn about the RQBE by exploring the new *SQL SELECT* command that underlies the RQBE. You learn the complete syntax of the SELECT command and how to use it to issue increasingly intricate queries on your own. This chapter also covers other searching and querying techniques, including FoxPro’s *Rushmore technology*, which enables you to retrieve subsets of data at startling speeds.

Chapter 8, “Organizing the Answers with BROWSE,” gives you an in-depth look at another one of FoxPro’s powerful commands: *BROWSE*. You learn to use BROWSE to view your data, including query results, on-screen, in almost endless configurations.

Chapters 9, “Putting the Answers To Work in Reports and Labels,” and 10, “Using the Report Writer and Label Designer,” teach you to put your data and query results to other productive uses, creating tangible output in any format you require.

Building FoxPro Applications

In Part III, “Building FoxPro Applications,” you learn to build programs to control the process of filling, maintaining, and querying databases by creating *applications* so that many people can use the same information in a consistent way.

Chapter 11, "Coordinating a FoxPro Application," is devoted to the principles of interface design. This chapter presents some model criteria for choosing among the bewildering array of options you have available in FoxPro and tells you how to decide which ones meet the needs of a particular project. This chapter also gives you a quick introduction to the power tools presented in Part III so you can see how each one helps you achieve your goals.

Chapters 12 and 13 cover the *Screen Builder*, in which you create visual formats for data entry and other communication. In Chapter 12, "Creating Application Elements," you learn to control this complex tool, and in Chapter 13, "Improving Screen Design with Complex Screen Sets," you find out how to coordinate your results with the other elements of applications.

Chapter 14, "Organizing and Packaging Your Applications," continues this process. Using the *Menu Builder*, you learn to provide users with choices of all the tasks your application can accomplish. Using the *Project Manager* and the *Distribution Kit*, you learn to manage your application's files for yourself and when you make them available to others. You also learn how to structure a program from its subsidiary elements, as collected in a Project.

Chapter 15, "Controlling Events and Tasks in Applications," takes everything you've learned about the Power Tools and shows how the various FoxPro features fit together under the surface of an application to allow the user maximum flexibility.

Chapter 16, "Discovering More FoxPro Productivity Features," covers a whole host of supporting tools available in the FoxPro interface and in the applications that you design (Resource files, the Filer, the color system, macro keystrokes, the desk accessories on the System menu, printer drivers, and the API).

Chapter 17, "Transporting FoxPro Applications across Versions and Platforms," gets you started with the information you need to bring data and programs into FoxPro 2.5 from earlier versions of FoxPro and other Xbase dialects, and provides strategies for maintaining applications across multiple *platforms* (computer environments) in FoxPro 2.5.

FoxProgramming: Enhanced Use of the Design Tools

In Part IV, "FoxProgramming: Enhanced Use of the Design Tools," you find out how to get the most out of FoxPro's application development process.

Chapter 18, "Understanding Program Structure," is your introduction to programming principles. You learn to plan a program, what its basic elements are, and how to accomplish the basic programming tasks required for your work in FoxPro.

Chapter 19, "Using Advanced FoxProgramming Techniques," continues this process. You learn to organize large-scale programs that incorporate many other programs—creating programs that are easily maintained and that can "flex" to accommodate the environments in which they are run. You learn how easily you can create *template* programs, which can generate other programs for you.

Chapter 20, "Enhancing the Applications You Program," covers tools of special interest to developers, including the creation of custom help systems, error handling during development and from within an application, and *FoxDoc*, a device to help you document and maintain your programs.

Getting To Know FoxPro Commands and Functions

In Part V, "Getting To Know FoxPro Commands and Functions," you get an introduction to the rich command language that is the basis for the power and capability of FoxPro. No attempt is made to cover every command available. You explore some techniques and related *families* of commands in depth so that you can proceed to investigate others in a similar manner when you are ready.

Chapter 21, "Using Commands and Functions To Manipulate Data," teaches you how single data elements are handled in FoxPro and how you move through the items in a table or database to locate and edit the ones you want. The chapter also provides information on commands and functions specific to handling multi-user needs (file and record locking for data integrity).

Chapter 22, “Using SQL Commands, Arrays, and the Low-Level File Functions,” teaches you how to create and manipulate arrays. Arrays are structures (similar to tables) that are stored in memory. This chapter also covers FoxPro’s low-level file functions, which allow you to directly read from and write to any type of file or communications port, and continues the exploration of FoxPro’s implementation of SQL, a query language, that you began in Chapter 7.

Chapter 23, “Controlling a Windowed Environment,” covers the rich variety of commands and functions that create, maintain, and reference *windows*, which are FoxPro’s primary interface element for managing and structuring individual database tasks.

Using the Appendixes and the Source Disk

The various Appendixes provide handy references to topics of special interest on using FoxPro in your environment.

Appendix A, “Installing FoxPro for DOS,” tells you how to take FoxPro out of the box and get the program working on your system, including the optional Distribution Kit.

Appendix B, “Optimizing FoxPro’s Performance,” tells you how to get the most out of FoxPro with reference to your hardware configuration and gives you some techniques to help you gauge and fine-tune performance.

Appendix C, “Customizing the CONFIG.FP File,” teaches you how to use the special configuration file that FoxPro reads on startup so that you can set your FoxPro environment up in your own style.

Appendix D, “Using Command Line Options and Loading FoxPro,” explains the different ways in which you can load FoxPro and what difference this makes to your use of the program.

Appendix E, “Key Codes, Key Labels, and Special Key Usage in FoxPro,” contains a comprehensive reference chart of the different ways keystrokes are interpreted and acted on by FoxPro, and information on keyboard-handling in the program.

Appendix F, "Installation Disk Files and File Extensions," tells you about the files you find when you have installed FoxPro on your disk and how to interpret the various file extensions that FoxPro uses for them and for the files you create yourself.

Appendix G, "Finding Available Help," tells you how to contact Microsoft and other people who work with FoxPro when you want to solve a problem or just share what you have been doing.

Appendix H, "Example Database Structures and Procedures," provides some short programs that support the sample tables and applications created in this book.

The programs in Appendix H, along with the procedures in all chapters of the book, are included as FoxPro source code files on the disk that comes with this book. You refer to the disk for the programming examples that are included in almost every chapter. The disk includes a model application built from scratch in Parts I - III of the book, and a second application that builds more advanced features from Parts IV - V into the original model. The disk also contains many stand-alone pro-cedures, illustrative code fragments, and utility programs, drawn from various discussions in the text that don't relate directly to the model applications.

What Hardware Does FoxPro Need?

According to Microsoft, FoxPro 2.5 requires at least 640K RAM in the Standard Version and at least 4M of RAM in the Extended Version. The Extended Version requires an 80386SX (or better) processor. Both versions run in MS-DOS 3.1 or higher. The total of all the basic files *for both versions and the Distribution Kit* is about 15M, and the additional sample files and source code for supporting FoxPro applications consumes up to 30M; as described in Appendix A, you can decide how much space to devote to these additional files when you install the product.

You also need disk space for FoxPro's temporary files used during processing. The program runs far more smoothly if you give it more memory by using LIM 4.0-compatible expanded or extended memory. The more RAM you give FoxPro, the greater the program's capability to handle many simultaneous activities in multiple windows to its fullest extent.

If you are using FoxPro on a network, each workstation should have this memory free after the network shell is loaded. Workstations do not need local hard disks, but they greatly enhance performance. Most currently available networks are supported.

To take full advantage of FoxPro's output capabilities, you also should have a printer and a mouse. FoxPro 2.x includes improved support for network printers.

Where Can You Go from Here?

No one book can cover all the aspects of FoxPro. As you get more serious about programming, you should have as many different perspectives as possible. If you develop cross-platform applications, *Using FoxPro 2.5 for Windows,* Special Edition, gives you valuable information about the FoxPro for Windows Power Tools and other features specific to the Windows environment.

Que's *Creating FoxPro Applications*, by George F. Goley IV, is an excellent companion volume to this book. Using the same engaging style for which he is known as a trainer, Goley takes you through the development of a complex project from start to finish, concentrating on techniques and practices unique to FoxPro.

Appendix G, "Finding Available Help," gives you more ideas about sharing your interests and discoveries, and broadening your resources, as you learn about FoxPro.

Let this book take you on your initial tour of the powerful tools and features of FoxPro. With this database management system, your ultimate destination is any place you want to go.

Introducing FoxPro

1

CHAPTER

Understanding FoxPro Fundamentals

In this chapter, you learn to navigate among FoxPro features by using the sample application programs provided on the installation disks.

An *application* is a collection of instructions and information designed to perform a specific task, such as accounting or telecommunication. (FoxPro itself is a large application.) The sample applications are convenient devices, including some organizers for personal information and facts. More importantly, taken together, these applications present an impressive display of the powerful tools available in FoxPro 2.5 for DOS.

After you explore some sample applications, you learn to create an application. This application includes a *table*—the basic database management tool for collecting information—that you use in later practice sessions in the book.

You don't need to be a programmer to create an application. You can *generate* an application by using *FoxApp*, one of FoxPro's special tools. Fox App writes the programs for you; it's easy and fun. Although you may choose to write programs in a style very different from Fox App's when you write them yourself later, you still can learn a lot about how a FoxPro application looks and behaves as you go through this exercise.

If you are a programmer, this section introduces you to some new methods you can use in FoxPro and to the polished and complex results you can produce with the relatively few lines of programming code you need to enter.

Getting Ready To Work

If your copy of FoxPro 2.5 for DOS is not already installed on your computer, refer to the installation instructions in Appendix A, "Installing FoxPro," to help you install the program.

CAUTION: If you are working on a network, your system should already be properly configured to share files with other users. If you are working on a stand-alone computer, or with files on a local drive rather than a network drive, you should ensure that SHARE is loaded as part of your system startup routine. If FoxPro is already installed, refer to Appendix A to learn about loading the DOS SHARE command.You need to use specific SHARE parameters that are appropriate for use with FoxPro. You need to learn to work effectively on a network, even if your applications are running on only one computer now.

You also can access your data from multiple sessions of FoxPro (or from separate sessions of different Xbase programs) on one computer by using a multitasking environment, such as Quarterdeck's DESQview or Microsoft Windows. For these reasons, the exercises throughout this book take advantage of FoxPro's *record- and file-locking capabilities*, which protect data when competing requests to change or use information are received. This protection will be effective *as long as both requests are received from programs that are aware of each other's locking schemes*. However, on a computer that is not connected to others on a network, SHARE must be loaded to activate FoxPro's multiuser safeguards and features.

Throughout this book, you create and store data files on disk, including scratch files that you may want to delete immediately and working files that comprise the model application you refer to frequently.

Create separate subdirectories on the disk to hold your data and practice files. If you explore the hard disk after installation, you may notice that FoxPro itself creates many subdirectories to hold its subsidiary sample files. Keeping your data files separate from the FoxPro program files as delivered on the installation disks makes it much easier to manage your disk. You will be able to make backups much more easily if you aren't also making copies of the program files, or other files that don't change frequently (such as FoxPro's own samples), at the same time.

DOS, the disk operating system that sends information back and forth between the different components of the hardware system, also runs slowly when it must find a single file in an overcrowded directory. As you examine the sample applications, you see that a single application may require a large number of files of different types. DOS can locate files faster if you keep each application's files in a separate directory and even put different types of files belonging to one application into subdirectories of their own.

FoxPro creates so many files that you may find you need as much help wading through them as DOS does! In Chapter 14, "Organizing and Packaging Your Applications," you learn to use FoxPro's Project Manager to catalog the files for an application. Although some of the files may be stored in separate subdirectories, and may even be shared by several different applications, the Project Manager will keep track of them for you.

TIP

If you have worked through the exercises in a different edition of this book (*Using FoxPro 2* or *Using FoxPro 2.5 for Windows*, Special Edition) you will be able to use the same *data* files for this one, with minor adjustments. However, you should create a separate subdirectory for the *application* files you create in this edition, because some of the beginning exercises will be easier to follow if you are creating fresh files rather than converting old ones. In Chapter 17, "Transporting FoxPro Applications Across Platforms," you learn to *transport* application files so that you can use them simultaneously in different environments and different versions of FoxPro.

To hold the practice files for this book, make a subdirectory by using the following procedures. Refer to your DOS manual if you have difficulty following these instructions.

After the computer is turned on and has gone through the startup sequence, make the drive holding FoxPro 2.5 for DOS the default drive. At the DOS prompt, type the drive letter, a colon, and then press Enter. This procedure looks like the following line:

```
C:\>C:
```

Now type the letters MD (for make directory), a backslash (\), the name of the FOXPRO main directory, another backslash (\), and the word MODEL. You may specify a different directory name than MODEL, but you should use something short and preferably all letters (no symbols or digits). You should not use any spaces. If you installed FoxPro 2.5 for DOS in a directory called FPD, for example, type the following line and press Enter:

```
MD\FPD\MODEL
```

During practice sessions, start FoxPro from this data directory. This practice will make saving information in this directory easier. To start FoxPro from a data directory (or any directory other than the main program directory), DOS must be able to find the FoxPro's program files on the PATH. Type PATH at the DOS prompt to see whether you already have a path installed. DOS returns a line that begins with PATH=, followed by a list of directories similar to the following line:

```
PATH=C:\;C:\DOS;C:\UTILS
```

Add the FoxPro main directory to the path by typing a line similar to the following:

```
PATH=C:\;C:\DOS;C:\UTILS;C:\FPD
```

If DOS didn't return a path, you can create a path by typing the following line:

```
PATH=C:\FPD
```

Substitute the appropriate drive and directory in the new path to fit your needs.

Now, when you are ready, start FoxPro from the MODEL data directory by typing the following lines at the DOS prompt and using the appropriate drive and directory, as in the following (CD is the DOS command for change directory):

```
CD\FPD\MODEL
FOX
```

The name FOX is one of several *loader* programs available to start FoxPro. You use the loaders and command-line switches to specify important configuration options at startup. Refer to Appendix D, "Using Command Line Options and the Loaders," for this information.

You can put the preceding lines in a *batch file* (starting with the PATH line) so that you can start FoxPro from DOS with one line or one letter. You can have several batch files to start FoxPro from different data directories.

You also can specify FoxPro as part of the DOS path when you start up the computer, by editing the AUTOEXEC.BAT, which is a special batch file that executes when the computer boots up.

FoxPro uses a mouse extensively. If you have a mouse, make sure that you install the driver software and that the mouse is working *before* starting up FoxPro. If your mouse is not installed in your AUTOEXEC.BAT file when you turn on the computer, you can add the command that loads your mouse driver to the beginning of the batch file you use to start FoxPro.

In Chapter 2, "Understanding the FoxPro Interface," you learn about the FoxPro Editor, which enables you to create and edit batch files and other text directly in FoxPro.

Exploring the Program

In this section, you take a tour of FoxPro. By making a few quick choices, you see how easily you can change the appearance of the screen, alter the default behavior of the program, or select an application to run.

Selecting Tasks in FoxPro

The FoxPro 2.5 for DOS sign-on screen presents eight choices in a row across the top, as shown in figure 1.1. The next chapter covers these choices and how you access them. Practice choosing a few options and see what happens.

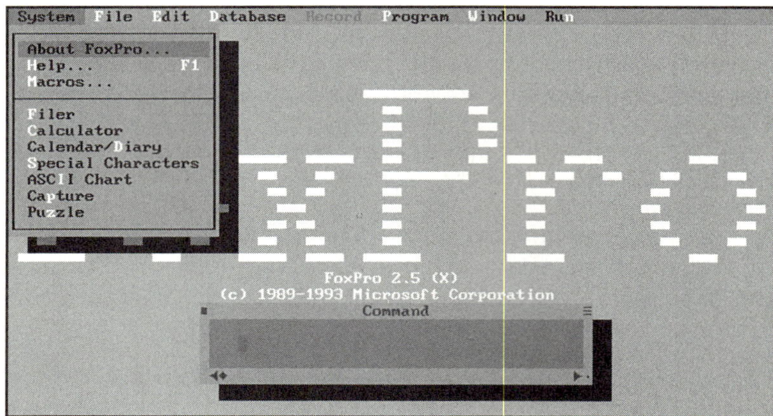

FIG. 1.1

The FoxPro 2.5 for DOS sign-on screen when the System option is accessed.

For now, you need to know only that you can use the keyboard to choose an option by pressing the Alt key simultaneously with a highlighted letter in the choice you want (the letter is shown on your screen in a different intensity or color). To access the first option (System), press Alt+S and a box of subsidiary choices appears. You then can press the single highlighted letter (without pressing Alt) of any subsidiary choices. Try this procedure and look at the list of choices (refer to fig. 1.1).

Mouse users also can click the words on-screen to activate the choices. Click means to press and quickly release the left mouse button (or right, when indicated). Double-click means to press the left mouse button twice in rapid succession. Drag means to move the mouse pointer while holding down the left mouse button.

Press Alt+W or click Window to access the Window choices. You see another list. Press V (or click View) to select the last item and then M (for Miscellaneous), and the screens in figures 1.2 and 1.3 appear in succession.

Communicating Choices to FoxPro

You can make many choices on the miscellaneous panel. One item (the box labeled Date) is highlighted, which means that you can edit the item in the box. Press the Tab key or the Shift+Tab keys, and you can cycle the highlight through the control objects on the Miscellaneous panel to edit the choices one at a time. (You also can click the choice you want.) Press the Tab key until the [ ] Clock check box is highlighted. After you press Enter or the space bar or click the item, the check box (the square brackets) contains an X, and the clock appears in the upper-right corner of the screen.

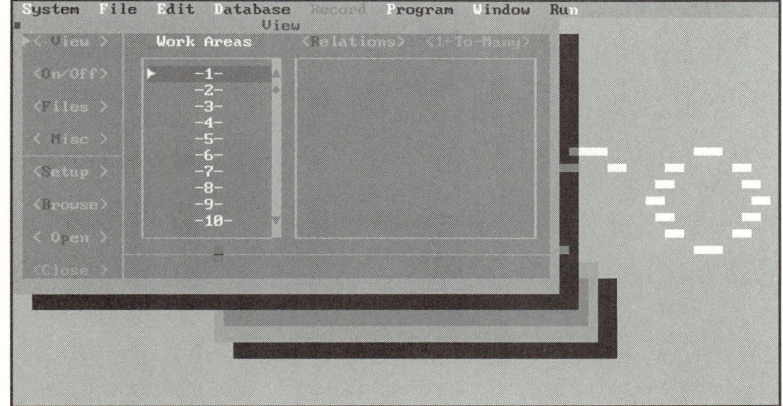

FIG. 1.2

View, accessed from the Window options by pressing Alt+W and then V.

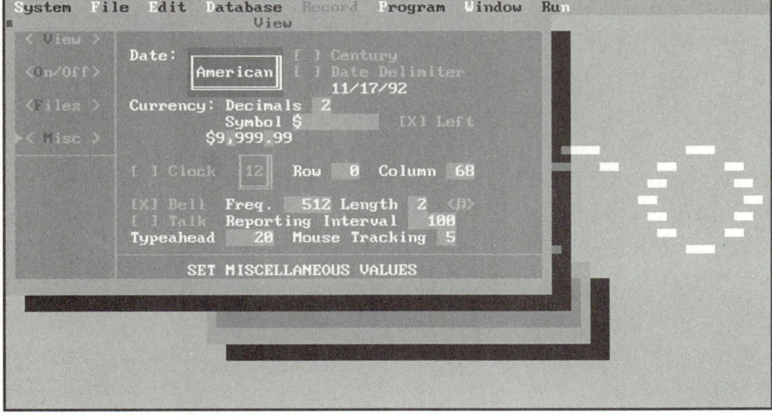

FIG. 1.3

View's Miscellaneous panel is selected.

If you don't like the clock's on-screen position, you can change the position by typing different numbers in the Row and Column items. (You learn how to change the colors in Chapter 16, "Discovering Additional FoxPro Productivity Features.") Figure 1.4 shows the clock turned on and moved slightly from the default position. The Enter key was pressed on the box initially labeled 12 to change the time format to military time. Using the arrow keys, move the highlight to the 24 as shown, and then press Enter or the space bar to select the box; or you can click 24 with the mouse.

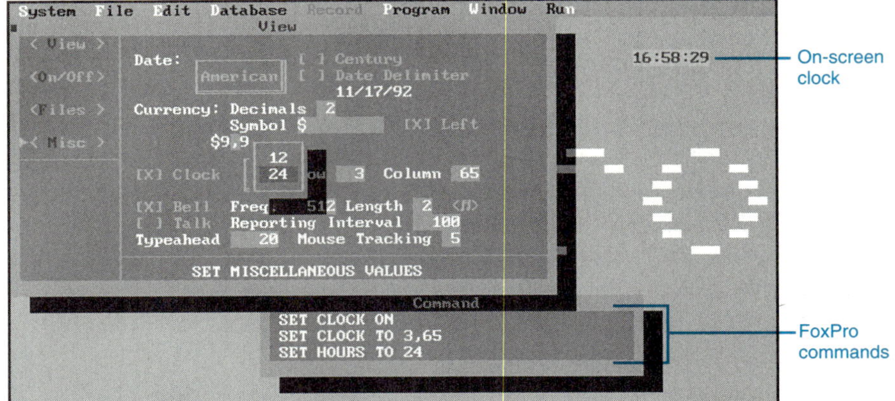

FIG. 1.4

Activating the clock.

In figure 1.4, words appear in a box close to the bottom of the screen as you make these selections. These words are FoxPro commands; all the decisions that you made about the clock caused these commands to be executed. FoxPro echoes commands so that you can read each command as it is executed. Noting these commands as you make the selections is a good way to learn how to issue commands directly.

If you use a mouse, you may want to try changing the Mouse Tracking setting, or value, before leaving the Miscellaneous panel. This value ranges from 1 to 10 (1 is the least responsive setting) and initially is set in the mid-range. Type different values and move the mouse around on the pad or desk; if you press 1, you must move the mouse much farther before the mouse cursor moves on-screen than if you type 10. Choose a value comfortable to you.

What happens if you make a mistake? Figure 1.5 shows a value outside the allowable range entered into the Mouse Tracking box and the error message that results. Just click or press any key, and then enter a new value (you can use the Backspace key to erase the previous value if necessary).

Press Esc and the View/Miscellaneous panel disappears. To load one of the sample applications, press Alt+N, accessing the Run choices, and then press A for Applications.

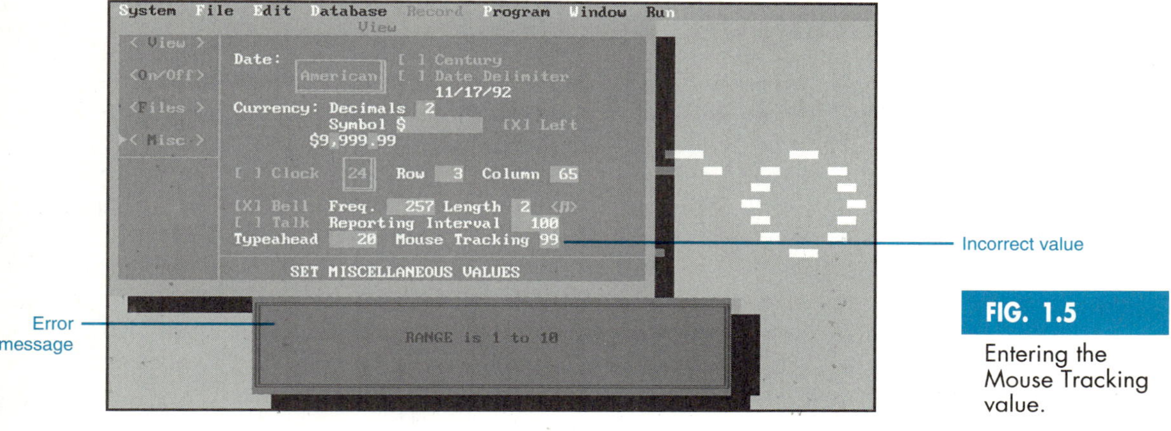

FIG. 1.5

Entering the Mouse Tracking value.

T I P

The Run choices were added to FoxPro after the initial release of FoxPro 2.0. Run is a convenient way to access all the *results* of your work in FoxPro, such as reports and applications that you have created, in one place. Running an existing Application is the same thing as pressing Alt+P (Program) and then D (Do). Later in this book, you learn to organize the system of choices available to you, which are termed FoxPro's *system menu*, so that they appear in any order you want.

Starting To Organize

When you choose to Run an Application, you move from FoxPro's default features to features determined by an *application* developer, or programmer. These features are limited and arranged by the developer to help you perform the application's special task. In this section, you explore one of the sample applications, Organize, which you can install with FoxPro.

Nothing about Organize's behavior is necessary or required in a FoxPro application; in fact, you might create a FoxPro application that performed exactly the same tasks in completely different ways. Running Organize simply gives you an idea of the freedom FoxPro gives you to tailor its features in your own applications.

Starting an Application

After you press A, you see a screen much like figure 1.6. If you started FoxPro from the MODEL data directory, as previously instructed, the upper-right box corner shows the current drive letter, and in the next box down (the middle right), the word MODEL (the current directory) appears. The long box at the left, under the words `Application to run:`, is empty. Press Enter with the [..] entry highlighted in this box, or double-click the brackets, to move up one level in the drive's directory structure. You are now in the main FoxPro 2.5 program directory. Use the mouse or the cursor keys to move the highlight to the SAMPLE directory, as shown, and then double-click or press Enter to access this directory.

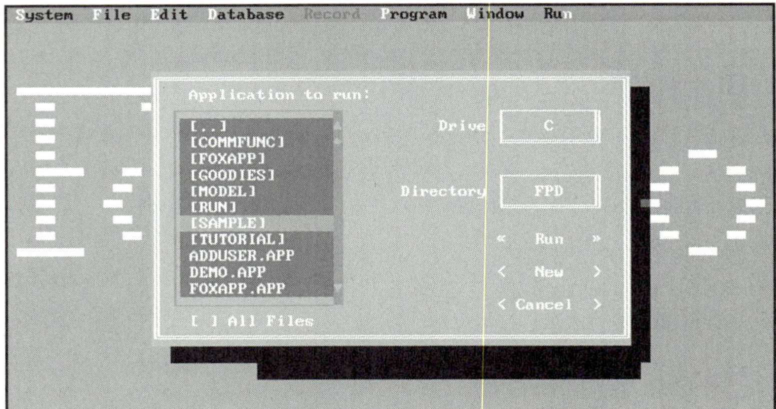

FIG. 1.6

Getting a list of Application files available to run.

After you locate and enter the SAMPLE directory's list of files, press the letter O. The highlight moves to the first file that begins with the letter O, as shown in figure 1.7. ORGANIZE.APP is the file you want, so after this filename is highlighted, press Enter to run the ORGANIZE application.

Using Common Application Features

The file list disappears, and you see a brief flash of the list of choices on the top line. A message appears in the center of the screen, with the message `Organizer is installed under System menu popup`, but the screen doesn't seem to change otherwise. The next key you press clears the message.

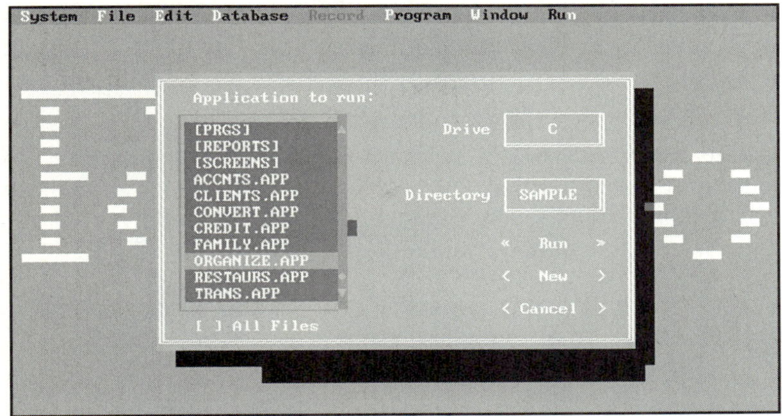

FIG. 1.7

The ORGANIZE.APP program is highlighted.

T I P

If you didn't start FoxPro from the MODEL directory or didn't create the MODEL directory under the main FoxPro program directory, as suggested, you may need to search for the SAMPLE files. Use the Drive and Directory items (press Enter after the items are highlighted and select, just as you did to change the time format for the clock). If you cannot find the SAMPLE directory and files under the main FoxPro directory, you may not have created these when you installed FoxPro. If necessary, refer to the installation instructions in Appendix A to add them now.

Using another FoxPro application, you also can install—at any time—a choice of optional products from *within* FoxPro. Use the preceding instructions to access the option to Run an Application, and then choose the main FoxPro drive and directory. Press Tab, or click the list of files you see on the left side. Press I, or use the cursor keys or mouse until the file INSTALL.APP is highlighted. Press Enter to start installation of optional files.

You also can run the INSTALL application any time you want fresh copies of sample data. The INSTALL process warns you if your computer lacks the free space to install all the optional files you select. Ignore this warning, however, if you are deliberately installing these files to replace existing copies.

Press Alt+S and look at the System options again. The two new options are now installed on the menu popup, under Puzzle. These options, Conversions and Organize, are two of the sample applications that come with FoxPro.

The Conversions menu option is a delightful program that functions as a desk accessory, much like the Calendar and Calculator programs native to FoxPro's System options. This option converts different kinds of measurements from one unit to another.

Organize is a group of programs that helps you manage personal information. When you press O, you see a list of Organize subsidiary programs: Restaurants, Client Manager, Family & Friends, and Money Manager, which also contains subsidiary programs (see fig. 1.8).

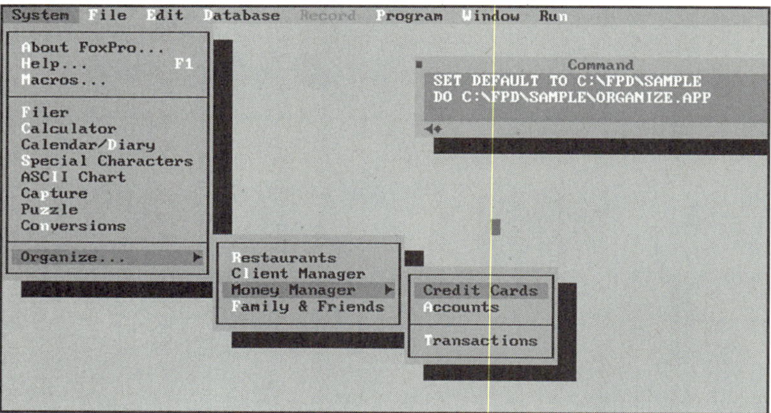

FIG. 1.8

The Organizer applications.

Press M to see the list of Money Manager applications, and then press the right- or left-arrow key to go back one level to the main Organize list. Explore all the Organize programs at your leisure; these applications all function in similar ways. For this exercise, press L to access the Client Manager. A screen similar to figure 1.9 appears.

> **CAUTION:** Some Organizer programs and features may not run on some systems, depending on the amount of memory the system has. If you see an `Insufficient memory` message from FoxPro while trying to follow some of the instructions, follow along by using the accompanying screen displays shown in the text. You can use the System About option to learn about your system configuration and the way FoxPro sees the memory available. To fine-tune the system for use with FoxPro, check Appendixes B and C, "Optimizing FoxPro's Performance" and "Customizing the CONFIG.FP File."

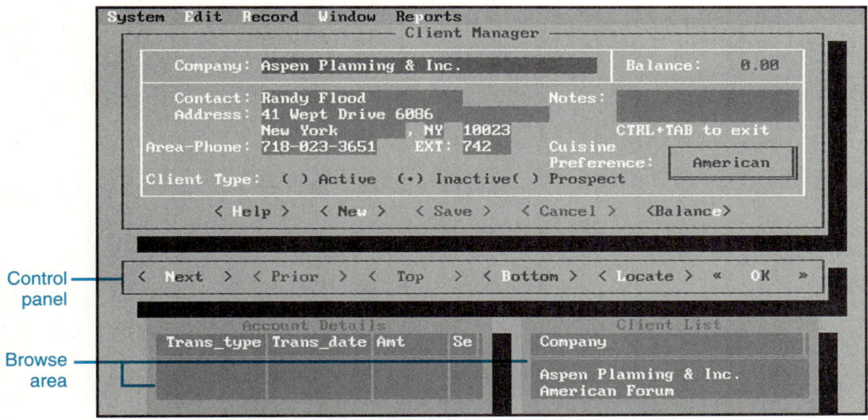

FIG. 1.9

The Client Manager application screen.

On the top section of the screen, you edit information for this client. The middle section contains a *control panel* of options that enables you to move through the records storing information about various clients in the Client table. The bottom section contains two examples of BROWSE, one of FoxPro's most versatile features for displaying lists of items. In one corner, you see the current Client Browse. In the other bottom corner, you see the Account Browse (empty in fig. 1.9) that provides you with a detailed perspective on the client's financial transactions.

Initially, the cursor is placed in the first item to edit (Company), as shown by the highlight. You can press Tab or click items that you want to edit.

When you select the Cuisine Preference box for editing, a list of choices pops up, similar to the time format options box for the Clock you previously edited. A similar list appears if you select the two-character State item.

The Notes box enables you to enter free-form information about a client.

You cannot directly edit the Balance figure as you press Tab to move through the items in the Client Manager. Before you have edited the Client record, or when you have Saved or Canceled any changes that you made to the Client record, you can calculate the Client balance by selecting the `Balance` push button. Specify month, and choose whether to calculate a balance for one client or for all records, and the program will calculate the Client's Balance.

To understand the Balance feature, select Balance and, while the Balance features are displayed, use the System Help option. A Help topic on the Balance option or an index to Help topics appears (see fig. 1.10).

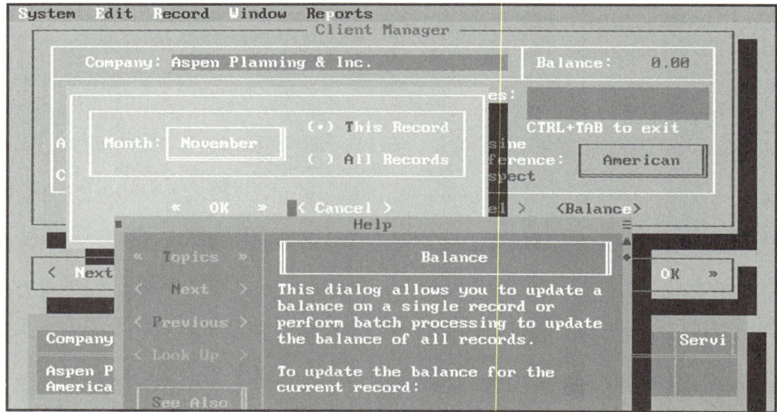

FIG. 1.10

The Balance feature and its Help topic.

Within the index, pick topics to read about by highlighting the topic and pressing Enter. Figure 1.10 shows the Balance topic help screen. (To see the screen exactly as shown in the figure, use the Window Move option from the top bar.) Read the information on Balance and on all other topics that interest you. You can access the index again by pressing T while in the Balance help screen. Press Esc to return from the Help screens to the Client Manager.

By pressing Ctrl+F1 or clicking different places, you can *cycle* through the different areas of the screen (you find the Cycle option under Window in the top bar). Use the cursor keys or the mouse to move through the different items in each area, and use the control panel to move through the different clients. As you do so, notice the changes in the Client and Account Browses.

Find a client for whom some transactions are listed, cycle to the Account Browse, and move the cursor to the Memo item under the Service heading. Press Ctrl+PgDn or double-click the Memo item to see another level of detail (see fig. 1.11). You access a box that contains the Service information which, like the Notes box in the Client table, can contain any free-form text you type.

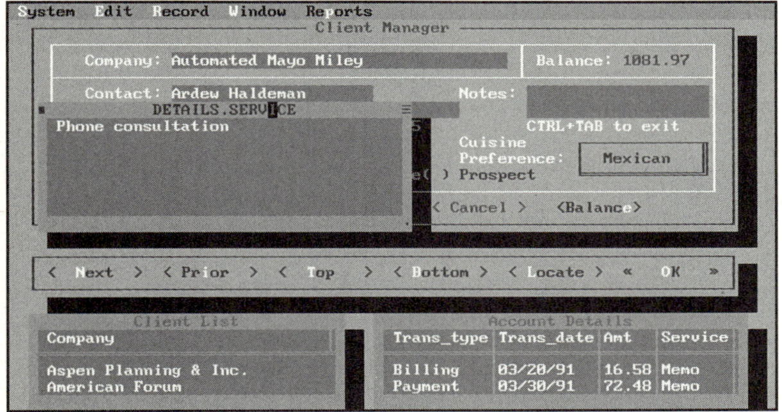

FIG. 1.11

The Service memo accessed through the Account Browse.

Press Esc, and the Service text disappears. From the top bar, choose the Reports option (Alt+P) and select Reports, Labels, and Mail Merge. For each subsidiary option, press Ctrl+Enter at the next screen to accept all the default choices. This exercise shows the versatility with which FoxPro displays and outputs information from data. Afterwards, press Esc to return to the Client Manager application.

In Chapter 3, "Exploring Databases and Tables," you learn more about maintaining tables. You can completely clear the Organizers of sample data and fill them with information for personal use, but you aren't limited to the structures provided by the Organizer tables. You can create similar applications from scratch, with tables that hold records in a format that you design.

If you still are in one of the Organizer Reports output options and you want to leave the Client Manager, press Esc and then press Esc again (or use the OK option).

Creating an Application

Press Alt+N and then A, but this time, instead of choosing a filename of an existing application to Run, select the New button. This action starts FoxPro's built-in application generator, FoxApp.

Now that you've seen FoxPro's sample Organize application, use FoxApp in this section to build a quick application from start to finish. FoxApp-generated applications include most of the standard features required in database management applications, organized in a generic framework. Generating and running the FoxApp-generated application will help you recognize these features so you can build the same capabilities into any application framework you design.

Designing the Data Table Structure

The FoxPro Application Generator screen appears, with the cursor positioned in an empty box waiting for a Database name to be entered. Type the path of your MODEL directory (the directory you use for all data) followed by a backslash (\), and the word PRODUCT, as shown in figure 1.12. It doesn't matter whether you type in upper- or lowercase.

NOTE Although you started FoxPro from your MODEL directory, you have now run the Organizer applications, which may have changed your *default directory* in FoxPro to point to their own data. To be certain that FoxApp sends the files to the appropriate place, type the full drive and directory of the files you want to create.

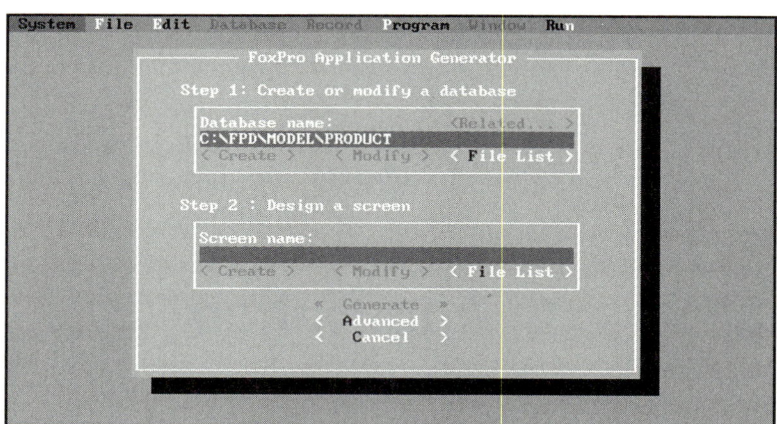

FIG. 1.12

Beginning work in FoxApp.

After you finish typing, press Enter. By replacing the file name with a line similar to C:\FPD\MODEL\PRODUCT.DBF, which includes .DBF as the default extension for a table, FoxApp confirms the name of the table you are creating. FoxApp also fills out the Screen Name box with the same file name and .SCX, the default extension for screens.

The Create item under the table name now is highlighted. Press Enter and a screen similar to figure 1.13 appears.

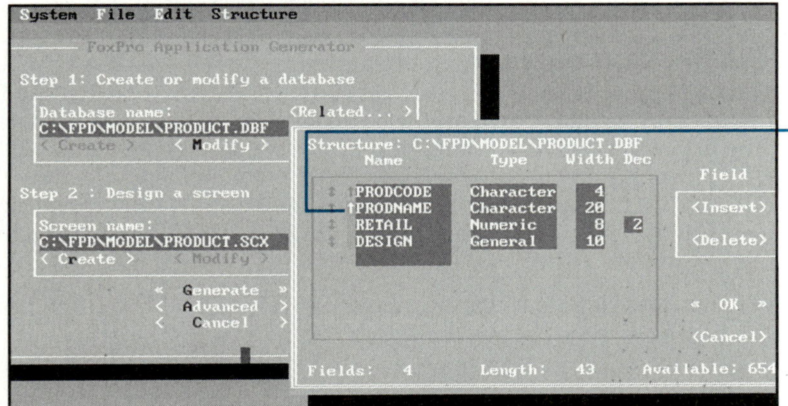

FIG. 1.13

Creating the Product table structure.

In this step, you actually describe the table structure to FoxPro. As you discover in Chapter 3, "Exploring Databases and Tables," a table is a kind of list, and each item on the list is a *record*. In the Product table, each record is an item in the product line of the imaginary Omnipresent Widget Company.

Each record can incorporate many different pieces, or *fields* of information about the item it represents. In the Product table, you store a name, a company code, and a price for each product. You also create a place to store a picture of each product in a special kind of FoxPro field, new to FoxPro 2.5, called a *General field*.

When you create a table in Chapter 3, you learn how to name fields, all of the kinds of fields available, and what these fields do. For this brisk run-through, however, just type the Name, choose the Type from the list that appears, and add the Width for the four necessary fields, as shown in the following instructions and figure 1.13. As you make each entry, press Tab to go to the next space (or click the available spaces for each entry) so that you put each Name, Type, and Width in the correct place.

- As the first field Name, type PRODCODE (FoxPro uses all uppercase, no matter how you type it). After you type the name, a small shaded box appears just to the left. Use the left-arrow key, or Shift+Tab while you're in the PRODCODE space, and press the space bar (or double-click the shaded box). A small up arrow appears instead of the shaded box. As you learn in the following chapters, this arrow represents an index, which enables FoxPro to show you the data in order by product code. Double-click the box again, and a small down arrow appears. Double-click again, and the arrows disappear, indicating that no index will be created. After cycling through these choices to see what they look like, repeat the double-clicking until you see the up arrow again for your final result. Leave the Type at the default of Character and type 4 for the Width.
- The second field is PRODNAME. Again, double-click the shaded box, or highlight it and press the space bar so that the small up arrow appears. This field also is a Character type, and the Width should be 20.
- For the third field Name, type RETAIL. Press Tab to move to the Type entry, and press the space bar or click it to choose Numeric from the list of data types that appears. Give this field a width of 8 with 2 Decimal places, as shown in the figure.
- The fourth field, which you give a Type of General, has the field name DESIGN. If you try, you find that you cannot add an index to this field. General fields take up a fixed width of 10 characters per record, although their actual entries may be widely varying in size, so FoxPro doesn't ask you to enter the width.

Now press Ctrl+Enter, a shortcut for choosing the default (chevron enclosed) *end task* option that you can use almost everywhere in FoxPro, or press Enter with the OK item highlighted (or click it with the mouse) to save the table definition. FoxApp asks whether you want to `Input data records now?` Press N or click No and you return to the main FoxApp screen. (After using FoxApp to generate the application, you plan to use FoxApp's application screen to enter the data.)

TIP

General fields are not directly used in FoxPro 2.5 for DOS. In Windows applications, they store objects using special formats that link them to other Windows applications. This general field will hold an object that can be read and displayed by Microsoft Paintbrush. As you learn in Chapter 17, "Transporting FoxPro Applications Across Versions and Platforms," the Omnipresent Widget application's files will be useful to people using FoxPro in several different environments at the same time.

You have the ability to create this field, while in the DOS product, for Windows users. If you were certain that your application would be used only on the DOS platform, you might prefer to make this field a memo field. Memo fields are another special type of FoxPro field, which can store literally anything you want. (The Notes field and Service field that you saw briefly in the Client Manager are both memo fields.) You can store scanned and digitized photographs of the products in the memo field, but you need a third-party utility to display these pictures. FoxPro for DOS cannot display the photographs on its own.

Although a table now exists, you can use FoxApp to modify this table if you need to make changes. If you are satisfied that you followed the instructions and that the table is structured as shown in figure 1.13, use the `Create` button to create a screen in which you can enter the Product records.

FoxApp places the cursor in the Screen Name space, in case you want to rename the file. Press Enter to accept the default name and press Enter again, if necessary, with the `Create` push button highlighted. You see a message from FoxApp that announces the screen is now created.

Modifying the Generated Entry Screen

Although FoxApp already did all the work, choose the `Modify` push button highlighted now and make at least one change in the prepared screen. After you click `Modify` or press Enter, the screen in figure 1.14 appears.

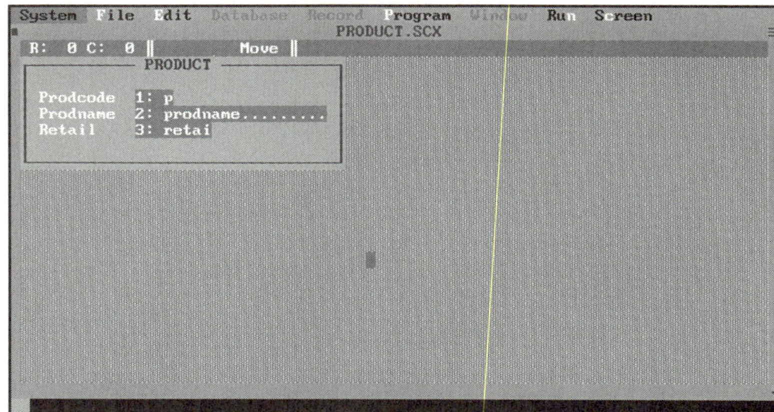

FIG. 1.14

The FoxApp-created Product data entry screen.

You see three of the field names you just created, each next to a space for you to enter data. Because you cannot do any direct data entry to the Design field, Fox App didn't create a place for you do to it in this screen.

The screen looks crowded. To make the screen look better, add some extra space. Access the Screen option on the top bar by pressing Alt+C and press Enter on Screen Layout to see the varied display of options shown in figure 1.15. (You learn more about these options in Chapter 12, "Creating Application Elements.") You can solve the space problem if you change the Height and Width items on the left. Type `9` for the Height, and `40` for the Width. After you type the numbers, press Enter, click `OK`, or press Ctrl+Enter to look at the adjusted screen layout (see fig. 1.16).

Now the screen looks unbalanced. To make the screen look better, highlight different items in the layout and press the arrow keys or drag the items with the mouse to move each individual item around on the layout. Press Enter or release the mouse button to fix an item in the new position. Do the same thing for the text labels on the left and for the data entry boxes on the right.

While you're at it, change the text labels to something more readable. Field names can't have spaces in them, but your screens don't have to be as cryptic as the actual field names. Delete the words Prodname and Prodcode, by highlighting them and pressing the Delete key, and type more descriptive labels directly into the layout. Follow the model in figure 1.16. After you type each label, press Enter. The label becomes another item you can move around on-screen as a unified object.

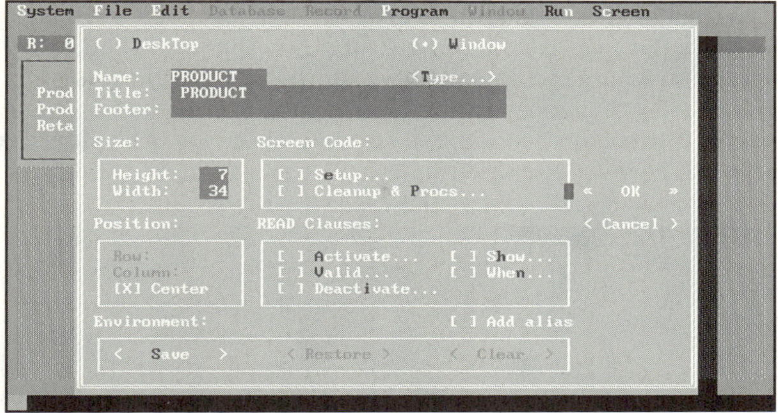

FIG. 1.15

The Screen Layout options.

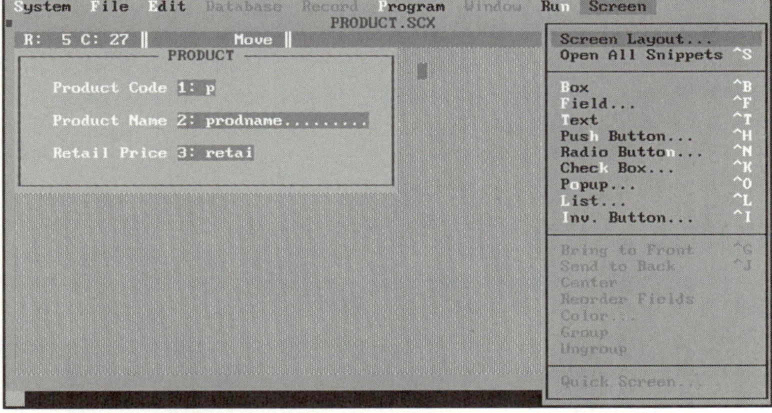

FIG. 1.16

The revised Product entry screen and the Screen Builder options.

Press Alt+F to access File options from the top bar and choose Close. After FoxPro asks whether you want to save the changes, select Yes.

You are now back at the main Fox App screen, and you can click the `Generate` push button on the bottom of the screen (or press Ctrl+Enter). Fox App asks for a name for the application with a file list similar to the one you used to find an application to Run. The name PRODUCT.APP is fine for this application, but make sure that you use the Drive and Directory options, if necessary, to get into the MODEL directory so that you save the file in the correct place. (If you prefer, you also can use the File list to move between directories.)

FoxApp then begins to generate the application, and you see a number of messages flash across the screen. After FoxApp is finished, a message tells you where the application is stored and that you can press any key or click the mouse to start the application for the first time. When you start an application, the screen you see looks like the screen in figure 1.17.

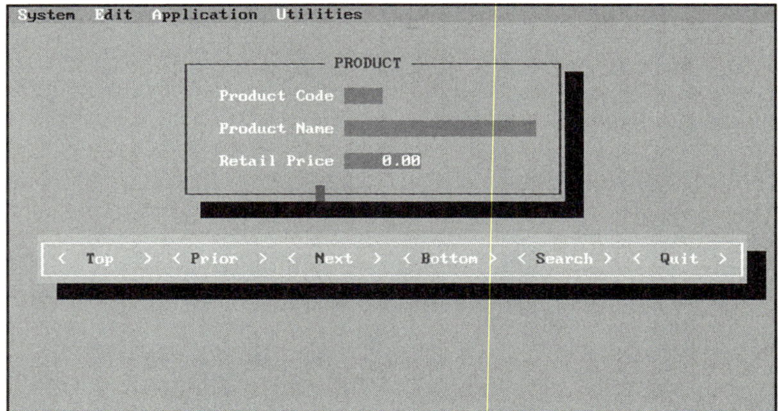

FIG. 1.17

The main screen for the Product application generated by FoxApp.

Entering Data by Using the FoxApp-Generated Application

The Product table application screen contains a data-entry area and a panel of controls that you use to move through the file. The screen also has a new list of options on the top bar. Table 1.1 lists the products manufactured and sold by Omnipresent Widgets. Type these items into the data-entry area now so that you can use them in examples throughout this book. As you type each record, use the option you find under Application on the top bar, as shown in figure 1.18, to Add a new record.

Table 1.1 The Ominipresent Widget Product Line

Record Number	Product Code	Product Name	Retail Price
1	WGT2	Mainframe Widgets	10000.00
2	WGT1	LapTop Widgets	2000.00
3	DSQ0	Dream Sequencers	79.95
4	BBM0	Bobometers	60.00

Record Number	Product Code	Product Name	Retail Price
5	LLD0	Log Ladles (pine)	25.00
6	JLD0	Jeli-Do Nuts & Bolts	2.50
7	WZL1	Pine Weazlettes	145.00
8	WZL2	Lemon Weazlettes	145.00
9	WZL3	Floral Weazlettes	145.00
10	WZL4	Unscented Weazlettes	155.00

NOTE

You don't type the *record numbers* in the preceding chart. Each record in a table has a number that FoxPro assigns internally. The record numbers are provided here for your convenience. Record numbers are not fixed and may change if some records are permanently removed from the table. But, at any time, the highest record number is the same as the *total* number of records in the table.

Make sure that you enter the information carefully. In particular, assign each product code three *capital* letters followed by a *digit*, as shown in the list. This is a convention used by most of Omnipresent Widgets' data codes. At this point, the generated application enables you to add any characters you type in either field. Soon, you learn ways of *validating* data, or of making sure that data fits certain criteria as you enter information. For now, however, this application is not protected by these techniques.

Searching for Data by Using the Application

Now that the table contains information, see what you can do. Use the Application Search option to explore or click the control panel to find some text within the available fields, as shown in figure 1.19.

Depending on what text you choose, FoxApp may give you a message to let you know that it needs to use a relatively slow search process to look for it. In figure 1.19, the text comes from the middle of a field and will require a more thorough search than would be required if letters from the beginning of the entry (Dre) were typed. Finding records by different criteria, and by multiple criteria, is one of FoxPro's greatest strengths. Throughout this book, but especially in Parts I and II, you learn methods for making such searches fast and efficient.

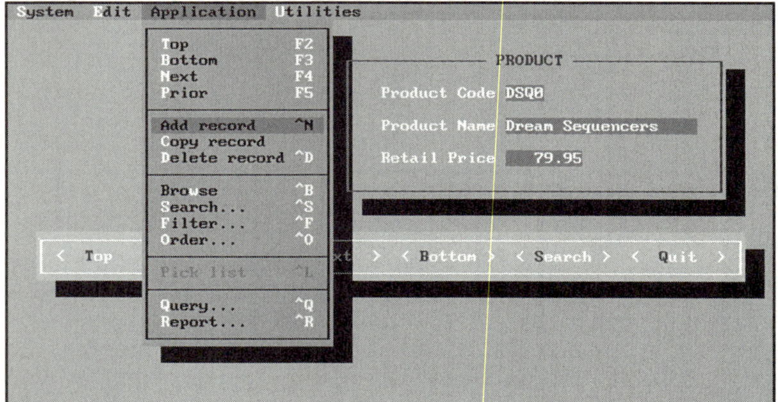

FIG. 1.18

The FoxApp-generated application options.

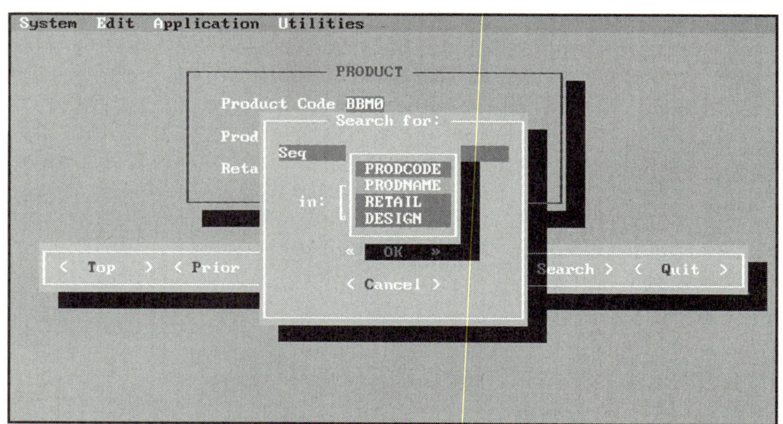

FIG. 1.19

The FoxApp-generated application search screen.

After you find a desired record, you may want to display this record in the context of the product list in various sequences, by using the Browse and Order options from the Application choices. Try the Browse option first; then change the Order, and Browse the product list again.

Next, try Application's Query option. You are asked to specify a Query name; you can accept the default of PRODUCT.QPR. You then see the screen shown in figure 1.20.

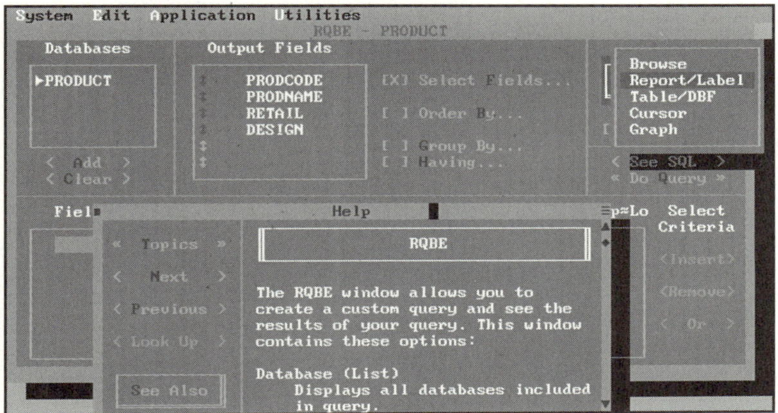

FIG. 1.20
FoxPro's RQBE with the Report/Label option about to be chosen and the Help screen available.

This screen is FoxPro's RQBE (Relational Query By Example) design screen. The RQBE enables you to select records by almost unlimited criteria and then display the selected record in many ways. You learn about RQBE and SQL (Structured Query Language), the command set that underlies FoxPro 2.5's RQBE, in several sections of this book. RQBE is worth a look during this tour because, along with the Screen Builder, with which you have briefly worked, this tool represents a powerful feature introduced in FoxPro 2.x. If you access the System Help option while the RQBE screen is showing, you can read a good synopsis of RQBE's elements.

For now, however, just click or press the Tab key to move to the Output To box in the top-right corner and press the space bar to choose Report/Label from the list of options that appears. Mark the Options check box. From the screen that appears next, press R and then Q to prepare an RQBE Quick Report (see fig. 1.21). Press Enter to accept the default layout. Press Ctrl+Enter to finish selecting Options, and you are returned to the main RQBE screen.

The sample records are entered in no particular order. Arrange the records in alphabetical order for the report. Press B (for Order By), and the screen in figure 1.22 appears. Use the down-arrow key or click the mouse to move the highlight to the Product.Prodname entry in the Selected Output list on the left side of the screen. Press Enter (or double-click the entry), or click the `Move` button that becomes available once you have chosen a field, and Product.Prodname moves to the Ordering Criteria box on the right side, as shown in the figure. Press Ctrl+Enter to return to the main RQBE screen. (Notice that in the Order By check box, an X now appears.)

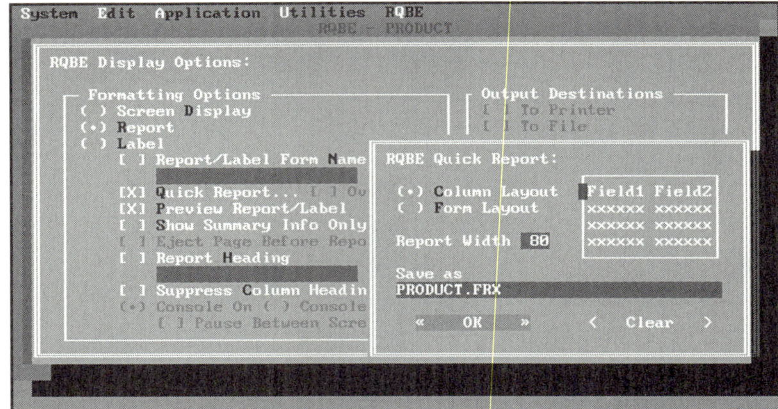

FIG. 1.21

Choosing RQBE output options.

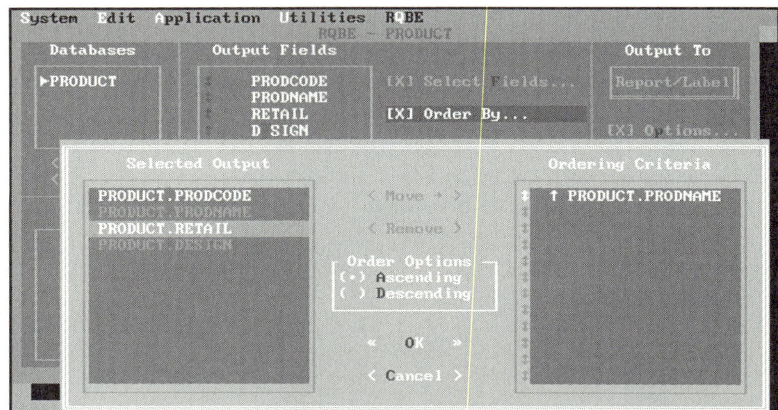

FIG. 1.22

Ordering output in the RQBE.

Now press Q, and the report is delivered to the screen, as shown in figure 1.23, with all records alphabetically ordered by product name. Enter the Options again and press P to remove the Preview Report/ Label option. Then press T to send the report To the Printer.

You have not exhausted the capabilities of a generated application in this quick tour, although a FoxApp-generated application represents only a small fraction of what FoxPro can do. Return to this application at your leisure and experiment with the different choices FoxApp provides.

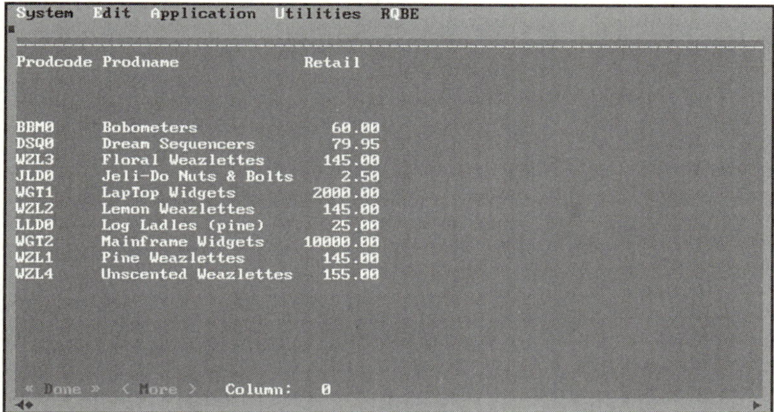

FIG. 1.23

The RQBE-generated Quick Report previewed on-screen.

T I P

If you already are comfortable with database table structures, look ahead to Chapter 3, "Exploring Databases and Tables," for the structure and data used in Omnipresent Widget's Budget table. You can generate a separate application, by using FoxApp's Advanced option screen, that relates the information in the Budget and Product tables and shows them working together in one data entry screen. (If you are new to database management, wait until you have completed Chapter 3 and Chapter 4, "Database Managment Fundamentals," to try this exercise.) Part III of this book examines a FoxApp-generated application, and you learn to create similar applications yourself, without Fox App and with more flexibility.

Fox App itself is just another FoxPro application, similar to the Product application you just generated *with* Fox App, and similar to the Organizers. If you use the Run Application sequence that you were using to search for files, and if you installed the necessary optional products, you find a FOXAPP directory under the main FOXPRO directory. The FoxApp directory and the sub-levels contain the source files for FOXAPP. Later in this book, you examine them directly to see how FOXAPP does the work.

Learning More about FoxPro

FoxPro's installation disks contain many other sample materials that this book cannot fully cover. Besides FOX APP, you find the following items under the GOODIES directory:

- A complete simple application in the LASER directory
- A directory, FNDATION, that holds sophisticated examples for programmers
- A HELPTREE directory that contains a program to add advanced features to the FoxPro 2.5 HELP system

Take a close look at the self-running DEMO.APP program you can DO from the main FOXPRO program directory (the same way you started Fox App). You find the source files in the DEMO directory, under GOODIES. DEMO.APP gives you a quick introduction to all the features and power tools available under FoxPro 2.5 for DOS.

Ending a FoxPro Session

You may decide that you practiced enough in FoxPro for the day or that you are ready to go to Chapter 2, "Understanding FoxPro Fundamentals," to begin to learn how these intriguing sample applications are created. When you leave FoxPro, however, use the Quit option on the File menu popup. Never turn off or reboot a computer without first Quitting FoxPro.

Occasionally (because of a program or disk crash or a power failure), you must end a FoxPro session abnormally. When this kind of disaster strikes, you will see a number of temporary work files with the extension .TMP on the disk. FoxPro usually deletes these files at the end of a session; the number and location of these files depend on the tasks you performed and on other aspects of the configuration. Refer to Appendix D, "Using Command Line Options and the Loaders," for the kinds of temporary files and how to manage these files by using a CONFIG.FP file. When you find these files, you can delete them. You also can run the CHKDSK command from DOS to clean up any lost clusters that may result from an abnormal exit. (See the DOS manual for details, or for more information, see *MS-DOS 5 User's Guide,* Special Edition or *Using MS-DOS 5*, both published by Que Corporation.)

Cleaning up temporary files is easy. But restoring precious data files, which may become corrupted in a disk crash or other abnormal exits from FoxPro, often isn't easy. Therefore, backing up data is as vital as using the Quit option to end a FoxPro session safely. Whether you use a special backup utility program or DOS commands to make a second copy of the data doesn't matter; just find a comfortable routine and develop the habit of backing up important data files.

Summary

In this chapter, you learned to navigate among FoxPro features by using some of the sample application programs. You learned to create an application. You practiced starting the program and entering data in the Product table that you created. In the next chapter, you step back a little to discuss the FoxPro 2.5 for DOS interface, the ways in which you interact with the program.

2

CHAPTER

Understanding the FoxPro Interface

In this chapter, you learn about the elements that make up the FoxPro interface. The interface of any computer program is composed of all the ways in which you and the program can communicate with one another. This interface, through which information travels between you and the program, includes the following characteristics:

- The items you can expect to see on-screen
- The language and formats or style of presentation the program commonly uses to ask you questions and inform you of tasks in progress
- The methods you can use to respond to the program's requests
- The clues (such as colors, positions on-screen, or sounds) that the program uses to help you understand the task you are currently doing and the options available to you

These items, formats, methods, and clues are in use no matter what task you are performing with the program. Therefore, the more comfortable you become with the interface, the more productive you become.

Some parts of the FoxPro interface may be familiar if you have used other computer programs, and other parts may be unique to FoxPro. Because of the rich assortment of choices in the interface, you have to take the time to understand how these choices are organized and presented.

If you like to dive in without much introduction, however, go right ahead. In the following chapter, "Exploring Databases and Tables," you can go right to work creating and using data. You can return to this chapter if some aspect of the interface puzzles you.

In subsequent chapters of this book, when you design FoxPro applications for other people to use, you find that you have powerful tools for creating application interfaces by using the same items, formats, methods, and clues that FoxPro uses. The better you understand the interface, therefore, the better you can design easily-understood applications.

Familiarizing Yourself with the FoxPro Screen

If you followed the introductory information in Chapter 1, you installed FoxPro and know how to load the program from the DOS command line. If you haven't installed the program, read Appendix A, "Installing FoxPro," to make sure that you are prepared to use the program.

Unless you have already done so, refer to Chapter 1 and create a subdirectory, \MODEL, of the main FoxPro directory (for example: C:\FOXPRO25\MODEL) to store the data and other files for practice sessions and for the model application. Include the main FoxPro directory in the DOS path, as described in Chapter 1. Now change the current drive and directory so that you are in the MODEL directory. Make sure that the mouse driver is loaded and load FoxPro.

NOTE

Remember that the *driver* (the software that interprets information from the mouse) is not part of FoxPro. By using a program provided by the manufacturer of the mouse, you need to make this driver available before you load FoxPro.

You can use FoxPro with or without a mouse, or other pointing tool. For many people, however, mouse use in FoxPro is both fun and intuitive. Even if you have never used a mouse, make arrangements to test one with this program. This book provides both keyboard and mouse alternatives for each action you take. With a little experimenting, you may find that a mixture of using the keyboard and the mouse best suits your work habits.

After you load FoxPro, you see a sign-on screen (see fig. 2.1).

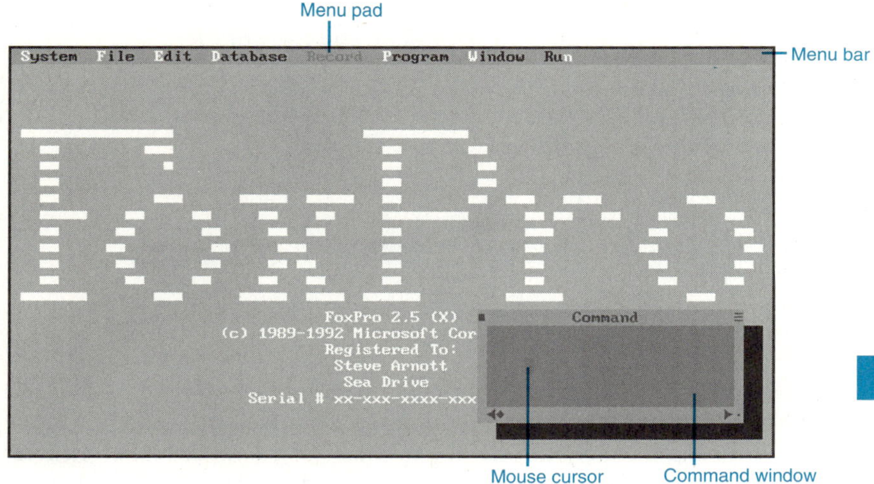

FIG. 2.1

The FoxPro sign-on screen.

Across the top of the screen, you see a line known as the *menu bar.* Like other software (and restaurant) menus, this menu presents a list of options available to you. Each option is a *pad* of the menu bar. In the next section, you learn how to choose options, or *menu pads,* and navigate through the choices contained in each.

In the bottom-right quarter of the screen shown in figure 2.1, and in approximately the same position on-screen when you load FoxPro, you see a small box with a border. This box is known as a *window.* FoxPro uses windows to present and separate different kinds of tasks and information. In this chapter, you learn about the different kinds of FoxPro windows, the kinds of information these windows contain, and the work you accomplish with each window.

The FoxPro window you now see is the *Command window.* As an alternative to making menu choices, you can type FoxPro command language instructions directly into this window. This chapter helps you learn the techniques you use to type and edit instructions in the Command window and elsewhere in FoxPro.

In figure 2.1, you also see a small rectangle in the bottom half of the screen. This rectangle is the *mouse cursor.* If you are using a mouse, the mouse cursor shows you where the mouse is currently positioned (otherwise, the mouse cursor doesn't appear). If you think the mouse is working but you do not see it, move the mouse around on the mouse pad or on a hard surface until you can see the cursor.

The mouse cursor may have a different shape than the rectangle in figure 2.1. Some PCs are equipped with graphics cards that display the mouse cursor as a graphical arrow cursor.

Understanding the FoxPro Menu System

FoxPro uses two kinds of menus. Some menus are simple lists of available options from which you make a choice and then continue with your business. Other menus are part of a menu system, which organizes the options according to the kind of function each menu performs. The menu bar in figure 2.1 is part of a menu system. Each pad in the menu bar represents a different kind of function that you can perform in FoxPro.

In this section, you investigate the FoxPro menu system, and you learn how to use the menus to communicate with FoxPro without knowing the FoxPro command language.

Learning How To Use the Menu System

A *menu system* has four components: a menu bar, menu pads, menu popups, and menu options. The *menu bar*, the glue that holds the menu system together, contains one or more menu pads, which divide the menu options into different categories. Menu *options* display in a *popup window,* which appears as though attached to the related menu pad.

Figure 2.2 shows the FoxPro menu system with the System menu popup active. Solid lines in the menu popup, such as the line between Macros and Filer, divide the options by function. Here, the solid line separates the desktop accessories, such as the Calculator and the Capture utility, from the other System menu options, such as Help.

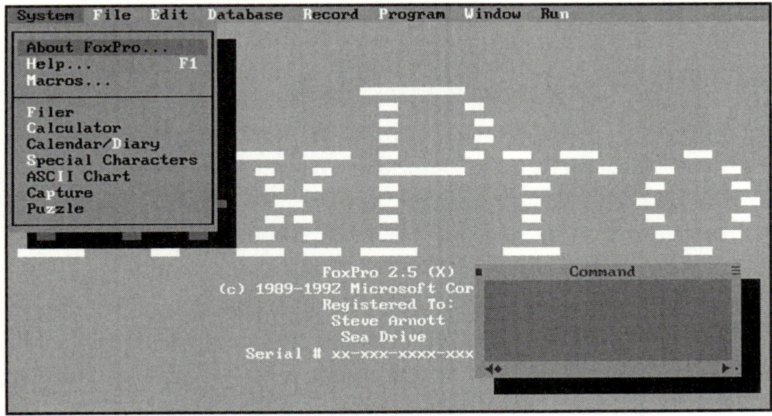

FIG. 2.2

The FoxPro for DOS menu system.

The ellipsis (...) that follows some options indicates that FoxPro requires more information about what you want to do. The method through which this additional information is collected is usually a *dialog.* Dialogs are explained in a following section of this chapter.

Notice that each menu pad name and option description contains a highlighted letter. If you are using a color monitor, the letter appears in a color different from the rest of the text. On a monochrome monitor, this letter usually appears brighter than the other letters. This letter is part of a *hot key,* which enables you to select the pad or option quickly. You learn more about hot keys later in this section.

TIP On some monochrome and EGA monitors, you may have to adjust the monitor's contrast setting to see the hot-key letter. Move the contrast control to the highest setting and then slowly reduce the contrast until you can distinguish the hot-key letter from the rest of the text.

You can select some menu options directly from the keyboard without activating the menu. If an option can be selected in this way, a *control-key shortcut* appears on the menu popup to the right of the option name. In figure 2.2, you see that pressing the F1 function key selects the FoxPro Help facility. You learn more about control-key shortcuts in the following section.

Selecting Menu Options

You have two ways to select a menu option in FoxPro. One way is to activate the menu and choose the option from a menu popup. You can perform this step by using the keyboard or the mouse. The other way is to enter the option's control-key shortcut (if a shortcut is available) from the keyboard.

The simplest way to activate the FoxPro menu is to press the Alt key or the F10 function key. These keys perform the same function as the slash (/) key in the Lotus 1-2-3 spreadsheet program. The menu bar becomes active, and the first menu pad is highlighted. From here, you can activate a particular menu pad and the related popup by moving the highlight bar to the pad name and pressing the space bar, or by typing the hot-key letter. You then can select the desired menu option in the same way, by highlighting the option name and pressing the space bar, or by typing the hot-key letter. Mouse users also can activate the menu bar by double-clicking the right-hand button.

You also can activate a particular menu popup by holding down the Alt key and pressing the pad's hot-key letter. For example, Alt+F activates the File popup. The F10 key, however, does not work in the same way and should not be used for this purpose.

You can deactivate the menu at any time by pressing the Esc key or by clicking the mouse on an area of the screen other than the menu system. FoxPro reactivates the previously active window. You also can deactivate the menu by pressing the Alt key or the F10 key again. Using the F10 key is preferable in multitasking environments, such as Windows and DESQview, which may interfere with the way FoxPro uses the

Alt key. When you switch to another program in DESQview or Windows and then come back to FoxPro, the menu bar is automatically activated.

After you activate a menu popup, you can activate other menus by using the left- and right-arrow keys to move from one menu pad to the next or by using their hot keys.

You can select certain menu options by using a control-key shortcut. Except for the FoxPro Help facility, which you select by pressing F1, keystroke shortcuts involve holding down the Ctrl key and pressing an assigned letter or function key. This step is the fastest way to access an option; however, the procedure requires that you memorize the assigned keystrokes. You may want to memorize only the shortcuts for the options that you use frequently, especially if you do not have a mouse.

The following quick reference guide lists the FoxPro control-key shortcuts that appear on the menu popups. Keep in mind that FoxPro also uses control-key shortcuts that do not appear on these popups, such as Shift+Ctrl+F9 to dock a window, and remember that the caret (^) means that you hold down the Ctrl key while pressing the appropriate key. Table 2.1 begins with the menu option shortcuts.

Table 2.1 Menu Option Shortcuts

Pad Name	Option	Key Shortcut
System	Help...	F1
Edit	Undo	^Z
	Redo	^R
	Cut	^X
	Copy	^C
	Paste	^V
	Select All	^A
	Find...	^F
	Find Again	^G
	Replace and Find Again	^E
Record	Continue	^K
Program	Do...	^D
	Resume	^M
Window	Move	^F7
	Size	^F8
	Zoom↑	^F10
	Zoom↓	^F9
	Cycle	^F1
	Command	^F2

You can easily activate a menu popup by using a mouse. Place the mouse cursor on the desired menu pad and click the left mouse button. Then move the mouse cursor to the desired option and click the left button again.

The FoxPro menu system is context-sensitive, which means that an option is enabled only when the option currently serves a useful purpose. When you first run FoxPro, for example, you cannot activate the Record menu pad because all the options on this pad's popup act on an open table. Because a table isn't open yet, these options serve no useful purpose and the Record menu pad appears dimmed. You cannot select dimmed pads or options.

For similar reasons, one or more options on a popup may be disabled. If you activate the Database popup when no table is open, most of its options are dimmed because those options need an open table on which to operate. The enabled options display the FoxPro Open File dialog which allows you to select a table.

FoxPro displays disabled options in a color (on color monitors) or intensity (on monochrome monitors) that makes the options appear dimmer than enabled options. The default colors for disabled options are cyan letters on a low-intensity white background.

Working with FoxPro Menu Options

The FoxPro menu bar usually contains eight menu pads. Each pad's menu popup contains options of different kinds.

In the following sections, you see an overview of each menu pad in the form of a table. Consider these tables to be reference guides to the menu options. Subsequent chapters cover use of the menus.

You also learn about various menu options whose uses may not be apparent. Where applicable, references guide you to the chapter in which these options are discussed in greater detail.

The System Menu Pad

The System menu popup shown in table 2.2 presents an eclectic group of options, the most important of which is the FoxPro Help facility. This feature provides instructions on the proper use of FoxPro's many commands and functions. The Help facility is covered in the final section of this chapter.

The System menu also contains desk accessories, such as the Filer and Calculator, and the keyboard macro utility, which enables you to save and replay keystroke sequences. Chapter 16, "Discovering Additional FoxPro Productivity Features," covers these desk accessories. Table 2.2 lists the System menu popup options.

Table 2.2 The System Menu Popup

Option	Purpose
About FoxPro...	View information about the version of FoxPro, Resource and configuration files in use, available memory and disk space, and so on
Help...	Access the FoxPro Help facility
Macros...	Create and edit keyboard macros; create, save, and restore sets of macros, including a special default set
Filer	Display file names; use such DOS file functions as Copy, Move, Delete, and Rename; search files for text strings
Calculator	Perform basic mathematical functions on-screen and store the results for pasting into a field or file
Calendar/Diary	Display a calendar for any month of any year; attach appointment and other notes to a particular date; store the date selected for use in a field or file
Special Characters	Insert graphic characters into a field or file
ASCII Chart	Display the complete ASCII character set
Capture	Mark and copy text from the screen or window to a field or alternate window
Puzzle	A FoxPro toy. Check out this game!

The File Menu Pad

The File menu popup enables you to create, open, save, and print files. File also enables you to quit FoxPro and return to DOS. Table 2.3 describes the options available on the File menu popup.

Table 2.3 The File Menu Popup

Option	Purpose
New...	Create a database, program, text, index, report, label, screen, menu, query, or project file
Open...	Open an existing database, program, view, text, index, report, label, screen, menu, query, or project file
Close	Close the active window
Save	Save a file with the current name
Save As...	Save a file with the current name or a different name; create a view file when the View window is open
Revert	Cancel all changes to the file in the current editing session
Printer Setup...	Set certain printer output options, such as the print device and page margins
Print	Print the contents of any open text window, a file, or the FoxPro Clipboard
Quit	Return to DOS

One file that you can create with the New... option is a query file. A query file contains search expressions, which you build by using the RQBE (Relational Query By Example) dialog. RQBE is a powerful searching tool. Chapters 5 and 6 cover RQBE and queries.

Notice that the Close option doesn't close a database file; Close closes the active window. If you are editing a text file in the window, the file closes as a result of your closing the window. If you made changes to the text file since you opened or last saved the file, FoxPro asks whether you want to save those changes.

Save and Save As... both save files by writing the files to the disk. Save As..., however, enables you to save the file with a different name, and on a different disk or directory. This feature is useful with files created without a specified file name (in which case, FoxPro assigns the name UNTITLED to the file). This option also is useful when you want to keep a file in original form and create a modified version. With Save As..., you can create a new file with a different name rather than replace the existing file.

Although the File popup menu contains a Print option, you usually use this option only to print straight ASCII text files, such as FoxPro programs. You print reports, labels, and other results from FoxPro tables by using the Report... and Label... options on the Database menu popup.

The Edit Menu Pad

Table 2.4 shows you the options on the Edit menu popup. In table 2.1, you see that most of these options have control-key shortcuts, which enable you to access quickly the editor's features from the keyboard. The primary purpose of the Edit pad, therefore, is to act as a reference guide for typists, and to provide mouse users with access to the editor's functions. The FoxPro editor is explored in a following section of this chapter.

Table 2.4 The Edit Menu Popup

Option	Purpose
Undo	Cancel the most recent change in a field or file
Redo	Reverse the most recent undone change
Cut	Remove text from a field or file and place the text on the Clipboard
Copy	Copy text from a field or file to the Clipboard
Paste	Insert the current contents of the Clipboard into a field or file
Clear	Delete text without placing the text on the Clipboard
Select All	Select all text in the current editing window or select the contents of a current field in a Browse or Edit window
Goto Line...	Move the cursor to a specific line number in a text file or memo field
Find...	Search a file or memo field for the first occurrence of a text string
Find Again	Find the next occurrence of the text string
Replace and Find Again	Same as Find Again, except that the located text is replaced by the replacement text entered in the Find dialog
Replace All	Replace all occurrences of a text string
Preferences	Set certain text formatting options, such as word wrap and tab spacing

Like other text editors, the FoxPro editor uses default settings, such as the number of spaces to insert into the file when you press the Tab key. You can configure the editor to use settings that are appropriate for a task through the Preferences option. You can specify that these new settings apply only to the current file or to all new files that have the same extension as the current file (for example, all files that end in .TXT).

The Database Menu Pad

The Database menu popup contains some options, such as Browse and Report..., that you use all the time and other options, such as Append From... and Copy To..., that you may use infrequently (see table 2.5). Among others, these options allow you to modify a table's structure, view and add records to a table, perform some mathematical calculations upon the data stored in the table, and permanently remove deleted records from a table.

Table 2.5 The Database Menu Popup

Option	Purpose
Setup	Set display options for the records in the current work area or modify the structure of the table
Browse	View/Edit records in the current table
Append From...	Add records to the current table from another table or from a file of a different format
Copy To...	Copy records from the current table to a new table
Sort...	Sort the records in the current table by using a specified field as the sort key
Total...	Create records in another table containing totals of numeric fields in the current table
Average...	Calculate the average of numeric fields in the current table
Count...	Calculate the number of records in the current table that meet a specified criterion

Option	Purpose
Sum...	Calculate totals of numeric fields in the current table
Calculate...	Perform financial and statistical operations on fields in the current table
Report...	Print reports by using an existing report form
Label...	Print labels by using an existing label form
Pack	Permanently remove records marked for deletion from the current table
Reindex	Re-create all open index files related to the current table

All these options work on an open table, and most of the options are therefore disabled when a table is not open in the current work area. The enabled options, such as Browse, bring up the Open File dialog so that you can select and open a table.

Browse is the real workhorse of FoxPro. If you are familiar with the limited functionality of the BROWSE command in dBASE IV or FoxBASE+, then you are in for a treat as you begin to learn the power of FoxPro's browse facility. The ways in which you can use Browse are limited only by your imagination. This remarkable FoxPro feature is covered in Chapter 8, "Organizing the Answers with BROWSE."

You use the Report and Label options to print reports and labels by using existing report and label forms. To create these forms, select the New... option from the File menu popup. Chapters 9 and 10 cover the features of reports and labels.

The Record Menu Pad

The Record menu popup enables you to perform basic database management operations—such as Add, Edit, Replace..., and Delete...—on one or more records in the current table. You also can locate a record by entering a search expression in the dialog that appears after you select Locate... or Seek.... Table 2.6 describes the various Record options.

Table 2.6 The Record Menu Popup

Option	Purpose
Append	Enable new records to be added to the current table from the keyboard
Change	Edit existing records in the current table
Goto...	Move the record pointer to another record in the table
Locate...	Find the first record that meets specified criteria
Continue	Find the next record that meets the criteria specified in the Locate command
Seek...	Use an active index file to quickly find a record
Replace...	Set the contents of one or more fields to a specified value
Delete...	Mark records for deletion at a later time
Recall...	Restore records marked for deletion to active status

Seek... uses a FoxPro index file. Indexed searches are fast (usually taking less than one second), regardless of the table's size.

Locate..., however, searches the database by scanning each record without using the active index. Although you can restrict the range of records to be scanned, search times using Locate... are proportionate to the size of the database and usually longer than Seek... search times. FoxPro's Rushmore technology, a data access technology that collects sets of records by using any of the available indexes rather than one active index, makes Locate... a better choice than Seek... under some conditions. Rushmore and the ways in which you use this technology are discussed in Chapter 7, "Querying with SQL and Searching with Rushmore."

The Seek... and Locate... options are used and discussed throughout the programs in this book.

The Program Menu Pad

The Program menu popup options listed in table 2.7 enable you to create, compile, and run programs. The Generate... option tells FoxPro to create a program by using a special screen or menu definition table that you create with the Screen Builder or Menu Builder. These tools are covered in Chapters 12, 13, and 14.

Table 2.7 The Program Menu Popup

Option	Purpose
Do...	Execute a FoxPro program
Cancel	Cancel a program paused by using the Suspend command
Resume	Resume execution of a paused program
Compile...	Create an executable version of a FoxPro program
Generate...	Create a FoxPro program from a screen or menu definition table
FoxDoc	Create technical documentation for a FoxPro program
FoxGraph...	Create two- and three-dimensional graphs from a table or database

FoxDoc is a powerful documentation tool for FoxPro programmers. After you tell FoxDoc the name of a project file or the name of the first program in the system, this tool creates formatted source code listings, a tree diagram, a variable cross-reference, and several other useful reports. Most FoxPro programmers consider FoxDoc an invaluable aid. The final section of Chapter 20, "Enhancing the Applications You Program," is devoted to FoxDoc.

The Window Menu Pad

The Window menu pad is FoxPro's window control center (see table 2.8). Besides the options shown in the following table, the Window menu popup lists the names of windows you previously defined and enables you to activate a window by selecting the window name from the menu.

Zoom↓ minimizes a window so that text and other objects aren't obscured on-screen, yet still remain visible and easily accessible.

You also can move a window out of the way by docking it. Docking and other methods of manipulating windows are covered in the following section.

Table 2.8 The Window Menu Popup

Option	Purpose
Hide	Remove the active window from the screen display
Clear	Remove all displayed text in the active window
Move	Move the active window to another position on-screen
Size	Change the size and shape of the active window
Zoom↑	Expand the active window to fill the screen
Zoom↓	Shrink the active window to its minimum size (all you can see is the title bar)
Cycle	Activate the next window in the list of defined windows
Color...	Use the FoxPro Color Picker to set the screen display colors
Command	Activate the Command window
Debug	Activate the FoxPro program debugging window
Trace	Activate the FoxPro program trace window
View	Activate the View window

The Run Menu Pad

A recent addition to the FoxPro menu bar, the Run menu pad allows you to print reports and labels quickly, create new queries and execute saved queries, and run FoxPro applications by selecting the desired file from a dialog (see table 2.9). Queries are covered in Chapters 5-7, Screens in Chapters 12 and 13, and Reports and Labels in Chapters 9 and 10. Chapter 14 discusses, in detail, building applications through the Project Manager; Chapters 18 and 19 cover the programming techniques that you use in your applications.

Table 2.9 The Run Menu Popup

Option	Purpose
New Query	Create a new query using the RQBE dialog
Query...	Run a query (.QPR) file that you previously created through the RQBE
Screen...	Run a screen (.SPR) program that you created through the Screen Builder
Report...	Run a report using a report definition (.FRX) table that you created in the Report Generator
Label...	Print labels using a label definition (.LBX) table that you created using the Label Generator
Application...	Execute a FoxPro program (.PRG, .FXP, .APP, or .EXE) file

The Run menu pad differs from the other pads in the menu bar in that it is not a native part of the menu system. A FoxPro application called FOXSTART.APP (located in the FoxPro home directory) adds the Run menu pad to the menu bar. Whenever FoxPro is loaded, it looks for a system variable named _STARTUP and executes the program whose name is stored in this system variable. By default, _STARTUP contains the fully qualified file name for FOXSTART.APP (for example: C:\FOXPRO25\FOXSTART.APP).

You can tell FoxPro not to add the Run menu pad to the menu bar by adding the configuration option _STARTUP = "" to the FoxPro configuration file, CONFIG.FP. Refer to Appendix C, "Customizing the CONFIG.FP File," for more information on using the FoxPro configuration file.

The Context-Sensitive Menu Pads

Occasionally, the menu pads that appear on the FoxPro menu bar may change. Some pads appear only when the options contained in the related menu popups are pertinent to the current screen. In addition to providing quick access to certain options, these popups also serve as a quick-reference guide to features related to the current task.

Figure 2.3 shows the FoxPro menu bar, with a Browse window open. The Browse menu popup shows you many options that add power and flexibility to the Browse editing mode. After you close the Browse window, the menu pad disappears from the menu bar.

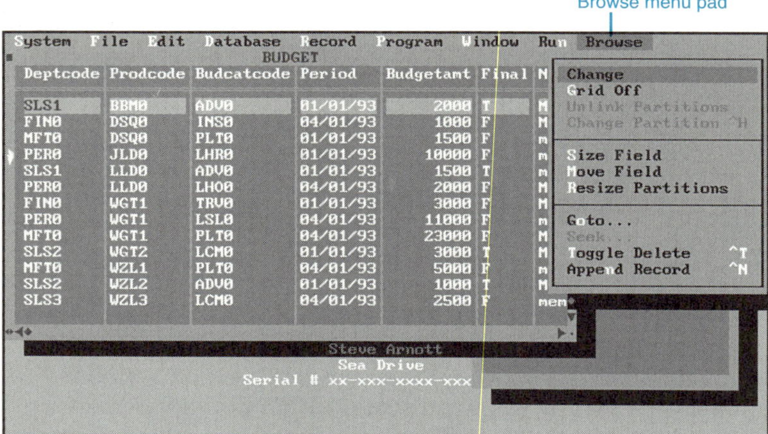

FIG. 2.3

The Browse menu popup.

In some contexts, FoxPro also eliminates some of the usual pads from the menu bar. These pads reappear when you can use them again.

Examining FoxPro Windows

You may have previously noticed that the menu popups you produce by selecting menu bar options sometimes cover up, but do not really erase other information on-screen. This condition occurs because menu popups are a special kind of FoxPro window.

Consider a window as a self-contained object. Many people find that thinking of the screen as a desktop is a good analogy, with the windows as pieces of paper or other items arranged on the desktop. You can move windows around and remove old or add new windows; you also can change a window's dimensions, contents, or other attributes without affecting the underlying desktop surface.

In this section, you learn to recognize and manipulate the various window elements and controls and to use these elements to distinguish among the different types of FoxPro windows.

Understanding the Parts of a Window

Figure 2.4 shows you a typical assortment of windows in use during a FoxPro session. As you can see, many FoxPro windows have shadows (a dark line to the bottom and the right of the window) to help you remember that these objects are separate from the screen. The windows also are surrounded by a border that serves as a visual boundary between this window and the screen and other windows that may be open.

Using the System pad on the menu bar, open the Filer and the Calculator as you learned in the preceding section. Then select New... from the File menu popup. In the dialog that appears, click the File option, or press F; then click OK, or press Ctrl+Enter. The UNTITLED text file window appears.

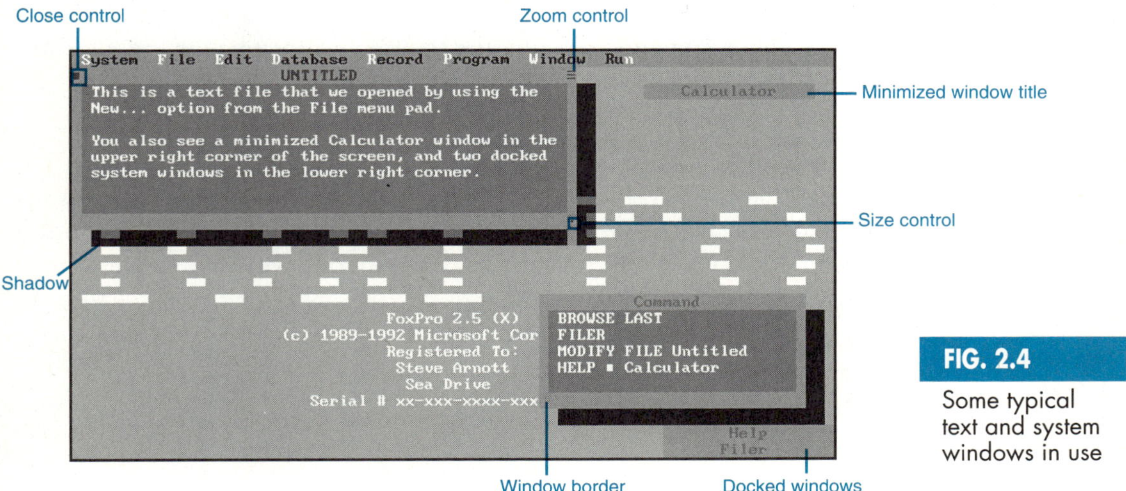

FIG. 2.4

Some typical text and system windows in use

Besides the Command window, you should now see three other windows on-screen. Each window probably appears on top of the previous window. As you activate these windows, notice that each has a title, centered in the top window border, that indicates the window's function. One window has a title differently colored or highlighted from the other windows (see fig. 2.4). This color marks the currently active, or in-use window. Only one window is active at a time. The last window you opened usually is the window on top of the stack and is active until you close it or make a new choice.

After you select the Window menu pad, you may notice that the newly opened Filer, Calculator, and UNTITLED file are added to the list of windows available. You can cycle through the available windows, making different windows active by performing one of the following procedures:

- Select the desired window from the Window menu popup (by pressing the highlighted letter in or next to the name; by using the up- and down-arrow keys to move the highlight bar to the desired name and then pressing Enter; or by clicking the name with the mouse).
- Select Cycle from the Window menu popup.
- Click directly the window that you want to activate with the mouse.
- Press Ctrl+F1 to move between the windows until you activate the window you want.

Try the different window-activation techniques by using the mouse and the keyboard in different combinations. You may find clicking the Window menu pad and selecting the window by highlighted letter a more natural way to perform this procedure, or you may prefer to select the Window menu pad by using Alt+W and then clicking the window name. Sometimes, you might prefer clicking directly on the window you want to activate, but in other situations, such as when the screen is crowded, you may use Ctrl+F1 to bring windows forward until you see the desired window.

You can make the Command window active by using a special keyboard shortcut. Press Ctrl+F2 at any time to bring forward the Command window.

Controlling the Window

You can do more with windows than simply open them and cycle among them. You also can move, size, hide, zoom, and dock windows. In this section, you learn to use menu options and special window elements to control the windows that appear on the FoxPro desktop.

Manipulating Windows

Using any of the techniques discussed above, activate the Filer. You see that the Filer provides many options for file management that you may want to keep readily available, even if you don't want the Filer cluttering the screen. An easy way to set up this kind of screen is to minimize the window so that the Filer remains on-screen but uses little space. Minimize the Filer now by performing one of the following actions:

- With the mouse, double-click the top border near the Filer title.
- From the Window menu popup, choose the Zoom↓ option.
- Press Ctrl+F9.

You bring the Filer back to the normal size by repeating one of the preceding actions.

You may prefer to keep the Filer on the desktop, either minimized or normal size, but want the menu out of the way to make room to edit the UNTITLED text file. You can move a window by performing one of the following actions:

- With the mouse, drag (press and hold down the mouse button as you move the mouse) the window's or box's top border.
- Activate the window, and then choose the Move option from the Window menu popup.
- Activate the window, and then press Ctrl+F7.

If you are moving a window by using the keyboard, the border flashes (blinks on and off), and you can press the up-, down-, left-, and right-arrow keys until the window is in the preferred position. Press Enter to end the move.

FoxPro uses a special technique, called *docking,* to minimize and push a window out of the way at the same time. When you dock a window, you stow the window neatly in minimized size in the lower-right corner of the screen. Figure 2.4 shows two docked system windows. If you dock more than one window, the windows stack in a vertical pile. You dock a window by double-clicking the window title while holding down the Shift key, or by pressing Shift+Ctrl+F9.

You just learned an important and consistent FoxPro interface principle. Adding a Shift key to the mouse click and to the keypress (where a keyboard equivalent exists) are equivalent actions.

FoxPro often uses the space bar to imitate a mouse click to select items, such as currently highlighted menu popup options. Wherever a double-click or a Shift-click enables you to perform an additional action, you can perform the same action with a double space bar or a Shift+space bar keypress.

To make a window consistently appear in a specific part of the screen, minimize and move the window to the desired position. The next time you minimize this window, the window moves to the selected position.

Using Window Controls

Activate the Command window. You see that, besides a differently colored title, an active window may have extra elements in the border, usually referred to as *controls.* These controls enable convenient window manipulation for mouse users.

The bottom border contains a small triangle facing left at the left corner, another triangle facing right at the right corner, and a diamond on the border between the two triangles. These three items make up a window's scroll bar. These characters indicate that you can move to the left and to the right to see more information in the window. The scroll bar at the bottom of the window is called the *horizontal scroll bar.* A window also may have a *vertical scroll bar* along the right border, which indicates that you can scroll up and down to see more information in the window.

You use the scroll bars by clicking with the mouse on either triangle to scroll smoothly through the window. Notice that the diamond (referred to here as the scroll bar's *thumb*) moves to provide a rough indication of the current position in the window, relative to the width or height of the information list. You also can click any point of the scroll bar or drag the thumb, which changes your relative position with rapid jumps.

You cannot activate the scroll bars directly from the keyboard, but all windows that show a vertical scroll bar enable you to move rapidly through the window contents by using the PgUp and PgDn keys. You also can move to the beginning or end of a file in a window that contains text by using the Ctrl+Home or Ctrl+End key combination.

Considering Other Window Controls and Options

The Command window border contains a few more controls that you need to recognize and learn to use. In the upper-right corner of the border, for example, is a small box composed of three horizontal lines (≡), which is the window's zoom control. Clicking the zoom control enables you to make the currently active window fill all the space available on-screen. This feature is useful for editing text on a full screen. Clicking the zoom control again returns the window to its original size.

You also can zoom a window to full screen size from the Window menu popup by using the Zoom↑ option, or by pressing Ctrl+F10. You can return a window to its previous size by repeating the action.

To change a window to a size other than the FoxPro default size (not a full-screen window), you can use the control that appears as a small dot (•) in the lower-right corner of the border. This control enables you to size the window any way you want. With the mouse, drag the control to stretch or shrink the window. Alternatively, you can size a window from the Window menu popup by using the Size option, or by pressing Ctrl+F8. After you take either step, the border flashes, and you can use the arrow keys to size the window, as you did when you moved the window. The cursor temporarily disappears while the arrow keys assume the sizing or moving function. When you finish resizing the window, press Enter.

An important difference exists between zooming a window and resizing a window. By storing information in the Resource file, FoxPro can remember a custom size that you give as a window's new default size. The FoxPro Resource file (discussed in Chapter 16), holds many other personal preferences besides window positions. Consider this file as the way FoxPro arranges the screen to suit your work habits. Zooming a window doesn't affect FoxPro's default size for this window.

Activate the Calculator window and notice the solid square control (■) in the upper-left corner of the border. This symbol is the close control. You can click this control to close a window, or you can choose the equivalent Close option from the File menu popup. After activating each window in turn, try both methods to close the Calculator and Filer windows. You also can close these windows by pressing Esc. Note that you can activate or close a minimized or docked window.

You also can hide a window by Shift-clicking the close control. Make the Filer window active and try this procedure. Alternatively, you can hide a window with the Hide option on the Window menu popup. You still can activate a hidden window for use even when the window is hidden. Choose the window from the current Window menu popup list, and the window reappears.

Activate the UNTITLED text file window now. Type your name in the window. Practice changing the size and hiding the window. Now bring back and try to close the window by using any of the preceding methods.

If you typed your name (or anything else) in the text file window before trying to close the window, you see a new kind of window with a message, as shown in figure 2.5. (The buttons in the figure appear only after the Esc key is pressed to close a text file after you make changes.)

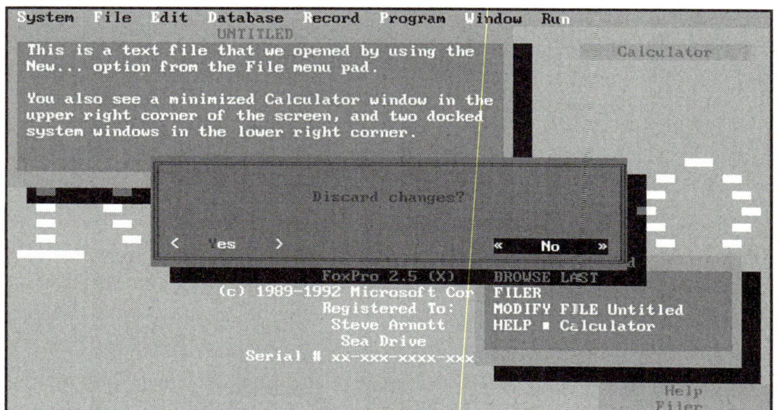

FIG. 2.5

A sample Alert with prompt and buttons.

Working with Different Window Types

The Alert box, although asking for information and a response, looks different from the dialog that opens a new file. The Alert uses different colors or intensities. FoxPro uses Alerts to tell you that something may be wrong. The preceding Alert wants to know whether you mean to save the information you typed to a text file before closing the window; if you do not save these changes, the information is lost. FoxPro asks a question, known as a *prompt* or message, and enables you to make responses by clicking buttons.

Depending on the method you use to try to close the text file window, the Alert may display a prompt or choices different from those in figure 2.5. Responding to an Alert, however, is similar in each case: like buttons on a physical machine, these buttons offer choices. You must press one button to signify your intent. You press a button by clicking it with the mouse, or by using the Tab key to move the highlight to the button and pressing Enter. You also have a default button, usually indicating the safest choice you can make, which you can choose by pressing Enter or Ctrl+Enter when you see the Alert. The default button is surrounded by *chevrons* (« »)—for example, «No». By pressing Esc, you can cancel the process that brought about the Alert.

TIP

FoxPro offers keyboard shortcuts that in one step close the window and save all the work in the window. Press either Ctrl+W or Ctrl+Enter to close and save. Refer to Appendix E and table 2.1 for more information on key combinations that close a window.

Not every Alert requires you to make a choice. You see an error message from FoxPro when you type a command in the Command window that FoxPro doesn't understand. Try activating the Command window, typing your name, and pressing Enter to see this kind of Alert message. This message requires that you read the message only, which you then remove by pressing any key that usually produces on-screen characters (Shift, Ctrl, CapsLock, and other keys that produce no output don't work), or by clicking the mouse anywhere on-screen.

Not all messages that FoxPro gives you are warnings. FoxPro has a special kind of dialog that contains informational messages or instructions that require minimal response. These items usually appear in a small window in the upper-right corner of the screen and look entirely different from Alerts. Again, by pressing any key, you can remove this kind of window after you read the contents.

To see an informational message window, activate the Command window, type `DISPLAY MEMORY`, and press Enter. FoxPro prompts you to `Press any key to continue` in a small message window which provides a pause so that you can read each screen of information.

You cannot resize Alerts, dialogs, other message windows, and some windows with special contents, such as the Filer. You can move those windows, however, by using normal methods. (You may want to move an Alert to examine a window or other object on-screen that is beneath the obscuring item before you answer the prompt.) Try moving an Alert, message window, or dialog by dragging the top border, or by pressing Ctrl+F7. Although these borders appear different from other window borders, the borders respond normally. You cannot specify new default positions, however, by moving dialogs and Alerts (when these items next appear, they return to the original position). To momentarily check the screen beneath all the open windows, such as when checking the memory display you just called on-screen, press the Ctrl, Shift, and Alt keys together. As long as you hold down this key combination, all open windows—even the menu bar—remain hidden.

Learning about More Window Options

You may want to tidy the screen after displaying memory variables on-screen or (as in an upcoming chapter, after you learn to direct FoxPro's output) in a window. Choose the Clear option from the Window menu popup, and the information disappears from the screen.

If you hold down the Shift key while you use either the mouse or the keyboard to select the Window menu pad, you see a subtle change in the options in the Window menu popup. The Hide option now reads Hide All, and the Clear item changes to Show All. (You cannot select both items at the same time.) This step is another effective way to banish clutter from the screen and yet keep working objects within easy reach.

You have yet another way in which you can affect the appearance of FoxPro windows: you can change window and object colors. Although you more fully investigate methods for changing the colors of FoxPro interface elements in a following chapter, you can immediately change the colors of all standard interface elements (if, for example, the present combination appears unpleasant or difficult to read on some hardware). Even if you use a monochrome monitor and video card, you may want to vary intensities to make certain elements more legible.

Choose the Color... option from the Window menu popup, and a special dialog, the Color Picker, appears. In the upper-right corner is a special popup control; pushing this kind of button makes a list of choices appear. Click this button with the mouse, or press the Tab key until the button is highlighted and then press Enter. A list of screen objects pops up, as shown in figure 2.6.

You see several kinds of interface objects that you may recognize, such as Alerts and dialogs. Select an object that you know by clicking it with the mouse, or by moving the highlight in the popup to the object and pressing Enter or the space bar while the object is highlighted. The popup closes, and the chosen object's name appears on the popup control.

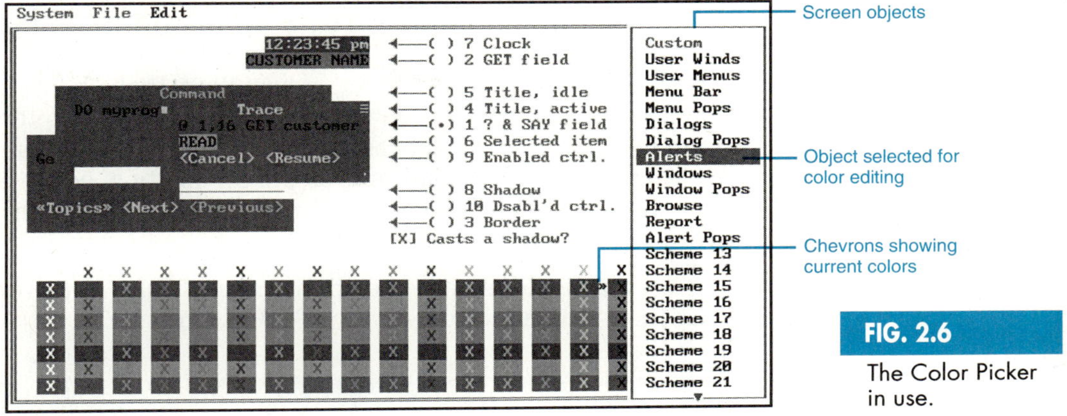

FIG. 2.6

The Color Picker in use.

A bullet (•) marks the object's element for which you are selecting colors (hot keys, text box, and the like), and the grid of color pairs includes one item marked with chevrons (» «) to indicate the current colors for the element.

From the keyboard, use the Tab key to move the highlight to the currently selected item, Normal text, and press the space bar. The chevrons blink, and you can use the arrow keys to move the selection to a new color pair. As you move among the pairs, watch in the sample window as the normal text sample changes colors. Pick new colors for normal text in this object by pressing the space bar or Enter.

You can more easily change an object element's colors with the mouse. Click the Normal text item, and then click the desired color pair. (The chevrons move to your selected color pair, but they don't blink.)

When the colors are set the way you want them, choose OK to register your changes (which will not be permanent). Call up a new instance of this kind of object in the interface. You see your new color selections reflected in the new dialog or Alert window that appears.

The new color selections remain in effect for this kind of object until you change them again or until you quit FoxPro. To save the selections more permanently, read the "FoxPro Color Control" section of Chapter 15.

Putting System Windows in Perspective

So far, the windows you have examined are windows that FoxPro creates internally and produces when needed. In following chapters, you learn to design windows that can have the same attributes as windows designed by the system, such as the capability of being moved, having a particular border style, or a window definition that includes any combination of these attributes.

Table 2.10 is a quick reference to the options available for both system-defined and user-defined windows in the FoxPro interface.

Table 2.10 Window Manipulation

Window Action	Menu Item	Key Shortcut	Mouse Method
Open a window	Various System menu pad options, Open dialog on the File menu popup	None	None
Cycle between windows	Cycle option of Window menu pad	Ctrl+F1 (Ctrl+F2 for Command window)	Click inside the window that you want to activate
Minimize a window	Zoom↓ on Window menu popup	Ctrl+F9	Double-click the top window border
Move a window	Move on Window menu popup	Ctrl+F7	Drag on top border
Dock a window	None	Shift+Ctrl+F9	Shift, double-click top border
Move quickly through window contents	None	PgDn, PgUp, Ctrl+End, and Ctrl+Home in window border	Scroll bars on bottom and right of text
Zoom to full-size	Zoom↑ on Window menu popup	Ctrl+F10	Zoom control on right corner of border
Size a window	Size on Window menu popup	Ctrl+F8	Size control on lower-right corner
Close a window	Close on File menu popup	Ctrl+W or Ctrl+Enter to save contents; Esc or Ctrl+Q to cancel last changes	Close control on upper-left corner

Window Action	Menu Item	Key Shortcut	Mouse Method
Close all windows	Close All on Shifted File menu popup	None	None
Hide a window	Hide on Window menu popup	None	None
Clear output from a window	Clear on Window menu popup	None	None
Hide all windows	Hide All on shifted Window menu popup	Ctrl+Shift+Alt (temporary)	None
Show all windows	Show All on shifted Window menu popup	None	None
Change window or window element colors	Color... on Window menu popup	None	None

Understanding Dialog Logic

A *dialog* is a special kind of FoxPro window that gathers information needed to complete a FoxPro command or expression. The box appears whenever you select a menu option followed by an ellipsis (...). Dialogs are visually distinguished from other kinds of windows by a double-line border and the special objects they contain. While in a dialog, you must finish one or more tasks before you can go to other options.

In this section, you learn to recognize the various components of a dialog and how to use a dialog to complete menu selections.

Identifying the Components of a Dialog

Dialogs consist of *control objects* that enable you to specify, confirm, and cancel actions. Each object has a different appearance, which provides a visual clue as to the function of the dialog.

The FoxPro Report dialog shown in figure 2.7 contains four kinds of objects: check boxes, radio buttons, push buttons, and text boxes.

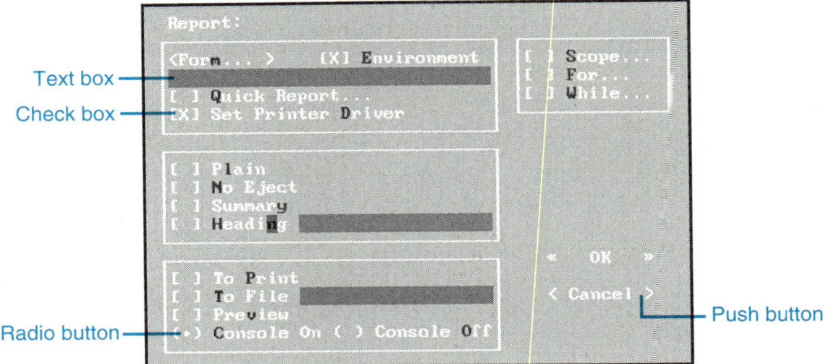

FIG. 2.7

The FoxPro Report dialog.

Check Boxes

A check box appears as a pair of square brackets followed by text. The text describes what happens if you check the box. A check box that is checked, or marked, shows an X between the brackets.

Check boxes enable you to turn on or off different options. Selecting a check box is like flipping a light switch. An option that is *on* is turned *off,* and vice versa.

Related check boxes are usually grouped together in a box drawn with a single solid line. Although related, each check box is a separate object. You can mark more than one check box in a group at the same time, and marking one box usually has no effect on the other boxes. A check box may become disabled, however, if another check box with which this option is incompatible is marked.

Radio Buttons

A radio button appears as a pair of parentheses followed by text. Radio buttons always come in groups of two or more. The selected button appears with a bullet (•) between parentheses.

Radio buttons enable you to choose among several related options. Unlike a group of check boxes, a group of radio buttons forms a single FoxPro object. Because only one radio button in the group may be marked at a time, each radio button responds to actions performed on the other buttons in the group. When you change a selection from one button in a group to another button, the selected symbol (•) moves from the old button to the new button.

Push Buttons

A push button appears as text enclosed by angle brackets (< >). A push button always triggers an action. If the text is followed by an ellipsis (...), another dialog appears after the push button is chosen. Most dialogs contain at least two push buttons, `OK` and `Cancel`.

Every dialog has one push button enclosed in chevrons. This button is the default action button. You can trigger the default action from the keyboard by holding down the Ctrl key and pressing Enter.

If the default action push button is disabled, you haven't provided FoxPro with at least one item of information, such as a file name, that the program needs to complete the command or expression.

Text Boxes

Text boxes enable you to enter text from the keyboard. These items usually appear in conjunction with another dialog object, such as a check box, to provide information that cannot be obtained through the menus or that is easier to specify directly, such as the name of an output report file.

Note that, although a text box may appear a certain width, you can type past the right edge of the box; the text scrolls to the left as you type.

Scrollable Lists

When FoxPro needs the name of a file or database field, the program presents you with a list. If the list contains more entries than can be displayed on-screen, you can scroll the list to bring the other entries into view. Scrollable lists contain up and down arrowheads and a diamond-shaped scroll bar to the right of the list. If you have a mouse, you can use these controls to quickly scroll through the list. At the top of a list of file names, for example, you see one or more items enclosed in square brackets. These items are the names of directories on the disk. The double period object (..) is a DOS convention that enables you to move up one level in the directory tree. The other directory names shown, if any, are subdirectories one level below the current directory. If you select a new directory name, the list changes to display the files in that directory.

You can select an item from the list by using the arrow keys to highlight the item name and then pressing Enter, or by double-clicking the name with the mouse.

Popup Controls

Popup controls appear as boxes drawn with a single line across the top and left sides of the box and a double line across its bottom and the right sides. You use popup controls to change the items shown in a list that appears when you select the control. This list is similar to menu popups, and you move through the options in the same way.

The popup controls shown in figure 2.8 enable you to change the drive, directory, and file type from which a list of files is constructed. In other dialogs, a Database popup control enables you to select a table from which to select a field.

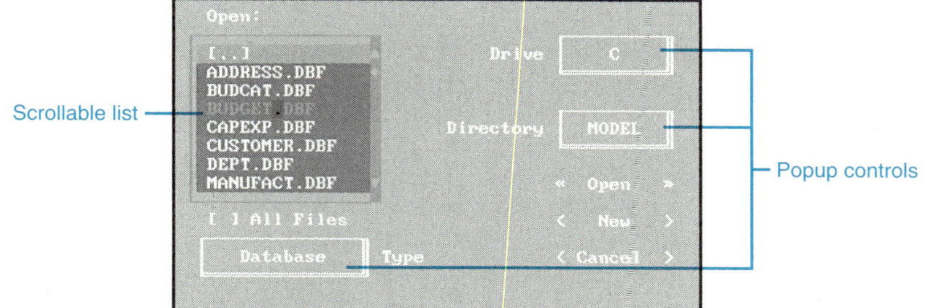

FIG. 2.8

The Open File dialog.

Using a Dialog and Confirming Choices

From the keyboard, you use the Tab key to move to the next object and Shift+Tab to move to the preceding object. When the highlight bar rests on the last object in the dialog, Tab takes you back to the first object. When the highlight bar is on the first object, Shift+Tab moves the highlight bar to the last object.

A mouse makes a big difference when you work with dialogs. Just position the mouse cursor on an object and click the left button to select the object. If you spend a great deal of time using dialogs, a mouse saves you both time and frustration. If you do not have a mouse, many dialog control objects have highlighted hot keys you can use from the keyboard, just as the menu popups do. After you activate the list, you also can move through lists by typing the initial letters of the choice.

TIP

The highlighted hot keys help you move from object to object. After you select an object that requires further typing (whether a box that accepts text or a list or menu popup that accepts characters to move through the choices), the hot keys are disabled so that typing isn't interrupted.

After you set up the dialog options, you tell FoxPro that you're finished by selecting the default push button, which is usually `OK`. You can select this button from the keyboard by using the Tab key or Shift+Tab key combination to highlight the button and then pressing Enter. Of course, you also can click the button with the mouse. If you decide to cancel the operation, press Esc or click `Cancel`. No matter where the highlight is in a dialog, you also can press Ctrl+Enter to activate the default closing option.

Editing Keystrokes and Mouse Movement

Until now, you have done little typing in FoxPro except to select menu options; and if you are using a mouse, you may not even have used the keyboard much for that procedure.

Entering text is an important part of database management. You type commands, express calculations, enter data, phrase queries, answer dialog questions, and write programs—all by entering text. Throughout this process, you use an *editor* (or you use certain consistent shortcuts to modify and manipulate the text as you enter the information). As usual in FoxPro, the editor's features are available to both mouse and keyboard users.

In FoxPro, editing shortcuts remain the same no matter what kind of text you are entering, although a few features differ slightly in different text-editing situations. In this section, you practice with FoxPro's editor in a text file that can contain any kind of notes, but remember that you soon can make good use of the same features in the Command window and during data entry.

Creating, Opening, and Saving a File

First, create a text file for editing practice. You previously used the File menu popup's New... option to open an UNTITLED text file. If the file is not still open, reopen it. With this text file as the active window, type your name.

File New... always opens a window that you see on-screen and is titled UNTITLED. In most cases, File New... also shows a default file extension. If you choose to create a new label, for example, the Label Designer window that appears is titled UNTITLED.LBX. (Default file extensions for different kinds of files are available from the on-line Help system discussed in a following section of this chapter.)

Try to close this editing window now by using the Close option on the File menu popup, or by clicking the window's close control. Because you made changes to the file, an Alert asks whether you want to save your changes before closing the file. Choose to save the changes, and the File Save dialog appears. You can access this dialog directly (without seeing the Alert) if you try to close the window by using the Save or Save As... menu options or by using any appropriate keyboard shortcuts previously described in this chapter.

Because this file was created with the New... option, FoxPro asks you to name the new file. You can assign any valid DOS file name and choose another file extension (if you want), and the dialog enables you to place the file in any drive or directory on your disk. Use the popup controls and the scrolling list described previously to choose the drive where the FoxPro files are located (here, use the default) and the MODEL directory. Type the file name `MODEL.TXT` (capitalization does not matter).

Because you saved the file after you initiated the close action, FoxPro now closes the file. You need to retrieve it, however, to practice a few more procedures.

Any previously created file is available with the File menu popup's Open... option. A dialog asks you to specify the kind of file for which you are looking and enables you to search through the drives and directory to find the file. (If you assigned a file extension that doesn't appear by default for this kind of file, use the All Files check box to make the file appear in the scrolling list.) Notice that, in figure 2.9, a file currently open appears in different colors, or different intensity, to indicate that the file is open and cannot be selected.

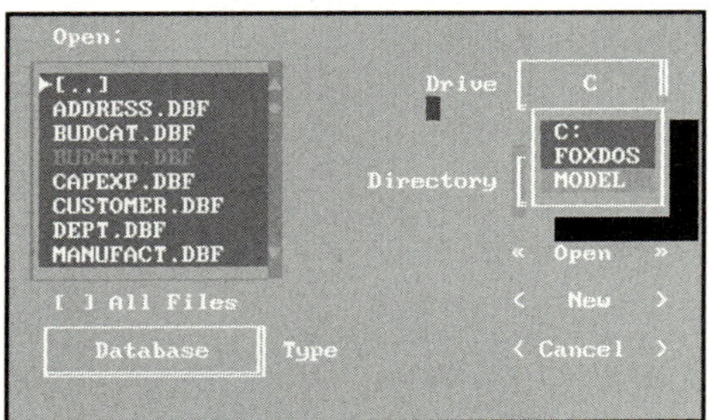

FIG. 2.9

The File Open dialog.

Practice opening and saving this file by using different interface techniques. You can save the same information under several different names (by using the File Save As... option to bring up the file-naming dialog you previously saw) and open several windows at once.

The FoxPro editor is flexible in the amount of text it can handle. The only real limits on the size of a file that you can edit, or on the number of items you can edit in different windows simultaneously, are imposed by the system configuration and available memory.

Like the editing techniques you learn in this chapter, this process of opening and saving files remains consistent for all kinds of FoxPro files. You select a different file type in the File New or Open dialogs. When you save a file, the file is saved in the appropriate format.

Moving through and Editing Text

If you already know another editing or word processing program, you may feel comfortable navigating in the FoxPro editor. Table 2.11 provides a handy reference for moving the cursor through the text.

Table 2.11 Cursor-Movement Reference Table

Move Cursor	Menu Item	Key Method	Mouse Method
One character	See note*	Right-, left-arrow keys	See note**
One word		Ctrl+right-, left-arrow keys	
One line		Up-, down-arrow keys	
One window		PgUp, PgDn	
Beginning of line		Home	
End of line		End	
Beginning of file		Ctrl+Home	
End of file		Ctrl+End	

* *The Edit menu popup has several items that enable you to move to any position in the file by searching for text. The menu popup also contains a Goto Line... option that enables you to move rapidly through the file in some situations.*

** *Mouse movement of the cursor to any position in the text is simple: click the mouse where you want the cursor to appear. You also can use the mouse to move rapidly through the text by using the scroll bars.*

With the MODEL.TXT text window active, and by using any technique in the preceding chart, move the cursor to the end of your name and type a few sentences describing yourself (without pressing Enter). Notice that the text *wraps* in the window (words too long to fit at the right margin of the first line jump down to the next line). Resize the text window and watch the word-wrapping feature change line lengths when the amount of room available changes.

The FoxPro editor defaults to inserting, rather than overwriting, text and uses a single line (_) as the cursor shape in Insert mode. Use the arrow keys to move the cursor between the first and last names. Type a middle name and note that the text to the right moves to the right to make room. Now press the Insert key; a solid block cursor (█) appears. Use the arrow keys to return the cursor to the first letter of your middle name and give yourself a new middle name by typing over the one you just typed.

Press the Backspace key, and you delete the characters to the left of the cursor (erasing your new middle name). You can press Ctrl+Backspace to erase the whole word at one time. Press the Delete key to delete a character directly under the cursor, moving characters on the right to the left to fill the gap created by the deletion. Pressing the Delete key repeatedly therefore erases characters to the right of the cursor.

Move the cursor to the end of your name. Press Insert (if you haven't already put the editor back into Insert mode) and insert a carriage return after your name by pressing Enter. Now, resize the text window; the first two lines don't flow together regardless of the space available. The word-wrap feature recognizes carriage returns that you enter so that you can press Enter to separate paragraphs and make sections of text distinct from one another.

Now that you know how to type and move around in the text, you can learn to select or mark sections of text of various lengths. Selected or highlighted text appears in a different color or intensity. You then can edit selected text by using the techniques described in this section. These techniques are summarized in table 2.12.

You select text from the keyboard by using the same cursor movements mentioned previously, but here you add the Shift key. With the mouse, place the cursor at the beginning of a text block that you want to mark; then hold down the Shift key and click at the end of the block. Alternatively, drag from the beginning of the block to its end. Both selection methods mark all the text between the original and new cursor positions.

Some other tricks are available for text selection with the mouse. You find these techniques listed in table 2.12.

If you type while text is selected, you replace the selected text (delete the selected text). Pressing the Delete, Enter, or Backspace key also deletes selected text. You can unselect text by moving the cursor.

A special kind of text removal, known as *cutting,* eliminates selected text from the current position, but instead of simply deleting the text, cutting also stores the cut text in memory. Press Ctrl+X to cut text. You can then paste the text (by pressing Ctrl+V) to another position in the same file or to another file you are editing in a different window.

You also can copy a selected block of text (by pressing Ctrl+C). This step does not change the selected block, but makes the same text available for pasting in another or multiple locations. Keep in mind that you also can select Cut, Copy, and Paste from the Edit menu popup.

> **CAUTION:** After cutting or copying a text selection, FoxPro stores this text in a system memory variable known as _CLIPTEXT, which is FoxPro's Clipboard. Only one selection can be present in _CLIPTEXT at a time (only one Clipboard is available). When you cut or copy a new selection, you replace the data contained in _CLIPTEXT with new material. Variables are explained in Chapter 16, which covers program structure, although you use these variables in earlier chapters. System variables are locations in memory that hold values that FoxPro uses for special purposes. FoxPro creates these variables without your intervention. You saw these system variables listed when you used the DISPLAY MEMORY command in a previous section of this chapter.

If you make a mistake when you delete or cut text, or regret an editing action, FoxPro's editor has an almost unlimited memory for past editing actions. You can undo and redo these mistakes with Ctrl+Z and Ctrl+R, respectively.

Table 2.12 Editing Techniques

Editing Action	Menu Item	Key Method	Mouse Method
Select Text, any length, from current position to new cursor position	None	Shift+editing keys from Cursor-Movement Table continuing to move the cursor while holding down the Shift key continues to change the length of the selection until another action is performed	Drag or Shift-click anywhere to select from cursor position to place you clicked
Select a word at a time	None	See above	Double-click (drag for additional whole words)
Select a line at a time	None	See above	Triple-click (drag for additional whole lines)

Editing Action	Menu Item	Key Method	Mouse Method
Unselect whole selection	None	Any key from Cursor-Movement Table	Click outside selected text
Select All Text	Select All on Edit menu popup	Ctrl+A	None
Delete text (and to the right)	None	Delete key	None
Delete text to the left	None	Backspace key	None
Delete selected text	None	Delete, Backspace, Enter, or type any text	None
Cut selected text	Cut on Edit menu popup	Ctrl+X	None
Copy selected text	Copy on Edit menu popup	Ctrl+C	None
Paste selected text	Paste on Edit menu popup	Ctrl+V	None
Undo last edit action	Undo on Edit menu popup	Ctrl+Z	None
Redo last "Undone" edit action	Redo on Edit menu popup	Ctrl+R	None

Searching for Text

One of the most productive techniques available in any text editor is the capability of finding and replacing specific text. Searching for text enables you to move instantly to any phrase or symbol in the text. If you specify a replacement phrase, you can change any or all instances of the search text.

Use Ctrl+F, or the Find... option on the Edit menu popup to activate the appropriate FoxPro dialog. As you see in figure 2.10, this dialog enables you to specify search and replace text and also the following options:

- Whether a search is case-sensitive (should *Edit* in the search phrase find *edit* in the text?)

- Whether the search text must match a *whole word* in the text (should *and* in the search phrase find *understand* in the text?)
- Whether the search goes forward or backward from the current cursor position in the file
- Whether the search should end or wrap around when the beginning or the end of a file is reached

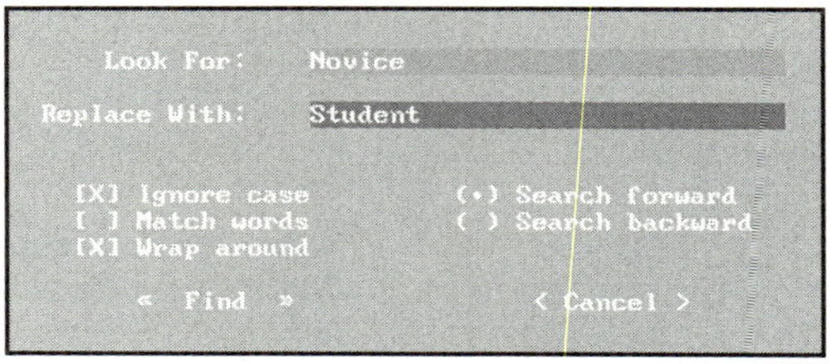

Look For: Novice
Replace With: Student
[X] Ignore case (•) Search forward
[ ] Match words ( ) Search backward
[X] Wrap around
« Find » < Cancel >

FIG. 2.10

The Find and Replace dialog with a search phrase highlighted.

After the search phrase is found, FoxPro marks the phrase in the text. Then you can press Ctrl+G to find the next incidence (the Edit Find Again option), replace the selected text by using Ctrl+E and move to the next incidence (the Edit Replace and Find Again option), or just continue editing from that point in the text. You even can use the Edit Replace All option to find and replace all occurrences of the search phrase in the text at one time. (If you perform a Replace or Replace All with no replacement text specified, the search phrase is deleted.)

Notice, in figure 2.10, that the search phrase is highlighted. As is common in FoxPro dialogs, if an item where you need to type contains text when you move into the dialog, the text is selected. Dialogs obey the editing rules just as other text entry situations do; if you start typing immediately when text is selected, you overwrite the old entry. If you use the arrow keys, the text becomes unselected for editing. You can reselect the text with Ctrl+A or paste in a previously copied phrase.

Try the selecting and searching techniques with the MODEL.TXT file. Under your name, type `FoxPro Novice`. Select the word *Novice* by any of the available methods and then press Ctrl+C to copy the word. Use any cursor-movement technique so that Novice is no longer selected. Press Ctrl+F to bring up the Find dialog and press Ctrl+V to copy the word Novice into the Look For text box. Choose a description of yourself and type this description as a replacement phrase. Confirm the choice and you return to the MODEL.TXT window with Novice highlighted. Press Ctrl+E, and the replacement phrase replaces *Novice*. A bell rings, and a small message window informs you that the search phrase cannot be found again.

Searching for and Typing Special Characters

You may often want to use special graphics characters and search in the text for these characters or nonprinting characters. You may want to use a graphics border around some text, for example, or search for the first incidence of a carriage return in the text. FoxPro provides methods for finding or using special characters.

By using one of the following FoxPro methods, you can easily search for nonprinting characters that you commonly use in text entry:

- Type `\r` to search for a carriage return
- Type `\n` to search for a line feed
- Type `\t` to search for a tab character
- Type `\f` to search for a form feed character

(Because the backslash is used to indicate the special nature of the character that follows, you must type `\\` to search for the backslash.)

Like many other editing programs and word processors, FoxPro enables you to type other special characters by combining the Alt key with the character's *ASCII value,* which you enter by using the separate numeric keypad on the keyboard and not the numbers that form part of the standard typewriter keyboard. ASCII is a code used by computers to represent text. You can use each character that is assigned a unique numeric value in the ASCII system. You enter the small graphics triangle (◄) used in figure 2.11 by holding down the Alt key while typing `17` on the numeric keypad. After you release the Alt key, the character appears at the cursor position. You can choose the ASCII Chart from the System menu popup to look up the ASCII value of characters (see fig. 2.11). You also can insert an ASCII character into a text-editing window by highlighting the desired character in the ASCII Chart and then pressing Enter, or by double-clicking the desired character.

Notice that in the ASCII Chart shown in figure 2.11, the same graphics character also can be expressed as a control character, and this procedure is often easier to remember than the ASCII value. In the chart, the control character is written as ^Q, which you usually type by pressing the key combination Ctrl+Q. Because, however, many control characters (including this example) are used with special meanings in FoxPro, the editor provides a method to enable you to type these characters. Type a left-single quote (‘) followed by the character (here, `Q`). Because of the special use of the ‘ character (similar to that of the backslash), you must type the character twice to enter a left-single quote.

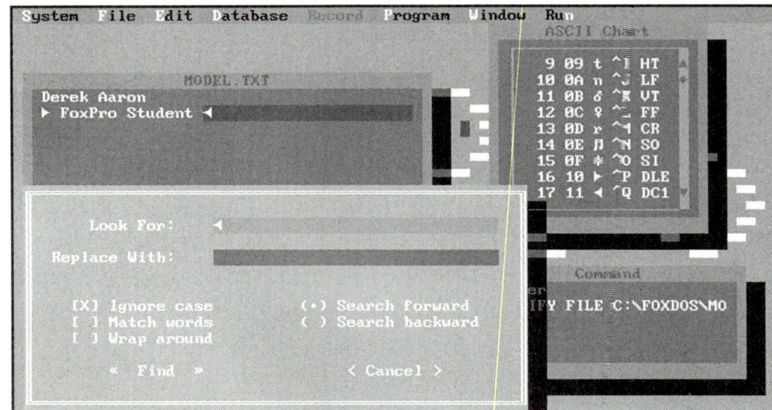

FIG. 2.11

The ASCII Chart helps you type special characters.

In a following section, "Using the FoxPro Help System," you find a quick use for typing some graphics characters.

Editing Options and the Edit Preferences Dialog

Until now, you were editing a text file with all the editor's default settings, but you can alter many of these features by using the Edit menu popup's Preference selections (see fig. 2.12).

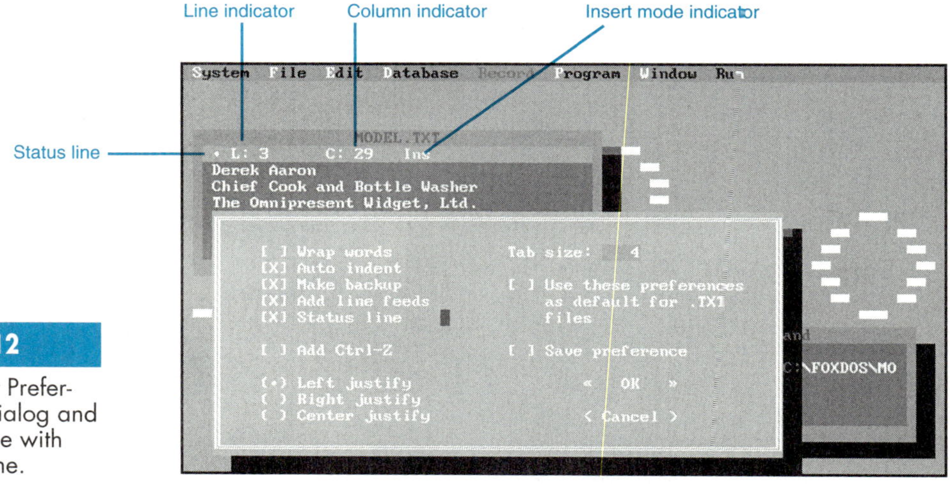

FIG. 2.12

The Edit Preferences dialog and a text file with status line.

Many settings are self-explanatory. You can tell Tabs to indent the text a number of spaces other than the default of 4, and you can turn off the word-wrap feature. You also can turn off the feature that backs up files by copying the last version of the file to another file name with a .BAK extension.

NOTE When the Wrap Words and Auto Indent check boxes are both marked (the default for text file editing), you can indent a whole paragraph by altering the position of the first character in the first line (by adding spaces or a tab, or by removing spaces or tabs with a Backspace). If you begin a paragraph with a number (for example, to write an outline) or other text followed by a tab, the wrapped paragraph is aligned with the text following the tab.

Mark the Status Line check box and return to the text file. You see a new line added to the text-editing window, as shown in figure 2.12. If you changed the file since the last save, a bullet (•) appears in the corner of the status line to remind you these changes aren't yet saved to disk. The C: followed by a number tells you the cursor's current screen *column* position (characters across, counted from the left), and Ins or Over tells you whether you are in Insert or Overwrite mode. If you turn off Wrap Words, as you do to write programs, an L: followed by a number tells you the cursor's position counted in lines from the top of the text (or *rows*, as FoxPro usually calls on-screen lines). After you turn off Wrap Words, you also can use the Goto Line... option on the Edit menu to move quickly to any line number.

The Edit Preferences dialog enables you to store all combinations of these features. You can make this feature set available for the current file only (by marking Save preference and confirming the dialog choices in the standard way) or for all files that you create or open with the same extension (by marking both Save preference and Use these preferences as defaults for .TXT files before confirming the choices).

If you are comfortable in another text editor or word processor now, you may be accustomed to different sets of keystrokes to accomplish many editing tasks. Or you may have some tasks that you do over and over for which the FoxPro editor has no shortcuts. In either case, you can further customize the editor by using *macros.* Macros assign sequences of keystrokes, including the editing keystrokes you learned about in this section, to a key combination that you can remember and use easily. You learn about macros in Chapter 16.

Typing Command Instructions

Besides selecting options from menus, you also can execute FoxPro commands by typing in the Command window. If you haven't used a command language before, you may feel a little intimidated at first.

Few commands you enter can harm the data, and FoxPro usually gives you a chance to cancel an action that results in the permanent loss of data, such as removing deleted records or overwriting a file. Be aware, however, that a way exists to tell FoxPro that you're sure you know what you're doing, and you don't want to be prompted to confirm actions. You do this by typing `SET SAFETY OFF` in the Command window, or by including this command in a program and then running the program. The default value for the SAFETY setting is ON, which means that FoxPro forces you to confirm a choice before executing the command. If you have doubts, type `SET SAFETY ON` in the Command window and press Enter.

Using the Command Window

The Command window is a special kind of FoxPro window. When you run FoxPro, the Command window appears on the desktop, ready to accept instructions.

In a previous section, you activated the Filer utility. You may have noticed that the word `FILER` appeared in the Command window. FoxPro enters the FILER command for you.

When you choose an option from a menu, FoxPro uses the selections to build a command language instruction. These command expressions usually appear in the Command window and then execute. Think of the Command window as the low-level interface to the FoxPro database engine, through which all requests are processed. The menu system is the high-level interface that constructs and then enters FoxPro commands in the Command window. If you note the expressions that FoxPro constructs for you, you can begin to learn the FoxPro command language, with FoxPro acting as a tutor.

You may wonder why you need to learn how to enter commands when FoxPro enters these commands for you. You need to learn to use the Command window to type commands for the following three reasons:

- Often you can type a command easier and faster than you can deal with menus and dialogs, especially if you don't have a mouse.
- Not all of FoxPro's more than 700 commands and functions are available through menu selections. Not enough room exists for all these commands. At some point, you may want to use the commands that you have to enter manually.
- The more you know about the command language, the more confident you become in mastering the intricacies of database management and FoxPro. If you decide to try writing FoxPro programs, you have the tools you need to get started.

Entering, Repeating, and Editing Commands

You enter commands on a single line, although you can tell FoxPro to regard a subsequent line as part of the current line. When you press Enter, FoxPro tries to execute the command on the same line as the cursor. The position of the cursor on the line is not important; FoxPro includes the entire line as part of the command.

The Command window is an editing window in which you move around by using the same keystrokes you learned in the section of this chapter that covered the FoxPro editor. All the editor's functions, such as Cut and Paste, are available to you in the Command window.

You can repeat a previously entered command by moving the cursor to the command and pressing Enter. You also can add or delete parts of a command. When you enter a command incorrectly, you don't have to retype the command. Just use the editor to correct the error and press Enter.

Some commands, such as BROWSE, have a multitude of options. The entire command may be so long that the text scrolls off-screen. FoxPro doesn't care about this situation and happily executes the command regardless of length, but you can break a long command into two or more lines to make it easier to read.

If you end a line with a semicolon, FoxPro doesn't try to execute the command and regards everything typed on the following line as a continuation of the preceding line. You can use any number of lines to type a command, but remember that the last line must not end in a semicolon.

TIP When you design queries with the RQBE (which you learn in Chapters 5 and 6), FoxPro writes lines of code for you that can be long and complex, nicely formatted as multiple lines. Examining a query is a good way to learn how to format long command lines.

Interpreting and Responding to Error Messages

The command language has strict syntax rules. You must correctly spell the command, and you must provide all information required to execute the command. If you use the COPY TO command to copy records from the current table to another, for example, you have to include the name of the other table. If you don't include the name, FoxPro displays a `Syntax error` message in an Alert window, as shown in figure 2.13. Press any key or click the mouse to clear the message from the screen and return to the Command window.

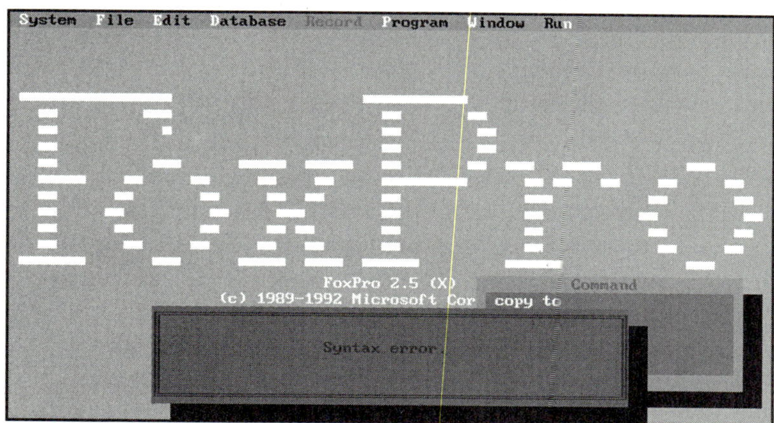

FIG. 2.13

A FoxPro error message in an Alert window.

When you make a mistake, FoxPro attempts to tell you what is wrong. Sometimes what you type appears correct, but FoxPro cannot execute the command because you use a field name that isn't part of the current table. This error usually results in a `Variable not found` message, and FoxPro tries to identify the incorrect word in the line by including the word in the error message. All the error messages are brief, and some messages can be rather cryptic until you learn what to look for when you see them.

If you receive an error message from FoxPro while entering commands in the Command window, first check what you typed for misspelled words, missing information, or missing commas in a list of field names. If you have doubts that what you typed is correct, try to execute the command by using menu selections and compare the entry that you typed with the entry that FoxPro enters in the Command window.

In the following section, you learn to use the Help file to aid you in tracking down problems. The Help file has one entry that contains a complete listing of all the error messages. The file has separate entries that show you the correct syntax for all the commands and functions and includes examples that help you learn how to use those commands and functions. You even can copy the examples from the Help window, paste them into the Command window, and press Enter to execute the command!

Using the FoxPro Help System

By now you realize that FoxPro contains many menu options and dialogs. You may at some point be asked to make a choice and have absolutely no idea what to do. Fortunately, help for the action you are currently performing is never more than a few keypresses away.

Open the Edit menu popup and press F1, the FoxPro help key, and you see a Help window with an entry on Text Editing similar to the window shown in figure 2.14. Except when the System menu is active, mouse users can press Alt while clicking the left mouse button to access the Help system. If you press Alt and click the left button while the System menu is active, FoxPro returns you to the last active window, and the menu deactivates.

This Help window contains information on one FoxPro topic. Down the left side are controls that enable you to access other topics in the Help Index. Among these controls is a `Look Up` button that you can press whenever you have text selected within the Help window or in any other text you may be editing. (Although you cannot modify the help text on-screen, you can select text and search within help text just like in any other FoxPro window.)

FoxPro's help system is *context-sensitive,* which means that FoxPro tries to give you information relevant to the text you select or the action you perform. If FoxPro cannot find a match, the Help Index appears, positioned as closely as possible to a matching entry. You can move around in the index with the usual cursor movements, or you can start typing the initial letters of the choice. The Index tries to find a match, until you select a topic to investigate. If the `Look Up` button can't find a match, a similar list appears from which you can choose a topic.

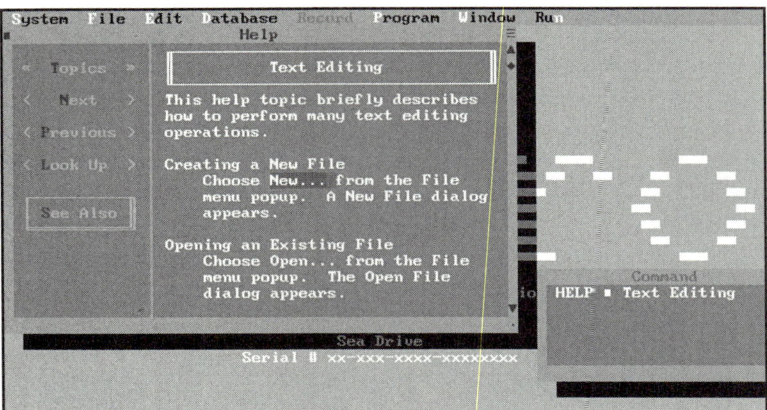

FIG. 2.14

The Help window.

The Help Index is complete. The Help file is revised when Microsoft makes changes to the product; the Help file is the most up-to-date source of FoxPro information available. Be sure that you use the topic "Changes Since Documentation" to annotate your copy of the manuals and to learn about new features added after the manuals went to press. FoxPro has an entry for every command or function, and also topics (marked with a ► at the top of the index), which are all introductory or general in nature. Topics marked with a ■, at the bottom of the list, are designed to describe different aspects of the FoxPro interface. In between these two groups are the individual commands and functions, arranged alphabetically, that make up the FoxPro programming language.

Figure 2.15 shows you an abbreviated version of the Help Index so that you can contrast the different kinds of Help topics. Take some time to look through the topics and practice moving through the Help file, using the `Look Up` function and the See Also popup control to jump to related topics.

While you are in the Help Index, also practice searching for a topic by typing the first few characters of the topic's name. You can easily reach the introductory topics by using one of the methods of typing special characters, which you learned in the text editing section. Press Alt and type 16 on the numeric keyboard (which generates the ► character), and you jump to the introductory topics section of the index.

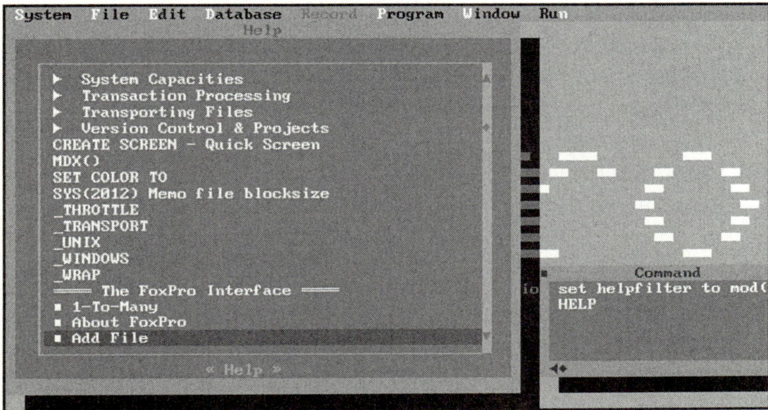

FIG. 2.15

Selections from the Help Index, showing different kinds of topics.

You also can ask FoxPro directly for help on any topic by typing `HELP` in the Command window and following the command with the topic name or the first few characters in the name. Activate the Command window and type `HELP HELP` and see what happens. Then type `HELP ■ F` (press and hold down the Alt key and type `254` on the numeric keypad to produce the small box character), and you are placed in the first matching topic (in the middle of the interface topic group). Try the `Next` and `Previous` buttons to look through other interface topics. Return to the Command window and type `HELP ► F` (use the Alt+16 key combination, or type ' followed by a `p`), and FoxPro returns you to the general introductory topic list where you can refer to the File Extensions list available.

Now that you have learned how to use the Command window, the text editor, and the Help file, you can begin to learn FoxPro commands. Most of the entries for FoxPro commands and functions in the Help file hold examples of the action's use, along with the explanatory text. You can copy and paste in the Command window and edit the example to suit your needs. If an Alert window appears because FoxPro didn't understand a command, just press F1 again and look for the answer.

Summary

In this chapter, you learned to interpret and respond to the various objects that make up the FoxPro interface.

You now know where to find options in the FoxPro menu system and how to summon the options you want. You are familiar with various kinds of windows that FoxPro uses to exchange information with you, and how the windows differ in use and appearance. You know how to change the appearance and positions of the windows to set up the FoxPro desktop as a comfortable workspace.

You now are aware of the editing keystrokes available in FoxPro and can begin to use these keystrokes to issue instructions in the FoxPro command language by using the Command window and Help system. You know how to open, close, and save all kinds of files.

You can put these skills together to do some real work. In the following chapter, you start to put raw data into a FoxPro database and pull out organized information.

3

CHAPTER

Exploring Databases and Tables

In Chapter 1, "Understanding FoxPro Fundamentals," you learned how to create a table (the Product table) by using FoxApp. You also learned that a table is a kind of list and that each item on the list is known as a *record*. Each record, in turn, consists of pieces of information contained in fields. A useful way to think of tables is as lists of items that have the same kinds of information.

The word *database* is often used interchangeably with the word *table*. As used in this book, however, a database is a collection of tables that work together to accomplish a common purpose.

Understanding What a Database Is and What It Does

A dictionary, for example, can be considered a database that holds information about words. Dictionaries usually contain a table of phonetic conventions, a table of abbreviations used in the word listings, a table of words and definitions, and a variety of specialty tables—such as commonly used abbreviations, historical names, fictional names, and other information the publisher thinks may fulfill the purpose of the dictionary. Although combining these extra tables with the definitions list is possible, arranging the tables separately from the list provides easier access to the information from any part of the dictionary application and conserves disk space.

In FoxPro, a database consists of the tables that hold all the data required to provide the information you need to accomplish a task, such as managing your business.

In figure 3.1, you see the components of a dictionary that are treated as separate tables in a database. In figure 3.2, you see how a FoxPro database looks. If you wrote a dictionary in FoxPro, its database would consist of tables similar to the tables in figure 3.2. The output of the database, however, could be made to look like any other dictionary.

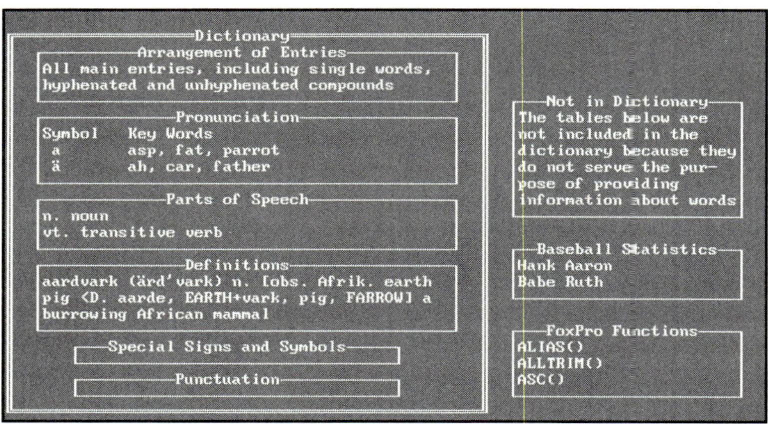

FIG. 3.1

The dictionary as a database.

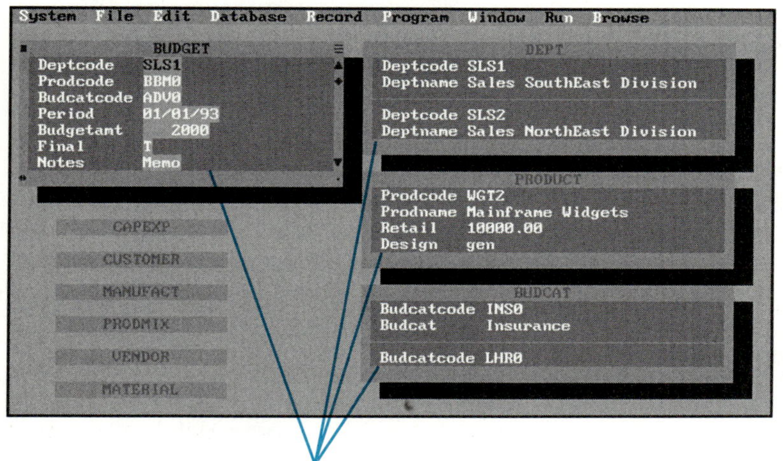

FIG. 3.2

How a database looks in FoxPro.

Understanding the Role of a Table in a Database

The purpose of the model application example used in this book is to provide the managers of the Omnipresent Widget Company with the information needed to manage the company. The complete application consists of many tables that represent all facets of the company. For now, however, this book concentrates only on the subapplication that helps the managers handle the ongoing budget process. To accomplish this task, the managers need budget information by product, by department, and by budget category. Four tables, therefore, are needed: one each for products, departments, and budget categories, and a table in which the budget information itself is stored.

You created the Product table in Chapter 1. The next table you must create is the main table, Budget. You use FoxPro's View window, rather than FoxApp, to create this table. No matter which way you create a table in FoxPro, however, you must understand a table's structure and elements.

Designing a Structure and Assigning Data Types

As discussed in Chapter 1, records in a table consist of pieces of information stored in fields. Designing a table structure involves creating fields to hold the pieces of information you collect for each record in the table. (This procedure, of course, assumes that you already know how you plan to use the table and what information you need to collect. You learn more about determining your needs in Chapter 4.)

You also must know two things about each piece of information collected: the *type* of the data (characters, numbers, dates, and so on) and its *possible ranges* (the smallest and largest, or shortest and longest, values you reasonably can expect the data to hold).

Different types of information are handled differently by FoxPro. FoxPro offers several options for manipulating most types of data. FoxPro can convert a field that contains a word or a phrase to upper- or lowercase or to a mixture of cases. FoxPro also can tell you the length of the phrase or the first three letters of the word or phrase. If the field contains numeric data, you can use FoxPro to perform arithmetic operations on the data. In this book, you find examples of data manipulation for each data type.

Understanding Data Types

To store your data correctly and with the most efficient use of disk space, FoxPro must know what *type* of data you are storing. You tell FoxPro the data type of each field as you create the table. If you open the popup list in the Type column of the Table Structure dialog, you see eight data types. You assign a data type to each field by choosing a type from the list.

Character fields are composed of letters, digits, punctuation marks, line drawings, and foreign alphabet and special symbol characters. Character fields are limited to 254 characters in a field. You can enter these characters from the keyboard by typing them directly, pressing the Alt key plus a number key on the numeric keypad, or by choosing the character from the Special Characters table, which you access by selecting Special Characters from the System menu pad.

The Alt+number combination generates a character based on the ASCII code number of the character—you can see the ASCII code for a character by referring to the ASCII Chart option on the System menu popup.

FoxPro treats character data as strings of individual characters. If you add together the contents of two character fields, you get a combined string of the two fields—*"dog"+"cat"*, for example, equals *"dogcat"*. (This process is known as *concatenation*.)

NOTE All computer information—program, text, image, and other files—is stored in binary format. The character symbols discussed here are a subset of binary data, or *ASCII characters*. ASCII is an agreed-upon convention in the computer industry that enables programs to share character data. For special purposes, a character field also can contain non-ASCII binary data, such as a series of special codes or instructions to be sent to the printer. Usually, however, you use the memo data type to store non-ASCII binary data, which is generally not manipulated directly by FoxPro, but imported from and exported to the hard disk to serve special needs.

Numeric fields contain only numbers, the minus and plus signs, and the decimal point. Numbers are limited to 20 digits (including signs, decimal point, and the number of decimals). FoxPro treats numeric data as numbers, which means that if you add two numbers, you get the sum of the numbers—that is, 2 + 2 = 4.

Although you can enter 20 numbers in a field, FoxPro tracks only the first 16 significant digits, which means that if you enter 17 digits, the number is not correct (digits after 16 are replaced by 0). You can, however, accurately enter 16 digits, a minus or plus sign, and a decimal point.

Do not assume, however, that you must place data in a Numeric field just because the data contains digits. If you plan no computations on this data, you are better off treating the information as a string of characters and putting the data in a character field.

U.S. ZIP codes and Social Security numbers, for example, are composed of digits, but finding and sorting such data is easier when these codes and numbers are entered in a Character field rather than in a Numeric field. If you have doubts about the eventual contents of the field, use a Character field. (You may, for example, need to store Canadian postal codes, which have both alphabetic and numeric characters.)

TIP Although you cannot manually enter more numbers than the digits allowed in a field, you can use FoxPro's REPLACE and INSERT INTO commands to place into a field a number larger than the field's actual size. You also can place into a field a number that has no mathematical value. (The result of dividing by zero, for example, has no mathematical value.) If a number is too large to fit or is the result of dividing by zero, FoxPro either fills the field with asterisks or displays on-screen a number such as .990E+03. This form is the number's scientific notation and is equal to the beginning number times 10 to the power indicated after the E. The result in this example is .990 times 10^3 (.990 times 1000), or 990. Unfortunately, having asterisks and scientific notation numbers in fields can lead to problems. The best approach is to make your numeric fields large enough to hold any numbers you need and to avoid dividing by zero.

Date fields can contain only valid dates, in numeric form, between 01/01/100 and 12/31/9999. FoxPro enables you to use many forms to represent a date. You can enter dates with the full century represented, as in 01/01/1993, or with only the last two digits of the year displayed, as in 01/01/93. You also can enter and display dates in American, British, Italian, or other formats. In a following section, "Adding Data by Using FoxPro Browse," you can experiment with different date formats and see how the dates change to reflect these formats. No matter which date form you use, however, FoxPro stores dates internally in the numeric form *YYYYMMDD*—the year (*Y*), in four digits; the month (*M*), in two digits; and the day (*D*), in two digits.

Because dates are stored internally as numbers, FoxPro can use dates to perform date math (such as figuring out what date is 30 days from today) and can convert numeric dates into character dates for reports (such as January 1, 1993).

Logical fields contain only the letter *T*, for true, or the letter *F*, for false. (You also can enter Y for true and N for false, but the field always stores the value as *T* or *F*). You can think of a logical field as an on/off switch to specify whether a certain condition is satisfied. The sample Budget table contains a Logical field named Final, which you use to determine whether you can edit a record.

Memo fields can contain text or any binary data, such as images or programs. FoxPro can perform a large number of simple and complex operations on data stored in Memo fields. For now, however, use these fields only to add additional free-form notes to the contents of a record.

NOTE The data you enter into a Memo field is stored in a separate file, which FoxPro opens whenever you open the table. If you view the table's data in a Browse window, FoxPro displays a *placeholder* that indicates the position of the Memo field in the table. If the companion memo file holds an entry for the current record, FoxPro displays a capital `M` in the placeholder field; if no entry exists for this record, a lowercase `m` is displayed.

General fields are included in FoxPro to make the program compatible with FoxPro for Windows. A General field is used to store Windows objects, such as pictures and sounds. You can add a General field to a table in FoxPro for DOS, but you cannot store data in the field.

Picture fields are included in FoxPro to make the program compatible with Microsoft's Macintosh products. You can create a Picture field in FoxPro for DOS by using the CREATE TABLE command, but as with General fields, you cannot store data in the Picture field.

NOTE The default extension for a FoxPro table is .DBF. If a table contains one or more Memo, General, or Picture fields, FoxPro creates a companion file (a memo file) with the same file name but the extension .FPT. (Regardless of how many Memo, General, or Picture fields are in a table, FoxPro creates only one memo file to hold all these fields.) Remember, if you move files from one location to another, you must keep the table and its related memo file together in the same directory. If you copy the table, you also must duplicate its memo file. After you open a table, FoxPro opens the related memo file. If the companion memo file is missing, an error message appears.

CAUTION: Although floating-point Numeric fields also are available as you create a table structure, FoxPro handles these fields as numeric data. For this reason—and because FoxPro may use these fields differently in the future—use regular Numeric fields.

Character and Numeric fields are limited to a field length that you determine, up to FoxPro's maximum length for each field type. The exact field lengths you choose depend on the values each field must contain. In a Character field for customer names, for example, you may need 25 to 30 (or more) available character spaces in which to enter the full name of a customer. Try to determine in advance as much as you can about the values that must fit in each field. Avoid using field lengths that are much larger than required to store the data; as you increase the field length, you also increase the amount of disk space each record requires. If you know, for example, that a Character field never holds more than 10 characters (such as one for a code you created), set the field length for no more than 10.

You can enter memos as large as your available disk space permits. Each Memo field takes 10 bytes per record in the .DBF file, but the associated entries in the .FPT file can vary in length.

Creating a Table by Using the View Window

You can create a table by using FoxApp, as described in Chapter 1, but using the FoxPro View window to create a table gives you greater flexibility and enables you to arrange other aspects of the work environment at the same time.

Figures 3.1 and 3.2 show two ways to visually represent the nature of a database. The FoxPro View window provides another, more useful way to display a database (see fig. 3.3).

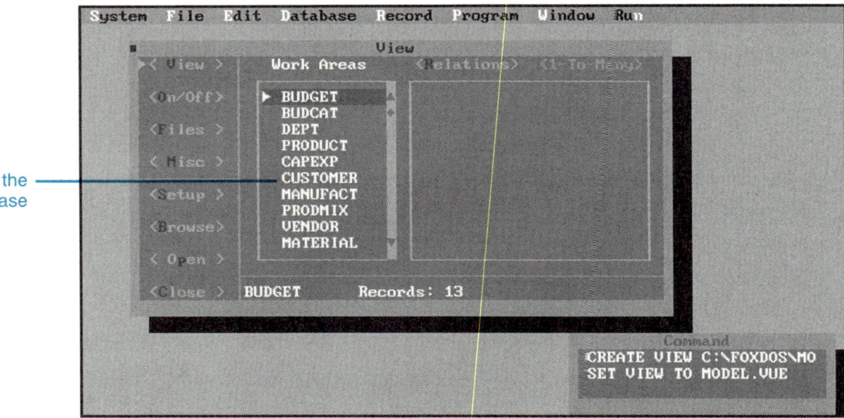

FIG. 3.3

The View window's display of a database.

Besides providing a view of your tables, the View window enables you to enter data, view table contents, create and modify individual tables, and combine individual tables to build a database. You also can use View to change a variety of miscellaneous FoxPro settings. You can think of the View window much as an alternative Command window.

In Chapter 1, you used the `Misc` push button of the View window to activate the clock and to change other settings. In the section "Adding Data by Using FoxPro Browse," later in this chapter, you see how changing settings affects how data is displayed on-screen and entered on the keyboard.

To use the View window, select View from the Window menu popup by pressing Alt+W and then pressing V or by clicking the Window menu pad and then clicking the View option on the menu popup. You also can type SET in the Command window to activate the View window. You then see an empty View window similar to the window shown in figure 3.4. In the upper-half of the left column are the View window's panel selection push buttons, with the View panel currently selected. The lower-half of the column contains the options you can select while working in the View panel. The center column shows a list of Work Areas, and the right column currently is empty.

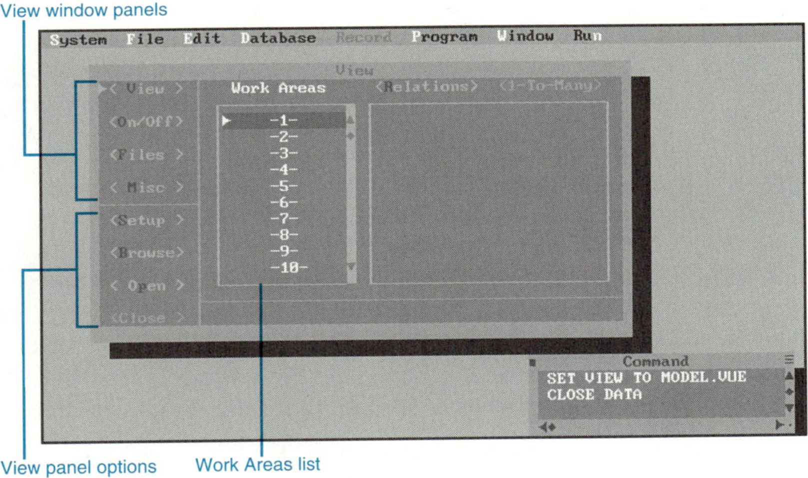

FIG. 3.4

An empty View window.

Working in the View Window's Panels

The View window has four panels that you can select by choosing the different panel selection push buttons. Each of the following panels displays a different set of options and information:

- *View*, shown in figure 3.4, displays FoxPro's available work areas in a scrollable list and provides you with options to `Open`, `Browse`, `Setup`, and `Close` tables. You also can use this mode to set `Relations` among the tables in a database.
- *On/Off* provides access to many of FoxPro's SET commands, which are either SET ON or SET OFF. If the box is checked, the option is SET ON; if unchecked, the option is SET OFF.
- *Files* enables you to specify your working drive and directory, as well as your current Help and Resource files.
- *Misc* enables you to configure many elements of your working environment, such as the currency symbol and date format FoxPro uses while displaying and printing your data.

Understanding Work Areas

In FoxPro, the various tables that comprise a database are opened (made available for use) in up to 225 possible work areas. You can refer to these work areas as 1 through 225 (as the View window does) or as A through J and 11 through 225. Each work area holds one table at a time.

NOTE

Only the Extended version of FoxPro for DOS provides 225 work areas. The Standard version is currently limited to 25 work areas, which you refer to as 1 through 25 or as A through J, 11 through 25. The additional work areas may be provided in a future release of the Standard version of FoxPro.

After a table is opened in a work area, the work area and the table become virtually synonymous. You can refer to or select either a table or a work area by using the table's *alias*. An alias is similar to a nick-name for a table or work area. If you use the View window, FoxPro shows you the table's alias when you open that table in a work area.

After you open a table from the View window, FoxPro by default assigns the name of the table as its alias. If, however, you open the same table in different work areas or open two different tables with the same name in different work areas, FoxPro distinguishes between the two files by assigning to the second table an alias that is composed of the table name and a letter. If you open the Product table in work area 1, for example, the alias becomes PRODUCT. If you switch to work area 2 and open the Product table again or open another Product table (say, one from a different DOS directory), the alias in work area 2 becomes PRODUCT_A. (Note that aliases are assigned this way only if you open tables from the View window.)

You also can open a table by using FoxPro commands, either in a program or in the Command window, and specify an alias different from the default alias name.

One work area is always the currently selected work area. From the View window, you can select a particular work area by using the Tab key to move to the Work Areas column and then using the up- and down-arrow keys to highlight the desired work area. After the desired work area is highlighted, press the space bar to make it the active work area.

You also can choose a new work area by clicking the work area you want. The currently selected work area is marked by a ► in the Work Areas column, immediately to the left of the Work Area designation or table alias (refer to fig. 3.4).

The table open in the currently selected work area becomes the controlling table for many FoxPro operations. In Chapter 4, "Database Management Fundamentals," you learn about the controlling table and how to establish connecting relationships between tables. These relationships are always established between the controlling table and other tables in the database.

Creating the Budget Table

Now you can use the View window to create the Budget table of the database. (First, however, you must make sure that the MODEL directory you created in Chapter 1 is the working directory. Use the Files panel to do this now.)

Designate work area 1 as the currently selected area, and choose the `Open` push button from the panel options. The Open File dialog appears, as shown in figure 3.5.

To open an existing table, you can select the table from the list of available files. Because you are creating a table, however, you must select the `New` button. The Table Structure dialog then appears, as shown in figure 3.6.

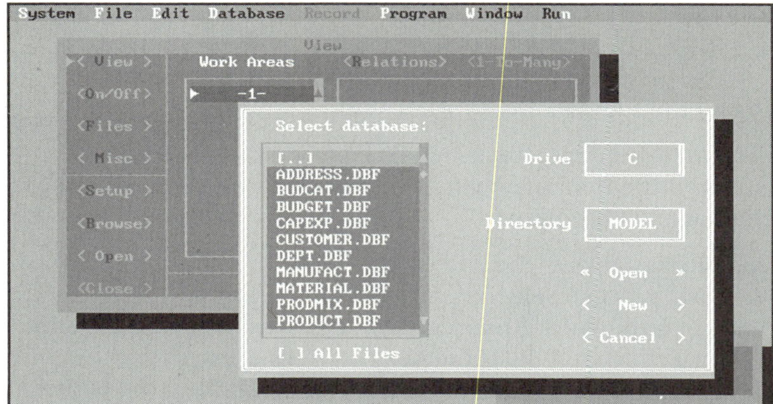

FIG. 3.5

The Open File dialog, used for table selection.

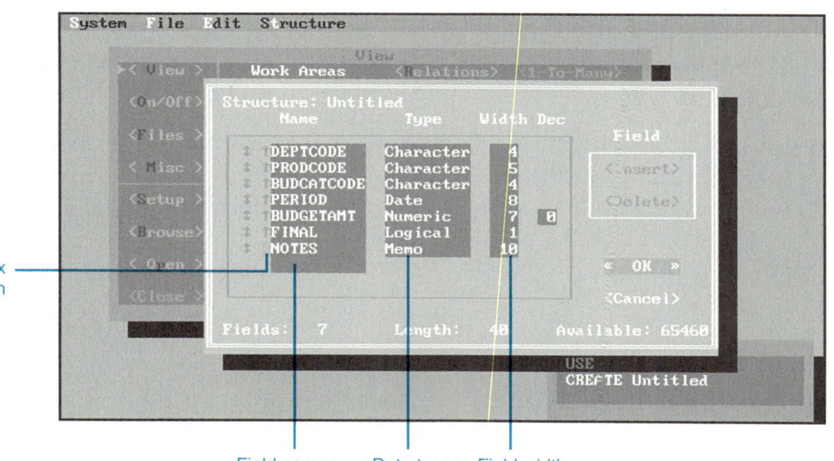

FIG. 3.6

The Table Structure dialog.

This dialog might look familiar because you used the same box in Chapter 1 to create the Product table. (The dialog currently is titled Structure: Untitled, because you have not yet named this table.)

Now create the fields in the table by entering the field names, type, width, and decimals (optional), as shown in figure 3.6. Remember that you can move from the name to the type to the width by pressing the Tab key (or Shift+Tab to move back) or by clicking with the mouse. After you enter several fields, you also can move up and down within each column by using the up- and down-arrow keys. Table 3.1 explains the characteristics of each field.

Table 3.1 The Structure of the Budget Table

Field Name	Type	Width
DEPTCODE	Character	4
PRODCODE	Character	4
BUDCATCODE	Character	4
PERIOD	Date	8*
BUDGETAMT	Numeric	7
FINAL	Logical	1*
NOTES	Memo	10*

** Widths are determined by FoxPro.*

The shaded box to the left of each field name in figure 3.6 represents an *index tag*. (Tags are explained in the "Quick Results to the Screen" section, later in this chapter.) You access this box by pressing Shift+Tab immediately after entering the name or, after all the fields are entered, by pressing Tab until you reach the box you want. You also can access this column by clicking it directly with the mouse. After you access an index tag, you can fill the box with an up arrow or a down arrow—or leave an empty shaded box—by pressing the space bar or the Enter key or by clicking the mouse. (Each time you press a key or click the mouse, you cycle through one of these three available options.)

You explore indexes in Chapter 4. From working with the Product table in Chapter 1, you already know that an index enables you to view the data in a different order than that of the *natural order* (the order in which the records are entered). The up arrow creates an *ascending tag* (lowest to highest), the down arrow creates a *descending tag* (highest to lowest), and the empty shaded box creates no index tag on that field. As you create the Budget table, you want to create ascending index tags for all the fields except the Memo field, which doesn't accept an arrow in the shaded box.

NOTE *Ascending* and *descending* have different meanings depending on the data type. For numeric data, the order ascends from the smallest number to the largest. For dates, the order ascends chronologically from the earliest date to the latest date. For logical data, the order ascends from false to true. For character data, however, this ordering is not as simple and intuitive. Character data ascends from the lowest ASCII code number to the highest. This order is not strictly alphabetical; rather, it is case-sensitive—that is, uppercase letters precede lowercase letters—and spaces precede both letters and digits, so "Micro Soft" would appear before "Microsoft." An example of ascending character order is shown in the following list. (The numbers in the list also are entered in Character fields.)

1
10
2
20
APPLE
GO THERE
GOPHER
apple
banana

Now you might better understand why so much computer data requires single-digit numbers to be entered as double-digit numbers (for example, 02) and codes and other information to be entered only in upper- or lowercase characters. (You may want to remember these conventions as you are indexing, although FoxPro, of course, provides features to simplify the process.)

As you enter the Period, Final, and Notes fields (date, logical, and memo data types), notice that you cannot adjust the width. Date type fields default to a width of 8, logical types to a width of 1, and memo types to a width of 10. Because of how date and memo types can be displayed and entered, however, these limiting factors may seem confusing.

As discussed earlier in this chapter, you can display and enter Date fields in many forms—including a full century form, such as 01/01/1993, which has a width of 10. Yet FoxPro uses a width of 8 no matter how dates appear on-screen, because FoxPro stores the date internally in the form *YYYYMMDD* (year, month, day). You can accept this default and still know that you can display or enter dates in the form you require.

Similarly, memo data types are limited in size only by the available space on the hard disk—certainly far greater than the default width of 10. The data in a Memo field, however, is actually stored in its companion memo file; the 10-character field in the main file is used by FoxPro only to make the connection to the memo file.

As you create field entries, you can change the order in which the entries appear. (Entries initially appear in the same order in which they are saved in the table.) To move an entry up or down in the list of fields, drag the double-headed arrow (↕) located to the left of a field and its index tag (refer to fig. 3.6). To use the keyboard to move an entry, press the Ctrl key plus the up- or down-arrow key after highlighting a field's information.

After the Table Structure dialog is completed so that it exactly matches the dialog shown in figure 3.6, press Ctrl+Enter or select `OK` to save your work. The Table Naming dialog appears, as shown in figure 3.7. Type the name `BUDGET` in the text box, and press Ctrl+Enter or select `Save`.

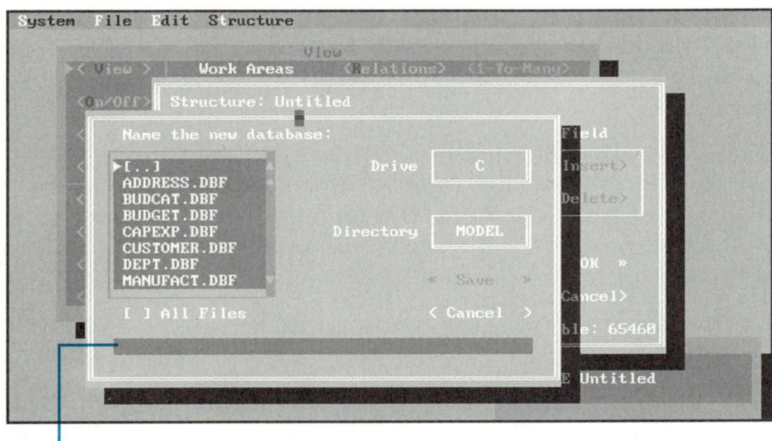

FIG. 3.7

The Table Naming dialog.

FoxPro asks if you want to input data now. If you click the `Yes` button, you can begin to add records to the table. (The "Adding Data by Using FoxPro Browse" section, later in this chapter, describes how to add records to this table.) For now, however, select `No` to exit to the View window.

The Budget table is now open in work area 1.

Saving Your Place by Using a View File

Now that you have created the Budget table and understand the different kinds of data a table can contain, you can create the rest of the tables in the model database. The structures and the index keys (or index orders) for each table are found in Appendix E. These tables also are included on the accompanying source disk.

Throughout this book, you are referred to many of these tables in the examples that you create for use in the practice sessions. You also draw on the tables that form the parts of the sample applications provided with FoxPro. Often you may want two or more tables open at the same time and to see the contents of these tables displayed in a particular order for a particular task.

Each time you start to work, you can open all the tables you need and set each table's order, much as you open the drawers of a desk and arrange notebooks, pens, and other tools for easy access. If you use a special type of file known as a View, FoxPro also enables you to "walk away and then come back" and still have all the tools just as you left them.

If you closed the Budget table after creating that table in the preceding section, use the View window to open Budget again now. Choose a second work area, and open the Product table. Create or open as many other tables in the model database as you want, using a new work area for each table.

Keeping the View window active, choose the File Save As... menu option. The Save View As dialog appears, as shown in figure 3.8. (Your screen may look different than the figure, depending on how many sample tables you have open and in what sequence you opened them.)

Type `model` as the file name and confirm the choice; the open files are now saved. If you look in the Command window for the executed command, you see that FoxPro has added the default extension .VUE, for a View file.

Now, if you want to begin work after you load FoxPro, you can use the File Open... menu option to open the View file, or you can enter the SET VIEW TO <filename> command in the Command window to restore these files just as you want them (along with other factors of what in FoxPro is known as the environment).

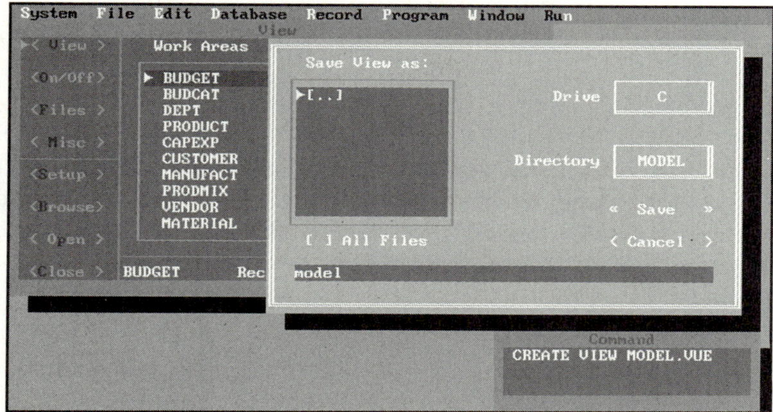

FIG. 3.8

The View window, with the Save View As dialog.

NOTE View files are unusual because you cannot use File New... to create a View file. You can access this capability only by using File Save As... while the View window is currently active or by typing the CREATE VIEW command in the Command window.

Exclusive and Shared Use of Tables

If you purchased any previous version of FoxPro, you bought either the single-user version or the multiuser version. All versions of FoxPro 2.5, however, are multiuser products. Although multiuser considerations are discussed at greater length elsewhere in this book, you should understand some of the following multiuser basics before you begin to enter data into tables.

Tables are opened for either exclusive or shared use. When a table is opened for exclusive use, no one else can open that table until you close it. If someone else tries to open the table, FoxPro displays the error message `File is in use by another.`

By default, FoxPro opens tables for exclusive use. To open a table for shared use, you must load the DOS SHARE program (unless you work on a network that does not require SHARE), and you must type SET EXCLUSIVE OFF or USE <table name> SHARED in the Command window. If you SET EXCLUSIVE OFF, all tables that you subsequently open are opened for shared use. (Tables that are already open remain in exclusive use.) Adding the SHARED clause to the USE command enables you to override the EXCLUSIVE setting for a particular table. If you want to open tables for shared use from the View window or through the File Open dialog, you must first SET EXCLUSIVE OFF, as these tools do not enable you to specify that a table is to be opened for shared use.

If the tables you use also are needed by others on a local area network, you almost always want to SET EXCLUSIVE OFF. Instead of doing this from the Command window each time you run FoxPro, however, you can insert the line EXCLUSIVE=OFF in your FoxPro configuration file, CONFIG.FP. (Configuration options are discussed in detail in Appendix C.)

Certain FoxPro commands require exclusive use of a table. These commands are shown in table 3.2.

Table 3.2 Commands Requiring Exclusive Use of a Table

Command	Comments
DELETE TAG	
INDEX ON ... TAG	Like tables, compound indexes are opened for exclusive use when you create them. After a compound index is closed, exclusive use is required to add a new tag to the compound index file.
INSERT [BLANK]	Do not confuse INSERT, which requires exclusive use, with the SQL command INSERT INTO, which does not.
MODIFY STRUCTURE	If the table is open for shared use, you can view the table's structure, but you can't change anything.
PACK	
REINDEX	
ZAP	

After a table is open for shared use, you must deal with the problem of record contention. For now, however, you only need to know that FoxPro handles most of these problems for you as you add and modify data interactively, as in the remaining sections of this chapter and in Chapter 4.

As you begin to enter or change a field's contents in a Browse window, for example, FoxPro tries to lock the record you are modifying so others cannot change it until you are finished. If no one else currently has this record locked, you obtain the required record lock, and your entries are accepted. If someone else already has the record locked, the message `Attempting to lock... Press Escape to cancel` appears in the upper-right corner of the screen. After the record becomes available, the message disappears, and you can edit the record. If you decide you don't want to wait any longer, you can press Esc and try again later.

In Chapters 5 through 10, you extract results from your tables rather than change the information the tables contain, so you don't have to worry much about arranging record and file locks. After you begin to create applications in Part III, however, obtaining record and file locks becomes very important.

To watch FoxPro lock files and records as you proceed through the examples in the remainder of this chapter, perform the following steps:

1. Make sure that the SHARE program is loaded, if required (as described earlier in this section).
2. Type `SET EXCLUSIVE OFF` in the Command window.
3. Type `SET STATUS ON` in the Command window.

After the Status bar is visible at the bottom of the screen, you can see the `Locked/Unlocked` status of the current record and table as you enter data.

If you are sure that EXCLUSIVE is SET OFF, but the Status bar still shows that the table is open `Exclusive`, either the SHARE program is not loaded, or the table was opened while EXCLUSIVE was SET ON, or the table in use was just created. A table that you create is opened for exclusive use until you close it. The next time you open the table, you can open it for shared use.

Adding Data by Using FoxPro Browse

Now that you have created the tables in the model database (or have copied them from the source code disk), you can begin to fill the tables with data. In this section, you learn some quick techniques for adding records to the files by using FoxPro's Browse feature.

Open the Product and Budget tables. If the View window is not currently available, make the View window active now.

Highlight the Product table in the list. If you press Enter, you open a Browse of Product records.

You also can double-click the Product table to open a Browse of the Product table. One click selects the Product table (makes Product the active work area), and the second click opens the Browse. Because the space bar is used in FoxPro to imitate mouse clicks for keyboard users, you also can press the space bar once to select the table and again to open the Browse. Watch the commands being executed in the Command window as you press the space bar.

As you can see, the Browse window is an arrangement of the Product records with the various fields listed across (in columns) and the various records listed down (in rows). You can use the usual editing keys to move around in the Browse window. The current record (the record you are editing) is highlighted in different colors or in a different intensity than the other records, and the current field also is presented differently. (Use the Tab key to move between fields.)

Because, for the moment, you are using the Product table only for reference, resize and then place its window to one side. Then select the Budget table and open it in a Browse window, just as you did with the Product table. (Try using the View window's `Browse` push button this time.) Resize the Budget Browse window so that you can comfortably see all the fields. The screen setup should now resemble that shown in figure 3.9.

Adding Data in the Browse Window

Notice that you now have a new option on the menu bar, the *Browse pad*. Browse is one of FoxPro's most powerful and versatile features, and you learn much more about how to arrange the Browse contents in subsequent chapters. For now, you just use the last two entries on the menu popup, Toggle Delete and Append Record, to add information to the file.

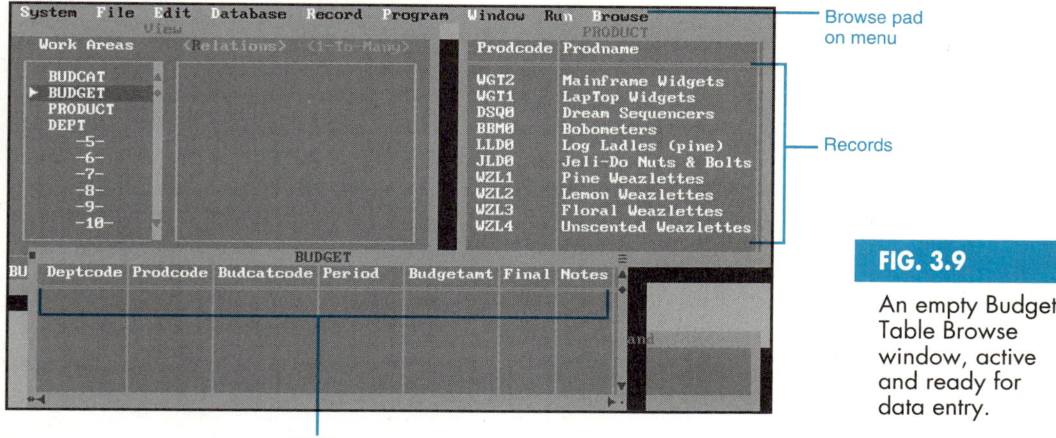

FIG. 3.9

An empty Budget Table Browse window, active and ready for data entry.

The key shortcut for appending, or adding, a new record to the table is Ctrl+N. The key shortcut for a toggle delete is Ctrl+T. The deleting process marks a record in a special way so that the record becomes invisible to FoxPro for many tasks, although the record is not physically removed from the database. (You learn more about deleted records in the following section, "Packing a Table.")

A *toggle* is a switch used to alternate between two mutually exclusive states. Here, you can delete a record by pressing Ctrl+T, and then you can turn off the delete marker by pressing Ctrl+T again. You can tell that a record is deleted in a Browse window because the record is marked with a bullet (•) to the left of the first field.

No mouse equivalent exists for Ctrl+N. You cannot, therefore, add records to a table directly with the mouse. You can toggle the delete state of records, however, by using a single click immediately to the left of the first field in the Browse. Clicking elsewhere on a record makes the record the current active record.

Figure 3.10 shows the Budget table with information added. Take time now to append records and type the sample information so you can use this data for display and queries in this and the following chapters. (A complete listing for the sample records is in Appendix H.) The Deptcode, Prodcode, and Budcatcode fields come from other supporting tables in the database, including the Product table currently on-screen. (You can refer to this Browse window as you type to see what each product code means.) In following operations, you use these codes to identify groups of records that belong together, so make sure that you type the codes accurately. Delete records to get rid of errors or simply to practice.

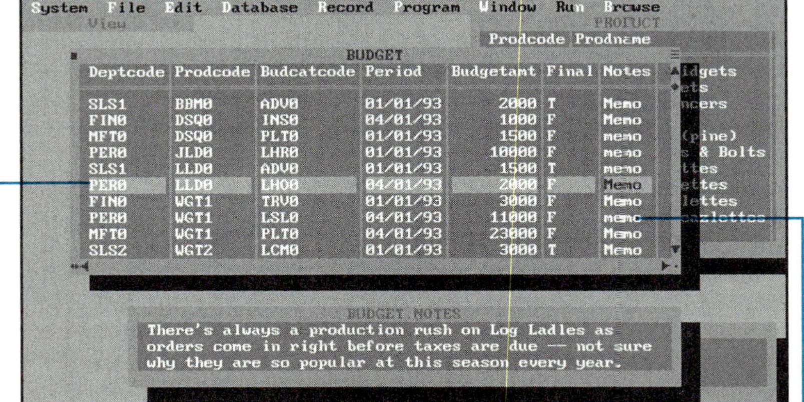

Deptcode	Prodcode	Budcatcode	Period	Budgetamt	Final	Notes
SLS1	BBM0	ADV0	01/01/93	2000	T	Memo
FIN0	DSQ0	INS0	04/01/93	1000	F	Memo
MFT0	DSQ0	PLT0	01/01/93	1500	F	memo
PER0	JLD0	LHR0	01/01/93	10000	F	memo
SLS1	LLD0	ADV0	01/01/93	1500	T	memo
PER0	LLD0	LHO0	04/01/93	2000	F	Memo
FIN0	WGT1	TRV0	01/01/93	3000	F	Memo
PER0	WGT1	LSL0	04/01/93	11000	F	memo
MFT0	WGT1	PLT0	04/01/93	23000	F	Memo
SLS2	WGT2	LCM0	01/01/93	3000	T	Memo

FIG. 3.10

The Budget Table Browse with information added.

The Period field is a Date field; all dates are shown as the first day of a fiscal quarter. Type a nonsense date, such as 13/13/91, in the Period field or some nonnumeric characters in the Budgetamt field to see the way FoxPro prevents you from typing an obviously invalid entry. The Final field is a Logical field that accepts only True or False values (although Logical fields also enable you to type Y or N, which are appropriately converted to True or False values).

In later chapters, you learn to perform much more complex validations of information by using criteria that you define. You do not have to type information into code fields such as Prodcode either; you can tell FoxPro to look up such fields in the support tables from which these fields originate.

Notice that the last field, Notes, is designed to enable executives to jot down reminders about the budget lines as these lines are entered. Because Notes is a Memo field, however, you cannot edit Notes directly in the Browse window. To edit this field, position the cursor in the four-character memo *placeholder* in the Browse window, and press Ctrl+PgDn to access a text-editing window in which you can type notes.

Using the mouse, you can double-click the memo placeholder to bring up the memo editing window. You can edit and save a Memo field as you save any other text. After you enter information into a Memo field, you can see that the placeholder in the Browse window now displays a capital `M` on-screen, indicating that the Memo field for this record contains data.

As you enter text in the Notes field, take a moment to look at the Edit Preferences menu option. You can see that the available options for a memo differ slightly from the options for a regular text file.

You can press Ctrl+F or use the Edit Find... option to search for information in a Browse window. Because this procedure can check all Character and Numeric fields, Edit Find... conveniently enables you to move quickly through a large table to find information. You can search only forward in a Browse window; however, the Wrap Around option in the Edit Find dialog enables you to find data in records that precede the current record. If FoxPro finds a match in its search, you can press Ctrl+G or select the Edit Find Again option to search for the next occurrence of the search term.

Setting Browse Display Options in the View Window

The View window contains many features you have not yet explored. Some of these features are useful for quick editing, such as in the work you are now doing in the Browse. Open the View window, and then click the `Misc` button to display the check boxes and other options in the Miscellaneous Settings panel, as shown in figure 3.11. The Bell, Date Delimiter, and Century check boxes are of particular interest to this Browse session. Change the settings of these features to see what happens to the Browse.

If you change the Bell Frequency or Length (instead of simply turning off the Bell), for example, you can choose the little musical note to the right of these items to immediately hear the change you make. If the Bell check box is marked (the default state), you hear this sound as you edit information in the Browse window—each time you completely fill a field and the cursor moves to the next field.

You also might want to experiment with the Mouse Tracking option, which can be set between 1 and 10 (a setting of 10 is the highest level of sensitivity). A high level of sensitivity means that small movements of the mouse result in large movements of the mouse cursor across the screen.

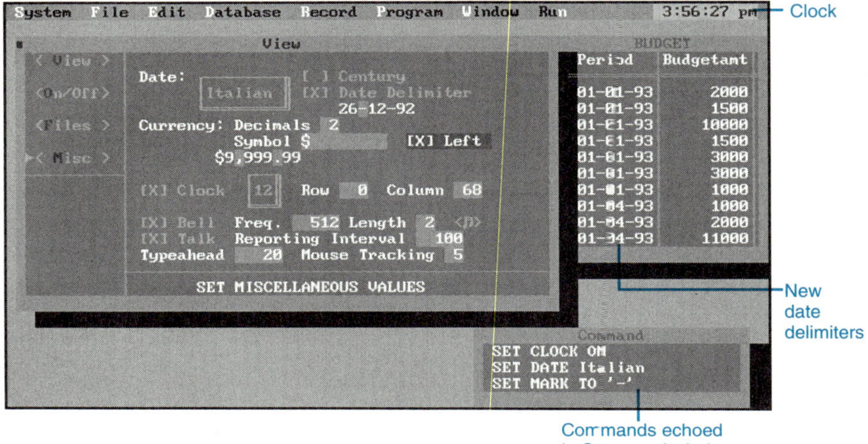

FIG. 3.11

The View window's Miscellaneous Settings panel.

Now choose the View window's `On/Off` button to access the On/Off panel. A number of the check boxes in this panel also have particular application to the editing session. Turn on DELETED (DELETED is on if the check box displays an X), and return to the Budget Browse window; the deleted records are no longer visible. Turn on CARRY and append a new record to this Browse; the information on the previous record is carried over. Set CONFIRM to on and go back to entering information in the Browse; when you reach the end of a field, you must now press Enter or Tab instead of simply moving on by default to the next field.

The View window also has a fourth panel, Files. Although you do not yet have to change these settings, look at them as you experiment with the View features. If you do not know what a particular item does, use the Help system. (If you do not know how to use the FoxPro Help system, refer to the section, "Using the FoxPro Help System" at the end of Chapter 2.)

You can express most of the options in the View window as commands that begin with the word SET, such as SET DELETED ON/OFF. (To find out about this setting, access SET DELETED in the Help file index.)

Packing a Table

You learned in the preceding section that you can delete records in a table, but that these records are not really erased. In this section you learn that, if you do not want deleted records accessed along with others, you can use the SET DELETED ON command. Using this command makes these deleted records invisible for the purposes of a count or for any other output you ask FoxPro to create.

Ordinarily, therefore, you do not need to physically remove deleted records from a table. This is important to know because actually removing records creates more work for FoxPro (and more interruption for you) for the following reasons:

- FoxPro must create a temporary file while removing records. If this file is large, you may not have enough disk space. (A good rule of thumb for the free space needed on a disk is three times the size of the file, including associated memo files.)
- Removing records takes time. (The exact time required depends on the size of the file and the speed of the system.)
- If you run FoxPro on a network, no one else can access this file until you complete the process of removing the unwanted records. If anyone else has the table open, or if you have opened the table for shared use, you are not able to PACK, as this operation requires the table to be open for exclusive use only.

As part of regular maintenance procedures, however, you may want to remove the records entirely from the table. The physical removal of such records is known as *packing* a table. This option is available from the Database menu pad.

You can pack the Budget table now (unless you do not have exclusive use of the table). If you left the TALK check box in its default setting of ON in the View window, FoxPro displays a message that tells you how many records remain in the file after packing.

The physical removal of deleted records can give you a significant savings in disk space. Packing a table has another benefit, however. If the packed table contains Memo fields, as does the Budget table, that table has an associated file in which memos are stored. (The associated file has the extension .FPT.) FoxPro assigns space to each Memo field in a standard unit of size known as the file's *blocksize*. Although you can adjust the blocksize for a given file, some space is always wasted as you add information to a particular Memo field. The space is wasted because each piece of information is not an exact blocksize, or a multiple of the blocksize, in length.

As FoxPro packs a table, it consolidates the entries in the table's memo file and eliminates this wasted space.

You may want a table's memo file entries consolidated even if you do not want to remove the deleted records. You can instruct FoxPro simply to consolidate the memo file by issuing the PACK MEMO command in the Command window. If for some reason you need only to remove deleted records from the file, but do not want to consolidate the memo file, you can issue the command PACK DBF.

Another reason to use PACK MEMO is that PACK MEMO removes wasted space without creating a temporary file, so you do not need extra disk space to use this command. If you do not have enough room on your disk for FoxPro to PACK the table, try using PACK MEMO first to compress the .FPT file. You then may have sufficient disk space to PACK the table.

Structural index files, discussed in Chapter 4, also can contain wasted space that the PACK command can reclaim.

Now that you have made the effort of putting data into the Budget table, the database is ready to work for you by pulling information back out of the table.

Getting Quick Results to the Screen and Printer

As discussed in Chapter 1 (and as covered in more detail in Chapter 8, "Organizing the Answers with Browse"), the Browse window in which you are currently working is a powerful tool for viewing information in tables. You also need, however, to print information and to display information on-screen in many different forms.

Quick Results to the Screen

If the View window and the Browse window for the Budget table are not currently open on-screen, open them now.

As you created the Budget file, you set index tags on all the fields except the Notes field (a memo field). This section demonstrates how these tags work in a Browse window.

Select the View window again, and choose the `Setup` push button. The Setup dialog appears.

In the left column, you see the table's structure, defined when you created the table. In the middle column, you see the fields you indexed; each indexed field displays an up arrow (an ascending tag) to the left of the field name, just as you set these fields when you created the table.

Just as you can currently select only one table or one work area, only one index at a time can order the records. A bullet (•) appears to the left of this index, which is known as the *master* or *controlling index*. If no bullet appears, the records in the Browse window appear in the original order in which these records were entered in the table.

You can see what the Browse looks like if you list the records in date order. Highlight the Period index, and select the `Set Order` push button; the bullet appears to the left of the name, as shown in figure 3.12. (Whenever the highlight bar is on the name of the current master index, the `Set Order` button changes to `No Order`.) Click the `OK` button to exit the Setup dialog.

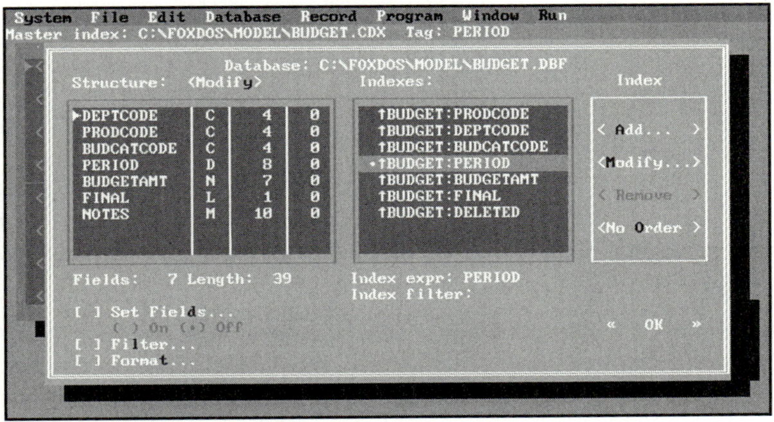

FIG. 3.12

The Setup dialog, with an index order by Period selected.

Now return to the Browse window. The records appear in *ascending date order* (from earliest date to latest date), as shown in figure 3.13. Return to the Setup dialog box, select another index, choose `Set Order`, and return again to the Browse window. The records now appear in ascending order (from lowest value to highest value) by whichever field you chose (such as Deptcode or Prodcode).

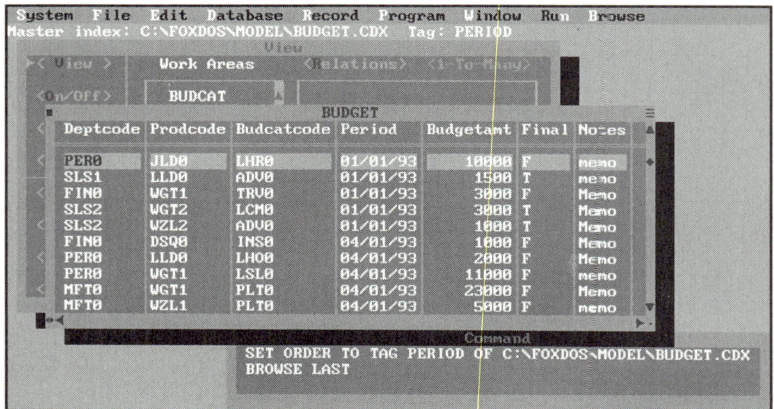

FIG. 3.13

The Browse window, displaying records in ascending date order.

Quick Results to the Printer

In Chapter 1, you saw a quick demonstration of how to print reports by using FoxPro's RQBE. In following chapters, you learn how to produce both easy and complicated reports by using FoxPro's Report Writer. Other printing options also are available for special situations.

FoxPro, however, provides a simple way to print the information you just saw in the Browse window. Press Ctrl+F2 to bring forward the Command window (or select the Command window from the Window menu pad). Make sure that the printer is ready. In the Command window, type `LIST TO PRINTER`, and then press Enter (see fig. 3.14). If you have a laser printer, type `EJECT` to tell the printer to eject the page. (On an impact printer, EJECT merely advances the page to the top of the next page.)

Now you can try some more LIST options. To print a report that shows only the Prodcode and the Budgetamt, type `LIST FIELDS Prodcode, Budgetamt TO PRINTER`. (If using a laser printer, add the EJECT command.)

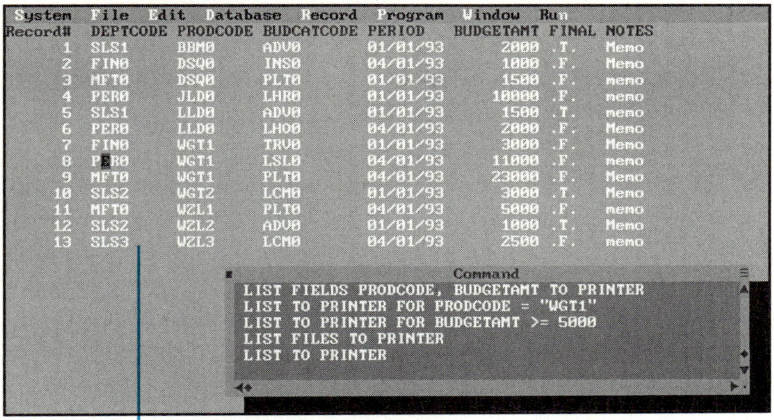

```
System  File  Edit  Database  Record  Program  Window  Run
Record#  DEPTCODE PRODCODE BUDCATCODE PERIOD    BUDGETAMT FINAL NOTES
      1  SLS1     BBM0     ADV0       01/01/93       2000 .T.   Memo
      2  FIN0     DSQ0     INS0       04/01/93       1000 .F.   Memo
      3  MFT0     DSQ0     PLT0       01/01/93       1500 .F.   memo
      4  PER0     JLD0     LHR0       01/01/93      10000 .F.   memo
      5  SLS1     LLD0     ADV0       01/01/93       1500 .T.   memo
      6  PER0     LLD0     LHO0       04/01/93       2000 .F.   Memo
      7  FIN0     WGT1     TRV0       01/01/93       3000 .F.   Memo
      8  PER0     WGT1     LSL0       04/01/93      11000 .F.   memo
      9  MFT0     WGT1     PLT0       04/01/93      23000 .F.   Memo
     10  SLS2     WGT2     LCM0       01/01/93       3000 .T.   Memo
     11  MFT0     WZL1     PLT0       04/01/93       5000 .F.   memo
     12  SLS2     WZL2     ADV0       01/01/93       1000 .T.   Memo
     13  SLS3     WZL3     LCM0       04/01/93       2500 .F.   memo

                                  Command
  LIST FIELDS PRODCODE, BUDGETAMT TO PRINTER
  LIST TO PRINTER FOR PRODCODE = "WGT1"
  LIST TO PRINTER FOR BUDGETAMT >= 5000
  LIST FILES TO PRINTER
  LIST TO PRINTER
```

Results of LIST TO PRINTER command echoed on-screen

FIG. 3.14

The LIST commands displayed in the Command window.

To produce a list for only records that use the Prodcode WGT1, type `LIST TO PRINTER FOR Prodcode = "WGT1"` (which means "Information in the field Prodcode is equal to or the same as the string of characters WGT1").

Notice that WGT1 is character data and must be enclosed in quotation marks. You use quotation marks to distinguish character data from FoxPro commands and from the names of fields. Notice also that, because the comparison is case-sensitive (that is, "WGT1" is not the same as "wgt1"), you must type `WGT1` in uppercase characters.

Now type `LIST TO PRINTER FOR Budgetamt >= 5000`. The `>=` is defined as *greater than or equal to*. Numbers need no quotation marks; FoxPro can work directly with numbers.

Type `LIST TO PRINTER FOR Period = {04/01/93}`. You must add curly braces around dates to distinguish them from numbers.

As you try these commands, you also can return to the Setup dialog and change the index order, as you did the Browse window. The order of records in your printed output changes in exactly the same way. If desired, continue to experiment with the Miscellaneous Settings panel's options in the View window, changing the CENTURY setting from OFF to ON or the date format from American to British. Now try changing the DELETED option in the On/Off panel of the View window; if you have any deleted records, you see these records disappear after DELETED is set to ON and reappear after the option is set to OFF.

Now highlight (that is, select as text) the word LIST from the commands in the Command window, and press F1. FoxPro's Help entry appears for the LIST command and all its different options (see fig. 3.15).

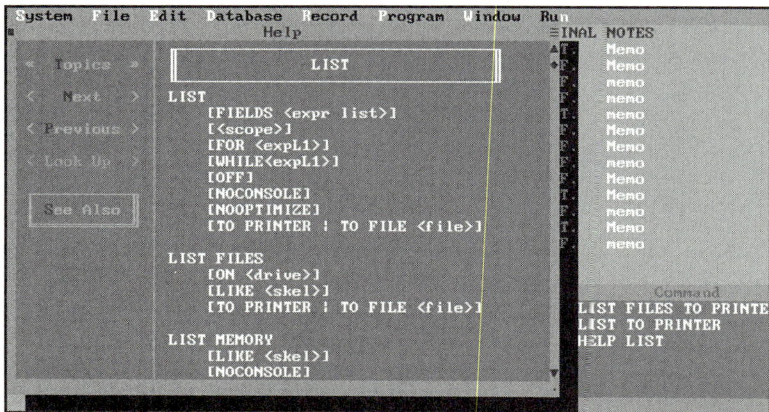

FIG. 3.15

The FoxPro Help entry for the LIST command and its options.

In the Command window, type `LIST FILES TO PRINTER`, and you print a list of all the tables in the working directory. Type `LIST STRUCTURE TO PRINTER`, and you print the structure of the Budget file.

The LIST command displays this same information on-screen during the printing process—or on-screen only if you omit TO PRINTER from the command. (You can use the NOCONSOLE keyword to print records but not to display the records on-screen.) If this display is not visible on-screen, press Ctrl+Alt+Shift (all three keys at the same time) to temporarily hide any windows that may be obscuring the screen.

NOTE Another convenient way to list the contents of tables to a screen is by using the DISPLAY command, which pauses after each screen or window of information. The DISPLAY command is nearly identical to LIST except that this command defaults to show the current record only; LIST displays on-screen or prints all records, subject to the conditions you previously set. Type `DISPLAY ALL` to see all records on-screen.

The LIST command does not show the contents of a Memo field by default. To display the contents of a Memo field, you must use the FIELDS clause and include the name of the Memo field in the FIELDS list, typing the command, for example, as `LIST FIELDS Budgetamt, Notes`. You also can print or display the contents of one Memo field with other fields by typing another FoxPro command used for output—the `?` (question mark). Switch back to the Browse window for the Budget file, and select an entry for which the word Memo in the Notes field begins with a capital M (which indicates that this memo contains text or other data). Now switch to the Command window and type the following commands:

```
SET PRINT ON
? Notes, Period
SET PRINT OFF
```

If you want to show the entry only on-screen, leave out the SET PRINT ON and SET PRINT OFF commands. The former command sends all output to the printer until the latter command is used to turn off the SET PRINT ON command.

Like LIST, the ? command has many options for producing output—some of which are quite sophisticated. Check the Help file for information on these options.

LIST and DISPLAY are both affected by the active printer driver setup, and a STYLE special clause on the ? command enables you to adjust the output even further if a printer driver is loaded. Refer to the "Printer Drivers" chapter in the *Developer's Guide* (and to Chapter 16) for more information on printer drivers.

Quick Results to a File

You often want a more permanent record of a report for subsequent use or to print at a later date. You can use the LIST command to send a report to a file on disk by using the TO FILE <filename> clause.

In the Command window, type `LIST TO FILE LISTFILE`, and then type `MODIFY FILE LISTFILE.TXT`. The file is displayed in an editing window as it is stored on disk. You now can edit the file. Notice that because you did not specify a file extension, FoxPro creates a file with the extension .TXT. You can create any file name you want by specifying the entire name, as in LISTFILE.PRN. Press Esc to exit the LISTFILE.TXT window.

To print the contents of the file, type the following commands in the Command window: `SET HEADING OFF`, followed by `TYPE LISTFILE.TXT TO PRINT`, followed by `EJECT` if printing to a laser printer. You also can print a file by choosing Print from the File menu pad. In the Print dialog that appears, use the `Windows` popup button to choose File, and then enter the name of the file to print in the File text box. Select the Page Eject After check box if you have a laser printer or to advance the paper to the top of the next page.

The TYPE command is affected by the printer driver you load. TYPE also has keywords that enable you to activate word wrap and indentation for Memo fields.

Rearranging and Extracting Data from Tables

By now, you know something about how indexes work. You learn more about how to create and maintain indexes in Chapter 4, but you can already see how useful indexes are for rearranging data. By using the FOR option of the LIST command, you begin to see how to extract data from tables so as to deal with only the specific range of information useful to you at the moment. Many ways of performing this process are available in FoxPro, but all rely primarily on the same concepts.

If extracting data, you set certain conditions that the data must meet before the data is included in the output. Essentially, you define a *subset* of all possible data.

In Chapter 1, you used FoxPro's RQBE feature to rearrange and extract data. You get much more practice using this feature in following chapters, and you learn that the RQBE handles many details of the process for you. This section, however, examines the rearranging and extracting of data as applied to FoxPro table commands such as the BROWSE and LIST commands discussed earlier in this chapter.

Extracting Records by Using a Scope Clause

A Scope clause tells a FoxPro command to limit its action to a specified range of contiguous records. (The records are contiguous as defined by the current index order.) If all conditions of the Scope clause are met, those records are included in the extraction process. (If you previously tried the DISPLAY ALL command, the ALL clause told DISPLAY to show all the records.) Table 3.3 lists the various Scope clauses available for FoxPro commands.

Table 3.3 The Scope Clauses

Scope Clause	Effect
ALL	Acts on all records in the table.
NEXT <n>	Acts on the next <*n*> (number) of records, starting at the current record. If you are located at the first record in an ordered table, the command LIST NEXT 10 gives you a list of the first 10 records. If you are at or near the end of the table, NEXT 10 gives you as many records as exist (up to 10 records) in this range.
RECORD <n>	Acts on only the one record number you specify. Therefore, LIST RECORD 5 lists only the information for record number 5. Warning: This clause acts on the physical record number 5, not on the fifth record in the current table order.
REST	Acts on all remaining records in a file, starting with the current record and continuing through the last record in the table.

Extracting Records by Using FOR, WHILE, and SET FILTER TO

FOR and WHILE clauses, like Scope clauses, instruct a FoxPro command to limit the actions of a command to only those records that meet certain conditions. SET FILTER TO is a FoxPro command that limits the range of records that other commands process.

The FOR clause tells a FoxPro command: "Work on all the records in this table FOR which the following conditions are true."

The WHILE clause begins at the current record and tells FoxPro to "Work on records in sequence WHILE the conditions are true" or "Work on records in sequence *until* the conditions are *no longer* true."

You use SET FILTER TO a little differently—to tell FoxPro to ignore all records that do not meet certain conditions. SET FILTER TO is used *before* a command so that the command sees only data that already meets certain conditions. This command works much like the FOR clause, except that SET FILTER TO selects the records before a command or series of commands is issued. These conditions stay in effect until removed by another SET FILTER TO command. (If you include no conditions, all records are again seen by the command.)

Not only are the conditions for each SET FILTER TO, FOR, and WHILE clause comprehensive and possibly complicated, but you also can combine the three clauses—with each other and with the various Scope clauses—to create extremely precise sets of conditions. One possibility is to create a combination of commands and clauses such as in the following example:

```
SET FILTER TO <conditions>
LIST NEXT 5 FOR <conditions> WHILE <conditions>
```

Designing these combinations can become complicated; in practice, however, a less complex combination of conditions can handle most needs.

> **CAUTION:** A filter created by using SET FILTER TO is not activated until the record pointer is moved. In practice, a good idea is to follow a SET FILTER TO command with a GO TO command, which moves the record pointer to the first record that satisfies the filter condition.

If you previously used other Xbase dialects, you know that SET FILTER TO and FOR clauses are seldom used because the database manager is forced to scan the entire table and evaluate conditions for each record. If a table contains several hundred records, this process can take a long time.

If you can phrase the conditions in the form of an expression that includes one or more index expressions, FoxPro can quickly extract the desired subset of records by using its exclusive *Rushmore* technology. You learn how this technology works in Chapter 7. For now, however, remember that FOR and SET FILTER TO clauses are efficient and usable options in FoxPro.

Defining Conditions

Conditions are a simple concept. Nearly every moment, you make choices based on whether certain conditions are met. If you dine out, you must first choose a restaurant and then select a number of items from a menu. You can phrase these conditions in the following way: "I want to eat Italian food, but I have only $10 to spend. I want to eat pasta with alfredo sauce, and I want to leave the restaurant by 9 p.m. so that I am home in time to watch a *Star Trek* rerun."

First, you narrow the available options from all the possible meals on earth to decide on the meals available in a certain restaurant. Then you winnow the food choices from all the meals available from the restaurant's menu. In "FoxProse," this kind of narrowing down may look like the following text:

```
SET FILTER TO FOOD = ITALIAN AND PRICES = INEXPENSIVE

EAT FOR ITEM = PASTA AND SAUCE = ALFREDO AND
PRICE <= $10 WHILE TIME <= 9 PM.
```

In the preceding listing, <= means *less than or equal to* (as >= means *greater than or equal to* in the LIST exercises). Of course, = means *equal to*. These examples are FoxPro *logical operators*—symbols that FoxPro interprets to make comparisons between data items.

In FoxPro, conditions are defined (or constructed) by comparing one or more data items in a variety of ways. You previously defined conditions in the LIST exercises by typing the commands directly into the Command window. FoxPro also provides a tool for defining conditions—the *Expression Builder.*

You can quickly see how to use the Expression Builder to define the conditions for a filter. If the View window and the Browse window for the Budget file are not currently open on-screen, open the Budget table in the View window, and then Browse the Budget table.

Choose the `Setup` push button from the View window to access the Setup dialog (refer to fig. 3.12). Select the Filter check box in the lower-left corner to activate the Expression Builder dialog, as shown in figure 3.16.

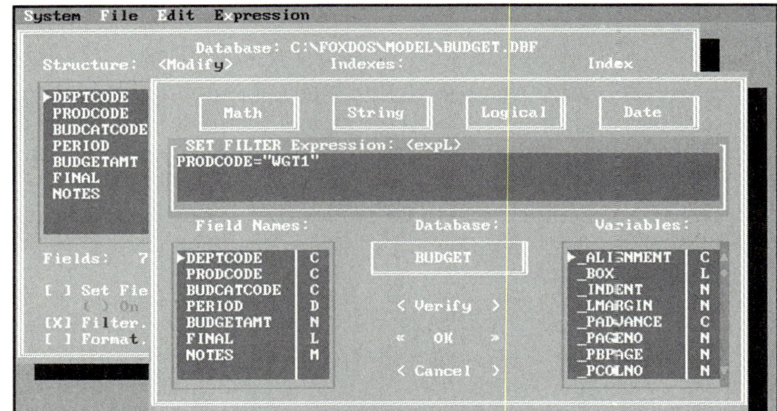

FIG. 3.16

The Expression Builder dialog.

Type `Prodcode = "WGT1"` in the SET FILTER Expression box. (Remember that you used this condition in the LIST exercises with the FOR option; the condition tells FoxPro to create a temporary table that includes only the budget items with product codes of WGT1.) Press Ctrl+Enter or click `OK` to save the work. After you return to the Setup dialog, you can see the condition displayed on-screen, beside the Filter check box. Return to the View window.

Select the Browse window again. Only items with WGT1 product codes are listed, and no other items are available. If you LIST ALL now, only the items visible in the Browse window print in the reports. To return to a listing of all the items in the table, return to the Setup dialog and reselect Filter; then reenter the Expression Builder dialog and delete the condition you set. Try this step now. After you return to the Browse window, you see that all the items are listed again.

You learn more about defining conditions and using the Expression Builder in Chapter 10. You also learn the syntax FoxPro uses for making comparisons.

For now, select the Database menu pad from the menu bar and select any option on the menu popup. You see that almost all the options—from Append From... through Label...—have Scope, FOR, and WHILE options that use the Expression Builder. The Setup option on the Database menu is the same as Setup in the View window, and you can use this option to set a filter the same way.

Summary

In this chapter, you began to take control of data tables. You saw how the tables fit into a wider picture of related tables, and you now know how to create a table to meet specific needs. You learned how to rearrange information for a particular purpose and how to extract subsets of data that meet specific requirements.

Using the mouse or keyboard to move around and to select menus, popup and drop-down menus, and boxes in FoxPro is fun, but the real point of using the program is that FoxPro gives you the power to control the information you need to do the job.

In Chapter 4, “Database Management Fundamentals,” you concentrate on ways to organize and define information, creating corrrectly structured tables and databases so that FoxPro can manage your data.

4

CHAPTER

Database Management Fundamentals

In this chapter, you learn to design a database by looking at a database as one part of an *information system.* The purpose of an information system is to provide you with the information you need to accomplish a specific objective, such as running your business.

Raw data has little value. An information system makes data useful by collecting, organizing, processing, and presenting the data in a way that makes sense to the user.

To design an effective information system, you must focus on the *results* you ultimately want to achieve, and realize that the purpose of the information system is to support you in managing a process or activity. Emphasizing results gives you a context in which to make decisions; this emphasis filters down to the smallest details of database design and management.

Information systems frequently fail because of an inadequate understanding and definition of the results. Results can be defined as both *comprehensive* and *detailed.* A comprehensive system design includes consideration of future growth, increasingly sophisticated information users, and potential changes in the operating environment. These changes may include both changes in the people who use the system and in the equipment used to run the system. A detailed system design includes an exacting analysis of what information is needed and a plan for the information's proper use.

In the model presented in this chapter, the Omnipresent Widget company is developing an information system that tells management how well the company is performing and provides the company with information that helps to identify both problems and opportunities. Omnipresent Widget uses this information to monitor growth and change so that the company can respond quickly and appropriately to changes in the marketplace. The company generates information that gives both a wide view of the company's performance and a narrow view of how individual products, salespeople, and departments are functioning.

The first three sections of this chapter show you how the Omnipresent Widget database designers—and you—can design the structure of a database and get all the elements to work together internally. In the fourth section, you learn how to set up the database management system to function as a whole within the information system that already exists within the company.

Constructing Databases

In Chapter 3, you learned that a database is a collection of tables that work together to accomplish a common purpose, and that tables are collections or lists of records, with each record holding individual pieces of information in fields.

How do you determine which pieces of information you want in a database? How do you determine the tables you need in a database? How do the tables work together to accomplish a purpose? What do you want to know, and how do you put together a system that gives you this information?

There are two approaches to constructing a database. In the *top down* approach, you define the results, define the specific purpose of the database in terms of supporting these results, and look at what you specifically want to know. In the *bottom up* approach, you organize specific pieces of information into increasingly larger groups. When constructing a complete database system, you must use both approaches at the same time.

Although this process may sound complicated, you already know how to do it. The process is often referred to as getting organized. The following mental exercise illustrates this process.

Suppose that a tornado sweeps through your home and office, picks up every scrap of paper, and deposits the whole mess on the living room floor. You now must sort through this chaos and reorganize all the information. Because the material may not have been as organized as you wanted it to be, and you also accumulated a great deal of junk, you can use this opportunity to start with a clean slate. Think about how you want to organize the material. Without the inertia of the old systems, you find a new freedom to create systems that work better.

You might start with a home pile and an office pile. These piles represent databases. You then can break down the home database into separate piles such as home finances, family matters, and community affairs. These piles are the *tables,* which you can break down into even more precise tables.

Note how you are thinking and making choices. You are organizing the material based on how you want your life organized—based on the results. Although you are putting together pieces of information one at a time (building *up* piles), you also are working *down* from a mental image of what you want to know and how you want to access the information. You probably aren't sorting all the blue pieces of paper into one pile and the yellow pieces into a second pile—such a sorting process, although a form of organizing, is not very useful.

Concentrating on Output

The purpose of a database management system is to produce useful *output,* or information that you can review and analyze. Computer systems provide output in many different forms, usually on-screen and on paper. Although the information with which you work is the same, you can present the data differently, as you saw with BROWSE and with the printed reports when you used LIST.

Before constructing a database, think of every report you imagine may be useful. A handy tip is to think in terms of printed reports. Design the system by sketching the reports on pieces of paper. Make these sample reports look exactly as you want to see the printed product. Think of the possible subsets of information and the order in which you want this information to appear. Be creative. Don't limit yourself at this stage; you always can make compromises later.

Suppose that you want a list of customers. One report may consist of a list of all customers in alphabetical order. Another report may be a list of only certain customers in alphabetical order. Another report may be a list of customers sorted by salesperson. You may want mailing labels (just another form of report) sorted by ZIP code, or you may want a list of all the products that each customer purchased in the preceding year.

You begin to see information you need in the output, and you can work back from these results to determine the information you need to collect (or input) to produce this output. You must collect information that does the following:

- Tells you something you want to know
- Gives you a means of ordering information
- Gives you a means of extracting subsets of information
- Gives you a means of relating, or connecting, one set of information to other sets of information
- Is used in processing other input (for example, calculating sales tax on a sale)

When you complete this process, you have determined all the pieces of information you need to output and most of the pieces of information you need to input or provide within an application. The following section looks at the task of organizing and distributing these pieces of information into tables.

Organizing Information into Tables

Suppose that you are again back on the living room floor with the piles of paper. You need to sort this data into fields, records, tables, and databases.

The goal is to organize information economically into tables (without unnecessary duplication or wasted space) and in a way that enables each table to operate as independently as possible. You may think that putting all the information into a single table is the most efficient sorting method. However, much of the power and flexibility of FoxPro depends on separate tables that work together.

Remember that a table is a collection of items that share common traits. These traits may differ from the way you organize paper files. In a paper-based system, for example, you may have a customer file that contains a variety of different kinds of information. You may have a cover sheet with name, address, assigned salesperson, and miscellaneous information, correspondence to and from the customer, and copies of all invoices, payments, and adjusting memos. This method has several problems:

- Duplicated information takes space. On a computer system, duplication takes up disk space, which is always at a premium.
- If you ever want to look at the correspondence of all customers (for example, to analyze the number of complaints about a certain product or the number of letters received by date), you may need to keep another file that contains a copy of every piece of correspondence. Similarly, if you want to extract information about invoices, you need a separate invoice file.
- Duplicated information makes changing data difficult. In a paper-based system, if you have a customer file and an invoice file—and both contain the customer's complete name and address—you must make changes in both files when the address changes. A better method is to make changes in one place, because the change is quicker and because the fewer changes you make, the fewer mistakes occur.
- Suppose that you are entering customer data on a form and you want to assign an available salesperson to this customer. You do not want to have to thumb through all the customer files to get this information. You want a separate list of salespeople to which you can refer.

In a relational database management system such as FoxPro, you create one table for each kind of information and *relate* the tables (similar to keeping cross-reference lists for paper files). You can easily present the information together—just as though all the information were in the same table. When you need to, you also can work with each table independently.

Deciding which kinds of information belong together in one table can take thought and perhaps some experimentation. This decision also depends a great deal on specific circumstances. *Customers* are generally the same kind of *items,* although different kinds of customers exist. Although you might have different kinds of customers, all customers usually can stay in the same table with a code that identifies each kind of customer entry. If you have a business in which you keep completely different kinds of information for each of two groups of customers, however, you might choose to create separate tables for the two customer groups.

In another example, you might consider sales and payments as different items that require separate tables. When you set up the tables, however, you see that the Sales table contains the same fields as the Payments table. You see that you can combine the two tables into one by adding a field to hold a code to distinguish between the different types of transactions.

To use record and disk space most efficiently, you occasionally may need to separate into different tables some items that seem similar. Addresses always require the same types and numbers of fields. Normally customers have one or two addresses (billing and shipping), so you might place fields in each customer record for both billing and shipping addresses. In some applications and in some cases, a customer might have seven addresses for different purposes. You might not know in advance how many addresses a customer has. If you set up separate fields for all possible address combinations and numbers, you waste disk space for all the customers who have only one or two addresses. You also may run up against FoxPro's limit of 255 fields per table. In this case, a more sensible approach is to put addresses into a separate address table. Each record in the address table contains one address and two additional fields that identify the customer to whom each address belongs and the kind of address of each entry.

A few additional considerations are best explained by looking at the Budget, Product, and Dept tables. Figure 4.1 shows the Budget and Product tables—and the Dept table, which you have not yet created—opened. The structure of the Dept table is similar to the structure of the Product table and the other tables that support the Budget table in the model database. (You create the Dept table in Chapter 12. To see the Dept table's structure, along with the structure of the other supporting tables, refer to Appendix H.)

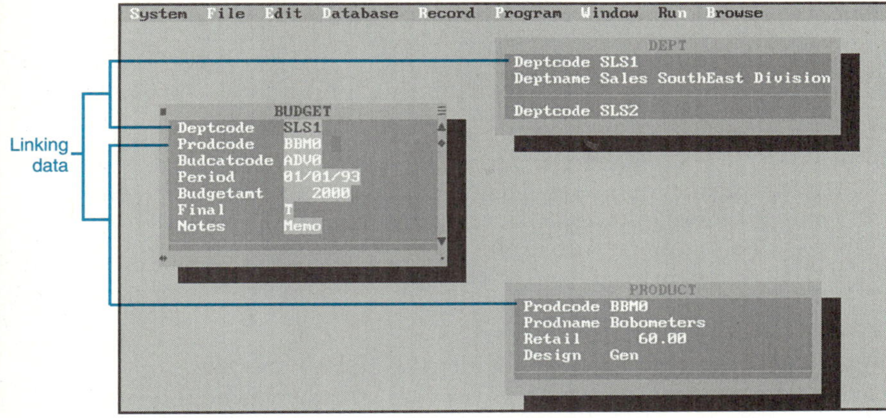

FIG. 4.1

Data in the Budget table forms the links to the Product and Dept tables.

Consider the Budget and Product tables in the context of the larger database. Why are these tables separate? Why do you need a separate Product table? Why don't you just store the product name in each record of the Budget table?

Theoretically (although with some difficulty), you can stuff all this information into one table, the Budget table, which is the center of activity for this particular database task.

The Product table contains the Design field, which holds a picture of the product's design specifications. If you don't have a separate Product table, you must store the design everywhere you store the product name, in case you want to display the picture. Pictures require large amounts of disk space, so it makes sense to store the picture once in a separate table that all the other tables can reference when necessary.

You also can save more disk space and data-entry time by eliminating the repetition of the long product names in the Budget table. Another argument for separate tables is that, during data entry, you might want to look up available products and choose a product from a list. A separate table makes this process simple. In a similar way, you may want to validate a product code as you type the entry, to make sure that you are using information that already exists and is defined as acceptable input. Otherwise, you may end up entering the same product name with different spellings or abbreviations, and the associated records may not be properly grouped together when you order or extract data.

You can use the following guidelines to help you decide when to place data in separate tables:

- Create separate tables for sets of information that are essentially *independent* of each other.
- Create separate tables to provide the most *economic* use of table and disk space. If many records in a table will not contain an entry for one or more fields, consider creating a separate table to hold the data for those records that will require entries.
- Create separate tables to hold data-entry lookup lists, such as products, styles, and colors.

Sorting information into tables is not a cut-and-dried process. In relational database terminology, this process is known as *normalization*. As you gain more experience with database management concepts, you might want to read more about normalization. For now, if you concentrate on economy and independence of tables and apply common sense, you are off to a good start.

Understanding How Tables Connect and Interact

If you read the preceding sections, you learned that often you must separate data into independent tables and that these tables also must work together to perform the tasks of a database. How tables work together is the subject of this section.

You provide connections between tables by creating cross-referencing links. In the Omnipresent Widgets database, you can link the Budget table to the Product, Department (Dept), and Budget Category (Budcat) tables by using information present in these tables. The Budget table links to the Product table by using a field that has the same name, Prodcode, in both tables. The two fields do not necessarily have to use the same name; however, the tables must share the contents of the field. The field values, such as WGT1—not the field name Prodcode—provide a connecting link between records in the two tables.

After you establish connections between tables, the way tables interact seems almost magical. As you scan through one table, the associated information from other tables connected to this table is immediately available and can be viewed, reported, or processed simultaneously. The equivalent in a paper-based system would be the ability to thumb through the customer files, have the selected invoices and correspondence for each customer pop up on the desk for immediate use, and then pop back into the files after you move on to the next customer's file.

NOTE In FoxPro, you create the connecting link between tables by using a *key expression* common to both tables. A key expression that links two tables is usually a field or combination of fields. You use key expressions to distinguish between records in the same table; the key identifier in the parent table evaluates to a value that is unique among all the records in that table. For example, each record in the Product table has a unique Prodcode. The key expression that links the Product table to the Budget table is the Prodcode field, which enables FoxPro to find those records in the Budget table that are related to the current record in the Product table.

To make the connection between tables, you give FoxPro instructions that can be translated into English as, "As you process records in a table, look for this reference in the connected table, and bring me the related information." In the "Creating Relations" section later in this chapter, you learn how to create these instructions, known as *relations*; you also learn the rules that govern the creation of inter-table relations.

Connections between tables are made in only one direction. The connection is established between the table in the currently selected work area and other tables and is active if you stay in this work area. You can temporarily activate the child table, or any other work area, and move among the records in that table. When you return to the controlling table, the connections are reestablished.

The controlling table can make connections with many tables at the same time and can look up individual records in these tables or sets of information. If the Budget table is the controlling table and is linked to the Product table, FoxPro finds only one record in the Product table that relates to the current Budget record, and more than one Budget record may relate to that Product record. This example is known as a *many-to-one relationship*.

If Product is the controlling table and you are looking up information in Budget, you might find several Budget records that relate to the current Product record. This example is known as a *one-to-many relationship*.

A one-to-one relationship, in which records in two tables are paired, is also common.

FoxPro uses indexes to look up information quickly in tables connected to the controlling table. Consequently, you must order the lookup tables by using an index expression that forms the connecting link. You can order the controlling table or leave the controlling table unordered, depending on your objective. You learn about indexes and index expressions in the "Using Indexes" section later in this chapter.

Organizing Information into Records

When you were "concentrating on output" in a previous section with that name, you discovered several kinds of information that you need to collect and enter into the system. The information that you store in record fields does the following:

- Tells you something you want to know. The fields store the actual data, such as name, address, and contact.
- Gives you a means of ordering the information in a table. If you want to alphabetize customers, you need a field that can be indexed to produce alphabetical output (for example, last names or an alphabetizing code). To produce mailing labels by ZIP code, you need a separate ZIP code field (rather than making the ZIP code a part of a long address line). You also can use a combination of fields in index expressions.
- Gives you a means of extracting subsets of information in the table. If you want to produce a report for each salesperson, you need a separate field for a salesperson name or code.
- Gives you a means of relating or connecting one table with other tables—the connecting links or keys discussed previously.
- Helps you process information in other tables. (If you don't have a lookup table that provides the sales tax percentage for each location, you have to enter this figure into each record.)

Create fields that enable you to fulfill all these purposes, assigning appropriate data types, optimum field lengths, and index tags (where appropriate) for all fields as you go along.

When you work in a table, you often want an easy way to locate the specific record with which to work so that you can change or delete some piece of information. To find a specific record, you need a unique identifying code for each record. You need to create this code only if you (or FoxPro) need to find one—and only one—record among many records. The Product table needs this code, called a *primary key*, because each physical product is unique, and you want to find a specific product to change or delete. When you relate the Budget table to the Product table, you also want FoxPro to find one and only one Product record with the right information for this Budget record.

Depending on how you want the system to work, you can mix and match the way you and FoxPro locate records. For example, when a user of the system enters data, you can use a searching method based on conditions to find several records that provide a *near match* rather than using a unique code that finds one exact match. The Budget table is a good example of a table in which you might want to find several possible matches as the result of one search.

When you choose to access records by using unique codes, make sure that the table order is set to the index expression that matches the primary key. This step enables you to use FoxPro's speedy indexes to find the record quickly.

Choosing the values the primary key will have is another area where you may need to think a bit and perhaps experiment. The main consideration is that you must choose values that provide unique keys for as many records as you think you may have. If you limit the key to one uppercase letter, you have at most 26 unique keys.

Furthermore, if you want to be able to use the primary key during data entry, choose values that you can easily remember (character-based codes are best for this purpose) and that are as short as possible. Product codes in the model project are based on three characters that identify a class of products, plus a digit that identifies products within the class (you can, for example, type `WGT1` for Laptop Widgets and `WGT2` for Mainframe Widgets).

NOTE In the OWL system, the user creates the Product code by entering the code in the FoxApp-generated entry screen you created in Chapter 1. In Chapter 12, you learn how to make sure the code entered by the user is unique for each record. This procedure is common when computer systems replace existing manual systems that already use many codes. However, computer systems also frequently create primary key codes without the user's intervention. (After all, in many systems, the user doesn't care about the code that represents a product; he or she is interested in the product's name only.) You learn one technique to generate such codes in Chapter 21, in the section titled "Converting Numeric Data to and from Character Data."

By now, you have most of the information you need to create tables. As you read the rest of this chapter, however, you discover other considerations that affect your table and record design.

Using Indexes

In Chapter 3, you saw how you can use indexes to order the data in a useful way for viewing and reporting. The capability of ordering data also is useful to FoxPro, especially for connecting tables and increasing processing speed. FoxPro's incredible speed and much of the ease of use result from the capability of creating and manipulating unusually efficient indexes to access data.

In this section, you learn more about what indexes are, how you open and select indexes, and how you can create simple and complex index expressions that enable you and FoxPro to link tables.

Understanding Indexes

You and FoxPro use indexes to

- Order data for processing or output
- Look up information quickly in tables

FoxPro has two types of indexes. Both index types are separate files from the data tables. The first type, the *compound index*, has the file extension CDX. This kind of index may contain multiple individual indexes, or *tags*. The second type of index file, the *individual index*, has the file extension IDX and contains only one individual index.

Indexes contain only as much information as is needed to perform the kind of search you specify in an index expression, plus *pointers* to the corresponding records in the table. When you open index files along with the table, FoxPro updates the information in the index when records in the table are added, edited, or deleted.

The compound index (CDX) is a very fast and efficient feature of FoxPro. A compound index's capability of containing multiple indexes enables you to open all of the indexes that a table requires by opening a single file. An added advantage is that these indexes require only one

MS-DOS file handle, which means that CDX files can decrease the burden placed on the operating system, which opens and manages files for FoxPro (and also all the other application programs).

FoxPro also has a special kind of compound index, called a *structural index*. You created a structural index in the Structure dialog when you created the Budget and Product tables. This index file always uses the same base file name as the table, and FoxPro opens this file whenever you open the table.

The individual indexes (IDX) are the type of index FoxPro once used exclusively. FoxPro 2.5 includes these indexes mainly to provide compatibility with FoxBASE+ and with FoxBASE+/Mac (which Microsoft continues to support as part of its Fox product line). However, IDX indexes can be useful if you need a quick index for a temporary purpose. When you create individual indexes, be sure that you always use the COMPACT option, which produces a smaller and faster index. However, if you create an individual index that must be used by FoxBASE+ or FoxBase+/Mac, don't use COMPACT, because these products cannot read compressed indexes.

Note that you cannot create an index of any type on Memo, General, or Picture fields. Fields of these types often hold large amounts of binary data and are not suited to FoxPro's indexing scheme.

Opening and Selecting Indexes

When you created the Budget table, you also created an index for all the fields except the Notes Memo field, which you cannot directly index. In many tables, however, you may have fields that you don't need to keep in any particular order. You may never want to order the data by street address or by customer contact person.

Because keeping all open indexes updated may slow FoxPro a bit, limit the number of tags in the structural index (or in other indexing schemes) to the fields you regularly need to order or search.

Similarly, although you can have multiple indexes of all kinds open with the same table, you might find that limiting this practice is usually more efficient. Because FoxPro can build indexes very rapidly, you usually use a structural index for the most common indexing needs and create temporary IDX indexes on the fly when needed.

If you often need to create several temporary indexes, consider using a nonstructural compound index, such as TEMP.CDX, and creating each temporary index as a tag in the compound index. That way, you only have one file to keep track of and erase when you no longer need these indexes.

To open multiple indexes for a table (remember that the structural index is opened automatically whenever you open the table), you can use the Setup dialog from the View window or the Database menu pad. You also can use the Setup dialog to create additional indexes that you can either add to a new or existing compound index or assign to an individual index. To open nonstructural indexes, type one of the following FoxPro commands:

```
USE <table> INDEX <index file list>
SET INDEX TO <index file list>
```

You use the first command to open the indexes at the same time the table is opened. You use the second command to open indexes for a table that is already open. In each case, the <index file list> consists of one or more index file names, separated by commas. Both these commands contain additional options that enable you to set the order of the indexes as you open them and to access a previously created ascending index in descending order (or a descending index in ascending order). The SET INDEX command also enables you to add new indexes to the current index file list, if you use the keyword ADDITIVE.

T I P

CDX files, both structural and nonstructural, have a complex format. When you add tags at different times or add large groups of records, CDX files can grow far faster than the new data being added may warrant, because some space is wasted. Chapter 3 explains how you can use the PACK command to remove this file bloat and wasted space in memo files. If you want to slim down the CDX files at other times, you can use the REINDEX command, or you can use the DELETE TAG ALL command (which erases the index file) and then re-create each individual tag. The latter approach, although seemingly convoluted, is preferable because you also can use this procedure to rebuild a CDX file that is missing or damaged. Adding and deleting tags to a CDX file, however, requires exclusive use of the CDX. When the CDX is a structural index, you also need exclusive use of the associated table. This can cause problems in a network environment, where files are normally opened for shared use. Weigh these factors for each situation when you work out your file maintenance practices.

In the "Understanding Index Expressions" section later in this chapter, you use the Setup dialog to create an additional index for the Budget table and to experiment with opening multiple indexes for the table.

Setting the Index Order

A table's current order is controlled by the master index, which is established when you choose Set Order in the Setup dialog, use the FoxPro command SET ORDER TO, or set the order with the USE and SET INDEX TO commands. Other open indexes, however, are active in the sense that these indexes are constantly updated as changes are made in the table.

> **CAUTION:** Remember that indexes that are not open when the table is edited are *not* kept current. You need to rebuild or re-create these indexes when you're ready to use them. Because FoxPro has compound structural indexes, no real reason exists to maintain indexes that you don't keep open and updated along with tables. Create temporary IDX file indexes for infrequent reports or other special purposes just before you need the index. Delete these indexes after you finish the task.

When a structural index is opened along with the table, FoxPro sets the order to 0 (natural order). FoxPro takes this approach for several reasons. Because tags are in the index in the order they were created, the first one may not be the one you want to order the data. Moreover, FoxPro performs many operations more efficiently when no order is in effect, because FoxPro doesn't have to access the index to determine which record comes next in the current ordering scheme.

In Chapter 3, you experimented with changing the index order for the Budget table in the View window's Setup dialog. You can continue to use the Setup dialog for this purpose and choose the desired order from among any of the open indexes.

The SET ORDER command and ORDER options of the USE and SET INDEX TO commands give you the option of referring to an individual index or tag within a compound index by its name, which is the most efficient way to perform this function.

To maintain compatibility with FoxBASE+ and FoxBase+/Mac, FoxPro also provides the option of referring to indexes by number. However, the numbering system can be extremely complex if you use a large number of tags and mix together index types. If you want to refer to indexes by number, look up (in the *Commands and Functions* volume of the FoxPro documentation) the CDX( ), KEY( ), TAG( ), and other associated functions that you use together to determine the order number of a given index expression out of all the indexes currently available.

In FoxPro, using the DESCENDING or ASCENDING keyword on the SET ORDER TO or SET INDEX TO commands enables you to flip the order of records in an index, no matter how the index was created. To check the original index expression, in the Command window or in a program, you can check the value returned by the following expression:

```
SET("ORDER")
```

If the index was created in descending order, this expression returns a string that includes `"DESCENDING"`.

Note that using the DESCENDING and ASCENDING keywords on SET ORDER TO and SET INDEX TO doesn't physically alter the index for future use (unlike the Setup/Index/Modify option of the View window). In addition to doubling the flexibility of each index, this feature provides additional speed in searches because you don't bloat your compound index files with an additional index tag.

Understanding Index Expressions

Although the indexes you previously created ordered the tables on the basis of a field name, indexes create orders on the basis of a key expression. The field names you used in previous indexes are known as *simple key expressions*.

A slightly more complex FoxPro index expression is a combination of fields. This kind of *compound* key creates a cascading index order. To display on-screen—or to print—the information for the Budget table in product order and in department order for each product, use the index expression Prodcode + Deptcode. These cascading orders can get much deeper, subject only to the overall limit on the length of an index key expression (this limit varies according to the kind of index you use; CDX indexes have a greater maximum length than IDX indexes). You can easily create an index that you first index by product, then by date, and finally by budget amount.

NOTE Compound index expressions must use the same data type components. You cannot mix a Character field and a Date field in these fields' native states. You can use various FoxPro functions, however, to translate one or more of the components into other data types. You see an example of this kind of translation in an index you create later in this section. You also learn in Chapter 3 that indexing character data can lead to unexpected results because character data is ordered by ASCII code number. To index on a Character field that may contain upper- or lowercase letters, you can produce a correct order (by most alphabetizing standards) if you use the FoxPro UPPER( ) function as part of the index expression. Using a function in an index expression does not change the data stored in the table; the function affects only the contents of the index.

Index expressions can be even more complicated and can include memory variables and user-defined functions. These functions are discussed in Chapter 10—where you learn to use these features in the Report Writer—and in even greater depth in the programming sections of this book. Index expressions may even contain fields from other connected tables. You also can create a *conditional index*, which enables you to include only records that meet certain conditions that you set. To create a conditional index, use the FOR clause of the INDEX ON command (or the equivalent selection in the Setup dialog). This command works in the same way as the FOR clause on the LIST command, which you used in Chapter 3 to extract a subset of data from a larger table.

Now you can experiment with creating additional indexes for the Budget table. If they are not already open, open the Budget table and the View window now.

Select the Budget table and choose Setup from the View window or the Database menu popup. Now create a completely separate index of the IDX type to see how this kind of index works. In the far right column, you see the Index options. Click the `Add...` button to add a new index to the existing list.

In figure 4.2, you see the Open Index dialog. So far, you have not yet created additional index files for the Budget table; you have relied on the structural index. Choose `New` to create an index, and you see the Index dialog shown in figure 4.3.

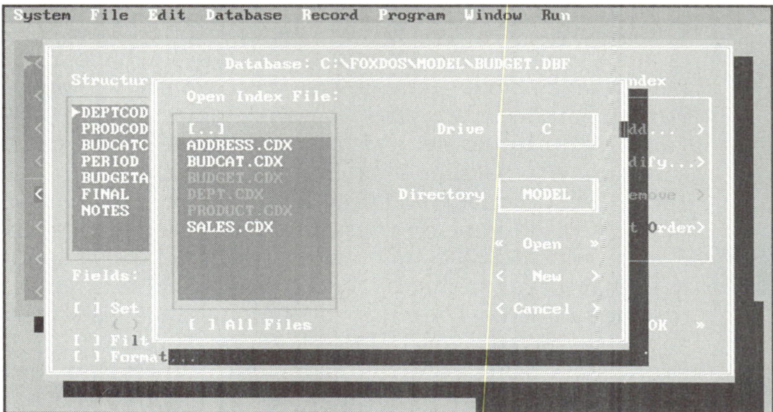

FIG. 4.2

The Open Index dialog.

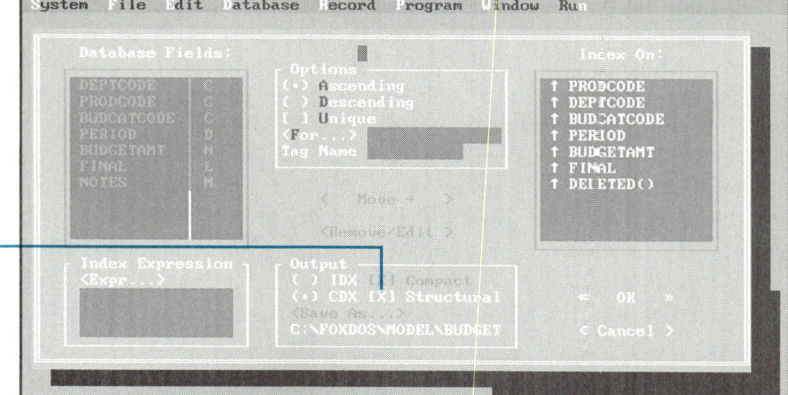

FIG. 4.3

The Index dialog.

You can use the Index dialog to add, delete, or modify index tags within the structural index, to create IDX indexes, or to create or modify additional CDX indexes. As you see, this dialog provides many options.

Notice that the Index dialog assumes that you want to add indexes to the existing structural index. In the upper-left corner of the window is the Database Fields list, which shows all the fields in the current table. The fields already used as index expressions are dimmed to indicate that you cannot select these fields. (The NOTES field is dimmed because you cannot index on a Memo field.) In the upper-right corner, the Index On list shows all the current index expressions. Indexes that consist of only field names correspond to the dimmed fields in the Database Fields list.

In the top and center of the Index dialog, you see the Options box. The selections in this box determine whether a specific index is ascending or descending, and whether the index is unique. A *unique* index type contains only one instance of each value for the key expression. In the Budget table, you can create an index similar to the following line:

```
INDEX ON Prodcode UNIQUE TO Budgprod
```

When this index controls the use of the Budget table, only one entry is shown (the first entry typed into the table) for each product. Likewise, if multiple records have a blank Prodcode field, only the first record is displayed on-screen. If some products do not appear in the indexed table, you know that *no* entries exist in the Budget table for these products.

The `For...` button in the Options box enables you to create a condition for a specific index, and the Tag Name is the name given to a specific tag within a compound index file. Usually, the tag name defaults to the field name. If you create a new or more complex tag, you are prompted to enter a new name.

Experiment with using only the sections of the Index dialog you have learned about so far. In the Index On list, select any index so that the index is highlighted. Now move to the top center and click the Descending radio button. You see the arrow for this field change to a down arrow. Now select the Ascending radio button, and the arrow changes back.

Select the `For...` button and you see the Expression Builder discussed briefly in Chapter 3 (subsequent chapters cover the Expression Builder in greater detail). If you enter an expression here, you build a condition. The index you create includes only records that match the condition. If you type `BUDGETAMT >= 5000`, only records whose budget amount is greater than or equal to 5,000 are included in the resulting index. Because you use these indexes in subsequent chapters, click `For...` again and delete any expression you entered.

Now, select any index in the Index On box and click the `Remove` push button. Notice that the index disappears from the list on the right side of the screen and appears as a selectable field name in the list on the left. Select the field in the left list and choose `Move`. The field name is again dimmed in the left window and shows up in the right window.

Look at the options in the lower part of the dialog. On the left is an Index Expression box, with a text box used to create a compound index key. In the center is the Output text box, where you name an index file if you don't want to use the structural index. Choose the IDX radio button, which creates an individual index, and notice how the dialog changes. In the Options box, only the Unique check box and For... button are selectable. All IDX indexes are created in ascending order and don't use tag names.

All the fields are now undimmed on the left, and no fields exist in the Index On list because you haven't yet used any fields in this new index file.

Move to the Index Expression box and use the `Expr...` button to bring forward the Expression Builder. Now you can create the Prodcode + Budgetamt index discussed previously. Type the expression `Prodcode + Budgetamt`, or select each field from the fields list on the lower-left and type + (the plus sign) between the fields. Choose `Verify` to see whether you created a valid index expression. You haven't, because Prodcode is a Character field and Budgetamt is a Numeric field; you can't mix the two in an expression. Retype the expression as follows:

```
Prodcode+STR(Budgetamt,7,0)
```

You type this line in the Expression Builder text box shown in figure 4.4. Select `Verify`—it works! You just used the FoxPro STR( ) function to transform a numeric field into character data. Now that all elements in the index expression are the same data type, the expression is valid.

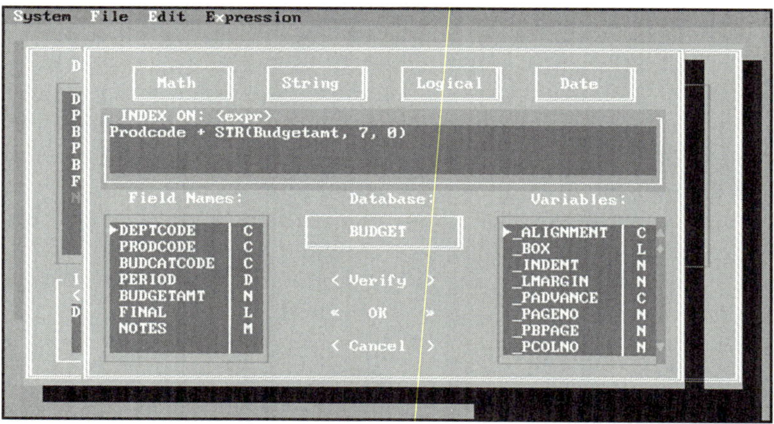

FIG. 4.4

The Index On Expression Builder dialog.

Select `OK` to complete the work here.

When you return to the Index dialog, you see the index expression you entered in the Expression Builder's Index Expression box. Choose `Move` to move the expression to the top right (Index On) list.

You have one more option. You can either name the new file in the Save As box or select OK. If you don't type the name of the new file in the Save As box, FoxPro prompts you to enter the file name by using the same Save File dialog you used for other types of files.

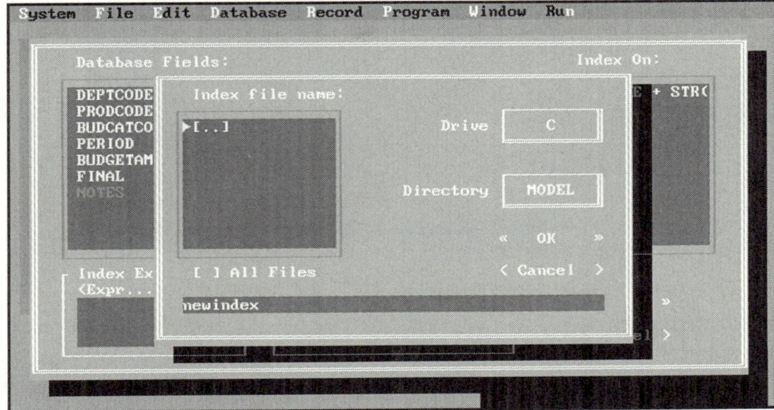

FIG. 4.5

The Index file name dialog.

When you return to the Setup dialog (see fig. 4.6), you see that the new index was added to the Indexes list, and the table's order is set to the new index (you see the ↑ character next to the new index file name). Return to the View window and select the Browse button to browse the Budget table. Note that the records are listed in product code order and that within each product code, the budget amounts are listed in ascending order.

Indexes are powerful tools; they also are the cornerstones on which many of FoxPro's other powerful tools are built. In the next section, you learn more about the important role that indexes play in FoxPro's relational scheme.

Linking Tables

Now that you understand how FoxPro uses data that two tables have in common to connect the tables, and uses indexes to find related records in connected tables quickly, you are ready to learn how to establish links, or *relations*, that connect tables. The ability to create relations enables you to transform your separate tables into a database.

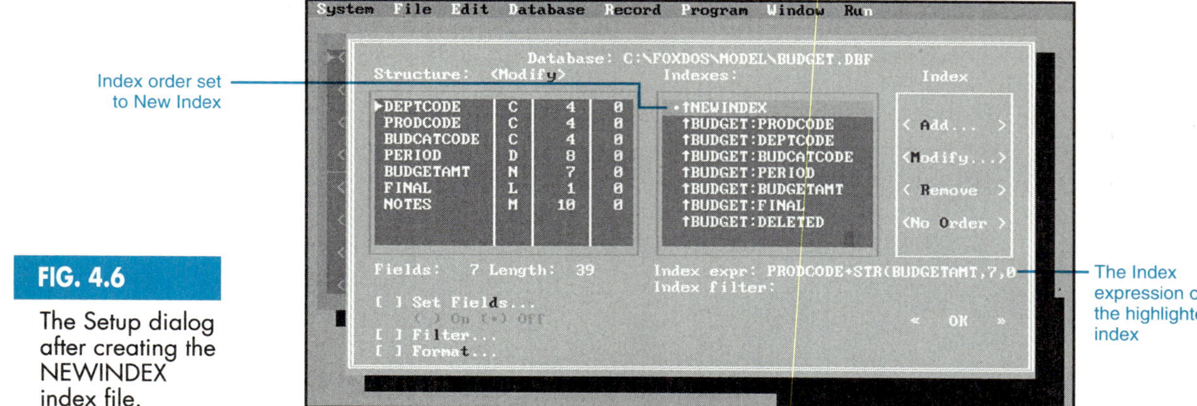

FIG. 4.6

The Setup dialog after creating the NEWINDEX index file.

In the examples that follow, you use the View window to create and modify inter-table relations. As you work through these examples, pay close attention to the commands that FoxPro echoes to the Command window at each step in the process. When you begin to develop FoxPro applications that require you to link tables without the View window's help, you need to know the FoxPro commands that establish and break relations.

Creating Relations

Open the View window and close all open tables.

Select work area 1 and open the Product table. Choose the Set Order option from the Setup dialog to set the order of the Prodcode index. Now select work area 2, open the Budget table, and choose the Set Order option from the Setup dialog to set the order of the Prodcode index.

You are going to set a relation *from* the Product table *into* the Budget table. For a relation to be set, the subsidiary table (in this case Budget) must be indexed on the connecting link. You are going to link by Prodcode, the only field that contains information shared by both tables.

The View window should now look like figure 4.7.

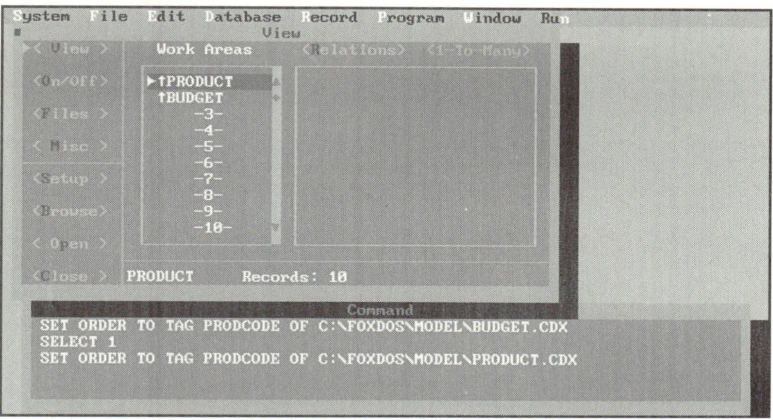

FIG. 4.7

The Product and Budget tables in the View window before linking.

As you learned previously in this chapter, the controlling table must be the table currently selected when a relation (connection) is established. This relation is active only when the controlling table is selected. You can select and work in the subsidiary table without removing the relation; the link is reactivated when you reselect the controlling table.

Select the Product table and choose `Relations`. The View window now looks like figure 4.8.

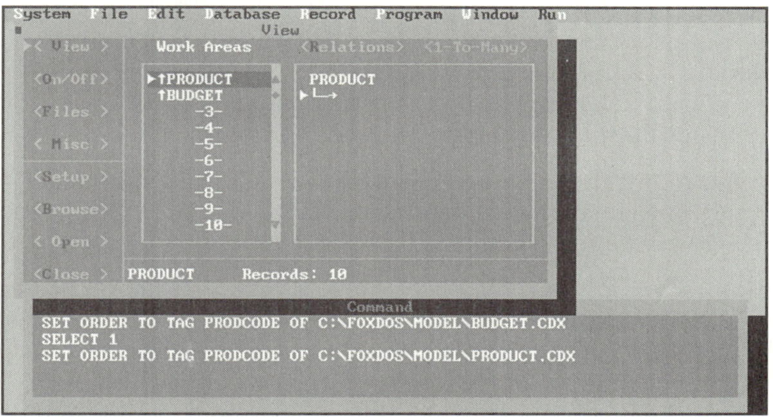

FIG. 4.8

The Product table, chosen as the controlling table.

The beginning of the relation is complete, with the Product table now established as the controlling table. Select the subsidiary table, Budget, by highlighting the name in the list and pressing Enter or by clicking the name with the mouse. The Expression Builder appears so that you can enter an expression on which to create the relation, as shown in figure 4.9.

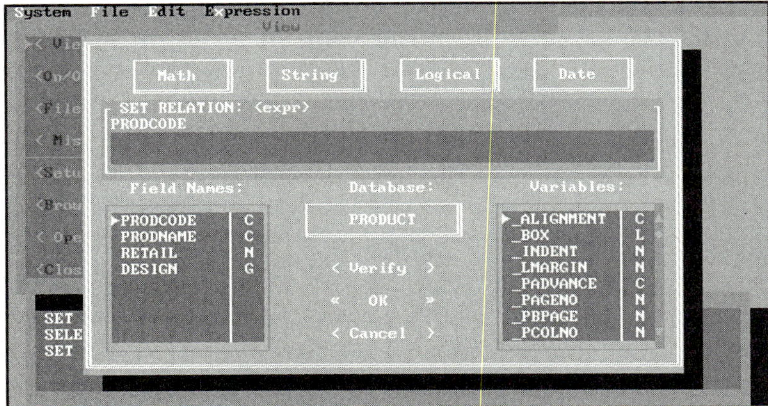

FIG. 4.9

Using the Expression Builder to set the relation.

Notice that the Expression Builder already contains the name of the Prodcode field. FoxPro used the following two pieces of information to *guess* that this field should form the link:

- Each of the tables being linked contains a Prodcode field.
- The subsidiary (or target) table is currently ordered by this field.

If FoxPro cannot determine the proper linking field, you enter the expression into the Expression Builder text box, either by typing `Prodcode` or by selecting the field name from the Field Names list. Now select the `OK` button to complete the task.

After you return to the View window, the screen resembles figure 4.10. Note the SET RELATION command that FoxPro entered in the Command window to create the relation.

Now look at what you accomplished. Select and then click `Browse` to browse the Budget table. Everything looks normal. Resize and move the table out of the way, but where you can still see it. Now select and then browse the Product table. The Budget Browse window has changed to show only the records that match the current product code in the Product table Browse window (see fig. 4.11). Select a new record in the Product table and watch the Budget table BROWSE change to show a different group of matching records.

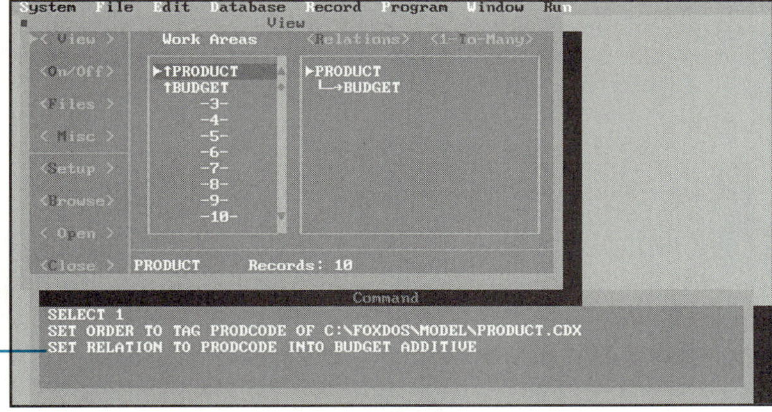

he FoxPro ommand at your ork in e View ndow oduced

FIG. 4.10

The View window displays a graphic representation of existing relations.

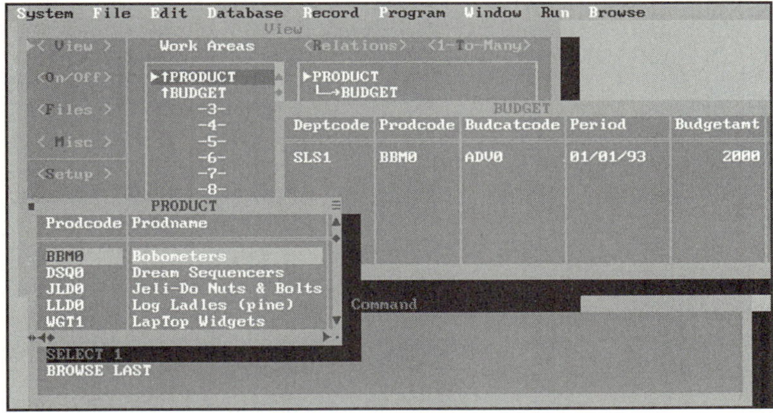

FIG. 4.11

The Product table related into the Budget table.

Remember that the connection is not maintained when the subsidiary table is the currently selected table. You can quickly see how this process works by returning to the View window, selecting the Budget table, and issuing a new Browse command by double-clicking or pressing Enter with Budget highlighted or by using the Browse push button. Notice that you now can see all the records in the table. Select the Product table Browse again, and you see the nonmatching records in the Budget table Browse disappear. (To see the change reflected on-screen, you must issue a new BROWSE command rather than select a Browse window.)

Keep the View window and the Product and Budget files open now, for use in the following section, or save the setup as a new .VUE file so that you can return to this precise setup shortly.

NOTE

Remember that it is *the result of an expression*, not a field name, that forms the link. Whenever you move from one record to another in the controlling table, FoxPro reevaluates the expression and searches the master index of the subsidiary table for a matching value.

To demonstrate this, try the following. First, save the current setup as a new .VUE file so you can easily restore the current work areas and index orders. Now select the Budget table and access the Setup panel of the View window. Select `Add...` and choose NEWINDEX.IDX, the IDX-type index you created previously, from the Open Index File dialog. Recall that NEWINDEX's index expression is Prodcode + STR(Budgetamt,7,0). Now select the Product table and follow the previously described procedure to relate Product into Budget, this time typing `Prodcode + STR(2000,7,0)` in the Expression Builder. When you browse the two tables again, you see that the Budget Browse window displays a matching entry only if the Budgetamt field contains the value 2000. When you move the highlight in the Product table to the record that contains BBM0 in the Prodcode field, FoxPro searches the Budget table's NEWINDEX index for BBM0 2000 (the three spaces in the middle of the expression are significant), finds a matching value, and displays the related record in the Budget Browse window.

Managing the One-to-Many Relationship

As you learned in the preceding sections, you can use SET RELATION to link two tables, and the tables move together in relationship. As you move through the *controlling* (or parent) file, the first record that matches in the *subsidiary* (or child) file is accessed. If more than one matching record exists, the other records aren't available from the current work area, even though you can see them in their Browse window.

The *parent and child* metaphor is useful because it implies that, although each parent might have many children, each child has only one parent.

In FoxPro, you modify the nature of the relationship by using the SET SKIP command, which enables you to access all the child records while remaining in the parent work area.

In this special version of the one-to-many relationship, each record in the controlling table is joined to all the matching records in the subsidiary table to create *virtual* records, consisting of the information in the controlling record and information from all the child records that match the controlling record. When you create a Browse window, a report, or other representation of a database, you see as many entries for one parent record as that record has corresponding records in the child table. (If no matching child records exist, however, one entry still exists for the parent.)

Some other features of FoxPro also provide the capabilities of the one-to-many relationship. Usually, you can get the same result with less effort by using the RQBE and SELECT statements, which are shown elsewhere in this book. Occasionally, however, creating virtual records with SET SKIP may prove useful—particularly when you process data in a particular order as opposed to extracting data for reporting purposes.

Return to the View window, with the Product and Budget table open and a relation set on the Prodcode field between the Product table and the Budget table. Make sure the Product table is the currently selected table.

Notice that, after you select the Product table, in the top-right corner of the screen the `1-To-Many` push button is active. Select this option now by pressing T, or by clicking the button with the mouse.

You now see the Establish 1-To-Many Relationship dialog shown in figure 4.12. Notice that the terminology used in this dialog relects the parent-and-child metaphor.

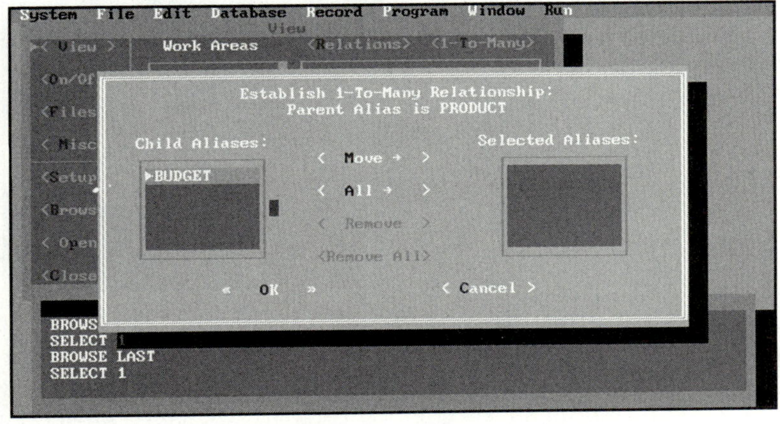

FIG. 4.12

The Establish 1-To-Many Relationship dialog.

You see only one entry in the Child Aliases list because you established a relation only between the Product table and the Budget table. You also can establish relations between the Product table and additional tables. If you establish these relations with other tables, the new aliases appear in the list. For now, however, you want to establish only the one-to-many relationship between Product and Budget. Select `All` to move Budget into the Selected Aliases list and then select `OK` to complete the work.

To observe the effects of a one-to-many relationship, you must issue a few instructions in the Command window.

Make sure that Product is the currently selected table. Activate the Command window and type the following command:

```
BROWSE FIELDS Prodcode, Prodname, Budget.Budgetamt, Budget.Period
```

Press Enter to execute the command. You learn more about the BROWSE command in subsequent chapters of this book. This command instructs FoxPro to create a Browse window that shows the product code and product name from the Product table and the budget amount and the period from the Budget table. In Chapter 3, you use a FIELDS clause to explicitly include a Memo field in a list. Here, you use a similar FIELDS clause specifying aliased fields from a related table so that these fields are included in the Browse. The Browse window is shown in figure 4.13.

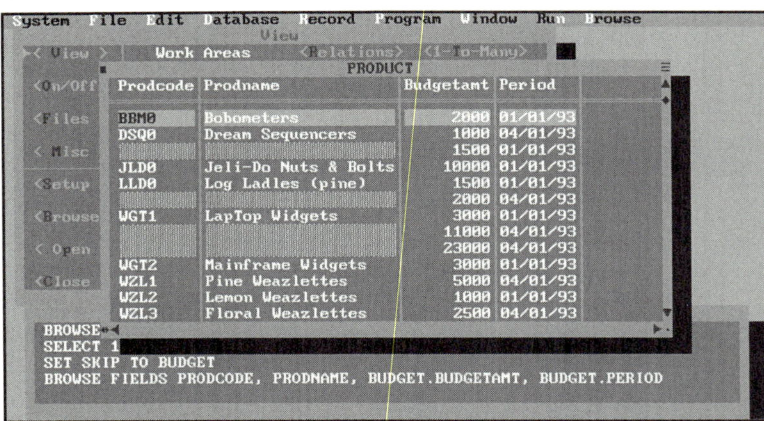

FIG. 4.13

The Product table linked to the Budget table in a one-to-many relationship.

As you see, the Browse window now treats both tables as if they are one table. For each record in the controlling (parent) file, additional entries are shown until all the child records are displayed on-screen.

(To help you distinguish between entries that belong to different parent records, these additional entries use shaded blocks instead of repeating the information in the parent table's fields.)

Maintaining Relational Integrity

By now you have a good feel for how the Product and Budget tables are connected when the Product table is the controlling table. Now consider the following question: What happens if you delete one of the products from the Product table or change a product code and do not make a corresponding adjustment in the Budget table?

If you change WGT1 to ABCD, all the records in the Budget table with the product code of WGT1 are now, in a sense, *orphaned*. When FoxPro looks up information in the Budget file, it cannot find these records or include them in reports or other output that is based on the WGT1 relationship.

The consequences of orphaned records can become serious. For example, in an accounting application, being unable to find specific records can lead to out-of-balance accounting files.

Maintaining viable links is called *relational integrity*. The most important rule of relational integrity is that whenever you change or delete a field used anywhere in an application to link to another table, make sure that the related tables are updated to reflect this change.

If you change WGT1 to ABCD in the Product table, go to the Budget table and change all occurrences of WGT1 to ABCD. If you delete WGT1, go to the Budget table and replace WGT1 with another valid product code.

NOTE In certain situations, orphaned records in a table are acceptable. For example, you may knowingly delete entries in a products lookup table when you no longer manufacture those products so that new orders for these products cannot be entered. Existing orders for these products would, at some point, be transferred to a history table and then removed from the orders table.

You may create orphaned records if you are absolutely clear that this kind of condition exists.

You have much more to learn about linking files and other ways to perform the linking. In special cases, you can link two files with identical sets of records by the record number—by using the RECNO( ) function—rather than with a key expression. You now have, however, all the basic tools you need to set, take advantage of, and maintain relations between tables.

Setting Up a Database Management System

The focus of this book is to use FoxPro to design database applications—for you, for an organization, or for clients. Yet, as indicated at the beginning of this chapter, a database application is just one part of a complete information system, and the best database application in the world can fail if improperly used.

This section addresses the issue of designing and implementing a database application so that the application can function properly in a real-world environment.

Understanding the Scope of the Project

You're now back to the central issue of what you want in a database management system. In a community or an organization, this issue really is, *what does everybody want?* For a database management system to succeed, all the people who need information must be able to get this information in a form and in a time frame that makes the information useful. All the people from whom information is collected—and all the people who enter the information into the computer—also need suitable tools and schedules so that the work can be completed. As you start the project of designing and implementing a new system, the task can be made considerably easier if you solicit the support, commitment, and participation of all who may be involved in the operation of the system. Although the support of top management is critical to the ultimate success of the system, the support of clerks and secretaries can be just as important. Often, top management can provide the big picture of what's needed, and the person who does the job can tell you how the work is really done. Top management may not understand how information is collected and prepared, and clerks may have no idea why they go through the routines. For the system to work well, you need to know both sides of the story.

Most people are cooperative if they feel that their contributions are appreciated and valued. People like to have a part in creating changes that influence their lives and usually want to participate in planning a new work system. You need to nurture this willingness to cooperate by including the input of other users when you consider these changes; keep everyone informed and solicit advice. If you approach people in an arrogant or condescending manner, you cut off the free flow of information—and this information is vital for the successful conclusion of the system design and implementation.

The following are the main steps of a database management project:

1. Design the system.
2. Write and document the application.
3. Implement the system.

In the following section, you look at some considerations these steps may entail, with an emphasis on the human aspects of the problem not covered elsewhere in this book.

Designing the System

The first step in system design is to determine the results you want this application to produce.

In a previous section of this chapter, you concentrated on output—especially printed reports—to determine the results you want an application to produce, and for a good reason. Although people basically want to cooperate, getting them to tell you what they really want from an application is often harder than pulling teeth.

You can encounter a million reasons why people do not or cannot tell you their needs. They might not know what is possible, or might not know the job well enough to explain the needs of certain tasks; the discipline of communicating needs in the detail required by a project of this nature might seem too hard; some might just not care; others might be afraid to tell you what they want in case they don't get it (or in case they *do* get it and are then committed to the results of the change); a few might occasionally withhold information to exercise power over you or over their surroundings; some might even consciously or unconsciously try to sabotage the project, either out of malice or because they feel threatened; others might believe their needs may sound stupid; and so on.

Communicating needs to others might be work, a risk, or a commitment. People often avoid work, risk, and commitment.

To get the information you need, listen closely to what the people who use the applications are saying (and what these people are not saying). Become sensitive to the situations and possible motives of others. Become a combination interviewer and therapist. Because you are (or soon may become) the database expert, you can help those with limited vision comprehend the possibilities of the system's design and application. You can draw on your previous experience in similar situations to point out alternative results that others might find useful.

Concentrating on output is a useful approach because data in this form isn't particularly threatening or personal. A report also is tangible and real: you and others can pick up, look at, react to, review, and analyze the material. People don't have to think hard to describe what they do if they can simply hand you the end product of their work.

Collect specific examples of desired output to help you analyze the systems currently being used and how and why they work—or how and why they do not work. When others are sure that you are listening to real needs and appreciating the importance of the work they produce, they feel encouraged to share with you their "wish lists" (such as reports these users don't currently get and the user tasks you can simplify).

TIP As you collect information about the existing system, be especially attuned to its weaknesses. If the manual system has serious design flaws, try to convince management that now is a good time to fix the problems. The worst thing you can do to a company is take a bad manual system and computerize it. The old data processing acronym *GIGO* (garbage in, garbage out) is as relevant now as ever.

How a system fits in with all the other systems in an organization also is important. You cannot totally change most organizations to a new system overnight, which means that the piece you are adding cannot disrupt other kinds of work that now function smoothly.

You should also design the system to handle problems caused when two or more users try to use the same record simultaneously. If your application updates more than one table with entered data, will you be able to complete the recording of the transaction or roll back the transaction if all the tables cannot be updated? Start planning for these problems now. Even if your application will be used only on a stand-alone computer now, you might be asked to make it available on a network in the near future. Providing for multi-user access at the design stage is far easier than incorporating file- and record-locking capabilities into a completed application later.

As you design the tables and the way the database fits together, remember also to design all required support systems. Remember that information is entered *into* a database system, is processed, and then is sent *out* of the database system in various ways. How exactly is the information going to be placed in the system? What forms are filled out? Can existing forms work, or do new forms need to be designed? Who collects, enters, and distributes information? What will the work flow be, and what schedules must be met? Are checklists planned to help perform the job or organize work flow? Who designs these checklists? When information comes out of the system, to whom does the information go, and when is the information needed? Are special forms, such as preprinted invoice forms, needed for output? Who designs these forms? How and when are the forms ordered? An appreciation of the importance of these details and a willingness to attend to or oversee a resolution to each detail is crucial if you are to win the acceptance of the people who use the system.

Writing and Documenting the Application

Throughout this book, you learn about creating the application as a process of designing menus, data-entry screens, and different kinds of output. As you design and produce these different elements, document your work, both for users and developers. Good or at least adequate documentation results in substantial savings in training and support over a system's lifetime. If written in concert with the writing of the application, documentation can assist measurably in refining the design of a system and in discovering potential problems.

Documentation is a strategic tool that pays off in the long term. Documentation helps you concentrate on the long-term needs and implications of the system as a whole instead of just using the development process to remedy the most pressing and immediate needs.

As you write the documentation, notice those aspects of the system that you have trouble describing. If you can't explain how the elements of the system function and interact, something may be wrong with the system design. Think it through again.

Testing a system is another integral part of the development process. You should perform testing at every step of development. When you consider an application complete, test the entire system again. Take the application through a complete cycle: installation, day-to-day operations, special month-end or year-end procedures, and maintenance procedures. If possible, use real data. Try to re-create the real operating environment as closely as possible. Besides seeing whether the system actually produces the desired results (for example, checking the arithmetic in the reports), note how the menus and data-entry screens feel when used. Consider how the system may feel to a data-entry clerk who must perform these tasks over and over again. Test the system on the equipment that will run it.

Good communication between you and the user of the system also must extend far beyond the development phase. If documentation and one-on-one assistance are not sufficient to instruct the participants in the use of the new system, develop training programs. Establish a system for monitoring and reporting program errors and suggestions for changes and enhancements. You can build into an application error-handling routines that can save details about the error and also give instructions to the user on how and what to report (see Chapter 20, "Enhancing the Applications You Program," for more details).

An effective online help system can be an important addition to the system documentation. Users feel less intimidated by a new application when they can view on-screen instructions that are context-sensitive to the task they are performing. In Chapter 20, you learn how to add a FoxPro-style help system to your application, and how to create your help file as you develop the application by using the Comment snippet for each input field in your data-entry screens.

Encourage users to submit requests for improvements and additional features. You might not be able to fulfill all the requests immediately, but you might find ways to incorporate improvements as you change the application for other reasons. Users appreciate a responsive attitude on your part and are usually excited about contributing to the improvement of the application. The more the users contribute, the more personally invested they feel in the work—and the more successful the system becomes.

Implementing the System

Before you begin the installation, ask yourself one final question: Have I achieved the *consensus* of everyone involved that the project is complete and the application meets his or her needs? If you can't answer this question affirmatively, then you aren't done.

When you have met the goal of consensus and are ready to install the application, make sure that everyone involved in the system's use is ready. Make sure that all the forms are ready, that equipment is installed and running, and that all users clearly understand the part they play in the system. Make sure that schedules are in place and that the flow of work is clear. Make sure that data to be entered into the system is ready and organized.

You might need to hire temporary personnel to assist in entering a large volume of existing data. Be sure that the source data these temporaries are given is organized and ready and that the rules for data entry are clear. You might need to develop a standardized data-entry form for entering customer names and other data. Alternatively, mark the source data with the codes needed for the computer system.

If you already have information collected on a computer, such as with a word processing, spreadsheet, or other database program, you might be able to import this information directly into FoxPro and save some (if not all) the time required for data entry. If you are designing this system for you, the organization for which you work, or a specific client, you might be able to use this method easily. If, however, you are designing a relatively generic application which can be used by many organizations that collect data through other computer programs, this method becomes less useful, or more expensive, to apply. You learn about importing and exporting data in the "Importing Available Data" section of this chapter.

Run the system *in parallel,* while the old system is still operating. Check the results of the new system with the results of the old system and make sure that the new system produces accurate and complete results. This stage of the project is difficult for everyone; some people may have two full-time jobs collecting and entering data into two separate systems. A useful alternative to running parallel in real time is to *run parallel backwards*—choose an earlier date (perhaps a month ago) and begin using the system as of this date. Because all the output from the earlier period is already available for cross-checking, you can usually enter a month's worth of data, and therefore verify the accuracy of the data (and the system) in a week or so.

When everyone is comfortable with the new system, and the design appears to work properly, someone must decide that the project is completed. The old system is abandoned, and the new system replaces the old.

Managing the Entire Project

Manage the design and implementation of a database system as you manage any other large project. Break down the entire project into specific goals and establish timetables. Assign responsibility to a specific person for each phase of the project and monitor results. Determine who has authority to approve the various aspects of the project. Who, for example, can approve the system design? Who determines that the project is truly complete?

In a database system project, concentrate specifically on the three main steps. Make sure that each step is completed before continuing to the next step.

Complete the design stage by making a presentation of the design in as much detail as possible. If you can, present a demonstration of the system that includes—at a minimum—the way menus and data-entry screens look and operate. Also, if possible, provide samples of all the reports the system generates. Try to get the approval, official or otherwise, of the people who use the system. As you see in subsequent chapters of this book, FoxPro's design tools make the creation of a mock-up system easier than you might think. Finally, get official, final approval of the system design.

Complete the writing and documenting phase with thorough testing. Test both the program and the documentation.

Complete implementation with another official, final approval. Then take everybody to lunch—they deserve it!

NOTE No database management application is ever really completed. You may know this already if you have reached this stage in a project. As you write the application and the documentation, you might see ways to improve the design of the system. As you write the application, you often might feel that you can do something more efficiently, but that you lack the time needed to implement the change. Both you and the application's users also may see ways to improve areas while implementing the system, and beyond. Depending on the circumstances, you might improve some areas and not others, some areas right away and some areas later, but you soon learn that the refinement process is always a trade-off.

Importing Available Data

The preceding section explains that you can import existing computer data into a FoxPro application. You also can export data from the FoxPro table format to file formats that other programs can use.

Again, being close to the environment in which the program operates makes a difference when you use the import and export capabilities of FoxPro. Even if you are remote, however, this feature can enhance an application to include importing and exporting capabilities that support the most popular word processing, spreadsheet, and database programs.

You are still at an early stage in your FoxPro education to be introduced to all the possibilities and complexities of importing and exporting data, but you might find a broad outline of some of the available features useful.

In Chapter 3, you learn that you can export text to a disk file that any word processor can then read. You export the text by using FoxPro's LIST TO command or the Print to File option of FoxPro's File menu. FoxPro provides a number of these kinds of utilities, including the SET PRINTER TO <filename> command, which sends the results of printing statements to a file, and the COPY MEMO <memo fieldname> TO <filename> command, which sends the contents of a Memo field to a separate file on disk.

Although the FoxPro command language is rich with text-creation and export features, exporting text files that include the internal formatting commands of specific word processing programs can get a little complicated. Although creating a preformatted word processor file is difficult, creating fully formatted files for desktop publishing programs, such as Ventura Publisher (which uses embedded character codes for formatting purposes), is relatively easy.

Importing and exporting data, as opposed to text, is an entirely different story. FoxPro can import information from word processing, spreadsheet, and other database programs.

If you are importing data from another database program that is part of the Xbase family (for example, dBASE III+/IV, Clipper, and Arago), the conversion process is both quick and painless. FoxPro transparently reads all Xbase (.DBF) data files, including files created on Macintosh computers. To add records to a FoxPro table from another Xbase table, you use the APPEND FROM command. To limit the records that are added, use APPEND FROM with the FOR <expr> clause. If the other table's field names are different from the ones in the FoxPro table, you can USE the other table, COPY TO <tempfile>, and then modify the structure of the temporary table to match the field names of the FoxPro table. Select the FoxPro table, and use APPEND FROM <tempfile> to add the new records.

NOTE

When using APPEND FROM FOR <expr>, be aware that FoxPro evaluates the FOR expression in the context of the target table, not the source table. For example, if you create a temporary table to hold only those records in Budget that have a department code of SLS1, you might decide that the temporary table does not require the Deptcode field, because all the records it holds will be for department SLS1. However, when you use

```
APPEND FROM Budget FOR Deptcode = 'SLS1'
```

FoxPro returns the following error message:

```
Variable 'DEPTCODE' not found.
```

The FOR expression is evaluated with regard to the temporary table. Because this table does not contain the Deptcode field, an error occurred. You can work around this limitation by using COPY TO <file> FOR <expr> to create a temporary table that holds only the desired records and then APPENDing FROM the temporary table to your target table.

Importing data from a word processing program requires that the text be formatted in one of two ways: delimited with a special character (usually a comma or tab) or in a fixed field length (known as SDF format). If you understand how to create these files with a word processor, you can import data by using FoxPro's APPEND FROM command, which can be in either of two forms:

```
APPEND FROM <filename> DELIMITED WITH <character>
```

or

```
APPEND FROM <filename> TYPE SDF
```

First, you create a FoxPro table in which to import this data. The table must contain fields long enough to accept the longest item in each of the imported file's columns. If you are importing from a delimited file, the fields can be longer than the longest data element because the delimiter character tells FoxPro where each data element begins and ends. However, if you are importing from an SDF file, the fields must be exactly the same length as each of the columns in the text file, because FoxPro uses the field lengths to determine where one text column ends and the next begins.

The easiest way to see how this process works is to export an existing FoxPro table to two separate text files by using the COPY TO command with first the DELIMITED and then the SDF option. To reverse the process, you need a text file that looks like the results of either of these COPY TO procedures. You then use APPEND FROM with the proper option, DELIMITED or SDF, to add records containing the data in the text file.

NOTE

FoxPro can APPEND character data to Character fields (in the delimited option, you usually need to enclose the data in quotation marks to distinguish these characters from numbers) and numeric data into Numeric fields. However, date fields can import only data that matches FoxPro's internal date structure of YYYYMMDD. If you cannot easily change the source data to reflect this convention, import the dates into a Character field and then process the table to convert this Character data into a date-type field by using CTOD( ) and other date functions FoxPro provides for this purpose. Refer to Chapter 22 for more information about conversion of data from one type to another.

The APPEND FROM ... DELIMITED command has a keyword (WITH) that confuses many people. A delimited file actually contains *field separators* and also *delimiters*. In the following default format, the commas are field separators, and the quotation marks are delimiters:

```
"Bob","Jones","Suite 140, 123 Elm Street","Omaha"
```

continues

In the street address, the comma is properly interpreted as data because it is placed between paired quotation marks. Sometimes, however, the data also can contain quotation marks as well as commas. You can use the DELIMITED WITH <character> option or (where convenient) WITH TAB or WITH BLANK to specify a delimiter other than quotation marks. (Although field separators are commonly used, these characters aren't required in FoxPro except where no delimiters at all are used.)

If you are importing data from a spreadsheet or from a non-Xbase database program, FoxPro's IMPORT command can provide you with an even easier conversion process. The IMPORT command can create a FoxPro table from many of the most popular spreadsheet packages, including Lotus 1-2-3, Excel, Symphony, Multiplan, and Framework, as well as from Paradox tables. Unlike APPEND FROM, the IMPORT command creates the table for you. FoxPro imports columns as fields and rows as records, using the data in the first row of the spreadsheet to determine the width and data type of each of the fields in the new table.

FoxPro imports the data from the spreadsheets, but not the underlying formulas. If you are fairly sophisticated in using spreadsheets and use different regions of the spreadsheet for lookup tables or subtables that feed information into the main table, you might get unpredictable results when you import spreadsheet data into FoxPro. For this reason, before you import spreadsheet data, make sure that the spreadsheets you import are as simple (row- and column-wise) as possible. This might require that you extract and copy portions of the spreadsheet into a temporary spreadsheet for the purpose of exporting this data to a table.

To combine these two approaches, you can use the IMPORT command to create a table (in FoxPro format) and then use APPEND FROM or other FoxPro commands to transfer specific records and fields from the new table into an existing table. Using IMPORT also can give you information you need as you try to design a table that can efficiently append data thereafter.

Finally, as you learned in Chapter 3, FoxPro Memo fields can contain any data you can store on a computer, including graphics files (pictures, photos, and so on), tables, programs, digitized sound, and so on. Presently, you can't use FoxPro for DOS to do much with nontextual Memo fields, such as pictures and sound, although you can export the contents of Memo fields intact to the hard disk and therefore make this information available to programs that can import this information.

FoxPro also can run external programs that use sound or pictures (or both), which enables you to access the contents of these Memo fields as part of FoxPro's applications. (FoxPro for Windows can work directly with Object Linking and Embedding, or OLE, objects stored in General fields, which can include pictures and sounds created in other applications.)

FoxPro uses the APPEND MEMO <memo fieldname> FROM <filename> command to place nontextual data into a FoxPro Memo field and the COPY MEMO <memo fieldname> TO <filename> to send a file to the hard disk for use by other programs. (Note that the COPY TO command does not copy Memo and General fields to a foreign format, even if you specify the field name in the FIELDS list.) The external programs are run either directly by DOS (using FoxPro's RUN command), as binary modules (using FoxPro's LOAD and CALL commands), or through use of the API and FoxPro's SET LIBRARY command. The use of these external programs is briefly discussed in the "Using External Library Routines" section in Chapter 16.

Summary

In this chapter, you learned how to approach the job of designing a database system. The suggested approach emphasizes how to determine which tasks you want the system to handle and how to put the system together so that you accomplish your goals.

You saw the importance of broadening and refining your approach to information systems, and how constantly having both the big picture and the details before you can help you design and implement a superior system.

You learned how the elements of FoxPro—fields, records, tables, and databases—are created and work together.

You also began to consider the implications of the real world, in which every person is different and every operating environment has an ecology, and the way database information systems must fit gracefully, efficiently, and usefully within these constraints. In designing a database information system, one important goal to achieve is that of consensus. You learn about other important design goals in Chapter 11.

With so many constraints and goals to consider, you're probably wondering how you can ever take care of everything. In Part II, "Getting Productive with FoxPro Databases," you start using the unique FoxPro productivity tools that help you perform this job.

Getting Productive with FoxPro Databases

5

CHAPTER

Using the RQBE as the Gateway to Queries

After you set up the tables and enter the data, you want to be able to extract information from the tables. Finding some information can be a straightforward operation: you can search by BROWSEing the tables. Eventually, however, you may need to extract more complex answers from the data than BROWSEing allows. If so, the *RQBE,* or *Relational Query By Example,* comes into play. *RQBE* is an interactive tool that enables you to extract and organize the data stored in tables. With the RQBE, you can derive answers that once required you to write complex programs.

In this chapter, you gain facility with the RQBE and learn to create some simple queries. In Chapter 6, "Investigating Your Data with Advanced Queries," you expand your knowledge of the RQBE and learn how to use the RQBE to phrase more complex questions.

Before you get into the RQBE, make sure that the Budget table is open in the current work area. Select New Query from the Run menu, or open a Query file from the File New... dialog. You see the RQBE screen with the Budget table selected, as shown in figure 5.1.

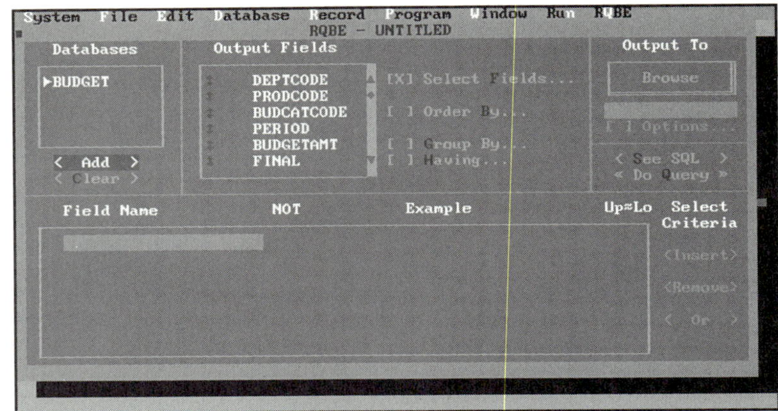

FIG. 5.1

The default settings of the RQBE window, with a single table selected.

Now select the `Do Query` push button by clicking the button, pressing Ctrl+Enter, or pressing the Do Query hot-key combination, Ctrl+Q. The result should look like the screen shown in figure 5.2.

System File Edit Database Record Program Window Run

QUERY

Selected 13 records in 0.11 seconds

Deptcode	Prodcode	Budcatcode	Period			
SLS1	BBM0	ADV0	01/01/93	2000	T	Mem
FIN0	DSQ0	INS0	04/01/93	1000	F	Mem
MFT0	DSQ0	PLT0	01/01/93	1500	F	mem
PER0	JLD0	LHR0	01/01/93	10000	F	mem
SLS1	LLD0	ADV0	01/01/93	1500	T	mem
PER0	LLD0	LHO0	04/01/93	2000	F	Mem
FIN0	WGT1	TRV0	01/01/93	3000	F	Mem
PER0	WGT1	LSL0	04/01/93	11000	F	mem
MFT0	WGT1	PLT0	04/01/93	23000	F	Mem
SLS2	WGT2	LCM0	01/01/93	3000	T	Mem
MFT0	WZL1	PLT0	04/01/93	5000	F	mem
SLS2	WZL2	ADV0	01/01/93	1000	T	Mem
SLS3	WZL3	LCM0	04/01/93	2500	F	mem

FIG. 5.2

A simple query.

Congratulations! You just created and executed your first query. The Browse window you see is not too different from all the other views of the data you previously used. You may be more impressed, however, when you see how easily you can modify RQBE's default values to create valuable results.

You can control the Browse window that your query created in the same way you control other windows. The Zoom, Size, Split, and Close controls are all visible and active. You also can reposition the Browse window. The query-created Browse, however, is unusual in an important way: this Browse is *readonly* (you cannot change the data that appears on-screen). For now, just close the Browse window—by clicking the Close control or by pressing Esc—so you can continue exploring the RQBE.

TIP

In the RQBE and at any other time, you can press the F1 key to call up FoxPro's context-sensitive help system. The RQBE help entry gives you a quick refresher course on the different features of the RQBE window.

Major Components of a Query

The RQBE window is divided into five sections. Each section plays a different role in the task of creating the query, as described in table 5.1.

Table 5.1 The Parts of the RQBE Window

Section	Primary Function	SELECT Clause
Databases	Maintain the list of tables that participate in the query.	FROM <table list>
Output Fields	Control the fields that appear in the query output.	SELECT <field list>
Output To	Specify where the RQBE sends the query results.	INTO <query dest>
See SQL/Do Query	Display the SELECT command that the RQBE builds as you select options (`See SQL`), and execute the query (`Do Query`).	
Select Criteria	Build expressions that join the tables and filter the records that the RQBE includes in the result.	WHERE <expression list>

The Databases list, found in the upper-left corner of the RQBE window, lists all the tables that the query is currently using. In this example, only the Budget table is displayed. You can add more tables with the `Add` button, and you can remove tables one at a time with the `Clear` button.

When you open the RQBE window to create a query, you are presented by default with the table that is open in the current work area. If no table is open in the current work area when you enter the RQBE, FoxPro asks you to select a table through the Open File dialog. When selected, a file becomes the default table for this query. If you choose Cancel in the Open File dialog, you still are allowed into the RQBE, but no tables are selected and most of the RQBE's options are unselectable. You must use `Add` to open a table before you can create a query.

The Output Fields section is found in the upper-middle part of the RQBE window. A list shows the fields currently selected for output. You can change the order of the fields in this list, and the order in the query output changes to match. Several check boxes to the right of the list enable you to make further adjustments to the fields and records that appear in the query result.

If you check the Select Fields... box at the top of the Output Fields section, you can control the fields that appear in the output. The Order By... dialog, where you can set the sort order for the data, is the next control, followed by a third check box for the Group By... dialog, which controls groupings and subtotals. Finally, the bottom check box provides access to the Having... dialog, where you can set filter criteria to eliminate groups.

The default settings for these check boxes are: no Order By, no Group By..., and no Having... . As you saw in the first query, if a table is open when you first enter the RQBE, all fields in that table are selected for output, in their natural order in the table.

You see the Output To popup control in the upper-right corner of the RQBE window. With this control, you can choose where to send the results of the query. You can send the results to a Browse window (as you did with the simple query, by using the default), a Report/Label, a Table/DBF, a Cursor, or a Graph. (You must own a separate graphing product to use the Graph output option.)

The bottom half of the RQBE window is the Selection Criteria section. This section has two purposes: to tell RQBE which records to include or exclude and to tell RQBE how to link multiple tables when applicable. Because you have only a single table selected and have not yet entered any filter conditions, this box is currently empty. When this box is empty, all records in the table are included in the query.

The small box below the Output To section contains two buttons: `See SQL` and `Do Query`. Because the real output of the RQBE is a SQL SELECT statement that FoxPro executes to produce the output you see, clicking the `See SQL` button shows you the SQL SELECT statement that the RQBE executes when you select `Do Query`. You can look at this statement at any time as you build the query, although you cannot edit the statement at this point.

You can pronounce SQL as *sequel. SQL* is an acronym for *Structured Query Language* and is the name of a language entirely separate from FoxPro. SQL is specifically designed to query databases, just as you are doing here. FoxPro's implementation is a specially enhanced subset of the SQL language that doesn't require you to leave FoxPro—or go into a special mode—to access.

You can use a SQL statement in any FoxPro program, and you can enter this statement directly into the Command window, the same way you enter any other command. When you save a query you created in the RQBE, the query is saved as a normal text file (with a .QPR extension), ready to edit or to add to a program you are writing.

Viewing the SELECT statement helps you learn SQL and also helps you understand how the RQBE works. Each section of the RQBE (not including the See SQL/Do Query section) controls one or more parts of the resulting SELECT command, as shown in table 5.1. For example, the FROM clause comes directly from the list of database tables. Every time you add a table to the Databases list, the FROM clause of the SELECT command expands to include the new table.

Select the `See SQL` button now to see the SELECT statement that produced your first query. This simple command selects all the fields and records in the Budget table and displays them in a Browse window. The asterisk (*) is a shorthand SQL notation for "all fields." You learn more about the construction of the SELECT command in Chapter 7, "Querying with SQL and Searching with Rushmore," but you can learn a lot simply by watching the ways that the SELECT command changes in response to your choices in the RQBE. When you are ready to go beyond what you can accomplish with the RQBE, you will have a firm grasp of the effects of the various SELECT clauses on the query results.

The Do Query button executes the query. You can choose this button when at least one table is shown in the Databases list and at least one Output Field is selected. These are the minimum requirements for the RQBE to construct and execute the SELECT command successfully.

You also can choose most of the RQBE options from the RQBE menu pad, which appears on the system menu when a RQBE window is active. The RQBE menu popup also contains Comments, an option not found elsewhere in the RQBE. Comments are notes of unlimited length, which are for reference only and are saved with the query file in the same way other program comments are saved (in lines that begin with an asterisk, which are ignored by FoxPro). These comments appear before the SQL SELECT statement that the RQBE builds. You can view these comments at any time by selecting See SQL or by reopening the Comments editing window.

TIP

Because viewing the SELECT command that the RQBE constructs is so instructive, you may want to keep the window in which the command is displayed in view as you work through the examples in the following section. You can do this by arranging your screen to match the screen shown in figure 5.3. To do this, first move the RQBE window down six rows on the screen. Select See SQL and resize the UNTITLED.QPR window until its bottom border is on the same row as the RQBE window's top border. Finish resizing the .QPR window by stretching it until it is as wide as the RQBE window, and then reselect the RQBE window. The only option you cannot select with the RQBE window in this position is the Or push button, which you do not use until Chapter 6, "Investigating Your Data with Advanced Queries," and even this option is still selectable from the RQBE menu.

Details, Details

Now that you have looked around the RQBE, the various options may no longer seem particularly mysterious. In previous chapters, you learned methods of selecting and ordering records, and you learned how you can link tables together by using SET RELATION. In the following sections, you explore each of the RQBE components and you learn how to make these components work together to accomplish the same things (and more) in the RQBE.

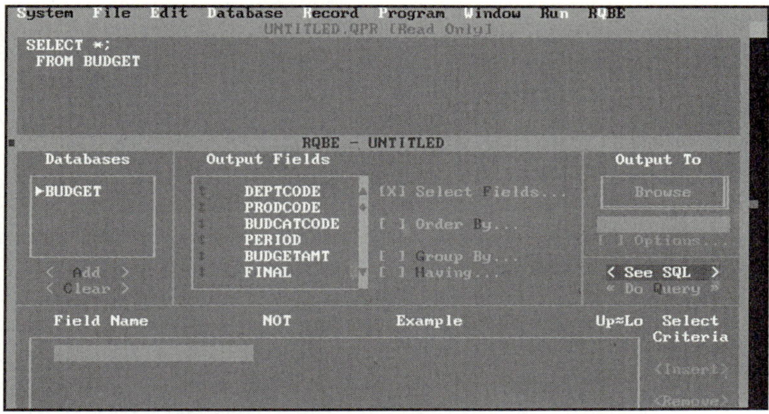

FIG. 5.3 Arranging the RQBE window to show the SQL SELECT command.

Selecting Fields

You may not need all the fields in the Budget table to appear in the query output. Mark the Select Fields... check box in the Output Fields section of the RQBE to see the dialog in figure 5.4.

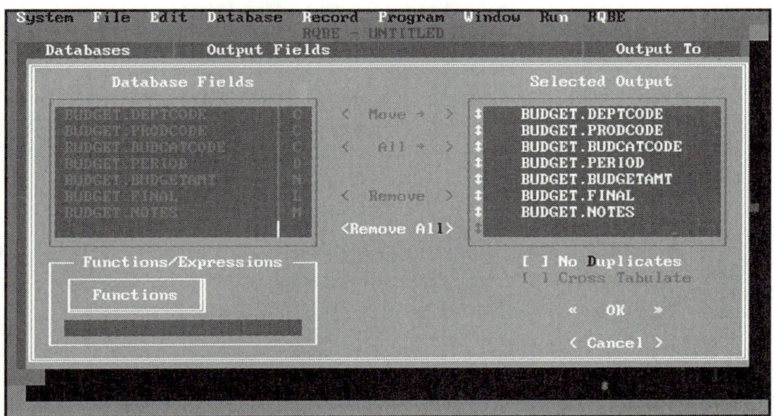

FIG. 5.4 The Select Fields... dialog.

In the Select Fields... dialog, the Database Fields list on the left side of the dialog contains all the fields you can choose from the tables shown in the Databases list. The Selected Output list on the right side of the dialog shows all the fields currently selected for output into the query.

NOTE The fields currently selected as output are disabled in the list on the left. Also, notice that the table name Budget precedes the field names. If multiple tables are involved, the table name distinguishes the fields from others that may have the same name, such as Budget.Deptcode and Dept.Deptcode.

You can remove any or all fields from the Selected Output list. If you are using a mouse, double-clicking a field name moves the file from Selected Output to the Database Fields list. If you are using the keyboard, highlight the field you want to move and press Enter or press the space bar rapidly twice (FoxPro's keyboard equivalent of double-clicking a mouse). You also can mark multiple field names by using the Shift key and the space bar—or by using mouse clicks—and then selecting `Remove` to remove all the marked fields at one time. You also can remove all the fields at one time without marking them if you select the `Remove All` button. You can move fields to the Selected Output list in a similar way, by clicking `Move` rather than `Remove` and `All` rather than `Remove All`.

In the following example, you want to see only a few fields. Rather than individually removing the fields you do not want, you can use `Remove All` to remove all the fields and then choose the few fields you want. Using either method, select the following fields:

BUDGET.DEPTCODE

BUDGET.PERIOD

BUDGET.BUDGETAMT

In this and the following chapter, table and field names are often shown in all uppercase letters, because the RQBE displays table and field names in uppercase.

Select `OK` to confirm the selection and return to the main RQBE dialog. Now select `Do Query`. The Browse window displays only the fields you chose, as shown in figure 5.5. When you finish viewing the results of the query, close the Browse window.

If you don't like the order in which the fields are displayed, you can change the order in several ways. You can alter a field's relative position in the Selected Output list of the Select Fields... dialog. You move items in this list in the same way you learned to move items in the Setup dialog of the View window when you created the Budget table.

With a mouse, drag the double-headed arrow to the left of the field name. From the keyboard, highlight the field name and then use Ctrl+PgUp or Ctrl+PgDn to reposition the field in the list.

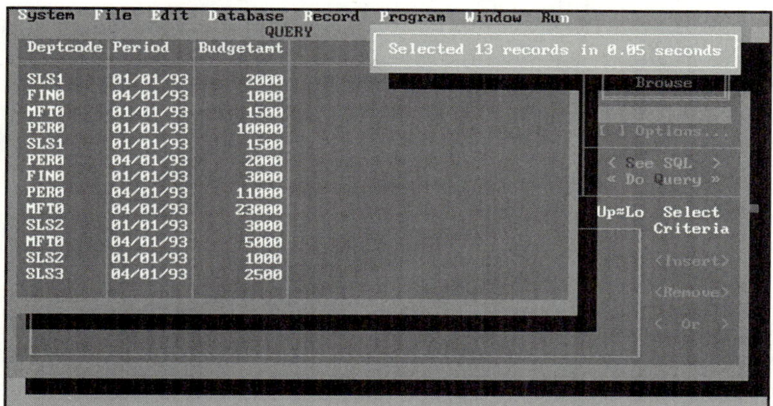

FIG. 5.5

Limiting the query output to selected fields.

You can reshuffle the output fields in the main RQBE window's Selected Output list by using the same keystrokes. A third alternative is to change their sequence in the Browse window, as you learn in Chapter 8, "Organizing the Answers with BROWSE." Changes you make in the order of the fields in the Browse window are temporary, however. The next time you select `Do Query`, the fields once again appear in the order shown in the Output Fields list.

The different ways in which you can change the order of the output fields are an example of the freedom that FoxPro's event-driven environment gives you. You aren't restricted to making every decision in a precise, rigid order. You can make changes as you work, until you get exactly what you want.

Now convert the dates displayed on-screen in this Browse window to calendar quarters. To perform this step, you add an expression to the Selected Output list. Returning to the Select Fields... dialog, access the Function/Expression text box in the lower-left corner of the dialog.

To convert these dates to the calendar quarter, use FoxPro's CEILING() function, which rounds numbers up to the nearest whole number, and the MONTH() function, which extracts the number of the month in a date you supply. You learn more about FoxPro expressions and functions as you progress in this book. The following expression is the key to the conversion you need:

```
CEILING(MONTH(date) / 3 )
```

If the date you supply is 5/15/93 (in MM/DD/YY date format), the preceding expression returns the number 2 for the second quarter. To display this number with the year, however, you must convert the number into a string of characters. When you create reports and labels in Chapter 9, "Putting the Answers to Work in Reports and Labels," and Chapter 10, "Using the Report Writer and Label Designer," you see many more conversions of this kind, and these conversions are discussed more thoroughly later in the book. For now, however, type the following expression in the Functions/Expressions text box. FoxPro scrolls the contents of the text box as you type to allow more characters to fit; do not press Enter until you finish typing the entire expression.

```
'Q' + STR(CEILING(MONTH(Budget.Period)/3),1) + ' ' +
    STR(YEAR(Budget.Period),4)
```

(If you read the preceding string from left to right, you can interpret the expression to mean "Start with the letter *Q*, then add the character equivalent of the number you calculated as the calendar quarter of the Date field Budget.Period. Now add a space to the end of this string, and then add the characters of the year for the field Budget.Period.")

Now select the `Move` button to add the expression to the Selected Output list, then select `OK` to exit the dialog. After you select `Do Query`, you see a more meaningful representation of the Period field.

If you see an error message when you select `Do Query`, you probably typed the preceding expression incorrectly. Check the expression for accuracy, then select `Do Query` again.

T I P

By selecting the Save option from the File menu pad of the menu bar, you can save a query any time you are in the RQBE window. As you learned when you saved new files of other kinds, if the query is still UNTITLED, FoxPro prompts you for a file name. For the query name, type `CHAP5001` (FoxPro adds the extension .QPR). You can exit the RQBE at any time by pressing Esc. If the most current version of the query on which you are working is not saved when you press Esc, FoxPro gives you an opportunity to save the current query before you exit the RQBE window.

To open a previously saved query, choose Open from the File menu popup and select Query for the file type. You see a list of the available queries. Pick the query with which you want to work, and FoxPro returns you to the RQBE screen—right where you left off with this query.

To tidy up the display, go back to the Select Fields... dialog and remove the Budget.Period field from the output, because this field is redundant now that you can see the calendar quarter. Also, remove the Budget.Deptcode field and add the Budget.Prodcode field. You also can change the order of the fields so that the product code is the first column and the date expression is the second column displayed in the query output.

Select `OK` to exit the Select Fields... dialog, and select `Do Query` to examine the results of your labor. Your screen should resemble figure 5.6.

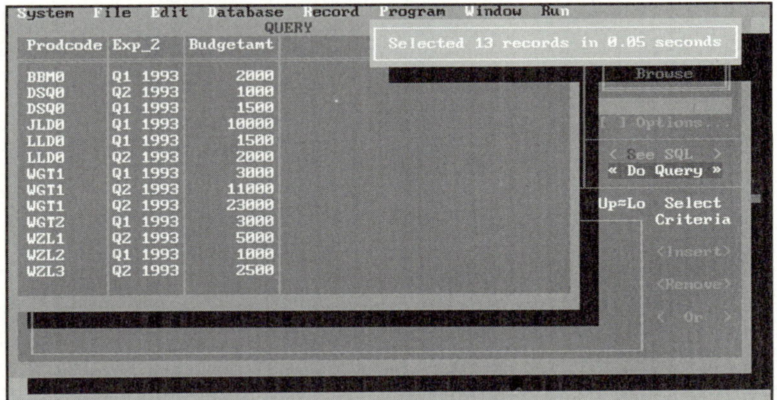

FIG. 5.6

A query that uses an expression to convert dates into calendar quarters.

Adding More Tables

With this query, you are forced to remember the rather cryptic product codes. What you really want to see are the product *names*. You make this information available to the RQBE by *joining* the Budget table with Product, the table that holds the product names.

The first step of the join process is to add the Product table to the query. Select `Add` under the Databases list. You see the Open File dialog, in which you choose the PRODUCT.DBF table. Adding a table to the query triggers the RQBE Join Condition dialog, as shown in figure 5.7. The RQBE must know how the Product table relates to the Budget table. Both tables hold a field that contains the product code. You must tell the RQBE that this relationship exists. Because the product code field has the same name (Prodcode) in each table, the RQBE offers this field as a likely candidate to form the link.

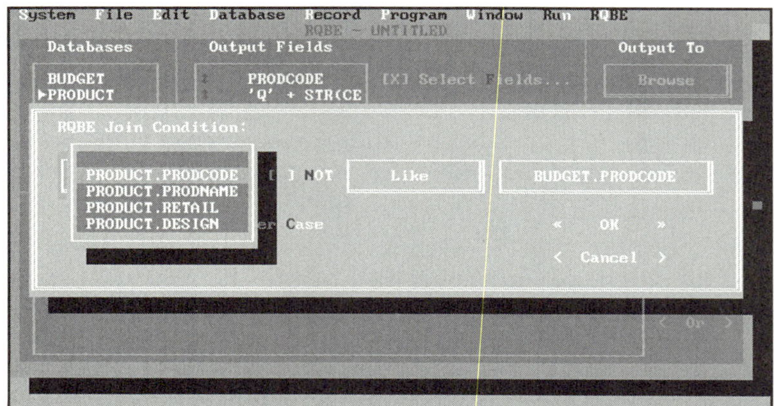

FIG. 5.7

The RQBE Join Condition dialog.

The fields that link the tables are shown as the current values in popup controls on either side of the dialog. In this case, the RQBE has correctly guessed that Prodcode is the linking field. If the tables did not use the same field name for this information, you would use the popup controls to select the linking fields from a list of all fields in the tables.

After you select OK to confirm the selection, the Join Condition dialog disappears, and you return to the RQBE screen, which now looks a bit different (see fig. 5.8). In the Select Criteria section of the RQBE window, you see the same linking expression you just selected in the Join Condition dialog. To the left of this phrase, you see a small double-headed vertical arrow character (↕) that indicates a join condition.

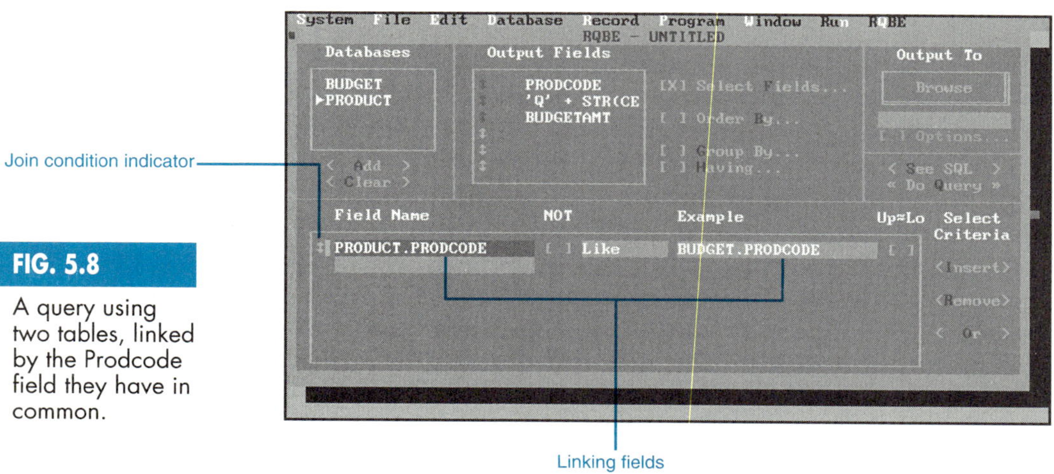

FIG. 5.8

A query using two tables, linked by the Prodcode field they have in common.

CAUTION: If you have more than one table and do not specify a join condition for each table, then select `Do Query`—FoxPro attempts to join every record of every table with every record of every other table. If you have two tables with 100 records each, this combination produces meaningless output of 10,000 records. If you have three tables with 100 records each, the output has a *million* records!

FoxPro detects this condition when you select `Do Query`, and warns you that without a join condition for each table, the query may take a long time. Heed this warning.

Now that you have linked the two tables, you can choose Output Fields from both tables as if you are working with one combined table. Return to the Select Fields... dialog. In figure 5.9, notice that the list on the left contains fields from both the Budget and Product tables. Now add the product description field, Product.Prodname. With the product name present, the Prodcode field becomes unnecessary, so you can remove the code field from the output list. Finally, move the Prodname field to the top of the list. The screen should now look like the one in figure 5.9. Select `OK` to exit this dialog.

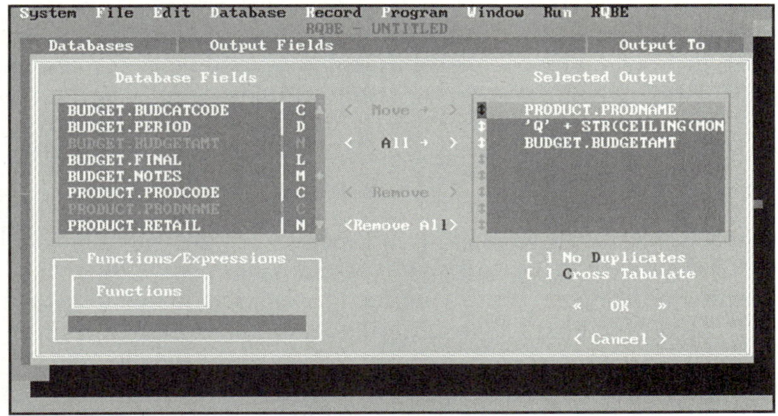

FIG. 5.9

Selecting fields from multiple tables.

Select `Do Query` and notice that the Browse window has become much more informative. After exiting from the Browse window, select Save from the File menu and save this query as CHAP5001. (Remember that you do not have to type .QPR; FoxPro adds this extension.)

Sorting Your Output Records

Presenting information in a sorted order makes the output of a query more readable. In this example, you order the Budget records by product name, and by descending calendar period within each product. To bring up the RQBE Order By... dialog shown in figure 5.10, select the Order By... check box.

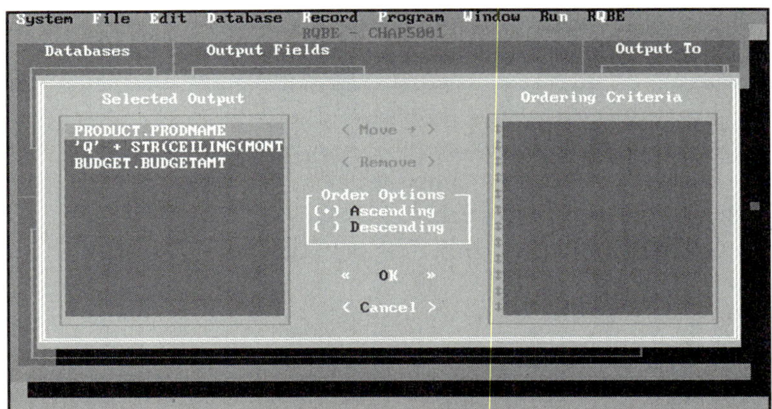

FIG. 5.10

The RQBE Order By... dialog.

You can sort output by each output field in ascending or descending order. The RQBE limits your choices to the fields selected for output. (For advanced queries, you can use the SQL SELECT command to sort by fields *not* selected for output. You learn more about using SQL in Chapter 7, "Querying with SQL and Searching with Rushmore.")

You want to sort the output by the Prodname field in ascending order, and the calendar quarter expression, which you created earlier, in descending order. Start by moving the Product.Prodname field from the Selected Output list to the Ordering Criteria list. The Ordering Criteria list works in the same way the Select Fields... dialog does—and much like the index-creation procedures you learned about in Chapter 3, "Exploring Databases and Tables," and Chapter 4, "Database Management Fundamentals." You see the Product.Prodname field appear with an up-arrow character (↑) to the left of the field. The ↑ indicates that the order is *ascending* (product names beginning with *A* appear first, and names beginning with *Z* appear last). Now change the Order Options radio button to Descending and `Move` the calendar quarter expression field over to the Ordering Criteria list, where it appears with a down-arrow character (↓) to its left.

When you change the ascending/descending order status, you must know which objects are affected. The ascending/descending radio button status affects any tagged item. (Tagged items are marked with a triangle to the left of the item.) As tagged selections in the Selected Output list are moved to the Ordering Criteria list, they are set to the ascending/descending status currently in effect. If any current ordering criteria are tagged, the selections' ascending/descending status changes if the Order Options radio button is changed.

Select `OK` to return to the RQBE screen. Before you run the query, notice the 1↑ beside PRODNAME, and the 2↓ beside "Q"+STR(CE in the Output Fields list (see fig. 5.11). These notations tell you that the data is sorted in ascending order by Prodname and descending order by calendar quarter within Prodname.

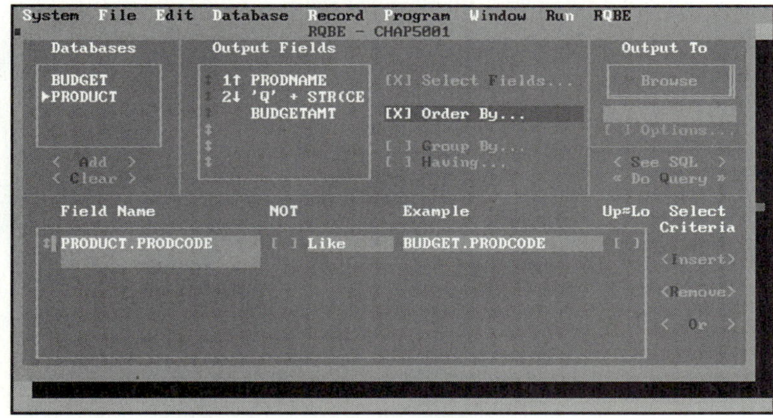

FIG. 5.11

Arrows next to field names in the Output Fields list show you the sort order of the query results.

Now, select `Do Query` to examine the results of your work. As shown in figure 5.12, the product names are in ascending alphabetical order, and the quarters (shown in the column labeled Exp_2) are in descending order within product. Exp_2 is a rather cryptic name for the field. RQBE assigns similar field names to all the expressions you create.

TIP

In a later section of this chapter, you learn to create *report forms* by using the RQBE. You can then use the Report Writer to change the report format in almost any way imaginable, including replacing the field names assigned by the RQBE. However, you can use a trick to make the field names created by the RQBE more understandable, even without sending the SELECT statement to a report.

In Chapter 7, you learn about the AS clause of the SELECT command. This clause enables you to specify an alias for any field in a query. This alias is then used as the title for the output column. Although the RQBE does not provide direct access to the AS clause, you can add this clause to the SELECT command that the RQBE constructs when you use the Select Fields... dialog to create the field expression. In the previous example, you can simply add the phrase AS Quarter to the end of the expression that displays the calendar quarter. The expression now appears as follows:

```
'Q' + STR(CEILING(MONTH(Budget.Period)/3),1) + ' ' +
STR(YEAR(Budget.Period),4) AS Quarter
```

You could also use this trick to specify column titles for each of the fields. Rather than selecting the fields from the Database Fields list, enter them into the Functions/Expressions text box and add the AS clause to the field name (for example, Product.Prodname AS Product).

This technique is of limited value, however, if you need to save the query and later modify the fields list for the query. Because the RQBE doesn't recognize the AS clause, when the RQBE reads the .QPR file to construct the fields list, it ignores the AS clause and simply adds each field or expression to the fields list, removing the AS clause in the process.

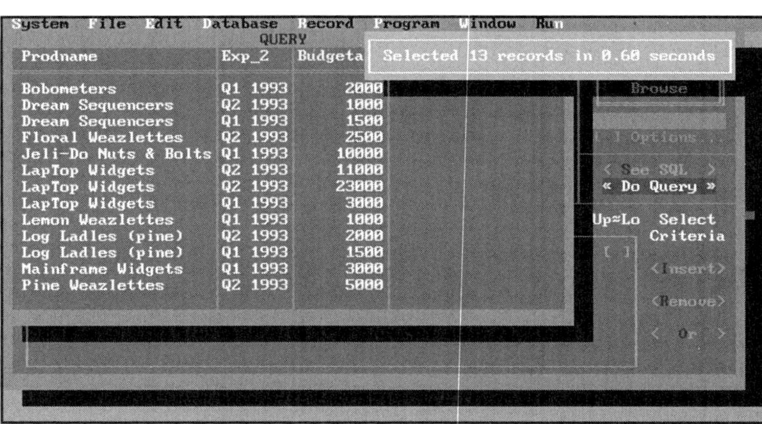

FIG. 5.12

The query results ordered by product name and calendar quarter.

After closing the Browse window, save this query as CHAP5002. (You can do this with the Save As command from the File menu. Remember that the .QPR extension is provided by default.)

Grouping Your Data into Summaries

When analyzing data, you often want only a summary of the information. You may not want to see every budget entry for each product; you may want to see only the total budgeted amount—by product—which is where the Group By... option comes into play. To see how Group By... works, you first create a query. If you have not already done so, close the CHAP5002 query and close all open tables. Create a new query as you did before, then select BUDGET.DBF from the Open File dialog.

Go to the Select Fields... dialog and unselect all fields except BUDGET.PRODCODE. (You may find that using `Remove All`, then selecting BUDGET.PRODCODE, and then using `Move` to move BUDGET.PRODCODE to the Selected Output list is easier than removing fields one by one). For this example, you want the sum of the amount budgeted for each product. To include this information in the query results, select the `Functions` popup button (in the Functions/Expressions section of the dialog). You see a list of the available SQL column functions (also shown in table 5.2) and a list of the fields contained in the selected tables (see fig. 5.13). Because you want to sum the budgeted amounts, select SUM(). In the current list, the only Numeric field is BUDGET.BUDGETAMT. Because BUDGET.BUDGETAMT is the only field that can use this function, all other fields on the list are unselectable. To select this field, press Enter.

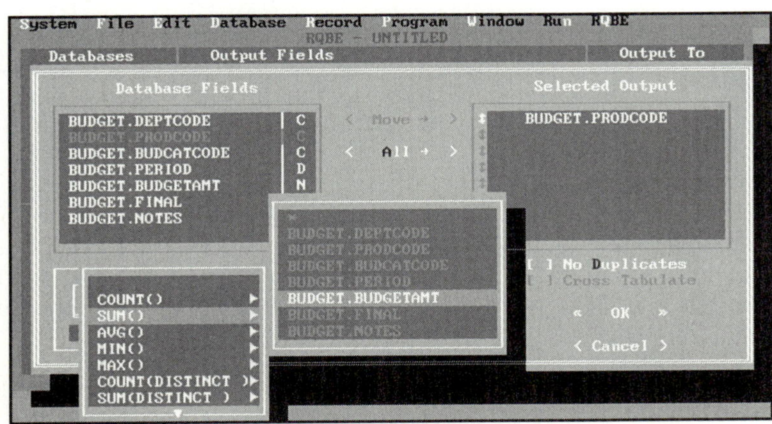

FIG. 5.13

Creating an SQL column function expression.

Table 5.2 SQL Column Functions

Function	Definition
COUNT( )	Counts the number of records processed.
SUM( )	Sums a Numeric field.
AVG( )	Calculates the arithmetic average of a Numeric field.
MIN( )	Returns the lowest value of a field.
MAX( )	The opposite of MIN( ); returns the largest value of a field.
COUNT(DISTINCT)	Counts the number of unique values found in a field. If the values in the table are 1, 2, 3, 3, and 4, the result of COUNT(DISTINCT) is 4.
SUM(DISTINCT)	Sums values, similar to the SUM( ) function, except SUM(DISTINCT) sums only one occurrence of each value. If the values in the table are 1, 2, 3, 3, and 4, the result of SUM(DISTINCT) is 10.
AVG(DISTINCT)	Works like SUM(DISTINCT), except AVG(DISTINCT) computes an average, not a sum.

Note: Each function listed in table 5.2 is calculated separately for each group if you specify any groupings of the data.

The expression SUM(BUDGET.BUDGETAMT) appears in the text box just below the Functions popup. Note that the `Move` button at the top of the dialog is now enabled. Use `Move` to place this expression in the Selected Output list, and select `OK` to leave the dialog.

NOTE If you forget to move the expression to the output list and then select `OK`, FoxPro senses that an expression is pending and asks whether you want to include this expression in the output list.

If you select `Do Query` at this point, you only get one output record, which has the name of the last Prodcode in the table and the sum of all the budgeted amounts for all products. The total budget for all products may be a meaningful number, but that isn't the information you want to see right now.

You want the RQBE to subtotal on—or Group By—the product code. To do this, mark the Group By... check box. The Group By... dialog looks and acts like the Order By... dialog, without the Order Options radio buttons (see fig. 5.14).

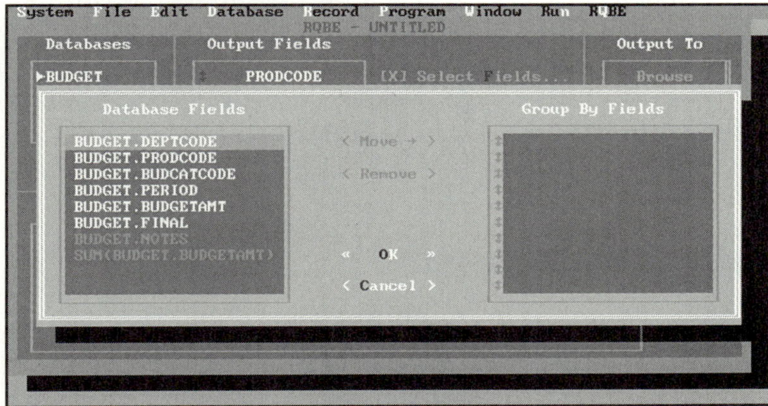

FIG. 5.14

The Group By... dialog.

The BUDGET.NOTES and SUM(BUDGET.BUDGETAMT) fields are not selectable because Notes is a Memo field and SUM() is a SQL function. You cannot Group By Memo fields, General fields, or SQL functions. (You also cannot Order By or join two tables by these types of expressions.)

NOTE The initial release version of FoxPro 2.5 for DOS is somewhat inconsistent in its treatment of General fields. Although you cannot select a General field in the Order By... dialog, for example, you *can* select a General field in the Group By... dialog. When you select `Do Query`, FoxPro informs you that the General field is an invalid Group By... expression. If you have a later version of the product, you may not see this problem.

`Move` the BUDGET.PRODCODE field to the Group By Fields list, because this field is one you want to subtotal on. Return to the main RQBE window by selecting `OK`. When you select `Do Query`, you see a list of unique product codes with the total budget for each product.

Once again, however, you would rather see the product names than the codes. You can perform this substitution as you did in the CHAP5002 query. Doing so again now will help you to become more familiar with the joining process. Again, you perform this procedure in the following manner: select the Add button from the Databases section of the RQBE and open the Product table. For the RQBE Join Condition, join the PRODUCT.PRODCODE field with the BUDGET.PRODCODE field. Next, return to the Select Fields... dialog, add the field PRODUCT.PRODNAME to the Selected Output, and remove the field BUDGET.PRODCODE. Exchange the position of the two selected fields so that the PRODUCT.PRODNAME field is first, then select OK to return to the RQBE. When you select Do Query, you finally have the information in the desired format. Save the query as CHAP5003 and then exit the RQBE.

Filtering Your Data

Another major feature of the RQBE is its capability to filter tables so that only records that meet certain criteria appear in the output. For example, you may want to see the Budget information for a single product.

Open the query CHAP5001.QPR, which you saved previously.

You enter filtering conditions in the Select Criteria section, located in the lower-half of the RQBE window. This section is the heart and soul of the RQBE. Recall that *RQBE* stands for *Relational Query By Example.* In the Select Criteria section, you *R*elate the tables and enter the *E*x-amples *B*y which the RQBE constructs a *Q*uery that answers your question.

Select the blank text region below the box that contains PRODUCT.PRODCODE. This action triggers a popup with the list of fields, shown in figure 5.15. Note that a bar separates the fields from each table. Select the field PRODUCT.PRODNAME.

NOTE You can also enter filtering conditions by using the Having... dialog, but filter expressions entered in the Having... dialog eliminate *groups,* not individual records. If you use the Hav-ing... dialog but haven't specified any fields to Group By, FoxPro selects records by joining the tables and applying any filter conditions entered in the Select Criteria section, without regard for your Having filter conditions. FoxPro then applies the Having condition or conditions to each record in the intermediate query result as though each record is a separate group. Although the result is the same,

FoxPro may take much longer to process the query in this fashion. Unless you are sure that your filter conditions should eliminate groups rather than records, enter your filter conditions in the Select Criteria section of the RQBE window.

You learn more about the Having... dialog in Chapter 6, "Investigating Your Data with Advanced Queries," and Chapter 7, "Querying with SQL and Searching with Rushmore," covers the HAVING clause of the SELECT command.

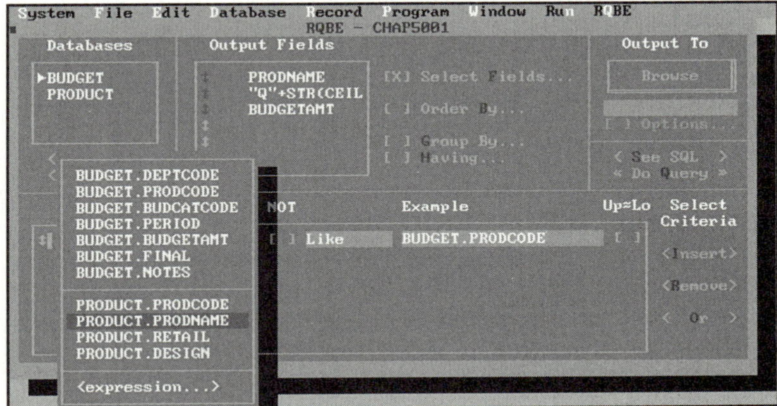

FIG. 5.15

Choosing the field for a filter condition.

If you use the keyboard to select PRODUCT.PRODNAME, you are placed in the NOT check box. This check box works with the text field to the right to specify how the filter discriminates between records. For now, leave NOT unchecked. Select the text box on this line with the word Like in it. The popup that appears contains a list of available connectors, described in table 5.3.

Table 5.3 RQBE Join/Filter Connectors

Like	The SETting of ANSI affects Like. ANSI, unlike most other SETtings in FoxPro, can only be changed from the Command window, with the SET ANSI ON and SET ANSI OFF commands. The default for SET ANSI is OFF. With ANSI set OFF, Like checks whether the beginning of a shorter Character field matches the longer one and continues to compare characters until one of the strings is exhausted. For example:

continues

Table 5.3 Continued

	`"JIM" Like "JIMMY"`
	`"JIMMY" Like "JIM"`
	`"JIM  " Like "JIM"`
	`"JIM" Like "JIM"`
	The preceding comparisons are all considered matches but `"JIM " Like "JIMMY"` is not a match.
	With SET ANSI ON, FoxPro adds spaces to the shorter field to make this field the same length as the longer string before comparing. For example, with `"JIM" Like "JIMMY"`, FoxPro actually compares `"JIM"` Like `"JIMMY"` ..., so this comparison is not considered a match.
Exactly Like	Checks for exact matches.
More Than	Checks whether the field on the left is greater than the field on the right.
Less Than	Checks whether the field on the left is less than the field on the right.
Between	Checks whether the field on the left is between two values, separated by commas, on the right.
In	Checks whether the field on the left is in the list of values supplied on the right.

You are interested only in records where the product name is the same as, or Like, the text "Dream Sequencers." Select Like from the popup and type `Dream Sequencers` in the Example text box. Take care to type the text in proper case, because RQBE performs a case-sensitive search by default. To carry out a case-insensitive search so that (in this example) all entries of *DREAM SEQUENCERS* or *dream sequencers* are found, check the check box below the Up∞Lo column heading.

NOTE If you are viewing the SELECT command that the RQBE constructs as you select options, or if you now select `See SQL`, you will notice that checking the Up∞Lo check box encloses the field name on the left side of the connector within the UPPER( ) function and converts the comparison text on the right side to all uppercase letters.

You also can type only the first part of the string for which you are searching. If you type `Dre`, RQBE finds *Dream Sequencers*. However, RQBE also finds *Dreadnoughts*, if Omnipresent Widgets makes them. You can disable this feature by using Exactly Like rather than Like.

When the screen looks like figure 5.16, you are ready to select `Do Query`. When you execute the query, you may see a message box with the following message as FoxPro tries to use the window Preference, which is stored in the Resource file from the prior query's Browse window:

```
Invalid BROWSE setup - default setup used
```

Press Enter to ignore the message, and the query appears. Note in figure 5.16 that no join condition indicator appears because this expression is not a join condition.

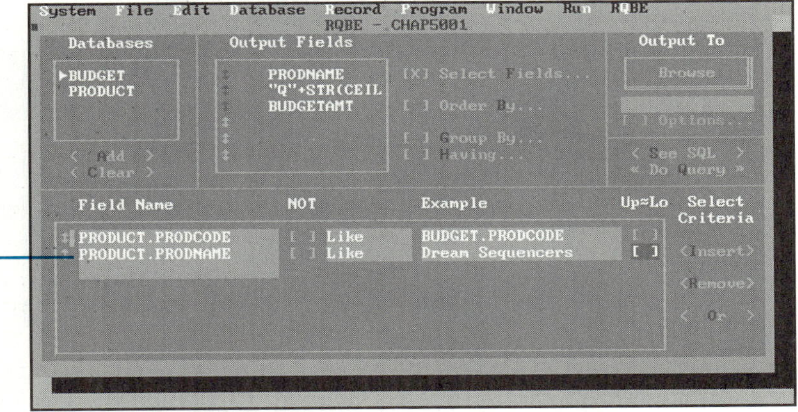

FIG. 5.16

A completed filter example.

Suppose that you want to see records for both Dream Sequencers and Bobometers. Just change Like to In. Edit the field that contains the words *Dream Sequencers* by typing a comma after the string and then the word `Bobometers`. This corresponds to the English instructions, "Select all products in the list Dream Sequencers, Bobometers." To see the records for all products *except* Dream Sequencers and Bobometers, check the NOT box. When you Do this Query, you see records for Log Ladles, Weazlettes, and so on, but no records appear for Dream Sequencers and Bobometers.

Continue to experiment by adding more complex filtering conditions. When you are satisfied with the selected conditions, save this query as CHAP5004.

Directing Your Query Output

Until now, all the query output was directed to a Browse window. You can now get fancy with RQBE output. Sending query results to a printed report is easy because the Report Writer is integrated with the RQBE. Using the Output To popup control, choose Report/Label as the output type. This choice enables the Options check box beneath the Output To control.

Now select the Options box. You see the RQBE Display Options dialog, as shown in figure 5.17.

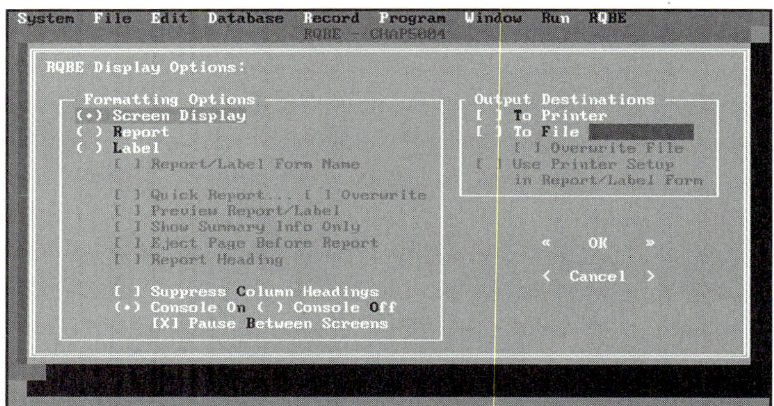

FIG. 5.17

The RQBE Display Options dialog.

The RQBE Display Options dialog presents a wealth of options. To produce a printed report, select the Report radio button. Now most of the options in the Formatting Options section of the dialog are available. Select the Quick Report check box. You now see the RQBE Quick Report dialog, which enables you to format the report by using either the Column or Form radio button (see fig. 5.18). Selecting either button updates the layout guide picture on the right side of the RQBE Quick Report dialog. For this example, leave the default Column Layout radio button pressed. You also can specify the Report Width, but leave this setting at 80 columns. The last item in the dialog is the Save As text box, which defaults to the same name as the query. To exit the Quick Report dialog, select `OK`, and you return to the Display Options dialog.

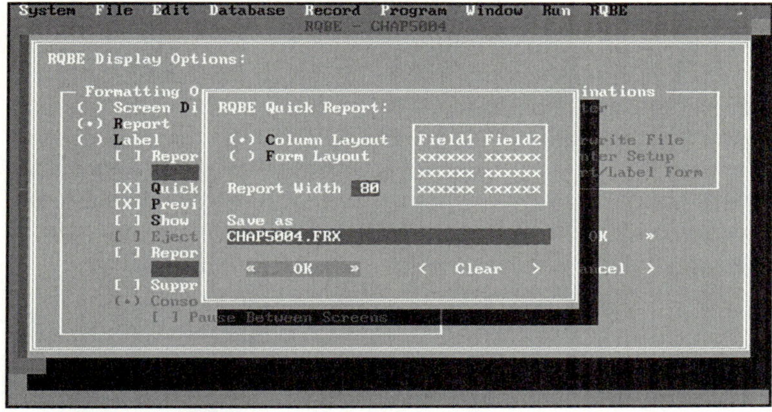

FIG. 5.18

The RQBE Quick Report dialog using Column Layout.

Notice that the Preview Report/Label check box is checked. This check box enables you to see the report on-screen before you print. Select `OK` to exit the dialog, and then select `Do Query` to preview the report (see fig. 5.19).

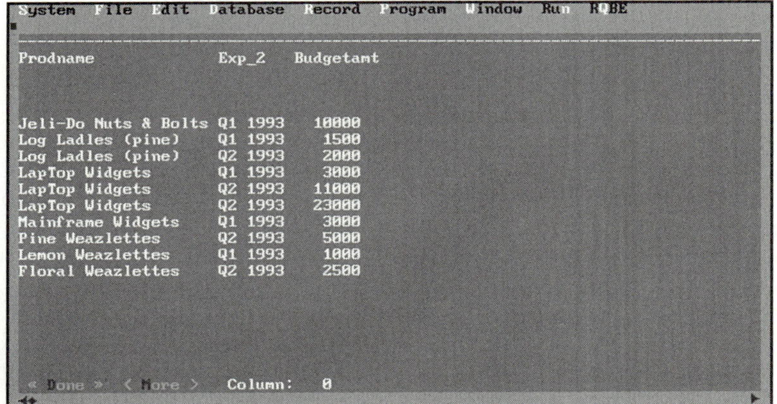

FIG. 5.19

The FoxPro Report Writer's Page Preview called from the RQBE.

You are now in the Report Writer's Page Preview mode. You have now created a report that you can edit (add headings, totals, and so on) with the Report Writer, which is covered in Chapter 9, "Putting the Answers to Work in Reports and Labels," and Chapter 10, "Using the Report Writer and Label Designer." All changes made to the report form in the Report Writer are reflected when you run the query again.

To print the report, return to the Display Options dialog and unselect the Preview Report/Label check box. Doing so enables you to check the To Printer check box. Now mark the Report Heading check box, and the Expression Builder dialog appears on-screen. This complex dialog, which you use throughout FoxPro, enables you to choose a field or variable or to type another expression to serve as your report title. You learn more about the Expression Builder in the following chapters. For now, just type `"Budgets by Product and Quarter"` (including the quotation marks), as shown in figure 5.20.

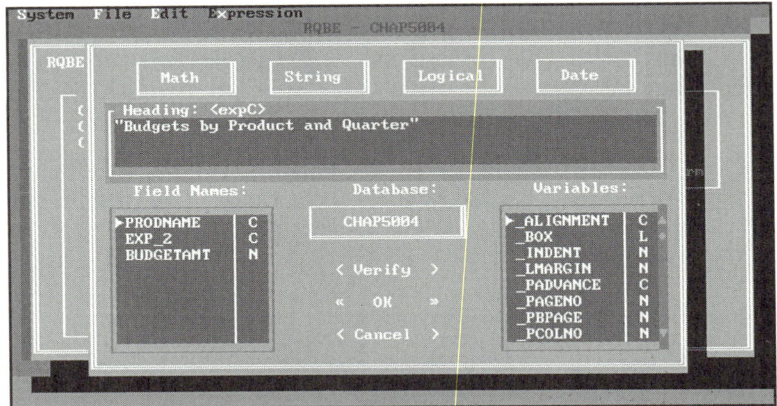

FIG. 5.20

Creating a report heading with the Expression Builder.

Select `OK` to leave the Expression Builder. (You can first select the `Verify` push button to ensure that you typed a valid expression. If an error message appears in an Alert window, you may have forgotten to enclose the heading in quotation marks.) To print the report, mark the To Printer check box. Select `OK` to leave the dialog. Select `Do Query`, sending the report to the printer.

As you learn in Chapters 9 and 10, labels—although similar to reports in FoxPro—use a simpler set of options. Therefore, you have fewer options from which to choose in the RQBE Display Options dialog. Because no Quick Label feature is available in FoxPro, you cannot create labels until you are introduced to the Label Designer in Chapter 9. Then you can specify the name of a preexisting label as your query output.

CAUTION: When you specify the name of a preexisting label or report as your query destination, be sure that any alias referenced in the label or report form is removed or edited to be appropriate for the temporary table, or cursor, used by the RQBE as an interim place to store the results. (This problem is presented in greater detail in Chapter 7, "Querying with SQL and Searching with Rushmore.")

Screen Display, the default Report option, is simply the DISPLAY or LIST command that shows the query results on-screen or directs output to a file or the printer. This operation is similar to the way you used LIST and DISPLAY to show records in Chapter 3, "Exploring Databases and Tables," and Chapter 4, "Database Management Fundamentals."

If you haven't already done so, use Save As to place this query on disk in the present form, as CHAP5005. If you also want to save a copy of the data that results from this table, you can send the data to another table on the disk. Select Table/DBF. A File Save dialog appears with various naming options available. For now, accept the default. When you return to the main RQBE dialog, note that the text box just above the Options check box changes from CHAP5005 to CHAP5005.DBF.

By selecting Cursor as the output type, you can send the results to a temporary readonly file without immediately viewing the results of your query. Throughout this chapter, the RQBE has been outputting your results to a Cursor. You learn more about Cursors in the following chapters. For now, just remember that Cursors are temporary tables that FoxPro automatically removes from the disk when you close them.

If you own and have installed FoxGraph, you also can send the query results directly to a graph by selecting Graph and running the query. If you have another graphics package, you also may be able to link this software to FoxPro's RQBE. FoxPro's API (Application Programming Interface) makes writing the necessary routines possible, as is discussed briefly in Chapter 16, "Discovering Additional FoxPro Productivity Features." Chapter 21, "Using Commands and Functions to Manipulate Data," covers the API more extensively.

Summary

With the RQBE, you can create complex queries to extract information from tables in a matter of minutes. Before FoxPro 2.0, experienced programmers took many hours to create hundreds of lines of program code to accomplish the results that one FoxPro query can provide. For many complex queries, the most sophisticated program code does not execute as fast as the SQL SELECT created from FoxPro's RQBE—largely because of SQL's use of the *Rushmore* technology, which is discussed in greater detail in Chapter 7.

In this chapter, you learned to manipulate the RQBE as a tool. Now that you know how to use this feature, you are ready to take on some real work. In the following chapter, you learn to construct more intricate queries by accessing the power of additional clauses of the SQL SELECT command.

6

CHAPTER

Investigating Your Data with Advanced Queries

In Chapter 5, you learned about most of the simple features of FoxPro's RQBE. You have seen only a sliver of its potential, however. In this chapter, you begin to see the power of the RQBE by learning to use its tools to create more complex queries.

Because the Budget and Prodcode tables you used in Chapter 5 are not sufficient to demonstrate some of the more powerful capabilities of the RQBE, you now use some of the sample tables provided with FoxPro. These tables are located in the Tutorial directory, under the main FoxPro directory.

NOTE

If you did not install the Tutorial files when you installed FoxPro, you must install them now if you want to follow the examples in this chapter. To install the Tutorial files, move to the FoxPro directory and run the INSTALL program in *one* of the following ways:

- At the DOS prompt, type the DOS command `FOX INSTALL`.
- Enter `DO INSTALL` in the Command window.
- Choose `INSTALL.APP` from the Run Application dialog or the Program Do dialog.

Because you already installed FoxPro, you do not proceed exactly as you did during the initial installation. Choose No when asked whether you want to overwrite your FOXUSER file. Choose the tutorial files from the Supplemental Product list. You then are prompted to insert the correct disk.

Creating Complex Filter Conditions

More often than not, you want to filter data from your tables by using more than one criterion. In Chapter 5, you filtered records by using only one criterion: product name. In this section, you learn how to filter more selectively.

Asking Questions with AND and OR

To begin, open a new query (from the File New dialog), and select the CUSTOMER.DBF table from the Tutorial directory. Don't use the CUSTOMER.DBF table in the Model directory. Use the Directory pop-up of the Open File dialog to move back to the FoxPro home directory, and then select Tutorial from the directory list. Select the CUSTOMER.DBF table from the list of tables in the Tutorial directory.

The first action you want to take is to eliminate some of the fields from the Output Fields list. (This step will probably apply to most of your queries.) From the Select Fields... dialog, select only the following fields for output:

CUSTOMER.COMPANY

CUSTOMER.STATE

CUSTOMER.YTDPURCH

If you do not see these fields on your Select Fields... list, you are using the wrong Customer table. Go back to the main RQBE dialog, select the `Clear` button to clear this table, and then select `Add` to add the correct Customer table from the Tutorial directory.

NOTE You can look in the RQBE's Select Fields... dialog or the Setup panel of the View window to understand the structure of this and other tables from the Tutorial directory that you use in this book. To get a good sense of the entire Tutorial database and the way its tables are interrelated, refer to the chart at the beginning of the "Using SQL SELECT" section in your *Developer's Guide*.

Suppose that you are interested only in customers based in New York State. To select those customers, set a filter in the Select Criteria section of the RQBE window. Select the popup beneath the Field Name heading, and select CUSTOMER.STATE from the popup. Leave the NOT box empty and leave Like in the joiner box. In the Example heading, type `NY`. After you select `Do Query`, a Browse window of all customers in New York appears. Your screen should look like that shown in figure 6.1.

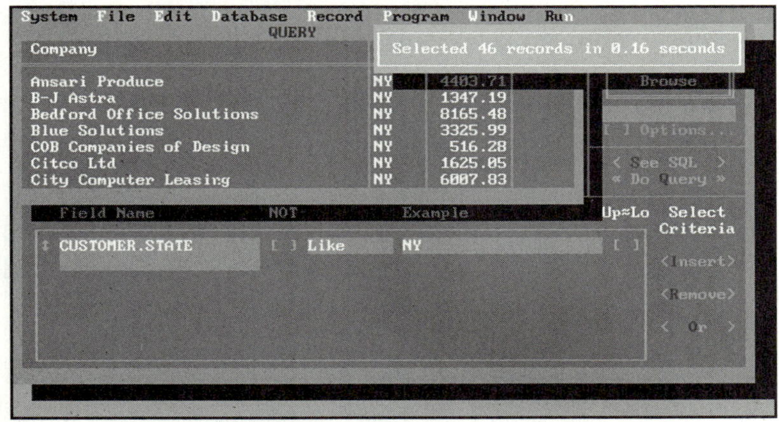

FIG. 6.1

All customers in New York State.

Perhaps you want to see only your best customers from New York—those with year-to-date purchases of $5,000 or more. To see these customers, add another filter below the one you just entered, specifying that CUSTOMER.YTDPURCH is not less than 5000.

After you finish, your screen looks like the one in figure 6.2.

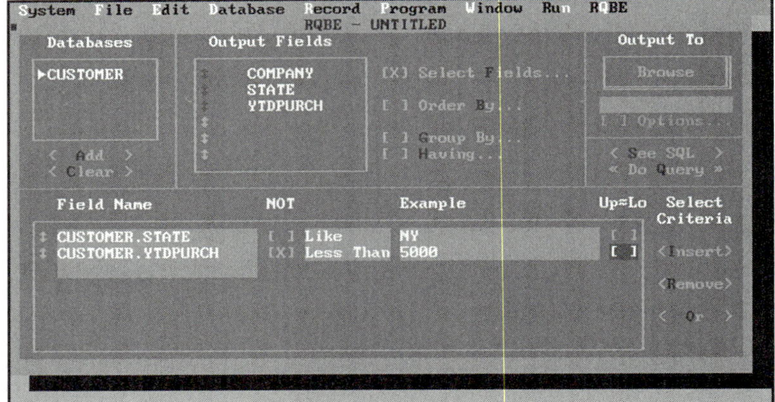

FIG. 6.2

Filtering by state and year-to-date purchases.

Notice that even though you are interested in customers with year-to-date purchases of $5,000 or more, you selected customers in New York with year-to-date purchases of not less than $5,000. This procedure may seem a bit backward; however, had you selected customers with purchases of more than $5,000, you would have missed customers whose purchases were exactly $5,000.

If you select `Do Query` now, your Browse window contains only your best customers from NY, as shown in figure 6.3.

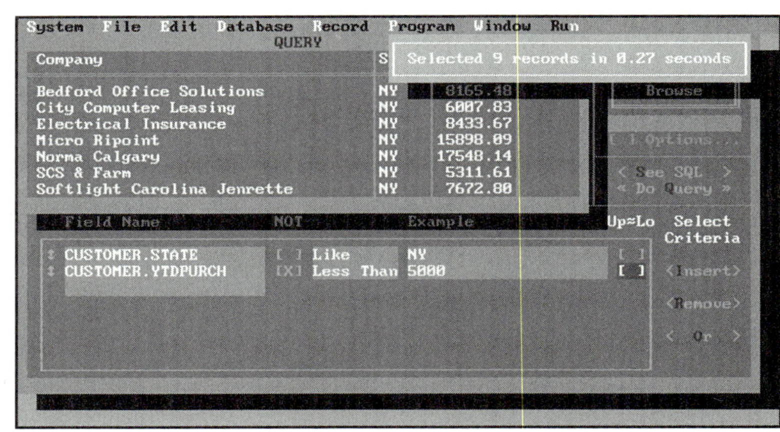

FIG. 6.3

The best customers in New York.

Perhaps you want to see your best customers (those with $5,000 or more in year-to-date purchases) *and* your worst customers (those with less than $100 in year-to-date purchases). This query seems pretty straightforward. Just add another filter, specifying CUSTOMER.YTDPURCH less than 100, and your screen looks like that shown in figure 6.4.

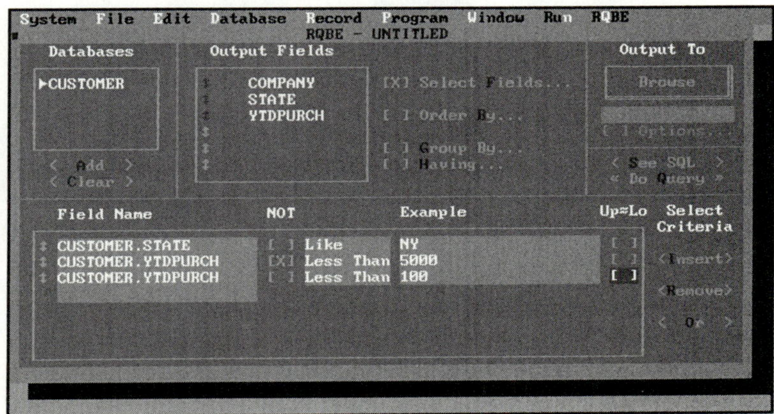

FIG. 6.4

The best- and worst-customer filters.

If you select `Do Query` at this point, the command doesn't work correctly—no output records are produced even though you know, from the previous example, that you have nine good customers. The problem here is that the RQBE is doing exactly what you told it to do, not what you want it to do. The following shows how FoxPro translated the query:

```
Select all customers whose state is New York,
AND whose year-to-date purchases are not less than $5,000,
AND whose year-to-date purchases are less than $100.
```

The trick is knowing that FoxPro asks this three-part question of every customer. For any given customer, all three parts cannot be true.

What you really want to say to FoxPro is the following:

```
Show me all customers from New York
whose year-to-date purchases were $5,000 or more,
OR whose year-to-date purchases were less than $100.
```

To write the query correctly, you need to add OR. Select the `Or` button (its hot key is O). The RQBE places a line with the word OR in it beneath the CUSTOMER.YTDPURCH filter, as shown in figure 6.5.

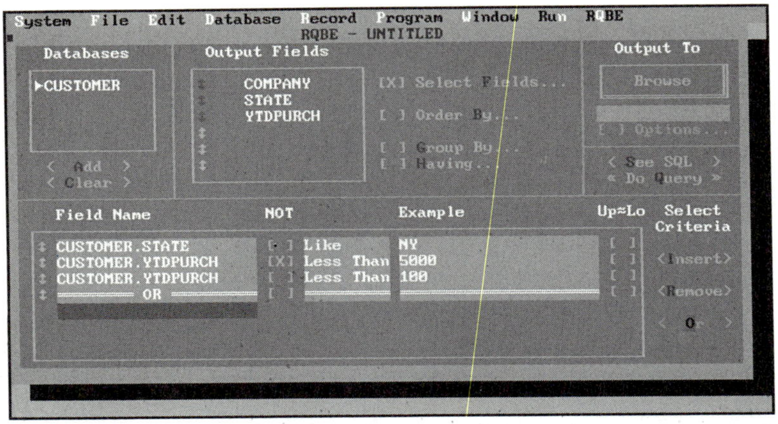

FIG. 6.5

The OR line.

Move the OR line so it is between the two CUSTOMER.YTDPURCH filters. The OR line can be moved by using the Ctrl+PgUp and Ctrl+PgDn keys, or by dragging the doubled-headed arrow character at the far left. This is the same way that fields are moved in the Output Fields list and in other similar lists. After you have moved the OR line, your screen looks like that shown in figure 6.6.

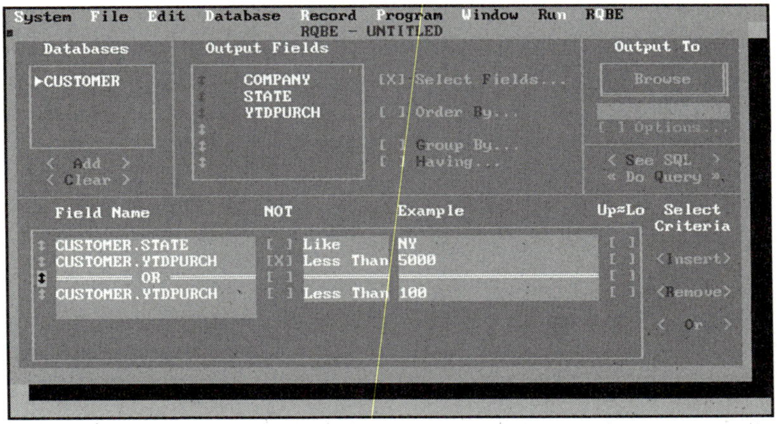

FIG. 6.6

The OR line moved.

Now select `Do Query` again, and you see your best New York customers and worst customers from all states in the same Browse window— almost what you want. The RQBE is connecting filters on both sides of the OR line. For all customers, FoxPro makes sure that they are in NY and have purchases of $5,000 or more. If this test fails, FoxPro determines whether the customer's purchases are less than $100. The second test knows nothing about NY. To correct this problem, add a new filter condition at the bottom exactly like the first filter condition. After adding the filter, your screen looks like that shown in figure 6.7.

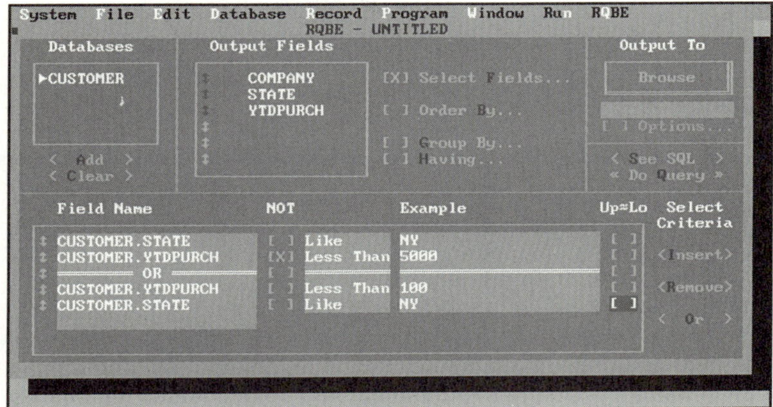

FIG. 6.7

Duplicating filters to determine your best and worst customers.

After you select `Do Query`, you see the information for which you are searching. However, your worst customers are interspersed with your best customers. To segregate them, order by CUSTOMER.YTDPURCH, set the Order Options to Descending, and then select `Do Query`. Now your best customers are at the top of the Browse window and your worst customers are at the bottom, as shown in figure 6.8.

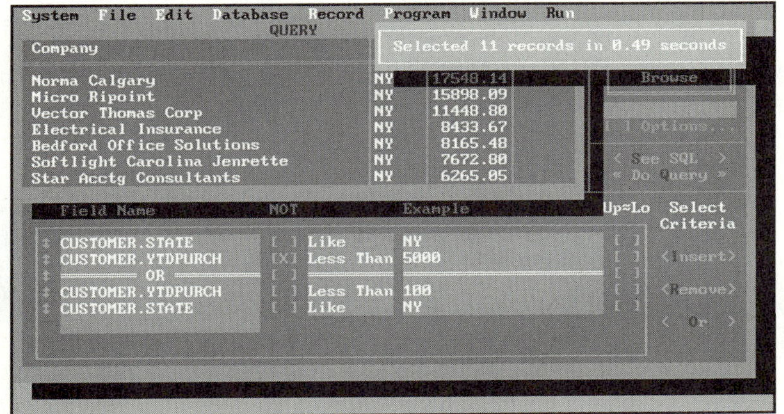

FIG. 6.8

The worst and best NY customers in sales order.

At this point, you should save your query. Saving this file is not as simple as before, however, because you used tables outside the current directory. When you bring up the File Save dialog, you see that the Directory is Tutorial because the table you used is in the Tutorial directory. Because you want to save your query in the Model directory, change Tutorial in the Directory popup by going up one level to the main FoxPro directory and selecting Model from the list. After that, type the name for your query: `CHAP6001` (FoxPro adds the default extension, `.QPR`).

> **CAUTION:** The RQBE does not save the directory name of the tables with the query file. Consequently, if you close a query and its associated files and then try to reopen it, FoxPro cannot find the proper tables. Instead, FoxPro opens the Customer table in the Model directory. Because this table does not have the correct fields, FoxPro gives you an error, and you can't access your query. Whenever your tables are in a different directory than the query file, you have to open the tables yourself before you open or execute the query.

Deciphering AND, OR, and NOT

AND, OR, and NOT are simple words in English sentences, but using them properly in filter expressions can be confusing. Look closely at the way these operators work.

Filters are made up of *logical expressions*. In other words, the expressions can be either TRUE or FALSE. The filter expressions are evaluated for every record. If the expression is TRUE, the record is included in the query result. If it is FALSE, the record is excluded. Table 6.1 shows how TRUE and FALSE conditions work with AND, OR, and NOT.

Table 6.1 AND, OR, and NOT Logic

Operator	Description
AND	When two items are joined by AND, both must be true to obtain a result of TRUE. TRUE AND TRUE = TRUE TRUE AND FALSE = FALSE FALSE AND TRUE = FALSE

Operator	Description
	FALSE AND FALSE = FALSE
OR	When two items are joined by OR, only one must be true to obtain a result of TRUE. TRUE OR TRUE = TRUE TRUE OR FALSE = TRUE FALSE OR TRUE = TRUE FALSE OR FALSE = FALSE
NOT	The NOT function (check box in RQBE) reverses a TRUE or FALSE. NOT TRUE = FALSE NOT FALSE = TRUE

In mathematics, similar types of expressions are evaluated from left to right; that is, in their order of appearance. In RQBE, logical filter expressions are evaluated from top to bottom. In the last example, your final filter looked like the following:

```
CUSTOMER.STATE                      Like          "NY"
CUSTOMER.YTDPURCH      NOT          Less Than     5000
=========OR========    ====         ========   ==========
CUSTOMER.YTDPURCH                   Less Than     100
CUSTOMER.STATE                      Like          "NY"
```

Each record in the customer table was tested with the preceding filter rules. The items immediately next to each other were joined with AND. The OR separator divided two sets of AND clauses. If either of the two AND sections resulted in TRUE, the entire expression was considered TRUE.

No matter how many filter expressions you use, all these expressions can be divided into sets of AND clauses, separated by OR clauses. By using the preceding table, you can pick apart the filters to determine exactly what is happening. Often in complex situations, studying the SQL SELECT command that FoxPro constructs (by selecting the `See SQL` button) helps you understand just what your query does.

If you are experienced in earlier Xbase dialects, you might notice that the operators AND, NOT, and OR are not written with surrounding periods (.AND., .OR., and .NOT.) as they would be in other Xbase syntax. The periods are not required with these operators in FoxPro 2.x, although the logical values TRUE and FALSE still require them (.T. and .F.).

NOTE You can use the `See SQL` button at any point to view the SQL SELECT statement that FoxPro uses to execute the query, as well as any other FoxPro commands used to display the query results, such as BROWSE. This way, you can use the RQBE to learn the syntax of the SQL SELECT command and determine how simple FoxPro commands are used to enhance the basic SQL SELECT. Remember that the .QPR file created by the RQBE is simply a regular program composed of normal FoxPro statements, which you can issue singly from the command window or in programs in combination with any other commands you wish. In FoxPro, SQL is not a separate mode; it is completely integrated into the language.

Along with helping you get accustomed to SQL syntax, a quick look at `See SQL` every now and then helps you understand how the different controls on the RQBE work. You can use the RQBE tools to learn SQL, and in turn, SQL commands can help you learn about the RQBE.

Filtering Groups with the HAVING Clause

In Chapter 5, you learned how to set groupings. You also learned how to filter your data by entering selection criteria. This filtering eliminates the unwanted records before any other work or grouping is performed.

On some occasions, you might want to filter your results after the grouping has taken place. For example, using the same customer file you used in the last example, you might want to produce a listing of the year-to-date purchases by state in which the total purchases in each state exceed $50,000. Because the filter is based on the state *grouping*, you have to use the Having... dialog. Create the following query to see how this dialog works.

If you have not already done so, close the CHAP6001.QPR query. Make certain that the Customer table from the Tutorial directory (the same one you used before) is open in the current work area. Then open a new query.

Because you are interested in year-to-date purchases by state, you don't have to see most of the fields in the Customer table. From the Select Fields... dialog, adjust the Selected Output so that only the following fields are selected:

CUSTOMER.STATE

SUM(CUSTOMER.YTDPURCH)

Remember, to create the SUM() expression, use the Functions popup in the lower-left section of the Select Fields... dialog.

Next, from the Group By... dialog, move CUSTOMER.STATE into the Group By Fields list. The current query should list each state and its year-to-date purchases. Do this Query to make sure. Your screen looks like the one in figure 6.9. FoxPro makes it easy to select `Do Query` at any time so you can determine whether you are on the right track.

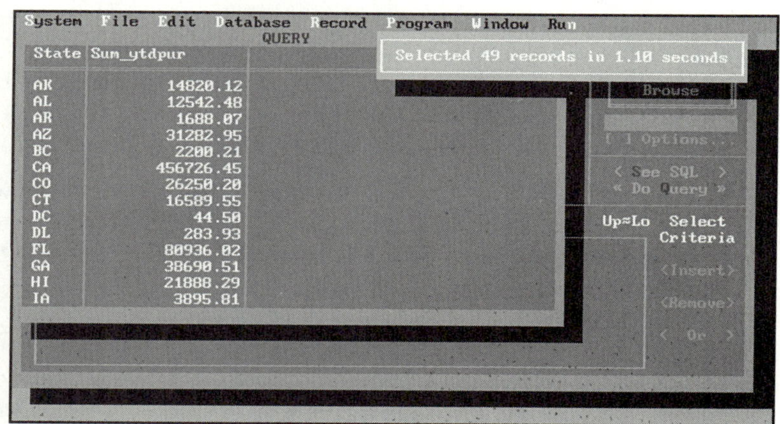

FIG. 6.9

Year-to-date purchases by state.

So far, this query is doing exactly what you want. Next, rule out states in which the year-to-date purchases are less than $50,000. Exclude these states by using the Having... dialog, which you see in figure 6.10. To access the Having... dialog, select the Having... check box (use its hot key, H).

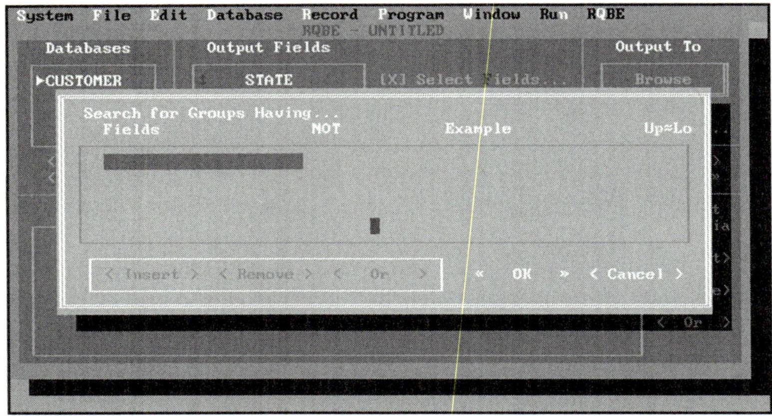

FIG. 6.10

The Having... dialog.

The Having... dialog works much like the Select Criteria section. Select the popup under Fields to see a list of expressions and fields that can be used in filters. In this example, you want to limit the output based on the sum of the year-to-date purchases, so select SUM( ), which limits the fields you can choose to the numeric fields. Select CUSTOMER.YTDPURCH as the field to SUM( ). Check the NOT box, change Like to Less Than, and then enter `50000` in the Example text box. As before, you want all groups not less than $50,000. If you select more than $50,000, you miss any states with exactly $50,000 in purchases.

Also notice that you can have multiple Having... criteria connected with implicit ANDs. You can also connect the criteria with OR lines. These conditions are logically connected in the same way as they were in the Select Criteria section of the RQBE window.

Your screen now looks like the one shown in figure 6.11.

Now, select `OK` to leave the Having... dialog, and then select `Do Query`. Your output looks like that shown in figure 6.12.

Based on this query, you may want to move your headquarters to California, which would reduce costs immensely!

Save this query as CHAP6002.QPR. Make sure that it is saved in the Model subdirectory and not in the Tutorial subdirectory.

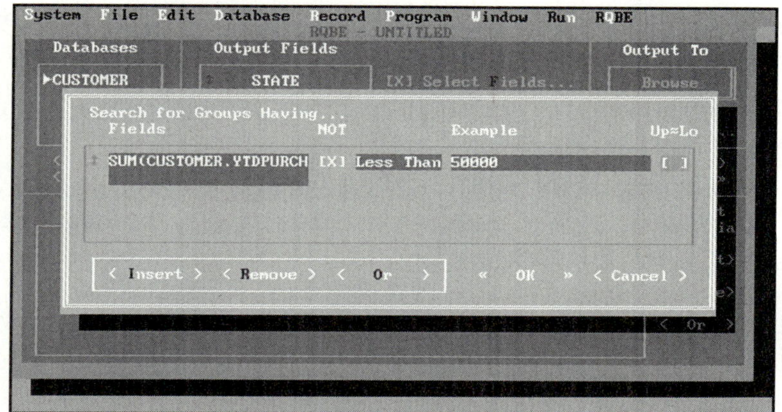

FIG. 6.11

Using the Having... dialog to filter groups.

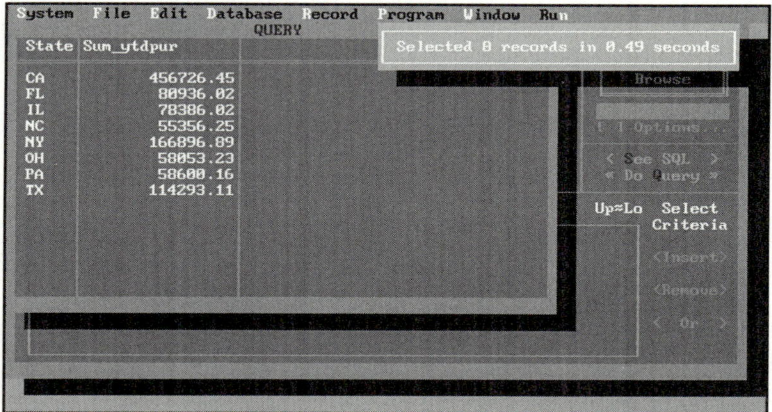

FIG. 6.12

All states with year-to-date purchases of $50,000 or more.

Joining More Than Two Tables

In this example, you want to see those customers who have purchased five or more of any part. In addition to their names, you want to see how many of each part they have purchased.

Because you are looking for parts-per-customer, you have to join the Customer table with the Parts table. Because no common fields exist between the Customer table and the Parts table, the tables cannot be joined directly. However, they can be *indirectly* joined. To do so, join the Customer table with the Invoices table (by CNO). Then join the Invoices table to the Detail table (by INO). Finally, join the Detail table with the Parts table (by PNO).

Using the SET RELATION command, you can express the same type of indirect relationship in a series of commands, such as the following:

```
SELECT 0
USE parts
INDEX ON pno TAG pno
SELECT 0
USE detail
INDEX ON ino TAG ino
SET RELATION TO pno INTO parts
SELECT 0
USE invoices
INDEX ON cno TAG cno
SET RELATION TO ino INTO detail
SELECT 0
USE customer
SET RELATION TO cno INTO invoices
SET SKIP TO invoices, detail, parts
BROWSE FIELDS CUSTOMER.COMPANY, PARTS.DESCRIPT
```

In the RQBE, however, you can solve the problem more easily. If you have not already done so, exit from the RQBE and close any open tables. Now open a new query. FoxPro prompts you for a table. If the listed directory is not Tutorial, change it to Tutorial, as before, and select the CUSTOMER.DBF table.

Now, select `Add` to add the other tables you need (INVOICES.DBF, DETAIL.DBF, and PARTS.DBF). As you add each table, RQBE invokes the Join Condition dialog. Because each table has a field with the same name as a field in one other table, the RQBE correctly determines all the correct linkages. Accept each of the join conditions that the RQBE proposes.

After you have finished and return to the main RQBE screen, your screen looks like the one in figure 6.13. Now you should understand why the table name must be placed in front of the field name in the RQBE popups. If multiple tables are used, the table name clarifies which fields are referenced—even if the field names are identical.

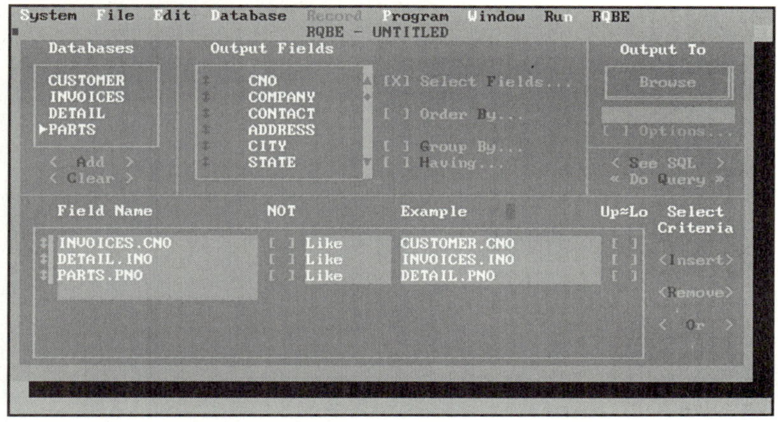

FIG. 6.13

A four-table join.

Before you select `Do Query`, you might want to choose Select Fields... for output. Because RQBE is still in its default state, it simply would output every field from the Customer table and none from the other tables. This step makes the other three tables superfluous; you don't learn anything from them. Open the Select Fields... dialog and select the following fields for output:

CUSTOMER.COMPANY

PARTS.DESCRIPT

Now select `Do Query`; your results should match figure 6.14. You might notice that this query takes longer than those in the previous exercises. Depending on your available memory and hardware, this query might take long enough for FoxPro to display a thermometer as it runs the query. This query takes longer because, by default, no indexes exist in the Tutorial tables, so you have forced SQL to create them on the fly. (In the equivalent example using RELATIONs from the View or Command window, you had to create those indexes as well.) You learn how to fine-tune your queries for the best possible performance in Chapter 7.

Save this query as CHAP6003.QPR in the Model directory. The query has produced one line of output for each part each customer purchased. This query would be even more useful if it showed how many of each part each customer had purchased. That determination is your next step.

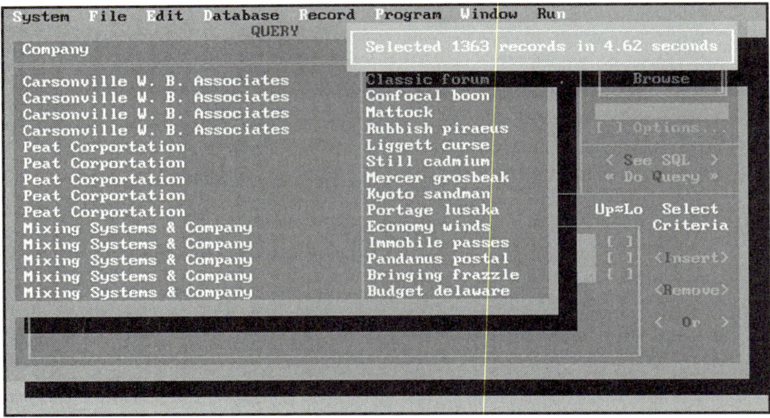

FIG. 6.14

The results of a four-table join.

You have to subtotal (group) the Detail.Qty field by customer and then by part, which requires two groupings. Open the Group By... dialog and add the following groupings:

CUSTOMER.CNO

PARTS.PNO

After you add the groupings, select `OK`.

NOTE

You also can group by DETAIL.PNO instead of PARTS.PNO, which would produce the same result because you have only one matching part record for each detail record. Although changes like this may not alter the output, often they can have performance implications. In this case, however, the change doesn't have an ill effect.

This step instructs the RQBE to group by part number (Pno) within company, enabling you to calculate a separate SUM(Detail.Qty) on each part number for each company. Thus you are asking the question, "How many of each part did each customer purchase?"

Now you have to add a field to the output to display the summed quantity field. Open the Select Fields... dialog. You need a sum of the Qty field for each grouping, so activate the Functions popup and select SUM( ). Doing so produces the popup of fields, and only the Numeric fields are available for selection. Select the DETAIL.QTY field and close the Select Fields... dialog.

Now select `Do Query`. One of the things you might notice is that the output is too wide to fit in the default Browse window. You can use the

Tab key to see the hidden fields, or you can resize the Browse window to fit the fields. If you resize the Browse window, your output looks something like that shown in figure 6.15.

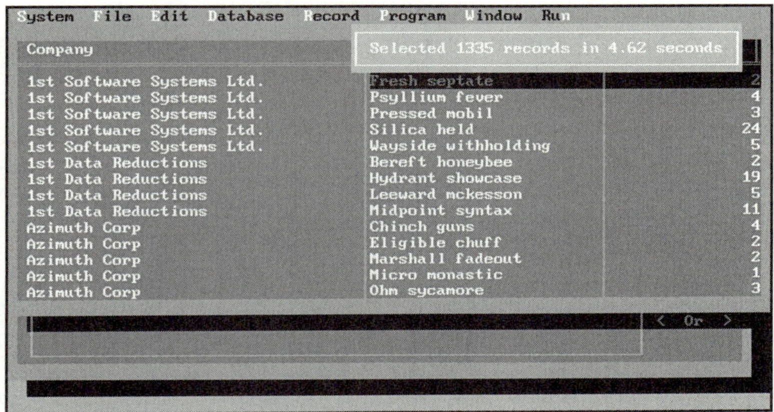

FIG. 6.15

How many of each part that each customer purchased.

The last action you must take to answer your original question is to limit the output to five or more parts purchased per customer. This step is a job for Having... because Having... works on Groupings instead of on individual records. Open the Having... dialog and add the following criteria:

```
SUM(DETAIL.QTY)      More Than      4
```

You can also specify not less than 5, but because the QTY field does not hold fractions, you don't have to do this. Select `OK` to leave the Having... dialog. Now, select `Do Query` again; your output looks like that shown in figure 6.16.

You have now met your original goal. You did it in simple, discrete steps and were able to check yourself every so often by using `Do Query`. Save this query as CHAP6004.QPR in the Model subdirectory.

Creating One-to-Many Relations with RQBE

You created *one-to-many* views of your data by using the SET RELATION and SET SKIP commands in Chapter 4. It is even easier to create one-to-many relations with the RQBE. You cannot, however, achieve the intuitive look of the integrated one-to-many Browse windows that FoxPro creates from direct commands—with shaded blocks indicating the extent of each parent's child records. With RQBE, however, you can obtain the same information in fewer steps by enabling FoxPro and SQL to do some of the work for you. Also with RQBE, you need not have any indexes on the tables as you did with the SET RELATION method (although the presence of indexes improves the speed of queries).

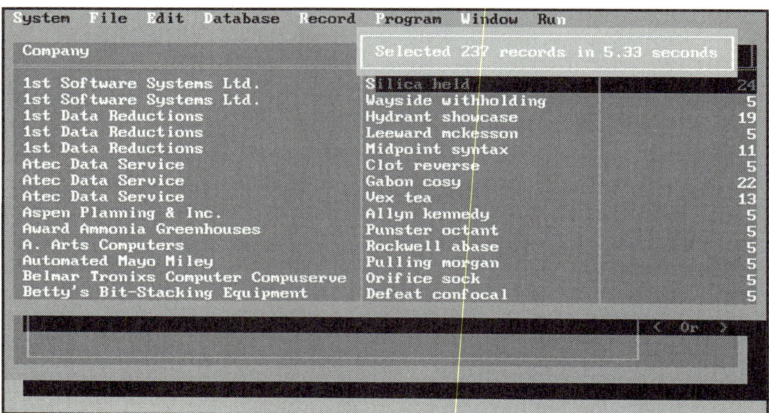

FIG. 6.16

Parts popular with particular customers.

To see a short example of one-to-many views, you have to create a new query. If you have not already done so, save and close the CHAP6004 query and close any open tables. Next, create a new query. When FoxPro prompts you for a file, move to the Tutorial directory and select the CUSTOMER.DBF table.

In this example, you look at all customers and their invoices. Each customer has one or more invoices: the one-to-many relation.

You now have a query with the Customer table open. Because you want to relate the Customer table to the Invoices table, you have to add the Invoices table and join them on their common customer number (Cno) field. Once again, the RQBE recognizes this relationship, so you simply have to select OK in the Join Condition dialog.

Next, to obtain useful output, open the Select Fields... dialog and select the following fields:

CUSTOMER.COMPANY

INVOICES.IDATE

INVOICES.ITOTAL

If you were to select `Do Query` now, you would receive a random list of companies and their invoices—you could not determine how many invoices a particular company had. Ordering by company, however, places all the invoices for each company next to each other. To do this, open the Order By... dialog, move CUSTOMER.COMPANY to the Ordering Criteria list, and then return to the RQBE screen. Select `Do Query` now; your output looks like that shown in figure 6.17. Save this query as CHAP6005.QPR in the Model directory.

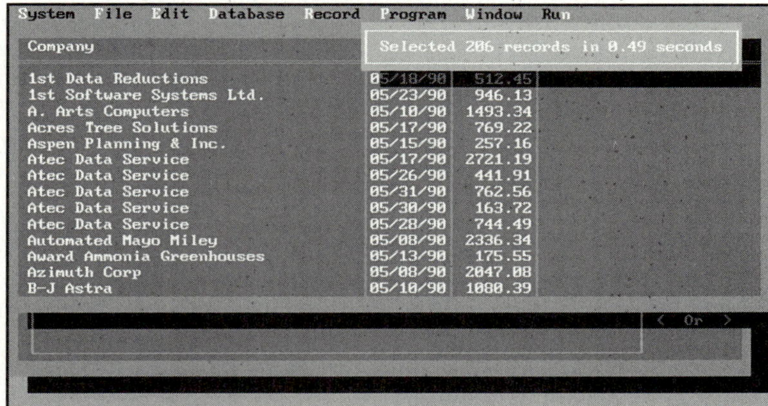

FIG. 6.17

A one-to-many relationship created with the RQBE.

Adding a Dimension to Your Output with Crosstabs

The query you created in the preceding example listed customers, the amount of their invoices, and the date of their invoices. This type of data often is stored in spreadsheets. The useful format of spreadsheets is a major reason for their popularity.

FoxPro offers a spreadsheet format that displays the preceding query with customers on the side, invoice dates across the top, and invoice amounts at the intersecting cells. This format is called a *crosstab*, and it is created by a FoxPro program called GENXTAB.PRG. You don't have to know anything about the GENXTAB program or how it works, although you might enjoy studying it. (GENXTAB was written by Walter J. Kennamer, the author of the FoxDoc program documentation utility described in Chapter 20.)

GENXTAB has an interface built into the RQBE. If you study the following example, you'll get an idea of the types of reports you can create with crosstabs.

If you have not closed the CHAP6005.QPR query, you're all set. Otherwise, reopen it. (Remember, you must *first* open the CUSTOMER.DBF and INVOICES.DBF tables from the Tutorial directory, because they are not in the Model directory with the query file.)

Open the Select Fields... dialog. Notice that the Cross Tabulate check box (under the Selected Output list) is enabled. Remove INVOICES.IDATE from the Selected Output list—notice that the Cross Tabulate check box becomes disabled. Crosstabs can be created only when exactly three fields are selected for output: one each for the Row headings (the first field), the Column headings (the second field), and the data that fill the intersecting cells (the third field). None of these fields should be a Memo field.

A spreadsheet with invoice dates across the top can have a tremendous number of columns unless the columns were months. To make your columns months, select the Functions/Expressions text box and enter the following expression:

```
MONTH(Invoices.Idate)
```

After you enter the expression, move it to the Selected Output list.

Field names are always preceded by their table names. This convention is used to prevent FoxPro (or you) from confusing more than one table with the same field name. If you are referencing a field name unique to a particular table, you need not specify the table name. In this example, the expression MONTH(Idate) is unique because only the Invoices table has an Idate field. You can save some typing this way, but including the table name is a good habit to develop.

Now, rearrange the Selected Output list so the fields are in the following order:

CUSTOMER.COMPANY

MONTH(INVOICES.IDATE)

INVOICES.ITOTAL

Exactly three fields are again selected for output, so the Cross Tabulate check box is enabled. Check it now and then select OK to exit this dialog.

Notice after returning to the main RQBE window that the Order By... and Group By... check boxes have been checked and disabled. To create a crosstab, you must order the table by the Row field and then by the Column field, and group it on these two fields. Because the RQBE does this automatically, these controls are disabled.

Now, select `Do Query`. If you've never used GENXTAB before, you see a message that FoxPro is compiling the GENXTAB program. While GENXTAB is creating the crosstab, it displays a thermometer to advise you of its progress. When the crosstab is complete, your screen looks like the one in figure 6.18.

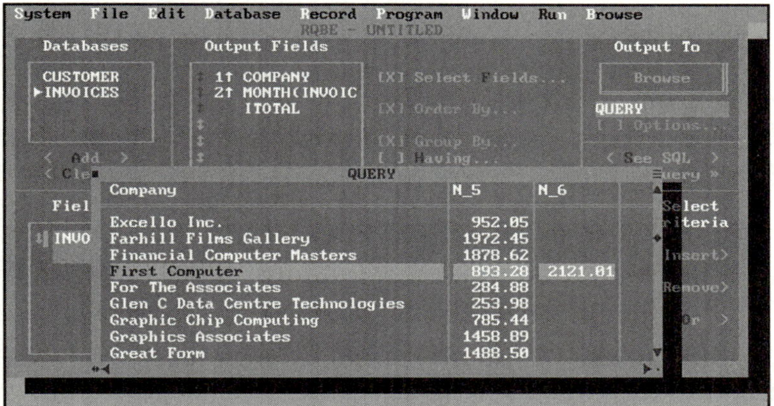

FIG. 6.18

A crosstab query displays your data in spreadsheet format.

The column headings are N_5 and N_6. The N indicates that the column heading was constructed from a number (the value returned by the MONTH( ) function), and the digit is the actual number. In this case, the column headings represent May and June. If you scroll down the Browse window, you see some data in the June (N_6) column. If there had been invoices from other months, they also would have columns.

Save this query as CHAP6006.QPR in the Model directory, and then exit the RQBE. Do not close the Customer and Invoices tables; you need them for the following exercise.

Although this sales information is useful, it's missing something that would almost certainly be included in a spreadsheet: a cross-totals column. GENXTAB can create a cross-totals column, but you can't specify that you want this feature through the RQBE. To do this, you have to create the query and then manually call GENXTAB, either from the Command window or from a program.

In a text-editing window, open the query file you just saved by typing the following command in the Command window:

```
MODIFY COMMAND CHAP6006.QPR
```

You also can open the query file with the File Open dialog, but you must select Program from the Type popup control before you select the file from the scrollable list. If you open the QPR as a Type Query file, the RQBE window opens, which is not what you want to happen here.

Modify the next-to-last line so that it matches the following line:

```
DO (_GENXTAB) WITH 'QUERY', .T., .T., .T., 1, 2, 3, .T.
```

Be sure to place a period before and after each of the Ts. Also be sure to separate each of the Ts and the digits with commas. Save this modified file as CHAP6007.QPR in the Model directory; then return to the Command window.

Each of the items in the list that follows WITH is a *parameter* that you pass to GENXTAB. You use these parameters to change GENXTAB's default behavior. The final .T. in the parameter list instructs GENXTAB to create a cross-totals column. (You learn more about parameters in Part IV of this book, which covers FoxPro programming.)

Now run the new query with one of two methods:

- By selecting Query... from the Run menu and then selecting CHAP6007.QPR from the list of available .QPR files that FoxPro presents in the Query to Run dialog.
- By typing `DO CHAP6007.QPR` in the Command window.

When GENXTAB has finished creating the crosstab, you see that the Browse window now has an extra column called Xtotals, which contains the total amount of the invoices for each customer, as shown in figure 6.19.

If you want GENXTAB to create cross-totals by default, you can modify GENXTAB.PRG. Because the RQBE calls GENXTAB without changing any of GENXTAB's default settings, these changes affect crosstabs created within the RQBE.

Type `MODIFY COMMAND (_GENXTAB)` in the Command window or use the File Open dialog to locate GENXTAB.PRG in the FoxPro home directory. (_GENXTAB is a FoxPro system variable that holds the fully qualified file name of GENXTAB.PRG.)

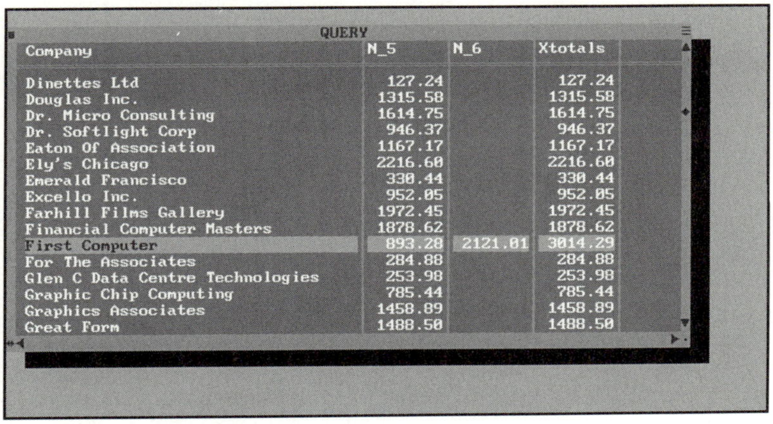

QUERY

Company	N_5	N_6	Xtotals
Dinettes Ltd	127.24		127.24
Douglas Inc.	1315.58		1315.58
Dr. Micro Consulting	1614.75		1614.75
Dr. Softlight Corp	946.37		946.37
Eaton Of Association	1167.17		1167.17
Ely's Chicago	2216.60		2216.60
Emerald Francisco	330.44		330.44
Excello Inc.	952.05		952.05
Farhill Films Gallery	1972.45		1972.45
Financial Computer Masters	1878.62		1878.62
First Computer	893.28	2121.01	3014.29
For The Associates	284.88		284.88
Glen C Data Centre Technologies	253.98		253.98
Graphic Chip Computing	785.44		785.44
Graphics Associates	1458.89		1458.89
Great Form	1488.50		1488.50

FIG. 6.19

Adding a cross-totals column to a crosstab.

Now find the following lines and change the line that reads `"m.xfoot = .F."` to read `"m.xfoot = .T."`, as shown:

```
IF PARAMETERS() < 8
   * Create a total field?
   m.xfoot = .T.
ENDIF
```

If you don't feel comfortable modifying programs, don't worry. You build your programming skills in Part IV. For now, you can always add a cross-total column to individual query files, as you did previously.

Using User-Defined Functions with RQBE

A *user-defined function* (UDF) is a FoxPro procedure that returns a value that you can use in a program. UDFs can be used almost anywhere that built-in FoxPro functions can be used. You learn more about UDFs as you continue reading in this book. For now, however, just know that (like other FoxPro functions) you can enter UDFs into queries from the Functions/Expressions text box of the Select Fields... dialog and that you should be cautious about using them with queries.

From within a UDF, you can use any FoxPro command. Among other actions, you can open tables, close tables, change record pointers, and change the data in fields. However, doing anything of this sort in a UDF called from an SQL SELECT statement can have unforeseen side effects. Because FoxPro determines the best way to perform a query when it is executed, there is no way to determine how these actions will affect the outcome of a query.

For example, you can write a UDF that changes the currently selected work area and then include this UDF in a field expression in a query. Although this query might work perfectly every time, it just as easily might produce incorrect results at any time. FoxPro keeps detailed information about your data and, based on this information, determines the best way to perform the query. If you add, remove, or change the data in any of the tables, FoxPro can change how it builds and optimizes the query. This feature can cause a query that had worked in the past to produce incorrect results, simply because of an errant UDF.

> **CAUTION:** The only thing you can assume about the FoxPro environment and how it is altered by queries, whether for the purpose of adding a UDF or for any other reason, is that you can assume nothing.

When you begin to write your own UDFs, especially when you're designing a report or a screen, you can manipulate your FoxPro environment with impunity from functions that you write. Just remember that, because the internal optimizer (used by FoxPro to process the query) operates with relative autonomy, you do not have the same freedom in a query.

Doing a Query from a Program

After you have saved a query, you can DO it from within a program by using the following command:

```
DO <query file>.QPR
```

Substitute the name you assigned to your query for <query file>. For example, you can include the following command in a program:

```
DO CHAP6002.QPR
```

To make this an even more useful feature, you can use *variables* in a query. For example, you can add a filter to a query, such as in the following command (StateVar is a variable name):

```
CUSTOMER.STATE     Like     StateVar
```

Then, in a program, you can include lines something like the following:

```
StateVar = "NC"
DO StateQry.QPR
```

With these commands, the query looks only at customers in North Carolina.

The variable StateVar must exist when you enter the filter expression in the Select Criteria section. If it doesn't exist, the RQBE thinks you are looking for a state called StateVar and encloses the string in quotation marks ("StateVar"). For the purposes of entering the filter expression in the RQBE, it is enough to enter `StateVar = ""` in the Command window before opening the query.

As discussed in the last section, queries can change your environment. You should therefore save your environment before you execute a query and restore your environment afterward. You learn more about these features in Chapter 18, "Understanding Program Structure."

Using the RQBE Wisely

You have seen a sampling of what the RQBE can do to select, group, subtotal, and order information. The following are a few suggestions to help you get the most out of the RQBE and some warnings to help keep you out of trouble.

Constructing Queries

By now, you should realize that using the RQBE is not difficult. What can be difficult is informing the RQBE how to construct the query that answers your question. Constructing queries proficiently, whether through the RQBE or through direct use of the SQL SELECT command, requires a good deal of practice.

Although the RQBE enables you to query a database without becoming a programmer, it's still just a tool. You can't simply type your question in a text box and have the RQBE derive the answer. You have to meet the RQBE halfway by telling it which tables contain the data, how those tables are related, which SQL column functions to use to create subtotals, and how to group the results.

Consider using the following step-by-step approach to construct your queries:

1. Use a diagram of your database to locate the required data.

   You can't tell the RQBE which tables to include in the query if you don't know which tables hold the required information or how these tables relate to each other. A diagram, such as the one at the beginning of the "Using SQL SELECT" chapter in your *Developer's Guide*, can be very helpful. Save your creativity for the problem-solving part of the query.

2. Select and join the required tables.

   If your tables use the same field names for the same information (such as Customer.Cno and Invoices.Cno), the RQBE usually does a good job of constructing the proper join condition when you use Add to add a table. However, remember that the RQBE doesn't actually understand anything about your data. It simply searches the open tables for a field with the same name as a field in the table you are adding. You should always verify that the proposed link field is correct.

   For example, if you open the Customer table in the Tutorial directory and then add the Salesman table, the RQBE proposes to join the tables on the Address field, which is clearly incorrect. The field that links these two tables is the Ono (Office number) field, not the Address field.

3. Select the output fields and SQL column functions you need.

   If your natural-language query contains words like "total" or "average," you probably want to add at least one SQL column function (such as SUM( ) or AVG( )) to your output fields list. A corollary to this rule is, if your output list contains a column function, you should also have at least one field in your Group By Fields list. Otherwise, your column function calculates the SUM( ) or AVG( ) of all records in the virtual table. This is not usually what you want.

4. Add any required grouping fields to your Group By Fields list.

   The other side of the corollary stated previously is, if your Output Fields list does not contain any column functions, your Group By... fields are performing the same task as the DISTINCT clause. RQBE adds the DISTINCT clause to the SELECT command when you check No Duplicates in the Select Fields... dialog. The value of any Numeric field in your Output Fields list that doesn't use a column function is simply the value of that field in the last record of the specified group.

This fact leads to another important caveat. When you are grouping by one or more fields, remember that any output fields that are not included in the Group By Fields list and are not column functions simply show the contents of that field in the last record of the group. These contents might be different from the field's value in other records in the group. When you add an additional subgroup level, be aware of output fields that might no longer be relevant to your query.

5. Decide which records to eliminate from the query result and enter the proper filter condition(s) in the Select Criteria section.
6. Add any required Having... filter to remove certain groups from the output.

   Be careful to distinguish between filtering records and filtering groups. You filter records in the Select Criteria section, and you filter groups in the Having... dialog. If your question is "Which customers purchased five or more Log Ladles?" you eliminate sales records for products other than Log Ladles in the Select Criteria section, and then eliminate customers who have purchased fewer than five Log Ladles in the Having... dialog.
7. Set the desired Order for the output.
8. Select `Do Query`.

Creating Query Skeletons

You can save time by creating query skeletons. A *query skeleton* is a query that can be used repeatedly with only minor changes. For example, you might have a query with a filter that restricts the output to customers in a particular state. This query can be brought up at any time; the state changed; and the query reexecuted. Other filters can be added or removed. You can add expressions and fields to the output and use Save As... to save your modified query, thus leaving the skeleton intact for further use.

Using Variable Names in Filters

You can use variable names in query filters, which can be useful for queries called from a FoxPro program. You can take the example query, CHAP6002.QPR, in which you listed states with year-to-date purchases of $50,000 or more, and make it more general. You can replace the

Having... filter of 50000 with a variable name. (Create the variable in the Command window before replacing the filter!) You can then have your program prompt the user for the desired dollar limit, store the answer in the variable the query is using, and activate the query.

Using Queries To See the Forest and the Trees

When you use a query to gather and summarize information from your tables, the output is usually summary information. What is missing at the end of these summary lines is a Total line. If you send the output of a query to a report, you can add totals and other calculations from the Report Writer. The Report Writer is discussed in detail in Chapters 9 and 10.

Seeing Double with Multiple Queries

FoxPro enables you to have multiple RQBE windows open at the same time. Sometimes it's useful to compare the results from different queries.

If you send your query to a Browse window and try to select an item outside this window, the Browse window closes. It can be reopened from the View window or from the Command window (with the BROWSE command). You can open your first query, select `Do Query`, and then close the Browse window. You can then reopen it immediately! Next, open a second RQBE file, activate it, and see the two results on the same screen.

If your hardware supports one of the extended screen modes, using it can be helpful. Check the on-line help for the SET DISPLAY command to determine whether any of these modes works for you.

Keeping Your Records in Order

You may notice that grouping a table automatically structures the table in ascending order of the grouped fields. On rare occasions, this sorting does not occur, often depending on how FoxPro optimized the query. If you want to be sure that your output is ordered, you must use the Order By... dialog.

Getting Your Queries Out Fast

You can do a few things to ensure that your queries run quickly. The single most effective measure you can take is to have the indexes necessary for Rushmore optimization present when you select `Do Query`. *Rushmore optimization* requires that the comparisons used in filter conditions have exact counterparts in index expressions. You already learned to create indexes in Chapters 3 and 4; in Chapter 7, you learn to be certain that Rushmore can use them.

If you have a slow query that uses UDFs, you might try to redesign the query to work without the UDFs. Many times UDFs do not noticeably affect the performance of a query. Other times, however, they slow down a query greatly.

> **CAUTION:** Never close a table used in a query while the RQBE is open. Doing so can cause you to lose your query.

Cleaning Up after Yourself

If you output to a *Cursor* (discussed in the next chapter), you don't have to worry about cleaning up after yourself. Although a Cursor acts like a Readonly table, in reality it is much different. When a Cursor is closed, it is removed from the disk. It won't sit around taking up valuable space.

If you choose to output to the Browse window, to a Report/Label, or to a Graph, the RQBE actually sends the output to a Cursor, and then browses, reports on, or graphs the cursor. Because a Cursor was created, you don't have to worry about deleting it. If you send your reports to the screen, you don't have to worry about disposing of the output either.

If you output to a Table or DBF, that is another story. The table created by the query remains on your hard disk until it is overwritten or deleted. If you don't want it sitting around, you have to delete it.

Cleaning Up after the RQBE

After working in the RQBE and doing several queries, take a look at the View window. You see that the RQBE leaves some files behind, as shown in figure 6.20. These files are usually Cursors, but they look and act like regular tables. When you create an *untitled* query, the Cursor's name is usually *query;* otherwise its name is usually the name of your query. If you create many different queries without closing these files, you can run out of work areas; only 25 are available. Closing Cursors removes them from the hard disk, making them easy to clean up.

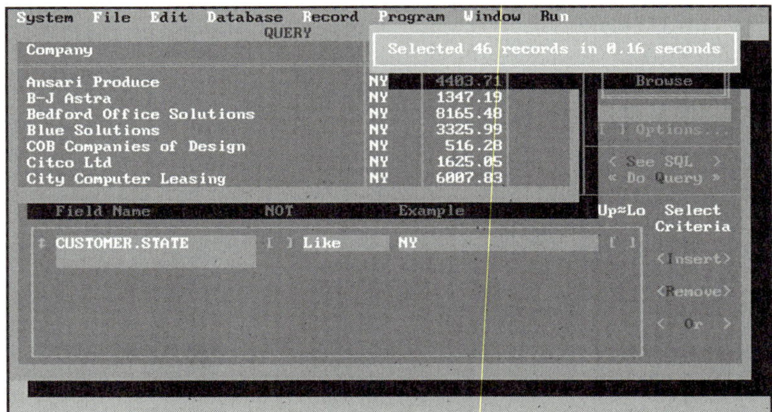

FIG. 6.20

Leftover files from RQBE.

Querying One Step at a Time

Often, complex queries can be easier to design as several, simpler queries. This procedure can be done easily if the first query outputs to a Table or DBF. Unlike a Cursor, Tables are permanent and can be used by subsequent queries. Of course, if you do this, remember to delete the temporary tables when you're done.

Keeping Expressions Consistent

When using expressions and UDFs that return character data for output fields in a query, make sure they always return values of the same length. For example, if you want to produce the name of a month, use the following expression:

```
CMONTH(SomeDate)
```

This function returns months such as January, February, and March. This function returns between three characters (May) and nine characters (September). Depending on how your data is organized and how

FoxPro optimizes the query, you might get only three or four characters for this field in your output. If four characters are assigned to the field, for example, the user sees months such as Octo, Janu, and Febr. In this case, you can use the PADR( ) function, which adds spaces to the right of an expression. This function's syntax follows:

```
PADR(CMONTH(SomeDate), 9)
```

In this example, FoxPro pads the CMONTH expression to nine characters by placing spaces on the right. Be sure that you know the proper length to which the string should be padded. Strings that exceed the specified length are truncated.

Summary

In this chapter, you built on the basic skills you acquired in Chapter 5. You learned how to join tables, create complex filter conditions, eliminate groupings that don't meet your criteria, and create cross tabulations that display your query results in a spreadsheet format.

Although the RQBE is a wonderful tool, you cannot create every possible query through its dialogs. In Chapter 7, you gain direct control over the RQBE's engine: the SQL SELECT command. If you think the RQBE is powerful, hold on to your hat! You can design entire applications around SQL SELECT.

In Chapter 7, you also learn about the Rushmore technology and various performance optimization techniques. You benefit from these performance enhancements throughout your work in FoxPro, but Rushmore and optimization techniques have special relevance to SQL queries.

7

CHAPTER

Querying with SQL and Searching with Rushmore

In Chapters 5 and 6, you work with FoxPro's Relational Query By Example, which is an interface between you and the SQL SELECT command. SQL, or *Structured Query Language,* is a concise and powerful language developed to maintain databases. The SELECT command is the main tool SQL uses for database queries. In this chapter, you learn more about the SELECT command, how this command's components relate to the RQBE, and how to use SELECT to exceed the RQBE's capabilities.

You also look at FoxPro's Rushmore technology, which can accelerate database searches. Rushmore, which many native FoxPro commands use to boost performance, is the key to the lightning speed of FoxPro's implementation of SQL SELECT.

If you have not yet read Chapters 5 and 6, you should do so before continuing. Even if your goal is to write queries that you include in programs rather than execute interactively, you must be familiar with the basic SQL concepts presented in these previous chapters. You might also find that you can use the RQBE to construct quickly most of the query statement, which you can then save as a .QPR file and enhance with any options that the RQBE does not support. Constructing queries in this fashion has two additional benefits: selecting fields from a list is much faster than typing their names, and you avoid introducing typing errors into your query.

Examining the SQL SELECT Command

When you use the RQBE to create a query, you are indirectly using SQL, or at least the version of SQL's SELECT command that is built into FoxPro. SELECT is an important part of FoxPro's capability to perform fast and flexible database searches.

In this section, you examine the clauses available with SQL SELECT that contribute to this command's flexibility. The following is the full syntax of the SQL SELECT command:

```
SELECT [ALL ¦ DISTINCT]
   [<alias>.]<select_item> [AS <column_name>]
   [,[<alias>.]<select_item> [AS <column_name>]... ]
FROM <table>[<local_alias>] [, <table>[<local_alias>]...]
[[INTO <destination>]
   ¦[TO FILE <file>[ADDITIVE] ¦ TO PRINTER ¦ TO SCREEN]]
[PREFERENCE <name>]
[NOCONSOLE]
[PLAIN]
[NOWAIT]
[WHERE <join_condition>[AND <join_condition>...]
   [AND ¦ OR <filter_condition>[AND ¦ OR
   <filter_condition>...]]]
[GROUP BY <group_column>[, <group_column>...]]
[HAVING <filter_condition>]
[UNION [ALL] <SELECT command>]
[ORDER BY <order_item> [ASC ¦ DESC]
   [,<order_item> [ASC ¦ DESC]...]]
```

Table 7.1 summarizes the usage of each clause of the SELECT command.

Table 7.1 Summary of SQL SELECT Clauses

<table>
<tr><th>Clause</th><th>Use</th></tr>
<tr><td>ALL</td><td>Include duplicate rows or records.</td></tr>
<tr><td>DISTINCT</td><td>Eliminate duplicate rows or records.</td></tr>
<tr><td>[<alias>.]<item>
[AS <column_name>]</td><td>Specify output columns (usually a field list) in a list separated by commas, and for each column, optionally specify the name given to the column.</td></tr>
<tr><td>FROM<table>
[local_alias] ...</td><td>Specify the source tables in a list separated by commas, and for each table, optionally specify a local name that refers to the table in the rest of the SELECT command.</td></tr>
<tr><td>INTO ARRAY |
INTO CURSOR |
INTO DBF/TABLE |
TO FILE <name>
[ADDITIVE] |
TO PRINTER |
TO SCREEN</td><td>Specify the destination of the query results. DBF and TABLE are used interchangeably (that is, INTO DBF is the same as INTO TABLE).</td></tr>
<tr><td>PREFERENCE <name></td><td>Display the Browse window using the attributes specified for <name> in the Resource file, and update the window's attributes when the Browse window is closed. If the Preference does not exist, it is created.</td></tr>
<tr><td>NOCONSOLE</td><td>Prevent output from appearing on-screen.</td></tr>
<tr><td>PLAIN</td><td>Omit column headings in output.</td></tr>
<tr><td>NOWAIT</td><td>Omit pauses between screens of output.</td></tr>
<tr><td>WHERE <conditions></td><td>Specify join conditions (similar to SET RELATION commands) and filter records to specify further which records are included in the output. Multiple WHERE conditions are separated by AND or OR.</td></tr>
<tr><td>GROUP BY <column> ...</td><td>Specify columns of output, used to summarize or group the records, in a list separated by commas.</td></tr>
<tr><td>HAVING <condition></td><td>Specify filters to be used to eliminate some groups from the output.</td></tr>
</table>

continues

Table 7.1 Continued

Clause	Use
UNION [ALL] <SELECT>	Combine the results of one SELECT command with another. This eliminates duplicates by default; if you want duplicates, include the optional ALL keyword.
ORDER BY <item> [ASC | DESC] ...	Sort the output based on information from one or more columns, which are specified in a list separated by commas. By default, the data for each indicated column is sorted in ASCending order, but you can specify DESCending order.

The SQL SELECT command has several options that you cannot tap from the RQBE. Table 7.2 lists some of these additional capabilities, and points you to the related SELECT clause. You learn how to tap each of these capabilities in the discussion of the related clauses.

Table 7.2 Query Options Not Available through the RQBE

Option	Related SELECT Clause
Order the output by fields not selected for output.	ORDER BY
Perform subqueries with nested SELECTs.	WHERE ... ALL | ANY | EXISTS | IN (SELECT...)
Specify output field names, which also become column headings.	AS
Connect multiple SQL SELECTs.	UNION

The remainder of this section examines each component of the SELECT command separately. The syntax of each clause is shown again so you don't have to flip pages, and the examples show you some different ways you can use SELECT in your programs. Each example is a complete SELECT command that you can type into the Command window, execute, and modify to learn more about how the different SQL clauses work together to produce different query results.

Creating Simple Queries

Syntax:

```
SELECT [ALL ¦ DISTINCT]
       [<alias>.]<select_item> [AS <column_name>]
       [,[<alias>.]<select_item> [AS <column_name>]... ]
   FROM <table>[<local_alias>] [,<table>[<local_alias>]...]
```

Examples:

```
1) SELECT * FROM Budget

2) SELECT DISTINCT Prodcode FROM Budget

3) SELECT Product.Prodname, Budget.* ;
      FROM Product, Budget ;
      WHERE Product.Prodcode = Budget.Prodcode

4) SELECT A.Prodname, B.Budgetamt ;
      FROM Product A, Budget B ;
      WHERE A.Prodcode = B.Prodcode

5) SELECT Product.Prodname AS Product, ;
          SUM(Budget.Budgetamt) AS Budgeted, ;
          COUNT(*) AS Count ;
      FROM Product, Budget ;
      WHERE Product.Prodcode = Budget.Prodcode ;
      GROUP BY Product
```

If you remove all the optional clauses (those that are enclosed in square brackets) from the full SELECT syntax listing, you see that the following is the minimum syntax of the SQL SELECT command:

```
SELECT <select_item> FROM <table>
```

In any query, you must specify at least one output field for the query, and the table that contains this field. This is the SELECT form you see when you create a new query and choose See SQL in the RQBE.

The <select item> Variable

Each <select_item> in the list can be one of the following:

- The name of a field contained in one of the tables included in the query

- A constant value
- Any valid FoxPro expression, which may include SQL column functions, FoxPro functions, and user-defined functions

These fields and expressions become the columns of the query result, and each column appears in the same order as it appears in the output list. The rows of the query result are the records that meet the query conditions, as specified by the filtering clauses, WHERE and HAVING.

The table's alias name may precede the field names. If you use the same field name in more than one of the involved tables, you must use the alias to distinguish among them. In the preceding examples, you have the option not to use the tables' aliases with the Prodname and Budgetamt fields, because each field exists in only one of the two involved tables. Specifying the table alias is a good habit to develop, because doing so documents which table each field comes from and relieves you of the responsibility of ensuring that all field names are unique.

If you assign a local alias to a table in the FROM clause, you must use that alias when referring to fields from that table in the <select_item> list. (See the discussion of the FROM clause for more information on using local aliases.)

You also can include constant values in the output list. When a column that is specified as a constant is added to the output, all rows contain the same value in the column. The "Combining Queries with UNION" section, later in this chapter, covers some good uses for constant values.

The output list also can include one or more of the following SQL column functions (table 5.2 in Chapter 5, "Using the RQBE as the Gateway to Queries," describes what each column function does):

```
AVG([DISTINCT] <select_item>)

COUNT([DISTINCT] <select_item>)

MIN(<select_item>)

MAX(<select_item>)

SUM([DISTINCT] <select_item>)
```

The values that these functions output into columns are reset based on the fields you include in the Group By fields list.

The DISTINCT Keyword

The DISTINCT keyword tells SQL to eliminate duplicate rows from the output. ALL, the default, includes duplicates instead. DISTINCT or ALL may appear only once in the SELECT command and applies to all items in the output list. Although you can place the keyword before or after the output list, you cannot place it within the list unless you use it as part of a column function. For example, the following clause triggers an error:

```
SELECT Budget.Prodname, DISTINCT Budgetamt
```

You can use an asterisk (*) as shorthand to tell SQL SELECT to include in the output list all fields from all tables listed in the FROM clause rather than specify a fields list. All fields from a particular table are included if you specify <alias>.*, as shown in Example 3. The COUNT column function also can take the asterisk as its <select_item> because you are asking for the number of records in the table without regard to the contents of any particular field. Example 4 shows you this form of the COUNT column function.

The AS Clause

The AS clause enables you to specify the name of any output field, overriding SELECT's default name. This new field name also becomes the column title in the Browse window in which you view the query result. Use AS to provide meaningful column titles for expressions you create by using SQL column functions and other FoxPro functions. Using substitute names also gives you another way (other than using the column number) to GROUP BY and ORDER BY expressions that you cannot directly include in the GROUP BY or ORDER BY clause.

Because the output of a SELECT is often a table and, in that case, the name you assign to the column becomes the field name in the result table, column names must conform to FoxPro's field-naming conventions. Column names must begin with a letter and consist only of letters, digits, and the underscore character.

The FROM Clause

The FROM clause tells SQL which tables to include in the query. You can use either the file name or the table's alias to specify tables already open. If any tables you specify in the tables list are not open, FoxPro must be capable of finding the tables in the current directory or on the FoxPro search path. You can specify unopened tables by using an explicit file path, such as C:\FOXPRO25\MODEL\BUDGET.

Using a Local Alias

Whether you specify open or closed tables, and whether you specify tables by alias or file name, you have the option of assigning a special *local alias* for use in this SELECT command, as shown in Example 4. A local alias doesn't change the way you refer to the table in other FoxPro commands, or even in other queries. If you must refer to a table several times in a long SELECT command, a short local alias can be very convenient. If you decide to use a local alias, however, you *must* use the assigned alias every time you refer to the table throughout the SELECT command.

Directing the Query Output

Syntax:

```
[[INTO <destination>]
   ¦ [TO FILE <file> [ADDITIVE] ¦ TO PRINTER ¦ TO SCREEN]]
[PREFERENCE <name>]
[NOCONSOLE]
[PLAIN]
[NOWAIT]
```

Examples:

```
1) SELECT Product.Prodname, Budget.Budgetamt ;
      FROM Product, Budget ;
      WHERE Product.Prodcode = Budget.Prodcode
      INTO CURSOR query

2) SELECT A.Prodname, B.Budgetamt ;
      FROM Product A, Budget B ;
      WHERE A.Prodcode = B.Prodcode
      TO PRINTER NOCONSOLE
3) SELECT Product.Prodname, Budget.Budgetamt ;
      FROM Product, Budget ;
      WHERE Product.Prodcode = Budget.Prodcode
      PREFERENCE query
```

As you can see in the syntax listing, all the clauses are optional. By default, SELECT in FoxPro 2.5 sends its output to a cursor and then displays the cursor's contents in a Browse window. (This behavior is different from FoxPro 2.0, which did not create a cursor and sent its output to the screen by default.) When working interactively in FoxPro, this default is often sufficient and is the quickest way to see your results.

In a program, however, you usually want more control over the display of the results. Even if you want to use a Browse window, you might want to use some of the BROWSE command's many options to tailor the display. For example, you might want to use a custom window title and more descriptive column headings. In this case, you use the INTO or TO clause to direct your results and suppress the default Browse window display.

The INTO Clause

The <destination> of INTO can be any of the following:

```
CURSOR <cursor_name>

ARRAY <array_name>

TABLE <table_name>

DBF <table_name>
```

Specifying CURSOR as the destination is usually quicker than sending output to a TABLE. *Cursors* are temporary tables that FoxPro automatically removes from the disk when you close them. If the data in the source tables is changed, the values in a CURSOR can be affected (a potentially significant consideration in multi-user situations), but they are not directly editable. (Chapter 22, "Using SQL Commands, Arrays, and the Low-Level File Functions," discusses another SQL command, CREATE CURSOR, which is included as part of FoxPro's SQL implementation. Cursors created through this command, rather than through a SELECT command, can be edited.)

You can send the output of a SQL SELECT to a memory array by specifying ARRAY <array_name> as the destination. Remember the following points when you use an ARRAY as the destination:

- If the array exists before the SELECT is executed, any information the array held before the SELECT is lost when the SELECT re-creates the array.
- If the array does not exist before the SELECT is executed, and no output is generated from the SELECT (such as when no records in the database match the filter conditions), the array is not created. You can check the system memory variable _TALLY to see whether the query produces any output. If no records are selected, this variable contains the value 0 immediately after the SELECT is executed.
- If the array previously existed and the SELECT produced no output, the array is not deleted. Again, you must check _TALLY to determine whether the SELECT produces output.

The keywords TABLE and DBF are interchangeable and used to store the results of a query to a table on the disk. If the table name already exists and SAFETY is set ON, FoxPro asks you to confirm that you want to overwrite the file before proceeding.

The TO Clause

Using the TO FILE syntax creates a text file with the output of the query. When the ADDITIVE keyword is specified, the results are appended to the end of the text file if the file already exists; if ADDITIVE isn't used, the existing file is overwritten. TO PRINTER sends the output to the printer, and TO SCREEN sends the output to the screen or to the active user-defined window.

If both TO and INTO are specified, INTO is honored and TO ignored. When you send the results TO FILE or TO PRINTER, the output of the SELECT is echoed to the screen. Including the NOCONSOLE clause suppresses the screen display of the output.

The PREFERENCE Clause

If you don't specify where to send the query results, the output appears in a Browse window. You can use the PREFERENCE clause to save the Browse window's attributes, including its size and position, in your Resource file. When you include the Preference name in a subsequent query, FoxPro applies the saved Preferences to the resulting Browse window. You learn more about Preferences in Chapter 8, "Organizing the Answers with BROWSE."

The PLAIN, NOCONSOLE, and NOWAIT Keywords

Including the PLAIN keyword prevents SELECT from showing the field headings on the output. NOCONSOLE suppresses the screen display of the output. PLAIN and NOCONSOLE do not apply to queries output to TABLE, CURSOR, or ARRAY destinations, but are meant for use when the TO clause is specified.

Unless you use the NOWAIT keyword when output is directed or echoed to the screen, you are prompted to press a key before data scrolls off-screen.

Using WHERE To Join and Filter Tables

Syntax:

```
[WHERE <join_condition>[AND <join_condition>...]
   [AND ¦ OR <filter_condition>[AND ¦ OR
   <filter_condition>...]]]
```

Examples:

```
1) m.deptname = "finance"   && you would usually GET
                           && this from the user
  SELECT B.Prodname ;
      FROM Budget A, Product B, Dept C ;
      WHERE A.Prodcode = B.Prodcode ;
        AND A.Deptcode = C.Deptcode ;
        AND UPPER(C.Deptname) = UPPER(m.deptname)

2) SELECT Prodname ;
      FROM Product ;
      WHERE UPPER(Prodname) Like "%WIDGET%"
```

The WHERE clause serves two purposes with SELECT: it joins multiple tables and specifies filter conditions. You can have multiple join conditions and filters. You must connect these options by using ANDs.

The <join_condition> Expression

To create a join condition with WHERE, you use an expression of the form

```
fieldname_1 operator fieldname_2
```

where fieldname_1 and fieldname_2 are the related field names of the tables being joined, and operator is any of the following words or symbols:

=

<> or != or #

==

>

>=

<

<=

Although you can use any of these operators to join tables, you almost always want to use the = operator to join the tables that form a relational database.

String comparisons respect ANSI conventions when ANSI is SET ON. With ANSI SET OFF, these conventions work in the same way as with all other FoxPro commands. (For an explanation of ANSI string comparisons, see the Like condition listing in table 5.2.)

The <filter_condition> Expression

Filter conditions also are entered with the WHERE command. The following line shows the simplest form of filter conditions:

```
WHERE <field1> operator <field2> ¦ <expression1>
```

where field1 and field2 are database fields and expression1 is any valid FoxPro expression, including user-defined functions (UDFs). (From the discussion of UDFs in Chapter 6, "Investigating Your Data with Advanced Queries," remember that you must be careful when invoking UDFs in an SQL SELECT statement.) The following is an example of a filter condition:

```
WHERE State = 'NY'
```

You can connect filter conditions with AND and OR, as in the following command:

```
WHERE State = 'NY' AND (Ytdpurch >= 15000 OR Ytdpurch <= 20000)
```

Wild Card Searches

The LIKE comparison is new to FoxPro and usable only with the SQL SELECT command. Almost the same as =, LIKE also can use the % and _ wild cards. (The % and _ characters are treated as normal text when a comparison uses other operators.)

When a query uses the LIKE operator to compare character strings, the characters _ and % serve as wild cards (similar to the ? and * characters in MS-DOS commands). The underline character (_) represents a single character, and the percent sign (%) represents any number of characters. The following expressions all evaluate to True:

```
'Bobometer' Like 'Bobometer'

'Bobometer' Like '___omet__'

'Bobometer' Like 'Bob%'

'Bobometer' Like '__b%'
```

You can type a string of characters surrounded by two % characters (for example, %obo%) to find the string no matter where the string is positioned in another string. Looking for a character string inside another string is known as a *substring search*. You can use the wild-card characters to perform substring searches in the LIKE conditions you create in the RQBE and in queries you write directly with SQL SELECT commands.

The BETWEEN and IN Clauses

You can specify a range by including a BETWEEN clause in a filter condition, as in the following syntax:

```
WHERE <field> BETWEEN <low_value> AND <high_value>
```

When you use the BETWEEN clause to specify a range of values, the preceding filter condition changes to the following:

```
WHERE State = 'NY' AND Ytdpurch BETWEEN 15000 AND 20000
```

The following command uses the IN clause to search a list for a value:

```
WHERE Product.Prodname IN ("Dream Sequencers","Bobometers")
```

This clause finds all products named *Dream Sequencers* or *Bobometers*.

Nested SELECTs

You can nest one SELECT statement inside another. The results of the *inner* SELECT query form a set which is then processed by the *outer* SELECT. The clauses used with these kinds of nested SELECTs are ALL, ANY/SOME, EXISTS, and IN. Although FoxPro allows only one level of nested SELECTs in all but the most complicated situations, one nested SELECT is sufficient. Nested SELECTs are best explained with the following examples.

The following filter condition finds all customers whose year-to-date purchases are greater than the combined sales volume of all salespersons:

```
WHERE Customer.Ytdpurch > ALL ;
   (SELECT Ytdsales FROM Salesman)
```

The following filter condition finds all customers whose year-to-date purchases are greater than the dollar amount of goods that any one salesperson sold during the year:

```
WHERE Customer.Ytdpurch > ANY ;
   (SELECT Ytdsales FROM Salesman)
```

EXISTS returns True if the subquery returns any rows; otherwise, EXISTS returns False. Therefore, the following filter condition finds all salespersons with a customer within the salesperson's ZIP code.

```
SELECT * ;
   FROM Salesman ;
   WHERE EXISTS ;
      (SELECT * FROM Customer ;
          WHERE Customer.Zip = Salesman.Zip)
```

Notice that the subquery seems to violate one of the rules you learned for constructing queries: the subquery refers to a table (Salesman) that is not included in its FROM list. In a subquery, when FoxPro sees a table that is not listed in the subquery's FROM list, it looks to the outer query for the table reference and executes the subquery for each record in that table. This is called a *correlated query*. In the preceding example, the inner query is executed for each record in the Salesman table. Although the WHERE clause of the inner query resembles a join condition, it is evaluated as a filter condition comparing the current value of the Salesman.Zip field to the Customer.Zip field in each record of the Customer table. If the subquery result is not empty, the current record in the Salesman table is included in the result of the outer query. You can read more about correlated queries and other advanced SQL topics in Melissa Dunn's book, *FoxPro 2 and SQL,* listed in the bibliography at the end of this chapter.

You can use the IN clause to see whether a value is contained in a subquery. The following query finds all products that have a record in the Budget table:

```
SELECT Product.Prodname ;
   FROM Product ;
   WHERE Product.Prodcode IN ;
      (SELECT Budget.Prodcode FROM Budget)
```

To get a list of all the products that are *not* in the Budget table, preface IN with the NOT operator, as follows:

```
SELECT Product.Prodname ;
   FROM Product ;
   WHERE Product.Prodcode NOT IN ;
      (SELECT Budget.Prodcode FROM Budget)
```

Although the preceding SELECT appears cryptic, you can read this expression as "List all products in the Product table where the product is not in the Budget table." The inner (nested) query (SELECT Budget.Prodcode FROM Budget) builds a list of all the product codes found in the Budget table. Then the outer SELECT searches the Product table for records whose Prodcode is NOT IN the list that the inner SELECT created.

Using GROUP BY To Summarize Your Data

Syntax:

```
[GROUP BY <group_column>[, <group_column>...]]
```

Examples:

```
1) SELECT Product.Prodname, ;
          SUM(Budget.Budgetamt) ;
      FROM Product, Budget ;
      WHERE Product.Prodcode = Budget.Prodcode ;
      GROUP BY Product.Prodname
```

```
2) SELECT Product.Prodname, ;
          SUM(Budget.Budgetamt),;
          PADR(CMONTH(Budget.Period),9) ;
      FROM Product, Budget ;
      WHERE Product.Prodcode = Budget.Prodcode ;
      GROUP BY 3, Product.Prodname

3) SELECT Product.Prodname AS Product, ;
          SUM(Budget.Budgetamt) AS Budgeted, ;
          PADR(CMONTH(Budget.Period),9) AS Month;
      FROM Product, Budget ;
      WHERE Product.Prodcode = Budget.Prodcode ;
      GROUP BY Month, Product
```

Use the GROUP BY clause to specify groupings. The group_column can be any field name in the selected tables. The grouping fields do not have to be—but usually are—included in the output.

The group_column cannot be an expression. For example, using the following GROUP BY clause in Examples 2 and 3 produces the error `"SQL queries of this type are not supported at present"`:

```
GROUP BY PADR(CMONTH(Budget.Period), 9)
```

However, you can group by an expression by specifying the expression's column number. The query shown in Example 2 groups by the expression being output in the third column.

Similarly, although you cannot use an expression directly in the grouping, if you use the optional AS clause to give this column a new name, you can specify the column by name rather than by number. The query in Example 3 uses this alternative approach.

In most cases, grouping the output has the side effect of ordering the results on the grouping columns. You cannot rely on this always happening, though. If your results must be in order, be sure to use the ORDER BY clause.

Using HAVING To Eliminate Groups

Syntax:

```
[HAVING <filter_condition>]
```

Examples:

```
1) * List customers who purchased five or more
   * Log Ladles, and the average price they paid
   SELECT Customer.lastname, Customer.firstname, ;
          AVG(Sales.Price);
```

```
   FROM Customer, Sales, Product;
   WHERE Sales.Custcode = Customer.Custcode;
     AND Product.Prodcode = Sales.Prodcode;
     AND Product.Prodname = "Log Ladles";
   GROUP BY Customer.Lastname, Customer.Firstname;
   HAVING SUM(Sales.Quantity) >= 5

2) * List all salespersons who have sold
   * more than $5,000 this year.
   * Note that the tables used in this
   * query are located in the FoxPro
   * TUTORIAL directory.
   SET DEFAULT TO <FoxPro-tutorial-directory>
   SELECT Sls.Name, SUM(Inv.Itotal) AS Sales ;
      FROM Salesman Sls, Invoices Inv ;
      WHERE Sls.Salesman = Inv.Salesman ;
      GROUP BY Sls.name ;
      HAVING Sales > 5000
```

The HAVING clause is used to specify filters on groupings. The filter_condition usually is based on one of the groupings. Because groupings are typically used to create subtotals or perform other calculations on a set of records, a HAVING clause usually includes a column function, although not necessarily the same function that appears in the output list, as shown in Example 1.

Ordering the Results with ORDER BY

Syntax:

```
[ORDER BY <order_item> [ASC ¦ DESC][,<order_item> [ASC ¦ DESC]...]]
```

Examples:

```
1) SELECT Ad.Company, Cu.Lastname, Cu.Firstname;
      FROM Customer Cu, Address Ad ;
      WHERE Ad.Addrcode = Cu.Addrcode;
      ORDER BY Ad.Company

2) * Order the results by using a field that is not
   * selected for output. Note that you cannot
   * do this in the RQBE.
   SELECT Product.Prodname, SUM(Budget.Budgetamt), ;
          PADR(CMONTH(Budget.Period), 9) ;
   FROM Budget, Product ;
   WHERE Budget.Prodcode = Product.Prodcode ;
   GROUP BY 3, Product.Prodname ;
   ORDER BY Budget.Period, Product.Prodname
```

Use the ORDER BY clause to tell SQL SELECT the order in which you want to sort the output. The <order_item> can be a field name in one of the selected tables, the position number of one of the output fields, or the name you assigned to an output field by using the AS clause, just as in the GROUP BY clause.

By default, or if you specify ASC, the output is sorted in ascending order. You can change the sort order for any of the output items to descending with the DESC keyword.

The SELECT command shown in Example 2 lists the products and the products' total budgeted amounts for each month, ordered by month. Note that the first ORDER BY field, Budget.Period, does *not* appear in the output list. If you are using the RQBE, you cannot ORDER BY a field that does not appear in the output list; instead, you must order by the expression

```
PADR(CMONTH(Budget.Period, 9))
```

which sorts the months alphabetically (April appears before January) rather than by calendar order.

You cannot actually ORDER BY an expression such as PADR(). Although you can select the expression from the Selected Output list, the RQBE uses the expression's column number to construct the ORDER BY clause, which it inserts into the SELECT statement.

Combining Queries with UNION

Syntax:

```
[UNION [ALL] <SELECT command>]
```

Example:

```
* Create a mailing list of customers
* and salespersons
SET DEFAULT TO <FoxPro-tutorial-directory>
SELECT "C" AS Code, PADR(Contact, 30) AS Addressee, ;
       Company, Address, City, State, Zip ;
   FROM Customer ;
UNION ;
SELECT "S", Name AS Addressee, ;
       SPACE(35), Address, City, State, Zip ;
   FROM Salesman ;
ORDER BY Addressee ;
INTO CURSOR Maillist
```

The UNION clause links multiple SQL SELECT commands to create a result set that a single SELECT cannot achieve. FoxPro appends the result of the second query to the results of the first. Additional queries linked by UNION are processed in the same manner.

Without the ALL clause, a UNION clause discards duplicate records from the two SELECT statements. In this situation, which is common in mailing applications, using UNION without ALL enables you to "merge/purge" two parallel lists of duplicate entries. If, however, you do not want the duplicates eliminated, you can use UNION ALL.

For UNION to work, you must follow these rules:

- SELECTs linked with UNION must have an identical format for the output expressions of both statements.
- Only the last SELECT can have ORDER BY and INTO clauses.
- UNION cannot join nested SELECTs.

FoxPro uses the first SELECT to create the format of the output (the number of columns, and the name, width, and data type of each column). The output of SELECTs that a UNION joins to the first SELECT must have exactly the same number of columns. Each column must be the same width and data type as the related column in the first SELECT.

If you have both a Customer and a Salesman table and want to print mailing labels for all records in both tables, you can use the query shown in the preceding example. This query produces a cursor with the names and addresses of all customers and salespersons. If duplicates exist, they are eliminated. You then can print the labels with the FoxPro label generator.

Note the example's use of PADR( ). The Customer.Contact field is not the same length as the Salesman.Name field. You can combine fields of different lengths and data types by using the FoxPro data conversion functions. PADR(Contact, 30) adds spaces to each of the Contact entries in the Customer table so that they have the same length as the entries in the Salesman.Name field. You can use STR( ) to convert numbers into character type data, and VAL( ) to convert strings of digits into numbers.

Occasionally, a field from one table isn't available in the other table (such as in our Salesman table, which doesn't have a Contact field). You still can create the union by inserting a literal expression that contains the same number of spaces as the Contact field in the customer table. In the example, SPACE(35) creates a placeholder field of the required length in the second SELECT's output.

Similarly, you can use numbers as placeholders for Numeric fields. You can use any number, even 0, but this replacement can cause confusing output and must be used carefully. Logical fields can be simulated with .F. and date fields with { }.

You can place as many UNIONs in one SELECT statement as you want. However, if you have many UNIONs or if your UNIONs are complex, you might exceed the 2,048 character limit for a single FoxPro command statement. Even if a long statement is short of the 2,048 character limit, you still might receive the following message indicating that an internal FoxPro limit has been exceeded:

```
Compiled statement too long
```

Simulating an Outer Join

When two tables are joined, records in either table that have no corresponding record in the other table are ignored. Some SQL implementations enable you to specify that you want to include these orphan records in the result set. Such a query is called an *outer join.* Although outer joins are not directly available in FoxPro's SQL SELECT, you can simulate an outer join in FoxPro by using the UNION clause. Consider the following query:

```
SELECT Product.Prodname, Budget.Budgetamt ;
   FROM Budget, Product ;
   WHERE Product.Prodcode = Budget.Prodcode
```

This query doesn't output a record for the Unscented Weazlettes product, which appears in the Product table but not in the Budget table. To make sure that all products are listed—even if no Budget records are prepared for these products—you can simulate an outer join with a UNION clause by using a second SELECT, like this:

```
SELECT PRODUCT.PRODNAME, BUDGET.BUDGETAMT ;
   FROM BUDGET, PRODUCT ;
   WHERE PRODUCT.PRODCODE = BUDGET.PRODCODE ;
UNION ;
SELECT PRODUCT.PRODNAME, 0 ;
   FROM PRODUCT ;
   WHERE PRODUCT.PRODCODE NOT IN ;
      (SELECT BUDGET.PRODCODE FROM BUDGET)
```

The UNION added the second specification to the original one. The second SELECT outputs all products *not listed* in the Budget table.

Although this usage of UNION enables you to achieve your goal, remember that this approach is a workaround that compensates for FoxPro's lack of support for outer joins. As with most other workarounds, there are some drawbacks:

- The query is complicated to write and conceptualize, which increases the chances of making mistakes and achieving results that may not be what you want.
- This type of query is not executed quickly (although more quickly than the task is otherwise accomplished).
- All products not in the Budget table appear to have a budget amount of 0. Although these products are indeed unbudgeted, there is a difference between a product with records that have no budget amounts entered and a product with no budget records. The SELECT does not record this difference.

You can use any number to match the Budget.Budgetamt column; perhaps 9999999 is a better choice to point out items as nonbudgeted. (You can use a character string, a logical .T. or .F., or a dummy date as a placeholder where necessary to simulate output fields of other data types.) The Report Writer provides the flexibility to check for these nonbudgeted records. You can specify all records that show a 9999999 Budgetamt, that also show the budgeted amount as 0, and that are flagged as nonbudgeted items. You learn how to perform this procedure in Chapter 10, "Using the Report Writer and Label Designer."

Going Places with the Results

The SQL SELECT statement can send the output to the screen, the printer, a cursor, a table, a text file, or an array. Usually you send the output of the SELECT to a cursor. Cursors are useful because you can use them to report on, display, graph, browse, create crosstabs, print labels—anything you can do with a regular table—and you can easily dispose of them when you are finished. Because the cursor contains a preselected set of fields and records, possibly joined from several related tables and formatted exactly the way you need for a single use, getting the output to look exactly the way you want is often more convenient if you create the cursor first instead of trying to output directly from the table or tables.

Generally, programs send SELECTs to an array. You learn more about the use of arrays later in this book. All arrays created through an SQL SELECT command have the proper number of rows and columns to hold the query's output (unless no records are SELECTed by the query, as explained in the description of ARRAY as a query destination earlier in this chapter).

Unlike reports, labels cannot be created by the RQBE because FoxPro has no Quick Label feature to generate a generic label format. However, you can send the output of an SQL SELECT to a preexisting label form (you learn how to create these forms in Chapters 9 and 10). Just put the command LABEL FORM <labelname> after a SELECT statement whose output was sent to a cursor or table. Immediately after the SELECT is executed, the output cursor or table becomes the current work area, and the query's output fields are used to print the labels.

You also can send query output to labels from the RQBE (by using the Report/Label Options dialog). The RQBE does not run the query unless you specify an existing label form name.

CAUTION: When you use the RQBE or issue a SELECT directly to send output from a table to a report or a label form, remember that the SELECT statement sends results to a cursor first and then issues a REPORT FORM or LABEL FORM statement. If you specify a preexisting report or label for the output, you probably created the report or label form by using the original table as a model. If the report or label form includes the alias of this table in the references to fields, the output is incorrect when you try to use the report or label with the cursor, even though the field names are the same.

After the SELECT statement, the original table is opened in another work area and information from the current record in the original table is repeated for each record in the cursor, while the report or record moves the pointer through the cursor to generate output.

You can easily fix this problem by removing the alias from the field expressions in the report or label. Because you cannot know in advance the alias that may be used for a cursor created by the SELECT statement, make sure that each report and label designed to work with queries does not include aliases.

Rarely, you might create a report or label that uses a cursor in a work area other than the current area. In such an instance, you must reference the fields with an alias, so check the cursor's ALIAS() before you issue the REPORT or LABEL FORM command and store the alias to the variable. Use this variable as part of the field reference.

In Chapter 6, you create a *crosstab* report by using an option in the RQBE. You also can create a crosstab based on a query that uses some of the SQL SELECT options not allowed directly by the RQBE. To do this, you call the GENXTAB program after the SQL SELECT produces an appropriate table or cursor. GENXTAB.PRG is simply another FoxPro program.

The table or cursor must have at least three fields, not including Memo and General fields. By default, the first field is used for Rows, the second field is used for Columns, and the third field becomes the data contained in the intersecting Cells. The table must be ordered by the field that will be used for the Row. You also can change some of GENXTAB's default behavior by calling the program with some parameters to take more control of GENXTAB behavior than the RQBE allows.

The following list shows the complete syntax for calling GENXTAB:

```
DO GENXTAB WITH <out_file_name>, ;
                [<cursor_only>], ;
                [<close_input>], ;
                [<show_thermometer>], ;
                [<row_field>], ;
                [<col_field>], ;
                [<cell_field>], ;
                [<xfoot>]
```

GENXTAB follows the rules of parameter passing used by all FoxPro programs, which you learn about in Chapter 18, "Understanding Program Structure," and Chapter 19, "Using Advanced FoxProgramming Techniques." The important information to remember here is that, to use any parameter, you also must pass all prior parameters, specifying behavior otherwise used by default if you omit parameters. The parameter's position in the parameter list tells GENXTAB which option you want to change.

<out_file_name>, the first parameter, is the name of the file or cursor that you want GENXTAB to create. The default for this parameter is XTAB.DBF.

<cursor_only> is a logical parameter. If you do not specify the parameter, the output becomes the same type as the input. If the input is a cursor, then the output is a cursor. If the input is a table, then the output is a table. Typing .T. here forces the output to be a cursor, and .F. tells GENXTAB to create the output as a table. This may not be your intended result (you would think that specifying .F. should be the same as not specifying the parameter), but such is the way that GENXTAB currently works. This may change in a future release of FoxPro.

<close_input> also is a logical parameter. If the parameter is .T. or not specified, the input table/cursor (the table or cursor from which the crosstab is created) is closed when GENXTAB is finished. Otherwise, the input table or cursor remains open.

<show_thermometer> displays or hides the thermometer graphic that measures GENXTAB's progress. If you set the parameter to .T., the thermometer appears on-screen. This is also the default behavior. Set this parameter to .F. to turn off the thermometer.

<row_field> is the field number in the input table/cursor that corresponds to the Row. The row should be the first field in the input to GENXTAB, and the value of this field number should be 1. This result is the default.

<col_field> represents the field number in the input of the Column. The column is usually the second field in GENXTAB's input. The default value of this parameter is 2.

<cell_field> is the field number of the data cell in the input to GENXTAB. This field is usually the third (and final) field. The default for this parameter is 3.

<xfoot> is a logical parameter that defaults to .F.. If you specify .T., GENXTAB creates a column at the end of the crosstab table with a cross-total for each row. To specify cross-totals and output to a cursor and use default behavior otherwise, use the following syntax:

```
DO GENXTAB WITH '<filename>',.T.,.T.,.T.,1,2,3,.T.
```

Enhancing the Performance of SQL SELECTs

At the end of the preceding chapter, you learned some general do's and don'ts for wise RQBE use. Similarly, keep in mind the following principles as you continue to expand your understanding of—and explore new ways to use—SQL SELECT's potential. Do not consider these principles as absolute constraints on the use of this powerful command; just use them to guide the course of your investigation.

Create Indexes SELECT Can Use

SQL SELECT statements, for the most part, are fast. Complex queries often execute faster with SQL than with procedural FoxPro code. The most significant step you can take to wring the best performance from SQL is to make sure that the appropriate indexes are available.

Usually, if you are joining multiple tables, having indexes or index tags on the joining fields helps. Having indexes or index tags that correspond to fields used in filter conditions also helps considerably. Occasionally, SQL determines that building indexes on the fly and on its own is faster than processing a query without indexes. If you ensure that the index is available, you save the time it would take FoxPro to create the index.

Structural indexes are particularly useful if you allow SQL to open the tables. If the indexes to a table are not structural and SQL opens the tables, SQL doesn't see the indexes and therefore doesn't realize the indexes are available.

Avoid Nested SELECTs When Possible

You can construct many queries in more than one way. If you have a query with a nested SELECT that also can be processed without a nested SELECT, the latter method almost always executes faster. Practice with SQL SELECT syntax to look for similar alternatives.

Include UDFs Only When Necessary

You can include UDFs in the selected output list of a SELECT and in filter conditions specified in the WHERE clause. You also can GROUP BY UDF expressions if you use the GROUP BY <position> syntax and use the UDF for output. This FoxPro SQL SELECT feature is powerful, but tends to slow down processing considerably. A query executed without a UDF almost always executes more efficiently than the same query with a UDF.

Monitor HAVING and WHERE Clauses

When you have no GROUP BY, you can use either HAVING or WHERE to get the same results, but the speed of execution differs. On rare occasions, specifying filter conditions in the HAVING clause rather than the WHERE clause results in a faster query. However, such occasions are likely to become even more rare in future versions of FoxPro as the internal methods by which FoxPro optimizes the SQL processing are continually improved. Use the WHERE clause by preference unless you are specifying filter conditions on a grouping.

Optimize Indexes and Orders

You can more quickly complete some SQL SELECTs that must be in a certain order by not specifying the ORDER BY in the SELECT command and INDEXing the result of the SELECT. Although you see the results of the query more quickly, processing the indexed table is slower because FoxPro must use the index file to find the next record in the table. Experiment with different approaches to discover the best way to handle a particular situation.

Remedying Some Common SQL Errors

When FoxPro encounters an error while executing a query, FoxPro displays an error message. Some of these messages clearly describe the problem; others, such as `"SQL invalid aggregate field"`, are both cryptic and unilluminating.

Table 7.3 lists the SQL-related error messages contained in the FoxPro help file, along with the related description of the problem, as Microsoft sees it. As with the error messages themselves, some of these descriptions are very helpful, but others provide little insight into the problem.

If the error's entry in the table contains a number in the Text Reference column, refer to that number in the text that follows this table for what should be a clearer explanation of the possible cause and remedy of the problem.

Table 7.3 SQL Errors

Error Text (Number)	Help File Description	Text Ref.
<cursor> must be created with SELECT ... INTO TABLE. (1815)	Some cursors cannot be used in successive queries.	1
<field> | <variable> is not unique and must be qualified. (1832)	The field or variable in the SQL SELECT command you have specified cannot be found.	2
<name> is not a memory variable. (225)	A file variable (field) was used where a memory or array variable was required.	3
Cannot GROUP by aggregate field. (1846)	There has been an attempt to GROUP one of the aggregate functions MIN(), MAX(), SUM(), AVG(), COUNT(), NPV(), STD(), or VAR().	None
SELECT's are not UNION compatible. (1851)	Data types or sizes of fields being projected in each SELECT are not identical.	None
SQL aggregate on non-numeric expression. (1811)	There was an attempt to perform an average, sum, standard deviation, or variance on a non-Numeric field.	None
SQL canceled operation. (1839)	There was an attempt to SELECT into a table when SAFETY was ON and the user chose not to overwrite the table.	None
SQL column <field> | <variable> not found. (1806)	The field or variable you have specified cannot be found.	4
SQL could not locate database. (1802)	The database specified could not be found.	None
SQL err building temporary index. (1831)	A temporary index could not be built, possibly due to insufficient disk space.	None
SQL Error Correlating Fields. (1801)	An outer-reference can only be in syntax similar to the following: X = Y Syntax such as X = Y + 1 or X = 5 produces this error.	5

continues

Table 7.3 Continued

Error Text (Number)	Help File Description	Text Ref.
SQL expression too complex. (1845)	FoxPro ran out of memory when it tried to expand the SELECT statement to analyze it.	None
SQL illegal GROUP BY in subquery. (1828)	When using one of the six operators +, -, *, /, <, and >, there can be only one row of output.	None
SQL index not found. (1830)	FoxPro could not find the existing index.	None
SQL Internal Error. (1800)	An internal error has occurred. If this error occurs, call Microsoft Product Support.	None
SQL invalid * in SELECT. (1820)	There was an attempt to use * in one of the aggregate functions of MAX( ), MIN( ), AVG( ), or SUM( ).	None
SQL invalid aggregate field. (1822)	There has been an attempt to do aggregation on a Memo field.	None
SQL invalid DISTINCT. (1819)	There must only be one distinct used per level.	None
SQL invalid GROUP BY. (1807)	There is an error in the GROUP BY clause.	6
SQL invalid HAVING. (1803)	There is an error in HAVING clause, for example the clause does not contain a logical expression.	None
SQL invalid ORDER BY. (1808)	One of the fields chosen for the order by is not in the SELECT list. This only occurs when using numeric indexing, for example: SELECT a,b,c FROM database ; ORDER BY 4 The number chosen exceeds the number of fields selected.	None
SQL invalid SELECT statement. (1804)	There is an error in the projection list.	None

Error Text (Number)	Help File Description	Text Ref.
SQL invalid SELECT. (1826)	There has been an attempt to select more than one field in a subquery.	None
SQL invalid subquery. (1825)	Something in the subquery is erroneous.	None
SQL invalid WHERE clause. (1833)	There is an error in the WHERE clause.	None
SQL invalid use of subquery. (1810)	A subquery was used in a place where it wasn't expected.	None
SQL invalid use of union in subquery. (1813)	UNION is not supported in subqueries in FoxPro 2.5.	None
SQL no FROM clause. (1818)	There must be a FROM clause in the SELECT command.	None
SQL out of memory. (1809)	FoxPro has run out of memory while trying to process your SELECT command.	None
SQL queries of this type are not supported at present. (1814)	There was an attempt to perform a query that is not supported by FoxPro 2.5.	7
SQL statement too long. (1812)	The object code is too long to be compiled.	None
SQL subqueries nested too deep. (1842)	FoxPro 2.5 does not support nested subqueries.	None
SQL too many columns referenced. (1841)	There must be no more than 256 columns total referenced in any SELECT command.	None
SQL too many subqueries. (1805)	The number of subqueries allowed in FoxPro 2.5 is two per SELECT.	None
SQL too many UNIONs. (1834)	The maximum number of UNIONs (10) has been exceeded.	None
Unrecognized phrase/keyword in command. (36)	A phrase beginning with an invalid keyword was used in a command line.	8

1. `"<cursor>" must be created with SELECT ... INTO TABLE.` (1815)

   Cursors don't always have a disk presence. Sometimes the cursor is nothing more than a filter of the source table. Because SQL opens tables to extract the required information, the source must usually be an actual table. For example, the following code causes this error:

```
SELECT * FROM Budget INTO CURSOR Query1
SELECT Prodcode FROM Query1
```

If you see this error, follow the instructions: output the results INTO TABLE rather than into a cursor. Remember that, because SQL creates a table on disk, you are now responsible for erasing the table.

2. `"<field> ¦ <variable>" is not unique and must be qualified.` (1832)

   This is one case where the error message is more helpful than Microsoft's explanation of the problem. The problem is not that the field cannot be found; the problem is that you have not specified a table alias for a field that appears in more than one table involved in the query. Use the table alias to specify the table that contains the field.

3. `"<name>" is not a memory variable.` (225)

   This error is often caused when you forget to include in the FROM list a table that is referenced in a WHERE join or filter condition. Without the table name in the FROM list, FoxPro assumes you are referencing a memory variable.

4. `SQL column "<field> ¦ <variable>" not found.` (1806)

   Your query probably refers to a nonexistent field in a table, such as Dept_code when the actual field name is Deptcode, or to a memory variable that does not currently exist or is hidden within the current procedure.

5. `SQL Error Correlating Fields.` (1801)

   If you didn't intend to create a correlated query, you probably neglected to include in the subquery's FROM list one of the tables in the subquery. SQL found the table in the outer SELECT's FROM list and decided you are creating a correlated query.

   If you did intend to create a correlated query, the expression that contains the table from the outer SELECT's FROM list is probably involved in a calculation, such as Budgetamt * 0.5, that is illegal. The outer reference's job is simply to move the pointer in the table to which it refers so that the subquery is performed for each record. Try to rephrase the query so that the calculation is outside the subquery; immediately following the WHERE is a likely candidate for the proper position.

6. `SQL invalid GROUP BY.` (1807)

   The reason for this error is usually the same as for the "SQL invalid ORDER BY" error; that is, you have instructed SQL to GROUP BY a nonexistent column number.

7. `SQL queries of this type are not supported at present.` (1814)

   The most common cause of this error is an attempt to GROUP BY or ORDER BY an expression, such as the following:

   ```
   GROUP BY PADR(CMONTH(Budget.Period), 9)
   ```

   Use the number of the column in which the expression appears, or use AS to assign a name to the column, and then GROUP BY the column name.

8. `Unrecognized phrase/keyword in command` (36)

   A common cause of this error is a missing comma between the fields in your output fields list. Of course, the error message may be correct; you may have misspelled or misused a clause in the SELECT, so check for typos and verify the proper syntax of the command.

Searching with Rushmore

During the development of FoxPro's patentable data-retrieval mechanism, Fox Software used the code name *Rushmore,* a tongue-in-cheek reference to the Alfred Hitchcock movie, *North by Northwest.* The name persists in FoxPro's official vocabulary, however, because the name is both appropriate and memorable.

Rushmore searches for sets of data by intelligently using all available indexes, including all FoxPro index types: standard .IDX files, compact .IDX files, and compound .CDX files.

Before FoxPro 2.0, SET FILTER, LOCATE FOR/CONTINUE, COUNT FOR, SUM FOR, and similar commands were far too slow to use on large tables. These commands individually examined all the records in a table, so indexes were of no help. With Rushmore, however, these commands become very useful with tables of any size—even tables with millions of records.

The first example uses the same CUSTOMER.DBF table you used in Chapter 6 (in the TUTORIAL directory, not the MODEL\CUSTOMER table). You see how Rushmore can help find all the customers in New York with year-to-date purchases of $15,000 or more.

Working with Rushmore

Using the sample tables, FoxPro, even without the aid of Rushmore, is too fast to demonstrate the difference Rushmore can make. If you have spare disk space and want to see Rushmore in action (as opposed to just believing what you read), you must create a larger table. You can do this in a few easy steps, and you learn a few new FoxPro commands along the way.

First, open the table \TUTORIAL\CUSTOMER, which is under the main FoxPro program directory. Make sure that the default directory remains the MODEL directory so that the example files are saved there. If you're not sure, type the following command in the Command window:

```
WAIT WINDOW SET("DEFAULT")+SYS(2003)
```

If the drive and directory for the MODEL files don't appear, type the following command in the Command window, substituting the actual drive and directory for the MODEL files:

```
SET DEFAULT TO C:\FOXPRO25\MODEL
```

Now use the Database menu popup's Copy option, or type the following instructions in the Command window, to create a new table:

```
COPY TO Bigcust FIELDS Company, State, Ytdpurch
```

You are copying the Company, State, and Ytdpurch fields from the currently selected table (the TUTORIAL Customer table) to a new table, Bigcust.dbf in the MODEL directory. (You copy selected fields to save disk space and to simplify the examples.)

Next, close the Customer table and open the Bigcust table you just created by using the View window. You can do the same thing by typing the following line in the Command window:

```
USE Bigcust
```

Notice that the USE command closed the Customer table because the table was in the current work area. The Bigcust table holds 500 records, just like the Customer table. You can enlarge the table by appending more copies of the table to itself. Use the Append option of the Database menu popup or enter the following command in the Command window:

```
APPEND FROM Bigcust
```

If you have the View window open, you see that the Bigcust table now has 1,000 records. You can enter the APPEND FROM Bigcust command as many times as you like—if you have enough disk space—and FoxPro continues to double the number of records each time you APPEND. (In the Command window, just move the cursor to the line you typed and press Enter as many times as you want to repeat the command.)

The larger you make the table, the more noticeable is Rushmore's effect. Entering the command four times results in an 8,000 record Bigcust.dbf; if you have a fast computer, you may have to make the table this large, or even larger, to appreciate Rushmore.

NOTE

If you are familiar with Xbase, you might be surprised to learn that you can APPEND records from a table into itself. Because FoxPro now can APPEND records FROM a table open in another work area and because FoxPro also can open several instances of one table in different work areas (with the USE AGAIN command), this capability is not too surprising. APPENDing from a table into itself is a handy way to create large tables for other tests.

To create a Browse of all the customers whose year-to-date purchases are $15,000 or more, type the following command in the Command window:

```
BROWSE FOR Ytdpurch >= 15000
```

After a few seconds, a Browse window appears with all the requested customers listed. (If the screen's appearance is nearly instantaneous on your computer, you might want to issue another APPEND FROM Bigcust command to increase the table size.)

This wait isn't too bothersome, but now limit the Browse to the customers from New York with $15,000 or more in purchases. To do this, type the following command:

```
BROWSE FOR State = 'NY' AND Ytdpurch >= 15000
```

Remember that here, as usual, FoxPro understands commands regardless of the mixture of upper- and lowercase letters you type. The character data you type, `NY`, however, is searched with case sensitivity; be sure that you type the character data in uppercase.

This time, you probably waited a while before FoxPro completed the cycle.

You can see the difference Rushmore makes if you make sure that indexes are available for use. Add a structural index with two tags: a tag on the State field and another tag on the Ytdpurch field. If you add these tags from the View window's Setup/Index Add dialog, the tags by default use the same name as the fields on which they are based. You also see the equivalent command echoed in the Command window. You can assign any other tag names; Rushmore finds the needed data based on the contents of the key expression, not on the tag names.

If you created the index tags from the View window, use the `No Order` push button to set the index order off. If you created the index tags from the Command window, issue the equivalent SET ORDER TO command. The significance of having the table in natural order is explained in the "Increasing the Performance of Rushmore" section of this chapter. Try the last BROWSE command again.

This time, the Browse popped up much more quickly. This enhanced speed demonstrates Rushmore in action. If the table holds a million records, a similar search may take hours without the indexes, but with the indexes, the search probably doesn't take noticeably longer than with an 8,000- or 16,000-record file.

NOTE

The time Rushmore takes to retrieve a set of records depends more on how many records meet the searching criteria than on how many records are in the table. If 25 customers in New York exceed purchases of $15,000 and you have a million records in the Customer table, Rushmore can find the 25 good New York customers in a few seconds. The more customers that match the search criteria, the less effective Rushmore becomes. If the search criteria matches all records in the table, Rushmore becomes virtually useless except for the purposes of a COUNT FOR.

Consequently, the more specific you make the search definition, the more refined and prompt is the response. This situation is almost the opposite of the rules you have to use for other search techniques, in which you trade off benefits of a narrowly targeted search with the lengthy search times this kind of search can require.

How Rushmore Works

Watching Rushmore work is a lot of fun, but to use Rushmore properly you need to understand some of the details of *how* it works. Remember that any command or series of commands that you execute here as interactive instructions to FoxPro also can be used to enhance programs that you write in FoxPro.

When can you use the help provided by this technology (usually referred to as Rushmore *optimization*)? Rushmore is available any time you issue a FoxPro command by using a FOR condition for which a matching index or tag is available. Note that APPEND FROM is not included even though it has a FOR clause. Table 7.4 lists the commands that use Rushmore to optimize searches. Note that APPEND FROM is not included even though it has a FOR clause. As explained in Chapter 4, "Database Management Fundamentals," FoxPro evaluates the FOR expression in the context of the target table, not the source table, and therefore does not use the source table's indexes to aid in the search.

To understand why SET FILTER is included even though no explicit FOR is issued, think of a FOR condition as a request to FoxPro to check *all* the records in a table against the requirements you specify. Commands that can take a FILTER into account as they move through a table also can benefit from Rushmore—even if the commands have no explicit FOR clause.

Table 7.4 Commands that Benefit from Rushmore Optimization

AVERAGE	DISPLAY	REPORT
BROWSE	EDIT	SCAN
CALCULATE	EXPORT	SET FILTER TO
CHANGE	LABEL	[SQL-]SELECT
COPY TO	LIST	SORT
COPY TO ARRAY	LOCATE	SUM
COUNT	RECALL	TOTAL
DELETE	REPLACE	

Working with Optimizable Expressions

Suppose that you have index tags on State and Ytdpurch only, but you want to find the records where Company = 'Micro'. Because Rushmore works with indexes, you expect (correctly) that Rushmore doesn't help in this search. At other times, however, you might expect Rushmore to have an effect, but the effect doesn't occur. In this section, you examine the conditions under which optimization takes place.

A FOR expression can be Fully Optimizable, Partially Optimizable, or Not Optimizable. All fully optimizable expressions are made up of one or more Basic Optimizable Expressions, which are usually found in this form:

```
Index-Like Expression <joining operator> Search Expression
```

In this expression, the Index-Like Expression component is a field name or a concatenation of field names, exactly matching an index key; <joining operator> is a FoxPro operator; and the Search Expression is the string for which you are searching. Table 7.5 shows you the FoxPro operators that you can use in optimizable expressions.

Table 7.5 Rushmore-Optimizable Operators

Operator	Description
<	Less than
>	Greater than
=	Equal to
<=	Less than or equal to
>=	Greater than or equal to
<>	Not equal
#	Not equal (same as above)
l!=	Not equal (same as above)

If you are familiar with the FoxPro operators, you might notice the absence of == (*exactly equals*), which is not optimizable in the present version of FoxPro. Several other FoxPro operators also cannot be optimized (notably the $ for finding the incidence of one character string as a part, or *substring* of another string).

Although == is not generally optimizable, SQL SELECT, whether used directly or through the RQBE, successfully employs Rushmore in queries that use the == (Exactly Like in the RQBE) operator.

Creating Fully Optimizable Expressions

The Bigcust table you created currently has two index keys, on the fields State and Ytdpurch. Therefore, the following expressions are fully optimizable:

```
State = 'NY'

'NY' = State

State <> 'NY'

State = 'NY' OR State = 'CA'

State = 'NY' AND Ytdpurch > 15000

State = 'NY' AND NOT (Ytdpurch > 15000)

State = 'NY' AND (Ytdpurch > 15000 AND Ytdpurch < 16000)

(State='NY' OR State='CA') AND (Ytdpurch > 50 AND Ytdpurch < 80)
```

Notice that the more complicated expressions are built from simpler, basic optimizable expressions. The last expression in the list is constructed from four basic optimizable expressions:

```
State = 'NY'

State = 'CA'

Ytdpurch > 15000

Ytdpurch < 16000
```

You can continue adding basic optimizable expressions without compromising Rushmore's capability of quickly finding the matching records. Notice that parentheses are used to indicate the expressions that are evaluated first.

Note also that FoxPro is "smart" enough to recognize that

```
(Ytdpurch >= 50 AND Ytdpurch <= 80)
```

is the same as

```
BETWEEN(Ytdpurch, 50, 80)
```

The following expression is optimizable:

```
(State='NY' OR State='CA') AND BETWEEN(Ytdpurch, 50, 80)
```

Recognizing Nonoptimizable Expressions

Some expressions are not optimizable by using the index tags you have so far created for the Bigcust table.

The following expression is not optimizable because the Company field has no index:

```
Company = 'Micro'
```

The following expression finds all companies whose names begin with Micro in the state of New Jersey:

```
State + Company = 'NJ' + 'Micro'
```

You already know that, to be useful for a search of this field, Rushmore needs a tag on the Company field. However, even this tag cannot help you in this search.

With EXACT left at the default setting of OFF, this expression finds all the appropriate records, but Rushmore isn't available to speed up the search. For Rushmore to work, the expression must *exactly match* an index key. You can create another tag on State + Company, but this step is unnecessary. With a tag on each of the fields involved, the expression State = 'NJ' AND Company = 'Micro' is used and optimized. These separate tags provide more flexibility for other searches. You also can now perform, for example, an optimized search for a company alone or for companies with a particular Ytdpurch amount.

The expression

```
Ytdpurch * 1.10 > 15000
```

is not optimizable for the same reason that the other expressions are not: Ytdpurch * 1.10 has no index. If an index did exist, you then could optimize the search for this criterion.

The following case is unusual. The expression is optimizable when EXACT is set ON but not when EXACT is set OFF. When EXACT is OFF, the expression is guaranteed *never* to find a match, but with EXACT ON, the statement matches any record in which the State field is equal to "N ":

```
'N' = State
```

To understand this limitation, you must understand how FoxPro compares character expressions in different cases. Table 5.3 shows you the difference between LIKE and EXACTLY LIKE in the RQBE, as used to make comparisons in an SQL SELECT statement, and how SET ANSI ON/OFF affects LIKE.

Other (non-SQL) FoxPro commands compare character strings by using slightly different rules, in which both the order of the strings examined and the command SET EXACT ON/OFF play a role.

When EXACT is set OFF, FoxPro compares character expressions left to right until a character that does not match is found or until the expression on the *right* ends. This situation means that when EXACT is OFF, the following list applies:

`'NJ' = 'NJ'` is true

`'NJB' = 'NJ'` is true

`'N' = 'NJ'` is false

and

`'N  ' = 'NJ'` is false

`'N' = 'NJ'` is false

When EXACT is set ON, FoxPro returns False if both character expressions are of different lengths, but ignores trailing spaces, as shown in the following examples:

`'NJ' = 'NJ'` is true

`'NJB' = 'NJ'` is false

`'N' = 'NJ'` is false

`'N  ' = 'NJ'` is false

but

`'N' = 'N  '` is true

Notice that the last expression here is considered equal with EXACT ON, but unequal with EXACT OFF. In this case, EXACT ON is less exact than EXACT OFF.

The == operator applies the most rigorous test. This operator considers two character expressions to be equal only if the expressions are identical, including trailing blanks.

> **CAUTION:** The preceding rules generally apply to most comparisons you make in FoxPro (or in Xbase). The difference between the right and left side of an expression can be useful when you search tables. You must remember, however, that SQL SELECT is an exception to this rule. In SQL SELECT comparisons, the order in which two expressions surround the operator makes absolutely no difference.

To return to the previous example, in a non-SQL SELECT comparison and with SET EXACT OFF, State = 'N' matches any state that begins with the letter *N*. However, 'N' = State finds no matches because State is a two-character field.

If you SET EXACT ON or (in SQL SELECT) SET ANSI ON so that the shorter string ('N') is padded with blanks to match the length of the other, then 'N' = State is optimized. Rushmore uses the tag on the State field and compares the tag to the character string you supply. Of course, no records are found to match.

This example gives you a chance to explore the subtleties of a FoxPro character search. Look at some other forms of comparisons that cannot be optimized, such as the following:

```
UPPER(State) = 'NJ'
```

This comparison is not optimizable, because the index does not contain the UPPER() function. Just as you can create a tag on Ytdpurch * 1.10, you can create a tag on UPPER(State). You then can perform optimizable, case-insensitive searches on States.

Assuming that there is no index tag on Company, the following expression is not optimizable because every record in the table still must be examined in the search:

```
State = 'NJ' OR Company = 'Micro'
```

Although Rushmore can build a set of records that includes only records for which the first condition is satisfied, every record in the rest of the table still must be checked for the second condition.

Combining Fully Optimizable and Nonoptimizable Expressions

The preceding expression—in which an OR combines an optimizable expression with a nonoptimizable expression—is not a typical example of how Rushmore handles complex expressions.

Often, combining fully optimizable expressions with nonoptimizable expressions produces partially optimizable expressions. If you combine a partially optimizable expression with another partially or fully optimizable expression, you get another partially optimizable expression. Rushmore is completely ineffective only when you use an OR to connect a nonoptimizable expression to others, or when all components of a complex expression are nonoptimizable.

Rushmore, on encountering a partially optimizable expression, first searches the indexes for all the records that match the fully optimizable portion of the expression and then evaluates only those records against the nonoptimizable portion of the expression.

This section shows some examples of partially optimizable expressions, such as the following:

```
State = 'NY' AND Company = 'Micro'
```

Based on the index, Rushmore finds all customers from NY and then looks at these NY customers to rule out customers whose company name does not begin with Micro.

```
(State = 'NY' OR State = 'CA') AND Ytdpurch > 15000 AND Company = 'Micro'
```

In the preceding expression, Rushmore first finds all the NY and CA customers—based on the State index tag—and then uses the Ytdpurch index tag to find which of the NY and CA customers match. So far, the search is fully optimized. Without a tag to match the rest of the query, Rushmore then checks the actual records in the subset already collected to see which records have companies with names beginning with Micro.

This sequence may not be exactly the way in which the expression is evaluated. Rushmore may determine that checking the Ytdpurch index is faster and proceed accordingly, but the idea and results are the same. Table 7.6 shows all the possible ways in which you can combine optimizable and nonoptimizable expressions.

Table 7.6 Combining Basic Optimizable and Nonoptimizable Expressions

Basic Expression	Connector	Basic Expression	Optimization
Optimizable	AND	Optimizable	Full
Optimizable	AND	Nonoptimizable	Partial
Optimizable	OR	Optimizable	Full
Optimizable	OR	Nonoptimizable	None
Nonoptimizable	AND	Nonoptimizable	None
Nonoptimizable	OR	Nonoptimizable	None

Increasing the Performance of Rushmore

You can take several steps to help Rushmore deliver the best performance.

SET ORDER TO 0 Whenever Possible

Commands that produce output which other FoxPro commands either display, print, or process will benefit more from Rushmore optimization if the table is left in the natural order and Rushmore is left to decide which tags best suit a search. If the ORDER is SET to a particular index—perhaps because you are outputting a report in customer sequence or labels in ZIP code order—Rushmore must process the table in the order specified.

FoxPro always processes a table faster in natural order when you are moving through all the records. This attribute, although not unique to Rushmore, can significantly affect your perception of Rushmore's value.

Table 7.7 lists commands that perform better when ORDER is SET TO 0. This list is a subset of the commands in table 7.4.

Table 7.7 Commands that Perform Better When ORDER Is SET TO 0

BROWSE	LABEL
CHANGE	LIST
COPY TO	LOCATE
COPY TO ARRAY	REPORT
DISPLAY	SCAN
EDIT	SET FILTER TO
EXPORT	TOTAL

** This table applies regardless of whether Rushmore is involved.*

Note that SQL SELECT is omitted from this list. You can use SQL SELECT or the RQBE (which uses SQL) without concerning yourself with the current order of the table.

Use a DELETED() Tag If You SET DELETED ON

SET DELETED ON tells FoxPro to ignore deleted records and acts just like a filter. Rushmore treats any operation as partially optimizable at best when SET DELETED is ON. This occurs because FoxPro must look outside of the index, to the actual table, to find out whether a record has been deleted. Fortunately, you have a way around this: if DELETED( ) has an index tag, then Rushmore uses the tag to optimize SET DELETED.

Avoid Using NOT and FOR in Index Tags

Rushmore doesn't recognize indexes that contain NOT or ! in an index key, such as in the following:

```
NOT DELETED()
NOT Animal = "CAT"
```

This kind of key is sometimes used to group all records not matching the condition, followed by all records matching the condition (because these expressions always evaluate to False or True). If an index contains NOT, Rushmore cannot use this index. If you create the indexes without NOT, Rushmore can use the indexes, and, when necessary, these indexes perform the same service for you. (You can reverse the group that appears first in the index by using the DESCENDING keyword when you SET ORDER.)

In Chapter 4, you learned that you can create a conditional index by using the FOR clause, which filters the records so that only a subset of the file appears in the index. Programmers often create conditional index expressions, such as the following:

```
Id_code FOR NOT DELETED()
Zip FOR animal = "CAT"
```

Rushmore does not use conditional indexes. Instead, use a regular index tag to create these filters by using FOR clauses on the table-manipulating commands or by using the SET FILTER command, as in the following clauses:

```
INDEX ON Id_code TAG Code
INDEX ON DELETED() TAG Del
SET DELETED ON
SET FILTER TO Id_code = "XYZ"

INDEX ON Zip TAG Zip
INDEX ON Animal TAG Animal
SET ORDER TO Zip
REPORT FORM Statusrpt FOR Animal = "CAT"
```

In the second example, ORDER is not SET TO 0, because the report is printed in ZIP code order. Rushmore, however, still provides a benefit in selecting the "CAT" records to be processed.

Use Rushmore Selectively

Rushmore can speed up many operations in FoxPro, but relying too much on this technology can hurt performance. With a little work, you can perform some procedures faster without Rushmore. The following examples use SCAN/ENDSCAN, a programming construct with which you might be unfamiliar. Review SCAN/ENDSCAN if necessary after you read Chapter 16, “Discovering Additional FoxPro Productivity Features.” You must understand only that when you SCAN records in a program, FoxPro moves through all the records in the table, performing the operations you specify for each record before moving to the next one.

Using the Bigcust table, the following example is much faster with Rushmore than without Rushmore:

```
SET ORDER TO
SCAN FOR State = 'NY'
     ....
     do something with the record
     ....
ENDSCAN
```

The following is still faster, although you might not notice the difference unless you process very large files:

```
SET ORDER TO State
SEEK 'NY'
SCAN WHILE State = 'NY'
    ....
    do something with the record
    ....
ENDSCAN
```

However, change the line

```
SCAN FOR State = 'NY'
```

in the first code segment to

```
SCAN FOR State = 'NY' AND Ytdpurch >= 15000
```

and change the line

```
SCAN WHILE State = 'NY'
```

in the second code segment to

```
SCAN WHILE State = 'NY' FOR Ytdpurch >= 15000
```

and you find the first method much faster than the second method.

With these kinds of elaborate conditions, Rushmore's advantage is most apparent because the SEEK can use only one index order at a time, and Rushmore uses multiple tags. Usually, in a situation in which you must squeeze every last bit of speed from the code, you should try several different methods to see which works best for your situation.

Pick the Right Index Format

Rushmore works with any of the three index types provided by FoxPro. Better performance usually results from using either the compact or compound indexes because these indexes are smaller (all compound indexes also are inherently compact). The more efficiently information is stored in an index, the more index information FoxPro can keep in memory at one time, which in turn reduces disk accesses. (Accessing the disk is one of the slowest processes of database operations. You learn more about this factor in Appendix B, which covers the relationship between FoxPro's performance and computer hardware.)

Rushmore works as quickly with noncompound compact indexes as with compound indexes. As you already learned in Chapter 4, however, compound indexes offer other advantages and are usually the best choice, unless you are building a temporary index intended for one-time use.

Compound indexes also have a few disadvantages. Chapter 4 mentions the index file bloat phenomenon. Related to (and a partial cause of) this problem is *compound index fragmentation*. In standard and compact index files, all information concerning each index key is stored together. In compound indexes, this kind of storage, however, is not always the case. Information about an index key may be scattered all over the file. This scattering forces FoxPro to perform far more disk accesses than is otherwise necessary, which can slow operations considerably. You can reduce this problem by occasionally rebuilding the compound index files, either by REINDEXing or by deleting and rebuilding all the tags individually.

Working without Rushmore

You might think that you must do everything possible to optimize each search or filter condition. But sometimes you must decide not to use Rushmore. When Rushmore encounters a command that uses FOR with an optimizable expression, Rushmore determines which records match the expression *only once*—when the FOR condition is first encountered. The command works only on the records Rushmore finds. If the data is changed while the Rushmore set is still in use, it is inaccurate because the information is not updated as are active indexes.

Be particularly aware of this condition when you use FoxPro on a network, where many people may be editing the table in which you are working at the same time.

If you encounter this situation, use the NOOPTIMIZE clause on the commands usually subject to optimization, or SET OPTIMIZE OFF, which turns off Rushmore for *all* operations until you SET OPTIMIZE back to the default state of ON.

In FoxPro for Windows and the Extended version of FoxPro for DOS, the size of Rushmore-optimizable tables is limited only by the amount of memory in your computer. However, when you use the Standard version of FoxPro for DOS (either because you are running on a 286 or lesser machine, or because the 386 doesn't have sufficient memory for the extended version), Rushmore becomes unavailable when the tables include 500,000 or more records. Rushmore may also turn itself off if your computer does not have enough memory to process your query efficiently.

If Rushmore doesn't operate because one of these limits is exceeded, a FoxPro message informs you that not enough memory is available for Rushmore optimization. FoxPro then executes the command (without Rushmore) while you take a coffee break.

Summary

In this chapter you closely examined the effect Rushmore has on the SQL SELECT command and other FoxPro search methods. When you ask FoxPro to present a set of records that satisfy criteria you set, think of each request as a series of comparisons of records against the criteria. You now know that the results of these comparisons, the format in which FoxPro presents them, and the speed with which FoxPro responds to requests to produce these comparisons can vary significantly, depending on how you phrase the request.

Working with SQL SELECT syntax represents an enormous increase in the search vocabulary and the fluency with which you can make these kinds of requests of FoxPro. You now have a working knowledge of some of the unique capabilities of FoxPro searches; you also learned about these capabilities' inherent limitations.

A significant limitation in FoxPro's implementation of SQL SELECT is a lack of direct support for outer joins. Outer joins are not part of the ANSI SQL standard but are included in many other SQL implementations.

ANSI, the American National Standards Institute, is an organization that sets standards for programming languages and other engineering disciplines. ANSI standards exist for many programming languages—such as C, FORTRAN, COBOL, and SQL—used on personal computers and mainframes. As this book is being written, Xbase vendors are working to develop an Xbase ANSI standard. Because most SQL implementations respect the ANSI SQL standard, you can write an SQL SELECT in any SQL implementation and then use the statement on another computer. Many FoxPro SELECT statements you used produce the same results in ORACLE or other languages.

The FoxPro SQL SELECT, however, has some clauses that ANSI SQL doesn't support, such as INTO DBF and INTO ARRAY. These clauses were added to help make SQL easy to use with the rest of FoxPro.

This situation is probably not of great concern to you at the moment. As you explore SQL SELECT in FoxPro, however, you might become interested in the way SQL is used in the larger database management community.

In fact, with the introduction of the Microsoft FoxPro Connectivity Kit, slated for release in the second half of 1993, this use of SQL SELECT may form an integral part of the way FoxPro uses information from—or communicates results to—other database systems. If you find yourself thinking about these issues, you can consult some of the following sources. These books also help you to organize your thoughts and find new approaches as you use SQL SELECT from FoxPro:

FoxPro 2 and SQL, Melissa Dunn. Pinnacle Publishing, 1992.

The Practical SQL Handbook, Sandra L. Emerson, Marcy Darnovsky, and Judith S. Bowman. Addison-Wesley, 1989.

SQL: The Structured Query Language, Dr. Carolyn J. Hursch and Dr. Jack L. Hursch. TAB, 1988.

8

CHAPTER

Organizing the Answers with BROWSE

BROWSE is FoxPro's most useful command for viewing and editing records contained in one or more tables in a database. You can display the records in a columnar, spreadsheet-style format or in a vertical format, or in both formats at the same time. You also can limit the display to certain records and fields, and can rearrange the size and position of each field.

In this chapter, you learn how to use the FoxPro menu system and the Command window to access the power of BROWSE for interactive use. Although you work interactively, the techniques you learn in this chapter (especially the many options of the FIELDS clause) apply equally to your use of BROWSE in FoxPro programs. Remember that almost any command you type in the Command window can be included in a program.

In Parts III and IV of this book, you learn about some additional BROWSE features specifically designed for browsing tables in a FoxPro program.

Opening and Closing a Browse Window

You can use several methods to open a Browse window:

- Select Browse from the Database menu.
- Click the `Browse` push button in the View window.
- Output the results of a query to a Browse window.
- Type `BROWSE` in the Command window.

Figure 8.1 shows a Browse window in the default Browse format, together with the Browse menu that appears in the system menu bar whenever a Browse window is active.

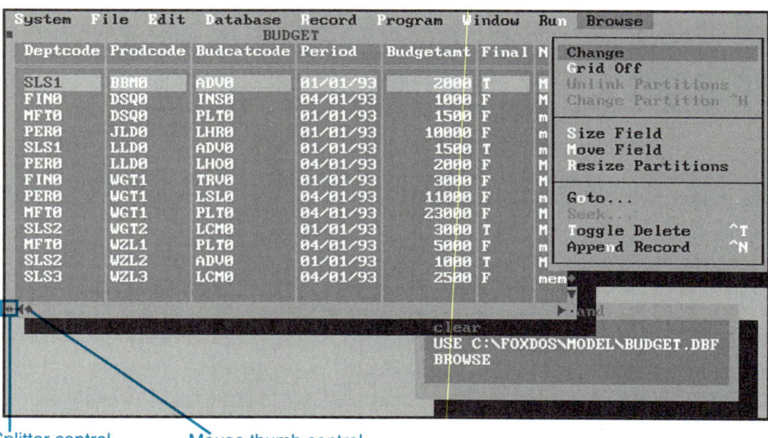

FIG. 8.1

A Browse window in Browse format, and the Browse menu options.

Selecting Browse from the Database menu issues a BROWSE LAST command, which opens a Browse window that looks the same as it did the last time you browsed the current table.

Clicking the `Browse` push button in the View window also issues a BROWSE LAST command but gives you more flexibility by enabling you to set a filter, specify a list of fields to appear, or use a format file to control the display format. If you need these options, select the `Setup` push button in the View window before selecting Browse. For more information on using the View window, see Chapter 3, “Exploring Databases and Tables.”

As you learned in Chapter 5, "Using the RQBE as the Gateway to Queries," you can output the results of a query to a Browse window. This method is a powerful way of limiting the display to those items that provide the answers you are seeking. Because a copy of some of the records is created in a separate table, you can use the RQBE to create multiple views of data, and use BROWSE to switch from one view to the other without affecting the original tables.

Finally, you can work directly from the Command window. This approach gives you the greatest degree of flexibility in specifying the exact combination of BROWSE options that result in the display format and editing criteria you want.

BROWSE always works on the table in the current work area. If no table is currently open in this area, FoxPro asks you to select a table through the Open File dialog. After you make the selection, FoxPro opens the table and displays the Browse window.

You can have more than one Browse window open at one time. As you saw in Chapter 3, you can have a separate Browse window for each work area if the computer has sufficient memory. You can move from one window to another by clicking the one you want with a mouse or by using Ctrl+F1 to cycle among the open windows.

To close an active Browse window, press Esc or Ctrl+W or click the close box. Closing a Browse window does not close the related table.

Arranging the Browse Window's Appearance

Browse, a special kind of FoxPro window, has several unique options that enable you to change the way in which the data is displayed. You can access these configuration options through the Browse menu, or you can use the mouse and the window's several control objects.

In this section, you learn the ways in which you can create a customized look for Browse windows. In the following section, you learn how to save and restore this look in later Browse sessions with the same table.

Sizing and Rearranging Fields

In the default Browse format, each field is displayed as a separate column. The fields appear from left to right in the order in which they exist in the table. The width of each column is the same as the size of the associated field, unless more room is needed to show the name of the field.

You can change the order in which the fields appear so that the most important fields are grouped together and visible. With a mouse, just drag a field name to the desired position. From the keyboard, select Move Field from the Browse menu. If the field you want to move is not currently selected, use Tab or Shift+Tab to select the field you want, and use the left- and right-arrow keys to position the field. Press Tab or Shift+Tab to select another field to move, or press Enter to complete the operations.

You also can change a column's width so that more or fewer columns are visible together. This technique is useful when you are viewing wide fields that typically end in blank spaces, such as first and last names, and you want to bring additional information into view. With a mouse, drag the vertical line to the right of the field name, resize the column width by moving the mouse cursor to the left or the right, and release the mouse button. From the keyboard, select Size Field from the Browse menu and use the left- and right-arrow keys to decrease or increase the column's width. Select another field to size with Tab or Shift+Tab, or press Enter to complete the operation.

Moving and resizing a column affects only the display of the data. The field's length, contents, and physical position within the table remain the same.

Using Change To See the Whole Record

Browse's columnar format is great for displaying many records at once, but tables often have more fields than can be displayed horizontally. When you want to see all the information for a particular record, the Change/Edit format is more useful (Change and Edit are synonymous in the context of a Browse window).

FoxPro's Edit format displays each record in a vertical format, with each field on a separate row (see fig. 8.2). The last field of one record is followed by the first field of the next.

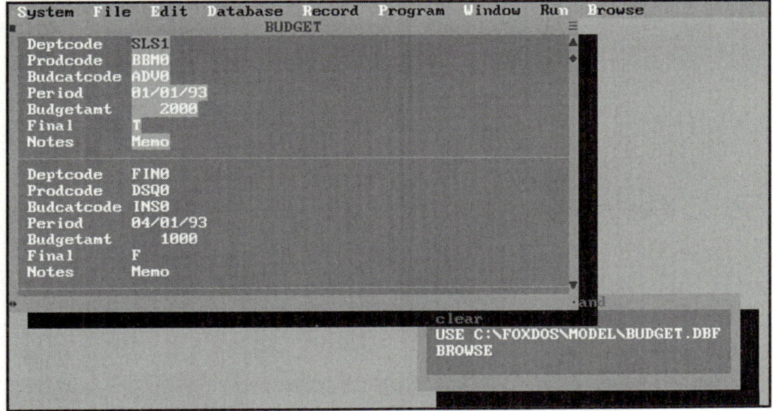

FIG. 8.2

Viewing records in Change/Edit format.

To switch the display format from Browse to Edit, select Change from the Browse menu. When you activate the menu the next time, you see that the Change option is replaced by Browse. This menu option toggles between Browse and Change, enabling you to switch from one format to the other. From the Command window, you can issue either the CHANGE or the EDIT command to use the vertical format; these commands are identical.

Splitting a Browse Window

As you can see, both of Browse's display formats are useful at different times. You can use both of them together, however, by splitting the Browse window into two partitions.

To split a Browse window, you use the *splitter control,* which is located in the lower-left corner of the Browse window. Activate the splitter with a mouse by dragging the splitter control to the right. From the keyboard, select Resize Partitions from the Browse menu and use the right-arrow key to move the splitter to the right. Moving the splitter changes the relative sizes of the two partitions in the window. As you move the splitter to the right, the middle bar (which is the left border of the right partition) moves with the splitter. When the partitions are sized the way you want them, release the mouse button or press Enter. Figure 8.3 shows a split Browse window.

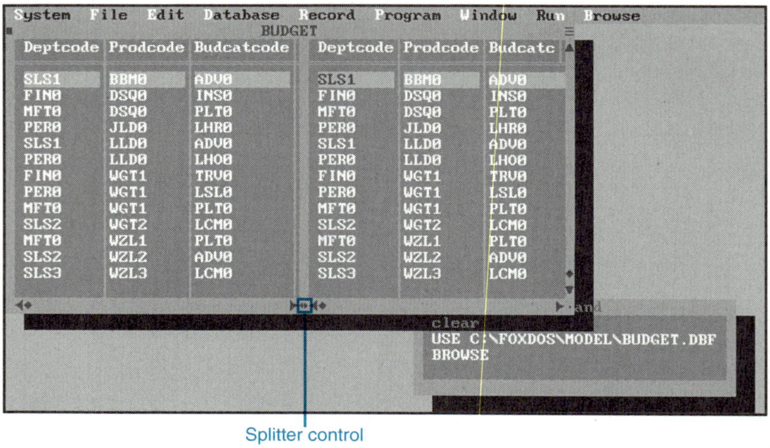

FIG. 8.3

A Browse window split into two partitions.

Splitter control

After you first split the window, both partitions have the same format (Browse or Edit), and the right partition is active. When you toggle the display format, the change affects only the currently active partition. Thus you can have one partition that uses the Browse format and another that uses the Edit format, as shown in figure 8.4.

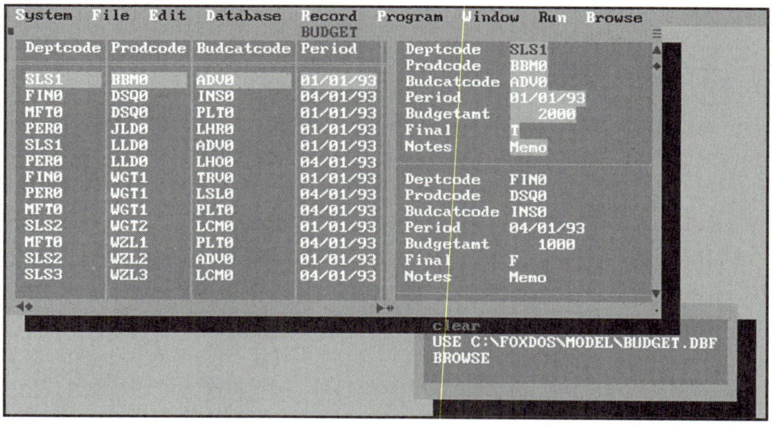

FIG. 8.4

A split Browse window with a different format for each partition.

You switch from one partition to the other by clicking a field (not a field name) in the other partition, by selecting Change Partition from the Browse menu, or by using the menu option's control key shortcut, Ctrl+H.

Change the format of one of the partitions now so that one side uses Browse and the other uses Edit. Then activate the side currently in Browse mode. As you move the cursor from one record to another, notice that the highlight in the other partition moves in unison because the partitions are *linked*. Both parts of the window show the current record.

Unlink the partitions by selecting Unlink Partitions from the Browse menu. You can now scroll each partition independently of the other partition. However, a table has only one record pointer. The current record is always highlighted in the active partition. Unlinking the partitions just tells FoxPro not to update the inactive side of the window to display a different set of records. When you activate the other partition, the window is refreshed, and the current record is highlighted.

Although each partition may display a different set of records, a change in a field's position on one side also is reflected on the other. In fact, the entire process of moving the field is shown in both partitions.

Editing Memo Fields

If you browse the Budget table, you see the Notes Memo field. As you learned in Chapter 3, Memo fields are stored in a separate file that has the same name as the table, but a different extension (.FPT). Each record in the table contains a reference that enables FoxPro to find the data for that record in the memo file. The Browse window displays a placeholder for each Memo field. "Memo" (note the capital *M*) indicates that the Memo field contains an entry; "memo" tells you that the Memo field is currently empty.

Memo fields are displayed and edited in a window separate from the Browse window. To open a Memo field in an editing window, you either move the cursor to the field and press Ctrl+PgDn, or you double-click the placeholder. If the table has more than one Memo field, you can open each in its own editing window. As you move through the records in the table, the memo editing windows are updated to show the contents of the memos for that record.

You can size and position memo editing windows, like other windows, however you prefer, as shown in figure 8.5. If you select Preferences from the Edit menu while a memo editing window is active, you see that you can set certain display options for the window, such as the text justification and tab size.

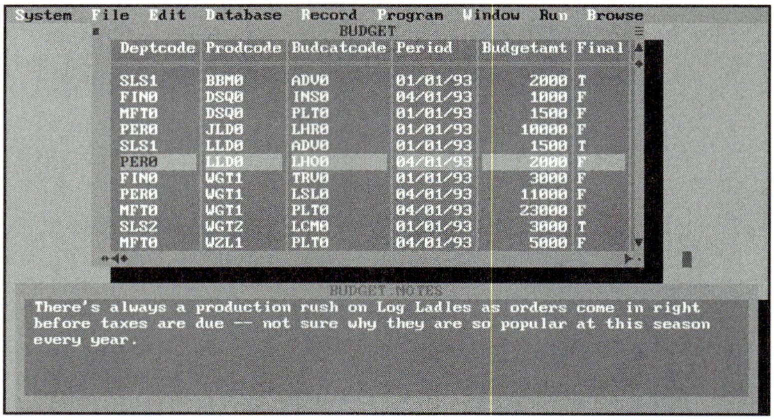

FIG. 8.5

The Budget.Notes field opened in a memo editing window.

When you close editing windows, or when FoxPro closes them because you exited the Browse window, FoxPro saves each window's size, position, and other characteristics in a special file. You learn how to restore these attributes in the next section of this chapter.

Saving a Browse Window's Look in a Preference

As easy as rearranging the appearance of a Browse window is, you still don't want to have to perform this step every time you browse a table. Fortunately, FoxPro has two methods for restoring the look of a Browse session. Both methods use a special FoxPro table known as the *Resource file.*

Using BROWSE LAST and BROWSE PREFERENCE

Every time you exit a Browse window, FoxPro saves in a Resource file certain information about the status of the Browse window and any memo editing windows that were open at the time. By default, the name of this file is FOXUSER.DBF. If FoxPro cannot find the Resource file, it creates the file in the current working directory.

After you select Browse from either the Database menu or the View window, BROWSE LAST appears in the Command window, and the command is executed. LAST indicates that you want to use the same Browse settings you used the last time the currently selected table was browsed. After you exit the Browse window, the Resource file is updated with the current settings.

To have more than one view of the table, or if more than one person uses the table and each user wants a different look, you can create a *preference* in which to store the Browse settings as a separate record in the Resource file. From the Command window, type a command that uses the following syntax:

```
BROWSE PREFERENCE <preference name>
```

Substitute the name of the preference for <preference name>, as in BROWSE PREFERENCE Custpref1. A preference name can consist of up to 24 characters.

If the preference does not exist yet, FoxPro creates the preference record. Adjust the Browse window to look the way you want; then close the window, using any of the available methods *except* Ctrl+Q. The preference is stored in the Resource file. When you tell FoxPro to use the Custpref1 preference, by again typing `BROWSE PREFERENCE Custpref1`, FoxPro restores the Browse window to the way this window looked when you last created or made changes to this preference.

Users of FoxPro 2.0 should note that FoxPro 2.5 stores the size of a *zoomed* Browse window in the Resource file. In FoxPro 2.0, the size and shape of a Browse window are saved in the Resource file only if you sized the window either by using its size control or by selecting Size (or pressing its hot key, Ctrl+F8) from the Window menu.

FoxPro also creates a separate preference record for each memo editing window. These preference records are updated whenever you open the Memo fields or when you edit the window's preferences by using the Preferences option of the Edit menu.

However, the attributes of memo editing windows are not stored along with preferences you create with the PREFERENCE keyword. These preferences apply to the Browse window only; the memo windows' attributes are the same as they were when the memo windows were last closed.

Changing Preferences in the Resource File

Keep in mind that Resource file is simply a FoxPro table that has a particular structure. You can view and edit the Resource file just as you can any other FoxPro table. To view the contents of the Resource file, you first close the file by unchecking the Resource check box in the View window's On/Off panel or by typing `SET RESOURCE` the Command window.

After the file is closed, you can open the Resource file just as you can open other tables. Try opening the file now.

NOTE

FoxPro has several ways to tell you the name of the Resource file in use. You can use the About FoxPro option on the System menu or the `Files` button in the View window. You also can type the following command in the Command window:

```
WAIT WINDOW SYS(2005)
```

The full path name of the Resource file then appears in the upper-right corner of the screen. Note the name of the file, then press any key to clear the message window. You can have FoxPro find and open the Resource file for you by simply entering `USE SYS(2005)` in the Command window. Refer to Chapter 16 for more information on the Resource file.

Figure 8.6 shows the contents of a typical Resource file. The Type field indicates the version of FoxPro that created the preference. Preferences created with versions of FoxPro previous to 2.0 have PREF in the Type field, and later versions have PREF2.0 (FoxPro 2.0), PREF2.5 (FoxPro 2.5 for DOS), or PREFW (FoxPro 2.5 for Windows).

The Resource file is discussed in greater depth in Chapter 16. There you learn that you can USE a Resource file with the AGAIN keyword while the file is active. As a rule, however, editing the active Resource file isn't a good idea.

FoxPro uses the Id field of the Resource file to distinguish among the different kinds of preferences that you can create. Browse window preferences contain WINDBROW in the Id field and either the table alias or the name of a user-created preference in the Name field. Memo editing window preferences contain WINDMEMO in the Id field, and the name of the Memo field (including its table alias) in the Name field.

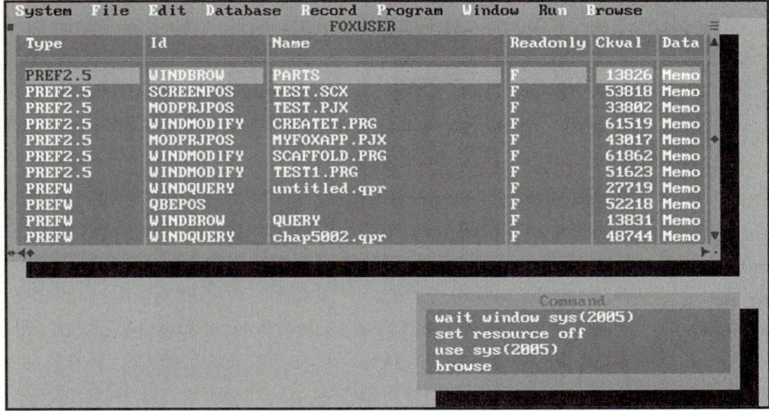

FIG. 8.6

Browsing the FoxPro Resource file.

The primary reason for examining the Resource file is to edit the Readonly field. This logical field usually is set to False (F), which indicates that the current settings for this preference may be updated at any time. After you create a preference and make all the adjustments you need, you can prevent accidentally overwriting the new preference by changing the Readonly value from False to True (T) by typing `T` in the field.

NOTE

There is one other reason for learning how to modify the Resource file's Browse preference records: you have no way to use and make changes to an existing preference and then create a preference by saving the existing preference with a new name. (You cannot use LAST and PREFERENCE together in a single BROWSE command.)

To create small variations of the basic preference, you can copy the preference in the Resource file by following these steps:

1. Browse the Resource file and highlight a basic preference.
2. Activate the Command window.
3. Create memory variables that contain the current contents of this record by typing `SCATTER MEMVAR MEMO` in the Command window.
4. Create a new record by typing the command `APPEND BLANK`.

continues

5. Move the data from the memory variables into the record's fields by typing `GATHER MEMVAR MEMO`.

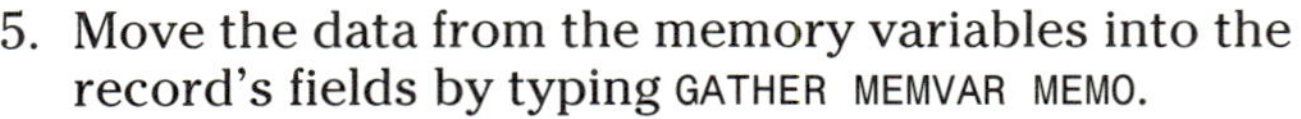

   You have now created a copy of the basic preference.

6. Create additional copies by using APPEND BLANK and GATHER MEMVAR MEMO for each one.

7. Browse the Resource file again and enter a unique preference name in the Name field for each new preference. You now can refer to each new preference by name, and you can use and modify all preferences separately.

8. Close the table and then reactivate it by typing the command `SET RESOURCE ON`.

You now have multiple, identical preferences that you can modify to fit your needs by browsing the table, using the name of each preference, modifying the table's appearance, and then closing the Browse window.

Creating a Subset of Records in Browse

A database can store a huge amount of information; however, a file cabinet can do the same. What makes a computerized database a better storage medium is the capability of creating a subset of the data. This subset can be based on any combination of criteria.

If you have a company-wide personnel file, you can easily tell FoxPro to show you only married people in San Francisco with two or more children. Try this sorting job with a file cabinet full of forms arranged in alphabetical order by last name!

You can restrict the table to certain records by using the SET FILTER TO command, but that filter affects *all* operations you perform on the table until you turn off the filter. Browse's filtering options remain in effect only as long as the Browse window is active.

BROWSE has two options, FOR and KEY, that enable you to restrict the records that you display. To use these options, you must activate the Browse window from the Command window.

BROWSE KEY uses an active index file to find quickly the first record and the last record that satisfy the filter expression. You can use a single value or a range of values.

You can use BROWSE KEY to display only records in the Budget table that have SLS1 in the Deptcode field, for example, by typing the following lines in the Command window:

```
USE Budget AGAIN IN 0 ALIAS Budget
SELECT Budget
SET ORDER TO TAG Deptcode
BROWSE KEY "SLS1"
```

Now modify the command to include a range of values, as in the following example:

```
BROWSE KEY "SLS1", "SLS3"
```

The most important things to remember about KEY are that the table must be indexed on the field for which you are specifying a value or values, and that this index must be the current master index. If you are not getting the results you expected, use the Setup panel of the View window to check the table's index settings. Refer to Chapters 3 and 4 for more information on indexes.

BROWSE FOR is more general in scope and doesn't require an active index, although FoxPro's Rushmore technology uses one or more of them, if available, to optimize a search. (Chapter 7, "Querying with SQL and Searching with Rushmore," covers Rushmore in depth.)

BROWSE FOR enables you to specify any number of criteria that a record must satisfy to be included in the subset. The FOR condition is specified in the same manner as the FOR clause in the LIST command. FOR is a logical expression, which is evaluated as True or False for each record in the table.

You can display the data for department SLS1 by typing the following lines in the Command window:

```
SELECT Budget
BROWSE FOR Deptcode = "SLS1"
```

The Browse window shows only the data for department SLS1.

You can limit the subset even further. Activate the Command window and edit the BROWSE command to match the following line:

```
BROWSE FOR Deptcode = "SLS1" AND Budgetamt > 1500
```

Note that the subset is reduced further by adding another filter criterion. If no records in the table satisfy the FOR expression, an empty Browse window appears.

Although the case of a command is not significant, the case of the filter expression *is* significant. That is, BROWSE KEY "SLS1" is equivalent to browse key "SLS1", but *not* equivalent to browse key "sls1".

When working with character data, such as first and last names, however, you usually don't care about the case of the entries. To see the data for everyone whose last name is Jones, you don't want to exclude a record because the operator typed JONES. You can tell FoxPro to ignore the case of the data in a BROWSE FOR (*not* in a BROWSE KEY) command by converting the characters to a particular case for the purpose of performing the comparison to the filter expression. So, to ensure that you see all the Jones entries, you can use the UPPER( ) and LOWER( ) functions, like this:

```
BROWSE FOR UPPER(Deptcode) = "SLS1"
```

or

```
BROWSE FOR LOWER(Deptcode) = "sls1"
```

As FoxPro tests each record, the program converts the field contents to the specified case before comparing the field to the match criterion. This conversion does *not* change the table's data in any way. The conversion is done entirely in memory.

This technique works only with BROWSE FOR. BROWSE KEY uses an index, which you cannot change "on the fly" in this manner. If you know beforehand that you don't want the case to be significant, you should use the UPPER( ) or LOWER( ) function as part of the expression used to create the index, as in the following example:

```
INDEX ON LOWER(Deptcode) TAG Deptcode
```

Now, when you want to search the table or view only certain records, you must remember to use lowercase letters in the search or filter expression, because the index is composed of all lowercase letters:

```
BROWSE KEY "sls1", "sls3"
```

Again, if you are getting unexpected results, such as an empty Browse window when you know that some matching records should exist, use the View window to verify that the master index is the correct index and that the index expression matches the filter expression.

NOTE Remember from Chapter 7 that Rushmore uses an index only if the index expression *exactly* matches your search expression. In the preceding example, the index expression is LOWER(Deptcode). Therefore, although

```
BROWSE FOR UPPER(Deptcode) = "SLS1"
```

finds the same records as

```
BROWSE FOR LOWER(Deptcode) = "sls1"
```

only the second command enables Rushmore to use the index. With a large table, the search times for these otherwise identical commands may be vastly different.

Taking Control with FIELDS

BROWSE has a FIELDS clause that enables you to specify exactly the fields with which you want to work, how you want the data to appear, and what kind of entries are allowed in each field.

The FIELDS clause always is followed by a field name list, which contains the name of each field you want displayed on-screen. The field names must be separated by commas, as in the following example:

```
BROWSE ;
   FIELDS Prodcode   :H="Product", ;
          Budcatcode :P="AAA9" ;
   FOR Deptcode = "SLS1"
```

Note that the last field name is not followed by a comma, even though that name is not the end of the command. Also, you don't need to include a space between field names, but spacing makes the command easier to read.

To each field in the list, you can attach one or more options that control the field's display format, column width, column heading, and range of acceptable entries. You also can use options that prevent any changes to the field or that accept changes only under certain conditions.

The multitude of FIELDS options—and the ways in which you can combine these options—may seem a little bewildering. Table 8.1 lists each of the options along with the required syntax and an example of how each is used. You might want to refer back to this table as each option is discussed in this chapter.

Table 8.1 The FIELDS Clause Options

Option	Name	Syntax	Example
:P	Picture	:P=<expC>	:P="!!!!"
:H	Heading	:H=<expC>	:H="Department"
:B	Boundaries	:B=<exp>,<exp>[:F]	:B=0,10000
:R	ReadOnly	:R	:R
:<n>	Column Width	:<n>	:10
:V	Valid	:V=<exp>[:F][:E=<exp>]	:V=!EMPTY(Deptcode)
:W	When	:W=<expL>	:W=!EMPTY(Deptcode)

Using :P (The Picture Option)

The :P option enables you to create an editing template for the field. You might want the field to contain only uppercase characters, for example, regardless of the case in which the characters are typed. In a telephone number, you might want to enclose the area code in parentheses without having to type them. To save disk space, you might choose not to store the parentheses in the field, using them only for display purposes. These choices are but a few of the ways in which you can control the display and editing format of a field.

FoxPro has two kinds of field formatting codes. *Function codes* act on all characters in the field and are preceded by the at symbol (@). *Picture template codes* act on a single character.

You can use all the picture and function codes available in the @ SAY/GET command by using the :P option. Table 8.2 is a complete list of available picture template codes, and table 8.3 lists the function codes. Note that these codes affect only the display, not the contents, of the data.

Table 8.2 BROWSE Picture Template Codes

Code	Description
A	Allows letters only.
L	Allows True (T or Y) or False (F or N) only; can be entered in upper- or lowercase.
N	Allows letters and digits only.

Code	Description
X	Allows any character to be entered.
Y	Allows only True (Y or y) or False (N or n). Lowercase entries are converted to uppercase (Y or N).
9	If the data is of character type, only digits are allowed. If the data is numeric, digits and signs are allowed.
#	Allows digits, blanks, and signs.
!	Converts lowercase letters to uppercase letters.
$	Displays the current currency symbol. By default, the placement of the symbol is immediately before or after the field, depending on the placement required by the particular symbol. However, you can change the currency symbol and its placement (SET CURRENCY), the separator character (SET SEPARATOR), and the decimal character (SET POINT).
*	Shows asterisks in front of a number.
.	Shows a decimal point.
,	Shows a comma.

Table 8.3 BROWSE Function Codes

Code	Description
A	Allows letters only.
B	Left-justifies numbers.
C	Displays a CR (credit symbol) after a positive number. In a Browse, this code can be used only with calculated fields, in the picture template of the TRANSFORM( ) function. See the text for more information.
D	Uses the current SET DATE format (for example, BRITISH, GERMAN, and so on) to edit dates.
E	Edits dates using the European (BRITISH) date format.
I	Centers text in the field.
J	Right-justifies text in the field.
K	Selects the field contents on entry into the field. The effect is the same as pressing Ctrl+A on entering the field. If you type any character, the field's contents are deleted and replaced by the typed character.

continues

Table 8.3 Continued

Code	Description
L	Displays leading zeros rather than spaces in numeric values.
M <list>	Specifies multiple preset choices. <list> is a comma-delimited collection of items. Press the space bar to cycle through the list, or type the first letter of the first word in an item. If more than one item begins with the same letter, typing the letter repeatedly cycles through the items that begin with that letter. Note that M must be separated from <list> by at least one space.
R	When used with formatting characters, shows but does not store the extra characters in the field. You can use this code only with character data. The R must be separated from the first formatting character by exactly one space. Any additional spaces are considered part of the display format.
S<n>	Limits the display width to <n> characters, where <n> is a positive integer. After the end of the displayed field is reached, the characters scroll to the left to enable you to enter or display the remaining characters, up to the defined length of the field. You can use this code only with character data. Note that there is no space between S and <n>.
T	Trims leading and trailing blanks.
X	Displays a DR (debit symbol) after a negative number. In a Browse, this code can only be used with calculated fields, in the picture template of the TRANSFORM( ) function. See the text for more information.
Z	If the value of a numeric field is 0, displays the field as blanks.
(	Encloses negative numbers in parentheses. In a Browse, this code can only be used with calculated fields, in the picture template of the TRANSFORM( ) function. See the text for more information.
!	Converts letters to uppercase.
^	Displays numbers, using scientific notation.
$	Displays numbers in the current currency format. The currency symbol appears before or after the field value, depending on the current setting of SET CURRENCY. Because the currency symbol is not stored in the field, the column's display width should be at least 1 greater than the width of the field.

The C, X, and (function codes are designed to work exclusively with display commands, such as @ SAY and ??, rather than with editing commands, such as @ GET and BROWSE. Although you cannot apply these function codes to actual fields in a Browse, you can use them to display calculated fields by including them in the picture template of FoxPro's TRANSFORM( ) function, as follows:

```
* Display Accounts Payable balances (usually stored as negative
* numbers) as positive numbers. Display DR after debit balances.
BROWSE FIELDS Balance = TRANSFORM(Balance * -1, "@X 9,999,999.99") :15
```

Part of the trick to getting this to work is understanding that you must leave room for the formatting characters. In the preceding example, the Balance field is N(10,2). The calculated field is forced to a width of 15 to account for the five extra formatting characters (the two commas, the space after the amount, and the letters DB).

Some of the examples shown in table 8.4 contain characters other than those that actively participate in the picture, such as the parentheses in (999) 999-9999. These characters are *formatting characters.* Don't try to type these characters because FoxPro automatically skips over them. Formatting characters are stored along with an entry, so the field must be wide enough to hold both the formatting characters and the data. If you don't want to store the extra characters, use the @R function clause, as shown in table 8.4.

Table 8.4 Some Examples of Using Picture Clauses in BROWSE

Picture/Function	Description
:P="@!"	Converts any and all lowercase letters to uppercase letters.
:P="AAA999"	In an invoice number field, requires that the first three characters be alphabetic and that the last three characters be digits.
:P="@! AAA999"	Same as preceding example, but converts the alphabetic characters to uppercase.
:P="(999) 999-9999"	In a North American telephone number field, accepts only digits and formats the display for easy viewing.
:P="@R (999) 999-9999"	For the same telephone number field, tells FoxPro not to store the formatting characters along with the data. Because the extra characters are not being stored, the field need be only 10 characters long.
:P="999,999.99"	In an invoice amount field, separates the thousands, hundreds, and cents.

The last example shown (:P="999,999.99") works fine with existing data, because numbers are displayed right-justified in the field. Data entry always starts at the left of the field, however, even when the field is numeric. FoxPro inserts a comma after you type the third digit, even though the number you are entering may be less than 1,000. After you press Enter, the number is right-justified, and the commas (if any) appear in the correct positions.

You can combine some functions within a single picture clause as long as they don't conflict with each other. "@A!" is a permissible combination, for example, but "@IJ" is not, because you can't have data both centered and right-justified at the same time.

Using :H (The Column Heading Option)

By default, FoxPro uses the field name as the column heading. Because they are limited to 10 characters, field names often don't tell you what kind of information the fields are supposed to contain. A Social Security number field, for example, may have SSNO as a name. You can replace the default column heading of Ssno with Soc. Sec. #, which is easier to read, by using this command:

```
BROWSE FIELDS SSNO :H="Soc. Sec. #"
```

Of course, you must balance the desire to use descriptive headings with the need to not waste a great deal of screen space, because the column width is adjusted if the specified heading is longer than the field size. In the case of a Social Security number, the field must be at least nine characters long (if you choose not to store the dashes), so changing the field name to Soc. Sec. # increases the length of the column by two at most.

BROWSE has a separate WIDTH clause (not to be confused with the :W FIELDS option), which is used to limit the displayed width of all fields in the Browse window. FoxPro does not override the WIDTH clause to display a column heading that is longer than the specified value. The program does override WIDTH, however, if you attach the :<n> option to the field.

Using :B (The Boundaries Option)

The :B option enables you to specify a range of acceptable entries for the field. This option works the same way :V does but is much more limited in scope. You cannot have a user-defined function, for example, as part of a boundary condition.

FoxPro lets you type any value in the field and then checks the entry against the specified range. If the entry doesn't fall within the range, the FoxPro message `"Invalid input"` appears and you are forced to change the entry before you can move to the next field.

The data type of the boundaries must be the same as the data type of the field. Therefore, if you're entering data in a field of date type, be sure that you enclose all literal boundary expressions within curly braces ({}), the delimiters for dates in FoxPro.

By default, the boundary conditions are checked only if you changed the contents of the field. If you previously typed data in the field, FoxPro doesn't force you to change this data. To force existing data to be checked for validity, include the :F (force) option. Note that the cursor must enter into the field for the :F option to take effect.

Using :R (The ReadOnly Option)

You can prevent changes to a field by using :R, which makes the field temporarily a Readonly field. The field is shown on-screen as usual, but you cannot edit the field, and FoxPro beeps at you if you try to make a change.

The :R option is used most often within a FoxPro program but also is useful when you work from the Command window. If you're setting up a Browse window for others to use, you might want to ensure that someone typing from a form doesn't inadvertently change certain information without realizing that the cursor is in the wrong field.

Using :<n> (The Column Width Option)

FoxPro uses either the field's length or the length of the column heading, whichever is greater, as the default column width. To use a different width, include the :<n> option, replacing <n> with the desired size of the column.

The sample Budget table, for example, contains the Budcatcode field. The field's length is only four, but its field name is 10 characters. To reduce the column width from 10 to four, you can resize the column from the Browse window, as previously discussed, or you can use the :<n> option, as in the following example:

```
BROWSE FIELDS Deptcode, Prodcode, Budcatcode :4
```

Making this change also truncates the column heading to BUDC, which may not be acceptable. As with the column heading option, you have to balance the need to conserve screen space with the need to use descriptive column headings.

Using :V (The Valid Option)

More than any other factor, the capability of validating entries is responsible for the adoption of BROWSE as a data-entry vehicle by people who program in the Xbase language. The BROWSE command in dBASE III PLUS and FoxBASE+ did not have this feature and generally was used only for interactive data entry and simple record displays.

The validation expression is any legal FoxPro expression that evaluates to True (.T.), False (.F.), or 0. This expression can be a simple test for whether the field was left blank, or it can be a call to a *user-defined function* (UDF) that may perform hundreds of operations before returning to the Browse window.

If the expression is True, the cursor moves to the next field. If the expression is False, the cursor remains in the field, and an error message is displayed. If the expression evaluates to 0, the cursor remains in the field, but no error message appears.

The following subsections provide a few examples.

Preventing Blank Entries

In the sample application, several of the tables have the Deptcode field in common. The entries in this field enable you to link the tables. If the Deptcode field were allowed to be blank, FoxPro could not create the linkage.

Using a validation clause, you can prevent users from blanking out the Deptcode entries. Use a validation clause similar to one of the following:

```
BROWSE FIELDS Deptcode :V=!EMPTY(Deptcode)

BROWSE FIELDS Deptcode :V=(Deptcode != SPACE(LEN(Deptcode)))

BROWSE FIELDS Deptcode :V=(Deptcode != "    ")
```

All three of these commands do the same thing and differ only in the way they express the fact that Deptcode must not be blank. Of the three, the first command is both the easiest to read and the most general way of expressing the condition, because the EMPTY( ) function works on all categories of data. The validation clause in the second command is preferable to the third because it remains effective if you change the width of the Deptcode field.

NOTE The third command's validation clause is an example of a *hard-coded* value (it only works if Deptcode is four characters wide). Avoid using hard-coded values whenever possible. If you include this BROWSE command in a program and then change the width of the Deptcode field, you must remember to change this validation clause. The first and second commands adjust to the new field length automatically because they let FoxPro determine the current width of the field.

Attaching a Custom Error Message

As is the case with :B, the boundaries option, an entry that doesn't satisfy the validation expression causes an `"Invalid input"` message to appear. Because this message isn't very informative, you can attach a custom error message to the :V option. Use :E=<character expression>, replacing <character expression> with the text of the error message to appear, as in the following example:

```
BROWSE FIELDS Deptcode :V=!EMPTY(Deptcode) ;
                       :E="Department may not be blank!"
```

Now, when the field is left blank, the user understands the problem and—after reading the message and pressing a key to remove the message window—knows how to make the correction.

Forcing Evaluation of Validation Expressions

You can force the validation expression to be evaluated, whether or not the data is changed, by including :F as part of the option. The validation is forced, however, only if the field is entered.

Ensuring the Entry of Valid Codes

An in-depth discussion of commands and functions is beyond the scope of this chapter, but seeing an example of what you can do with a user-defined function attached to a BROWSE field validation option may whet your appetite.

What if, rather than leaving the Deptcode field blank, you typed SSL1 rather than SLS1? Making this kind of error is as bad as leaving the field blank, because FoxPro cannot find the matching records in the other tables.

What you really want to do is ensure that a *valid* department code is entered. All the valid department codes are contained in the Dept table. The following paragraphs give you a look at a user-defined function that ensures that only valid entries are made in the Deptcode field.

Activate the Command window and type the following command:

```
MODIFY COMMAND VAL_DEPT.PRG
```

Now, type the following lines in the FoxPro editor window, just as they appear here:

```
* FUNCTION val_dept
* This UDF ensures that only valid department
* codes are entered in the Deptcode field of any table.
PARAMETERS mdeptcode
RETURN SEEK(mdeptcode, "Dept")
```

Save the program by clicking the window's close box, by selecting Save from the File menu, or by pressing Ctrl+W.

This simple UDF searches the Dept table for a record that has the same department code as the one you entered. This job is performed by FoxPro's SEEK( ) function, which returns True if a match is found and False if one is not found. The communication between BROWSE and the UDF is handled by the PARAMETERS command, which accepts information from BROWSE, and RETURN, which passes information back to BROWSE. In this case, the success or failure of the SEEK( ) function is returned.

To use the UDF in a Browse window, you first must open both the Dept and Budget tables. Then activate the Command window and type the following lines:

```
SET ORDER TO TAG Deptcode IN Dept
SELECT Budget
BROWSE ;
   FIELDS Deptcode :V=VAL_DEPT(Deptcode) ;
                   :E="No such Department Code!", ;
          Prodcode, ;
          Budcatcode
```

TIP

Remember that you can type a single command on more than one line by placing a semicolon at the end of any line that should be continued on the next line. Breaking up the command in this fashion makes reading the command easier and enables you to find errors more easily. This formatting style is used in the remainder of this chapter.

When an invalid entry is made in the Deptcode field, you should see the custom error message displayed in the upper-right corner of the screen. Press any key to clear the message. FoxPro does not let you exit the field until you either enter a valid code or press Esc to cancel the entry and close the Browse window.

Note that, in the preceding example of using a UDF in the BROWSE :V clause, you could accomplish the same validation by simply using:

```
:V=SEEK(Deptcode, "Dept")
```

However, by using a UDF, you make it easier to add extra features to your validation requirements. For example, you may want to display the valid Department codes in a popup window or in a separate Browse window. This method requires that you know a little bit about programming in FoxPro. More advanced validation techniques, such as the preceding technique, are covered in Parts III and IV of this book.

Using :W (The When Option)

The :W option works much like :V. Both options are followed by an expression that triggers an action, and the expression can include a call to a user-defined function. The :W expression, however, is evaluated *before* the field is entered rather than as you exit it.

If the expression evaluates to False (.F.), the cursor skips over the field and moves to the next one. If every field has a :W expression that evaluates to False, the cursor appears in the first field, but you cannot enter or change anything.

The :W option enables you to add some intelligent behavior to the Browse window. When entering a customer's address, for example, skipping the second address line if the first was left blank makes sense. The following example shows how you can use the :W option to enforce that rule:

```
USE Address AGAIN IN 0
SELECT Address
BROWSE ;
   FIELDS Addrcode, ;
          President, ;
          Company, ;
          Address1, ;
          Address2 :W= !EMPTY(Address1), ;
          City, ;
          State, ;
          Zip, ;
          Phone
```

If you leave the Address1 field blank, the cursor skips to the City field, bypassing the Address2 field.

As is the case with :V, :W can include a UDF as part or all of the expression. You might use a UDF to present the available choices in a popup window and enable the user to select one. You then can stuff the choice into the field. This technique also requires some understanding of programming and is covered in Part IV of this book.

Using Calculated Fields

FoxPro can display the result of a calculation as if this result were a field in the table. You also can use this feature to verify the accuracy of entries or to mark certain records based on the value of one or more fields.

Suppose that you are entering invoices into the Sales table, working from handwritten order forms. The table has a Quantity field to hold the number of units ordered and a Price field to hold the price per unit.

Because you can calculate the total charge for the item by multiplying Quantity times Price, you don't need to store the total as a separate field in the table. The capability of comparing the calculated total to the total that the salesperson entered on the form, however, can be useful.

To create a calculated field, you must assign it a field name. For the invoice example, you can use Total:

```
BROWSE ;
   FIELDS Invoice, ;
          Prodcode, ;
          Datesold, ;
          Quantity, ;
          Price, ;
          Total = Quantity * Price, ;
          Salesman, ;
          Custcode
```

Figure 8.7 shows the results. When you make an entry into either the Quantity or Price field, the new value of the calculated field Total is displayed.

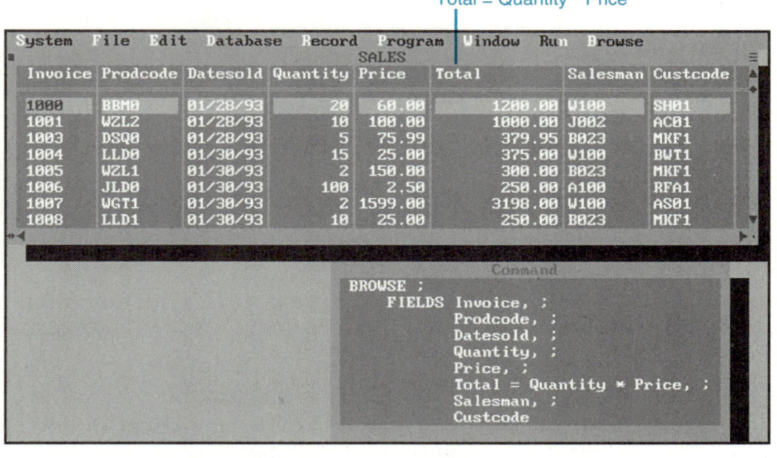

Invoice	Prodcode	Datesold	Quantity	Price	Total	Salesman	Custcode
1000	BBM0	01/28/93	20	60.00	1200.00	W100	SH01
1001	WZL2	01/28/93	10	100.00	1000.00	J002	AC01
1003	DSQ0	01/28/93	5	75.99	379.95	B023	MKF1
1004	LLD0	01/30/93	15	25.00	375.00	W100	BWT1
1005	WZL1	01/30/93	2	150.00	300.00	B023	MKF1
1006	JLD0	01/30/93	100	2.50	250.00	A100	RFA1
1007	WGT1	01/30/93	2	1599.00	3198.00	W100	AS01
1008	LLD1	01/30/93	10	25.00	250.00	B023	MKF1

```
BROWSE ;
   FIELDS Invoice, ;
          Prodcode, ;
          Datesold, ;
          Quantity, ;
          Price, ;
          Total = Quantity * Price, ;
          Salesman, ;
          Custcode
```

FIG. 8.7

Using a calculated field.

You also can use a calculated field to *flag* certain records. Figure 8.8 shows an example of how you can use a calculated field in the Budget table. In this example, the check-mark symbol (√) is used as the flag character, but you can pick any character you prefer. A FoxPro event-handling command (ON KEY LABEL) also is used to trap the keystroke used to mark the record. You learn more about this command and other similar techniques in upcoming chapters.

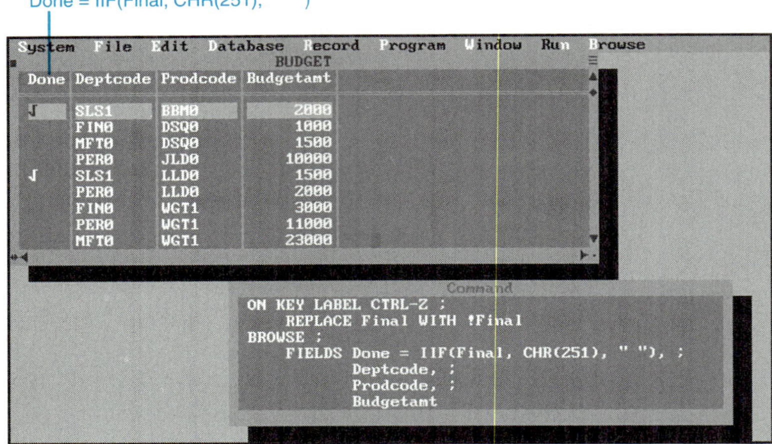

FIG. 8.8

Using a calculated field to flag records in a Browse window.

To set up this calculated field, open the Budget table and type the following lines in the Command window:

```
ON KEY LABEL CTRL+Z REPLACE Final WITH !Final
BROWSE ;
   FIELDS Done = IIF(Final, CHR(251), " "), ;
          Deptcode, ;
          Prodcode, ;
          Budgetamt
```

Final is a logical field, meaning that the field can hold only one of two values, either True or False. Done is a calculated field that gets its value from the current state of Final. If Final is True, a check mark appears in the Done column; otherwise, the field is blank.

Two advanced techniques are used in this example. One technique is the use of FoxPro's IIF( ), or *immediate if,* function. IIF( ) evaluates a condition (is Final True or False?) and returns one value (CHR(251), the check-mark character) if the condition is True, and another value (" ") if the condition is False. Using IIF( ) enables you to incorporate some simple IF...THEN...ELSE logic into a Browse window without using a user-defined function.

The second technique is the use of FoxPro's ON KEY LABEL command. Every time the specified key is pressed, FoxPro executes the specified command. In the preceding example, when the Ctrl+Z key combination is pressed, FoxPro replaces the Final field with the opposite of its current value. Ctrl+Z therefore acts as a toggle. When you move the highlight bar to a different field or record, the contents of the Done field change to reflect the current state of Final.

Part IV of this book explores these kinds of techniques in detail.

Using BROWSE To View Related Tables

FoxPro is a relational database management system. Thus you can link a table to one or more other tables, using a field that each table has in common to create the linkage. The table from which the link, or *relation,* is created is called the *parent* table. Each table related to the parent is called a *child* table.

After you link tables, you can treat them as if they were part of a single table. You can create a single Browse window, for example, that shows fields from each of the related tables. You do so by preceding each of the field names with the alias of the work area in which the table is open. The alias tells FoxPro from which table to take the data. If you don't specify an alias, FoxPro assumes that you're referring to the table in the currently active work area, which is usually the parent.

Using SET RELATION

The following example should help to clarify some of this information about linking tables. Open the Budget and Dept tables. Use the View window to open the tables so that you can use this window to link the tables. By linking Budget to Dept through the common Deptcode field, you can display data from both tables in a single Browse window or in two related Browse windows.

If the View window is not active, make View the active window and select Budget as the parent table. Select the `Relations` push button and notice that Budget then appears in the Relations box beneath the push buttons. The ↪ symbol indicates that a relation is being formed between Budget and another table. To complete the link, select the Dept table by clicking the table name or by highlighting Dept and pressing the space bar.

What happens next depends on whether the index order for Dept is set. If you opened the tables as part of this exercise, the index order probably isn't set. In this case, the Set Index Order dialog appears. Select the Deptcode index, and the Expression Builder appears, with Deptcode as the default expression. Accept this field as the link between the tables, as you accept any other default in FoxPro, and notice that Dept then appears next to the ↳ symbol in the Relations box of the View window, indicating that the two tables are related (see fig. 8.9).

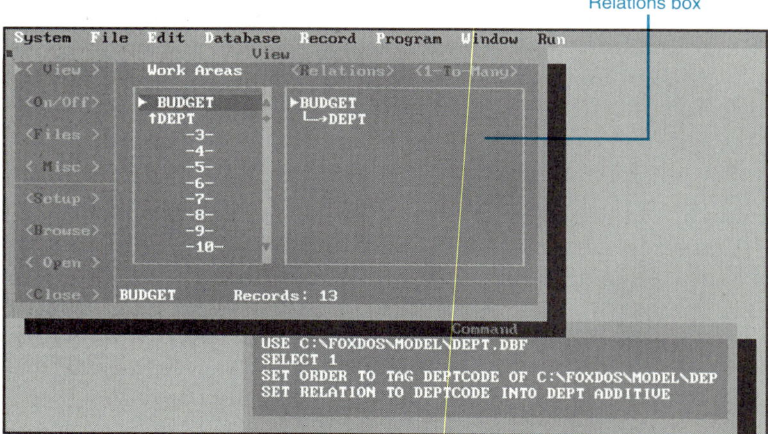

FIG. 8.9

A relation set in the View window.

If you had set the index order for Dept, the Set Index Order dialog would have been bypassed. If the field on which the child table currently is ordered has the same name as a field in the parent, that field automatically becomes the default expression.

Look at the commands FoxPro used to create the relationship. Activate the Command window. You should see entries similar to these:

```
USE C:\FOXPRO25\MODEL\BUDGET.DBF
SELECT 2
USE C:\FOXPRO25\MODEL\DEPT.DBF
SELECT 1
SET ORDER TO TAG DEPTCODE IN DEPT
SET RELATION TO DEPTCODE INTO DEPT ADDITIVE
```

The relation was created by the SET RELATION command, which has the following syntax:

```
SET RELATION TO [<expr1> INTO <expN1> ¦ <expC1>
   [, <expr2> INTO <expN2> ¦ <expC2> ... ]   [ADDITIVE]]
```

<expr1> is an expression that FoxPro evaluates and searches for in the child table. The child must be indexed on an expression that evaluates to the same result, and the index must be the child's master index. Ninety-nine percent of the time, the expression is simply the name of a field that the two tables have in common. However, recall from Chapter 4 that it is the *data,* not the field name, that forms the link.

The SET ORDER command sets the index to the proper tag. <expN1> ¦ <expC1> is the work area or alias of the child, which in this case is Dept. The View window sets relations one at a time, using the optional ADDITIVE keyword to create new relations without breaking existing ones, but you can set more than one in a single SET RELATION command by separating the relations with commas.

Now that you have set the relation, you can find out what this relation enables you to do. Open a separate Browse window and size both windows so that you can see both of them at the same time, as shown in figure 8.10.

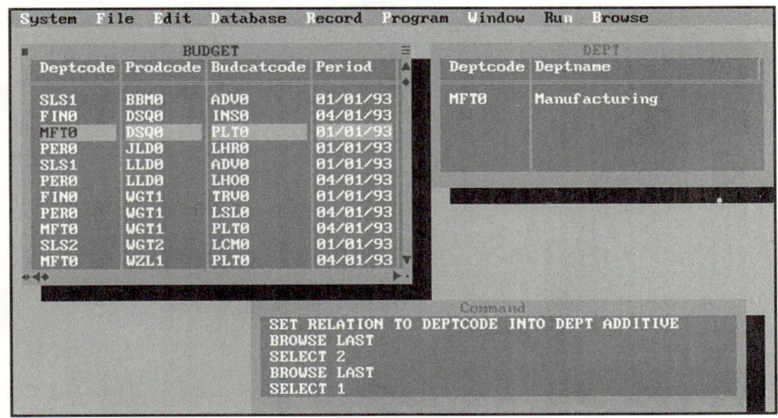

FIG. 8.10

Displaying related Browse windows.

Activate the Budget window and move the highlight bar from one record to another. As you move the record pointer in the parent table, the record pointer in the child table moves to the first record that contains the same value in the field on which they are related—in this case, the Deptcode field. Remember the way FoxPro operates here; this feature is important to an upcoming part of this discussion.

If the child has no record of the same value in the related field, the child's record pointer moves to the end-of-file (EOF) position, and the child's Browse window appears to be empty.

Now create a single Browse window that contains data from both tables. Close both Browse windows, activate the Command window, and type the following lines:

```
SELECT Budget
BROWSE ;
   FIELDS Deptcode, ;
          Dept.Deptname, ;
          Prodcode, ;
          Budgetamt
```

Because Budget is in the selected work area, you do not need to precede its field names with an alias, although you can. However, for FoxPro to execute the command, you must specify that the Deptname field is part of table Dept, because Budget has no such field.

The resulting Browse window, shown in figure 8.11, shows four fields: three from Budget (Deptcode, Prodcode, and Budgetamt) and one from Dept (Deptname).

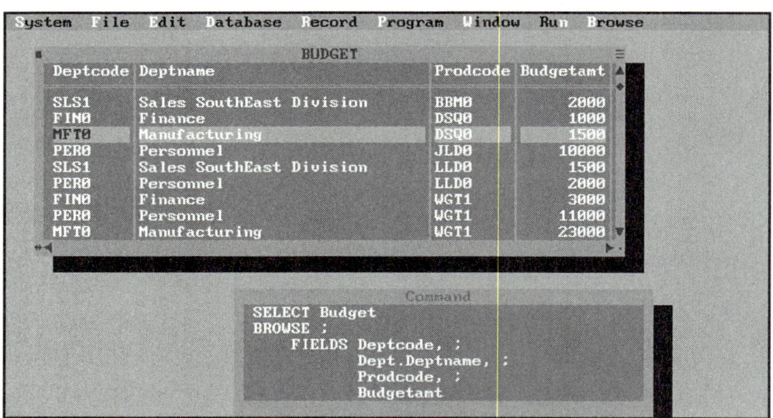

FIG. 8.11

A single Browse window with fields from two related tables.

The name of each department has been pulled from the Dept table and is displayed next to the related department code.

Displaying data from more than one table in a Browse window really has nothing to do with setting relations. FoxPro pulls in the value of the current record in any open table if you tell the program which table you want to access. The difference here is that because you have linked the tables, the record pointer in the child is updated as FoxPro moves through the parent to display the records.

TIP

If the field values pulled from a child table into the Browse window are all the same, the tables probably aren't linked. The relation may not have been created properly, or perhaps the relation was inadvertently broken. Use the View window to verify this situation and, if necessary, to re-create the relation.

Using SET SKIP

The relation that you just created between Budget and Dept is a *many-to-one relationship*. That is, the parent (Budget) can have many records that use a particular department code, but the child (Dept) has only one record for each department code.

A more natural way to think of the data is as a series of *one-to-many relationships*. A report showing sales by customer code, for example, is more informative than a listing in simple invoice number order. To create a report by customer, you need the capability to relate each unique customer code in the Customer table to those invoices in the Sales table that have that customer code.

FoxPro gives you this capability with the SET SKIP command, which you learn about in Chapter 4. Using SET SKIP, you can create Browse windows and reports that show a unique parent table value, followed by any number of related child table records, for each record in the parent table.

This section investigates another example of related tables from the Omnipresent Widget database and extends the way you can manipulate the relation in a Browse. Create the Customer and Sales tables in your \MODEL directory and add the sample records. Appendix H lists the structures and sample data for these exercises. (The source disk that accompanies this book also contains these tables.)

Activate the View window and open the Customer and Sales tables. Select and then link Customer to Sales on the Custcode field. (As with any relation, the child must be indexed on the field that relates the two tables. If necessary, index Sales on the Custcode field before trying to link the tables.)

Notice that the `1-To-Many` push button is enabled. When selected, the 1-To-Many dialog appears. The list on the left shows the alias names of any child tables. In this case, only one exists: Sales. To create the one-to-many relationship, simply move Sales from the Child Aliases list to the Selected Aliases list on the right by selecting the `All` button. Then confirm the choices to exit the dialog.

The square box to the right of Customer indicates that the table is a parent involved in a one-to-many relationship with one or more of this table's children.

Close the View window and activate the Command window. The last line should be SET SKIP TO SALES. SET SKIP is the FoxPro command that transforms a many-to-one relationship into a one-to-many relationship. This command tells FoxPro to process your keystrokes in the Browse window as if the child rather than the parent were the controlling table. The record pointer in the parent table moves in sync with the current record in the child rather than vice versa.

Now look at what this feature does for you. To open a Browse window that pulls data from both Customer and Sales, type the following lines in the Command window:

```
BROWSE ;
   FIELDS Customer.Custcode, ;
          Customer.Lastname, ;
          Customer.Firstname, ;
          Sales.Invoice, ;
          Amount = Sales.Quantity * Sales.Price
```

The records now appear as *record blocks* (see fig. 8.12). Each block consists of a single record from the parent and one or more records from the child. If the child has more than one related record, the parent's records are separated from each other by a hash pattern that fills the fields taken from the parent. Whenever the cursor is in a field of the parent table, you can move from one block to the next by pressing Ctrl+down arrow and to the previous one with Ctrl+up arrow.

NOTE

When the cursor is in a field (a Browse column) that belongs to a child table, Ctrl+down arrow and Ctrl+up arrow move the cursor to the next and previous record, respectively, in the *child,* not to the next and previous record in the parent.

If you want these keystrokes to move among record blocks regardless of which field the cursor is in, you can use ON KEY LABEL to instruct FoxPro to call a procedure that does this for you whenever Ctrl+down arrow or Ctrl+up arrow is pressed. Appendix H contains an example of such a procedure, SKIP_IT.PRG.

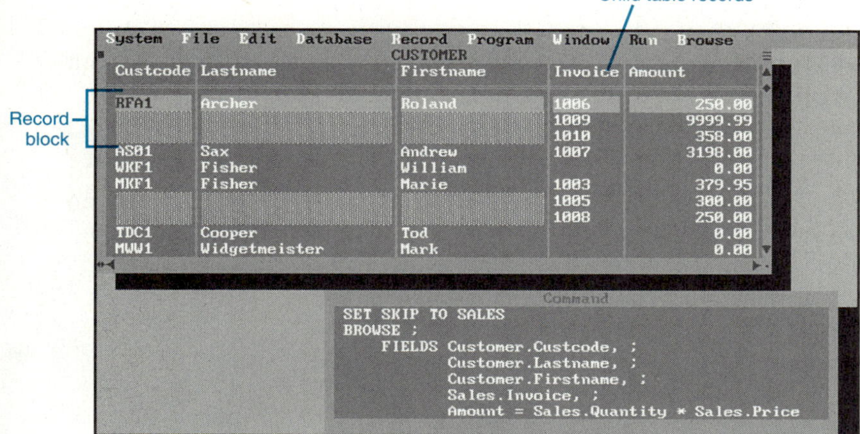

FIG. 8.12

Browsing with a one-to-many relationship.

Breaking Up Relationships

You can break up these happy romances as easily as you created them. Select the parent table (Customer) and type the following line in the Command window:

```
SET RELATION OFF INTO Sales
```

Now activate the View window. Notice that the table names no longer appear in the Relations box. You also can dissolve this relationship from the View window by modifying the relation and then deleting the linking field name from the Expression Builder.

You also can use relations to replace the user-defined function you used in the :V expression of the FIELDS clause earlier in this chapter. Remember that the purpose of the UDF is to ensure that only valid entries were made in the Deptcode field of the Budget table. The UDF used the SEEK( ) function to move the record pointer in the Dept table. If the entry was invalid, the record pointer moved to the end-of-file (EOF) position.

Remember that the child's record pointer also moves to end-of-file position when the child does not contain a record that matches the current record in the parent. You can use this fact to rewrite the Deptcode validation clause in the following way:

```
BROWSE ;
   FIELDS Deptcode :V= !EOF("Dept") ;
                   :E="No such Department Code!", ;
          Prodcode, ;
          Budcatcode
```

Rather than calling a UDF to perform the validation, you can use FoxPro's EOF( ) function to tell whether the record pointer in the child (Dept) is positioned at the end-of-file position. If the pointer is at this position, the entry doesn't exist in the child and therefore must be invalid.

The lesson to learn from this example is that you often have more than one way to perform a task in FoxPro. If you find yourself working too hard, step back from the problem and make sure that you haven't overlooked an easier way to accomplish your objective.

Using Implicit and Explicit Record Locks in a Browse

As you learned in Chapter 3, you can open a table for exclusive or shared use. By default, tables are opened for exclusive use. You open a table for shared use by SETting EXCLUSIVE OFF before opening the table or by using the SHARED keyword with the USE command.

When you browse a table that is in exclusive use, you don't have to worry about record locking; no one else can access the table. When the table is accessible to others on a local area network, however, you must prevent others from changing the data at the same time you are making changes. You do this by locking the record you are changing.

When you browse a table, FoxPro usually handles the record locks for you. As long as you are simply viewing the data, the records in the table are unlocked and available to all users. As soon as you initiate an editing session by typing in a field, however, FoxPro tries to lock the record. If someone else has the record locked, you cannot obtain the record lock until the other user has finished modifying it; otherwise, you obtain the lock, and no one else can modify it until you complete your changes. When you move to another record, FoxPro releases the lock.

This is known as *implicit* record locking, because FoxPro does it for you. When working interactively in FoxPro, this level of protection is usually sufficient. However, under certain circumstances, you might need to lock a record *explicitly* in a Browse.

If any of the clauses you have attached to your BROWSE command result in FoxPro switching to a work area other than the one you are browsing, or if you interactively select a different work area, you lose any implicit record lock that FoxPro has set for you. This is necessary from FoxPro's standpoint, because FoxPro does not "know" whether or not you intend to return to this work area, and cannot leave records locked for indeterminate periods of time.

If you require FoxPro to maintain a lock while you switch to another work area (perhaps to perform some type of data validation), you must explicitly lock the record before leaving the current work area. To do this, you use the LOCK( ) or RLOCK( ) function (they are identical). If you switch work areas in a validation routine, you can LOCK( ) the record in the procedure. If you change work areas interactively (through the View window, for example), you can type the following ON KEY LABEL commands in the Command window before browsing the table:

```
ON KEY LABEL F9 WAIT WINDOW NOWAIT ;
   IIF(RLOCK(), "Record Locked", "Unable to Lock")
ON KEY LABEL F10 UNLOCK
```

Note the semicolon at the end of the first line; the second line is a continuation of the first. When you press F9, the current record is explicitly locked; FoxPro maintains this lock even if you move to a different record or to another work area. To release the lock, press F10.

By default, FoxPro locks only one record at a time. When you lock a different record, the lock on the first record is released. To lock more than one record at a time, you must SET MULTILOCKS ON, either by typing the command in the Command window or by checking the Multilocks box in the View window's On/Off panel. Note that UNLOCK releases all record locks in the current work area.

When you are done, remember to restore the function keys to their default settings by typing `ON KEY` in the Command window.

You learn more about explicit record-locking functions and multi-user environment settings in Part IV.

Exploring Other BROWSE Options

BROWSE has a few other options of which you should be aware. Most of these options are used more often from within FoxPro programs than from the Command window or the menus, but you might find some of these options useful. Other than FORMAT, all the options are saved in a preference when you exit the Browse window.

Using BROWSE LOCK

Sometimes you might need to keep in view certain information, such as a person's first and last names, while moving the other fields in and out of view. You can control the view in this way with the LOCK option. You simply specify how many of the left-most fields should be placed in their own partition.

To see how LOCK works, open the Customer table and type the following lines in the Command window:

```
BROWSE ;
   FIELDS Firstname, ;
          Lastname, ;
          Greetname, ;
          Custcode, ;
          Addrcode, ;
          Phone, ;
          Phone_ext ;
   LOCK 2
```

The LOCK 2 option tells FoxPro that you want the first two fields in the list, Firstname and Lastname, to appear by themselves in the left partition of a split Browse window. The right partition is active. These two fields also appear in the right partition so that you can still edit the fields without switching partitions.

Although this technique is useful in an interactive editing session, moving the fields around and creating the partitions by using a mouse or the menus is almost always easier than typing all this information in the Command window. Unless the fields that you want to keep in view are the first ones in the table field order, you must use the FIELDS clause to put them together and at the left of the Browse window, which means that you have to type the name of every field you want to view.

As with the FORMAT clause, LOCK has been largely superseded by more powerful and flexible methods of achieving its goal. Because compatibility with earlier versions is an important consideration, however, LOCK will probably exist for some time to come.

The FREEZE clause is another BROWSE option retained from earlier Xbase dialects. FREEZE is often used with LOCK and is handy for quick, interactive editing. FREEZE is followed by a single specified field name and permits editing only on the specified field, no matter how many fields are displayed in the BROWSE.

Using BROWSE TITLE

Just as each field name is used as the default for column headings, the table's alias is used as the default for the title of the Browse window. You can create a custom title by using the TITLE clause.

Just follow the TITLE keyword with a character expression or any expression that evaluates to a character string. You can, for example, create a more descriptive title for the Budget table by using these lines:

```
BROWSE ;
   TITLE "Budget For Fiscal Year Ended December 31,1993"
```

or

```
BROWSE ;
   TITLE "1993 Budget As Of " + DTOC(DATE())
```

Figure 8.13 shows the Budget table with a new title. As you can see, DTOC(DATE()) results in the current date.

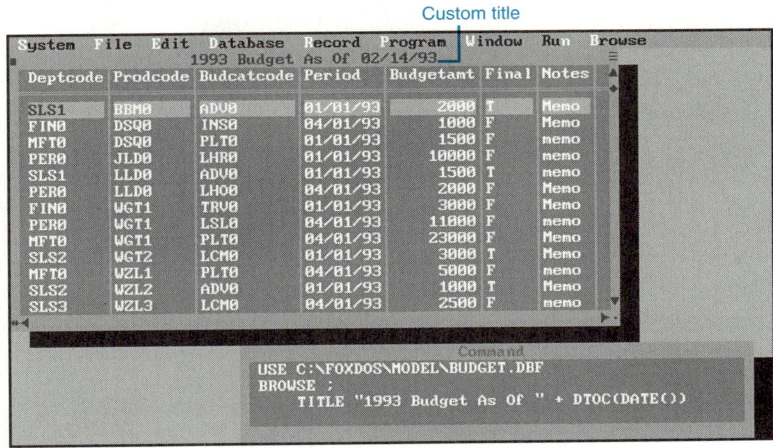

FIG. 8.13

A custom Browse window title showing the current date.

In the first example, the title is a simple character string, which must be enclosed in single or double quotation marks. In the second example, you use a character expression formed by concatenating the result of the DTOC( ) function and the character string "1993 Budget As Of ". If you always use BROWSE LAST, or if you save the title information in a preference, the Browse window always shows the current date as part of the title.

Using BROWSE WIDTH

FoxPro uses the greater of a field's column heading (which is, by default, the field's name) and its physical length (the Width you assigned to the field when you created the table) to determine how many screen columns to use when displaying each field's contents. The WIDTH clause enables you to specify a maximum width for each column in the Browse window. This feature is useful when you want to view many fields at once without having to type a field list.

The Address table, for example, contains many wide fields, such as Company and Address1, that greatly limit the amount of information you can view at once. Figure 8.14 shows the view of the Address table in the Browse window.

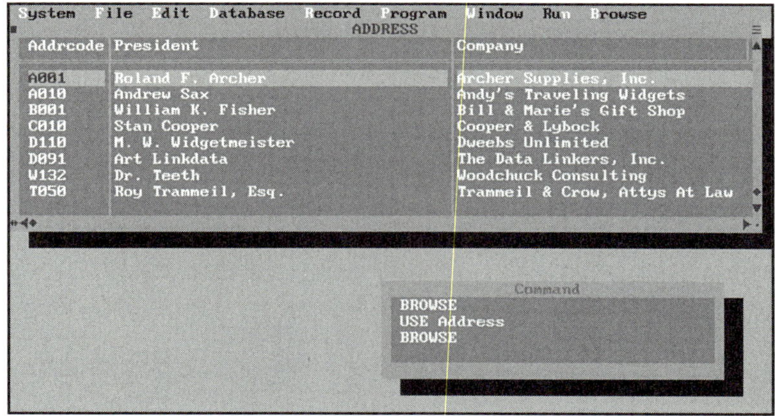

FIG. 8.14

Browsing the Address table with default column widths.

Because you usually can identify a company name without seeing the entire field, you might want to limit each column's width to something less than its maximum. You can use the following command, for example, to limit each column's width to 15 characters:

```
BROWSE ;
   WIDTH 15
```

Figure 8.15 shows the results in the Browse window. Now you can see enough of each field to identify it, and more of the information is visible at once.

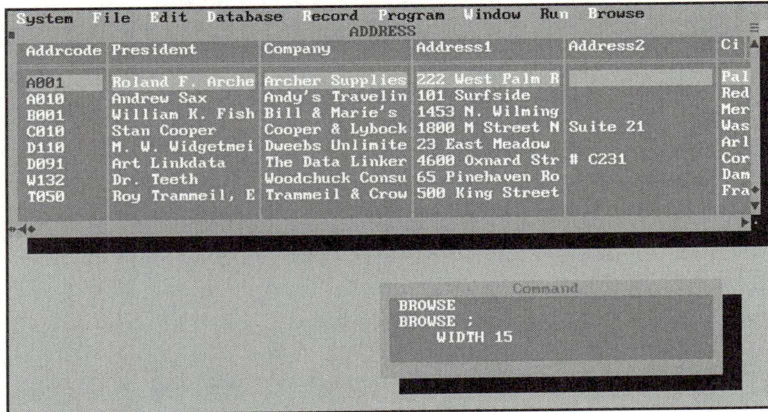

FIG. 8.15

Using the WIDTH clause to limit column widths.

Notice that the Addrcode column is still only nine characters wide (eight for the title plus one to show the "deleted" marker). The WIDTH clause specifies a *maximum* width. If the default width is less than the maximum, the default is used.

Remember also that if you are using the :W option of the FIELDS clause to specify a width for a particular field, that width overrides a global column width set with the WIDTH clause.

Using BROWSE COLOR or BROWSE COLOR SCHEME

FoxPro makes intelligent use of colors to distinguish among the different elements of the Browse window. The most obvious example is the highlight bar, which must use distinct foreground and background colors so that you can tell which record you're currently working on.

Each kind of FoxPro window has a default *color scheme*. BROWSE takes its colors from Color Scheme 10 unless you use the COLOR or COLOR SCHEME clause to use a different set of colors.

Color schemes and the *color picker*, which enable you to create and edit color schemes interactively, are discussed in Chapter 16. For now, just be aware that you're not limited to the colors shown so far in the BROWSE command.

You can see some of the color combinations that make up the various color schemes by using the COLOR SCHEME clause with different numbers. Try Color Scheme 8, for example, with any of the tables that you currently have open. Type the following command:

```
BROWSE ;
   COLOR SCHEME 8
```

The results look much like the default Color Scheme 10 except that the highlight bar uses a different color pair.

To use a particular color pair for a particular window element, you can use a *color pair list* rather than a color scheme. A color pair list can have up to 10 color pairs. Each pair is separated from the others by a comma. To take advantage of this feature, you first must know which color pair affects which window element. Not every interface object uses all 10 available pairs. As you see in table 8.5, which lists the color pair positions and shows the window element that each pair controls, BROWSE doesn't use the last two pairs.

Table 8.5 The Browse Window Color Pairs

Pair No.	Affected Browse Window Element
1	All records other than the current record. The second color is the grid background.
2	The current field of the current record.
3	The window border. The second color is the grid foreground.
4	The window title when the window is active.
5	The window title when the window is inactive.
6	Selected text in the window.
7	Fields of the current record other than the current field. The second color is the delete marker.
8	The window's shadow (if any).
9	Not used.
10	Not used.

A color pair consists of a foreground color and a background color. This coloring works the same way here as you see with printed text. The text you're reading right now, for example, uses a black foreground (the letters) on a white background (the paper on which the letters are printed).

You don't have to specify all the color pairs in the color pair list. You have to specify only the pairs you want to change from the defaults. Commas are used as placeholders for any color pairs that you skip, however, so that FoxPro applies only the pairs that you change to the proper window elements.

To change only the colors of the highlight bar in fields other than the current field, for example, type this command:

```
BROWSE ;
   COLOR ,,,,,,W+/R
```

FoxPro then uses bright white letters on a red background for the highlight bar. The + means bright or high intensity and can be used with any color.

You can use only four "colors" on monochrome monitors: white, black, underlined (U), and inverse video (I). Of course, underlined and inverse video aren't actually colors. However, you refer to each of these codes as a "color" in the command syntax.

In Chapter 16, table 16.1 lists all the colors (and the related codes) available in FoxPro.

Using BROWSE FORMAT

The FORMAT option enables you to use a separate file known as a format *file* to control the format of the Browse window's display. The format file contains a series of @ SAY and @ GET commands and can include VALID, WHEN, PICTURE, and RANGE clauses for each field.

Format files don't provide the same power of expression and control available with the FIELDS clause, but they do provide downward compatibility for anyone who used them in dBASE III PLUS or FoxBASE+.

Although you can use a format file with BROWSE, this file originally was designed to control the display and editing format of a full-screen edit, using the READ command. As such, the format file contains screen positioning instructions (@ <row>, <column>) for each field. BROWSE ignores these instructions, but you must include them to use the format file successfully.

The following is a format file that you can use with the sample Budget table:

```
* BUDGET.FMT
* This is a format file you can use with the Budget table in
* a BROWSE FORMAT command.
@ 0,0 GET Deptcode VALID !EMPTY(Deptcode) PICTURE "@!"
@ 0,0 GET Prodcode PICTURE "@! AAA9"
@ 0,0 GET Budcatcode PICTURE "@! AAA9" WHEN !EMPTY(Prodcode)
@ 0,0 GET Budgetamt PICTURE "9,999,999" RANGE 0, 1000000
@ 0,0 SAY IIF(Final, CHR(251), " ")
```

When you include @ SAY in a format file, BROWSE treats this expression as a calculated field and shows on-screen the result of the next expression. All GET statements' validation and formatting clauses are respected by the corresponding BROWSEd fields.

To use a format file with BROWSE FORMAT, you first must SET FORMAT TO the format file. To use BUDGET.FMT with the Budget table, type the following command in the Command window:

```
SELECT Budget
SET FORMAT TO BUDGET
BROWSE FORMAT
```

In Chapters 12 and 13, you learn how to use FoxPro's Screen Builder to generate @ SAY...GET statements by using the Screen Builder's template program, GENSCRN.PRG. GENSCRN doesn't create files that you can use as default Format files. Because GENSCRN is a program written in FoxPro, however, you can create an alternative version that can generate Format files that BROWSE FORMAT can use. In Chapter 19, you learn about the text-merge commands used by GENSCRN and how to edit a template program.

Using EDIT FORMAT

BROWSE and EDIT are identical commands, right? BROWSE displays the records in columnar format, and EDIT displays the records in a vertical format, right? So except for the field layout, EDIT FORMAT is the same as BROWSE FORMAT, right?

Wrong. If you look at the EDIT command's entry in the FoxPro *Language Reference* manual or in the Help file, you see no mention of a FORMAT clause. Although FoxPro 2.5 includes both BROWSE FORMAT and EDIT FORMAT for downward compatibility with older Xbase products, they are very different. Although BROWSE FORMAT disregards row and column coordinates, EDIT FORMAT uses them to position text labels and GETs in the same manner as the READ command.

In fact, EDIT and EDIT FORMAT are completely different commands. EDIT FORMAT does not use the BROWSE display format at all; after placing the text labels and fields on the screen or active window, it invisibly issues a READ command. (If you doubt this, run the EFORMAT.PRG program in Appendix H and check the value returned by the RDLEVEL( ) function as you move through the records.)

As a READ-type command, EDIT FORMAT has some intriguing aspects. For example, you can use the Screen Builder to create a screen (.SPR) file, SET FORMAT TO <the screen file>, and then use EDIT FORMAT as a simple data entry mechanism. (If you forget to use SET FORMAT TO, FoxPro disregards the FORMAT clause, and displays a normal Edit/ Browse window.)

To create a format file that works with EDIT FORMAT, however, you must use the Screen Builder's #NOREAD generator directive to prevent GENSCRN from including a READ command in the screen file. Chapters 12 and 13 discuss the Screen Builder and the GENSCRN program.

Unlike READ and READ CYCLE, the special form of READ used by EDIT FORMAT moves the record pointer to the next record in the table when you press PgDn, Tab, or Enter in the last GET. When you press Esc or move past the last record in the table, the EDIT ends.

Also unlike READ, EDIT FORMAT does not use FoxPro's implicit record locking. If you use EDIT FORMAT in a multi-user or multitasking environment, you must issue explicit record locks before editing a record.

Read the comments included in the EFORMAT program in Appendix H for more information about EDIT FORMAT. Keep in mind, however, that because this command is no longer documented, future versions of FoxPro may abandon it.

Summary

In this chapter, you have learned to use FoxPro's BROWSE command to view tables, restrict the display to certain fields and groups of records, validate data input, create and save customized Browse window "looks," and link one or more tables. In the process, you also learned much about using the View window and the Command window together, and you now know how to determine which window is appropriate for the task at hand.

Setting relations among tables is a powerful tool. Getting relations right requires a little experience with manipulating tables and an understanding of database design principles. The time you spend planning the database layouts pays handsome dividends in the form of easy access to all the information through inter-table relationships.

Although you can customize the appearance of a Browse window to a great degree, Browse still limits the ways in which you can display your data. In the next two chapters, you learn to use FoxPro's powerful Report Writer to create custom layouts that enable you to view and print your information in almost any way imaginable.

9

CHAPTER

Putting the Answers To Work in Reports and Labels

In Chapter 8, "Organizing the Answers with BROWSE," you learn how to use BROWSE to review data on-screen, which can differ greatly in appearance from the contents of the records in the tables. Now that you are familiar with the flexible display capabilities of FoxPro, you may want a more permanent kind of output to help you evaluate, use, and share the information in the data files.

You learned that the LIST command can send quick snapshots of the tables to the printer or a file, but you begin to tap the real power of FoxPro for output when you use the Report Writer and Label Designer. These two tools give you the same flexibility in the creation of printed results as FoxPro BROWSE provides on-screen.

Typically, a *report* is output that is composed of many records and arranged in a format that lists the fields across and the records down, one record per line. A *label,* however, usually contains information about only one record and is formatted more as a CHANGE/EDIT. Because label formats are meant to accommodate mailing labels you can buy in sheets or rolls, you can designate the number of labels you want to print across the page, and FoxPro prints one record for each label.

FoxPro does not have hard-and-fast rules for report and label formatting. You can format a report exactly like you format a label (in *form* rather than in *column* layout), and each report can contain information about only one record. You may find this feature useful for printing mail-merge letters or even for formatting addresses for continuous-form envelopes. You also can use a label format on normal paper to print information about many records when information about multiple records on each line is desirable.

The following two chapters describe ways to create and use labels and reports so that you can experiment with the differences of each procedure as you learn the techniques shared by the versatile FoxPro Report Writer and Label Designer.

This chapter concentrates on the Label Designer and Report Writer as tools because using these tools may differ from other kinds of editing you have done with a computer. If you have used desktop publishing programs on the PC or the Macintosh computer, however, you may quickly become comfortable with these tools; the editing approaches of the desktop publishing programs are similar to those of the FoxPro tools. With FoxPro, you manipulate the elements of labels and reports as objects which you can move, size, and attach to each other.

First you create a Quick Report, using the Report Writer as a learning tool to introduce you to these objects. Next you learn about the different kinds of objects you can use, you learn to manipulate these objects in a Report layout, and you learn ways to change the report layout as a whole.

After you become familiar with these options, you look at the file formats that FoxPro uses to make the options available. Finally, you apply the same techniques and principles in creating labels with the Label Designer.

Designing a Quick Report

If you use the Quick Report feature, FoxPro makes designing your first report easy—without requiring you to know anything about the way the Report Writer works. After you create this report, you can examine and alter its components to suit your needs.

If you have not already done so, open the Budget table. (In the following chapter, you also use the Product table with the relation set to the Prodcode field as you learn in Chapter 3, "Exploring Databases and Tables.") If you created a View with these two files related, you may prefer to use either SET VIEW TO <viewname> or the File Open dialog to access that View file. The Budget table is opened as part of the View.

Use the File New dialog to open a Report file. A new kind of window, the Report Layout screen, appears. The window shows that you have created a new and unnamed file, UNTITLED; the Report file's extension is .FRX. Notice that the menu bar has a new pad, Report. Choose this pad, and the options listed in figure 9.1 appear.

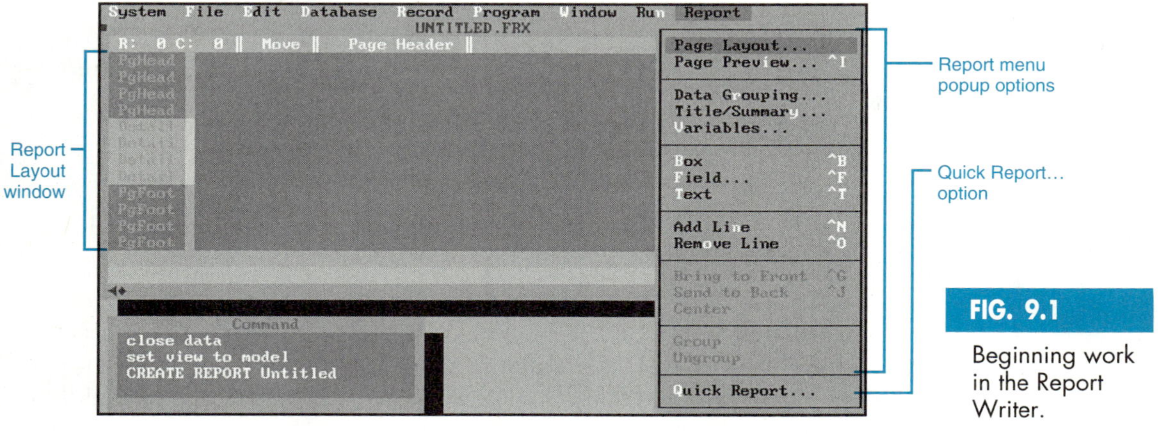

FIG. 9.1

Beginning work in the Report Writer.

Choose the Quick Report... option listed at the bottom of the popup. (You can use the Quick Report feature only when you are working with a blank report.)

The dialog on the upper-left corner in figure 9.2 has two radio buttons for specifying Column Layout or Form Layout. Select the Form button; the diagram to the right of the radio buttons changes to the layout you have chosen. Then return the layout to the default of Column.

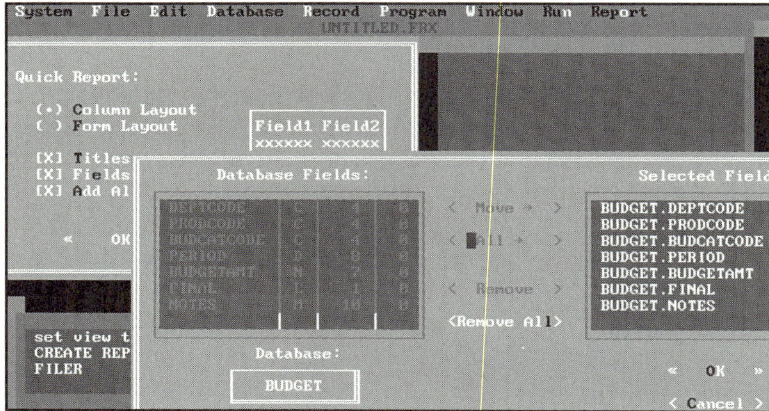

FIG. 9.2

The Quick Report dialogs.

In the Titles check box, you can specify whether you want the columns to have headings. Quick Report supplies headings by using field names. If you mark the Add Alias check box, the Report Writer adds a reference to the appropriate table when data contained in fields is referred to. Leave both of these options at the default setting.

Mark the Fields check box to see the Field Picker, a standard FoxPro Mover dialog, active in figure 9.2. Choose the `All` push button; all the fields from the Database Fields list on the left side of the dialog then appear in the Selected Fields list on the right. This list is the default fields list that you get by using Quick Report if you did not select the Fields check box. Notice that each item is prefaced by Budget, the current alias by which you can refer to the file from where these fields come. A period (.) separates the alias from the field name.

In the Selected Fields list, you may want to rearrange the order of or delete some fields. Mark the fields that appear on the list by clicking the mouse button or by pressing the space bar and holding down the Shift key for additional fields (if you want to mark more than one field at a time). A character appears to the left of all selected fields. Click the `Remove` button to delete these marked fields; the fields again become available for use in the Field Picker list on the left. Now mark the fields on the left and click the `Move` button to move the fields, one at a time, back to the rightmost box in the order you want the fields to appear (left to right) in the report. For this sample report, make sure that you select all fields; you can tell that you have selected all fields when all the entries on the left side are dimmed, as shown in figure 9.2.

Besides pressing the `Move` button while fields are selected in the Database Fields list, you can press Enter, double-click, or press the space bar twice to move any field into the Selected Fields list. (If you have selected more than one field, hold down the Shift key as you press the space bar twice.)

Confirm the choices in both dialogs. The Layout window appears with the designed report. If what you see makes no sense to you yet, use the Page Preview... option from the Report menu popup (or press Ctrl+I) to look at the output produced by this layout, as shown in figure 9.3. (To check the results of each action you take, you may want to use Page Preview... repeatedly during the following exercises and while you design other reports.)

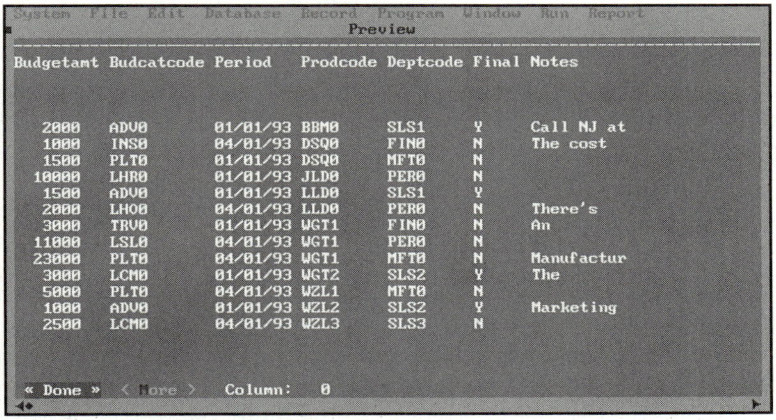

```
System  File  Edit  Database  Record  Program  Window  Run  Report
                              Preview

Budgetamt Budcatcode Period   Prodcode Deptcode Final Notes


   2000    ADV0       01/01/93 BBM0     SLS1     Y     Call NJ at
   1000    INS0       04/01/93 DSQ0     FIN0     N     The cost
   1500    PLT0       01/01/93 DSQ0     MFT0     N
  10000    LHR0       01/01/93 JLD0     PER0     N
   1500    ADV0       01/01/93 LLD0     SLS1     Y
   2000    LHO0       04/01/93 LLD0     PER0     N     There's
   3000    TRV0       01/01/93 WGT1     FIN0     N     An
  11000    LSL0       04/01/93 WGT1     PER0     N
  23000    PLT0       04/01/93 WGT1     MFT0     N     Manufactur
   3000    LCM0       01/01/93 WGT2     SLS2     Y     The
   5000    PLT0       04/01/93 WZL1     MFT0     N
   1000    ADV0       01/01/93 WZL2     SLS2     Y     Marketing
   2500    LCM0       04/01/93 WZL3     SLS3     N


 « Done »  < More >  Column:   0
```

FIG. 9.3

A Page Preview of a Quick Report.

Examining the Report Layout Screen

The Quick Report is a good way to start designing a layout, but FoxPro offers several methods for improving this report. To use these methods, you must understand and learn to edit the components of a FoxPro report form.

In a FoxPro report, each horizontal line (or row) belongs to one of several kinds of *report bands*. Each band represents a part of the report page (see fig. 9.4).

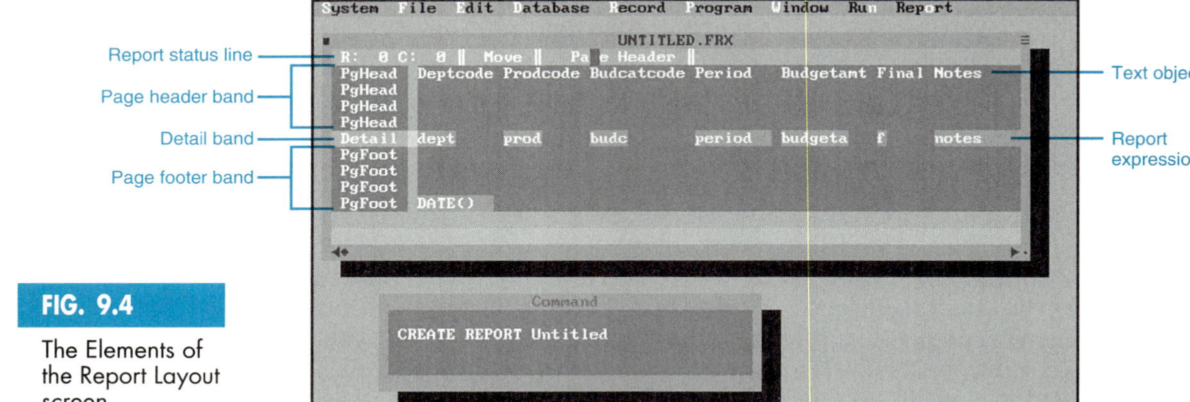

FIG. 9.4

The Elements of the Report Layout screen.

On the left side of the Report Layout screen, each row is designated as a line in a PgHead (page header), a Detail, or a PgFoot (page footer) band. Lines in the page header and footer bands appear at the top and bottom of each page. By using the appropriate Report menu options, you also can add Title and Summary bands that appear only at the beginning and end of each report. (Other band designations, indicating *data groupings,* also may appear as you work. These designations are discussed in the following chapter.)

In the middle of the Report Layout screen is the Detail band. Although you currently see only one line, this band actually generates most of the lines in the Page Preview shown in figure 9.3. When you produce a report, the Report Writer moves through a table, record by record, and generates a set of items for the detail band for each record. The Report Writer leaves room for the page footer band on each page, starts a new page by reprinting the page header lines, and then continues with the next available record until reaching the end of the table (or the scope you supplied).

Each band can hold more than one line. A report can have as many as 255 distinct detail lines. The Report Writer prints all the detail lines for one record and then prints a new detail band (or set of detail lines) for the next record.

Report bands contain three different kinds of report objects: *field, text,* or *box,* as described in this chapter. Each object is a self-contained unit that you can edit or alter. Each band can contain objects of any kind or, if you desire, objects of all three kinds.

Look at the report layout, to the right of the band designations, in figure 9.4. Notice that the items in the page header (the field names supplied by the Quick Report as column headings) are displayed in different colors or intensities than the detail band items or the item in the footer are displayed. The Report Writer is differentiating between *text objects,* which appear exactly as typed, and *report expression objects,* which the Report Writer evaluates. When FoxPro evaluates an expression, the results of this expression rather than the expression itself display in the report.

Notice that the report expression in the page footer is the FoxPro function DATE( ). If you look in the Help file, you see that the result of this function is the current system date and that date is what the Report Writer displays wherever this expression is positioned in the report. (FoxPro formats this function according to the current default you set either in the View Misc panel options or in the SET DATE command in the Command window.)

Each report expression in the detail band is the name of a field in the Budget table. For each detail line, the Report Writer evaluates each expression by asking: "What is the current value of this expression?" At the appropriate position, the Report Writer places the contents of the field for the current record in the report.

Don't be alarmed if only a few letters of each field name appear in the report expressions listed in the detail band. The Report Writer is displaying how much space the results of the report expression require within the report (in this example, the width of each field in the Budget table). The actual expression producing this result may be much longer.

The sample page header band, however, contains some text objects that the Report Writer literally copied into the report; the Report Writer did not evaluate the text in these objects as expressions. Each text object appears on-screen as it prints out in the report.

An object of box type, like text objects and unlike report expressions, appears in the layout exactly as the object appears in the report. *Box* objects consist of lines and boxes that you can draw to enhance a report. The report layout shows box objects in the same colors or intensities as text objects. The Quick Report layout does not have box objects.

NOTE The top line in the Report Writer is the *report status line*. On the left, the status line tracks the current cursor position, which is useful as you decide where to fit a new item in the layout. The next item in the status line tells you the action you are currently performing. Here Move is displayed on-screen, but Box (when you draw a line or box object), Text (when you type a text object into the layout), or Field (when you manipulate report expressions) also may appear. The final status line item is a reminder of which report band the current action is going to affect.

Making Simple Layout Adjustments

Now that you understand the elements of the Report Writer layout, you can adjust the default appearance Quick Report provides. You can resize and reorder the objects in the layout and use additional graphics elements to draw attention to the most important data in the report.

Adjusting Band Size

The first thing you may want to do in the sample report is to remove the empty lines in the page header and footer bands. Place the cursor in an empty line in the page header band and use the Report menu Remove Line option (or press Ctrl+O) until only the line with the field names is left. (If you make a mistake and try to remove a line that contains data, the Report Writer asks you to confirm the choice.) You can use the same method to delete the lines in the footer band.

Suppose that you decide that the empty line between the data and the date in the page footer is a good idea. To insert an empty line, place the cursor in the line that contains the DATE( ) expression and then choose the Add Line menu option or press Ctrl+N. A blank line appears above the cursor.

You also may want to separate the column headings in the page header band from the data with at least one blank line, or perhaps you want to draw a line between the two bands. To do so, place the cursor on the line that contains the page headings, press Shift while you access the Report menu or press Ctrl+N. On-screen, the option changes to Add Line After.

Mouse users have another way to add and remove lines. Place the mouse cursor in the area to the left, where the band titles are located. Drag the mouse down to add lines to or up to remove empty lines from the band in which the cursor is located. Hold down Shift while you drag the mouse up or down to affect the band *above* the band in which the cursor is located.

Adding Lines To Distinguish Headings

Now draw a line between the column headings and the data. To do so, place the cursor in the middle of the blank line you added to the page header, and select the Box option from the menu popup (or press Ctrl+B). A small flashing box appears. Although invisible, the cursor is now at the lower-right corner of this box. You can change the shape of the box by using the arrow keys or by dragging the mouse; you make the box wider by moving the cursor to the right; taller, by moving the cursor down; narrower, by moving the cursor to the left; and shorter, by moving the cursor up. If you move the cursor to the same row in which you began the box drawing, the box becomes a horizontal line. When you move the cursor to the same column in which you started drawing, the box becomes a vertical line. The box continues to change, as shown by its flashing, until you press Enter, click the mouse, or press the space bar.

Notice that you cannot draw the line or box above or to the left of the original cursor position. When you size the box, you use a technique known in FoxPro—and in other programs—as *rubberbanding* or *stretching*. In FoxPro, you usually stretch an object down and to the right.

Suppose that the line you drew didn't start far enough to the left (under the Deptcode heading). You can select this line or any other object in the Report Layout screen by clicking the line or by pressing the space bar while the cursor is on the line. After making the selection, you can move an object by using the cursor keys or by dragging it. Now move the line further to the left. When you have positioned the object, press Enter or the space bar, or click elsewhere in the layout to unselect the line. When no object is selected, click the mouse, use the cursor keys, or press Tab to move to other objects in the layout.

Resizing Objects

Because you moved the line to the left, the line may no longer extend far enough to the right. You can resize the line by holding down the

Ctrl key while you select the box with the space bar or the mouse. After the object begins to flash, you can release the Ctrl key and use the cursor keys for the resize operation.

Continue moving the cursor to the right, stretching the box. Notice that the scrolling movement does not stop at the window border. You can stretch the line until you reach the right margin of the page, which by default is a wider area than the report layout window can show at one time. (You learn how to change the report margins in the following section.) As you continue to move the cursor to the right or down in the layout window, you probably will become accustomed to the scrolling that takes place (and to the movement of the thumb in the scroll bar in the border).

After you reach the right margin of the report, you see two more objects in the page footer that were not previously visible. One object is the text object Page. Beside Page is a report expression that holds the system variable, _PAGENO, which FoxPro uses to internally track the page count for the report you are running. The Quick Report... option inserts the DATE( ) expression to the far left and these two page numbering expressions to the right. For this report, suppose that you want to place the page number in the page header (you may want to add a page header line for this procedure). You already know how to select one object; you select multiple objects by holding down the Shift key as you select additional objects by clicking the mouse or by pressing the space bar. (Hold down Shift and click again or press the space bar again to unselect a particular item while you keep the other items selected.) Now you can simultaneously move the two objects, Page and _PAGENO, to the top of the report.

Grouping Objects

You may want to move these objects often; you also may always want to move these objects together. After selecting them, you can use the Report menu option to group the objects. The next time you select one of these objects, both objects are selected by default.

Mouse users have an alternative method for selecting multiple objects. Place the mouse cursor in the report (but do not place the cursor on any report object), and then drag the mouse. A box with dotted lines appears; you can stretch and size this box, called a *selection marquee*. Do not place the cursor on any report object when you begin to size the selection marquee; otherwise, the click selects only the report object. Fortunately, you can stretch this box in all directions, not just to the right and down; without this feature you could not use the selection marquee on objects in the upper-left corner of a report.

When you release the mouse button, all objects (even objects partially within this box) are selected. Figure 9.5 shows how a selection marquee appears during the selecting of multiple objects. To unselect inadvertently selected objects, hold down the Shift key and click them, or press the space bar. You then can choose to group the selected objects as you did before.

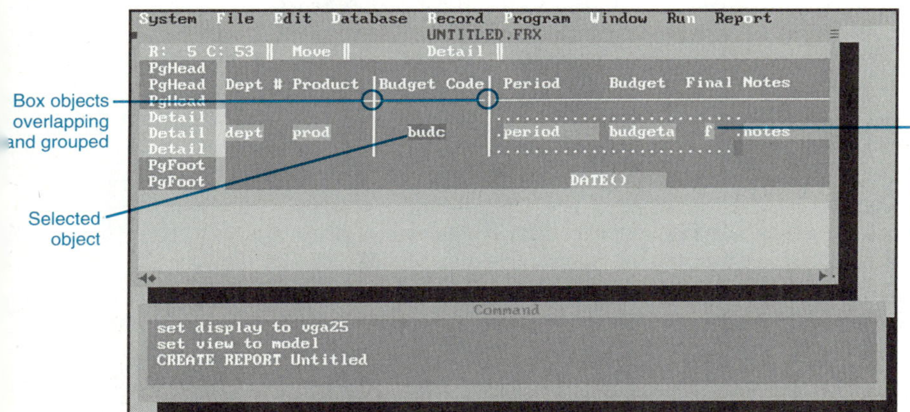

FIG. 9.5

The Report Layout screen during editing.

Removing Objects

You also can remove from the layout any object or group in the report just by selecting the object or group and then by pressing Backspace or Delete. You can copy, cut, or paste all objects by using the usual editing shortcuts (Ctrl+C, Ctrl+X, and Ctrl+V). When you paste the object into the new location, FoxPro includes any formatting and other attributes that you previously defined for that object. Practice moving the DATE() expression to different places on the page and then return the expression to the page footer band.

Moving Objects among Layout Windows

You can open several report layout windows at one time, just as you can open several text editing windows. You may want to copy a report object or several objects from one report to another. You can easily copy a standard page heading for your company from layout to layout.

TIP Marking, copying, pasting, and deleting report objects use the same key shortcuts and procedures that you use for editing text in FoxPro, but the edited items are not the same. The Report Writer Clipboard is separate from the text Clipboard for the FoxPro Editor because it has to handle specialized information about each object it holds, not just a string of characters. (In Chapter 12, "Creating Application Elements," you learn that the Screen Builder has a separate Clipboard for its own objects, too.) Suppose that you want to use an old report that was printed in a word processor or some other computer system as a model for your FoxPro report. Because the objects are not interchangeable, you cannot just mark and copy text from a text file and paste it into your report layout, even as a text label. (Even report text labels are specialized objects, not regular text.) You can trick FoxPro into adding text to your Report (or Screen) Layout by adding a hot key or menu shortcut which executes the following command:

```
KEYBOARD _CLIPTEXT
```

When you press the hot key, FoxPro sends the characters from the text Clipboard (using the system variable _CLIPTEXT, which holds the contents of the text Clipboard) to the Layout, as if you typed the characters individually. They will appear as a text label in the Layout. You learn more about the KEYBOARD command and how to assign such a command to a hot key or menu shortcut in later sections of this book.

As you practice selecting different objects, occasionally check the Report and Edit menu popups. Depending on whether an object is currently selected, you see various items become available or unavailable on the menus as items do when you edit a text file.

Changing Object Alignment

With the DATE( ) expression selected, you may want to try an additional option on the Report menu—Center. (FoxPro does not have shortcuts or mouse equivalents for this option.) Grouping takes on a special significance with the centering option; if you select more than one object, each object is centered individually, relative to the central character in the line. If two or more objects are in the same row, FoxPro lays all objects in a stack—on top of each other. Although you cannot see all of them in the Page Preview, all the grouped objects are present and print over each other.

If you want these objects to be centered together on the line, however, group the objects before you choose the Center menu option. The order in which you select the objects before grouping does not affect the order in which they appear on the line after centering; the objects remain in the same right-to-left order. The distance between the items also remains the same as before centering.

Grouping objects has a special significance when box or line objects touch each other: you can change the characters at the connection points so that the boxes or lines are joined. The difference between intersecting but separate lines and grouped lines is shown in figure 9.5. If you need to edit only one object from a group, you must first Ungroup the objects by using the Report menu.

Changing Report Headings

If you frequently check the Page Preview, you may see a number of improvements you can make. The column headings, for example, are still raw field names that you can edit to English words with the usual text-editing strokes. With the cursor directly on a text object, press Ctrl+T. You see the word Move change to Text in the status line. You can continue to edit text until you press Enter to return to Move status.

Edit the first column headings to read Dept #, Product, and Budget Code. You may want to shift the Product and Budget code columns and headings to the right or left as you change the width of the headings.

Changing the Display of Data in Report Expressions

The next column, Period, is an easily understood heading. However, suppose that you want to show all four digits of the year in the date. Use the Window View Misc panel to check off the Century option, then return to the Report Layout window, and do another preview. Although the change was made, it was not completely successful—the dates read 01/01/19 and 04/01/19, but they don't show the year. You have to make room for the extra digits in the Period report expression. Luckily, you can resize a report expression in the same way you resized the box object. Move other objects to the right side of the screen to make room for the extra digits, as necessary.

Place the cursor inside the Period report expression and select the expression while pressing the Ctrl key. The column indicator on the status line immediately shows the last column occupied by this object, regardless of where the cursor was when you selected the expression. Watch the status line indicator while you resize the object to two columns wider. Then use the same method to resize the DATE( ) expression in the page footer. Now choose Page Preview... to see the results.

You may want to make other changes to the Notes report expression. If you typed new entries into the Notes Memo field, the entries are cut off after only a few words in the report. Although you can resize the Notes report object by a few characters, a Memo field is unlimited in length so you cannot possibly provide for all the Memo fields in this manner.

Expanding the Detail Band Vertically

Because you have limited room to expand a report expression horizontally, the solution is to stretch the expression holding the Notes Memo field vertically. Before you expand this expression, make the problem a little more interesting by adding a box around the Notes report object. Add two detail lines and move the current detail expressions to the middle line of the three, either by selecting the expressions in the usual way or by using the selection marquee. With the extra detail lines, you can draw the box object around the Notes report expression. Resize the Notes field to take as much room as you can without overwriting the box.

Double-click the Notes field or place the cursor on the field and either press the space bar twice or press Enter. The Report Expression dialog appears (see fig. 9.6). The following chapter covers this feature more fully. Mark the Stretch Vertically check box, which tells the Report Writer that you want this field to continue for as many lines as necessary so that it can contain the Notes for each record.

To coordinate the box dimensions with this change, you need to tell the Report Writer that the box that surrounds the Notes must adjust for the Notes field length. You bring up a dialog for styling box objects by using the same techniques on the box object that you used on the field object. This dialog enables you to make an object Float as Band Stretches, which means that FoxPro places the field one line below the last line of the stretched character field (see fig. 9.7). If you don't select this option, FoxPro places the field on the report at the position you defined in the Layout; if character field stretches, the data overwrites the bottom field.

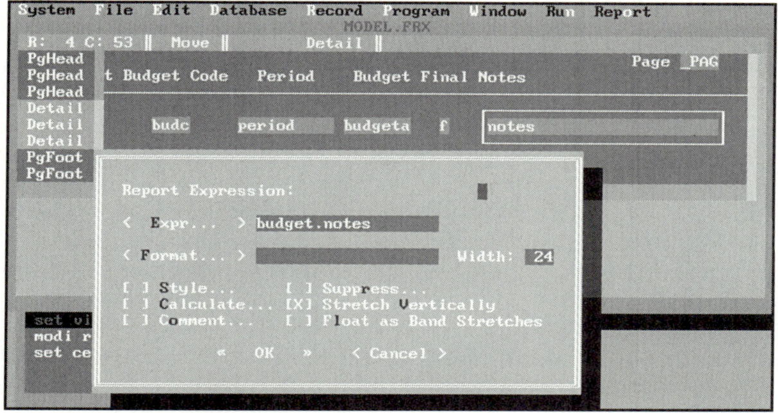

FIG. 9.6

The Report Expression dialog.

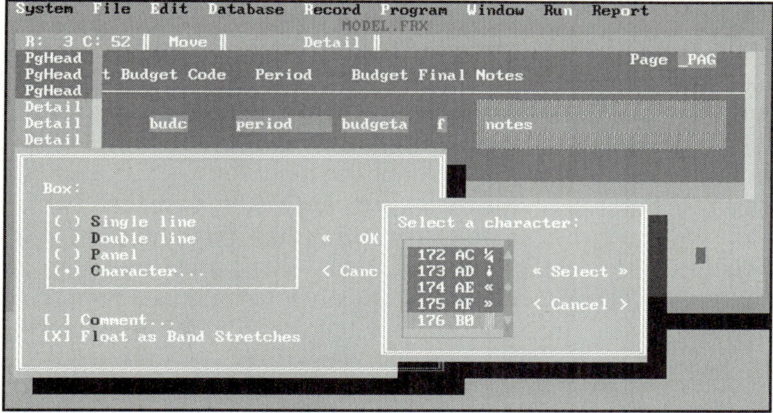

FIG. 9.7

The Box Object dialog and associated ASCII character list.

Figure 9.7 shows options to modify the style of the box object; radio buttons enable you to pick a double line or panel for the box, as opposed to the default single line, and provide an opportunity to form the box from any character from a version of the ASCII character list that appears. The figure also shows the results you can achieve with the Character... radio button; remember that if a box is formed from a character in this list, the box has no true corner characters when boxes are grouped, as boxes formed from Single or Double lines or the Panel radio button option.

TIP As you practice grouping boxes and lines, you may have some difficulty getting the corner characters properly displayed. Make certain that all the objects you plan to join are first ungrouped from any other previous groupings. Select all the objects at the same time, and then choose Group from the menu popup. If they still don't appear to be joined properly, you may have to Ungroup them again and adjust their positions slightly. Grouped boxes also may fail to join properly if you unwittingly add an object that isn't a box to the selected group. Ungroup the objects, press Shift+space bar or press Shift and click the offending text or report expression, and then group the boxes again.

Adding Text under an Object

You may want to place a text object under the box to indicate that this box can include handwritten memos jotted down in the box's empty space (if no notes are added to this record's Memo field). Expand the detail band to include an additional line for the text object and type the words `Make notes here` directly under the box. Double-click this text object, press Enter, or press the space bar twice (as you can for the line and report expression object types); a dialog that affects the style and position of text objects appears (see fig. 9.8). Mark the Float as Band Stretches check box because this object also must move relative to the Notes field. (The options to stretch and float are active only in the detail and page header bands of a report.)

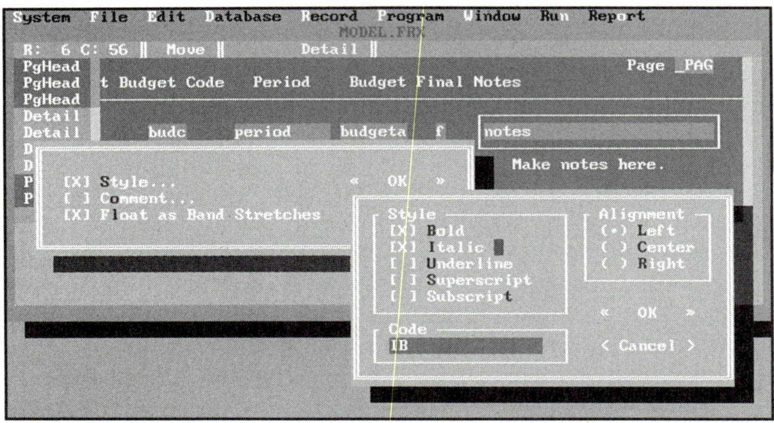

FIG. 9.8

The Text Object and Style dialogs.

If you also mark the Style... check box, you can select printer enhancements, subject to the printer driver you previously installed. The enhancements you check from the Style list on the left and the Alignment list on the right appear as codes underneath, to which you can add custom codes if you have written a printer driver or use a printer driver that can handle these style and alignment options. (You find information on printer drivers in Chapter 16, "Discovering Additional FoxPro Productivity Features.")

NOTE Style dialog enhancements differ from other formatting changes you can make because these enhancements are specific to printed output, which includes printing to a file for later use with a printer. When you send a report to the screen, the Report Writer ignores style enhancements. In addition, you cannot see the results of these changes in this dialog when you choose the Page Preview... option.

All three kinds of object dialogs have an additional Comment... check box. If you select this box, a text editing window appears. Whatever you type in the window serves as notes on the creation and use of this report object; this information does not appear in output. The Comment feature is especially useful if you are copying objects between two reports.

Making Changes that Affect the Entire Report

So far you altered different kinds of individual report objects. You may want to make some global changes that affect the report as a whole, however. You can find these selections under the Page Layout... option of the Report menu popup (see fig. 9.9).

Figure 9.9 also shows the Page Layout dialog and the associated Options dialog. Except for the `Environment` text buttons discussed later in this section, the items you can choose here are self-explanatory. The report layout dialog includes a text box for the report's right margin; using this option, you can affect the page margins by typing `132` as a right margin for a report in standard compressed pitch type.

One default setting you often want to change is the Page eject before printing option. This option is most appropriate when people share a printer that is located in another area. In this situation, you eject a page before beginning a report to make sure that your report doesn't start in the middle of a page left in the printer by the last job. If you set up the printer yourself or if your programs always eject a page when they are finished printing, you don't need to waste the extra piece of paper.

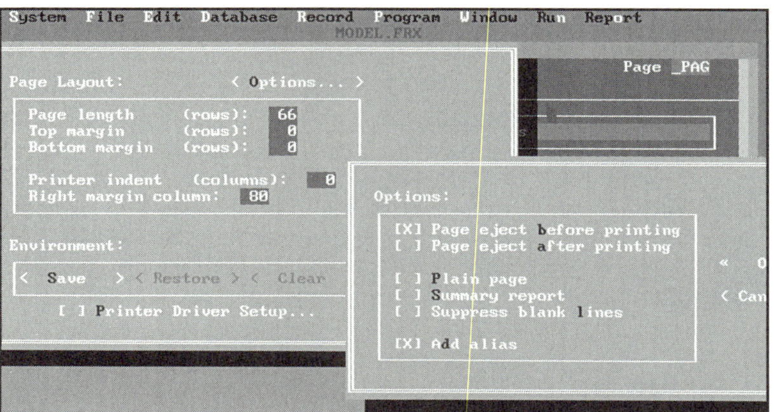

FIG. 9.9

The Page Layout dialog and its associated Options dialog, showing default settings.

With the Suppress blank lines check box in the Options dialog, you can specify that all completely blank lines in the detail band do not appear. (This feature doesn't suppress lines with numeric fields in which 0 prints or lines that hold no objects. It suppresses detail lines in which *all expressions evaluate to spaces or null strings*. You learn more about suppressing blank lines in reports and labels in the following chapter.) The Summary report check box suppresses all detail lines, which is useful if you grouped the data and want information only on each group. Usually, however, you get more flexibility if you do not mark this box; you always can make a given instance of a report a summary report by using the SUMMARY keyword in the REPORT FORM command or by choosing the appropriate Report dialog check box. If you have a report for which you never want details, you can check this box or simply leave the detail band empty. Either method creates a permanent summary report.

When the Page Layout settings are the way you want them, save this report using any of the methods for closing and saving that you learned for text file windows. FoxPro requests a file name and assigns the extension .FRX to the name you choose. Save the file as MODEL.FRX. (You will return to this report in the following chapter and continue to modify it.)

When you save a report for the first time, you get an alert that reminds you to save the work before exiting. This alert also asks whether you want to save the report environment. Choose `Yes` for the MODEL report.

A report's *environment* is a special way of saving the information required to run the report or of previewing the report data while you are editing. FoxPro saves the required information (the files that must be open, the relations that must be set, and the order in which you want to see the data) in the report file itself rather than in an independent .VUE file.

You normally choose to save this information when you first create a report. If you save the environment, you can later edit the report. Then each time you open the report, FoxPro opens the appropriate files. You may decide that you need another file or that a different index is useful. In either case, you can use the Save option in the Page Layout dialog to save the new environment information to the report form, or you can decide that the new information is only temporary. You use the other Page Layout... options, `Restore` or `Clear`, to restore the original environment information or to clear the environment information attached to the report form.

> **CAUTION:** The word *Save* in this dialog is misleading. When you use the Page Layout... Save option to save the environment, you affect only the copy of the report form currently loaded in memory; the new saved environment is saved to disk only when you save the entire report. If you cancel the entire editing session, the new environment is not saved.

Rather than separately choosing SET VIEW before you run the report, you can mark the Restore environment check box in the Report dialog. The options MODIFY REPORT or REPORT FORM from the Command window also include clauses you use to restore the environment. (Open the MODEL.FRX file from the File Open dialog without the Restore Environment box checked. Note that the MODIFY REPORT MODEL.FRX line echoed in the Command window includes the keyword NOENVIRONMENT.)

The Printer Driver Setup... option brings you to the same Printer Driver Setup dialog available throughout FoxPro. If you want the Report Writer to use any style enhancements to report objects (or if you want Report Writer to issue other printer-specific instructions), you must have a currently active printer driver. In Chapter 16, "Discovering Additional

FoxPro Productivity Features," you learn how to ensure that the printer driver you load supports the enhancements you select.

When you load a printer driver, you make a special change in the FoxPro environment. The Report Writer saves this information with the current report (similar to the way View information is saved). When you are ready to print a report, you can use the PDSETUP keyword to choose to load the printer driver with which the report was saved—rather than the currently active driver or no driver at all.

Looking Closely at Report and Label Files

NOTE Eventually, you may settle on several standard features for the reports you produce: you may never want a page to eject before the report begins to print; you may use the same heading on all reports; and you may save report environment information for all or none of the reports. The printer also may use a standard number of lines that differs from FoxPro's default, especially if you have a laser printer. In addition, you may want to set standard margins to other than the defaults.

In all these cases, you may want to set up and save a blank report with a special name. When you are ready to design a new report, you can open and then save this *template* report to a new file name. To avoid overwriting this special report file, you can set the file attributes to readonly. (Use FoxPro's Filer, described in Chapter 16, "Discovering Additional FoxPro Productivity Features," to set the file attributes.)

You already observed that reports are composed of various kinds of objects and that you can assign each object different attributes. The attributes accompany the object as you move or copy the object from one location to another.

FoxPro stores the objects and assigned attributes by saving information about a report or a label in a database table. This table is like other tables you design and use, with the following exceptions:

- FoxPro assigns the extension .FRX by default, and the associated Memo field uses the extension .FRT (the extensions are .LBX and .LBT for a table that stores information about a label).

- FoxPro internally sets a required structure (in FoxPro 2.5, this structure is the same for reports and labels).

When you work in the Report Writer or the Label Designer, FoxPro stores a copy of this table in memory. As you add and delete objects and the assigned attributes, FoxPro adds and deletes records in the table and fills out the table fields.

If you open MODEL.FRX, you can examine the structure of the .FRX in the same way you can examine any other table. Choose File Open, select Database type files, and mark the All Files check box. When you browse this table, you see that it contains an Objtype field. If you examine the contents of each record, you soon realize that the different Objtype fields correspond to the report objects you are examining. The first record, OBJTYPE 1, holds the report's global information; notice that the record's Height and Width fields hold the report dimensions. Each record has a number of Memo fields used to store an object's expression, styles, and other attributes—including the associated Comments you may have added. Not all fields are in use for all kinds of objects, of course.

NOTE The structure of the .FRX/.FRT and the .LBX/.LBT tables is available in the FoxPro documentation. As you learn to manipulate FoxPro tables, you will become comfortable in altering or directly viewing the information in .FRX or .LBX. You may find that creating a report to access the information in the .FRX and .LBX tables is useful. Because the file structure of these tables never varies, you can use such reports to keep records of all the reports or labels you created—and what these reports and labels contain.

So far this chapter has discussed report forms. Many of the features you learned in the preceding sections, however, are important when you design and use labels.

First, you can edit and style label lines by using procedures similar to those used for editing and styling report objects. In addition, storing a master label form that saves the general attributes your company wants for all the labels is a good idea. You also can open several label layout windows and move expressions between the windows. Finally, labels share the reports' capability of containing environment information without using a View file.

That FoxPro labels are internally maintained as tables, similar to report form tables, is a key to this process. In following chapters, you learn that other FoxPro tools maintain information in a similar way.

Designing Basic Labels

The FoxPro Label Designer is a tool that is similar to the Report Writer but that contains far fewer options. Perhaps for this reason, no analog of the Quick Report feature is available in the Label Designer. Still, if you use the skills you already have, standard mailing labels are simple to prepare.

For the next exercise, you can use any standard address file. You have several files available for your use. If you have created all the tables in the model database by using the structures and data found in Appendix H, "Example Database Structures, Data, and Miscellaneous Procedures," you can follow the examples in this section; the examples use the Omnipresent Widget Address table. You also may have constructed your own FoxPro address table (by using the procedure you learned in Chapter 4, "Datebase Management Fundamentals"), or you may have imported address information from another data format. You also have appropriate address data in several of the FoxPro sample applications (the Organize applications use a Clients table). Practice creating labels with any table of address data that you prefer and follow along in the exercise, substituting new field names as necessary.

First open the address file you plan to use. Then use the File New dialog to open an UNTITLED Label file; its extension is .LBX by default. The Label Layout window appears (see fig. 9.10).

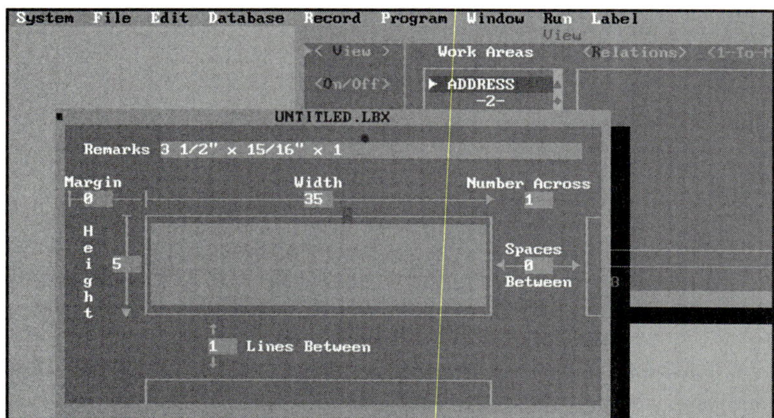

FIG. 9.10

The Label Layout window.

The first thing you need to do when you design a label is to figure out the label's dimensions according to the following limits:

- The number of labels you print across the page
- The size of each label
- The number of lines between the bottom of one label and the top of the next
- The number of characters between the sides of the labels

These dimensions are usually decided by the kind of labels the printer can handle and the kind of labels you purchase. You can vary label dimensions tremendously in FoxPro, however. A single label can be 255 lines long and 255 characters across. You also can place up to 120 labels across the page. These capabilities come in handy if you use the Label Designer to create special report forms.

As shown in figure 9.11, the Label menu popup that appears when you open a label layout window seems to be a much simpler version of the Report popup options. Three options are available, however, that enable you to select, save, and delete standard label layouts.

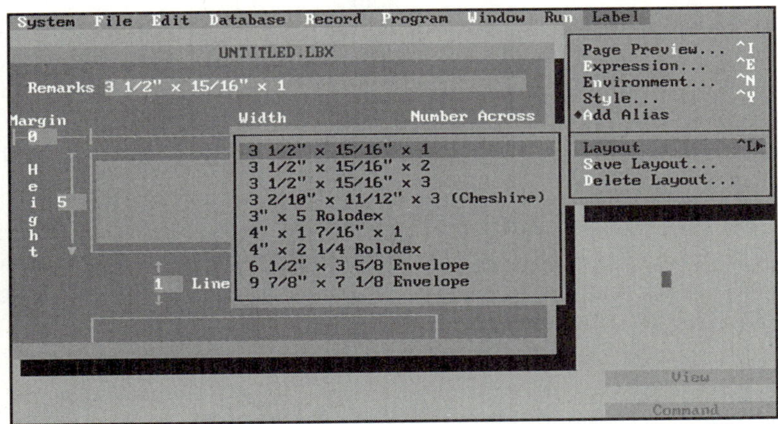

FIG. 9.11 The Label menu options and Sample Layout popup menu.

Because Label Layouts options are designed to handle the dimensions so basic to label output, these options are handled separately from the label environment and printer setup information. The Environment... option on the Label menu popup handles these two features.

If you choose the Layout option from the menu or press Ctrl+L, you see a popup list of standard layouts. Choose a few items from this list.

Watch the label layout window to observe the changes that occur to the various dimension assignments and to the Remarks box that reminds you of the current label type. After you find a label type you use regularly, you may want to edit the Remarks information to include a label stock number. You also can edit the dimension-assignment boxes to fit another standard label type, edit the Remarks box to describe the label, and then use the Save Layout... option to add the label to the available layouts. The figures in this section use the 4" x 1 7/16" x 1 label layout.

The standard label layouts and the label dimensioning process are meant for printers that handle labels in rolls or in continuous form. (You can use the envelope layouts either with continuous form envelopes or with single envelopes sent through the printer from special envelope feeders.) Each label must be exactly the same distance from the next label; no direct provision is available for changing the top and bottom margins for the group of labels almost universally required by label sheets that are used in laser printers.

In FoxPro, however, you can use a printer driver (described in Chapter 16, "Discovering Additional FoxPro Productivity Features") or other printer instructions to designate the top and bottom margins that the printer should use to fit these laser labels (although you cannot tell the Label Designer about these dimensions directly). You then can design the label layout to fit the dimensions of the label you are using, including a number for the option Lines Between labels that matches the distance between labels within one label sheet. The printer takes care of ejecting the sheets.

In Chapter 16, you also learn about the ways to use the printer drivers to create setups appropriate to Hewlett-Packard LaserJet and compatible printers for commonly used label stock and tips on creating setups for other printers and for special needs.

Placing Your Label Expressions

Unlike the Report Writer, the Label Designer has no provisions for text or box objects. FoxPro evaluates each label line as an expression in its entirety. Because FoxPro doesn't have to distinguish between expressions and other kinds of objects in labels, you can type the expressions directly into the label lines.

In the following chapter, you learn how to construct and verify complex expressions; in this chapter, you use the fields in the address table as expressions. Place a Browse or Edit of the address table on-screen so that you can more easily refer to the field names, as shown in figure 9.12. Then type the field names in the label layout.

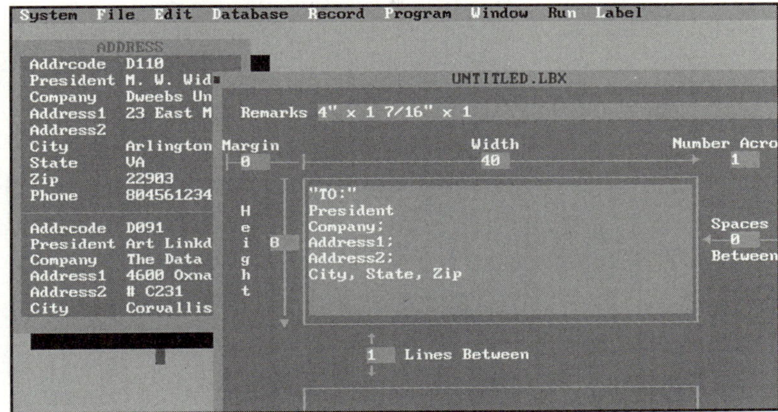

FIG. 9.12

Editing a label.

Look at the line in which you typed `City, State, Zip`. Because each label line must be an expression that FoxPro can evaluate, you must *concatenate*—or add together—the fields in some way to form a valid expression if you want to place more than one field on a line. In FoxPro, you usually concatenate fields or expressions by typing plus signs between the fields or expressions, such as City + State + Zip. With the Label Designer, however, you can conveniently use commas to concatenate. Each comma eliminates blank spaces from the right end of the expression before you add the first expression to the following expression and places exactly one space between the two expressions.

Note that you also place `TO:` in the first line of the labels. This word is not a valid expression. The quotation marks around the word indicate that the report data is a *literal,* or a string of characters, that require no further evaluation.

The lines holding the expressions Company, Address1, and Address2 end in a semicolon. The semicolon at the end of a line suppresses that line if the expressions on it evaluate to complete blanks. (A line with no expressions may be included on a label, of course, if you want a blank line to appear.) In contrast, the President line does not have a semicolon. If the Address table does not have an individual's name as the

President (or main contact) for this company, this line remains blank on the label. In the next chapter, you learn ways to enter an expression such as President or CEO for those labels not having an individual listed. Alternatively, you can prevent the printing of labels for companies that do not have a contact listed by using the FOR clause, SET FILTER, or executing a SQL SELECT command to exclude them, as you learned in earlier chapters.

After you type the label layout, use Page Preview...—as you did in the Report Writer—to check the work. Your screen should be similar to the example in figure 9.13, depending on the address data you are using.

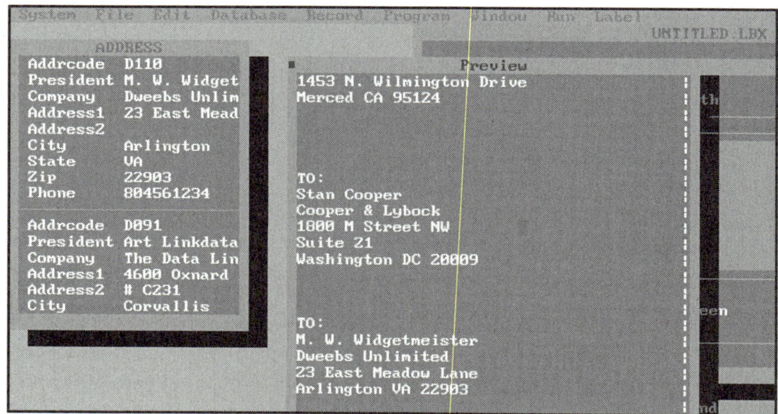

FIG. 9.13

Previewing label output.

Try typing the first and last label lines without the quotation marks and commas to see the difference. Experiment by moving items around in the layout, cutting and pasting selected expressions. Because each label line is an expression, where you type the expression within the line doesn't matter. FoxPro ignores spaces typed before the field name just as it ignores spaces in a command typed in the Command window. Try indenting the Company line. To indent, you must create an expression that indents (perhaps by adding two spaces between the quotation marks), such as the following line:

```
"  "+Company
```

Another result of the fact that each complete label line is an expression is that you use the Label menu option or press Ctrl+Y to choose a style for each label line as a single object. The Style options and Alignment options, the procedures for saving label files and the associated environment, and setup information are similar to those in reports.

Sending Labels and Reports

Now that you can create simple labels and reports, you need a way to deliver these items. First, save the label you have created as MODEL.LBX.

The Database menu pad contains two options, Report... and Label..., which have associated dialogs for this purpose. Chapter 2, "Understanding the FoxPro Interface," introduced you to the Report dialog. You also learned ways to specify records to be considered (the Scope) and the conditions for which a command should act (FOR and WHILE clauses and the capability of SET FILTER command), when you used the LIST command in the Chapter 3, "Exploring Databases and Tables." Now you can put these dialogs to good use. Remember that you can use the `Form` button to specify the name of the report or label, and you can use the Environment check box to open all required files without using further commands.

Notice that the Preview option on the Report dialog also gives you the same capability as the Page Preview... options of the Label and Report menu popups. This option is useful for checking the scope or conditions you selected or for verifying that you identified the correct report or label file.

NOTE To have a more flexible view of the report or labels onscreen, use the To File check box to specify a file name. You then can open the file you created (which has a .TXT extension by default). You can scroll through, search through, and even edit or import the file into a word processor, just as you can with all other text files. Usually, when you open a text file created in this manner, you should choose Edit Preferences so that you can turn word wrap off. You also can just open the file as a program (and not as a text file), and word wrap is turned off by default.

As shown in figure 9.14, the Label dialog offers one extra option to print Sample labels. Continuous-form labels usually must be positioned very carefully in a printer, both horizontally and vertically. FoxPro provides this option so that you can run a sample label, or as many samples as needed, composed of lines of asterisks that match the full dimensions of the label you specified. (In figure 9.14, you also see three sample labels echoed to the console behind the dialogs.) You can adjust the label stock in the printer and print more samples until you have the asterisks correctly placed. Each time you print a sample, you may be asked whether you need more samples, whether you want to do labels, or whether you prefer to choose `Cancel`. Start the print run after you are satisfied with the position of the stock.

The SAMPLE option works best when you're using *continuous form* labels rather than the individual sheets used by laser printers. Printing labels from FoxPro for DOS requires some special instructions to be sent to laser printers to accommodate the laser label sheets' top and bottom margin. Refer to Chapter 16 for more information on sending these instructions to the printer.

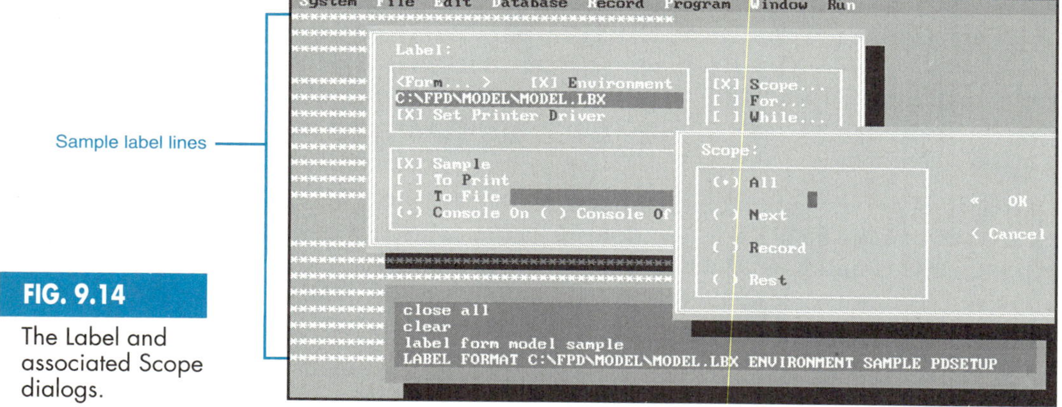

FIG. 9.14

The Label and associated Scope dialogs.

Summary

Reports and labels are the true representatives of your database management skills. By using the Report Writer and the Label Designer, you can quickly create, test, and rearrange countless formats in which you can present database information on-screen and on-paper.

Creating this kind of output—even on the rudimentary level you have achieved so far—once required many hours of tedious programming. In the following chapter, you learn to produce more sophisticated label and report formats by using these two powerful tools and a little more effort.

10

CHAPTER

Using the Report Writer and Label Designer

As you continue exploring FoxPro output, you need to draw on all you have learned about database systems (related tables, data order, and so on). Although the data sets available to you are still relatively limited, the options for displaying on-screen and printing these data sets are almost unlimited when you use the Report Writer and Label Designer.

Using Related Tables in a Report or Label

In the last chapter, you created a MODEL.FRX report form to learn how to manipulate the Report Writer as a tool. This report is analogous to a simple BROWSE command; it displays information about a single database table. As you learned in Chapter 8, a Browse window can be much more informative if the window displays the information from two or more tables from the database. You establish a relationship between both tables by using information common to the tables to link records from one table to those of the other. You can then use BROWSE to show this linked information for both tables together.

Similarly, a report is more useful if that report includes information about two or more tables from a database. In this section, you create report form expressions and layouts that demonstrate this principle. You can start with the basic MODEL.FRX from Chapter 9, or create a Quick Report by using the Budget table on which to practice; for these exercises, do not be too concerned with the *appearance* of the report elements or the report layout.

Reopen the MODEL.FRX report form so that you can continue to make changes; or open the Budget file, choose to create a New Report from the File menu popup, and use the Report menu popup's Quick Report option as described in Chapter 9.

Because you are examining budget items in relation to the model product line in this session, open the Product table and set the Product table order to Prodcode. With the Budget table in the currently selected work area, set a relation on the Prodcode field from the Budget table into the Product table. As Chapter 4, "Database Management Fundamentals," discusses, this step ensures that the record pointer in the Product file moves to information appropriate to the current record in the selected file—in this case, a Budget file. In figure 10.1, you can see this relationship illustrated in the View window. As the View window shows, other tables in the Omnipresent Widget database that are related to the Budget table (Budcat and Dept) also have been opened and related to Budget. Although Budget remains the selected table, all the other related files' record pointers move to correspond to the current Budget record.

Because you are creating a report that concentrates on the Products and the associated budget lines, add a few page header lines and use Ctrl+T, or just start typing in an empty space to add a Text Object to serve as a title that indicates the purpose of this report. If the title doesn't end where you want it to, move it or center it.

Because the data about departments is not necessary in the report, you can remove it and then move the Product field expression and heading to the left. At this point, the product code isn't too informative unless the report's recipient knows the codes for the Widget product line. However, you have the Prodname field, with English descriptions of each product, available in the Product table. You can add a new report expression under the product code by placing the cursor under the product code by using the Report Field menu option or by pressing Ctrl+F. The Report Expression dialog you saw in the preceding chapter appears (see fig. 10.1). Select the `Expr...` (Expression) push button, and the Expression Builder dialog appears (see fig. 10.2).

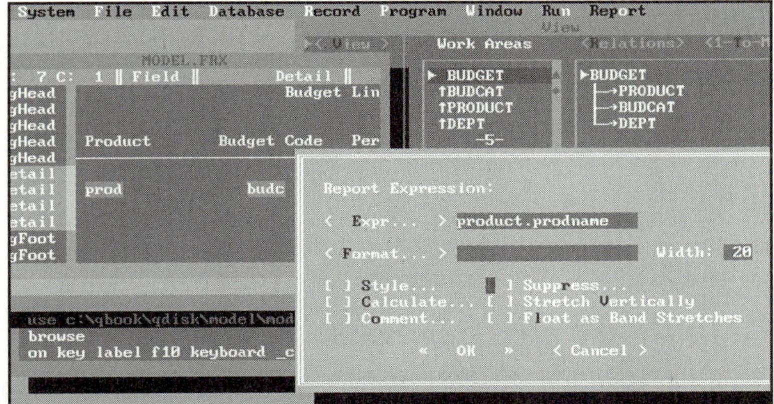

FIG. 10.1

A report expression from a second table shows in the Report Expression dialog.

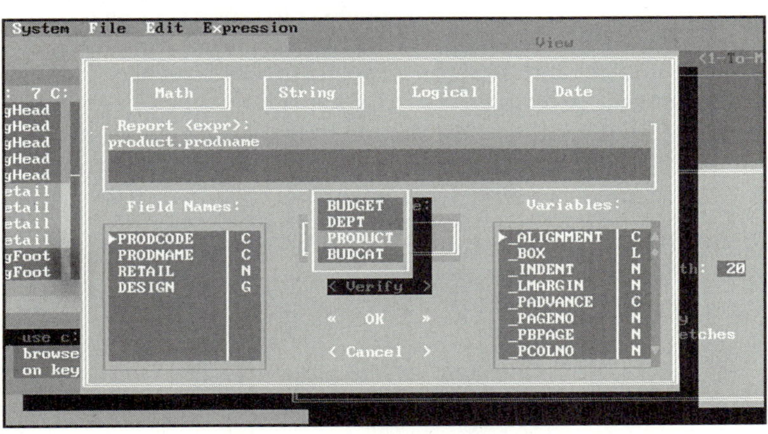

FIG. 10.2

Creating the report expression in the Expression Builder.

You first encountered the Expression Builder while building FOR and WHILE conditions for a LIST command or for report and label output. You also saw that this dialog is available to SET a FILTER on the records. (The filter condition limits your display of records from a table, and if you issue any commands, the commands only affect records appropriate to the filter.) You can use the Expression Builder throughout FoxPro as a way to create complex expressions for all purposes. The popup controls at the top of the window are labeled with the different kinds of functions and operations available to act on each data type. In the lower-left corner is a Field Picker list, enabling you to add database fields to an expression. Use the Database popup to see fields from any currently open tables. To the right, you see a list of the variables currently in memory, including all variable names to which you assigned values and the system variables that FoxPro creates. These variables begin with the _ (underscore character).

You can select fields, functions, and variables from all these Expression Builder sources. These items then appear in the *expression box* titled Report <expr>, in the middle of the Expression Builder. This area is where you build the expression. You also can type directly into this box, and you can edit the contents in the same way you can edit other FoxPro text.

In this chapter, you use the Expression Builder extensively to create increasingly sophisticated expressions for reports and labels. To begin using the Expression Builder, select the Product Table and then place the Prodname field in the expression box, as shown in figure 10.2.

Note that the table alias, Product, is placed in the expression box with the field name; a period separates the alias from the field name. When you are forming expressions or creating output from different sources, you must add the aliases so that FoxPro knows where to find each item.

Confirm this choice, and then the Report Expression dialog appears with the expression box filled out. (If you prefer, you can type the information directly into the box.) Note that the expression *width* also is filled out; by default, this number is the length of the field you chose. Confirm this choice as well.

The Report Layout window appears, displaying a new report expression object. If necessary, move the expression to a position under the Prodcode expression. Your screen looks like the screen in figure 10.3.

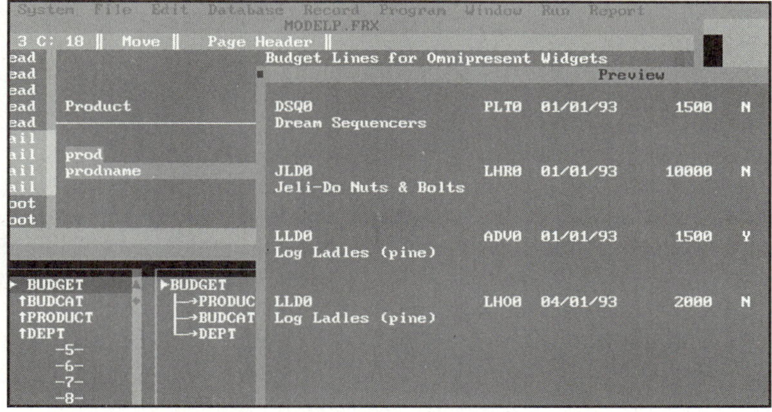

FIG. 10.3

A Report that uses Related tables.

If you want to return to the original version of this report at a later date, save it to a new name MODELP. Be sure to save its new environment along with the report.

You can easily see how you can repeat the same process in a label form. The Omnipresent Widget Customer table, for example, is related to an Address table by the field Addrcode, which indicates the address and company of a certain customer. (Although the Address table holds one main contact and phone number for a company, many contacts and their personal phone numbers may be related to each company.)

Suppose that you want labels for all customers meeting certain criteria. The criterion for inclusion in a mailing may be part of the Customer table (such as the person's title, age, or the first letter of his last name), or selection criteria may include information from the related Address table (such as all people in a particular ZIP code). Complex conditions can incorporate information from other tables; you may relate a Sales table, for example, and find out which individuals in a particular ZIP code have bought items from Omnipresent Widgets between specific dates. To trace the results of your mailing, the label could include a sales code indicating what products your customers have purchased or the date of their most recent invoice. Select the Customer table for your work area. For the first label line, use Prefix, Firstname, Lastname, because as you learned in the last chapter, labels use commas to concatenate expressions that have exactly one blank space between them. Another label line may read Sales.Datesold, followed by Address.Company, and the rest of the label is filled out with information from the Address table as before.

As explained earlier, you can add aliases to the fields from the selected table used in expressions (Customer.Prefix, Customer.Firstname, Customer.Lastname) for clarity. Just as when you use related tables in a multitable BROWSE FIELDS list, however, you must add table aliases for fields from tables in other work areas (Address.Company, Sales.Datesold).

In the report and label described in this section, the Product and Address tables are functioning as *lookups* in many-to-one relationships with the Budget and Customer tables. If a table is used as a lookup, this table is used to store information that otherwise would be entered repeatedly in another table. In the current report about Budget items, many Budget records share information from one Product entry. Although you have not created the data for other lookup tables yet, after the Omnipresent Widget database is complete, each Budget record also gets information from other lookups into the Dept and Budcat tables.

Lookups prevent wasting both valuable disk space and data-entry time. You can retrieve the information in labels, reports, and other output only when you need it. Other cases may exist, however, where the relationship between the tables in a report or label is not quite so straightforward.

Using One-to-Many Relationships in a Report

The Omnipresent Widget system has an Address table in which each company address record may be related to many Customer or Contact records, each of which in turn may be related to many Sales records. You may need to generate an invoice for each company, but the record pointers in the related tables must move many times for each company record. In other applications, you might have a Customer account table related to an address table that has several possible addresses for each account (for shipping, billing, and home office purposes). When you generate mailing labels for a marketing release, you can send each customer a flyer at each address that you have on record.

You know that FoxPro can handle this kind of situation by using the SET SKIP command, which you can execute by defining a one-to-many relationship between tables in the View window. In this section, you learn to express this type of relationship in a FoxPro report.

The tables you currently have open can handle a one-to-many relationship between Products and the associated Budget entries, so you can use these tables for the following example.

In the View window, first eliminate the current relationship between the Budget and Product tables. Leaving this relationship in place can cause a cyclical relation error because only one of two tables at a time can control the relationship between the tables. In the Relations box of the View window, select the Product table (currently pointed to by a relation from the Budget table). The Expression Builder appears with the Prodcode field, on which the relation was set, displayed in the expression box. The field is already selected, as indicated by the highlight; press the Backspace or Del key so that the expression box is empty. Confirm the choice. When the Expression Builder disappears, the relation between the Budget and Product tables is no longer set.

Make the Product table the current work area; a triangle appears next to its name in the Work Areas list. Then press R or select the `Relations` push button, and set a new relationship from the Product table into the Budget table. You need to set the order of the Budget table on the Prodcode field and accept the default of Prodcode when the Expression Builder asks on which expression the relation is to be set.

After you return to the View window, press T or select the `1-To-Many` push button. If you have several tables open and other relationships set, as shown in figure 10.4, you are asked for a related table (or tables) to which you want the one-to-many relationship set. Designate the Budget table. In the Work Areas list, a ■ symbol appears to the right of the Product table entry, indicating that this action was taken.

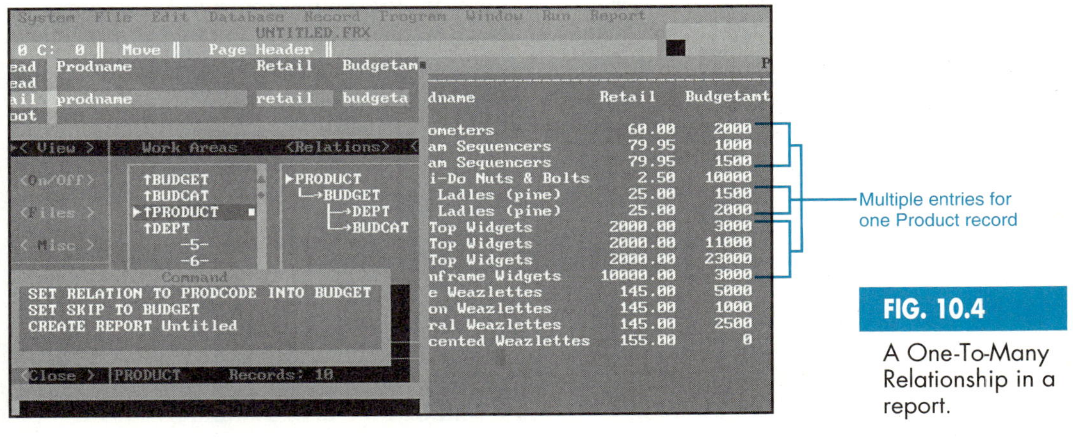

FIG. 10.4

A One-To-Many Relationship in a report.

Next generate a Quick Report for the Product table, using the Prodname and Retail fields. As you learned to do in the last section, add a detail entry (and a heading if you prefer) for a field from the related Budget table. The example uses Budget.Budgetamt.

As you see in figure 10.4, with the one-to-many relationship set, there are as many detail entries for each Product table record as Budget table entries exist for the product. Remove the one-to-many relationship from the View window, preview the report again, and you can see the difference; only one detail entry shows for each product. Reinstate the one-to-many relationship and save this report to a new name (MODELS), using the File Save As... menu popup option.

Adding Complex Label and Report Expressions

Although each report expression you have used has been a single field or variable, more complex report expressions can use many fields and variables combined with FoxPro functions and operators. To explore more ways of refining the report expressions you can produce, return to the MODELP report and the product lookup information and environment saved earlier in this chapter. Make sure that you restore the environment to the File Setup and relationships this report requires, including the many-to-one relationship. (Because you are reversing the relationship between the Budget and Product tables again, CLOSE DATABASES from the Command window or use the View window to remove their current relationship. By taking either of these actions, you avoid a "cyclical relation" warning as FoxPro attempts to place the Budget and Product tables in the relationship defined by your saved report environment.)

Formatting Expressions in the Report Writer

After you select the Product.prodname expression for editing (by double-clicking it or by pressing the space bar twice), the report expression dialog reappears. Below the `Expr...` button and text box, you see another button and text box for expression formatting. Select the `Format...` button. A dialog displaying several formatting options appears (see fig. 10.5).

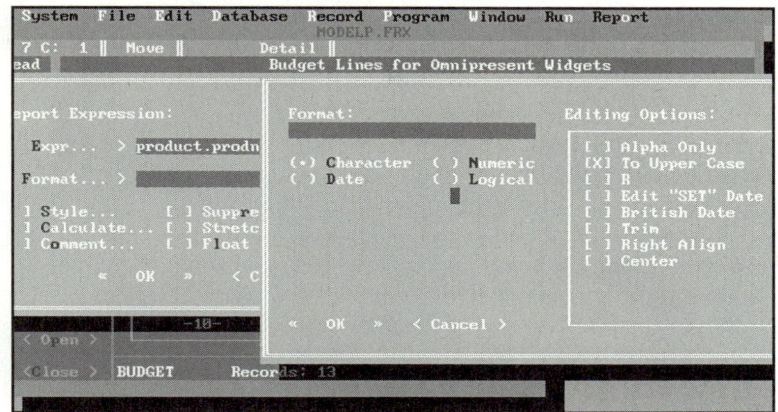

FIG. 10.5

The Format dialog for a character-type expression.

Because Prodname is a character-type field, FoxPro assumes that the expression you are building is a character-type expression and gives you options appropriate for formatting character data. As you build more complicated expressions, you find that FoxPro takes a best guess at the kind of data the expression eventually returns. This guess, however, isn't always correct, so FoxPro provides radio buttons for specifying the kind of expression you are creating. Select a different radio button, and the formatting options change.

In figure 10.5, the format check box To Upper Case is selected. When you return to the report expression dialog, the appropriate codes appear in the Format text box. You also can type these format codes, along with picture templates, directly in the text box or in the Format dialog. By typing these format codes and picture templates, you can make more formatting decisions about the way the expression looks than are available when you create from the check box choices. The check boxes simply provide a convenient list of the most commonly used format codes so that you do not need to remember the codes.

If you access the Help file from the Format dialog, you see a more complete list of the codes and templates available for you to type into the Format box. You may recognize this list from the formatting functions and pictures available for BROWSEd fields discussed in Chapter 8, "Organizing the Answers with BROWSE." You use the same formatting options in BROWSEs and reports—and also in data-entry screens you design in Chapters 12 and 13.

Practice using the format options available by clicking the check boxes for each data type. You have already altered a character expression (Product.Prodcode). To see the way the formatting changes affect the report, practice formatting fields of other types—using Budget.Period for date, Budget.Budgetamt for numeric, and Budget.Final for logical—and use the Report Preview option.

TIP The Right Align format option is not equivalent to the Right Alignment style you encounter in Chapter 9, "Putting the Answers To Work in Reports and Labels." Styles affect only printer drivers, not the formatting of the object when the report is run. If you use the Right Alignment style for any object, make sure that you also select Right Align in the Format dialog for the same object so that it appears right-justified whether or not a printer driver setup is used.

FoxPro does not have check boxes to make format options for a logical-type report expression directly available to you. The Budget.Final expression, however, shows a format template—the letter *Y*. If this letter is used, logical data appears as either Y for *yes* or N for *no* rather than the .T. for *true* and .F. for *false* that otherwise appears. The Quick Report creates this format for logical data without your intervention.

Remove the Y format and use the Page Preview... option to see the difference in formatting. You see only a period showing in each detail line under the Final heading. When you create custom expressions or adjust the format for an expression, you often need to adjust the expression Width as well. To make room for the expression, type **3** in the Budget.Final Width box provided in the Report Expression dialog.

If the model report is arranged like the report in figure 10.3, you also may want to adjust the width of the Product.Prodname field. The report looks sloppy because the field's right edge does not come all the way under the Budget.Budcatcode beside it. You can shorten the field by a few characters and lose any whole word that doesn't fit, or you can use the Stretch Vertically option, and the expression wraps to the next line. In this case, the latter idea is better because you know the memo field in the report often adds a number of detail lines to each report entry.

So far you still are adjusting the look of a single field, but both the Report Writer and the Label Designer handle more sophisticated expressions as report objects. Both tools use the Expression Builder to handle this task.

Using the Expression Builder in the Label Designer and the Report Writer

In the Expression Builder, you use database fields, constant values, values stored in memory variables, and the functions and operators of the FoxPro language to literally build an expression which FoxPro evaluates. You then can return the result of this evaluation as the report or label object you want to print.

In Part IV, "FoxProgramming: Enhanced Use of the Design Tools," and Part V, "Getting To Know FoxPro Commands and Functions," of this book, you develop a better sense of the wide variety of actions you can take to manipulate different kinds of data. To take full advantage of the Report Writer and Label Designer, however, gradually accustom yourself to using more FoxPro functions to define output expressions.

As previously stated, the four popup controls divide relevant functions by data types for easy reference (see fig. 10.6). Then the Expression Builder can help you develop your knowledge of FoxPro's data-manipulating capabilities. You can select these functions from the popups or type the function names directly in the expression box in the following quick practice samples.

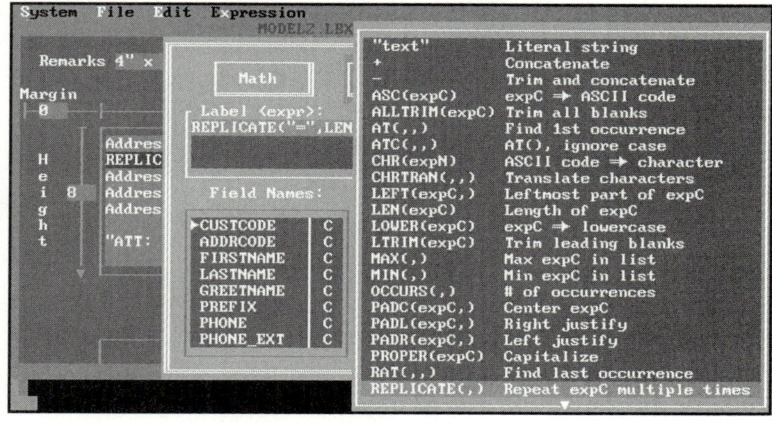

FIG. 10.6 One of the Expression Builder's popup controls provides the functions available for use on character-type data.

Using the Expression Builder with Character-Type Data

A FoxPro function usually consists of a *keyword* (a word with a special meaning in the FoxPro language) followed by a set of parentheses.

These parentheses can enclose one, more than one, or no *parameters* (items of data or other instructions you give the function). If the function requires more than one parameter, you must use commas to separate the parameters. Using these instructions, each function performs a particular action and returns a value. The value is then used for output or examined by still other functions until you have the desired result. If you use more than one function in an expression, the function in the innermost set of parentheses is acted on first, followed by the next innermost, until the outermost level is reached, and the expression returns a value. When an expression includes other expressions, the expressions are referred to as *nested*.

Consider the somewhat alarming-looking expression in figure 10.7. The expression is really simple when you examine what the expression does.

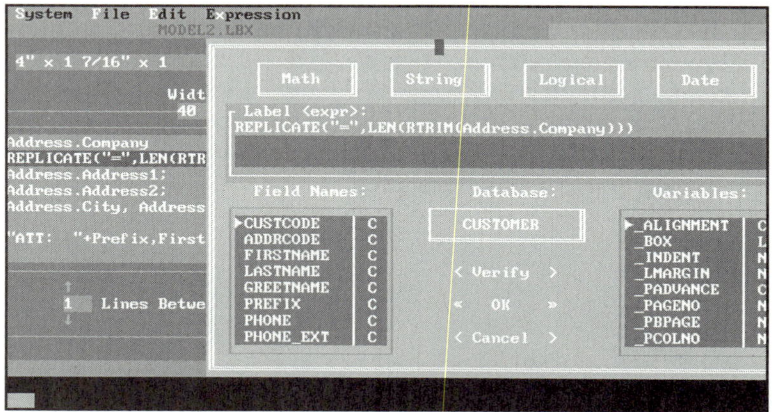

FIG. 10.7

The Expression Builder at work in the Label Designer.

The label layout shown has been adjusted to provide results for each customer, as suggested earlier in this chapter. (Customer is the selected work area, with a many-to-one relationship into the Address table.) The company name is now first. The following string and the contact name are now placed in a lower line of the layout:

```
"ATT:   "
```

These items are concatenated with the + sign to form a valid expression. (Note that the string concatenation, using +, works together in one label expression with the Label Designer's special use of a comma between fields.)

The goal here is to draw a graphics line in the Label Designer, which doesn't share the box and line-drawing capabilities of the Report

Writer. In the second line, a line has been added beneath the company name. You want this line to vary in length to match the company name entry. To create this effect, open the Label Expression Builder by using the Expression option of the Label menu or pressing Ctrl+E. (To edit any label expression after you create the expression, select the expression and access the Label Expression Builder again, as shown in the example.)

As the innermost function, you type the following expression:

```
RTRIM(Address.Company)
```

The RTRIM( ) function removes trailing blanks from the expression passed to it. The preceding expression takes the Company field and removes all blank spaces that may follow the company name.

The LEN( ) function then takes the character expression passed to it (the result of the RTRIM( ) function) and returns the *number* of characters in the expression. You then know how long the line should be.

The REPLICATE( ) function takes all characters received as the first parameter and repeats this passed information a number of times, according to the second parameter, the result of the LEN( ) function. (Note that you use the graphics character "=", using the quotation marks so that FoxPro interprets the character literally. You also can express this character as an ASCII value by typing the CHR( ) function CHR(205).)

When an expression is unwieldy, you can shorten most FoxPro functions and commands to four characters. The completed label expression might look like the following:

```
REPL("=",LEN(RTRIM(Address.Company)))
```

Note that, unlike FoxPro internal keywords, the alias and the field name, which you created yourself, must not be abbreviated.

Figure 10.8 displays the results of the expression in the Label Page Preview.

TIP

When you used the Expression Builder, you may have made at least one typing mistake, such as leaving out one parenthesis in a pair of parentheses. Click the `Verify` push button in the Expression Builder to check your work. Verify's error messages are not especially enlightening, but you can still save a great deal of time if you make sure that FoxPro understands what you have typed before you continue with the report or label design session.

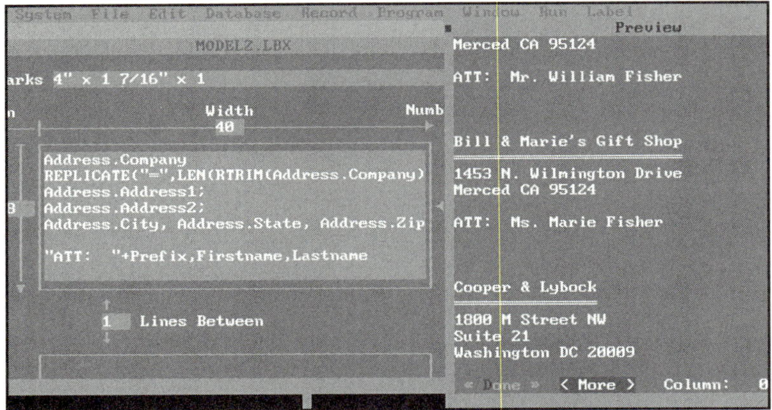

FIG. 10.8

The Expression Builder's results in the Label Preview.

Formatting a Report Expression by Using the Expression Builder

For another example of the Expression Builder at work, open any saved version of the model report. If you look at the page number of any Quick Report or MODEL.FRX in the Report Preview, you notice that the report has an unsightly gap between the word Page and the actual number provided by the system variable _PAGENO. As created by the Quick Report feature, Page is a text object, and the page number is a numeric expression next to it. The numeric expression defaults to a width of 4, so you can easily prepare a Quick Report of up to 9,999 pages—but the resulting page number in the report is not very attractive. There are too many spaces between the word Page and the page number.

For the word and the page number to flow together, they must be part of the same object. First remove the Page text object. (If the objects were grouped when you previously edited the report, you need to ungroup the two objects first.) Then select and edit the report expression that contains the _PAGENO variable. Create an expression that includes the word "Page " as a literal, using the quotation marks again. You can use "P. " or "Pg. " or any other word or set of words you like, but you should include a single space at the end. Concatenate this string with the _PAGENO expressed as a string of characters by using the following expression:

```
"Page " + ALLTRIM(STR(_PAGENO))
```

The STR( ) function converts the number you pass as the parameter to a string of characters, and the ALLTRIM( ) function that surrounds the string removes all leading and trailing blanks. Change the width of the expression to allow for several more characters. (Should you receive an error message such as `Width must be between 1 and 4` after you save the expression, you have attempted to add more characters than the number of characters between the leftmost column of the expression and the right margin. Change the width to a smaller number until you no longer get the error message.) Any extra characters in the expression width are placed on the right side, where they don't interfere with the expression's appearance. You are now ensured a well-formatted page number whether you are on page 1, page 100, or page 1000, and you did so with one report object that you can easily reposition on the page without grouping.

NOTE The preceding technique—changing a number to a character format—is extremely useful for solving a wide variety of output problems. Experiment with the TRANSFORM( ) function, and also STR( ), to get a better idea of all the possibilities. A fundamental rule for creating valid expressions that you concatenated from several parts, as is done in the Expression Builder, is that all the elements added together must be the same data type. You often must convert parts of an expression to match the other parts, as you did here.

Formatting Dates with the Expression Builder

A good use of the Expression Builder is to format dates for display and for reports. The model report uses the DATE( ) function, which checks the system clock and returns a current date for display. FoxPro has an easy-to-use function to show the date in a more legible way. To create a more readable date, use the following expression:

```
MDY(DATE( ))
```

In this expression, the MDY( ) function evaluates the system date and produces a *Month-day-year* format, which may not provide exactly what you need. Single-digit days of the month, for example, appear like the following line:

```
June 06, 1993
```

IF CENTURY is SET OFF (check the setting in the View Window Miscellaneous Panel), the result is even less attractive:

```
June 06, 93
```

By using the following expression, you can produce a much more pleasing *dateline* for the reports:

```
CDOW(DATE( ))+", "+CMONTH(DATE( ))+" "
+ ALLTRIM(STR(DAY(DATE( )))) + ", "
+ STR(YEAR(DATE( )),4,0)
```

FoxPro evaluates this expression, reading the associated elements from left to right, in the following way:

- Returns the day of the week, followed by a comma and a space.
- Adds the month of the system date, expressed as a string of characters, followed by a space. (Another function, MONTH( ), is available that returns the *number* of the month for the date evaluated.)
- Adds the day of the system date, converted to a string and with all leading and trailing spaces removed, followed by another comma and a space.
- Adds the year of the system date, converted to a string and including four characters with no decimal places.

As an added advantage, the final STR(YEAR(DATE( )),4,0) element of this expression correctly includes all four digits of the year, regardless of the current state of the SET CENTURY switch previously discussed.

Selecting Printer Enhancements for Expressions

Note that you used no semicolons to type this long line, as you usually do to make the line manageable in the Command window (and as you subsequently do when you write programs). In the Expression Builder, an expression too long to fit on one line wraps. All lines in the expression box are part of the same expression even if you use carriage returns.

This expression obviously has a variable length, depending on the system date. Make sure that the width you use provides enough space for the longest possible date. When you mark the Format Center check box for this kind of variable length expression, centering the report object in the layout is not really sufficient because FoxPro doesn't always return the same number of characters as the full width of the object. If you select the Format Center check box, you are centering the actual expression *within the width of the report object.* You then can correctly center the resulting object in the layout by using the Center menu option.

Using Delimiters in Expressions

So far you have dealt mostly with character and numeric data in expressions, using care to convert some elements to different data types to make sure that you can concatenate all the elements into one expression. FoxPro accepts a literal string of characters, such as a comma and a space, as part of a character-type expression if you *delimit* (or enclose) the characters with quotation marks. You also can use single quotes (by typing the right single quote character, `'`, only) or brackets (`[]`) to delimit literal character strings. You can use a literal date in an expression by enclosing the date in curly braces (`{}`), as the following example shows:

```
MDY({12/01/91})
```

Be careful that you express the date according to the current DATE format SET in your system, which you learned to check and adjust in the View Misc panel.

In a similar way, you delimit logical data by using a period on either side so that FoxPro interprets the .T. as *the value True*, rather than as the letter T.

Controlling Field Output with Variable Conditions

A valuable function in the Expression Builder is the IIF( ) (or "Immediate If") function. These parentheses must enclose the following three parameters, separated by commas:

- The first parameter checks a condition and evaluates to a logical value (true or false).
- The second parameter is returned if the condition is true.
- The third parameter is returned if the condition is false.

In the model report, the instruction `"Make notes here"` is included adjacent to the box that holds the Notes memofield data. This instruction, however, isn't really useful if the box is filled with text. Delete and replace this text object with the following report expression:

```
IIF(EMPTY(Budget.Notes),"Make notes here","")
```

This expression indicates to the Report Writer that if the Notes field has nothing in it for this record, Report Writer prints some instructions. Otherwise, Report prints nothing. *Nothing* is expressed in the third parameter by the *null string* (`""`).

An important fact illustrated here is that a Report Writer or Label Designer expression doesn't need to return anything to be printed; the expression can simply evaluate a condition or do other work, including issuing printer instructions, without creating visible results.

If you place this expression underneath the Notes field and stretching box, remember to select Float as Band Stretches as you did for the original text object. You may also want to choose Suppress Blank Lines from the Page Layout options screen, as discussed in the preceding chapter.

Always be careful that you adjust the Width text box or resize the object width in the layout for any expression that has variable widths under different conditions, because FoxPro cannot guess the eventual width. An expression must have *some* width. If you know that the expression never returns anything as output, type a width of `1`. This step, although it may seem unnecessary or annoying, is actually very convenient because it enables you to see and manipulate this expression object within the report layout.

Suppose that you are interested in reading the Notes field (and taking up a correspondingly large number of lines in your report) only when the budget item concerns a significant amount of money. You can use the following for the IIF( ) function in place of the Notes field report expression in the model report:

```
IIF(Budget.Budgetamt > 2000, Budget.Notes,
"Minor budget item.")
```

You can specify how significant the item has to be for the report to include Notes if you replace the literal 2000 in this expression with a variable, such as in the following:

```
IIF(Budget.Budgetamt > big_item,Budget.Notes,
"Minor budget item.")
```

Before you run the report, assign a value to this variable in the Command window, as in the following example:

```
big_item = 2000
```

You can adjust the assigned value for every report you run, if necessary. If you forget to assign a value to this variable, the FoxPro error message `Variable 'big_item' not found` appears in an alert window when you try to run the report. (Later in this chapter, you learn a trick to avoid this error by using report variables.) If you assign a value to the variable in the Command window, however, note that you can select big_item from the Variables list in the Expression Builder, as shown in figure 10.9, to include the variable in a report expression. You also can Preview the report and use the `Verify` push button to verify the expression successfully once the variable has been assigned a value.

Figure 10.9 shows another IIF( ) expression; an asterisk is placed in front of the same significant budget items. Note that this expression returns a character string (the "* " concatenated with a converted Budget.Budgetamt field) in one case and a number (the Budgetamt field value) in the other. Having an expression return values of different types at different times is perfectly proper; however, you usually need to be careful that you assign a width and all required formatting to the return value.

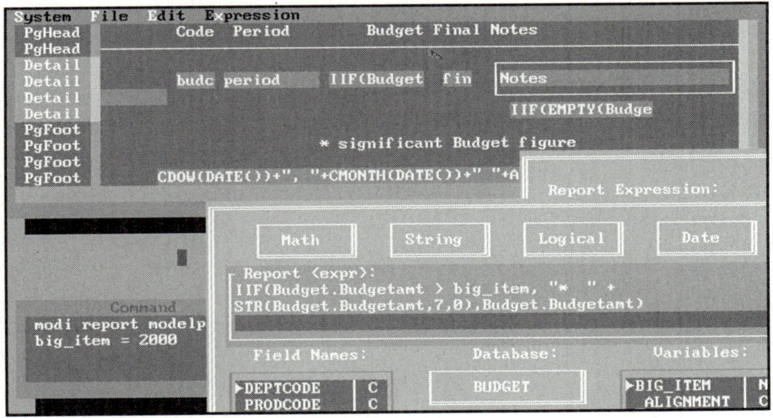

FIG. 10.9

Designing an expression with the IIF( ) function.

Figure 10.10 shows the result of some suggested changes you made in this report.

This Preview was created with the screen set to 50 lines, using the command SET DISPLAY TO VGA50, available on systems with VGA video monitors and boards.

In Chapter 7, "Querying with SQL and Searching with Rushmore," you create an SQL SELECT statement that uses the UNION clause to simulate an outer join. Remember that a placeholder value was added for all products that had no Budget table entry. For a report on the results of this query, you can replace the placeholder item with a more meaningful entry, as follows:

```
IIF(budgetamt=9999999,"Unbudgeted!",budgetamt)
```

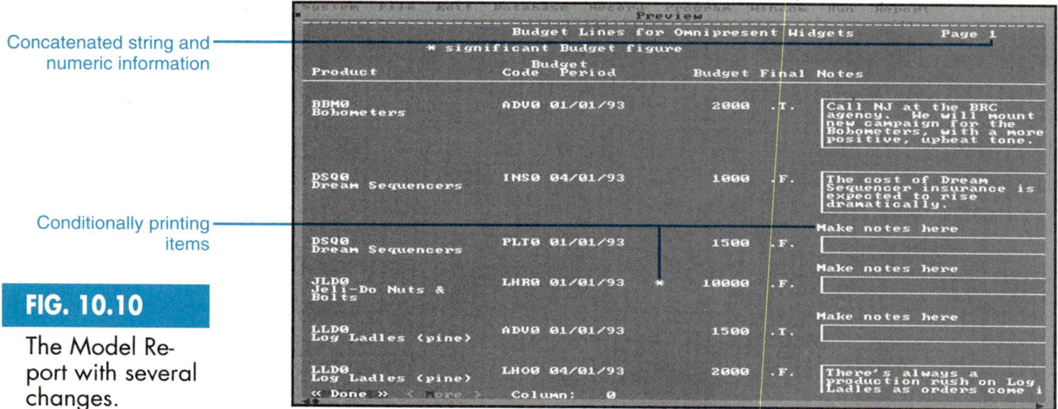

FIG. 10.10

The Model Report with several changes.

If you designed the query to leave the Budgetamt at 0, you may have added a different kind of placeholder field, as in the following SELECT statement:

```
SELECT Product.Prodname,;
    Budget.Budgetamt ,;
    .T. as Budgeted;
  FROM Budget, Product ;
  WHERE Product.Prodcode = Budget.Prodcode ;
UNION ;
  SELECT Product.Prodname, ;
      0, ;
      .F. as Budgeted;
    FROM Product ;
    WHERE Product.Prodcode NOT IN ;
    (SELECT Budget.Prodcode FROM Budget);
INTO CURSOR CHAP7004
```

This placeholder field (Budgeted) can be used directly in the report as a logical, or it can form the condition for your IIF( ) expression.

Remember that using the Expression Builder can be equally varied in the Label Designer. A common use of the IIF( ) function is for addressing. Suppose that you have an address table in which you can store the full names of two different individuals. To address a label correctly, you need to format the names differently when two individuals are listed. You also may need to check whether both individuals use the same last name. The following expression uses two nested IIF( ) functions to accomplish both these checks; as usual, the innermost element is evaluated first:

```
IIF(EMPTY(fname2),
     ALLTRIM(fname1),
     IIF(ALLTRIM(lname2) = ALLTRIM(lname1),
          ALLTRIM(fname1) + " & " + ALLTRIM(fname2),
          ALLTRIM(fname2) + " " +
          ALLTRIM(lname2)+ " & " +
          ALLTRIM(fname1))) +
" " + lname1
```

No matter how complicated this expression looks, you can evaluate one section at a time, just as FoxPro does and just as you did with simpler expressions. Other sections of this chapter present additional tricks for using the IIF( ) expression.

Using User-Defined Functions

In spite of the bewildering variety of tools available to you at the touch of a popup control in the Expression Builder, you still may want to perform some actions or to manipulate data in ways that FoxPro functions do not directly provide.

You can write short programs or procedures that can be called in report or label expressions just as the internal FoxPro functions are called. These procedures are known as *user-defined functions*, or *UDF*s.

If you have used FoxPro Version 1, be aware that you have less need to create UDFs for reports than ever before because of FoxPro 2's new *report variables*, described in a following section of this chapter. Situations may still arise, however, in which you may want to call external functions that you design.

One reason to use UDFs is that the Expression Builder limits you to 254 characters for a given expression. As you evaluate data in the process of creating a single item of output, you may want to exceed this length.

Another reason to use UDFs may be that you need to break down the task you want to accomplish into several steps. In a UDF, you can issue a long sequence of commands before you return a result.

Designing and creating a UDF is covered more thoroughly in Chapter 18, "Understanding Program Structure." In this chapter, simple examples show you how to include UDFs in reports and labels.

If the printer uses single sheets rather than continuous forms or if you feed single letterhead sheets to a printer that otherwise uses a bin, the

Report Writer has no internal provision for a pause until you insert each additional page. You can add this feature with a UDF. In the Command window, type the following command:

```
WAIT WINDOW
```

Press Enter to issue the command. A small system window appears in the upper-right corner of the screen, similar to other notices you have received. The system window vanishes when you press any key or click the mouse. This window and pressing the required key is FoxPro's way of providing the kind of pause you need. All you need to do is to alert the report form to issue the pause.

From the File New... menu popup option, choose the Program option to create a program. A text-editing window opens. This window looks like any other text-editing window, except that the name of the file you are editing has a default extension of .PRG. (The file name appears in the window's title bar and is UNTITLED.PRG at present.)

In this editing window, type the same two words that you typed in the Command window and add a second line:

```
WAIT WINDOW
RETURN ""
```

End each line by pressing Enter. (Programs are not word wrapped.) Then save and close the file, typing `WAITPAGE.PRG` as the name.

NOTE You just wrote a program. If you never have tried programming, you may think that the process is terribly complicated, but a program is just a text file that holds a sequence of actions you want to perform. Each action is like a command you type in the Command window or a command generated in the Command window after you make a menu choice. When you are ready to run this sequence of actions, issue a command to DO the program. FoxPro reads and then executes the commands, one after the other.

Position the cursor in the first position of the first pageheader line of the report and create a report expression object at this position. In the expression box, type the following expression, in the same way you type any function belonging to the FoxPro language:

```
Waitpage( )
```

Give this expression the width `1`. This UDF, Waitpage( ) function, which has no parameters, executes the WAIT WINDOW command and then returns the null string to the report for output. Because you placed the function in the first position of the page, you caused the report to pause at this line when you take the printer off-line and position a new sheet of paper. When you are ready to continue and the printer is on-line again, press any key or click the mouse. The report continues printing the rest of the page. You can even see the process work in Page Preview mode.

Suppose that sometimes you need a pause between pages (when you feed single sheets to the printer) and at other times, you don't need the pause between pages (perhaps when you use a different printer). You can reopen the WAITPAGE.PRG program and edit the file to read:

```
IF pause
    WAIT WINDOW
ENDIF
RETURN ""
```

Then all you need to do before running the report is to create a variable called *pause*, just as you created the variable big_item, and assign the value of true or false to the variable, as in the following:

```
pause = .T.
```

or

```
pause = .F.
```

Using the IF/ENDIF construct, which is explained in a following section, the revised Waitpage function checks whether to interrupt the report.

NOTE While running a report, FoxPro must find all included UDFs. To verify an expression that includes a UDF, the Expression Builder also must have access to the UDF. In this example, you have made Waitpage( ) available by saving the UDF as a separate file in the directory in which you are working (with the model reports and database). In Chapter 14, "Organizing and Packaging Your Applications," you learn how to include this separate file in a project, and in Chapter 18, "Understanding Program Structure," you learn about other ways FoxPro can find UDFs within a larger program file.

You may want to rewrite, as a UDF, the complicated nested IIF( ) expression you created that formats two individuals' names for a label line. Maintaining this kind of expression (or far more complex expressions) as a UDF often is easier than maintaining it as a report or label expression. You can create a program, NAMELINE.PRG, similar to the following example. The lines that begin with asterisks are *comments*—not part of the program—that help you understand what the program does. Lines beginning with asterisks are ignored by FoxPro as it interprets the program:

```
mreturn = ""
* create a variable to hold the string
* the UDF will eventually RETURN to the label or report

IF EMPTY(fname2)
   * is there only one person at this address?
   mreturn = ALLTRIM(fname1)
   * put the one person's first name into the string
ELSE
   * two people exist
   IF ALLTRIM(lname2) = ALLTRIM(lname1)
       * do they share one last name?
         mreturn = ALLTRIM(fname1) + " & " + ;
         ALLTRIM(fname2)
       * put the two first names into the string
   ELSE
      * two last names exist
         mreturn = ALLTRIM(fname2) + " " + ALLTRIM(lname2);
            + " & " + ALLTRIM(fname1)
      * put the second person's whole name and
      * the first person's first name into the string
   ENDIF
ENDIF

* take the string we have created and add
* the first person's last name to the end
mreturn = mreturn + " " + lname1

* send the string back to the label
RETURN mreturn
```

The label line expression then simply becomes the following:

```
Nameline( )
```

If you have other output involving this address table, you can use the same UDF to format the output names properly in each case, without rewriting the program.

TIP

When UDFs in a report do a lot of processing or evaluating of expressions such as Nameline( ) does, you may sometimes see some of the intermediary results of these steps echoed in the report. Use the command SET TALK OFF and run the report again; this undesirable side effect of UDFs disappears. SET TALK determines whether command processing of any type is echoed by FoxPro, usually to a window or the screen. For the duration of a report, however, all output (including such command processing) is directed to the report destination, whether it is the screen, a file, or the printer.

Suppressing Blank Lines in Reports and Labels

One common problem in reports and labels is that you may need to suppress blank lines. Suppose that a household address table contains not only names for two individuals but also two fields for address information (to leave room for apartment numbers and so on to be entered separately from a street address). When both address fields are not used, you want to close the label or the address portion of an invoice so that you don't leave a blank line in the center of the address.

In the Label Designer, you easily made this correction by using a semicolon at the end of all lines that would possibly be left blank. In this example, the label definition looks like the following:

```
Nameline( )
address1;
address2;
RTRIM(city)+", "+state+"     "+zip
```

The procedures to accomplish the same result, however, are more varied and more complicated in the Report Writer.

As mentioned in the preceding chapter, the FoxPro check box option in the Page Layout Options dialog enables you to Suppress blank lines. For some kinds of reports, this option works well to suppress detail band lines with missing information.

Users frequently want to put address information in the page header band of a statement or invoice, however, or they want an address on the left side of a detail band and other information about the customer on the right side. In the former case, the Suppress blank lines option doesn't apply because the affected lines are not in the detail band; in the latter case, the lines aren't suppressed because there are additional (nonblank) expressions in the same line.

NOTE Suppress blank lines does not consider an expression consisting of only null characters (ASCII 255 or CHR(255), as you would express this in a report) to be completely blank—a useful fact when you want some blank lines in a report omitted and others left alone. This option also does not suppress a detail line in which you have placed no expressions. Therefore, you still can place completely blank lines in a report as visual separators when you want them. However, expressions composed solely of space characters CHR(32) or even nonprinting characters such as carriage returns and line feeds (CHR(13)+CHR(10)) are all suppressed.

Paradoxically, the way to close this kind of blank is to concatenate all the expressions involved into one long expression and force line breaks in this expression where needed. Type the special Format instructions `@;` to tell the Report Writer to interpret all semicolons enclosed in quotation marks as a request for a line break. When you use this format, the expression Stretches Vertically without your choosing this option. You need to tell any other objects on the same or following detail lines to Float as Band Stretches, however.

The address information is reported as two, not four, report expression objects in the Report Writer. The first object contains the following expression:

```
Nameline( )+
   IIF(EMPTY(address1),"",";" + address1) +
   IIF(EMPTY(address2),"",";" + address2)
```

This object is given the width of the longest of the three possible lines and is assigned the Format @;. The second object contains the following expression:

```
RTRIM(city) + ", " + state + "     " + zip
```

This expression is identical to the last line of the label definition. In the Report Writer, however, the expression needs to Float as Band Stretches to accommodate the changing size of the preceding object.

You also can take care of more complicated situations by using a UDF that examines each part of the expression and decides where and when the line breaks occur. The UDF's name then appears in the expression box, and you can use the same @; Format.

TIP

In a twist on this problem, you can use the REPLICATE( ) function to return any number of ";" strings to the Report Writer if you want to force extra line breaks or a page break. The system variable _PLINENO can tell you where on the page you are currently positioned. You can evaluate this information with a UDF and decide how many extra lines you need to move down the page at any point. After the semicolons, be sure to add at least one CHR(255) or other *nonblank* character to the returned expression (i.e., REPL(";",nlines)+CHR(255)), or the Report Writer discounts all the extra line breaks. If the report using this tip also requires the Suppress Blank Lines option for other formatting reasons, you must add a nonblank character to each forced line to prevent the line being suppressed, as follows:

```
REPL(";"+CHR(255),nlines)
```

Adding Groups and Totaling to Reports

You may frequently want to examine data grouped on the basis of one or more criteria. You learned that, by putting data in a certain order, you can examine all Budget items for one product and then for the next product, for example. If you change the order, you can report on Budget items for one period or department at a time.

With FoxPro, however, you can perform certain actions relative to each group of items, setting up *group headers* that appear when a new group is reached and *footers* that follow the end of the group. As with page headers and footers, these group headers and footers contain information that concerns the whole group (not individual detail items) and can be formatted differently from the detail lines.

In the Report Writer, this kind of grouping is known as a *control break*. A control break literally instructs FoxPro to stop printing detail lines and to do something else when the conditions are met.

You usually define a group or control break by using the same expression you used in the tag or index that controls the data order for this report. Return to one of the Budget reports you worked on earlier. Use the View window Setup panel to choose the Order the Budget data by Product option.

With the Report Layout active again, choose the Data Grouping... option from the Report menu popup. Then choose the Add a group option. The Group Info dialog appears, as shown in figure 10.11.

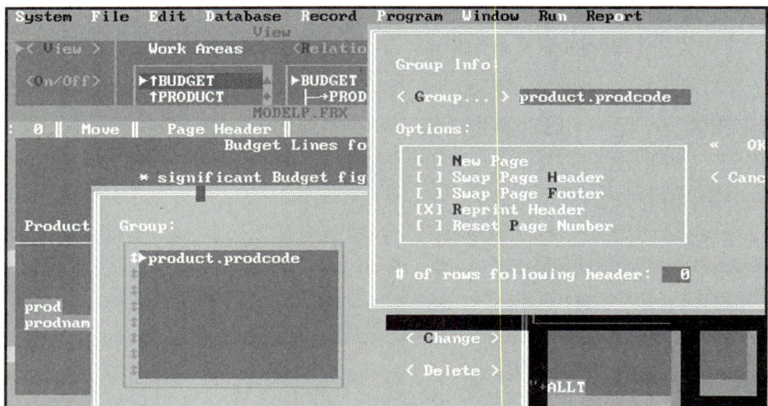

FIG. 10.11

The Group and Group Info dialogs.

You can type the same expression that is used in the current controlling index or tag, or you can click the `Group` button to select and edit the appropriate fields and other information using the Expression Builder.

Look at the Options list available in the Group Info dialog. Every time a new group is reached, you can instruct FoxPro to begin a new page. You can use the Swap Page Header or Swap Page Footer options to use the group headings rather than page headings when a new group is reached; this setting selects New Page by default because doing the swap makes no sense if the groups start midpage.

You also can choose to Reset Page Number so that every new group begins with the page number 1 (this setting also forces groups to start new pages), or you can choose Reprint the group Header when a group spans two pages, as happened in this example. You also can use the # of Rows Following Header option to ensure that group headers are not left at the bottom of a page, with no room left for detail items.

When you return to the report layout, the new bands were added. You then can add lines that print heading and summarizing information for this group.

In the group header band, you often may place information that displays the current reporting group. When you know this information is the same for each item in the group, for example, reporting the Product name in each detail band is unnecessary. Place an expression that includes the Product.Prodname field in the group header band. Remove this information from the detail band, and move the other objects in the detail band to suit your needs. Notice that the column headings may not be easy to relate to the data because a group header is intervening. Accordingly, you can add extra group header lines and move the column headers into the group band. Choosing Reprint Header from the Group Info dialog, as shown in figure 10.11, ensures that column headers appear on a new page even when a group spans pages.

A common procedure is to calculate data by group and to display the results in a group footer band. Because you want a subtotal of the budget amounts for each group, the expression is the field Budget.Budgetamt. Highlight and copy this field to the group footer band, or create a new expression in the group footer using this field. For this new object in the group footer, select the Calculate... option from the Report Expression dialog, choose to Sum this expression, and use the Reset popup control to end the calculation on the group expression (Budget.Prodcode in this example).

Add an appropriate defining text label for this calculated object in the group footer band (the report in the figure uses "Total Budget "+Product.Prodcode+":"). Because this numeric expression is a total, it should have room for more digits than the original field had, but the figure may not always need all the space. To make the number follow the text label immediately, without unsightly spaces in between, you can concatenate a STR( ) version of it with the text as a character expression—or, as shown in figure 10.12, you can choose the Left Justify format for the budget sum figure.

Select and copy the two objects by pressing Ctrl+C. Then, using the Title/Summary option from the Report menu popup, create a *summary band* for the end of the report. Paste a copy of these objects in the summary band by pressing Ctrl+V and then edit the object's Calculate settings to Reset on End of Report. Edit the text label to remove the reference to an individual product (the label may read simply "Total Budget:"). You then have a grand total of the budget. (The results of these changes are shown in figures 10.14 and 10.15, in the following section of this chapter.)

You may have noticed that you also can use any of the Calculate... options to create page-level calculations, but you may want to use another similar object even to put calculations in the detail band. Paste another copy of the summary band object into the detail band (which, like the original version, still is set to reset on a group level). Choose Page Preview, and you see that this object keeps a running total of the budget amounts in a group, or if you change the Reset option, throughout a report.

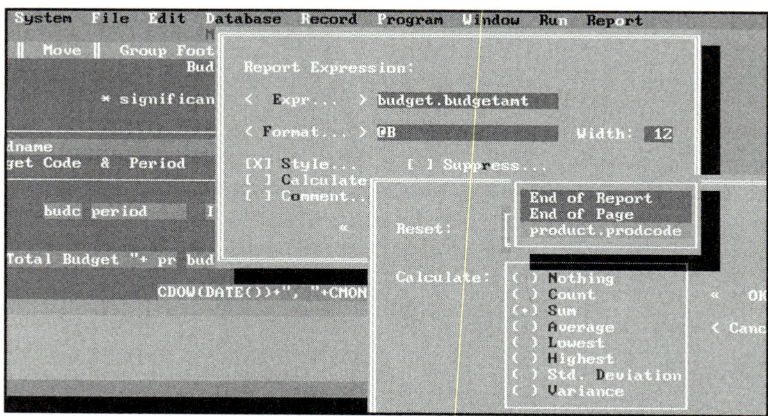

FIG. 10.12

The Calculate options for a Report Expression, choosing to Reset at the end of a group.

The Calculate... option is handy for creating item numbers on a report—within a page, for example. Define a report expression, which is the numeric value 1 (although almost any other expression works), mark the Count radio button, reset the value on a page, and then place it in the detail band, formatted as you would format any numeric expression.

You even can instruct the Calculate feature to give a conditional count. Suppose that you want to report the number of budget items that have a budget amount higher than 1000. Define a report expression similar to the following:

```
IIF(Budget.budgetamt > 1000, 1, 0)
```

Mark the Sum radio button. You can place the expression in any of the footer bands, reset it appropriately, and produce an answer. The following section, “Understanding Report Variables,” presents variations of this problem and the resulting output.

You aren’t limited to one level of subtotals or other calculations in a FoxPro report; you can have as many as 20 nested group levels. If you want to report on the budget by department and within each department by period, you can create an index or tag by using the following expression:

```
deptcode + DTOS(period)
```

The DTOS( ) function converts the Date field, Period, into a character form so that you can concatenate and correctly order this field with the Deptcode field. Add one group level, the *outer* (or more important) level, by using the expression Budget.Deptcode. Create another, inner level to start a new group within the department listing when a new period is reached. Then assign headers and footers to each level of grouping again.

Groupings do not necessarily have to take the form of database fields. In FoxPro, you can create an index expression that includes a UDF, which means that the ways you can group data are almost unlimited.

On rare occasions, you may want to create groupings that have nothing to do with the index expression. In certain special cases, setting a group to start a new page is a good way to force a page break. A common reason for this step is to avoid splitting up a long memofield between two pages. Use a UDF in the detail band of a report to evaluate these conditions and to change the value of a variable when the conditions are met. Create a group on the variable and have this grouping level start a new page. In FoxPro 2.x, this procedure is easy when you use report variables (see the following section).

Understanding Report Variables

So far you have touched on only a few of the extensive settings in the Calculate... option. Besides the settings' usage with numeric values, you find that several settings (Highest, Lowest, and Average) also work well with date-type expressions.

The Calculate feature of report expression objects has a major limitation, however: after you choose to use the feature, you cannot further manipulate the result before putting it into the report. You cannot use TRANSFORM( ) to change the result for special formatting, concatenate the result with other expressions, or—most important—perform several calculations and create another expression by doing a computation that involves the calculated results.

To return to a previous example, suppose that you need to keep a certain amount of cash on hand, a percentage of all budget items. You know how to calculate and sum the amount, as shown in the following expression:

```
budgetamt * .15
```

You also know how to restrict the calculation if you are required to perform this calculation only for significant expenditures, as in the following expression:

```
IIF(budgetamt >= big_item, budgetamt * .15, 0)
```

Suppose that you want to compare this calculation's result to the amount of money you deposited in the bank; this information is derived from another table. You may want to print a line in the summary band of the report to reflect a shortfall. If the deposited money is sufficient to cover the requirements, a different message is printed.

In versions of FoxPro prior to 2.0, you handled this kind of situation with a UDF in a group-, page-, or report-level summary band. Rather than using the internal Calculate Sum feature, you wrote instructions to move through all the records of the file (or perhaps just through the records of one group), check certain criteria, and arrive at an answer. The UDF either returned the correct output directly to a report expression or placed the total into a variable that you created before running the report, which was then used in other report expressions.

Besides being fairly complicated, this method is wasteful because you make at least one extra pass through the records in the file. FoxPro is already moving through the file to print the lines that you see in the detail band in the report. In FoxPro 2.x, *report variables* do this kind of calculation along the way. The Report Writer performs each operation you designate—for each report variable and each report object in the detail band—for each record in the report.

Choose the Report Variables menu popup option to access the dialogs shown in figure 10.13. As you see, you choose to add a variable and give it a name and an initial value. By using the Value to Store... option, you create an expression or assign Calculate options in the same way you have created other report expressions. FoxPro evaluates the Value to Store and assigns the result of this evaluation to the report variable, at the beginning of the detail band instance for each record of the report's controlling table. You also assign a level (group or page) on which the report variable is reset to its initial value.

The difference is that you can now *use* this created variable in another report expression or even in the calculation of another report variable.

In figure 10.13, note how performing the task suggested in the example works—by creating the variable you name *deposit* and instructing the Report Writer to sum the budget amount percentages. Because you intend to use this information in the summary band, choose the Reset at the End of Report option. You then can create expressions such as the following in the summary band:

```
IIF(deposit > bankacct.deposit,
   "Additional deposit required: ", "")
IIF(deposit > bankacct.deposit,
   deposit - bankacct.deposit, "")
```

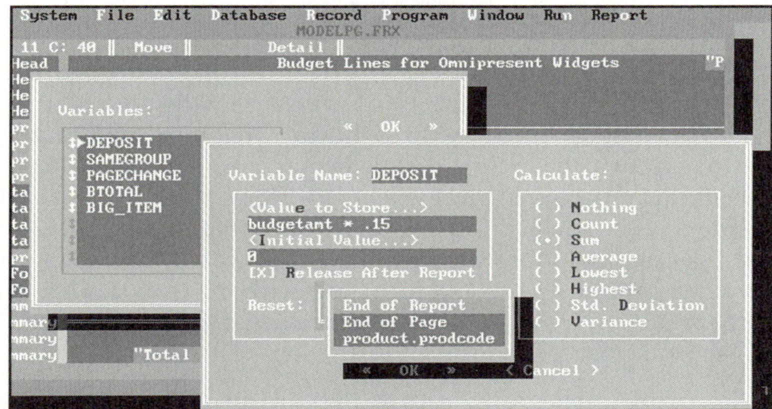

FIG. 10.13

The Report Variable dialogs.

NOTE You can easily concatenate these two expressions by using STR() or TRANSFORM(), but keeping the two expressions separate in cases where you may have more than two possibilities is more convenient. You return to this example in a following section, "Overlaid Report Objects."

Report variables also can *persist* after a report is run. If you uncheck the default Release After Report option, you can send a message to the screen with the *results* after the report is run, or use these values in other reports. You also can store report variable values to a table that stores information about report runs, or use a sequence of page numbers that is carried from one report to the next, as chapters in a larger report. An example of this process is included in Chapter 20, "Enhancing the Applications You Program."

Expanding Use of Report Variables

A calculation that involves other calculations is the most obvious reason for creating report variables. If you return to the model reports, however, you can perform many other tricks with additional report variables.

Printing Group Messages

You have used the Reprint Header option for a group that spans more than one page. When this occurs, you may want to add a message to the header and footer of the group to indicate that more information for that group is available than is showing on the current page. You don't want this message to print when you switch groups but are still on the same page. You also don't want the message to print when you switch pages and groups at the same time. You want the message only when you've switched pages but have not switched groups. This procedure requires a check to see exactly when pages and groups switch, a simple feat for report variables.

Create a variable, samegroup, with an initial value of .F. and store the value .T. to the variable. If this variable is reset on the group level, you can check to find out when the group changes.

Create another variable, pagechange, with an initial value of .T.; store the value .F. and choose Reset at End of Page.

The following expression creates a message, when needed, in the *group* header during a reprint at the top of a page:

```
IIF(samegroup AND pagechange,
   ALLTRIM(Product.Prodname)+
   " details continued from the previous page... ",
   Product.Prodname)
```

The following expression creates a message in the *page* footer, when needed:

```
IIF(samegroup,
   ALLTRIM(Product.Prodname)+" details continued
   next page...", "")
```

TIP

You also can use a similar technique to suppress certain page-level band information at the beginning or end of a report when this information may be redundant because of title and summary band material. _PAGENO = 1 tells you when you are at the beginning of the report. If you output the results of a temporary table from an SQL SELECT statement, as you learned to do in Chapter 5, "Using the RQBE as the Gateway to Queries," and Chapter 6, "Investigating Your Data with Advanced Queries," you can use the expression RECCOUNT() = RECNO() to see whether you are at the end of a report (when you reach the last record of the table). If you are reporting on a table that may be ordered or filtered or if you are using FOR or WHILE conditions, however, you can check the record number of the last record you are selecting before you begin the report run by storing the number to a variable. Compare the RECNO() to this variable in an IIF() expression to decide when to suppress page-level information.

Figures 10.14, 10.15, and 10.16 show the resulting report with the conditional page band objects implemented. In figures 10.15 and 10.16, the conditional page headers and footers are designed to continue groups across pages and to suppress redundant page information just before a summary band. To show the variation in page bands, the number of lines per page was reduced, using the appropriate Page Layout item. The option # of rows following header in the Group Info dialog was changed to 4 to avoid stranding group headers at the bottoms of pages.

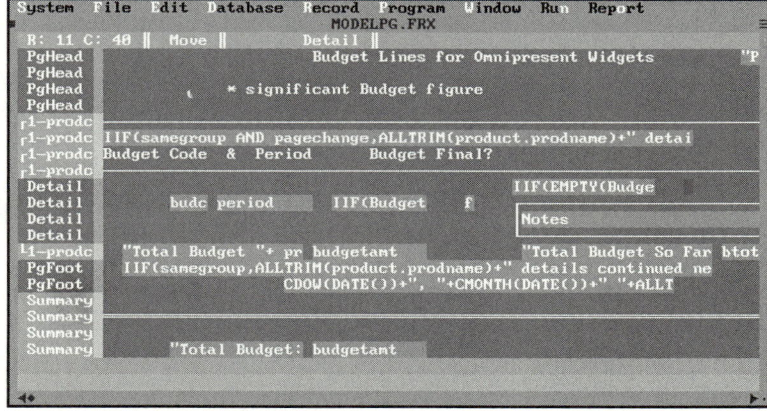

FIG. 10.14

The Model Report Layout Revised.

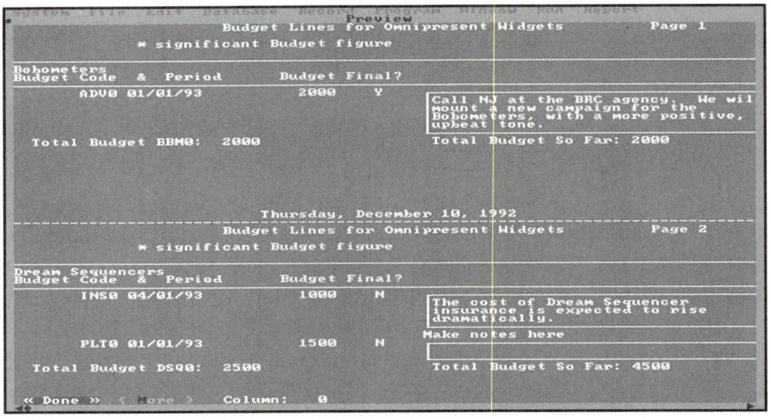

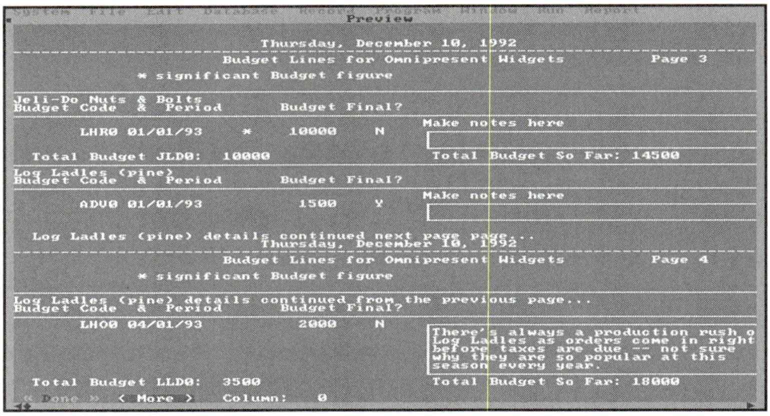

FIGS. 10.15 and 10.16

The revised report in Page Preview, using report variables.

The item labeled Total Budget So Far in figure 10.16 is a report variable named btotal, which stores the value of the Budgetamt field and uses the Sum and Reset at the end of report options. You can choose to increment or otherwise calculate a report variable as a manual operation (rather than use the Calculate options), however. In this example, you use btotal+Budget.Budgetamt as the value to store rather than mark the Sum radio button.

This kind of expression gives you more flexibility to affect the value of the report variable. You can use a UDF in the expression that creates the value to store, as you did with report expressions. The expression Xtotal+Your_UDF( ), for example, can increase the value of the report variable Xtotal by a different figure or percentage for each department or each product line. For convenience, you can do all calculations on a report variable by using UDFs and letting FoxPro initialize the variable.

Running Percentage of Group Total

Suppose that you want detail lines to show each budget item as a percentage of the total budget for the group. The report expression object may look like the following line:

```
STR(budgetamt/totalbudg * 100,3)+"%"
```

To evaluate this expression, you need the total budget figure for the group before FoxPro goes through the records providing the detail items for the group. The only way you can determine this figure is by using a UDF in the group header line. This procedure requires an extra pass through the table, which was previously mentioned as a practice to avoid; you cannot avoid this step in this instance.

At the start of the group, the UDF saves the current RECNO( ) to another variable. The command CALCULATE WHILE then moves through the records of the group to store the total of the Budgetamt fields to the totalbudg variable. Then the UDF uses the GO command and the now-saved record number to return the record pointer to the beginning of the group. The report then can process the detail lines.

Initializing Report Variables

In previous versions of FoxPro, you had to initialize the variable totalbudg before the report was run by typing the command `totalbudg = 0` in the Command window or in the program that ran the report. If you didn't initialize the variable, the report generated the error message `Variable not found`. By choosing to create totalbudg as a report variable, you ensure that this command is *bound* to the report, and you avoid the error.

You can use a similar trick to avoid an error even if the value of a variable is usually set by a calling program but may not be set during testing. Use the TYPE( ) function to determine whether this variable already exists. For the big_item variable used to decide when to print Notes earlier in the chapter, create a report variable with the same name, initialized to the following value:

```
IIF(TYPE("big_item") = "N", big_item, 500)
```

When the TYPE( ) function returns "N" (for "Numeric data type"), this expression assigns big_item the value of the existing big_item variable. Otherwise, big_item is assigned the default value of 500.

You must realize, however, that FoxPro usually expects to assign values to report variables; the program reevaluates these variables every detail line, using the information you assigned in the Value To Store option. When you don't want FoxPro to interfere with the manipulation of a report variable, such as big_item or totalbudg, use the variable's own name as the Value to Store, and nothing is changed.

Using IIF( ) in Report Variable Calculations

When used with UDFs, the IIF( ) function is useful in report variable calculations. As discussed, you can use the Count option to include line numbers or item numbers in a report. You also can use IIF( ) to give a conditional count based on certain factors. If you put all these functions together, you have an easy way to distinguish the parent records in a one-to-many relationship as you examine the detail lines of a report.

Return to the simple Products report on Products presented in this chapter when you were learning about one-to-many relationships. (Be sure to restore the file relationships as needed for this report; use CLOSE DATABASES first if necessary.) Add a report variable, prec, that has the initial value of 0 and stores the expression RECNO("product"), the record number of the controlling table. Add a second variable, newrec, also initialized to 0, and then store the following expression to it:

```
IIF(RECNO("product") = prec, 0, 1)
```

Choose the Calculate option to Sum this variable. Then change the order of the report variables in the list that appears in the dialog so that the variable you named newrec is first.

When you use report variables that reference each other, the order in which the variables appear in the list is vital to achieving the correct results. In this example, you instruct the Report Writer to evaluate newrec before the value of prec changes. Putting the variable first in the list accomplishes this task.

Figure 10.17 shows the difference between a straight count of the detail items (under the heading # Budget Lines) created in a report expression and a count of the parent records (under the heading # Products) created with the newrec and prec report variables. The straight count was done on a report expression of .T. to illustrate that any expression will provide a Count in the Report Writer, whereas Sum and the other Calculate... options must be performed on numbers or dates. Both # Products, the Product Name, and the Retail Price columns use the option Suppress Repeated Values option in this report to make the difference between the straight count and the conditional count of the parent records easier to see. These techniques, which indicate when the parent record has changed, have many uses in reports.

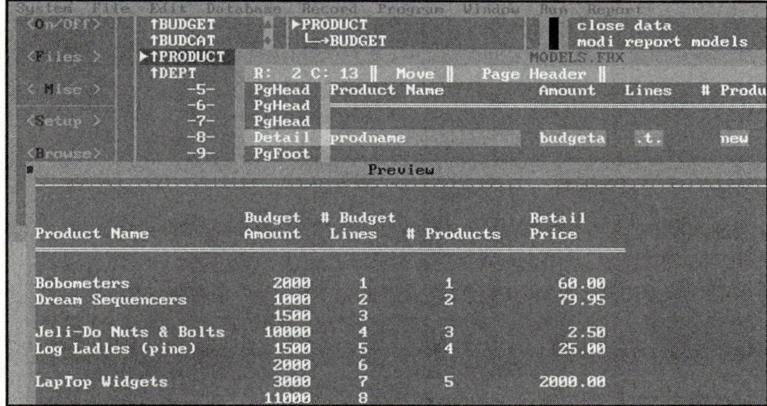

FIG. 10.17

Using Report Variables in a one-to-many relationship.

Overlaying Expressions

You have made frequent use of the IIF( ) function, which is limited to two choices for any one expression. By using several different *overlaid* expressions in the same physical location of the report layout, however, you can easily accommodate more possibilities than the two return values provided by one IIF( ) expression.

When moving objects around the layout, you may have noticed that two or more objects can occupy the same physical space. When you print a report, all the objects print, even though not all objects are visible at the same time in a Page Preview or when you send reports to the screen. By using the Bring to Front (press Ctrl+G) and Send to Back (Ctrl+J) options of the Report menu popup, you can designate the object that appears on-screen.

Remember the previous example of the budget figures that you compared to money on hand in a bank account. You may want to expand this example to have three overlaid objects by using these instructions at one position:

```
IIF(deposit > bankacct.deposit,
   "Additional deposit required: ", "")
IIF(deposit < bankacct.deposit,
   "Additional money available: ", "")
IIF(deposit = bankacct.deposit,
   "Bank deposit covers present requirements.", "")
```

You can expand two overlaid objects at another position by using the following instructions:

```
IIF(deposit > bankacct.deposit,
   deposit - bankacct.deposit, "")
IIF(deposit < bankacct.deposit,
   bankacct.deposit - deposit, "")
```

In this example, the IIF( ) expression evaluates the situation so that only the correct information prints in each report that you run.

At other times, you may want more than one item to print at one position, and the Report Writer will print each overlaid expression in turn. You can print a line of shaded blocks overlaid with a text heading as part of a form design, for example. Use a box object with the proper graphics character designated, or use the REPLICATE( ) function, discussed in one of the label designs, to accommodate variable-width text. To create a shaded box for a memofield in a report, use REPLICATE( ) and the Stretch Vertically option.

CAUTION: When objects overlap in the same row, the object that begins in the lowest column prints first. If two or more objects start at exactly the same position, all objects are sent to the printer with the one in the back first, in order, until the front object is sent. This process is important if you use any of these objects to send printer instructions.

To pause a page at the right moment, the Waitpage( ) function, which introduced you to UDFs in this chapter, always must be in the first row and first column of a report, but you can now see that you can put another report object in the same position. Just use the Send to Back option on the Waitpage( ) object to ensure that the object containing

Waitpage( ) is evaluated, calling the function, before anything else on the page is sent to the printer.

Summary

The two preceding chapters covered the features of FoxPro's Label Designer and Report Writer in some detail, but you have barely touched on the capabilities available. As you practice with these tools and as you learn more about FoxPro's special features in other parts of this book, consider the following possibilities to extend your reach.

You can use one report or label with different files by using an ALIAS. The last chapter mentioned that you may want to set up a report in which you open a label or report table and examine the objects the file contains. You may create a second table as a *lookup* for report or label files, with expanded versions of the field names more meaningful to you than the ten characters allowed in .DBF field names. If you use different .FRX and .LBX files with the same alias, the same report works for all files with one structure.

Design a single report with an all-purpose alias, such as REPTFILE, for reports or labels designed to work with the results of SQL queries. If you output the results of queries to a temporary table with this name, the report works for all queries.

Use labels to create columnar reports. Experiment with page headers and footers that surround a LABEL FORM command that uses a NEXT scope suitable to the number of labels you can fit on a page. Investigate the PRINTJOB/ENDPRINTJOB programming construct discussed in following chapters.

Use reports for quick setup and detailed formatting of information that you export to an SDF (columnar) format.

Use labels to create merge files suited to various word processors, easily including any merge codes required, or investigate FoxPro's text-merge capabilities and use a report form to handle mailmerge completely within FoxPro.

You can accomplish these and many other specialized tasks with the Report Writer and Label Designer. As you develop dexterity with these tools, you gain skills that are equally valuable as you explore other important tools in FoxPro.

Building FoxPro Applications

11

CHAPTER

Coordinating a FoxPro Application

Although a triumph of gear ratios, the machines [mechanical representations of the solar system called orreries] did commit a grave sin of information design—Pridefully Obvious Presentation—by directing attention more toward miraculous contraptionary display than to planetary motion.

Edward R. Tufte, *Envisioning Information,* p. 16

In the preceding chapter on the Report Writer and the Label Designer, you found that you can add style and formatting enhancements—including boxes and other graphics elements—to database output. Remember that having these capabilities, however, is not the same as needing to use them in every report you create.

In fact, this kind of decoration may run counter to the real purpose of effectively communicating the information you derive from collected data. Without the benefit of thoughtful design, indiscriminately *gimmicky* reports can distract from the truly interesting content they are supposed to present.

Part III deliberately begins with a note of caution. You are about to encounter other tools in FoxPro, which are the building blocks of *applications*, systems that can include tailored data-entry screens, output procedures, and the underlying tables that constitute a database. In this part of the book, you investigate the following tools:

- The Screen and Menu Builders you use to accept entry from and give choices to the people who need to use and add to data.
- The Project Manager you use to integrate all the entry, output, and utility tasks of a system into one structure.
- The Distribution Kit you use to present the new FoxPro application to the outside world.
- A number of additional devices you can use to enhance and embellish applications.

Interface Design and FoxPro

In some ways, these FoxPro tools make the business of *programming* applications more efficient and easier than ever. You are not, however, relieved of the responsibility to work hard on *designing* applications.

Like any owner of a sparkling new set of tools, you may be bewildered by the array of options in front of you. Because so many tools are available, you may find isolating and using the features to effectively help the user accomplish difficult tasks.

For this reason, the following section offers thoughts for helping you approach the FoxPro design tools with some discrimination. A full-scale discussion of the principles of application design is obviously beyond the scope of this book. However, in this short introduction, you find some helpful and provocative directions for a continued exploration of these topics. This chapter also attempts to provide a perspective on the impact FoxPro's tools have on your approach to applications design.

Although interface design in FoxPro 2.x bears an evolutionary relationship to FoxPro 1.x and FoxBase Mac, the actual design tools and the way these tools are integrated with the programming language represent a fairly complete departure from previous versions of Xbase.

Developing Criteria for Interface Design

Return for a moment to the list of interface elements with which you began the chapter on the interface of FoxPro. In building the interface of applications you create, you need to work with the following components:

- The items you present on-screen
- The language and formats the program commonly uses to ask questions and give information
- The methods by which the program can accept responses
- The clues (such as colors, sounds, or positions on-screen) the program uses to indicate the current task and options

These items, formats, methods, and clues require you to make design decisions about the on-screen display, how best to display the different items, and how to establish effective two-way communication with a user that makes transparent what everything in the application means. You must evaluate the effectiveness of each decision by using a consistent set of standards.

Achieving Design Consensus with Users

In Chapter 4, "Database Management Fundamentals," you investigated the process of dividing your data into fields and tables and learned some practical steps to ensure the smooth *implementation* of your new system after it is designed. At the beginning of the design process, you need the cooperation of many people to understand what elements the system must include, and at the end, you also need their interest and approval—or the system will never be used.

As you work to design your database and, later to put it in place as a device to help people get their work done, measure your work against a standard of *consensus*. Ask yourself, "Have I gathered information and opinions from everyone who needs to use the application? Does everyone understand what they need to do to participate? Do they have sufficient information to understand the progress so far? Have they expressed satisfaction with the progress, and with the projected results? Does my understanding of their tasks, and its translation into application procedures, seem to fit their normal work habits?"

If the answer to these questions is "No," you haven't finished your work; no matter how perfectly *designed* your application is. If the people who have to use it aren't involved, the application won't succeed.

For consensus to be achieved, people must feel that they can direct the computer to do what they want easily. They must be able to follow directions given by the computer easily, too. (Otherwise, users get *less* work done, instead of more, because of the computer—and feel humiliated and confused in the bargain.) These goals require you, as designer, to pay close attention to the *user interface* of your application.

Your primary mandate is to facilitate the *reliable* collection and storage of data. Don't make the mistake of ignoring the real needs of the people who collect the data, if you want to reach this goal. To understand how data errors happen, learn what *a user's* priority is at the time he or she enters the data.

Suppose that you want to collect extra demographic data, for future promotions, on the people who come to a store. You might decide the process would be most efficient if you attach it to a point of sale system, so that the salesperson collected the marketing data at the same time he or she entered the details of the order form.

But the salesperson is intent on processing the order smoothly and perhaps on collecting another commission from the next customer at the counter. If the demographic data required is at all complex, he or she may see this extra duty as an imposition; you are almost guaranteed faulty and incomplete data entry, no matter how carefully you safeguard the application with data validation.

By contrast, browsers in the store will probably enjoy spending a few minutes with a computerized questionnaire themselves, if it is attractively designed and displayed. They will complete the questions more efficiently than the employee, who was going to have to take their time anyway, asking them the questions and interpreting their responses.

The goal of data integrity, without which the information collected is unusable, depends on the data being collected in a reasonable way. The users must agree with the designer that this goal is important and that the application's interface allows them to reach it without undue effort.

The following section suggests additional standards of *comfort*, *clarity*, and *consistency* and attempts to describe the use of these standards in the interface design process.

Offering Comfortable Choices

Comfort for anyone is largely found in familiarity. You provide comfort by providing situations, language, and objects to manipulate that the users already know and understand.

For example, the word *password* is often used in computer systems that require security clearance to access some or all functions. This word literally means a countersign spoken between two people before one of them can enter a specific area. In a computer system, the user is not actually entering a secure room; no word is spoken; and no second person is involved. Yet the *metaphor* of password is understood, and the user knows exactly what task is accomplished by *giving a password* to the computer. Think how much less comfortable you become if, instead of being asked for a password, you are required to *enter a security identification #.*

Metaphors are often used so that people can identify computer tasks with chores they already know how to perform. When you use metaphors, whether with a visual representation of a familiar object on-screen or with metaphoric language, think about how *suitable* the metaphor is to the task at hand. Does the metaphor help you imagine the necessary images and words, or is the concept that the metaphor represents too abstract or otherwise difficult to represent? If you need to add to this task later, is the metaphor easily extended to include possible new uses? What other connotations may the metaphor represent?

You also must be certain that whatever metaphor you choose is suitable to the potential audience—not just to you. This kind of correspondence is often heavily dependent on age or cultural background. For example, the *desktop* metaphor that FoxPro uses—with calculator, diary, and notes arranged and rearranged over a desk—may not be as comfortable for children using an application as a *toybox* that contains items that can be taken out, used, and then put back into the box.

Apart from metaphor, another easy way of maintaining a high level of comfort is to reproduce the exact language—and even exact representations—of existing manual systems. You can use the Report Writer and Screen Builder to precisely mimic standard manual order forms, and you can arrange tasks on an application menu exactly in the order in which they are performed in the office. Even if these tasks and forms are going to change in the system, you can continue using the same language to describe them wherever possible. In the preceding example, if the expression *security identification #* is presently in use, continuing to use this expression in the system can provide a higher level of comfort than asking for *passwords*.

Where no possibility of familiarity with a task or a situation exists, you still can maintain comfort *if the user is aware that all actions they take are reversible*, or at least (where complete reversal can't be provided) that any harm done by choosing an action is minimal. You can maintain this high comfort level if you communicate clearly with the user about the choices available and make the results of a given action predictable and consistent. The steps you can take to provide and maintain comfort for the user are described in the following section.

Presenting Information Clearly

When you need to communicate information about the application to the user—either because you need to ask the user a question or because you want to answer a question—you may need to go beyond the bounds of the familiar. If the user needs to *understand* or *learn* something, your job is to make the information comprehensible.

Despite the current interest in graphical interfaces, icons, and other nonverbal methods of using a computer to communicate, effective use of language remains one of the best tools at your disposal to exchange information.

NOTE Although FoxPro for DOS is a text-based program, you also can use symbols to communicate your intentions. *Be careful, however, when using symbols.* Like metaphors, symbols are open to interpretation and must be tested for clarity just as words must be. For a real-world example, consider the following symbols, which are found on the buttons in some elevators:

These symbols do not indicate the buttons' functions as clearly as do the words *close* and *open*—although apparently, in at least one elevator designer's mind, the symbols seem preferable to words and sufficient. Perhaps the best choice here is to use both the words and the symbols together to mutually reinforce the meaning.

If you avoid the often murky connotations of graphics, you still must use language that fits *what the recipient of the message knows and understands—not what you know and understand.* This criterion is crucial at all phases of applications development. Suppose that you are designing an accounting application to be used internationally. Whether you are giving instructions to another programmer who works overseas or the end user of your program, you still must be aware of the differences in terminology and accounting practices in different countries; Accounts Receivable may be an asset in the United States, while it is treated as a liability in Japan!

You can't foresee every contingency, so the process of *acceptance testing*, discussed in a later section of this chapter, should include as many people of as many different backgrounds as possible. This book recommends that you plan for shared use of your applications even if you are not currently on a network. For similar reasons, in the author's opinion, you should keep an open mind about the *conceptual framework* of users of your application, as well as the eventuality that other programmers may have to maintain your work.

You can plan for other programmers' understanding of your application by using structured programming techniques and appropriately *documenting* your application, as described in Chapters 18, 19, and 20. For the benefit of users, you work hard to make your interface as flexible and as clear as possible.

Use appropriate language in all communications, and be certain that your words conform to the following criteria:

- Do not assign blame to the user. When a procedure fails, make sure that the *error messages* say that the *system*, not the user, made a mistake. `Cannot locate file: <filename>` is better than `File specified does not exist.`
- Without assigning blame, try to suggest that the user is in control of the system whenever possible. `Enter filename when ready:` is better than `Filename required:`.
- Avoid computer jargon. Choose language with which the users of your application are comfortable, as described in the preceding section. Also, avoid unnecessarily harsh language (`Abort procedure` or `Kill history file`) that may alarm the user about what happens to the data.

Make all questions and answers for the user follow these principles. Moreover, when the user is expected to provide a response, the language must clearly indicate all possible choices and explain what results to expect from each choice.

Beyond questions and answers, be certain that your applications provide constant *feedback* messages to let the user know what the system is doing, especially during lengthy procedures. (In FoxPro 2.x, the SET TALK command is enhanced to make this process easy.)

You also need to use language appropriately to produce *help text* for the users' reference. In Chapter 20, "Enhancing the Applications You Program," you learn to create help systems for applications with the same format and functionality as the FoxPro helpfile. For now, however, you only need to use words and to organize information in categories familiar and clear to the users.

By now, you are beginning to realize that building an application involves designing very frequent and even densely layered instances of communication. Many people think that software interfaces should avoid *information overload*, which they interpret as *too many* words or images. This confusion, however, is not directly proportional to the number of items a person must read or understand. Whether words or images are involved—and no matter how few or how many words or images appear—confusion occurs if these elements are not appropriately chosen by the designer.

Data also can be extremely complex. When you try to gather this data in an entry screen, organize the data in a report, or exhibit all the tasks required to maintain the data in a menu, communicating all this complexity is hard work. Simple reduction of the data, however, by eliminating a level of the detail or otherwise omitting some of the data's aspects, is not the answer. These techniques not only limit the value of the application by limiting the variety of tasks the application can handle; these omissions also show a disrespect for the abilities and intelligence of the users. A patronizing attitude inherent in the design is obvious to the users and can seriously damage their attitude toward your work.

Consider, therefore, offering some organizing structure in the design that gives the users a *macro view* (a general impression) of the data if this information is all they want and a *micro view* of all conceivable detail when needed.

You previously accomplished this task in the Report Writer when you learned how to group data in Chapter 10. Report groups provide up to 20 levels of summary, subtotal, and expanded detail. In the Screen Builder, you can group sections of data entry visually by enclosing the sections in boxes and then labeling the boxes, as you learned in the Organizer application screens. You also can separate sections of data into different windows, creating a *screen set*, with the initial window that holds the items that always need attention and with other windows, which are *brought forward* as the need for the subjects—or as the user's interest—arises. In the Menu Builder, you can organize options into menu pads with understandable titles and create subordinate menu popups that appear in a sequence logical to the user. When both menus and screens are unnecessary, you also can make items unselectable, further organizing the current task in the user's mind.

Using a Consistent Interface

When words that must be repeated and objects that look alike always mean the same thing and always produce similar results, the interface is termed *consistent*. Consistency is important because, besides performing comfortable and familiar actions, the users must develop confidence that a new and unfamiliar action proceeds according to past experience.

The more confident a user is that the system's meanings and responses follow a defined pattern, the more the users feel they are gaining skills and competence while they perform tasks. As a result, users are more open to exploring new features you may add to the system and are more willing to teach other users how to use the system.

Besides developing confidence, consistency has the added benefit of making users more sensitive to small variations. If you always use the same audible tone to indicate that the printer is not ready, and the user suddenly hears a different tone, the user is prepared for a different kind of alert.

The preceding chapter suggested that you create a *master report*, with the defaults for your company by saving the format to a special name. If you also use particular style enhancements or other indications to indicate grand totals in one report, use the same enhancements in every report. If you use a particular column heading for certain kinds of information in one report, repeat the column heading for every report in which this information appears.

Similarly, if you create one format for error messages in the Screen Builder, use the same format for all alerts. The following sections show how easily you can edit the window dimensions or text while leaving the basic *style* of the window (colors, border type, title) intact and save the window to a new name. Create a different format for informative messages that are *not* alerts—use different colors, borders, or placement—and the user quickly learns that each kind of window requires a consistently appropriate response.

You also can be certain that language remains consistent from screen to screen. Make abbreviations, the style of capitalization, even the general sequence of movement through data-entry items relative to their placement on-screen, the same throughout all the screens. If choosing the word Cancel on one screen reverses all current changes, consistent design requires that Cancel produces the same effect wherever you place the word in the application.

Compared to the profusion of menu systems available in previous versions of FoxPro and in the other Xbase dialects, the Menu Builder almost enforces a consistent interface style for the applications you create. Try, however, to extend this advantage by making shortcuts and hot keys behave consistently from one menu to the next. If Alt+D means *delete an entry* on one screen, Alt+D should never mean *enter the current date* on another screen!

You often can maintain this consistency across applications, although you must always consider the users for whom each system is designed. Besides a regard for the language and facts with which users are familiar, also make sure that you consider the method of input preferred by each user.

Is a particular user, for example, more comfortable with a mouse or with the keyboard? To be both safe and consistent, make sure that users can perform each task in the system with either device and that both key presses and mouse clicks give dependable results.

Sometimes you may need to depart from a consistent interface to make a major modification in an application. The users may tolerate new interface features and objects—in fact, the new objects and language can be boldly transformed, alerting users to the importance of the change and preparing them to learn these changes—if you have helped the user develop confidence during previous experiences with the application.

Pursuing Consensus, Comfort, Clarity, and Consistency

All the preceding suggestions require that you, as a designer, remain open to change and are able to acknowledge some false starts. Just as the users need feedback as they use the system, you need feedback from the user as you work to create or revise the application.

In this process, known as *acceptance testing*, you can involve as many kinds of potential users as possible—users with different needs, expectations, levels of skill and even of physical ability. Try to maximize the comfort of the process for each of the users. Explain that you are testing the *system*, not the *user*, and that if something goes wrong, you make changes or corrections to the system, not to how the user works with the system.

You can make acceptance testing a creative part of the design process if you begin early in the design stage, and the users feel encouraged to share their perceptions and wish lists with you. Users also become more convinced of the value of the new system because they have a personal investment in the design. Far from a simple process of uncovering bugs, testing provides yet another way that empowers users and lets them know that they are *in control* of the system.

The FoxPro tools encourage you to remain willing to change the design throughout the creation of an application. The ease with which you can make changes in a report, a menu, a screen, or a query, and also gather the necessary elements in projects, represents a high degree of compliance with the standards of good interface design that you see within FoxPro.

Introducing the FoxPro Design Tools

> Learning to program has no more to do with designing interactive software than learning to touch-type has to do with writing poetry.
>
> Ted Nelson, "The Right Way to Think About Software Design," *The Art of Human-Computer Interface Design*, p. 243.

The FoxPro interface does occasionally violate some of the design principles discussed in the preceding section. Perhaps you are bewildered by FoxPro error messages or have difficulty locating or understanding items in the Fox help file. Viewing the FoxPro interface (or a FoxApp-generated application or the sample applications) with a critical eye is a constructive exercise that helps you develop a strong design sense.

Studying FoxPro *as* an application helps you understand that no program is ever perfect, and every program can be improved. The process of design never really ends.

On the whole, however, the FoxPro design tools provide a comfortable, clear, consistent working environment and spectacular conditions under which you can create the same kind of environment for others.

The nature of the design tools enables nontechnical people to become involved in the design process. As you saw in the Report Writer, and as you are about to see again in the Screen Builder, page or screen layout in FoxPro is similar to graphics design work in a desktop-publishing program; objects are *drawn*, *stretched*, *colored*, and *placed*.

Encourage the appropriate design professionals to participate in this part of the work and to lend their talents to the application. You will notice that they exercise restraint in the number of font style and colors, of pictures, and of other embellishments they add to any particular design, compared to beginners, who may feel an urge to try out every new capability in their first attempt. Watching the professionals *choose*, and discriminate among, special effects, is one of the best ways to cultivate a unique design sense of your own.

If you read the first chapter of this book, you got a glimpse of the Screen Builder, and by now you must realize that this feature is strikingly similar in design to the Report Writer. You also may have previously run DEMO.APP, which is found in the FoxPro main program directory. Now is a good time to run DEMO.APP once more. For the first time or as a repeat, DEMO's quick display of all the FoxPro features can give you a panoramic view of the information presented in the following section (see fig. 11.1).

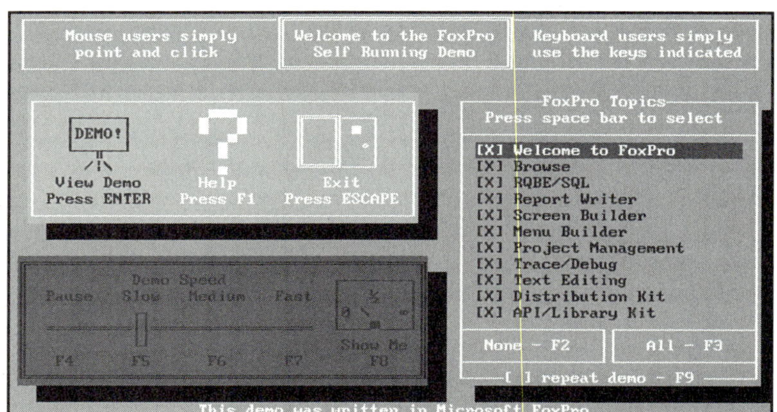

FIG. 11.1

The FoxPro Self-Running Demo's initial screen.

Because the Menu Builder and the Screen Builder, like the Report Writer and Label Designer, make creating and altering interface objects easy, you are free to concentrate on design goals while you use these tools.

In Chapter 14, you see how the Project Manager plays a key role in overseeing the developer's environment. Take a moment now to look at any projects provided on the FoxPro installation disks—even the PRODUCT.PJX project that FoxApp created for you in Chapter 1. To open a project, just use the File Open option from the menu and select files of Project type from the popup control, or type `MODIFY PROJECT ?` in the Command Window and a .PJX file. The following figures show LASER3.PJX, a sample project that you find in the GOODIES\LASER directory below the main FoxPro for DOS subdirectory.

TIP

If you try to open one of the sample projects from the installation files, you may see a message like the one in figure 11.2. When you open a project you did not create, FoxPro gets ready to reestablish the locations of the component files in your disk's directory structure. Among the other housekeeping chores, a project tracks the location of all the project's files on the disk, navigating from what FoxPro calls the project *home directory*.

When you open a project that was created by another person on a disk with a different directory structure than yours, you see this message as the project prepares to relocate the elements into the directory structure you selected. This talent of the Project Manager's is integral to the capability of coordinating the application when you distribute the completed application to users.

After you open a project, move the highlight to different files in the list and choose Info to learn how a project maintains information on the contents and the history of the file (see fig. 11.3). Select Edit for any entry, and learn that you can open the component screens, menus, programs, and databases of a project with this simple action. As you notice in figure 11.4, editing a screen set within a project enables you to make many choices about a screen's use specific to this application. These choices enable you to use—again and again—such screens as the *control panels* you saw in Chapter 1 and tailor a screen's use in each system you design.

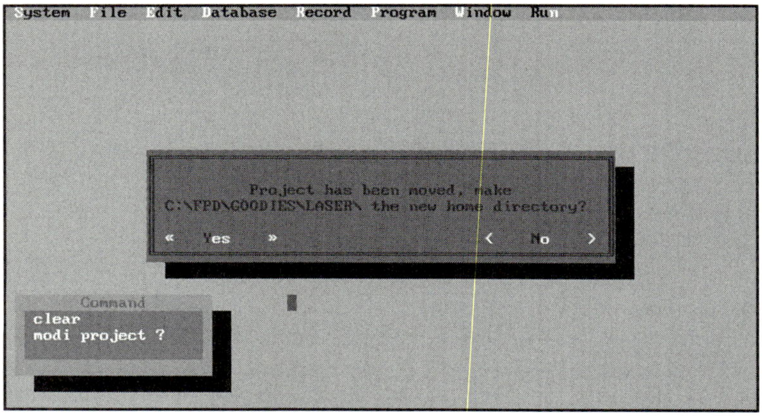

FIG. 11.2

The message that appears when you try to open a project you did not create.

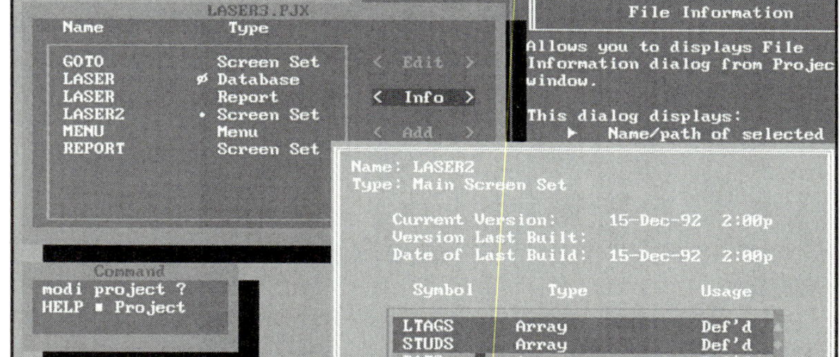

FIG. 11.3

The information on a file maintained in the project.

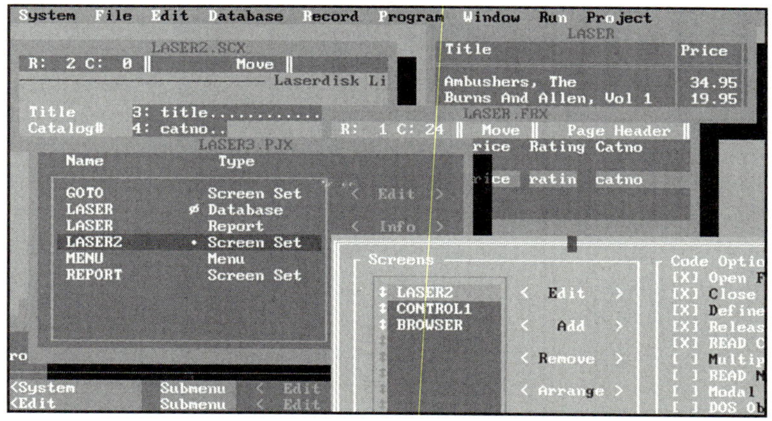

FIG. 11.4

Opening and editing different kinds of files in the project.

Finally, select Build and access the dialog that is truly a project's *raison d'être* (see fig 11.5). A project *builds* applications by putting together all the component files to compile an APP file, such as the files you previously learned to DO to run applications or (with the addition of the Distribution Kit) to generate two kinds of *executable* files, which are covered in Chapter 14, "Organizing and Packaging Your Applications."

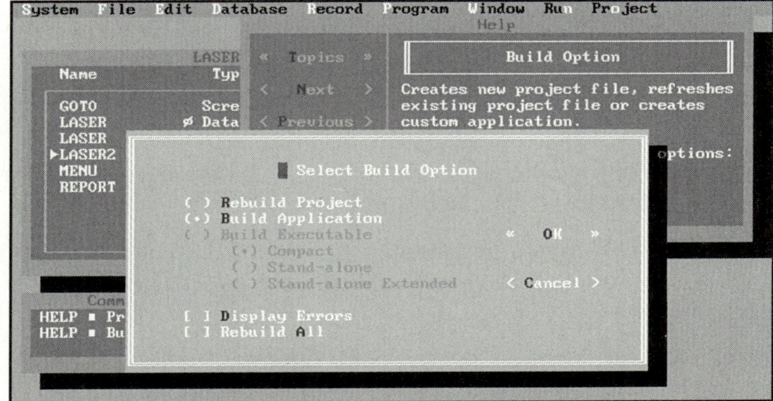

FIG. 11.5

The Project Manager's Build dialog.

Summary

Applications design is one of the most creative parts of using any database management system, and FoxPro is no exception. You should go on to enjoy this aspect of working with FoxPro, and continue to expand your thoughts on these issues as you explore the FoxPro design tools in Part III of this book and beyond.

Sources for new design ideas are all around you in the real world. The books listed next, from which many of the recommendations in this section are drawn, are just a few places to start.

Interface Design Issues: a Short Bibliography

Apple Human Interface Guidelines: The Apple Desktop Interface. Addison-Wesley, Reading, MA, 1987 (and revised editions).

"The Ziggurat Zone," Peter C. Coffee, *PC Tech Journal*. October, 1988, pp. 147-152. (Also see other issues that contain his "Outfitting the End User" column.)

The Elements of Friendly Software Design, Paul Heckel, Warner, New York, 1984. (Besides the subject in the title, to which Heckel provides a good general introduction, this book contains among the best analyses of how software developers—and other creative people—work together in collaborative design processes.)

The Art of Human-Computer Interface Design, Brenda Laurel, ed., Addison-Wesley, Reading, MA, 1990. (An anthology of views from diverse sources.)

The Windows Interface: An Application Design Guide, Microsoft Programming Series, Microsoft Press, Redmond, WA, 1991.

The Design of Everyday Things, Donald A. Norman, Doubleday, New York, 1990. (Previously published in hardcover as *The Psychology of Everyday Things*.)

Designing the User Interface: Strategies for Effective Human-Computer Interaction, Ben Shneiderman, Addison-Wesley, Reading, MA, 1987.

TOG on Interface, Bruce Tognazzini, Addison-Wesley, Reading, MA, 1991.

Envisioning Information, Edward R. Tufte, Graphics Press, Cheshire, CT, 1990. (Also see Tufte, *The Visual Display of Quantitative Information*.)

12

CHAPTER

Creating Application Elements

In the first chapters of this book, you learn a quick and easy way to enter data by using the BROWSE command to navigate in a table. BROWSE and its companion tool, EDIT/CHANGE, provide powerful means to format and enter data. However, data entry and other screen displays can take many forms in FoxPro.

The multifaceted READ command gives you almost unlimited access to the same interface objects for the data-entry designs that FoxPro uses. Chapter 2 introduces you to these objects, which you manipulate from the first action you take in the program. In the next two chapters, you learn how to use these interface objects as a developer using the versatile Screen Builder.

You use the Screen Builder to paint and arrange these objects on-screen so you can concentrate on creating an ideal layout. Similar to the Report Writer, the Screen Builder requires careful study. Although your initial efforts with the Screen Builder may produce useful and attractive results, attaching a few lines of programming instructions to some of these objects (just as you added UDFs to the reports) provides far greater control over both the content and the appearance of screens.

For data-entry screens, this control often involves some form of data validation. Data validation techniques make sure that information entered into a field or fields meets certain criteria you set. You can make the information in one field, for example, dependent on the information in another field. Or you can make sure the field contains one of the choices stored in a lookup table, a concept you encountered when you worked with reports and labels.

In a multiuser or multitasking environment, the concept of data validation extends to cover another category of data integrity. You design your application with additional goals: to ensure that two users don't try to change the same information at the same time and that the information each user views is as up-to-date as possible.

Of course, the Screen Builder can produce other application elements that aren't strictly data-entry forms. For example, you can design logos and other background screens, informational displays, alerts, dialogs, database-managing control panels, and all other forms of communication a system needs.

This chapter introduces the Screen Builder as a tool. The experience you had with the Report Writer has prepared you for many of the features with which you are going to work in this chapter and Chapter 13. Refer to Chapters 9 and 10 for detailed information on how to place, move, and size objects on the form layout. This chapter offers more advice on objects specific to screens, which you have not encountered in reports. You concentrate on enhancing the screens with various forms of data validation. You find out how and why you build more than one window into a screen set like the one in PRODUCT.APP. The process of enhancing screen sets continues in the following chapters, with examples of more complex screen sets and data validation.

If you're new to program writing, several programming concepts introduced in this chapter may intimidate you. Take the time to work through these concepts; don't try to complete all the exercises in one sitting. Rather, practice creating the interface objects using the techniques described in this chapter and the following chapter, without adding all the validation codes. To further help you understand the material, return to this section after you read the chapters on programming.

Even if you're well-versed in programming, you may have difficulty getting used to the Screen Builder. For many programmers, this tool represents a radical departure from standard methods of program design, creation, and maintenance. Expert programmers may find difficulty in relinquishing their edge on experience and expertise to adapt to completely new working conditions.

However, whether you are a novice or a veteran, your investment is repaid many times over if you give time and attention to the Screen Builder.

Using the Screen Builder

In Xbase terms, the objects you place on-screen to provide the user with information are SAYs, and the objects you use to collect information from the user are GETs. In this section, you create a simple screen layout of SAYs and GETs and explore some of the Screen Builder's options for enhancing these objects.

Starting To Build the Screen

As usual, start FoxPro from the MODEL directory. However, if you are already working in the data directories, you can access the practice files by issuing the following command in the Command window (substitute your drive and path if different.):

```
SET DEFAULT TO C:\FPD\MODEL
```

Examine the screen that FoxApp built and you edited slightly in Chapter 1. Open the MODEL.VUE file and use the View window to make the Product table the selected work area. Or type the following command in the Command window:

```
USE PRODUCT
```

In the File Open dialog, open the screen-type file PRODUCT.SCX (note the default extension), or type the following command in the Command window:

```
MODIFY SCREEN PRODUCT
```

The screen-designing window you see is similar to the Report Writer. The window includes some text items (in this screen, the field names) and different-colored or highlighted field expressions (in this screen, the Product table fields). You can select and move objects around, resize objects, or use a selection marquee and group objects.

Examining the Screen Builder Options

If you select an object and access the Screen menu pad from the menu bar, you see the following groups of options on the Screen menu popup, as shown in figure 12.1:

- The first group contains a Screen Layout... option that presents a dialog in which you make decisions that influence the overall look and behavior of the screen. The Open All Snippets option gives you access to the code snippets, which are attached to this screen. Code snippets are lines of programming instructions that can belong to a single screen object or give you screen-wide control. As you see in a following section, snippets are similar to the UDFs you created for the reports, but snippets are stored internally in the screen file.
- The second group on the menu popup are options for each kind of screen object that you can use. You are already familiar with Box and Text objects from reports, and you used all the other options as you explored the FoxPro interface.
- The third group of options on the Screen menu popup influences the behavior of a selected object or objects. (The items are enabled here because the text object Product Code was selected.) Although most of these options are familiar from the Report Writer, some options take on new significance when applied to screens.
- The fourth, or last, group has only one option, Quick Screen..., which is disabled in figure 12.1 because a Quick Screen generates only when you work with a completely empty screen. The original FoxApp-generated PRODUCT.SCX, before modification as shown, was a Quick Screen created by a programming command.

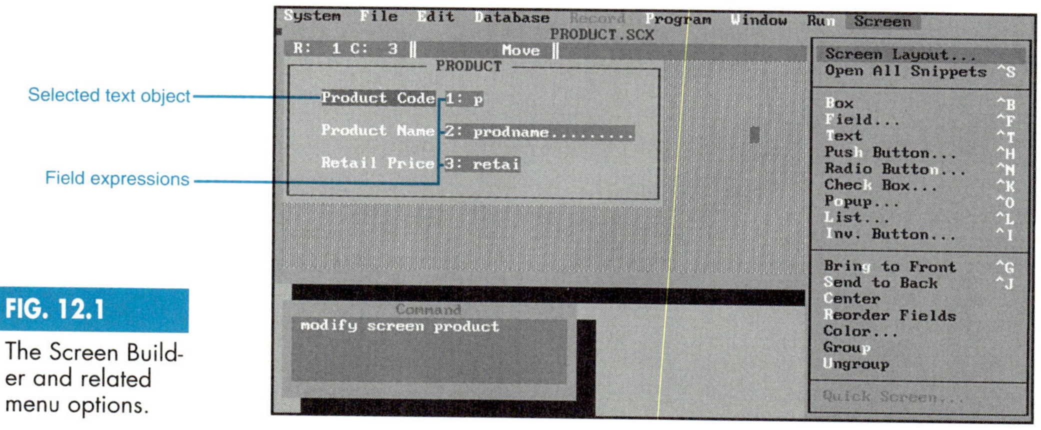

FIG. 12.1

The Screen Builder and related menu options.

Practice moving the objects around and perhaps changing the text objects to make them more understandable. Notice that pressing Ctrl+T or typing text on-screen puts you into text mode as opposed to the default move mode. You see the difference in the screen's status line. Pressing Enter while creating a text object puts you back in move mode and affixes the text object in the screen.

If you like, you can add a Box object by using Ctrl+B. After drawing the box, double-click or double-space to select the box's style using a set of radio button options (Single line, Double line, Panel, or Character) similar to the options you used in the Report Writer (see fig. 12.2). Notice that you see no Float option because this option makes no sense in a screen. Instead, you can use the `Fill Character` push button to fill the box with any character you choose.

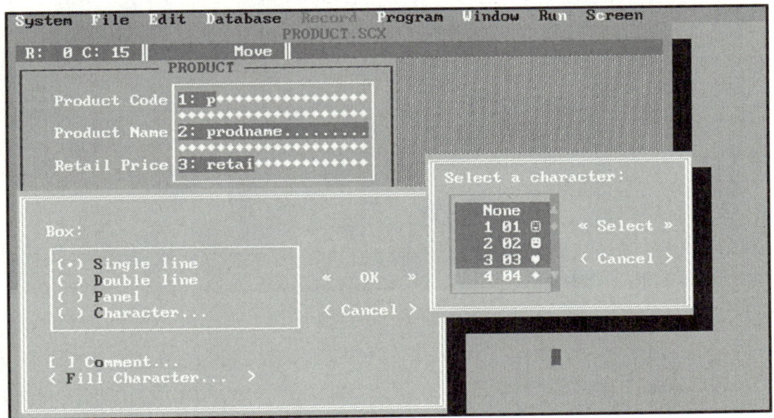

FIG. 12.2

A single line box, filled with a graphics character, overlaid by text and field objects.

After you create and fill a box, you may need to select the box object and use the Send to Back option before you can see the text objects again. This concept is familiar, too, although in reports you use Send to Back differently for printing effects.

You also may notice that the box doesn't add significantly to the elegance of the screen display. Select the box again and press Del; the box disappears.

Using the Field Expression Dialog

Selecting the field expression labeled by the text object Product Code for editing opens a dialog with a few familiar features. But in this dialog you begin to see the real differences between a report (which is entirely output) and a screen (where the user may edit some objects).

As shown in figure 12.3, the top set of radio buttons in this dialog enables you to designate the field expression as a SAY, a GET (shown here), or an EDIT. In a screen, a SAY is an expression that appears as a label, similar to a column heading in a report. The EDIT and GETs, in contrast, are the items into which the user places new information. EDIT expressions are, like Memo fields, variable in length, and GET expressions provide text boxes for data entry.

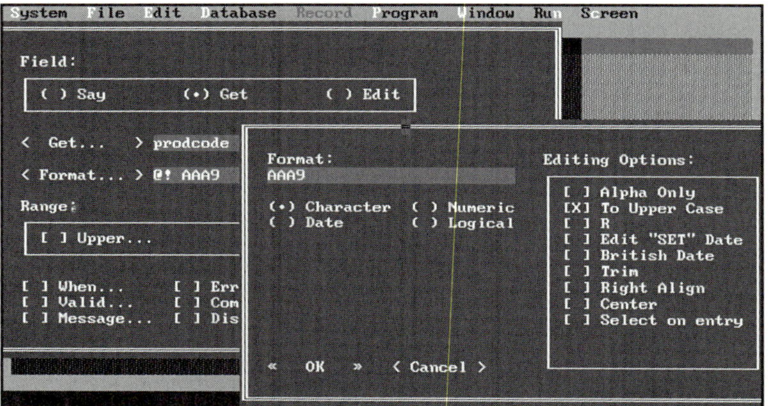

FIG. 12.3

Formatting the product code.

Besides the text box GETs and the EDIT expressions available from the Field Expression dialog, you have access to other, specialized forms of GETs through other options in the Screen menu popup (Push Button..., Radio Button..., Check Box..., Popup..., List..., and Invisible Button...). You know how these forms work from FoxPro's dialogs and system windows. In following sections of this chapter and following chapters, as you create examples of these specialized objects and explore the distinctive properties of each object, consider the actions that each type of GET is best suited to perform.

If you change the radio button selection from Get to Say or Edit, the other options in the dialog become enabled or disabled, as appropriate for the different field expressions. You learn more about the other options in a following section of this chapter. For now, return the selection to Get.

Beginning To Validate GETs

The Prodcode field expression currently enables you to enter any characters, but the data-entry screen is more useful if you can ensure two items:

- Every product code follows a particular format; the Omnipresent Widget product line uses three capitalized alphabetic characters followed by one digit.
- Every product has a unique code to provide the correct lookups for the Budget and other tables.

These criteria are examples of simple *data-validation requirements*. An application with data-validation capabilities limits the data that can be entered by the user or imported from other data sources. If an entry or imported data item does not meet the application's specifications, the application rejects the data or modifies it to fit the criteria before storing the information in the database.

To provide the first kind of data validation for the Prodcode field, click the `Format...` button. You see a new dialog, also shown in figure 12.3. Checking the To Upper Case box and typing the format `AAA9` gives you the Format shown in the Field Expression dialog's text box.

You can press F1 at any time to get context-sensitive help on a current action. You need not remember all the possible Formatting template characters. As you see when you access the Help file, the template AAA9 means that the first three characters must be letters and the last character must be a number.

The second problem is more complicated. To make sure every product code you enter is unique and every product name has a code, attach a code snippet to the field expression by using the Valid check box.

A GET's VALID clause works the same way as a BROWSE field's :V switch, which you learn about in Chapter 8. The VALID clause is a logical expression evaluated when a user enters new data into that field and then tries to leave the field. If the expression evaluates to False, the contents of the field are not valid, and the user remains in that field. If BELL is SET ON, which is the default, the bell sounds. If NOTIFY is SET ON (also the default), a window with an error message appears. The default message is `Invalid Entry`. You can provide more informative error messages by using the ERROR clause, like the BROWSE field's :E switch, for which you also see a check box.

As in a BROWSE, a VALID clause does not handle data entry in a field concluded by pressing the Esc key, which indicates cancellation of the entry (the GET reverts to the data the field held before editing). You should treat this kind of cancellation separately and consistently throughout the system.

Unlike a BROWSE field's :V switch, a VALID clause also can return a positive or negative number, as well as a .T. or .F. result. A positive number advances the cursor that number of GETs forward, and a negative one forces the cursor backward. In a following section, you return to this way, and other ways, of influencing the order that GETs are entered.

A VALID clause can contain a simple expression, such as the following line:

```
! EMPTY(Prodcode)
```

You can use the exclamation point (!) interchangeably with the word NOT in FoxPro expressions. The clause also can call a single UDF or more complicated expressions—such as the work you created by using the Expression Builder—that include multiple UDFs.

If you use the Valid check box to create an Expression (by marking the Expression radio button in the Valid dialog), you can type the expression directly or use the Expression Builder. You also can use Valid to create a Procedure (see figs. 12.4 and 12.5). This process enables you to write a set of instructions, which you attach to this object, that FoxPro creates as a UDF (as you see when you examine the program you generate later). This method is a convenient way to avoid worrying about what you named, or where you stored, the UDF. Advantages exist in creating an Expression, however, which you see in the following sections.

NOTE Screen files (tables with the default extension .SCX) can hold procedures to be used in conjunction with these files' related elements, but report files (.FRX tables) cannot. Screen files have this capability because they are sent through a generating template, which produces complete programs that you include with the applications you create. The attached procedures are generated as parts of these programs. The generated programs must then be compiled, like other programs that you can DO, so that FoxPro can interpret them. Report files, however, do not produce programs to be used at run-time; FoxPro interprets reports directly in table form. All procedures run in conjunction with report files, therefore, must exist outside the files so FoxPro can compile these procedures separately. .FRX tables cannot generate code, but this seeming limitation has a compensatory advantage. Because reports need not be compiled, users can modify and create reports with applications you create. In Chapter 14, where you explore various ways to distribute the applications you create, the significance of this difference becomes clear.

When you mark the Procedure radio button you see a small text-editing area in which you can type. However, you may prefer to select the `Edit...` option, as shown in figure 12.4. `Edit...` opens a full-scale editing window for the snippet and puts you back at the Field Expression dialog. Select `OK` or press Ctrl+Enter, and you enter the snippet-editing window, as shown in figure 12.5.

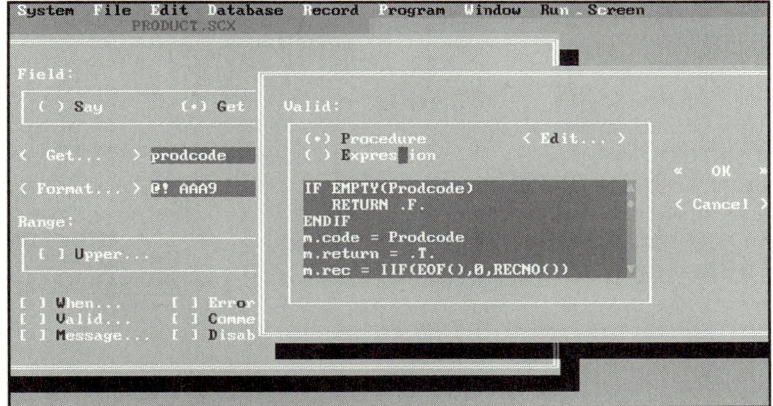

FIG. 12.4
Accessing the VALID clause and choosing to create a Procedure snippet.

The instructions to validate the product code are relatively complex. These instructions, however, contain several tricks worth learning, because creating unique codes like these is a task required in almost every relational database system.

Remember that FoxPro ignores lines in a program that begin with an asterisk (*). These lines provide comments. By reviewing the comments in the following lines of code, you can follow and reproduce this procedure for programs you write. Check the *Language Reference* volume of the FoxPro documentation (or the Help file) to understand unfamiliar capitalized keywords.

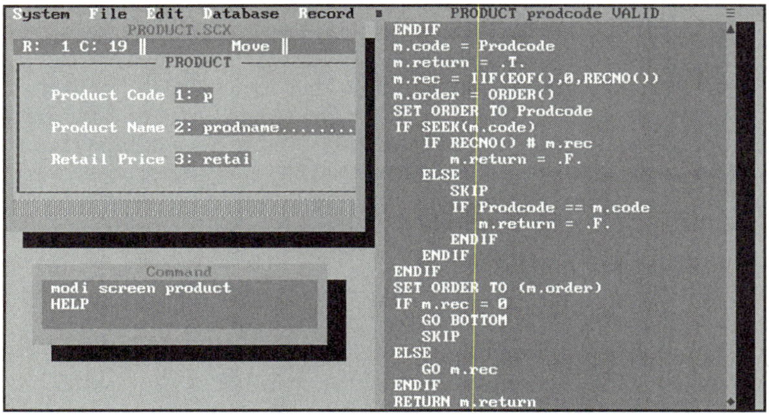

FIG. 12.5

The VALID clause Procedure snippet in an editing window.

■ Prodcode VALID snippet

```
IF EMPTY(Prodcode)
   * it should not be blank
   RETURN .F.
ENDIF

m.return = .T.
m.code = Prodcode
* save the entered value into
* a variable, 'm.code', and
* set up a variable, 'm.return',
* to hold the RETURN value

m.rec = IIF(EOF( ),0,RECNO( ))
* save the current record number
* so you can return to it after
* moving around in the table
* set it to 0 if you're at the end of
* the file

m.order = ORDER( )
SET ORDER TO Prodcode
* save the current table order
* so you can set up the order the way you want
* but restore it afterwards

IF SEEK(m.code)
   IF RECNO( ) # m.rec
      * this code is in another record!
     m.return = .F.
   ELSE
```

```
      * we found the record we are now editing
     SKIP
      * is there a second record in the index
      * with this code?
     IF prodcode==m.code
       m.return = .F.
     ENDIF
   ENDIF
ENDIF

* now put things back the way you found them
SET ORDER TO (m.order)
IF m.rec = 0
   * go to end of file
   GO BOTTOM
   SKIP
ELSE
   * go to original record
   GO m.rec
ENDIF

RETURN m.return
```

A simpler procedure, shown in figure 12.6, enables the two error conditions you identified to produce different error messages. Use the Error check box in the Field Expression dialog and choose to Edit a Procedure. Enter the following code in the editing window:

■ **Prodcode ERROR snippet as a Procedure**

```
IF EMPTY(Prodcode)
   RETURN "Product Code field cannot be empty."
ELSE
   RETURN "Product Code already in use."
ENDIF
```

Alternatively, because only two possible messages exist, you also can Edit an Expression. The Expression Builder appears, and you create the following expression, shown in figure 12.7.

■ **Prodcode ERROR snippet as an Expression**

```
IIF(EMPTY(Prodcode), "Product Code field cannot be empty.",
    "Product Code field already in use.")
```

As you see in figure 12.7, the small editing space available to edit an expression word wraps lines of code that don't fit, an attribute the Code Snippet editing window shares with the Expression Builder. Although you may add extra spaces for clarity (as the figure illustrates), do not add carriage returns by pressing Enter.

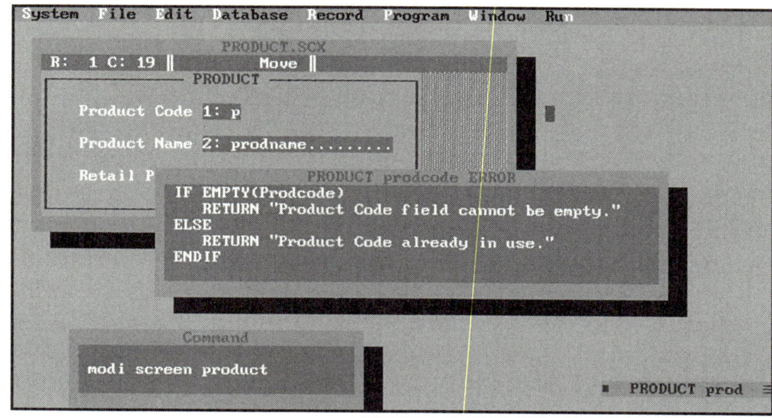

FIG. 12.6

The Screen Layout window with Prodcode VALID snippet docked and available while you edit the Prodcode ERROR snippet as a procedure.

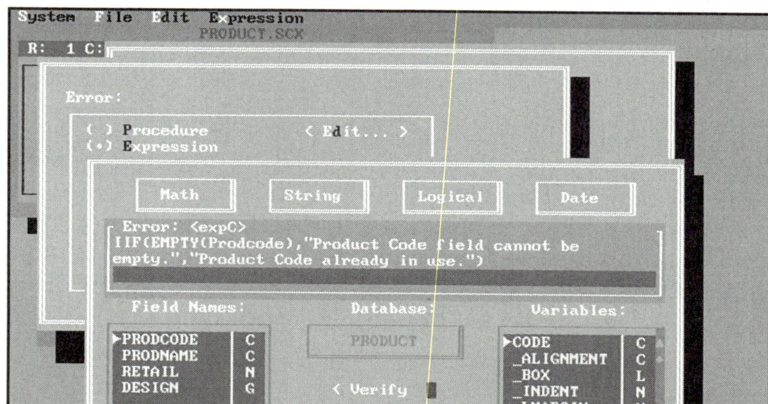

FIG. 12.7

Editing the Prodcode ERROR snippet as an expression.

TIP After you create at least one snippet, you can use the second option on the Screen menu popup to Open All Snippets at the same time as you work. (Use Ctrl+S as a shortcut.) You may find that keeping all snippets open in docked form is convenient as you work with a screen. Remember that you can resize the layout window to make room on-screen, as shown in many of the figures in this chapter. If you save a screen with snippets open, these snippets open and are ready for use when you want to modify the screen. If the screen looks too cluttered, access the Screen menu popup with Shift+Alt+C or a shifted mouse click to change the option to Close All Snippets. If you're in the Layout window, use Shift+Ctrl+S as a shortcut to hide all snippets.

Generating and Running the Screen Program

After you are satisfied with your screen design, you want to start using the results. Unlike the Report Writer, the Screen Builder does not have a Preview option, so you have not been able to get frequent glimpses of the final product as you have worked on the layout. You must execute the screen program in its final form to see how it looks and to discover whether your data validation code works as you expect.

If you use the Run menu popup's Screen... option, however, you notice that the standard Open File dialog that appears does not present .SCX files, like the screen file you just edited, from which you choose the Screen To Run. Instead, the dialog suggests files with an .SPR extension.

As you learned earlier in this chapter, an .SCX file holds descriptions of all the objects you have added to the screen, including program code you have attached to these objects. The .SCX, however, must be run through a generator program to create a program file that FoxPro can execute. The extension .SPR is the default extension for this generated program file. This section shows you how to create and execute an .SPR program from the .SCX you edited in this chapter.

Saving the Environment before Generating

To view the results of the work you did, access the Screen Layout option from the Screen menu popup, and use the dialog's Environment option on the Screen menu popup to Save the Environment. If you are creating this screen from scratch, you can save the environment the first time you save the screen, by using a dialog similar to that shown in figure 12.8. This step is familiar to you from your work with the Report Writer. If you are editing the screen FoxApp created, however, the command that CREATEd a Quick Screen in FoxApp did not save the environment in the screen file. Because FoxApp saved the screen previously, you do not get the special dialog that appears only when you save the screen for the first time. You should now deliberately save the state of the files by using the Screen Layout dialog's Environment option.

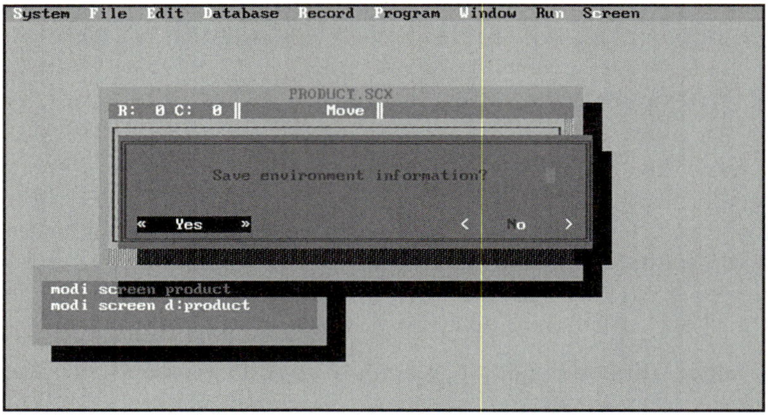

FIG. 12.8

Newly created screens that give you a choice when you first try to save the screen file.

When you work on this screen again, you can change the environment saved with the screen using the option in the Screen Layout dialog. If you try to open the screen file at a later date and you are missing a necessary index or other part of the environment, you get an error message, but you still can edit the screen. If this situation occurs, adjust and then resave the environment in the Screen Layout dialog.

With the screen on which you are working as the active window, access the Program menu popup and notice that the Generate… option is now enabled. If you press Ctrl+F1 or otherwise activate the Command window or one of the other system windows, or you open any text file in the usual way, the Generate… option is disabled again. Activate the screen design window to reactivate the option. Select the Generate… option and, because you made changes since the last time you saved the screen, you now can fix the changes on-screen and save the screen. In response to the alert that appears, as shown in figure 12.9, select `Yes`. The screen saves, and the generation of the new screen program, PRODUCT.SPR, begins.

CAUTION: If you want to DO the generated application again in the original state and you do not choose another file name to which you save the screen, you need to rebuild the Product project file, a process you learn about in a following chapter. To continue using PRODUCT.APP and its project in its original form, therefore, use the File option Save As…, and choose `No` when asked whether you want to overwrite. Save the screen as PROD-UCT1. Use this name in the following instructions.

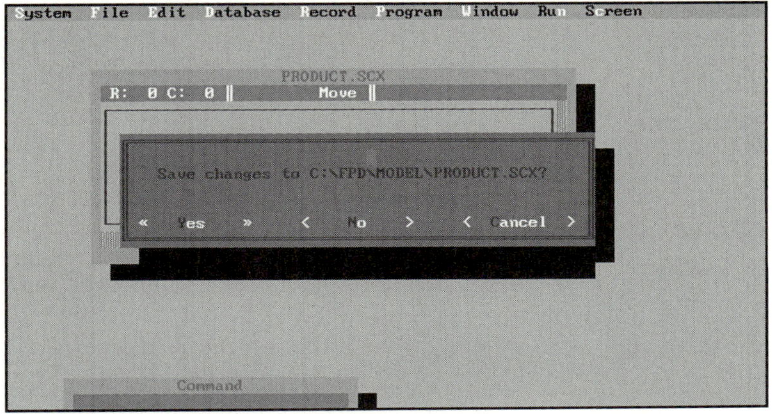

FIG. 12.9

Preparing to generate a screen program.

The first step is to select from the wide range of options as shown in figure 12.10. For now, press Ctrl+Enter to accept all the defaults.

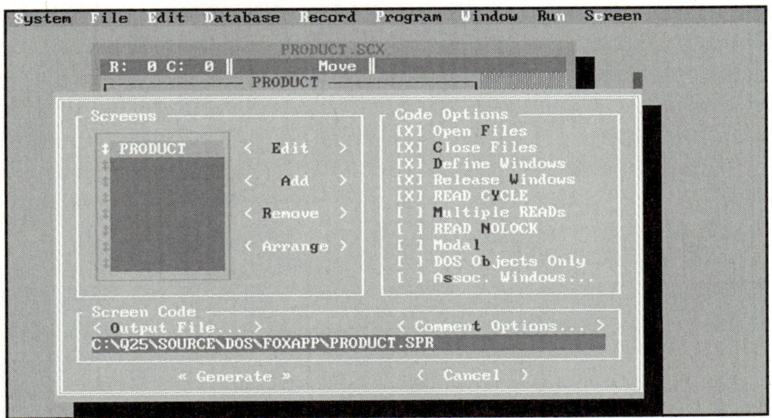

FIG. 12.10

The screen generation options dialog showing default settings.

You may receive a message asking whether you want to overwrite the old FoxApp-generated PRODUCT.SPR file. If you saved the screen to PRODUCT1.SCX, you don't see this message because no previous PRODUCT1.SPR exists in the directory.

A thermometer appears that shows you FoxPro's progress in generating the program. You saw a similar thermometer if you generated a crosstab report in the Query chapters or created an index on a large file. You also may have seen a similar thermometer during the FoxPro installation procedures, as described in Appendix A. If you are generating a screen for the first time since installing FoxPro, you see an additional thermometer as FoxPro compiles the program GENSCRN.PRG used to produce the screen code. (GENSCRN is a template, or program-creating program, supplied with FoxPro. In a following chapter, you learn that GENSCRN is another set of FoxPro instructions that you must compile the first time you run the instructions so FoxPro can interpret this template as a program.)

Don't be alarmed if the thermometer doesn't appear to progress at a constant rate. Some parts of screen program generation involve many more lines of code than others, so the indicator may seem to pause for a while.

Compiling the Generated Program

Before you try to run PRODUCT.SPR, compile the generated program. By default, FoxPro compiles the program the first time you try to DO the program, but compiling the program before a DO allows you to check for errors you may have made in typing the snippets when you edited the screen. After selecting the Compile... option from the Program menu popup, highlight and select PRODUCT.SPR from the file list in the Compile dialog and accept all other default settings as shown in figure 12.11. If typing errors exist, you see an error message similar to the message shown in figure 12.12.

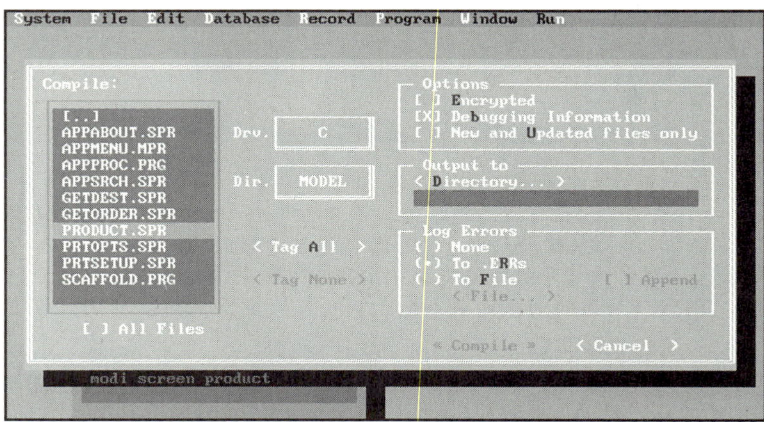

FIG. 12.11

Compiling a screen program.

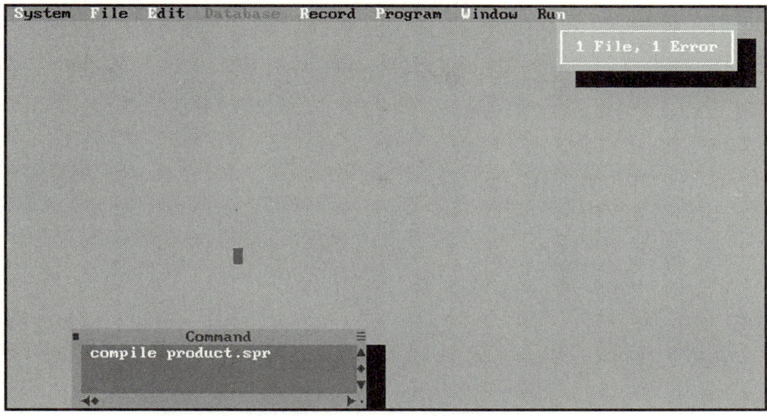

FIG. 12.12

A typical error message from the Compiler.

As you see in figure 12.13, you then can look for a file name with the extension .ERR by using the File Open... menu option or (a faster way) by typing the following command in the Command window:

```
MODIFY FILE *.ERR
```

This command finds a file that contains the instruction(s) FoxPro wasn't able to interpret. The best thing to do, as shown in figure 12.14, is to reactivate the screen you were building, open the snippets, and look for the error that caused the problem. (Don't forget to highlight and copy the error in the .ERR file first, and use the FoxPro editor to Find this text in the snippets.)

After you find and edit all errors, save, generate, and compile the program again. To see whether more errors exist, type the following command:

```
MODIFY FILE *.ERR
```

If all the errors have been corrected, this command results in a `File does not exist` error message because FoxPro erases the old error file during the compilation process.

NOTE The process of finding and fixing errors in programs is called debugging the code. FoxPro has sophisticated tools, the Debug and Trace windows, which you learn about in Chapter 20, "Enhancing the Applications You Program." These tools are indispensable in large systems that contain many programs. For now, however, this simple error-correcting method suffices.

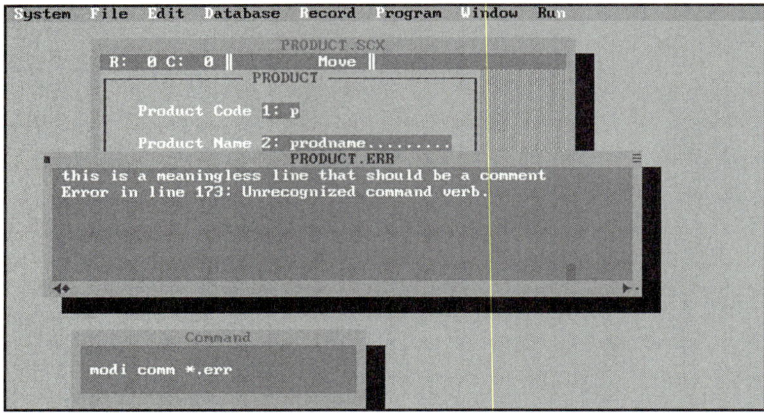

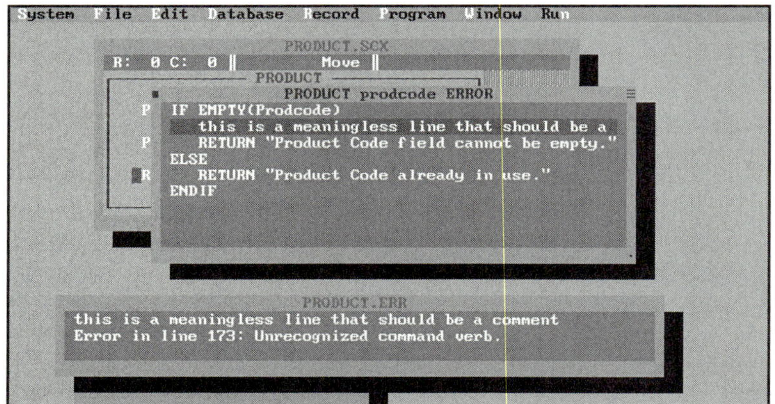

FIGS. 12.13 and 12.14

Finding and fixing errors in the screen file.

Running the Program

After you correct all errors, you can use the Program Do… option to run the PRODUCT.SPR program. As you can see in figure 12.15, attempting to edit the product code for a record (Floral Weazlettes) to a code already in use for another product (Dream Sequencers) results in a useful error message, as does an attempt to enter a blank code.

But something is missing. How do you add records? How do you move off the first record in the file?

In the FoxApp-generated program, you added new records by using a menu entry, and you moved around in the table with a second window, called a control panel. You can provide both of these capabilities, and many others, in a control panel, placing the control panel with the data-entry screen in a screen set.

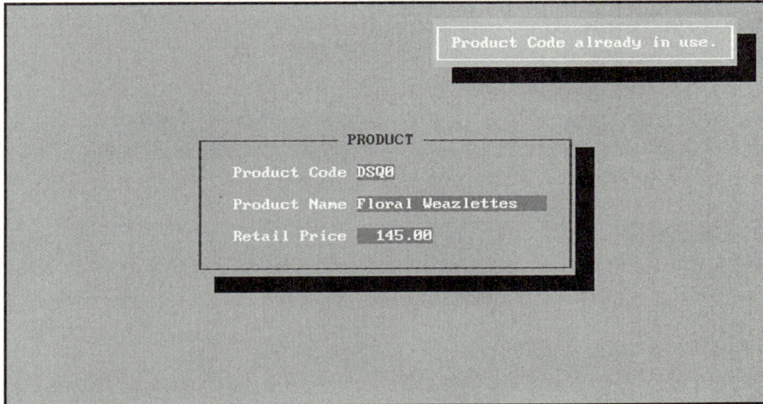

FIG. 12.15
Product table data entry with validation.

In the next chapter, you create a more sophisticated data-entry screen for the Budget table, and you can try all the tantalizing interface objects assembled in the Screen menu popup. First, however, create a few more simple screens by using some of the other lookup tables in the model database (Budcat and Dept). This process gives you a chance to explore these basic database management needs.

Gaining Proficiency in Screen Builder Use

Now that you know how to create a screen and generate an executable screen program, this section introduces you to some standard screen design techniques and code snippets that you should find useful in the applications you create for your own data.

You enter data in the Budget table in Chapter 3 and the Product table in Chapter 1. If you have not yet created or entered information in the Budcat and Dept tables, you can enter the information by using your newly designed screens following this section. You need the data in these tables to perform data validation in the Budget data-entry screen in Chapter 13. In the following section, the examples refer to the Dept table and DEPT.SCX, but you should repeat this process and create a screen set for the Budcat table after you finish with the Dept table.

Tables 12.1 and 12.2 give you structures and sample records that provide lookups for all the records you created previously in the Budget table.

Table 12.1 Structures for the Budcat and Dept Tables

BUDCAT.DBF

Field	Field Name	Type	Width	Index
1	Budcatcode	Character	4	Asc
2	Budcat	Character	20	Asc

DEPT.DBF

Field	Field Name	Type	Width	Index
1	Deptcode	Character	4	Asc
2	Deptname	Character	30	Asc

Table 12.2 Records for the Budcat and Dept Tables

Omnipresent Widget's Budget Categories (BUDCAT.DBF)

Record Number	Budget Code	Budget Category Name
1	INS0	Insurance
2	LHR0	Labor, Hourly Reg
3	LHO0	Labor, Hourly Over
4	LSL0	Labor, Salary
5	LCM0	Labor, Commission
6	TRV0	Travel
7	ADV0	Advertising
8	PLT0	Plant

Omnipresent Widget's Departments (DEPT.DBF)

Record Number	Dept Code	Department Name
1	SLS1	Sales Southeast Division
2	SLS2	Sales Northeast Division
3	SLS3	Sales Western Division
4	FIN0	Finance
5	MFT0	Manufacturing
6	PER0	Personnel

Create the structures shown in table 12.1 as you created the Budget table. (Use the View window to select an unused work area, choose Open, and then choose New when asked to select a file.) Create tags on both fields in each table.

Select the new lookup table, DEPT, to begin the screen-creation process. Choose to Open a New screen file, which you can save to the same name as the table (DEPT.SCX), and then select the Quick Screen... option to access the dialog shown in figure 12.16.

Modifying Tables with Direct and Indirect Reads

When users modify records in a table, you need to provide them with a way to cancel the changes they have made. Your method depends on whether your data-entry routine employs direct reads or indirect reads. In the Screen Builder, you make this choice by checking the Memory Variables check box (indirect read) or leaving it unchecked (direct read).

In a direct read, the user's entries are stored directly into the field values. You preserve the existing entries by copying them into memory variables with the SCATTER MEMVAR command. In an indirect read, you also use the SCATTER MEMVAR command to copy the record's field values into memory variables, but the user now modifies only the contents of the variables; the actual field values remain unchanged until the user verifies that the changes are acceptable.

If you use the indirect read method, the record's original values are automatically protected. If the user decides that the changes are correct, you copy the values stored in the memory variables into their related fields using the GATHER MEMVAR command. If the user does not want to save the changes, you simply leave the record's field values the way they were before the editing session began.

If you use the direct read method, the user's changes have already been placed into the fields. You need a way to restore the previous values if the user changes his mind and cancels the edit. You restore values using the GATHER MEMVAR command to overwrite the user's changes with the previous contents of the record's fields, which you stored into memory variables with the SCATTER command.

Note that the Screen Builder does not generate the SCATTER MEMVAR and GATHER MEMVAR commands for you. You must place these commands in the code snippets that are executed before and after the editing session. You learn how to place these commands later in this section.

Both indirect and direct READ methods have advantages. FoxApp and the revised PRODUCT.SPR use direct editing of a record. In this example, choose to edit memory variables instead and explore the way this protection works.

As shown in figure 12.16, you should use Quick Screen's check box labeled Memory Variables, which is not the default. (Notice that when Memory Variables is checked, the Add Alias check box becomes disabled.) Quick Screen now creates GETs that are memory variables rather than fields. These variables are referenced by the Screen Builder and by the procedures you write using the names of the fields prefaced with *m.* in each case. After choosing this option, you can accept the other defaults and create the Quick Screen.

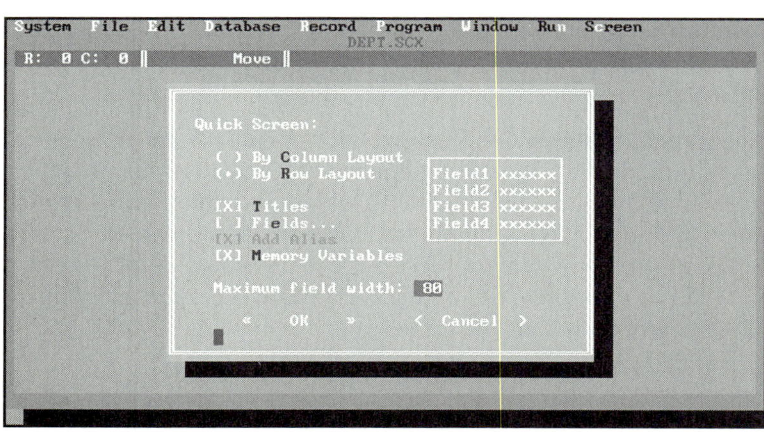

FIG. 12.16

The Quick Screen dialog, choosing to GET to memory variables.

Changing the Entry Window Style

As you did with the FoxApp-generated screen, you want to move the items around slightly. Access the Screen Layout... options next and size the window more appropriately for the two-field table data entry.

First, notice in figure 12.17 that the radio buttons on the top row default to a Desktop screen, which means that the GETs and other items are placed directly on-screen. Click the Window radio button and the window Name, Title, Footer, and the Type options become enabled. Type a Title for the window's top border and a Footer if you like, and use the Height and Width options to size the window more appropriately. Click the `Type` button and look at the resulting dialog.

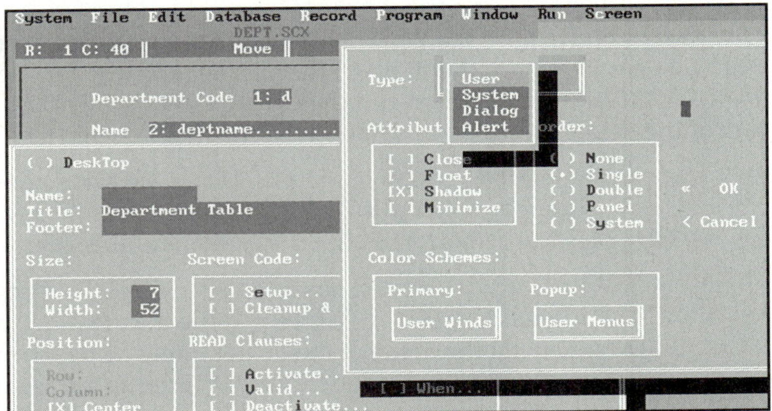

FIG. 12.17
Adjustments in the Screen Layout dialog and the Window Type dialog.

> **TIP**
>
> A good way to change the size of a window is to drag its lower-right corner directly in the screen layout window. If the window still is defined as its default of Desktop rather than Window type, you can resize the entire layout window and then change to a Window type in the Screen layout dialog. The window you are designing automatically adjusts to the current size of the layout window. You see the Height and Width change immediately in the Screen layout dialog.

Although you do not change much for now in the Screen Layout dialog, take a moment to access the Window Type dialog from its push button. You can use this dialog's other option to change the colors of the window overall. Or use the Type popup control to assign colors and other characteristics (Border and Attributes) to match the patterns you learned for System, Dialog, and Alert windows in the FoxPro interface. If you change from one type of window to another in this dialog, you see that not all attributes or borders are available for each kind of window. This feature is FoxPro's attempt to encourage you to become consistent in interface design.

Refining Your Understanding of Data Validation

Next, you need to attach the same kind of data validation to the Deptcode (or Budcatcode) field as you used in the Product table. These codes all share the same structure and the codes all are determined the same way.

Because you can have more than one screen open at one time, open the PRODUCT screen file to use the @! AAA9 formatting template for the Prodcode GET. Copy the template and then paste it into the Format text box of the field expression m.deptcode in the new screen.

Instead of copying an edited version of the VALID and ERROR clauses for each of the two other lookup tables, you can make the process more generic by creating a short UDF that many similar tables share.

Each table can use the same validation scheme because the FoxPro functions VARREAD( ) and EVALUATE( ) give you the information you need. VARREAD( ) tells you the name of the current field or memory variable into which you are entering data. EVALUATE( ), as the name suggests, evaluates a character-type expression and returns the result of the evaluation. If VARREAD( ) is currently deptcode, EVALUATE(VARREAD( )) is the current value of Deptcode, which may be SLS1 or FIN0.

TIP If you're experienced in other Xbase dialects, you may recognize EVALUATE( ) as something like a macro-substitution. This process is another way to treat the contents of a variable as a character string literal and evaluate the variable's contents at run-time. Tests show that this new EVALUATE( ) function is significantly faster in execution than macros in some circumstances. Rushmore optimization, discussed in Chapter 7, is unavailable when the conditions include EVALUATE( ); so if you are collecting sets of records, use a macro. Usually, however, EVALUATE( ) is faster if the expression is to be expanded once, as in this example.

First, see how this process works with the simpler ERROR clause. After marking the Error check box in the Field Expression dialog for the m.deptcode object, enter the following UDF that you are evaluating as an Expression (not a Procedure):

```
errcode( )
```

■ **Deptcode/ Budcatcode ERROR expression**

Now, create a program file by choosing New… from the File menu popup and then Program, or by typing the following command in the Command window:

```
MODIFY COMMAND errcode
```

You can type the entire UDF into the text editing window, as shown in figure 12.18, by entering the following listing:

■ **FUNCTION errcode**

```
IF EMPTY(EVALUATE("m."+VARREAD( )))
   * if the current contents of the variable
   * being READ is blank

   * Note that you add the "m." to VARREAD( ) to
   * distinguish the variable deptcode
   * from the field Deptcode --VARREAD( ) can't do
   * this by itself

   RETURN PROPER(VARREAD( ))+;
       " field cannot be empty."
   * Use a message with the name of the variable
   * that explains the problem.
   * The PROPER( ) function capitalizes the name of
   * the variable appropriately for the message.
ELSE
   * The error was that the code is already in use
   * -- you need an appropriate message for that, too:
   RETURN EVALUATE("m."+VARREAD( ))+;
        " already in use in "+;
        PROPER(VARREAD( ))+" field."
ENDIF
```

Of course, you also use the code field's Valid check box, and the Expression it should hold is the name of another UDF, ChkCode( ). Following are the contents of CHKCODE.PRG, using VARREAD( ) and EVALUATE( ), which also refers to a variable, addmode, that you use in the screen set to tell this UDF what you are trying to do.

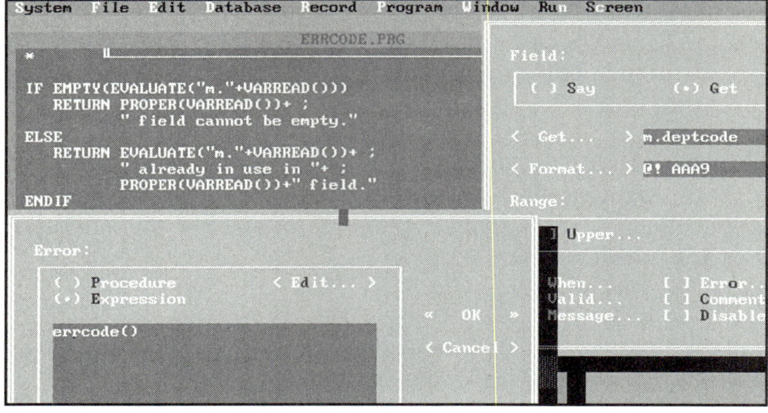

FIG. 12.18

Editing ERRCODE.PRG and using it as a UDF in an ERROR clause expression.

Because ChkCode( ) is almost the same as the procedure you used in PRODUCT.SCX, the following comments are limited to explaining the changes that make the code generic:

FUNCTION ChkCode, used as the Deptcode/ Budcatcode VALID expression

```
the_var = VARREAD( )
* store the name of the variable being READ

IF EMPTY(EVALUATE("m."+the_var))
   * check to see if the variable is empty
   * using "m." again to distinguish the variable
   * from a field of the same name
   RETURN .F.
ENDIF

IF RECCOUNT( ) = 0
   * if we're adding the first record of the table,
   * we can skip the whole check
   RETURN .T.
ENDIF

m.code = EVALUATE("m."+the_var)
* store the contents of the variable

m.return = .T.
m.rec = IIF(EOF( ),0,RECNO( ))
m.order = ORDER( )
SET ORDER TO (m.the_var)
* reference the name of the variable
* to set the order
```

```
IF SEEK(m.code) AND (m.addmode OR RECNO( ) # m.rec)
   * if you are trying to add a record
   * NO record in the table should
   * have this code, regardless of what
   * record you're on in the table
   * when you're NOT adding, a record with
   * a different record number than m.rec
   * represents a problem, as it did before
   m.return = .F.
ENDIF

SET ORDER TO (m.order)
IF m.rec = 0
   * you're at the End-of-File marker, not a
   * regular record
   GO BOTTOM
   SKIP
ELSE
   GO m.rec
ENDIF

RETURN m.return
```

Now, you may begin to see why you want to create this kind of procedure as a UDF and why you want to call this procedure as an expression instead of building the procedure as a snippet within a screen file (again see fig. 12.18). Although complex, this program also can handle validation for most of the lookup codes in a system. You need to write this program only once. With few changes, the same UDF can handle the same kind of validation for direct READs rather than for memory variables.

NOTE In the past, you may have wanted to put a generic UDF like Errcode( ) into a procedure file to make the UDF available throughout an application. In FoxPro 2.x, you can attach the UDFs to the screen file by placing them in the Cleanup snippet, effectively turning the screen file into its own procedure file. You also can create UDFs as little programs, and the Project Manager (covered in Chapter 14) takes care of building the application from all the procedures you may reference, no matter where you keep them.

Adding the Editing and Navigation Control Panel

The plan for data entry calls for the capability of moving through the table at will, adding and editing records, and saving or canceling changes you make. This capability requires adding features to this screen. You return to add these features after you integrate a second screen with the first screen. The second screen is a control panel based on the panels you already know from the sample programs that Microsoft supplies.

In the Command window, type `MODIFY SCREEN ?`, or choose Open… from the File menu popup and select screen-type files. Look through the sample directories at the different screens available. Several directories have screens with the file-name skeleton CONTROL?.SCX, and all these screens follow the same basic principles. The screen you want to adapt for this example is CONTROL3.SCX, located in the TUTORIAL directory under the FoxPro root directory. Then you modify CONTROL3.SCX and save the file to a new name, CONTROLM.SCX, in the MODEL directory. Before you make the name change, however, you need to make a few adjustments.

As you see in figure 12.19, this control panel is a narrow rectangle with a group of push buttons that enables you to move through a table. You need to make this window longer to provide room for two more choices in the group. Use the Width and Height options in the Screen Layout dialog again, but don't worry about the Row and Col placement of the window on-screen. As you see in a following section, you can control the relative placement of the two windows when you bring together these windows in a screen set.

Use the Screen Layout dialog option to give this window a Name. (The examples in this section use the name Controls to refer to this window.) Notice that a GET window's name is not the same as the title, which appears in the top border, although in this case you have used the same word for both. You use a window name when you DEFINE the window, giving dimensions, colors, and attributes. As the term suggests, the Screen Builder uses DEFINE to define the window for you and GENSCRN generates a name for the window. However, because you refer to the window by name in some of the code snippets, use the Screen Layout Name text box to assign the window a name that you can recognize easily instead of allowing GENSCRN to generate a random name.

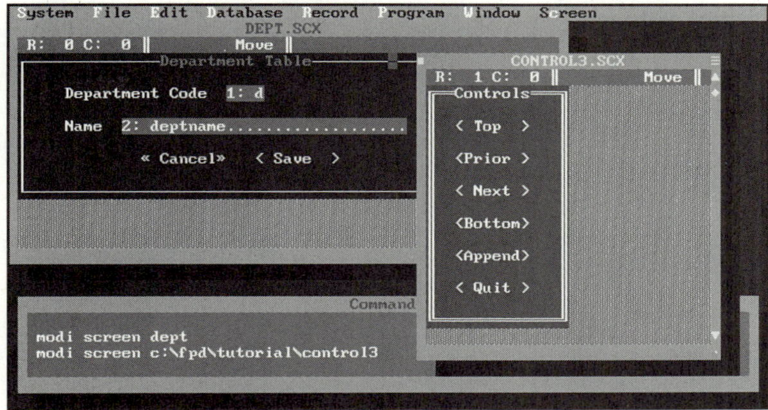

FIG. 12.19

The original TUTORIAL\ CONTROL3.SCX control panel.

After you lengthen the window by at least two lines, select the push button object. Because these buttons are a set, providing a value for a single variable, pressing the space bar twice or double-clicking any button accesses the dialog shown in figure 12.20. As you can see in the dialog, the buttons are Horizontal or Vertical radio buttons. You control the Spacing between the buttons. You Choose a Variable in which to store a button choice (this option can bring up the Expression Builder if you want to see which variables are currently defined), or you can type a variable name in the text box.

The on-screen heading Variable: is a little misleading. You can store the button choice to a memory variable, a field, or an array element. (You learn about arrays in subsequent chapters.) In any case, you must store the choice as a numeric or character data type. If you allow FoxPro to create the variable for you, as you do in this example, instead of manually initializing the variable with a default choice, the variable is of numeric type and a number corresponding to the number of the chosen button is stored to the variable. The variable for this button set happens to be act2. Buttons also can be designated as Terminating, which means that making a choice from this group terminates the READ. In the example, you do not want the buttons to terminate the READ; rather, you want the user to continue to make new choices and edit new records until choosing to leave the screen.

Besides these options, you also see the check boxes When..., Valid..., Message..., Comment..., and Disabled available for field expressions. Of course, the buttons also need prompts, which you create in the box on the left.

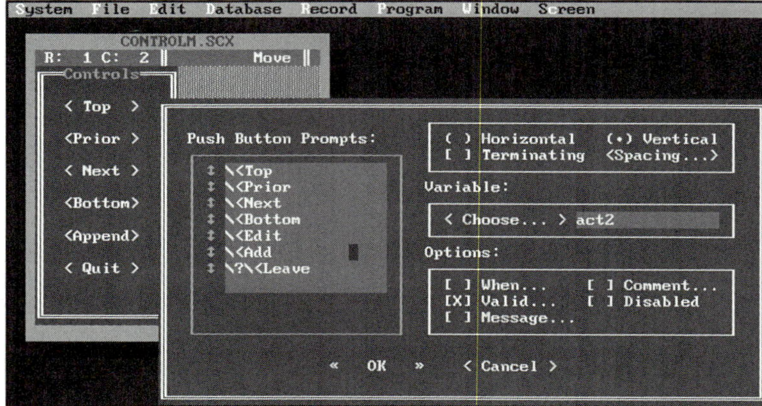

FIG. 12.20

The revised control panel as you edit the push buttons.

In figure 12.20, you have edited the list of prompts to contain a new prompt, `Edit`; changed the `Append` prompt to `Add`; and changed the `Quit` prompt to `Leave`. (Type these new prompts at the bottom of the list, and then select and move them as you usually move fields in structure-modifying dialogs.) The new prompts do not show in the screen layout yet, because you are still in the dialog. You also have placed the characters \< before the initial letters of each prompt, which highlights and designates the prompts as hot keys. Notice that the characters \? before the final entry (which you edited from `Quit` to `Leave`) were maintained from the original Control screen, designating this prompt as an escape button. Because of the \? characters, choosing this entry is the same as pressing the Esc key. You can have only one escape button in a set.

Quit is not a good name for an escape button because in Xbase, Quit usually means leaving the entire application, not just one screen. That is why you change the prompt on this button to Exit, Leave, Finished, or some other word you like better. Remember that you should use the same word as your escape button prompt for all screens of this type in your application. You also changed `Append` to `Add` because Appending is a computer term. The user envisions the application in terms of adding information to the data he or she has stored, not appending records to the table.

TIP

You may be surprised that you don't add a `Delete` button to this control panel to go with the `Add` and `Edit` buttons. Recall that this screen manages data entry for several lookup tables. As you learned in the "Maintaining Relational Integrity" section in Chapter 4, entries in lookup tables are the parents in one-to-many relationships in a database. Records in the main tables may have entries dependent on these lookup items. Avoid deleting entries in lookup tables unless you are very careful to give its child records viable links to a different lookup record as part of the deletion process. In many cases, unnecessary entries are best left in the lookup table, which is usually not large in size (unlike the main data tables). Many systems also do not enable editing of lookup codes after they are created, unless all child tables have been checked for entries. You can use the SEEK() function on the Budget table to add this check to ChkCode() when editing, and you can revise FUNCTION ErrCode to give an appropriate error message.

You also need to make sure that hotkeys don't repeat from one button to the next. Of course, you can designate a different character than the initial letter of a prompt as a hotkey to avoid hotkey duplication. Your first goal is consistency and comfort for the user, however, and such scattered hotkeys can be hard to remember, making them more hindrance than help.

Now is a good time to save the revised control panel screen file to a new name (the example uses CONTROLM.SCX) in the MODEL directory. After you save the file, you can return to editing this screen, knowing that you aren't overwriting the original CONTROL1.SCX needed by other programs.

Edit the VALID clause attached to the push button set.

If the Valid check box appears disabled, the related snippet is already opened in an editing window somewhere. As you learned previously, this situation can be true when you haven't previously accessed a snippet if the screen file was saved with the editing window open. Check the list of windows from the Window menu popup list; the snippet may be docked or hidden behind the Screen Layout window.

By now, you probably have a good idea of what is happening in this procedure. The CASE structure, which you explore in Chapter 18, checks the value of the variable, act2, into which the button choice was placed. Depending on the choice, the procedure moves the record pointer in the file and issues a SHOW GETS command, which makes sure that information from the appropriate record appears on-screen. If the user selects `Leave` or `Quit`, the READ is CLEARed and the code RETURNs a value of 0 so that in other cases you remain in the control panel instead of moving to another GET.

You need to add another CASE to fit the new `Edit` push button choice, and edit the `Add` push button CASE. The new lines of instructions do not move the record pointer, but they change the value of two variables, m.addmode and m.editmode, to tell you what task the user is performing. Figure 12.21 (in a subsequent section) shows this snippet and the other snippets you create for this screen, with CASEs act2 = 5 and act2 = 6 storing .T. to editmode and addmode, respectively. The `Quit` (now `Leave`) button moves to the end and is now CASE act2 = 7.

Adding Record Locks

The `Edit` choice has one more task besides changing the value of the m.editmode variable. The `Edit` choice must lock this record or discover that this record cannot be locked because another user in the system is making changes to it. Because this screen edits memory variables, the user can view the variables freely until choosing to begin an edit. Then he or she must own, or lock, the record. The entire code snippet follows:

The Control panel act2 push button set VALID snippet

```
DO CASE
CASE act2 = 1
   go top
CASE act2 = 2
   skip -1
   if bof( )
      go top
   endif
CASE act2 = 3
   skip 1
   if eof( )
      go bottom
   endif
CASE act2 = 4
   go bottom
CASE act2 = 5
   IF RLOCK( )
       m.editmode = .T.
   ELSE
```

```
        WAIT WINDOW ;
                      "Sorry -- some one else is editing "+ ;
                       "this record!"
   ENDIF
CASE act2 = 6
   m.addmode = .T.
CASE act2 = 7
   CLEAR READ
ENDCASE
SHOW GETS
RETURN 0
```

In our previous screen, PRODUCT.SPR, the READ command locked the record involved in the current GETs. FoxPro has an automatic locking system for direct READs and edits occurring in BROWSEs. If the record cannot be locked, FoxPro's error-handling system is triggered. If you take advantage of the automatic locking feature, you write an error-handling program to translate the problem of the record's being unavailable. You issue an appropriate message so the user can decide what to do. (You learn how to add an error handler to your application in Chapter 20, "Enhancing the Applications You Program.")

When you edit memory variables, however, the automatic record locking doesn't occur. The preceding RLOCK( ) function, which is an explicit lock, returns .F. if the function cannot place a lock on the record that the user chooses to edit by using the `Edit` push button. The code then informs the user that this record cannot be edited right now.

The preceding strategy is only one way to handle record locking. The most pessimistic strategy is to lock a record as soon as the user looks at it, rather than when he or she chooses the `Edit` push button, to ensure that the on-screen data is current. The most optimistic strategy is to avoid locking the record until the user signals that the edit is complete. The pessimistic method prevents other users from gaining access to a record this user may have no intention of editing. In the optimistic method, the developer makes one of three assumptions:

- No one else has changed the data in the meantime.
- The user does not need to worry about this possible change and can confirm his own edit without concern for what has happened in the meantime.
- The system is doing additional checking against separate memory variables or array elements, so the user can choose to accept the original information in the file, the previous edit, or his own changes as final.

Which method you use depends on the number of users or concurrent sessions, the type of network environment, and the nature of the application. Obviously, an application that tracks sales of supplies or tickets, of which you have a finite supply, cannot practice the most optimistic type of locking because inventory figures against which orders are placed must be up-to-date. On the other hand, if a doctor's office is registering information about a patient's medical insurance, the chances of the same patient (or even a member of the same patient's family) giving this information at the other office across town, at the same instant, are slim.

NOTE Your opportunities to pick a locking strategy do not end if you decide to edit table fields directly. The READ command has a NOLOCK clause you can use to make a direct READ behave like an indirect READ of memory variables. Instead of locking each record as the user views it, the READ NOLOCK issues all the GETs that directly affect the contents of fields as readonly (the user can type or change nothing). You issue an explicit SHOW GETS LOCK when the user chooses to begin editing or adding a new record, and you UNLOCK when the edit or add is confirmed.

Initializing Variables in the Setup Snippet

The two variables m.editmode and m.addmode must be available to all the various parts of the screen program because you check these variables frequently. You initialize these variables by creating another snippet in the Setup code option of the Screen Layout dialog, where you store the initial value .F. to both variables. The code is simple:

■ Setup code placed in CONTROLM screen

```
m.addmode = .F.
m.editmode = .F.
```

The Setup code is part of the main program, which calls all the procedures and expressions in the screen snippets. If you try to initialize the variables in any of the other snippets, the variables are not usable by the other routines that the screen requires.

As you see later, the Setup code for a screen set containing multiple windows is put together and executed before the rest of the screen program occurs. You choose to put this initialization in the Setup of the

CONTROLM screen rather than the DEPT screen because the variables are required whenever CONTROLM is used, no matter which data-entry screen uses the control panel.

The same reasoning works for many of the other snippets that affect the READ as a whole; a generic .SCX should be packaged with the code it needs. If the code itself is generic enough to be associated with many screens, the code should be free-standing in separate programs, like CHKCODE.PRG, where all the screens can find the code easily.

Completing the Screen Procedures with SHOW and DEACTIVATE Clauses

You need two more snippets. The READ SHOW clause handles the display of GETs on the screen after the user moves to a new record. The READ DEACTIVATE clause handles the user's choice of a task as he moves between windows.

The SHOW GETS command that you issue in the button's VALID clause activates a procedure that you store in the READ SHOW clause. Like the Setup code, and like other clauses global to a READ rather than specific to one GET, the Show option is in the Screen Layout dialog. FoxPro calls the SHOW clause internally when you issue the SHOW GETS command, no matter how often or where you issue the command.

The SHOW clause for this program uses the following instructions, commented to explain the tasks performed:

■ SHOW clause for CONTROLM.SCX

```
IF m.addmode
   * if you are adding a new record

   SCATTER MEMVAR BLANK
   * create memory variables with nothing
   * in them, but with the same characteristics
   * as a record in the current table

ELSE

   SCATTER MEMVAR
   * create memory variables holding the data
   * from the current record in the currently
   * selected table

ENDIF
```

continues

```
* now when the GETs in the dept screen are shown, they
* have blank memory variables if you're adding
* or show the data of the current record

IF m.editmode OR m.addmode
   * if you're about to start editing or adding a record,
   * remove the capability to move around in the table
   * until you're through editing or adding:
   SHOW GET act2 DISABLE

ELSE
   * you're not editing or adding when the SHOW GETS
   * is called
   UNLOCK
   * release any lock that may have been placed
   * previously on the record to perform an edit
   * and re-enable movement through the table
   SHOW GET act2 ENABLE

ENDIF
```

The final snippet for this screen goes into the READ DEACTIVATE clause. The DEACTIVATE clause is called when you change the active window, Tab through the fields, or select a new window (using the menu Cycle option of Ctrl+F1, clicking the new window with the mouse, or choosing the new window from the Window menu popup list). If the DEACTIVATE clause issues a RETURN .T., the READ is terminated. You want this snippet always to RETURN .F. because the `Leave` button provides the only means of termination you need. Before you reach the RETURN line, however, the following DEACTIVATE clause gives you another chance to call the SHOW clause and make sure options are appropriately displayed when the user switches windows:

DEACTIVATE clause for CONTROLM.SCX

```
IF UPPER(WONTOP( )) = "CONTROLS"

   * WONTOP( ) tells you what window is
   * "on top," which window has been activated.
   * Here's the reason you needed to know the
   * window's name!

   * it's always a good idea to use
   * the uppercase version of the window
   * name compared to the uppercase version
   * of what the window functions return,
   * just in case.
```

```
   * Now that you know you are in the control panel:

   m.addmode = .F.
   m.editmode = .F.
   * turn off both the record-changing tasks

ELSE
   * you're in a record-editing window

   IF ! m.addmode
      * in case you got here by switching windows,
      *  choose to edit by default

        IF RLOCK( )
         * as in the Editing push button choice,
         * make sure we can grab the record
         * for the edit
           m.editmode = .T.
        ELSE
           WAIT WINDOW ;
                    "Sorry -- someone else is editing "+ ;
                     "this record!"
           _CUROBJ = OBJNUM(act2)
             * setting _CUROBJ to the OBJNUM( ) of the act2
             * button will force the cursor back to the button
         ENDIF
   ENDIF

ENDIF

* now get a new set of memory variables and properly
* enable or disable the control panel as before:

SHOW GETS

RETURN .F.
```

Figure 12.21 shows the snippet for the DEACTIVATE clause, the SHOW clause, the revised VALID clause for the buttons, including the new choices, and the Setup code snippet.

Notice that all these instructions are completely generic, like the CHKCODE.PRG function you wrote previously. After you decide on an approach for these data-entry screens, you can use the same approach over and over again without re-creating the code.

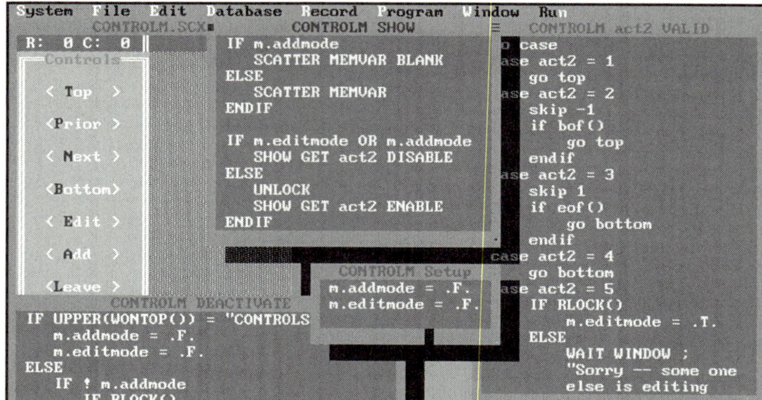

FIG. 12.21

The revised control panel and its associated snippets.

Adding Save and Cancel Buttons

You still need to make a few more changes to the editing screen, DEPT.SCX. Resize the window slightly if necessary and add a push button set to this screen (press Ctrl+H as a shortcut). The strategy here is to ask the user to confirm (Save) or Cancel the record in the process of being added or edited. Figure 12.22 shows the prompts and the VALID clause for this button set. Notice the \?\! before the `Cancel` prompt, which makes this push button the escape option and also the default.

Use the button's Spacing... option to leave space between the buttons, and arrange or center the buttons in the window as you like. Then add the VALID clause.

The VALID clause for the new push buttons checks to see whether you got a confirmation of changes. If you did, and if the user is adding, you INSERT the MEMVARs that the user edited. INSERT INTO <table> FROM MEMVAR creates a new record, locking it and making it the current record in one step. If the user is not adding, you GATHER the contents of the memory variables into the current record. Resetting m.addmode and m.editmode and issuing a new SHOW GETS returns you to the control panel and releases a lock if any had been placed on the record for an edit:

■ DEPT/BUDCAT.SCX m.saveit VALID snippet

```
IF m.saveit = 2
   IF m.addmode
      INSERT INTO Dept FROM MEMVAR
       * use INSERT INTO Budcat as appropriate
   ELSE
```

```
        GATHER MEMVAR
    ENDIF
ENDIF
m.addmode = .F.
m.editmode = .F.

SHOW GETS
```

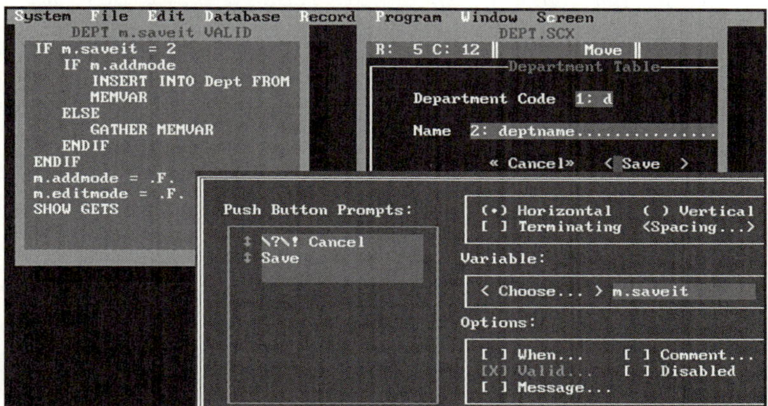

FIG. 12.22

Push buttons in the data-entry screen enabling you to save or cancel changes.

The SHOW clause in the CONTROLM.SCX is executed, because of the SHOW GETS command in this snippet, after the two screens are tied together in one READ, so you do not need to add any special code to redisplay the GETs in this window. Before generating, however, you should edit the VALID clause for the Deptcode field to hold the following expression:

```
LASTKEY( ) = 27 OR ChkCode( )
```

This expression enables you to press the Esc key, seen by the LASTKEY( ) function as 27, to get you out of the field. Otherwise, pressing Esc while attempting to add a record doesn't take you out of the field because the current m.deptcode is empty. Of course, the ERROR clause should still hold the ErrCode( ) UDF you designed previously.

If you are working on both the BUDCAT.SCX and DEPT.SCX at the same time, create the basic layout for the second of the two screens. Then mark, copy, and paste the new `m.saveit` button from the first screen, complete with VALID, into the second screen. Edit the VALID clauses to handle any screen-specific requirements, and you're finished.

Generating and Running a Modified Entry Screen

Finally, you're ready to generate a screen set from the data-entry form and the control panel. Choosing the Program Generate option, this time you want to Add the second screen to the Screens list in the upper-left corner, as shown in figure 12.23. Make the control panel the first screen on the list because you want this window to be the first window accessed during use. (Figure 12.23 also shows the Comments Options being filled out. Choose this dialog to affect the look and location of the generated program, which you examine more closely in the following chapter.)

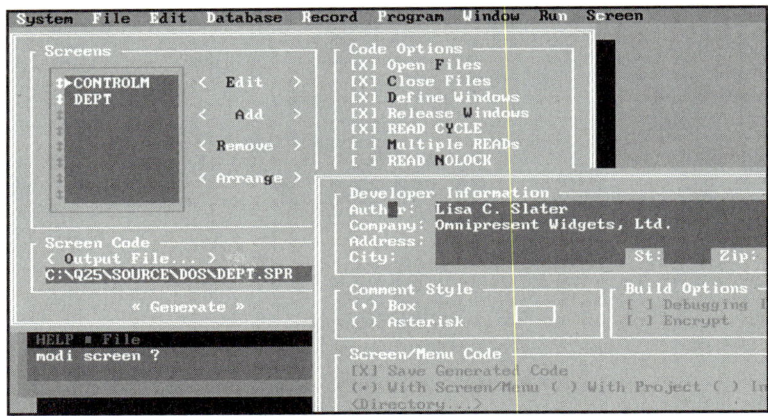

FIG. 12.23

Getting ready to generate screen code from multiple screens and using the Comment Options dialog.

You also must use the Arrange option in the screen-generating dialog to set the windows' relative positions. As shown in figure 12.24, the available options are simple, and the arrangement is easy to perform. Just move the windows as you move other windows in FoxPro. Save the arrangement and then choose `Generate`.

When you DO the resulting DEPT.SPR file, a simple data-entry system appears and provides for valid entries for the lookup table, as shown in figure 12.25. Notice the disabled controls that require you to complete or cancel editing for one record before going on to affect others. Try pressing Esc at different points and switching windows using the keyboard or the mouse to see what happens. Think about ways you may want to improve this system. Investigate the other control panels included in sample applications with Finding, Browsing, and Ordering capabilities, and design ways in which you can add those features to the control panel.

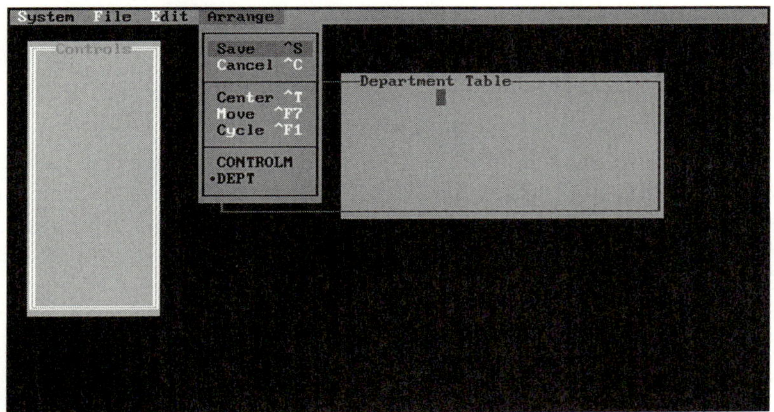

FIG. 12.24

The screen-arranging options that are part of the code-generation process.

If you are running FoxPro on a network or can run two sessions of FoxPro under Windows or another multitasking system, you can test the record-locking capabilities of this system, as shown in figure 12.25. If you have not already done so, SET EXCLUSIVE OFF to enable more than one user to access the same file. You also should SET REPROCESS TO 1 to avoid additional error messages from FoxPro. If you forget to change REPROCESS from its default value of 0, the system still works, but you need to press Esc to make FoxPro stop trying to lock the record.

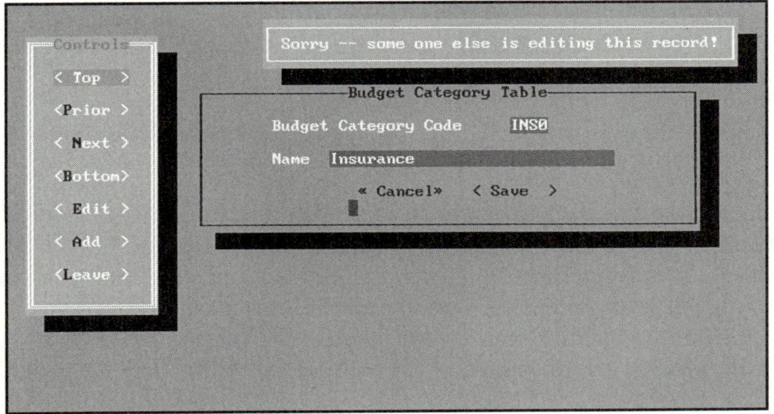

FIG. 12.25

The mini data-entry application with validation and record-locking.

If you like, continue to work with the control panel and add features to it. Generate mini-applications for each of the Budcat and Dept tables that use the custom controls. Use the new applications to enter the information shown in tables 12.1 and 12.2. Now the lookup tables necessary for proper management of the Budget table are complete.

After you enter this data, set the order of each of the three lookup tables to a tag on the respective code fields, select Budget, and set relationships to each of the three other tables on the code fields. The three lookup tables and the View window should then match figure 12.26. If the View file (MODEL.VUE) doesn't match this setup, you may want to use the File Save As... option to resave the View to these specifications for further use. (Knowing which file is in which work area is immaterial if all the files are open and the relationships are set as shown.)

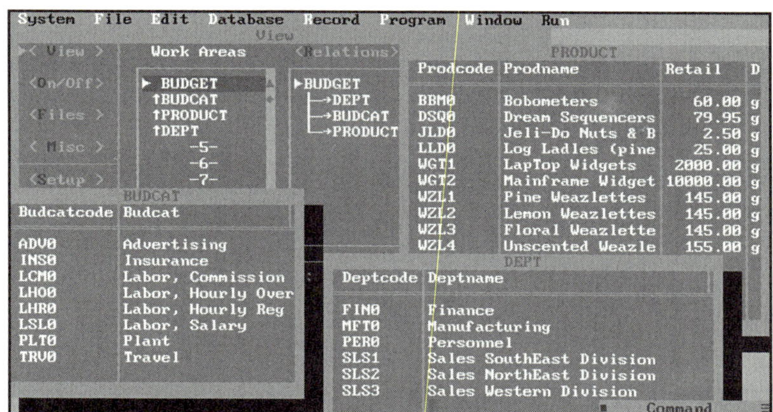

FIG. 12.26

The model application environment and its lookup tables as they appear when filled with data.

Summary

As you realize, through successive revisions and improvements to these data-entry systems, you have only begun to tap the power of the Screen Builder. You learned a little about code snippets and other ways to attach procedures to GETs and other objects in a READ, and you learned the difference between editing tables directly and editing memory variables. You developed some facility with the Screen Builder tool. You probably have begun to think about all the ways you can validate and control the entry of data in the systems you design. You also may be eager to use radio buttons, scrolling lists, and the other useful features the Screen Builder puts within reach.

In the following chapter, you create a Budget table-entry screen that uses many more of the interface objects. You investigate the inclusion of BROWSE commands and memo-editing within a screen set and get a sense of the way the READ-level clauses interact with one another.

13

CHAPTER

Improving Screen Design with Complex Screen Sets

In the preceding chapter, you built screens by using the Screen Builder. As you built them, you became aware of an interim step: the template program *generated* screen programs, which were then compiled by FoxPro and interpreted when you executed the programs. Yet you never actually wrote the programs.

In the past, writing screen programs was a programmer's most time-consuming and painstaking task. So far in this book, however, you have not been asked to look at the programs you created (the files with .SPR extensions) with the Screen Builder's help. Microsoft doesn't recommend that you edit the generated programs in any way. Rather, you should make changes directly through the Screen Builder and regenerate the programs. You don't need to be proficient with the syntax for the different kinds of GET objects.

Nevertheless, in the following section, you examine a generated program. Knowing the structure of a generated program can help you understand the relationship between the snippets and the different READ objects and clauses. You also see examples of the window-defining commands and window-manipulating functions you use more and more as you develop intricate screen sets, such as the budget data-entry system you create in the following section and the relational screen sets you create in Chapter 15.

Understanding the Generated Screen Program

As you learned in the last chapter, the .SPR file represents an interim product of the FoxPro screen-creation process. Your source code is the .SCX file you edited in the Screen Builder, but FoxPro executes the .SPR, which is a file of instructions generated from the .SCX's screen description by GENSCRN.PRG, when you're ready to execute the screen program.

Ordinarily, you never look at the .SPR. You certainly don't edit it; any changes you make to the .SPR are lost when you use the Screen Builder to add new features to the .SCX and then re-generate the program. However, in this section, you look at the .SPR so you understand how GENSCRN prepares this file from your .SCX. Once you're aware of how GENSCRN operates on the contents of the .SCX, you'll find it easier to understand why, how, and where you attach code to the various snippets in the Screen Builder.

Type `MODIFY COMMAND DEPT.SPR` in the Command window or open the program DEPT.SPR from the File Open option. The first thing you see is a program header, created by GENSCRN. The header names and dates the program and provides a copyright notice, as specified in the Generate Comment options.

The Program Header Section

Following the header, you see several sections of setup code that follow a different order, depending on what you placed in the Setup code snippet. You can precede some or all of the Setup code snippet with a *generator directive* so that the snippet is placed ahead of all other lines in the program.

A generator directive is an instruction that GENSCRN uses as it creates a program. FoxPro doesn't use these directives in actual program execution. The appropriate generator directive to put setup code before all the other generated code is #SECTION 1. For example, you may want to pass *parameters* (values or variables determined by a calling program) to the screen program. A PARAMETERS statement must be the first line in any program that receives values from a calling program. Therefore, this part of your setup code must occur before any other program lines GENSCRN creates.

Without a #SECTION 1 directive, GENSCRN places the code in your Setup snippet after the code it generates to DEFINE WINDOWs. You may have additional sections of your setup code that must execute only after the WINDOWs for the screen set are DEFINEd; in this case, if you used a #SECTION 1 for the first part of your setup, precede the rest of your setup code with a #SECTION 2 directive.

Table 13.1, at the end of this section, lists the generator directives. You use any of these directives by placing them in the Setup snippet of a screen. In addition, as the table shows, you can place #INSERT and #NAME directives in any of the other snippets in the screen. (In order to use these two directives, however, you must use the snippets as procedures rather than expressions.)

The Program Environment Section

Following any code you create in the Setup snippet with the #SECTION 1 directive is the program environment code that GENSCRN always creates. This code defines some regional variables that are used to save the state of the factors GENSCRN is about to alter so that you can restore these factors at a later time.

Regional variables are specific to each window within a screen set. GENSCRN assigns a region number to each .SCX included in a set and uses the number to distinguish the screen layout code and procedures that belong to each screen or window in the set when the .SPR that includes all the procedures is generated. If you initialize any variables as REGIONAL, the compiler then generates variable names specific to each region. These names tie the variables to the appropriate window. In this way, you can use the same variable names in code that belong to different windows within each set, and the names don't conflict with each other.

The variables created by GENSCRN in the program environment code, however, are used by the entire screen set. GENSCRN precedes these variables with a #REGION 0 compiler directive to indicate this condition. You learn more about how regional variables work in Chapter 19.

The File-Opening and Window-Defining Sections

The file-opening code is generated only if you previously saved the environment with the screen and if you left this option checked in the Generate dialog. Next comes the window-defining code, also created only if you choose the appropriate option in the Generate dialog. Part of the window-defining code is visible in the fragment of DEPT.SPR shown in figure 13.1. Notice the DEFINE WINDOW command, which you use shortly, and the WEXIST( ) function, an example of a useful assortment of window-checking functions that FoxPro provides.

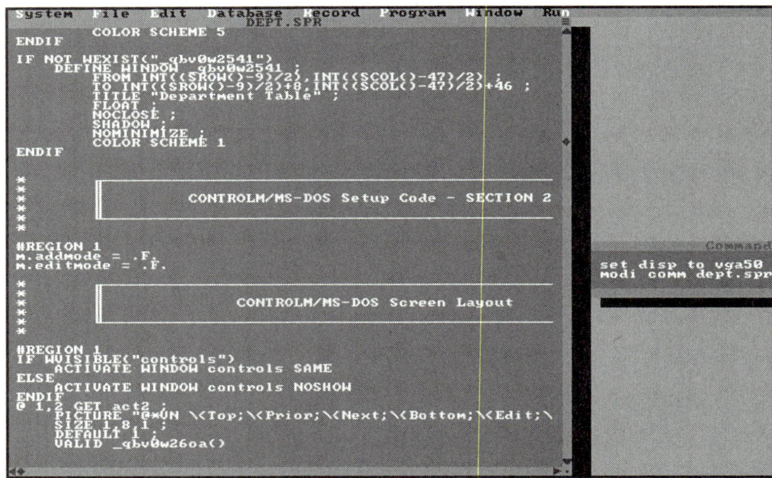

FIG. 13.1

A fragment of a generated screen program, showing part of the window definitions, setup code, and a screen layout.

Next comes any code you put in the Setup snippet if you did not use the #SECTION 1 directive. If you used #SECTION 1 earlier, GENSCRN inserts any Setup code you prefaced with #SECTION 2 at this point in the program. After the #SECTION 2 Setup code, as shown in figure 13.1, the windows are activated one at a time and filled with GETs. If you choose multiple READs in the Generate dialog, each window has a specifically related READ command, controlling the GETs in that window. Otherwise, after the final window in the set is ready, one READ command is issued for the entire set. This READ command includes READ-level clauses and keywords you created in the Screen Layout or specified by using the #READCLAUSES described in table 13.1.

As you look at the code, notice the differences between the VALID and ERROR clauses you created as expressions for m.deptcode, the generated procedure names in the saveit VALID clause, and the READ DEACTIVATE and SHOW clauses.

The Cleanup Section

The READ is followed by various kinds of cleanup code, as determined by the Generate dialog settings. First, you see window-releasing code and then file-closing code, and finally the program environment is restored. All code that you added in the Cleanup code snippet, including UDFs that you attached to this screen set, comes next. (The DEPT.SPR program you generated in the last chapter doesn't include UDFs because you created CHKCODE.PRG and ERRCODE.PRG as standalone programs to make this code available to multiple screen sets.) Finally, the generated procedures—such as the saveit VALID—are put at the end.

Remember that all code that precedes the READ is executed before the user sees a data-entry screen and before the READ is activated. The code that follows the READ statement in the Cleanup snippet can contain commands that execute when you exit from the READ.

The Cleanup code snippet, however, can provide a convenient place to hold many subprocedures called before and during the READ while the clauses on objects and the READ command are evaluated. If you choose, you could write CHKCODE and ERRCODE as functions in the Cleanup of this screen set. You separate each one from the rest of the code by naming it with a line such as the following:

```
FUNCTION ChkCode

* Your code goes here

* If you don't put a RETURN
* statement at the end of the
* function FoxPro assumes a
* RETURN .T.
```

continues

```
* for any execution of the function
* that hasn't resulted in a RETURN
* at some earlier point in the function's

* code.
```

You have no reason to bury CHKCODE.PRG and ERRCODE.PRG in the cleanup of this one screen set or any other, however, because you designed them generically to work in many different sets. The next chapter explains different ways of incorporating these functions into your application's files.

In FoxPro 2.5, you have the alternative of using the generator directive #INSERT to force GENSCRN to generate the code for such generic functions directly in the cleanup of a screen that calls it; yet you have the convenience of editing the code as a separate program file. Refer to table 13.1 for instructions on using #INSERT.

The READ Interrupts and READ Clauses

Clauses on each object, such as the VALID ChkCode( ) you placed on the Deptcode field, are evaluated every time the user tries to alter the object. The clauses on the READ are sometimes called *interrupts* because they contain instructions which interrupt or alter the user-controlled process of data entry activity and the normal sequence of program events. These clauses can be evaluated whenever the user does one of the following:

- Enters the READ (the READ-level WHEN, ACTIVATE, OBJECT, COLOR/COLOR SCHEME, LOCK/NOLOCK, NOMOUSE, TIMEOUT, and SHOW clauses)
- Attempts to move between windows (the ACTIVATE, DEACTIVATE, MODAL, and WITH clauses)
- Attempts to exit the READ (the READ-level VALID, DEACTIVATE, CYCLE, and SAVE clauses)

As shown in the preceding chapter, the READ SHOW clause also can be brought into play any time you issue a SHOW GETS command.

In the preceding chapter, you learned how to use the SHOW and DEACTIVATE clauses, which are significant for the control panel approach to selecting and editing records. In the Budget table-entry screen, you use SHOW again and investigate the use of the ACTIVATE clause to provide integration of a BROWSE in a screen set. This provides you with a different way to move through a table. The BROWSE WHEN clause and a number of tailored object-level procedures assist in creating a graceful data-entry process in the Budget screen set.

Even with these two different techniques, you are not going to learn everything about the extensive READ options in this chapter. You have many more directions to explore, and you will want to experiment a great deal more. You return to these options in Chapter 15, after learning more about other FoxPro tools you need to create complete applications in Chapter 14.

Table 13.1 helps you gain a better understanding of GENSCRN. As you use the directives and other options of the Screen Builder, the Generator dialog, and READ, you may find that building a special practice screen that uses a trick can be valuable. To do this, put the WAIT WINDOW command, followed by the name of each clause and other valuable information, into each of the code snippets, as shown in the following line:

```
WAIT WINDOW "Deactivate Clause "+WONTOP( )+" "+WLAST( ) NOWAIT
```

As you tinker with the screen and generate different versions to try out, the WAIT WINDOW helps you become familiar with the exact actions that initiate the various clauses, under exact circumstances, at any given time.

Table 13.1 The GENSCRN.PRG generator directives

Directive	Meaning to GENSCRN	Examples and Instructions for Use	Place in What Snippet?
* #INSERT <text filename>	Generate the contents of the named file as part of the generated program, at the point the directive appears.	#INSERT ChkCode.PRG #INSERT Comments.TXT * Be sure to use the entire file name, including extension! * Use straight text files only. * Include the full path, unless the file is on your DOS or FoxPro PATH. * If the file isn't found, GENSCRN adds a comment to the generated program.	At any point of any snippet, used as a procedure

continues

Table 13.1 Continued

Directive	Meaning to GENSCRN	Examples and Instructions for Use	Place in What Snippet?

#ITSEXPRESSION <single char>	Treat information placed in format clause and window titles and footers as expressions rather than as literal strings of characters.	#SECTION 1
		#ITSEXPRESSION ~
		PARAMETERS wtitle
		
		* Now use
		~ *wintitle*
		in the Screen Layout to represent the window title, and call the screen like this:
		
		`DO the_screen WITH ;`
		`"Confirm Changes"`
		* or
		`DO the_screen WITH`
		`"Add an Entry"`
		
		* More examples will appear in later sections of this chapter.
		
		* Note the space between the directive and the character you choose to represent expressions.
			Setup snippet only

* #NAME <procedure name>	Use a specific name for the generated procedure, which GENSCRN places in the Cleanup of the generated code.	#NAME ChkCode * Placed in the VALID snippet of the Prodcode field, with the snippet used as a procedure, this directive would cause the GET to have a VALID ChkCode( ) clause and the snippet to be generated with the name FUNCTION ChkCode in the Cleanup. * *Caution:* Because you name the function yourself rather than allowing GENSCRN to generate a unique procedure name, you must check for duplicate procedure names yourself!	At the beginning of any snippet, used as a procedure—*not* as an expression

Directive	Meaning to GENSCRN	Examples and Instructions for Use	Place in What Snippet?
* #NOREAD	Generate only the code without the READ statement, so the programmer can add the READ line following with whatever embellishments are necessary at run-time. With the PLAIN keyword, generate only the @... SAY, @...GET, and @...EDIT portion of the code.	#NOREAD #NOREAD PLAIN * *Note:* a file generated with #NOREAD PLAIN can be used as a FORMAT file for EDIT FORMAT but not for BROWSE FORMAT. All the different GET objects may be activated in the file. However, EDIT FORMAT is included in FoxPro 2.x for backward compatibility and its behavior is problemmatical. See Appendix H for details and for a sample program (EFORMAT) demonstrating its use.	Setup snippet only
#READCLAUSES <expressions>	Generate whatever follows the directive as part of the READ line in the generated program.	#READCLAUSES OBJECT 1 * This directive permits the addition of keywords for which no provisions exist in the Screen Builder. It may be used dynamically, with a macro expanded expression: #READCLAUSES &my_clauses The variable my_clauses is either a PARAMETER for the screen or a variable initialized earlier. The READ clauses that commonly fill my_clauses or are specified directly with the #READCLAUSES directive are * COLOR <exprC>/COLOR SCHEME <exprN> (changes the color of the current GET from the default—works only with text boxes.)	Setup snippet only

continues

Table 13.1 Continued

Directive	Meaning to GENSCRN	Examples and Instructions for Use	Place in What Snippet?
		* NOMOUSE (turns off the mouse for this screen, perhaps because you must have items entered in a precise order.) * OBJECT <expN> (specifies, by number, which GET is initially selected for editing when the READ is issued. Individual buttons within a set have individual object numbers.) * SAVE (prevents the clearing of GETs after exit from the READ so you can reissue the READ without reissuing the GETS.) * TIMEOUT <exprN> (exits the READ after a specified number of seconds if no editing occurs, generally to release a record lock.)	
#REDEFINE	Generate window-defining code without performing checks to see whether the window previously exists.	#REDEFINE *An example of a requirement to use of this directive occurs in the next chapter, when the Budget screen is included in a larger application.	Setup snippet only
#SECTION 1 <codesection1> #SECTION 2 <codesection2>	Generate setup code following the #SECTION 1 directive before any other code in the file. Generate code following the #SECTION 2 directive after the file-opening and window-defining code.	#SECTION 1 PARAMETERS param1,param2 #SECTION 2 MOVE WINDOW getwind TO 3,3 SEEK param1 IF param2 * etc. * *Note:* If these directives are not used, all setup code is normally generated in the SECTION 2 position.	Setup snippet only

Directive	Meaning to GENSCRN	Examples and Instructions for Use	Place in What Snippet?
* #WCLAUSES <expressions>	Generate whatever follows only the directive as part of the DEFINE WINDOW line in the generated program.	#WCLAUSES GROW * This directive is similar to #READCLAUSES; use it to add DEFINE WINDOW clauses for which there are not opportunities within the Screen Builder. You find a reason to add the GROW keyword later in this chapter, where you use the Screen Builder to add BROWSE-image windows to your screen set. Because it can be used with a macro-expanded expression, it can be used to specify a window's attributes dynamically at run-time.	Setup snippet only
#WNAME <window name>	Substitute the GENSCRN-generated unique window name for any references to this window name in the code.	#WNAME my_window * This directive isn't very useful, although it ensures the unique names of windows in a large application. Because you are not aware of the unique names that GENSCRN creates (which are different every time you generate the code), you can't refer to this name intelligently in your code if you need to refer to it outside this program, as you will often want to do. Instead, specify window names yourself in the Screen Layout dialog and use your own techniques to ensure uniqueness.	Setup snippet only

* *New to Version 2.5.*

Improving Screen Design

In this section, you create a Budget entry screen, containing different kinds of objects and controls than you used for the Dept and Budcat screens in the last chapter. You'll learn how such objects can make data validation easier to arrange, while providing a more attractive and simpler interface for the user.

To begin creating a Budget entry screen, you could generate a Quick Screen as you did in previous chapters. Because you plan to define different kinds of objects and controls, however, the related vanilla GET objects may not be helpful.

To start on the design, you need an easy reminder of the structure of the Budget table, which defines the information you want to GET. You create this reminder, similar to a notepad, with your first use of the DEFINE WINDOW command.

The DEFINE WINDOW command is not available from the FoxPro menus. When you read the generated DEPT.SPR program, you may have noticed that this command has many clauses you can use to create windows that mirror the windows FoxPro creates.

Using the following lines, create a short program called STRUCT.PRG:

```
IF ! WEXIST("struct")
   * no need to redefine window if you
   * created it previously

   DEFINE WINDOW struct FROM 1,1 TO 80,55;
      SYSTEM FLOAT MINIMIZE CLOSE;
      COLOR SCHEME 10;
      TITLE "Structure"

   * You define the window by giving it a name,
   * coordinates, and other attributes
ENDIF

ACTIVATE WINDOW struct NOSHOW
* make this window the active-output window

LIST STRUCTURE
* list the structure of the SELECTed table

ZOOM WINDOW struct MIN AUTO
* place the window, docked, on-screen

SHOW WINDOW struct
* pop up window, filled and ready for use
```

Save this program and from the Command window or the menus, SET VIEW TO MODEL. (Refer to the last figure in the preceding chapter and make sure that the appropriate tables and relations are ready for the work you plan to do. The Budget table should be in the SELECTed work area.) From the Command window, the Program menu's Do option, or the Run menu pad, activate the DO STRUCT command.

You see the window docked and ready for reference. If you press Ctrl+F9 or double-click the window, you see something like the screen in figure 13.2.

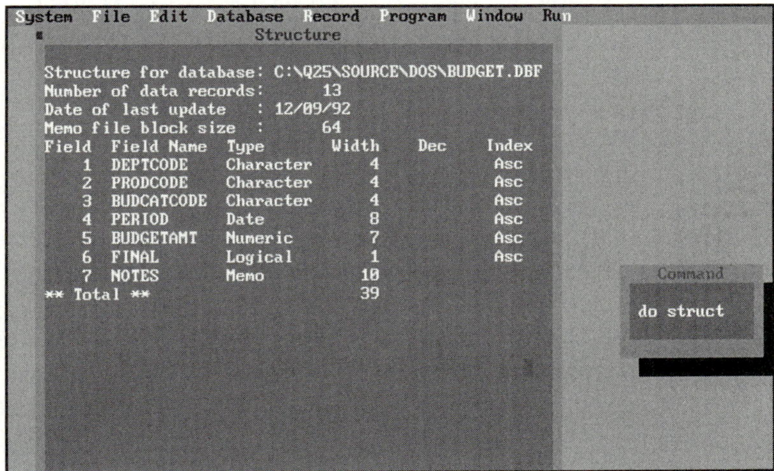

FIG. 13.2

The Budget table structure, ready for reference in a notepad.

TIP

This handy trick is included not only because it is useful during a screen design session, but also because it shows normal window command usage. After you read the programming sections of this book, you may want to expand the idea by using a FOR...ENDFOR loop to check all tables open in FoxPro's work areas and list all the structures in a similar notepad. As a final hint, list all the file structures using LIST STRUCTURE TO <filename> ADDITIVE in the FOR...ENDFOR loop, and then MODIFY FILE <filename> WINDOW STRUCT for a scrollable display of the information you sent to the file.

Planning the Data-Entry Window

The following paragraphs define the strategy as you begin to design the Budget table entry screen.

This table structure includes three code fields (Deptcode, Prodcode, and Budcatcode) that should be restricted to information contained in the three lookup tables. Now that all three fields are complete with data, you can use them to make the budget entries.

This strategy calls for the Final field to provide you with an important criterion for the editing of the rest of the record. After a record is marked Final, the information contained in the record cannot be changed (although you can choose to allow editing of the Notes field at any time). After a record's Period date falls in a past quarter or within the present quarter, the record is automatically marked Final if the record was not marked Final by the user at an earlier date. The Budget table records are used for projecting costs and cannot be altered after the quarter in which the fall has begun.

Blank entries are allowed in the Budgetamt field, in case an event that causes no financial change requires Notes of some kind, but you must assign a Period date and department, product, and budget category codes to every added record.

You want to move through the table by using a BROWSE, but records are designed to be editable only in the screen you design. You GET information into memory variables again, as you did in the Dept and Budcat tables in the last chapter, and GATHER the data to the current record if the editing is confirmed.

Editing the current record takes place on one portion of a relatively large data-entry window. This window, however, also holds several controls that enable you to change the order in which you view data and to query the data immediately, so that you can see your progress as you carry out the budgeting process.

NOTE

In the following example screen, you use three different methods of providing lookups. Usually, you don't mix techniques in this way in one screen or in one system—this procedure is completely contrary to the rules of consistent design explained in Chapter 11, "Coordinating a FoxPro Application." Similarly, the Budget table data-entry screen contains almost every kind of interface object available in FoxPro. Again, you normally don't combine a screen like this with the radically different screens you designed earlier for the lookup tables' data entry. It is especially unusual for one database application to combine direct and indirect READs, as was the case in the preceding chapter.

These demonstrations of different techniques are created only to introduce you to as many options as possible within one small sample application. Continue with whatever personal combinations of techniques you like after learning about them here with this caveat in mind; remember that these techniques are rarely mixed in real programs.

Sketching a Layout Screen

To begin creating BUDGET.SCX, start with the Screen Layout, accessible from the first choice on the Screen menu popup. As before, you need to click the top radio buttons to choose a Window—rather than DeskTop—layout. (You want a movable window, not objects directly on the screen.)

Because you have the Model view open, Save the Environment, which is already set up the way you want this screen. Uncheck Add Alias, because you are READing to memory variables. Type the name `budget` for this window and add a title. The layout requires a Height of `18` and a Width of `78`. You can Position the layout at Row `1` and Column `1` after unchecking the default of Center, but it's easier to leave the window Centered and Arrange it in this position when you generate the code later.

Next, choose the `Type` button. Although you maintain the default type of User window, change the Color Schemes, setting the Primary scheme to Windows and the scheme for Popups contained in this window to Window Pop. These two schemes coordinate well with each other and with the BROWSE you are using in the screen set. As shown in figure 13.3, add more Attributes to this window to include Float and Minimize, in case you want to devote attention at times to the BROWSE, resized to take up most of the screen.

Return to the design window and draw a box to define the record-editing portion of the screen. Add an explanatory title for this box, as well. You can type the title wherever you want and then select and move the title to overlay the upper-box line. You can use one of the techniques covered in Chapter 2 to add the graphics characters to the text object and window title (see fig. 13.4). Now is a good time to use the left-quote character trick: If you type `'P`, the right-facing triangle is displayed; and if you type `'Q`, the left-facing triangle is displayed.

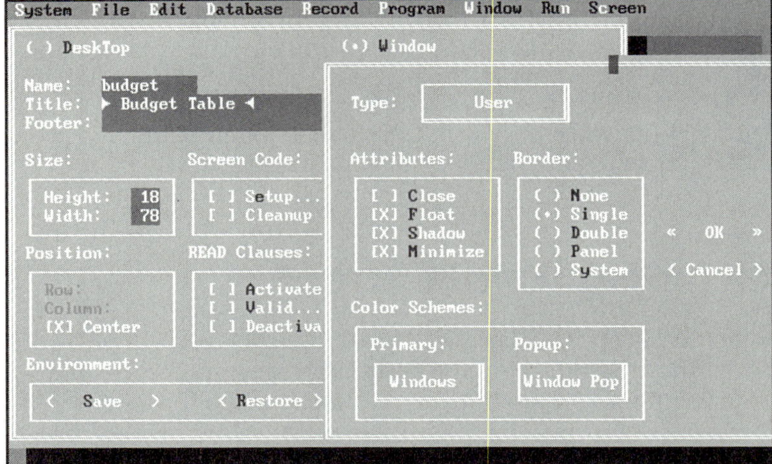

FIG. 13.3

Basic screen layout and window Type dialogs for the Budget table data-entry screen set.

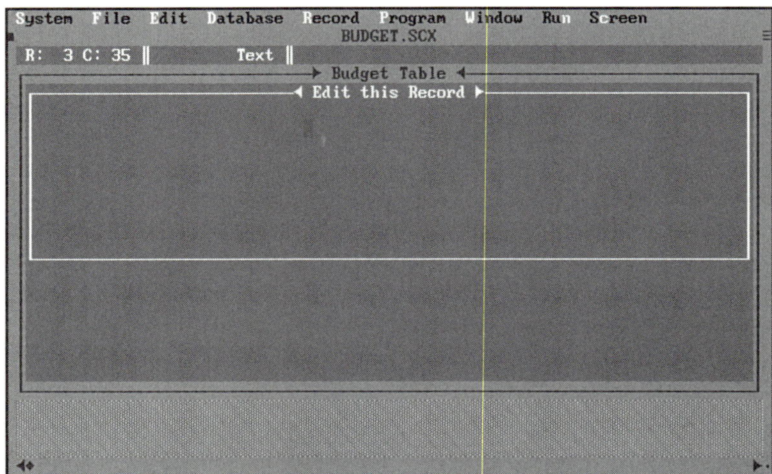

FIG. 13.4

The window has its own title, but you can define an area within a window, with its own titled box.

Notice that when you type the title, the Screen status bar shows that you are in Text mode. You can use the normal FoxPro cursor key combinations and the mouse to select and and delete portions of the text. When you press Enter, you are back in Move mode, and the text becomes a unified object that you can affect as a whole. Move it to overlay the top line of the box you drew, and, with the object or title selected, choose Center from the Screen menu popup. Now the selected item is positioned on the line correctly. After you finish defining these characteristics, the Screen Builder design window should resemble that shown in figure 13.4.

Performing Actions with a Check Box

Now create a check box (use the Ctrl+K shortcut or choose the option on the menu popup). This object enables the user to indicate that a budget entry is Final. Check boxes are best for logical, or on-off, fields. Because the Final designation determines whether the other fields in an entry are editable, you put the check box on the bottom boundary of the window box, centered directly under the title.

As you see in figure 13.5, a check box has a prompt, similar to a push button. You type `\<Finalize Entry?` as the prompt; the `\<` characters indicate a hot key. You are going to GET to SCATTERed memory variables again, and the SCATTER command will create a variable named m.final for the Final field, so you type this variable name in the Variable text box.

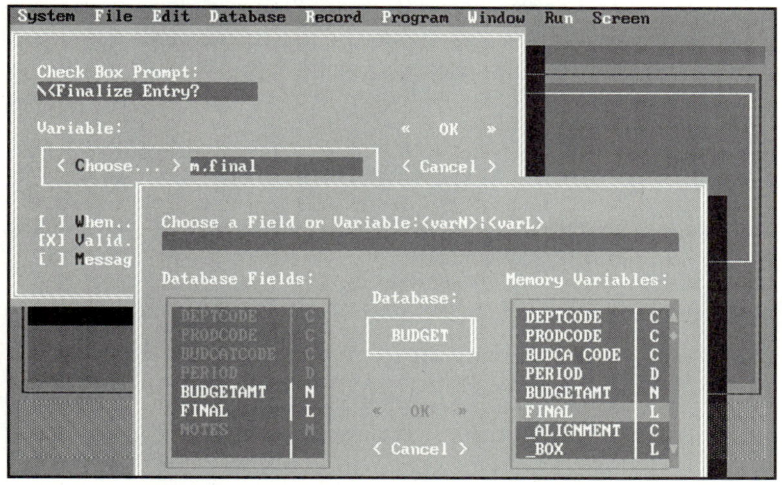

FIG. 13.5

The Expression Builder can be used to pick a variable for the Check Box.

Using the Expression Builder To Pick a Variable

You don't have to type the variable name if you prefer to access it through the system dialogs. If you have the Budget table properly selected in your environment, you can SCATTER MEMVAR or SCATTER MEMVAR MEMO from the Command window, just as your program will perform this action when you run the code later. Now the appropriate variables for this screen, including m.final, appear in the Expression Builder's list if you press the `Choose` button in the Check Box dialog.

As you notice in figure 13.5, the Expression Builder has two entries that both read FINAL (one in the fields list on the left, and one in the variables list on the right).

Regardless of the setting of Add Alias in the Screen Layout dialog, if you double-click the entry in the variable list, the Expression Builder will not add the m. in front of the word. When the code runs, if the name final is used for both a field in the current work area and a variable, FoxPro will see the reference as pertaining to the field, so be careful to add the m. yourself or you won't be GETting to the variable you SCATTERed.

Notice, also, that the figure shows several of the Budget fields as unavailable for selection here. A check box can be used only for logical or numeric values; its on-off values are stored as either .F. and .T. or 0 and 1, respectively. Several of the Budget fields are inappropriate data types. By contrast, all the variables in the list on the right are available because in Xbase, a variable may change its type.

Validating and Inter-Relating GETs

The check box's VALID clause will perform two functions if the user chooses to Finalize a record:

- Change the availability of several other fields for editing purposes
- Tell the user what's going on

As shown in figure 13.6, if m.final is set to .T., you perform this action with the following code in the VALID snippet:

m.final VALID snippet

```
IF m.final
   WAIT WINDOW  NOWAIT;
      " Finalized Budget Entries are not editable. "
    * disable some GETs:
   DO no_edit
ENDIF
```

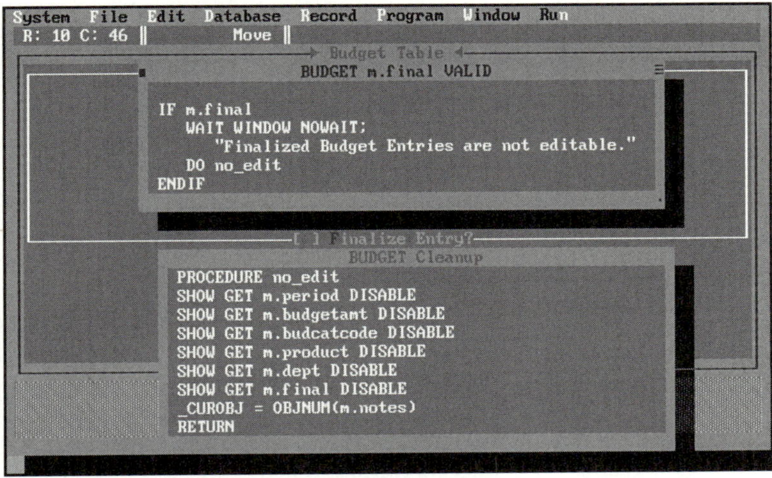

FIG. 13.6

The code supporting the m.final check box appears in its Valid snippet and the Cleanup section.

You don't need to plan for any actions if the user turns off the Final check box because the rules of this system specify that a record cannot be recalled to editable status once it is Finalized. (Later in this chapter, you learn how to make this requirement a little less alarming for the user.)

TIP

Why DO no_edit, instead of simply disabling the relevant GETs directly in this VALID clause? Recall that there are other reasons why a record might become Finalized; the system automatically changes its status if the record period is changed to a date earlier than a set limit. Moreover, the Finalized nature of each record must be determined each time a new record's values are placed in the screen by the SHOW clause. Rather than repeat this code each time, you call the same procedure at each location requiring these actions. If you need to edit the procedure, you edit it only once. You learn more about this approach to programming in Chapter 18, "Understanding Program Structure."

The no_edit procedure is placed in the Cleanup code section and looks like the following lines:

PROCEDURE no_edit from the Cleanup snippet

```
PROCEDURE no_edit
SHOW GET m.period DISABLE
SHOW GET m.budgetamt DISABLE
SHOW GET m.budcatcode DISABLE
```

continues

```
SHOW GET m.product DISABLE
SHOW GET m.dept DISABLE
SHOW GET m.final DISABLE
_CUROBJ = OBJNUM(m.notes)
RETURN
```

The line preceding the RETURN line puts the cursor in the Notes field. You may instead prefer to place the cursor in the Save/Cancel Edit object you create by using the following line:

```
_CUROBJ = OBJNUM(m.saveit)
```

Notice that _CUROBJ refers to GETs by number rather than by name. A GET's number is determined by the order in which GETs are accessed on-screen by using the keyboard (the mouse can access GETs in any order). You always can refer to GETs by number rather than by name by using the SHOW OBJECT command, which performs the same functions as a SHOW GET—for example:

```
SHOW OBJECT OBJNUM(m.dept) DISABLE
```

CAUTION: The Screen Builder uses a second numbering system on-screen in the layout. Don't use these numbers when referring to GETs by numbers in your programs! This second system differs from the GETs' object numbers, which determine order of GETs in the running program, in several ways:

- The layout numbers include SAYs along with GETs. The cursor never moves to a SAY in the running program.
- A button set is treated as a unit, whereas in the running program, each button in a set has a unique number. (If it didn't, you couldn't move _CUROBJ to a specific button in a set in your code.)
- The layout doesn't show numbers for GET control objects, such as button sets, although it assigns numbers to these objects.

Always use OBJNUM(<the_variable>) in your programs to determine the number of a particular object. If you want to refer to the third button of a button set, its number is OBJNUM(<button_set_variable>)+2.

You can create some GETs as sets of objects, such as the `Save/Cancel` buttons you added to the Dept table editing screen in the last chapter. Although the group of buttons determines the value of only one GET variable, each button has a special object number. You can SHOW a group as a set by using SHOW GET <the_variable>, or you can redisplay any individual member of the group by using SHOW OBJECT <number> or SHOW GET <the_variable>,<number>. SHOW GET's second option, <number>, indicates the button's position within the group.

After you check the Structure notepad, you see that you need to define a GET for the Date field named m.period. This GET is a normal field expression, similar to expressions you created in the preceding chapter, but much of the other editing depends on this GET's contents. If you edit m.period to contain a date in the current or past quarters, you want to mark this entry as Final to prevent further editing.

The VALID clause, therefore, executes a UDF that you create and place in the Cleanup code, which checks the date and sees whether all requisite fields are filled out. If no necessary fields are blank and if the date is now in a current or a past quarter, this clause takes appropriate action. The UDF, named to_final( ), is called as a function so that you can use the RETURN value (which tells you whether the entry is Final) to determine what to do next. The procedure for the VALID is shown in the following listing:

m.period VALID snippet

```
IF ! to_final( )
   DO can_final
ENDIF
RETURN .T.
```

This procedure first checks to see whether to_final( ) automatically makes the entry final. If not, this procedure runs another procedure named can_final, to see whether all requisite fields are filled out. If these fields are filled out, can_final allows the user to make the entry final.

NOTE

No matter what to_final( ) returns, and no matter what action takes place in can_final, the m.period VALID always RETURNs .T.. Very often, code used in the VALID clause does not perform any normal data validation. Similarly, code may be placed in an object's WHEN clause that never prevents entry into the object (the WHEN clause always RETURNs .T.).

The WHEN and VALID clauses are useful because of when they occur. You can use these interrupts to cause events whenever a GET is accessed or exited, even when you don't need to forbid entry or validate the contents of the GET. The READ command also has WHEN and VALID clauses, which you can use to perform similar tasks on the READ-level.

Can_final is a simple procedure placed in Cleanup, as shown in the following listing:

PROCEDURE can_final from the Cleanup snippet

```
PROCEDURE can_final
IF EMPTY(m.prodcode) OR EMPTY(m.deptcode) OR ;
   EMPTY(m.budcatcode) OR EMPTY(m.period)
   SHOW GET m.final DISABLE
ELSE
   SHOW GET m.final ENABLE
ENDIF
RETURN
```

Following is the to_final( ) UDF for you to place in Cleanup:

FUNCTION to_final from the Cleanup snippet

```
FUNCTION to_final
m.return = .F.

IF m.final
   * if the entry is already final,
   * as it will be in some circumstances
   * when this function is called

   DO no_edit
   * disable some GETs selectively

   m.return = .T.
   * let the calling procedure know

ELSE

   IF ! EMPTY(m.period) AND (m.period < DATE( ) OR ;
      (YEAR(m.period) = YEAR(DATE( )) AND ;
       pd(m.period) = pd(DATE( )) ) )
      * if you got a date and it's either earlier than
      * today's date or it's in the same year and the
      * same quarter, which you determine with the
      * UDF PD( ), you finalize the entry yourself:

      STORE .T. TO m.final

      WAIT WINDOW NOWAIT "Entry in past or present " ;
          +"Periods must be Final."
      * remember that users can still Cancel the
      * edit if this is unacceptable to them
      DO no_edit
```

```
      m.return = .T.
      * let the calling procedure know

   ENDIF

ENDIF

RETURN m.return
```

The UDF Pd( ) used in FUNCTION to_final, which also goes in Cleanup and RETURNs the quarter in which a date occurs, is shown in the following listing:

■ FUNCTION pd from the Cleanup snippet

```
FUNCTION pd
PARAMETERS the_date
* pass the date you want to check
RETURN CEILING(MONTH(the_date)/3)
```

The only step left to do for the GET object m.period is to give it the Format of Select on Entry, which appears as @K. When editing a date, you use the @K because having the entire original date wiped out by the new keystrokes is usually the most convenient method. The @K is used for any item when editing the item usually entails a completely new entry. You see the way it works in the FoxPro System dialogs wherever a default filename is supplied.

Position this GET and a text label that indicates what it is in the upper-left corner of the record-editing box. Put another one below the first for the GET m.budgetamt. The second one will have a Numeric format, and you can choose to have it Selected on Entry as well. You also can choose a Currency format (choosing both appears as @K$).

No clauses are needed for this GET (no restrictions apply to this field). Size it by referring to the Structure window and giving the same number of places (seven) as the BUDGETAMT field. If you start by placing the object in Column 1, the status line column figure reflects the object's current length for easy resizing. Next, move the object to the desired position. The new object looks like figure 13.7.

Adding Lookups and Edits

Notice that the Screen Builder sizes the m.period field with eight places. Although the PERIOD field, like all dates, also is eight places wide, the GET includes two extra characters for the delimiters between the month, day, and year (in the order you are currently presenting the date). You may want explicitly to SET CENTURY OFF in the Setup code to accommodate these extra characters or size the GET to 10 places. SET CENTURY ON (a better choice, as we near the year 2000!) if you want all four digits of the date to show.

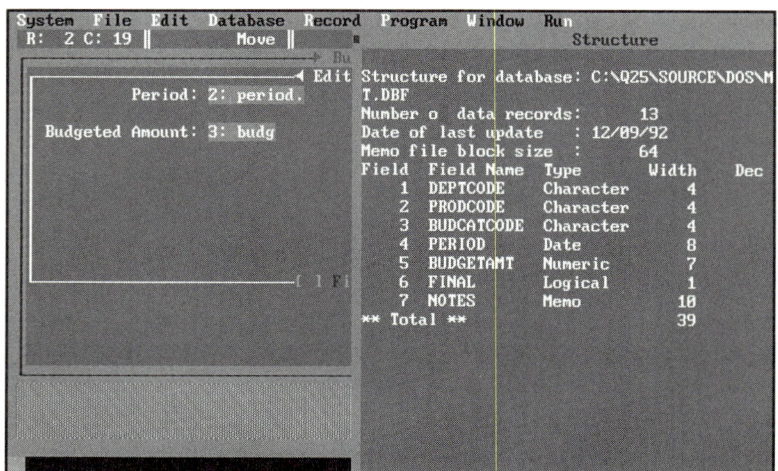

FIG. 13.7

Sizing GETs in accordance with the Budget Table Structure List.

The next GET is the first lookup you create. First, add a regular text label and field expression for m.budcatcode. You probably remember from the preceding chapter that the Format is @! AAA9. But now, you're checking both on the way into and the way out of the object (by using the WHEN and VALID clauses) to see whether the value held within also is found in the Budcat table. If not, your code will pop up a list of values from the Budcat table and ask the user to pick a value. One UDF accomplishes this feat in both instances. The popup appears in the WHEN if the variable, m.budcatcode, is empty (if you are adding a record). The user, who may be familiar with the budget category codes, can edit the code manually or just confirm the popup choice. If the user edits the code, either at this point or when subsequently re-editing the record, the VALID serves to ensure that the code still is a value in the Budcat table after the edit.

The WHEN clause contains the expression valbudcat(). This UDF, which you can place in Cleanup with all the other UDFs, takes the following form:

```
FUNCTION valbudcat
IF EMPTY(m.budcatcode) OR;
   ! SEEK(m.budcatcode,"budcat")
```

FUNCTION valbudcat, used in the m.budcatcode WHEN as an expression and in the m.budcatcode VALID snippet, is located in the Cleanup section.

```
   * if the variable is empty or if the value
   * can't be found in the budcat table

   ACTIVATE POPUP budcat
   * When the POPUP is DEACTIVATEd, code
   * execution continues here.
   * The record pointer in the Budcat table
   * has moved to correspond to the user's
   * choice from the popup.
   * You place the value of the code
   * into the appropriate variable
   * and the NAME of the budget category
   * into another one created just to
   * provide visual confirmation of the choice

   SELECT Budget
   STORE Budcat.Budcatcode TO m.budcatcode
   STORE Budcat.Budcat TO m.budcatname
   SHOW GET m.budcatname DISABLE

ENDIF
RETURN .T.
```

The VALID clause should contain the following snippet as a Procedure:

m.budcatcode VALID snippet

```
= valbudcat( )
DO can_final
```

Again, the procedure can_final determines whether you have all requisite fields filled out and can make this entry final.

As noted in the comments in the code for FUNCTION valbudcat, you create another variable, m.budcatname, and put it in the data-entry window to show the name that goes with this code. As you see in figure 13.8, you place this variable in the screen like other objects, although it is colored differently because you choose the Field Expression option to DISABLE the variable (because this expression is never directly editable by the user).

TIP

If you don't like the disabled object's colors in the layout, change the colors by selecting the object and choosing the Color option from the Screen menu. Be sure that the object remains differentiated from editable text, no matter what color you pick.

continues

continued

Because this object will display the category name from the Budcat table, give it a size of 20 characters to match the appropriate Budcat field. You don't have the opportunity to give it a Width of 20, as you did with Report expressions. If you have difficulty making the size exactly 20 characters, position the object so that its first character is in column 1 (watch the status line). Now resize the object until the status line reads `C: 20` after you release the object and click a space in the layout in the same column as its ending character. Now you can move the object into its appropriate position in the layout.

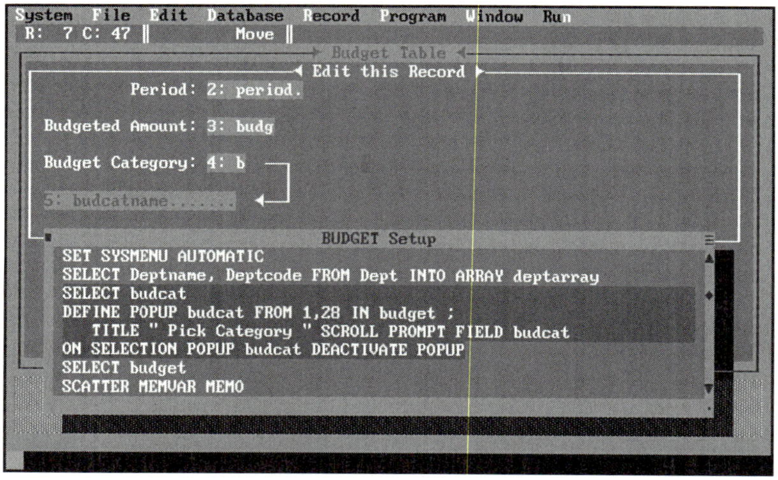

FIG. 13.8

The budget category field and text label, along with a disabled GET that holds the budget category name.

Figure 13.8 also shows part of the screen's Setup snippet. In the figure, the highlighted portion of the Setup code defines the popup activated by valbudcat( ) and determines the popup's behavior. The entire Setup code is reproduced near the end of this chapter.

The arrow between m.budcatcode and m.budcatname is actually four separate objects. First, use Ctrl+B to create two short horizontal lines and one vertical line (in other words, two small 1-row boxes and one 1-column box). Then select the objects, along with the option to Group Boxes, and smoothly join the three into one. Next press the Alt key and type `17` to create the graphics character on-screen. (Alternatively, you can type `'Q` by using the left quote method or the special characters or ASCII chart, as you did in Chapter 2.) Finally, select and move the character into position, overlaying the bottom left edge of the grouped box/line figure. You can now Group the character together with the box/line figure so that if you need to move the figure later you don't disturb the arrangement.

Next, you create a scrollable list (shortcut Ctrl+L) to hold the Product choices. Here, you don't actually show the user the product codes. The list contains entries from the Product table's Prodname field. As shown in figure 13.9, this list's prompts are created by a popup of one of several types the Screen Builder can automatically create for you.

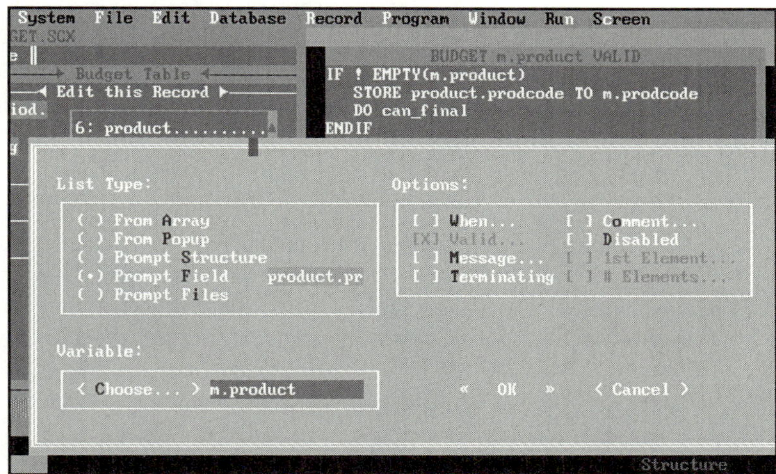

FIG. 13.9

Creating a scrollable list.

In the List dialog, choose a List Type of Prompt Field and indicate in the matching text box that the field to be used is Product.Prodname. You store the results in a Variable named m.product. Then, by putting a Procedure in the Valid snippet, check to see whether the user made a choice. If so, the record pointer in the Product table will have been moved to the appropriate record, and you can use the Prodcode field to fill the m.prodcode value with the right value. You then call can_final again to check whether all appropriate fields have values, and this entry is permitted to be finalized. The following listing is the entire procedure for the snippet (also shown in figure 13.9):

m.product VALID snippet

```
IF ! EMPTY(m.product)
   STORE Product.Prodcode TO m.prodcode
   DO can_final
ENDIF
```

When you return to the design screen, size the list object until the box shows at least three entries and is wide enough to show the product names adequately.

You are using only one of many choices when you define the Product scrollable list with the Prompt Field option, as you can see in the list dialog shown in figure 13.9. Be aware that this may be the most flexible of the new GET objects available in FoxPro. The Prompt Field option used here can use an expression and a field name. The little text box in which you typed product.prodname scrolls. You can type as many characters as you like for the list prompts. For example,

```
product.prodcode+":  "+product.prodname
```

If, instead, a list is created From Array, the list may hold almost anything you can imagine. You use an array for the next lookup you design in this screen, which is a popup control to designate a department for the Budget entry.

If you choose to create a scrollable list popup From Array, the 1st Element and # Elements check boxes are enabled. In a two-dimensional array, like the deptarray array described later in this section, the 1st Element is the column of the array you want to display in the list, and the # Elements is the number of rows, or items, to be included in the list.

Among the sample files included with FoxPro 2 are GETFILE.SCX and FLDLIST.SCX (in the \GOODIES\SCREENS directory), which are good models for the use of this GET object. Written by Sherri Kennamer, these screens provide all the functionality of the FoxPro system file and field-picking dialogs.

CAUTION: As you investigate these sample dialogs and watch the behavior of list objects you create, you notice that their behavior is different from other GET objects. The WHEN clause will be called each time the user scrolls between choices in the list, and the value of the corresponding variable will change at the same time. The user doesn't have to make an explicit choice in the list for these actions to occur.

This behavior is not a bug; at times, you do want control over every movement through the list, using the WHEN of the list much as you use the WHEN clause on the BROWSE later in this chapter. However, in the Budget screen, you use the VALID clause to accept new Product information into the budget record only if the user makes an explicit selection.

Although scrollable lists and popup controls can receive their list of choices from a DEFINEd POPUP, be aware that not all DEFINE POPUP attributes will appear in the GET objects. Most importantly, you cannot use DEFINE POPUP's MULTI keyword to allow multiple selection of objects in a scrollable list or popup control.

Programmers who used FoxPro 2.0 in the past should be aware of a change in scrollable list properties. In 2.0, if the user clicked the upper or lower border of the list to scroll the choices, a list might have no highlighted object at a given moment. FoxPro 2.0 considered this state, in which no choice is showing on the screen, as indicating that no choice was made; therefore, the value of the corresponding variable was reset to zero at this moment. In FoxPro 2.5, if the scrollable list border (in DOS) or the right-side arrows (in Windows) is clicked to scroll choices, no choice may show on the screen but the value of the variable is not reset.

You create the last lookup to retrieve a department code for this budget record, as a popup control (shortcut Ctrl+0). You can create popup controls either as a List-type or as an Array-type. In a List-type popup, you type the prompts, as you do for a set of radio or push buttons. You might choose an Array popup because you need not know the prompts to design the screen. An array, similar to a small table, has rows and columns of elements (although, like a table, an array also may have a single row or a single column). The array is a structured set of memory variables. FoxPro contains a number of commands and functions designed expressly to manipulate arrays (explained in Chapter 22). You create the array that fills this popup using a simple SQL SELECT statement in the Setup snippet:

```
 SELECT deptname,deptcode FROM dept ;
    INTO ARRAY deptarray
* fill the array with the department names and codes
* in the first and second column, respectively
```

Now you need to tell the popup the name of the array that you are using (deptarray) and the variable in which you want to put the choice. The array popup prompts are taken from the first column of elements in this array. The variable is numeric and represents the number of the choice the user makes from the displayed list of items.

Choose to name the variable m.dept and, as shown in figure 13.10, you again create a VALID clause that evaluates the choice, fills the variable that stands in for an actual Budget field, and checks to see whether you can make the entry final:

m.dept VALID snippet

```
IF ! EMPTY(m.dept)

   STORE deptarray(m.dept,2) TO m.deptcode
   * m.dept tells you what choice was made
   * (i.e. what row)
   * The item in the second column of that
   * row is the appropriate department code.

   DO can_final

ENDIF
```

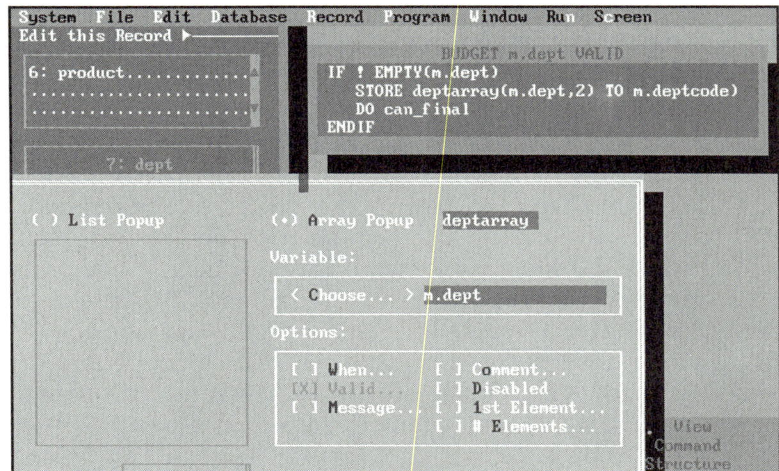

FIG. 13.10

Creating an array popup.

For the Memo field, Notes, you use an Edit Field expression for the first time. Press Ctrl+F and choose the Edit radio button. Type `m.notes` as the variable to edit. Choose the option for a scroll bar to have this familiar feature accompany this object, as shown in figure 13.11. The option to Allow tabs is enabled for Edits because, by default, you can cycle through Edits with the Tab key just like all other screen objects. If you want to allow tabs within the Edit, choose to Allow tabs and then you can leave the field by pressing Shift+Tab or Ctrl+Tab, instead.

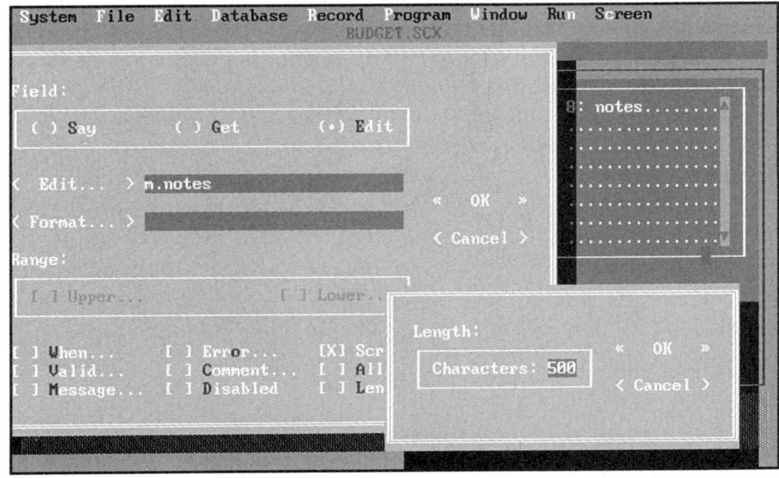

FIG. 13.11

Adding an edit.

T I P

As you see in the figure, this Edit object will use the option to limit the Length of the m.notes object to a specified number of characters. The m.notes variable in this screen is created with the SCATTER MEMVAR MEMO command, which means that it must be maintained entirely in memory; the Length feature limits the amount of memory that may be required.

In other situations, the editable Memo field may be of much greater size, and you may not be certain that the memory available can support such a variable. Yet you still want to edit indirectly rather than directly to the record's Memo field. In that case, you forgo the use of the MEMO keyword on the SCATTER MEMVAR command. Instead, you use the following code in the setup of your screen:

```
SCATTER MEMVAR
CREATE CURSOR scratch (onefield m)
* use additional fields if you have additional memo fields
APPEND BLANK
REPLACE scratch.onefield WITH budget.notes
* substitute appropriate memo field from your file here
```

Now you use this cursor record for your temporary memo edit, letting FoxPro worry about when to maintain it in memory and when to write it to a temporary file on disk. When you move to a new record, you use this REPLACE command along with each new SCATTER statement. (In most cases, you should not REPLACE into a non-selected area, but the procedure is safe in this case.) When you GATHER a confirmed edit into the record in your table, you add a REPLACE budget.notes WITH scratch.onefield.

Using Buttons To Control Your Table

After you resize the Edit and, if necessary, the Department popup control, you have ended placement of the Budget table items to be edited. A few controls, however, still aren't created. The first control is composed of push buttons, with which you are familiar from the preceding chapter. As you see in the figures throughout this section, you create a similar set of `Cancel/Save` buttons to revoke or confirm editing changes. The buttons have slightly different prompts and are arranged vertically instead of horizontally. The real difference, however, is in the following VALID clause you use:

Budget screen m.saveit VALID snippet

```
m.return = .T.
IF m.saveit = 2
   * if they chose to confirm changes

   IF EMPTY(m.deptcode) OR EMPTY(m.budcatcode) ;
     OR EMPTY(m.period) OR EMPTY(m.prodcode)
      * you can't accept an incomplete record;
      * they may have deleted some information

      WAIT WINDOW " Fill out all information "+ ;
         "before Saving, or Cancel Edit " NOWAIT

      * keep them here
      m.return = .F.

   ELSE
      GATHER MEMVAR MEMO
      * notice the extra keyword to
      * account for the Notes memo field

      SHOW GETS
      * will call the SHOW clause on the READ
      * which will SCATTER a new set of memory
      * variables and refresh all the GETs

   ENDIF
ELSE

   WAIT WINDOW " Editing Cancelled " NOWAIT
   IF LASTKEY( ) = 27
      * the user pressed ESC and is ready to
      * leave the data entry screen
      CLEAR READ
```

```
   ELSE
      SHOW GETS
      * see above comment
   ENDIF

ENDIF

RETURN m.return
```

Although you are choosing to RETURN .F. if the edit cannot be saved because a requisite field wasn't filled out, you can send the user to the first field in the group of four still empty. If you make this choice, without GATHERing anything, you RETURN .T. from this procedure at all times. The following CASE statement determines the object that comes next:

Budget screen m.saveit VALID snippet alternative code

```
* IF the user wants to save but
* you got an incomplete record,
* use the same WAIT WINDOW, and then
* check the important fields in order:
   DO CASE
   CASE EMPTY(m.period)
         _CUROBJ = OBJNUM(m.period)
   CASE EMPTY(m.budcatcode)
         _CUROBJ = OBJNUM(m.budcatcode)
   CASE EMPTY(m.prodcode)
         _CUROBJ = OBJNUM(m.product)
   CASE EMPTY(m.deptcode)
         _CUROBJ = OBJNUM(m.dept)
   ENDCASE
* continue as before with the
* ELSE
*    GATHER MEMVAR MEMO
```

TIP

Rather than creating these two buttons as a set, you may prefer to create each button individually, each with a specific variable and VALID clause. This approach has an added benefit of making resizing individual buttons easier. If you prefer a set, you notice that you cannot size buttons by typing spaces at the beginning of prompts. Instead, use the blank character (created by holding down the Alt key and typing 255 on the numeric keypad).

Now, create a set of radio buttons (shortcut Ctrl+N) to change the order in which you view the data at any time. Creating radio buttons is like creating a set of push buttons, as you can see in figure 13.12. Following is the Valid procedure snippet for these buttons:

m.order radio button VALID snippet

```
DO CASE
CASE m.order = 1
   SET ORDER TO 0
CASE m.order = 2
   SET ORDER TO period
CASE m.order = 3
   SET ORDER TO deptcode
CASE m.order = 4
   SET ORDER TO budcatcode
ENDCASE
* Show the Browse again so that the new order shows
SHOW WINDOW Pick REFRESH
```

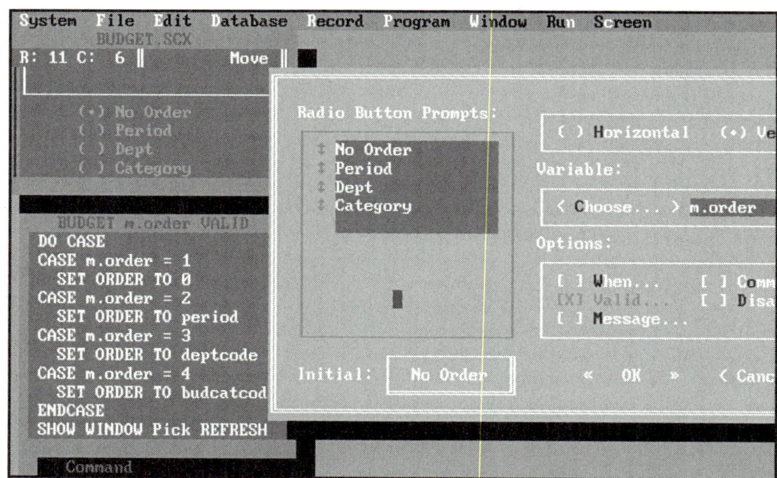

FIG. 13.12

Creating a set of radio buttons.

The final controls on this screen are two invisible buttons (shortcut Ctrl+I). Invisible buttons are areas on-screen that you can size and select like other objects. Invisible buttons function like push buttons, initiating an action. In a graphical interface, you overlay these areas with an icon or other indicators that tell the user what happens when this area of the screen is clicked or selected by other means.

In FoxPro, you can devise this kind of representation with the graphics characters available, or you can overlay these areas with a text description of what the invisible buttons do, as you do here. With a text overlay, consider these invisible buttons as push buttons—except the prompts aren't required to have angle brackets. Because the prompts on push buttons can look unbalanced if you have a set with unequal-length prompts (because the angle brackets are the same distance apart on each button in a set, as required by the longest prompt), invisible buttons can provide a handy alternative to other on-screen buttons.

Invisible buttons also can be used to arrange the user's choices in a visual display that uses the physical proximity of the elements in a meaningful way. These buttons, for example, can represent a map of locations about which reports are available, or underlay text in an embedded menu of Help file subjects, as described in Chapter 20.

The invisible buttons on the Budget data-entry screen enable users to run two simple queries at any time. You create the buttons' overlay text as Field expressions (SAYs) rather than as text objects so that when the GETs are refreshed on-screen with a SHOW GETS command, the buttons are not on top of the labels.

The invisible buttons are defined separately, although you can design them as a set of two, if you prefer. As shown in figure 13.13, you assign each button a variable (you used m.query1 and m.query2). The VALID procedure for each button is as follows:

Invisible button VALID procedures to process queries

```
DO budget1.qpr
* DO budget2.qpr for the second button
ACTIVATE SCREEN && prevent BROWSE from
                && landing in the data entry window
* prevent BROWSE from landing in the data entry window
* the query used for this screen could make good use of
* the PREFERENCE clause added to the SELECT command
* in 2.5  to control the appearance of this BROWSE
BROWSE
SELECT Budget
```

When you select the button, the query is executed. The VALID procedure must then reSELECT the Budget table because any query may leave you in a different work area.

If you define these buttons as a set, just assign one variable and use CASEs in the VALID to test the result and decide which query to run. Whether you define the buttons singly or as a set, you should keep the button areas as large as you have room for and of consistent sizes, so the user does not have trouble clicking them with the mouse.

Now create the SAYs expressions that overlay the buttons. The two SAYs are as shown in figure 13.14. The following expressions are one method of achieving the desired results:

■ **SAYs to label invisible buttons**

```
CHR(251)+" Dept Totals for Pd"
```

and

```
CHR(251)+" Product Totals For Yr"
```

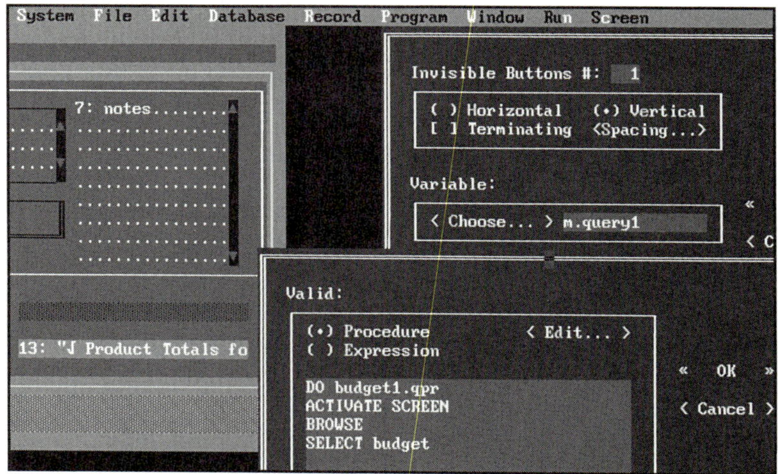

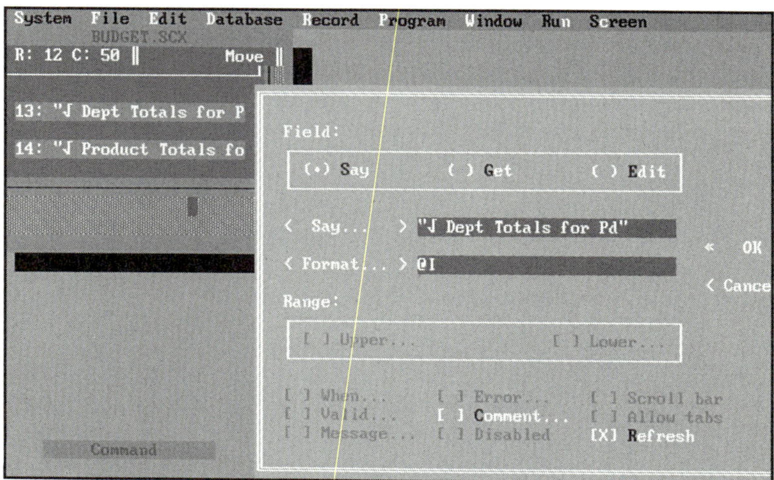

FIGS. 13.13 and 13.14

Creating invisible buttons and SAYs to label them.

The first character represents ASCII 251, which is often used to represent a check mark. If you prefer, you can type the character directly in the SAY expression inside the quotation marks, holding the Alt key down as you type 251 on the numeric keypad, so it appears as shown in the figure. Notice that you have surrounded each label with quotation marks so that it can be seen as a literal character string.

Just as in the Report Writer, where you built report expressions from a combination of functions, strings, variables, fields, and operators, you can use the Expression Builder to design any kind of SAY you want.

TIP

The SAY expressions literally name the two queries the buttons process, which is not necessary. You can make the SAY expressions "Query1" and "Query2" if you like and allow the users to substitute any queries they prefer for the sample queries you provide. You can even have each SAY contain a variable so that the users can provide labels for each of two queries they prefer. The queries themselves can be kept in a table and placed in a Memo field, with a Character field that holds the label for each one. In this way, each user may draw two favorite questions from a bank of useful queries to be immediately available on-screen as they work on the budget process.

Build the queries run by these two buttons in the RQBE and save them as .QPR files with the appropriate names. You can type these queries directly by using the command MODIFY COMMAND budget1.qpr and then MODIFY COMMAND budget2.qpr. You also can use these samples as an RQBE exercise—go backward from the syntax through the RQBE to achieve the same results. Notice that you should explicitly name the cursor each query will produce to avoid the queries creating BROWSE PREFERENCE records which will be inappropriate for each other (because of differing FIELDS lists).

To work on these queries in the RQBE, first initialize the variable m.period in the Command window by STOREing a date value to it or by SCATTERing MEMVAR FIELDS Period, which gives the variable an existing value from the Budget table, as your code will do when the screen program is run.

The following listing is BUDGET1.QPR, as created by the RQBE:

SQL queries to be run by invisible buttons

```
SELECT DEPT.DEPTNAME, BUDGET.PERIOD, ;
      SUM(BUDGET.BUDGETAMT) ;
   FROM BUDGET,DEPT ;
   WHERE DEPT.DEPTCODE = BUDGET.DEPTCODE ;
```

continues

```
   GROUP BY BUDGET.PERIOD, BUDGET.DEPTCODE ;
   HAVING BUDGET.PERIOD = m.period ;
   ORDER BY BUDGET.PERIOD ;
   INTO CURSOR BUDGET1
```

The following listing shows BUDGET2.QPR:

```
SELECT PRODUCT.PRODNAME, BUDGET.PERIOD, ;
       SUM(BUDGET.BUDGETAMT) ;
   FROM BUDGET, PRODUCT ;
   WHERE PRODUCT.PRODCODE = BUDGET.PRODCODE ;
   GROUP BY BUDGET.PRODCODE, BUDGET.PERIOD ;
   HAVING YEAR(BUDGET.PERIOD) = YEAR(m.period) ;
   INTO CURSOR BUDGET2
```

Using the variable m.period in the query allows the user to type any date in the edit window and use the query processor to find out something about it (the user can always cancel the edit afterward). If you prefer, you can use the actual data from the Budget table (Budget.Period) in place of m.period in each query.

Ordering Objects On-Screen

All the screen objects are now created. However, if you recall, you created the Finalize check box as the first GET. You certainly don't want this item to be the first entered by the user, so you need to reorder the objects in a more logical progression on-screen. To reorder, select all objects (while holding down the Shift key) in the order you want the items accessed.

You may need to move the long query text labels laterally so that you can select separately both the label and the related push button. (The order in which the two SAYs and the disabled m.budcatname GET are accessed isn't crucial to the data-entry process, but the order of the SAYs with respect to the invisible buttons makes a difference to the design process—just as with report objects, their relative position determines which object you can see as you work.)

Starting from the m.period GET, choose the objects by going down the columns within the data-entry area and then across to the next column: m.period, m.budgetamt, m.budcatcode, m.budcatname, m.product, m.dept, and m.notes. Next (still holding down the Shift key so everything remains selected), select the m.final GET and the m.saveit (the controls that actually affect the data-entry process). Last, select m.order and the query objects, selecting each button before its accompanying SAY.

Be careful that you don't move all the selected objects as you perform this procedure (although you can move them back when you finish). After objects are selected in the proper order, use the Screen menu popup option to Bring to Front (shortcut Ctrl+G) and you see the assigned object numbers change. Use Send to Back (or Ctrl+J), and you can watch the object numbers change to a reverse order.

> **CAUTION:** You just reordered the fields in a sequence appropriate for data entry in the screen. In a screen, fields are initially ordered in the same sequence in which you define them. You can select all groups of objects on-screen and choose the option to Reorder Fields from the Screen menu to reorder the selected objects left-to-right and top-to-bottom, an order inappropriate here but possibly convenient at other times.
>
> Grouping objects (which you can do to move or otherwise manipulate them as a set as you did in the Report Writer) also affects the objects' sequence. Grouped objects are by default reordered left-to-right and top-to-bottom within the group, with consequences you may not expect or desire. You can Ungroup all objects and then explicitly choose all objects and reorder these selections as you prefer when you finish designing a screen.

After you have reordered the objects (and repositioned the SAYs laterally, if you moved them during the reordering process), the completely designed screen should look like figure 13.15.

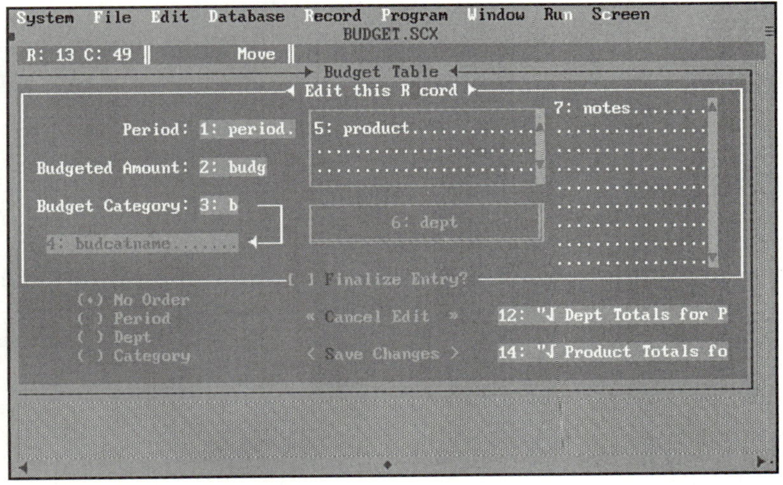

FIG. 13.15
The completely designed Budget screen.

TIP The two SAYs show on top of the buttons when GETs are refreshed by a SHOW GETS command by including them in the ordering process. However, in other situations, a SAY's contents may change dynamically during the course of a READ; for example, a calculated value may be dependent on the contents of one or more other editable GETs. You can use the Refresh option shown in the field expression dialog to refresh the value of the SAYs. GENSCRN provides this feature by rewriting the @... SAY code directly in the SHOW clause. However, using the global SHOW GETS command simply to refresh the value of a SAY (in this example, in the VALID or VALIDs of the editable GETs determining the calculated value) is inefficient, because all the other code in the SHOW clause must be run. Instead, use a disabled GET (or a GET WHEN .F.) as you did for the budget category name earlier. Now when the value of the putative SAY changes, you can issue a specific SHOW GET <getname> to refresh this one object.

Combining Objects into a Polished Screen Set

Although all the objects are created, you still have work to do before you can generate the BUDGET.SPR and run the code. Recall that you are going to have a BROWSE appear in this screen set; you take care of this feature in the Setup snippet of code, and you also need to add a few more screen-wide code sections by using the options in the Screen Layout dialog.

Setting Up the Screen

Although you have already seen much of the Setup snippet in previous sections of this chapter, the following listing reproduces the snippet in its entirety:

Setup Snippet for BUDGET.SCX

```
SET SYSMENU AUTOMATIC

* SYSMENU is ON by default but does not
* show on-screen during programs until the user
* presses ALT+F10, or double-clicks the
* right mouse button,
* unless the preceding line is added.
```

```
* Remove the preceding line if you don't want
* SYSMENU showing at all times,
* and replace it by
* SET SYSMENU ON

* Look at the program environment code to see
* how you might save the old value of SYSMENU
* and restore it in Cleanup, too.

* Because this program uses SYSMENU shortcuts to
* add and delete records (from the BROWSE pad)
* do NOT SET SYSMENU OFF!

* If your system does not take care of these environmental
* details earlier, you may want to SET REPROCESS TO 1
* here to avoid unlimited retries when the program attempts
* to lock a record.

* You can choose to have the Screen Builder generate
* file-opening statements by using the
* environment saved with the screen, so everything
* should be set up for you to do the following in the
* normal SECTION 2 position of Setup code:

SELECT Deptname,Deptcode FROM Dept ;
     INTO ARRAY deptarray
* fill the array with the department names and codes
* in the first and second column, respectively
* set up the array for the m.dept object

SELECT Budcat
DEFINE POPUP budcat FROM 1,28 IN WINDOW budget ;
   TITLE " Pick Category " ;
   SCROLL PROMPT FIELD Budcat
ON SELECTION POPUP budcat DEACTIVATE POPUP
* set up the popup for the m.budcatcode object

SELECT Budget
SCATTER MEMVAR MEMO
* here, again, the extra MEMO keyword is used
* to account for the NOTES memo field
* You must initially set up these variables
* to be available to all parts
* of the program, although the SHOW routine
* refills them with the initial values.
```

continues

```
* Do the same for the special object-variables
* below. If there is any chance of these
* variables reappearing in other screen sets
* that may be active at the same time as this one,
* you should declare the variables
* REGIONAL, as GENSCRN does with the variables
* it creates in the program environment section
* of the code before storing the initial values to them.

* If you're not on a blank record, use the
* RELATIONs that have been SET to get the
* budget category name from the Budcat table and the
* product name from the Product table, as follows:
m.budcatname = IIF(EMPTY(m.budcatcode), ;
                      SPACE(20),          ;
                      Budcat.Budcat)

m.product = IIF(EMPTY(m.prodcode),     ;
                    " ",                ;
                    Product.Prodname)

* Get m.dept from the row number of the
* array deptarray in which m.deptcode can
* be found:
m.dept = IIF(EMPTY(m.deptcode),           ;
                  0,                              ;
                 ASUBSCRIPT("deptarray",;
                   ASCAN("deptarray",    ;
                          m.deptcode),   ;
                   1)                    )
* Initialize the m.order variable
* and make it appropriate to the current order
DO CASE
CASE UPPER(ORDER( )) = "PERIOD"
  m.order = 2
CASE UPPER(ORDER( )) = "DEPTCODE"
  m.order = 3
CASE UPPER(ORDER( )) = "BUDCATCODE"
  m.order = 4
OTHERWISE
  * order may not be set,
  * or it may be set to one you're not
  * allowing access to in this screen
  SET ORDER TO 0
  m.order = 1
ENDCASE
```

```
* Depending on the situations in which you
* call this program, you may want to
* save ORDER( ) in a variable first, so you
* can restore it in cleanup.

* comments on the BROWSE
* and WINDOW brow follow below
BROWSE SAVE NOWAIT NOEDIT WINDOW brow ;
  TITLE " Pick Budget Entry " ;
  WHEN Do_Show( ) ;
  VALID :F Do_Unlock( )
```

Using Browses in a Screen Set

At the bottom of the Setup snippet is the first time you see a programmatic use of a BROWSE command. The SAVE keyword means that the BROWSE is kept open when you cycle through the windows in the READ. The NOEDIT keyword means, as you may expect, that the BROWSEd records are not editable directly. The NOWAIT keyword means that the program does not remain in the BROWSE after creating it, but continues with the rest of the programmed instructions.

The WINDOW brow clause means "open this browse with the characteristics defined by the WINDOW named brow, which you previously defined." However, you haven't yet defined a WINDOW named brow anywhere. To make GENSCRN generate a definition of this window along with the rest of the screen set, create a separate screen for it, as shown in figure 13.16.

Notice that you explicitly name this window (brow), and that the #WCLAUSES generator directive provides the characteristics of ZOOM and GROW for the window. These characteristics aren't available from the Window Type dialog along with other attributes; windows with GETs in them, which are the Screen Builder's main concern, cannot change in size as BROWSEs can.

In the Budget data-entry program, you need to refer to the BROWSE window just as you needed to refer to the control panel window in the last chapter as you wrote the Dept and Budcat screen programs. The TITLE clause is important in this context—you can refer to a BROWSE window in a program by referring to the BROWSE window's title (or by the first word in the title, if the title includes non-alphabetic characters). If the window has no title, you can refer to the BROWSE window by the title given to the WINDOW (if you defined the WINDOW with a TITLE clause). Failing this, if the BROWSE was defined IN WINDOW (a separate clause you do not use here) and that window was defined with a title, you can use this window's title to refer to the BROWSE in window functions. If none of the above situations apply, you can refer to the BROWSE window by the alias of the controlling table, which you will see reflected in its title bar.

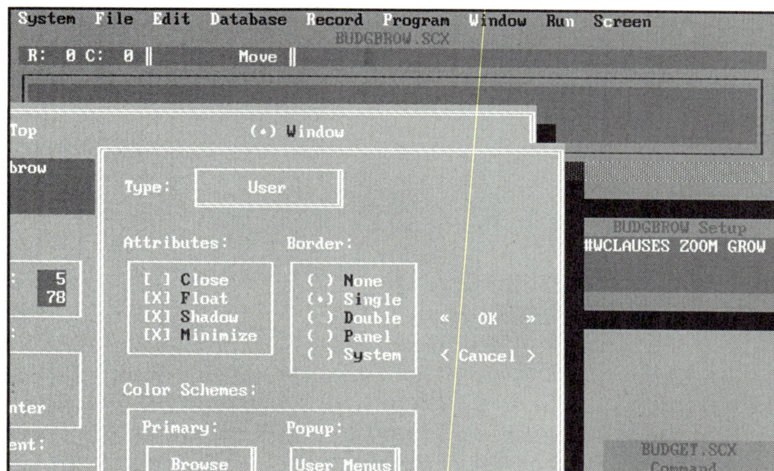

FIG. 13.16

Creating a BROWSE image-window for the Budget screen set.

TIP

If you find the preceding paragraph confusing, rest assured that you are not alone. The important point is this: A single DEFINEd window may give attributes to many different BROWSEs, and none of them actually exist in that window. They each have their own window and each window must have its own name. Each name can be deduced from the title you see on the BROWSE, although not all the characters in the title will be significant. Because referring accurately to a BROWSE window is important, however, take some time to get a sense of how this works by using a WAIT WINDOW trick, similar to the trick you used to learn about READ clauses:

```
ON KEY LABEL F10 WAIT WINDOW WONTOP( )+" "+WTITLE( )
```

Using this command in the Command window, try defining, titling, and windowing the BROWSEs in different ways and issuing BROWSEs. While each BROWSE is active, press F10 and check the current status of these two functions, watching for the changes.

When you finish, issue the command ON KEY LABEL F10 (with nothing following it) to cancel the previous instruction. You learn more about ON KEY LABEL commands in the chapters that cover programming.

The BROWSE WHEN clause is evaluated when the user moves between records (or rows) in the BROWSE. With a SHOW GETS in the WHEN clause, the Budget table data-entry window is refreshed as the user changes the current record by using the BROWSE. Because it RETURNs .F., the record currently being moved to is unavailable for editing (this record is readonly). You need to take these steps, even with the NOEDIT keyword, because a BROWSE NOEDIT still can have records added to it with Ctrl+N, and these records still are editable. You are taking advantage of FoxPro's native method of appending (and also deleting) records in this program. You also can use the keywords NOAPPEND and NODELETE to make these options unavailable or even NOMENU to make all the native BROWSE menu options unavailable. You then can devise new menu options or ON KEY LABEL options for the users to add and delete records under your control. Records added using this alternative are automatically uneditable without a WHEN clause RETURNing .F., like all others, in a BROWSE NOEDIT.

NOTE

Many reasons exist to prefer programmatic control over record-adding, instead of the simple method you use here. You may want to add a unique identification number for each record as the record is added or to check for recyclable deleted records before you choose to add one. You also may want to allow the user to choose certain fields for automatic entry of particular values throughout one data-entry session (creating a custom version of the SET CARRY command).

You can use the NOMENU clause on a BROWSE to gain full control. You then replace the options on the menu popup that usually appears when a BROWSE is the active window, with similar options of your own. Adding records may be done by SCATTERing MEMVAR MEMO BLANK and using the SQL INSERT FROM... VALUES... command when the edit is confirmed for a new record, as you did with the EDIT screen in the previous chapter. You still can allow adds only while in the BROWSE screen, using a check for IF WONTOP("Pick").

BROWSE has many other features you can explore. Besides the keywords and clauses that you learned about in Chapter 8, equally useful for interactive and programmatic use are the row-level Browse VALID clause and the various clauses that you can issue to determine a BROWSE's look in a program: LPARTITION/RPARTITION and PARTITION, NOLGRID/NORGRID, and NOLINK are among features introduced in FoxPro 2.0.

You stow the simple BROWSE WHEN clause UDF in the Cleanup snippet, as follows:

BROWSE WHEN clause, in Cleanup code

```
FUNCTION do_show
SHOW WINDOW Pick REFRESH SAME
IF NOT RLOCK( )
   WAIT WINDOW NOWAIT ;
        " Sorry -- " + ;
   "this record is unavailable for edit at the moment!"
   SHOW GETS DISABLE
   SHOW GET m.order ENABLE
   SHOW GET m.query1 ENABLE
   SHOW GET m.query2 ENABLE
ELSE
   SHOW GETS
   SHOW GET m.saveit ENABLE
   SHOW GET m.notes ENABLE
ENDIF
RETURN .F.
```

The SHOW WINDOW <browse window> REFRESH command makes sure that all new records added appear in the proper order, in case an index order is currently in use. The RLOCK( ) locks each record as the user comes to it, returning .F. if the record is already locked by another user. Unlike the Dept and Budcat screens, here you don't provide a method of initiating an edit after viewing (each record becomes editable as soon as it is displayed on-screen). Therefore, you lock each record in turn.

If a record cannot be locked, you DISABLE all GETs throughout the screen and then selectively ENABLE the GETs that are not tied to the record (the file-ordering and querying capabilities). Although leaving these non-destructive capabilities available even on an uneditable record is a nice touch, you have a second reason to ENABLE them: You need at least one editable GET in the READ. Otherwise, when a user clicks the READ window from the BROWSE, the READ will automatically end!

If the record can be locked, you use the global SHOW GETS command to determine which GETs may be enabled, and then explicitly ENABLE the two GETs (m.saveit and m.notes) that the SHOW clause does not ENABLE internally.

You may wonder why these two GETs are singled out for special treatment. Recall that the Notes field is editable, according to the system's specifications, even when a record is Finalized and otherwise uneditable. The SHOW clause, discussed later in this section, ENABLEs and DISABLEs GETs selectively based on these specifications, not on the ability of the user to lock the record. You could certainly choose to handle the system's record-locking attempt and its consequences within the SHOW clause, along with the specifications. In this model system, however, record-locking and its consequences have been separated from other system requirements for clarity.

NOTE Because the BROWSE is driving the record pointer in the Budget table, the BROWSE clauses are a natural place to handle record locking and requirements peculiar to a locked record (such as disabling the m.notes EDIT object) in this case. You could also decide to place these considerations in the ACTIVATE and DEACTIVATE clauses, using a system similar to the locking technique you used in the last chapter. This decision has the advantage of avoiding the record lock until the user moves from the BROWSE to the data-entry window but does not provide immediate feedback about which records are available for editing as the user moves through the BROWSE entries. Different techniques serve you well in different situations.

The BROWSE VALID clause function, also stored in the Cleanup section, is even simpler, as follows:

BROWSE VALID clause, in Cleanup code

```
FUNCTION do_unlock
IF UPPER(WONTOP( )) = "PICK"
   UNLOCK
ENDIF
RETURN .T.
```

The BROWSE VALID clause uses the :F (forced VALID) switch, which means the clause is called even if no editing has occurred (no editing ever occurs in this particular BROWSE). This ensures the unlocking of each record as the record pointer moves, regardless of whether the larger system allows multiple records to be locked with SET MULTILOCKS ON. Checking for the current window ensures that the record stays locked if the VALID is called because the user has moved to the data entry window, rather than moving to another record in the BROWSE.

Adding More READ-Level Clauses and Integrating the BROWSE

The Budget data-entry screen requires a simple but extremely significant READ ACTIVATE clause, which consists of the following lines:

Budget ACTIVATE clause

```
IF ! WVISIBLE("Pick")
   CLEAR READ
ENDIF
```

The ACTIVATE clause is evaluated when a new window is chosen during a READ; the window, however, must be participating in the READ with normal GETs rather than a BROWSE, MODIFY MEMO, or desk accessory window. This procedure reads as "If the browse window is no longer visible"—remember that you are going to refer to the browse by the title—"end the READ."

You also can choose to make the opposite assumption. If the user closed the BROWSE, the closure was accidental and the READ should not be CLEARed. You may decide that you want to allow an exit from the readonly by using a Quit option that you included as a button in the data-entry window. Rather than using the preceding ACTIVATE clause, you may want to use the following code:

Alternative Budget ACTIVATE clause

```
IF ! WVISIBLE("Pick")
   BROWSE SAVE NOWAIT NOEDIT
      TITLE " Pick Budget Entry ";
      WHEN Do_Show( ) ;
      VALID : F Do_Unlock( )
ENDIF
```

Here, you redefine and re-issue the BROWSE if it no longer exists.

The screen also requires an even simpler READ-level WHEN clause, which executes directly before the READ becomes active. The following is the entire clause:

Budget screen WHEN clause

```
RELEASE WINDOW brow
=Do_Show( )
```

The requirement for RELEASing WINDOW brow is explained in the next section. The call to FUNCTION Do_Show performs the record-locking duties for the first record in the READ, subsequently handled by the same function's use in the BROWSE WHEN clause. In Do_Show( ), listed above, the calls to the SHOW clause do the real work of giving the memory variables the correct values and editable status for the current record. The following lines show the entire SHOW clause:

Budget screen SHOW clause

```
IF ! Budget.Final AND ! EMPTY(Budget.Period) AND ;
   (Budget.Period < DATE( ) OR ;
   (YEAR(Budget.Period) = YEAR(DATE( )) AND ;
    pd(Budget.Period) = pd(DATE( ))))
```

```
   * If the actual record has not been marked 'final'
   * yet, but the date is within the current or past
   * quarters:

   REPLACE Budget.Final WITH .T.
   WAIT WINDOW NOWAIT "Entry in past or "+  ;
      "present Periods must be Final. "

   * (change the value in the actual record).
   * This part of the procedure will be in use
   * when the SHOW GETS command is called by
   * the BROWSE WHEN. In fact, you should see
   * the message quite a bit the first time you
   * run the BUDGET.SPR and cursor through the
   * BROWSE, especially if you typed the dates
   * shown in Chapter 3 for the sample data and you
   * are using this book in 1994 or later!
   * A useful strategy is to add a button
   * to SET FILTER TO !final in this screen in case
   * the users want to see only editable records.

ENDIF

* Now create appropriate values for the current record
* for all the variables, as you did in the setup code.
* You don't need to reset m.order just because you
* are moving between records, however:

SCATTER MEMVAR MEMO
* be sure to remove the MEMO keyword if you
* choose to edit to a scratch cursor record as
* described previously; REPLACE the value in
* the cursor memo field here

m.budcatname = IIF(EMPTY(m.budcatcode), ;
   SPACE(20),             ;
   Budcat.Budcat)

m.product = IIF(EMPTY(m.prodcode),      ;
                " ",                    ;
                Product.Prodname)

m.dept = IIF(EMPTY(m.deptcode),          ;
                   0,                    ;
                   ASUBSCRIPT("deptarray",;
```

continues

```
                        ASCAN("deptarray", ;
                              m.deptcode), ;
                   1) )

IF m.final
   DO no_edit
   * disable some GETs
ELSE
   DO can_edit
   * selectively enable GETs
ENDIF
```

The SHOW GETS command, besides calling the SHOW clause, also refreshes by default the GETs on-screen (which shows all the new values you may have given). Any SAYs for which you have chosen Refresh Output Field are also refreshed (GENSCRN rewrites the SAY code in the SHOW clause). However, often it is better to use a disabled GET or a GET WHEN .F., as you did for the budget category name in BUDGET.SCX, instead of a Refreshed SAY. A readonly GET can be refreshed explicitly with a SHOW GET <getname> command, at times when you don't want to run the rest of the code in the SHOW clause. (You encounter this situation in the WHEN and VALID of m.budcatcode; you issue a SHOW GET m.budcatname DISABLE explicitly when the user changes the value of the related budget category code without needing any of the other tests and procedures contained in the full SHOW clause.)

SHOW GETS is flexible, powerful, and has several optional keywords you can use to change default behavior. You previously saw the ENABLE/DISABLE keywords, available both globally using SHOW GETS and for the single SHOW GET command. You also can use the LEVEL <ExpN> clause to SHOW GETS at a particular level if you have *nested* READs (you learn more about a nested READs in the following section) or—if you have more than one GET window—the WINDOW <window name> clause to SHOW GETS in a particular window.

You may decide to SHOW GETS WINDOW Controlm DISABLE, for example, to prevent the user from moving to another record while you edit a record in the Dept screen set you designed in Chapter 12. The COLOR or COLOR SCHEME clause can SHOW GETS or SHOW a GET in any colors required to alert the user to a change in status at any time.

You may want to call the SHOW clause at some point without refreshing the GETs, which you can do with the OFF keyword, or refresh the GETs and not execute the SHOW clause's commands, using SHOW GETS ONLY. In a multiuser system that directly edits fields rather than memory variables, you use SHOW GETS LOCK when you have been browsing through the records with a READ NOLOCK and wish to secure a lock on the record you want to edit.

> **CAUTION:** The one unacceptable syntax is the use of the global SHOW GETS command (with no clauses) in the SHOW clause itself. Because this command triggers the SHOW clause, issuing the SHOW GETS in the clause starts a recursive loop, with the clause calling the command, which calls the clause again, which calls the command, and so on. Don't do it!

The Budget table screen set's SHOW clause uses one new procedure, can_edit, because, as you remember, the Budget table strategy calls for GETs to be enabled selectively according to some complex relations between them. Here is the can_edit procedure, the last one you need to place in the Cleanup snippet:

PROCEDURE can_edit used in the SHOW clause and stored in the Cleanup section

```
PROCEDURE can_edit
SHOW GET m.period ENABLE
SHOW GET m.budgetamt ENABLE
SHOW GET m.budcatcode ENABLE
SHOW GET m.product ENABLE
SHOW GET m.dept ENABLE
_CUROBJ = OBJNUM(m.notes)
DO can_final
* check to see whether the m.final
* GET can be entered yet
RETURN
```

Now, you only need to take care of the Cleanup snippet. This code should precede all the procedures and functions you typed into the Cleanup snippet. For clarity, you can end this code with a RETURN command (as shown in the following lines), although FoxPro doesn't require this step. This RETURN statement is the RETURN from the .SPR back to the calling program. The final cleanup code contains the following lines, to be executed after the READ:

Cleanup (post-READ) code

```
* re-set SYSMENU
* and re-SET REPROCESS if you have
* changed these settings at the beginning
* of the program

RELEASE WINDOW Pick
* get rid of the BROWSE if you exited the
* READ from the data entry window
```

continues

```
RELEASE POPUP budcat
RELEASE deptarray
* you don't need them and they don't need
* to continue taking up memory

* The following is not necessary because you
* are allowing the program to close the database
* tables, but will become necessary in situations
* where you do not close the tables when the data
* entry program ends,
* since the user may have exited the READ from
* the data entry window rather than the BROWSE:
UNLOCK

RETURN
```

Following these lines, you should have (in any order) all the PROCEDUREs and FUNCTIONs you created above, to be used and called by different objects and clauses in the program. Here is a checklist. Make sure that you have them all:

List of procedures and functions found in the Cleanup code, following the post-READ code

```
PROCEDURE no_edit
PROCEDURE can_edit
FUNCTION valbudcat
FUNCTION to_final
PROCEDURE can_final
FUNCTION pd
FUNCTION do_show
FUNCTION do_unlock
```

Using the Screen Set

Now, you are ready to generate the code, check for errors, and DO BUDGET.SPR.

Accept all the defaults in the Program Generate dialog, and add to the screen set the image window for the browse. Use the Arrange option in the dialog to arrange the two windows appropriately, as shown in figure 13.17.

If you have followed closely in this chapter, what you see when you run the BUDGET.SPR program should look much like figures 13.18 through 13.21. In figure 13.18, the user added a record and then changed the Order to Dept. After the file is put into Dept order, the new record is now positioned at the beginning of the BROWSE because a blank department code still exists. The GETs are now enabled, except for the capability of Finalizing the Entry. The Finalize GET remains unavailable until the required fields are no longer blank. For the same reason, when the user tries to Save Changes, the message displayed in the figure appears.

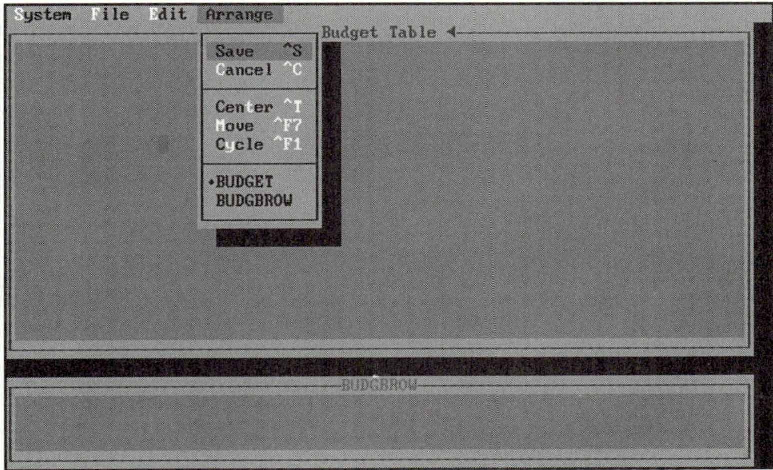

FIG. 13.17 Arranging the Budget screen and the browse image window.

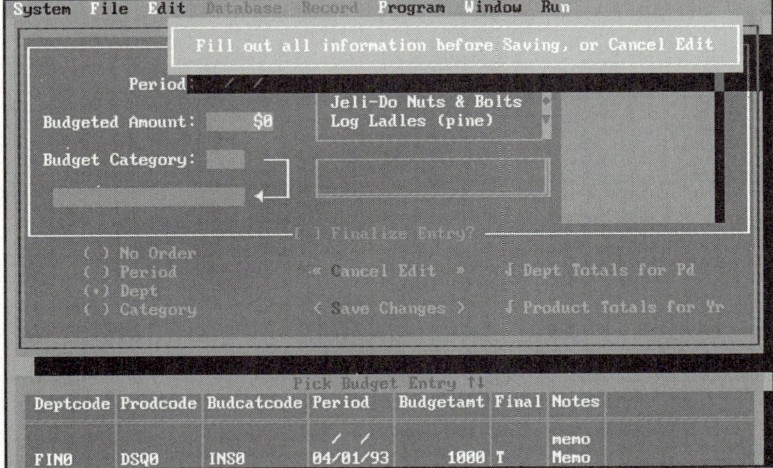

FIG. 13.18 The Budget Entry system after the user has tried to save an unfinished entry.

In figure 13.19, the user has cursored into an old entry in the BROWSE, which was added from an outside system. Noting that the record has escaped being Finalized earlier, the system informs the user that the entry must be marked Final and changes the record. Note the disabled GETs in the record-entry section, although queries still may be run, order still may be set, and notes still can be entered in the EDIT.

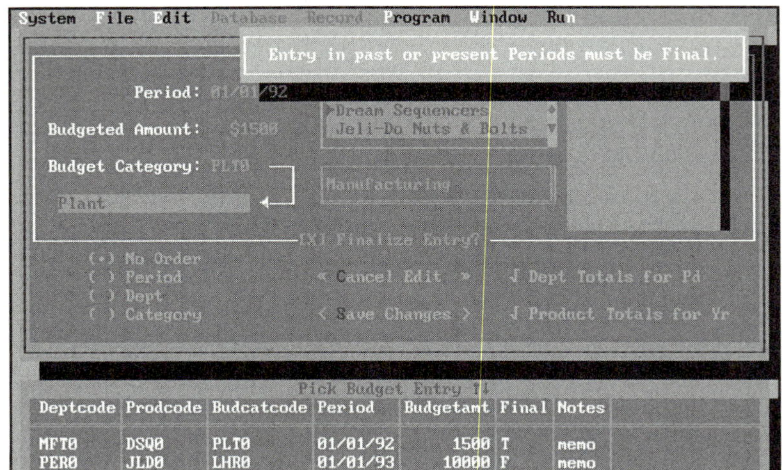

FIG. 13.19

The Budget Entry system, showing an automatically Finalized record.

In figure 13.20, a query was run against the data in the current entry. The results of the query, the total budgets for each department during this period, show in a separate BROWSE.

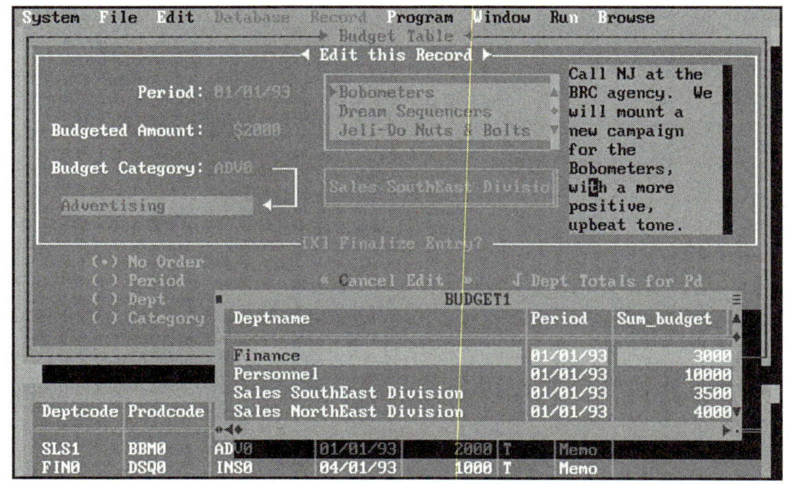

FIG. 13.20

The results of a query in the Budget Entry system.

In figure 13.21, the user has BROWSEd to a record that is locked by another user. The m.notes EDIT is unmodifiable along with the other record-specific objects, although the user may still change the order of the BROWSE or run the queries.

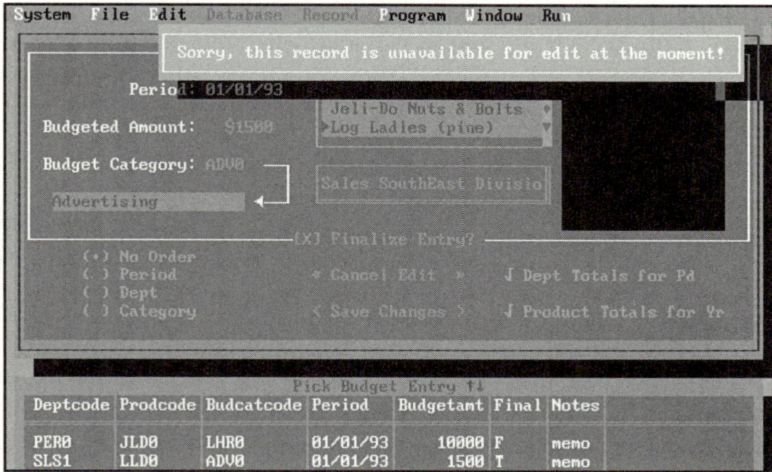

FIG. 13.21
The Budget Entry system handles a record currently being edited at another station.

You have to play with this screen for a while to observe all the features of this system in action. Yet, again, it displays only a fraction of the capabilities of the Screen Builder and screen sets.

Advancing Your Comprehension of FoxPro's READ Command

The Setup of the Budget data-entry screen set shown here uses a common technique integrating a BROWSE with READ windows. This approach, however, does not enable you to begin a data-entry session in the included BROWSE window. Another capability you want in many screen sets is a BROWSE of a related table. You can use the SET SKIP and SET RELATION commands you learned in Chapter 4 to provide a BROWSE of child records when you are editing the parent table or a BROWSE of parent records from which you decide which children to edit.

Fully understanding how to make multiple windows work together requires using the FoxPro design tools together in a coordinated manner and getting a clear picture of the tasks your program should perform. You are introduced to how the tools are coordinated and how tasks are identified in Chapter 14, which teaches you about the Menu Builder and Project Manager. Then, in Chapter 15, you return to increasingly complex screen sets and the editing of multiple files in one screen set.

As you work with the practice system and build new systems, you can find many ways to incorporate in screen sets existing window objects—including BROWSEs and MODIFY MEMOs, and also desk accessories, such as the calculator (a fixture on the System menu popup). Occasionally, however, you may not want all windows equally available to users. You need to direct users to perform tasks in a certain sequence, keeping them in one mode of action at a time. The FoxPro interface contains modal dialogs, similar to the Report option on the Database menu popup. Modal dialogs are windows whose tasks you must finish before you can go on to choose the next action.

The opposite of modal systems are modeless or nonmodal, where you can move at will between activities the same way you cycled between the Filer, the Command Window, and text-editing windows in the first chapter. (Some Macintosh users and programmers prefer the term *modaless* to describe systems that behave in this manner.)

So far, all the READs you have created have been nonmodal. But you may or may not have realized how careful you were to keep them that way. Did you notice the WHEN clause of the READ, in which you RELEASEd WINDOW brow? This window is the image-window you defined to set attributes and size for the Browse window and would have been an awkward participant in the set of windows available if you had not removed it.

You could have chosen to DEACTIVATE the WINDOW, which is usually a better choice, in case you need to reissue the BROWSE later, as suggested in the alternative READ ACTIVATE snippet. However, in this case, you have not made provisions for protecting the user from choosing the image window from the list available from the Window menu popup. You learn about tailoring the system menu in the next chapter.

At times, you need to communicate questions that the user must answer before work can proceed. You also may encounter times when you must limit users to a discrete set of windows, although you defined other windows needed for certain utility tasks. The READ keyword

MODAL, together with the associated WITH clause, are provided to help you with this problem.

In the Budget data-entry system, the users can choose to Finalize a record long before the record's Period field and the system's internal rules require the record to be unchangeable. If the user chooses this option, you provide a message, along with confirming visual clues (most of the GETs on the screen become uneditable). With these reminders, the user can choose to Cancel the edit, and no harm is done if the option was chosen in error.

However, this situation can be handled with a greater degree of comfort for the user if the user is given an immediate, explicit opportunity to change the decision he or she made to Finalize the record, just as FoxPro asks you to confirm your decision when you choose to PACK a table or to perform other critical tasks. Just as FoxPro does, you use a modal dialog in this situation by calling or nesting a new READ from within the current data-entry task. The nested READ must use the MODAL keyword to prevent the user from clicking back on the Budget window or the BROWSE before answering the question.

The following code, replacing the current VALID clause on the m.final GET, calls the modal dialog:

```
IF m.final
   IF Ask("Are you sure you want to Finalize?")
      WAIT WINDOW  NOWAIT;
      " Finalized Budget Entries are not editable. "
       * disable some GETs:
      DO no_edit
   ELSE
      * reset the value:
      m.final = .F.
   ENDIF
ENDIF
```

Notice that the dialog is called by Ask( ), a UDF, rather than by a procedure. Calling the generated screen program as a function provides the convenience of using its RETURN value (in this case, either .T. or .F.) as part of another expression. To use the program as a UDF, replace the extension of the generated program name, which defaults to .SPR, with .PRG, in the Program Generate dialog.

The Ask( ) function is also called with an argument (the question to be answered). You provide this capability by using a PARAMETERS statement in the #SECTION 1 of Setup, as described earlier in this chapter.

MODAL dialogs such as Ask( ) are typically designed as generically as possible so that you don't have to create new ones for every possible situation. You want generic dialogs to handle many system tasks, such as picking options for a report. However, there is a limit to how changeable a dialog can be; for example, you can't change the size of a GET each time the dialog appears. Appendix H contains an Ask( ) dialog designed to overcome this limitation with a few tricks.

The MODAL command, when used alone, limits a READ to the windows in the particular screen set. Any attempt to bring other windows forward with a mouse results in a beep and no other change, just as when you try to click the Command window while still in the Report or Search dialog. You then can add the WITH clause (the word WITH, followed by a list of windows) to enable selectively certain other windows to be accessed without harm, as in the following example:

```
READ CYCLE MODAL WITH Brow, Calculator, Calendar
```

This command enables the three named windows (which includes two System pad desk accessories) to come forward.

Again, you see how important knowing how to make an exact reference to a window can be, especially with a BROWSE and the related, complicated window-referencing rules.

Apart from the READ-level options, you haven't fully explored all the object-level options for each kind of GET and the other screen elements. Some of these features are mentioned in following chapters, but this is another direction in which you should continue to experiment.

As you learn about the syntax used in creating GET and EDIT objects, you will see a DEFAULT clause in use. This option is not available in the Screen Builder and is, in the authors' opinions, of limited utility. In explanation, and so that you are not confused when you see the DEFAULT values in clauses GENSCRN inserts for each GET or EDIT in the generated .SPR files, these values are used only to generate memory variables, if you include a GET or EDIT to an item that does not already exist.

If you GET directly to fields, or if you GET to memory variables and SCATTER MEMVAR (whether BLANK or filled with the contents of the current record), the DEFAULT clause is ignored. When you create GET controls that involve memory variables not directly related to a record, and therefore not created by a SCATTER, you should initialize them, as you initialized m.dept and m.product in the Setup code and in the SHOW clause of the Budget screen.

Although the example code initializes the variables to blanks if the user adds a new record, explicitly initializing these variables gives you a chance to indicate the default values you prefer. You can even maintain a table with each user's preferred defaults and RESTORE these memory variables from there if the user added a record.

Other GET-level options not directly supported by the Screen Builder are far more useful than DEFAULT. You may want to use the NOMODIFY keyword on an EDIT so that you can scroll and read, but not edit. You may want to use the COLOR clause, although, as you learn in Chapter 16, other ways are available to address color issues in FoxPro that may feel more natural in the Screen Builder.

Just as the #READCLAUSES generator directive enables you to add keywords and clauses to a READ that doesn't specify Screen Builder options, you can attach extra code on the object level. The easiest place to put this code is in the Format text box. Just use the #ITSEXPRESSION directive described in table 13.1 to get GENSCRN to treat whatever you place in the text box as an expression instead of a literal string to be bounded by quotation marks. (Remember that you place the #ITSEXPRESSION directive, followed by the character of your choice, in the Setup snippet with any other generator directives you use.)

Because GENSCRN prefaces the information in the Format check box with the word PICTURE, just enclose the real format information within brackets or, if the GET or EDIT has no picture, add a pair of brackets with nothing between them. Suppose that the #ITSEXPRESSION character is ~, as shown in the example in table 13.1, and you have a Memo field that should be viewable but not edited in a certain screen. The Format text box should contain the following line:

```
~ [] NOMODIFY
```

GENSCRN then generates the following line of code:

```
@ r,c EDIT your_memo PICTURE [] NOMODIFY
```

If you have a password GET designed to accept only uppercase characters and you want the word displayed in black-on-black so that the password cannot be read as typed, you can use the following Format:

```
~ [@!] COLOR ,N/N
```

GENSCRN generates the following code:

```
@ r,c GET your_pass PICTURE [@!] COLOR ,N/N
```

In this way, you can add to the generated code anything not directly included in the Screen Builder options.

Summary

With all these opportunities, mentioning that you still have other alternatives for screen design and generation in FoxPro may seem almost cruel. If, however, you do not like the programs generated by the Screen Builder, you can change GENSCRN.PRG.

To write screen programs, GENSCRN uses FoxPro's textmerge commands, which are described in Chapter 19, "Using Advanced FoxProgramming Techniques." Text-merge commands are extremely powerful yet easy to use. You can customize GENSCRN or build as many special-purpose generator programs as you like with different names. When you are ready to generate a screen, just supply the appropriate generator program name to FoxPro by storing the name in the _GENSCRN system variable.

Because the screen files are tables, you easily can investigate these files' structure to help you understand GENSCRN.PRG and for other reasons, as well. You can USE BUDGET.SCX like other tables and directly REPLACE ALL colorpair WITH a value you prefer FOR all objects of a certain kind. At times, this method may be quicker and more convenient than using the Screen Builder.

The two previous chapters covered a great deal of ground in a short time. You moved from painting a few objects on the canvas of the Screen Builder to creating complicated multiple-window screen sets (using almost every feature of FoxPro) and learning and working with queries to arrays and many new programming instructions.

In the following chapter, you investigate other tools, including the Menu Builder and the Project Manager, that help you assemble full-fledged data management systems. You are introduced to foundation READs, which you can use to maintain a system's tasks in a delicate balancing act, and other thoughts on ways to integrate, enhance, and share these various elements of FoxPro applications.

Then you go on, in Chapter 15, to address the ways these tools are combined to organize, integrate, and switch between the many tasks of an application.

14

CHAPTER

Organizing and Packaging Your Applications

Your exploration of the Screen Builder was productive but arduous. FoxPro's other power tools, which you approach in this chapter, may loom in your imagination like a range of mountains you have yet to climb. These FoxPro components, however, are easier to master than the Screen Builder is.

Knowing about the tools' development can give you some insight into the nature of the Screen Builder. During seven months of FoxPro 2.0 beta testing, the initial FoxPro Screen Builder underwent a complex evolution. Testers struggled, much as you have, to master the Screen Builder and to develop new programming procedures. These testers made numerous suggestions for new features. Fox Software responded both to the difficulties observed and to the requests for enhancements—and, as you have seen, Screen Builder emerged as both an intricate and an extremely powerful tool.

By contrast, the Menu Builder changed little in the same period. Although equally new, Menu Builder was adopted with relative ease by almost all the testers. The Menu Builder's features and options are limited in comparison to the features of the Screen Builder, but still provide almost unlimited flexibility in handling the tasks for which this tool is designed.

The Project Manager also underwent relatively minor adjustments. At first, testers found the Project Manager's pivotal role in coordinating the pieces of an application somewhat perplexing. The Project Manager, however, is as simple to learn as the Menu Builder is. This tool's advantages and purpose become obvious soon after you begin to use it and become increasingly apparent as time goes on.

The Distribution Kit, the third tool discussed in this chapter, is even simpler to use than the first two. The Distribution Kit is not sold with FoxPro as part of the base product. You must purchase the Distribution Kit separately if you want to develop and distribute applications to people who do not own copies of FoxPro. (Different versions of FoxPro require separate Distribution Kits.) The Project Manager alone is sufficient to build applications for distribution to other registered users of FoxPro. The Distribution Kit provides the capability of creating applications that work "without wires," that is, without the underlying FoxPro development tools. Because this tool's task is essentially subordinate to the Project Manager's, the Distribution Kit is treated as an option of the Project Manager in FoxPro; therefore, these tools are covered here together.

Building Your Own Menus

FoxPro's menu system is usually called SYSMENU. In FoxPro, you can use SYSMENU's native pads and options (the System pads and menu names in the documentation) when creating new menus. You can remove all pads and options you don't like or need and add others you do want; SYSMENU is completely customizable in FoxPro and in programs. Although all the menu systems and commands available in FoxPro 1.0x still are available to use, none of these items can remain active and accessible during a READ, as SYSMENU can. Because SYSMENU is so powerful and configurable, you may never need to resort to other menu systems in FoxPro.

By default, SYSMENU is ON in all programs, which means that the user can access SYSMENU by pressing F10 or Alt, or by double-clicking the right mouse button. If you decide not to use SYSMENU or to make SYSMENU temporarily unavailable, you can SET SYSMENU OFF. If, however, you want SYSMENU constantly available, as in the interactive environment, you SET SYSMENU AUTOMATIC. After you finish working on a particular task or in an application, you can return SYSMENU to the original set of pads and popups provided by FoxPro; just SET SYSMENU TO DEFAULT.

The Menu Builder is the design tool that enables you to customize SYSMENU. Like the Screen Builder, Menu Builder builds a table from options you designate. The template program GENMENU.PRG (similar to GENSCRN) then employs standard FoxPro procedures on the menu table (a file with the extension .MNX). Menu Builder generates a program (with the extension .MPR) that DEFINEs the MENU to specifications.

You DO the generated .MPR program just as you can DO an .SPR or .PRG command file, or you can incorporate the program into a larger application, as is shown in the section of this chapter that deals with the Project Manager.

A certain blurring of the distinction between *interactive* and *programmatic* use of FoxPro results from the capability to tailor SYSMENU. Remember from Chapter 1 that the Organize application attached itself to the System menu pad, and you were returned to the Command window. Unlike conventional applications, Organize did not prevent you from continuing to issue interactive commands that USEd other databases, executed other programs, or performed other tasks—yet Organize always remained available as a discrete application.

After you chose an Organize option, SYSMENU became restricted to Organize-specific tasks and you were, in the conventional sense, definitely placed inside a running application.

If, however, you look at HELPTREE.MPR, you see a program that expands even further the envelope of what you may consider an application. HELPTREE.MPR is a stand-alone menu program (found in the \GOODIES\HELPTREE directory, under the main FoxPro program directory). If you installed this program among the FoxPro optional files, use the Program Do… menu popup option now to execute HELPTREE.MPR. As you see in figure 14.1, Helptree is an organizing tool for FoxPro's Help file. Although installing this program on the SYSMENU bar adds a Helptree pad, just as Organize adds itself to the System popup, when you use Helptree you remain completely within the interactive environment.

If you choose the Helptree Search option, shown in figure 14.2, you see a dialog similar to FoxPro's native dialogs. (This dialog is patterned exactly after the Filer's Find dialog, as you learn when the Filer, one of

FoxPro's additional productivity features, is discussed in Chapter 16.) Just as when you access the native dialogs, SYSMENU features inappropriate to the current task become unavailable, but otherwise the environment remains unchanged.

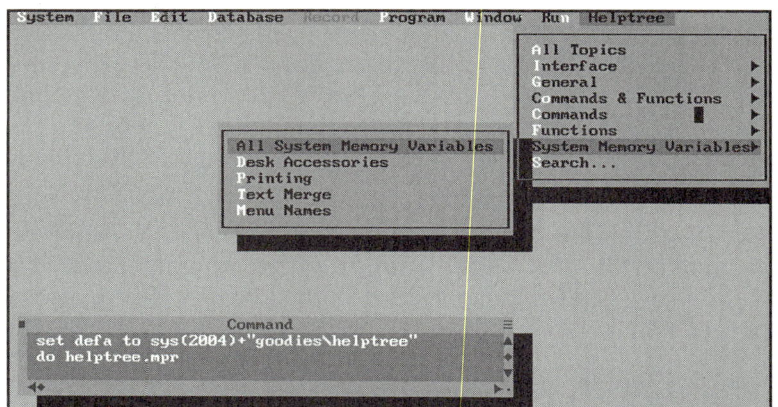

FIG. 14.1

HELPTREE.MPR in use.

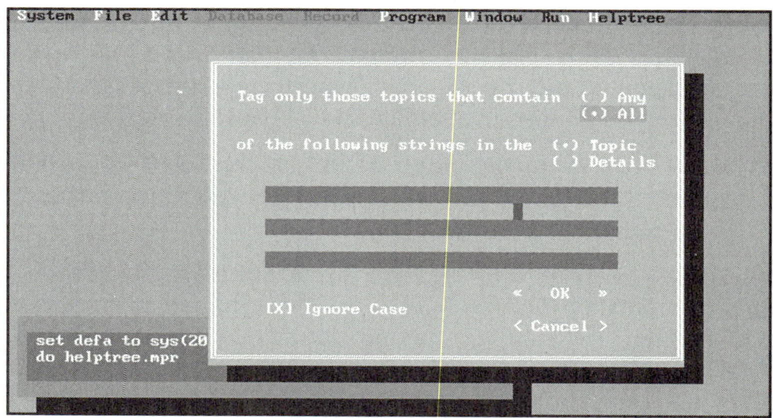

FIG. 14.2

Helptree's Search option, which is a modal dialog like the native FoxPro dialogs.

The Command window still is available in the Helptree application (which functions in the interactive environment), although you can't execute a command until you exit the dialog.

At the other end of the spectrum (and as you also saw in Chapter 1) is the version of SYSMENU in use during a FoxApp-generated application, such as the PRODUCT.APP you created. All options are completely tailored to the needs of the currently executing program. The Command window is never available, and you can't USE other tables or perform any other interactive functions.

Deciding whether the menu is part of the interactive environment or included in a self-contained program may be the most pivotal choice you make as you begin to design the interface of the program, but this choice still is only one of many choices. Because manipulating the Menu Builder is relatively easy, this section first discusses menu design in some depth. Determining the options to add to the menu and how to organize these options is one of the most difficult and most significant parts of the menu creation process.

Planning a menu in FoxPro or in any other computer software is a task that shares many attributes with the real-world object on which the *menu* metaphor is based. Whether an offering of hundreds of choices or a simple plan for a family dinner, a menu must be balanced (include everything necessary) and inviting (encourage people to try the items offered). The courses also must follow a progression that seems logical to onlookers.

If the consumers of this application don't like the menu, you don't necessarily have to throw out all the results of the cooking, but (as parents have said to children for time immemorial) how can you discover whether you like something if you don't try it?

As in Chapter 11's discussion of interface design, some guidelines are offered here for you to remember when you plan menus. Also remember the principles suggested there—consistency, clarity, and comfort.

All menu choices should be easy to follow. The Menu Builder enables you to build submenu upon submenu; a menu pad can lead to a popup, a choice from the popup can make another popup appear with further options, and so on in a *cascade* of choices. Don't descend through more levels than you absolutely need. These kinds of hierarchies are difficult for users to remember, and making the users search unnecessarily to perform tasks isn't the best way to provide choices.

Whenever possible, avoid creating separate menu options that the user must accomplish in a rigid sequence. You may need to post transactions, for example, before a certain month-end procedure can be executed. At the least, the application must provide an iron-clad check so that it refuses to run the month-end closing while transactions remain unposted. Users, however, may get frustrated if, after choosing an option and setting up a printer with the appropriate forms and making other preparations, they are told that they cannot complete the job.

A second, somewhat better choice is to disable the month-end option while any unposted transactions remain in the files. However, the user may receive no immediate and obvious clues from the system about how to gain access to this option again.

The most suitable plan for this situation may be to have the month-end option look for unposted transactions, inform the user of the situation, and ask directly for further directions in a friendly manner, as in the following on-screen message:

```
Unposted transactions remain in the file.
Do you want to post the transactions now, or continue later?
```

The posting option is then run directly from the month-end option if the user desires.

Occasionally, as this posting example shows, a menu can present a single task in multiple ways to give the user greater flexibility and control. When you consider which tasks to assign to menus, as opposed to control buttons in the screen sets, the advantages of a certain degree of redundancy become even more apparent.

FoxPro's documentation suggests using controls for reversible, commonly used options, reserving menu choices for less commonly used and more permanent changes. If you think about the standard SYSMENU Edit choices, which are reversible and commonly used, you see at once that you cannot possibly be consistent about this rule. (Implementing the Edit features through procedures you write is very difficult, whether for a menu popup option or a control button on a screen. Your versions of SYSMENU must almost certainly incorporate some of Edit's features by retaining the features in native form.)

A better rule of thumb is to restrict permanent and seldom-used choices to the menu while repeating the choices you want to make especially convenient as control buttons and menu popup options. The user then can select the choice instantly from the screen or use the hot key that a menu popup option affords.

How then do you decide what tasks belong on the menu? Resolving this decision is not too different from deciding what chapters belong in a book or—as is suggested in Chapter 18, where you start exploring programming in detail—from organizing the structure of a program. Usually, you begin by attempting to list all the jobs you want to accomplish in the application. You then rearrange and add to this list, noting which jobs are subprocedures of others and which jobs must be split into separate actions. An outline format can help you here. You revise the outline as needed when new requirements must be met and new tasks are added to the system.

After you know what the tasks are, how do you physically arrange these tasks in a menu? The outline you prepared can serve as a basis for menu organization. Some attention to language also can provide you with an implicit organizing principle. You can think of tasks in an application as simple imperative sentences, much like FoxPro commands. Tasks start with a verb, the action to be taken (such as add, edit, or copy) and end with a predicate, or object, on which the verb's action impacts (usually files and records).

In most well-designed application menus, these verbs and objects are consistently placed. If a menu pad initiates an action, such as Report, the associated popup contains the objects available for use with the action (in this case, all the output formats available for reporting). If, however, the menu pad is a noun, such as Product, the associated popup contains all the actions you can take that involve the Product table.

Another possible approach is to create a menu pad name as a noun that represents a *group* of objects with all the popup options containing other nouns that are members of this group. In the menu you design later in this chapter, for example, you create a Tables menu pad that contains a popup bar for each table in the database. Each bar enables the user to perform the same action, data entry, for one table. Each bar's prompt is the name of the table to which it provides access.

When you design menu options to add to SYSMENU, these options should incorporate logic that disables and enables them appropriately, according to other tasks being performed. This feature also must appear consistent. If you disable the month-end procedure in the previous description while the user is adding a transaction record, you may want to disable this procedure when records in the client file and other tables are being added, too, even if the disabling isn't equally crucial in all cases.

Previous experience with the default SYSMENU may have made you aware that no menu can be 100-percent faithful to these rules. Luckily, hunting through the choices in a menu is not an entirely unrewarding experience; on the occasions when you meandered around SYSMENU looking for a correct option for the task at hand, you probably discovered one or two handy features you had not previously seen. Users of your applications can enjoy this experience too, as long as they perceive the feeling of uncertainty as a momentary exception rather than as a rule.

Most database management systems include the following basic tasks:

- *Input*, in which records are added and edited to the basic tables or are incorporated from other computer file formats, or both
- *Output*, in which queries are processed and results are sent to reports, labels, summary tables, other computer file formats, and so on
- *Setup* and *utilities*, in which files, directories, and system parameters necessary to run the application are established, security passwords are recorded, and lookup files are filled
- *System maintenance*, in which files can be reinitialized and indexes can be rebuilt if necessary, and error logs can be accessed (Refer to Chapter 20 for information on error handling within an application.)

Every application also takes care of housekeeping chores that the user does not initiate, such as opening the files needed for the application. These chores are discussed in Chapter 18, where you learn about program structure; you also see some ways you can integrate the chores into the application when you use the Project Manager in a following section of this chapter. Here, you see how the chores of which the user is aware—the application's visible responsibilities—become part of the System menu.

The Menu Builder Options

Begin the creation of a menu file, as usual, by choosing the File menu pad and then the New... option and choosing Menu as the type, or type the command CREATE MENU in the Command window. You also may notice, with some relief, that the number of available options on the Menu pad are fewer than you saw in the Screen Builder. As shown in figure 14.3, General Options that correspond to the Screen Layout are available, are menu-wide in their effect, and are available from the first menu popup choice. The second choice is labeled Menu Bar Options, which are instructions that affect this menu level as a whole.

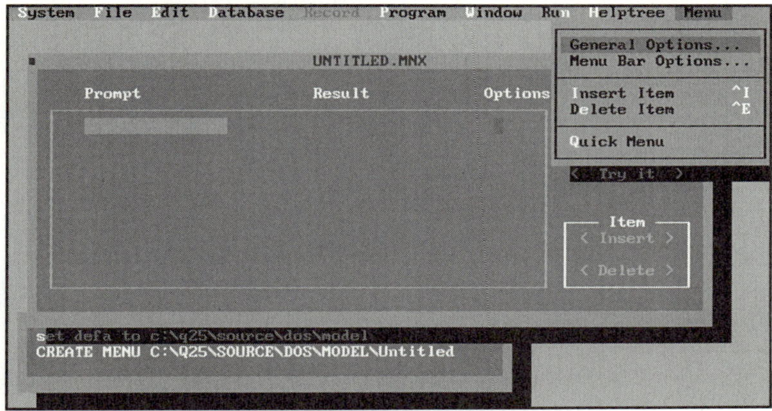

FIG. 14.3

Getting ready to create a menu by using the Menu popup options.

This second choice changes as you define and edit different menu levels. The Menu Bar is SYSMENU's top level, the pads defined for the top row of the screen. A menu popup activated when you choose a pad is the second level. A popup activated when you choose a menu popup option is the third level. The second Menu popup choice enables each subsidiary level to have a procedure, a mark character, and a color scheme assigned to all the elements, as a group. Each procedure, mark, or color scheme, however, can be superseded by instructions for individual elements at the next lower level.

This hierarchy is simpler to manipulate, and more useful, than the rule sounds. Figure 14.4 contains a rather frivolous example that graphically demonstrates the way these instructions change work. The mark is turned on (SET TO .T.) for the entire menu and set to the character ♫. This instruction is superseded for the File pad, which is set to the character ↨. The Window popup elements also are marked as a group, but this instruction is superseded with individual instructions for the Hide bar (which has a different mark) and for the Zoom ↑ bar (where the mark is turned off).

Similarly, you can activate one global procedure for every menu item or every option on a single popup and then *countermand* the procedure for specific elements assigned to each item's unique instructions. For convenience, you may want to create one such procedure to perform task routing for every menu option. This procedure examines the current status of the menu and determines what action to take. The status of the menu and the menu choice that called the procedure can be evaluated from a number of FoxPro functions, including PAD(), PROMPT(), PRMBAR(), MRKBAR(), and POPUP().

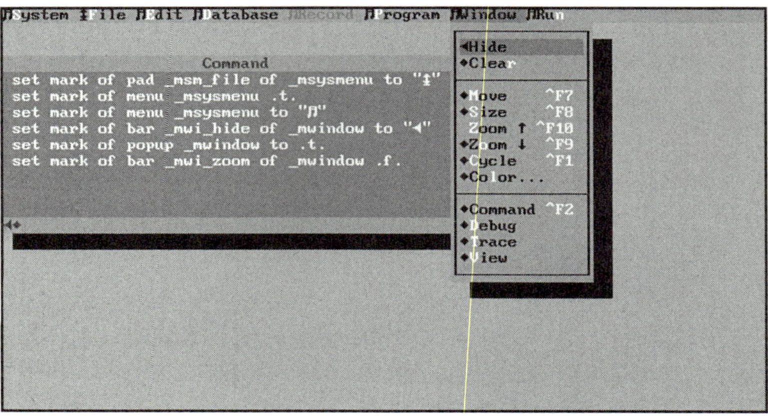

FIG. 14.4

The SYSMENU is marked as a whole, and individual pads, popups, and bars also receive mark instructions.

The Quick Menu

You start by using the Quick Menu option, which creates a duplicate of the default SYSMENU, complete in every respect. Like Quick Report... and Quick Screen..., this option is available only when the menu you're designing still is completely empty. Unlike these options, however, after you choose Quick Menu you are faced with no more choices or dialogs. The result is shown in figure 14.5; this result should look familiar. The items in the Prompt column are all the pads available on the default SYSMENU, with which you have worked since you first loaded FoxPro. The version created by Quick Menu is similar to the default SYSMENU, except for four differences. The File menu popup's Close All option and the Window menu popup's Hide All and Show All options are available on the default SYSMENU only when it is accessed with the Shift key, but are provided by Quick Menu as standard options along with their non-shifted partners (Close and Hide). The fourth difference is that the Run menu pad does not appear on the Quick Menu, for reasons that you explore later in this chapter.

Special Menu Prompt Instructions

The Prompt list may look familiar in another way: the \< characters are used here, as they were in prompts for control objects in a screen, to highlight a letter in the prompt and indicate that this character is the hot key, or is combined with Shift keystrokes for the hot key for this option. You also can type \- alone in a prompt when defining popup bars to separate the popup options into meaningful groups with dividing lines (although doing this on the menu bar, rather than on a popup, makes little sense). You also can type \ at the beginning of any Prompt name to make the item unselectable, which is the equivalent of using the Disable option for an object you define in the Screen Builder. More convenient ways are available to disable a menu item conditionally, however, as you see in following sections.

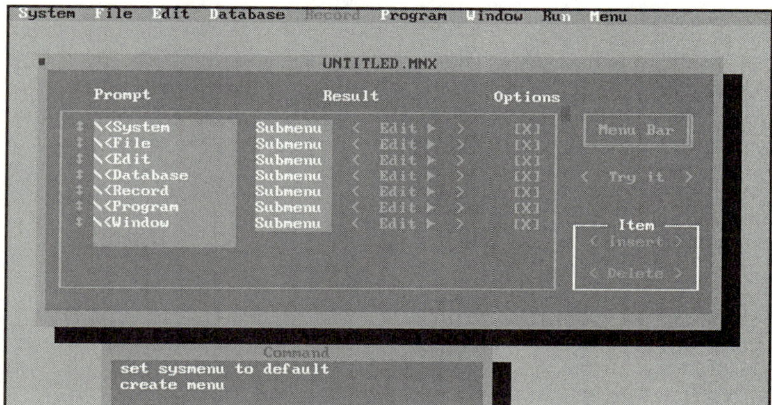

FIG. 14.5

The Quick Menu clones the System Menu.

T I P

Only one letter can be the highlighted character in a prompt. If you use \< twice or more, only the leftmost instance of \< creates the highlight. Also, the leftmost instance of a particular character receives the highlight. If, for instance, you use "This is a te\<st" as a prompt, the first "s" (in the word "This"), not the "s" you preceded with the \< instructions (in the word "test"), receives the highlight.

Variable Menu Prompts

Your menu requirements may include a need for variable menu prompts. Suppose that you want to enable the users of an application to change the prompts to any task titles that they find comfortable and easy to remember, rather than force them to use what you feel are appropriate designations for each choice. You can use the Menu Builder and GENMENU.

GENMENU surrounds any words you place in the Prompt text box with double quotation marks, as follows:

```
DEFINE PAD My_Pad OF _MSYSMENU PROMPT "My Prompt" COLOR SCHEME 3
```

To DEFINE a PROMPT using a variable, you must concatenate your variable with an extra set of quotation marks so that the variable appears surrounded by null strings when the code is run. If your users' prompt choice for a particular bar is placed into the variable barprmpt1, you type the following into the Prompt text box:

```
"+barprmpt1+"
```

GENMENU generates the code to look as follows:

```
DEFINE PAD My_Pad OF _MSYSMENU PROMPT ""+barprmpt1+""
```

You can include literal strings along with your variable prompt. If you place

```
Option 1:  "+m.prmpt1+"
```

in the Prompt text box, GENMENU generates

```
DEFINE PAD My_Pad OF _MSYSMENU PROMPT "Option 1:  "+m.prmpt1+""
```

All you have to do is make sure that the variable is properly initialized with the users' choice, and the menu prompt reads the way they want it to.

With this understanding of GENMENU, you can shoehorn an option MESSAGE clause into the prompt string, using prompts like the following:

```
This is my prompt" MESSAGE "This is my message
"+variable_prompt MESSAGE variable_message +"
```

Notice that, in each of the preceding examples, the prompt strings are arranged to work with the double quotation marks GENMENU adds to each end of the prompt.

NOTE FoxPro 2.5's menu table (.MNX) has a Message Memo field, but this field is not accessible from the FoxPro for DOS Menu Builder. You can USE the table and enter message contents in this field directly for the appropriate records, and GENMENU uses the contents to generate a MESSAGE clause. The contents of this field are placed directly after the word MESSAGE without delimiting quotation marks; GENMENU assumes that the Message field contains an expression. If you want to use a literal message string, put the surrounding quotation marks in the Memo field.

Assigning Results to a Menu Prompt

To the right of the Prompt column and its list of labels in the Quick Menu, you find the Menu Builder's Result column. Here, you define the consequences that result from choosing any individual menu option. All the pads on the menu bar in the menu currently have Submenu as a Result, because each default pad on SYSMENU leads to a menu popup.

TIP

To look at the options available from the File menu popup, perhaps because you want to see the Close All option created by Quick Menu, use the `Edit` button in the same row as the File prompt. You go down a level in the menu structure. Don't press Esc to go back up a level in the menu, as you would if you were actually accessing the menu popup and wanted to return to the menu bar. This action is natural if you're comfortable with FoxPro's menu system, but in the Menu Builder it acts as an escape from the entire menu, which is (after all) only an editing window similar to the Screen Builder or Report Writer. Luckily, you get the usual FoxPro dialog asking if you want to save or cancel your changes to the edit in progress, but having to cancel the Esc press and return to the menu-editing session is a minor annoyance. Use the popup in the right corner of the window to return to the menu bar level of the menu you are designing.

To create a new item, use the `Insert` push button or Menu option (the shortcut is Ctrl+I) anywhere you like in the list. You see that the Result is set to Submenu by default, but the push button to the right of Submenu reads `Create` rather than `Edit` because you haven't yet assigned popup bars for this item. Press the Tab key or otherwise move the cursor into the text box that reads Submenu and select it to see the list of other possible Results, as shown in figure 14.6.

If you choose Command as the menu option result, the `Create` button changes to a text box. Here, you can type any FoxPro command you like, and when this option appears on SYSMENU, the command is executed when the user chooses this menu option. (Although this box appears limited, you have as much room as you need; as you type, the text scrolls.)

Pad Name is the Result selection that enables you to assign one of FoxPro's native system options to the new prompt. At lower menu levels, this result changes to Bar #. You type the pad or bar name in a text box just as you might type a command.

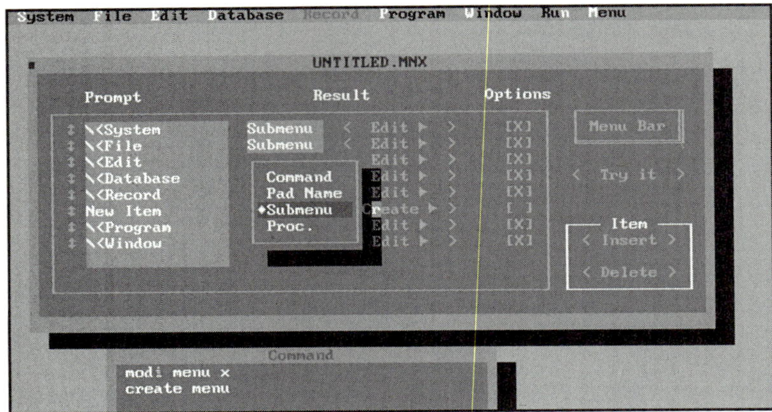

FIG. 14.6

The Menu Results selections available.

NOTE

If you look back at figure 14.4, you see the commands used to assign the various menu marks in the Command window, referring to the different bars and pads by special names. Each native element of SYSMENU is assigned a special *pad* or *bar name,* beginning with an underscore, that you and GENMENU.PRG can use to reference the element. All the bar names are available in the on-line Help file under the Menu System Names topic, as well as a complete chart in the *Language Reference* manual under an entry of the same name. FoxPro's SYS(2013) also returns a complete list of these names, should you ever need to check them quickly or need them as part of a program. Nevertheless, if you generate a Quick Menu as you are doing here, these names are entered for you. You can cut and paste the names from the Quick Menu or from the Help file without bothering to remember these names.

SYS(2013) does not provide bar, popup, and pad names for what are sometimes called the *conditional* menu pads in FoxPro. These options appear and disappear from the default SYSMENU as you work, depending on the task in which you are engaged. When you are MODIFYing a LABEL, REPORT, SCREEN, MENU, PROJECT, or STRUCTURE, each of these tasks has an associated menu popup. When you use the Diary, a Browse window, the Filer, Expression Builder, or Macros, each of these interface elements has an associated menu popup with specialized choices.

FoxPro does not offer any access to these menu popups or any way to remove them from your SYSMENU (short of SETting SYSMENU OFF) when you are performing one of these functions. The only partial exception is Browse, possibly because programmatic equivalents exist for the Browse menu options. You cannot access the bar names on the Browse menu, but you can issue a Browse with the NOMENU clause and then arrange the Browse any way you prefer, using the command's numerous clauses and switches. You can create your own Browse menu popup offering these options to your users.

The fourth Result selection is Proc. (procedure). If you choose Proc., the rightmost column again contains a push button with the prompt `Create`. If you select the button, the `Create` prompt changes to `Edit` and a text-editing window appears, as shown in figure 14.7. The editing window enables you to add a code snippet—just like the snippets in which you typed procedures for various objects and clauses in the Screen Builder—which is executed when you later choose this menu item.

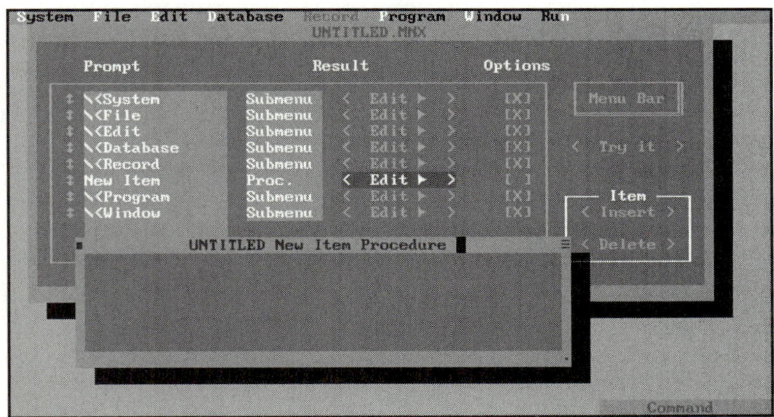

FIG. 14.7

Creating a procedure for a menu option.

In FoxPro 2.5, GENMENU uses the same #INSERT and #NAME generator directives as GENSCRN (refer to table 13.1 for instructions). Using the capabilities to #INSERT an external text file provides instructions for a common procedure. Giving a procedure an explicit #NAME ensures that your program can call the procedure. Both these features are particularly handy features in a menu.

Placing Prompts on the Screen

At the far left of the Prompt column in the Quick Menu, you see double-headed arrows typical of a FoxPro list that contains items you can shuffle. You may need to alter the relative positions of menu items many times before you are satisfied with the order. To move the menu items up and down in the list, you can drag the arrows, or press the Ctrl key and the up- or down-arrow key when the cursor rests in any column.

Assigning Other Attributes

One more column, labeled Options, is located at the far right side of the screen. If you select a check box from this column, the Options dialog appears so that you can assign more attributes to this menu choice.

Assigning Menu Shortcuts

A *menu shortcut* dialog is shown in figure 14.8, along with the Options dialog. Unlike menu hot keys, which you can use only when the menu is currently active (after you press Alt or F10, or double-right-click the mouse so that FoxPro expects the next keystroke to belong to the menu), menu shortcuts are active all the time, as long as the menu choice to which they belong is not disabled. For this reason, you cannot use single letters and other keys as shortcuts. Shortcuts are always combination keypresses, such as Alt+S, the default for the System pad, or Ctrl+A, default shortcut for the Select All text option. (Imagine assigning the single keypress *A* as a shortcut and then trying to type in an Edit region!)

When you press the combination of keys you want to assign, the combination appears in the Key Label text box. Then you can move the cursor into the Key Text box with the Tab key or the mouse and type the reminder of the shortcut that you want to appear in the menu popup next to the prompt.

TIP Be sure to assign menu shortcuts (usually Alt plus an initial letter) to the menu pad options you designate with the \< prompt option. Using \< highlights the next letter, but the highlight is cosmetic and does not assign the menu shortcut automatically.

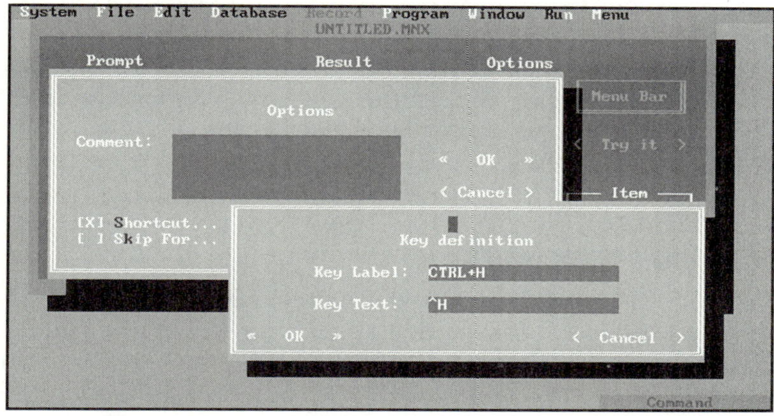

FIG. 14.8

The Menu Item Options and the subsidiary shortcut dialogs.

Setting the Menu Skip For Option

Choosing Skip For from the Options dialog brings up the Expression Builder, which you have already used in the RQBE, the Report Writer, and the Label Designer. This expression should evaluate to a logical value. When the expression evaluates to .T., the menu option becomes disabled, and when the expression evaluates to .F., the menu option becomes available for use.

You have many different ways to test for the suitability of a menu option. The window functions can be helpful here. For certain edit or dialog windows, you can disable some items if the WVISIBLE( ) function returns .T. You also can disable an option if a test of RDLEVEL( ), the function that tells you how many nested READs are currently in progress, returns a result greater than a particular number. You can disable an option if certain tables are either USED( ) or NOT USED( ). The important thing, as previously indicated, is to disable and enable options according to a logical pattern both discernible and predictable from the users' point of view.

NOTE The Skip For Options dialog feature generates a SKIP FOR clause on a menu option-defining command. Don't confuse the SKIP FOR clause with the command SET SKIP OF <menu option > <logical expression>. The SKIP FOR clause, available through the Menu Builder in the Options dialog, is evaluated dynamically, which means that as the value of the condition changes, so does the enabling or disabling of various menu options. SET SKIP OF conditions are evaluated

continues

once, at the time the command is issued. If the value of these conditions changes later, the pad or bar doesn't change to match. If you use both the SKIP FOR clause and SET SKIP command for the same menu option, the SKIP FOR clause always takes precedence because it's constantly reevaluated.

Setting the Menu Mark

The Mark check box was discussed in a previous section of this chapter. Use it to assign a character that appears on-screen when you SET MARK of this menu option TO .T.. Choosing this check box brings up the same modified ASCII table you used to pick special characters for Box objects in the Report Writer.

Assigning the Pad Name or Bar

The Pad Name option (replaced by a Bar # option in other menu levels) is similar to the Window Name option in the Screen Builder. By default, GENMENU creates names for all the elements of the menu, just as GENSCRN creates window titles and procedure names, but the Menu and Screen Builders enable you to name the items if you want to refer to these names in procedures you write. If you choose Pad Name or Bar # for the Result type (if you use the native SYSMENU elements), the pad name in the Options dialog is the same as the Result unless you edit it for reasons described in the following section.

Attaching a Menu Comment

Another option available for each single menu item is Comment, which functions in the same way here as it does in Reports, Labels, Queries, and Screens. You can keep notes to yourself here; as you'll learn in Chapter 20 when building a Help system, these notes can become the basis of a custom-designed Help file for your system. If you edit GENMENU to include new capabilities, the Comment text entry also can hold information for use in menu-generating procedures that you design.

Traversing Menu Levels

Now return from the Options dialog to the main Menu Builder window and notice in the upper-right corner the popup control that you use to move up a menu level if you are in a submenu. To move down, you select the `Edit` push button for any option that has a Submenu result. Tour the Quick Menu now and become acquainted with the structure, noticing the shortcuts in use, the hot keys, and the hierarchy of items with which you are already familiar. If you check the Menu popup frequently, you see that the second choice changes to provide a level-wide set of options appropriate to each submenu you investigate. As previously indicated and as shown in figure 14.9, level-wide options include the assignment of a popup Name, a Procedure to be used for this entire popup (except for entries on it that have Results of their own assigned), a Color Scheme, and a Mark character.

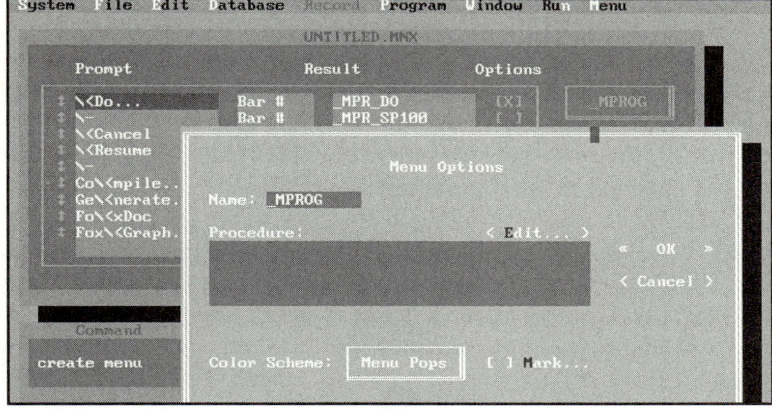

FIG. 14.9

Submenu-wide options in the Menu Builder.

Setting Menu Colors

So far, little time has been spent discussing colors and the color scheme system in FoxPro. Chapter 16 discusses the basic concepts of the color scheme system, which you can apply throughout FoxPro. In the discussion of SYSMENU, however, remember that you can choose a color scheme individually by submenu. This capability is a relatively arcane feature; different color schemes for different menu popups integrated into one SYSMENU are warranted only in special circumstances.

If you choose to alter the colors of all or part of your menu system, you may decide not to avail yourself of the Menu Builder's capability. You may want your menu or a particular popup to change colors dynamically in response to certain conditions. GENMENU is written to DEFINE each menu element with an explicit COLOR SCHEME clause. Each element's colors are fixed until that element is reDEFINEd. You can use the FoxPro color control commands to alter the color scheme that governs the menu bar and menu popups (schemes 3 and 4), and the colors of menu elements are altered immediately if you reDEFINE the appropriate menu items or respecify the colors in the appropriate schemes and reexecute the .MPR.

Setting General Options

The final options of the Menu Builder are contained in the General Options dialog. If you access this dialog now (which is available from any menu level), you find options only slightly more extensive than the choices available for submenus. Here, you can create the Procedure that executes for all menu options which have no set of instructions. You can set a Mark globally for the menu. You also can specify the Location—relative to the existing version of SYSMENU—of the menu options you are defining. The default is a complete Replace of the current SYSMENU. All other choices enable you to alter the existing SYSMENU instead. You saw how Append works when ORGANIZE and HELPTREE attached themselves to the SYSMENU. If you choose Before or After, as shown in figure 14.10, a list of the native SYSMENU pads appears so that you can place all new options exactly where you want them.

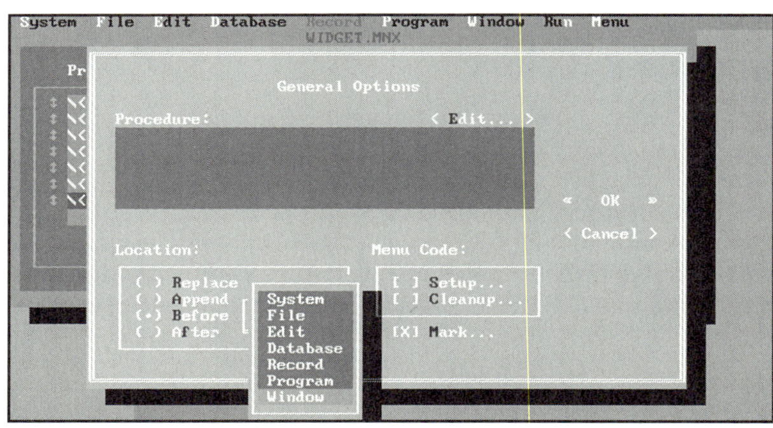

FIG. 14.10

General Options dialog in the Menu Builder.

The General Options dialog also uses check boxes that enable you to create Setup and Cleanup snippets for the SYSMENU. The Setup code for a menu can be similar to the code of a screen or screen set; you can initialize values and set up conditions that force various menu options to be enabled or disabled. (Remember that you cannot reference and alter menu elements in the Setup code because these elements aren't defined at this point of the generated program.)

The Cleanup code, however, does not function in quite the way you may expect. In screens, all the action takes place at a READ command that precedes the Cleanup code. UDFs tacked on the end of cleanup are available as subroutines of the .SPR program, which continues to be active for a long time. Menu code, in contrast, DEFINEs the components of the new SYSMENU and the action taken when you choose any of the components. Then the Cleanup code is immediately executed, and in most cases the .MPR program is no longer active. Control returns to the calling program or the interactive environment. Therefore, if you have a menu option with a Command result and if the command is to DO a procedure that you placed in the Cleanup code for the menu, you must issue the command in the following manner:

```
DO my_proc IN my_menu.mpr
```

Now, FoxPro can find the procedure when the menu option calls it, although the program MY_MENU.MPR ceased to be active as soon as the menu was DEFINEd.

If your application changes the default directory from the directory in which MY_MENU.PRG is kept, or if your menu items are meant to be added to an interactive environment, your menu commands must provide some help for FoxPro to find this program again. FoxPro provides the LOCFILE() function to enable your programs to ask the user to find files when they are not found where expected.

Look at LOCFILE()'s syntax in the file-opening code generated by GENSCRN in Chapter 13. You should use this syntax in commands you use as Results in menu code. In the preceding example, your command would be as follows:

```
DO my_proc IN LOCFILE ( "my_menu.mpr","mpr¦mpx¦app","Where is my_menu?" )
```

All LOCFILE()'s parameters are enclosed in quotation marks. The first parameter is the file that should be used. The other parameters are optional. The second is the list of extensions that FoxPro should check for files to be displayed in the LOCFILE() dialog. The third parameter is a question that can appear in the dialog to help prompt the user as he or she attempts to locate the appropriate file.

If you are distributing applications to other users, as you learn to do using the Project Manager and Distribution Kit later in this chapter, you include the .APP extension as one of the choices in LOCFILE()'s second parameter. However, for FoxPro to find a procedure included in a larger program within an .APP file, the procedure must be contained in the project's main file. Keep this restriction in mind as you build menus and decide where to position the procedures they require.

TIP If you design your menu for interactive use, adding the menu's directory to your FoxPro PATH statement is another good solution. The following code checks for a current FoxPro PATH. It tacks the directory containing the program currently running onto the end of the PATH:

```
PUBLIC m.newpath
m.newpath = SUBSTR(SYS(16),1,RAT("\", SYS(16)))
IF ! EMPTY(SET("PATH"))
   m.newpath = SET("PATH")+","+ m.newpath
ENDIF
SET PATH TO &newpath
```

If you use this procedure to change a FoxPro path for a particular operation and then want to restore the path afterwards, you use the following code:

```
IF "," $ m.newpath
    SET PATH TO (SUBSTR(m.newpath,1,RAT(",",m.newpath)-1))
ELSE
    SET PATH TO
ENDIF
```

You should alter this procedure if other programs might have changed the FoxPro path as well. (Try the STRTRAN() function to help you accomplish the job.)

Building a Sample Menu

Had enough touring? You now have looked at all the options and facilities of the Menu Builder. Exit the General Options and return to the main Menu window, where you will quickly build a rudimentary menu for the Omnipresent Widgets application. To start with a clean slate, use the `Delete` push button or the Menu popup option (the shortcut is Ctrl+E) to remove the New Item practice pad from the main menu bar.

Beginning with the System menu popup, you do not use the internal bar name _MST_HELP for Omnipresent Widget's Help system. The reasons for this step are discussed in Chapter 20, but at the moment you have not yet written a Help file for this application. Change the Help option's Result to a Command and, as the command to be run, type the following line:

```
WAIT WINDOW "Help System not yet available." NOWAIT
```

NOTE Besides providing an example of a menu option that executes a command, with this line you demonstrated a typical technique used in menu design for large systems. Although not all features are finished and available when the first changes are implemented, fleshing out the menu as fully as possible right from the beginning is helpful for both developers and users. Developers use these mock-ups to provide reminders of tasks not yet accomplished, but more important, the mock-ups help to determine the general flow of the application. Users become aware of the jobs they can eventually expect to be able to do and can provide early feedback if they spot missing pieces or task-grouping that seems to make no sense.

Because you made the first real adjustment to this menu, now save the adjusted menu to the name WIDGET.MNX.

Move to the File menu popup, where you are going to eliminate all the options here except the last three options—Printer Setup..., Print, and Quit (most of these File options become disabled while an application runs anyway). Although you are temporarily running the application menu in the interactive environment, in the Project Manager section you integrate this menu into a larger program. Removing SYSMENU options that you never plan to enable is a good idea because users otherwise find these options perplexing. These options also confuse the issue for you when you are concentrating on the menu design process.

Highlight the \<Quit and press Ctrl+C to copy it. Go back to the end of the System popup list and press Ctrl+V to paste a copy of the Quit there. Notice that the Bar # and name are not pasted along with the prompt; any connected options also are lost in the copying process. Unlike attributes of report and screen objects, you must copy these menu attributes separately (they are not attached to the prompt).

Here, you do not use the default Result of Command, nor do you use the Bar # associated with FoxPro's native Quit option. Choose Procedure for the result and enter the following code snippet:

```
IF "Support Library" $ VERSION(1)
   * DO any necessary cleanup
   QUIT
ELSE
   SET SYSMENU TO DEFAULT
   ACTIVATE WINDOW Command IN SCREEN
   * DO other cleanup
   CANCEL
ENDIF
```

If you type `WAIT WINDOW VERSION(1)`, this command (as shown in figure 14.11 along with the code snippet you are creating) returns the version and serial number of the FoxPro versions you are currently running. This simple test looks for identification "Support Library", which is found in all VERSION(1) returns under FoxPro's Distribution Kit, discussed in a following section of this chapter. If this menu is run under any of the Distribution Kit facilities rather than under the development version of FoxPro you are now using, a QUIT command takes the user directly to DOS. (The comment in the code reminds you to do any necessary cleanup first; you learn more about the kinds of chores likely to be included, in following sections of this chapter and in Chapter 18.) The Distribution Kit options enable users to run precreated and compiled programs, and no interactive environment exists here to drop back into.

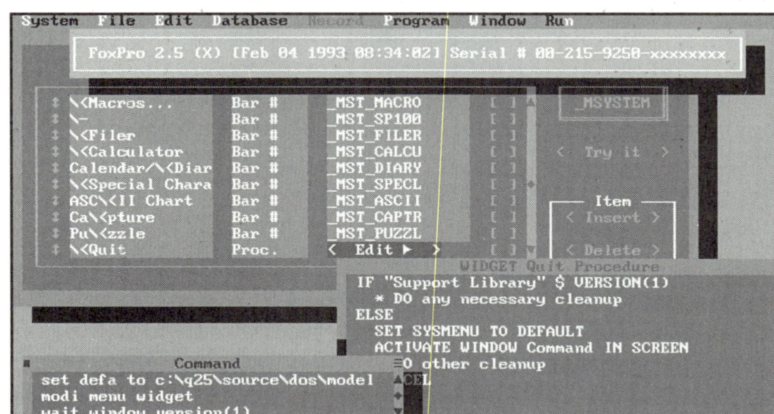

FIG. 14.11

Creating a Quit procedure in the menu.

T I P

Although for the moment the menu may not do much good outside the development version environment, providing for distributed applications separately is a good habit to form. A common approach is to create two Quit options: an Exit to Fox choice and a Quit to DOS choice. You can add "Support Library" $ VERSION(1) as the Skip For condition of the Exit to Fox option, which disables this choice when the menu is executed under a distributed application.

There is a second, vitally important reason to check VERSION(1) for distributable applications: if the support library files for a distributed application are not from the same version or *build date* of FoxPro as your development copy, changes made to the product can produce unexpected (and infelicitous) results. If you distribute applications, always make sure you acquire an updated Distribution Kit whenever you update the development version of FoxPro. Your distributed applications should also check VERSION(1), unless they are stand-alone executable files (which are distributed without support library files, as explained later in the chapter). Otherwise, the applications may run with a different set of support files than you intended.

If the user is running the development version of FoxPro, as you are doing now, an extremely important provision you must make is to provide at least a minimal recovery path after you edit SYSMENU. Without explicitly restoring the Command window, as you do in the ELSE portion of the preceding example procedure, you may lose access to the Command window if you remove references to this window in SYSMENU! Set up a special hot-key procedure as a panic button, by typing the following command in the Command window before you start testing the revised window:

```
ON KEY LABEL Alt-F9 SET SYSMENU TO DEFAULT
```

(Substitute any key combination you prefer.) The Quit option may suffice, and you can set up a shortcut to perform the same function as the previous ON KEY LABEL command.

Always separate the Quit option from other menu choices; insert another bar before it and type `\-` as the Prompt. You don't need to make any other change; the Result is irrelevant to a separator bar.

Returning to the File popup option, highlight and copy the Bar # for the Print option (_MFI_PRINT). You also are going to move this option to a new position on the menu, and now that you know the entire line is not pasted together, you may as well save yourself the trouble of remembering the Bar designation because the prompt is easier. On the main menu bar, insert a new pad. Type the prompt `\<Utilities` and accept the default Result for a main menu pad, Submenu. Use the Options dialog to assign a shortcut of Alt+U to this pad (it doesn't matter what the key text says because the reminders won't show on the main menu bar). Now edit this submenu by providing the submenu with the first bar: type `\<Print...` for the prompt, assign a Result of Bar #, and finally, press Ctrl+V to paste the bar name into the accompanying text box. Repeat the procedure to add a Printer \<Setup... bar to this popup.

TIP

You use this menu in the interactive environment, but the behavior of _MFI_SETUP, like the native bar _MST_HELP, is problematic under programmatic control. The option is enabled only when a text-editing window (such as a MODIFY MEMO) is foremost. Refer to the section on printer drivers in Chapter 16 for information on SET PDSETUP TO, a more flexible programmatic equivalent for summoning the printer driver dialogs.

You now can delete the File pad from the menu bar. Eliminate the Program pad completely, too, but keep the Edit popup unchanged because you might edit Memo fields and other text in the application. The Edit options are valuable during any text editing.

On the Record pad, you want to keep all the entries that search for data because you provided no mechanisms for this procedure in these programs. You can eliminate the entries that edit data (Append, Change, Replace, Delete, and Recall). You can add the Pack and Reindex options from the Database pad in the same way you moved Print. Perhaps you also should make a change in the Prompt of this pad to make it plural; Records better describes the function. For the Window pad, you may change more than the prompt (for which the plural might be better, as with the Records pad); you also may change the way in which FoxPro refers to the Windows pad. Edit the Pad Name in the Options dialog. This new version will behave differently from the native Window menu popup; it will not provide the names of all the active windows on the popup. (You may not want the user switching windows by using the menu.) A menu name is required, but any name will do for this pad, except the native system name. Move this pad to the bottom of the pad list (which puts it on the right end of the menu).

You are probably eager for a look at the revised menu. In the Menu Builder, you do not look at a canvas on which you arrange the objects as you do in the Screen Builder and Report Writer. The Menu Builder's format does not permit you to see the results of the work as you proceed, and visualizing the effects of each change you make is crucial in the design process. Fortunately, you don't have to regenerate a menu program file whenever you want to check the work. Notice the `Try it` push button in the main menu design window. If you select `Try it` now or at any time, the current SYSMENU appears to become the menu you are building. You can click all options and see all the submenus. If you select an option with a Command result, the Try It dialog displays the associated command. These are images only; you cannot run this altered SYSMENU until you generate and install this new menu in place of the default. When you choose Done from the Try It dialog, the real SYSMENU reappears, and you are placed in the Menu window again (see fig. 14.12).

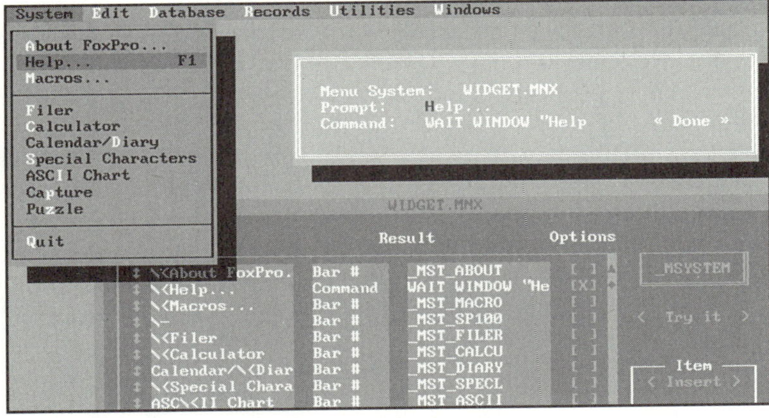

FIG. 14.12
Using the Try it option in the Menu Builder, you can check your work.

As you probably have figured out, you need a menu pad that enables you to access the screen sets and perform data entry in this system. Insert a pad between Edit and Database, typing `\<Tables` at thePrompt. As the first entry in the submenu, type `\<Budget Entries` and assign it the Command result DO BUDGET.SPR. You separate it from data entry for the lookup tables with a separator bar (\-) and then add similar entries for \<Products, Budget \<Categories, \<Departments, and all the other tables in the database (you can find a list of these tables in Appendix H). Type the appropriate command for the tables that have screen sets already built for them. Assigning a WAIT WINDOW

command to each bar that doesn't have an associated screen set would be silly, however; just edit the Table Menu Options as a whole to supply a Procedure for this menu level (type `WAIT WINDOW "Data Entry not yet available for this Table."`), and you make the change for all the tables. Remember that any individual bar instructions supersede this procedure.

Returning to the top level of the menu, use the Options dialog for the Tables pad to provide a shortcut by pressing Alt+T. You also use this dialog's option to supply a Skip For condition; when the Expression Builder appears, type the expression `RDLEVEL( ) > 0`.

The RDLEVEL() > 0 expression prevents more than one screen set from being active at a time. With more sophisticated methods, you can edit multiple screen sets at the same time. For now, you need a safeguard to prevent multiple READs from causing a problem.

Now move the Database pad between the Records and Utilities items and rename this pad to Resu\<lts because you will retain the pad options that may properly be considered output, and you are adding the other forms of output here. Notice that the letter *L* is used as the highlighted shortcut key because you already used the initial letter—and all the other letters found in the word Results. Giving two different menu options the same shortcut name is bad program design. Don't forget to add the shortcut Alt+L in the Options; just designating the highlighted letter doesn't work. Change the Pad Name here, too, so that the behavior is controlled by you and not by the internal system definition.

From the Database options, you keep Browse, Average, Count, Sum, and Calculate. Note that these options are available only when you are not currently involved in a READ operation. If no table is open, using the native Browse option enables you to open one of these options but gives you no mechanism for choosing another, so you must add immediately below Browse a Close \<Table bar that performs a simple USE command. This choice is not automatically disabled when you are in a READ because the choice isn't a native System option, so add a Skip For condition of RDLEVEL() > 0 as well.

NOTE Because having an active BROWSE doesn't increase RDLEVEL() and doesn't prevent accessing the Tables pad—and because of the way you named the windows—a slight bug exists in the menu as currently set up. If you are BROWSing the Budget table and then choose to enter Budget data, BUDGET.SPR will crash. The application already sees a window defined with the name Budget because this name also is the title of the system-created Browse window and doesn't DEFINE a new window. You can remedy this problem easily by regenerating the BUDGET.SPR file after adding the following line at the beginning of the BUDGET.SCX's Setup snippet:

```
#REDEFINE
```

Refer to table 13.1, on the Screen Builder generator directives, if you need help.

Setting an order in the table you were BROWSing, without going to a great deal of trouble about it, might be a nice choice. You may remember a choice like this in FoxApp-generated applications. This feature was produced by a screen named GETORDER, which you can find in the \FOXAPP\SCREENS directory under the main FoxPro program directory. If you generated PRODUCT.APP in your MODEL directory, following instructions in Chapter 1, you already have a copy of this screen in your MODEL directory.

If you don't have this screen in your MODEL directory, you can type `MODIFY SCREEN ?` in the Command window to find and then use the screen to generate a GETORDER.SPR; when you name the output file, be careful that you specify the MODEL directory in which you keep the application!

Add a new option to the Records popup by typing `\<Order...` for the prompt and `DO GETORDER.SPR` for the command, and you're finished. This way, you give the users a quick way to check any table in the system and use the other (calculation) options on the pad while the table is active.

Ordinarily, you also may want to offer a Reports option similar to FoxApp's, which can specify an output device, enable the user to choose reports, and enable the user to indicate whether to use the associated printer driver setup, no setup, or a different setup when the output is sent to the printer. You can look at FoxApp's GETDEST, PRTOPTS, and PRTSETUP screens for some examples of dialogs that offer these choices to users. You also may want to think about creating a special table that holds all the report, label, and query names, and perhaps even holds the model report and label files in Memo fields so that users can edit these files and add new entries. You can use a description field as the PROMPT FIELD for a POPUP that can be ACTIVATEd to enable the users to choose available entries.

Many other additional items exist that you can put on the application menu; you can create a *Filter-builder* like the one in the BROWSER.SCX in the LASER sample application. You also can make other Utilities pad entries, enabling you to create files in a user-specified data directory and to perform other tasks previously suggested. You have already built a great deal of flexibility into the application menu, and you practiced with all the options the Menu Builder offers. You can gradually expand your knowledge of this tool as you build more complex menus for your applications.

For now, just put one Budget report on the Results menu and opt to send the results to the screen. Add Budget \<Report by Product, or a similar prompt, to the bottom of the Results submenu. If the last-saved MODELP.FRX contains the variable big_item, which you initialized outside the report to mark certain items, make sure that the feature is available as part of the reporting Procedure, as shown in the following example:

```
* first find out if the variable exists; they
* may have already created one and you don't want
* to override the current value if they have
IF TYPE("big_item") = "U"
   big_item = 0
ENDIF
* Now find out what value they want to use; this
* screen file is a generic "question"-asker to which
* you pass a question, the name of the variable to
* hold the answer (which you initialize first), and
* a PICTURE clause if you want to use one to format
* the answer. It can look like anything you want,
* and you'll find the simple snippets it requires listed
* in Appendix H.
* DO ask.spr WITH "Smallest entry to mark:", ;
    big_item,"99999"
* Or, if you generate the ASK.SCX screen with
* the extension PRG, you can use ASK as a UDF:
big_item = ASK("Smallest entry to mark:", ;
               big_item,"99999" )
REPORT FORM Modelp PREVIEW ENVIRONMENT
```

You now are ready to generate and install the menu code. If you're in the main Menu window, the Generate... bar should be active on the Program menu popup. Select the Generate... option, and the dialog in figure 14.13 appears. (The last code snippet—the procedure for the Budget Report option—shows at the bottom of the screen.) Again, fewer choices are available here than you have with the Screen Builder; after making sure that the output file is going to the appropriate directory and specifying Comments style as you did before (if you want to use this feature), go ahead and generate the menu code.

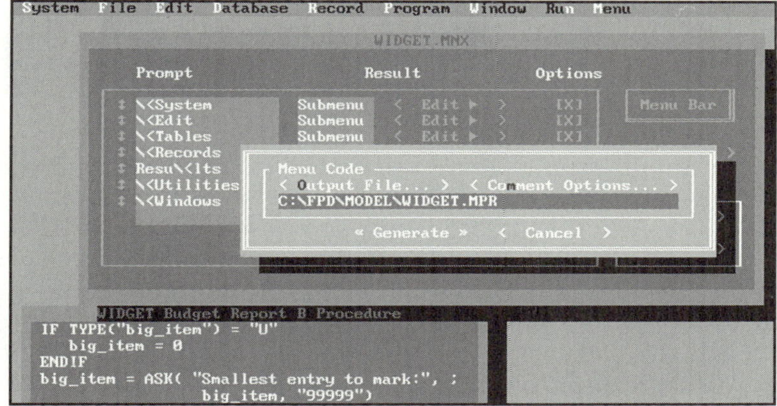

FIG. 14.13

GENMENU's Option dialog.

You can type the command MODIFY COMMAND widget.mpr to look at the structure of a generated menu program. This code is straightforward, although SYSMENU's component menu approach requires quite a few different commands. Helptree has a suboption that enables you to peruse, as a group, all the Menus And Popups commands and functions.

For now, however, you probably want to DO widget.mpr instead and see what happens.

You still have access to the Command window, but this altered SYSMENU makes some options accessible and others inaccessible, depending on the current action. In figure 14.14, the Tables menu pad is disabled because you are currently involved in a READ, and the two options on the Utilities pad also are disabled by default. The Command window looks as though you can use it—you can click and type in the Command window—but no commands are executed while the READ is in progress.

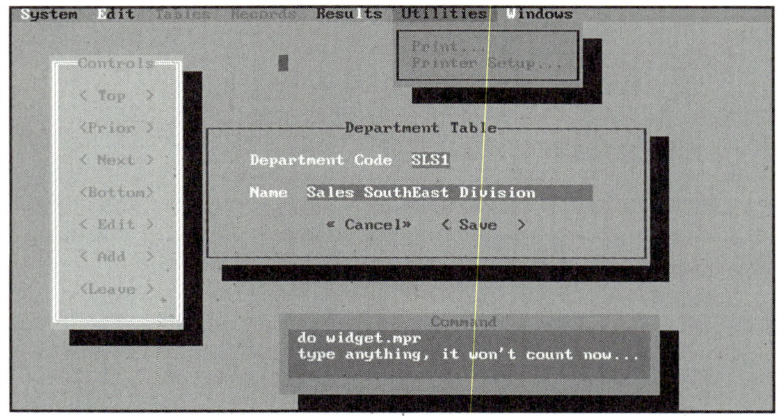

FIG. 14.14

Data entry in the revised SYSMENU. Note that the Utilities options are unavailable because a READ is in progress.

As you try out the menu options, you probably notice that the Product table's data-entry system should be redesigned to match the two lookup tables, Budcat and Dept, whose screen sets you designed, so that you can add records in the table's data-entry system. (None of these screen sets are designed with deletion of records available because lookup codes should rarely be removed from a system. If you want to add this capability, always be sure that none of the related tables contain records that use the lookup code you are removing.)

When you BROWSE the Budget table using the Results menu popup option, you may receive an error (`"DO_SHOW.PRG does not exist"`) if you have previously run the Budget data-entry program. The error occurs because the native BROWSE bar (_MDA_BROW) issues the command BROWSE LAST. As you learned in Chapter 8, BROWSE LAST is a special type of BROWSE PREFERENCE command, which looks for a PREFERENCE record with the same Name as the current table's alias (Budget, in this case). If this PREFERENCE record has been stored automatically in the Resource file during the execution of BUDGET.SPR, the record contains a reference to DO_SHOW(), the WHEN clause for the BROWSE in that screen. Since DO_SHOW() is a UDF in the BUDGET.SPR file, rather than a stand-alone program in the MODEL directory, the BROWSE LAST can't find the function.

You have two choices: you can move DO_SHOW() from the cleanup code of the .SPR file to a stand-alone .PRG named DO_SHOW.PRG, or you can change the menu option to a Command Result, which issues the command BROWSE. Without the LAST clause, the problem will not occur.

Although a WHEN DO_SHOW() clause will not do any harm for the Budget BROWSE as issued by the BROWSE LAST, changing the native bar _MDA_BROW Result to the Command Result of BROWSE is the better choice since you then have the flexibililty to add other options to this Result later if you want to fine-tune the menu option's behavior. In experiencing this problem, however, you have learned a basic rule about the native bar options: they often have built-in behavior that isn't optimal in an application. Although you start off using these native options, as you develop skill with the Menu Builder you find that they all can be replaced by Commands and Procedures you can control without concern for unintended side effects. You see another example of native menu option behavior, and its replacement by much better FoxPro commands, in Chapter 20's discussion of the FoxPro Help system.

In figure 14.15, however, you BROWSE the Budget table, and the Print option is available (as the figure shows, you even can print the contents of the current Memo field because the field is open in a window). The Command window also is perfectly usable, except when a dialog is active (this behavior is normal). While you BROWSE, you can choose the Order option or any other option from the Records pad or the calculation options, which are part of the Results. You may like to try using the Average option to store the average of the Budget.Budgetamt field values to the variable name big_item. As shown in figure 14.16, you then can run the Report on Budget entry with this number as the default amount; all budget items greater than or equal to the average amount are marked on the report.

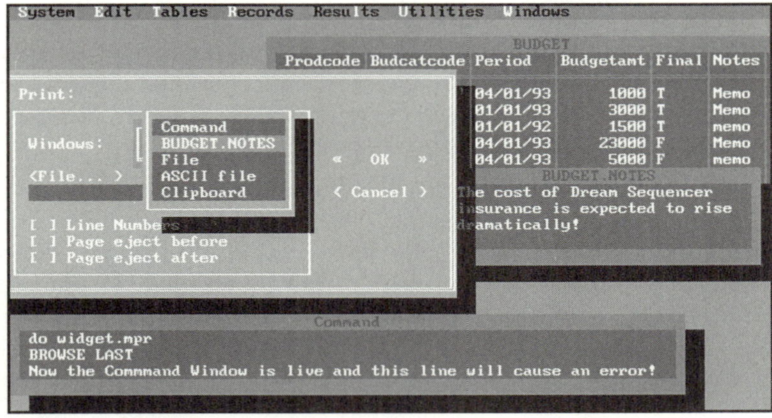

FIG. 14.15

Choosing the Print option while a BROWSE is in progress.

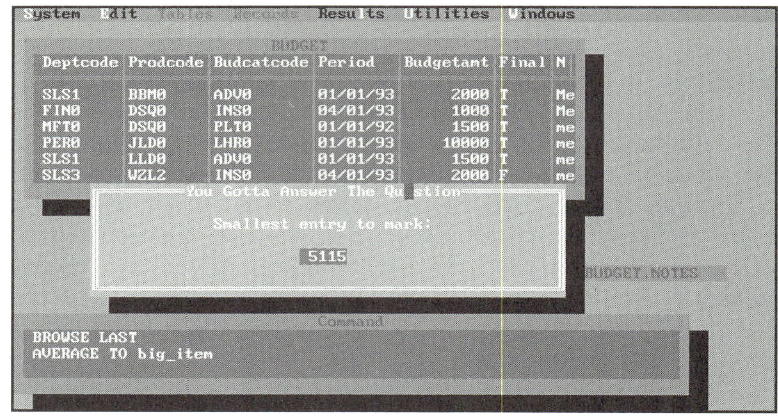

FIG. 14.16

After preparing an average Budget amount, the user prints a report from a menu option and gets a modal dialog requesting a number required by the report.

Techniques for Making an Altered Menu Available

You may need a little time to get used to which System options are disabled during a READ, which additional options you created that ought to be disabled, and which options can safely work together. You already noted that a modal dialog or READ requires a conclusion before further work can be done. All other choices in the FoxPro interface, including menu options that start new tasks, are disabled. You also may find a need to create modal READs in your own programs, with similar behavior.

SYSMENU's options are disabled when you issue the READ MODAL command, except for some that are universally relevant (for example, the Edit features). However, you can reenable other menu options deliberately by executing the .MPR program again in the WHEN clause of the modal READ.

If you take this step, you must make sure that no inappropriate actions can be taken, by disabling single menu items selectively. Alternatively, design a special, limited pad just for the modal READ, using the Menu option to append to the current menu rather than replacing, much as the native FoxPro activities, such as the Report Writer, add a pad to SYSMENU. DO this special .MPR in the READ WHEN clause, and RELEASE the extra PAD in the Cleanup of the modal READ. You see that the previous menu options are disabled, but the special pad with activities pertinent to this READ are accessible.

You have still a third approach: leave the special modal READ's menu at the default of Replace and use the READ WHEN to execute this menu.

When you exit the READ, your original menu magically reappears. Modal READs have a special property: they automatically send the current menu to a *stack* in memory and restore the menu from that stack when the READ concludes. This property is probably the means by which the MODAL READs accomplish their automatic menu-disabling; the menu works when executed in the READ WHEN because the internal PUSH MENU has already occurred.

At times, you may want to manipulate the menu stack yourself. The explicit commands to save a menu definition to a stack and restore it later, matching the behavior of READ MODAL, are PUSH MENU _MSYSMENU and POP MENU _MSYSMENU. (Similarly, you save and restore ON KEY LABEL assignments with PUSH and POP KEY, as you learn in the next chapter.)

The Quit procedure you wrote in the Widget application menu SETs SYSMENU TO DEFAULT; you can replace this command with POP MENU _MSYSMENU, with a corresponding PUSH MENU _MSYSMENU in the Setup code of the menu program. This approach enables you to restore any customizing of the menu.

SET SYSMENU TO DEFAULT, however, does not necessarily restore to a static version of the System menu. FoxPro also contains a SET SYSMENU SAVE command, which makes the current version of SYSMENU the one restored with a SET SYSMENU TO DEFAULT command. Personalize the System menu with your favorite tools in the positions you prefer, SET SYSMENU SAVE, and SET SYSMENU TO DEFAULT always brings you back to this version of the menu. (Use SET SYSMENU NOSAVE to return SYSMENU to its original state when you next use the SET SYSMENU TO DEFAULT command.)

TIP

Fox Software added SET SYSMENU SAVE to the language several months after the initial version of FoxPro 2.0 to facilitate adding the Run pad to the basic System menu. The Run pad isn't really part of the base product; it's a FoxPro .APP created to bring together all the ways of executing FoxPro options in one place. The Run pad also gave FoxPro users menu access to FoxApp for the first time.

The Run pad may not be a significant improvement to the product. Although we don't receive the source code, you could create your own Run pad easily enough, with menu bar Results of commands such as the following:

continues

continued

```
REPORT FORM GETFILE("frx","Report to run:","Run",1)
```

The improvements that were made to the base product to support the Run pad, however, are far more significant. FoxPro now looks for an .APP to run on startup as it loads. By default, this .APP is called FOXSTART.APP, and the FOXSTART.APP Microsoft supplies defines the Run pad and issues the SET SYSMENU SAVE command. You can, however, use the _STARTUP= option in your CONFIG.FP to change the name, location, and contents of this file to anything you want.

These features join the venerable COMMAND= option to enable you to perform activities when Fox loads, with an important difference: whereas COMMAND= is obviated by a program you tell FoxPro to execute from the DOS command line, the _STARTUP/FOXSTART application you designate still executes before the other program runs. Use it to set up your SYSMENU and other initial working conditions any way you want.

Understanding the significance of the menu stack and its connection to modal READs is about as complicated as FoxPro menus get. After you create one or two menus and develop a personal style, not even this point can pose much of a problem. Generating a menu in the Menu Builder makes one of the most tedious and time-consuming parts of developing an application an enjoyable exercise.

You move on now to the Project Manager to learn how to acquire control over other kinds of details during the development cycle.

Keeping Files Together with the Project Manager

When you look back over this investigation of the other tools, you realize that you created a motley collection of small files with all kinds of extensions and all kinds of formats. How can you know which files you need to create a transportable application that you can share with others? The Project Manager does this for you, and so easily that you're probably going to laugh out loud the first time you try it.

One or two tricks are available that you cover in the following chapters, but you can build the first project right now, before you learn more new techniques or the meaning of a single Project Manager control or option.

Create a new file of Project type, as you previously created menus, screens, and other files. In figure 14.17, you see the window, which isn't much except an empty box ready to display the Name and Type of this application's files after you add them. The Add button is the only button currently available. The shortcut is Ctrl+A (usually the Select All keypress, but you can't edit anything right now). Choose the button or the shortcut to add a file.

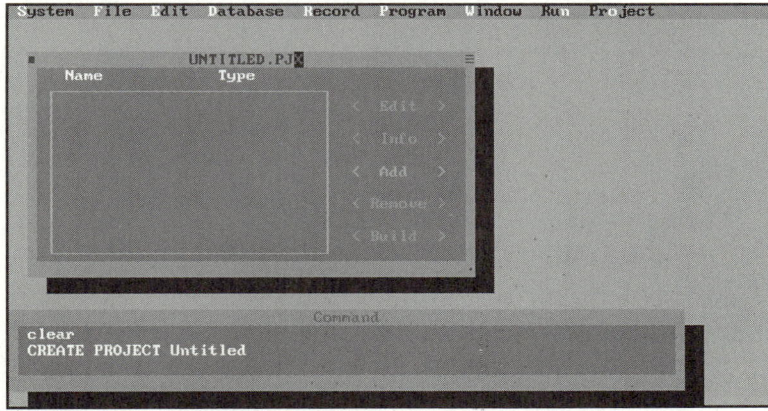

FIG. 14.17
Beginning work in the Project Manager.

A file dialog appears. From the files of Menu type, select the file WIDGET.MNX and confirm the choice. The name WIDGET and the type Menu appear in the main Project window. A character between these words indicates that this file is currently the *main file* for the project.

You are, for all intents, done. You may think you still have to tell the Project Manager about all the other files, but this tool finds out about these other files by checking the references to other files in the menu file. Select the Build push button, and the Build dialog appears. You return to this dialog later; for now, however, just accept the default choice (Build Project). You are asked to supply a name for the file. The name WIDGET is fine, and the Project Manager supplies the default extension of .PJX.

Confirm the choice and watch the Project Manager begin to work.

When the Project Manager finds a reference to GETORDER (the screen you borrowed from FoxApp), it gets stuck unless GETORDER.SCX is in the MODEL directory. The Project Manager needs access to the original source files, which are tables in the cases of menus and screens, not the generated programs. You may even have added GETORDER.SPR to the MODEL directory, but the Project Manager must find the .SCX file so that this file can be checked later. The Project Manager regenerates the .SPR anytime you have made changes to it—without your needing to do it yourself.

When you see the screen shown in figure 14.18, choose the `Locate` option. You have an opportunity to point the Project Manager towards GETORDER.SCX in the \GOODIES\FOXAPP\SCREENS directory.

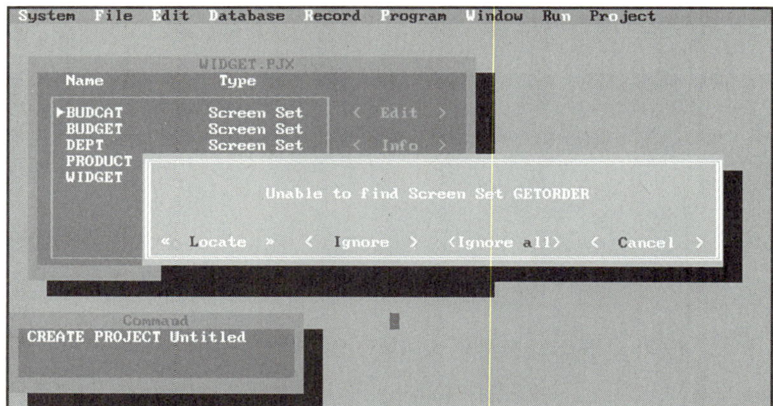

FIG. 14.18

The Project Manager needs you to choose Locate to find the GETORDER.SCX file in the FOXAPP subdirectory.

After you find the GETORDER.SCX file, the Project Manager continues the Build process. As you see in figure 14.19, all the files are here—even the UDFs in the screen code snippets and reports! Figure 14.19 also shows a screen of Project Information (with the shortcut Ctrl+J) available from the Project menu pad, which provides a handy summary of the kinds and the status of files you are using in this application. Using the shortcut (Ctrl+I) or the information push button (`Info`) also displays on-screen detailed information on any file that you highlight in the project.

NOTE

If you move files around in the directory structure, you must repeat the Locate process. Fortunately, after you locate one file in a previously unknown directory during a Build process, the Project Manager is smart enough to check in this directory for other files as it works (you don't need to use the Locate feature for each file in the directory).

If you take over a project from another developer, you may need to go through the same process. The Project Manager has a *home directory* feature that makes the search slightly more automatic. This feature is discussed in a following section.

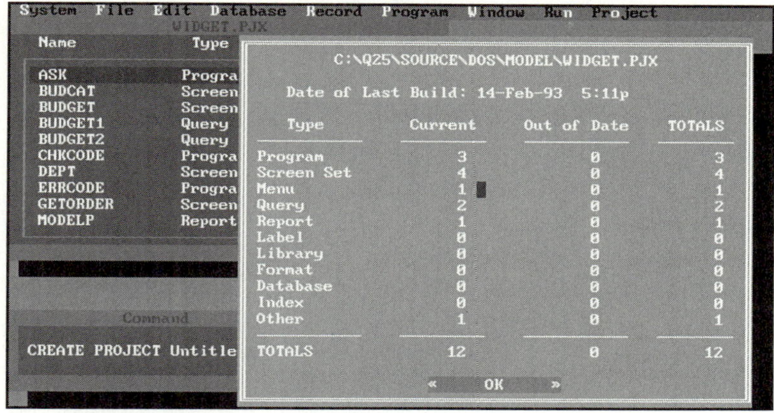

FIG. 14.19

The Build process is completed, and the Project contains the files needed to execute the Widget application.

Selecting the highlighted file (double-click or press Enter), however, enables you to edit the file, regardless of the type, from within the Project Manager. Editing files in this manner has several advantages, including the overview and perspective you can maintain on the application's development. Another important benefit of editing while in the Project Manager is that screen set options are saved through the Project Manager. You may remember that, although you used default settings for the screen options (Define Windows, Open Files, and so on), you had to rearrange the windows in their relative positions and remind GENSCRN that you wanted to add the control panel as a second screen in the set each time you regenerated the .SPRs by using the Generate... option of the Program menu popup. Screen files do not save settings because a given .SCX file may be used with many different applications. Each project saves these settings instead and generates the appropriate .SPR code.

Create screen set options now for the DEPT.SCX and BUDCAT.SCX files, making sure that the screen lists appear as shown in figure 14.20. This means that the CONTROLM screen should appear first, followed by the appropriate data-entry screens. (Using the `Edit` button in the dialog shown in figure 14.20, you can access the Screen Builder and open each screen in the set for further modifications if necessary.) You should check the following Code Options: Open Files, Close Files, Define Windows, Release Windows, and Read Cycle. Arrange the screens to your liking, as well.

For the BUDGET.SCX file, make sure that the same Code Options are in effect. If you did not add the extra line of code suggested previously for the Setup snippet, you can edit the screen now. Add the BUDGBROW.SCX image window to the screen set (this time, the order of the screens doesn't matter) and choose `Arrange`.

Isn't knowing that you never again have to perform these steps for this particular screen set a reassuring thought?

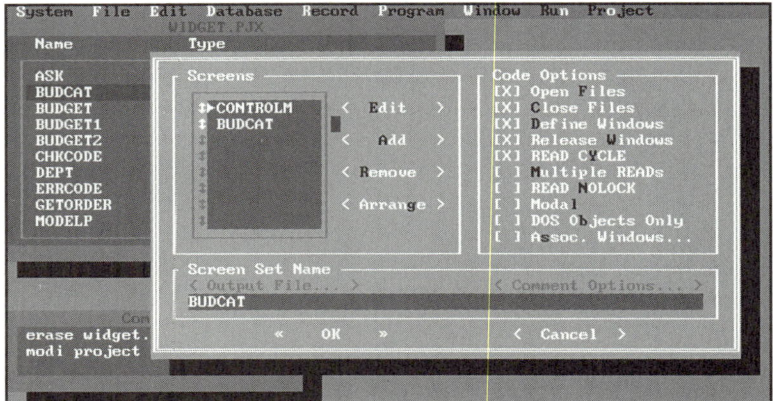

FIG. 14.20

By creating screen set options through the Project Manager, you permanently save the options.

CAUTION: You can BUILD PROJECT <project name> FROM <main file> in a program or in the Command window, giving the Project Manager the main file name to start with and any others you want to include explicitly. If you perform this step, all the screen settings and all other options you previously set for this project will be lost! Use this command when you really want to build a project from scratch or when you are in a low-memory situation. If you get a memory error message when you choose Rebuild Project in the Project Manager dialog, you can issue a BUILD PROJECT command instead. You then can enter your screen settings and options for any new screen sets that the Project Manager has pulled in for the first time because of new references to these screen sets in your programs. If necessary because of extremely limited memory, USE the project as a table and edit your settings directly in its records.

After you finish editing the screens, choose Rebuild Project again. You see that the Project Manager is very selective in the files chosen to regenerate. This option generates only the .SPR files because you performed no edits of the menu.

Now you need to take one more step. As you see in figure 14.21, the second radio button in the Project Build dialog is Build Application. You must "build" the application from the project's files to be able to DO the application.

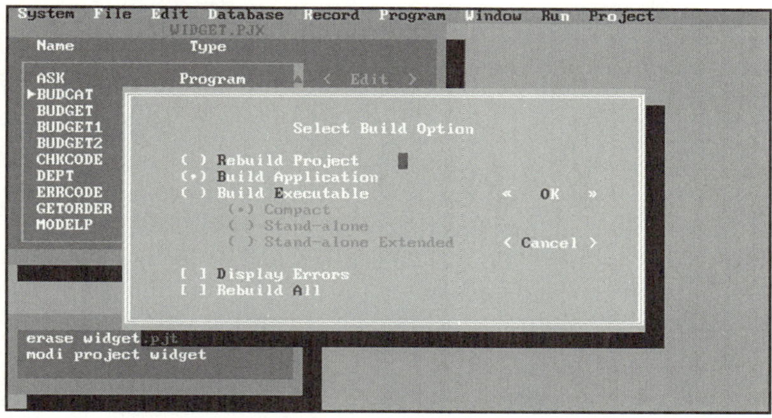

FIG. 14.21

The Project Build dialog.

This option is where the .APP files you used among the FoxPro sample applications and the FoxApp-generated application are created. An .APP file is a compiled version of all the programs necessary to run an application. You need to distribute only this file—as opposed to a collection of compiled .SPXs (compiled screen files), .FXPs (compiled programs), .MPXs (compiled menus), and so on—to the users of this application.

When you build an application, you see a request for a file name. You can accept the default (which is the name of the project accompanied by the .APP extension), and the Build process begins. Building an application is all you need to do!

Building an application incorporates all the file regeneration required by any editing you have done since your last build. Just like Rebuild Project, Build Application is selective and never regenerates files that have not changed. It is more convenient to go directly to Build Application and omit the Project Rebuild step entirely. Also, the BUILD APPLICATION command, which you can issue from the Command window, does not destroy your Project setting as the BUILD PROJECT FROM <main file> command does. You can BUILD APP <filename> FROM <project filename> from the Command window for a safe, convenient way to rebuild a project at any time.

TIP

Like BUILD PROJECT, BUILD APP from the Command window takes less memory than loading the Project Manager and accessing the Build dialog. If you run FoxPro (whether the DOS or Windows version) as the fifth or sixth program in your Microsoft Windows environment, you'll appreciate the difference.

Project Options and Alternatives

Although the preceding section implies that Project contains all the files needed for the application, this statement is, in two senses, not strictly true.

First, the Project does not actually contain the source code (the .SCXs, .PRGs, and so on), but contains *references* to the code, when the code was last edited and where the code is kept, so that the code can be used for version comparisons and application generation. If you want others to work with your project and be able to edit the source code, you must supply the source files along with the .PJX/.PJT.

Second, you may notice that the Project does not even contain references to the data files. By default, a Project is concerned with the *readonly* files used to build the .APP file. You can hardly compile editable files into the .APP file as if these files were programs because the user cannot modify the .APP file. You need to give users copies of all editable files, separately, along with the .APP file unless your installation procedures create the data files.

The Project Manager guesses at which files are readonly and which are editable when the project is being built, omitting tables and indexes and including just about everything else. If you have a readonly table or a modifiable report form, just overrule the program's judgment! Use the `Add` (Ctrl+A) option to explicitly include the readonly table. (The application's Help file is a good candidate.) Don't, however, be too quick to use the `Remove` (Ctrl+V) option to take out the .FRX file; remember that it is very convenient to keep tabs on an application's requirements by storing information about all the necessary files in the Project table. You can incorporate the editable files into a Project and prevent these files from becoming a readonly part of the .APP by using the Exclude option for any file. If you mistakenly exclude a file, just include the file again. Press Ctrl+C to toggle a file's status between Include and Exclude. You may find it convenient to add all the data files to a project and mark them as excluded.

TIP Although the Project Manager usually is considered a developer's tool, its capability to manage all the files needed for one task or database can make it valuable—even if you never compile an application. Because you can select any files (including data tables) for editing from the Project Manager's file list, a Project can be thought of as a super View window that is not restricted to table setup. If you have worked in early versions of Xbase, you may be familiar with the SET CATALOG command, a close cousin to SET VIEW. FoxPro's Projects perform the same function as Catalogs, in a more sophisticated way.

Whether you use the Project Manager to organize your own personal database tasks or to distribute applications, you find an added bonus in that the .PJX files it uses are just ordinary FoxPro tables, like .SCXs and .FRXs. If you list all files (including editable tables and indexes) in your Project, you can use it to help you figure out what files are required if you need to move your database to another computer. You can USE the .PJX and read from it to get a list of the files you need and where they are currently located. Then create a DOS batch file (using the low-level file functions and techniques described in Chapter 22) that create a compressed file (or perhaps one file per directory) from them all, using a file utility such as PKZIP or LHARC. Be sure to add any associated memo files (.FPTs) for the tables in your Project. Then add your Project's .PJX and .PJT to this file, and you are ready to move.

Figure 14.22 shows the Project with the tables and index files added. Excluded files are shown with the mark φ (phi) immediately to the left of the file type.

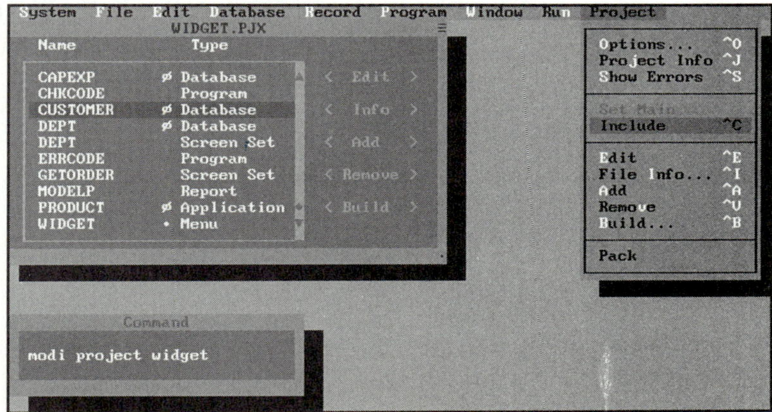

FIG. 14.22

The WIDGET.PJX Project file with tables and index files, and the PRODUCT.APP subsidiary application added and marked excluded.

One more type of file automatically is marked excluded by the Project Manager. Recall that your Tables option on the Widget menu is the "raw" PRODUCT.SPR, which doesn't have options to move through the table. This screen was designed as part of a FoxApp-generated application. Change the WIDGET.MNX option for editing the Product table to DO PRODUCT.APP, making the entire FoxApp Product application a *subsidiary* part of the Widget application. The next time you build the application or project, PRODUCT.APP shows on the project's file list, but it is automatically marked excluded. The subsidiary .APP file must exist separately on disk to be used by the parent application.

.APP files can be explicitly included in the .APP, bound in as File type rather than Application type and then copied to disk during installation. You can provide the same procedure for library files (.PLBs). Although these files can be used while bound into the .APP, you must copy their FoxPro for Windows equivalents (.FLLs) to disk, so cross-platform applications should include provisions for them.

T I P

Instead of manually including all these files in your project one by one, you can include an INSTALL.DBF in the product as a readonly file. The INSTALL.DBF should have some description fields your application uses to distinguish between records, and a Memo field. The Memo field for each record holds one file your application needs for installation (use the command APPEND MEMO <memo field name> FROM <filename> to put the file into the field and use the command COPY MEMO <name> TO <filename> during installation). For data tables installed in this manner, you may need three records (one for the .DBF, one for the structural .CDX, and one for the .FPT file). Other files that benefit from this treatment include a *seed* version of the application's Resource file; in Chapter 16 you find out why you should have this inviolate copy of the Resource file. Besides being useful for installations, this INSTALL.DBF can create new copies of any files corrupted in a power outage or other application disaster as part of error-handling procedures. Refer to Chapter 20 for an example of the kind of error routine into which you might incorporate file-creation procedures.

NOTE This practice creates the opportunity for *incremental installation.* You don't have to copy files out to disk in one tedious exercise when the application is first installed. You might have a large number of editable report files in a vertical market application, some of which a typical user never selects. If the error handler is designed to copy the files out from INSTALL.DBF whenever the files are not found, only the reports the user selects are ever copied to disk.

If you want to bind a custom CONFIG.FP file into your application, this file obviously cannot be located in the INSTALL.DBF (unless you don't need these configuration options the first time the application runs). FoxPro has several ways to specify different locations and file names for its CONFIG.FP (configuration file), which you learn about in Appendixes C and D. If the CONFIG.FP is a part of the .APP file, however, FoxPro cannot recognize the file within the application unless it has the default name (CONFIG.FP).

You also can include readonly copies of the editable application data tables. This application's installation process can then reproduce these files in editable versions on the user's disks. Unless these files should start out populated with default sets of data, however, using the commands CREATE TABLE and INDEX is an easier way to create the editable files during installation. This approach has the added benefit of helping to document the structure of the application directly in the code.

The Project Manager can become confused during the Build process if you use *indirect references* or *macro expressions* to refer to files in the code. You can tell the Project Manager to Ignore the problem and continue to build without resolving the reference, but an EXTERNAL command also exists, used only by the Project Manager, to point towards the real name of the file being referenced. You use EXTERNAL with a second keyword that describes the kind of file you want to reference, as in the following example:

```
* set up a variable
mreport = "Budget"
* here's the generic "question" screen again:
DO ask.spr WITH ;
   "Choose a <B>udget or <P>roduct Report?", ;
   mreport,"@M Budget, Product"
* tell the Project Manager about the choices
EXTERNAL REPORT budget
EXTERNAL REPORT product
REPORT FORM (mreport)
```

You use the EXTERNAL ARRAY command in a similar manner to point the Project Manager towards needed elements, which is necessary when an array is passed to a subprocedure. You use EXTERNAL ARRAY when an array is referenced in a procedure that did not create the array. The called procedure needs an EXTERNAL ARRAY statement that shows the array name used when the array was created; otherwise, the Project Manager sees the array reference as a UDF it can't find. You can read more about these procedures in the *Language Reference* manual in the entry on the EXTERNAL command. You may want to wait before you try to use this command until you read the programming sections of this book, in which you learn more about the ways arrays are used.

If you use arrays in reports, the reports don't have a place to store the EXTERNAL ARRAY instructions for the Project Manager, which causes an irritating error during Project and Application builds. You can get around the problem by creating a special program that declares all such arrays PUBLIC inside a code construct which ensures these PUBLIC declarations are never executed:

```
IF .F.
   PUBLIC array1(1)
   PUBLIC array2(1)
ENDIF
```

You can enlarge this special INCLUDE.PRG to hold all your EXTERNAL instructions (report file names and so on) for convenient maintenance.

The Project Manager has few additional options. As in any other table, entries that you remove (Ctrl+V) are not really removed from the file but simply marked deleted. A Pack option is provided on the Project menu popup to remove the unwanted entries completely from the table and to control the size of the associated memo file. A Show Errors (Ctrl+S) option displays on-screen all errors the Project Manager finds during the previous Build procedure. (As when you compiled program files directly, you also can find these errors written to a file of the same name as the project and having an .ERR extension.) A Set Main option enables you to designate the main file on which the other files in a project depend, either because you are adding the files to a project manually (rather than letting the Project Manager perform an initial Build) or because you changed the structure of the application in some way.

Before you continue with the application structure discussion, finish this investigation of Project options by looking at the Project Options dialog, which has the shortcut Ctrl+O, as shown in figure 14.23.

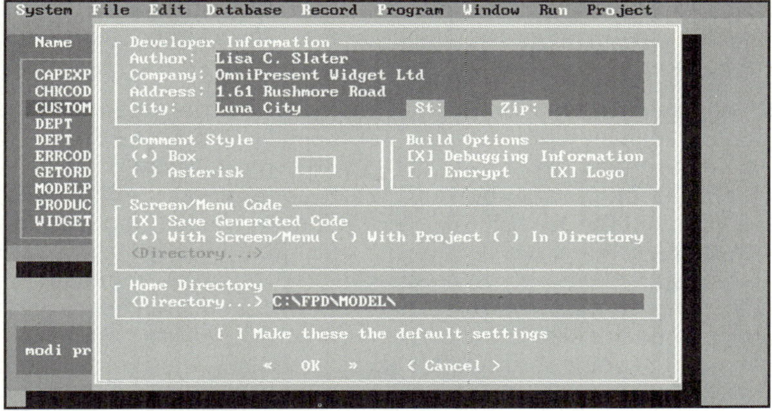

FIG. 14.23

The Project Options dialog.

Many of these items, such as Comment Style, Developer Information, and the opportunity to affect the default settings, are the same as the items you previously saw when you generated programs by using the Program menu option. Now you can apply these options to the project as a whole. The Project Manager, however, also enables you to make additional decisions about the way the code is generated, as shown in the following list:

- You can remove the Debugging Information from the code (by clicking the check box of the same name). FoxPro-compiled code contains a few extra bytes of information per line that enable line information to be provided if an error is found and also enable the Trace window to display each line on-screen and highlighted as the code runs. (You learn about the Trace window in Chapter 20.) If you are distributing the application and do not need this information, you can make the compiled file smaller by choosing this option.

- You can encrypt the code (by marking the Encrypt check box). Figure 14.24 shows the same program compiled with and without encryption. Without encryption, some messages and variables remain readable. It also is possible for someone to *decompile* a compiled file. Decompiling an encrypted compiled file is a much more difficult, if not impossible, task. If security is an important issue, you can protect the source by using this option.

- You can suppress the Microsoft Fox Logo when loading FoxPro by marking the Logo check box. If you always Do the application from inside FoxPro, this option may not matter to you, but if you use the Distribution Kit, or if you or the users start Fox with the application file name as a parameter at the DOS command line, you can control the display of the trademark sign-on screen and

Normal Shut Down message when you quit with this option. This option is equivalent to the -t command-line switch discussed in Appendix D.

- You can choose whether and where to save the generated menu and screen code by marking first the Save Generated Code check box and then toggling one of the With Screen/Menu, With Project, or In Directory radio buttons. When you generate .APP files, you don't need the .MPR files and .SPR files to run the application; these files' compiled versions are contained in the .APP file and are displayed merely as an interim step. It can be convenient, however, to check snippets and other elements of screen and menu code occasionally by typing `MODIFY COMMAND *.spr or *.mpr` instead of going through the Screen or Menu Builder for a quick look. You can use this option to save the generated file wherever the screen/menu resides (the default), wherever the project is located on disk, in another directory that you specify, or not at all. Save the source in the same directory as the .APP file if you want to use the Trace window later (see Chapter 20).

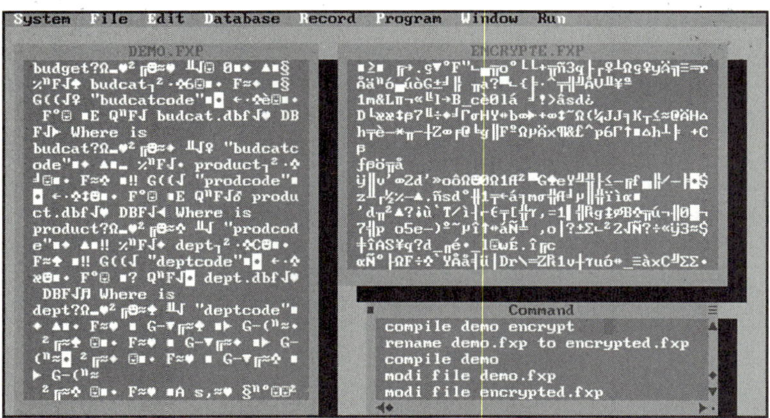

FIG. 14.24

A comparison between two compiled versions of the same program shows the effect of the Encrypt option.

Closely related to the last choice you can make about code generation is the final decision you can make in the Projects Options dialog: the project's *home directory*. Although you saved all the practice files for this book in one directory, you probably noticed that each sample project was installed by Fox with the project file in one directory and in separate subdirectories for screens, programs, menus, reports, and underlying database files. A project remembers the *relative path*, or the files' locations in subdirectories relative to the directory in which the project is placed, for all the component files. If you move these files to another developer's hard disk and use the same *relative* subdirectories for the subsidiary files, that the project is in a new directory or even on a different drive doesn't matter. The Project Manager can find all the pieces after the new home directory is confirmed.

Project Structure for Different Types of Applications

You just explored the Project Manager as thoroughly as this tool can be explored. Like the Menu Builder, the Project Manager is simple to learn; the real challenge comes when you try to structure a project to maximum effect.

With the Project Manager, this structure is no less than the actual structure of the application. The Omnipresent Widget application, with a menu program as the main file, is simple and fairly typical of applications designed to be available alongside interactive work in FoxPro.

Using a menu program as the main file in an application designed to be run as a stand-alone application, however, is unusual because menu code DEFINEs and ACTIVATEs the menu and then—having no more work to do—returns you to interactive mode. A far more typical design for a self-contained program uses a .PRG file as the main file. This main program includes four steps, described in the following sections.

Setting Up Code: DO SETUP.PRG

First, the program calls a *setup procedure* to open files and establish various system-wide parameters. The kinds of chores you do at this point in the program are discussed in Chapter 18, where you examine program structure more thoroughly. In the current WIDGET.APP, you may just SET VIEW to an appropriate file, but sometimes more elaborate setup procedures are required.

These setup procedures take the place of file-opening and file-closing code in the various .SPRs, or ENVIRONMENT keywords on LABEL or REPORT FORM command. Although you used the automatic methods of making files available so far in this book's exercises, typically you design your program to handle these chores with more flexibility. If the program opens the files, for example, you can specify different data directories at different times, without the user having to locate the files.

In your setup program or directly in your main program, you initialize the variables needed globally (throughout your application). If the variables are initialized in the SETUP.PRG rather than in the main program, they must be declared PUBLIC. Among these global variables should be one that indicates when the user wants to leave the application:

```
m.quitting = .F.
```

Defining a Menu: DO WIDGET.MPR

Second, the main program calls a *menu program* to set up the options for the application.

Waiting for the User To Take An Action: A Foundation READ

The third, and most crucial, step is that a READ is initiated. READ can be in an .SPR file that establishes the logo or a password screen for this application or just the READ command issued directly in the main program, as follows:

```
READ VALID handler()
* or
DO FNDATION.SPR
```

Either way, this READ is the application's *foundation READ*, which remains in force until the application is ready to shut down. The VALID clause, or sometimes the DEACTIVATE clause, contains a UDF that launches all the other tasks of the application in response to requests made by menu options or other events, checking the tasks in progress and handling all adjustments that must be made. The foundation READ's managing clause continues to RETURN .F. until a quit command of some kind is received.

A foundation READ is a more flexible and complicated management scheme than the RDLEVEL() check supplied in the current WIDGET.APP. Be sure that you investigate the applications in the \GOODIES\FNDATION sample file directory—and the GETLESS.TXT and GETANS.TXT files contained there, which summarize Microsoft Fox's ideas about event handling and the reasons for creating foundation READs.

When you read GETLESS.TXT and GETANS.TXT, you may get the impression that foundation READs are difficult to use and shouldn't be attempted without a great deal of preparation. Foundation READs are just an efficient method of placing users in a “wait state” at the menu between menu choices.

The examples provided by the Microsoft Fox team in the \GOODIES\FNDATION directory, especially EX2, can seem bewildering. Keep in mind that they were designed to suggest ways to handle *event-driven* programming in FoxPro. In event-driven programming, the program responds gracefully to every action of the user, no matter in what sequence the user decides to make his or her choices. You can think of the goal of event-driven programming as a completely modeless interface. In FoxPro, event-driven programming requires a great deal of backstage management to provide what looks like an effortless performance.

The foundation READ VALID clauses in EX1 and EX2 have to assess the current state of any READs in progress and shut them down intelligently before initiating another one. The VALID UDF does this while preserving the illusion that an unlimited number of READs are taking place at the same time, even though FoxPro is currently limited to only five READ levels. You learn more about the FNDATION directory examples and alternatives in the next chapter.

If your application provides mostly modal activities (and many common computer tasks, such as accounting, have inherently modal aspects), you can use a foundation READ in a far simpler way than is shown by the example applications. You can use a SKIP FOR clause on your menu options (using RDLEVEL() > 1, allowing one level for the foundation READ this time, or checking the current windows available with WONTOP() and WVISIBLE()) to decide when it isn’t safe to bring another READ or task forward.

When an option is not disabled, it can DO a procedure directly (program tasks don’t have to be initiated in the READ VALID clause). During any specific editing activity, you can provide some nested modal READs (perhaps a "Confirm Edit?" dialog or a Print setup dialog) without worrying that you will run out of available READ levels. Meanwhile, your READ VALID handler() function keeps checking the m.quitting variable. You have a Quit option on your menu that is different from the WIDGET.MPR version:

```
m.quitting = .T.
* Handle any GATHERing or confirming quit.
* Check the current activity and
* do other chores necessary to close up the
* current activity smoothly.
CLEAR READ
RETURN
```

Your READ VALID then is called. In this example, the expression does not even have to call a UDF; it can be as simple as the following:

```
READ VALID m.quitting
```

Keep in mind that this sequence of events (a CLEAR READ invoking a READ VALID clause) is specific to a *getless*, or foundation READ. If you issue a CLEAR READ during one of your *getful* (or normal editing) READs, the VALID clause on that READ is not called. If you are in the middle of an editing session that is a nested READ of a foundation READ, both READs are cleared when the CLEAR READ is issued. Therefore, the VALID clause on the foundation READ is the first item to be evaluated after the CLEAR READ statement.

More than two levels of READ nesting work differently, however. Presumably, you are in a modal dialog of some sort, and a RDLEVEL() test returns a number greater than 2. When you issue a CLEAR READ, you don't CLEAR the other READs of which this one is a "grandchild"; you only leave the dialog. You can still use the CLEAR READ ALL command to fall through to the foundation READ.

Cleaning Up and Leaving: DO CLEANUP.PRG

Finally, when the foundation READ ends, another procedure is called to end the application properly. You find a number of suggestions for appropriate cleanup procedures in Chapter 18. You also can look at the simple setup and cleanup routines included as part of ORGANIZE.APP, in the program UTILITY.PRG, and a pair of programs named SAVESET.PRG and SETSET.PRG in the \GOODIES\MISC directory. In the cleanup program, you check for the version of FoxPro under which the application is running, as your Quit option did in WIDGET.MPR, and decide whether to QUIT or CANCEL.

Locating the Foundation READ in the Application

Where should you place your application's foundation READ? Using a menu program as the main file in an application that includes a foundation READ is certainly possible. You add the foundation READ to the menu program in the Cleanup snippet, followed by all the other Cleanup code and procedures. The order is unimportant. You place the Setup code in the menu program's Setup snippet.

You also can specify a screen program as the main file. Here, the setup and a call to the menu program are made in the screen's Setup snippet;

the screen program's READ is the foundation READ; and all cleanup is placed in—or called from—the screen's Cleanup snippet.

Although no rules exist against burying the foundation READ and surrounding main components of the application in snippets, doing so can make the program structure difficult to comprehend and maintain. A .PRG file that contains the previously mentioned elements seems to work best.

NOTE Using a .PRG as the main file can have a minor side effect that you may want to counter if you distribute source along with programs. Remember that FoxPro 1, FoxBASE+, and other Xbase dialects all use .PRGs just as FoxPro does. If the main program uses an obvious name (MAIN.PRG or STARTUP.PRG, for example), users running other Xbase software may begin to run your program and then crash when they come up against the first FoxPro 2.5-specific instruction. Add a test to the very start of your application to make sure the program is executed under any version of FoxPro your application requires. Such a test can check the contents of VERSION(1), as you did earlier to find out whether the program was exiting under the Distribution Kit or the full Developer's version. This test also can check TYPE("_DOS") or any of the four system variables introduced to keep track of the four platform-specific versions of FoxPro 2.5. If the TYPE() of these variables is not "L", you're not running FoxPro 2.5. Having ascertained by this check that you are running FoxPro 2.5, you can evaluate the variable for the platform this program needs (_DOS, _MAC, _WINDOWS, or _UNIX) for a value of .T.. You learn more about these variables and developing multiplatform FoxPro applications in Chapter 17.

Packaging Options with the Distribution Kit

After you become comfortable with the FoxPro tools, develop a good sense of program structure, and learn to assemble stand-alone applications that you feel are polished and complete enough to share with others, you may want to create programs that do not rely on the FoxPro development files. If so, you can purchase the *Distribution Kit,* which Microsoft Fox created for this purpose.

Understanding the Distribution Kit

When you look at figure 14.21, you see several options under the heading Build Executable. These options are dimmed until you install the Distribution Kit files along with the development files.

The options that become enabled are determined by the Distribution files you install. See Appendix A, "Installing FoxPro," for more information about this process. For now, concentrate on the different distribution options the kit offers.

The simplest option is the *run-time* application. To distribute a run-time program, you must supply users with the .APP file, all editable files not created by the program, and the *run-time support* library files. The support library files are FOXD2500.ESL and FOXD2500.ESO for the standard version of FoxPro and FOXDX250.ESL for the extended version. You also need to distribute the run-time *loader* program, which is a small file named FOXR.EXE. (Appendix D provides more information about this file and the FOX.EXE, the other Fox loader.)

If you decide to create *compact executable files,* the Project Manager creates .EXE files, which are similar in content and size to .APP files and require the same support library files to be distributed. You can start the .EXE files, however, directly from the DOS command line, without the aid of FOXR.EXE.

Both compact executables and FOXR.EXE starting run-time applications can determine whether they are loading in an environment appropriate to the extended version of FoxPro and use this environment if both support libraries are present. If you know the environment the application uses, you need to distribute only the support library files for the appropriate version of FoxPro.

Compact executables and run-time applications share another important feature: the license to distribute these creations is unlimited if you distribute the applications in your organization. However, you may distribute only the support library files to users outside your organization as part of applications you prepare and sell. These users' licenses to use the support libraries are limited to the applications with which they received these files from you. (Users of your distributed applications can't distribute the support libraries to other users in turn.) This requirement is not an onerous one but read the small *Distribution Kit* handbook carefully to be sure that you understand the rules.

The other distribution mechanism, *stand-alone* or *monolithic executables*, differs a great deal from a run-time application. You must specify the standard or extended version when you generate the file, and you may find that this distribution mechanism creates a large file even for a simple program. The file is large because it contains all the parts of FoxPro needed to run the program. No secondary support files are required.

The compiler works with a certain degree of *granularity*, which means that if the program does not use certain broad areas of FoxPro, the compiler doesn't incorporate these areas into the executable file. Most of the sophisticated commands and features in FoxPro are supported by a number of other features, however, so the compiler cannot pick and choose among the necessary capabilities with a high degree of precision. The compiler's attempts to discriminate also can, in some circumstances, cause features you are actually using to be omitted. Suppose that all the SQL SELECT statements in an application were contained in macro expressions, as shown in the following example:

```
DO CASE
CASE PROMPT() = "Query"
   do_action = "SELECT "+from_tables + ;
      have_cond   + ;
      group_cond     && etc
CASE PROMPT() = "Execute"
   do_action = "DO "+prog_name
CASE PROMPT() = "Report"
   do_action = "REPORT FORM "+rept_name  && etc
ENDCASE

&do_action
* the above line executes your command by
* expanding the macro expression at run time
```

If the compiler cannot see an instance of the SQL SELECT command, the compiler may omit the capability of using SQL SELECT. In this example, the command is invisible to the compiler.

If the executable file returns the error message `Feature not available`, and you know the line that causes this error is not one of the unsupported commands for a distributable application, place a line of code in the program to trick the compiler into noticing that this feature is incorporated, as part of the INCLUDE.PRG suggested earlier in this chapter to handle EXTERNAL arrays and other references for the Project Manager's benefit. Although the code in the special program never executes, the trick is sufficient to make sure that the SELECT command is seen when the executable file is built.

You can reduce the size of a stand-alone executable file to a certain extent if some of its sections are contained in supporting .APP files. You need to distribute these files along with the main stand-alone .EXE; they serve as *overlays* to the main file.

Separating your program into modules in this manner, however, can lead to a similar problem as macro expansion. To make sure that the compiler links in the appropriate FoxPro capabilities needed to support the features used in your subsidiary .APPs, you must add these .APPs to your Project. They are marked as excluded by the Project Manager, but their presence alerts the compiler of the features they use, which may not be needed anywhere else in your application.

TIP Always use .APPs (not compact .EXEs) as subsidiary modules because the only difference is an extra header tacked onto the .EXE so the file can execute from the DOS command line. Because the subsidiary module is called from a file that has already executed from the DOS command line, there's no reason to add this bulk to the module file.

Choosing a Distribution Path

Which distribution path should you take? Each method has its advantages. .APPs and compact .EXEs require much less disk space and time to compile and are easier to transport if you need to supply updates for your program. On the other hand, stand-alone files carry a certain connotation of professionalism for many developers. Because they do not require support files, they can never be mistakenly run with support files that carry a VERSION(1) different from your development files.

TIP Both the Standard and Extended versions of the base product can create either Standard or Extended stand-alone executables if you have installed the Distribution Kit to permit all options. Microsoft has stated that using the Standard product to create Extended stand-alone .EXEs (the largest of the distributable file types and the most time-consuming to build) can free up some extra memory for the *linker program* that builds these files, speeding the Build process.

Although .EXEs are meant to be executed from the DOS command line, you also can run these files while in FoxPro by typing the command `DO <your_program>` in the Command window. By preference, FoxPro runs the executable application—if an executable application is found—then the .APP file or, finally, an .FXP file of the same name.

> **CAUTION:** FoxPro can execute only .EXE files created in this way. Use the RUN command for other (non-FoxPro) executables. If the distributed application uses the RUN command's /<numeric expression> switch to specify the amount of memory FoxPro makes available for external programs, be aware that you need to distribute the file FOXSWAP.COM with the application. You can find this file in the main FoxPro program directory. Like other accessory files for an application, you can place FOXSWAP.COM in an INSTALL.DBF's Memo field and copy it to disk during installation.

Distribution Mechanism Limitations

All the distribution mechanisms share some limitations when compared to the development version of FoxPro. Only part of FoxPro's SYSMENU, for example, is available in a distributed application. Except for the Filer option, the System menu pad is available, the Edit pad is completely available, and the Window and File options appropriate to a noninteractive environment are available. (You can see that the WIDGET.MPR requires some revision for distribution.)

Many development commands have no meaning in a distribution application, so—besides not appearing on SYSMENU—attempts to invoke these commands in distributed programs are ignored. You cannot, for example, ACTIVATE WINDOW COMMAND or BUILD PROJECT in a distributed application. Check the *Distribution Kit User's Guide* for a complete list of commands and features not supported by the Distribution Kit.

The most striking absences, however, are the Screen Builder, the Menu Builder, and the RQBE. Although you can create and modify labels and reports in a distributed application, you cannot use the other power tools because these tools generate code that requires compilation, which is impossible without a full development version of FoxPro.

Of the three omissions, only the lack of the RQBE is likely to be important in a distributed application. You can create dialogs that give your users wide latitude in the queries they issue. SELECT statements can include variables that are *macro-expanded* at run-time. Your query dialogs fill these variables with values based on the user's responses and then execute the custom query.

You must balance these omissions against the control a distributed application provides (in comparison with a program run under the development version), over exactly what is done with the data the program is collecting. An important point to note here is that you must think carefully about each user's level of sophistication, with regard to the user's understanding of database management, before you recommend (to anyone) either a distributed application or the powerful development version of FoxPro.

Another important difference between the distributed application and the full development edition of FoxPro is the number of *simultaneous users* licensed for the program. When you distribute a run-time application, you can give your users unlimited license without any royalties to Microsoft; however, the full development edition is licensed for a specified number of users. (Again, the rules are complicated, so consult the license agreement that came with your copy of FoxPro.) In most cases, considering the complexity of FoxPro, many large organizations choose to buy a limited number of licenses for their FoxPro developers, who then write applications to be used, under the support library, by the rest of the company.

Protecting against Problems in Distributed Applications

When you decide to share applications that you have written for yourself with other people, no matter which distribution mechanism you choose, you face some new development problems. Procedures that work for you on your computer may fail on someone else's. If another user has the full FoxPro package, he or she may have his or her own default macro sets that conflict with your application's. Perhaps he or she uses a different monitor type or keyboard, or has limited disk space or memory.

Chapter 22 presents a sample procedure to be used as part of your application's installation process and examines any existing CONFIG.SYS file to make sure that its FILES and BUFFERS settings enable your program and FoxPro to run. This factor is only one of many that you must consider when you distribute an application—the wider your distribution, the more possibilities—and the suggested approach is not foolproof. (If, for example, the user has a memory manager such as Quarterdeck's QEMM installed, these settings in the CONFIG.SYS file can be deceptive.) You cannot anticipate, much less successfully guard against, problems of this kind.

In Chapter 20, you learn about recovering gracefully from errors that you cannot always predict and how to keep your users informed at all times. These capabilities are just as crucial to the professional distribution of your application as the Distribution Kit.

Creating Demonstration Editions of Your Applications

Often you need to let users get a feel for your application before you can convince them to buy it. In earlier versions of FoxPro, you installed FoxPro and the Distribution Kit using an *activation key*, which could be set to a demonstration-use level to provide this "try before you buy" capability. The base product and the distributed applications you created could be limited to 120 records per data table using the demonstration activation key. Additional activation keys available from Fox Software could create limits of 30 or 240 records.

Because using these different keys meant keeping extra copies of the support libraries tuned to each of the limits, even if Microsoft were disposed to provide the same service, in FoxPro 2.5 you would run out of disk space and patience keeping track of various copies of library files for various FoxPro platforms! As in every other situation you face as a FoxPro developer, however, FoxPro provides an alternative if you're willing to do a little work yourself: install a similar check of your own on table sizes. You can check for a total limit of records in any single file (as Fox's demonstration keys did), or you can create a special variable or other condition and selectively use a SKIP FOR demo clause on menu options.

A third possibility is the creation of a *self-running demonstration program*. This kind of demo does not really enable the user to work with or edit files, but rather takes the user on a tour of the system of which keystrokes, system responses, and output are simulated. If you execute DEMO.APP, you see the self-running demo supplied with FoxPro. This demo is an attractive showcase for the features of the application. In Chapter 16, you learn about *macros*, or recorded keystrokes, and the ways you can use macros in programs to create this kind of demo.

Summary

This chapter concludes your introduction to the principal FoxPro *power tools*. Next, Chapter 15 brings together the products of these tools in additional sample applications that demonstrate a number of important application-building and event-handling approaches in FoxPro. Chapter 16 discusses a number of other supporting features unique to FoxPro that can add significantly to the functionality and the style of applications you create, concluding your exploration of the FoxPro interface agents. In Chapter 17, concluding Part III, you learn how to use these interface elements in *cross-platform* FoxPro application strategies, applying the power of FoxPro to diverse computer environments.

15

CHAPTER

Controlling Events and Tasks in Applications

In Chapter 12, "Creating Application Elements," you designed data entry systems for lookup tables—Product, Budcat, and Dept—which contain information needed by other tables in Omnipresent Widgets' relational database. In Chapter 13, "Improving Screen Design with Complex Screen Sets," you created a data entry system for the Budget table, one of the main tables in the database, and learned how to validate entries. Each Budget entry must reference an existing product, budget category, and department, as defined by available choices in the lookup tables.

The data entry task of editing the Budget table differs fundamentally from editing the Product table. The Budget table may have many repeating entries, but no Product record should repeat. Budget records may be added and deleted easily, but the Product records are rarely added and seldom, if ever, deleted. Yet the users of the Omnipresent Widget application don't see these activities as different—they even may want to accomplish both goals at the same time.

Users may not know or care about the organization of the underlying information (the normalization of the database tables); they simply want to get a job done. If this job includes adding a new Budget record, and halfway through the Budget data entry process, the user realizes that the record concerns a new product, the user needs to add the new product to the Product table without missing a beat. The application is responsible for taking care of the details.

You have already used some FoxPro features that allow the application to fulfill this responsibility. Almost all the .SPR programs you generated used more than one window to provide full data-entry capabilities. (PRODUCT.SPR is the exception, but the Omnipresent Widget application uses the FoxApp-generated PRODUCT.APP instead.) When you created the department and budget category data entry screen sets, you learned to use the DEACTIVATE clause on the READ command to let your program know when the user moves between windows, and to decide what the program does next. When you created BUDGET.SCX, you learned to use the READ ACTIVATE command to perform a similar task.

As you become more comfortable designing complex screen sets, you find that multiple windows are logical subsets of the information represented on-screen. Because the ACTIVATE and DEACTIVATE clauses tell your program when the user chooses a new window, these clauses can help the program make all necessary adjustments for the action to which the user has turned his or her attention. This chapter expands these kinds of capabilities, showing you additional ways to manage multiple files and windows.

The techniques described in this chapter integrate FoxPro projects and menus, which you learned about in Chapter 14, "Organizing and Packaging Your Applications," with data entry READs. Menus work together with screen sets and the screens' associated READs to provide an effective, smooth interface. Projects are essential to coordinating this process.

As you learned in previous chapters, you must write some programs, usually in the form of short UDFs and code snippets, to make productive use of the FoxPro Power Tools. If you're new to Xbase, you may need to return to this chapter after reading the programming sections of the book—but you can, and should, learn how to organize a FoxPro application even if you do not yet grasp all the programming details.

Understanding FoxPro Events and Tasks

To accomplish any big job, break the job into small pieces. You already learned this rule to help you organize information in separate tables. After the tables are properly organized, you bring the information together in a relational database. Similarly, when you write UDFs and FoxPro expressions, you find that each complex result is derived from many simple steps, each step is easy to understand.

To design an application, follow the same principle: take the job the user wants to accomplish—such as managing Omnipresent Widget's budget—and analyze the smaller jobs (*tasks*) required to accomplish it—entering and editing valid budget entries, keeping the lookup tables which provide validation up-to-date, and receiving reports on the results, with a variety of selection and ordering criteria.

Each task the user chooses may require the *interruption* of another task. Each choice made by the user is an event that the application must be prepared to handle. When you write a program, you must anticipate these events and manage the application's responses to each event effectively.

If the user enters information into a GET, for example, and chooses to leave the GET (by clicking another object, pressing Enter, or ending the READ), this choice is an *event*. You write instructions in the GET's VALID clause to interrupt the user's choice until your validation code confirms the entry. A menu choice is another type of event, which can request practically any action from the application. Your menu code must evaluate any task currently in progress, and decide how to coordinate such a task with the user's new request.

Collecting User Instructions during a Program

At some moments, usually when the program is executing a series of steps on a range of records, the program isn't receptive to user input. At most times, however, a FoxPro program waits for user instructions, responding to each user-initiated event as it occurs. The state in which the program waits is known as, appropriately enough, a *wait state*.

As you learned in Chapter 14, if no other task is in progress, you can place FoxPro in a wait state by using a *Getless* READ, which Fox programmers often term a *Foundation READ*. The user waits at the system menu until signalling the beginning of a task (usually by selecting a menu option).

A wait state also can take the form of a BROWSE or the use of one of FoxPro's desk accessories, such as the Calculator. The program may be receptive to multiple keystrokes or terminate with a single mouse click (if the wait state is a simple WAIT WINDOW). A function such as GETDIR( ) or GETEXPR may allow complex input, but the input may be limited to a defined type or structure.

The most common wait state for a FoxPro task that requires user involvement is a READ with GETs (or *GETful* READ). FoxPro's varied GET objects enable the READ to collect information from the user with almost unlimited flexibility. If the READ's GETs are insufficient, the READ can initiate or incorporate some of the other wait states while the READ remains active.

CYCLEing through a READ

When FoxPro 2.0 added the keyword CYCLE to the READ command, this change caused a fundamental shift in the manner in which FoxPro programs handled tasks. In previous Xbase programs, tasks began and ended in a straightforward manner. Users entered the READ in the first GET, as designated by the programmer, and when they exited the last GET, the users also exited the READ. This straightforward path was necessary because the program had no method to move the record pointer in a file during the READ. When the user finished editing GETs and exited the READ, the program then could save the information and add a new record or move the record pointer to a different record, issuing a new READ, with GETs filled by the values in the appropriate record.

As you learned in Chapters 12 and 13, the user doesn't exit the FoxPro READ CYCLE to edit a different record. Instead, when the user indicates that an edit is complete, the program saves the information, moves to a new record if necessary, and again displays the GETs with a SHOW GETS command. The READ continues; when the user exits the last GET, the cursor moves back to the first GET in the READ. If GETs are in separate windows under one READ, different windows come to the top as different GETs become current. The user can continue to edit the GETs in the READ, paging up and down between the different windows in the set or clicking different windows as desired, until some event occurs that explicitly ends the READ's task.

Before a READ-terminating event occurs, the program must handle diverse events that do *not* terminate the READ, temporarily interrupting—yet not disturbing—the CYCLE.

Responding to Events during Different Categories of Tasks

You often hear the term *event-driven* used approvingly to describe an application in which the user makes choices in a natural way. In an old-fashioned, rigid program, the user has to work on one task at a time, finishing the task before going on to the next, which isn't a natural method of work. Most people have to answer the phone, follow directions from a co-worker, and leave one task half-finished because a task with a higher priority comes up. These people don't have patience for programs that expect them to work any other way.

The term *event-driven programming*, however, isn't meaningful; all programs (and all people) are driven by events. Some people, and some programs, only handle a wider range of events at one time—and more successfully—than others. When using this term, developers express this goal: to give the user as broad a range of actions as possible, at any particular time. Programmers and applications designers want programs to respond as gracefully to interruptions as possible to mirror the way efficient people work.

This graceful response is called *modeless* behavior (or *modaless* behavior, by Macintosh programmers) on the part of the program.

No program and no person has infinitely graceful responses. No matter how well users can juggle tasks, they know that sometimes they have to turn off the phone and the beeper and attend to one family occasion or one work deadline. In the same manner, some computer tasks cannot be interrupted; users understand this necessity. In Chapter 13, you briefly explored uninterruptible tasks (*modal dialogs*). In FoxPro's native interface, you perform modal tasks every time you access a system dialog.

When you design an application and separate the application's main goal into separate, smaller tasks, categorize each task by asking several questions. The first specification is "Can I allow this task to be interrupted safely?" If you decide that the task can be interrupted before completion, you then ask, "What interruptions and events may occur, and how does my program respond to each one?" If you find that the task is inherently modal and *never* should be interrupted, you ask, "What steps do I take to prevent interruption?" You already have learned some answers to these questions in previous chapters of this book; the remainder of this chapter is devoted to additional strategies you can use for different application interfaces.

The second task specification is "To what other tasks is this activity related?" In the Omnipresent Widget budget system, as described previously, entering a Budget record is related to adding a Product record, in the sense that the Budget record cannot exist for a product until the product is entered in the Product table. These activities, however, are essentially separate (the user could enter Budget records all day without needing to edit the Product table). Allowing the user to edit both the Product and Budget tables is a convenience, not a necessity, for the user.

In contrast, some activities are inherently subsidiary to other activities. Confirming the value of the big_item variable used to run a report in Chapter 10, "Using the Report Writer and Label Designer," for example, only occurs when the user chooses to run the report. The user never enters a value for big_item except after choosing to run the report. The Budget data entry screen includes a subsidiary query activity, which is dependent on the current value of the m.period GET or other current information. This activity only occurs in the context of the Budget data entry process, as the user runs *what-if* scenarios on the data.

These kinds of subsidiary tasks are intrinsically modal in FoxPro. (The reverse is not always true; some modal activities are not subsidiary tasks.) The value of big_item must be known before the report runs, and the Budget query must complete and display the results before the user can continue with Budget data entry. After a task is characterized as subsidiary, therefore, you don't have to work hard to coordinate this task with other tasks. You know exactly when this task should be available, and you know that no other task should begin until this task completes.

The challenge of event handling in FoxPro, therefore, is to increase the user's ability to access *independent but related tasks* with the least possible restriction or interference by the program.

Because coordinating independent activities is a convenience, rather than a necessity, for the user, you don't need to achieve a particular level of modelessness to have a running application. The Widget applications designed in Chapter 14, "Organizing and Packaging Your Applications," use a RDLEVEL( ) check on menu items to prevent more than one data entry activity from going on at the same time. You can use this system until you become comfortable using any of the techniques described in this chapter.

Initiating New Tasks during a Program

FoxPro increased the complexity of handling tasks and task interruptions in an application because many different ways are available for the user to communicate requests in a FoxPro program. The program also can initiate new tasks without a user request.

During a normal data entry READ, the user may type information into the current GET, press Tab to access a new GET, or click a new location on the screen, or use the mouse or space bar to indicate a choice. The user also may decide to end the task with a terminating keystroke or a terminating GET control.

Additionally, the user may interrupt the data entry activity by accessing a menu option or by pressing a key to which an ON KEY LABEL command was assigned. (You first encountered an ON KEY LABEL assignment in Chapter 8, "Organizing the Answers with BROWSE," to toggle the contents of a calculated field in a BROWSE. In a following section of this chapter and in the programming sections of this book, you see that assigning a procedure to a keystroke by using ON KEY LABEL commands is a powerful method of initiating events in FoxPro.) The menu option or ON KEY LABEL command may start a new task or affect the current task.

The program has other ways to initiate a new task directly. For example, as you discovered in the Budget screen, a VALID on a push button control can DO a program. By returning .T., the READ DEACTIVATE clause can CLEAR the current READ automatically. The program also can imitate user input with the PLAY MACRO and KEYBOARD commands, sending keystrokes, which are interpreted by FoxPro during the wait state as if the user typed the same keys or key combinations. The keystrokes can terminate the READ or add information to a BROWSE or GET. If the keystrokes are assigned to a menu shortcut or ON KEY LABEL, the characters sent by the program can execute a menu option or a command.

Using READs To Support Tasks and Events

After a READ is initiated, the following events can occur to start a new task without ending the READ:

- A GET- or READ-level WHEN or VALID clause can trigger a program or execute a command. Any clause that issues a SHOW GETS statement also triggers the SHOW clause, which also may contain instructions to start a new task.
- The user or program can shift the focus to a new window, triggering the READ-level ACTIVATE or DEACTIVATE clause, which may initiate some activity.
- A menu option can trigger a program or execute a command.
- A keystroke or key combination pressed by the user (or sent by the program in imitation of a keypress during one of the events in this list) can trigger a program or execute a command.

When first beginning to program in FoxPro, many users try to create a modeless interface by allowing some or all of these interruption-events to start new tasks. Inevitably, this tactic requires some of the events to issue new READs. When one READ is issued during another, the second READ is *nested* within the first READ. FoxPro allows only five nested READ levels, so allowing READs to be issued indiscriminately by events that occur at the user's discretion causes a program error quickly. In Chapter 14, the SKIP FOR RDLEVEL( ) <operator> <ExprN> checked for each READ-issuing menu option, thus providing insurance against the error.

This approach requires the user to exit every READ or task before beginning another activity. Although an application that uses this check is safe, the result isn't very flexible from the user's point of view.

When FoxPro 2.0 was introduced, Fox Software included some example programs to demonstrate a more flexible alternative. These applications, EX1 and EX2, are distributed with Microsoft FoxPro 2.5 in the \GOODIES\FNDATION directory. In the following section, you learn how this alternative works.

Investigating the GETless Foundation READ

Using the Run Application option from the system menu, start the EX1 application. You see the system menu change, but no task starts (the screen is blank). Until the user chooses a task, the program waits at a Foundation READ.

Examine the choices on the altered system menu and note that the data entry tasks for the application are clustered on the Application menu popup (see fig. 15.1).

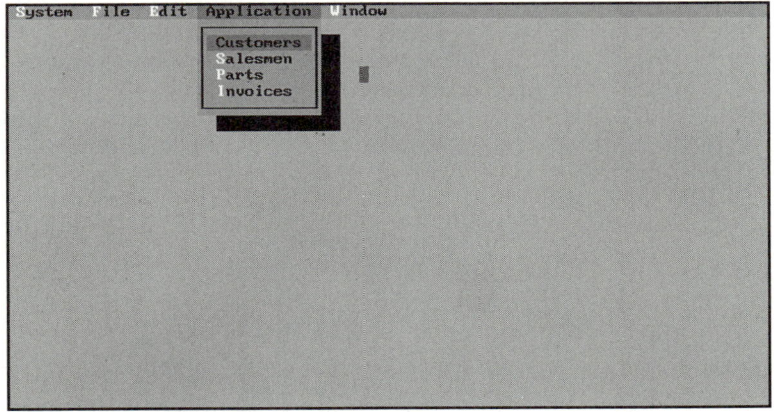

FIG. 15.1

EX1.APP waits at a Foundation READ for the user to begin an application task.

Choose any application task, and access the Application menu again. You notice that the other data entry tasks are not dimmed on the menu (see fig. 15.2). In fact, you can choose each task in turn, bringing up all the data window screens at the same time. You can select any task by choosing a window (cycle through the windows by using Ctrl+F1, the mouse, or the Window menu popup list).

The control panel window, which allows movement through the tables, corresponds to the currently active data entry window; if you press the `Next` button while editing Invoices, you move to the next Invoice record, but if you press the `Bottom` button when editing Customers, you move to the bottom of the Customer table instead.

Because you investigated control panels in Chapter 12, "Creating Application Elements," the behavior of the control panel is familiar. You already know that the button code, which moves the record pointer, is designed to work with multiple tables (this code doesn't name a table explicitly). This feature of a generic control panel allows you to adapt the code to work with multiple Omnipresent Widget tables in the exercises in Chapter 12.

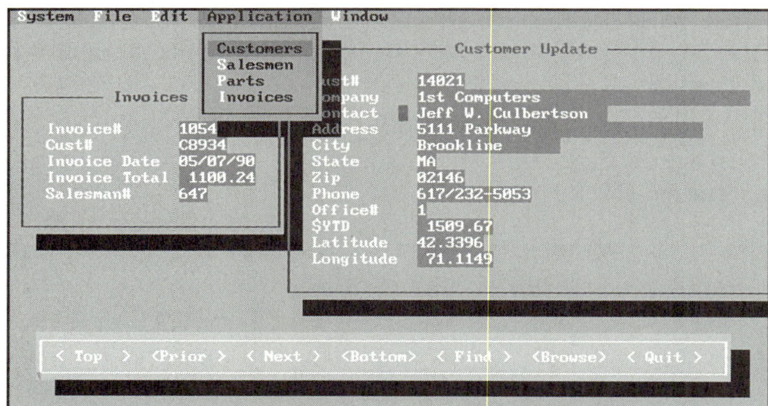

FIG. 15.2

Multiple tasks are accessible simultaneously in EX1.APP.

The new feature is the capability of accessing multiple tasks without first exiting a task. EX1 provides this behavior without nesting READs past the limit of five because *not all tasks on-screen are simultaneously in progress*. Use the Window menu to place the Debug window on-screen and enter the expression `RDLEVEL( )` in the Debug window's left panel (see fig. 15.3). The Debug window is a programmer's tool you learn more about in Chapter 20, "Enhancing the Applications You Program." The panel on the right displays the current value of this expression while the program runs. No matter how many Application menu popup options you access in EX1, this value continues to be 2.

The Foundation READ is one of the two READ levels—when you first start EX1 and are waiting at the empty application screen, RDLEVEL( ) = 1. When at least one of the EX1 data entry windows are visible, the topmost window is part of an active READ, and this READ is the second READ level. Although the other windows appear to be active, the READs of these windows have been CLEARed.

As you learned in Chapter 14, "Organizing and Packaging Your Applications," an option in the Program Generate dialog for screen sets permits a window to remain on-screen after the READ exits (un-check the default of Release Windows). Although the GETs still appear active, these are just painted in the window. If the user chooses this task again, the READ must be issued again.

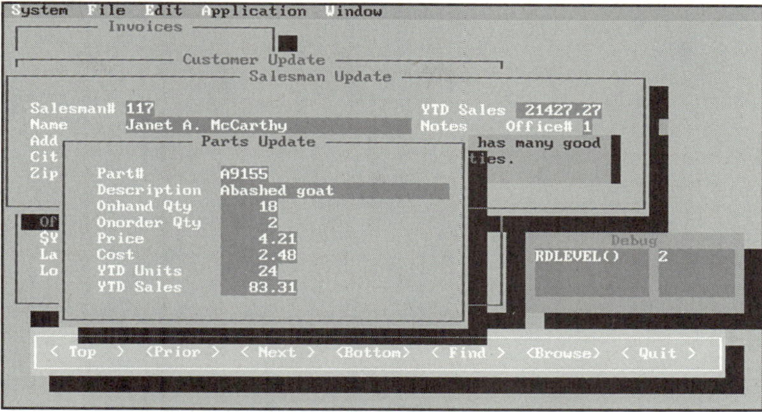

FIG. 15.3

RDLEVEL( ) does not match the number of tasks that appear to be in progress in EX1.APP.

How does EX1 reissue the READ when the user chooses a task that appears to be in progress on-screen, having turned attention to a different task for a while? The user can choose a task in two ways:

- Choose the task's menu option
- Choose the task's window

EX1 uses a slightly different method to handle each of these possibilities. To investigate these methods, exit from the EX1 application by using the Quit option on the File menu popup and opening the EX1 project.

If you open the EX1 menu file, you discover that each option on the Application menu popup runs the same procedure, Mhit, which you find in the menu Cleanup code (see fig. 15.4). Each option sends Mhit the name of the related task (expressed as an .SPR file name for its data entry screen set). The Mhit procedure checks RDLEVEL( ). Mhit executes the .SPR, *only if RDLEVEL( ) = 1*. If RDLEVEL( ) is greater than 1, another data entry READ is in progress. Mhit stores the name of the .SPR in a variable, *tobedone*, and CLEARs the current READ. The current data entry window remains on-screen, so the user is unaware that the old task no longer is available.

Because the nested data entry READ was cleared, the program now returns to the Foundation-level READ. Because this READ has no GETs, the Foundation READ VALID clause executes immediately. The VALID clause for EX1 is a UDF, Myhandler( ), which you find in the main program for the application (EX1.PRG).

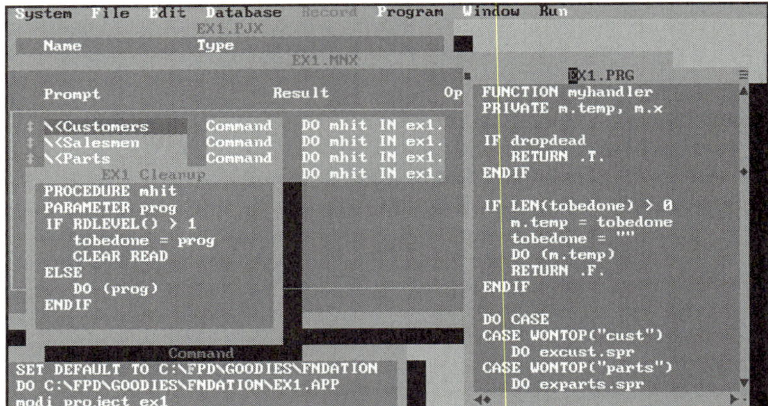

FIG. 15.4

The menu event handling code in the EX1 project files.

Myhandler( ) checks another variable, *dropdead,* to see if the user has chosen to quit EX1 entirely. If quitting the application is not the user's choice, Myhandler( ) checks the menu option variable, tobedone. If tobedone contains a value (the user made a menu choice), Myhandler( ) stores this value in a temporary variable and clears tobedone so that it is empty for the user's next action. Then Myhandler( ) executes the program name contained in the temporary variable.

Notice that the execution of the .SPR, which launches a new READ, has been removed to a safe place. When the code in the Foundation READ VALID is executed, RDLEVEL( ) always is 1.

While more than one data entry window is on-screen, the user may choose a new activity by cycling to a new data entry window. Instead of the menu procedure Mhit CLEARing a current READ, EX1 uses the old window's DEACTIVATE clause to decide on the next action. All the tasks in EX1 use a function named Stopread( ), which you find in EX1.PRG. Stopread( ) checks to see if the DEACTIVATE clause was called, because the user closed the current data entry window or because the user chose another window. In the former case, Stopread( ) RETURNs a value of .T.. In the latter case, Stopread( ) uses the WREAD( ) function to decide whether the new window belongs to the current READ (the current data entry READ may include several GET windows, along with the control panel). If the new window is not part of the current READ, Stopread( ) RETURNs .T..

As you may recall from Chapter 12, "Creating Application Elements," *the current READ terminates when the DEACTIVATE clause RETURNs .T..*

If the new window chosen belongs to the current READ, the DEACTIVATE clause RETURNs .F. and the READ continues. Otherwise, the DEACTIVATE clause's RETURNs .T., which CLEARs the READ, and automatically sends the program back to the Foundation-level READ VALID.

Once again, the Myhandler() function checks to see what event brought the program back to this level. This time, because this event was not a menu choice, the variable tobedone doesn't contain a program name (it's a null string). Instead, Myhandler() goes through a series of CASEs to determine what window is currently WONTOP(), or active—refer to Chapters 12 and 13 for other examples of WONTOP() use and Chapter 23, "Controlling a Windowed Environment," for a discussion of FoxPro's extensive window-handling commands and functions. Using the window name, Myhandler() determines which .SPR to execute to again launch the appropriate data entry task. The user remains unaware that this READ was not active all the time.

Although the method used in Myhandler() to decide which screen program to launch may seem cumbersome, you can streamline the EX1 approach considerably with a few improvements. Many programmers name their windows and their .SPR files in tandem, using naming conventions that allow the Foundation READ VALID code to determine when a new task is required. Using this approach, you don't need a separate CASE statement for every task in your system.

The method still is flawed, however, by its reliance on the DEACTIVATE clause to CLEAR a READ in progress because leaving a non-GET window does not trigger the DEACTIVATE clause. If the application includes BROWSEs or desk accessories, the EX1 approach does not work without additional gyrations.

If the application does not rely on non-GET windows, the EX1 method is useful. Investigating EX1 also gives you a deeper understanding of FoxPro READs and READ levels and the way menu and window events work together in a FoxPro system.

Some applications, however, cannot comply with the limitations of the EX1 method. Although scrollable lists and EDIT regions, which are true GET objects, may take the place of BROWSEs and MODIFY MEMO windows, non-READ windows have additional capabilities. Unlike list objects, BROWSEs are editable and can handle huge numbers of records without significant loss of speed. As you learned in Chapter 8, BROWSE clauses allow the programmer to display records in varied ways, unavailable in a list (more BROWSE tricks are included in a following section of this chapter).

Similarly, MODIFY MEMO windows—unlike EDIT regions—are true edit windows that you can resize or move with more flexibility than EDITs. In FoxPro for Windows, or in applications written in the DOS product but used on both platforms, a MODIFY MEMO also gains access to the conditional Text menu, like other text editing windows. The user can choose to spell check the text or change fonts—two features unavailable in an EDIT region.

Investigate EX2, the second example project in the \GOODIES\FNDATION directory, to learn how you can expand Myhandler( ) to take care of non-GET windows in a READ. You soon see that the method becomes far more unwieldy, and that all attempts to make the READ VALID work generically (without a separate CASE for every possible event) become hopelessly tangled.

The following section presents an alternative method for integrating non-GET windows into READs. However, you learn some valuable principles from the EX1 and EX2 procedures that control events (Stopread( ), Myhandler( ), and Mhit), which apply to any method you choose in FoxPro. These principles can be summarized as follows: Many different events can initiate a new task in FoxPro—these events are listed in the preceding section. *However, when a READ task already is in session, no new READ should be initiated unless it is MODAL and returns directly to the READ task already in progress.*

The central rule of FoxPro event processing is this: when a READ task currently is in session, initiate no new READ—unless the task initiated is MODAL and returns directly to the READ task already in progress.

Examining the GETful Foundation READ Alternative

Return to the FoxApp-generated PRODUCT.APP you created in the first chapter of this book, or use the Run menu's option to create a new application, for any data file available. Run the application with the Debug window displayed on-screen, as you displayed it for EX1.APP, to see the value of RDLEVEL( ). (You must activate the Debug window before you start the FoxApp-generated application, because this option isn't on FoxApp's custom menu.)

In the FoxApp application, only one task exists—editing the Product table. The first level READ that continues through the application contains the GETs for this task, rather than being GETless and holding the application at a wait state until the user chooses a task. RDLEVEL( ) increases beyond the value of 1 only when a subsidiary task is chosen, and this task is always MODAL. In figure 15.5, RDLEVEL( ) has climbed to 3. The user chose to Search for a record from the control panel; the Search dialog is a modal dialog (READ level 2). A third READ is launched by the Search dialog, with a dialog that informs the user that a relatively slow search mechanism will be employed. This dialog gives the user a chance to confirm or cancel the Search task. This *confirm or cancel* dialog is the highest READ level the FoxApp-generated application reaches, because no other activity is permitted at this point. At the conclusion of the search, the two dialogs disappear and RDLEVEL( ) returns to 1.

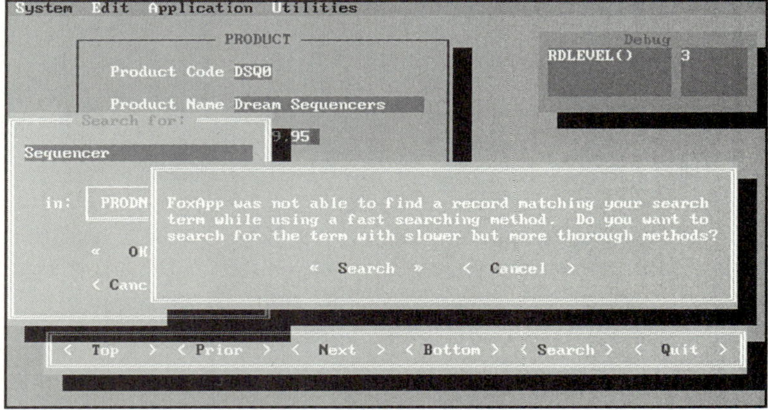

FIG. 15.5

In a FoxApp application, a GETful Foundation READ plus two nested dialogs attain a RDLEVEL( ) value of 3.

PRODUCT.APP and other FoxApp applications are simple but demonstrate a way to use the Foundation READ level productively to perform a task, rather than using a GETless placeholder READ. To create a more complex application, you can add much more activity and many related tasks to this one READ.

Expanding the GETful Foundation READ Model for Relational Screen Sets

This section presents guidelines to help you get started with complex READs. No technique suggested here is required for working with multiple tables, although the suggestions can streamline the process of designing a relational data entry screen set.

When you work on a screen set with more than one or two components, you want to add each .SCX and arrange the windows only once, although you often need to generate and compile the code numerous times before you are satisfied with the results. Always use the Project Manager, which—unlike the Program menu's Generate option—can save the .SCX file names, window arrangements, and additional READ options you specify in the screen set's Generate dialog. Your project may contain only one screen set, so the .APP you build is the same as an .SPR, but the convenience while testing still is considerable.

TIP Remember that you don't need to keep the project open while you work with the screen set. After the screen set options are specified in the project, close the project and BUILD APP <application name> FROM <project name> in the Command window. This method often is faster than using the Project dialog—and much faster than respecifying options in the Program menu Generate dialog—for multiple trial builds, because you can cursor up to a previous command in the Command window and press Enter for additional compiles.

As you start to design the set, create one .SCX for the information about each table. As stated previously, this design approach provides logical subsets of the data, from the user's point of view, and also allows the program to use the window-level READ clauses to make crucial distinctions.

If your tables have matching field names, the field names allow the View window and the RQBE to prompt you helpfully when you relate or join the tables. Omnipresent Widget's Product and Budget tables, for example, are related on the commonly-named Prodcode field. Matching names, however, can cause problems if you edit both tables under one indirect (to memory variables, rather than to fields) READ. If you SCATTER MEMVAR, how does the program know what m.prodcode means at a given moment in the program? Using separate windows for separate tables' information, you can use the REGIONAL variable declaration so that like-named variables in different windows, which the compiler considers separate *screen regions*, don't interfere with each other. Although helpful, this strategy cannot work if your variables are referenced in other regions.

If a SHOW clause defined by a common control panel, for example, refers to m.prodcode, the control panel is a separate window, so the program can't tell to which m.prodcode the code refers.

REGIONAL variables can cause other problems, if you use VARREAD( ) to perform the kinds of tricks you used in the ChkCode( ) function in Chapter 12, "Creating Application Elements," or if your help system uses VARREAD( ) to determine which help topic is appropriate. In Chapter 20, "Enhancing the Applications You Program," you learn that your applications can have a help system similar to FoxPro's. Just as the native FOXHELP file displays different information depending on the current action, the help file can display different information according to many environmental factors, including the current GET.

In the example code listed in this section, each data entry screen uses a REGIONAL declaration for the `Save/Cancel` push button variable (m.saveit) because, except by the current window, this variable is never referenced. However, all the data entry GETs are array elements, using the SCATTER TO <arrayname> command instead of SCATTER MEMVAR. GATHER FROM <arrayname> saves an edit, and INSERT INTO <table> FROM ARRAY <arrayname> supplies the code to add a record. Each window is responsible to initialize its variables in the Setup code, as shown in the following listing:

Data entry window-specific Setup code

```
* Setup for Budget data entry window
* for CONTROLR.SCX multiple file screen set:
REGIONAL m.saveit
SELECT Budget
SCATTER TO Budget
m.edbudget = .F.
```

With these housekeeping details tied to individual .SCX files, you can make repeated decisions about which windows—or which related tasks—to include in a single screen set without major code adjustments. When generating the .SPR file for the set, GENSCRN concatenates all the Setup code, assigning each window a region number.

Notice that the array name matches the alias of the corresponding table, and that another variable (m.edbudget) also is initialized. Each window has a corresponding variable that indicates whether an edit has begun in the current record (this variable stands for either an add or an edit). The variable name follows a similar naming convention as the array does—m.ed, plus the alias. This convention is continued in other areas of window maintenance; each window name corresponds to the alias of the table.

Naming variables and windows according to the affected table provides significant advantages in event handling because the generic code can easily tell which information corresponds to which related data entry task.

This example continues to use the control panel you edited in Chapter 12 to hold the generic code. Because of the slight edits needed here, save the screen file to a new name (CONTROLR.SCX is used in the example). You still use m.editmode and m.addmode, initialized in the control panel's Setup because these variables are needed no matter what data entry windows are involved in the READ. As before, the DEACTIVATE clause signals a change in the active window and calls the SHOW clause to handle the new window's requirements. However, this time each data entry window gets its own DEACTIVATE snippet, as follows:

Data entry window-specific DEACTIVATE code

```
* Budget data entry screen DEACTIVATE code
IF UPPER(WONTOP( )) ="CONTROLS"
   m.edbudget = .F.
ENDIF
```

This code ensures that the edit for the current window is canceled by a return to the control panel, because choosing the control panel in this system signals a desire to move to another record. GENSCRN concatenates all the DEACTIVATE code together with the following code, placed in the control panel's DEACTIVATE clause:

READ-wide DEACTIVATE code

```
* DEACTIVATE code for CONTROLR.SCX
IF UPPER(WONTOP( )) = "CONTROLS"
   STORE .F. TO m.addmode, m.editmode
ELSE
   SELECT (WONTOP( ))
   IF ! m.addmode
      IF RLOCK( )
         m.editmode = .T.
      ELSE
         WAIT WINDOW ;
        "Sorry -- someone else is editing this record!"
         m.editmode = .F.
      ENDIF
   ENDIF
ENDIF

SHOW GETS

RETURN .F.
```

The new line is SELECT (WONTOP( )). Notice that this command makes use of the naming convention in which the window name also is the table alias. If you prefer, you can use a CASE statement that lists each window name individually, but you can see that this one command is much easier.

For this method, the control panel is always placed *last* on the list of .SCXs in the Generate dialog, so the DEACTIVATE clause code is in the correct order, ending with the control screen's SHOW GETS and RETURN .F.. Yet, the control panel still is the first GET the user enters in the READ, because of the way the revised SHOW clause deactivates all other GETS by window, as shown in the following code listing:

SHOW clause for a complex READ

```
* show snippet, CONTROLR.SCX
* first, check if an edit is already in progress
* for this table -- if so, don't
* re-SCATTER and lose edit! --
IF NOT EVAL("m.ed"+ALIAS( ))
   IF m.addmode
      SCATTER MEMO BLANK TO (ALIAS( ))
   ELSE
      SCATTER MEMO TO (ALIAS( ))
   ENDIF
   * the following could be taken care of with an
   * #INSERT <filename>
   * and the file could hold different app-specific
   * information in each development directory
   IF UPPER(ALIAS( )) == "BUDGET"
      m.product = Product.prodname
      m.dept = Dept.deptname
      m.budname = Budcat.budcat
   ENDIF
ENDIF
IF m.editmode OR m.addmode
   SHOW GETS WINDOW Controls DISABLE ONLY
   SHOW GETS WINDOW (ALIAS( )) ENABLE ONLY
   STORE .T. TO ("m.ed"+ALIAS( ))
   * see comment above regarding an #INSERT
   IF UPPER(ALIAS( )) == "BUDGET"
      IF Budget(6)
         DO no_edit
      ELSE
         DO can_edit
      ENDIF
   ENDIF
ELSE
```

continues

```
    UNLOCK
    SHOW GETS DISABLE ONLY
    SHOW GET act2 ENABLE
ENDIF
```

The CONTROLR.SCX's SHOW clause contains code specific to the Budget window edit, rather than moving the code to the budget screen, to make sure that this code executes at a precise moment during the clause. This code does no harm if it's never used (if no window in the set has the name reserved for the Budget screen). To keep the control panel completely generic, however, you can use an #INSERT generator directive and refer to a file that contains different applications-specific information in each development directory.

TIP

If you do not disable all other GETs besides the control panel push buttons, you can still be certain that the push buttons are the first GET the user enters, no matter where the control panel .SCX is placed in the list; just determine the value of the first current object in the READ WHEN clause, like this:

```
_CUROBJ = OBJNUM(m.act2)
```

You need to use the OBJNUM( ) function because you don't know how many GETs will exist in the READ, as you move .SCXs in and out of the READ set, and you don't know where m.act2 will fall within this sequence. You might think a #READCLAUSES generator directive would be a better choice (the OBJECT clause seems designed to fulfill this requirement). Unfortunately the OBJECT clause is evaluated before the GETS have assigned sequence numbers. In the OBJECT clause for the READ containing the m.act2 GET, OBJNUM(m.act2) is always 0! In the WHEN clause, OBJNUM( ) returns the appropriate sequence number.

The DEACTIVATE code uses the naming convention to find the table alias to SELECT by checking the WONTOP( ) (name of current window). The SHOW code uses the reverse of this convention by checking the alias to know which window and memory variables to adjust. Without this convention, you could use a CASE structure to handle each window and file separately.

The DEACTIVATE and SHOW code have undergone minor changes, but they follow substantially the same path that the control panel code took in the Chapter 12 version. The control panel Setup and the control panel button code (the m.act2 VALID) work for all the tables on-screen—this code didn't change from the Chapter 12 version. The crucial adjustment is allowing the current work area and window to determine which task is current.

The task-specific code for each data entry screen also remains substantially the same. You need to make only one more critical change to allow related tables to function together in this method.

The Budget screen needs a relationship to the lookup tables to show appropriate product, budget category, and department names, and the Budget entries' product, budget category, and department code fields must be validated against these tables. Yet, the lookup tables' record pointers must remain coordinated with the related data entry edits, which may not correspond to the Budget relation.

The USE... AGAIN command, introduced in FoxPro 2.0, is the secret to fulfilling this requirement. (This command now is even more useful in FoxPro 2.5, with 225 work areas available in both FoxPro for Windows and the Extended version of FoxPro 2.5 DOS.) The Budget entry screen requires the environment represented by the MODEL.VUE file you used in various chapters of this book, but each lookup file is USEd .... AGAIN with a different ALIAS, in a separate work area, for a separate data entry window. This second alias is used for the array, window name, and variables that represent this data entry task, as shown in the following example:

```
USE Product AGAIN ALIAS Productr
```

The corresponding Setup code is shown in the following listing:

```
* Setup for Product data entry window
* for CONTROLR.SCX multiple file screen set:
REGIONAL m.saveit
SELECT Productr
SCATTER TO Productr
m.edproductr = .F.
```

The `Save/Cancel` buttons for each data entry screen have slightly altered code to coordinate with this change, as shown in the following code:

```
* m.saveit VALID for Product data entry window
* used in CONTROLR.SCX multiple file screen set:
IF m.saveit = 2
   IF m.addmode
      INSERT INTO Productr FROM ARRAY Productr
   ELSE
```

continues

```
      GATHER FROM Productr
   ENDIF
ENDIF
m.addmode = .F.
m.editmode = .F.
SHOW GETS
```

Although this code performs the INSERT INTO and GATHER to the file ALIASed as Productr, underneath this table still is Product (the table just has a different record pointer and, potentially, a different order). All changes made to this incarnation of the table are reflected in the version used as a lookup by the Budget data entry screen.

Figure 15.6 shows this method in action. The example screens look different from the screens you created in Chapters 12 and 13 but contain the same validation schemes, requiring little adjustment. Notice that both the Budget editing window and the Budcat editing window are in the process of active edits, although the budget category entries in the two windows don't match. If the Product and Department windows are chosen by the user, these windows too become editable, until the user moves between records by choosing the control panel.

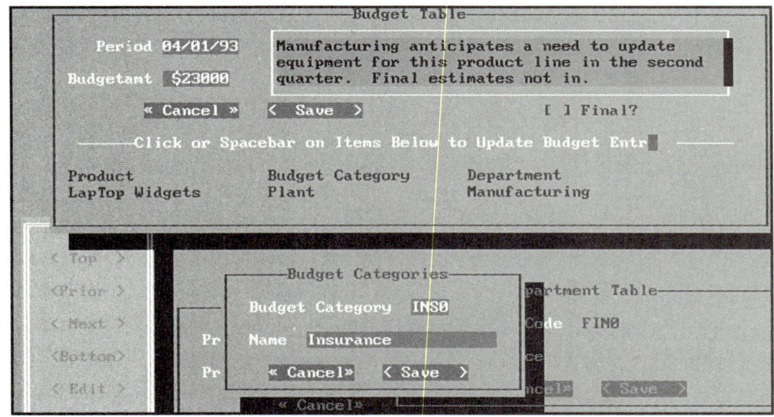

FIG. 15.6

A complex screen set in action.

The example in figure 15.6 uses a control panel to create a counterpoint to EX1, in which all the GETs participate in the same READ, and to highlight advantages of generic file-handling by using name conventions. A control panel, however, is emphatically not required for a complex READ approach. In fact, without the control panel, the code is simplified considerably, and the resulting behavior may be more intuitive for the user. A simple ACTIVATE clause can SELECT

(WONTOP( )), once again providing insurance that the currently-edited window corresponds to the SELECTed work area. Then, simple ON KEY LABEL assignments or menu shortcuts provide the movement through the file, as shown in the following code:

Keystrokes to provide an alternative to a control panel

```
* ON KEY LABEL PgUp DO Go_back
* or equivalent menu option with a PgUp shortcut

* ON KEY LABEL PgDn DO Go_forth
* or equivalent menu option with a PgDn shortcut

* procedures similar to the following could be
* assigned to Ctrl-PgUp and Ctrl-PgDn, providing
* access to the top and bottom of the file:

PROCEDURE Go_back  && PgUp
PUSH KEY CLEAR
IF EVAL("m.ad"+WONTOP( )) OR EVAL("m.ed"+WONTOP( ))
   IF Ask("Save work on this record?")
       GATHER MEMVAR
   ENDIF
   SHOW GETS WINDOW (WONTOP( )) DISABLE
   SHOW GET m.edit_or_add ENABLE
   STORE .F. TO ("m.ad"+WONTOP( )),("m.ed"+WONTOP( ))
ENDIF

SKIP -1
IF BOF( ) OR ;
   (WTITLE( ) = "Sales Records" AND ;
    custcode # Customer.Custcode)
   ?? CHR(7)
   SKIP 1
ENDIF

SCATTER MEMVAR
SHOW GETS
POP KEY
RETURN


PROCEDURE Go_forth  && PgDn
PUSH KEY CLEAR
IF EVAL("m.ad"+WONTOP( )) OR EVAL("m.ed"+WONTOP( ))
   IF Ask("Save work on this record?")
       GATHER MEMVAR
```

continues

```
   ENDIF
   SHOW GETS WINDOW (WONTOP( )) DISABLE}
   SHOW GET m.edit_or_add ENABLE
   STORE .F. TO ("m.ad"+WONTOP( )),("m.ed"+WONTOP( ))
ENDIF

SKIP 1
IF EOF( ) OR ;
   (WTITLE( ) = "Sales Records" AND ;
    custcode # Customer.Custcode)
   ?? CHR(7)
   SKIP -1
ENDIF

SCATTER MEMVAR
SHOW GETS
POP KEY
RETURN
```

This method, with no control panel, causes less disruption to the user's data entry process; the user stays in one window while concentrating on editing the window's information. If the file movement keystrokes are assigned to menu shortcuts of PgUp and PgDn, this method has the following added virtues:

- The PgUp and PgDn keystrokes usually take you through the windows of a READ, much as these keys might move you through pages of a written form. This behavior doesn't make sense in a complex READ, however, where the sequence of windows and files may not correspond to the sequence of actions the user usually wants to take. Assigning these keys to another responsibility, such as paging up and down through a single file's records without leaving the window, often is far more comfortable for the user. (This assignment is similar to the behavior of an interactive EDIT or EDIT FORMAT.)
- The menu options automatically provide a mouse alternative to the keystrokes, without added objects on-screen.

Additional requirements or restrictions are easy to include in the code. In the example procedures above, the WTITLE( ) check accommodates a situation you have not encountered in previous exercises: a set of child records through which the user wants to move, yet which should remain restricted to the set of records belonging to a parent record. In this case, the parent is a Customer table, and the child records are Sales table records for each customer.

Using Complex READS in Extensive Applications

You learned about one-to-many relationships by seeing these relationships graphically displayed in BROWSEs in the first section of this book. The users of your applications may have an easier time visualizing these relationships if the screen sets have BROWSEs, too. In addition, if you use BROWSEs to move through data tables, as you saw in the Budget data entry screen in Chapter 13, you eliminate the code necessary to reposition the record pointer.

In the following section, you add non-GET windows to the complex READ, although you now know the basic principles to make this kind of a READ work, with or without BROWSEs.

The central concept of an application that corresponds to a single READ, with many carefully categorized and related tasks operating at the same time, is limited by the memory this kind of READ may take. Each window and memory variable uses memory. The EX1-style application also requires memory in quantity, because the DEFINEd WINDOWs that aren't RELEASEd don't return memory to the available pool. In FoxPro as in all things, the more you want to accomplish, the more resources you need.

You can build the READ with a maximum number of tasks, test thoroughly, and eliminate a window at a time, until you see what works for your system. Remember, however, the goal is to make life simpler for the user. Cramming every task into one READ, or using the EX1 system to make all tasks seem available at the same time can be more confusing than useful. Instead, group tasks intelligently in modules, which are placed separately on the menu as a separate complex READ. Each READ contains several related tasks, although no READ contains the entire spectrum of activity of the application.

In an accounting application, the modules are Accounts Receivable, Accounts Payable, Utilities (lookup file maintenance), and so on. Some tables, such as the Address file, may be accessible in each module, but in each case you give a slightly different view of the file's information, by emphasizing different fields for editing and setting different table relationships. In a Utilities module, you may edit the Address table in a prominent GET window, but during the Invoicing procedure, the same table may serve as a lookup, in a BROWSE format.

Using the RDLEVEL( ) > 1 menu check discussed in the previous chapter and one extra Foundation READ, the complex application's modules *are modal with respect to each other.* The user can't access the full Invoicing module at the same time as Utilities. Still, while the user enters invoices, addresses and other customer information incidental to these invoices can be adjusted. The appropriate lookup BROWSE can be edited, or more commonly, a nested modal READ can be summoned for the current Address record when necessary.

Because the program accommodates the user's job in a flexible manner, the user doesn't feel restricted in this approach. Each module is *modeless internally.*

Each module in the application is similar to a separate application under a multitasking operating system, such as DESQView or Windows. In this kind of operating system, each module can be started as a separate instance of FoxPro. Modules are available simultaneously, and the operating system takes care of variables, window definitions, and program processes separately for each module, as if the modules were running on separate networked machines. This capability is one reason why your programs always should assume multiple-user access.

The complex READ system also mirrors the FoxPro interactive environment, in which the Command window serves the same function as the application's Foundation READ. The user can move between tasks in the same way you move between BROWSEs, desk accessories, and other activities from the interactive system menu, although some choices initiate a modal dialog and temporarily suspend your ability to perform other tasks. The difference between this approach for applications and the developer's interactive environment is that, in most cases, you restrict the tables and relationships, defining all the available activities in advance.

Integrating Multiple non-READ Windows in the Complex READ

When adding BROWSEs, MODIFY MEMOs and FILEs, and desk accessories to a READ, you accept a basic FoxPro rule: the window-level clauses (DEACTIVATE and ACTIVATE) which intercept and interpret user choices only apply to windows with GETs. If the current window—as returned by the WONTOP( ) function—is GETful and the user moves to a new window, the choice triggers the READ's DEACTIVATE clause, but if the current window is a GETless window, the DEACTIVATE code does not execute. If the new window chosen by the user is GETful, the ACTIVATE code executes, but if the new window is GETless, the ACTIVATE clause isn't triggered.

As a practical result of this rule, you must limit the DEACTIVATE code to activity necessary as the user leaves a GET window, and you only assign the ACTIVATE clause tasks necessary when a GET window becomes current.

This limitation is crucial to EX1.APP and EX2.APP because the applications rely on the DEACTIVATE clause to CLEAR a READ. If the user leaves a BROWSE to enter another window, the DEACTIVATE clause isn't triggered, so the application doesn't know that a window belonging to a different READ was accessed. In the complex READ approach demonstrated in this chapter, however, the problem doesn't occur.

The DEACTIVATE code presented in the previous examples performs two basic tasks, the code SELECTs an appropriate work area for the current data entry window and attempts to lock the current record. A non-GET window doesn't require these actions. A BROWSE SELECTs the appropriate work area and locks a record when the user begins an edit, a MODIFY MEMO doesn't need to SELECT but performs the lock, and the Calendar/Diary and Calculator don't need either adjustment.

Because these activities are necessary *for GET windows only*, move the DEACTIVATE code to the ACTIVATE clause. The code executes appropriately, because the ACTIVATE clause always is triggered when the user moves to a GET window.

CAUTION: You may be tempted to use the ACTIVATE and DEACTIVATE clauses more extensively, using the BROWSE WHEN and VALID clauses to perform the same functions for a BROWSE window. This approach isn't reliable. The BROWSE VALID clause has a switch, :F, to ensure that the VALID code executes every time the user leaves the record. By contrast, the WHEN clause is designed to execute when the record pointer moves in the BROWSEd file. WHEN code is *not* always executed if the user leaves the BROWSE and returns to the same record upon return to the BROWSE window. In addition, MODIFYed text windows—whether MEMOs or FILEs—and desk accessories do not have analogous clauses.

Categorizing the Roles of a GETless WINDOW

The example in this section uses tables from the Omnipresent Widget database that illustrate the roles a BROWSE can perform in a READ. This complex READ demonstrates the following BROWSE types:

- *A driver BROWSE.* In this example, the main data entry window is the Customer table, and a BROWSE of the same table—similar to the Budget BROWSE in Chapter 13, "Improving Screen Design with Complex Screen Sets"—allows the user to pick a Customer record for edit.
- *A parent BROWSE.* The Customer table is linked to the Address table, which stores address and company-wide information. (One company address can have many Customer records.) This BROWSE, a pick list, must allow the user to move freely through Address table, so the table is USEd ... AGAIN, like the lookup tables in the previous example, while another copy of the table is related to the Customer table for validation.
- *A child BROWSE.* The Customer table is the parent in a one-to-many relationship with Sales table records. With the relation set, only Sales records for this Customer show in the BROWSE.

Because this system is designed to perform indirect READs, all three BROWSEs are issued with the NOEDIT and NOMENU keywords (otherwise, the user needs to edit the tables directly). To edit each table, provide each BROWSE with a nested MODAL READ using a menu shortcut or ON KEY LABEL assignment. (The BROWSEs in this kind of a system can be edited directly, if you prefer direct READs.)

Figure 15.7 shows the READ in progress. The Setup for the screen issues a BROWSE NOWAIT SAVE for each of the tables. The Customer driver BROWSE, and all other BROWSEs paired with a data entry screen in the READ, use a WHEN clause similar to the Budget BROWSE in Chapter 13, which is shown in the following listing:

WHEN clause for a driver BROWSE

```
FUNCTION Do_Show
* move to a new record
* signals a cancel of
* any edit in progress:
m.editmode = .F.
m.addmode = .F.
SHOW GETS WINDOW (ALIAS( ))
RETURN .T.
```

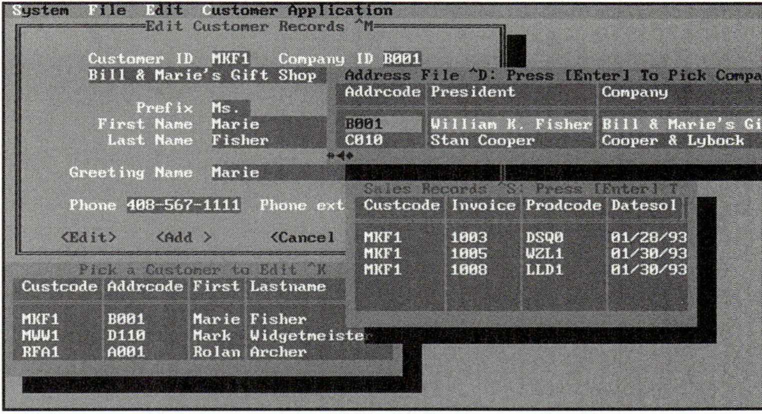

FIG. 15.7

A READ showing multiple BROWSEs serving as driver (Customer), child (Sales), and parent (Address).

The Setup initializes variables as you have learned to do in Chapters 12 and 13, and also provides a custom menu for this application task. The Setup code concludes with the following steps:

Setup code to assign tasks to keystrokes

```
PUSH KEY CLEAR

ON KEY LABEL Ctrl-W DO quitread
ON KEY LABEL Ctrl-End DO quitread
ON KEY LABEL Ctrl-Q DO quitread
ON KEY LABEL ESCAPE DO quitread

ON KEY LABEL ENTER DO browchoice WITH UPPER(WONTOP( ))
```

PUSH KEY CLEAR removes all previous ON KEY LABEL assignments for later restoration after this task completes. The next four statements assign READ-terminating and BROWSE-ending keystrokes to one procedure, which ensures that the READ ends in the same way every time the user uses the keystrokes, even if the current window is not a GET window. The Quitread procedure, placed in the Cleanup of the screen, checks the current window. If the window is a desk accessory or another window that may be closed without ending the READ, Quitread KEYBOARDs the Esc key with the PLAIN keyword, which means that a normal escape press occurs without triggering the ON KEY LABEL assigned procedure again. Otherwise, Quitread ends the READ, as shown in the following listing:

Exiting from a READ with non-GET windows

```
PROCEDURE quitread
IF INLIST(UPPER(WONTOP( )),"CALENDAR","CALCULATOR")
   KEYBOARD "{ESCAPE}" PLAIN
```

continues

```
ELSE
   IF NOT EMPTY(WOUTPUT( ))
      ACTIVATE WINDOW (WOUTPUT( ))
   ENDIF
   CLEAR READ
ENDIF
```

In this application, an Enter keypress in the Address BROWSE signals a new company address for the current Customer record, but an Enter keypress in the Sales BROWSE indicates that the user wants to edit a Sales record for this customer. The Enter key works properly in other windows. The final ON KEY LABEL assignment in the Setup code passes the current window's name to a procedure that evaluates the current window and decides what to do next. In the following code, note the PUSH KEY CLEAR/POP KEY command combination, which turns off all key assignments again until this procedure RETURNs. This step is extremely important, to prevent another Enter keypress—or the user holding the Enter key down for a while—from calling the procedure again:

Assigning window-specific behavior to a keystroke

```
PROCEDURE Browchoice
PARAMETERS currwind
PUSH KEY CLEAR
DO CASE
CASE currwind = "ADDRESS" AND ;
               (m.editmode OR m.addmode)
   STORE Address.Addrcode TO m.addrcode
   _CUROBJ = OBJNUM(m.addrcode)
   * restore the relationship, since
   * the tables are related on the field
   * Customer.Addrcode, which has not
   * changed, and the Company name
   * should reflect the variable
   * m.addrcode, which has been changed:
   GO RECNO("Address") IN Addressr
   SHOW GET Addressr.Company
   KEYBOARD "{CTRL-M}"
CASE currwind = "SALES"
   * launch a nested READ MODAL to
   * edit Sales records for this customer
   DO SALES.SPR
OTHERWISE
   KEYBOARD "{ENTER}" PLAIN
ENDCASE
POP KEY
RETURN
```

The KEYBOARD "{CTRL-M}" from the Address BROWSE in the first CASE above doesn't refer to an ON KEY LABEL CTRL-M assignment. This keystroke is assigned to a menu shortcut, as part of a window-control technique described in the next section.

The simple ACTIVATE clause is crucial to a complex READ

The ACTIVATE clause for this screen is SELECT (WONTOP( )). As in the preceding example, by assigning the Customer data entry window the name Customer to match the table's alias, you ensure that the user will be in the right work area no matter which BROWSE was selected earlier.

Two button sets, the VALID clause for m.act starts an edit or an add, indicate the user's desire to initiate an edit or an add of the current Customer record as shown in the following listing:

Buttons manage the editing process

```
* m.act VALID clause
IF m.act = 1
   IF RLOCK( )
       m.editmode = .T.
   ELSE
       WAIT WINDOW ;
          "Sorry -- some one else is editing this record!"
   ENDIF
ELSE
   m.addmode = .T.
ENDIF
SHOW GETS
```

As in previous examples, the following m.saveit provides cancel or save of an edit or an add in progress:

```
* m.savit VALID clause
IF NOT ChkAddr( ) && check all validation before
                 && allowing a save
    m.addrcode = Customer.addrcode
    SHOW GET m.addrcode
    SHOW GET Customer.company
    _CUROBJ = OBJNUM(m.addrcode)
    RETURN .F.
ENDIF
IF m.saveit = 2
   IF m.addmode
      INSERT INTO Dept FROM MEMVAR
      SHOW WINDOW Pick REFRESH SAME
   ELSE
```

continues

```
      GATHER MEMVAR
      SHOW WINDOW Pick REFRESH SAME
   ENDIF
ELSE
   GO RECNO( )
ENDIF

m.addmode = .F.
m.editmode = .F.
SHOW GETS
```

The GO RECNO( ) line, executed by the m.saveit VALID code if the edit or add was cancelled, is required to refresh the relationship between Customer and the Addressr copy of the Address file. At the end, as usual, the SHOW GETS command calls the SHOW clause to handle most of the work. The following code for the SHOW clause is simple and will be familiar from previous exercises:

The SHOW clause maintains the GETs

```
IF m.addmode
   SCATTER MEMVAR BLANK
ELSE
   SCATTER MEMVAR
ENDIF

IF m.editmode OR m.addmode
   SHOW GETS WINDOW Customer ENABLE ONLY
   SHOW GET m.act DISABLE
ELSE
   UNLOCK
   SHOW GETS WINDOW Customer DISABLE ONLY
   SHOW GET m.act ENABLE
ENDIF
```

Controlling the Current Window during the Complex READ

Often, you want to direct the user's attention to a particular window or activity. In previous examples, you used the capability of GET windows and GETs to respond to the value of _CUROBJ and SHOW GET(S) ENABLE or DISABLE to change the current focus. Desk accessories and other GETless windows also do not affect, or respond to, the value of _CUROBJ and the SHOW GETS command during a READ.

You often may want to force the user to make a valid lookup choice as part of validation. In the screen set you are currently studying, the user may enter an invalid Company ID (the Addrcode field that serves as a link between the Customers and the company address to which they correspond). You can RETURN .F. from the Addrcode's VALID clause if no match is found, but then the user has to enter a new value. You might prefer to move the focus to the Address BROWSE and let the user choose an existing company. You can allow the user to add a new entry or to edit the current record, while BROWSEing, by pressing a hot key; you issue a nested modal READ of the Address file.

If you try to ACTIVATE a GETless WINDOW from within the VALID of a GET, you find that the VALID clause ties the focus to the current GET, and control returns to the GET window after the VALID clause executes. You need a different tactic to summon the BROWSE windows programmatically.

The trick is to KEYBOARD a menu shortcut or ON KEY LABEL key combination that will ACTIVATE the WINDOW. FoxPro recognizes the KEYBOARDed strokes when the program execution *returns* from the VALID and is back to the READ wait state—just as if the user typed these keystrokes. Because the VALIDation is complete, the READ is no longer tied to the current GET and its WINDOW.

Menu code handles window-switching

The CUSTOMER.APP has a menu pad with several options, each of which performs this task for a different window. Each menu item has a Command result, which is simply ACTIVATE WINDOW <the window name>.

As you see in figure 15.8, the native option to Cycle through the windows, using the Bar result of _MWI_CYCLE and the usual Ctrl+F1 shortcut, also resides conveniently on the application menu popup. Any other window-handling native system bars, such as Zoom, also can be added here, or placed elsewhere on the limited system menu provided for this application.

TIP

For convenience, the menu for this application is defined by two separate .MNX files. After a command to PUSH MENU _MSYSMENU, so that the previous system menu is restored later, a limited system menu (System, File, Edit pads) replaces the current menu. This limited menu is generic, which you use in all your applications (and users know where to find each program's standard utilities and accessories). Next, DO a second .MPR which uses the Menu Builder option to Append one or more application-specific pads to the generic pads.

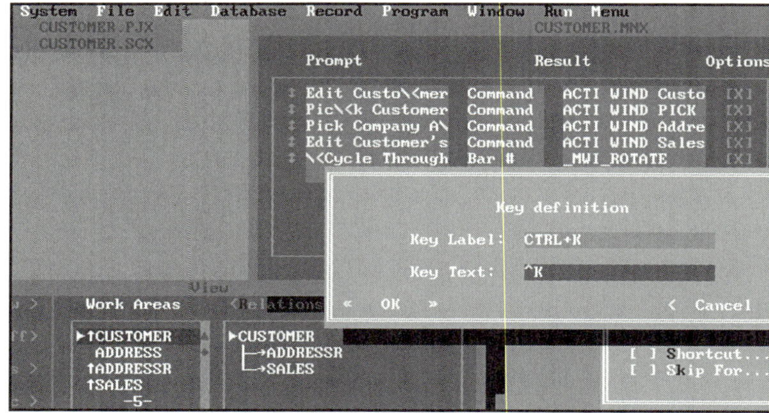

FIG. 15.8

The Menu Builder edits the Customer Application menu, and the View window shows the application's file relationships.

Notice, in figure 15.9, that each menu shortcut is reflected in the title of the related window, as an extra reminder, although menu shortcuts have the advantage of providing a handy list on the menu popup. Both the user *and* the program can use these shortcuts to change windows at any time. The VALIDation code for m.addrcode is a simple example of this technique, and is shown in the following code:

Including window-switching in GET validation

```
IF NOT ChkAddr( )
   KEYBOARD "{CTRL-D}"
ENDIF
```

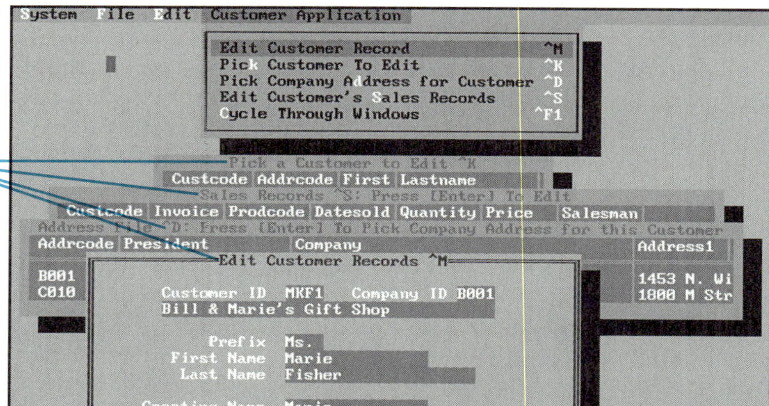

FIG. 15.9

The application menu pad for CUSTOMER.APP.

Segregate the actual validation of the address code in a UDF (ChkAddr( )) so that you can reuse this code in the previous m.saveit code:

```
FUNCTION ChkAddr
IF NOT SEEK(m.addrcode,"Addressr")
   WAIT WINDOW ;
      "Need a valid Company Address ID!"
   RETURN .F.
ELSE
   SHOW GET addressr.company
ENDIF
```

After developing this method of validating the linking Addrcode for the Customer record, you may decide that the user never enters the code. Instead, a button in the Customer screen can move the focus directly to the BROWSE if the user needs to edit company address choice. The button's VALID KEYBOARDs the menu shortcut as before. When the user then chooses to add a Customer record, the Customer.Addrcode can default to the current value in the BROWSE or repeat the previous Customer record's Addrcode value, or the program can check for an EMPTY(m.addrcode) when the user presses the `m.saveit` button to post the new record to the file.

The user doesn't have to see all the windows at one time. In the Setup code, you can MOVE the WINDOWs off-screen until you KEYBOARD the related shortcut in response to a validation requirement or a user request for the BROWSE. Place windows at negative coordinates to make sure they don't appear. (You may be surprised to realize that windows can be DEFINEd at, or MOVEd to, rows and columns with negative numbers, but you can do it. Since FoxPro's coordinate system starts with 0,0 in the upper-left corner, negative-numbered rows exist "above" the screen area, and negative-numbered columns exist to the left of the screen area. See Chapter 23, "Controlling a Windowed Environment," for more information about calculating and changing window positions.) Users also can rearrange the windows to suit their desktop style, just as you do in the interactive environment.

You can test for windows that the user has stowed away temporarily by using the WMIN( ) function, and you can use the ZOOM WINDOW <window name> NORM command to call the user's attention back to any window.

You may prefer to issue the BROWSE statement only when you need it, rather than leaving the BROWSE on-screen all the time or moving the BROWSE in and out of the visible screen area. In this case, you don't use the SAVE and NOWAIT clauses on the BROWSE. If the user enters an invalid address code, or presses a button indicating a desire to see an address list, for example, your code resembles the following:

```
PRIVATE m.select
m.select = SELECT( )
SELECT Address
PUSH KEY CLEAR
ON KEY LABEL ENTER DO PickBrow WITH "Addresses"
WAIT WINDOW NOWAIT ;
     "Pick an Address by pressing Enter..."
BROWSE && with a FIELDS list and any other
       && clauses
POP KEY
SELECT (m.select)
```

This BROWSE statement is modal *automatically*. Without the NOWAIT keyword, the user remains in the BROWSE (program execution doesn't continue until the BROWSE is exited). If the user clicks another window, the BROWSE closes because you didn't use the SAVE keyword.

> **CAUTION:** Never issue a BROWSE statement without the NOWAIT keyword unless you are sure that no BROWSE already exists for this work area. Issuing multiple BROWSEs for one alias is one of the fastest ways to crash a FoxPro application. The error message is often the bewildering `Transgressed handles`, which—according to Microsoft Fox technical support—indicates that FoxPro's memory is "somehow confused." Although you may receive this message in other ways, your BROWSE handling is the first place to look when attempting to resolve the problem.
>
> One solution is to add a test for WEXIST(<browse window name>) before you issue the BROWSE command. Here, as always, you must be careful to name the BROWSE properly. Refer to the section, "Using Browses in a Screen Set," in Chapter 13 to refresh your understanding of BROWSE windows and names. Rather than relying on these kinds of checks, however, you'd do better to use a consistent strategy. A particular BROWSE should be designed to be regularly available, should be a BROWSE NOWAIT SAVE, shouldn't leave before the READ ends—even if moved off-screen occasionally—and it never should be reissued. If the BROWSE has a discrete and limited purpose, issue the BROWSE as if it were a modal dialog and resume the normal flow of the READ after the BROWSE is gone. This strategy works equally well for MODIFY MEMO and FILE windows as for BROWSEs.

Using Sophisticated Window Strategies

After you become comfortable with non-GET windows on-screen and window control in a READ, you will find many ways to enhance the techniques presented here. Just as a menu shortcut or ON KEY LABEL keystroke, for example, can initiate a READ MODAL to edit a child record, a keypress in a BROWSE can initiate a dialog to change the BROWSE's order. You find that ACTIVATEing the dialog window on top of the BROWSE and DEACTIVATEing the dialog refreshes the BROWSE display with the new order, or with newly edited records, without further effort. Conceivably, another modal dialog may search for a particular record, asking the user for search directions. (In Chapter 16's section on using an API library you find an alternative search method that provides the same *incremental seek* feature for BROWSE as you use in scrollable lists and popups, so the user can begin typing a choice and the BROWSE's current record reflects the typing.)

Because you can KEYBOARD the keystrokes to make a BROWSE active at any time during the READ, KEYBOARD in the READ WHEN to *begin* the READ with a driver BROWSE as the active window. Understanding how to perform this feat, which puts the user in the best position to pick a record to edit, is one of the questions most frequently asked by developers who use multiple windows in a READ—yet, now that you know the trick, beginning the READ in a BROWSE, or any other specified window, is a trivial problem.

You can KEYBOARD a menu sequence to bring up the desk accessories during a READ (assigning menu shortcuts to the Calendar/Diary and Calculator makes this procedure look smoother). In the following simple example, the Calendar/Diary is part of date validation, and the user's choice replaces the inappropriate date upon return from the desk accessory:

```
* NEW_CAL.PRG
  CLEAR
  SET TALK OFF
  SET CENTURY ON
  DEFINE WINDOW entry FROM 1,1 to 9, 30 ;
         COLOR SCHEME 10 ;
         TITLE "My Data Entry Window"
```

continues

```
ACTIVATE WINDOW entry
stuff_date = .F.
@ 1,2 SAY "Whatever " GET other DEFAULT " "
@ 3,2 SAY "Enter Date" ;
      GET this_date ;
      WHEN ! stuff_date OR getdate( ) VALID vdate( ) ;
      ERROR "This date can't be blank!" DEFAULT {} ;
      PICTURE "@K"
@ 5,2 SAY "More Stuff " GET something DEFAULT "   "
READ CYCLE
RELEASE WINDOW entry
RETURN

FUNCTION vdate
mreturn = .T.
IF EMPTY(this_date)
  KEYBOARD "{ALT+S}d"
  * these keystrokes are default for the
  * Calendar/Diary, but if you give the option
  * a menu shortcut, you won't see the menu flash
  * when the KEYBOARD summons the desk accessory
  stuff_date = .T.
  _CUROBJ = _CUROBJ
  mreturn = .F.
ENDIF
RETURN mreturn

FUNCTION getdate
IF EMPTY(this_date)
   this_date = _DIARYDATE
   stuff_date = .F.
ENDIF
RETURN .T.
```

NOTE

Notice the `_CUROBJ = _CUROBJ` line in Vdate( ) in the preceding code. Usually, when a validation function RETURNs .F., the current GET doesn't change (the cursor stays in the same field until the VALID clause RETURNs .T.). In this case, however, activating the desk accessory causes the current object to be the first GET in the READ on return from the UDF. This behavior only applies to READ CYCLE and may change in future releases.

In a different application, you may allow the user to decide when (if ever) to use the Calendar/Diary. In the ACTIVATE clause, however, you can check the last window before the GET window that triggers the ACTIVATE code, using the WLAST( ) function. If you find that the Calendar/Diary was the last window and the current GET is a date-type field or memory variable—using the expression TYPE(VARREAD( )) = "D"—you can ask the user if they want the Calendar date (_DIARYDATE) to replace the value in the current GET. The following chapter provides a different way to access the desk accessories during data validation, using a nested MODAL READ to hold the program at the non-GET window.

Summary

FoxPro's capability of juggling windows and information displayed in windows, especially in the powerful BROWSE, has a paradoxical effect: you will continue imagining new problems that you want to solve, just because you continue to find the solutions within your reach. Appendix H shows additional examples of such special purpose solutions—including a READ with BROWSEs and other non-READ windows, but no GETs to manage the READ, a record marker for an inactive BROWSE, a BROWSE pick list in which the choices turn color according to a condition you set, and a BROWSE with an editable check box field.

Don't feel obliged to find a way to use all these tricks in every application you write—or even to understand their underlying code immediately. In Chapter 16, you learn about other supporting features unique to this extraordinarily rich environment. Although not as central to the development process as the power tools you explored in the last four chapters, the features covered in the following chapter can all add significantly to the functionality and the style of the applications you write. Chapter 16 concludes the exploration of FoxPro interface agents, and Chapter 17 shows how to use these agents to design applications for multiple FoxPro platforms.

In Part IV, you begin a focused study of the FoxPro programming language, the powerful and extensive set of commands and functions that provides the support and vehicle for all you have accomplished so far.

16

CHAPTER

Discovering More FoxPro Productivity Features

As you practiced with the FoxPro application-building power tools described in the preceding chapters, you rearranged the screen desktop to your liking. You may prefer to stack the files and code snippets you are editing, similar to pending documents in an *In* file basket. You also may prefer these packets of data in a tiled arrangement, as if the papers were spread across a desk. Finally, you may want to keep open but inactive windows docked in a corner, like folders pulled from a file cabinet, closed but ready for use.

You may want the Command window to stay in the default position on-screen, or you may prefer a Command window that stretches the entire width but sits on the bottom of the screen, approximating the *dot prompt* command interface used by older Xbase dialects.

How does FoxPro track the elements and arrangement of the desktop? A special table, the *Resource file,* stores information about what Fox sensibly and literally labels *preferences* for differing work habits and tool use.

In Chapter 8, you learned about Browse preferences, which enable you to save an intricate Browse arrangement of fields and formatting to use again at a later date, without reissuing the same complex Browse command. You investigated the actual Resource file, to see the manner in which FoxPro stores these preferences. You also BROWSEd and edited the Resource file as you do other tables.

In this chapter, you investigate the other preferences and related records maintained in a Resource file. You also learn about the following FoxPro features, many of which use Resource preferences and all of which provide enhanced personal productivity as you work in FoxPro:

- The *Filer,* which helps you manage files and directories without exiting from FoxPro.
- The *Color System,* which provides almost unlimited control over the colors you see for FoxPro system interface objects and the objects you design for applications.
- *Macros,* which enable you to store and replay complex sequences of keystrokes to automate tasks.
- The *Calculator, Diary,* and *Special Characters* and *ASCII charts* form a package of desk accessories, which have the same functions as the physical desk accessories with the same names. The *Capture* utility, which is an analog to a copy machine, completes this group of minor but helpful tools.
- *Printer Drivers,* and the *printer driver setups* that you store for individual printers as preferences in the Resource file, which provides printer-specific information as FoxPro creates output from files and data.
- The *API* (Application Program Interface), which serves as a gateway to special capabilities not directly available in FoxPro. You can use routines written in C and assembly language just as if these routines were native FoxPro functions.

All these special-purpose tools have implications for work in FoxPro's interactive environment, and you also can use many of these tools to enhance the applications you distribute to other users.

The Resource File

As with almost everything else in FoxPro, you can customize a Resource file and even SET RESOURCE OFF, closing the file. However, if you installed FoxPro and the program still is in the default state, the SETting of RESOURCE is ON, and the Resource file you use, FOXUSER.DBF, is found in the main FoxPro directory.

If you are not sure what Resource file is in use on a system, or wonder if RESOURCE may even have been SET OFF by another user, use the Files panel of the View window to check. In figure 16.1, you see a View window that shows the RESOURCE is ON (the Resource box is checked), but is set to a different file name, D:\Q_USER.DBF.

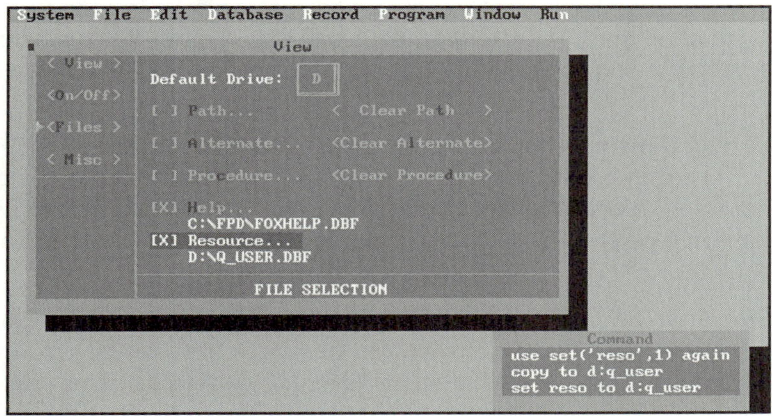

FIG. 16.1

The Files Panel of the View window shows the status of the Resource file.

Understanding the Resource File

As you perform the following exercises, you use the file that was, until now, the Resource file. If RESOURCE was previously SET OFF in the system, look for a FoxUser file in the main FoxPro directory or in the directory from which you started FoxPro. In the unlikely event that you have no Resource file on the disk, the SETting of OFF may have been specified for RESOURCE in the CONFIG.FP file with the RESOURCE=OFF line, as described in Appendix D. Without this instruction, if you start up FoxPro and a Resource file cannot be found, FoxPro creates a new FoxUser file in the current directory.

You also can create an empty Resource file at any time, with the following command in the Command window:

```
CREATE TABLE <filename> (Type         C(12), ;
                         Id           C(12), ;
                         Name         C(24), ;
                         Readonly     L    , ;
                         Ckval        N(6),  ;
                         Data         M,     ;
                         Updated      D)
```

You also can create a Resource table with this structure through the FoxPro interface, by using the View window or the File New dialog. A Resource file may have any legal file name, but the structure and field names must be in this exact form. You cannot add extra fields for new comments, for example, and have FoxPro recognize this file for Resource use.

As you may remember from Chapter 8, RESOURCE should be SET OFF or SET TO another file name before you can open the Resource table. You can use the `On/Off` panel of the View window to SET RESOURCE OFF, or you type `SET RESOURCE OFF` directly into the Command window.

Using the Resource check box in the `Files` panel of the View window enables you to SET RESOURCE TO a different file name instead. This method works only if you have another Resource file already available on disk; you cannot use the Open File dialog to generate a new, on-the-spot Resource file. If you specify a file name in this dialog but the file you choose is not a valid Resource file, the Resource file doesn't close or change (you don't see an error message).

Similarly, the SET RESOURCE TO <filename> command in a program or the Command window requires that the named file is available and of the correct format. The SET RESOURCE TO <filename> command SETs RESOURCE ON, provided that the named file is a valid Resource file. When the command is issued unsuccessfully, you see an error message, and RESOURCE is SET OFF.

When you have SET RESOURCE OFF or TO another file, you can USE Foxuser (or the name the original Resource file was called).

TIP

In figure 16.1 you also see the file currently in use as Fox's Help file. As you learn in Chapter 20, investigating the FoxPro Help file calls for techniques similar to the techniques you use with Resource files. Both kinds of file can be SET OFF or TO any FoxPro table with the appropriate file structure. Neither file type appears in a work area when in use, and neither file type uses a structural index file that you can modify—although the Resource file has a special, internally generated and erased index you see if you check the `View Setup` panel while the file is in USE.

You can open both file types while in use with the USE AGAIN syntax. The Help file is not editable when opened in this manner. Although the active Resource file does appear to be editable when USEd AGAIN, you may experience inconsistent results if you attempt to edit the file.

On the other hand, you can USE the active Resource file AGAIN (include the NOUPDATE keyword for safety) and keep a BROWSE NOEDIT open while you work. You can learn a great deal about Resource files by watching the active file's records change in the Browse while you interact with FoxPro.

By typing the following commands, you can use the Command window and some FoxPro functions to open the current Resource file at the same time you learn of the file's name and location:

```
SET RESOURCE OFF
USE SET("RESOURCE",1)
* SET("RESOURCE",1), like SYS(2005), tells the name of
* the current Resource file even if RESOURCE is OFF.
* The USE command takes this information as a reference
* to a file name and opens the file.
BROWSE TITLE FULLPATH(DBF())
* The browse window title tells you
* exactly what file you are in.
```

No matter how you decide to open the file, look carefully at the contents of the Resource file in a Browse. As you can see in figure 16.2, records are specified, by using the Type field, as either a preference (PREF) or a DATA type record. The Resource file stores separate Types for FoxPro 1.0, 2.0, 2.5 DOS, and 2.5 Windows PREFerences and DATA; the Q_USER.DBF in the figure shows the records from its use in all three environments. Within each Type, the Id field tells you the use of each record. PREFerences can have Ids that contain the letters POS, which denote records that hold position and size information for individual Menu Layouts, Projects, and Screen Layouts for different files, including the state of attached code snippets. Other POS records hold position and size for the Report and Label windows, the desk accessories, and other system windows. Notice that you can maintain a SCREENPOS record for an open snippet, such as TEST.SCX's m.button VALID snippet in the figure, as well as the .SCX Layout window.

System File Edit Database Record Program Window Run

Q_USER

Type	Id	Name	Readonly	Ckval	Data	Updated
PREF2.5	SCREENPOS	CUSTOMER.SCX	F	53818	Memo	01/21/93
PREF2.5	WINDBROW	ADDRESS	F	36039	Memo	01/21/93
PREF2.5	WINDCMD		F	47636	Memo	01/21/93
PREF2.5	VIEWPOS		F	21692	Memo	01/21/93
DATA2.0	PDSETUP	ProPrinter		55666	Memo	01/21/93
PREF2.5	DIARYPOS		F	33451	Memo	01/21/93
DATA	DIARYDATA	19930112	F	21684	Memo	01/21/93
PREF2.0	HELPPOS		F	1994	Memo	10/29/92
PREFW	REPORTPOS		F	49155	Memo	01/07/93
PREF2.0	WINDBROW	THREADS	F	6675	Memo	11/14/92
PREFW	WINDSCREEN	test - m.button Valid	F	1078	Memo	10/23/92
PREFW	SCREENPOS	test.scx	F	56115	Memo	10/23/92
PREFW	MODPRJPOS	test.pjx	F	56150	Memo	10/23/92
PREF2.0	GETEXPR					
PREF2.5	WINDMODIFY	userid.c				
PREF2.5	COLORSET	NEWCOLOR				
PREF2.5	CALCPOS					
DATA2.5	CALCULATOR					

Q_USER.DATA

Command

FIG. 16.2

Using BROWSE on the contents of the Resource file.

Other records use the Id of WINDBROW to hold characteristics used for a default BROWSE LAST for all files you BROWSEd in the past and also all special BROWSE PREFERENCEs you previously designed and saved. WINDMODIFY records save preferences for editing a particular file or files with a particular extension. WINDMEMO records hold preferences for editing a particular memo or all Memo fields. Each COLORSET record holds one complete set of references to colors for all the objects that make up the FoxPro interface.

The Edit menu popup's Preferences dialog discussed in Chapter 2, which affects Text Editing defaults, is where you give FoxPro the information stored in a WINDMODIFY record or records. The related Preferences dialog for Text Editing in Memo fields creates WINDMEMO records. When you use the Expression Builder and the Calculator, the Preferences option on the Edit menu popup also is enabled and presents a specialized group of Preference options for these two tools. The two dialogs are shown in figures 16.3 and 16.4; each box has a separate record in the Resource file to store the selections you make.

Where a PREF or DATA record has an Id that can be shared by many records, such as SCREENPOS or WINDBROW, the Name field is used to identify each specific record. DATA records with the Id PDSETUP, for example, hold printer setups you previously defined; the name you give to each setup shows in the Name field.

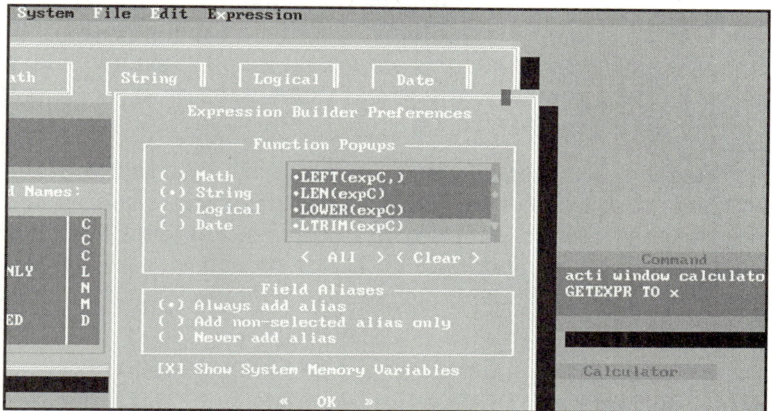

FIG. 16.3

The Expression Builder Preferences dialog.

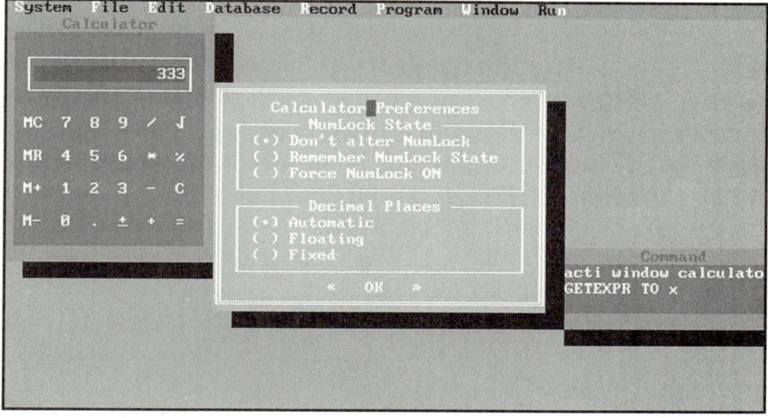

FIG. 16.4

The Calculator Preferences dialog.

Other DATA-type records store information obtained by each desk accessory. The most recent value displayed by the Calculator, the value held in Calculator memory, and the entries you make in the FoxPro Diary all are stored in the Resource file to which you can return in this and in future FoxPro sessions. All Label Layouts you define, and also the default labels available, are stored in DATA-Type records with the Id LBLLAYOUT.

Along with Name, the remaining fields in the Resource file structure are used in the same way by both PREF and DATA records. You can edit the logical Readonly field by changing the value to .T. as you did in Chapter 8, to make sure that a BROWSE setup, a Label Layout, or the position of a particular window is always the same when invoked, no matter how where you move the window on-screen or otherwise alter the window during use.

FoxPro uses the Ckval (checkvalue) field to make sure that the information in this record is accurate before the field is used to supply information about an interface element. With one exception (described in the following section), you never should have a reason to modify this field directly. The Updated field indicates the date of the last change made to this entry.

The Data Memo field contains the instructions that FoxPro uses to store the PREFerence or DATA information. In figure 16.2 you can see that, in the memo-editing window at the bottom right of the figure, this Memo field can contain a binary, rather than an ASCII text, entry. Except for DIARYDATA, all Resource records store data in a format that you should not modify directly by using the text editor.

If, like the Q_USER.DBF shown in the figure, the Resource file was in use under several versions of FoxPro, the file contains records for all the versions; but the formats of the Data Memo fields for these records are not interchangeable. If you created COLORSET records under FoxPro 2.0, you can create equivalent PREF2.5 records by using the FIXUSER program (under the main FoxPro 2.5 DOS directory in \GOODIES\MISC). If you created COLORSET records under FoxPro 1.0x, FoxPro 2.5's FIXUSER won't convert these records or add 2.5-format copies; you first must convert these records to 2.0-format using FoxPro 2.0's version of FIXUSER.

COLORSET records created under 2.0 are readable by both FoxPro 2.5 DOS Extended and Windows. The 2.0 COLORSET records, however, don't show up in the FoxPro 2.5 DOS Color Picker accessory, and FoxPro 2.5 Standard can't read them. Run FIXUSER to create PREF2.5 copies of the color sets instead (the new records appear in the Color Picker).

CAUTION: In some tests, FoxPro 2.5 for DOS Extended loaded information from a 2.0 COLORSET record in response to a SET COLORSET TO <setname> command, in *preference* to a 2.5 record with the same name. Because 2.5 doesn't always read the 2.0 records perfectly—especially for the screen color—and because you also can edit this COLORSET in 2.5 and want the changed color set to be the one FoxPro 2.5 uses, you may want to rectify this problem in one of two ways by opening the Resource file as a table, using any method described in this section:

- If you want to use this Resource file with both versions of FoxPro, change the names of the 2.5 COLORSET records so that these names don't match the 2.0 records after running FIXUSER.
- If you no longer use 2.0 or never use 2.0 with this Resource file, delete the 2.0 COLORSET records. This approach is preferable, especially if you maintain applications that refer to the color sets by name.

Although FoxPro 2.5 DOS Extended and Windows can read older FoxPro versions' COLORSET records, FoxPro DOS can't read color sets created under FoxPro Windows, and FIXUSER doesn't translate these records between the two 2.5 formats.You also must recreate and resave older FoxPro BROWSE preferences and other Resource data in new records for each 2.5 platform you use (the platforms don't share PREFerence information). LBLLAYOUT records for the DOS Label Designer cannot be used interchangeably with LABELLYT information for the Windows Report Writer.

Diary entries are the only exception to the rule that the Resource file doesn't share data easily between platforms and versions. The Data Memo fields for Diary entries are ASCII text, like all other memo fields you can edit. The Type remains DATA (rather than DATA2.0, DATA2.5, or DATAW) and needs no conversion. If you choose to edit these Memo fields directly, however, you must ensure that the Ckval fields continue to match by using the following approach:

```
REPLACE Ckval WITH VAL(SYS(2007, data))
* use a scope appropriate to the scope of records whose
* data field you have edited
```

NOTE FoxPro documentation is inconsistent about the proper value to use for the CKVAL field. In several instances, the documentation uses the formula VAL(SYS(2007, SUBSTR(Data,3))). This second formula is correct for non-DIARYDATA Resource file entries (as previously stated, you have no reason to edit these entries) but doesn't appear to work with diary entries. The formulas differ, perhaps, because the other Resource items' version information is stored in the first two characters of the Data field.

Managing Your Resource File

If you have been doing the exercises in this book and did not SET RESOURCE OFF, the Resource file contains more records than when you last examined the file in Chapter 8. FoxPro stores preferences for every window that appears on the desktop, even if you use the associated file only once.

For this reason, Resource files are subject to bloat. If you always use the same Resource file, you constantly add new records. After a time, printer setups you created for a test, preferences for text files with an extension you never use, BROWSE LAST setup for every sample table you investigate, and even old FoxPro 1.0x Resource records remain in the file. This practice not only wastes disk space but also causes FoxPro to perform more slowly as it wades through the Resource file to find needed data.

Trimming the Resource File

Regularly SET RESOURCE OFF, USE the Resource file, and delete all unnecessary records. As always, in a BROWSE you can delete records by clicking the mouse in the extreme left column or by pressing Ctrl+T. Be careful that you do not delete default or saved label layouts or other needed DATA records you labored to construct. You may find that deleting all no longer needed records of a certain Type and Id is convenient, either from the Delete... option of the Record menu popup or in the Command window. To perform this kind of group deletion, use the following formula:

```
DELETE ALL FOR Id = "MODPRJPOS"
* get rid of MODIFY PROJECT window positions
```

After you are sure that you have deleted all records you no longer need, PACK the file to reduce the size and to speed FoxPro operations (remember to USE the file EXCLUSIVEly to perform the PACK).

Although you probably don't want to delete diary entries as you do other Resource records, you occasionally may archive these records to trim the Resource file. Suppose that you want to archive all diary information for dates older than two months. Assuming that you have no other deleted Resource entries now, you can perform this process with the following code:

```
olddate = DTOS(GOMONTH(DATE( ), -2))
* The Name field stores the diary date for the entry
* in string form.
DELETE FOR Id = "DIARYDATA" AND Name < olddate
* Notice that you don't use the Updated field,
* which stores information about when
* the editing was done and not
* about the date to which the entry pertains.
COPY TO Olddiary FOR DELETED( )
PACK
```

To perform the same process for the following month, however, you want to add to OLDDIARY.DBF rather than replace the file with the next archival set of records. Instead of COPY TO Oldiary, add the following extra steps and a few SQL SELECT tricks:

```
SELECT Foxuser
m.olddate = DTOS(GOMONTH(DATE( ),-2))
DELETE FOR Id = "DIARYDATA" AND Name < m.olddate
SELECT *, .T.;
      FROM Foxuser ;
   WHERE DELETED( ) ;
   INTO CURSOR Temp
m.tempdbf = DBF( )  && Store the DBF name
                    && of the cursor
SELECT Olddiary     && Open the archive file
APPEND FROM (m.tempdbf) && You use the DBF name
                        && in APPEND FROM
SELECT Temp             && You use the ALIAS name
                        && in the SELECT command
USE                     && Get rid of the cursor
SELECT Foxuser
PACK                    && Get rid of the old records
```

In this procedure, you added an extra field (the .T.) to the field list in the SQL SELECT command. When you perform a SQL SELECT with only one source table (the FROM clause), the resulting cursor has the name you specify with the INTO CURSOR clause as the alias and doesn't have a different DBF( ) name from the original source table. FoxPro is saving time and disk space by creating a *map* to the matching records in the original table, rather than creating a table on disk. Because the APPEND FROM command uses the DBF( ) name of the table for the related source file, you are APPENDing FROM the original file and getting *all* the records from the source Foxuser table, rather than just the records marked DELETED( ).

Adding any constant to the end of the field list solves the problem. This addition forces SELECT to treat the cursor as a table with a new structure, requiring a temporary table on disk. This temporary table receives its own DBF( ), which you store to a variable and then indirectly reference—using parentheses—in the APPEND FROM command. The temporary table's DBF( ) usually is similar to F:\QUE\58599707.TMP, but you use the variable instead. The extra field is ignored during the APPEND FROM; because the Olddiary table has the same structure as your real Resource file, Olddiary has no room for this information. After the APPEND FROM is accomplished, you close the cursor, and FoxPro disposes of the temporary table.

CAUTION: You learned about APPEND FROM in Chapter 4. As explained there, APPEND FROM's DELIMITED ... WITH clause is confusing to many people who want to use the command to import data from other formats. APPEND FROM's behavior is perplexing even when the source file is another .DBF, as is the case in the preceding example. Because in FoxPro, you can APPEND FROM a table currently open in a work area, many users are surprised that APPEND FROM always reads the file on disk. The command doesn't recognize the open table or the related alias as an appropriate source for the records.

APPEND FROM reads the disk file mechanically, as if the records were in any foreign format, such as DELIMITED or SDF—even when the source is a .DBF. *FoxPro cannot evaluate information in a record intelligently, in the way it treats fields and records in a .DBF, until the target table has accepted the record.* For this reason, the APPEND FROM's FOR clause can evaluate only information that is accepted into the target. Never use the APPEND FROM ... FOR clause with filtering conditions that don't become part of the new record, such as RECNO( ), or DELETED( ), or any fields that are not included in the APPEND FROM ... FIELDS list.

Backing Up Your Resource File

After you are satisfied that the Resource file is clean, save a copy of the file to a separate name in the main FoxPro directory. Use the COPY TO <a new filename> command to create this template Resource file, and then use the SCATTER MEMVAR MEMO, APPEND BLANK, and GATHER MEMVAR MEMO commands to add new permanent records to the file from time to time, as you develop color sets, printer setups, and other Resources. By taking this step, you provide an extra layer of security for the FoxPro working environment and also a starting point from which you can create program- and user-specific Resource files for application and network use.

Keeping the Resource File Clean

Another way to stop a Resource file from bloating is to make the entire file, rather than specific entries, readonly. In the following section of this chapter, you learn how to mark files as readonly directly in FoxPro by using the Filer to reset the file's DOS attributes. You also can make a Resource file readonly for applications you create by including the file in the new .APP file (as you may recall from Chapter 14 and from working with the Project Manager, all tables contained in the .APP are readonly).

If a Resource file is readonly, you get the advantages of the material saved in it (color sets, label layouts, editing preferences, and printer setups) but you cannot add to the file. As you work with FoxPro, your use of the interface and tools matures. You continue to perform regular maintenance on the Resource file but eventually find that you no longer need to add new permanent records to the special template copy. You then can SET RESOURCE TO a readonly copy of this template file and eliminate the need for future maintenance.

In FoxPro 2.x, many people on a network also can share readonly Resource files. Editable Resource files must be used by only one person at a time, which means that each user must have a separate copy of the file.

Each approach has advantages and disadvantages. Readonly Resource files are especially good in situations where disk space is at a premium or when you need tight control over the configuration in which multiple BROWSEs and other windows appear in an application. Editable Resource files give users the greatest degree of flexibility.

Occasionally, a combination approach works best, especially if you plan to make diary entries. You can use an editable Resource file but mark many records as readonly by using the logical field provided. To maintain this file, you can enter the following code:

```
DELETE FOR ! Readonly AND ! (Id = "DIARYDATA")
BROWSE FOR DELETED( ) ;
   FIELDS Readonly, Id, Name, Updated ;
   FREEZE Readonly
* The FREEZE allows only the Readonly field to be changed,
* so you can quickly change this field for the one or two
* new records that you really want to keep.
* You can RECALL other DELETED( ) records individually
* during the BROWSE, also to preserve some editable records
RECALL FOR Readonly
PACK
* get rid of the rest
```

On a network, a combination approach allows all users common access to a readonly Resource file, yet SETs RESOURCE TO separate editable files when editing diaries. A maintenance routine, performed by the network administrator, can update the DIARYDATA entries in the Common file on a daily basis by using a procedure that performs the following steps:

- The administrator first makes an editable copy of the Common file (so the user can continue to access the Common file while maintenance is performed). Each user Resource file is USEd AGAIN, and the records are checked for Updated entries with the ID DIARYDATA. The Name field of the copy of the Common file is checked for corresponding diary date entries, to which new records are added where no current entry for this date is FOUND( ), by using SCATTER MEMVAR MEMO from the user file and INSERTing these VALUEs into the Common file.
- REPLACE common.data WITH user_a.data ADDITIVE is used to create the cumulative diary entry if a record for this date already exists—a comment line between entries can indicate each user's contribution to a given diary entry. REPLACE Updated WITH DATE( ) marks each change. Finally, the Common file copy has the edited records completed by REPLACing the related CHKVAL field WITH VAL(SYS(2007, data)), and PACK MEMO eliminates file bloat.
- The new copy of the Common file then can be rotated into active, readonly Resource status on the network.

This procedure is useful even in a copy of FoxPro not on a network, if you maintain separate Resource files for all the people who use FoxPro on a single computer but want to share a common calendar. You can work out a marking system for personal diary entries with symbols indicating that you can add certain entries to the common file while others are kept private.

This process is described in general terms, rather than just reproducing the program, because a key detail—opening and selecting user Resource files—changes, depending on how you keep records of users and user Resource files. After you finish reading about programming in Parts IV and V of this book, you may decide this procedure is a worthwhile exercise.

Creating Application-Specific Resource Files

Whether you plan to make the Resource file editable or readonly, provide a copy of the file in the .APP file of any application you distribute. You can make an editable copy of this readonly file during the installation routine. The readonly copy in the .APP can provide backup in case the editable copy is destroyed or lost. This backup file also provides the template Resource file copy as new users of a system are added.

CAUTION: To avoid confusion between which Resource file is in use, don't use the same name for the template Resource file bound into the .APP and the copy on disk.

If you decide to use the readonly copy in the .APP as the Resource file (perhaps to allow printer driver setups to be shared in a multiple-user application that doesn't need editable Resources), be sure that you use the line RESOURCE = OFF in the configuration file for the application. Otherwise, although you SET RESOURCE TO <filename> with no path, FoxPro looks for a drive and directory that matches the developer's disk and returns an error rather than first checking the .APP's contents.

As you learned in Chapter 14, you also can bind the configuration file (CONFIG.FP) to the .APP file. Read Appendices C and D for more information on using and specifying this file for different situations.

continues

When you SET RESOURCE to the file bound to the .APP, the contents of SET("RESOURCE",1) also erroneously contain the drive and directory information for the developer's copy of the file! When restoring the Resource file after any change in the environment, specify the file name explicitly if you use a bound-in Resource file.

If your application sometimes uses the bound-in file and other times uses a Resource file on disk, save the Resource file information with SET("RESOURCE",1) before changing Resources. When restoring the Resource file from the saved information, use a procedure such as the following (remember that the bound-in file and file on disk always should have separate names):

```
IF FILE(m.old_r_name)
   SET RESO TO (m.old_r_name)
ELSE
   SET RESO TO <bound in Resource file's name>
ENDIF
SET RESOURCE &old_r_state
* set the state after setting the filename, since
* SET RESOURCE TO <name> automatically
* SETs RESOURCE ON
```

A Resource file for a custom-designed application usually is far smaller than the file you use for development. This file doesn't need all the available color sets or label layouts if you settled on one or two settings for the program. A vertical market application Resource file—an application meant for sale in a particular industry, rather than custom-designed for one location—however, may need dozens of color sets and specialized printer setups to handle as many hardware configurations as possible.

As always, you gauge the sophistication and the needs of users when deciding how many options to make available in a Resource file. Can 20 color sets make finding at least one set that displays well on every laptop screen easier, or will the users find so many choices bewildering?

Pay particular attention to the Calculator preferences if the program you are creating allows access to this FoxPro feature. You may set Decimal Places to Fixed for an accounting application but change to Floating for a program that handles statistical surveys. You may want to set the Calculator to Force Numlock ON for some keyboards, but prefer not to alter the state of Numlock for other keyboards.

Similarly, if the application uses the GETEXPR command to get user input for queries or other output, you must use the Expression Builder preferences to tailor this complex dialog appropriately. Do users need to see the System Variables, or if you included this information and the users don't know what these variables are, will this addition only confuse the users? Do you remove some functions offered on the data popups to direct users toward other, more useful functions for the kinds of information they want to derive? Do you allow users to edit Resource files? You must consider these individual design decisions for each application.

If the application uses BROWSE PREFERENCE commands, place records providing the PREFERENCE definitions in the template Resource file bound into the .APP. You can choose to allow users to edit the PREFERENCES by leaving the Readonly field at the default of .F. in the editable Resource file copy in use by the application. If the users don't like the results, however, your application can provide a utility for users to restore the information for a PREFERENCE from the template file. Just USE the template file, SCATTER the contents of the appropriate record (don't forget the MEMO keyword!), and GATHER these contents into the PREFERENCE record in the editable version.

You have a second critical reason to provide these records if you use the BROWSE PREFERENCE command in your applications: once the PREFERENCE record exists, this command sometimes gets confused by an explicit FIELDS list. The FIELDS list, complete with switches that show heading and validation for each field, is necessary to *create* the Resource file record and the initial BROWSE, but afterwards the PREFERENCE record stores information for the BROWSE FIELDS list in the record's Data field. The record's information should control the placement and sizing of fields in the BROWSE, but the FIELDS list in the command may have competing descriptions of field order and width. One result of this confusion, which most people notice first, is that calculated fields don't appear in the proper position in the BROWSE—in fact, their position appears arbitrarily assigned, rather than corresponding to *either* the last use of the PREFERENCE *or* the FIELDS list! Unfortunately, this problem doesn't disappear if the Resource file record, or even the entire Resource file, is readonly. Although the problem seems to have been alleviated by changes to the BROWSE PREFERENCE record in FoxPro 2.5, making sure the record is always available is still a good precaution.

One solution is to provide the following code each time your application issues a BROWSE PREFERENCE command:

```
m.oldselect = SELECT( )
SELECT 0
USE <resource filename> AGAIN
LOCATE FOR Type = <this platform> AND ;
           ID   = "WINDBROW" AND ;
           Name = <this preference name>
m.existpref = FOUND( )
USE
SELECT (m.oldselect)
IF m.existpref
   BROWSE PREFERENCE <this preference name>
ELSE && first time!
   BROWSE PREFERENCE <this preference name> ;
          FIELDS <fields list>
ENDIF
```

You can see that just making certain that the BROWSE PREFERENCEs are installed, either by using an inviolate .APP-bound Resource file or by making sure that a template Resource file contains the proper records, is more efficient.

CAUTION: If your Resource file contains the proper records, your application never issues a full BROWSE PREFERENCE ... FIELDS <list> command. *Always document your full BROWSE command thoroughly.* The Resource file's Data field is in a cryptic binary format. If you don't track the full BROWSE command, you cannot re-create the BROWSEs in the event something happens to your Resource file or if Microsoft changes the PREFERENCE data structure again in a future release of FoxPro. Without this kind of documentation, you may not even understand what the BROWSE is supposed to accomplish when you look back at your program—and another programmer assigned to maintain your work certainly won't understand!

Writing a short program that creates an empty Resource file, USEs all the necessary tables in appropriate relationships, and then issues all the full BROWSE commands for each PREFERENCE within an application is the best way to maintain this documentation. If for any reason you don't want to distribute a template Resource file, this program even can be part of your installation procedures, creating the necessary records on the spot.

The Filer

In the preceding section, you archived diary data from the Resource file by using a COPY command, which is unlike the equivalent DOS command. This command copies the data contained in a table to a new table, including the table's Memo fields if any exist, and accepts a scope and conditions. Other optional clauses of this command create data files in non-.DBF file formats. You find Copy on the Database menu popup.

The FoxPro command COPY FILE, however, performs the same function as a DOS command. FoxPro has an ERASE command, which is similar to DOS's ERASE or DEL. A RENAME TO command, similar to DOS's RENAME, also is available.

Although these commands offer limited file management, the Filer tool is expressly provided to enable you to conveniently perform more extensive file and disk management tasks within FoxPro.

The Filer is available only for interactive FoxPro use. If you include the FILER command or attempt to ACTIVATE WINDOW FILER in an application created and distributed by using the Distribution Kit, a `Feature Not Available` message appears on-screen.

Nevertheless, the Filer is useful when you work in FoxPro. The Filer displays information about the files on disk and enables you to perform DOS functions with a handy visual representation of file-maintenance tasks as they are performed. You also can mark (or tag) both files and directories to perform these tasks on groups of files efficiently. You can use file masks to display only files that match certain criteria or in a particular order. You can display and edit the contents of any file on disk.

No menu shortcut exists for opening the Filer, although if you use Filer frequently, you can add a shortcut to a developer's version of SYSMENU. You also can dock the Filer on the desktop at all times, as suggested in Chapter 2. For now, open the Filer by using the System menu popup option, or by typing `FILER` in the Command Window. The Filer window appears, as shown in figure 16.5.

Most of the Filer window is taken up by a file list similar to file lists you see in Open File and other dialogs. This list, however, gives you far more information about each file than other lists usually give. The information is the same you see if you issue a DIR command to DOS, and the list also indicates the DOS attribute setting for each file. As in all FoxPro file lists, brackets with two periods ([..]) indicates that you are in a subdirectory and can move up a level in the disk's directory tree by choosing this entry. To the right, the familiar drive and directory popup controls enable you to investigate other files in the system.

Below the popup controls, you see an indication of the file mask that applies to the file list you see. By default, the indication reads *.*, which means that you see all files. You can change the mask to look at only program files by typing `*.PRG`, or at all files that pertain to the Budget table by typing `Budget.*`.

As usual in a FoxPro list, you can tag entries singly or in groups and then perform actions on the tagged entries. In the file list, you toggle the tag by clicking or using the arrow keys to highlight a file and then pressing the space bar. The familiar triangular mark appears as you select and tag entries. Use Shift+click or Shift+space bar to tag multiple entries. Below the file mask, you see three push buttons that enable you to tag and untag the files in the listing as a group. Try changing the file mask to *.PRG and select the `Tag All` push button. Then change the file mask back to *.*; all .PRG files remain tagged. Select the `Invert` button, and all files except the .PRG files are tagged. Select the `Tag None` button and all tags disappear.

TIP

You can activate the Filer from the Command window with a file mask already in place by using the FILER LIKE <file mask> clause. A file mask created in this manner or in the Filer Files Like text box may contain more than one skeleton, separated by semicolons, such as the following example:

```
FILER LIKE *.txt; C*.; str??.fxp
```

In this example, the Filer displays all files with a .TXT extension, all files that begin with C and have no extension, and all files with five-character names that begin with STR and end with an .FXP extension.

Below the file list, a double row of action buttons enables you to manage files. Most of these buttons are designed for use when files are tagged. Now that you used the `Tag None` button, for example, select the `Edit` button and the message `No files are tagged` appears. If a file (or files) is tagged, selecting the `Edit` button brings up one FoxPro text-editing window for each tagged file.

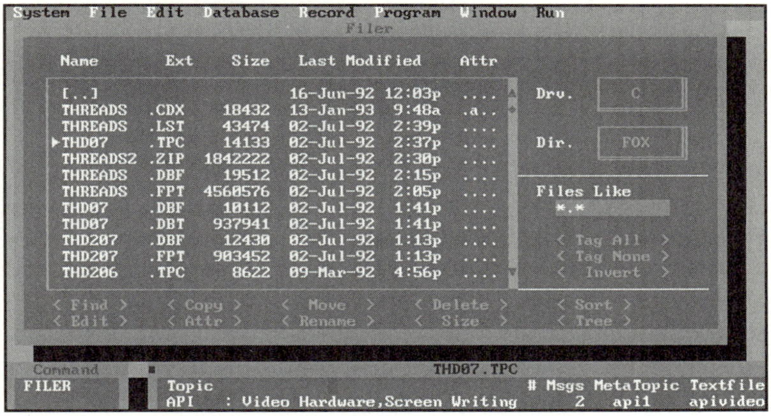

FIG. 16.5

The Filer in Files view.

The `Size` push button shows statistics on the files you tagged so that you can decide, for example, whether the file can fit on a floppy disk before you try to Move or Copy the file.

> **CAUTION:** In the FoxPro Filer, you may not always see all the files you tagged (unlike many other file-management programs you may have used). Tags persist even after you change drives and directories. Always use the `Tag None` button before you change directories, or check tagged file statistics with the `Size` button before choosing to perform file management operations. With the `Edit` button, the worst that can happen is that you run out of memory before FoxPro can open editing windows for all the tagged files. You can lose a great deal of valuable information quickly, however, by unthinkingly choosing to Delete All in response to the confirming dialog the Filer provides when you press `Delete`.

As shown in figure 16.6, you can use the `Attr` push button to change the DOS file attributes for a file or files. The capability of marking a file as readonly makes this option especially useful for Resource file maintenance.

The Filer cannot perform this action or any other on a file currently open in this session of FoxPro, including FoxPro's own temporary files and system files—notice that several files are dimmed in figure 16.6. The Filer, however, doesn't know about files required for *other* applications that may be running at the same time in a multitasking environment. Take care not to delete or edit these files accidentally!

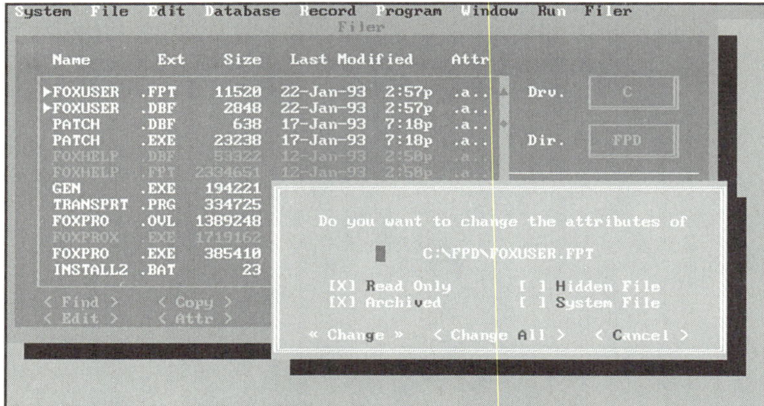

FIG. 16.6

The Filer Attributes dialog.

Along with the capability of limiting the files you see provided by the file mask, the `Sort` button enables you to view files in different orders. In figure 16.7, you see the Filer Sort dialog, specifying a Date Descending order. This particular order is handy to see files on which you have recently worked.

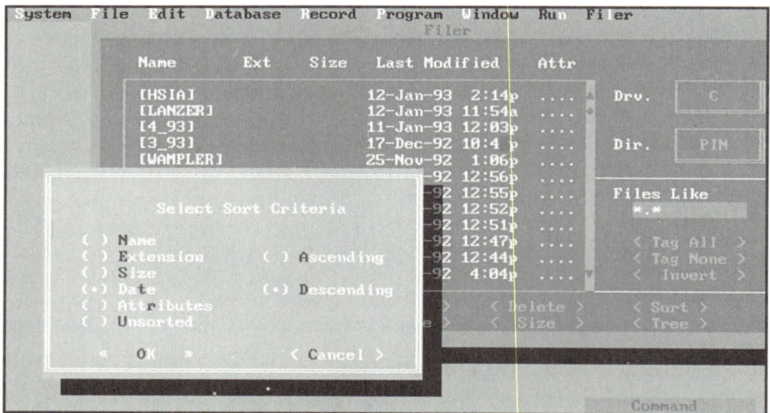

FIG. 16.7

The Filer Sort dialog.

The `Find` button can help you locate and tag for editing any text string in files of any format. Recall that you used a variable named big_item in a report in Chapter 10. Suppose that you want to see all procedures that make a reference to this variable. As shown in figure 16.8, the Find dialog tools enable you to specify up to three text strings and whether any or all of the strings must be found for a file to be tagged. As usual, in a FoxPro Find dialog, you can specify case sensitivity.

Initiating the search as shown in figure 16.8 in the MODEL directory, you find that several files are tagged. If you select the `Edit` button, all tagged files open in edit windows, with the first instance of the search string highlighted. Here, you do not want to edit the files directly because these files are not ASCII text files, but you still can view the files to provide enough clues for you to open the relevant files with a MODIFY SCREEN or MODIFY MENU command and quickly locate the changes that you need to make.

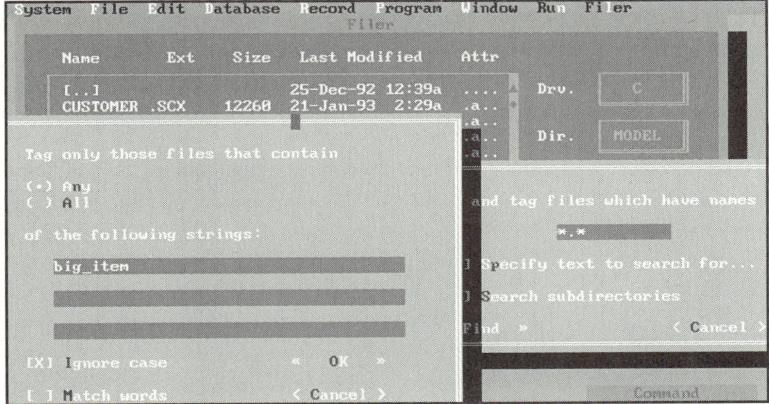

FIG. 16.8

The Filer Find dialogs.

Using the `Find` push button in the Filer changes the current search string in the Find dialog you access from the Edit menu popup, so finding other instances of the target in any file you open is easy. You open all tagged files for editing by pressing Ctrl+E.

The `Find` button has a separate file mask, which you can maintain separately from the file mask used to display files in the Filer list. You can even tag files not currently displayed. If you Search subdirectories, a small arrow appears to the left of a subdirectory name in which files were tagged in a search.

The Filer window is crowded, and maneuvering among the buttons with the Tab or arrow keys may be awkward. Fortunately, although the buttons do not have hot keys, menu shortcuts are provided in the Filer menu popup for *all* button options. Press Ctrl+L now—the equivalent to selecting the `Tree` push button—to switch from a Files display to a Tree display.

Figure 16.9 shows the Tree and the Filer menu popup. Notice the menu shortcuts, which make the Filer much easier to navigate by keyboard.

Also notice that, while in the Tree display, the buttons at the bottom change to a set appropriate to directory management. Many options in the menu popup also are disabled. In Tree mode, you can tag a directory or directories just as you previously tagged files. You can perform operations on entire directories, including any subdirectories just as you did on files. You also can create new directories and move whole directories of files to the new directory, preserving subdirectory structure as you do so. The `Size` button gives you at-a-glance information about whole directories.

A small dot indicates the current directory on the drive in view. You can use the `Chdir` push button to change the current directory on this drive. If you SET DEFAULT TO this drive, the chosen directory becomes the default FoxPro directory.

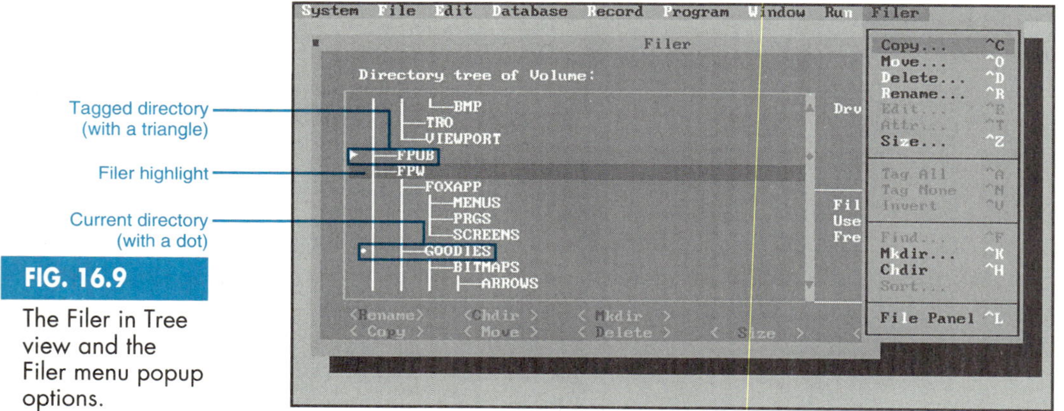

FIG. 16.9

The Filer in Tree view and the Filer menu popup options.

FoxPro Color Control

Most people familiar with DOS feel comfortable in the Filer because the screen is similar in feel and operation to other utility programs available outside of FoxPro. The advantage is that you don't have to leave FoxPro to use the Filer.

The FoxPro color system, however, which has no obvious analogs in other computer programs, is a another world entirely because the system is designed specifically to handle the FoxPro interface. The color system gives you complete control over the colors used to display every element of each interface object. For this reason, newcomers to FoxPro often consider the color system an arcane subject suitable only for experts.

You may never need to adjust FoxPro's default colors. Using color in programs, however, is a subject that affects every user at every moment, and therefore, this system is worth study. This section starts with a few notes on color's effect on interface design. You then learn to implement these principles by using the FoxPro color system. Because each interface element can have colors specified separately, you find that manipulating the color system requires patience and exacting syntax—but the system is not very complicated to use.

Understanding Color's Effect on the Interface

Paul Klee, whose art achieved a rare level of communication by using simple forms and images, once airily described his work by saying, "To paint well is simply this: to put the right color in the right place." Although putting this much emphasis on color—either in painting or in computer interface design—may be an exaggeration, color has a significant role in keeping people happy. When you decide on the colors you want to use for different screen objects in a program, you may think you are making a highly personal decision. You can apply a few basic standards and principles, however, to ensure that other people also are pleased with the colors you select.

Use strong colors sparingly and always on dull background tones. Striking colors can provide annotation to the general content of a screen, highlighting important facts while the muted background keeps the screen calm and harmonious. In large doses, strong colors can confuse the eye; the viewer or user cannot spot what is important.

Never rely on color alone for communication. Remember that some users are color blind and that other users may see certain colors but not respond well to this particular cue. To avoid relying on color to present a message, develop the interface with the understanding that some users have only monochrome or gray-scale monitors.

As in all other elements of interface design, make the colors consistent. If a particular color is reserved for the background of memo-editing windows in all modules, the users get used to memo-editing conventions—keystrokes, preferences, and closing methods—when this color appears.

Look around you—not just at computer screens—and take note of color combinations that both please and displease you. Edward R.

Tufte's, *Envisioning Information*, cited in Chapter 11, includes many examples of distinctive and extraordinarily beautiful color combinations. He also provides other examples that show how color can inflict active damage when used carelessly. Be warned, as he notes, that "...some color applied to display screens has made what should be a straightforward tool into something that looks like a grim parody of a video machine." One example of irrational and displeasing color usage includes a screen shot used in a FoxPro 1 advertisement!

Learning about Color Assignments

As you think about color assignments, remember that this subject also affects users of monochrome monitors. In monochrome systems, FoxPro provides fewer choices with which to work, but the same principles apply. You can set an object in reverse video; you can intensify the brightness; you can make the object blink; or you can underline text. You can use these differences in the same way that you use colors in color systems.

To use colors in a computer program interface, you assign colors to different interface elements. The FoxPro color system enables you to assign colors on three levels: color pair, color scheme, and color set.

The most basic unit in this system is the color pair. A *color pair* consists of two colors, the foreground and background colors for a single element of single display objects, such as the clock, the hot keys on a menu, or the border of a window.

The middle level unit is the *color scheme*, which consists of the color pairs required to display a single screen object. A color scheme consists of 10 numbered color pairs, although you don't need to use all 10 pairs with a given screen object. In Chapter 8, for example, you learned that the color scheme for the object "Browse" uses these 10 pairs in the following way:

- The first color pair is used for displayed records, and this background color provides the background color of the Browse grid.
- The second pair is used for the current field.
- The third pair is used for the border, and this background color provides the foreground color of the Browse grid.
- The fourth and fifth pairs create the title (in active and inactive states).

- The sixth pair is used for any text selected with text-editing methods.
- The seventh pair is used for the current record, and this background color provides the color for the DELETE bullet.
- The eighth pair provides the shadow color.
- The ninth and tenth pairs are unused.

The object "Menu Popup" uses the 10 color pairs in this scheme to handle these completely different elements:

- The first pair is used for disabled options.
- The second pair displays enabled options, and so on.

A chapter in the *Developer's Guide* volume of the software documentation contains charts that list the way each major interface object uses a color scheme. Various entries in the *Commands and Functions* manual that pertain to the definition of particular interface objects, such as the entries for @ GET controls, supplement these charts with more information.

When you work in FoxPro, you have 24 color schemes in use, each with the 10 pairs. These 24 schemes comprise a single color set. A *color set*, therefore, is the upper level of the color system, a collection of all the color schemes necessary to define the use of color in one application.

Just as color pairs of a scheme are assigned numbers within the scheme, the available schemes also are numbered within the set. Each interface object is assigned a default scheme, one of the first 12 schemes of the set. By default, Browses take colors from Scheme 10, and Menu Popups use Scheme 4. Schemes 13 through 16 have no interface objects assigned but are reserved for internal use by FoxPro.

Although only one color set is active at a time, you can change the default assignments for the color pairs of any scheme in the active set. You can save new assignments as completely separate color sets. Each saved color set has a unique name and an entry in the FoxPro Resource file.

CAUTION: The reserved color schemes are unused in FoxPro 2.5 for DOS, but FoxPro 2.5 for Windows uses Schemes 13 and 14 for permanent storage of external Microsoft Windows colors. The assignments for these schemes *cannot* be changed in FoxPro for Windows—attempting to do so causes a program error—although you can access the schemes to find out what these values are.

continues

> For this reason, avoiding the reassignment of colors in any of the reserved schemes is a good general rule. Although color sets are stored in separate preference records for the two platforms, this rule helps you prepare for writing programs in which commands assigning colors may be interpreted on both platforms.

When you DEFINE an interface object such as a WINDOW, if you do not issue specific color instructions, the object is given the default colors for the related object type, using the default scheme number and the color scheme currently loaded. You can change these defaults by performing one of the following steps:

- Changing the color pairs in the object's default scheme
- Defining the object with instructions to use a different color scheme or with an explicit list of color pairs
- Loading a different color set (usually not done within an application, except during setup procedures)

Editing, Saving, and Restoring Color Sets

You may think you must memorize the various color scheme and pair assignments or use cryptic codes to refer to the sets. The FoxPro interface, however, provides several ways to choose colors without remembering which pairs and which schemes go with each object. The following sections discuss these methods and cover the color codes, and also the manner in which you assign these codes in programs.

The FoxPro Color Picker

The Color Picker is FoxPro's native dialog for making color changes. In Chapter 2, you used the Color Picker briefly. As you return to this tool, you certainly recognize many more of the interface objects to which the Color Picker refers.

The Color Picker, like the Filer, has no menu shortcut. No command exists to invoke this tool; the Window menu popup option is the only way you can access the Color Picker, so use this option now. Notice that the popup control in the upper-right corner enables you to specify the scheme for which you want to pick color pairs. Select the scheme popup and the screen shown in figure 16.10 appears. Chevrons show selected colors.

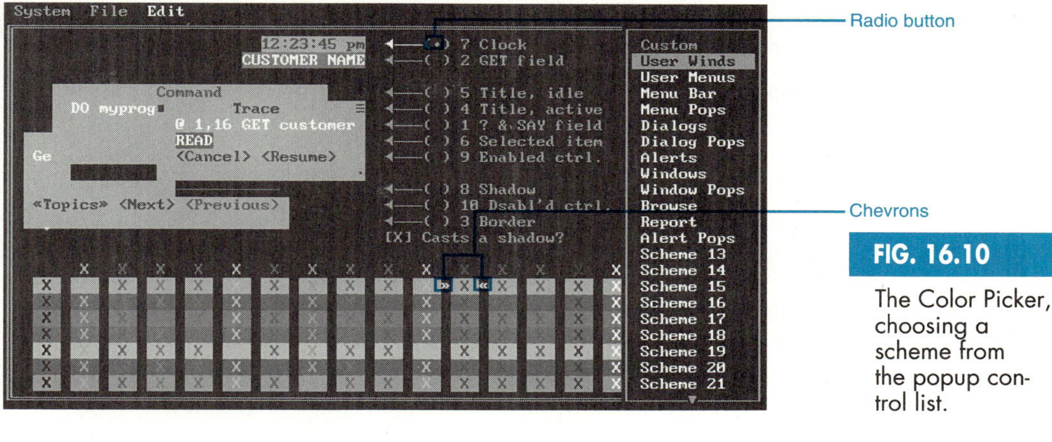

FIG. 16.10

The Color Picker, choosing a scheme from the popup control list.

As you see in this dialog, FoxPro really doesn't expect or even encourage you to remember the number of the scheme to which each interface object defaults. Rather than scheme numbers, you choose a scheme by the name of the related characteristic object. When you invoke the Color Picker, the popup control is preset to the kind of object currently in the active output window. If you select the popup control and choose a different object, the list of radio buttons displays the pair assigned for this scheme, as applied to the scheme's default object.

Numbered schemes, which do not have interface objects assigned by default, follow Alert Pops (Schemes 13 through 24). When you create custom schemes, remember to avoid the reserved schemes from 13 through 16.

All the unused schemes (13 through 24) are currently set by default to the same colors as Scheme 1 (User Windows). Select User Windows from the popup control and look at the colors used in the sample windows on the left. These colors are what you see if you DEFINE a WINDOW without setting colors.

You also see a scheme labeled Custom, above the first (User Windows) scheme in the popup control. Unless you have DEFINEd one or more WINDOW, this scheme is disabled. If you have DEFINEd one or more WINDOWs, while you are working interactively, this scheme can be used to reference the window. The Custom label in the popup control changes to a user window's DEFINEd name whenever that window is the active output window. When a different object is active, the Custom scheme is disabled again. You cannot use this Custom scheme in a program, and you cannot refer to this scheme in any way by using a FoxPro command.

Notice the two check boxes in this dialog. The Casts a Shadow box applies to the scheme as a whole and indicates whether objects DEFINEd with this COLOR SCHEME cast a shadow by default. You can override this option with the SHADOW/NOSHADOW keywords when you DEFINE the object. The Blink/Bright check box applies to all color pairs in the scheme whose color characteristics are being defined in the dialog. If BLINK is SET ON (the default setting), you can make the object that uses any color pair blink on and off. If BLINK is OFF and you use an EGA or VGA monitor, you can change the intensity of the background color of any pair to a brighter version of the same color. Use these two options sparingly, because bright backgrounds and blinking objects can become tiring to view.

Start by changing the colors of one color pair in Scheme 1. Most people prefer to set the clock colors differently from the default. As you see from the radio button list in the middle of the dialog, the clock colors are determined by color pair 7 of this scheme, which is the first selection on the list.

Use the mouse to select the radio button for the clock, or press the Tab key to move to the button and then press the space bar. You can now use the color pair grid at the bottom of the display to choose new colors for the clock. The chevrons indicate the active color pair among the choices on the grid (see fig. 16.10). Click the mouse on a different color selection. With the keyboard, after you press the space bar, the current colors are highlighted in the grid; you use the cursor keys to move the highlighted chevrons and press Enter when you are satisfied with your choice.

This change represents an alteration on the first (color pair) level of the color system.

But as you change the color of the sample clock object, you notice that the hot keys for the Enabled Ctrl. radio button (otherwise controlled by color pair 9) also change. Color pair 7 actually controls more than one element of the interface in this scheme.

Suppose that you want to DEFINE a WINDOW in default User Window colors, either by yourself or through the Screen Builder, and you want the clock to show, but you don't want the push button hot keys to reflect the same colors as the clock. You can assign new colors for the push button object directly from the Screen Builder (you see how to perform this step in the following section), but a more typical method is to make the change by using the middle level of the color system, which changes the SCHEME responsible for this window. You can perform this change easily through the Color Picker.

You see what looks like a modified version of SYSMENU at the top of this dialog. If you try to access the menu popups, the only options available are Copy and Paste from the Edit menu—and Paste is disabled until you use Copy in the Color Picker. Press Ctrl+C or select the Copy option to copy the color assignments for this scheme. Use the popup control to select Scheme 17 and press Ctrl+V (Paste). The colors in the sample objects, including the clock colors, change to the colors you picked for Scheme 1. Now select color pair 7 in this scheme, and change to a color pair that looks better as push button hot keys.

If you issue the following commands and have a READ with push buttons in this window, all button hot keys change to the colors you want while the clock continues to respond to the instructions of Scheme 1:

```
SET CLOCK ON
DEFINE WINDOW <window name> ;
FROM <row1,col1> TO <rol2, col2> COLOR SCHEME 17
ACTIVATE WINDOW <window name>
```

Use the `Save` push button to change the third level of the color system: save the edited schemes to a color set. After the list of available color set names appears, you can overwrite an existing set or save these changes to a color set with a new name. As previously explained, you create or edit an entry in the Resource file when you perform this procedure. To access a custom color set later, or in other FoxPro sessions, the same Resource file entry must be available. You can use the `Load` button in the Color Picker and select this color set, or you can use the following command in a program or the Command window:

```
SET COLOR SET TO <your set name>
```

NOTE FoxPro contains many commands kept for compatibility with older Xbase dialects that set colors of items of the interface as a separate step. You can SET COLOR TO or SET COLOR OF TITLES or INFORMATION TO explicitly named color pairs. When you do this, however, you change the colors in the active color set and you change the colors of other elements in the interface you didn't mean to affect. Use the Scheme system directly rather than these older commands.

FoxPro's Default Colors

When you load FoxPro, a default color set is loaded. The default color set is determined by a COLORSET-Type record with the Name DEFAULT in the active Resource file, if one exists for this version of FoxPro. One of the standard COLORSET records was given this Name when you installed FoxPro and chose a Monitor Type, as described in Appendix A.

If your CONFIG.FP contains the line RESOURCE=OFF or RESOURCE=<filename>, naming a particular Resource file that doesn't have a DEFAULT record, FoxPro checks your video hardware to determine whether to use a basic color or monochrome set. You can create a color set with the name DEFAULT at any time—and if contained in the Resource file active at startup, the color set is loaded along with FoxPro. You also can load an alternate color set along with FoxPro by placing the following line in your CONFIG.FP file:

```
COLOR SET = <name of color set you want>
```

If you create or edit the DEFAULT color set so that the set no longer contains the default values for your video hardware, you can recreate these defaults by using the following sequence of steps in the Command window:

```
SET RESOURCE OFF
SET COLOR SET TO
SET RESOURCE ON
CREATE COLOR SET DEFAULT
```

Substitute a different color set name in the CREATE COLOR SET command if you want these hardware-default colors available, but don't want these colors loaded when you start FoxPro.

Alternatives for Color Picking in Applications

After you assign colors to an application, be sure that your color control remains receptive to user changes. As you should infer from the color guidelines stated previously in this chapter, color control is not an exact science and you can't please everybody—or satisfy every combination of user, video hardware, and application elements—with your initial color assignments.

The Color Picker is unavailable in applications you build and distribute with the Distribution Kit. A sample application included with FoxPro,

ProColor, provides an example of ways you can give users these same capabilities.

ProColor's premise is more suitable than the Color Picker for a distributed application.

ProColor checks the Resource file you designate for available color sets and lists these sets. You select the color set you want to edit. Using a standard FoxPro dialog approach, ProColor provides complete examples of different interface objects, each in a related default scheme. Each object's elements are labeled clearly.

ProColor's help file includes the complete listings of the color pairs, the pair schemes, and relationships to interface objects. You can use the file while you run ProColor (as part of the .APP) or investigate the file, and the rest of ProColor's source code, in the \GOODIES\PROCOLOR directory under the main FoxPro directory. You will find these listings a useful reference, even if you do not use ProColor.

This tool, however, is intended for developers who work on color sets for their programs. Users are not concerned with decisions about individual interface *elements*; they want to make decisions about the way colors work together. Providing examples similar to ProColor's, you can demonstrate one complete color set after another, and users can indicate the set they like best. If you collect and distribute a wide variety of color sets, this may be all the color-tinkering your users need.

You also can enable users to choose a *base* color, from which you derive a complete color set of properly related and contrasting colors. This *relative color* approach is suggested by Bruce Tognazzini (in *TOG on Interface*, cited in Chapter 11). This idea allows the user to make sweeping changes without making many trivial and tedious decisions and yet allows the designer to be sure that all interface elements remain harmonious. The *effect* of this approach is similar to adjusting a base style in Word for Windows; a change in Normal style ripples through all the other styles based on Normal. Like all things intended to provide effortless and unconstrained choice for the user of a FoxPro application, however, the *implementation* of a relative color system requires the system designer to do extensive work behind the scenes.

A number of third-party utilities exist to provide finer control without overwhelming the user with the complete details of his or her color element choices. If you decide users should alter color sets or pick colors for all the elements of a new color set, use the CREATE COLOR SET <name> command to save the results to a Resource file entry.

TIP

At start up, FoxPro checks the video board in the system to see whether colors are supported. When you create setup procedures for new applications, you have access to the same kinds of checks by using the ISCOLOR( ) and SYS(2006) functions. FoxPro, however, may see the system's *video board* as supporting color, while the *monitor* displays in monochrome or gray scale only. In this situation, you may not see all interface elements. Use the Color Picker or ProColor to choose one of the nondefault color sets immediately or tinker with the color pairs for various objects until all objects are visible.

Programs you create may have trouble setting default color sets for the same reason. Rely on ISCOLOR( ) and SYS(2006) only long enough to ask the users some setup questions. These setup questions can use the same approach that ProColor uses: create sample objects and make sure that all elements are clearly visible to the user.

Color Use in the Application-Building Tools

When you studied the Screen Builder in Chapter 13, you learned how to give color instructions within a screen so that GENSCRN generates the proper color clauses. You DEFINE a WINDOW with COLOR SCHEME instructions by using the Type dialog available as a Screen Layout option. This dialog enables you to specify both a general scheme and a scheme for all popups contained in this screen.

When you select a GET or GETs, the Color option is enabled on the Screen menu popup. You can generate a COLOR SCHEME clause to make an object responsive to color instructions in a scheme other than the one you specified for the screen as a whole. You also can select multiple objects, or group objects, and assign colors to all the objects at the same time.

Remember that no matter what scheme you specify, a GET or other interface object always uses the same color pair within the scheme. A selected option in a dialog popup, for example, always responds to color pair 6, in whatever color scheme is used.

When you select a SAY, a text object, or a box object in a screen, you have the added option of selecting a color pair directly. Figure 16.11 shows the modified Color Picker that appears if you use the Color pair check box in the Color dialog (a SAY object was selected in the screen).

You may wonder why you cannot choose color pairs directly for other screen objects. Two good reasons explain why this option is not supplied:

- A single color pair is insufficient for most screen objects. You usually need to pick several pairs to define all the various attributes, and the scheme system is expressly designed to handle this procedure.
- Defining color pairs directly is not recommended under most circumstances because the effect, depending on the current hardware and color set in use, may be different than you expect. Always define colors relatively, rather than explicitly, so that the selections coordinate with other colors in use. You explore ways to define colors in the following section.

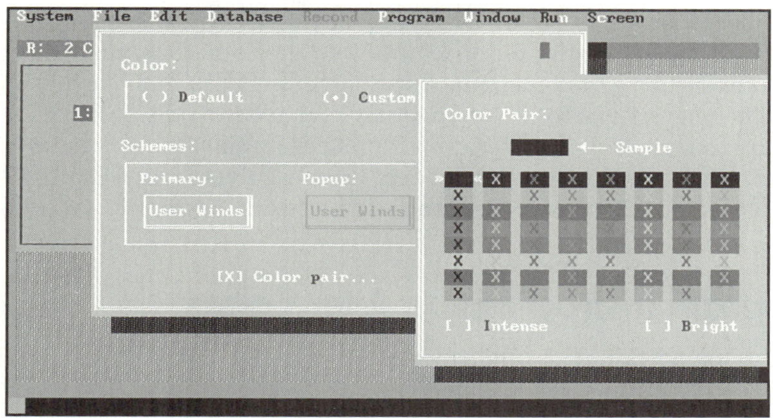

FIG. 16.11

Screen Object Color dialogs.

You can use the generator directive #READCLAUSES, described in Chapter 13, to add a COLOR clause to a READ statement for a screen file. This clause changes the colors of the current GET object as you move through the objects in the screen. The COLOR clause, like single object color assignments, can be either a COLOR SCHEME or a list of color pairs, as described in the following section. Only the second pair—used for GETs—of the scheme or list is used for the READ-level COLOR clause.

In rare cases where you must attach a color clause to a GET or EDIT, you can use the #ITSEXPRESSION trick described in Chapter 13 to include this clause in the Format text box, or you can use similar tricks to include it in any GET clause you want, assigning this clause an

Expression (rather than Procedure) type. A WHEN clause expression, for example, may read

```
your_when( )COLOR SCHEME 3
```

Or the clause may even read

```
.T. COLOR g/b
```

The Menu Builder offers you access to color control by scheme for the menu bar and also for each associated menu popup. You specify the color scheme you want to use in the Menu Option of the Menu popup (the second bar, which gives you options specific to the particular level you are editing). Take care if you change the scheme for one or more popups in a menu; click the `Try It` push button several times to make sure that you like the effect produced. Chapter 14 gives you additional hints on color definition and redefinition for menus.

Although the Report Writer and Label Designer don't support color schemes directly, you can create special Style codes that issue printer-specific instructions for color printers. You need to edit DRIVER.PRG, which is a part of the printer driver application GENPD.APP, or create a new driver to handle the style codes. Printer Drivers and GENPD.APP are discussed in a section near the end of this chapter.

Program Instructions To Alter Colors

As previously stated, setting color pairs explicitly isn't recommended in FoxPro programs because users' color choices conflict with your instructions, and you cannot use the same instructions to fit different hardware. Just as you refer to windows indirectly, without knowing their names, by using WONTOP( ) and other functions, you can use indirect and relative color instructions to set a single pair or a scheme. The keys to this process are the SCHEME( ) and RGBSCHEME( ) functions and the SET COLOR OF SCHEME command.

To match another scheme, you can use the following command:

```
SET COLOR OF SCHEME <scheme number> TO <scheme number>
```

This step is the same as using the copy and paste options in the Color Picker, but the SCHEME( ) function also enables you to adjust each color pair individually.

With one numeric parameter, the SCHEME( ) function returns a string of all the color pairs in the scheme that correspond to the number in the active color set. If you are using a color system and the color set is in the default state, you can use the following command:

```
WAIT WINDOW SCHEME(1)
```

You see the following string of characters on-screen:

```
W+/B,W+/BG,GR+/B,GR+/B,R+/B,W+/GR,GR+/RB,N+/N,GR+/B,R+/B,+
```

This string is composed of the scheme's 10 color pairs, separated by commas, in numerical order from left to right. Scheme 1 provides the default colors for user-defined windows.

With two numeric parameters, SCHEME( ) returns information for a specific color pair. Issue the following instruction:

```
WAIT WINDOW SCHEME(1,5)
```

The window shows the foreground and background colors of the fifth color pair in Scheme 1, used for the border and title of the window while inactive, as follows:

```
R+/B
```

FoxPro uses the designations shown in table 16.1 for different colors available in the interface.

Table 16.1 FoxPro Character Color Codes

Code	Color	Used by
N	Black	Color and Monochrome
X	Blank	Color and Monochrome (used for passwords)
W	White	Color and Monochrome
U	Underline	Monochrome
I	Inverse	Monochrome
B	Blue	Color
GR	Brown	Color
BG	Cyan	Color
G	Green	Color
R	Red	Color
RB	Magenta	Color
GR+	Yellow	Color

Notice the plus sign (+) after the code GR in the table, used for Yellow. In a FoxPro color code, the + symbol denotes intensity for a foreground color (yellow is considered an intense brown). On a color monitor, after SET BLINK is OFF, you can use an asterisk (*) to brighten or intensify a background color. After SET BLINK is ON, the asterisk makes the object or element that uses this color pair blink.

On monochrome monitors, an asterisk used with a color pair always makes the foreground blink and a plus sign always makes the foreground bright, regardless of how you SET BLINK.

Foreground and background colors in the pair always are separated by a slash, and pairs always are separated by commas. Where you place the asterisk in relation to the color pair really doesn't matter. On a color monitor, for example, all the following codes—and all other variations you try—produce the same effect:

```
*+W/G
*W/G+
+W/G*
W/G*+
W*/+G
```

NOTE In figure 16.11, you see two check boxes labeled Intense and Bright in the uppermost dialog (the modified Screen Builder Color Pair picker). Both check boxes actually refer to the same color attribute: the Intense check box specifies the level of the foreground color's brightness or intensity, and the Bright check box refers to the level of the background color.

In the default SCHEME(1) string, you also see an extra plus sign after the 10th color pair and comma. This sign indicates that objects defined with this scheme cast a shadow if no SHADOW/NOSHADOW instructions are issued. Although officially a scheme has only 10 pairs, you can use SCHEME(<scheme number>,11) to get this information.

Because a FoxPro program may be used under both the DOS and Windows versions, the alternative RGBSCHEME( ) function gives you information about colors in a Windows-standard system. In this system, each color value is defined by a set of three numbers, which range from 0 to 255. Issue the following instruction:

```
WAIT WINDOW RGBSCHEME(1,5)
```

The window shows this result:

```
RGB(255,0,0,0,0,128)
```

This expression includes six numbers; the first three numbers designate the foreground value (R+) and the last three numbers designate the background (B).

Each number represents the levels of three component colors (red, green, and blue) that are mixed together. The higher each number, the higher the proportion of the component color in the result. When the number of any component is approximately 128, the component color is mixed in normal intensity. High-intensity colors result when at least one component color is greater than 191.

The RGB notation looks intimidating at first, but the design is logical and can even make the FoxPro character code system easier to understand. Cyan, the background color for FoxPro system windows, for example, has the RGB values 0,128,128. The high-intensity version of the same color has the values 0,255,255. You can see immediately that cyan is composed of equal parts of green and blue—which explains why the character code for cyan is BG.

When all the components are approximately equal, the resulting color appears to have no color. At the low end of the scale (all components are less than 32), the result is black. At the upper end of the scale (all components greater than 191)—just as red, green, and blue spot lights may be used together to provide a white light—the resulting color is bright or high-intensity white. At the middle of the scale (all components approximately 128), the resulting color is low-intensity white, which appears as gray on computer monitors.

You may expect this system to allow subtle variations of colors; for example, you may think that the RGB values 90,90,90 provide a slightly deeper shade of gray than 128,128,128. In FoxPro DOS, when you designate RGB values—using the same procedures described in following text to SET COLORs to character code values—the numbers are rounded off to the nearest available color in the limited DOS palette.

In FoxPro for Windows, however, the same designations give you much finer shadings of color. For this reason, programs meant for cross-platform use should use the RGB system to designate colors explicitly or the Windows version won't always provide the correct results. Let the DOS version take care of translating the RGB numbers into character codes for you.

To use what you learn from SCHEME( ) to edit a color set in a program, suppose that you have a SAY in a screen that indicates whether the current record was deleted. This SAY expression may look like the following line:

```
IIF(DELETED( ),"Deleted Record",SPACE(14))
```

The SAY is marked Refresh so that when you issue a SHOW GETS command as you change records, either the "Deleted Record" comment or nothing appears in the appropriate position.

This window is designed in User Window colors, but suppose that you want the user to really notice this comment, rather than being the same colors as other SAYs. Because this window contains a *warning* comment, you may want to give the windows colors you usually reserve for Alerts.

If you decide to use the normal text colors from an Alert for this SAY, use the Color popup control to assign this SAY object to the Alert scheme. This step just tells FoxPro to use the same color pair (color pair 1) from Scheme 7 rather than the Scheme 1 colors used for the rest of the screen.

Suppose that you want to use the Alert-enabled control colors for this SAY. You have a special control in the window that you can use to toggle the DELETED( ) state, and you want both states to have the same colors. You also want the "Deleted" warning to blink. If you explicitly set these colors for the SAY, you cannot edit—or enable users to edit—these Alert colors without destroying the subliminal connection between this Deleted warning and the other Alert messages.

Instead, determine the current colors for an Alert control in the setup snippet for the screen and place the values into a memory variable. Use this memory value to determine the colors for a custom color scheme. In the following code, notice that pairs are separated by commas, and that commas are added between pairs to act as *placeholders* for the pairs not changed:

```
PRIVATE colorvar
* set up the memory variable to hold the information

* Then set up a string to represent this information,
* using the Alert color pair 9 and a "blink" asterisk for
* color pair 1 (the SAY), adding Alert button colors for
* pairs 6,7,9, and 10, which is used by the related button
```

```
colorvar = SCHEME(7,9)+"*"+    ;
           REPLICATE(",",5)+   ;
           SCHEME(7,6)+","+    ;
           SCHEME(7,7)+","+    ;
           ","            +    ;
           SCHEME(7,9)+","+    ;
           SCHEME(7,10)
* string colorvar now holds: W+/R*,,,,,W+/N,GR+/R,,W+/R,W/R
* store it to a scheme with an indirect reference
SET COLOR OF SCHEME 18 TO (colorvar)
SET BLINK ON
* so the SAY will blink rather than be bright
```

You now can designate Scheme 18 for this one SAY and for the one related button through the Screen Builder. No matter what Alert colors you change, if the colors are consistently defined with Scheme 7, they match.

The same procedure under both FoxPro for DOS and Windows uses the RGBSCHEME( ) function, as shown in the following code:

```
PRIVATE colorvar
colorvar = RGBSCHEME(7,9)+     ;
           REPLICATE(",",5)+   ;
           SCHEME(7,6)+","+    ;
           SCHEME(7,7)+","+    ;
           ","            +    ;
           SCHEME(7,9)+","+    ;
           SCHEME(7,10)
```

This procedure isn't an exact duplicate of the preceding procedure. You can't add the + or * symbols to RGB values to affect their intensity or blinking, and colors in FoxPro for Windows don't blink regardless of the setting of SET BLINK. The RGBSCHEME( ) version of the procedure provides a low-intensity background in Windows, as contrasted with a high-intensity background in from the SCHEME( ) version. The RGBSCHEME( ) version would provide a nonblinking background in FoxPro for DOS.

To make the procedures completely the same, you need to use the information provided by RGBSCHEME( ) at a more detailed level, examining each number and incrementing the highest value of the three components to a value over 191. As you see in the following example, you aren't restricted to using the information provided by SCHEME( ) or RGBSCHEME( ) one complete pair at a time, either. You can separate out a color pair into foreground, background, and attribute components.

Such color manipulation only rarely is necessary in FoxPro. The less you tinker with the color set chosen by the user, the more consistent your application's interface appears, especially if you always DEFINE user objects according to the related default schemes (dialogs as Scheme 5, Alerts as Scheme 7, and so on).

If you manipulate colors in cross-platform applications, you should be aware that in Microsoft Windows' graphical interface your intervention may not provide any obvious effect. You cannot control system-defined objects, such as the system menu, push buttons, and window borders and mouse controls by FoxPro color commands, although you can obtain their values from the appropriate SCHEME( ) or RGBSCHEME( ).

You may have occasion, however, to use an *invisible GET* that doesn't appear on the background of a screen; perhaps the related WHEN clause performs a check of some kind, or you are entering passwords. You can use the "X" (blank) color code, but this selection provides the same effect on color monitors as N/N (black). By using the color schemes, you can create a chameleon object without knowing the colors you are using in the surrounding screen or expecting any visual impact on the user.

First, find out the current color used for the background of the current window. Assuming that you still are working in a window DEFINEd with COLOR SCHEME 1, you find it using the following:

```
PRIVATE m.backcolor
m.backcolor = SCHEME(1,1)
* get the first pair, used for normal
* text and the general window background -
* by default, this would be W+/B

m.backcolor = SUBSTR(m.backcolor,AT("/",m.backcolor)+1)
* find the position of the slash and
* take only what comes after it (B is the default)

* build a new pair using only this color
m.backcolor = m.backcolor+"/"+m.backcolor
* new pair is B/B in the default
```

You now can put this new color pair to work with the following lines:

```
* add a comma in front, so you can represent the
* second pair in a scheme, used by GETs
m.backcolor = ","+m.backcolor

* set up a scheme that will be designated for
* your dummy GET to use
```

```
SET COLOR OF SCHEME 19 to (m.backcolor)
* same as saying SET COLOR OF SCHEME 19 to ,B/B
* scheme 19 now holds:
* W+/B,B/B,GR+/B,GR+/B,R+/B,W+/GR,GR+/RB,N+/N,GR+/B,R+/B,+
```

After you designate Scheme 19 for this GET through the Screen Builder, the GET becomes invisible.

The following procedure generalizes this method; the return value provides a completely invisible color scheme, starting with any scheme you designate as the PARAMETER:

```
* INVISIBL.PRG
PARAMETER whichscheme
PRIVATE m.backcolor
m.backcolor = SCHEME(whichscheme,1)
m.backcolor = SUBSTR(m.backcolor, AT("/",m.backcolor)+1)
m.backcolor = m.backcolor + "/" + m.backcolor
m.backcolor = REPL(m.backcolor+",",9)+m.backcolor
RETURN m.backcolor
```

Typically, you pass Invisibl( ) the active window's color scheme and assign its return value to one of the upper color schemes, calling the function in code similar to the following:

```
newcolor = Invisibl(5)            && active window is a dialog
SET COLOR OF SCHEME 18 TO (newcolor)
* SCHEME 18 now holds:
* RB/RB,RB/RB,RB/RB,RB/RB,RB/RB,RB/RB,RB/RB,RB/RB,RB/RB,RB/RB
```

Subsequent to this code, any item in a dialog-scheme window that should be invisible can be defined with COLOR SCHEME 18 until COLOR SCHEME 18 is assigned new colors. When desired, the SHOW GET and SHOW OBJECT commands can be used with the COLOR SCHEME 18 clause to provide temporary invisibility.

You can see that the corresponding procedures for FoxPro for Windows *must* use RGB values to create a truly invisible GET, because the character codes are inexact representations of the subtle color shades available in the Windows environment.

Although system objects can be colored again in FoxPro for DOS, one inconsistency exists between user-defined objects and system objects, such as FoxPro error message alerts, dialogs, or the Command window: any change you make to an active color scheme affects the next appearance of a system object in the interface. A user object, however, receives the color instructions at the time you DEFINE the object. The user object doesn't change colors if you adjust the color scheme to which the object responds unless you reDEFINE the user object, which sets new color instructions. You can use the SHOW GET or SHOW OBJECT command with the COLOR SCHEME clause to make a particular READ object respond to all changes you make to the scheme colors.

Macros

Compared to the FoxPro color system, FoxPro macros are similar to utilities you may know from other computer programs. Macros are sequences of keystrokes produced in response to a single key combination. Macros are useful to automate repetitive tasks and to simulate keyboard input in an application.

You can store up to 1,024 keystrokes in one FoxPro macro, and macros can call other macros to produce even longer sequences. You cannot, however, repeat mouse clicks and mouse movements in a macro. When you define a macro, always use the keyboard equivalent for actions that you usually perform with a mouse.

To consider ways in which macros are useful, consider the status line, a feature of the FoxPro editor. Windows opened for editing (MODIFY either FILE or PROGRAM) do not include the status line by default. You can save a preference for the status line to appear for all files of a certain extension, but you may want to open and edit files of many extensions. A macro can make repeating this sequence unnecessary every time you start editing files with a new extension.

Creating a Macro

You define, or record, a macro by pressing the exact keystrokes you want replayed when the macro runs. Create the exact same situation that will exist when the macro replays so that these keystrokes have the proper effect. To create the proper environment, open a text file for editing. Press Shift+F10 to begin defining a macro. The dialog in figure 16.12 appears. Press a key combination you want to use for this macro, and the macro name appears in the Defined Key text box.

You can use the Ctrl or the Alt key in combination with most keys, plus multiple shift combinations (Shift+Ctrl, Shift+Alt, Shift+Ctrl+Alt) with the alphabetic keys and function keys. You can use Alt+F10 with the alphabetic keys. You also can use certain nonalphanumeric keys as macros without shift combinations. In *The User's Guide* volume of the documentation, you see a list of keypresses valid for macros. All invalid keypresses for macros are not accepted in the Defined Key text box.

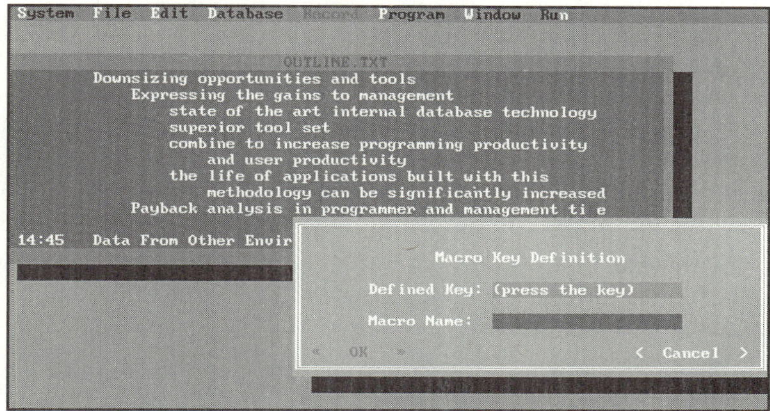

FIG. 16.12

The Macro Key Definition dialog.

Use multiple-shift combinations for macros because so many single-shift combinations are already used by the standard SYSMENU.

If you want to create an easily remembered macro for the Status Line, a good choice may be Ctrl+Alt+S. Alt+S invokes the System menu popup, and Ctrl+S is a menu shortcut in a number of the conditional menu popups. (In Appendix F, you find a list of the single-shift combinations, with notes on how each combination is used in the FoxPro interface.)

> **CAUTION:** Never use macros from another person's FoxPro environment or from examples such as the ones in this section without first checking for conflicts with key assignments in *your* environment. Remember that SYSMENU is configurable, so any macro that accesses menu options may have a different than expected effect. More important, this key combination may have an assignment in the outer environment if you run FoxPro under a multitasking system, or the key combination may even have an assignment through the CPU or a programmable keyboard.

After you press Ctrl+Alt+S, Ctrl_Alt_S appears as a default name for this macro in the Macro name text box. Because you use the macro name as a reminder of what the macro performs, change this name to something understandable. Use the mouse to click, or tab to the Macro name text box. (No other key works; if you try the down-arrow key, you define a macro for the DNARROW key. You cannot define macros for the Tab or Shift+Tab key, although these keystrokes can be used within a macro sequence of keystrokes.)

Macro names can be up to 19 characters long but cannot contain spaces. Macro names are saved in all capital letters, no matter how the name is typed. Type `status_line` as a macro name and confirm your choice with the `OK` button. A message window indicates that you are now recording a macro—unlike normal WAIT WINDOWs, which this window resembles, the window doesn't disappear as you begin to type.

Now type the exact keystrokes you want used in the macro. To create a macro for status lines in the editor, press Alt+E for the Edit menu popup and N for the Preferences dialog.

As you see while recording, the Preferences object highlighted is, initially, the number of spaces per Tab. Press the Tab key and the space bar to check the box that indicates that you want to use these preferences for all files with the current extension. Then press Tab and the space bar to mark the Save Preference check box. Press several more Tabs and a space bar to mark the Status line check box.

After making these changes, add a pause to the macro so that you can check to make sure that the structure is exactly as you want. You don't know whether these space bar presses haven't *unchecked*, rather than checked, the boxes; perhaps this macro was previously run for this file extension, or perhaps the change was made manually. To include the pause, again press Shift+F10. The dialog in figure 16.13 appears. Choose P or click the `Insert Pause` push button. In the default state—Key to Resume—a FoxPro macro pauses here to enable you to make manual adjustments until you press Shift+F10 again.

The Pause\Key to Resume option is a useful feature for data entry, enabling you to combine boilerplate phrases in a macro with inserted keystrokes or words unique to each entry. The other Pause alternative, Pause\Seconds, which pauses the macro for a specified amount of time and then continues, often is used for creating self-running demonstration programs. A Pause\Seconds also can make sure that a keystroke that takes a moment to conclude—such as a Ctrl+A which is highlighting all of a file or Memo field that may be lengthy—is finished before the next macro keystroke takes place.

A final choice available in the Stop Macro Recording dialog is `Insert Literal`. This choice enables you to record the literal keystrokes of the next keypress, rather than playing the keystrokes of another macro assigned to this keypress. The choice is similar to the PLAIN option on the KEYBOARD command, about which you learn in the programming chapters of this book.

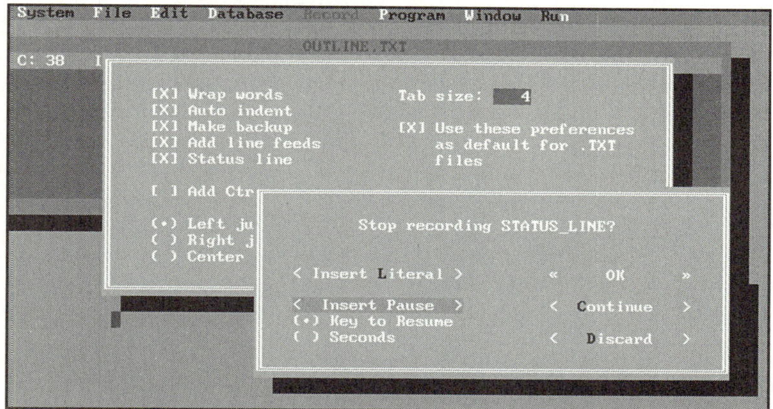

FIG. 16.13

The Stop Macro Recording dialog.

Returning to complete the macro after the pause, record more Tabs back to the `OK` button and a press of Enter on the button to save the editing preference. Press Shift+F10 again and choose the macro dialog's `OK` button to stop recording the macro.

Testing and Editing the Macro

To test the macro, open a new editing file with a different extension and press Ctrl+Alt+S.

Does the macro work the way you expected? If not, you can edit the macro, rather than re-recording from the beginning. Use the System menu popup Macros… option to access the Macros dialog you see at the upper-left in figure 16.14. Select the STATUS_LINE macro from the list and click the `Edit` push button. The Macro Edit dialog at the bottom right of figure 16.14 appears.

The Macro Edit dialog enables you to change the keypress, name, or recorded sequence to which the macro is assigned, that appears in the large text box, such as in the following example:

```
{ALT+E}n{TAB}{SPACEBAR}{TAB}{SPACEBAR}{TAB}
{TAB}{TAB}{TAB}{TAB}{TAB}{TAB}{SPACEBAR}
```

```
{PAUSE KEY}{TAB}{TAB}{TAB}{TAB}{TAB}{TAB}
{TAB}{TAB}{ENTER}
```

As you see, special key labels such as the Alt+E keypress you used to access the Edit menu popup appear in curly braces; where regular keypresses such as the lowercase *n* you used to access the Preferences dialog from the menu popup are shown alone. Special instructions, such as the PAUSE KEY, also are shown in curly braces. A Pause\Seconds looks like this: {PAUSE 0.25}. The Insert Literal looks like this: {LITERAL+CTRL+C}.

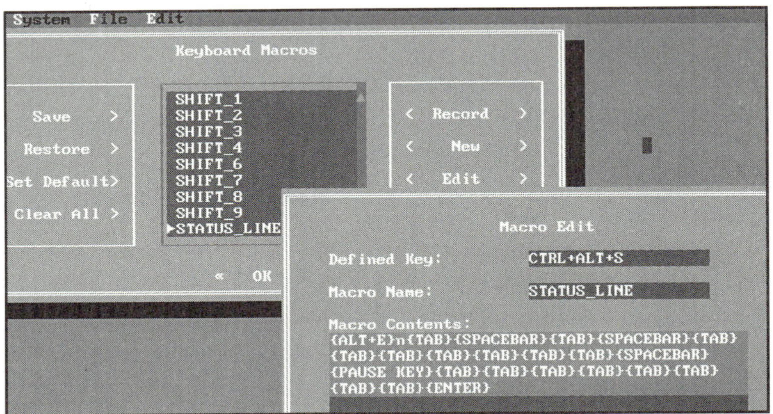

FIG. 16.14

The Macros dialog and Macro Edit dialog.

You can edit the macro sequence in the same way you edit other text in FoxPro, adding and deleting keypresses by using key labels, special instructions, and regular keystrokes as needed. The key labels and special instructions are case-insensitive like FoxPro commands, but the regular keypresses that represent straight typing are played back exactly as typed.

Key labels for all the special keys are shown in the chart in Appendix F. Note that the curly braces are given key labels ({LBRACE} and {RBRACE}) so that you can type these braces and not have these braces understood by FoxPro as key-label delimiters. If you use the semicolon character (;), the character is replaced by the key label {SEMICOLON} when you save the macro—FoxPro uses the semicolon as a continuation symbol.

Saving Macros

After you are satisfied with this and other macros, you can save the current macro set for later use. Returning to the Macros dialog from the System menu popup, you can click the `Save` button to save these macros to a new name. If you look quickly at the rest of this dialog, you see options to Restore a macro set from an existing file. `Restore` is an *additive* option in FoxPro; although older macros are overwritten by new ones assigned to the same keypresses, when you use `Restore`, the existing macro set is added to, rather than cleared out. To remove all existing macros, use the `Clear All` button.

The `Clear` button in the Macros dialog enables you to delete one macro at a time. The `New` button enables you to directly type (rather than recording) a new macro sequence. As in the Filer, this dialog uses no hot keys but the Macros menu popup has menu shortcuts for all the options.

Using Macros in Applications

The Macros dialog isn't available in distributed applications, but the Record and Stop Recording Macros dialogs are available. You can change the Shift+F10 keypress to invoke these dialogs to a different combination by using the SET MACKEY TO <key label> command. You can turn off the macro capability by using the SET MACKEY TO command, followed by no key label. The Macros dialog is replaced programmatically by the RESTORE MACROS FROM, CLEAR MACROS, and SAVE MACROS TO commands. You can store macros in both a Memo field and a file.

You can share .FKY files between FoxPro 2.0 and FoxPro 2.5 Windows and DOS. Not all macros, however, work the same way because many of the system dialogs are arranged with different options and different shortcuts.

If you allow the users to restore personal sets of macros from Memo fields or files, you can CLEAR MACROS, RESTORE MACROS FROM these personal sets, and then RESTORE MACROS FROM the application's default set. Because of the additive nature of the RESTORE MACROS command, this order ensures that the macros the application needs are available and that no required macros have been overwritten by new macros defined by the users.

How FoxPro Loads a Default Macro Set

The files that store FoxPro macros use the extension .FKY. When you load FoxPro, if a file DEFAULT.FKY exists, the related macros load. FoxPro has a default set of macros loaded if no DEFAULT.FKY file exists. These macros include common FoxPro commands for function keys 2 through 9—such as SET and LIST, each followed by a press of the Enter key to execute the macros. You can easily remove these macros for the macro sets used by programs you create. The default set also has macro definitions for the shifted version of the numeric keypad so that you can use the shifted numeric keys to select text in the FoxPro editor. If you use the shifted numeric keypad to type numbers or if you have separate cursor and numeric keypads, you also need to remove these macros. Use the SAVE MACROS command or the Set Default option in the Macros dialog to save the preferred set to the file name DEFAULT.FKY.

The Macros dialog Set Default option creates a DEFAULT.FKY in *the same directory* as the current Resource file (not the FoxPro home directory or the current default directory, as you may expect). This approach is carried over from FoxPro 1, in which each user on a network had a Resource file in a different personal directory. This setup can be problematic with the new shared Resource files, however; different users will overwrite each other's default macro sets.

In a distributed application, the Macros option is not available on SYSMENU. The menu option you create to set default macro sets for individual users must create .FKY files with names tied to individual users or store macro sets in Memo fields in a table that holds records for each user.

If, however, you use FoxPro 2.x interactively on a network and share a readonly Resource file, consider altering the default version of SYSMENU to omit the Macros dialog. Users still have the option of creating macros, and the new version of SYSMENU includes options to save new macro sets to individual default files.

A convenient way to safeguard each user's default macros is to assign each a separate user directory that contains his CONFIG.FP file. You can use the -C switch or a DOS environmental variable to specify this

CONFIG.FP file for each user. Although FoxPro does not automatically load a DEFAULT.FKY file in the same location as the active CONFIG.FP, you can use the CONFIG.FP's COMMAND = option described in Appendix C to indicate a startup program that runs as soon as FoxPro loads:

```
COMMAND = DO STARTUP
```

The STARTUP.PRG can be kept in the main FoxPro directory because this .PRG file is the same for every user. This program contains the following lines, along with any others you want to add for additional customizing of your FoxPro environment:

```
IF FILE(LEFT(SYS(2019),;
   RAT("\",SYS(2019)))+"DEFAULT.FKY")
   * Use the SYS(2019) function to find the
   * name and location of the active CONFIG.FP
   * file. Add the filename DEFAULT.FKY to
   * the same filepath and use the FILE( )
   * function to see if such a file exist.
   * If so:
   CLEAR MACROS
   RESTORE MACROS FROM ;
   LEFT(SYS(2019), ;
      RAT("\",SYS(2019)))+"DEFAULT.FKY"
   * Use that file as the macro default file.
ENDIF
* Complete with a command to DO an MPR file,
* which customizes your SYSMENU to SAVE MACROS
* to the same SYS(2019) directory when the
* user chooses to save default macros.
* The MPR program may be the same for all users,
* in which case it too can reside in your main
* FoxPro directory, or you can have personal
* SYSMENUs designed for each user, stored and
* launched with the same SYS(2019) trick.
```

Always supply a generic DEFAULT.FKY file in the main FoxPro program directory; this file is loaded if no personal DEFAULT.FKY exists in the user's directory.

When and Where To Use Macros in Programs

You can use macros to make FoxPro's interface, especially the text editor, more closely resemble keystrokes with which users are comfortable. This default set can include editing keystrokes from the user's customary word processing program. A special macro file,

FOXPLUS.FKY, is provided in the \GOODIES\MISC directory to change the editing keystrokes in FoxPro to match the editing keystrokes in FoxBASE+. If you use programs written in FoxBASE+ that check for these keystrokes, use this set of macros as the default set.

FoxPro's DEMO.APP has a Browse module that shows another common way to use macros in a program, which creates a self-running demonstration that looks as though a user is running the program directly. You use the PLAY MACRO <macro name> command in programs you created to run macros without a user keypress. You can use the TIME <expN> clause to create delays between the keystrokes for a demo, where expN is a number of seconds from 0 to 10 (you can include fractions in decimal form).

The following example shows an interactive use of the PLAY MACRO command, which allows any word under the cursor to be looked up in the current help file, without the word being highlighted. You can PLAY this MACRO from an ON KEY LABEL assignment or a menu option with a shortcut key combination:

```
PROCEDURE Lookhelp

PLAY MACRO Helpfind

* This macro marks to the end of the word, and
* copies the contents of the word into the clipboard.
* Then it presses the help key.

* Here are the contents of the macro:
* {SHIFT+CTRL+RIGHTARROW}{PAUSE 0.25}{CTRL+C}
* {PAUSE 0.25}{F1}

* The pauses may not be necessary on all equipment
* and the {F1} should be adjusted if you change
* this menu shortcut in your system.

* The following variant goes back to the beginning of
* a word for a cursor placed in the middle of the word:
* {RIGHTARROW}{CTRL+LEFTARROW}{
* SHIFT+CTRL+RIGHTARROW}
* {PAUSE 0.25}{CTRL+C}{PAUSE 0.25}{F1}

RETURN
```

You learn more about adjusting the FoxPro help system in Chapter 20.

If you use the PLAY MACRO command to execute several macros in a row, realize that no macros are played until FoxPro is in a *wait state* (in a READ, BROWSE, or memo- or text-editing window, or at a menu). PLAY MACRO statements issued in a VALID clause UDF, for example, are all considered *pending* until the UDF returns to the READ. If several pending PLAY MACRO statements exist, the last statement is executed first, and the others execute in reverse order until the first statement is played.

You also need to know that if you define a macro for a key combination, the macro definition takes precedence over the same key combination assignment as a menu or popup shortcut. Be careful not to repeat combinations.

The Desk Accessories

Macros are useful general purpose tools. To macros, FoxPro adds several features commonly found in computer programs—*desk accessories*. In Chapter 2, you learned about ASCII and Special Character charts. You know that you can mark, copy, and paste from either of these charts to add graphics characters and control characters when you are editing.

Along with the other FoxPro methods for adding the characters described in Chapter 2 (Alt+ the numeric keypad, left-quote method for control characters, and pressing Enter on the desired character in either character chart), however, pasting special characters that use low ASCII values may not work in a Browse. You still can set up a hot key to paste these characters into the Browse by temporarily storing the characters as literal strings or as ASCII values to _CLIPTEXT and then pressing Ctrl+V to paste the characters to the BROWSE field. This method is useful when editing printer escape codes, which (as you see in the section on Printer Drivers in this chapter) you can store in a table.

The Capture utility, FoxPro's *copy machine*, helps you save all or a portion of a screen to the FoxPro Clipboard (_CLIPTEXT). When you access Capture from the System menu popup, you set the upper-left corner of the area by using the cursor keys. After you press Enter to anchor the corner of the box, you set the lower-right corner of the box, again by using the cursor keys. Press Enter again, and the area bounded by the corners is saved to _CLIPTEXT. A message window confirms that you captured the screen or partial screen and that _CLIPTEXT now contains the information.

You may find Capture useful as you create documentation for programs. You can go through the entire process of using an application, saving screens as you go, as *notes*. These notes provide a natural order in which to document the application's tasks. A hot key after each screen capture stores successive screens to a text file by using the following procedure:

```
* PROCEDURE capscrn
STORE SET("memowidth") TO oldwidth
SET MEMOWIDTH TO SCOLS( )
* it's very important to set memowidth to the same number
* of columns as your screen
SET PRINTER TO screens.txt ADDITIVE
SET PRINTER ON
SET CONSOLE OFF
? _CLIPTEXT
SET CONSOLE ON
SET PRINTER OFF
SET PRINTER TO
SET MEMOWIDTH TO oldwidth
RETURN
```

When you finish creating the screen captures, the file SCREENS.TXT won't be available for you to print or use in other programs until you SET PRINTER TO another device.

The FoxPro Calculator is similar to many other *popup* calculators available for computer programs. Calculator retains a single value in memory and can perform basic calculation functions. The Preference dialog that corresponds to the Calculator is covered in a previous section of this chapter (see figure 16.4).

The Calculator has no menu popup or shortcuts, but the related functions all have single-letter keyboard equivalents, as shown in table 16.2.

Table 16.2 Calculator Keystrokes

Press on the Keyboard	Calculator Option	Calculator Task
Q	√	Square root
R	MR	Value displayed restored from value in memory
N	±	Change sign of displayed value

Press on the Keyboard	Calculator Option	Calculator Task
A	M+	Add value displayed to value in memory
Z	MC	Clear value in memory
S	M-	Subtract value displayed from value in memory
C	C	Erase current displayed value
CC	CC	Erase current value and operator

The Calendar/Diary is another tool used in a straightforward manner. You can use the cursor keys, the mouse, or hot keys to move through the dates on the calendar, or you can use the Tab key to move to the diary to write notes for a selected date. In the section on the Resource file, you learned how diary entries are stored and maintained and how you can archive old diary information. As you see in figure 16.15, you also can use a special option on the Diary menu popup to delete diary entries. If you select a date on the calendar and choose this option, you can delete all diary entries prior to the selected date.

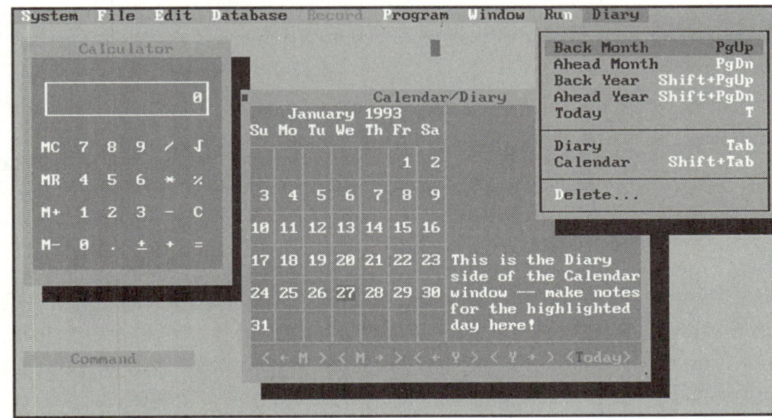

FIG. 16.15 The Calculator and the Calendar/Diary and its menu popup options.

Using the desk accessories within programs usually is a matter of including these programs on the application's version of SYSMENU. As explained in Chapters 13 and 14, however, a READ MODAL needs special help to allow access to menu options. Accessories must be made available on the version of SYSMENU executed in the WHEN clause of a MODAL READ. If you are creating a special, limited version of SYSMENU for this READ, make sure that the SYSMENU contains all desk accessories you want to provide. The READ MODAL also must have a WITH clause that lists the names of the windows for these desk accessories so that the accessories are included in the windows brought forward during this READ.

Table 16.3 shows a list of window names for these accessories, exactly as returned by the WONTOP( ) and WTITLE( ) functions. These return values are anomalies for the window functions because these values include spaces and nonalphanumeric characters. For the READ MODAL WITH clause, however, you must use only the characters before the first nonalphanumeric character in the window name or enclose the entire name in quotation marks.

Table 16.3 Window Names for the Desk Accessories

ASCII Chart
Calculator
Calendar/Diary
Filer
Special Characters
Puzzle

Besides allowing access to the desk accessories through options that invoke the related system bar names on SYSMENU, you can use the ACTIVATE WINDOW <window name> command to access these accessories as part of a hot key procedure during a READ.

For the ACTIVATE WINDOW command, use only the legal part of the window name or enclose the full name in quotation marks. The same naming strategy is used in the HIDE, MOVE, and SHOW WINDOW commands.

NOTE When you ACTIVATE a window or make other references to a window in these commands, the window references are not case-sensitive. However, adjust any comparison of the window name to the return value of WTITLE( ) or WONTOP( ) for case, to make sure the strings match. For example, compare LOWER(WONTOP( )) with a lowercase string.

To ACTIVATE the desk accessories by default, as part of a VALID procedure, rather than give the user an option to ACTIVATE by keypress, you learned a KEYBOARDing procedure in Chapter 15. However, some situations exist in which you may not have the desk accessory available on the system menu, and you cannot summon the KEYBOARD statement:

- You may have SET SYSMENU OFF.
- READ MODAL temporarily may have eliminated the part of the system menu that contains the desk accessory.

If you don't have the desk accessory you want available through the menu, you can use an ACTIVATE WINDOW command and a special nested READ to *hold* the user at this point—without the nested READ, the user is returned immediately to the READ in progress. The following procedure demonstrates this kind of nested READ:

```
* FINDDATE.PRG
* thanks to super betatester Barry Chertov
* for help refining this one
CLEAR
ACTIVATE SCREEN
SET TALK OFF
this_date = {}
@ 1,1 GET this_date VALID vdate(this_date) ;
   ERROR "This date can't be blank!"
READ
FUNCTION vDate
PARAMETERS tempdate
mreturn = .T.
IF EMPTY(tempdate)
   PUSH KEY CLEAR
   ON KEY LABEL ESCAPE DO getdate
   ON KEY LABEL CTRL-W DO getdate
   ON KEY LABEL CTRL-Q DO getdate
   ON KEY LABEL CTRL-END DO getdate
   ON KEY LABEL F2 DO getdate
   ON KEY LABEL LEFTMOUSE DO chkmouse ;
   WITH MROW(""), MCOL("")
   * F2 is our chosen "quit-key";
   * all the other ones are other FoxPro ways to
   * close a window that must be controlled
   WAIT WINDOW ;
      " Press F2 to select a date. " NOWAIT
   ACTIVATE WINDOW Calendar
   mquit = .F.
```

continues

```
   READ MODAL WITH "Calendar" VALID mquit
   * this READ is limited to the Calendar window
   WAIT CLEAR
   * just in case they closed calendar without
   * moving to a different diary entry first
   ON KEY
   POP KEY
   IF LASTKEY( ) # 27
   * 27 is value of ESCAPE press
   this_date = _DIARYDATE
   * store the new date to the GET
   ELSE
   * ESCAPE here will cancel
   mreturn = .F.
   ENDIF
ENDIF

RETURN mreturn

PROCEDURE getdate
* here's how we leave the special READ
mquit = .t.
DEACTIVATE WINDOW Calendar
CLEAR READ
RETURN
PROCEDURE chkmouse
PARAMETERS mouserow, mousecol
IF mouserow = WLROW("Calendar") ;
    AND mousecol = WLCOL("Calendar")
   * was mouse positioned on close icon?
   DO getdate
ENDIF && otherwise, just pass the mouse click on
      && to be used in the calendar -
      && a mouse click does not get "used up"
      && when it is trapped by an ON KEY LABEL
      && command as all other keystrokes are
RETURN
```

This procedure is more complicated than the simple KEYBOARD. Only use this procedure if the desk accessory is not available from the menu. If the user chooses the desk accessory while the ACTIVATE WINDOW command has the same window displayed on-screen, the procedure can produce an error in rare circumstances—a second reason to make sure that normal access is unavailable when this procedure is employed!

This example procedure uses a system variable, _DIARYDATE, to determine the user-selected date. FoxPro includes two system variables for the values obtained in the Calculator (_CALCVALUE and _CALCMEM) and _DIARYDATE for the Calendar/Diary. You can use these variables to transfer information from the accessories to a program's data-entry objects. The variables always hold information from the most recent use of the accessories.

You can use a procedure to assign a hot key or menu option, which pastes the Calculator value into a current GET, if the current GET is appropriate. You also can call the procedure by default after an ACTIVATE WINDOW Calculator statement, in the same manner as you just used _DIARYDATE, with the following example:

```
* ON KEY LABEL ALT-Z DO Pastecalc WITH VARREAD( )
* or make this a menu option
* this procedure only uses 2 decimal places of _CALCVALUE
* PROCEDURE Pastecalc
PARAMETERS thisvar
PUSH KEY CLEAR
* remove OKLs while this procedure is running, prevent
* interruption and recursion
calcno = IIF(_CALCVALUE = INT(_CALCVALUE), ;
             ALLTRIM(STR(_CALCVALUE,25,0)), ;
             ALLTRIM(STR(_CALCVALUE,25,2)))

private toolong
toolong = .F.
* check the data type of the current VARREAD( )
DO CASE
CASE TYPE(thisvar) = "N"
   IF LEN(calcno)  <= FSIZE(thisvar)
      REPLACE (thisvar) WITH _CALCVALUE
   ELSE
      toolong = .T.
   ENDIF
CASE TYPE(thisvar) = "C"
   IF LEN(calcno)  <= FSIZE(thisvar)
      REPLACE (thisvar) WITH calcno
   ELSE
      toolong = .T.
   ENDIF
CASE TYPE(thisvar) = "M"
   REPLACE (thisvar) with calcno ADDITIVE
OTHERWISE
   * date or logical field or maybe no VARREAD( ) at all
   WAIT WINDOW NOWAIT ;
    "Sorry -- Calculator value can't be pasted here."
ENDCASE
```

continues

```
IF toolong
   WAIT WINDOW NOWAIT ;
    "Calculator value is too long for this field: "+calcno
ENDIF
POP KEY
* bring back key assignments

RETURN
```

Printer Drivers

The printer driver system in FoxPro 2.x for DOS is somewhat paradoxical; the system is both more extensive and powerful in capability than most people ever need, and yet less immediately flexible and comprehensive out of the box than most people may prefer. Similar to FoxPro's power tools, the printer driver system requires some effort to learn—but after you make this effort, you can accomplish almost anything you can imagine.

The default system is based on the use of a table, P_CODES.DBF, which contains one record for each printer. Each record holds Character fields that contain the codes needed to give the printer particular instructions, such as enabling or disabling a particular print style or changing the page orientation. A second table, FONTS.DBF, holds information specific to PostScript printers and the HP LaserJet III's scalable font system, with one record that describes each font the printer recognizes.

Of course, you can add records to P_CODES.DBF and FONTS.DBF for all printers or fonts not included in these tables in the installed form. You see a procedure for adding these kinds of records in a following part of this section.

Each printer entry in P_CODES.DBF or font entry in FONTS.DBF does not, however, constitute instructions to the printer that FoxPro interprets by default. Instead, a FoxPro program provides an interface with which the user selects entries and printer attributes. The same program manipulates, in the active Resource file, both the entries and all related information. Another program sends the results, through FoxPro, to the printer. FoxPro's internal participation in this process is limited to calling the relevant procedures in this second program at appropriate moments during printing.

FoxPro is shipped with a sample application to perform the necessary tasks. GENPD.APP provides the interface that enables you to specify the printer record you want to access, and which characteristics you use from this record for a particular printing situation. GENPD.APP uses P_CODES.DBF or FONTS.DBF to store printer information in a special system array named _PDPARMS. This array also stores the specifications you selected to a record in the active Resource file.

Within GENPD.APP and the GENPD project, DRIVER.PRG and PS.PRG show you how to write FoxPro programs to hold the procedures with special names called by FoxPro during printing. These procedures use the elements of _PDPARMS to build strings of control characters sent directly to the printer at different moments. For example, PROCEDURE PdDocst returns a string used to initialize the printer at the beginning of a document.

DRIVER.PRG and PS.PRG are not really used by GENPD.APP; rather, this application uses API library versions of these files, written in the C language. If you look in the GENPD project in the \GOODIES\PDRIVERS directory, you see these libraries—DRIVER2.PLB and PSAPI.PLB—included in the Project file list. Library files are discussed in a following section of this chapter.

Just as you can replace GENSCRN.PRG and GENMENU.PRG custom template programs, with the associated names stored to the system variables _GENSCRN and _GENMENU, you can replace GENPD.APP with an application you write. You store an application's name to the system variable _GENPD, which provides an interface for the user. You set up the array _PDPARMS to use all the elements you need and fill the array with the information in P_CODES.DBF and FONTS.DBF (or replacement tables that you design), using any system you prefer. Your GENPD replacement can add records to the Resource file, as GENPD.APP does, or to a separate *printer preferences table* that you design.

Your printer driver application specifies a program that you write to replace the actual printer-code-passing procedures in GENPD.APP's driver programs by storing the program's name to the system variable _PDRIVER. The _PDRIVER program uses this version of _PDPARMS to find and return the correct codes to FoxPro during printing.

Although not used by GENPD.APP, DRIVER.PRG and PS.PRG are provided for use as models for _PDRIVER programs you create. If you decide to use GEN_PD.PRG, the part of GENPD.APP that provides the interface, but you want to change the driver programs from the API versions to edited version of DRIVER.PRG and PS.PRG or to new programs, you must edit GEN_PD.PRG to store the custom driver program's name to _PDRIVER. Search for _PDRIVER in GEN_PD.PRG; concise comments in the code tell you how to make this change.

The version of _GENPD you create is mostly unrestricted, except that you must include a PARAMETERS statement in the form expected by the command SET PDSETUP and the Printer Driver Setup check box. Consider the check box option only if your application allows access to the Report Writer, the Label Designer, or the system bar _MFI_SETUP (which provides the Printer Setup... menu option). The command SET PDSETUP represents the proper programmatic alternative for access to the printer driver system.

FoxPro passes two parameters to any program specified in _GENPD. The first parameter indicates the conditions under which the program was called, and the second parameter indicates the name of a specific printer driver setup (as shown in the Resource file) with which the program was called. If you write a printer driver interface and generation program to use as the custom _GENPD, read about these parameters and related information in the Printer Drivers chapter of the *Developer's Guide*. Also read Part IV of this book, or otherwise be sure that you are familiar and comfortable with programming in FoxPro.

Most people don't want to spend a great deal of time creating printer drivers. People want to designate a printer driver and want this driver to work. Now that you see the Microsoft Fox team's conception of—and the way you can extend—the printer driver system, look at the default behavior under the sample programs, and consider ways in which you can use the existing system provided by GENPD.APP. The following discussion refers to a sequence of events that can be completely different if you create a different application and store the application's name to the _GENPD variable.

NOTE Because the default programs are FoxPro applications, Microsoft can decide to change the behavior in different release builds, just as you can decide write programs to replace them. (The following information is current as of the first release version of FoxPro 2.5 for DOS.) If your results don't match what you read here and you have a later version, read the relevant Foxhelp entries. You will find a special topic on printer driver hints and another one with information about the latest changes to the product.

Specifying a Printer Driver Setup

The File menu popup enables you to access a Printer Setup dialog. This dialog, like the Label Environment dialog and Report Layout dialog, has a check-box option from which you can choose a Printer Driver Setup. Each printer setup consists of specifications for a particular printer, the appropriate information from the related P_CODES.DBF entry or—for a PostScript printer or LaserJet III—the FONTS.DBF entry for a particular printing situation.

You can create many printer driver setups for one printer, each setup giving instructions for different kinds of output. You may use one setup to generate 12-pitch print in Portrait orientation and another setup for compressed print in Landscape.

If you have a Resource file open, after you use the check box, you see a list of the previously saved printer driver setups like the list in the dialog shown in figure 16.16. If you create a New setup or decide to Edit an existing setup, the Printer Setup dialog shown in figure 16.17 appears. If no Resource file is open, this dialog appears without the intermediary dialog shown in figure 16.16. Here, you can specify—but you cannot save for future use—a printer driver setup for the current session.

From the Command window or within a program, you can set a printer driver with the command SET PDSETUP TO. Follow this command with the name of the printer driver setup you want in a string. Follow the command with nothing, or with a character expression that evaluates to a null string, to release the printer driver setup without installing a new driver. If you use a printer driver setup name unavailable in the present Resource file, you see the available list of drivers (see fig. 16.16) so that you can choose an existing or create a new driver.

You can invoke this list deliberately during a program or from the Command window, by using the following command:

```
SET PDSETUP TO " "
```

(Notice the single space between the quotation marks; you also can use any character string that doesn't match an existing setup name, as long as you *don't* use a null string.) If you issue the SET PDSETUP TO <non-null character string> command and no active Resource file is available, you see figure 16.17 without the intermediary list, just as if you accessed the Printer Driver Setup options from the menu option.

Using the SET PDSETUP TO command or specifying a printer driver setup through the menu option fills the array _PDPARMS with the appropriate values, as you see if you DISPLAY MEMORY LIKE _PDPARMS from the Command window. This command also puts the printer driver setup name in the system variable _PDSETUP. (When you remove the printer driver without specifying a new driver, _PDPARMS is released from memory, and _PDSETUP contains the null string, "".)

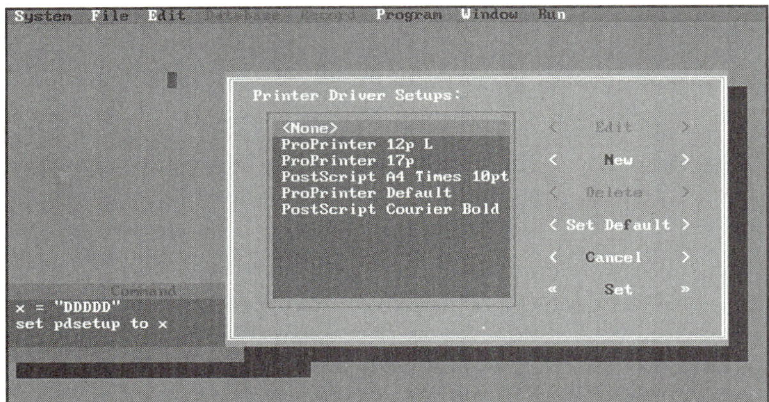

FIG. 16.16

The Printer Driver Setup dialog.

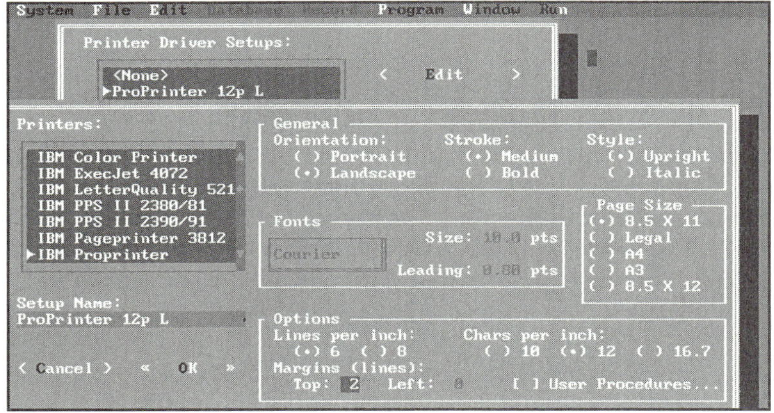

FIG. 16.17

Setting up a printer.

You can use the Printer Driver Setup dialog's `Set Default` button to specify a default printer driver to load when you load FoxPro. Making a printer driver setup the default doesn't change the related version of _PDPARMS. If you open the related Resource file, you see the default printer driver setup has a hyphen (-) included as the first character of the name entry. When loaded along with FoxPro, GENPD.APP looks for and uses this character to set the default. The default printer driver setup doesn't change when you change Resource files. (Remember that this behavior is specific to GENPD.APP and that you can replace this behavior with new default-setting procedures by editing or replacing GENPD.APP.)

Although no comparable command exists to designate a default printer driver setup, you can edit a Resource file directly with FoxPro commands to provide the same results, as shown in the following procedure:

```
LOCATE FOR Id = "PDSETUP" and LEFT(Name,1) = "-"
* find a current default, if any
IF FOUND( )
   REPLACE Name WITH SUBSTR(Name,2)
   * remove the first character
ENDIF
* now locate or create the record you prefer
* as a default setup and in this record:
REPLACE Name WITH "-"+Name
```

TIP

If you do not have a default printer driver setup, you can place the following line in your CONFIG.FP file to prevent FoxPro from searching for one. This line makes FoxPro load more quickly:

```
PDSETUP = "-"
```

Just as a shared Resource file can create conflicts if many people want different DEFAULT.FKY files (macro sets), a shared Resource file on the network can contain only one default printer driver setup for everyone. You can override the default printer driver setup as designated by the Resource file, however, by typing the following line in your CONFIG.FP file:

```
PDSETUP = <"your setup name">
```

Each user can have a separate CONFIG.FP file.

Even if you use the default GENPD.APP program to create a printer driver setup interface and _PDPARMS, you still can provide different driver procedures to send the control strings to the printer. In GENPD.APP's printer driver setup dialog, you can specify custom procedures for a printer driver setup on an individual basis. Click the User Procedures check box at the bottom right of the Printer Setup dialog to see the User Procedures dialog, shown in figure 16.18. You can use this dialog to specify procedures that you write for each event during printing that cause FoxPro to call the driver program.

TIP You don't need to specify user procedures for all the choices in this dialog. Often, you need only one or two user procedures. Avoid creating user procedures on the object level, rather than on the page or document level, because FoxPro has to interrupt the progress of the report each time a user procedure is called. Think of this kind of procedure as a UDF called for *every* object printed!

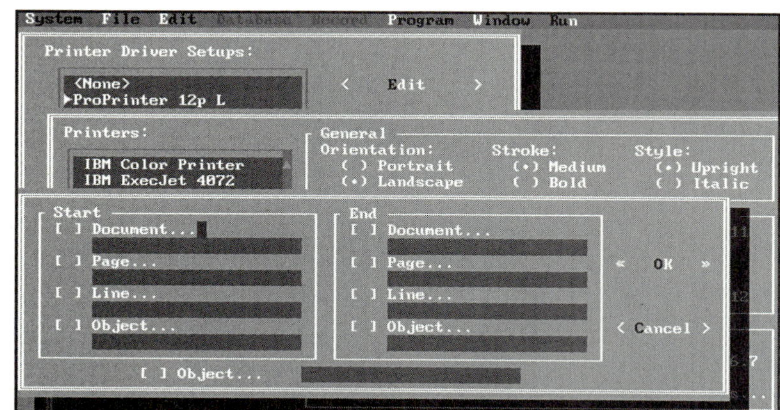

FIG. 16.18 The User Procedures dialog for the printer drivers.

GENPD.APP stores procedure names you specify to elements in _PDPARMS, along with the other printer driver setup information. During printing, the driver program builds special control code strings for each printing event. If the appropriate _PDPARMS element contains the name of a custom procedure, the driver passes the created string to the custom procedure. You can write anything you want to rewrite or add to this string. The driver program passes the edited string back to FoxPro, which sends the string to the printer.

Using Printer Driver Setups Effectively

When a printer driver setup is loaded, you affect FoxPro's instructions to the printer in many different situations. The commands affected by an active printer driver are shown in the following list:

- Issuing a REPORT or LABEL FORM command TO PRINT or TO a file, or causing a report or label to print by using the Database menu popup Report... and Label... options
- Using the TYPE command TO PRINT or TO a file
- Using DISPLAY or LIST commands, in all forms, TO PRINT or TO a file
- Using the ? and ?? commands to display output if PRINT is SET ON and the STYLE clause is used
- Using all choices in the File menu popup's Print option (the contents of a file, an open window, or the Clipboard), except for the ASCII file option

You may override the active printer driver setup with instructions stored in a label or report form. If you use the Printer Driver Setup option in the Report Layout dialog or the Label Environment dialog, you can access the same dialogs you see in figures 16.16, 16.17, and 16.18 while you edit a report or label. When you save the form, the name of the printer driver setup you specify is saved in the .LBX or .FRX table. (To see the results, USE an .LBX or .FRX table and LOCATE a record with OBJTYPE 21—the printer driver record. The name of this setup is stored in the related NAME field.)

To use this stored setup rather than the active setup, when you output labels or reports, use the PDSETUP keyword on the REPORT or LABEL FORM command or the Set Printer Driver option in the Database menu popup's Report or Label dialog. This step is the equivalent of issuing a SET PDSETUP TO <setupname> command separately. If the Resource file isn't open or doesn't contain the setup whose name is stored with the table, the printer driver dialogs appear so that you can recreate the setup before output is sent to the printer.

When you use the RQBE to send results of a query to a report or label, the RQBE Display Options dialog has a check box to Use Printer Setup in Report/Label Form. This option adds the PDSETUP keyword to the REPORT or LABEL FORM command generated in the QPR.

CAUTION: Be aware that the PDSETUP keyword or Set Printer Driver option loads a new printer driver without regard for the previously active setup, just like a SET PDSETUP command. You are responsible for restoring the old setup, if needed, afterward. You can store the contents of _PDSETUP to a variable before creating output and then SET PDSETUP TO <your variable name> after the output command is executed.

After a _PDPARMS array is filled by the active printer driver setup, all the preceding printing techniques cause FoxPro to call the _PDRIVER program's special procedures and any user procedures you added, in the process. You also can use the elements of _PDPARMS, however, for other kinds of control.

Not all the printing techniques to which printer drivers apply use the drivers in the same way. In the preceding list, you see the *?* and *??* commands. The ?? command sends an expression to the current output device; ? sends the expression preceded by a carriage return and line feed. These commands' use of printer driver setups is limited to the STYLE clause; the document initialization and ending strings and other procedures are not triggered by ? and ?? commands. Suppose that you switch on the printer, SET PRINT ON, and SET PDSETUP TO a 12-pitch type setup, and the printer's default is 10-pitch. Use the following command:

```
? "This is a test"
```

The printer still uses 10-pitch type. You also may use the following command:

```
? "This is a test" STYLE "B"
```

If you use this command, the printer honors only the STYLE clause (this example prints in 10-pitch bold type) because the instructions for 12-pitch type are sent as part of document initialization, not available to a ? command.

Suppose that you want to print the output with ? and ?? commands, but you want to use the active printer setup. You can use the *???* command, which sends instructions directly to the current PRINT device, to send the proper initialization string because the string is stored in _PDPARMS.8

To find out which element of _PDPARMS to use, look at the program GEN_PD.PRG. As you can see in figure 16.19, the file contains lines of comments that explain exactly how _PDPARMS is used by this program.

Look at DRIVER.PRG, also in the project, and check the procedure PdDocSt, for an example of the way the driver procedures use the _PDPARMS array elements. You see that the document initialization string sent by PdDocSt uses many different items of information provided by_PDPARMS, including the following elements:

_PDPARMS(7)	lines per inch
_PDPARMS(8)	characters per inch
_PDPARMS(10)	portrait/landscape orientation
_PDPARMS(25)	global style
_PDPARMS(26)	global stroke weight
_PDPARMS(28)	document height
_PDPARMS(29)	document width
_PDPARMS(30)	user procedure for the start of a document
_PDPARMS(41)	top margin in lines
_PDPARMS(44)	font size
_PDPARMS(45)	font command
_PDPARMS(47)	horizontal dots per page
_PDPARMS(48)	dots per column
_PDPARMS(49)	point size in inches
_PDPARMS(50)	graphic character width

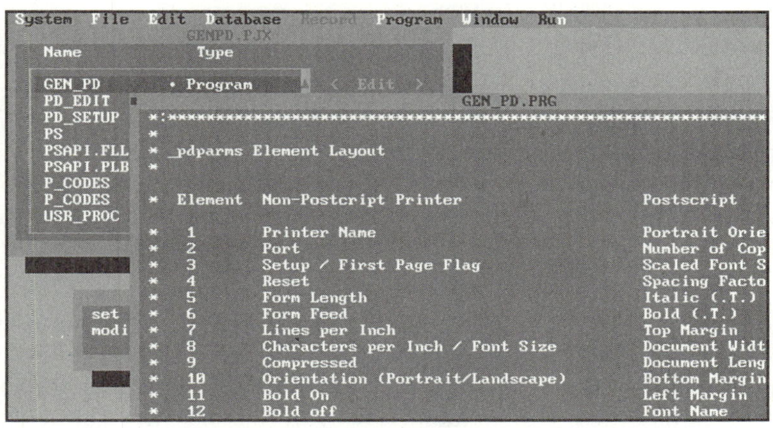

FIG. 16.19

The Comments in the GEN_PD.PRG show you the default _PDPARMS array used for both DRIVER.PRG/ DRIVER2.PLB and PS.PRG/ PSAPI.PLB.

You can combine all these instructions as PdDocSt does, if needed, to send to the printer with ???. In the preceding example, however, and in most cases, you use simpler instructions:

```
??? _PDPARMS(8)
* set pitch according to current printer driver setup
```

You can even open P_CODES.DBF as a table, and get the instructions directly from the fields, bypassing the current driver entirely except to check the currently specified printer, as shown in the following code sample:

```
SELECT P_CODES
IF TYPE(_PDPARMS(1)) = "C"
   * make sure that a printer setup is active
   * see note on Postscript use below
   LOCATE FOR P_name = _PDPARMS(1)
   * the first element of _PDPARMS holds printer name
   ??? P_setup+P_reset+P_12cpi
   * use P_CODES information to initialize the printer and
   * send instructions to print in 12-pitch.
ENDIF
```

Just as you send _PDPARMS elements or P_Codes fields directly to the printer by using ???, you can add these items to a report or label as expressions. In a label, concatenate the additions with other information on the same line, making sure that you have P_Codes open in some unselected work area:

```
"Normaltext"+P_codes.P_boldon+"Boldtext"+P_codes.P_boldoff+"Etc"
```

Or use the following line:

```
"Normaltext"+_PDPARMS(11)+"Boldtext"+_PDPARMS(12)+"Etc"
```

In a report, create a report expression wide enough to hold all the characters of the control codes that may be sent and insert the codes at appropriate positions in the report layout. Recall that you can overlay report expressions so that the instructions do not interfere with the positions of the expressions you want printed. Refer to Chapter 10 to determine the order in which expressions are evaluated and sent to the printer when overlaid.

Although using this technique enables you to apply styles separately to different items on the same line of a label, ordinarily you need not use the technique for reports. Assign styles to report objects individually. You can extend the P_Codes table, however, to store information about other styles not included by default, such as double-wide printing. Rather than bother changing _PDRIVER to an edited version of DRIVER.PRG that handles the new enhancements, you can pull these codes directly from the added P_Codes fields at printing time, while the default driver takes care of other styles.

TIP

All the preceding examples refer only to non-PostScript printers. Look at PS.PRG for equivalent PostScript printer information on elements of _PDPARMS and which elements are used by which printer procedures. Before you use _PDPARMS or P_CODES.DBF directly, check TYPE(_PDPARMS(1)), as you did prior to the LOCATE statement in the preceding code example. This command returns a "U" (Unknown) if no printer driver setup is active. If a PostScript driver is active, you see an "L" (Logical), because the PostScript driver uses _PDPARMS(1) to store .T. for Portrait and .F. for Landscape orientation, rather than a printer name because printer names are irrelevant to PostScript.

PostScript document initialization requires a long *header*, or Prolog, of instructions, which are sent to the printer, as you see in PS.PRG in PROCEDURE PdDocSt. If you initialize a PostScript printer, copy the Prolog instructions and follow the rest of the procedure closely. If you change fonts for single objects, follow the additional procedures in PS.PRG for the instructions you pass to the printer.

The final section of this chapter uses PSAPI.PLB to send driver procedures directly to the printer during ? and ?? printing to a PostScript printer. This approach probably is the easiest way to initialize a PostScript printer.

You can store new information to various elements of _PDPARMS, which you then can use during FoxPro's default use of the printer driver setup, and also instructions to the printer that you send. This practice, however, doesn't work with the default _PDRIVER programs (the library programs DRIVER2.PLB and PSAPI.PLB), which load the array only once. Use DRIVER.PRG and PS.PRG as the _PDRIVER programs. Remember that you need to edit GEN_PD.PRG to coordinate this change, as previously explained.

If you plan to distribute an application as a stand-alone executable file and want to give the users access to the GENPD.APP dialogs and drivers, add GENPD.APP to the project. As an .APP file, GENPD.APP is by default excluded by the Project Manager, but adding this file to the project ensures that all FoxPro features the file uses are contained in the executable. Also, add the Resource file that contains the printer driver setups that you want to supply with an application you create (excluded if you want the Resource file to be an editable file).

When you distribute the application, you must supply some additional files. You must place these files in the same directory as the executable application file. GENPD.APP is required, and you also should include a copy of the Resource file if the file is not readonly and if you don't create an editable copy during the installation procedures.

Occasionally, you may want to bypass the printer driver system for a particular printing need. FoxPro still supports an assortment of FoxPro printing system variables, which were added to the language before printer drivers were implemented. You can see these variables if you DISPLAY MEMORY (all these variables begin with _P). These variables also are listed in the *Commands and Functions* manual.

You must use some of these system variables within a PRINTJOB/ ENDPRINTJOB loop, which is indicated by a See Also reference to PRINTJOB/ENDPRINTJOB in their Commands and Function entries, but you can use other system variables at any time. Although these variables don't permit control of individual printers as precise as that for the printer drivers, you don't always need to make adjustments printer-specific, and the system variables often do the job well.

Suppose that you want a report that uses a nonstandard page length. Many continuous-form invoices used by dot-matrix printers are 7 inches long rather than 11 inches long. Continuous-form checks may be other lengths. If you create a report form 42 lines long (rather than 66 lines) by using the Report Layout option, you see that the printer still advances 11 inches at the end of each page where the printer expects to find the top-of-form. This unwanted advance occurs because by default a report form sends EJECT commands to the printer as a *form feed*, and the printer isn't instructed that the top-of-form is changed.

You can send the instructions through the printer drivers, of course, but you must first create these instructions for each applicable printer. This step may require a number of additional printer driver setups, or even separate printer entries, which you can add as described in the following section. You can, however, avoid adding setups or printer entries and instruct FoxPro to handle the job generically with the following commands:

```
_PLENGTH = 42
* default is 66
_PADVANCE = "LINEFEED"
* default is "FORMFEED"
```

Set the page length as before to 42 in the Report Layout option, but now, FoxPro sends *line feeds* to the printer until the line counter reaches 42 lines at the bottom of each report page, or until an EJECT or EJECT PAGE command is encountered in the program.

TIP

Just as ? and ?? don't send document-initializing instructions, because label forms never officially begin a document, label forms don't send page-level printer driver instructions. The Label Designer was created to handle continuous-form labels, not laser sheets. LABEL FORM commands don't understand that labels on one sheet are equidistant from each other, but the last label on one sheet is a different distance from the first label on the next page, and .LBX tables make no internal provisions for this difference.

If the laser labels don't start at the top of the page, the printer drivers have an option to specify a top margin. However, because the labels don't go all the way to the bottom of the sheet, you need a mechanism to force the LABEL FORM command to eject a page exactly at the bottom of the last label. If the page is ejected at the last line on the page, rather than the last line on the last label, the top-margin instructions don't intervene at precisely the right moment and printing on the next page of labels doesn't start at the right line.

With the proper page length, derived from the _PLENGTH and a _PADVANCE of "LINEFEED", the printer drivers' top margin provides the correct placement of the top line on subsequent label sheets.

When you try to adapt the printer drivers, and especially when you prepare a printer driver program for distribution with an application you created, you often need to check the results of your tinkering. Notice the consideration given to a PostScript driver, using a check for TYPE("_PDPARMS(1)") = "L" because listing the information about the printer driver while a PostScript driver is active is futile. The following procedure is a handy check on the current printer driver system information:

```
* PDCHECK.PRG

IF TYPE("_PDPARMS(1)") = "C"
   LIST MEMO LIKE _PDPARMS TO pd_test.txt
ENDIF
SET PRINTER TO pd_test.txt ADDITIVE
SET PRINTER ON
SET CONSOLE OFF
IF TYPE("_PDPARMS(1)") = "L"
  STORE _PDSETUP TO ps
  SET PDSETUP TO ""
```

continues

```
  ? "*** POSTSCRIPT DRIVER ***"
  ? "setup         = "+ps
ELSE
  ? "setup         = "+_PDSETUP
ENDIF
? "driver        = "+_PDRIVER
? "PD app        = "+_GENPD
? "resource file = "+SET("RESOURCE",1)
? "resource is set:"+SET("RESOURCE")
? "config.fp file :"+SYS(2019)
?
? "FP launch dir  :"+SYS(2004)
? "PD app is here :"
?? SYS(2004) $ _GENPD
?
? "curr directory :"+SET("DEFAULT",1)+SYS(2003)
? "PD app is here :"
?? SYS(2003) $ _GENPD
?
SET PRINTER TO
SET PRINTER OFF
SET CONSOLE ON
MODI FILE pd_test.txt NOMODIFY
ERASE pd_test.txt
IF TYPE("ps") = "C"
   SET PDSETUP TO ps
ENDIF
RETURN
```

Creating Printer Entries

Whether you distribute applications or only maintain a single-user printer driver system, you may need to create new printer entries in P_CODES.DBF or add extra fonts to FONTS.DBF. Perhaps you own an unusual printer not on the available list and incompatible with other printers on the list. Perhaps the printer was introduced to the market after the list was created. Perhaps the PostScript printer you own is capable of handling a far larger assortment of fonts than contained in the default set.

You may want to add another entry for the printer, with different instructions, even if the printer is on the list. If you look on the list, you see two entries for the Hewlett-Packard LaserJet II. One entry includes the phrase (60 lpp), which is default for the LaserJet. The other entry includes a nonstandard set of instructions in the P_codes.P_6lpi field, which reduces the amount of vertical space between lines to force the number of lines per page to 66.

This latter setup enables you to create a report form that works equally well with both dot-matrix and laser printers because dot-matrix printers usually default to 66 lines per page. The former setup usually is better for standard laser label formats, which were developed for the LaserJet's default vertical spacing. Use this printer entry with a top margin that matches the label forms as the basis for a special printer driver setup with a name that indicates you intend to use the driver for labels.

Even with two setups available, you may want to edit the LaserJet entries in P_codes. The LaserJet is shipped with a default character set that includes no line-drawing characters. To get the same graphics characters shown in the Report Layout when you draw box and line objects or use special characters, you can change the default character set by using instructions found in the LaserJet manual. You may have other applications, however, that depend on the original default set, and you may want to change the printer's behavior only for FoxPro. If so, edit the two LaserJet entries in P_codes to give these instructions by changing the P_codes.P_setup field. At the end of the default entry, type `(10U` to instruct the printer to choose the proper character set.

If the printer is not on the list of supported printers and you want to add a new entry, try to find a record similar to start with. An early model of the printer, or another printer with which this printer is compatible for most purposes may be on the list. If you see a similar printer listed, SCATTER MEMVAR, APPEND a BLANK record, and then GATHER MEMVAR. Edit the P_name field and all other fields that must be changed. If you can't find a similar entry, just APPEND BLANK and add information to all the fields.

Before you use the new or edited printer entries in P_CODES.DBF or font entries you have added to FONTS.DBF, remember that these tables are included in GENPD.APP as readonly files. (If the files were not readonly, you would need to distribute the files separately, along with GENPD.APP when you distributed an application.) For entries to be *recognized* by GENPD.APP, therefore, you must rebuild GENPD.APP from the GENPD project. Only then is the new version of the P_codes and Fonts tables contained in the project.

Understanding External Libraries and the Application Program Interface

The FoxPro programming language contains more functionality than most users need in a database management system. You may discover certain facilities, however, that you either need or may want available from within FoxPro, but are not provided by the internal commands and functions. To address these needs, FoxPro provides the capability of using external API libraries and binary routines (.BIN files).

The *External Routine Application Program Interface*, or *API*, is an interface definition that enables C and assembly language programmers to extend FoxPro's native capabilities by creating function libraries. These functions can be used in the same manner as built-in FoxPro commands and functions.

The API enables a programmer to access FoxPro's internal *engine*, or the FoxPro internal routines that handle memory management, file input/output, window management, error trapping, and so on. A library function usually executes faster than an equivalent FoxPro program, especially when the function performs an operation that may require the FoxPro program to call numerous different FoxPro functions.

Versions of FoxPro before 2.0, and also FoxBASE+, enabled you to LOAD and CALL binary routines to perform tasks such as checking for the presence of a disk in a floppy disk drive. Functions contained in an API library do the same things as binary files but have the advantage of working just like FoxPro's functions. You can use a library function as part of an index expression or as the test condition in an IF statement.

In this section, you learn about the API from the perspective of using external libraries created by others, rather than from the perspective of creating custom external libraries. You also learn how to use binary routines. Because the API is relatively new, times may arise when a library routine cannot be found to meet a need and a binary routine can do the job.

Using External Library Routines

How do you use an external library, and how do you actually execute the library's functions?

To use a library, you need to know the name of the library file, how to load the library, the names of the functions the library contains, and how to use these functions.

The library is a file with a .PLB extension. If you see a .PLB file on the library disk, you can load this kind of file by typing the following command in the Command window:

```
SET LIBRARY TO <library filename>
```

In this command, replace *library filename* with the name of the library file that you want to use. The default printer driver system, discussed previously in this chapter, uses DRIVER2.PLB and PSAPI.PLB files—so, whether or not you know it, you already own two library files! SET LIBRARY TO one of these files, either SETting DEFAULT TO the appropriate directory or using the file's full drive and path.

NOTE FoxPro 2.5 for DOS and Windows cannot use the same library files. FoxPro for Windows library files have the extension .FLL (or FoxPro-specific *dynamic link libraries*, which usually have the extension .DLL for Windows programs). Vendors who supply a library for one version of FoxPro 2.5, however, usually supply both the .PLB and .DLL files.

With the library loaded, you can use the DISPLAY STATUS command to see the names of the library's functions. After all the other information is shown, FoxPro displays the API library status information, which appears as shown in figure 16.20.

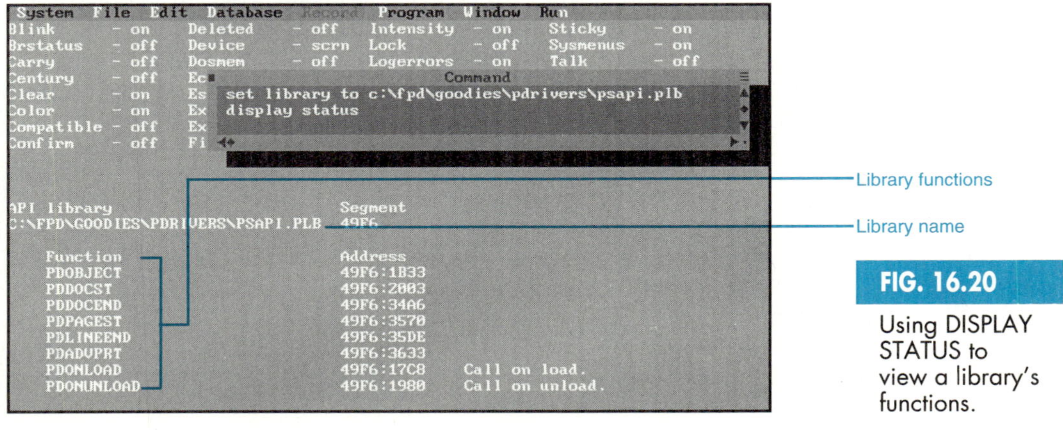

FIG. 16.20

Using DISPLAY STATUS to view a library's functions.

Each name shown under the Function column is a library function that you can use wherever you can use a FoxPro command or function, with the exception of functions marked Call on load or Call on unload. These marked functions, such as PDONLOAD and PDONUNLOAD in figure 16.20, are special internal library routines that execute only when the library is loaded and unloaded, respectively. These routines are not intended for your use.

You need to know the proper use of each function. As with FoxPro, each function expects to receive zero or more arguments, and all arguments passed to the function usually are a particular data type (character, numeric, and so on). Each function also returns both a value and a particular data type.

In this example, you use the PSAPI function PdDocSt( ) and PdDocEnd( ). As you learned in the preceding section, the ? and ?? commands don't send document-level instructions, and a PostScript printer requires document-initialization and document-ending information. To use ? and ?? with a PostScript printer, you send the information through the library functions.

The FoxPro environment for the following task must include a current PostScript driver, which the procedure turns off and restores as necessary, and you must SET TALK OFF—otherwise, the PostScript printer can get confused by results of the functions being echoed to the printer.

Your first job is to load the library. The code checks to see whether the library is already loaded. If not, the code looks for the library in a default location. In this case, PSAPI.PLB is included in FoxPro's home directory, represented by SYS(2004). If the library isn't present in its usual place, the program asks the user to find the file, using the GETFILE( ) function. When the presence of the library is assured, the SET LIBRARY command in the following sequence loads the library:

```
SET TALK OFF
SET PDSETUP TO "PS AvantGarde 10 on 8"
PRIVATE m.library, m.ps_set

* check to see if the library is already loaded:
IF NOT "PSAPI" $ UPPER(SET("LIBRARY",1))
   m.library = ""
   IF FILE(SYS(2004)+"PSAPI.PLB")
      m.library = SYS(2004)+"PSAPI.PLB"
   ELSE
      m.library = ;
          GETFILE("PLB","Where is PSAPI.PLB?")
```

```
   ENDIF
   IF EMPTY(m.library)
      WAIT WINDOW NOWAIT ;
           "Couldn't find Postscript library file!"
      RETURN .F.
   ELSE
      SET LIBRARY TO (m.library) ADDITIVE
   ENDIF
ENDIF
```

Notice the ADDITIVE keyword on the SET LIBRARY command. Without this keyword, all other libraries currently loaded are *unloaded* by the SET LIBRARY command! You may want to save information about current libraries, unload all the libraries, and reload the libraries later, in some limited memory situations. More often, however, you want to use the ADDITIVE keyword, which leaves the current libraries undisturbed.

You now are almost ready to use the functions in the library to initialize the printer. A small setup for the printing job is necessary, first, as shown in the following code:

```
STORE 0 TO _PLINENO, _PCOLNO
STORE 60 TO _PLENGTH, _RMARGIN
SET PRINT ON
m.ps_set = _PDSETUP
SET PDSETUP TO
```

The last line above turns off the current PostScript driver, having saved the driver's name for later use. You eliminate the driver right before you use the PSAPI function because you want the function instructions to go to the printer *exactly as sent* (not formatted as a line to be printed on a PostScript printer, but as commands).

When you purchase a library, the vendor provides you with instructions on how to use the package. In this case, a chart in the *Developer's Guide* tells you what values each procedure expects as parameters. These values usually are sent to the procedure directly by FoxPro during printing, but here you call the procedure with the relevant values. As you see in the chart, and in the description of the function on subsequent pages, PdDocSt( ) has two numeric parameters—the report height and the report width. You have conveniently stored these values in the _PLENGTH and _RMARGIN system variables so that when the following line calls the function, the function computes the proper instructions for a PostScript printer and RETURNs these instructions. Because PRINT is ON, the ? command sends the function's RETURN string to the printer:

```
? PdDocSt(_PLENGTH,_RMARGIN)
```

Now, your printer is ready for the lines you want to send to print. You set the PostScript driver back on in the following sequence, and then the driver takes care of describing each line's position, font, attributes, and so forth to the printer:

```
SET PDSETUP TO (m.ps_set)
* sample for a test print:
FOR x  = 1 TO 10
    ? "This is a test" AT 20
    ?? "bold test" AT 40 STYLE "B"
    ?? "underlining here!" AT 10 STYLE "U"
ENDFOR
```

When you finish printing, you send the document's trailer, setting the driver off again to send the PostScript commands exactly as computed by the PdDocEnd( ) function (you see from the FoxPro documentation that you don't pass PdDocEnd( ) anything):

```
SET PDSETUP TO
? PdDocEnd( )
SET PRINT OFF
```

One job remains; the entire page was described to the printer in PostScript terms, but you need the page released from the printer. You turn the driver back on to enable FoxPro and the printer driver to interpret the normal EJECT command in terms a PostScript printer understands, as shown in the following code:

```
SET PDSETUP TO (m.ps_set)
EJECT
```

Now the printer can employ the loaded PostScript driver for other uses, such as a REPORT FORM. However, if you don't expect to call the PSAPI functions again for more ? and ?? commands, you can remove the library from memory at this point by adding the following line:

```
RELEASE LIBRARY (m.library)
```

You may be surprised that RELEASE LIBRARY doesn't affect the printer driver's internal use of the same library. The printer drivers use a separate copy of the library, which don't show up when you DISPLAY STATUS, and which you cannot use directly.

You learn about the printer driver .PLBs in this section because these .PLBs are already available for use and are called in a standard style. The useful task illustrated here, using the ? and ?? commands with a

PostScript printer, is a FoxPro printing task that many people don't know how to accomplish. The following example, however, shows a more typical third-party library to perform a task *not* available as a FoxPro native feature.

Several sections of this book have mentioned the superiority of the BROWSE over popups and scrollable lists as a pick list; the BROWSE is more configurable, it is editable, and it handles far more pick list choices without causing degradation of speed or requiring all its choices to be loaded into precious memory. One capability of popups and lists not included as a capability of BROWSE, however, is *incremental seek*: you used this feature when you typed the initial letters of choices in the Help topic list, or in popups and lists, and the choices scrolled to match your selection.

Providing this feature for a BROWSE is a perfect application for a third-party library. The \MISC directory on the source disk for this book includes the JKEY library written by Joseph A. Gotthelf for this purpose. (The library is shareware; register for the most recent version of this useful tool by using instructions that Joe includes with the files for the library.)

When you read JKEY's accompanying text file, you find that the library consists of several functions. These functions are listed, just as the functions would be in the *Commands and Functions* manual, with the arguments the functions take and the FoxPro environment factors that affect the functions' performance.

Joe has used, for example, the value in the system variable _DBLCLICK to determine what delay between two keypresses will cause JKEY to start a new incremental search rather than continuing the current search—DEFINEd POPUPs use _DBLCLICK for the same purpose. As the text file also explains, JKEY also is affected by the SETting of BELL, TALK, and NEAR.

After the library is loaded, and a BROWSE begins, the program you created calls the JKeyInit( ) function to start a search. After this routine is called, most keypresses result in a SEEK that uses the current index on the current table. The BROWSE window is updated accordingly. If TALK is ON, the current search is displayed in a normal TALK window (see fig. 16.21).

JKeyInit is called with the following syntax:

```
=JKeyInit([<case> [,<key prefix> [,<talk prefix>
[,primary_window]]]])
```

Remember that arguments enclosed in brackets ([]) are optional. JKeyInit( )'s arguments permit you to specify the following characteristics:

- The case sensitivity of the search
- Search characters to prefix the keypresses for the SEEK expression
- An expression to appear in the TALK window
- A window to which JKEY's search may be limited (all other windows will accept keystrokes in the usual manner)

After the search is over, you return the keyboard to standard behavior by using another JKEY function:

```
=JKeyCanc( )
```

The demonstration program for JKEY.PLB in the following listing uses a copy of the Customer table from the book's sample files, which allows the user to toggle JKEY on and off, alternately searching through a BROWSE and editing entries in the BROWSE. JKeyInit( ) is called with "L" as its first argument, which tells JKEY to convert all the keypresses to lowercase for the SEEK (the user doesn't have to worry about matching the case of the field entry). Consequently, this program requires a tag on LOWER(lastname).

```
* LIB_DEMO.PRG
PRIVATE m.oldtalk, m.seekon
HIDE WINDOWS ALL
CLEAR
m.oldtalk = SET("TALK")
SET TALK OFF
SET ESCAPE OFF
IF NOT USED('Customer')
   USE Customer AGAIN IN 0
ENDIF
SELE Customer
* INDEX ON LOWER(lastname) TAG lastname
SET ORDER TO lastname
SET LIBRARY TO JKey ADDITIVE
PUSH KEY CLEAR
ON KEY LABEL F10 DO seektoggle
m.seekon = .F.
SET TALK ON
SET SYSMENU OFF
BROWSE FIELDS ;
```

```
              phone :H="Edit Phone:" :P="@R 999-999-9999", ;
              phone_ext :H="Ext:", ;
              name = TRIM(firstname)+" "+lastname ;
       TITLE " F10 To Toggle Incremental Seek "
=JKeyCanc( )
POP KEY
SET SYSMENU AUTOMATIC
SET TALK &oldtalk
RELEASE LIBRARY JKEY
SHOW WINDOWS ALL
RETURN

PROCEDURE seektoggle
IF m.seekon
   =JKeyCanc( )
ELSE
   =JKeyInit("L","","Find Last Name:  ")
ENDIF
m.seekon = ! m.seekon
RETURN
```

In this example, the expression on which the SEEK is performed (LOWER(Lastname)) is not displayed in the BROWSE. The name happens to be displayed in the calculated field *Name* (see fig. 16.21), but in fact doesn't have to be there, or could be in the BROWSE and editable. JKEY is working with the index, not with the visible BROWSE, so whether the SEEK expression is present and whether the expression is the leftmost expression in the BROWSE make no difference.

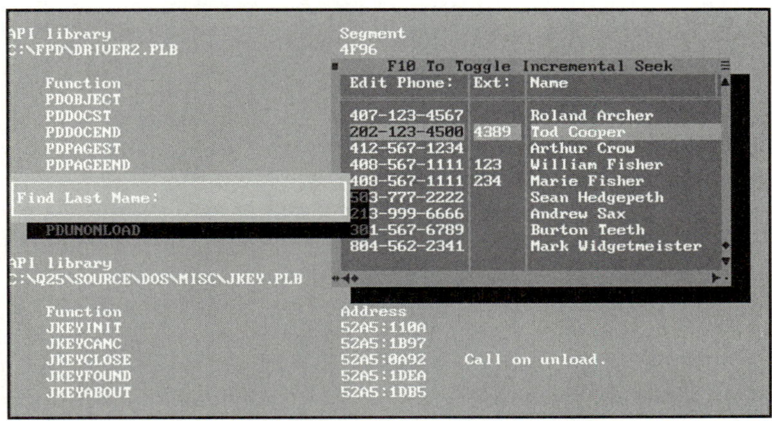

FIG. 16.21

The library JKEY provides incremental search in a BROWSE, while functions loaded by two external libraries show on-screen after a DISPLAY STATUS.

To have the same incremental search in a popup, the POPUP must be DEFINEd with the PROMPT FIELDS TRIM(Lastname)+", "+"Firstname", plus the phone number if you want to show this field. The prompts cannot be as readable as the form in which they are presented by the BROWSE—and the phone numbers cannot be edited—nor would the popup have a talk window that confirms the user's present search, the capability of being turned on and off, or any of JKEY's other configurable options.

JKEY's features are an excellent example of the functionality that libraries can add to the native capabilities of FoxPro. Other likely uses for third-party libraries include providing access from within FoxPro to external devices such as image scanners and providing communications facilities such as automated file transfers between a corporate headquarters and production sites.

Using Binary Routines

Because of the API's capability of making external functions work seamlessly with FoxPro, most capabilities provided by binary routines (or .BIN files) are likely to be replaced eventually by external libraries. This change, however, may take some time. Meanwhile, you still may need the functionality provided by the numerous .BIN files written to supplement the capabilities of FoxPro and the other Xbase dialects, so you need to know how to load, unload, and use a .BIN file.

BIN files are loaded with LOAD, used with CALL, and unloaded with RELEASE MODULE. If JKEY were a .BIN file, you would load the library by typing the following command in the Command window, or by including the following line in a program:

```
LOAD JKEY [SAVE ¦ NOSAVE]
```

The optional SAVE keyword (NOSAVE is the default) tells FoxPro to save the current contents of the video RAM in the FoxPro desktop upon return from a CALL to the binary routine. This step is important only if the binary routine modifies the screen. If the routine does modify the screen (and assuming that the routine writes directly to video RAM), FoxPro treats what was written by the binary routine as though FoxPro had written the information and therefore can protect the routine's output from erasure by objects you subsequently may move or drag across the screen. This protection occurs, however, only if you use the SAVE keyword with either the LOAD or the CALL command.

JKEY includes several separate functions, including JKeyInit( ) and JKeyCanc( ). Binary routines cannot contain separately addressable functions. You can CALL only a binary routine, although you can pass a parameter to a binary routine, and this parameter can contain code that tells the binary routine your intentions. You can tell the fictional JKEY.BIN, for example, to initialize a search, by using the following line:

```
CALL JKEY WITH ".I" + ".L"+"."+".Find Last Name"
```

Of course, the binary routine needs to know that ".I" at the beginning of the string means *start the search* and that the other parameters that the initialization of the search require are delimited with periods within the binary routine's one parameter. Likewise, you can type the following command to invoke the cancel routine in the binary file:

```
CALL JKEY WITH ".C"
```

A CALL command also can contain the optional SAVE ¦ NOSAVE keywords. If you use one command or the other, the default setting established when you LOADed the binary routine is overridden.

Finally, you unload a .BIN file by using the RELEASE MODULE command. To remove the JKEY file from memory, type the following command in the Command window:

```
RELEASE MODULE JKEY
```

Summary

This chapter concludes the study of FoxPro's powerful interface-driven tools. Beginning with Part II and your investigation of the RQBE, you were gradually introduced to the concepts and statements of the FoxPro command language.

You executed many FoxPro commands in the Command window. The lines you typed in the Command window also may have been executed from a program. As a *program*, or procedure, these lines are saved to a file to be executed at a later time, in the order you specify, as a deliberate and repeatable sequence of instructions.

You learned to write short procedures to provide support for the screens, menus, and output you produced, mostly in the form Microsoft Fox refers to as *code snippets*, or short sequences attached to a menu or screen file. In this chapter, you reviewed more examples of such procedures.

When you learned about the Project Manager, you glimpsed the manner in which you can combine these procedures to create an entire application. In the following chapter, you learn about using these procedures and the tools that support them in applications that in turn support different versions of FoxPro. Then, in the following part of this book, you begin to examine programming structure and the FoxPro language in detail. You learn to use various groups of commands and functions that perform a wide range of database management tasks and provide FoxPro's true power and depth.

17

CHAPTER

Transporting FoxPro Applications across Versions and Platforms

From the introduction of FoxBASE to the present, the sterling reputation of Fox Software (now Microsoft Fox) products has rested on two major factors:

- Each version was *faster* and more efficient than the version it replaced. Dr. Dave Fulton sold the original FoxBASE by introducing it at a dBASE III conference. He urged developers to run their dBASE III code under his product; they were stunned by the difference in speed.

- Each version was *backward compatible* with the version it replaced. The dBASE III developers also were amazed (and relieved) to learn that their applications ran unmodified under FoxBASE; they didn't have to do a lot of work to achieve new speed.

These priorities have been critical to the Fox development process, but their influence is limited by practical considerations. FoxPro 1.0 and FoxPro 2.0 each had a faster database engine than its predecessor, but their advanced windowing and screen design capabilities caused screen displays to paint slowly on older machines. The Fox team didn't reject the advanced screen and window capabilities because the new features conflicted with their concern for speed. The Fox team also has altered the behavior of certain commands and functions whose past behavior was inefficient or anomalous. Inevitably, these decisions conflicted with the criterion of backward compatibility; some of the changes cause developers to make compromises and rewrite some portions of their code when they upgrade to a new version of a Fox product.

FoxPro 2.5 represents a new and special dilemma for Fox developers with respect to compatibility. Upgrading applications to match a new version of the language ordinarily happens once, and then the major effort is over. FoxPro 2.5 is designed to work *across* platforms, however, in several different versions for DOS, Windows, UNIX, and the Macintosh. You may need to move your application from FoxPro 2.0 or some other Xbase environment; as usual, you make any necessary adjustments once and continue to develop in FoxPro 2.5 without a backward glance. In contrast, other adjustments must be *maintainable*, to enable simultaneous development and use of the application on two or more platforms.

This chapter discusses the FoxPro 2.5 tools for moving your applications from FoxPro 2.0 into 2.5 and then maintaining these applications cross-platform.

Approach this topic with an open mind. Microsoft's preannouncements and marketing for FoxPro 2.5 stress the product's backward compatibility and the ease of cross-platform use. The company's strategy is understandable, but the reality is more complex. By accepting this reality (instead of feeling cheated when you realize that the product's backward or cross-platform compatibility is not total), you gain rather than lose flexibility.

In an interview in *Dr. Dobb's Journal*, Bjarne Stroustrup, the author of the C++ language, addressed the compatibility issue in terms we can apply to FoxPro:

> *Portability is an economic issue. You're portable if it's cheaper to modify the program to run somewhere else than it is to build a new program from scratch.... People who are thinking about 100 percent portability are deluding themselves. You can only get 100 percent portability provided you port between two systems that are very similar. I don't think the environment of a Cray should be the same as the environment of a 386 to the point where you could guarantee that every program that ran on the one would run on the other. The people who use the one kind of machine have one kind of concerns, and the people on the other have other kinds of concerns.*

Rather than seek a goal of 100-percent compatibility between the versions, you should use all the features of each platform as they were designed (and as the users of that platform expect them) to be used. Instead of expecting 100-percent backward compatibility, you can accept the fact that some advances require change. As Stroustrup put it:

> *. . .100 percent portability is a very dangerous idea, a return to the Middle Ages where everything is what it was in my father's time, and nothing changes. That's a caricature of the Middle Ages, true. If it had been like that, we would never have gotten the Renaissance.*

Moving Applications to FoxPro 2.5

You should assess the wisdom of incorporating code that you have already written in earlier versions of Fox, or in other Xbase dialects, with reference to Stroustrup's criterion. An application is portable if incorporating its code into a new version is more efficient (a better investment of your valuable time) than rewriting the application from the ground up. Each individual developer must make this assessment, although as Stroustrup noted, the more similar the two environments, the easier the port becomes.

Porting from Other Xbase Languages and Fox Versions

The portability of code written in other Xbase dialects to FoxPro 2.5 is largely dependent on the style of the developer. Some people have little difficulty moving their code; others, who rely on different strengths or features in the other dialect, find that much of their code must be reworked for FoxPro.

The best strategy for Xbase developers moving to FoxPro is to create a new FoxPro project, designate the application's top-level program as the main program for the project, and let the Project Manager Build the Project, gathering its necessary components as usual. Investigate the files that the Project Manager included to see what's missing. (If you refer to programs indirectly in your code, consult Chapter 14 for information about EXTERNAL references and other ways to make sure the Project Manager recognizes and includes all the necessary programs.)

Then use the Project Manager's Build Application option to compile the application. The resulting error list will tell you which features of the other dialect are not supported by FoxPro. Begin your conversion process by rewriting the lines of code that produced these errors.

The next step is to understand that some features are supported, but don't work quite the same way in each dialect. Consult the *Language Reference*'s SET COMPATIBLE entry for a good initial guide to the commands and functions affected by these differences. The SET COMPATIBLE listings will not anticipate every possible problem, however, and comparing your application against the entries is no substitute for testing your application thoroughly under FoxPro.

Microsoft Tech Support gathers additional information on version and dialect differences, and you also can get a lot of help from your fellow developers in users' groups and CompuServe's FOXFORUM (see Appendix G, "Finding Available Help," for more information).

Having accounted for aspects of your application that may cause erratic behavior under FoxPro 2.5, you turn your attention to adding FoxPro 2.5-specific features. This process can be gradual, as you learn about the product. You probably want to start with the performance-enhancing features of FoxPro: switching your indexing scheme to FoxPro structural compound indexes, rewriting your database-querying modules to use SQL-SELECT and Rushmore, and changing file-opening procedures to take advantage of FoxPro's 225 work areas in programs that will not need to run in FoxPro 2.5 for DOS's Standard version.

TIP

Microsoft also has developed a special add-on tool for developers moving applications from dBASE IV. This tool provides conversions for screen files and other aspects development of a FoxPro application that should integrate use of the Power Tools, so you don't have to MODIFY SCREENs and other application elements from scratch. Along with creating FoxPro .SCXs and other system files, the tool will "step through" a dBASE IV procedure or program in a manner similar to FoxPro's Trace window, offering suggestions for alternatives to lines of code that will not run or will not run efficiently under FoxPro. This book was written before the official introduction of this migration kit; contact Microsoft directly to find out how to get the kit disks and documentation.

When you are ready to modify your application's interface, start with the addition of SYSMENU. Having a "live" menu during other database management tasks will change the way you organize your data entry procedures; in addition, as described in Chapter 14, you can use the Menu Builder as an outline tool to organize your modifications. Slowly, each task on the menu (executing READs in screen sets, and outputting reports and labels) can be rewritten using FoxPro-specific methods.

Porting from FoxPro 2.0

If your applications are written in FoxPro 2.0, using the FoxPro Power Tools, your situation is different from those of other Xbase developers. Each application already has a project and FoxPro 2-style reports, labels, screens, queries, and menus.

The *compiled version* of each project (the .APP file) must be recompiled in FoxPro 2.5 to run under FoxPro 2.5, and this process requires that the project files (the .PJX and .PJT files) undergo conversion to FoxPro 2.5 format.

NOTE

Any subsidiary compiled files used by the application—whether they are .APPs, FoxPro-produced .EXEs, or library files (.PLBs)—must be recompiled before they will run under FoxPro 2.5. The .PLBs must be recompiled under the 2.5 DOS version of the Library Construction Kit, a separate product, which is described briefly in Chapter 16's section entitled "External Libraries and the Application Program Interface."

When a project file is converted to 2.5 format, FoxPro 2.0 will not be able to read the project file again. Before editing any project in 2.5, copy it to a new name or to a new directory—unless you will never need the 2.0 project again.

The same caution applies to editing the other system files based on .DBF tables (.SCX/.SCTs for screens, .FRX/.FRTs and .LBX/.LBTs for reports and labels, and .MNX/.MNTs for menus). Each of these system file types has a different table structure for 2.5. (.QPR files for queries are in ASCII format, rather than tables, and don't require conversion between FoxPro versions.)

Simply compiling the 2.5-style .APP does not convert these component tables to 2.5 format, except for the project file. When you open a specific 2.0 screen, report, label, or menu for modification for the first time, the conversion occurs. You have an opportunity to refuse the conversion, as shown in figure 17.1, when you choose to edit the file, whether you select it from the Project list, open it from the File menu popup, or use the MODIFY command in the Command Window. (A similar alert appears when you choose to BUILD APP <name> FROM <project name> from the Command window, which requires the same conversion as when you MODIFY the PROJECT.)

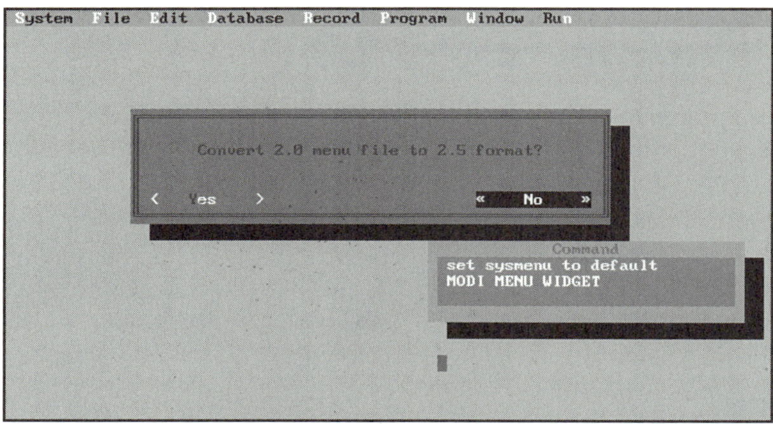

FIG. 17.1

Choosing to edit a FoxPro 2.0 system file under 2.5 requires a conversion.

TIP You may find the process of converting each screen, report, menu, and label inconvenient or annoying, since the process occurs on an individual basis for each file. You can write a short program similar to the following to take care of all the files in a project at once. First, create the 2.5 version of the project (by converting the 2.0 project, or by copying it to a new name and converting the new project). Next, BUILD the .APP for the project to make sure that all the necessary system tables are located where their project entries expect them to be. Then DO the following Convert program WITH the name of the project file:

```
* CONVERT.PRG
PARAMETERS which_pjx
PRIVATE m.select, m.error, m.olderror, m.this_pjx, ;
        m.type_file, m.fcount
m.select = SELECT()
m.olderror = ON("ERROR")
m.error = .F.
m.this_pjx = IIF("." $ which_pjx, ;
                which_pjx, ;
                TRIM(which_pjx)+".PJX")
ON ERROR m.error = .T.
USE (m.this_pjx) AGAIN IN 0 ALIAS This_pjx
ON ERROR &olderror
IF m.error = .T.
   WAIT WINDOW NOWAIT ;
   "Couldn't open "+m.this_pjx+"!"
   RETURN
ENDIF
SELECT This_pjx
SCAN FOR INLIST(Type,"s","R","B","M")
    DO CASE
    CASE Type = "s"
        m.type_file = "SCREEN"
        m.fcount = 79
    CASE Type = "R"
        m.type_file = "REPORT"
        m.fcount = 74
    CASE Type = "B"
        m.type_file = "LABEL"
        m.fcount = 74
    CASE Type = "M"
        m.type_file = "MENU"
        m.fcount = 23
    ENDCASE
    USE (TRIM(This_pjx.Name)) IN 0 AGAIN ALIAS This_file
    IF FCOUNT("This_file") < m.fcount
       USE IN This_file
       KEYBOARD "Y{CTRL-W}"
```

continues

continued

```
        MODIFY &type_file (TRIM(Name))
        * Instead of MODIFYing each file,
        * you can also call the _TRANSPORT program
        * described in later sections of this chapter
        * to convert screens, reports, and labels,
        * but it doesn't convert menus !
    ELSE  && already in 2.5 format
        USE IN This_file
    ENDIF
ENDSCAN
USE
SELECT (m.select)
RETURN
```

If you don't need to edit the screens and other system files, there's no need to convert them. Whether they are converted or not, their behavior is identical under FoxPro 2.0 and FoxPro 2.5 for DOS. The changes the files undergo during conversion are only apparent during *cross-platform* development, described in the next section.

Assessing Cross-Platform Strategies

When data and programs are used on a network, users want different types of computers to share these applications. In other situations, developers want to sell their commercial applications to as many different users, running as many different types of computers, as possible. Both cases require the developer to write code to handle differences between the computer environments.

The developer can write completely separate applications for each environment. The procedure that each operating system uses to start FoxPro names a different application or specifies a different home directory holding a different environment-specific copy of the application.

Separate applications require elaborate installation routines, or reliance on system adminstrators to insert the appropriate instructions into the startup routines. Although this approach appears to simplify development, because each application contains only the code for one platform, it causes nightmares for the programmer who has to maintain separate versions of the code for each platform. If a new validation rule is built into the application, the programmer must change each separate application to comply with the rule. The chances for errors and the testing requirements multiply accordingly.

Installing Applications on Different Platforms

A developer can write a small header application that removes the burden of installation and system startup from the user. Much as the FoxPro loader file FOX.EXE checks available memory and the processor to decide whether to run the Standard or Extended version of FoxPro, the header application can be designed to check the current environment and decide which subsidiary application to run.

FoxPro 2.5 has made this task easier by adding four special system variables (_DOS, _WINDOWS, _UNIX, and _MAC) that have the value of .T. in their respective environments and have the value .F. for code that is currently running in another version of FoxPro 2.5.

Don't try to fool FoxPro for any reason by attempting to assign a different value to these variables; you can't change them.

The header application might look something like the following:

```
DO CASE
CASE _DOS
    DO DOSapp
CASE _WINDOWS
    DO WINapp
CASE _UNIX
    DO UNIXapp
CASE _MAC
   DO MACapp
ENDCASE
```

The header application simplifies installation, providing a convenience for the user by hiding the main files for the four separate applications inside one shell. Still, a header application is only one step in the right direction. This CASE statement represents a primitive form of *bracketing* code in a control structure that permits the program to decide which procedures are appropriate to the current environment.

Each time the application is modified, the programmer still has to decide which modifications require separate adjustments in separate programs. The greater the percentage of the application's code that is maintained in common for all the platforms, the fewer are the program modifications that require multiple adjustments in each platform-specific code segment. The most efficient strategy places code brackets at the lowest possible level of the program, exactly where needed, rather than in the main program, as shown in the preceding example.

In this book's Omnipresent Widget Limited applications, for example, all general setup code (opening database tables, setting orders, defining system-wide variables) will be the same for each platform. A main program issues one DO SETUP command for all versions.

Almost all menu choices will be used on each platform, too. Instead of a different menu for each platform, a single DO WIDGET.MPR will suffice.

Within the menu or the setup program, some choices may not be applicable cross-platform. A table holding OLE objects used in Windows-style reports, for example, is not needed for the DOS application. The setup code might read as follows:

```
IF _WINDOWS
   USE Ole_obj IN 0
ENDIF
```

Similarly, a menu choice that permits a user to specify a picture file for the Product.Design field (a General field) might have a SKIP FOR clause containing the condition NOT _WINDOWS.

The database management tasks that are most platform-specific are screen display and printed output, because these tasks depend on capabilities of the environment and hardware. Screens, reports, and labels are therefore the files that undergo the most cross-platform adjustment.

You could solve the problem by bracketing the code used to DO an .SPR or execute a REPORT or LABEL FORM command. Each platform would have a separate set of these files, and the bracketing code for a menu option that initiated a data entry procedure might look like the following:

```
DO CASE
CASE _DOS
   m.scrn = "dscrn_1"
CASE _WINDOWS
   m.scrn = "wscrn_1"
```

```
CASE _UNIX
   m.scrn = "uscrn_1"
OTHERWISE
   m.scrn = "mscrn_1"
ENDCASE
DO (m.scrn+".SPR")
```

However, FoxPro 2.5's screen, report, and label tables allow information for multiple platforms to be maintained within a single form. The bracketing mechanism to differentiate between platforms occurs on a still lower level. The next section explores the way the FoxPro system tables accomplish this feat.

TIP

The disabled menu option should stay on the DOS menu; there's nothing wrong with users seeing that some capabilities are unavailable in their current environment. (Owners of FoxPro see the option to Build an Executable disabled in the Project Manager Build dialog if they haven't installed the Distribution Kit.) If you disagree with this design principle, however, you still don't have to maintain separate menu files. Instead, add the following code to the Cleanup of your menu:

```
FOR xx = 1 TO CNTBAR(<padname>)
   IF NOT _WINDOWS AND :
        INLIST(PRMBAR(<padname>,xx),;
                    <list of Windows-specific options>)
      RELEASE BAR xx OF <padname>
   ENDIF
ENDFOR
```

This technique can be extended to cover different security levels, or other selections of application features besides cross-platform development. Using a table to hold pad names and menu prompts, you can make the RELEASE process generic and even user-defined.

Transporting Screen Forms

Of the four FoxPro platforms, two (DOS and UNIX) are character-based and two (Macintosh and Windows) are graphics-based. When developing for multiple FoxPro platforms, realize that the graphical environments offer more display and output features. Do not try to move a graphical screen or report to a character-based platform. The examples in this section assume that your cross-platform development starts in a DOS application and moves to a Windows application when the basic features of the project are in place.

This assumption is appropriate for people moving from FoxPro DOS 2.0 to FoxPro 2.5, but it is also appropriate for people who are maintaining FoxPro 2.5 cross-platform applications without starting in 2.0. If you're working in both DOS and Windows, design the DOS form first. In many cases, you simply compile the screen or execute the report or label form, without performing any further conversion.

Figure 17.2 shows the Budget data entry screen from Chapter 13, developed and compiled under DOS and running in FoxPro for Windows. Because the DOS code that DEFINEs the WINDOW for the GETs doesn't have Windows-specific information, this window automatically defaults to FoxFont, a special font designed to make all the GETs and SAYs fit exactly into the window as they would under DOS. The buttons and the window title are special sizes to fit DOS sizing constraints, as well.

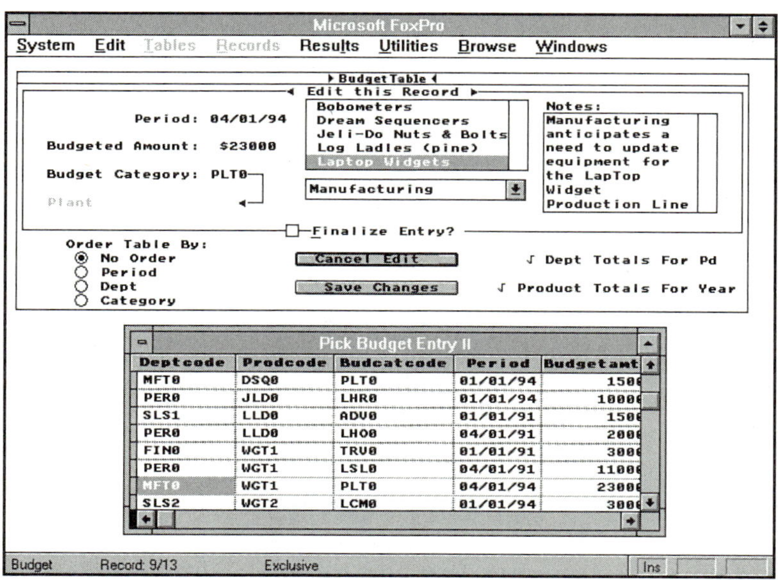

FIG. 17.2

The unmodified DOS Budget screen running under FoxPro for Windows.

If you use the Desktop-type window for GETs under DOS (representing the screen in a DOS application, or the main FoxPro application window in FoxPro for Windows), the Desktop may be given a different font by the user, by using an option on the Text menu popup, when the program is run in FoxPro for Windows. You can solve this problem by changing your Desktop windows to User Window type under DOS (size the new window as large as the screen, with no border). Alternatively, insert the following code before DOing your .SPR to ensure that FoxFont is appropriately used for your SAYs and GETs and that the FoxPro application window is large enough to hold all your Desktop information:

```
MODIFY WINDOW SCREEN FONT "FoxFont"
ZOOM WINDOW SCREEN MAX
```

This solution is sufficient to run the DOS code under Windows. If you need to edit the screen file, you can edit in DOS and be assured that both platforms will reflect your changes.

However, you may want a more Windows-specific looking screen for Budget data entry. Using Windows attributes requires you to modify the screen with the FoxPro for Windows Screen Builder. At this point, FoxPro must alter the underlying screen table. The tool FoxPro provides to alter the table is a program known as the Transporter.

TIP

The default Transporter program TRANSPRT.PRG is located in your main FoxPro directory. Similar to GENSCRN.PRG and GENMENU.PRG, this program's name and location is stored in a system variable, _TRANSPORT; you can edit TRANSPRT.PRG, move one copy to a single location for all your FoxPro platforms by altering the value of _TRANSPORT, or even supply a different FoxPro program to be used as your development Transporter.

When you choose to open a DOS screen file under Windows, the Transport dialog in figure 17.3 appears. Figure 17.4 shows the Budget screen after an initial session in the Transporter.

The Transporter does a pretty good job of importing all the DOS objects, but you may notice a few items you need to edit. The window size in this example is slightly too small, and some of the GETs should be resized, as well. The default MS Sans Serif font does not display certain graphics characters as the same symbols that appear on the DOS screen. You can change the font of these items (to FoxFont, FoxPro Window Font, or FoxPrint), or reinsert the characters using separate SAYs or text labels in a Windows Symbol or Wingdings font.

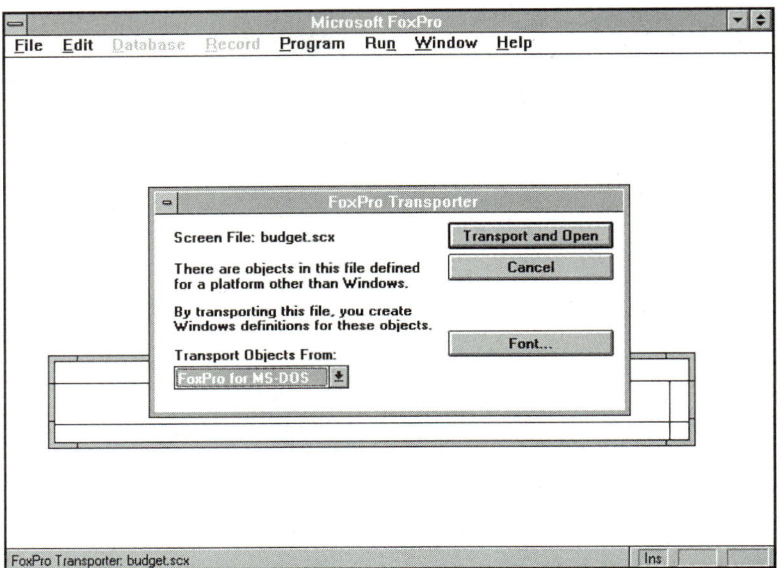

FIG. 17.3

The Transporter dialog.

NOTE The Transporter defaults to the font MS Sans Serif in 8 point, Bold for text labels and regular for GETs. If you prefer a different base font for your Windows screen, you can use the Transporter's `Font` button to select a different font, but try to keep its point size consistent with the default choice.

You may also choose to add Windows-specific features to the screen at this point. Add a picture, for example, or change the Budgetamt GET to a spinner-type field that is unavailable to DOS (see fig. 17.5). When you finish your initial Windows edit, save the screen.

USE the BUDGET.SCX as a table, and BROWSE the table. The first three fields of the table, as shown in figure 17.6, are used by the Transporter to do its work.

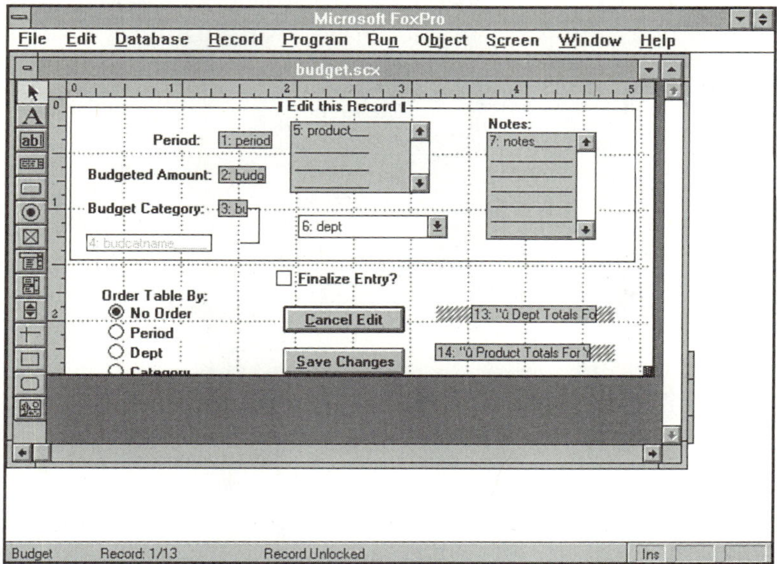

FIG. 17.4

The transported Budget screen.

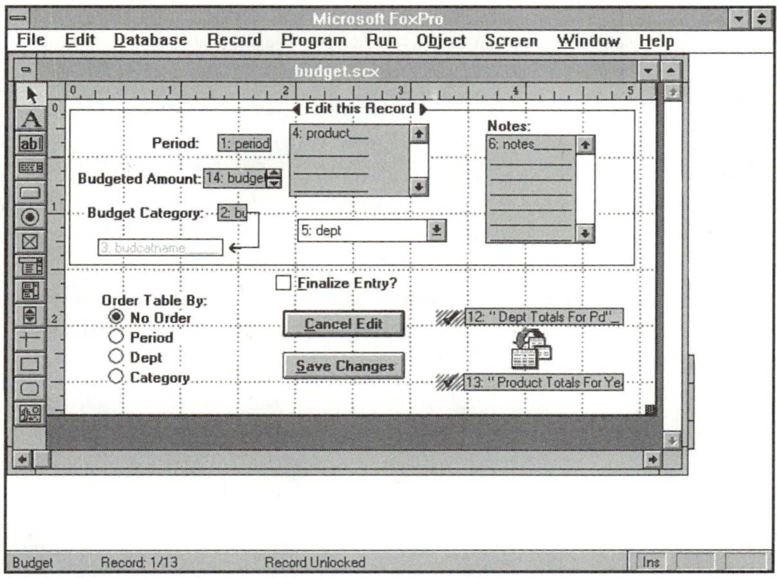

FIG. 17.5

A DOS screen with some Windows features after editing.

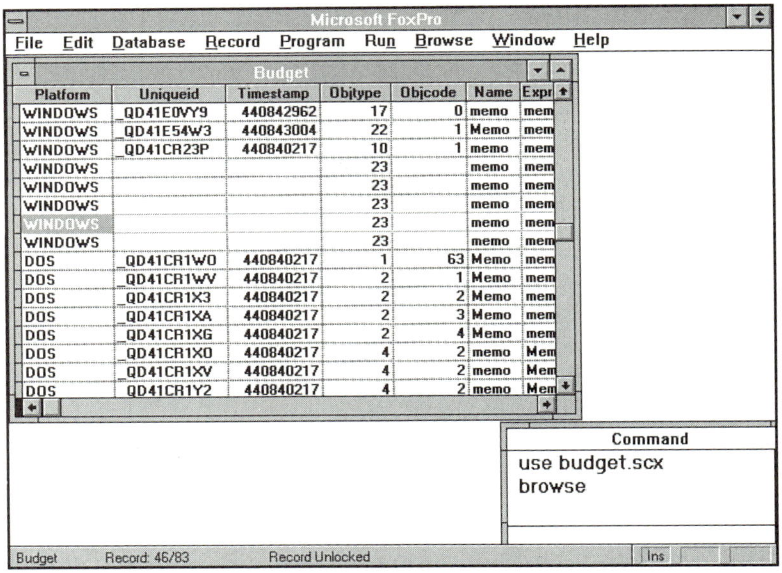

Microsoft FoxPro

File Edit Database Record Program Run Browse Window Help

Budget

Platform	Uniqueid	Timestamp	Objtype	Objcode	Name	Expr
WINDOWS	_QD41E0VY9	440842962	17	0	memo	mem
WINDOWS	_QD41E54W3	440843004	22	1	Memo	mem
WINDOWS	_QD41CR23P	440840217	10	1	memo	mem
WINDOWS			23		memo	mem
WINDOWS			23		memo	mem
WINDOWS			23		memo	mem
WINDOWS			23		memo	mem
WINDOWS			23		memo	mem
DOS	_QD41CR1W0	440840217	1	63	Memo	mem
DOS	_QD41CR1WV	440840217	2	1	Memo	mem
DOS	_QD41CR1X3	440840217	2	2	Memo	mem
DOS	_QD41CR1XA	440840217	2	3	Memo	mem
DOS	_QD41CR1XG	440840217	2	4	Memo	mem
DOS	_QD41CR1XO	440840217	4	2	memo	Mem
DOS	_QD41CR1XV	440840217	4	2	memo	Mem
DOS	_QD41CR1Y2	440840217	4	2	memo	Mem

Command

use budget.scx
browse

Budget Record: 46/83 Record Unlocked Ins

FIG. 17.6

The .SCX fields responsible for cross-platform maintenance.

The first time you transport a screen to a new platform, the Transporter creates a new record for each object in the screen (including a global record to DEFINE the WINDOW with all necessary attributes). The old record's Platform field contains the identification of the old platform (DOS in this case), and the new record's Platform field contains identification of the new platform (WINDOWS here). The records for the same objects contain identical information in the second field, Uniqueid, and identical information in the memo fields holding various object snippets (WHEN, VALID, MESSAGE, and so forth). In addition, the Transporter adds size and position information to the new record, and font information where applicable, to correspond with the requirements of the new platform.

TIP

While you're experimenting with cross-platform development, you can try out different fonts and arrangements along with other Windows features. You can start over again from your base DOS screen, with all snippets intact: USE the .SCX file EXCLUSIVEly, and DELETE ALL FOR Platform = "WINDOWS". After you PACK the file and close it, you can MODIFY the screen again, and the Transporter will give you fresh copies of the Windows objects.

The third field, Timestamp, is critical to cross-platform maintenance. Close the screen data table again, and MODIFY the same screen in FoxPro 2.5 for DOS (remember that you won't be able to open this screen in FoxPro 2.0 again). The DOS Transport dialog appears, as shown in figure 17.7.

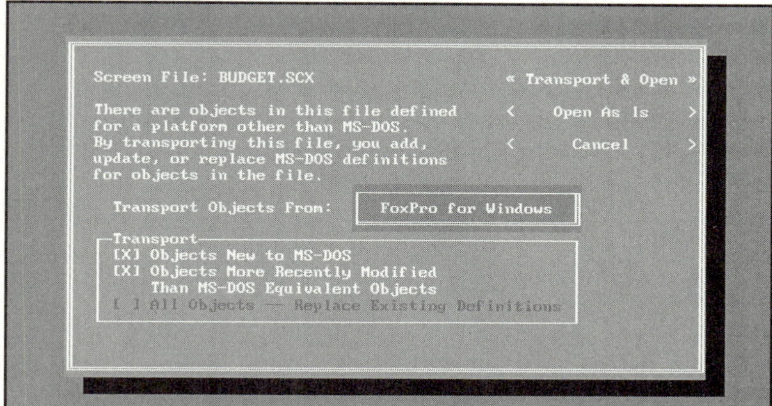

FIG. 17.7
The DOS Transport dialog.

The Transporter has compared the Timestamp field for DOS objects against the Timestamp for objects in other platforms with matching IDs. The program also notes that some objects now exist in the screen table for which there are no matching IDs in the DOS platform. Accordingly, the dialog suggests that you choose to transport objects that are more recently modified on another platform, or that are new to the DOS platform.

If you uncheck both these default options, a third check box enables you to transport all objects, without exception. You rarely use this choice. When you accept the defaults, you see the dialog in figure 17.8 with a suggested list of objects. You can omit some objects in the screen from the transport process by pressing Enter or double-clicking the listed objects you don't want to transport.

In this case, the new or changed objects all represent Windows-specific improvements, mostly to account for different symbol characters in the Windows font. So none of the objects should be transported this time; uncheck all the entries. We could have chosen the previous dialog's Open As Is choice to accomplish the same task. The Open As Is choice prevents any transfer of information about objects between the platforms; the DOS screen is opened exactly as it was before you edited the screen under Windows.

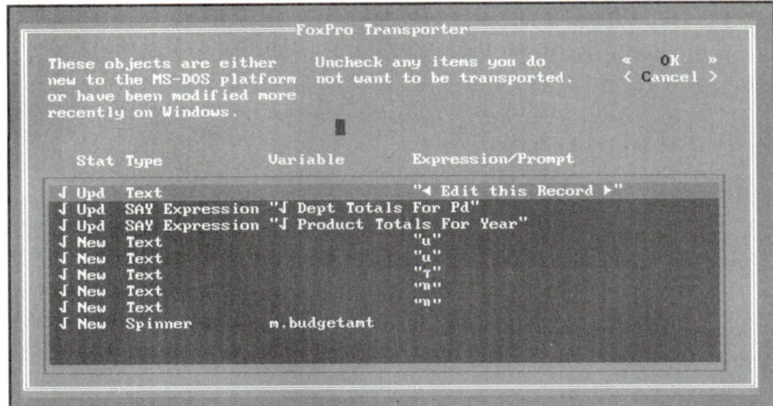

FIG. 17.8

Choosing which objects to transport.

If you choose to transport the spinner, however, you find that this GET becomes a normal text box in the DOS screen. You notice that the picture you added to the Windows screen, which has no DOS equivalent and does not materially affect the data entry process, is not even offered as a Transport list item.

At other times, you may add another snippet to an existing item, or include a new GET on-screen. Transporting these screen elements updates a second platform's information; you don't have to remember to add the new snippet to the second platform's object or screen table record. When you update a screen element by adding a new snippet, only the new snippets are transported. The GET's positioning information, which is usually customized for each platform, will not be transferred inappropriately along with your validation code.

In some instances, the same GET may require different validation codes for different platforms. Pursuing the principle of keeping platform-specific code at as low a level as possible for ease of maintenance, you should bracket CASEs for each platform within one snippet for that GET, instead of creating different snippets on each platform and trying to remember which GETs should not be transported.

When you're ready to generate program code from the screen table or tables, you can choose to generate code for the current platform only, by using an option in the Screen Set Generate Options dialog. By default, however, GENSCRN produces code for all platforms for which it finds records, generating CASEs that bracket platform-specific code for you.

CAUTION: If for any reason you decide to keep different snippets for one object in different platforms, do not use the Procedure option and the #NAME generator directive to name the functions yourself, unless you are sure you have given each platform's snippet its own function name. When GENSCRN doesn't generate unique procedure names for you, the program can't check to make sure you haven't used a UDF name twice.

Transporting Reports and Labels

Report and label forms, like screens, do not need to be transported at all if you don't need the extra features of a graphics platform. The reports and labels that you design in FoxPro 2.0 or 2.5 for DOS, and continue to modify under FoxPro 2.5 for DOS, will run under FoxPro for Windows just as they do under DOS.

If you need to transport a report to the FoxPro for Windows Report Writer, however, the benefits of continued cross-platform transporting are less significant than they are with screens. (Labels cannot be retransported at all; once they are brought into a new environment, you must make all modifications separately under each platform.) Because reports are entirely display- or output-centered and have no need to apply common validation rules to data, reports on different platforms tend to diverge far more than screens do. The FoxPro Windows and DOS Report Writers also diverge in their capabilities, far more than do the platforms' Screen Builders. Although report expressions and report variables are evaluated the same way on both platforms, various characteristics of the report bands are incommensurate.

The best solution is to leave the reports in character-based format whenever reports or labels are meant to be comparable and to substitute a CASE statement that can issue platform-specific REPORT FORM or LABEL FORM commands whenever graphical output or the use of General fields is required from the Windows application. If the Windows application sends REPORT or LABEL FORMs TO a file, the cross-platform developer who uses separate DOS and Windows reports can avoid problems by sending the separate DOS report TO the file instead.

This solution doesn't work, however, if a report contains both DOS and WINDOWS platform objects; the REPORT FORM command used in the Windows product will use the WINDOWS platform objects for its output. If a cross-platform report must be sent TO a file, use a SQL SELECT statement to create a temporary report table holding only DOS objects (SELECT the objects FROM <the FRX table> INTO the temporary table WHERE Platform = "DOS"). Then execute the REPORT FORM .<temporary table's name>... TO FILE command. In this strategy, the DOS objects may be combined with a DOS printer driver (PDSETUP); or more commonly, no printer driver is used, thus creating a straight ASCII file.

Programs designed for cross-platform use should avoid incorporating the MODIFY LABEL and MODIFY REPORT commands. These commands are available for distributed programs (unlike MODIFY SCREEN and QUERY), but if the user opens the report or label under a different platform, the user must cope with the same cross-platform issues that the developer faces in this chapter. If you give users the ability to access the Report Writer or Label Designer by using these commands, you must cope with cross-platform use in one of the following ways:

- Include TRANSPRT.PRG in your application. Microsoft allows you to distribute the Transporter program, but you probably do not like the idea of users encountering its dialogs in the midst of your otherwise carefully planned interface.
- Write your own Transporter, with new dialogs, storing its name to the _TRANSPORT system variable and designing it to use the same parameters that FoxPro passes to TRANSPRT.PRG internally.
- Adapt TRANSPRT.PRG so it runs without the user seeing its dialogs; this solution prevents the user from omitting certain elements from the transport process.
- Limit access to the MODIFY REPORT and LABEL commands very carefully, monitoring report and label file names in a table and designing all reports separately so that all files opened under FoxPro for DOS are DOS-only reports and labels, and all files opened under FoxPro for Windows are Windows-only reports and labels. If you choose this method, your documentation and the surrounding code should ensure that the user makes all necessary changes to each copy of a file after he edits the copy for a single platform—or the calling program should perform a limited Transport procedure (without dialogs) after each edit to transfer the changes.

Coping with Special Problems of Cross-Platform Applications

Now you have an idea of the basic method of creating and maintaining cross-platform application elements. You must realize, however, that you have many other factors to consider in cross-platform work. Whatever percentage of your code can be maintained in a common version, in common FoxPro system tables across multiple platforms, you still need to develop some code in unique versions for each platform to deal with each platform's unique needs and to exploit its unique capabilities.

The very fact that your code is responsive to the requirements and features of more than one platform places new burdens on your application development skills. This section provides you with some indications of the skills you can expect to exercise—and the questions you need to ask—as you work to make your applications and interfaces fit multiple platforms.

Keeping the Compiled Application within Memory Limits

When you look at the code generated by GENSCRN, you realize that bracketed code can create programs perilously close to the 64K limit for a single compiled procedure, even though much of the code isn't used on a specific platform. All the different procedures place additional burdens on the program to create variables holding platform-specific values. FoxPro 2.5 includes some *preprocessor directives* to limit the size of the compiled program and to minimize the number of variables required by the different conditions of multiple platforms.

The #IF... #ELIF... #ELSE ... #ENDIF preprocessor directives look like a normal Xbase IF... ENDIF structure, but these directives function more like a CASE ... OTHERWISE ... ENDCASE structure. As you have seen in the snippets used in the previous chapters of this book, and as you will investigate more thoroughly in the next chapter, conditions in a CASE structure are evaluated for each successive CASE until one CASE evaluates to .T.. When the conditions for one CASE evaluate to .T., the instructions for this single CASE execute; the rest of the CASE statements following the executed instructions are ignored. If no CASE evaluates .T. and an OTHERWISE set of instructions is included, the OTHERWISE instructions execute.

All the CASEs are compiled into the program. The CASEs are evaluated at run-time to decide which CASE code should execute.

Think of #IF as the DO CASE and first CASE of a similar structure; however, this structure is evaluated during compilation rather than at run-time. When the #IF... #ENDIF structure is used, only the instructions in one part of the structure are compiled. #ELIFs are the additional CASEs, #ENDIF performs the same job as ENDCASE, and #ELSE represents an OTHERWISE.

A typical #IF... #ENDIF structure for a cross-platform application might read as follows:

```
#IF "DOS" $ UPPER(VERSION(1))
   REPORT FORM drpt_1
#ELIF "WINDOWS" $ UPPER(VERSION(1))
   REPORT FORM wrpt_1
#ELIF "UNIX" $ UPPER(VERSION(1))
   REPORT FORM urpt_1
#ELSE
   REPORT FORM mrpt_1
#ENDIF
```

This structure results in a single line of code (different for each platform) in the compiled version of the program.

You may expect the #IF structure to use the system variables determining platform, rather than the VERSION(1) checks in the previous example. Unfortunately, the system variables, or conditions including them are not evaluated during compilation; these variables only have values at run-time.

Dealing with Display Size Differences

Another effect of cross-platform development and the increased flexibility of fonts in a graphical environment is the need to keep track of platform-specific information to include in display formulas. The original screen font with which a screen was developed, for example, influences the AT clause that GENSCRN generates on the DEFINE

WINDOW command. When WINDOW is later DEFINEd and ACTIVATEd, the window does not appear at the expected position if the user has changed the screen font.

Using the MODIFY WINDOW SCREEN command (suggested earlier for DOS screens that you want to run unedited in the Windows environment) is one way to solve this problem. Run the command before each screen program is executed, after you save the user's screen font choice for later restoration by using Windows-specific font-investigating functions. Another solution is to MOVE the WINDOW in #SECTION 2 of the screen's setup, after GENSCRN's generated code DEFINEs the WINDOW. Determine the coordinates for the MOVE WINDOW command by using a formula to relate its old position to the new screen font. Both solutions, however, require that the original screen font, with which the screen was created, be known to the program.

You could create variables to hold this information. By the time you have saved the information, and other analogous information, for every screen in your system, however, you have saddled yourself with an overwhelming number of extra variables—none of which ever changes during the course of the program.

To avoid the overhead of these variables, you can use the preprocessor directive #DEFINE, which substitutes constant values for variable names you use in your code. Like #IF... #ENDIF, however, #DEFINE is evaluated at compile time rather than run-time.

The following sample procedure, designed for use only under Windows, shows the way the original screen elements can be preserved in the program as constants, using the #DEFINE preprocessor directive:

```
* MOVEWIND.PRG
#DEFINE sfont_name   "System"
#DEFINE sfont_size         6
#DEFINE sfont_style       ""
#DEFINE wrow              10
#DEFINE wcol               6
MODIFY WINDOW SCREEN FONT "System",6
DEFINE WINDOW a_window SIZE 5,20 AT 10,6 ;
      SYSTEM TITLE "Here's a window..."
ACTIVATE WINDOW a_window
WAIT WINDOW "Notice the window position"
MODIFY WINDOW SCREEN FONT "Ariel",24
DEFINE WINDOW a_window SIZE 5,20 AT 10,6 ;
```

continues

```
      SYSTEM TITLE "Here's a window..."
ACTIVATE WINDOW a_window
WAIT WINDOW ;
  "Notice the window position; "+ ;
  "the DEFINE WINDOW statement was exactly the same!"
MOVE WINDOW a_window TO ;
     wrow * ;
     ((FONT(1,sfont_name, sfont_size, sfont_style)+;
       FONT(5,sfont_name, sfont_size, sfont_style)) /  ;
     (FONT(1,WFONT(1,""), WFONT(2,""), WFONT(3,""))+;
      FONT(5,WFONT(1,""), WFONT(2,""),WFONT(3,"")))) , ;
     wcol * ;
     (FONT(6,sfont_name, sfont_size, sfont_style) /  ;
      FONT(6,WFONT(1,""), WFONT(2,""),WFONT(3,"")))
WAIT WINDOW ;
 "The window position has been adjusted for the new screen font."
```

#DEFINE's substitutions occur only with the same program in which you place the #DEFINE statement; the compiler leaves any other instances of the same variable names untouched. To extend the preceding example, you could have a different #DEFINE sfont statement in each .SPR (because each screen set may have been designed with a different screen font). Other programs in the same application also may use the variable name sfont and may not include a #DEFINE statement; these instances of the variable would remain in the compiled code.

For most purposes, the FoxPro Power Tools cope admirably with the requirements of cross-platform development. Aside from the rather inflexible treatment GENSCRN gives windows with respect to screen position, many of the annoyances of transporting objects are trivial. For example, the positioning of joined line and box objects is rarely satisfactory when transported, but the objects are easy to re-create in the second platform.

Additional, nontrivial problems occur if you try to code screens and reports without using the Screen Builder and report or label forms. Keeping track of different display positions or font requirements on your own will convince you to use the Power Tools, even if you were satisfied using FoxPro 2.0 without their help.

Some areas of the product do not involve the Power Tools directly, yet their impact on display and printed output requires different decisions for different platforms. Refer to Chapter 16 for information on many of these system resources, especially the different color systems and printer driver approaches in use under DOS and Windows.

Handling Keystroke Differences for Different Platforms

In Chapter 2, you learned to navigate the FoxPro interface and discovered that a particular keystroke moves the window focus from object to object in a standard dialog or a Browse window and that a different keystroke always closes the window with predictable effects. These keystrokes are different for FoxPro for DOS and FoxPro for Windows. FoxPro for Windows includes a special command, SET KEYCOMP TO DOS | WINDOWS, which you can use to change the keystrokes that handle window navigation, object selection, and so on, to the DOS equivalents. SET KEYCOMP TO DOS if you have individual users who run the same program in both environments so that they don't need to learn two sets of keystrokes for each platform.

SET KEYCOMP TO DOS also if you use editable BROWSEs in your applications. The Windows keystrokes assigned to BROWSEs are, quite simply, unacceptable for extended data entry sessions, because each field is selected (highlighted) after the focus moves to the field. (As you already know, if you start typing with the field selected, all previous data is erased.)

If you want to present a standard Windows interface in your application and your users never run a program under FoxPro DOS, you may prefer SET KEYCOMP TO WINDOWS for dialogs and SET KEYCOMP TO DOS just before issuing an editable BROWSE (SETting back TO WINDOWS after the BROWSE).

Be aware, however, that SET KEYCOMP TO WINDOWS does not present the user with completely standard Windows keystroke behavior; in a real Microsoft Windows dialog, pressing Enter cannot be used to move from text box to text box. (Enter closes the dialog if the dialog has a default terminating button.) After you press Enter in a FoxPro for Windows data entry window or other dialog with a text box, and you SET KEYCOMP TO WINDOWS, the focus moves to the next GET (the window does not close). Although this compromise makes data entry much easier, true Windows adepts may find the behavior confusing. You should include attention to keystroke behavior as an integral part of the acceptance testing process described in Chapter 11 and draw your conclusions about how to SET KEYCOMP based on your users' access to both possible keystroke systems.

Dealing with ASCII Character Value Differences

One critical area of incompatibility remains between the platforms: not all ASCII character values have the same representation in the DOS character set (OEM) and the common Windows character set (ANSI). For display elements such as line-drawing characters, this problem is easily solved by confining these elements' Windows font to FoxPrint, which contains the correct graphics characters to match the DOS set. Non-English speakers, however, use accented characters which are represented by different values above 128 in the OEM and ANSI sets. (These characters are commonly known as *extended ASCII*, although they aren't technically ASCII characters, according to Microsoft.)

If the data and application are ported from FoxPro 2.0 or another Xbase dialect solely for use under Windows, the data can be converted to ANSI values using the OEMTOANSI( ) FoxPro for Windows function. Thereafter, the data will display properly and be appropriately editable for the international characters in FoxPro for Windows. FoxPro also contains a translation function, SYS(20), designed to allow the proper sorting of accented German characters for indexes and other purposes. The difficulties with sorting and displaying international character sets in multiple fonts, however, are quite separate and not anwered by these solutions. A Windows-only application with international character sets should be installed without giving the user access to FoxPrint and FoxFont or other fonts with character assignments that are anomalous in Windows.

By contrast, an application with data to be shared between DOS and Windows must display and edit all data in FoxPrint and FoxFont; otherwise, the data will not be readable in DOS. Use these fonts for all GETs and report expressions. If your international and cross-platform application allows editing during a BROWSE, take care to use the NOMENU keyword on BROWSE commands so that the user cannot change fonts from the Browse menu popup. Use @... EDIT instead of MODIFY MEMO to ensure that the user cannot choose a font from the Text menu popup while in the memo text-editing window. Because a MODIFY FILE has no equivalent keyword to NOMENU, also use @... EDIT with a cursor record, later converted to a disk file, to avoid the Text menu popup's availability during a MODIFY FILE editing session.

One more limitation must be imposed on Windows users if the international application is to work seamlessly across platforms: The Edit menu popup's Find... option should be removed from SYSMENU. The cross-platform application demands a DOS-compatible OEM font, but the Find dialog will always appear in the Windows System font, which uses the ANSI character set. Users can search their BROWSEs and text-editing windows by using the Alt key with the numeric keypad to type the ASCII equivalents of the characters they want, but the characters will not look like the characters they want; so the benefit of the Find dialog becomes questionable, at best.

Obviously, not using true Windows fonts and normal FoxPro features such as the Find dialog is a workaround of last resort for the Windows product. Unfortunately, there is no better solution to cross-platform use of international character sets in FoxPro in the initial shipping version of FoxPro 2.5. Microsoft is aware of this grave problem and is at work, along with other Xbase vendors, on new standards and new strategies that will permit .DBF tables to incorporate more information about the character sets with which their data has been defined. Depending on when you're reading this book, the solution may already have been incorporated into the product.

Summary

This chapter does not evaluate the behavior of every FoxPro command for backward and cross-platform compatibility. A comprehensive treatment of this subject would require a treatise on the evolution of Xbase and is beyond the scope of this book. The strategies presented in this chapter are simply recommendations for efficient conversion of programs for FoxPro 2.5 use and for efficient cross-platform maintenance of FoxPro 2.5 programs.

These strategies are not immutable rules. Perhaps more than any other aspect of the product, these techniques and workarounds are subject to change in future versions of FoxPro. Their difficulty, and the likelihood that changes will occur, may lead you to conclude that FoxPro has unnecessarily complicated its cross-platform approach and that better solutions will come easily. To the contrary: the Microsoft Fox team should be commended for a brave beginning on several problems that other database management products do not attempt to explore.

oxProgramming: nhanced Jse of the Design Tools

18

CHAPTER

Understanding Program Structure

In most books about database management programs that contain a command language, this part of the book would be your first introduction to the programming language. You already have done a fair amount of programming in FoxPro, however, because the program allows you to attach user-defined functions and code snippets to objects, such as fields defined in the Report Writer and the Screen Builder. On the other hand, most of the programs that you have written so far have had a limited scope and have been designed to accomplish a narrowly defined task, such as validating the data entered into a field.

These chapters explore the FoxPro programming language in depth. Rather than provide you with a simple reference guide, which would repeat much of the material contained in the FoxPro manuals, this discussion focuses on *how to use* the language to achieve your database management goals.

The current chapter introduces you to programming concepts, program design, and some of the author's opinions concerning programming style (a heated topic if ever there was one!). Along the way, you learn to control program execution and branching and to create subroutines that break tasks into manageable pieces.

Later chapters in this part of the book present more advanced programming techniques. These chapters divide some of FoxPro's commands and functions by category and explore the ways in which you can use them—from the Command window and from within programs.

Learning What a Program Does

At its most basic level, a computer program is a combination of words and other symbols that can be "read" by a computer. A computer program is written in a specific language. Each language has its own rules and conventions, which enable the computer to understand your words and symbols and perform the tasks that you intend it to perform.

The FoxPro language uses English-like words. The commands do what someone who understands English would expect them to do. For example, STORE saves a value somewhere, and REPLACE replaces the current contents of a field with another value. The FoxPro language, therefore, is very readable. Even if you don't know how to manipulate the commands, you often can read a FoxPro program written by someone else and understand what that program does.

Throughout this chapter, and those that follow, the discussion emphasizes the *readability* of the programs that you write. Always keep in mind that writing a computer program is a form of *communication*, not only between you and the computer, but also between you and those who later will read your program to understand, enhance, and maintain that program.

Moving Commands You Type Repeatedly into a Program

You can think of typing a command in the Command window as creating a program that has one line and that is executed by pressing Enter. Each command may be part of a series of commands that has one objective, like finding and displaying the records for a particular customer in an orders table.

If you understand the sequence of events required to produce a certain result, you can design and write a program. To try a simple example, enter a few commands in the Command window and then use the FoxPro editor's cut-and-paste feature to move the commands into a program (.PRG) file. Activate the Command window and then type the following commands:

```
SELECT 0
USE Sales AGAIN ORDER Custcode
BROWSE KEY "MKF1"
```

This series of commands selects the next available work area, opens the Sales table (AGAIN if it is already open in another work area), orders the entries by customer code, and displays the orders for the customer whose code is MKF1 in a Browse window. Now create a program file by typing the following in the Command window:

```
MODIFY COMMAND SHOWORDS
```

A blank window titled SHOWORDS.PRG appears on-screen. Without closing the new program's window, activate the Command window. Select the three lines that will make up the program and paste them into the SHOWORDS.PRG window. (Refer to the discussion of the FoxPro editor in Chapter 2, "Understanding the FoxPro Interface," if you don't know how to do this.) Save the program (press Ctrl+W, or select Save from the File menu popup), and return to the Command window.

Now that you have transferred your command sequence from the Command window to a program file, you can run the program by entering the following command:

```
DO SHOWORDS
```

This program is not very useful because it always displays only the records for customer MKF1. Working from the Command window, you can view other customers' records by modifying the BROWSE command to use a different customer code. You can accomplish the same thing in a program, but first you need to learn more about the structure of a program.

Examining a Program for Structure and Style

Take a few moments to review the following program, RUN_APP.PRG. (This program is identical to the APPSHELL.PRG program which was part of the FoxApp system included in FoxPro 2.0.)

```
* RUN_APP.PRG
* This is a routine to display a list of APP files
* and prompt the user for the one to run.
* It does not display the list of files if a file
* name is passed as a parameter.

PARAMETERS fname
SET TALK OFF
IF PARAMETERS() = 1
   DO (fname)
ENDIF

more = .T.
DO WHILE more
   fname = GETFILE('APP','Application to run')
   IF !EMPTY(fname)
      DO (fname)
      CLEAR PROGRAM
      more = .T.
   ELSE
      more = .F.
   ENDIF
ENDDO
```

Although short, this program contains features that you use in every application you write:

- A PARAMETERS statement that accepts information from another program
- An environment modifier—SET TALK ON
- An assignment statement—more = .T.
- A conditional branching construct—IF ... ELSE ... ENDIF
- A conditional looping construct—DO WHILE ... ENDDO

Using just these few tools, you can write many useful programs. The following discussion examines what the program does and how the structure and style make reading and understanding the program easier.

The first thing you should notice is that lines following a conditional statement such as IF or DO WHILE are indented to make the program easier to read. The computer doesn't care whether these lines begin in column 1 or in column 100, but people require reading aids. Just as each new thought in a book begins with a new sentence, each set of statements to be executed under a certain condition should be set off from those executed under a different condition. Programmers define statement blocks by indenting them at the same level. Although you may not yet understand the following commands, you can see that they are executed if the memory variable fname contains a value, that is, if fname is not EMPTY ( ):

```
DO (fname)
CLEAR PROGRAM
more = .T.
```

If you don't know what a memory variable is, don't worry. This chapter explains memory variables in detail. For now, just understand that memory variables are names that you can use to hold values and that you can compare those stored values to constants (like the number 2) and other variables to determine whether to take an action.

Just as related thoughts are grouped into paragraphs, related statements in a program usually are separated from other statements by one or more blank lines; FoxPro ignores blank lines. In fact, when FoxPro compiles your program, it removes all blank lines and spaces not required to separate one command from the next.

Using Pseudocode To Clarify Your Approach

Programs that proceed in a straight-line fashion in performing a simple task, such as the SHOWORDS program, usually can be written from start to finish without a separate planning stage. More ambitious, complicated programs require that you gain a good understanding of the steps that the program will take in achieving its objective, before you find yourself mired in the intricate details of writing the actual code.

To effectively plan a program, you need to use a *high-level language,* one in which a few words can convey your objectives. Spoken languages, such as English, are high-level languages because a few well-chosen words can quickly convey a wealth of meaning and information. Spoken languages, however, often introduce an unwelcome amount of ambiguity. Because computers do what we say rather than what we mean, ambiguity must be avoided.

What you need in order to express your ideas for creating the program is a pseudo-language, one that combines the expressiveness of a spoken language with the precision of a programming language, like FoxPro's command language.

Pseudocode (as the term is used here) is a language with no rules. You invent your own version. You mix and match English words and phrases with those of the FoxPro language to express clearly the steps that your program needs to take to achieve your goal. If you are a beginner, your first attempts at using pseudocode will consist mostly of English. As your knowledge of FoxPro increases, you will use a greater percentage of commands in place of English words and phrases.

The following example of pseudocode uses RUN_APP.PRG and presents the program in English:

```
Purpose:

Runs application programs (those ending in .APP). Lets the user
specify the name of the first application to run. If no application
is specified, displays a list of application (.APP) files and
prompts the user for the one to run. Continues running applications
until the user chooses to stop.

Steps:

accept the name of an application to run from the calling program

make sure that the TALK feature is off

if the user specified an application to run,
   run it now

if an application was not specified, or after it was completed
   let the user specify one / another one

if the user selected an application
   run it
   go back and get another one to be run
otherwise
   end the program and return to the calling program
```

Now, without losing the expressiveness of your original ideas, try to rephrase this pseudocode so that you get a little closer to the actual FoxPro commands that you need to use in your program:

```
Steps:

store the name of an application to run in a variable called fname

set TALK off
```

```
if the fname variable is not empty
   run the application whose name is stored in fname now

until the user chooses to stop
   get the name of an application to run and store it in fname

   if fname is not empty
      run the application and then clear it from memory
   else
      s/he wants to stop

end the program and return to the calling program
```

The final step in the process is to write the program. Rather than start from scratch, use your pseudocode to create the program as follows:

- Convert each line of pseudocode *that represents a single FoxPro command or function* into the actual code.
- Use the remaining lines as *comments* for the sequence of commands or functions required to complete the task. (Place an asterisk at the beginning of the line to tell FoxPro that what follows is a comment.)

```
* A modified version of RUN_APP.PRG
parameters fname
set talk off

if !empty(fname)
   do (fname)
endif

do while .t.
   fname = getfile('APP','Application to run')
   if "" != fname
      * run the application, and then clear it from
      * memory
      do (fname)
      clear program
   else
      EXIT
   endif
enddo

return
```

Wait a minute! That's not the same as RUN_APP!

The preceding program is not the same because its programming style differs from that of the person who wrote the RUN_APP program. The two programs are *functionally* identical. The difference is in the appearance of the code (mostly lowercase here, instead of mostly uppercase in RUN_APP.PRG) and in the specific commands, functions, and techniques used.

Programming style is largely a matter of personal preference. Some programmers will tell you that the EXIT command (which causes the program to break out of an enclosing DO WHILE, SCAN, or FOR loop) is to be strictly avoided. Others (including the author of this chapter) find the use of flags, such as the variable *more,* to be inelegant and to add little to the readability of the program.

Which style you choose is not important. What is important is that you be *consistent* in your usage of a style. If you use uppercase letters for commands and lowercase letters for variable names in one program, be sure that you use them in the same fashion throughout your program. If you use different styles within the same program, you will not only confuse others who read your code, but you also will find your own programs difficult to read six months from now.

When properly used, pseudocode almost always decreases the amount of time required to design, write, and debug an application. Although it's often not easy, you must avoid the temptation to start coding before you have mapped out the logic of any nontrivial program.

Organizing the Tasks of a Program

The first step the authors took in the task of writing this book was to prepare an outline. We listed all the topics we felt were needed to help you learn to use FoxPro, divided the topics into chapters, and then grouped related chapters into separate parts.

Developing an application requires the same kind of planning and structuring. You break down the overall task into subtasks and group the related subtasks into modules. The medium used to provide access to the different modules is the *menu.* Just as FoxPro's features are organized into different menu pads, your application's features should be organized in a menu.

If you didn't skip the chapter on the Menu Builder, you are aware that you can incorporate your own menu options into the FoxPro system menu bar, along with as many of FoxPro's menu options as you want the users of your application to be able to access.

FoxPro 2.0 introduced a new way of accessing the tasks of an application. Central to this new philosophy is the READ command, which enables you to do the following:

- Have GETs active simultaneously in more than one window
- Have windows not usually associated with READ, such as Browse and Modify Memo windows, participate in the READ along with active GETs
- Create an event-driven interface, like that of FoxPro, in which applications are launched from the system menu bar

In addition to activating GETs, READ can be used to insert a *wait state* into your program, in much the same way as the Command window is FoxPro's "wait state." From the Command window, FoxPro recognizes and acts upon your keystrokes and menu selections. Your applications can respond to events, such as selections made by the user from the System menu. Because you can incorporate modules of your application into the System menu, you can create a truly seamless environment in which the user can access the features of FoxPro and your application, while retaining control over what is available and when it is available.

Most of the required interaction among your menus, screens, and other programs is coordinated for you by the Project Manager, covered in Chapter 14.

The following section discusses the tasks required to establish the framework of your application and to provide a smooth transition to and from the user's environment. The next section, "Developing Programming Techniques," covers some of the FoxPro commands that you can use in the programs activated by making selections from your menus.

Saving, Setting, and Restoring the Environment

When you rent a summer cottage, it's considered polite to leave things the way you found them. (Perhaps the owner has a good reason for keeping the dishes in the washing machine!)

If, upon exiting your application, the user can return to the interactive FoxPro environment or to another FoxPro application that uses yours as a module in a larger application, you must restore the environment settings to the values they held before your application was run.

Consider the SAFETY setting, which controls whether FoxPro asks your permission before overwriting or erasing an existing file. From within an application, you usually are in control of which files can be erased with impunity, such as when you erase temporary files. Therefore, you usually should SET SAFETY OFF at the top of your program. You cannot make any assumptions, however, about the proper setting for SAFETY outside your application. The best practice is to leave the SAFETY setting the way you found it.

FoxPro has several built-in functions that return the current value of a setting. The most versatile of these functions is SET( ), which enables you to save the current SETting of most, but not all the many SET commands.

The syntax for the SET( ) function is as follows:

```
SET(<expC> [,1])
```

The only reason to save a setting is that you are going to set it to some value that may be different from the current value. Because SET( ) always returns the current setting, you have to save what it returns to a variable before you change it. You then use this variable to restore the previous setting.

In RUN_APP.PRG, TALK is SET OFF to suppress the screen display of the assignment statements' values (e.g. more = .T.) that follow in the program code. You can amend this program to save and restore the current TALK setting as follows:

```
PARAMETERS fname
IF SET("talk") = "ON"
   SET TALK OFF
   curr_talk = "ON"
ELSE
   curr_talk = "OFF"
ENDIF

* (the rest of the program goes here)

IF curr_talk = "ON"
   SET TALK ON
ENDIF
```

SET( ) has an optional second argument (the number 1) that can be used to return additional information about what the setting has been SET TO. Even with cases in which this argument is not documented, it can be used for almost every SET command that is SET TO a value in addition to or instead of ON/OFF. For example, to save the name of the current Help file:

```
curr_help = SET("HELP",1)
```

You cannot use this argument to find out about the BELL tone and duration settings or about SET commands that are more than one word, such as SET COLOR SET.

So far, this section has covered saving the environment settings at the top of the application and restoring them before exiting. The types of settings that you usually would save in this manner include TALK, SAFETY, and BELL.

You will want to save, change, and restore other settings often throughout your application. One such setting is presented in Chapter 12, which covers the Screen Builder. In the data-entry validation code snippets, you save the index order of the particular lookup table, set the order to what you require to do your lookup, and then restore the index order to its previous value before returning. To do this, you use FoxPro's ORDER( ) function, which returns the master index file name or master tag name for the table in the currently selected work area:

```
morder = ORDER()
SET ORDER TO Prodcode
* save the current table order
* so you can set it up the way you want to
* but restore it afterwards

IF SEEK(mcode)
.
.
.
ENDIF

* now put things back the way you found them
SET ORDER TO (morder)
```

FoxPro has several other functions that enable you to put things back the way they were. Some of the most often used are the following:

- ALIAS( ) Returns the alias of a work area
- RECNO( ) Returns the number of the current record
- SELECT( ) Returns the number of the selected work area

Part V, "Getting To Know FoxPro Commands and Functions," explores some of the ways in which you use these functions.

Selecting Work Areas and Opening Tables

Before you can work with a table, you have to open it in a work area. You can open a table in one of two ways:

- Restore the environment (including open tables and index files) that you saved with the CREATE VIEW command by using SET VIEW TO <view file>.
- Use the USE command.

Chapter 3, "Exploring Databases and Tables," discusses CREATE VIEW and SET VIEW TO. From within a program, it is more typical to open the specific tables and indexes that the application requires. This section discusses the USE command and its options.

If you are coming to FoxPro 2.5 from dBASE III, FoxBASE+, or FoxPro 1, be advised that the simple USE command found in those products has acquired a few new features, among them the capability to open a table in more than one work area. Although this chapter covers most of the typical uses of the command, you should refer to the FoxPro *Language Reference* manual or the Help file for complete information on this enhanced command.

Unless you specify a particular work area, USE opens the table in the current work area, which defaults to 1 if you haven't yet selected any other work area. You can use the IN clause to specify a particular work area. Work areas are referred to by number (1-25 in the Standard version, and 1-225 in the Extended version). You also can reference work areas 1-10 by using a letter (A-J).

Work area 0 does not exist, but you can use IN 0 as a code to tell FoxPro to select the next available work area, whatever its number may be. You learn more about letting FoxPro manage the available work areas for you in Chapter 19.

FoxPro can open the same table in more than one work area. This capability is useful when you want to view the table in more than one Browse window simultaneously.

Each work area is assigned an *alias,* which you can use to reference the open table in that work area. The default alias is the name of the table. If you open a table in more than one work area using the AGAIN clause, the work area letter (or a combination of "W" and the work area number for areas above 10) is assigned as the alias.

Using the following statements, open some of the tables used in the Omnipresent Widget application, each in its own work area:

CLOSE DATA		Closes all open tables and selects work area 1.
USE Budget	IN 1	Assigned alias is Budget.
USE Budcat	IN 2	Assigned alias is Budcat.
USE Customer	IN 0	Opens Customer in next available work area, which is area 3; assigned alias is Customer.
USE Customer	IN D AGAIN	Customer is now open in two work areas; its alias in area D is D.
USE Dept	IN 5	Assigned alias is Dept.
USE Sales	IN 11	Assigned alias is Sales.
USE Sales	IN 12 AGAIN	Sales is now open in two work areas; its alias in area 12 is W12.

The work areas used in the above examples were chosen for illustrative purposes only. Usually, there is no good reason to use both numbers and letters (1 and D) when referring to work areas, nor does it usually make sense to assign tables to work areas in anything other than a sequential fashion.

Use the View window to view the current status of the open work areas. Note the alias assigned to each work area.

You can assign an alternative alias to a table with the ALIAS clause, as long as that alias has not already been assigned to a table in a different work area. Assigning an alternative alias can be especially useful when opening a table in two work areas, such as the Sales table. When the Sales table was opened in work area 12, for example, you could have assigned it an alias such as Sales_A:

```
USE Sales IN 12 AGAIN ALIAS Sales_A
```

Notice that if the Sales table were opened in a second work area, using the View window, FoxPro would assign Sales_A as the table's alias in that work area.

The whole point of alias names is that you don't have to know, or care, in which work area a particular table is. You now can refer to the second instance of the Sales table as Sales_A, rather than have to remember that you opened the table in area 12. Using alternative aliases becomes particularly important when using SQL SELECT statements, either in your program or through the RQBE facility, because SQL SELECT opens tables in work areas indiscriminately.

NOTE

You should be aware of a little-known fact concerning aliases. Some legal DOS file names cannot be translated into a legal alias. Table names that begin with a digit, for example, are assigned the work area letter as their default alias, rather than the table name.

Create a table, for example, called *1993DATA.* Now activate the View Window. Notice that the new table's alias is the work area letter, not 1993DATA as you may have expected. If you try to select the table with SELECT 1993DATA, FoxPro displays an error message because no such alias exists.

After entering the USE commands in the Command window, type `DISPLAY STATUS`. Notice that each of the tables has an open index file, even though you didn't specify any INDEX clauses in your USE commands. These indexes are *structural indexes,* created when you first created each of the tables in the Omnipresent Widget sample application. Structural indexes open when the related table opens. For that reason, structural indexes are preferable to stand-alone index files.

Keep in mind, however, that when a table with a structural index is opened, none of the index tags are set as the controlling, or *master* index. To set a specific tag as the master index, use the ORDER clause. The following command, for example, sets the Deptcode tag as the controlling index tag:

```
USE Dept IN 1 ORDER Deptcode
```

You can use the DESCENDING keyword with the ORDER clause (or with the SET ORDER TO command) to order the records from highest to lowest, as in the following example:

```
USE Dept IN 1 ORDER Deptcode DESCENDING
```

The Dept table is now ordered from Deptcode SLS3 to FIN0.

FoxPro 2.0 was the first version of FoxPro to use structural indexes. Earlier versions were limited to using stand-alone index files, which must specifically be opened along with the related table, using the INDEX <.idx file list> clause of the command or the SET INDEX TO <.idx file list> command. The following command, for example, opens the index files MYDATA1 and MYDATA2 along with the table MYDATA:

```
USE MYDATA INDEX MYDATA1, MYDATA2
```

The first index in the index file list, MYDATA1 in this case, automatically becomes the master index. Structural index files, on the other hand, require that the desired index order be specified with the ORDER clause or the SET ORDER TO command.

Refer to Chapter 4, "Database Management Fundamentals," for more information on the different types of indexes you can create with FoxPro.

Using Menus To Present Choices

The environment has been set—like a backdrop; the tables, like actors, have been called to take their places. Now you can establish your menu, which provides the series of acts for the play about to be performed.

You learned how to create a menu system in Chapter 14, "Organizing and Packaging Your Applications." If you create your menus through the Menu Builder system, as most people using FoxPro do, enabling your menu is a simple matter of adding the following command at this point in your program:

```
DO the_menu.mpr
```

FoxPro also can create many other forms of menus—from simple popups to complete menu systems. Whichever menu form you choose, your program executes its main menu now.

A FoxPro application is like certain forms of improvisational or experimental drama; the actors and the audience (the users) can determine a different order for the acts every time the program is performed. Your menu system should be flexible enough to enable your users to do their work in a way that seems natural to them, rather than the way that seems natural to you.

Developing Programming Techniques

Earlier in this chapter, you moved some commands from the Command window into a program file and ran the program. Placing the commands into a program enabled you to achieve your objective, without having to retype the commands each time you wanted to use them.

You could just as easily have stored these commands in a *macro* file and played the macro. You wouldn't have had to retype the commands, and you could have inserted a pause in the macro to enable you to type the desired customer code.

What makes a program more powerful than a macro is the ability it gives users to take different actions based upon the truth or falsity of a *condition*. The condition may be set by an action that the user takes during the program execution, or the condition may depend on the current values of the data in your tables.

This section explores FoxPro's *structured programming* commands and functions that are used to control program execution and branching within a FoxPro program. The following commands and functions are discussed:

- IF ... ENDIF
- IIF( )
- DO WHILE ... ENDDO
- SCAN ... ENDSCAN
- DO CASE ... ENDCASE
- FOR ... ENDFOR

The discussion provides one or more examples of how to use each of these commands. As you gain in your knowledge of and experience with the FoxPro programming language, you will begin to recognize the situations in which one command may be preferable to another.

Trying to control program execution without understanding *memory variables* is like trying to drive a car without a steering wheel. This section defines memory variables (in a linguistic and a programmatic sense) and shows you how to use such variables in your programs.

This section also covers commands that use a Scope, a FOR, or a WHILE clause to perform an action on a group of records in a table. Among these commands are COUNT, SUM, and REPLACE.

Last, but not least, the section introduces you to *procedures* and helps you to expand your knowledge of *user-defined functions* (UDFs), some of which you already have used as code snippets in the Screen Builder and Menu Builder chapters. Procedures and UDFs are indispensable allies in the battle to produce readable, verifiable, and maintainable code.

Understanding and Using Memory Variables

If you followed along with the examples in Chapter 10, "Using the Report Writer and Label Designer," you already have seen and used memory variables. Think of a memory variable as a bucket, to which you affix a gummed label with the name "My_Bucket" printed on it. Into this bucket, you put three marbles. When your mother asks you, "Have you lost your marbles?" you reply, "No, they're in My_Bucket!"

When you want to refer to those three marbles, you can use the name My_Bucket in place of the contents of the actual bucket. When you type `IF My_Bucket = 3`, FoxPro looks in the variable My_Bucket, sees the value 3 stored there, and evaluates the expression as follows:

```
IF 3 = 3
```

This statement is true. Because the expression evaluates to true, FoxPro executes the commands that follow IF and precede ELSE (if you specified an ELSE) or ENDIF (if you did not specify an ELSE).

As the word implies, a variable may be changed at any time. You can increment a variable, decrement a variable, store a completely different value to a variable, or copy a variable's value to another variable. The following list describes some of your alternatives:

mvar = 0	Create the variable mvar and set it to 0.
mvar = mvar + 1	Add 1 to mvar and save the result back to mvar.
mvar = mvar - 1	Subtract 1 from mvar and save the result to mvar.
My_Bucket = mvar	Create the variable My_Bucket and copy the value of mvar to it.

After entering these commands in the Command window (without the comments), My_Bucket equals 0, so maybe your mother was right!

NOTE

FoxPro provides two ways of assigning values to memory variables and array elements, = and the STORE command. The STORE command has the following syntax:

```
STORE <expression> to <memory variable list> ¦ <array>
```

Both = and STORE do the same thing. Which one to use is mostly a matter of personal preference. Some programmers prefer STORE to =, as this command is more descriptive of its function: to store values. Those who have programmed in other languages usually are more comfortable with =.

The one clear advantage of STORE over = is its capability to store a value to more than one variable. Because STORE accepts a list of variables or array elements, multiple assignments of the same value to more than one variable or array element can be accomplished with a single line of code, as in the following:

```
STORE .F. to mvar1, mvar2, mvar3
```

FoxPro, as well as most of the other Xbase dialects, differs from many other languages in that you need not define a variable and specify its data type before you actually create the variable. In the preceding example, the first time you assign a value to *mvar,* FoxPro creates the variable if it does not already exist.

You also can change the data type of a variable after it has been created, something that is prohibited in most languages. You can change the data type by assigning to the variable a value of the new data type. To demonstrate this procedure, activate the Command window and type the following lines:

```
mvar = 0
WAIT WINDOW TYPE('mvar')
```

FoxPro displays N in the upper-right corner of the screen, indicating that the variable mvar is of numeric type. Press a key to clear the message window, and then type the following:

```
mvar = "Hello, world!"
WAIT WINDOW TYPE('mvar')
```

As you can see, mvar is now of character (C) type.

NOTE

In computer science terms, the Xbase language has "weak type checking," which means that the compiler cannot catch your mistake when you unintentionally assign a value of the wrong data type to a memory variable. The compiler cannot flag the assignment as an error because you may have *intended* to change the variable's data type. The capability to change a variable's data type can be used to great advantage, but this capability also can get you into trouble.

This weak type checking also applies to arrays, but does not extend to fields in tables. You cannot change the data type of a field by REPLACEing the value with a value of a different data type. If you try to store a value of the wrong data type to a field, you will trigger an error.

You need to understand the following rules when creating and using memory variables:

- Memory variables must begin with a letter or the underscore (_) character. Avoid beginning memory variable names with the underscore character, however, because your variable names may conflict with FoxPro's system memory variables and menu bar names.
- You can use a name longer than 10 characters, but only the first 10 are significant. To avoid error and confusion, limit your variable names to 10 characters.
- You can create a memory variable with the same name as a field in the currently selected table. Indeed, FoxPro does this when you use the SCATTER MEMVAR command. When you use a command that can take its arguments from the field or the memory variable, however, precede the memory variable name with the M. or M-> prefix to tell FoxPro to use the value of the memory variable. Otherwise, FoxPro gives precedence to the field and uses the field value.
- You can store the contents of a memo field as a character string in a memory variable, but keep in mind that a character string has a length limitation. The exact limit depends on which version (Standard or Extended) of FoxPro you are using. In the Standard version, character strings can be a maximum of 64K (65,536 characters). In the Extended version, character strings have a theoretical maximum of *2 gigabytes* (slightly more than 2 billion bytes). The practical limit is the amount of available RAM (random-access memory) in your computer.

Now that you understand what memory variables are, you can use them to construct conditional expressions that FoxPro's structured programming commands can evaluate.

Using Commands That Evaluate Conditions

You already have seen some simple examples of using IF ... ENDIF and DO WHILE ... ENDDO to test for certain conditions and to perform actions suitable to each set of circumstances. Knowing when you need to evaluate a condition is the easy part. The hard part is understanding how to properly express the condition, or combination of conditions, to be tested.

The condition always takes the form of a *logical expression*, one that can be evaluated as true or false. You can construct a logical expression by using one of the following alternatives:

- A table field of a logical type
- A memory variable or array element that holds a logical value
- A function (built-in or user-defined) that returns a logical value
- Other expression types (character, numeric, or date) separated by a *relational operator* (such as <, >, =, <=, or !=)

You also can use .T. or .F. to construct a logical expression.

To illustrate some of these, refer to the RUN_APP.PRG example one more time:

```
* RUN_APP.PRG
* This is a routine to display a list of APP files
* and prompt the user for the one to run.
* It does not display the list of files if a file
* name is passed as a parameter.

PARAMETERS fname
SET TALK OFF
IF PARAMETERS() = 1
   DO (fname)
ENDIF

more = .T.
DO WHILE more
```

```
   fname = GETFILE('APP','Application to run')
   IF !EMPTY(fname)
      DO (fname)
      CLEAR PROGRAM
      more = .T.
   ELSE
      more = .F.
   ENDIF
ENDDO
```

This program uses three of the five means of constructing a logical expression. RUN_APP.PRG uses a function that returns a logical value (EMPTY( )), an expression that evaluates to a logical value (PARAMETERS( ) = 1), and a memory variable (more) that contains a logical value.

The version of RUN_APP that grew out of the pseudocode example uses a pair of nonlogical expressions compared to each other using a relational operator (in this case !=) and a logical value (.T.):

```
do while .t.
   fname = getfile('APP','Application to run')
   if "" != fname
      * run the application, and then clear it from
      * memory
      do (fname)
      clear program
   else
      EXIT
   endif
enddo
```

Examine the IF construct first. If the user presses Esc while in the Getfile dialog, the GETFILE( ) function returns the null string (""), which is stored into variable fname. You then can compare fname to the null string to determine whether to run another program.

> **CAUTION:** Be careful when comparing strings; if EXACT is SET OFF, "" = fname is very different from fname = "". With EXACT off, fname = "" is always true!
>
> Refer to the "Recognizing Nonoptimizable Expressions" section in Chapter 7 for a detailed discussion of the rules that FoxPro uses to compare character strings.

What does `do while .t.` mean? This instruction specifies a logical value, rather than an expression that must be evaluated to a logical value. You can just as easily say do while 3 = 3. You are telling FoxPro, "This is not the right time to decide whether to continue. I'll let you know somewhere else when I want to leave this loop."

This type of construct is called an *infinite loop*. Without some other means of exiting, a program with an infinite loop goes on forever. As its name implies, the EXIT command enables you to break out of the infinite loop. When the user presses Esc in GETFILE( ), the expression "" != fname becomes false (fname now contains the null string); the ELSE is activated; and EXIT is executed.

Using IF ... ENDIF To Choose Your Path

By now, you have seen many examples of how to use the IF ... ENDIF construct to make a decision. IF ... ENDIF has two formats:

Format 1: IF ... ENDIF

```
* Evaluate a condition, and perform one or more steps
* only if it is true
IF <condition>    <optional comment>
   commands to be executed if <condition> is true
ENDIF   <optional comment>
```

Format 2: IF ... ELSE ... ENDIF

```
* Evaluate a condition
* Perform one series of steps if it is true,
* and a different series of steps if it is false
IF <condition>    <optional comment>
   commands to be executed if <condition> is true
ELSE   <optional comment>
   commands to be executed if <condition> is false
ENDIF   <optional comment>
```

You can place comments at the end of any line. Comments that appear on the same line as a command or expression must be preceded by a double ampersand (&&), which tells FoxPro not to evaluate the remainder of the line. A comment that appears on a line by itself must be preceded by a double ampersand, the word NOTE, or more traditionally, by one or more asterisks (*).

IF statements also can be *nested;* that is, one or more of the commands to be executed may itself be an IF statement, which also can have one or more IF statements nested within it:

```
* GLADHAND.PRG
* An example of a nested IF
*
input "How old are you (in years) ? " to your_age
if your_age < 40
   if your_age < 30
      if your_age < 20
         ? "Gee, I wish I was a kid like you again!"
      else
         ? "Your twenties are the best years of your life!"
      endif
   else
      ? "Your thirties are the best years of your life!"
   endif
else
   if your_age > 49
      if your_age > 59
         ? "Gee, you don't look a day over 30!"
      else
         ? "Your fifties are the best years of your life!"
      endif
   else
      ? "Your forties are the best years of your life!"
   endif
endif
return
```

When each condition in an IF ... ELSE ... ENDIF performs the same operation with a different expression, you can use the IIF( ) (usually read as "Immediate If") function to evaluate the condition and return the desired expression. IIF( ) requires three arguments and is structured as follows:

```
IIF(<condition>, <expression1>, <expression2>)
```

The condition is evaluated. If the condition is True, <expression1> is returned; if it is False, <expression2> is returned. Because the returned expression is not very useful by itself, you assign the expression to a variable or pass it along as the argument of another command or function. You can rewrite the GLADHAND procedure using IIF( ) as follows:

```
* GLADHAND.PRG
* An example of a nested IF using IIF()
*
input "How old are you (in years) ? " to your_age
? iif(your_age < 40, ;
   iif(your_age < 30, ;
      iif(your_age < 20, ;
```

continues

```
            "Gee, I wish I was a kid like you again!", ;
            "Your twenties are the best years of your life!"), ;
         "Your thirties are the best years of your life!"),;
      iif(your_age > 49, ;
         iif(your_age > 59, ;
            "Gee, you don't look a day over 30!",;
            "Your fifties are the best years of your life!"),;
         "Your forties are the best years of your life!"))
return
```

This program looks much more complicated, but the logic is the same. The real difference is that this program is harder to read because the ELSE is *implied* in the construction of the IIF( ) function's arguments, rather than printed in the appropriate place in the program. Actually, if you adopt a formatting convention like the one shown in the preceding example and use that convention every time you use IIF( ), the program becomes just as easy to read as an IF ... ELSE ... ENDIF:

```
IIF(condition, ;
   expression to return if condition is true, ;
   expression to return if condition is false)
```

The logic of the GLADHAND program is clear and fairly easy to follow. In a more complicated case, the use of multiple nested IFs can make the program hard to understand.

FoxPro has a command, DO CASE, that makes it much easier to follow the logic of a program that must choose among more than two possible cases.

Making Multiple Choice Decisions with DO CASE

FoxPro's DO CASE command is similar to the CASE command in Pascal and the SWITCH( ) function in C. DO CASE evaluates a series of conditions and performs the ones that follow the first condition, if any, that is true:

```
DO CASE
   CASE <condition 1>
      [<statements>]
   [CASE <condition 2>
      [<statements>]]
   ...
   [CASE <condition n>
      [<statements>]]
```

```
   [OTHERWISE
      <statements>]
ENDCASE
```

The brackets ([and]) indicate that these parts of the construct are optional. A DO CASE can contain one CASE to be evaluated, in which case it would be functionally identical to an IF ... ENDIF. However, DO CASE is rarely used in this fashion.

The following restructure of the GLADHAND program is a more typical usage of DO CASE:

```
* GLADHAND.PRG
* An example of using DO CASE
*
input "How old are you (in years) ? " to your_age
do case
   case your_age < 20
      ? "Gee, I wish I was a kid like you again!"
   case between(your_age, 20, 29)
      ? "Your twenties are the best years of your life!"
   case between(your_age, 30, 39)
      ? "Your thirties are the best years of your life!"
   case between(your_age, 40, 49)
      ? "Your forties are the best years of your life!"
   case between(your_age, 50, 59)
      ? "Your fifties are the best years of your life!"
   otherwise
      ? "Gee, you don't look a day over 30!"
endcase
return
```

When a condition that evaluates to true is found, the conditions that follow it are not evaluated; unlike C, in which the program *falls through* to all the other statements in the SWITCH( ) function call.

The optional OTHERWISE clause enables you to specify a default series of steps to be taken. The commands that follow OTHERWISE are executed only if none of the stated conditions evaluates to true.

Using Commands That Operate on a Range of Records

When using commands that operate on records in a table—such as REPLACE, COPY, and COUNT—you usually can limit the records the command processes to a certain range. The records to be included in the range are specified by attaching a *scope*, FOR, and/or WHILE clause to the command. If the range to be affected by the command can be specified in this manner, you should do it this way, instead of using one of the looping constructs to skip through the table, because FoxPro only needs to evaluate the condition once.

Table 18.1 shows the commands that take a *scope*, FOR, and WHILE clause. Table 18.2 shows the *scope* clauses you can use with these commands.

Table 18.1 Commands That Use a Scope, FOR, and WHILE Clause

Command	Command	Command	Command
AVERAGE	COPY TO ARRAY	LABEL	SCAN
BROWSE	COUNT	LIST	SORT
CALCULATE	DELETE	LOCATE	SUM
CHANGE	DISPLAY	RECALL	TOTAL
CONTINUE	EDIT	REPLACE	
COPY TO	EXPORT	REPORT	

Table 18.2 The Scope Clauses

Clause	Range of Records Affected	Record Pointer Lands at
ALL	All records in the table	End of file
NEXT <n>	The next <n> records, beginning with the current record	Last record processed
RECORD <n>	Only the record whose record number is <n>	Record <n>
REST	From the current record to the last one in the table	End of file

BROWSE, CHANGE, and EDIT are included in table 18.1 primarily because they use the FOR clause; these commands do not use the WHILE clause and have limited scoping capability.

Keep in mind that the order in which the records are processed is affected by the master index, if any. If you use the command REPLACE NEXT 3 ..., the replacements are made in the current record and in the two records that follow it in the current index order.

Be especially careful when using the REPLACE command to change the value of any field contained in the current master index expression. Because REPLACE updates all active indexes, a *scope*, FOR, or WHILE clause should never be used with REPLACE when updating any field that is part of the master index expression.

Repeating Your Actions with DO WHILE, SCAN, and FOR

FoxPro has three commands (DO WHILE, SCAN, and FOR) that enable you to repeat certain actions as long as some condition remains true. While these commands are similar in function, each is more appropriate than the others in certain circumstances.

The venerable DO WHILE command is the most versatile of the looping commands and has the distinction of being able to replace the other two under all conditions.

The format of DO WHILE ... ENDDO is the same as that of IF ... ENDIF. The following evaluates a condition and executes one or more commands if that condition is true:

```
DO WHILE <condition>
   commands to execute while condition is true
ENDDO
```

The difference is that, after the commands have been executed, FoxPro reevaluates the condition and keeps executing the commands until the condition evaluates to false. When that evaluation happens, program execution control passes to the line that follows ENDDO.

SCAN works much like DO WHILE, but is designed specifically for moving through a table. SCAN automatically advances the record pointer on each successive loop. This command also reselects the table it is working on if you change the active work area within the loop. The default scope for SCAN is ALL, meaning that you don't have to explicitly position the record pointer at the top of the file. You also can specify any of the other scope clauses (REST, NEXT <n>, or RECORD <n>) to restrict SCAN to the records in a range. Because it works only on tables, SCAN is more limited in what you can do with it than is DO WHILE.

The first of the following code fragments uses DO WHILE and is functionally identical to the second fragment, which uses SCAN:

```
SELECT 1
GO TOP
DO WHILE !EOF()
   SELECT 2
   < some commands >
   SELECT 1
   SKIP
ENDDO
SELECT 1
SCAN
   SELECT 2
   < some commands >
ENDSCAN
```

Although not required, you can explicitly reselect work area 1 before repeating the loop in the second code fragment. You must remember, however, not to use SKIP with SCAN, unless you are sure that you actually want to skip over the next record.

FOR ... ENDFOR executes one or more commands in a loop a specified number of times. To use the FOR command, you have to set a memory variable, which acts as a counter, to some initial value and specify a limit value that causes the FOR to be exited when the limit value is exceeded by the counter. By default, the counter is incremented by one after each pass through the loop. If the counter variable does not exist, FoxPro creates the counter variable for you.

You can increment the counter by a value other than one by specifying a STEP value. You can STEP downward from an initial value by specifying a negative increment.

FOR, shown in the following examples, is easier to illustrate than to explain:

```
* turn off the function keys F1 through F10
FOR j = 1 TO 10      && STEP 1 is implied
   SET FUNCTION j TO *
ENDFOR


* display the letters from "A" to "Z"
FOR j = ASC("A") TO ASC("Z")   && STEP 1 is implied
   ? CHR(j)
ENDFOR
```

```
* display every other letter from "A" to "Z"
FOR j = ASC("A") TO ASC("Z") STEP 2
   ? CHR(j)
ENDFOR
* display only the consonants, in reverse order
* from "Z" to "A"
vowels = "AEIOU"
FOR j = ASC("Z") TO ASC("A") STEP -1
   IF ! (CHR(j) $ vowels)
      ? CHR(j)
   ENDIF
ENDFOR
```

In each case, the counter *j* is initialized to some value and incremented by the STEP value after each pass through the loop. The commands in the loop are executed as long as the counter is less than or equal to the limit value. If you have specified a negative STEP value, the counter must be greater than or equal to the limit.

Just as you can use DO WHILE in place of SCAN, you also can use it to accomplish things for which you use FOR:

```
* turn off the function keys F1 through F10
j = 1
DO WHILE j <= 10
   SET FUNCTION j TO *
   j = j + 1
ENDDO
```

The FOR command is preferable in this instance, however. Not only is the program that uses FOR two lines shorter, its form also more clearly states the objective of the loop.

As a general rule, choose SCAN or FOR over DO WHILE whenever they can do the job, because SCAN's or FOR's more limited functionality clarifies the objective of the routine.

Changing the Program Flow with LOOP, EXIT, and RETURN

Each of the looping commands has two clauses, LOOP and EXIT, that enable you to alter the normal sequence of events within the loop.

LOOP tells FoxPro to disregard the remaining statements in the loop and to return to the DO WHILE, SCAN, or FOR line to reevaluate the condition. LOOP often is used within an IF statement that tests for a condition that, if true, obviates the intended function of the remaining statements in the loop. The following code example shows LOOP used in an IF statement within a SCAN command:

```
* process the Sales table, disregarding "house" accounts
* House accounts begin with a "Z"
SELECT Sales
SCAN
   IF UPPER(LEFT(Custcode,1)) = "Z"
      LOOP
   ENDIF
   * it's not a house account, so process it
   < statements >
ENDSCAN
```

EXIT, which is used in the sample version of the RUN_APP program, transfers program control to the line that follows the ENDDO, ENDSCAN, or ENDFOR line. EXIT often is used to break out of an infinite loop created by DO WHILE .T..

RETURN transfers control to the program that called the current program or to the Command window if the current program is the first (or only) module in your application. When RETURN appears at the end of a procedure or UDF, the command does not alter the natural flow of the program. When one program ends, it is natural for the program that called the terminating one to resume execution.

When RETURN appears within the body of a program, however, FoxPro disregards all the subsequent statements in the program. You can think of RETURN used in this manner as a LOOP that works with programs and subprocedures, rather than with the various looping commands. As with LOOP, RETURN is most often used when some condition exists that makes it unnecessary to continue with the program. An example of this is when a PACK routine is called, and the table to PACK is empty.

You should understand that you never have to use any of these program control altering devices. You always can write a program so that they are not needed. Writing a program without these devices, however, sometimes requires you to use a large number of IFs, which can become nested to an uncomfortable level.

When, or whether, to use LOOP, EXIT, and RETURN is a matter of personal preference, although their judicious use can enhance the readability of your programs. If well-defined conditions under which you don't want to proceed appear, just say so, and get out of there! Try writing some routines that use LOOP, EXIT, and RETURN, as well as some routines that avoid using them, to see which ones seem more natural to you.

Using Structured Programming Commands: an Extended Example

You may wonder why the discussion of commands that act on a range of records, such as REPLACE, is positioned between the discussion of the different types of structured programming commands. The reason is that DO WHILE also can operate on a range of records, but provides you with much more flexibility in determining which records, are processed and which processes are applied to them.

The condition (Custcode = "MKF1") is evaluated *once* when you use a command such as the following:

```
REPLACE salesman WITH "B023" FOR Custcode = "MKF1"
```

The Custcode field of each record in the Sales table is compared to "MKF1". If they are the same, the replacement is made.

The condition specified in a DO WHILE command, on the other hand, is evaluated the first time it is encountered in the program and on *each successive pass* through the loop. The elements that make up the condition can be changed by any of the commands contained between the DO WHILE and ENDDO, giving you a much greater degree of control over which records are processed.

For example, if you want to calculate the commission due to the sales manager on house accounts for the previous fiscal quarter, you can write a program to perform the calculation. The rules for calculating the sales manager's commissions are the following:

- The manager's commission percentage is a flat 8 percent of gross sales to house accounts.
- All house accounts start with Z in the CUSTCODE field.
- The total commission for the quarter cannot exceed $10,000.
- The commission earned on any one account cannot exceed $1,000.

The following example illustrates one way to write this program in pseudocode:

```
* CALCCOMM.PRG

Purpose:
To calculate the commission due to the sales
manager for a specified fiscal period. The rules to be used in
the calculation are:
(restate the above rules)

Steps:
accept the fiscal period from the calling program

open the Sales table

create a temporary index so that the sales are limited to those
made in the specified fiscal period to house accounts

initialize memory variables to hold the commission rate, the
maximum commission amounts, and the commission balance

while there are more sales records to be processed, and the total
commission for the quarter has not exceeded the maximum

   keep track of the current account

   while you're on the same account

      if the commissions for this account have not
      exceeded the maximum for each account

         add the commission rate * the amount of the
         sale to the running total for this account

if     the commission for this account
   +   the commission for all accounts
   <=  the maximum total commission

      add the commission for this account to the running
      total for all accounts

otherwise

   set the total commission equal to the maximum commission

erase the temporary file and return
```

Refined closer to the actual program code, the preceding example now appears as follows:

```
accept the fiscal period from the calling program

if the Sales table is not open
   open it in the next available work area
endif
select the sales table

get a temporary file name for your temporary index

index Sales on upper(Custcode) for sales made in the
   specified fiscal period to customers which are house
   accounts to (temporary file)

initialize memory variables to hold the commission rate,
the maximum commission amounts, and the commission balance

do while there are more house accounts to be processed,
   and the total commission for the quarter has not
   exceeded the maximum

   keep track of the current account
   scan the records for this account
      if the commissions for this account have not
      exceeded the maximum for each account

         add the commission rate * the amount of the
         sale to the running total for this account

      endif

   endscan

   if       the commission for this account
      +  the commission for all accounts
      <= the maximum total commission

      add the commission for this account to the running
      total for all accounts

   else
      set the total commission equal to the maximum
      commission

   endif
```

continues

```
enddo

erase the temporary file
return the commission amount due
```

Now you are ready to write the program:

```
* CALCCOMM.PRG
*
* Calculate and return the commission due to the sales
* manager for the fiscal period specified, as an
* integer, in parameter mperiod.
*
parameters mperiod
if !used('Sales')
   * open the sales table in the next
   * available work area
   use Sales again in 0 alias Sales
endif
select Sales

* get a unique file name for our temporary index
temp = sys(3) + ".$$$"

* limit the records to sales made in the previous fiscal
* period to customers which are house accounts
index on upper(Custcode) ;
   for     upper(left(Custcode,1)) = "Z" ;
       and pd(Datesold) = mperiod ;
   to (temp)

* initialize memory variables to hold the commission rate, the
* maximum commission amounts, and the total commission balance
comm_rate =  0.08
max_comm  = 10000
max_each  =  1000
tot_comm  =     0

do while     !eof() ;
      and tot_comm < max_comm

   curr_cust = Custcode
   this_comm = 0

   scan while Custcode == curr_cust
```

```
      if this_comm <= max_each
         * add the commission rate * the amount of the
         * sale to the running total for this account
         this_comm = this_comm + comm_rate * Quantity * Price
      endif
   endscan

   if this_comm > max_each
      this_comm = max_each
   endif

   if this_comm + tot_comm < max_comm
      tot_comm = tot_comm + this_comm
   else
      tot_comm = max_comm
   endif

enddo

set index to    && close the temporary index
erase (temp)    && erase the temporary index file

return tot_comm
```

NOTE The UDF PD( ), used to determine which fiscal period a particular date is part of, comes from examples in Chapter 13 in which the UDF is part of a VALID clause code snippet.

Notice that a good deal of the work occurs before the DO WHILE loop because of the construction of an index that limits the table's visible records to those that may be needed to calculate the commission. This step reduces the task to a matter of skipping through the records by customer group, performing calculations, and testing simple conditions along the way.

Using Subroutines To Manage the Tasks

Procedures and UDFs are programs, just like any other program. A program is called a *procedure* when used by another program to perform a particular task, and a *UDF* when used to calculate and return a value to a calling program. Procedures and UDFs have more in common than they have differences, so this discussion refers to both as procedures.

A procedure can be part of a program file, part of a separate procedure file, or a stand-alone program. Unless it is a stand-alone program, a procedure must start with a label that enables FoxPro to find it. You assign a label to a procedure by preceding the label with PROCEDURE or FUNCTION (e.g. PROCEDURE My_Proc).

Which label prefix you use is not important. Procedure My_Proc may be labelled as FUNCTION My_Proc or PROCEDURE My_Proc. Likewise, both PROCEDUREs and FUNCTIONs may or may not explicitly return a value. For style and readability, use PROCEDURE for routines that do not explicitly return a value and FUNCTION for those that do.

Starting with version 2.0, all procedures return a value. If you do not explicitly RETURN a value, the procedure returns .T. (True).

Communicating with Subroutines through PARAMETERS

At the beginning of this chapter, you created a program called SHOWORDS by moving some commands from the Command window into a separate program file. SHOWORDS is limited to displaying the records for a single customer because you *hard coded* the customer number into the program. To use this program to display sales records for other customers, you need to include a PARAMETERS statement.

The PARAMETERS statement serves as a communication link between a procedure and the programs that call the procedure. The PARAMETERS statement must be the first line in the procedure and must be followed by a list of one or more variable names. PARAMETERS creates *local memory variables*, or arrays using these names, and assigns to each the value passed to the procedure by the calling program.

The data type of each variable or array is the same as that of the value in the same position within the list of values sent to the procedure. The list that follows a PARAMETERS statement can be longer than the list of parameters actually passed to the procedure. Any parameter names that cannot be filled with data from the calling program are created as logical variables and are set equal to .F.. If your parameter list has three names, for example, but you call the procedure with a list of only two values, the third parameter is set equal to a logical False.

You can modify SHOWORDS to use parameters and then call SHOWORDS with a parameter list:

```
* SHOWORDS.PRG
*
* Accept the order of the index to be used
*   to perform a BROWSE KEY, and the "key" value to be
*   displayed, from the calling program.
*
* The table to be used is currently selected.
*
PARAMETERS morder, mkey

* if the second parameter was not passed
if type('mkey') = 'L'
   * set mkey to the null string, which will cause
   * BROWSE KEY to display all records in the table
   mkey = ""
endif

* set the proper index as the master index
set order to morder

*display the desired records
browse key mkey

return
```

To use the new version of the program from the Command window, type the following:

```
SELECT 0
USE Sales AGAIN
DO SHOWORDS WITH "Custcode", "MKF1"
```

Then try the following command:

```
DO SHOWORDS WITH "Custcode"
```

You now have transformed the rigid command sequence into a useful program that displays any or all index key values, as long as you tell the program which structural index tag to set as the master index.

The PARAMETERS statement in the procedure created the variables *morder* and *mkey* and then stored into each variable the value of the related item in the parameter list of the calling program (or Command window, in this case). You also can create the variables in the Command window and not use the PARAMETERS statement. In the

Command window, you can type the following and delete the PARAMETERS statement from SHOWORDS:

```
morder = "Custcode"
mkey = "MKF1"
SELECT 0
USE Sales AGAIN
DO SHOWORDS
```

So why should you use parameters? Using parameters enables you to do the following:

- Use procedures and UDFs without having to remember the names used to refer to the values that you want the procedure to manipulate (*morder* and *mkey* in the example)
- Hide the variables that you are using in the program from the procedure and prevent their values from being changed by the commands contained in the procedure

Calling a Subroutine

FoxPro provides you with two ways to call a subroutine. Which of these ways you use depends on whether you want to use the subroutine's returned value.

When you want a subroutine to perform a task without using its returned value, you use the following format:

```
DO <procedure name> [ WITH <argument list> ]
```

When you want to use the subroutine's returned value, you can use the following format:

```
<UDF name> ([ argument list ])
```

The value returned by the UDF usually is assigned to a memory variable or used as an argument to a built-in FoxPro command or function. Not all of FoxPro's commands, nor all clauses of those that do, accept a UDF. Refer to the "User-Defined Functions (UDFs)" entry in the FoxPro *Language Reference* manual for a complete list of the commands and clauses that support UDFs.

The return value of built-in functions and UDFs also may be discarded by using the = command, which evaluates an expression consisting of one or more function calls. You may choose to use this command if you are only interested in a *side effect* of the function, such as moving the record pointer to a specific record in a table.

Passing Parameters by Value and by Reference

One possible side effect of a procedure or UDF is that it may change the value of any of its parameters within the body of the subroutine. If the modified parameter received its original value from the calling program in the form of a memory variable or an array (as in DO SHOWORDS WITH morder), as opposed to a constant (such as DO SHOWORDS WITH 'Prodcode'), the memory variable or array may or may not retain the changes when the subroutine ends.

If parameters are *passed by value,* the subroutine makes a *copy* of the original variables for use within the subroutine. When the subroutine ends, these temporary variables are released from memory. The original variables are not affected.

If parameters are *passed by reference*, the subroutine does *not* create a copy of the original variables but refers to them by the names used in the parameter list. Any changes made to the parameters within the subroutine actually are made to the original variables.

Which type of parameter passing is used for a particular subroutine call depends upon one or both of the following factors:

- The form used to call the subroutine (DO <procedure name> WITH <parameter list> or <function name> (<parameter list>))
- The current SETting of UDFPARMS

Variables passed to a subroutine using DO <procedure> ... are always passed by reference, unless you specify that pass by value should be used for a particular variable by enclosing its name in parentheses. Variables passed to a subroutine using <function> (<parameter list>) are passed by value, unless UDFPARMS is SET to REFERENCE or the variable name is preceded by the AT symbol (@). The default setting of UDFPARMS is VALUE.

Arrays also are affected by the calling format and by UDFPARMS. Although the rules are not difficult to understand, the manipulation of arrays passed as parameters is an advanced subject covered in Chapter 22, "Using SQL Commands, Arrays, and the Low-Level File Functions." For now, just be aware that a single element of an array (as opposed to the array itself) is always passed by value.

Summary

This chapter covers many of the FoxPro programming basics. You learned about the structure of a program, how to use pseudocode to outline the steps the program will take, and how to use FoxPro's structured programming commands to test conditions and repeat actions.

You also learned more about memory variables: what they are, when they are created, and how you can use them in programs. Finally, you learned the basics of using procedures and user-defined functions to break the tasks of the program into smaller pieces that make the application easier to read and to debug.

In the next chapter, the discussion expands on the knowledge and skills you gained in this chapter and introduces you to some more advanced programming techniques.

19

CHAPTER

Using Advanced FoxProgramming Techniques

Chapter 18 introduced some programming structure and design concepts. Pseudocode was used to clarify the steps that a program needed to take, and a few programs that used FoxPro's structured programming techniques were examined.

This chapter reinforces all the concepts and techniques used to this point and introduces you to a few more advanced techniques. This chapter also introduces you to FoxPro's text merge features, which you can use to create program templates.

This chapter begins by discussing the two types of memory variables that you can create and the circumstances under which you would use each of them.

Using Public and Private Variables

Chapter 18 defined memory variables and gave you some rules for using them. To manage memory variables in an application, you must know more about how FoxPro resolves potential conflicts between variable names that are used more than once in different routines of your application.

Consider the following code fragment:

```
PROCEDURE mainproc
   x = 1
   y = factorial(5)
   ? x     <== the current value of x is now 120!
return

FUNCTION factorial
   *
   * return the factorial of mnum
   *
   parameters mnum

   x = 1
   for j=mnum to 1 step -1
      x = x * j
   endfor
return x
```

(Notice that FACTORIAL handles the special case of 0 but does not handle negative numbers correctly.)

Procedure MAINPROC stores the constant value 1 to a variable called *x*. If FoxPro encounters this statement, FoxPro looks for *x* in its internal list of variable names. If FoxPro doesn't find the variable, the program creates the variable and stores the desired value to it. The variable *x*, therefore, is created in procedure MAINPROC.

If FoxPro encounters the statement *x*=1 in function FACTORIAL, FoxPro again looks in its internal list. This time, the name *x* already is present in the list, so FoxPro does not need to create the variable. FoxPro simply changes the value of *x* from whatever the previous value was to the new value—in this case, the constant value 1. FACTORIAL increments *x* by *x* times *j* until *j* becomes equal to one. After FACTORIAL returns control to MAINPROC, *x* is equal to 120.

When you called FACTORIAL, you did not know that the function referenced a variable named *x*. To prevent unintentional changes in variables, you can keep your own list of variable names currently in use and make sure that you never use the same one twice. Alternatively, you can tell FoxPro that *x* is really two different variables that have the same name.

FoxPro is an example of a *block structured language*. A procedure is a block of program statements. Variables created in a particular procedure are visible only in the current procedure. Because the procedure might contain calls to other procedures, however, the procedure's variables also are visible to all its subroutines unless you specifically hide the variable names from the subroutines. You hide variable names by using the PRIVATE command, as follows:

```
PRIVATE <memory variable list>
```

PRIVATE instructs FoxPro to create a separate instance of any variable contained in the <memory variable list> the first time a value is stored to the variable name in the current procedure. The PRIVATE command does not create the variable. The command simply hides the name of previously defined variables that have the same name as a variable in the list. This is done so those variables are not changed by the current procedure or by any subroutines called by the current procedure.

The code fragment in the preceding example can be rewritten so the value of *x* in MAINPROC is not affected by any changes made to a variable of the same name in MAINPROC's subroutines. Rewrite the code as follows:

```
PROCEDURE mainproc
   x = 1
   y = factorial(5)
   ? x         <== now the value of x is still 1!
return

FUNCTION factorial
   *
   * return the factorial of mnum
   *
   parameters mnum
   PRIVATE x, j  && don't change any other x's or j's

   x = 1
   for j=mnum to 1 step -1
      x = x * j
   endfor
return x
```

If FoxPro encounters the statement *x*=1 in FACTORIAL, the program creates a new variable named *x* and uses this variable to store the values assigned to *x* in the body of FACTORIAL. After FACTORIAL terminates, its private copies of both *x* and *j* are released from memory, and references to *x* in MAINPROC again refer to the copy of *x* created in MAINPROC.

This approach works well but creates a few problems of its own. Occasionally, you might want each procedure in an application to refer to the same copy of a variable name. You can, for example, have users enter their names and then display the current user's name at the top of each screen. You want to be able to access the variable in which the user's name is stored. You can make sure that this variable is available throughout the application in two ways.

First, by applying the rules of block structure, you can ensure that the variable name is visible to all routines in the application by creating the variable in the top-most procedure—the one first called by FoxPro as the application runs. This approach has some advantages—variables used throughout the application are declared up front—but also has some disadvantages. If, for example, the application has many such variables, the main program can become cluttered with variable declarations.

The second way to ensure that variables are available throughout the application is to use the PUBLIC command, as follows:

```
PUBLIC [ARRAY] <memory variable list ¦ array list>
```

As opposed to the PRIVATE command, PUBLIC actually creates the memory variables and arrays. Public (or global) variables and arrays are initialized to False (.F.). A variable that has been declared public is visible to all procedures in the application, regardless of the nesting level of the procedure in which the variable was created.

Declaring a variable public doesn't prevent you from declaring a private variable by the same name. The public variable is hidden from view in the procedure that creates the private variable. After the procedure terminates, the private variable is released, and the public variable is visible again.

On the other hand, if you try to declare a public variable or array that has the same name as an existing private variable or array, you see the error message `Syntax error`.

Public variables and arrays are not released by the RELEASE ALL command, and they are not released after you return to the Command window. Public variables can be removed from memory only by including their names in the memory variable list used with RELEASE <memory variable list> or by using the CLEAR ALL or CLEAR MEMORY commands.

Using Regional Variables

A *regional variable* is a special type of private variable. Regional variables conform to the same scope rules as do private variables. In conjunction with the #REGION compiler directive, however, regional variables can coexist in the same program with other regional variables that have the same name.

Regional variables mainly are useful when creating screen sets with the Screen Builder. Each screen in the set can use variables that have the same name as variables in one or more of the other screens.

After the screen program generator, GENSCRN, creates the single screen (.SPR) program from the screen information tables (.SCX), GENSCRN resolves any conflicts between regional variables declared in other parts of the screen program. GENSCRN resolves these conflicts by padding the name of the second variable with underscores followed by the number of the region in which the variable was declared. So if variable myvar, for example, is declared as a regional variable in both region 0 and region 1, the myvar in region 1 is created as the private variable myvar____1.

Regional variables are not very useful in areas of the program over which you have direct control and need not be discussed further in the context of writing programs.

Using Subroutines To Describe the Steps of Your Program

The section of Chapter 18 that covered pseudocode suggested that you use pseudocode statements that cannot be translated into a single statement as a comment for the series of statements required to perform a task. If the task requires few statements, and its function is specific to a particular program, this type of program structuring usually works quite adequately.

At other times, however, a task might require many steps, or the task might be required in other parts of your application. In either case, consider moving the statements into a subroutine. By doing so, you accomplish the following:

- You keep your main program small so that the objective of the program is not lost in the code required to accomplish ancillary tasks, such as saving and restoring the current environment settings.
- You localize the functions of your program so, if the code requires changes, you must change it in only one place.

After reviewing the sample programs included on your FoxPro disks, you might notice that some of them begin with many lines of setup statements—such as statements for saving the existing environment and for opening tables. Although necessary for the program to function correctly, these setup statements have no direct bearing on the purpose of the program.

Rather than include these details of the program setup at the top of the program, you can move the statements to one or more subroutines. You can use descriptive names for the subroutines to indicate their functions and then quickly get into the meat of the program.

The following code is an example of a typical program with the setup details included in the body of the main program:

```
* save user's environment
if set("TALK") = "ON"
   set talk off
   talk_stat = "ON"
else
   talk_stat = "OFF"
endif
safe_stat = set("SAFETY")
set safety off
<other environment-saving statements>

* set global variables
PUBLIC m.g_var1, m.g_var2, m.g_var3
m.g_var1 = 1
```

```
m.g_var2 = 2
m.g_var3 = 3

* open tables
use BUDGET in 1
use BUDCAT in 2
<other table-opening statements>
*
* body of program goes here
*

* restore user's environment
if talk_stat = "ON"
   set talk on
endif
<other environment-restoring statements>
```

You can move the setup details from the main program into subroutines by using the following code instead:

```
do save_env       && save user's environment
do set_global     && set global variables
do open_data      && open tables
*
* body of program goes here
*
do rest_env       && restore user's environment

PROCEDURE save_env
   *
   * save user's environment
   *
   public talk_stat, safe_stat, ;
          <other environment-saving variables>

   if set("TALK") = "ON"
      set talk off
      talk_stat = "ON"
   else
      talk_stat = "OFF"
   endif
   safe_stat = set("SAFETY")
   set safety off
   <other environment-saving statements>
return
```

continues

```
PROCEDURE set_global
   *
   * set global variables
   *
   public g_var1, g_var2, g_var3

   g_var1 = 1
   g_var2 = 2
   g_var3 = 3
return

PROCEDURE open_data
   *
   * open tables
   *

   use Budget in 1
   use Budcat in 2
   <other table-opening statements>
return

PROCEDURE rest_env
   *
   * restore user's environment
   *
   if talk_stat = "ON"
      set talk on
   endif
   <other environment-restoring statements>
return
```

Notice that when you use this approach, the procedure SAVE_ENV must declare its variables as PUBLIC so these variables are not released after SAVE_ENV terminates and so the variables are available for use by REST_ENV.

One way to look at this method is that you use subroutines the same way that you use built-in FoxPro commands. You do not, for example, care how the PACK command works; you care only that PACK removes deleted records from a table. After you write your own procedures that save and restore the user's working environment (SAVE_ENV and REST_ENV in this example), you can treat them as built-in commands.

The previous example uses statements that usually are executed only once in your application. Many of the programs and subroutines that make up your application, however, perform tests for certain conditions that, if true, make the remaining statements in the program unnecessary.

You might, for example, have a program that uses FoxPro's low-level file functions to open an input file, verify that the input file contains some information to be processed, and then create an output file to save the results of the operations you performed on the input data. You can write the following code to perform this procedure:

```
private in_name, out_name, in_handle, out_handle

in_name  = "INPUT.TXT"
out_name = "OUTPUT.TXT"

* open the input file, and store its file handle
* in in_handle
in_handle = fopen(in_name)
if in_handle < 0
   wait window "Unable to open file " + in_name + "!" ;
      timeout 5
   RETURN
endif

* make sure that the input file is not empty
if feof(in_handle)
   wait window "File " + in_name + " is empty!" ;
      timeout 5
   = fclose(in_handle)
   RETURN
endif

* create the output file, and store its file handle
* in out_handle
out_handle = fcreate(out_name)
if out_handle < 0
   wait window "Output file " + out_name + ;
      " could not be created!"
   = fclose(in_handle)
   RETURN
endif
```

You can move the above file-opening and error-checking code into subroutines by writing the code in the following manner:

```
private in_name, out_name, in_handle, out_handle
```

continues

```
in_name  = "INPUT.TXT"
out_name = "OUTPUT.TXT"
store 0 to in_handle, out_handle

if    ! open_file(in_name, @in_handle) ;
   or file_empty(in_name, in_handle) ;
   or ! make_file(out_name, @out_handle)

      = fclose(in_handle)
      RETURN

endif

FUNCTION open_file
   *
   * open the f_name file, and store its file handle
   * in f_handle; return the success or failure of
   * the operation
   *
   parameters f_name, f_handle

   f_handle = fopen(f_name)
   if f_handle < 0
      wait window "Unable to open file " + f_name + "!" ;
         timeout 5
   endif
return f_handle > 0

FUNCTION file_empty
   *
   * is the f_name file empty?
   *
   parameters f_name, f_handle

   if feof(f_handle)
      wait window "File " + f_name + " is empty!" ;
         timeout 5
   endif
return feof(f_handle)

FUNCTION make_file
   *
   * create the f_name file, and store its file handle
   * in f_handle;
   * return the success or failure of the operation
   *
   parameters f_name, f_handle
```

```
   f_handle = fcreate(f_name)
   if f_handle < 0
      wait window "Output file " + f_name + ;
      " could not be created!" timeout 5
   endif
return f_handle > 0
```

This revised version of the code informs you that three conditions exist under which you do not want to proceed; it describes those conditions by using descriptive procedure names; and then it informs you at a glance what the program does if any of these conditions is true. The code also gives you some generic file-handling routines that you can use in any application you write.

This approach to program structure is an example of the concept of *abstraction*. The following section explores this important concept further and shows you how to use abstraction to create programs that are easily understood and maintained.

Using Abstraction To Create Readable Programs

The programs you create in FoxPro should be both readable and maintainable. *Readable* means that you or another person can easily understand the program's objectives and the methods used to achieve these objectives. *Maintainable* means that you or another person can adapt the program to handle additional requirements without rewriting the entire program.

To make a program readable, you use variable names and procedure names that help describe the purpose of the variable or subroutine; you use comments if your purpose cannot be so succinctly expressed.

To be maintainable, a program must be able to adapt to changes in its working environment. Used here, the term *working environment* includes input devices (such as the keyboard), output devices (such as the display screen), and the data the application manipulates.

The following section discusses using variables and the #DEFINE preprocessor directive to create constant values, and introduces you to some built-in FoxPro functions that give you control over the ever changing FoxPro environment.

Avoiding Hard-Coded Values in Your Programs

Do you know what number is returned by the LASTKEY( ) function when you press the Backspace key? If not, you can look it up in the FoxPro manuals whenever you need this information, or you can create your own reference table by mapping to a variable name each of the keystrokes commonly used in your applications. The following procedure creates these global variables:

```
PROCEDURE set_keys
   *
   * map inkey( ), lastkey( ) and readkey( ) values used
   * in the application to descriptive variable names
   *
   PUBLIC ik_enter, ik_esc, ik_up, ik_down, ik_left, ;
          ik_bksp, ik_pgup, ik_pgdn, ik_home, ik_end, ;
          ik_del, ik_clear, ik_ctlend, ik_tab, rk_esc

   ik_enter  =  13
   ik_esc    =  27
   ik_up     =   5
   ik_down   =  24
   ik_left   =  19
   ik_bksp   = 127
   ik_pgup   =  18
   ik_pgdn   =   3
   ik_home   =   1
   ik_end    =   6
   ik_del    =   7
   ik_clear  =  25
   ik_ctlend =  23
   ik_tab    =   9
   rk_esc    =  12
return
```

In applications that include the above SET_KEYS procedure, you can now determine whether the user pressed the Esc key with the following code:

```
IF LASTKEY( ) = ik_esc
```

Storing constant values to variables serves the following three purposes:

- Reduces the constant to an abstraction. (You want to know whether the user pressed Backspace; you do not care what number FoxPro's INKEY( ) function returns.)

- Makes your application more portable to other environments, such as UNIX, which may or may not use the same values.
- Makes your program more readable. (The reader doesn't have to know that LASTKEY()=27 means that the user pressed Esc.)

In Chapter 23, "Controlling a Windowed Environment," you learn to use FoxPro functions such as SROWS() and WCOLS() to avoid hard-coded values if referring to screen and window positions.

Using the Preprocessor Directive #DEFINE

FoxPro 2.5 introduces two preprocessor directives, #DEFINE and #IF. #DEFINE enables you to create compile-time constants, and #IF enables you to conditionally include source code in your programs. In Chapter 17, you learned to use these directives to minimize some of the problems inherent in maintaining an application across multiple platforms, such as DOS and Windows. In this section, you learn more about #DEFINE and how to use this directive in your applications.

The syntax of #DEFINE is as follows:

```
#DEFINE <constant_name> <expression>
```

#DEFINE instructs the compiler to store the name and the expression that follows the name in an internal table and to insert the expression into the compiled program wherever the name is encountered. Consider, for example, the following directive:

```
#DEFINE   THE_MAX   100
```

This instructs the compiler to substitute the value 100 for the name THE_MAX wherever this name is encountered in the program currently being compiled. The directive must appear in the program before any lines for which this substitution is to be made. The compiler substitutes 100 for THE_MAX, for example, if it encounters the following line:

```
for j=1 to THE_MAX
```

The compiler then creates the following line in the compiled program file:

```
for j=1 to 100
```

But why use this preprocessor directive instead of creating a variable called the_max and setting that variable equal to 100? Three reasons exist to use constants created by #DEFINE instead of memory variables:

- Memory variables are just that—values that must be stored in memory. If you force FoxPro to hold a value in memory, FoxPro cannot use that memory for any other purpose, such as creating a window.
- Every time FoxPro encounters a variable in your program, it must look in its name table for the variable name and retrieve the current value of the variable. Although this process takes place very quickly, it still takes more time than is required to evaluate a constant value that can never change, such as the value 100.
- If you use #DEFINE, you document that the name is a constant and that it is to be used only as a constant. You also prevent unintentional changes to the constant value.

Because the compiler substituted a number for the name in the compiled program, the following statement triggers an error:

```
the_max = 10
```

The error occurs because the compiler converts this statement into the following assignment:

```
100 = 10
```

This assignment is illegal. Notice that the_max is the same as THE_MAX. Because the compiler is performing a simple text substitution, the case of the constant name is unimportant.

Notice the following characteristics of #DEFINE that might not be obvious:

- The compiler only performs the substitution within the program in which the #DEFINE directive appears. Therefore, the compiler performs the substitution in procedures and UDFs that are contained in this program file, such as in the Cleanup code of a screen (.SPR) program, but not in other programs that are called by this program. You cannot, for example, use #DEFINE to create constants in place of the global variables you created in the preceding section because these variables are used in many different program modules.
- The compiler performs a simple text substitution of the expression for the name. The compiler does not evaluate the expression and substitute the value that the expression holds at compile time.

The second point bears elaboration. You can see how this works if you include the following lines in a program:

```
mvar1 = 10
#DEFINE   mvar2   mvar1
mvar2 = 20
```

The compiler does not evaluate mvar1 and substitute the value 10 in place of mvar2 in the third line. It simply replaces mvar2 with mvar1 in subsequent statements. As opposed to the previous example, in which the substitution expression was the constant value 100, this code fragment does not cause a program error to occur.

Finally, you can instruct the compiler to stop the text substitution at any time by placing the following line in the program at the point where you want the text substitution to stop:

```
#UNDEF <constant_name>
```

Using LEN( ) and FSIZE( ) To Determine the Length of a Field

Sometimes you need to know the length of a particular field in a table. You may want to pop up a window, GET a value into a memory variable, and eventually replace the field with the value of the variable. You want the GET to be sized correctly to hold the required data.

FoxPro has two functions that return the length of a field, LEN( ) and FSIZE( ). FSIZE( ) can be used only with database fields; LEN( ) can take either a database field or a memory variable as an argument. LEN( ), however, can be used only with character expressions; FSIZE( ) also returns the size of a Numeric field. (You do not have to determine the size of Date, Logical, and Memo fields; these fields are always 8, 1, and 10 in length, respectively.)

Although these functions can be used interchangeably with Character fields, the correct usage of LEN( ) differs from that of FSIZE( ). The following example demonstrates the difference by getting a value to a memory variable, using each of these two functions. The example uses LEN( ) to determine the size of the Character field (Prodcode) and FSIZE( ) to determine the size of a Numeric field (Quantity).

```
*
* GET the product code and quantity manufactured
* for a new entry into the Manufact table
*
```

continues

```
m.prodcode = space(LEN(Manufact.Prodcode))
m.quantity = 0

do while empty(m.prodcode)
   activate window get_win    && previously defined
   @ 0,1 say "Product code:    " get m.prodcode picture "@! AAA9"
   @ 1,1 say "Production qty: " get m.quantity ;
      picture replicate("9",FSIZE("Quantity","Manufact"))
   * the picture clause serves to determine the
   * proper display size of the GET for m.quantity
   read
   if mod(readkey( ),256) = rk_esc
      EXIT
   endif
enddo
```

If you choose to SELECT the Manufact table before issuing the GET commands so the reference to the table's alias name is not required, the only difference between the two functions is that FSIZE( ) requires that the field name be enclosed in quotation marks. If referencing alias names, however, FSIZE( ) takes the alias name as its second argument (also in quotation marks), and LEN( ) takes the alias as part of a full field name (the_table.the_field or the_table->the_field).

Selecting Available Work Areas by Using SELECT( ), SELECT 0, and IN 0

A table usually must be opened in a work area before that table can be used by the commands in your program. (Some SQL Commands are exceptions; the INSERT INTO command, for example, opens a table if the table is not already open.) In previous examples, you opened all your application's tables simultaneously near the beginning of the program and assigned the tables to work areas sequentially, starting with work area 1.

At some point in your program, you probably need to open one or more additional tables in an unused work area. You might, for example, want to create a temporary copy of selected records from a table and then manipulate the records in this temporary table. After you open the table, you must make sure that you are not using a work area that already contains an open table to avoid unintentionally closing that table.

In dBASE III PLUS, FoxBASE+, and FoxPro 1, the SELECT 0 command is used to tell the DBMS that you want to select the lowest available work area. You also can use this feature in FoxPro 2.x for this task. For example:

```
temp_dbf = sys(3) + ".$$$"    && get a unique file name
select Budget
copy to (temp_dbf) next 3     && create the temporary table
SELECT 0                      && select the lowest unused
                              && work area
use (temp_dbf) alias TEMP_DBF && open the temp table without
                              && closing any other table
```

In FoxPro 2.x, you can open a table by issuing the command USE <table_name> IN SELECT(1). This command opens a table in the *highest* available work area. In FoxPro 2.5, you also can open a table in the *lowest* available work area by using USE <table_name> IN 0.

Notice that these commands do not activate the new work area automatically. You must still select the work area by using its alias name, as in the following example:

```
temp_dbf = sys(3) + ".$$$"
select Budget
copy to (temp_dbf) next 3
use (temp_dbf) alias Temp_dbf in 0
select Temp_dbf
```

You also can use SELECT( ) without an argument or with an argument of 0—SELECT(0)—to return the number of the currently selected work area.

Combined with the use of work area alias names, SELECT 0, IN SELECT(1), and IN 0 enable you to place the responsibility for the management of work areas where it belongs, on the shoulders of the DBMS. Which work area a table is open in should not concern you.

Using SYS(3) To Obtain Unique Temporary File Names

In a single-user application, code fragments such as the following are not uncommon throughout the program:

```
* create a temporary index
index on <field name> to Temp
```

If only one person is running the application and the data files are segregated from those of other applications, this strategy for creating a temporary file works quite adequately. In a multiuser environment, however, temporary files with hard-coded names can get you into trouble.

To avoid this potential problem, always use the SYS(3) function to obtain a unique file name. SYS(3) uses the system date and time to return an eight-character name that you can use in creating temporary indexes and tables. SYS(3) does not, however, check the default drive for the existence of a file by that name. Use the FILE( ) function in conjunction with SYS(3), therefore, to make absolutely sure that the file is unique. The following example uses a user-defined function called UNIQFILE( ) to return unique file names:

```
* create a temporary index
tempidx = uniqfile( )
index on <field name> to (tempidx)
*
* other code goes here
*
* erase the temporary index file
if file(tempidx)
   erase (tempidx)
endif

FUNCTION uniqfile
   *
   * return a unique file name
   *
   private mfile

   mfile = sys(3) + ".$$$"
   do while     file(mfile)
      mfile = sys(3) + ".$$$"
   enddo
return mfile
```

Notice that you must store the name returned to a variable by UNIQFILE( )—or SYS(3) if you do not employ a user-defined function—so you can refer to it when you need to delete the file.

Using Macro Substitution, Indirect Referencing, and EVALUATE( )

Many of FoxPro's commands require you to supply these commands with a name or other character string literal. Occasionally, however, you do not know the literal's value—such as when you use the SYS(3) function to get a unique file name. You must, therefore, instruct FoxPro to use the contents of a memory variable or array element as the string literal. Macro substitution, indirect referencing, and the EVALUATE( ) function enable you to do this.

Of these three methods, macro substitution is the most flexible but also is the slowest to execute if a single macro substitution is performed. After a macro substitution is performed several times in the same routine, however, such as in a DO WHILE loop, the substitution can become very efficient.

The ampersand character (&) represents the macro substitution function. If a character-type memory variable or array element name is preceded by &, FoxPro treats the contents of the variable or array element as a character string literal and substitutes that value in place of the variable.

dBASE III PLUS does not support arrays. Advanced dBASE III PLUS programmers use macro substitution to simulate one-dimensional arrays. The following code fragment, for example, enables a programmer to GET input from the user in a row-and-column format, storing the data in memory variables with names constructed "on the fly":

```
x = 1                       && your "pseudo array" element counter
firstrow =  5               && start GETting values on row 5
lastrow  = 20               && don't go below row 20
mrow = firstrow             && start at the top
do while mrow <= lastrow
   * create the memory variable names
   * (e.g. arr_one1, arr_one2)
   curr_get1 = "arr_one" + ltrim(str(x))
   curr_get2 = "arr_two" + ltrim(str(x))
```

continues

```
   * now create and initialize the actual variables
   &curr_get1 = space(5)    && e.g. ARR_ONE1 = space(5)
   &curr_get2 = 0           && e.g. ARR_TWO1 = 0

   * issue the GETs
   @ mrow,10 say str(x,2)
   @ mrow,15 get &curr_get1 picture "!!!!!"
   @ mrow,25 get &curr_get2 picture "99999"

   * increment the element counter
   x = x + 1

   * move to the next screen row
   mrow = mrow + 1
enddo
READ
```

By using this technique, you not only can simulate arrays in dBASE III PLUS, but you also can simulate a Browse of a small table. The "table" is limited by the amount of memory that you can allocate to create all these variables.

Unlike dBASE III PLUS, however, FoxBASE+ supports both one- and two-dimensional arrays. As long as you have a good idea of the maximum size of the array and enough memory available to create an array of that size, pseudoarrays such as those used in dBASE III PLUS are unnecessary. In spite of this capability, macro substitution is still of great value in FoxBASE+.

Macro substitution most often is used to refer to files, whose actual names can vary, depending on the specific circumstances. If, for example, you must create a temporary table, you can use macro substitution to supply both the COPY command and the USE command along with the actual name of the file, as follows:

```
temp_table = sys(3) + ".$$$"     && get a unique file name
copy to &temp_table
select 0
use &temp_table alias temp_table
```

Although you can still use macro substitution to supply file names to commands in FoxPro, FoxPro 1.0 introduced a more elegant and efficient method—*indirect referencing*. You can use indirect referencing in any command or function that takes a name, such as a file name or a window name, as an argument. To use indirect referencing, simply enclose in parentheses the name of the variable that holds the string literal. Using this approach, you can open your temporary table as follows:

```
temp_table = sys(3) + ".$$$"     && get a unique file name
copy to (temp_table)
select 0
use (temp_table) alias temp_table
```

Indirect referencing is more limited, however, than is macro substitution. You cannot use indirect referencing to evaluate an expression and substitute the value of the expression in a program statement. Because FoxPro does not have to call its expression evaluator, however, indirect referencing executes faster and should be used in place of macro substitution wherever possible.

The EVALUATE( ) function evaluates a character expression and returns its result. EVALUATE( ), like indirect referencing, can be much more efficient than macro substitution and should be used in its place whenever FoxPro evaluates the expression only once instead of repeatedly for each item in a set of records or variables.

EVALUATE( ) cannot replace the & function in all cases, however. You cannot, for example, restore the previous setting of TALK by using the following code:

```
SET TALK ON
talk_stat = SET('TALK')
SET TALK EVALUATE(talk_stat)
```

Neither can you restore the previous setting of TALK by using the following code:

```
SET TALK ON
talk_stat = SET('TALK')
SET TALK EVALUATE('talk_stat')
```

In the first case, FoxPro tries to evaluate the name (ON), which is stored in talk_stat. Because no such variable exists, however, an error occurs. In the second case, FoxPro evaluates talk_stat itself, the value of which is ON. But you cannot use the following command:

```
SET TALK "ON"
```

This command results in a syntax error. You still must use macro substitution to SET TALK in a single command, as in the following statement:

```
SET TALK &talk_stat
```

Both EVALUATE( ) and macro substitution can be tricky to use correctly. If your statements are not producing the anticipated results, execute the statements in the Command window (after setting TALK to ON) and observe the results of each level of assignment.

Considering Some Advanced Techniques

FoxPro's *Language Reference* manual, although very complete in terms of specifying the syntax of the commands, does not give you very many real-world examples of how to create useful programs. In this section, you learn a few routines that show some of the ways you can use the power of the FoxPro programming language. All the routines come from working programs.

Most of these examples use several FoxPro commands and functions that may be unfamiliar to you. The comments in the code should be sufficient for you to understand the purpose of these commands, even if you do not yet understand how they work. If you have not already done so, begin familiarizing yourself with the *Language Reference* manual—you need it as you reach Part V of this book, "Getting To Know FoxPro's Commands and Functions."

We do not intend for you to slap these routines into your programs. They are food for thought. Critique their approaches to the problems the routines are designed to solve. Ask yourself the following questions:

- Are these approaches solid?
- Can you think of a better, clearer way to accomplish the task?
- Does the programming style enhance or detract from your understanding of the code?

Using INKEY( ) and ON KEY LABEL To Trap Keystrokes

INKEY( ) is one of several FoxPro functions that pauses for user input. Unlike most other functions, INKEY( ) waits for a single keypress and then returns a number indicating which key was pressed. You learned some of the return values of INKEY( ) earlier in the chapter as you mapped these values to memory variables.

ON KEY LABEL is different from INKEY( ). All the two have in common is that both react to a keypress. ON KEY LABEL is one of FoxPro's event-handling commands. It intercepts certain keystrokes and executes a specified command. The command can be a call to a UDF or may be something as simple as a STORE command.

In this section, two routines are presented—one that uses INKEY( ) to accept a user's password and one that uses ON KEY LABEL to remap the Enter key and mark records in a table from a Browse.

Using INKEY( ) To Simulate a GET

Access to an application that deals with sensitive information, such as a payroll program, is often restricted. One way to restrict access to the data is by locating the computer containing the data files in a room accessible to only certain people.

Sometimes, however, this approach is not feasible. A single computer may need to serve the needs of everyone in a small business. Even within the application, some people may have the authority to view, but not to change, the information.

Passwords have long been used to restrict access to an application to those with the appropriate authority. Valid passwords can be stored in a table, along with a related user identification code, and compared to a user's password entry each time the application runs. FoxPro is capable of accepting this information through a simple GET and READ. Why, then, would anyone want to use INKEY( )?

Because restricting the view of the screen to the person who is using the computer is often impossible, the actual characters that make up the password are never displayed. In applications written in the Xbase language, the display color often is set to the same color as both the foreground and background (such as blue on blue), preventing anyone from seeing the user's password entry. The only problem with this approach is that the user cannot see the password either and therefore cannot know whether each character of the password has been recognized and accepted by the computer.

The solution to this problem is to display a visual indicator, such as an asterisk, as a placeholder for each keystroke that has been accepted by the password routine. GETPASS( ) uses this approach and employs a hashing algorithm that encrypts the user's entry before storing it, as in the following code:

```
Structure for table: USERS.DBF
Field  Field Name  Type        Width
    1  ID          Character       3
    2  PASSWORD    Character       5
    3  FULLNAME    Character      30
** Total **                       39

FUNCTION getpass
   *
   * Get and verify the password for the user on whose
   * record in Users.dbf you are currently positioned.
   * If the user enters a valid password, return True;
   * otherwise, return False
   *
   private hours_stat, chour, mornafteve, ;
           trow, brow, lcol, rcol, mpass

   * what part of the day is it?
   hours_stat = set("hours")
   set hours to 24
   chour = val(substr(time( ),1,2))
   mornafteve = iif(chour < 12, ;
                 " morning, ", ;
                 iif(chour < 18, ;
                     " afternoon, ", ;
                     " evening, "))
   set hours to (hours_stat)

   #DEFINE WHEIGHT   4
   #DEFINE WLENGTH  40
   trow = (srows( ) - WHEIGHT) / 2
   brow = trow + WHEIGHT -1
   lcol = (scols( )-WLENGTH) / 2
   rcol = lcol + WLENGTH - 1

   define window pass_win ;
      from trow,lcol to brow,rcol ;
      none shadow color scheme 10

   do while .t.
      activate window pass_win noshow
      clear
```

```
      @ 1,1 say "Good" + mornafteve + Users.Fullname
      @ 2,1 say "Please enter your password: "
      show window pass_win

      * get the user's password and store it in mpass
      * if the user presses Esc, getkeys( ) will return
      * the null string
      mpass = getkeys(len(Users.Password))
      if "" = mpass
        * the user pressed Escape
        EXIT
      endif

      * user entered a password
      * hash the entered password
      mpass = hashit(mpass, len(Users.Password))

      * now compare the hashed password to the entry
      * stored in the Password field of the current record
      if mpass == Users.Password
         * you've got a valid password
         EXIT
      else
         ?? chr(7)   && ring the bell
         wait window "Incorrect password entered, " + ;
            "please start over." nowait
      endif
   enddo

   release window pass_win
return ("" = mpass)

FUNCTION getkeys
   *
   * get user's password, using the inkey( ) function
   *
   parameters max_len
   private j, mpass

   j = 0
   mpass = ""
   do while len(mpass) <= max_len
      j = inkey(0)           && get a keystroke
```

continues

```
      do case
      case      j > 0 ;
           and (isalpha(chr(j)) or isdigit(chr(j)));
           and len(mpass) < max_len
         * user typed a valid password character ;
         * acknowledge acceptance by displaying an asterisk
         mpass = mpass + lower(chr(j))
         @ $,$ say "*"

      case j = ik_esc or j = ik_enter
         * either you're done or the user wants to cancel
         * the password entry
         EXIT

      case j = ik_bksp
         * user wants to edit the entry ;
         * simulate the backspace key
         do case
         case len(mpass) = 1
            mpass = ""
            @ $,$-1 say " "
            @ $,$-1 say ""

         case len(mpass) > 1
            mpass = substr(mpass,1,len(mpass)-1)
            @ $,$-1 say " "
            @ $,$-1 say ""
         endcase

      otherwise
         ?? chr(7)          && ring the bell
         wait window "A valid password may contain " + ;
            "only letters and digits." nowait

      endcase
   enddo

   if j = ik_esc
      * zap the password entry
      mpass = ""
   endif
return mpass

FUNCTION hashit
   *
   * calculate hash code for password entered by user
   *
```

```
   parameters hashstr, str_len
   private j, hashcode

   hashcode = 0
   for j=1 to len(hashstr)
      hashcode = hashcode + asc(substr(hashstr,j,1)) * j
   endfor

   hashstr = str(hashcode * 11, str_len, 0)
return hashstr
```

If you took the time to look up the $ command in the *Language Reference* manual, you might be confused by how the command is used in this example. The $ command has a dual nature. $ can be used to mean "is a substring of" (as in IF 'A' $ vowels). The $ command also can be used, as in the preceding routine, as a shorthand notation for the ROW( ) or COL( ) functions. FoxPro determines the correct usage for the command, based on the context in which you use the command.

Notice that the HASHIT( ) function creates a string that can be the result of more than one possible password entry. The user's actual password, therefore, can in no way be reconstructed from the hashed password. If an unauthorized person uses either FoxPro or a DOS text viewer to view the contents of the Users table, the password that appears in the table bears no relationship to the user's actual password, rendering the latter virtually indecipherable.

This means, however, that if the user forgets the password, a new password must be assigned by someone who has supervisor or administrator status. A complete user-authorization system, therefore, must contain procedures that are not contained in this sample program.

Using ON KEY LABEL To Remap the Keyboard

One of the most important enhancements to the Xbase language that FoxPro 1.0 provides is the BROWSE command. BROWSE, which rarely was used in a program before, has become an important tool in every FoxPro programmer's tool kit, attaining near-equal status with the READ command.

The ON KEY LABEL command immediately became an indispensable supporting player to both BROWSE and READ. ON KEY LABEL enables the user to perform ancillary tasks without exiting the Browse window. Of equal importance, the Browse window reflected any changes made to the table after program control returned to the Browse window.

With the release of FoxPro 2.0, ON KEY LABEL lost some of its former luster. You can now customize the FoxPro system menu to include options that call the same subroutines an ON KEY LABEL can call, also without exiting the Browse. You can even assign the same control key shortcut to the menu option.

ON KEY LABEL still serves some very useful purposes, however. The command gives you control over the function of the Enter key, for example. (If you want the user of your application to select one or more items from a list, using the Enter key as a marking device seems very natural.)

Suppose that your application revolves around a personnel table containing such items as each person's first name, last name, and Social Security number. The user first selects a desired record from the table and then enters all available information about that person before going on to the next record.

Using BROWSE to display the personnel table to find the record for this person seems like a natural choice. You can instruct the user to move the highlight bar to the person's name and then press Enter to confirm the selection.

To use the ON KEY LABEL method of selection, you first must remap the Enter key to function the same as the Esc key. The following code remaps the Enter key accordingly:

```
select People
set order to tag Lastname
wait window "Highlight the desired name, " + ;
   "then press Enter" nowait
on key label enter keyboard chr(ik_esc)
browse ;
   fields Firstname :h="First Name", ;
          Lastname  :h="Last Name", ;
          Ssno      :h="Soc. Sec. #" ;
   nomodify noappend nodelete
on key label enter
```

After the user presses Enter, the command KEYBOARD CHR(ik_esc) is executed. (Remember that ik_esc is a memory variable you created earlier in this chapter to hold the number returned by pressing the Esc key.)

The KEYBOARD command stuffs the specified character into the keyboard buffer, as though the user had entered the character from the keyboard. After the user presses Enter, the Browse window responds to the presence of the Esc key in the keyboard buffer, and the Browse is exited, leaving the record pointer on the user's selection.

The following example also uses ON KEY LABEL to remap the Enter key. This time, however, pressing Enter does not exit the Browse window. The F7 function key is used for that purpose.

After the user presses Enter, a UDF named MARKREC is executed. MARKREC replaces the value of a logical field (Selected) in the current record with the opposite of its current state—True or False. The Enter key, therefore, becomes a toggle.

The table used is a Reports table, which has the following structure:

```
Structure for table: REPORTS.DBF
Field  Field Name  Type       Width
    1  CODE        Character      6
    2  DESCRIP     Character     50
    3  REPT_FORM   Memo          10
    4  REPT_MEMO   Memo          10
    5  SELECTED    Logical        1
**Total**                        78

Index tag:   DESCRIP      Key:  DESCRIP
```

All the reports used in this application are stored in this table. Each record represents a different report. The report form table (.FRX) is stored in the Rept_form Memo field, and the report form's memo file (.FRT) is stored in another Memo field, Rept_memo.

Rather than printing reports one at a time, the user selects as many reports as needed. Then, one by one, you copy the report's table and memo file to the disk and print the report. You can tell which reports have been selected by evaluating the current contents of the Selected field. To evaluate the Selected field's current contents, use the following code:

```
PROCEDURE print_rpts
   *
   * let the user select which reports to print;
   * for each selected report, copy the report table
   * and memo file to disk from the record's memo fields
   *
   private temp_form, temp_memo, conditions

   * get some temporary file names
   temp_form = sys(3) + ".$$$"
   temp_memo = sys(3) + ".$$$"
```

continues

```
* list the reports alphabetically by description
select reports
set order to tag Descrip

* tell the user what to do
wait window "Use the Enter key to select reports, " + ;
   "press F7 when done" nowait

* save the current settings of any function
* keys or ON KEY LABELs, and remap the Enter
* and F7 keys
push key clear
on key label enter do markrec
on key label F7 keyboard chr(ik_ctlend)

* display the available reports
define window rpt_list ;
   at 5,10 size 15,60
browse window rpt_list ;
   fields Check=iif(Selected, chr(251), " "), ;
          Descrip :h= "Report Description" ;
   freeze Descrip ;
   nomodify noappend nodelete

* restore default key actions
pop key

* print the selected reports
select Reports
scan for Selected
   * copy the report files to disk
   copy memo Rept_form to (temp_form)
   copy memo Rept_memo to (temp_memo)

   * build a string containing the user's report choices
   * e.g. "for State = 'CA'"
   * NOTE: function get_conds( ) is not presented as
   *       part of this example
   conditions = get_conds(code)

   * print the report, using macro substitution
   * to expand the conditions variable into the
   * string of desired report options
   report form (temp_form) &conditions
endscan
```

```
   release window rpt_list
   * erase any temporary files
   if file(temp_form)
      erase (temp_form)
      erase (temp_memo)
   endif
return

PROCEDURE markrec
   *
   * mark or unmark a record by replacing the "selected"
   * logical field with the opposite of its current value
   *

   * disable the Enter key until we're done here
   on key label enter *

   * "flip" the flag
   replace selected with !selected

   * move to the next record, or to the first
   * if we are on the last
   skip
   if eof( )
      go top
   endif

   * reset the Enter key to call markrec
   on key label enter do markrec
return
```

Using a Data Compression Technique

Through its Rushmore technology, FoxPro can handle huge databases. This capability makes downsizing mainframe applications to PCs feasible. Attempting to store on a PC's hard disk the tremendous amount of data that is typically generated by a mainframe application can, however, be a problem. One way to overcome the problem is to use a *data compression* technique.

A data compression algorithm encodes information in such a way that the information can be stored in fewer bytes than would otherwise be required. A related decompression algorithm is then used to translate and restore the data to its original form. This section explores one such data compression technique in depth.

Suppose that Omnipresent Widgets manufactures its own line of shoes. The company makes shoes in eight different sizes (5 through 12) and three different widths (narrow, medium, and wide). Whenever the company receives an order from a customer, its sales department needs to know whether each style on the order is made in the sizes and widths that the customer has requested.

To determine this, company personnel must store the combinations of sizes and widths for each style and then compare the ordered size and width combinations to those on the stored list.

If you designed a paper form to hold this information for each style of the company's shoes, you probably would start by setting up a grid that has the sizes running across the top of the page and the widths down the left side. For each combination of size and width, you put a check mark in the box if the style is available and leave the box blank if the style is not available. This method works for paper forms, but what if you must store this information in a database table?

The most apparent method is to create a table to hold a separate record for each combination of style, size, and width. You can use a structure for your table such as that of the following example:

```
Structure for table: STYLES.DBF
Field  Field Name  Type       Width
    1  STYLE_CODE  Character      6
    2  WIDTH       Character      1
    3  SIZE        Character      2
**Total**                        10
```

Because each record requires 10 bytes, and a maximum of 24 combinations of three widths and eight sizes is possible, each style's available size and width information can require as much as 240 bytes of disk space to store.

You might decide to store the data the same way the information appears on the paper form. The sizes become Logical fields in the table ("available" or "not available"), and the width remains a Character field. You require a record for each of the three widths for each style, so your table now has the following structure:

```
Structure for table: STYLES.DBF
Field  Field Name  Type       Width
    1  STYLE_CODE  Character      6
    2  WIDTH       Character      1
    3  S5          Logical        1
    4  S6          Logical        1
```

```
      5  S7          Logical        1
      6  S8          Logical        1
      7  S9          Logical        1
      8  S10         Logical        1
      9  S11         Logical        1
     10  S12         Logical        1
**Total**                          16
```

Although each record now requires 16 bytes, each style has only three records (one for each width), reducing your storage requirements to only 48 bytes per style. This reduction represents a significant saving of storage space—but you can do even better.

Look at the paper form again. If you erase the vertical lines separating the different size columns, your table seems to need only two fields in addition to the style code. You can store the size information in an eight-character string, with each position in the string representing a different size. If the style of shoe is available in a particular size and width, you indicate this availability by storing an X in the appropriate position in a Sizes Character field. Your table now assumes the following structure:

```
Structure for table: STYLES.DBF
Field  Field Name  Type       Width
    1  STYLE_CODE  Character      6
    2  WIDTH       Character      1
    3  SIZES       Character      8
**Total**                        16
```

This seems to be a good approach but still requires the same 16 bytes of storage space as the previous version of the table.

The only remaining way to significantly reduce the space requirement further is to find a way to store more than one piece of information in a single byte. In this case, you want to store all the available widths for each size of shoe in a single character position of a Size_grid field, thereby reducing the number of records for each style from three to one.

You can accomplish this reduction by replacing the X marker in the Sizes character field with a decimal number between 0 and 7. Each of these numbers represents the decimal number equivalent of a three-character binary string—a string composed only of the binary digits 0 and 1. (The binary string 101, for example, equals the decimal number 5.)

The key to employing this technique is realizing that the information to be stored is binary. That is, the information can have only two possible values—True or False, On or Off, or (as computers reason) 1 or 0. Just as each position in the Size_grid field represents a different size, so too can each position in the binary string represent a different width. The following chart illustrates this concept.

```
Sizes        5      6    7      8     9      10     11      12
Decimal#     0      0    3      0     5      0      7       0
             |           |            |             |
Binary      000         011          101           111
Widths      NMW         NMW          NMW           NMW
```

From this chart, you can see that this style of shoe is available in size 7 (medium and wide), size 9 (narrow and wide), and size 11 (all three widths).

The final version of the Styles table has the following structure:

```
Structure for table:      STYLES.DBF
Field  Field Name  Type        Width
    1  STYLE_CODE  Character       6
    2  SIZE_GRID   Character       8
**Total**                         15
```

No matter how many size and width combinations are available for each style, you can now store the information in only 15 bytes, a 94-percent improvement over the original 240 bytes of required storage.

This method, however, works only for up to three possible shoe widths. If Omnipresent Widgets develops an extra-wide shoe, the approach no longer works, because the decimal equivalent of the binary string 1111 (one binary digit per width) is 15, which requires two bytes (or character positions) instead of one.

The following program, GETSIZES, solves this problem by storing the decimal number as its related ASCII character. If you activate FoxPro's ASCII chart from the System menu pad, you see that the ASCII equivalent of 14 is a musical note (♫). If size five of a style is available in narrow, medium, and wide, but not in extra wide, the binary string is 1110; the decimal number is 14; and the Size_grid field for this style contains the ♫ character in the first position.

The conversions from decimal numbers to binary digits and back is handled by the NUM2BIN and BIN2NUM procedures, respectively. The conversion between decimal numbers and their ASCII equivalents is performed by using FoxPro's CHR( ) and ASC( ) functions.

In addition to the Styles table, the program uses a Widths table, which holds the available width codes. The Widths table has the following structure:

```
Structure for table:      WIDTHS.DBF
Field   Field Name   Type        Width
    1   WIDTH_CODE   Character       1
    2   DESCRIP      Character      10
** Total **                         12
```

GETSIZES requires some sample data to run. Create the Styles table and add a record to the table, filling in just the Style_code field. GETSIZES stores the proper information in the Size_grid field. Then create the Widths table and add three records using M, N, and W (Medium, Narrow, and Wide) as the Width_code entries. Entries in the Descrip field are optional. (These tables, complete with sample data, are included on the source disk that accompanies this book.)

```
* GETSIZES.PRG
* This program enables the user to enter the size / width
* combinations for the current style in a grid-like
* fashion, with sizes shown across the top and widths
* down the left side.
*
private the_grid, was_chgd, kp

* define constants
#DEFINE   IK_CTLEND         23
#DEFINE   IK_TAB             9
#DEFINE   MARK_CHAR   chr(251)

do set_env                 && save and set the environment
do open_data               && open the tables
the_grid = make_grid( )    && create the sizes grid;
                           && make_grid returns the alias
                           && of the grid table
do make_wins               && create the windows

do while .t.
   * fill the grid for the current style
   wait window "Filling the grid..." nowait
   = fillgrid(the_grid, Styles.Size_grid)
   select (the_grid)
   go top
```

continues

```
    activate window msg_win
    @ 0,0 say padc("Enter:Toggle Mark    F7:Done",wcols( ))

    * set a flag which will be set to True in markgrid
    * if the user made a change
    was_chgd = .f.

    * map Enter key and F7 function key
    on key label enter do markgrid
    on key label F7 keyboard chr(IK_CTLEND)

    * get size information
    select (the_grid)
    activate window size_win
    browse in window size_win ;
       nomodify noappend nodelete noclear

    * reset keys
    on key label enter
    on key label F7 *

    * save the key used to exit the Browse
    kp = lastkey( )

    * if any changes made, let user save settings
    if was_chgd
       wait window "Save these settings? (Y/n)" to choice
       if upper(choice) = "Y"
          do savegrid with the_grid
       endif
    endif

    * did the user press F7 to exit the Browse?
    if kp = IK_CTLEND
       wait window "Are you done? (Y/n)" to choice
       if upper(choice) = "Y"
          EXIT
       endif
    endif
enddo (while .t.)

do cleanup
return

PROCEDURE set_env
    *
    * save the current environment and set it
```

```
   * the way we want it
   *
   public talk_set
   if set("talk") = "ON"
      set talk off
      talk_set = "ON"   else
      talk_set = "OFF"
   endif
return

PROCEDURE open_data
   *
   * open the tables
   *
   if !used('Styles')
      use Styles again in 0 alias Styles
   endif
   if !used('Widths')
      use Widths again in 0 alias Widths
   endif
   select Styles
return

FUNCTION make_grid
   *
   * create a temporary table to hold the user's size and
   * width selections for a particular style
   *
   private j, k, struc_arr

   wait window "Creating size grid.  Just a moment..." nowait

   * create constants to hold the smallest and
   * largest sizes
   #DEFINE SMALLEST   5
   #DEFINE LARGEST   12

   * create an array to hold the structure of the
   * temporary grid table, and fill the array with
   * the table structure information
   dimension struc_arr[largest - smallest + 2, 4]

   * we need a field to hold the width code
   struc_arr[1,1] = "Width"
   struc_arr[1,2] = "C"
   struc_arr[1,3] =  2
   struc_arr[1,4] =  0
```

continues

```
    * we need a field for each size
    k = 2
    for j=SMALLEST to LARGEST
       struc_arr[k,1] = "S" + ltrim(str(j))
       struc_arr[k,2] = "C"
       struc_arr[k,3] =  1
       struc_arr[k,4] =  0
       k = k + 1
    endfor

    * create the grid table in fname
    fname = sys(2015)
    create cursor (fname) from array struc_arr

    * create a record in the grid table for
    * each available width
    select Widths
    scan
       insert into (fname) ;
          (Width) ;
          values(Widths.Width_code)
    endscan

    wait clear
return fname

PROCEDURE make_wins
    *
    * create the windows for the display
    *

    * create a window in which to display the grid
    wheight = min(reccount( )+4, srows( )-5)
    wlength = len("Width") + (fcount(the_grid)-1)*4 + 8
    define window size_win ;
       at 0,0 size wheight, wlength ;
       title "Available Sizes for " + trim(Styles.Style_code) ;
       none shadow color scheme 10
    move window size_win center

    * create a window in which to display a message
    if _WINDOWS and set("status bar") = "ON"
       public bar_on
       bar_on = .t.
       set status bar off
    endif
```

```
   msgline = set("message")
   define window msg_win ;
      from msgline,0 to msgline,scols()-1 ;
      none color w+/r

return

FUNCTION fillgrid
   *
   * fill the grid table with a check mark for each
   * currently selected size and width for the current style
   *
   * return the total number of available sizes and
   * widths for this style in fill_num
   *
   parameters gridfile, mgrid
   private n, j, k, nfields, nwidths, fill_num, ;
           b_str, grid_name, asize

   select (gridfile)
   nfields = fcount()
   nwidths = reccount("Widths")
   fill_num = 0

   for j=1 to nwidths         && for each width
      go j
      scatter to asize
      for k=2 to nfields      && for each size
         n = asc(substr(mgrid,k-1,1))
         b_str = num2bin(n,nwidths)
         asize[k] = iif(substr(b_str,j,1)="1", ;
                        MARK_CHAR, ;
                        " ")
         fill_num = iif(asize[k] = MARK_CHAR, ;
                        fill_num+1, ;
                        fill_num)
      endfor
      gather from asize
   endfor
return fill_num

PROCEDURE savegrid
   *
   * save the current grid table by converting the
   * check marks and spaces back into ASCII characters,
   * then saving the resulting string in the size_grid
   * field for the current style
   *
```

continues

```
   parameters gridfile, savefile
   private mgrid, nfields, nwidths, b_str, j, k

   select (gridfile)
   mgrid = ""
   nfields = fcount( )
   nwidths = reccount("Widths")

   * construct the new grid in mgrid
   for k=2 to nfields         && for each size
      b_str = ""

      * construct the binary string in b_str
      for j=1 to nwidths      && for each width
         go j
         scatter to asize
         b_str = b_str + iif(asize[k] = MARK_CHAR, ;
                             "1", ;
                             "0")
      endfor

      n = bin2num(b_str)
      mgrid = mgrid + chr(n)
   endfor

   select Styles
   replace Size_grid with mgrid
return

FUNCTION num2bin
   *
   * convert a decimal number between 0 and 255 (n) into
   * a string representation of its binary equivalent
   *
   * slen holds the number of "significant characters"
   * in the binary string
   *
   * e.g. 7 = "111"
   *
   parameters n, slen
   private s, x

   s = ""
   for x=7 to 0 step -1
      if n / 2^x >= 1
          s = s + "1"
          n = n - 2^x
```

```
        else
            s = s + "0"
        endif
    endfor
return right(s,slen)

FUNCTION bin2num
    *
    * convert the string representation of a decimal number
    * (b_str) between 0 and 255 back into its decimal equivalent
    *
    * e.g. "111" = 7
    *
    parameters b_str
    private n, x, j

    n = 0
    x = 1

    for j=len(b_str) to 1 step -1
       n = n + val(substr(b_str,j,1)) * x
       x = x * 2
    endfor
return n

FUNCTION markgrid
    *
    * toggle the state of the current field in
    * the temp grid table
    *
    private curfield

    * turn off the Enter key until we're done here
    on key label enter *

    if !(upper(field(1)) == upper(varread( )))
       * if we're not in the Width field,
       * toggle the check mark
       curfield = varread( )
       replace &curfield with iif(&curfield = MARK_CHAR, ;
                                  " ", ;
                                  MARK_CHAR)

       was_chgd = .t.
    endif
```

continues

```
   * stuff the Tab character into the keyboard buffer
   * to move the cursor to the next field in the Browse;
   * the key won't be "read" by FoxPro until the Browse
   * is once again active
   keyboard chr(IK_TAB)

   * remap the Enter key once again
   on key label enter do markgrid
return .t.

PROCEDURE cleanup
   * release the windows and erase the "cursor" table by
   * closing it
   release windows size_win, msg_win
   use in (the_grid)

   * close the other tables
   use in Styles
   use in Widths

   * if we're in Windows, did we set the status bar off?
   if type('bar_on') = "L" and bar_on
      set status bar on
   endif

   * restore previous environment settings
   if talk_set = "ON"
      set talk on
   endif
return
```

The GETSIZES program demonstrates that the FoxPro language provides you with a level of power and flexibility usually associated with "real" programming languages such as C. If you consider the additional capabilities of FoxPro's low-level file functions and its capability to link third-party utilities through the Application Programmer's Interface (API), you find very little that you cannot do in FoxPro.

Creating Templates Using FoxPro's Text-Merge Features

Template languages and program generators are nothing new. They have been around for a long time, and they're all limited in some fashion. You must do things their way, and there is always something you want to do that they don't provide for.

Microsoft, however, has given the FoxPro programmer complete control over program code generation by using the one language that all FoxPro programmers know—the FoxPro language!

Understanding FoxPro's Text-Merge Commands

FoxPro is not only a programming language, but also its own template language. If you can write a program in FoxPro using a text editor, you also can create a program template.

FoxPro's template-generation system consists of three commands and two system variables. The syntax of the three commands is as follows:

```
\ <text_line ¦ \\ <text_line>

SET TEXTMERGE [ON ¦ OFF]
              [TO [<file>] [ADDITIVE]]
              [WINDOW <window_name>]
              [SHOW ¦ NOSHOW]

SET TEXTMERGE DELIMITERS
   [TO <expC1> [, <expC2>]]
```

The \ and \\ commands tell FoxPro to output the text that follows these commands. These commands are similar to the ? and ?? commands you have already seen. \, like ?, outputs a carriage return and a line feed before the text. \\, like ??, appends its output to the current line.

SET TEXTMERGE controls whether FoxPro evaluates text enclosed in the text-merge delimiters, or treats any existing delimiters as simple text. This command also controls the target (screen, file, or user-defined window) of the text.

The SHOW and NOSHOW keywords of the SET TEXTMERGE command determine whether the output is also echoed to the screen when you direct the text-merge command's output to a file. You can combine SET TEXTMERGE clauses and keywords into a single command, as in the following:

```
SET TEXTMERGE ON TO mytext.txt NOSHOW ADDITIVE
```

When TEXTMERGE is SET ON, FoxPro searches the text line for delimiters which are defined by the SET DELIMITERS TO command. By default, these delimiters are the left and right double angle brackets, << and >>. Any text contained between the delimiters is evaluated and substituted for the text.

For example, if you previously defined a variable as

```
myvar = "This is the textmerge text stored in variable myvar"
```

FoxPro substitutes this text for myvar whenever TEXTMERGE is SET ON, and <<myvar>> appears in a line following the \ or \\ commands, as in the following example:

```
SET TEXTMERGE ON
myvar = "This is the textmerge text stored in variable myvar"
\myvar = <<myvar>>
```

You can use the SET DELIMITERS TO command to instruct FoxPro to search for delimiters other than the default double angle brackets. For example, you can tell FoxPro to search for double asterisks with the command:

```
SET TEXTMERGE DELIMITERS TO "**", "**"
```

Using the double asterisks as text-merge delimiters, you now rewrite the above code as follows:

```
SET TEXTMERGE ON
myvar = "This is the text merge text stored in variable myvar"
\myvar = **myvar**
```

FoxPro also uses two system variables in conjunction with the text merge commands. These system variables are _TEXT and _PRETEXT.

_TEXT stores the file handle of a file to which TEXTMERGE is SET. Just as the low-level file functions FOPEN( ) and FCREATE( ) return a number representing the handle of the opened file, so too does SET TEXTMERGE <file> store the file's handle in _TEXT. If you want to output text-merge text to more than one file in the same program, you can store the handle of each file you open with SET TEXTMERGE TO <file> into separate variables and then use these file handles to direct your output, as in the following example:

```
SET TEXTMERGE TO file1.txt
file1_handle = _TEXT
_TEXT = -1     && keep the file open while we open another file
SET TEXTMERGE TO file2.txt
file2_handle = _TEXT
_TEXT = file1_handle   && direct textmerge output to file1
```

```
\\"This is some text for file1"
_TEXT = file2_handle
\\"This is some text for file2"
SET TEXTMERGE TO
CLOSE ALL
MODIFY FILE file1.txt nowait
MODIFY FILE file2.txt
```

_PRETEXT stores a character expression that you want to precede any output of the \ or \\ commands. _PRETEXT is commonly used for indenting your text-merge output, using either a specified number of spaces or Tab characters. You can indent some text beneath a preceding paragraph, for example, by using a text-merge code such as the following:

```
\This is the main paragraph
_PRETEXT = CHR(9)    && CHR(9) is the Tab character
\This is the indented text
_PRETEXT = ""        && reset _PRETEXT to output nothing
```

FoxPro uses templates to create screen and menu programs from the tables in which it stores the choices you make in the Screen Builder and Menu Builder. GENSCRN creates screen programs, and GENMENU creates menu programs. You can learn more about the kinds of logical decisions you must make in deciding how best to construct a template by reviewing these templates. The templates are located in the main FoxPro directory.

After you feel comfortable using the text-merge commands, you can view the GENMENU.PRG and GENSCRN.PRG templates in a text-editing window to see how these programs create "table-driven" programs by writing lines of code from the information in each record of the .MNX or .SCX table. If either template does not fit your needs, you need only to edit that template until it does fit. (If you save your edited versions to new names, tell FoxPro to use your programs to generate menus and screens by assigning the new file names to the system variables _GENMENU and _GENSCRN.)

Using Text Merge To Create a Program

In the GETSIZES program shown in the preceding section of this chapter, the size grid is displayed in a Browse window. The column headings in the Browse are the names of the fields in the size grid table. These field names are S1 through S8, which are not very informative. The user must count the columns to determine which column relates to a particular size.

You can use the FIELDS clause of the BROWSE command to specify your own custom column headings for the sizes, but there is one other problem to consider. In addition to selling in the United States, Omnipresent Widgets sells its shoes in Europe through its Italian subsidiary, and European sizes are different from U.S. sizes. The U.S. size 7, for example, is a size 37 in Europe. When the Italian subsidiary runs the application, you want the application to display European sizes.

Rather than maintain two versions of the application, you can use FoxPro's text-merge commands to solve the problem. First you write a program that builds your application, using the BUILD APP command. Immediately before the BUILD APP command, you run a program (BLD_BROW.PRG) that uses text merge to create a program that contains the proper BROWSE command for this version (U.S. or European) of the application. The program that builds the application contains the following commands:

```
* BUILDAPP.PRG
parameters the_version

do bld_brow with the_version
build app shoe_app from shoe_app
if file('shoe_app.err')
   modify file shoe_app.err
endif
return
```

By default, BLD_BROW uses U.S. sizes. To override the default setting, you pass a parameter, a character string containing the name of the version you want to create, to BUILDAPP. BUILDAPP passes this string on to the BLD_BROW program, which contains the text-merge commands to create the proper BROWSE command. The code for BLD_BROW is as follows:

```
*
* BLD_BROW.PRG
*
* This program uses FoxPro's text merge commands to
* create a program that is then built into an
* application.  BLD_BROW uses the mtype parameter to
* determine if the application uses U.S. or European
* shoe sizes, and outputs a BROWSE command containing
* the appropriate column headings for the sizes.
*
* Example calls: DO BLD_BROW   && use U.S. sizes
*                DO BLD_BROW WITH "EUROPEAN"
*
```

```
parameters mtype
private fld_list

if type('mtype') = "L" or upper(mtype) = "U.S."
   * use U.S. sizes by default or if passed in mtype
   fld_list = "S1 :h=' 5', S2 :h=' 6', S3 :h=' 7', " + ;
      "S4 :h=' 8', S5 :h=' 9', S6 :h='10', S7 :h='11', S8 :h='12'"
else
   * use European sizes
   fld_list = "S1 :h='35', S2 :h='36', S3 :h='37', " + ;
      "S4 :h='38', S5 :h='39', S6 :h='41', S7 :h='42', S8 :h='43'"
endif

* Browprog.prg is included in the application's project
* file, and is called by GETSIZES to display the size
* grid in a Browse window
set textmerge on to browprog.prg noshow
set textmerge delimiters to

*
* Create the Browprog program
*

* Use \\ to avoid skipping a line in the text merge file
\\browse in window size_win ;

* indent the following code by one tab stop
_pretext = chr(9)

* Output the FIELDS clause, using the field list
* constructed above
\fields <<fld_list>> ;

* Add the remaining clauses of the BROWSE command
\nomodify noappend nodelete

* Reset _pretext for the next time
_pretext = ""

* Turn off text merging
set textmerge to
set textmerge off

return
```

BLD_BROW creates a program, BROWPROG.PRG, which GETSIZES calls to display the Browse of the size grid. To accomplish this, you replace this code

```
browse in window size_win ;
   nomodify noappend nodelete noclear
```

in the version of GETSIZES shown above, with the following command:

```
do browprog
```

Whenever you want to build your application, you DO BUILDAPP to create the U.S. version, or DO BUILDAPP WITH "EUROPEAN" to create the European version.

Although text-merge commands are most often used in mail merge applications, these commands also can help you solve a variety of programming problems.

Documenting Your Program as You Write

FoxPro includes a powerful program documentation utility, FoxDoc, that provides you with formatted source code listings, variable cross-reference reports, tree diagrams, and more. FoxDoc is the subject of the "Documenting Applications with FoxDoc" section in Chapter 20, "Enhancing the Applications You Program."

FoxDoc does not, however, document the logic of your program for you. That responsibility remains squarely on the shoulders of the developer.

This book has discussed the need to make your programs understandable and maintainable. You have learned some techniques for achieving this goal, such as using variable names and procedure names that describe what information these names store or what function they are intended to perform.

Comments also can provide information that make your program more understandable. However, there is no generally accepted method for commenting program code; you must develop your own style. Consider, therefore, the following thoughts on commenting:

- Comment your programs as you write them. You will never understand the logic of a procedure or block of statements better than you do as you are actually writing the code.
- Don't use comments to compensate for an obtuse code. If five lines of code require you to write 10 lines of comments to explain the code, something probably is wrong with your code.
- Commenting your program is a good way to check your understanding of the problem-solving process. If you cannot write a short comment that describes the process, you probably do not understand the process sufficiently. Check your code for flaws in logic or design.

Summary

This chapter has discussed the different types of memory variables and arrays and provided you with some guidelines for using them. You have learned the merits of using abstraction to avoid hard-coding values into your programs.

The programming examples presented have introduced you to some new commands, functions, and techniques. These examples should give you some perspective on the broad range of database management problems that you can solve by using the FoxPro language.

Finally, the chapter discussed using FoxPro's text-merge feature as a template generator. The simplicity of this tool, however, belies its power. By using the text-merge feature, you can create programs that conform to the requirements of almost any application.

The next chapter discusses how to use the FoxPro Help system as an adjunct to your applications, how to use FoxPro's Debug and Trace features to help you debug your programs, and how to use FoxDoc, a powerful program-documentation tool.

20

CHAPTER

Enhancing the Applications You Program

In the preceding chapters, you learned about the structure of a FoxPro program, the basics of program control and execution, and quite a few commands, functions, and techniques for developing applications. This chapter focuses on additional tools that smooth the process of designing and maintaining an application.

With FoxPro's integrated Help system, you can provide user support and document the requirements and intended usage of different elements in applications that you create.

With FoxPro's error-handling system, you can sleuth your way to the cause of the inevitable bugs that occur as you write the programs. You also can help users deal with any "infelicities" that remain after the application is in use. *Infelicities* is the Microsoft Fox team's term for the unintended consequences of programming; some people refer to them as *anomalies* or *bugs*. (The consequences of infelicities that remain in a program are known, less than affectionately, as *crashes* and *bombs*.) Because even the best-tested application is bound to have one or two infelicities, you should be prepared with procedures to handle them.

Finally, with FoxDoc and SnipFmt providing permanent and properly formatted documentation of systems, you have a superb means of maintaining your applications—and investigating someone else's—should you need to make modifications.

Adding FoxPro-Style Help Systems

The perfect user interface is self-explanatory. Every task, every control, and every object on-screen is effortlessly interpreted with no error by all who use the program. Because the perfect interface is an unreachable goal, however, most developers add *on-line help*, or explanatory text the user can call on, in the program.

An on-line Help system can be simple and, at the same time, provide an overview (macro-level) and a context-sensitive (micro-level) help. You can write a text file that explains the whole system. A menu option, complete with hot key, opens this file in a scrolling window that the user can read. You can use the MESSAGE clause for GETs, available through the Screen Builder for each kind of GET object. A one-line explanation of each item appears on-screen as the cursor moves through a data-entry screen. (If you used previous versions of FoxPro and FoxBase, you will appreciate FoxPro 2.x's capability of directing this message line to the appropriate window.)

FoxPro provides far more flexible and sophisticated options, however. You are already familiar with FoxPro's extensive on-line Help system. This section teaches you how to produce similar Help systems for applications that you create.

As you read this chapter's discussion of the ways in which you can design custom Help systems, remember that these systems are not intended as a *substitute* for, but rather as a *supplement* to, thoughtful interface design. Never assume that everyone is going to sit down and read all the Help entries (much less a printed manual) before beginning to use a program. Try to make the Help system as inviting and as accessible as possible so that users will access this feature often, thoroughly, and successfully.

Building and Organizing the Help File

In the View window's On/Off panel or in the Command window, SET HELP OFF. From the main program directory, open FoxPro's Help file, FOXHELP.DBF as a table. (Type `USE ?` in the Command window as a shorthand way of getting to the Open File dialog and then pick the file by name, or type `USE SET("HELP",1)` in the Command window.) BROWSE to look at the file structure and arrangement.

TIP

With HELP ON, you can actually open FoxHelp by typing the command USE FOXHELP AGAIN. There is no advantage to this technique when you want to *edit* the Help file; the copy of the file that you open with the USE AGAIN command is readonly. Develop the habit of using the SET HELP OFF command, or just SET HELP TO a different file before you begin working on a new help system.

You can write a quick program to perform this process. Save the state of HELP and the name of the current Help file. Then SET HELP OFF, USE the file for editing, and restore HELP to its original state by using the techniques you learned in Chapter 18, "Understanding Program Structure." This option is a good tool to add to the personally tailored version of SYSMENU you use during program development.

Structuring the Help File

As figure 20.1 shows, the FoxHelp table consists of three fields:

- *Topic*, a Character field that describes the contents of each Help entry and is used in the Help Index. A Character field of this nature is *required* as the first field in any Help file you create that uses FoxPro's built-in Help system. Although you can give the topic any name or length, this book refers to this name as *the Topic field* in the following discussion.
- *Details*, a Memo field that holds the actual text for each Help entry. This kind of Memo field also must be the second field in the Help files and is referred to as Details, but you can give the field any name you prefer.

- *Class*, a Character field that FoxPro's Help system uses to categorize and select appropriate help topics for any task you are performing. A Class field is not required, but you may create at least one field, and possibly several, that perform the same function for Help systems. You can have as many extra fields (of any type) as you need in the Help file. These fields must not precede the two required fields.

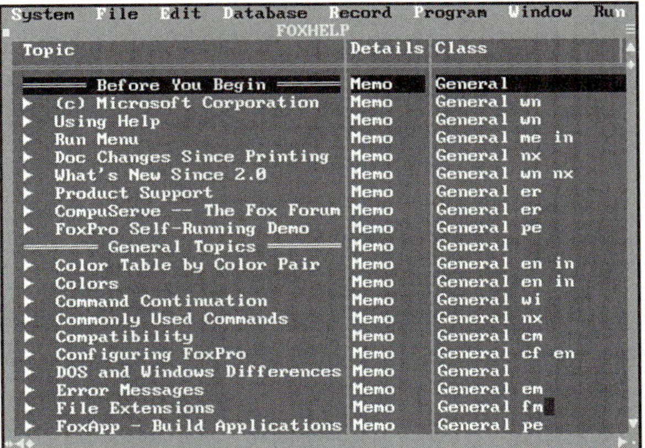

Topic	Details	Class
═══ Before You Begin ═══	Memo	General
► (c) Microsoft Corporation	Memo	General wn
► Using Help	Memo	General wn
► Run Menu	Memo	General me in
► Doc Changes Since Printing	Memo	General nx
► What's New Since 2.0	Memo	General wn nx
► Product Support	Memo	General er
► CompuServe -- The Fox Forum	Memo	General er
► FoxPro Self-Running Demo	Memo	General pe
═══ General Topics ═══	Memo	General
► Color Table by Color Pair	Memo	General en in
► Colors	Memo	General en in
► Command Continuation	Memo	General wi
► Commonly Used Commands	Memo	General nx
► Compatibility	Memo	General cm
► Configuring FoxPro	Memo	General cf en
► DOS and Windows Differences	Memo	General
► Error Messages	Memo	General em
► File Extensions	Memo	General fm
► FoxApp - Build Applications	Memo	General pe

FIG. 20.1

The structure and contents of FOXHELP.DBF, FoxPro's internal Help file.

A Help file you build—with the two required fields and with all other fields you want—can be *assigned* to access FoxPro's built-in Help system simply by using the following commands:

```
SET HELP ON
SET HELP TO <your filename>
```

Thereafter, the *help* key strokes (Alt+F1, F1, and Alt+click), as well as the System pad Help... option or any other menu option which was assigned the bar number _MST_HELP, accesses *your* file rather than FoxHelp until you reissue the SET HELP TO FoxHelp command.

Arranging and Ordering Help FileTopics

The topics in FoxHelp are carefully arranged, and yours should be too, so that the Help Index is useful. If you check the View window, you notice that FoxHelp doesn't have a structural index. The Help file topics, or actually the records, are always shown in the natural order of the table whether you are using the Help Index or paging through Topics with `Next` and `Previous` buttons. FoxHelp uses the graphics characters ► (Alt+16) and ■ (Alt+254) to segregate some topics at the beginning and end of the list and arranges the topics in between alphabetically, but the file was *sorted*, not indexed, on the Topics to maintain this order.

Creating a Help file with a structural index does not disturb the Help system in any way, however. You can work on the Help file just as you work any other table, creating a Class or Order field that (perhaps along with the Topic field) determines the exact final arrangement. INDEX ON the appropriate expression as a TAG. COPY TO a new table having SET ORDER TO the index expression you want, or SELECT INTO a new table. The new file then has the records in the order you want. The structural index on a Help file can continue to be useful even after the file is complete, as you will see shortly.

What kinds of topic arrangements are useful? Put yourself in the users' position as much as possible. When the users need help, their perspectives on the problem may be entirely different from your perspective.

Suppose that you are writing an accounting system and you choose to put all information about printer setups under a general printing topic. This topic includes checking the character set the printer is set up to use, and making sure that the graphics characters in your attractive invoice forms print properly. New users, however, may not realize that a problem that occurs when they generate invoices is a system-wide printing question. They may wonder why the topic Invoices does not explain how to get the pretty boxes to print the way they appear in the documentation samples. As they page through the `Next` and `Previous` topics surrounding Invoices—finding the topics Billing Procedures, Invoice Numbers, and so on—the users may wander further and further away from finding the right information.

Inserting See Also References

Because even a sophisticated computer user may face difficulties when exploring a new system or beginning a new task, FoxPro gives you the capability of providing alternative *paths* toward a topic—by inserting See Also references, which you have used in FoxHelp. You can place the See Also references after at least one carriage return (press Enter) at the end of the Help text in the second required field (the Memo field). Precede the list of references by the words See Also: (the colon is required) and separate the entries in the list of entries by commas. End the list with another carriage return. You can add spaces for readability and graphics characters to set off the list from the rest of the text, as FoxHelp does. FoxPro then places these entries in a popup control button in the Help window.

In the preceding example, you want any Help topic that provides information on printed output, such as Invoices, to include a See Also reference to the Printing topic.

To develop the Help file topics, the topic order, and suggestions for appropriate See Also references, ask for input from as many different people as you can. Include information that is appropriate to all the kinds of users of the system and add as many cross references as you can. Because the Help system is as easy to edit as other tables, correcting or even redesigning a Help system should never seem an insurmountable task.

When the users select a reference from the See Also popup control, FoxPro searches the list of topics for the *first* matching topic name. If the search finds a topic name that *begins* with the See Also reference, this topic is considered a match. You can see why uniquely identifying each record as a topic is important and why you must carefully arrange the topics. Not only the user's convenience, but also the internal help system's search through topics for references, is dependent on the order of the topics in the help file.

Gathering Help File Information from an Application's Screen Sets

The list of topics can and should include records for all the fields and memory variables that are GETs in the system's data-entry boxes and dialogs. Filling out all these Help entries doesn't have to be a last-minute undertaking when the system is completed. As you design the screens, you çan write Help text in the Comments snippets for each GET. Then you write a program to fill out the Help text for all the GET-level entries by accessing the screen files (.SCXs) as tables. Refer to the appendixes of the *Developer's Guide* for the structures of the project and screen files, especially the Type field in a project and the Objtype field in a screen as you read the following pseudocode for one method you can use:

```
SET HELP OFF
USE the helpfile
SELECT another workarea
USE the project file
SCAN FOR type = "S"
* look through all the
* screenfile records in the project
```

```
SELECT another workarea
USE the screen file (SCX)  ALIAS the_screen
SCAN the records in the screen file
   IF objtype = 1
      * it's the main (or header) record in
      * the screen file; this record
      * will provide screen-level help
      STORE the window name & title to memvars,
         make them all LOWER( ) case to make
         comparisons easier later
      SELECT the helpfile
      APPEND BLANK
      * add a record to the helpfile
      REPLACE the DETAILS field WITH
         the_screen.Name
      REPLACE extra fields WITH stored window
         name and title if you plan to use them
         to search for correct topics
      REPLACE TOPIC field WITH
         PROPER(screenfile name)
   ELSE
      IF BETWEEN(objtype,11,16)
      *these objtypes are the GET records
         SELECT the helpfile
         REPLACE DETAILS field from
           the_screen.Message (if used)
           + the_screen.Comments
         REPLACE extra fields using stored
           window name and title if you
           use them
         ************************************
         REPLACE an extra field WITH
            LOWER(the_screen.Name)
            * this item will be
            * what VARREAD( ) returns
         ************************************

         REPLACE Topic WITH
            PROPER(the_screen.Name field )
            * uniquely identify this GET in
            * the topic list
      ENDIF
      * ignore other records like BOXes or SAYs
   ENDIF
   * SCAN automatically SELECTs the_screen
   * and SKIPs to the next record
```

continues

```
    ENDSCAN
    USE
    * close the screenfile
    * SCAN reSELECTs project file
    * and SKIPs to next record
ENDSCAN
USE
* close the project file
```

In the preceding suggested pseudocode, you look at only the screens in the project; subsequently, you may want to do the same for other elements of the project (such as reports) to create more Help entries. You may want to BROWSE through the Help file, checking for empty Details field entries (to see if you neglected to include Comments for every GET, for example). You also may want to check and replace some Topic fields with friendlier topic titles where necessary. When you use the PROPER( ) function to standardize capitalization, for example, the BUDGET.SCX produces Topics like those in the following list:

```
Budcatcode
Query1
Saveit
```

You may want to make the Topics more readable by changing them to the following:

```
Budget Category Code
Budget Query #1
Save or Cancel Your Edit
```

These longer titles may be found in associated SAY commands, or you may choose the MESSAGE clause to create and display these titles consistently on-screen. Another possibility is to make this line the first in the Help text entry, repeating the Topic as a heading for the Details, as FoxHelp does. Using the following replacement lines, you can easily change the preceding code to more informative Topic entries, as shown in the following lines:

```
REPLACE Topic WITH the_screen.Message
```

or

```
REPLACE Topic ;
   WITH SUBSTR(the_screen.Comments,1,;
   AT(CHR(13),the_screen.Comments)-1)
   * take the portion of the comments field up to
   * the character just before the first carriage return
```

Look at the line in the pseudocoded procedure that is set off by lines of asterisks. You may remember that you used the function VARREAD( ) when you learned about the Screen Builder and data validation. VARREAD( ) returns the name of the current field, memory variable, or array element used in the current GET during a READ. Having an extra field in the Help file that matches this value is the key to providing context-sensitive help on the GET level. In the following section, you see just how you program the Help system to respond with the correct entry at the right time.

Making the Help File Accessible

FoxPro's internal use of the Help file uses some idiosyncratic methods to determine which topic to show you when you press F1. _MST_HELP, the system bar name associated with the Help system, checks for highlighted text in the front-most window first. If you have highlighted text, the Help system searches the topic list for the text. If you do not have highlighted text, the system searches topics using an internal reference to the name or title of the front-most window. If the user activates the system menu, the system uses the current bar rather than the front-most window. All the *interface* topics in FoxHelp are prefaced by the ■ (Alt+254) character. When FoxPro uses a window reference in its search for the current activity among the topics, _MST_HELP's internal procedure prefaces its search string with this character followed by a space. When FoxPro then checks See Also references from one interface topic, all the references are prefaced with ■; the result is that the interface topics can only reference other interface topics.

If you try to extend this method, as suggested by the *Developer's Guide* section "Customizing Help," you will find that this method has limited usefulness. As you may remember from working in the Screen Builder, Window referencing is always a complicated subject where BROWSEs are concerned and becomes even more complicated with the Help system. Although it checks a window title first and then a window name, _MST_HELP also can pick the *image* window you DEFINEd for a BROWSE WINDOW rather than the actual BROWSE title. _MST_HELP also may be confounded by the addition of other graphics characters to the window title. Even if you forgo the use of window titles, when you are permitting GENSCRN to generate window *names*, you have another problem—one which the #WNAME generator directive cannot resolve. Further, adding the ■ to the beginning of the topic may not suit you, or you may not like the effect this addition has on the See Also list.

F1, in the internally defined role as _MST_HELP's shortcut key, also performs somewhat inconsistently during a READ. If you DO FILENAME.SPR with no redefinition of the System menu at all, F1 no longer shows as the hot key for the Help option on the System menu pad. Although you still can press Alt+S and then press H to access Help, pressing F1 terminates the READ instead!

Fortunately, FoxPro provides better methods of making the Help system respond appropriately.

The simplest and most direct approach is to use the SET TOPIC command. You can SET TOPIC TO a character expression, and the Topic field (or whatever you named this field) is searched for a case-insensitive match to the expression.

To effectively use SET TOPIC, you must create a method of accessing Help. Rather than use the bar _MST_HELP, just program the Help... option on the SYSMENU to issue the HELP command. If SYSMENU is unavailable, an ON KEY LABEL F1 HELP command can accomplish the same thing. Even if you use SYSMENU, an additional ON KEY LABEL F1 HELP command can ensure that the hot key works consistently in a READ.

You also can SET TOPIC TO a logical expression, and the Help file is searched for a record that causes the logical expression to RETURN .T.. This expression is often complex and can reference the extra fields in the Help file, as shown in the following examples.

```
SET TOPIC TO <a character expression>
```

The preceding command is very similar to the following command:

```
HELP <the same character expression>
```

No matter which way you choose to SET TOPIC, remember that the rule you applied in the See Also Topic searches also applies here: the *first topic* that contains a match is the topic shown.

The SET TOPIC command, however, can be issued once (at the beginning of the program) and is *evaluated dynamically*. If the SET TOPIC expression (whether a logical or character type) contains functions or variables that you initialize in the program, the contents of the expression change—as does the current Topic. The current Topic depends on the conditions prevailing when Help is accessed. If the Help table includes extra fields for the name of the current window and the current variable, as suggested in the preceding example, you can use a SET TOPIC expression in the following manner:

```
SET TOPIC TO Wname = LOWER(WONTOP( )) AND ;
   Read_item = LOWER(VARREAD( ))
* Wname and Read_item are helpfile fields
```

NOTE Notice that in both cases the *shorter* expression is placed on the *right* side of the comparison—the fields Wname and Read_item may be longer than WONTOP( ) and VARREAD( ), which contain no trailing spaces. If you refer to the SET EXACT entry in the *Commands and Functions* manual or Chapter 7, "Querying with SQL and Searching with Rushmore," of this book, you find extensive discussion of *string comparisons*. As in other Xbase dialects, if EXACT is SET OFF, which is the default, when you type the single equal sign (=) to compare two character expressions, the expressions are compared only until *the one on the right side ends*.

In SET TOPIC expressions you find yet another use for the ubiquitous IIF( ) function. Suppose that you want to select a special set of Help entries when users are just looking through menu options and not actually performing one of the tasks in the system. You can create these entries with Topics to match your menu pads and use the following expression:

```
SET TOPIC TO IIF(RDLEVEL( ) = 0,                ;
                topic = PAD( ),                 ;
                wname = LOWER(WONTOP( )) AND ;
                read_item = LOWER(VARREAD( )))
```

This expression says "If you're not in a READ, find a topic that matches the current menu pad. Otherwise, use the active window and current GET to find a topic." (In Chapter 14, "Organizing and Packaging Your Applications," and Chapter 15, "Controlling the User Interface in Applications," and in the FoxPro documentation, you learn about Foundation READs, which remain active while the user waits in a menu. If you use a Foundation READ, you need to change the preceding expression to check RDLEVEL( ) > 1.)

You also may want to create a special Help topic that explains how to navigate in a BROWSE in the system. You can title all the BROWSEs consistently, for example, by using a graphics character you use nowhere else, such as in the following expression:

```
BROWSE WINDOW <window name> ;
   TITLE "↑↓"+PROPER(ALIAS( ))+ " Records  "
```

For the BUDGET.SPR BROWSE, the following window title appears:

```
↑↓ Budget Records
```

Now the SET TOPIC expression can be as follows:

```
SET TOPIC TO IIF("↑↓" $ WTITLE( ),              ;
                 "Browsing Records",           ;
                 Wname = LOWER(WONTOP( )) AND  ;
                 Read_item = LOWER(VARREAD( )))
```

The IIF( ) function limits you to only two methods of using SET TOPIC, however, and you may want a Help system that considers more than two situations. As you may expect, you can accomplish this with a CASE statement.

You can SET TOPIC directly TO a UDF( ) that RETURNs a logical or character expression based on the CASEs it evaluates, but having the Help menu option (or ON KEY LABEL command) DO a special help procedure is far better than simply calling HELP. This procedure can accept anything you need to establish your conditions as a list of passed parameters, for example:

```
Do My_help WITH RDLEVEL( ), WONTOP( ),;
   WTITLE( ), VARREAD( ), PROGRAM( )
```

The help procedure includes the following instructions:

- Accept passed conditions in the form of a PARAMETERS statement.
- Evaluate current conditions in a DO CASE structure and SET TOPIC accordingly.
- If necessary, use PUSH KEY CLEAR to move any ON KEY LABEL assignments to the stack. To select the currently highlighted record in a BROWSE for editing, for example, many people use the command ON KEY LABEL ENTER KEYBOARD CHR(23), which also can be expressed as KEYBOARD "{CTRL-W}", . This reassignment is awkward when the user tries to use the Enter key to select a Topic from the Help Index.

- Issue the HELP command.
- Use POP KEY to replace ON KEY LABEL assignments.

Using a specialized help procedure, you can add yet another feature to the Help system: you can use the SET HELPFILTER TO command, which takes a logical expression. SET HELPFILTER is placed before the HELP command to restrict the topics that appear in the index. You previously saw a sophisticated use of this command in the HELPTREE.MPR program provided with FoxPro under the \GOODIES directory. Chapter 14, "Organizing and Packaging Your Applications," briefly discussed the HELPTREE utility when you explored the Menu Builder. Take time to investigate HELPTREE.MPR, shown in figure 20.2, to get an idea of this command's potential for use with optional fields in the Help file's structure.

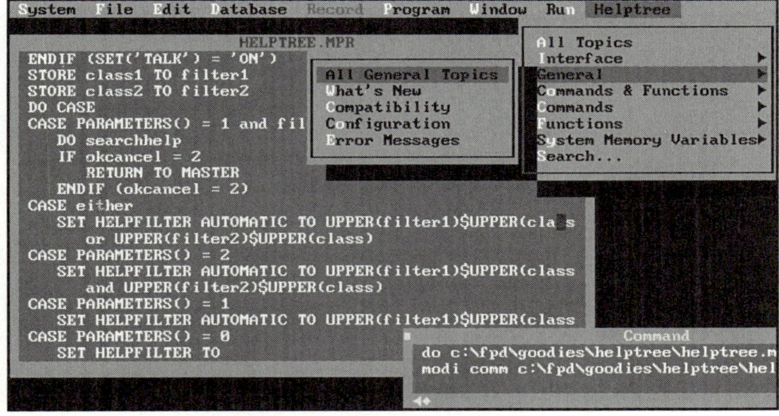

FIG. 20.2

HELPTREE.MPR and the resulting Helptree pad demonstrate using the SET HELPFILTER command.

In the example Help file structure, you may want to use the following command in at least one help CASE:

```
SET HELPFILTER AUTOMATIC TO LOWER(WONTOP( )) $ Wname
```

The keyword AUTOMATIC ensures that the filter is removed (that all topics are again accessible) after the Help window is closed. If you use AUTOMATIC, you avoid having to use a HELPFILTER in every CASE or having to SET HELPFILTER TO <nothing> to turn off the filter after the HELP command.

Giving Users Control of the Help System

If the application uses passwords or restricts access to some features in any way, you can include a check for appropriate access in the user-accessed printing procedure below and in the SET HELPFILTER command. The FoxPro Help system gives you many other ways to help users feel in charge of the Help system—and the application as a whole.

Just as the Help file is no substitute for proper interface design, don't rely entirely on on-line documentation. Many people prefer a manual that can be studied at leisure while they are away from the computer. You can easily include these user needs in your Help system plans.

Printing the Help File

Using report forms, you can create a paper version of the Help file. A UDF( ) in a MANUAL.FRX, for example, in the page header band, can transfer information about the output, including page numbers for the beginning of each topic (or groups of topics as defined by the report's control breaks) to another table while the report is created. You can choose to have this second table include one record for each page or one record for each topic or group. With such a table, imagine how easily you can create or revise a table of contents. The lists of See Also references, stored in one memo field of this support table, also can form the basis of an index. A special TAG in the Help file's structural index can reorder the topics for the manual, if necessary.

A special Memo field in the Help file can even store screen shots. If you used FoxPro's own Capture option to create them, the screen shots can be printed along with the Help text in the usual way. (Remember to make the report expression wide enough to print them.) If you use an external program to capture screens as graphics files, a Memo field in the Help file can still hold them so that they remain coordinated with the current topics. If you have the capability to print graphics files to disk, the extra Help file Memo field can store them as printing instructions, an even better alternative.

Because manuals are always getting lost, you can remind users that they can use the File pad's Print... option to get a hard copy of any open window, including the current Help topic. If the application's version of SYSMENU doesn't make this option available, you can easily create a program to let users choose topics to print. The following simple example presents a number of the techniques you have learned in this programming section:

```
old_prn = SET("PRINTER",1)
old_alias = ALIAS( )
* save state of printer and work you have done
SELECT 0
USE widghelp AGAIN
* open the helpfile in an unused area
* USE... AGAIN is okay here, because you're not editing
SET ORDER TO doc_ord
* having the structural index helps us out here -
* the natural order of the table, which is used for
* proper use of the help index and SET TOPIC/See Also
* may not be the order you want for this job
* here you might want to add an option
* for printing ALL topics without seeing the
* popup and choosing them one at a time
   DEFINE POPUP widghelp FROM 5,5 TO 20,42 ;
    PROMPT FIELD topic
* set up a popup showing all topics
IF m.output # "P"
   * You have previously determined whether the user
   * wants to print to a file or to the printer
   * If to a file, the user has specified a filename
   * It is erased if it already exists and the user
   * doesn't want to append information to it;
   * the ADDITIVE keyword will allow the append
   * if the file is there
   SET PRINTER TO (m.helptext) ADDITIVE
ELSE
   SET PRINTER TO
   * restore to default (or set to a particular port
   * if you prefer)
ENDIF
ON SELECTION POPUP widghelp ;
   REPORT FORM widgdoc TO PRINT NEXT 1 OFF
m.pgcount = 0
* the report form will use a UDF, pageno( ), below
* to print page numbers, because you will be printing
* topics as separate REPORT FORMs, one at a time
* You initialize the variable in the calling program
* Notes after the UDF offer an alternative approach
```

continues

```
DO WHILE LASTKEY( ) # 27
   * continue until the user presses ESC
   ACTIVATE POPUP widghelp
ENDDO
* put everything back the way you found it
RELEASE POPUP widghelp
SET PRINTER TO (old_prn)
USE
SELECT (old_alias)
RETURN

FUNCTION pageno
m.pgcount = m.pgcount + 1
RETURN ALLTRIM(STR(m.pgcount))
* this function is unnecessary if you design your report
* with persisting report variables, as described in
* Chapter 10. Initialize the report variable to
* m.pgcount+_PAGENO, and store
* m.pgcount+_PAGENO to it. This report variable
* becomes your page number in the report.
* Uncheck the option to Release After Report.
* In between report printings, change the value of
* m.pgcount to reflect the pages that have been printed,
* like this:
* ON SELECTION POPUP widghelp DO helpprint
* PROCEDURE helpprint
* REPORT FORM widgdoc TO PRINT NEXT 1 OFF
* m.pgcount = reportvar
* RETURN
```

Encouraging Users To Edit the Help File

You also can make sure that users feel in charge of the Help system by providing ways in which they can edit the file. Each user of the system can have a personal copy of the Help file, containing notes added by the user. Alternatively, you can add another memo field to the Help file that (like Post-it notes) can contain the comments of all the users. This memo field can be in the Help file or in a separate table; if it's in a separate table, the extra field is editable even when HELP is ON. When the user accesses Help, your help procedure includes a separate menu option or hot key to edit this additional field. The Help file, or its editable twin containing the extra field, can have a structural index with special filtered indexes (INDEX ON ... FOR ...) to allow editing of help text by department or password level, as necessary.

Your application's .APP file always contains the original (readonly) copy of the Help file, so no permanent damage can be done by users' editing. Remember that an edit of the Help file requires that you SET HELP OFF first. If you are sharing a Help file on a network, you must edit the file in a procedure similar to the one suggested in Chapter 16, "Discovering Additional FoxPro Productivity Features," for editing a shared Resource file.

Embedding an Introductory Menu in the Help System

A macro-level Overview topic that introduces the system users to the application can be a perfect place to give users an immediate sense that they are in control of the system. To do this, you can use an *embedded menu* that takes advantage of FoxPro's Look Up feature. Just write some friendly paragraphs describing the system and its features. In the beginning of this introductory entry, you can explain how to use the Help system and that users can find out more about many of the subjects mentioned. Use the actual names of some of the other Topics directly in the text, perhaps setting them off with special marks, as shown in figure 20.3. Like the See Also listings, embedded menus provide a fairly simple system of the type sometimes called *hypertext*. A hypertext system encourages users to explore text listings in many branching directions, rather than move in a linear fashion from the beginning to the end of a text.

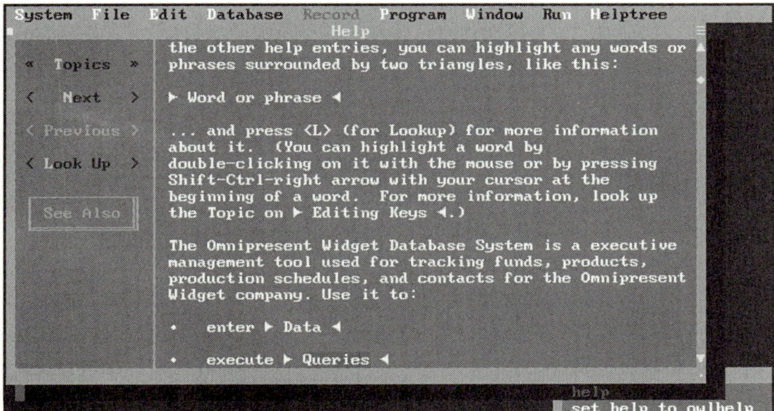

FIG. 20.3

An embedded menu-style introductory help topic.

Finding and Handling Program Errors

Perfect programmers never make mistakes. They have a complete conceptualization of all facets of the program to be written. They are in complete control of all inter-relationships within the program and never accidentally type > rather than <.

This level of performance is a worthy goal, but most programmers never attain perfection. Programs usually contain errors in both execution logic and language usage. The process of finding and correcting these infelicities (or *bugs*) is known as *debugging*.

Debugging a program usually has at least three separate phases:

1. Correcting errors flagged by FoxPro as the program is compiled
2. Correcting obvious logic errors
3. Correcting hidden logic errors

When you compile a program, FoxPro indicates how many errors it found in the program and saves the error messages in a text file that has the same name as the program or application but has an .ERR extension. You can view this error log by typing `MODIFY COMMAND <program name>.ERR` in the Command window or by opening the file, using the Open... option on the File menu. Correcting these errors is usually simply a matter of locating the offending lines and retyping the incorrect parts of the statements.

After you successfully compile the program and FoxPro does not find errors, you can move on to the next step, finding and correcting obvious logic errors. As you test the application's features, you may notice things that don't work as you intended, such as the positioning of windows and messages. You also may encounter run-time errors that cannot be flagged at the compilation stage, such as the program trying to use a logical variable in a function that requires a numeric argument or referring to a field name that is not part of the current table.

The final stage of debugging usually requires help from one or more people who weren't involved in the development of the application. Because you understand how the program is supposed to work, the application may have some errors that you can never catch. You may never have considered the possibility that a user may enter a negative order quantity in the New Sales Orders data-entry screen, for example, because you know that these adjustments are entered in the Credit Memos entry screen. If the program then uses the user's negative number in a function that accepts only positive numbers, the application may bomb. The inability of the developers to anticipate every way in which the application will be used or misused is one reason for the lengthy *beta test periods* that all major commercial applications undergo.

FoxPro has several tools that can help you debug programs. The most powerful tools are the Debug and Trace windows. With the Debug window you can inspect the current value of variables and expressions contained in a program and pause the execution of a program when one or more of these values changes. The Trace window displays program instructions and highlights each line as the line is executed. The Trace window or the Debug window may be used alone, or the two windows can be used together.

TIP

Because FoxPro enables you to remap the keyboard with ON KEY and ON KEY LABEL, you may need a way to enter a command without pressing Enter or the space bar if the program bombs after you have mapped one of these keys to do something other than the key's normal task. (Many developers let the user select a record from a Browse by remapping either the space bar or the Enter key to perform a KEYBOARD "{CTRL-W}", for example.)

If you suddenly find yourself in this position, don't panic. You can get around the problem by typing `ON KEY` in the Command window, and using Shift+space bar rather than the space bar between the words ON and KEY, and then Shift+Enter rather than Enter to execute the command.

Using the Debug Window

You can open the Debug window by selecting Debug from the Window menu or by typing `ACTIVATE WINDOW DEBUG` in the Command window.

The Debug window resembles an empty split Browse window in that the Debug window also has a left and right partition and all the Browse window's control objects, such as a window splitter and scroll bars.

Unlike a split Browse, however, only the left partition of a Debug window can be activated because this partition is where you type the expressions that you want to inspect. The current value of the expression is displayed in the right partition.

Although you can activate the Debug window at any time, the Debug window is usually activated either before running a program or from a running program that is *suspended* or paused in execution (see fig. 20.4). You can use one of several methods to suspend a program. You can insert the SUSPEND command into the program or you can set a *breakpoint* (discussed in the following paragraphs) in the Debug window. You also can suspend a program by selecting Suspend from the FoxPro error-handling dialog that appears when a program error is encountered or when you press Esc—if the command SET ESCAPE ON is enabled. FoxPro displays the message `Do suspended` in the system message window and returns you to the Command window.

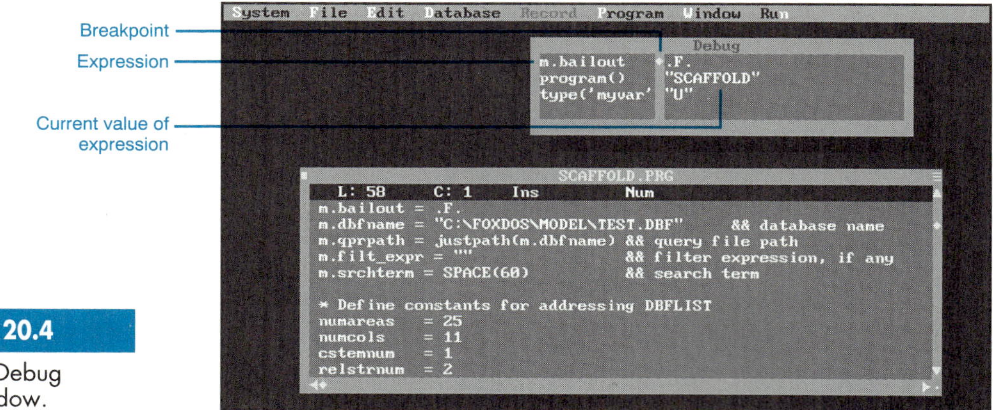

FIG. 20.4

The Debug Window.

To monitor the value of an expression, position the cursor in the left partition of the Debug window, type the expression, and then press Enter. If the expression is longer than the displayed width of the partition, the text scrolls to the left as you type. The expression usually is a variable name, but it also can be a FoxPro function, such as PROGRAM( ), which returns the name of the program currently executing.

If the expression is syntactically correct and if FoxPro can evaluate the expression, FoxPro displays the value on the same row in the right partition of the Debug window. If the expression contains a syntax error, the computer beeps when you press Enter. If the expression is valid but currently has no value, FoxPro accepts the expression but doesn't display anything in the right partition.

NOTE The Debug window cannot evaluate an expression that contains a macro substitution, such as *&field_name*.

You can resize the Debug window the same way you resize other windows. FoxPro assumes that you want to adjust the right partition and lengthens or shrinks the right side as you change the size of the window. You can adjust the relative size of the partitions by dragging the window splitter control or by using the Tab key to move to the window splitter and then using the left- and right-arrow keys.

You also can use the Debug window to set program breakpoints based on the value of an expression. Setting a breakpoint instructs FoxPro to pause the program when the value of the expression on which the breakpoint is set changes.

To set a breakpoint by using a mouse, click the breakpoint column (the column that divides the left partition from the right) to the right of the desired expression. From the keyboard, press Tab or Shift+Tab until a highlighted block appears in the breakpoint column. Use the up- and down-arrow keys to position the block to the right of the desired expression and then press the space bar. With either method, a diamond appears to indicate that you have set a breakpoint. Because a breakpoint is a toggle (either on or off), you clear the breakpoint by repeating this process.

With a breakpoint set, FoxPro suspends program execution when the value of the expression changes. If you set a breakpoint on an expression that currently has no value (a field name in a table that has not yet been opened), the program is suspended when the expression acquires a value and then again when the expression changes to a different value.

When a program is suspended, the System menu becomes active, *even if you turned it off from within the program*. You can use the View window to see the currently open tables, the currently selected work area, the current master index, and so on. You also can work from the Command window by typing commands such as `DISPLAY STATUS` to view the file search path, the default drive, open tables and indexes, and the current status of many FoxPro options. DISPLAY MEMORY lists the names and current values of all existing memory variables, including the system memory variables such as _PDSETUP and _CUROBJ.

Using the Trace Window

The Trace window is a useful tool for tracking down particularly elusive errors in program logic. Trace is often used in conjunction with the Debug window. You enter the names of variables and expressions that the program manipulates in the Debug window and then use the Trace window to *step* through the program, watching the values that the variables hold at certain problem points.

You can open the Trace window by selecting Trace from the Window menu or by typing `ACTIVATE WINDOW TRACE` in the Command window. The Trace window looks like a simple text-editing window but has a menu bar that contains some special options, as shown in figure 20.5. Each menu pad has a hot key, but unlike the System menu, you do not press the Alt key and then the hot-key letter to access the option. To activate the Trace window's Program popup, for example, just press the letter P. Alt+P still activates the Program pad that is part of the System menu.

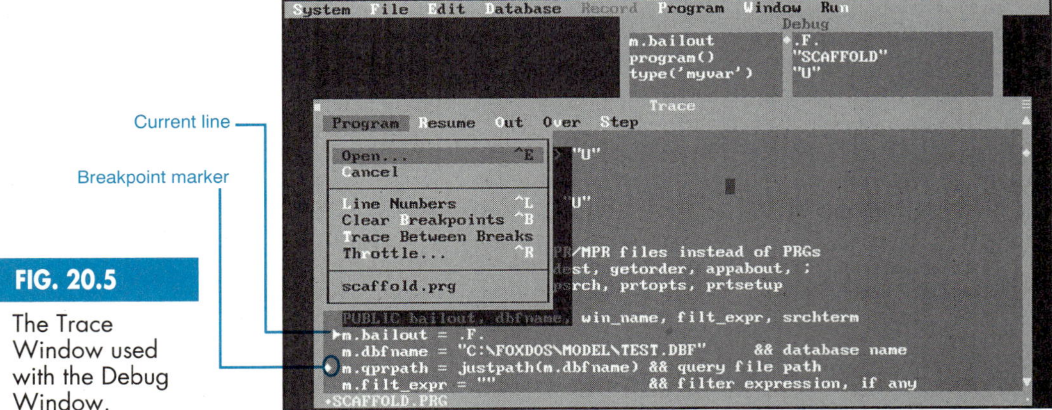

FIG. 20.5

The Trace Window used with the Debug Window.

The Program menu popup contains six options, as shown in figure 20.5. You can open a program file in the Trace window by selecting Open... from the menu or by pressing Ctrl+E when the Trace window is active and then selecting the file from the Open File dialog. The name of the program is displayed in the bottom of the window's border. You can select Cancel to stop the execution of a suspended program.

The Line Numbers option is a toggle that displays sequential line numbers before each line of the program in the Trace window. By default, line numbers are not displayed.

You can clear, one at a time, any breakpoints you previously set, or you can select Clear Breakpoints to clear all the breakpoints at one time. Keep in mind, however, that selecting this option clears the breakpoints in all the program files. FoxPro *remembers* where you set breakpoints in a program—even breakpoints you replaced in the Trace window with another program.

NOTE Breakpoints you set in the Trace window differ from those you set in the Debug window. In the Trace window, a breakpoint instructs FoxPro to suspend the program every time it encounters the line on which the break is set. In the Debug window, breakpoints are set on variables and other expressions, not on program lines; the program is suspended when the value of the expression *changes*, not whenever it is encountered in the program.

Trace allows you to execute the code between two breakpoints (or from the top of the program to the first breakpoint) without displaying each line in the Trace window. If you know that a problem lies in a particular segment of the program, you can quickly get to the segment by turning off the Trace Between Breaks option (the default state is ON) and then setting a breakpoint where you want to start the debugging session. Trace Between Breaks, like the Line Numbers option, is a toggle and is ON when a diamond (◆) appears immediately to the left of the menu prompt. When the option is ON, each line of the program is displayed and highlighted as the program executes.

With the Throttle... option, you can pause the program for a chosen number of seconds before moving from the current line to the next line. If you are debugging a large program, however, make sure that you set a breakpoint right after the code segment that you want to slowly step through. After you Do or Resume the program, all the menu options become disabled and, if you have SET ESCAPE OFF, you cannot pause or even cancel the program.

To set one or more breakpoints, open a program in the Trace window and then locate the first line on which you wish to pause the program's execution. Next click the line, or position the cursor on the line and press Enter or the space bar. The diamond that appears to the left of the line indicates that a breakpoint is set there. To clear a single breakpoint, repeat the steps you took to set it. As in the Debug window, you can toggle breakpoints on and off.

With the Do option, you can run a program. If you have loaded a program in the Trace window, FoxPro starts executing the program. If you haven't loaded a program, you can select the program to Do from the Open File dialog that appears by default. When a running program has been suspended, Do is replaced by Resume. Selecting Resume causes the program to resume execution one line after the line where the program was last paused.

Whenever a breakpoint is encountered, FoxPro suspends the program until you select Resume from the menu. While the program is suspended, you can scroll the Trace window to view other parts of the program. You also can open the Debug window, activate the Command window, and, in general, do anything you can do in the interactive FoxPro environment.

When you move off the currently executing line (which is always highlighted when the cursor rests on the line), FoxPro marks the position with a right arrowhead (►). To return to this point after reviewing other parts of the program and setting breakpoints, for example, press the Home key. You cannot change the point at which a program resumes execution. To reach a certain point in the program, FoxPro must execute all the preceding statements.

Whenever FoxPro suspends a running program, the Program menu popup expands to contain the chain of program execution, which is displayed beneath the Throttle... option. The name of the current procedure is shown at the top of the list, followed by the names of the procedures or programs called to reach this point. This listing can be useful when you are debugging a module that is called by other routines in the program and that seems to exhibit problems only at certain times, depending on which routine called the module.

The Out, Over, and Step options are the heart and soul of the Trace utility. These features greatly simplify the debugging process by allowing you to quickly (or slowly, in the case of Step) move through the program and locate the source of your errors.

The Over option *steps over* a call to another program. FoxPro still executes the called program or procedure but doesn't display the program's lines in the Trace window. If you select Over on a line that doesn't call another program, Over moves to the next line, just as if you had selected Step.

The Out option tells FoxPro to continue and complete execution of the currently executing procedure, function, or program, and then suspend program execution on the line that follows the line that called this program. This option is useful if you need to check the first few lines of a program to refresh your memory about what the program does and then, realizing that this program isn't the source of the problem, want to quickly return to the calling program. The Out option is only enabled when you are not in the top-level program of the application. You cannot step out to the Command window; you must use `Cancel` to do this.

The Step option *steps through* the program to the next line. This option is the Trace feature that you will use most often, in conjunction with the Debug window, to nail down problems after you isolate the part of the program where the problem occurs. Enter the variables that are set and evaluated by this portion of the program in the Debug window and note these values as each command is executed.

Error Trapping in an Application

A 0.00001 failure rate or a 15-year MTBF (mean time between failures) is totally meaningless when the product fails. Insofar as the user is concerned, the failure rate instantly becomes 1.0000 and the MTBF becomes 0 microseconds when the gadget quits.

"The Alternate View: Quality," G. Harry Stine, *Analog Magazine,* May 1991

By using the Trace and Debug windows and giving the program a thorough workout, you can catch many program errors so that users never see them. Just as you cannot design the perfect interface, however, you can never be sure (no matter how thoroughly you debug and how sophisticated the tools you use are) that the applications you create are 100 percent free from error.

Inevitably, you encounter situations in which applications you create fail during normal use. You cannot test an application under every imaginable set of conditions and, even if you could, you cannot imagine all the possible sets of conditions. Besides this limitation, some situations, such as hardware failures, occur that you can imagine but cannot control within the program. Because software *does* fail, you want to write applications that fail as gracefully as possible.

Allowing users to encounter FoxPro's internally generated error messages is definitely not a good strategy. If you refer to the interface design discussion on the subject of effective language found in Chapter 11, "Coordinating a FoxPro Application," you learn that FoxPro error messages don't always meet the criteria of blamelessness, reversibility of action, and clear-cut choice. When an error occurs during regular program use, you want to be especially sure that you communicate to the users that the program, *not the user*, failed, just as you want to give users this feeling during the acceptance testing period.

In a FoxPro application, you can intercept errors before FoxPro responds to them by using an *error-handling* program that you create to deal with all errors that occur. An error-handling program is called with the special ON ERROR command, usually with several parameters, that passes information about the state of the program at the moment the error occurs. This type of command is shown in the following example:

```
ON ERROR DO widgerror WITH ;
      LINENO(1), PROGRAM( ), ;
      MESSAGE( ), MESSAGE(1), ERROR( ) ;
      WLAST( ), WREAD( ), WONTOP( ), RDLEVEL( )
```

This list of parameters is by no means exhaustive. As you see shortly, an error-handling program can use many different FoxPro functions. A good general rule is to pass the function results that may be altered if the functions are called within the error procedure. If the error-handling procedure includes the recommended design of showing the user a message in an alert window, for example, you need to pass WLAST( ) and the other window functions so that these values aren't altered by the addition of the alert window. Some other functions passed in this ON ERROR example, such as MESSAGE( ), rarely change their return values within the error-handling program—unless, of course, an error exists in the error-handling program.

NOTE Debugging an ON ERROR routine can be the trickiest part of creating an application. In FoxPro, after you're inside the program called by ON ERROR, you cannot rely on the program's own error-handling nor can you call a second ON ERROR routine to handle errors for you. Fortunately, the logic and arrangement of an ON ERROR routine is simple and clear-cut, and you will probably be able to reuse a single ON ERROR procedure without significant change in every application you write.

The error-handling program usually contains a CASE structure, enabling the program to classify and handle errors according to type and severity. The CASE tests uses the ERROR( ) function to find out what has occurred. A number of similar errors may be handled by one CASE.

A good strategy for dealing with errors—how the CASEs handle each error—includes some evaluation of the error's *severity*, as well as the error type, as defined in the following list:

- *Trivial* errors, such as `Printer not ready`, that can be remedied by the user's adjusting the hardware and then continuing, can usually be handled with a polite message and a RETRY command.
- *Recoverable* errors, such as a missing or corrupted index, often can be handled by a standby message as the program takes necessary corrective measures (such as re-creating the index file), followed by a RETURN command.
- *Unrecoverable* errors, such as a corrupted database (due to a power failure, for example) or a corrupted program file, should be handled with an explicit and clear explanatory message. Explain to the users what has happened, what they can expect to happen next, and what to do about the error (especially where to look for help). Perform as "graceful" a cleanup as can be managed and then CANCEL or QUIT the program.

These classifications are not as clear-cut as they may look. Recoverable and unrecoverable errors may frequently overlap. Occasionally, a single procedure may not run properly, but you can give the users the option to continue with other program tasks. You can use the RETURN TO MASTER command in this case. Make sure that you initialize the program as if you were reloading the program.

If you use a Foundation READ, but it is in a backdrop-type screen called by your main program—or if it is not directly in the main program for any other reason—you should return to <filename>, explicitly specifying the program containing the Foundation READ rather than TO MASTER. With a Foundation READ, you also should be extremely careful to cancel any edits currently in progress. Your method of canceling these edits will vary, as described in Chapter 12, "Creating Application Elements," depending on whether you choose direct or indirect READs for your application.

Some special CASEs among the recoverable errors do not actually mean a problem was encountered, although an error condition is created. If you issue the command SCATTER MEMVAR with the MEMO keyword, you may have insufficient memory to store a large memo field as a memory variable. The variable is created but is .F. (logical type). If you see an `Insufficient memory` message (Error # 43, passed using the ERROR( ) function) and the program line contains the word SCATTER (the line is passed using the MESSAGE(1) function), you can create a temporary file with the COPY MEMO command. You then can edit this file rather than the memory variable. If you save these changes, you can use the APPEND MEMO command at a later time to replace the file's Memo field. (As you learned in Chapter 12 and Chapter 13, "Improving Screen Design with Complex Screen Sets," you also can avoid this error by using a cursor to indirectly edit a Memo field rather than use SCATTER MEMVAR MEMO.)

Unlike previous versions, Foxpro 2.x's MESSAGE(1) is useful even if you have distributed an application without source code. The command from the source code line will be returned. If a macro substitution was used to create the line of code, the entire line (the result of the macro substitution) will be returned. The LINENO( ) function also was enhanced with an optional parameter so that you can receive a line number relative to the current procedure rather than from the top of the entire program that you bound together with the BUILD APPLICATION command. In Appendix B, "Optimizing FoxPro's Performance," you find an interesting use for the LINENO(1) function within the DEBUG window.

Another special recoverable error that doesn't indicate a real problem with the program is the inability to lock a record or a file in a multiuser situation. You can use the error-handling routine to notify the user of the problem and RETRY the command until the record or file is locked or until the user decides not to proceed. This type of error should not occur with the explicit record-locking procedures recommended in Chapters 12 and 13 for data entry, but all such cases should be handled in the error routine, even if the protection seems redundant.

Every time the error-handling program is called and the cause is neither trivial nor one of these special cases, record the error for later examination. You can call a subprocedure in the appropriate CASEs to create this kind of log.

The following code is for one method of error logging, an ON ERROR routine called WITH the preceding example's parameters. Because an error program cannot make assumptions about what conditions prevailed when the error occurred, the program begins by establishing an environment.

```
PROCEDURE widgerror

PARAMETERS errlineno, errprog, errmsg, errline, ;
           errno, lastwind, readwind, topwind, readno

PRIVATE err????
PRIVATE lowmem, errstr, memscreen, nofiles
PRIVATE ALL LIKE ????_errs

* If you are in the habit of using SET PRINT, SET CONSOLE, or
* SET DEVICE, you may have to
* SET PRINT OFF
* SET CONSOLE ON
* SET DEVICE TO SCREEN
* here and restore state later as necessary.  (However, CONSOLE
* is automatically SET ON by an ON ERROR program, so there is
* no problem with the messages and WAIT WINDOWS herein being
* displayed.)  The procedures here and elsewhere in the WIDGET
* rely on the TO <target device> clauses and NOCONSOLE keyword
* in specific commands rather than SETting PRINT or CONSOLE or
* DEVICE, which obviates this problem to a great degree.
errpset = _PDSETUP

* The printer driver setup is removed and later
* restored in case a PostScript driver is installed,
* which would make the LISTings of MEMO and STATUS
* very difficult to read... see the PDCHECK program
* in the Printer Drivers section of Chapter 16
* for an expanded look
* at saving printer driver-related information at
* error time, or any time.  Much of that routine
* could be incorporated here, and the information could
* be stored in the Listing memo field.

errtalk = SET("TALK")
* one or two of Widget procedures may SET TALK ON temporarily
* such as PACKing or doing a SELECT...

errsafe = SET("SAFETY")
* some of the error procedures require SAFETY OFF

SET TALK OFF
SET PDSETUP TO ""
SET SAFETY OFF
```

continues

```
* Sound a distinctive bell, clearly different from
* other sounds in your application
* This particular "uh-oh" syntax is
* courtesy of Hallie Steiner Cooper,
* age 3 and a half:
SET BELL TO 328,3
?? CHR(7)
SET BELL TO 261,8
?? CHR(7)
SET BELL TO
```

Next, the program evaluates the error that occurred by comparing this error to various categories of FoxPro errors, as follows:

```
errstr = "/" + ltrim(str(errno)) + "/"
lowmem = (val(sys(1001))-val(sys(1016)) < 10000)

* add or edit the following list as necessary
memo_errs = "/43/1012/1149/1150/1151/1600/"
indx_errs = "/5/19/20/114/1707/"
disk_errs = "/1410/"
file_errs = "/1/15/41/111/1115/1294/1643/1644/1705/"
netw_errs = "/124/1705/"
lock_errs = "/3/108/109/110/1502/1708/"
prtr_errs = "/125/"
drvr_errs = "/1910/1643/1644/1717/"
```

After evaluating the error, the program can take care of any error considered trivial (according to the classification system described earlier in this system), as follows:

```
*  a trivial problem :
IF errstr $ prtr_errs
   * the following generic UDF is used throughout the
   * Widget applications -- code for it is in Appendix H
   err_ask = Ask("The printer is not ready; RETRY or CANCEL?",;
                "RETRY ","@M  RETRY, CANCEL")
   SET TALK &errtalk
   SET PDSETUP TO errpset
   SET SAFETY &errsafe
   IF "R" $ err_ask
      RETRY
   ELSE
      * you may want to set a public variable in
      * here that indicates that a print job was cancelled,
      * as below for the record locking
      RETURN
   ENDIF
ENDIF
```

Normal procedures that may trigger errors, such as the automatic locking system, are handled similarly to trivial errors, as follows:

```
IF errstr $ lock_errs
   err_ask = Ask("Record/file in use; RETRY or CANCEL?",;
                 "RETRY ","@M  RETRY, CANCEL")
   SET TALK &errtalk
   SET PDSETUP TO errpset
   SET SAFETY &errsafe
   IF "R" $ err_ask
      RETRY
   ELSE
      got_cancel = .T.
      RETURN
   ENDIF
ENDIF
```

NOTE

You may think that you don't need to use these error-handling procedures for the automatic locking system if you always use explicit locks in your data entry system. Certainly, an application does not usually contain both direct data entry READs and indirect READs as the Widget application does for demonstration purposes. (The FoxApp-generated PRODUCT.APP contains direct READs, and all the other screen sets you created in Chapters 12 and 13 are indirect READs.) It is even unusual for one programmer to use both direct and indirect READs in different applications which might require the same generic ON ERROR routine.

You must *always* handle a failure to obtain a file or record lock in the error handler, however, even if you think you have perfectly-designed explicit locks. You may not realize that a particularly obscure operation (such as SAVE MACROS TO MEMO <memofield>) will trigger the locking system, for example, and you may forget to put an explicit RLOCK( )/UNLOCK sequence around that command. In such cases, the automatic locking system intervenes and your error handler should handle the interruption smoothly.

After errors that can be handled with a RETRY have been dispatched, the program proceeds to evaluate some additional special cases. These cases include errors that require data files to be reconstructed and unrecoverable errors that should end the program immediately.

TIP In the second CASE below, note that the error handler is temporarily removed so indexes can be rebuilt by a subsidiary program. When a structural index is missing or damaged and you have SAFETY OFF enabled, the subsidiary program can USE the table anyway, and the structural index information is removed from the table's header. The index then can be re-created. *You must not have an ON ERROR program in use for this technique to work.*

If the subsidiary program cannot get EXCLUSIVE use of the tables necessary or encounters any other problem so that it cannot rebuild the indexes successfully, the error is unrecoverable. The CASE sets a flag variable to indicate this fact.

The following code handles these special cases:

```
no_files = .F.

WAIT CLEAR
SET COLOR OF SCHEME 5 TO SCHEME 7
* Set WAIT WINDOW colors to alert colors, for a clear difference,
* or create a standard ALERT.SCX and use that instead --
* An ALERT.SCX will allow you to provide a fuller explanation
* of the class of error that has occurred than the one-line
* standard WAIT WINDOW, but keep in mind that an ALERT.SCX
* will require more memory than the WAIT WINDOW if you choose
* to use it.

DO CASE

* take care of an important but recoverable problem like this:
CASE UPPER(errprog) = "FILEOPEN"
   * FileOpen would be a procedure that opened all
   * files for your system as necessary
   * Here, you create files not found,
   * This program should reset the value of no_files
   * if it's unsuccessful
CASE errstr $ indx_errs
   ON ERROR
   WAIT WINDOW NOWAIT ;
      "Index file error detected; re-creating indexes..."
   * put a rebuilding index program here
    * This program  resets no_files if it's unsuccessful
```

```
   ON ERROR DO widgerror WITH ;
      LINENO(1), PROGRAM( ), ;
      MESSAGE( ), MESSAGE(1), ERROR( ) ;
      WLAST( ), WREAD( ), WONTOP( ), RDLEVEL( )
   WAIT CLEAR

CASE errstr $ drvr_errs
   * printer driver errors will be handled differently
   * depending on the way you use FP's sample printer driver
   * system -- or if, instead, you write your own _GENPD or
   * _PDRIVER.  See comment about PDCHECK.PRG above (found
   * in Chapter 16) for appropriate items to check
   *  when printer driver problems are suspected.

* take care of unrecoverable errors such as out of
* memory, disk, corrupted problem files, like this:
CASE errno = 1309
   WAIT WINDOW ;
      "There is a problem with your program files.  "+ ;
      "Please reinstall."

ENDCASE
```

Then, in the following code which ends the program, the error handler checks for unrecoverable errors:

```
IF no_files OR lowmem OR INLIST(errno, 1309, 56)
                                 && make your own list!
   * write a limited log, as per instructions below,
   * to the printer if possible first
   WAIT WINDOW UPPER(PROGRAM(0))+;
            " cannot recover from this error; "+;
            "press a key to clean up & exit."
   CLOSE ALL
   * m.oldvue is a temporary file created by the Setup
   * procedures of this program
   * m.oldvue is a PUBLIC variable
   ERASE (m.oldvue)
   QUIT
ENDIF
```

If the error is not in the unrecoverable category, however, the next step is to log the error so that the programmer can examine the conditions causing the error. This procedure requires information to be written to disk, one reason why the `Out of disk` error, number 56, is unrecoverable. Following is the logging code:

```
WAIT WINDOW NOWAIT ;
  "A program exception has occurred; writing error log... "
err_sel = SELECT( )
err_rec = RECNO( )
IF USED("errlog")
   SELECT errlog
ELSE
   IF FILE("errlog.dbf") AND FILE("errlog.fpt")
      SELECT 0
      USE Errlog
   ELSE
     * first error at this installation!
      CREATE TABLE Errlog ;
             (errdate    d(8), ;
              errtime    c(8), ;
              snapshot   m(10),;
              underneath m(10),;
              listing    m(10),;
              usernotes m(10))
   ENDIF
ENDIF
APPEND BLANK
SAVE WINDOWS ALL TO MEMO Snapshot
ACTIVATE SCREEN
SAVE SCREEN TO memscreen
SAVE ALL LIKE memscreen TO MEMO Underneath
REPLACE Errdate WITH DATE( ), Errtime WITH TIME( )

* create listing memo field from chunks of data --
* do a couple of REPLACEs so that less memory is
* used for each step of this process

errdata =         'error number='+ALLTRIM(STR(errno))
errdata = errdata+CHR(13)+'error message='+errmsg
errdata = errdata+CHR(13)+'last error parameter='+SYS(2018)
errdata = errdata+CHR(13)+'program=  '+ errprog
errdata = errdata+CHR(13)+'lineno=  '+;
                          ALLTRIM(STR(errlineno))+":  "+errline
REPLACE Listing WITH errdata

errdata =          CHR(13)+'bof='+IIF(BOF( ),"YES","NO")
errdata = errdata+CHR(13)+'eof='+IIF(EOF( ),"YES","NO")
errdata = errdata+CHR(13)+'last window='+lastwind
errdata = errdata+CHR(13)+'top window '+IIF(EMPTY(topwind),;
```

```
                            'SCREEN ',UPPER(topwind))+;
                            IIF(readwind, '*is*','*is NOT*')+;
                            ' involved in current READ'
REPLACE Listing WITH errdata ADDITIVE

errdata =         CHR(13)+'read level='+ALLTRIM(STR(readno))
errdata = errdata+CHR(13)+ 'rec. no.='+ALLTRIM(STR(err_rec))
errdata = errdata+CHR(13)+ ;
          'diskspace='+ALLTRIM(STR(DISKSPACE( ),25))
errdata = errdata+CHR(13)+ 'os='+OS( )
errdata = errdata+CHR(13)+ 'ver='+VERSION(1)
REPLACE Listing WITH errdata ADDITIVE

errdata =         CHR(13)+ ALLTRIM(STR(VAL(SYS(1016))/1024))+;
                            "K memory in use by user objects"
errdata = errdata+CHR(13)+ ALLTRIM(STR(VAL(SYS(12))/1024))+;
                            "K memory remaining"
errdata = errdata+CHR(13)+ ALLTRIM(STR(VAL(SYS(1001))/1024))+;
                            "K total memory available to Fox"
errdata = errdata+CHR(13)+ IIF(EMPTY(errpset),"NO",errpset)+;
                            " Printer Driver Installed"
REPLACE listing WITH errdata ADDITIVE

errdata =         CHR(13)+ 'processor='+ SYS(17)
errdata = errdata+CHR(13)+ 'video card/monitor='+SYS(2006)
errdata = errdata+CHR(13)+ 'FILES='+SYS(2010)
errdata = errdata+CHR(13)+CHR(13)+REPLICATE('=',50)
errdata = errdata+CHR(13)+'            Status listing'
errdata = errdata+CHR(13)+REPLICATE('=',50)+CHR(13)
REPLACE Listing WITH errdata ADDITIVE

RELEASE errdata

IF TYPE("gramdisk") # "C"
   * gramdisk would be a variable you'd let
   * them specify a workdisk with during setup;
   * would have complete pathspec in it
   gramdisk = ""
ENDIF
errfile = gramdisk+SYS(3)+".tmp"
DO WHILE FILE(errfile)
   errfile = gramdisk+SYS(3)+".tmp"
ENDDO
```

continues

```
LIST STATUS TO (errfile) NOCONSOLE
APPEND MEMO listing FROM (errfile)
* APPEND MEMO is ADDITIVE by default

ERASE (errfile)

REPLACE Listing WITH CHR(13)+REPLICATE('=',50)+CHR(13)+;
                '             Memory listing'+CHR(13)+;
                REPLICATE('=',50)+CHR(13) ;
                ADDITIVE

LIST MEMORY TO (errfile) NOCONSOLE
APPEND MEMO Listing FROM (errfile)

* add blank user questionnaire of some type
* to the user-editable memo field

APPEND MEMO Usernotes FROM survey.txt

SELECT (err_sel)
ERASE (errfile)
WAIT CLEAR
SET COLOR OF SCHEME 5 TO
SET TALK &errtalk
SET PDSETUP TO errpset
SET SAFETY &errsafe
* reset system parameters here as necessary
* and, if you have been event-handling in several
* apparent READs saving state in all of them, cancel
* all changes and CLEAR READ ALL

* if your foundation READ is inside a Fndation.SPR called by
* your main program, which paints a logo before
* issuing the main READ, you would change the following to
* RETURN TO Fndation.SPR
RETURN TO MASTER
```

The log takes a few seconds to create and may seem unnecessarily thorough. Remember that this subprocedure may not be used often—but when you do need it, every piece of information you can gather may be helpful.

The error log table used by the preceding suggested procedure contains only a few fields, as shown in the following list:

- *Errdate* and *Errtime*, Date and Character fields that indicate when the error occurred.
- *Snapshot*, a Memo field that holds information about the windows on-screen at the time the error occurred. Use the RESTORE WINDOWS ALL FROM MEMO Snapshot command to look at the state of these windows when you want to investigate the error later.
- *Underneath*, a Memo field similar to Snapshot that stores the desktop activity under the DEFINE WINDOWs. To restore the state of the screen to examine the error later, the programmer first uses RESTORE FROM MEMO Underneath ADDITIVE, making the variable memscreen available, and then RESTORE SCREEN FROM memscreen. After the screen information has been re-created from the Snapshot and Underneath fields, the programmer sees exactly what the user saw at the time the error occurred, including any information the user input into the data screens just before the error. The windows can be moved or CLEARed one at a time to reveal any information in additional windows below.
- *Listing*, a Memo field that holds a text description of the state of the program at the time of the error.
- *Usernotes*, another Memo field, used either within the ON ERROR routine or later to enable the user to jot down any facts the user thinks may help track down the problem. Rather than leave this field empty when you create the error log record entry, you can fill the field with a helpful questionnaire for the user to complete. Because Memo fields are unlimited in length, the user can add additional unstructured comments, including any information that might be helpful, at the bottom of the questionnaire.

You can use a menu option to make this error log table accessible to users, just as you do with any other table. Typically, useful utilities for the error log include the following:

- A BROWSE of the file, with Usernotes as the only editable field. In this field, the user can add recollections or record a resolution of the problem, print the contents of the Listing field or give you pertinent information about the error over the phone.
- A REPORT on the contents of the file.
- Error log maintenance. Users can delete old records of resolved problems or copy the file to a floppy disk to send to you (see fig. 20.6).

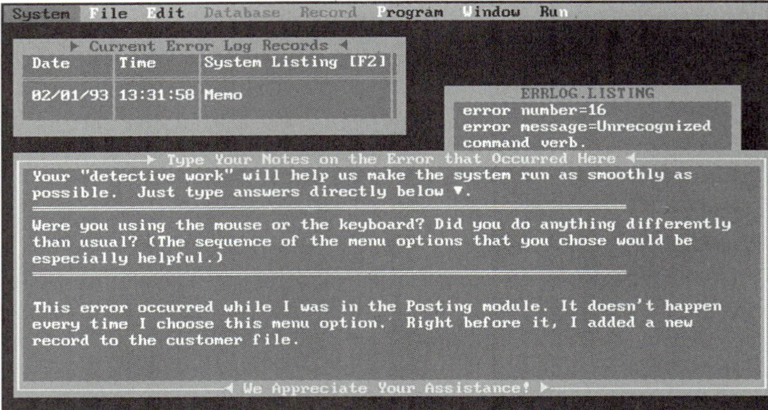

FIG. 20.6

An error log table edited by a user.

To prepare for a situation in which the problem is so severe that normal access through the application is impossible, you can create a special stand-alone procedure that, completely separate from the rest of the application, allows access to the error log and the associated utilities.

No error-handling procedures can guarantee you complete control of program behavior and a graceful exit under all conditions. When the error is `Insufficient memory` or `Out of disk space`, you probably cannot create the Listing memo field in the error log, but you can create an alternate log by sending information directly to the printer, after you check with the user to make sure a printer is available.

No matter how many layers of insulation from errors you provide, however, the obvious conclusion is that some kinds of errors require *preventive* checking to avert them at points of the program in which they are likely to happen. With both preventive and remedial error-handling, users can endure the rare total crash with good humor and a cooperative attitude.

Quality is an overused and even abused word. The Latin expression *sine qua non*—"without which nothing," an indispensable factor—may represent the most exact definition of quality. Most people do agree that products that aren't high quality shouldn't be built. The disagreement begins when you try to ascertain precisely what is indispensable to a high-quality product.

This section suggests that your definition of quality include an awareness and an acceptance of problems. This definition is indispensable to a constructive response—on the part of the application and also the users—when problems occur, as they inevitably will.

Documenting Applications with FoxDoc

FoxDoc is a FoxPro-specific version of SNAP!, a shareware program written by Walter J. Kennamer. FoxDoc is a marvelous program documentation tool. You simply supply FoxDoc with the name of the top-level program in the application (or the application's project name), set FoxDoc's options (or use the default settings), and run FoxDoc. FoxDoc then follows the program's execution from beginning to end and creates numerous useful reports, such as a variable cross-reference report, a database structure report, action diagrams, and a program tree structure diagram.

FoxDoc also can format the source code files, which makes the output more attractive and readable. FoxDoc can indent control structures (such as IF ... ENDIF blocks), capitalize and expand keywords, and add informative headings to each program and procedure in an application. Besides simple text (such as the program name, author, and copyright notice), the headings also include the names of files that this program calls and files called from this program.

FoxDoc is a stand-alone executable file (FOXDOC.EXE) and, as such, can be run from DOS by typing `FOXDOC` at the DOS prompt. FoxPro includes a *hook* into FoxDoc, which makes FoxDoc accessible from FoxPro. You can run FoxDoc while you are in FoxPro by selecting FoxDoc from the Program menu or by typing `FOXDOC` in the Command window.

If you have disabled the FoxDoc option on the Program menu, FoxPro cannot find the FoxDoc files. Refer to the "Getting Started" section of the FoxDoc chapter in the *FoxPro Developer's Guide* for a list of the required files. With the exception of CONFIG.FXD, all these files must reside in the FoxPro home directory.

FoxDoc always looks for the configuration file CONFIG.FXD in the current directory. If it finds this file, FoxDoc takes the default values from the file. If it doesn't find the file, FoxDoc uses the built-in defaults. You can and should create a configuration file for each of your applications and save the file in the application's main directory. Then when you run FoxDoc from the application's directory, FoxDoc automatically restores your saved settings.

To create a configuration file, run FoxDoc and fill in the fields on the system screen. Then press the F5 function key to save the entries. Accept the default configuration file name, and FoxDoc then creates the file. As you work through each of FoxDoc's option screens, always remember that you must save the settings if you want them used as the default values in the next FoxDoc session with this application.

The documentation for FoxDoc is located in Chapter 13 of the *FoxPro Developer's Guide*. The documentation is fairly straightforward and complete. FoxDoc also has a very complete context-sensitive Help system that you can always access by pressing F1. Rather than simply restate what you can learn about FoxDoc from reading the manuals and the help screens, the next section focuses on what may not be apparent from those sources and gives you a few pointers for getting the most from this impressive tool.

The FoxDoc System Screen

When you run FoxDoc, the first thing you see is a FoxPro logo screen. Press Enter, and the FoxDoc System screen appears. This screen is the only one in which you must enter information. FoxDoc requires the name of the *main*, or top-level program, in the application or the name of the application's project (.PJX) file. Enter the name of this file in the field below the copyright date.

If you haven't yet created a configuration file in the current directory, FoxDoc uses the current directory as the default value for all the paths. If any directories are incorrect, you must change them so that FoxDoc can find the files. In particular, you must set the line Path for FoxDoc files: to the FoxPro home directory (unless for some reason you have moved FoxDoc's files to a different directory). You can clear the current entry by pressing Ctrl+End and then copying the contents of the previous field into the current field by pressing Ctrl+D.

After you fill in all the information, press F10 to activate FoxDoc's main menu. FoxDoc then verifies that all the directories you specified and the top-level program of the application can be found; otherwise, you receive an error message. Press Ctrl+C to exit FoxDoc or press any other key to return to the System screen. If FoxDoc accepts all your entries, a screen similar to the one shown in figure 20.7 appears.

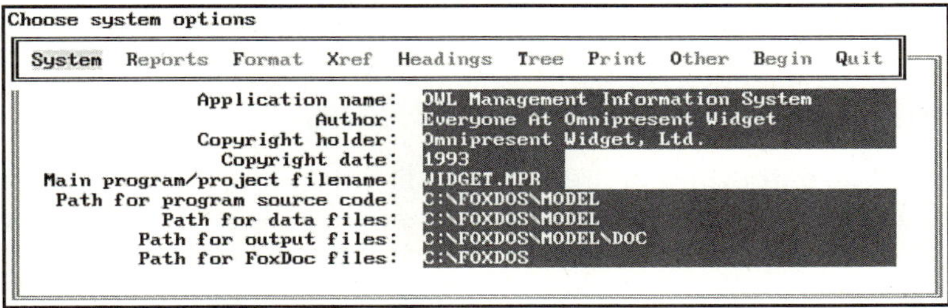

FIG. 20.7

The FoxDoc System screen and menu bar.

Remember that FoxDoc can process only ASCII source code (.PRG, .MPR, and .SPR) files and project (.PJX) files. FoxDoc cannot read compiled source code (.APP, .EXE, or .FXP) files. If you receive the error message `The main program must be a source code or project file`, the current directory probably contains only the compiled version of the program. If you specify the wrong file extension, FoxDoc scans the current directory, looking for source code files with the file name you entered. If you entered MAIN.APP as the main program file, FoxDoc looks for a related source code file, such as MAIN.MPR, and processes the menu file rather than informing you that the .APP file cannot be read.

> **CAUTION:** Always specify an *output files* directory different from the *program source code* directory. If you don't, FoxDoc overwrites the original source code files with the formatted output files. Although FoxDoc will save the original files with a .BAK extension, this protects you only once. When you next run FoxDoc on this application, the original source code files are overwritten and gone forever.
>
> You could direct FoxDoc output files to a subdirectory named \DOC beneath the directory that holds the program source code, for example. If the program source code is in C:\MYPROGS, direct the output files to C:\MYPROGS\DOC. If this directory does not exist, FoxDoc creates it for you.

FoxDoc Configuration Options

FoxDoc has a few dozen configuration options you can use to customize the reports, format source code listings, and output file names. The default settings usually work fine and do not need to be changed. In this section, you focus on the few configuration options that require you to decide what you want FoxDoc to do in certain situations.

Source Code Formatting Options

Run FoxDoc, enter the required information on-screen, and then press F10 to activate the main menu. Then select the Format option. A screen entitled FoxDoc Format and Action Diagram Options Screen appears. You must be sure that four options on this screen are set properly before you run FoxDoc.

By default, FoxDoc follows the Xbase formatting convention of using lowercase for tokens (i.e., variables, table names and other non-keywords) and uppercase for keywords (e.g., REPLACE). If your programming style doesn't follow this convention, then you need to change these settings. You can instruct FoxDoc to use all uppercase, all lowercase, uppercase for the first letter only (leaving the other letters unchanged), or no capitalization (leave everything unchanged).

FoxDoc also assumes that you want to re-indent control structures, such as DO WHILE ... ENDDO blocks. You can instruct FoxDoc to insert either Tab characters or spaces in the output file to accomplish this, or you can tell FoxDoc not to change your indentation.

As you write your programs, you probably capitalize and indent them the way you want. As you may have noticed in this book, the indenting style for programming constructs that contain multiple expressions is as follows:

```
DO WHILE     <condition 1> ;
         AND <condition 2>
```

If you don't want FoxDoc to change the program's appearance, be sure that you select N for all these options and that you use the F5 function key to save the settings in CONFIG.FXD.

One situation in which you definitely want to use FoxDoc's formatting options is when you are taking over a project from someone else whose formatting conventions may differ from yours or who didn't follow a consistent pattern of capitalization and indentation. Even if the listings aren't exactly the way you prefer, the consistent treatment of variable names and keywords makes the program much easier to follow.

The final formatting option you definitely should consider is the *Graphics, ASCII or other characters?* option. By default, FoxDoc uses the line-drawing characters in the IBM-extended ASCII character set to create the action diagram lines, linking the beginning of a control structure to the ending. If your printer does not support these characters, type A in this field. FoxDoc then uses standard ASCII characters in drawing the lines.

Cross-Reference Options

One of FoxDoc's most useful reports is the cross-reference report. This report shows you the program module and line number where a particular variable or keyword appears in the application and how the variable or keyword was used at that point in the program. If you use a variable named myvar, FoxDoc tells you that in procedure SETUP, myvar was declared PRIVATE on line 1 and had a value STOREd to myvar on line 10. This information can be extremely useful when you have changed a variable's name in one place (especially a PUBLIC variable's name) and want to make sure that you changed the name everywhere else. This report also is handy to ensure that any variable whose value is changed in a particular procedure is declared PRIVATE in this procedure so that you don't risk an inadvertent modification of a variable by the same name in a higher level procedure.

FoxDoc assumes that you want to cross-reference variables and other *tokens*, but not FoxPro keywords. To see where the keyword REPLACE is used in the application, change the Cross reference FoxPro keywords option from N to Y.

To create the global, system-wide cross-reference report, FoxDoc must maintain a table of all token names and locations in memory. In a large application, FoxDoc may lack enough memory to store all this information. You can work around this problem by setting the Local cross-references only? option to Y. This change tells FoxDoc to create a separate cross-reference report for each module in the application. You can see where the variable foo (FoxDoc's author's favorite variable name) was referenced within a particular procedure, but you will not get a listing of every occurrence of foo throughout the application.

Tree Diagram Options

Like the action diagrams, tree diagrams may use graphic characters or ASCII characters to draw the lines in the diagram. If your printer does not support the IBM line-drawing characters, set the Characters for tree (G/A/N)? option you see on-screen to either A (ASCII) or N (none).

If you select N, the diagram uses no lines to connect programs, but you still can tell which programs are called by other programs by the level of indentation they have in the diagram.

Printing Options

For many developers, FoxDoc's formatted source code listings are the program's most valuable feature. Although many FoxDoc screens may be left unchanged, you may want to change at least one of the default printer setup options before you print the source code listings.

Reviewing an action diagram is helpful in tracking down a nesting error in a program that contains multiple nested IFs and DO WHILEs, for example, but you don't always want to print these diagrams along with the source code. If you want to create but not print the action diagrams, set the Create action diagrams? option on the Format and Action Diagrams Options screen to Y so that action diagrams are created. Then set the Print action diagrams? option here to N.

FoxDoc's line width, page length, and margin settings are all configured for a wide-carriage, dot-matrix printer. If you use a laser printer, you may want to change most of the settings. Remember that the default page length for a Hewlett-Packard LaserJet is 60 lines per page rather than 66 and that you can print 132 characters across the page only if you use compressed print.

To use compressed print without resetting the printer's default setup, you can enter the proper LaserJet escape code sequence in the Printer setup string: field. Information you enter here is sent to the printer before printing begins. If you enter a setup string, you also need to enter a reset string in the field below the setup string. The contents of this field are sent to the printer after the print job is complete.

You can use the List option (F2) to pick a printer from a small list of printers for which Microsoft has provided appropriate printer settings and printer control codes. The printers currently supported are Epson and Hewlett-Packard LaserJets and close compatibles that use the same setup strings as these printers. The printer setup codes are contained in the ASCII text file FXDPRT.FXD, located in the FoxPro home directory. If this file is not on the disk or if you want to add a printer to the file, you can create or modify this file. You must follow these formatting conventions, however, for FoxDoc to *read* your setup. The following lines are at the top of the FXDPRT.FXD file:

```
* This is the FoxDoc printer default file. It is formatted like
this:
*  Printer name
*  Line width
*  Page length
*  Top margin
*  Bottom margin
*  Left margin
*  Right margin
*  Tab expansion
*  Print line numbers?
*  Form feed before print?
*  Form feed after print?
*  Setup string
*  Reset string
*
**********************************************************
Default printer
**********************************************************
999
66
8
8
12
1
3
Y
Y
Y
```

continues

```
************************************************************
Epson-pica
************************************************************
80
66
8
8
12
1
3
Y
Y
Y
\027@
\018
```

Note that the two blank lines that separate the last entry for Default printer and the row of asterisks above Epson-pica are part of the printer setup for "Default printer". The fact that these lines are blank indicates that this printer doesn't require a setup or reset string.

Formatting Snippets with SNIPFMT.APP

Code snippets that you create in the Menu Builder and Screen Builder are stored in a table with the other information for the menu or screen. When you generate the source code, these snippets form part of the .MPR or .SPR source code file. FoxDoc treats code snippets just like any other procedure and formats them, using the options you specified.

The original snippet still located in the menu or screen table doesn't change, however. FoxDoc's author, Walt Kennamer, has written a separate utility program, SNIPFMT.APP, in the FoxPro home directory, to format code snippets. The SNIPFMT utility is more limited in capability than FoxDoc, but SNIPFMT can indent your snippet code with tabs or spaces and can capitalize keywords and variables in whichever style you prefer.

Like the template programs, GENSCRN and GENMENU, as well as the GENPD printer driver system, SNIPFMT is just an application written in FoxPro. To change it, you MODIFY the project that you find in the GOODIES\SNIPFMT directory. You can change the SNIPFMT screen to add more options and then edit the FMT procedure, located in SNIP.PRG (SNIPFMT's main file), to process your new settings.

You use SNIPFMT by running the SNIPFMT.APP file. SNIPFMT presents you with a screen in which you enter the name of the file that contains the snippets and set your capitalization and indenting preferences (see fig. 20.8).

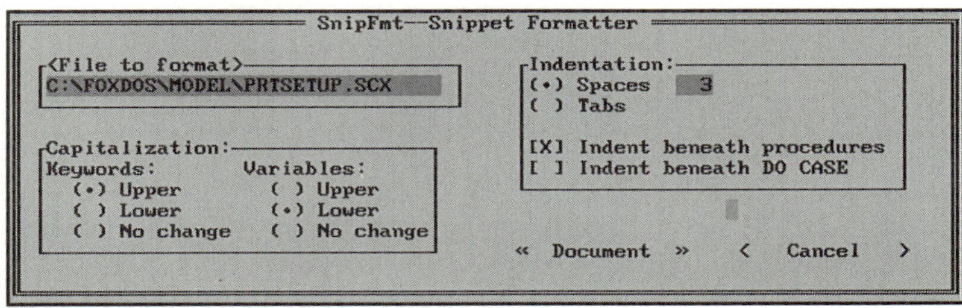

FIG. 20.8
The SNIPFMT.APP Configuration Options Screen.

When you select the `Document` push button, SNIPFMT loads the keywords file and formats each snippet in the selected file. SNIPFMT actually applies the formatting to a temporary copy of the original snippet but will not change the source code unless you select Save when the formatted text appears in a window. Review and then save the formatted snippet if you like what SNIPFMT did.

Summary

Help systems, Debug and Trace, ON ERROR, and FoxDoc—this chapter has covered some diverse features of FoxPro. All these features share one important characteristic: each is a high-quality tool designed for a distinctive role within the overall process of creating a superior application.

With these features and with the wide-ranging options discussed in Part III, "Building FoxPro Applications," FoxPro goes to great lengths to ensure that *you* always have the right tool for the job so that you can create systems that provide *your users* with the right tools for the job.

Supporting all these tools, and intrinsic to each one of them, are the commands and functions that constitute the FoxPro programming language. You began using some of them in Part I, "Introducing FoxPro," of this book, and you were gradually introduced to more commands and functions in the practice sessions in Parts II, "Getting Productive with FoxPro Databases," and III, "Building FoxPro Applications." In Part IV, "FoxProgramming: Enhanced Use of the Design

Tools," you have learned about the logic and structure that are essential to programming techniques. Part V, "Getting To Know FoxPro Commands and Functions," covers some categories of commands and functions in greater detail and provides suggestions for their use and sample procedures to assist you as you begin to develop custom programs.

21

CHAPTER

Using Commands and Functions To Manipulate Data

Many of FoxPro's commands and functions enable you to manipulate data elements of FoxPro's basic data types (character, numeric, date, and logical). You can convert lowercase letters to uppercase, extract a line from a Memo field, convert one type of data element to another type, and determine whether a sequence of characters is contained in a character string. The list of data manipulation functions that FoxPro provides is long, and the possible combinations of these functions is almost endless.

FoxPro also provides commands that make it easy for you to locate records and create subsets of your data. This chapter covers many of FoxPro's data manipulation commands and functions. Finally, this chapter discusses the commands and functions required to properly manage file and record lock contention in a multiuser environment.

Some of these commands and functions you have already seen in previous chapters. Others you will see for the first time. The goal is not to provide a reference manual to FoxPro's commands and functions, but rather to organize them by their intended use, to provide you with concrete examples of their use, and to show you some creative methods for employing them in your applications.

Manipulating Single Data Elements

This section covers the functions that manipulate single data elements, such as a memory variable or a single record in a table. For the most part, this section focuses on those functions that transform the data in some way. Because many of FoxPro's commands and functions require their arguments to be of a particular data type or in a certain format, data transformation is a very important subject.

Keep in mind that functions simply return values; the functions don't actually change the data. The UPPER( ) function, for example, doesn't change the case of its argument; the function simply makes the uppercase form of the data available for use by another command or function. To actually convert the data element to all uppercase, you must store the returned value of the UPPER( ) function back to the variable—for example:

```
m.Lastname = "smith"
SEEK UPPER(m.Lastname)
* m.Lastname is still"smith"
m.Lastname = UPPER(m.Lastname)
* Now, m.Lastname is "SMITH"
```

Manipulating Character Strings and Memo Fields

FoxPro excels at manipulating character strings. You can search a string for the presence of a substring, strip off file extensions, replace one substring with another, pad a string with spaces, and convert character strings to other data types. The list goes on and on. This section describes the commands and functions used with character-type data.

In the standard version of FoxPro for DOS, character strings can be up to 64K long; character strings can be much longer in the Extended version and in FoxPro for Windows (up to whatever length your system's free memory can accept). By contrast, Memo fields are limited only by your available disk space. For this reason, not all functions that you can use on character strings work properly on large Memo fields; some of the functions work on Memo fields only if the contents of the field remain within allowable string size. In tables 21.1 and 21.2, an asterisk indicates the functions that you can use on Memo fields *regardless of their size.* All memo handling functions, however, have no such limitation, so you can use them on character strings of any size.

Finding One String within Another

FoxPro has several functions that enable you to search a character string for the occurrence of a character or substring. Table 21.1 lists these functions.

Table 21.1 FoxPro's String Search Functions

Function	Description
*$	Returns .T. if a substring is contained in a string or Memo field.
*AT( )	Returns an integer representing the position in a string where a specified occurrence of a substring was found, searching from left to right. AT( ) is case-sensitive.
*ATC( )	Works the same way as AT( ), but is case-insensitive.

continues

Table 21.1 Continued

Function	Description
*ATLINE( )	Returns the number of the line in a Memo field where a substring was found. Although most often used with Memo fields, this function also works with character strings. The current setting of MEMOWIDTH determines how many characters each line contains, subject to the effects of word wrapping.
*ATCLINE( )	Works the same as ATLINE( ), but is case-insensitive.
*OCCURS( )	Returns the number of occurrences of a substring within a string or Memo field. OCCURS( ) is case-sensitive.
RAT( )	Works like AT( ) but searches the target string from right to left. This function is particularly useful when you must strip a simple file name from a fully qualified file name, using the \ character as the search substring. Because the rightmost \ character indicates the end of the path, you can strip the file name of its path by using RAT( ).
RATLINE( )	Works the same as ATLINE( ), but the search is performed starting with the last character and moving toward the first.

** Denotes functions that can be used on Memo fields of any size.*

The $ symbol, which Fox's documentation refers to as both a function and an operator, tells you whether one string is contained in another string. If it is, $ returns .T.; otherwise, it returns .F.. The AT( ) function does the same job, but also tells you where in the string the substring occurs. If the substring is not found, AT( ) returns 0. The following two lines are functionally equivalent:

```
IF "Johnson" $ Lastname

IF AT("Johnson", Lastname) > 0
```

If all you need to do is test for the presence of a substring, which function you use is mostly a matter of personal preference. If you are performing substring searches on Memo fields and the substrings can consist of more than one word, however, you should be aware of some special capabilities of $, explained in the ATLINE( ) example later in this section.

You use $ with two arguments in the following form:

```
<substring> $ <string>
```

This entire expression evaluates to either True or False. To test for the absence of a substring, you must apply a logical negative operator (! or NOT) to the entire expression, as follows:

```
IF ! ("Johnson" $ Lastname)
```

The enclosing parentheses are not required, but they make the function easier to read.

The AT( ) function really comes into its own when you need to extract a series of characters from a string. You might, for example, have enabled the user of your application to create a comma-delimited list of fields on which you will create an index tag for the current table. To isolate each field in the list, you can use the AT( ) function as follows:

```
* fld_list is in the form "Last, First, Company"
DO WHILE AT(",", fld_list) > 0
   * extract the field name from the beginning of the list
   index_fld = ALLTRIM(LEFT(fld_list, AT(",",fld_list)-1))

   * create the index on this field
   INDEX ON &index_fld TAG (index_fld)

   * now remove this field, and the comma that follows it,
   * from the list
   fld_list = SUBSTR(fld_list, AT(",", fld_list)+1)
ENDDO

* you now have a list that contains a single field name
* create the index on this field
INDEX ON &fld_list TAG (fld_list)
```

Because you know that each field name is separated from the next by a comma, you use the AT( ) function to determine the number of characters that make up the field name, the LEFT( ) function to store the current field name to a variable (index_fld), and the SUBSTR( ) function to remove this field name from the list when you don't need it anymore. LEFT( ) uses AT( ) to determine how many characters to include in index_fld, and SUBSTR( ) uses AT( ) to determine the first character of the old fld_list that should be included in the new fld_list. The next chapter describes LEFT( ) and SUBSTR( ).

The ATLINE( ) functions—and its relatives ATCLINE( ) and RATLINE( )—often are used with the MLINE( ) function to display or store the contents of a particular line of a Memo field. For example:

```
* find each record in the table that contains a certain
* string in the NOTES memo field, and display the first
* line in which the string was found
contact = "Jones"
LOCATE FOR contact $ Notes
DO WHILE FOUND()
   ? MLINE(Notes, ATLINE(contact,Notes))
   CONTINUE
ENDDO
```

The MLINE( ) function is covered later in this section.

The behavior of ATLINE( ) and its related functions are subject to word wrap, like all other Memo field handling commands. In the example above, if contact were "Bob Jones" rather than "Jones", the $ search would return .T.. However, if the words "Bob" and "Jones" were at the end and beginning of two separate lines, the ATLINE( ) function returns 0. Therefore, the technique shown in this example is limited to single words. Word wrap and behavior related to MEMOWIDTH are covered in greater detail in the following section.

Changing the Length, Case, and Contents of Strings and Memo Fields

Besides simply searching for strings, you also can change their contents. You can change a string's length and case and substitute one set of characters for another. Table 21.2 lists the FoxPro functions you can use for these purposes.

Table 21.2 FoxPro's String Manipulation Functions

Function	Description
TRIM( )	Strips trailing blanks.
LTRIM( )	Strips leading blanks.
RTRIM( )	Same as TRIM( ).
ALLTRIM( )	The same as LTRIM(RTRIM(<string>)).
PADC( )	Pads the string to the left and right so that it is centered within a specified character or characters.

Function	Description
PADL( )	Pads the string to the left with a specified character or characters.
PADR( )	Pads the string to the right with a specified character or characters.
REPLICATE( )	Returns a string consisting of a specified number of copies of a given expression.
SPACE( )	Returns a character string containing a specified number of spaces.
LOWER( )	Converts a string to all lowercase characters.
UPPER( )	Converts a string to all uppercase characters.
PROPER( )	Changes the first character of each word to uppercase and the remaining characters to lowercase.
*LEN( )	Returns the length of string.
LEFT( )	Returns a specified number of characters, beginning with the first character in the string.
RIGHT( )	Returns a specified number of characters, counting from the last character in the string.
*SUBSTR( )	Returns a specified number of characters, beginning at a specified position within the string.
*MEMLINES( )	Returns the number of lines in a string or Memo field as determined by the current setting of SET MEMOWIDTH.
*MLINE( )	Returns the contents of a specified line in a string or Memo field. The current setting of MEMOWIDTH determines which characters appear on the line.
CHRTRAN( )	Substitutes any occurrence of a character for a different one, using two character strings as a translation table.
STRTRAN( )	Works like CHRTRAN( ), but with entire substrings rather than individual characters. Any instance of the first substring is replaced by the second substring, or by the null string (" ") if a second string is not supplied.
STUFF( )	Works like STRTRAN( ), but replaces a specified number of characters, and the replacement begins at a specified character position.
TRANSFORM( )	Enables you to display formatted character or numeric expressions without using @ ... SAY/GET.

** Denotes function that can be used on Memo fields of any size.*

The *trimming* functions remove all blank spaces from one end or both ends of a string or Memo field. To ensure that two strings that are the same are not regarded as different because of extraneous spaces, strings are usually trimmed before a comparison operation. For example:

```
@ 10,10 SAY "Contact" GET contact DEFAULT SPACE(20)
READ
* user may have entered "  Bob Jones"
* use the LTRIM() function to strip any leading spaces
* before comparing the entry
IF LTRIM(contact) = "Bob Jones"
   <statements>
ENDIF
```

Note that the expression

```
IF LTRIM(contact) = "Bob Jones"
```

may not return the same value as

```
IF "Bob Jones" = LTRIM(contact)
```

because of the way that all Xbase dialects compare character strings. The current setting of EXACT (ON or OFF) also affects the expressions. If EXACT is ON, the expressions are considered the same; if EXACT is OFF, they are not. Refer to Chapter 7, "Querying with SQL and Searching with Rushmore," for a detailed analysis of the rules FoxPro follows to decide whether two strings are the same.

The converse of the preceding trimming functions, the *padding* functions, adds spaces (or any other character or characters) to a string. The only difference among the padding functions is where the characters are added.

PADC( ) (pad center) is useful for displaying a message centered within a window of unknown width, as follows:

```
ACTIVATE WINDOW win1
@ 0,0 SAY PADC("Reindexing tables...", WCOLS())
```

WCOLS( ) returns the number of columns in the active window (win1), and PADC( ) inserts the proper number of spaces before and after the message text so that the message is centered within the window. To pad the message with something other than spaces, specify the pad character(s) as the third argument in the function call. For example:

```
@ 0,0 say PADC(" Reindexing tables... ", WCOLS(), "*")
```

You can use PADR( ) (pad right) to ensure that a search expression has the same form as the current index expression. If, for example, you have the index key Lastname+Firstname, and Lastname is 20 characters long, the index entries look like the following:

```
Jones       Bob
Thompson    Michael
```

To find "Bob Jones" using this index, you must pad the last name with spaces so "Bob" appears in the same position in the search expression as it does in the index expression, as follows:

```
mlast  = "Jones"
mfirst = "Bob"
msearch = PADR(mlast, fsize('Lastname')) + mfirst
SEEK msearch
```

The case-changing functions are used primarily to overcome the case-sensitive nature of FoxPro's comparison operators and searching functions. When updating a customer table, for example, you might want to avoid having two records for Bob Jones, one in proper case and one in upper- or lowercase. The following procedure is an example of this type of validation:

```
* open the Customer table; the index key is
* UPPER(Customer)
USE Customer

@ 10,10 SAY "Customer " GET m.Customer DEFAULT SPACE(20)
READ

* user may have entered "Bob Jones", "bob jones" or
* "BOB JONES"; use the UPPER() function to convert the
* search expression to the same case as the index entries
IF SEEK(UPPER(m.Customer))
   ?? CHR(7)   && get the user's attention
   WAIT WINDOW "This customer is already on file!" NOWAIT
ENDIF
```

LEFT( ), RIGHT( ), and SUBSTR( ) all return a specified number of characters from a string or Memo field. The primary differences between the functions are the location in the string at which the substring to be returned will begin and the direction in which the number of characters are specified. LEFT( ) always starts at the far-left character and returns the specified number of characters to the right; RIGHT( ) starts at the far-right character and returns the specified number of characters to the left (though it retains the original left-to-right orientation of those characters); and SUBSTR( ) starts wherever you tell it to and returns the specified number of characters to the right.

Suppose that you have a memory variable that holds a fully qualified file name (C:\FOXPRO25\CONFIG.FP, for example). You can extract the various parts of the file name by using each of these substring functions, as follows:

```
* STRSLICE.PRG - slice up a supplied string to
* isolate the FoxPro configuration file's drive and
* subdirectory, base file name, and file extension
* store the name of the config file
Fullname = SYS(2019)

* Locate the last backslash character.
bs_pos   = RAT("\",Fullname)

* Locate the period in the file name.
pd_pos   = RAT(".",Fullname)

dirname  = LEFT(Fullname,bs_pos)
basename = SUBSTR(Fullname,bs_pos+1,pd_pos-bs_pos-1)
extname  = RIGHT(Fullname,len(fullname)-pd_pos)
*
* if fullname = C:\FOXPRO25\CONFIG.FP, then
*    dirname  = C:\FOXPRO25\
*    basename = CONFIG
*    extname  = FP*
```

MLINE( ) returns the contents of a single line of a Memo field or character string. MLINE( ) is like SUBSTR( ), but is specifically designed to respect word wrapping. The current setting of MEMOWIDTH determines how many characters are on each line. The following example demonstrates how MLINE( ) works and how it differs from SUBSTR( ):

```
DemoString = REPLICATE("Nothing runs like the fox! ", 150)
SET MEMOWIDTH TO 50
? LEN(DemoString)                       && 4050
? LEN(DemoString) / 50                  &&   81
? MEMLINES(DemoString)                  &&   84
? SUBSTR(DemoString,51,50)
   * ox! Nothing runs like the fox! Nothing runs like t
? MLINE(DemoString,2)
   * fox! Nothing runs like the fox! Nothing runs like
```

If the MEMLINES( ) function did not respect the MEMOWIDTH setting and the resulting word wrapping of the text, MEMLINES( ) would return the same value as LEN(DemoString) / 50. Instead, the function returns the number of lines that would be displayed on-screen if you entered `? DemoString` in the Command window.

SUBSTR( ) sees the memory variable DemoString as a simple string of characters, as follows:

```
         0         1         2         3         4         5
         12345678901234567890123456789012345678901234567890
  0      Nothing runs like the fox! Nothing runs like the f
 50      ox! Nothing runs like the fox! Nothing runs like t
100      he fox! Nothing runs like the fox! Nothing runs li
```

MLINE( ) and MEMLINES( ), on the other hand, see DemoString as a Memo field that has been opened in a memo-editing window, like this:

```
         0         1         2         3         4         5
         12345678901234567890123456789012345678901234567890
  0      Nothing runs like the fox! Nothing runs like the
 50      fox! Nothing runs like the fox! Nothing runs like
100      the fox! Nothing runs like the fox! Nothing runs
```

The MLINE( ) function has an optional third argument which can greatly enhance the function's utility by allowing you to specify an offset from a particular memo line. In addition, a new system variable (_MLINE) automatically tracks the current offset into a string or Memo field (relative to its beginning) returned by a previous MLINE( ) function call. When you print a series of lines from a Memo field, using 1 as the second argument and _MLINE as the third argument greatly improves the rate at which MLINE( ) returns Memo field lines.

The following program, PARSMEMO.PRG, shows how you can use the MLINE( ) function and _MLINE system variable to read a text file of commands and execute them by using macro expansion. The text file could contain single- and multiple-line commands and even SQL select statements. The user creates the text file (perhaps through a series of dialogs) and saves it as COMMAND.TXT. The program then uses APPEND MEMO to create a Memo field FROM the text file, and MLINE( ) and _MLINE to parse it:

```
* PARSMEMO.PRG
* By Lisa C. Slater

CREATE CURSOR parser (formula m)
APPEND BLANK
APPEND MEMO formula FROM command.txt
oldwidth = SET("MEMOWIDTH")
```

continues

```
SET MEMOWIDTH TO 2048   && limit for command line length
DO parsememo
SET MEMOWIDTH TO oldwidth

PROCEDURE parsememo
no_lines = MEMLINES(formula)
_MLINE = 0
thisline = ""
thiscmd = ""
FOR xx = 1 TO no_lines
      thisline = MLINE(parser.formula,1,_MLINE)
      * Note that we need to alias the formula field,
      * because we don't know what work areas the
      * formula might be SELECTing! The only restriction
      * is that the created formula must not move the pointer
      * in the parser table,
      IF EMPTY(thisline)
         LOOP
      ENDIF
      thiscmd = thiscmd + thisline
      thiscmd = TRIM(thiscmd)
      IF ! RIGHT(thiscmd,1) = ";"
          &thiscmd
          thiscmd = ""
      ELSE
          thiscmd = SUBSTR(thiscmd,1,LEN(thiscmd)-1)
      ENDIF
ENDFOR
RETURN
```

The STRTRAN( ) function is great for removing blank spaces from within a string or for swapping file extensions.

The trimming functions can easily strip blanks from the beginning and end of a string, but they can't help you when you need to remove spaces from within the string. You can use STRTRAN( ) to accomplish this task by specifying the null string (" ") as the third argument, or by not specifying a third argument, which tells FoxPro to use the null string as the replacement string. This feature can be very useful when you want to search a field that may contain any number of embedded spaces, as follows:

```
* search for a name in the Contact field; the user might
* enter "Bob Jones" as "Bob   Jones", so you need to
* strip out the embedded spaces; you actually search
* for "BOBJONES," with all uppercase and no spaces
@ 10,10 SAY "Contact " GET fullname DEFAULT SPACE(20)
READ
```

```
LOCATE FOR    UPPER(STRTRAN(Contact," ")) ;
           == UPPER(STRTRAN(fullname," "))
```

When you create a temporary copy of a table that has a Memo field, a memo file (FPT) also is created. If your application doesn't know whether the table has a Memo field, you should check for the existence of a memo file when erasing the temporary files. Because the memo file has the same base name as the database file, you can use STRTRAN( ) to change the extension of the file name stored in a memory variable, as follows:

```
* Get a unique file name and create a temporary copy
* of the current table.
tempfile = SYS(3) + ".$$$"
* This creates a file name like 55048985.$$$
COPY STRUCTURE TO (tempfile)
*
* Data processing commands would go here.
*
* Now you're ready to "clean up."

* Erase the temporary database file whose name is
* held in tempfile.
ERASE (tempfile)

* You must also erase any memo file created.
tempfile = STRTRAN(tempfile, ".$$$", ".FPT")

* tempfile is now something like "55048985.FPT"
IF FILE(tempfile)
   ERASE (tempfile)
ENDIF
```

You also can use the CREATE CURSOR command to create a temporary table that is erased automatically when you close it. The "Using FoxPro's SQL Commands" section of Chapter 22 covers the CREATE CURSOR command.

Converting Character Data to and from Other Data Types

FoxPro has several functions that convert character data to and from other data types. Table 21.3 lists these functions.

Table 21.3 Character Data Conversion Functions

Function	Converts From	To
CTOD( )	Character (using current SET DATE format)	Date
DTOC( )	Date	Character (using current SET DATE format)
DTOS( )	Date	Character (using YYYYMMDD format, suitable for indexing)
STR( )	Numeric	Character
VAL( )	Character	Numeric

This chapter's "Manipulating Dates" section includes examples of CTOD( ), DTOC( ), and DTOS( ), and the following section discusses STR( ) and VAL( ).

Manipulating Numeric Data

Many of FoxPro's numeric data handling functions perform mathematical, trigonometric, and financial operations on numeric data. Among them are ABS( ), which returns the absolute value of a number, and PAYMENT( ), which calculates the amount of each payment on a fixed-interest loan.

Most database applications have little need for the trigonometric and financial functions, and those that do require a more in-depth analysis of their usage than can be provided here. This book looks at the numeric functions that are generally more useful in database applications.

Using MAX( ) and MIN( ) To Define Boundaries

Often, you may need to select the largest or smallest in a series of values. Rather than comparing all possible pairs of values in the series by using a number of IF ... ENDIFs, you can use FoxPro's MAX( ) and MIN( ) functions. The MAX( ) function returns the largest of a list of expressions; the MIN( ) function returns the smallest of a list of expressions.

Both functions accept a list of expressions. Although they are categorized as numeric functions, their arguments can be of any data type, as long as they are all of the same data type (to verify this, try typing `? MAX(.T., .F.)` in the Command window). The return value is the same data type as the argument list.

The following example uses both MAX( ) and MIN( ) to determine the proper width for a data-entry window. The size of each field in the table is compared to a variable that holds the size of the largest field seen so far, and then the size of the largest field is compared to the number of available screen columns to ensure that the window is completely contained in the visible screen area:

```
* Create an array containing structure info on current
* table. AFIELDS() automatically creates the array if it
* doesn't exist.
= AFIELDS(fld_array)

* Determine the largest field.
max_len = 0
FOR j=1 TO ALEN("fld_array",1)
   * the field length is held in the third
   * "column" of the array
   max_len = MAX(max_len, fld_array[j,3])
ENDFOR

* Adjust max_len to account for the field descriptions,
* the window borders, and some extra spacing.
max_len = max_len + 16

* Store the lesser of max_len or the screen width in
* win_width.
win_width = MIN(max_len, SCOLS())
```

This example uses two of FoxPro's array-handling functions, AFIELDS( ) and ALEN( ), to provide the required information about the current table. The next chapter covers array-handling functions in detail.

Using the Rounding and Modulus Functions

You can round numbers up and down with ROUND( ), CEILING( ), and FLOOR( ) and drop the decimals from a number with INT( ). MOD( ) and % are equivalent functions that return the modulus of a number. Table 21.4 describes these functions.

Table 21.4 FoxPro's Rounding Functions

Function	Description
%	Returns the remainder obtained by dividing one number by another. Also called the modulus operator.
CEILING( )	Returns the nearest integer that is greater than or equal to the specified number.
FLOOR( )	Returns the nearest integer that is less than or equal to the specified number.
INT( )	Returns the integer portion of a number.
MOD( )	A function that performs the same task as the modulus operator (%).
ROUND( )	Rounds a number to a specified number of decimal places.

The % operator provides the same functionality as the MOD( ) function. Each function returns the remainder obtained by dividing two numbers. MOD(5,2), for example, returns 1, as does 5 % 2.

The traditional example of a use for the modulus functions is to determine whether a year is a leap year. A leap year is one which is exactly divisible by four, unless it is a centennial year, in which case it must be exactly divisible by four hundred. You can determine whether a year is a leap year as follows:

```
curr_year = year(date())
is_leap = iif(curr_year % 100 = 0, ;
curr_year % 400 = 0, ;
curr_year % 4 = 0)
```

You also can use % or MOD( ) to create a sample of records in a table. Suppose that you have a table of names and addresses of people from all over the United States that represents a mailing list. Before you spend money on postage and materials, you want to send a sample mailing to a cross section of people, and you want your sample to contain people from each of the different states in the same proportion as the entire table. To create a sample table, you can sort on the State field and then copy every *n*th record to the sample table, as follows:

```
PROCEDURE makesamp
   *
   * Create a sample table containing samp_size number
```

```
    * of records from Maillist
    *
    PARAMETERS samp_size
    PRIVATE tot_recs, samp_intvl, tempfile
    USE Maillist
    tempfile = SYS(3) + ".$$$"
    SORT ON State TO (tempfile)
    USE (tempfile)
    tot_recs = RECCOUNT()
    samp_intvl = INT(tot_recs / MIN(tot_recs,samp_size))
    COPY TO Sample FOR MOD(RECNO(), samp_intvl) = 0
    USE
    ERASE (tempfile)
    USE Sample
RETURN
```

This example uses the INT( ) function to make sure that you are always working with integers. You could have used

```
ROUND(tot_recs / MIN(tot_recs,samp_size), 0)
```

to obtain the same result. The MIN( ) function causes the procedure to return all the records from the Maillist table when the specified sample size is larger than the number of records in the table.

Converting Numeric Data to and from Character Data

FoxPro has two functions that are useful for working with numeric data you need to treat as a string of digits and for working with character data on which you need to perform a numeric operation.

STR( ) converts numeric data into a character string of digits. VAL( ) performs the opposite function, converting character data into its numeric representation.

STR( ) is useful when you need to include a number as part of a character expression. For example, an index expression must be of a single data type. You cannot index on an expression that contains character strings and numeric data. You can, however, index on a character string plus the character representation of a number, such as

```
INDEX ON Custno + STR(Amount,10,0) TO Invbyamt
```

In this example, STR( ) accepts two optional arguments with which you can specify the length of the string and the number of decimal places.

Use VAL( ) when you need to perform a computation on a character data element that consists, at least partially, of digits. A table, for example, can have a Character field that holds an invoice number. In an order-entry routine, you might want to display the next sequentially ordered invoice number as the default for the next order. Because you cannot increment a character string, you must convert the character string into a number, add 1 to it, and then convert the result back into character form. You use both VAL( ) and STR( ) in the process, as follows:

```
* Open the Sales table and order it by DESCENDING
* invoice number, which is a character-type field.
USE Sales ORDER Invoice DESCENDING

* Because the index is now in descending
* order, we're on the last invoice in the
* table; increment the last invoice number
* and use it as the default for the next order
minvno = STR(VAL(Invoice)+1, len(Invoice))
```

You might wonder why the invoice number is stored as a character string in the first place when it consists entirely of digits and you want to be able to perform a computation on it. There are a couple of reasons for this.

First, the invoice number also may include one or more letters.

It is not uncommon for an invoice number to be prefaced by an identifier, such as XX1234, where XX might be the code for a particular division of the company. If a company that had been using invoice numbers that consisted of digits decided to include an identifier as part of the invoice number, you would not easily be able to accommodate this change if you had been storing the invoice number in a Numeric field.

If you use an invoice numbering system of this nature, you strip the prefacing alphabetical characters from the invoice code before incrementing the invoice number in the earlier procedure, as in the following:

```
* Invoice numbering system is "XX1234"
* where XX represents the division.
minvno = m.Division + ;
         STR(VAL(RIGHT(Invoice),4)+1,4)
```

Second, although you might want to perform some type of computation on the invoice number, such as incrementing it by 1, you don't need to include the number in any table-wide computational database commands, such as SUM or AVERAGE. You never need to keep a running total of invoice numbers. Just as with a Social Security number, the digits don't really have any numeric significance other than to differentiate one record from the others.

Manipulating Date and Time Data

FoxPro provides a full complement of functions that manipulate dates. Many of the date functions return character strings that you can use in reports to display the current date as text (September 30, 1991, for example), rather than as digits (09/30/91). Other functions simply convert dates into character strings (perhaps for inclusion in a character index expression) and character strings into dates (for use in a "date math" calculation or for comparison to a Date field or variable).

FoxPro treats dates as a special type of numeric data. This explains why you can add or subtract one date from another. If, for example, you type the following in the Command window:

```
? CDOW({01/01/1901})
? CDOW({01/01/1901} - 1)
```

you will see that the first New Year's Day of the 20th century fell on a Tuesday, and that the last New Year's Eve of the 19th century fell on a Monday.

For an in-depth analysis of FoxPro's internal handling of dates, see *Developing FoxPro 2.0 Applications,* by P.L. Olympia and Kathy Cea (Addison-Wesley, 1991).

Displaying the Current Date and Time

FoxPro has built-in functions that return the current system date and time by reading the computer's system clock.

DATE( ) often is used to display the current date at the top of the screen and to print the current date on reports. DATE( ) also is used as the argument to those date functions that convert a date from digits to text, such as "January 1, 1992".

TIME( ) is used in much the same way as DATE( ). TIME( ) returns the current time, as stored in the computer's system clock. You also can display the current system time on-screen with the SET CLOCK ON command. You change the position with

```
SET CLOCK TO <row>, <col>
```

Manipulating Time Data

Another time function, SECONDS( ), returns the number of seconds that have elapsed since midnight. Using this function, you can determine, for example, how long it took FoxPro to execute a series of commands. Simply save the value returned by SECONDS( ) immediately before the first line of the block of commands and then display the difference between the current value of SECONDS( ) and the variable that holds the beginning time. You can convert the seconds elapsed to an hour-minute-second format by using the modulus function, described earlier in the chapter:

```
StartTime=SECONDS()
WAIT WINDOW
WAIT WINDOW "It took "+SHOWTIME(SECONDS()-StartTime) + ;
            " for you to press a key"

* SHOWTIME - convert numeric seconds to character HH:MM:SS
FUNCTION ShowTime
parameter nTime
return LTRIM(STR(INT(nTime/3600),10,0)) + ":" + ;
   PADL(LTRIM(TRANSFORM((nTime % 3600)/60,"99")),2,"0") ;
   + ":" + ;
  PADL(LTRIM(TRANSFORM(nTime % 60,"99")),2,"0")
```

Because you can manipulate both date and time variables as numeric data, FoxPro is ideal for use in time calculations such as times-series analyses.

Displaying Dates as Text and Extracting a Day, Month, or Year

Because dates are treated like numbers, it is possible for you to calculate any of the information provided by the functions shown in table 21.6, as long as you know the relevant information for some other date. For example, if you know that 12/31/1999 was a Friday, you can calculate the day of the week on which April 11, 2000 falls. Similarly, you can duplicate the functionality of many of the other functions. However, to do this, you might need to use many IF ... ELSE ... ENDIF or DO CASE constructs. In some variants of ther Xbase language, creating such complex functions is left to the developer.

Luckily, you don't have to calculate this information. The FoxPro date functions take much of the headache out of calculating and displaying dates. Of particular interest are the MDY( ) and DMY( ) functions, which you can use to display a date in fully spelled form, such as "October 12, 1991", or the equivalent European format "12 October 1991", respectively.

Because the uses of these functions are self-evident once you know what they do, table 21.5 simply describes the functions, and table 21.6 provides some usage information and sample output.

Table 21.5 Date Manipulation Functions

Function	Description
CDOW( )	Returns the day of the week for a specified date as a name, such as "Saturday".
CMONTH( )	Returns the name of the month for a specified date, such as "April".
DAY( )	Returns the day of the month for a particular date.
DMY( )	Returns a date in European day-month-year format. The month is displayed as a name, and the number of digits in the year depends on the current setting of CENTURY.
DOW( )	Returns the number of the day of the week for a date; Sunday is day 1.
GOMONTH( )	Returns the date that is a specified number of months before or after a date. GOMONTH( ) takes the differing number of days in the intervening months into account so that the date it returns always has the same day of the month as the date supplied.
MDY( )	Works the same as DMY( ) but uses American month-day-year format. With CENTURY set ON, MDY( ) and DMY( ) are useful for printing the current date on a letter.
MONTH( )	Returns the month of the year for a particular date.
YEAR( )	Returns the year of a given date. The year is always returned as a four-digit number, regardless of the setting of CENTURY.

Table 21.6 Using the Date Manipulation Functions

Function	Takes	Returns	Example	Displays
CDOW( )	Date	Char	? CDOW(DATE( ))	Saturday
CMONTH( )	Date	Char	? CMONTH(DATE( ))	October
DAY( )	Date	Num	? DAY(DATE( ))	12
DMY( )	Date	Char	? DMY(DATE( ))	12 October 93
	(with CENTURY set ON)			12 October 1993
DOW( )	Date	Num	? DOW(DATE( ))	7
GOMONTH( )	Date,Num	Date	? GOMONTH(DATE( ),3)	01/12/94
MDY( )	Date	Char	? MDY(DATE( ))	October 12, 93
	(with CENTURY set ON)			October 12, 1993
MONTH( )	Date	Num	? MONTH(DATE( ))	10
YEAR( )	Date	Num	? YEAR(DATE( ))	1993

Converting Dates to and from Character Data

You can convert dates to character strings and back by using the functions shown in table 21.7.

Table 21.7 The Date Conversion Functions

Function	Description
CTOD( )	Read as "character to date." Converts a character string, such as "01/01/91", to date type.
DTOC( )	Read as "date to character." Converts a date into its equivalent character string.
DTOS( )	Read as "date to string." Converts a date into an eight-digit string in the format YYYYMMDD, which is most suitable for ordering a table on a Date field.

CTOD( ) converts a character string to date type. One instance in which this feature is valuable is when you are filling a Date field with dates that are currently stored in an ASCII text file as character strings in MM/DD/YY format.

Suppose that you are converting an application from another database management system to FoxPro, that the other DBMS's file format is incompatible with FoxPro, and that the file format is not one of the file formats supported by the IMPORT command. You can export the data to an ASCII text file from the other DBMS and then append the text to a Character field in your FoxPro table by using the APPEND FROM command. For this example, assume that you have created an ASCII text file called OLD_DATA.TXT that looks like the following (of course, the ruler at the top is only for your reference):

```
0         1         2         3         4
1234567890123456789012345678901234567890123456789
Jones                William        052354
Smith                Roger          091562
Walters              Kenneth        100756
```

where the last column is a date in the format MMDDYY. To match the format of the text file, you create a table that has this structure:

```
Structure for database: <FoxPro Directory>\MODEL\PEOPLE.DBF
Field         Field Name          Type         Width     Dec    Index
 1             LASTNAME           Character    20
 2             FIRSTNAME          Character    15
 3             TEMP_DATE          Character     6
** Total **                                    42
```

Now you're ready to import the data. Type the following in the Command window:

```
APPEND FROM Old_data.txt TYPE SDF
```

A new record is appended to your table for each row in the text file, and the fields are filled with the appropriate data, because you sized them according to the number of spaces in each column of the text file.

Notice that the Date field, Temp_date, is actually a Character field. Because you cannot import text into a Date field unless it is in compatible format (a format to which you can SET DATE), you must perform the conversion in two steps. First, you import the text into a Character field, as you have just done. Then, you add a Date field to the table. Call it Birthdate. Now you can use the CTOD( ) function to fill the Date field with the intended date values, as follows:

```
REPLACE ALL Birthdate WITH ;
   CTOD(LEFT(Temp_date,2) + "/" + ;
        SUBSTR(Temp_date,3,2) + "/" + ;
        RIGHT(Temp_date,2))
```

To complete the conversion, just remove the Temp_date field from the table.

DTOC( ) converts dates to character strings. This function often is used to concatenate a Date field with one or more Character fields, as in

```
@ 10,10 SAY "Today's date is " + DTOC(DATE())
```

DTOC( ) accepts an optional second argument, the digit 1, that tells FoxPro to return the character string in the form of YYYYMMDD. This form is more appropriate than the MMDDYYYY form for creating an index that orders the records by a Date field.

DTOC(date( ),1) is equivalent to DTOS(date( )). Both return an eight-digit string in YYYYMMDD format, regardless of the current setting of CENTURY. Without the ,1 argument, CTOD( ), and DTOC( ) both respect the current CENTURY setting.

Using TYPE() and EMPTY() To Test a Variable

In an event-driven environment such as FoxPro, you often need to know whether a variable currently exists, and, in the case of a global variable, whether it has been assigned a value. TYPE( ) and EMPTY( ) provide this information.

TYPE( ) returns a single letter code for the data type of an expression: C for character, N for numeric, D for date, L for logical, and U for undefined.

TIP You also can use TYPE( ) to check for the existence of an array by specifying the first element of the array. If TYPE(arrayname[1])#"U", then the array exists. You must specify an array element number, or else TYPE( ) checks for a memory variable of the same name.

Because FoxPro enables you to modify the system menu, you can enable the user of your application to launch the application by selecting it from the system menu. Your application becomes an addition to FoxPro. When not in the application, the user has complete access to all of FoxPro's commands and functions through the Command window and the menu popups.

The example application for Omnipresent Widget works in just this way. It installs itself into the FoxPro system menu and peacefully coexists with the other FoxPro menu options. Each menu option runs a separate program contained in an application (.APP) file. Each of these programs must save any elements of the user's environment it needs to set a certain way and must restore the environment before exiting. Although the code to save the environment is contained within each of the programs, you can use a generic procedure called RESTENV to restore the environment. Each program calls this procedure before exiting.

RESTENV knows that each program that called it used the same name to save a particular environment setting, but RESTENV doesn't know whether the calling program actually created such a variable. RESTENV uses the TYPE( ) function to test for the existence and proper data type of each variable that it uses. For example, the following lines reset the previous setting of SAFETY and EXACT, but only if TYPE( ) verifies that a character type variable that stores the required information exists:

```
PROCEDURE restenv
   IF TYPE('safestat') = "C"
      SET SAFETY &safestat
   ENDIF

   IF TYPE('exacstat') = "C"
      SET EXACT &exacstat
   ENDIF
```

EMPTY( ) accepts an expression of any data type and returns .T. only if the expression is blank. The meaning of *blank* in this context depends on the data type of the expression. Table 21.8 defines *blank* for each of the data types, treating Memo fields as a special form of character data.

Table 21.8 Values That Cause EMPTY( ) To Return True

Data Type	What FoxPro Considers To Be a Blank
Character	Nulls, spaces, tabs, carriage returns, and line feeds
Numeric	0
Date	Null (for example, { / / })
Logical	False (.F.)
Memo	Empty (no memo contents, including no spaces, carriage returns, or characters of any kind)

FoxPro enables you to pass a variable number of arguments to a procedure or UDF. From within the procedure, you often need to know whether the calling program passed a parameter, and if so, whether it contains a value. The procedure CHIMES, for example, accepts up to five parameters. The pause parameter is optional. Any parameters that the calling program did not pass are initialized to .F., so you need to know whether pause contains a value passed by the calling program before you try to use the parameter:

```
PROCEDURE chimes
   *
   * ring bell, using different frequencies and durations
   PARAMETERS startfreq, endfreq, freqstep, duration, pause
   PRIVATE j, bellstat
   bellstat = SET("BELL")
   SET BELL ON
   FOR j=startfreq TO endfreq STEP freqstep
      SET BELL TO j,duration
      ?? CHR(7)
      IF !EMPTY(pause)
         = INKEY(pause)
      ENDIF
   ENDFOR

   * Restore bell SETtings.
   SET BELL TO 512,2
   SET BELL &bellstat
RETURN
```

If you are familiar with the PARAMETERS( ) function, you might wonder why it wasn't used rather than EMPTY( ). PARAMETERS( ) returns the number of parameters that were passed to the most recently called procedure, which is not necessarily the current procedure. If, for example, you had called a procedure to display a message in a window before executing the body of CHIMES, PARAMETERS( ) would thereafter have returned the number of parameters passed to the message-displaying procedure rather than the CHIMES procedure. If you choose to use PARAMETERS( ) in your programs, make sure that you save its value to a memory variable at the top of the procedure and use the variable rather than the current value of PARAMETERS( ).

Testing Lists and Ranges: INLIST( ) and BETWEEN( )

Two other functions, INLIST( ) and BETWEEN( ), do not fit neatly into our main categories of string, numeric, or date functions, because, unlike most FoxPro functions, they accept parameters of different types. INLIST( ) and BETWEEN( ) return a logical value, .T. or .F., based on whether the value to be tested (the first parameter supplied) is in the list of parameters or within the specified range of values, respectively. These functions can simplify testing for complex values and provide much easier to read programming code. The following are two examples using INLIST( ) and BETWEEN( ):

```
? INLIST(CDOW(DATE()),"Monday","Wednesday","Friday")

SCAN FOR BETWEEN(SaleDate,StartDate,EndDate)
```

Manipulating Records

In addition to manipulating single data elements, FoxPro contains commands and functions that move to or search for a particular record and that manipulate a group of records or an entire table. This section discusses these commands and functions.

Moving to or Locating a Particular Record

Each record in a table has a record number. The number of the current record is returned by the RECNO( ) function. RECNO( ) always returns a number between 1 and the number of records in the table (as returned by RECCOUNT( )) plus 1, unless the work area has no open table (in which case RECNO( ) returns 0). To position the record pointer on a particular record, you use the GOTO command, which is usually abbreviated as GO. Even the GO is unnecessary—simply type a record number to make that record the current one.

GO often is used with RECNO( ) to reposition the record pointer on a particular record after you have used some other data manipulation command, such as SEEK, that has moved the record pointer to another record or perhaps to the end of file (EOF) position. Before using any of the record-moving commands, you can save the current record position by storing the current value of RECNO( ) to a memory variable, as follows:

```
currec = IIF(EOF(), 0, RECNO())
```

The EOF( ) function, which tests for the end of file condition, returns True or .T. if the record pointer is positioned on what is known as the *phantom record*. The phantom record is a blank record beyond the last physical record stored in the table.

When positioned on the phantom record, RECNO( ) returns the number of records in the table plus 1. If you try to GO to that record, you receive the error message

```
Record out of range
```

Because no record in the table has a record number of 0, you store 0 to the variable currec as an indicator that you are currently at EOF. When you later want to reposition the record pointer, you can compare currec to 0 to determine whether you were previously at EOF before trying to move the record pointer to a particular record:

```
currec = IIF(EOF(), 0, RECNO())
*
* (other commands)
*
* Reposition the record pointer on the previously
* current record.
IF currec > 0
   GO currec
ELSE
   * You were previously at end of file,
   *  so go back there.
   GO BOTTOM
   IF !EOF()
      SKIP
   ENDIF
ENDIF
```

If the file contains no records, GO BOTTOM positions the record pointer on the phantom record, from which you cannot SKIP forward. You therefore must test for EOF after going to the bottom before you skip because you already may be at EOF.

SEEK has always been Xbase's searching workhorse. SEEK uses the currently active index to locate quickly the first record that matches the search expression. The search expression *type* and *format* must match the *type* and *format* of the index expression. If, for example, the index key *expression* of the current index is UPPER(Lastname), you must use the uppercase form of a search expression to locate the record, as follows:

```
USE Customer ORDER Customer
* The index key of tag Customer is upper(Lastname).
@ 10,10 SAY "Last Name " GET m.Lastname ;
   DEFAULT SPACE(LEN(Lastname))
READ
IF EMPTY(m.Lastname)
   RETURN
ENDIF
SEEK UPPER(m.Lastname)
IF FOUND( )
   * Commands to process record you've found go here.
ENDIF
```

The SEEK( ) function is a powerful combination of the SEEK command and the FOUND( ) function. Not only does SEEK( ) return a logical True or False, depending on whether the search expression was found in the current index, it also accepts a work area alias as an optional second argument. SEEK( ), therefore, can search an unselected table and position the record pointer in that table on the desired record. That record is then available to all of FoxPro's other table-accessing commands. You could rewrite the preceding example as follows:

```
USE Customer ORDER Customer
* the index key of tag Customer is upper(Lastname)
@ 10,10 SAY "Last Name " GET m.Lastname ;
   DEFAULT SPACE(LEN(Lastname))
READ
IF EMPTY(m.Lastname)
   RETURN
ENDIF
IF SEEK(UPPER(m.Lastname), "Customer")
   * Commands to process record you've found go here.
ENDIF
```

Where the record pointer is positioned after an unsuccessful search depends on the current setting of NEAR. If NEAR is set ON, the record pointer is positioned on the closest matching record to the search expression. If NEAR is set OFF, the record pointer is positioned at EOF.

Regardless of the setting of NEAR, RECNO(0) always returns the record number of the closest matching record after an unsuccessful search. The "closest matching record," in this context, does not mean a near match using an intelligent search, phonetic or otherwise. It simply means the first record with a key that is greater than the expression for which the SEEK was done.

In FoxPro 1.x and previous versions of FoxBASE+, the LOCATE command hardly ever was used because it always required that each record in the table be compared to the search expression. FoxPro 2.x, however, has optimized the use of the LOCATE command to use indexes and the Rushmore engine to speed searches whenever possible, resulting in retrieval speeds comparable to Rushmore-optimized SEEK performance.

CONTINUE tells FoxPro to find the next record in the table that matches the LOCATE FOR expression. Following is an example that uses LOCATE, CONTINUE, and GO. This example uses LOCATE/CONTINUE to find all the records in the current table that match a search expression. The record number of each matching record is stored in an array; each matching record is copied to a temporary table; the user selects a record from a Browse; and then the program uses GO to reposition the record pointer in the source table on the selected record. The key to the technique is the fact that the rows of the array correspond to the record numbers in the temporary table.

```
* Save the current work area.
source = SELECT( )

* Get the search expression.
@ 10,10 SAY "Last Name " GET m.Lastname ;
   DEFAULT SPACE(LEN(Lastname))
READ

* If the user pressed Esc or didn't enter a name,
* don't proceed.
IF LASTKEY( ) = 27 or EMPTY(m.lastname)
   RETURN
ENDIF

* Create a temporary table with the same structure
* as the current table.
tempdbf = SYS(3) + ".$$$"
COPY STRUCTURE TO (tempdbf)
USE (tempdbf) IN 0 ALIAS tempdbf
```

```
* Limit the number of matching records and create an
* array with this many elements to hold the record
* numbers.
max_recs = 100
DIMENSION recs_arr[max_recs]
j = 1

* Perform the search.
LOCATE FOR Lastname = m.lastname
IF !FOUND( )
   RETURN
ENDIF

* Copy the matching records to the temporary table
* and store their record numbers in an array
DO WHILE FOUND( ) AND j <= max_recs
   recs_arr[j,1] = RECNO( )
   SCATTER MEMVAR MEMO
   INSERT INTO tempdbf FROM MEMVAR
   j = j + 1
   CONTINUE
ENDDO

* Use the space bar to let the user select a record
save_key = ON('KEY', 'SPACEBAR')
ON KEY LABEL SPACEBAR KEYBOARD CHR(23)

* Browse the temporary table.
SELECT tempdbf
GO TOP
BROWSE ;
   TITLE "Press Space Bar to select, Esc for new search" ;
   PARTITION SCOLS( )-30 REDIT LPARTITION ;
   NOMODIFY NOAPPEND NODELETE ;
   COLOR SCHEME 10

* Restore the previous state of the space bar.
IF empty(save_key)
   ON KEY LABEL SPACEBAR
ELSE
   ON KEY LABEL SPACEBAR &save_key
ENDIF

* If the user selected a record, position the record
* pointer in the source table on the selected record.
mrec = recs_arr[RECNO( )]
```

continues

```
SELECT (source)
IF LASTKEY( ) != 27
   GO mrec
ENDIF

USE IN tempdbf
ERASE (tempdbf)
```

Creating a Subset of Records

FoxPro provides two methods for viewing a subset of the records in a table. The SET FILTER command compares each record in the current table to a filter expression that you supply, such as State = "CA", and includes a record in the subset only if the expression is True for that record.

The other method is to use INDEX ON ... FOR, again supplying a filter expression. Only those records that match the expression are included in the index, and only the indexed records are visible as long as the index controls the order of the records.

In FoxPro 1.x and FoxBASE+, the preferred method was to create an index. Although it took some extra time to do this, once the index was in place, subsequent access to the records in the subset was much faster than using a filter, because FoxPro had to evaluate records constantly against the filter condition.

Thanks to its Rushmore technology, however, FoxPro 2.x can use existing indexes to evaluate a filter condition, making SET FILTER the preferred method for creating a subset of your data if you already have created an index that matches your filter condition.

Chapter 3, "Exploring Databases and Tables," discusses SET FILTER; Chapter 4, "Database Management Fundamentals," covers INDEX ON.

Processing Multiple Records

Many database functions call for processing a large number of records, such as updating inventory records with a pricing increase. The simplest method of processing all records is by enclosing the repetitive steps within a SCAN ... ENDSCAN loop. Including FOR or WHILE clauses allows the selection of specific records or blocks of records. The selection of appropriate indexes and use of the SEEK command and WHILE clause will cause FoxPro to use only those records that fit specific criteria. The increased efficiency in reading or writing only a subset of the data can lead to significant performance improvements when you are processing a large update or complex analysis.

You must be careful when writing out data in multiple-file situations. Using the REPLACE command will not write data into the phantom record, mentioned earlier, and REPLACE does this by checking whether the *current database* is positioned to that record. If a SEEK( ) has failed or a GO BOTTOM and SKIP sequence has occurred in the current database, attempting a REPLACE (even when specifying another database alias) will fail without returning an error message. Therefore, when using REPLACE to replace fields in a record, you should select the database into which the REPLACE is occurring rather than use an alias name to reference the field; that is, don't REPLACE customer.custid WITH ... when customer is not the SELECTed database, but rather

```
SELECT customer
REPLACE customer.custid WITH ...
```

Managing File and Record Contention

Previous sections discussed how to manipulate your data and to locate the records on which you want to operate. Now that you have the data you want, you need access to printers to output it and to databases to save it.

In a network environment, users contend for network resources, such as a shared printer. The network software manages this contention. For example, most networks redirect output intended for the printer to a file on the network server. A separate program maintains a list of files in the queue and sends each to the printer in the order in which the files are created. This system prevents one user's output from being printed in the middle of another user's.

In a multiuser database environment, users contend for database resources, primarily tables and records. Database contention is managed by the database manager, in this case FoxPro. Although FoxPro can automatically (implicitly) manage simultaneous access to tables and records, the program also provides several commands and functions that enable you to lock and unlock tables and records explicitly and to tailor the way in which FoxPro responds when you try to access a resource currently in use. Table 21.9 lists these multiuser commands and functions.

Table 21.9 FoxPro's Multi-User Commands and Functions

Command/Function	Description
FLOCK( )	Attempts to lock a table; returns .T. if successful; returns .F. if another user currently has the table, or a record in the table, locked.
LOCK( )	Attempts to lock one or more records in a table; returns .T. if successful; returns .F. if another user currently has the record(s) or file locked. Whether you can lock more than one record simultaneously depends on the current SETting of MULTILOCKS.
NETWORK( )	Returns .T. for the network versions of FoxPro, including FoxPro2.0/LAN and all versions of FoxPro 2.5. This function *does not* tell you whether you are on a network.
ON ERROR	Specifies the error-handling routine, if any, that is executed when FoxPro cannot lock a table or record implicitly, such as when you try to edit a record in a Browse. The error routine is not activated when you use one of the explicit locking functions because the functions' inability to gain the lock is not considered to be an error.
RLOCK( )	Works the same as LOCK( ).
SET EXCLUSIVE	Determines whether tables are opened for exclusive use. Regardless of the SETting of EXCLUSIVE, you can explicitly open a table for exclusive use by including the EXCLUSIVE option with the USE command. By default, EXCLUSIVE is set ON. If you USE a file with EXCLUSIVE ON and then SET EXCLUSIVE OFF, the file continues to be USEd exclusively until it is closed.

Command/Function	Description
SET LOCK	Determines whether certain database commands that don't change any of the table's information try to lock the table before proceeding. The default setting of LOCK is OFF.
SET MULTILOCKS	Determines whether the current workstation can lock more than one record in a table at a time. By default, only one record at a time can be locked.
SET NOTIFY	If NOTIFY is set OFF, FoxPro does not display the message `Attempting to lock...` while attempting to place a lock.
SET REFRESH <ExpN1>, <ExpN2>	The first parameter determines when changes made by other users are reflected in a browse/edit window or in a modify memo window. The second parameter determines when data buffers are automatically FLUSHed. The default values are 0, 5, in seconds. SET REFRESH has no effect on active GETs or on data displayed in any other manner.
SET REPROCESS	Determines how long FoxPro continues trying to lock a table or record after an unsuccessful first attempt.
SYS(0)	Returns the network machine #/name for the current workstation. The network software must have set the machine #/name, and the network shell must be loaded.
SYS(2011)	Returns a character string containing the current file or record lock status. The text returned is the same as that displayed in the system status bar (for example, File Locked). Because SYS(2011) does not try to place a lock, unlike RLOCK( ) and FLOCK( ), SYS(2011) also does not report whether another user placed a lock previously. It just lets you know whether you have locked this record or file previously.
UNLOCK	Releases file or record lock(s).
USE ... SHARED	Opens a table for shared use, regardless of SETting of EXCLUSIVE.
USE ... EXCLUSIVE	Opens a table for exclusive use, regardless of SETting of EXCLUSIVE.

Considering Implicit and Explicit File and Record Locks

At its simplest level, whether two people can access a table simultaneously depends on the SETting of EXCLUSIVE. If EXCLUSIVE is set ON on either workstation, only the first person to open a table can use the table. This limitation also is in effect if the table is opened for exclusive use, regardless of the SETting of EXCLUSIVE, with the EXCLUSIVE clause of the USE command (for example, USE BUDGET EXCLUSIVE).

When a table is opened for shared use, implicit and explicit locks control each user's access to records in the table.

Implicit locks are those that FoxPro places on records and tables. An implicit lock is placed under two types of conditions:

- When you begin to edit a record in a BROWSE/EDIT or MODIFY MEMO window
- When you issue certain database commands, such as READ or REPLACE

A table opened for shared use can always be viewed in a Browse window, even if someone else locked the file. FoxPro does not try to lock a record until you begin editing it. At that point, FoxPro tries to lock the record to prevent anyone else's changes from overwriting yours (or vice versa). The record is unlocked automatically when you move the record pointer off the current record.

Whether issuing a database command results in a file lock or a record lock generally depends on the number of records that may be affected. FoxPro is smart enough to know that REPLACE or REPLACE NEXT 1 affects only the current record, although REPLACE ALL or REPLACE NEXT 10 affects more than one record. REPLACE locks only the current record, but REPLACE <scope> locks the entire table. Implicit locks are released after the command is executed.

Explicit locks are those placed by using the FLOCK( ), LOCK( ), and RLOCK( ) functions. FLOCK( ) locks the entire table, but LOCK( ) and RLOCK( ), which are functionally identical, lock one or more records. Records locked with LOCK( ) or RLOCK( ) are not released when you move the record pointer. Explicit record and file locks are released only by the following:

- Issuing an UNLOCK command releases file and record locks in the current table.
- UNLOCK ALL releases all file and record locks in all open tables.
- Locking a record releases the previous record lock, unless MULTILOCKS is ON.
- Changing the SETting of MULTILOCKS releases all locks in all open tables.
- Locking a table with FLOCK( ) releases any record locks in that table.
- Closing a table releases all locks in that table.

Using Automatic REPROCESSing

What FoxPro does when it cannot place a lock depends on the current SETting of REPROCESS, whether an ON ERROR routine is in effect, and whether the lock is being placed implicitly or explicitly. Table 21.10 shows the different settings of REPROCESS and how long FoxPro continues to try to place the lock.

Table 21.10 The Effects of Different REPROCESS SETtings

SET REPROCESS TO...	#/Duration of Retries	Esc To Cancel?
0		
with ON ERROR	0	N/A
without ON ERROR	Indefinitely	Yes
0 SECONDS	0	N/A
–1	Indefinitely	No
<n>	<n> times	No
<n> SECONDS	<n> seconds	No
AUTOMATIC or –2	Indefinitely	Yes

If REPROCESS is set to 0 (the default) and an ON ERROR routine is active, FoxPro does not retry the lock. Whether the ON ERROR routine is called depends on whether the attempted lock was implicit or explicit. If you try to edit a locked record in a Browse (an implicit lock), the error routine is called. If you try to lock a record with the LOCK( )

function (an explicit lock), the error routine is not called and the function returns the logical value .F.. These behaviors—an unsuccessful implicit lock triggering an error and an unsuccessful explicit lock returning .F.—will always occur after the REPROCESS-determined duration/number of retries. Therefore, your error-handling routine must anticipate and handle the errors that may occur.

Displaying Changed Data Using SET REFRESH

REFRESH controls how frequently a Browse/Edit or memo-editing window reflects the changes others on the network make to a table and how often data buffers are FLUSHed automatically (saving changes to disk). REFRESH has no effect on GETs activated with READ.

By default, the first parameter of REFRESH is set to 0, which means that others' changes are not reflected in your Browse unless you position the cursor on a changed record that the other user has unlocked. At that point, the changes made for that record become visible to you. Changes made to other records are still not reflected.

You can specify that a Browse/Edit or memo-editing window be refreshed at some interval by SETting REFRESH TO a value between 1 and 3,600, representing the number of seconds in the interval. Follow this procedure especially if the users of your application spend a great deal of time in a Browse window. However, keep the following considerations in mind:

- Regardless of the SETting of REFRESH, a user's Browse/Edit or memo-editing window does not reflect changes made by another user until that user unlocks the record.
- By including the NOREFRESH option in the BROWSE command, you can override the current REFRESH setting to disable the Browse window refreshing.
- Setting REFRESH to a low value, such as 1, forces FoxPro to spend a great deal of time *polling* the network and may slow down an intensive data-entry application.

Unless each user must be aware of changes as they are made, a REFRESH setting between 60 and 300 (1 to 5 minutes) should be a good compromise between data timeliness and program efficiency.

The second parameter of SET REFRESH is set to 5 by default. This setting determines how long FoxPro goes between FLUSHing (or saving changes that might have been stored in memory for faster access to the disk version of your tables). The same considerations previously described should be applied to your use of this value. Experiment with both settings in your own environment to determine their optimal values for your programs.

TIP

In previous versions of FoxPro, developers may have used the NETWORK( ) function to determine the proper SETting of EXCLUSIVE in the setup part of an application. Based on the return from the function, a developer could choose to SET EXCLUSIVE ON or OFF. Because FoxPro 2.5 is designed to be multi-user out of the box, the NETWORK( ) function always returns .T..

You learn in Chapters 1 and 3 that all programming code should be written to perform properly in a multi-user environment. If a situation arises in which you must determine whether file- and record-locking features are enabled (either through the use of a network or of SHARE, as discussed in Appendix A, "Installing FoxPro"), you can use the SYS(2011) function. SYS(2011) returns the current file and lock status. If you choose to USE a database specifying the SHAREd clause and then test the SYS(2011) function, a return value of "Exclusive" indicates a stand-alone system and "Record Unlocked" indicates that you must follow multi-user protocols.

Printing to Network Queues

Support for network queues was a significant change in multi-user FoxPro 2.0. Two forms of the SET PRINTER command provide this support:

```
SET PRINTER TO
  [\\<machine name>
     \<printer name> = <dest>]
SET PRINTER TO
  [\\SPOOLER [\NB]
       [\F = <expN>] [\B = <banner>]
       [\C = <expN>] [\P = <expN>]]
*       [\S = <server>] [\Q = <queue>]
```

Although the printer driver system does not directly support any kind of network printing assignments, you can tailor printer driver setups to the different printers available on a network.

Standard FoxPro dialog windows can give you the ability to choose among the available printers and then issue the appropriate SET PRINTER TO command. After output is directed to a printer, you can SET PDSETUP TO a printer driver setup appropriate for the printer you selected.

Numerous methods for handling multiuser printing have been developed. The source code for several of these programs is available in CompuServe's FoxForum libraries and message areas; see Appendix G, "Finding Available Help," for instructions on participating.

The Network message section is one of the liveliest Forum areas, and the Forum members and staffers have a wide and invaluable range of experience. Often, you might have difficulty telling whether FoxPro has anything to do with a network problem. Someone on the Forum probably has encountered a similar hardware and software setup and will be glad to share what he or she has learned.

Summary

FoxPro contains a dizzying number of commands and functions. This chapter introduced you to some that help you manipulate your data into different forms. You learned how to search strings and Memo fields, add and delete spaces in strings, convert one data type to another, and display dates as text in reports. You learned how to use FoxPro's record-positioning commands to locate individual records or groups of records in a table, and you learned the functions and commands to use for handling file and record contention after you find the data you want.

In the next chapter, you learn about the commands and functions that help you manage low-level access to files and how to use FoxPro's powerful array-handling functions. You also learn about the SQL commands that enable you to create permanent and temporary tables and to insert records into FoxPro tables.

Getting To Know FoxPro Commands and Functions

22

CHAPTER

Using SQL Commands, Arrays, and the Low-Level File Functions

The introduction of Structured Query Language (SQL) commands into FoxPro 2.0 was a major step in extending the capabilities and capacities of FoxPro-developed systems. In combination with the Rushmore technology, SQL gave FoxPro a significant performance edge over its competitors. The addition of standardized SQL also attracted many corporate developers and caused FoxPro to be considered for large corporate mission-critical systems previously not feasible on a PC platform. This chapter reviews those SQL commands not covered in depth elsewhere in the book.

FoxPro's primary data structure is the table. Storing data in a table has many benefits, including the capability to create an index, which provides almost immediate access to any record in the table, and the capability to relate one table to any number of other tables.

An array is a type of data structure different from a table, although an array can be manipulated in some of the same ways and, like a table, can be conceptualized as a collection of rows and columns. You already have seen some of the ways in which arrays can be used in FoxPro. In this chapter, you examine arrays in more depth and learn the array-handling commands and functions that FoxPro provides.

This chapter also covers FoxPro's low-level file functions, which give you direct access to files and which are comparable to the file manipulation functions of general-purpose programming languages, such as C.

Using FoxPro's SQL Commands

FoxPro supports four Structured Query Language commands that you can use in your programs to replace multiple FoxPro commands. These four commands are shown in table 22.1.

Table 22.1 FoxPro's SQL Commands

Command	Description
CREATE CURSOR	Creates a temporary table.
CREATE TABLE	Creates a table.
INSERT INTO	Appends a record to a table. The table can be open in the current work area, open in another work area, or closed.
SELECT	Retrieves data from one or more tables.

You can use a SELECT command anywhere you can use any other FoxPro command. It is just another, albeit powerful, FoxPro command. Although SELECT statements can be constructed interactively through the RQBE, SELECT also can be used within a program or from the Command window, where some of SELECT's optional clauses can be used to enhance SELECT's capabilities and readability. The SELECT command is covered in detail in Chapter 7, "Querying with SQL and Searching with Rushmore."

You can use CREATE CURSOR and CREATE TABLE to create a table. Like tables created with the interactive CREATE command, tables and cursors are first opened in EXCLUSIVE mode, regardless of the setting of SET EXCLUSIVE. CREATE CURSOR creates a temporary table that exists until you close it. Unlike a cursor created by a SELECT command, a cursor created by CREATE CURSOR is editable (although a cursor cannot be PACKed). The table created by CREATE TABLE is permanent.

In previous versions of FoxPro, as well as in FoxBASE+, you had two methods for creating a table. You could use the COPY STRUCTURE TO command to create an empty table with the same structure as the current table, or you could use the COPY TO ... STRUCTURE EXTENDED form of the COPY TO command, followed by CREATE FROM. Both of these methods can still be used in FoxPro 2.5, but CREATE CURSOR and CREATE TABLE have the advantage of not requiring an existing table from which to create the new table. Furthermore, because the table created by CREATE CURSOR automatically is deleted when it is closed, using this command relieves you of the housekeeping chores associated with erasing temporary tables created in other ways.

Both commands use the same syntax, as shown in the FoxPro Help file:

```
CREATE CURSOR <dbf_name>
   (<fname1 <type> [(<precision>
   [, <scale>])
   [, <fname2> ... ]])
   ¦ FROM ARRAY <array>

CREATE TABLE ¦ DBF <dbf_name>
   (<fname1> <type> [(<precision>
   [, <scale>])
   [, <fname2> ... ]])
   ¦ FROM ARRAY <array>
```

Although the syntaxes of other commands and functions have not been presented, the syntaxes for these commands are shown because the terminology used to describe them differs from that used for non-SQL commands.

Each field in the table is defined with a name, type, precision, and scale. These terms are equivalent to the field name, field type, field length, and number of decimals columns that you see when you use the CREATE command to create a table interactively. The terms used are different, but the idea is the same. The resulting table is identical to one that you might have created interactively.

Chapter 15, "Controlling the User Interface in Applications," presents an example of a SELECT- created CURSOR that is APPENDed FROM after some processing, using the DBF() function to reference it. CREATEd CURSORs can also be manipulated in this way. Use the DBF() function to reference a cursor, as shown in Chapter 15's example.

Appendix H, "Example Database Structures, Data, and Miscellaneous Procedures," contains the listing for a procedure that uses CREATE TABLE to create each of the tables in the Omnipresent Widget database. Please refer to Appendix H for examples of how to use CREATE TABLE. These examples work equally well with CREATE CURSOR.

INSERT INTO performs the same function as APPEND BLANK followed by a REPLACE command, but it doesn't require that the table be open in the current work area, or be open in any work area, for that matter. If the table is not currently open, INSERT INTO will open it in the next available work area. INSERT INTO reselects the prior work area after it is complete. Its syntax has two forms:

```
INSERT INTO <dbf_name>
   [(<fname1> [, <fname2>
      [, ...]])]
   VALUES (<expr1> [, <expr2>
      [, ...]])

INSERT INTO <dbf_name>
   FROM ARRAY <array>
   ¦ FROM MEMVAR
```

Because INSERT INTO performs an implicit REPLACE, you must supply at least one value if you use the first form of the command. The replacements are made in the order that the fields appear in the table unless you specify the optional list of related field names, one per value in the VALUES list. Because you cannot depend on which work area is selected within the INSERT command, any database fields referred to within the VALUES list should include a table alias:

```
INSERT INTO Test_Tbl ;
   VALUES (Customer.custno, Invoice.Invoiceno)
```

Notice that, like CREATE TABLE and CREATE CURSOR, the field names and VALUES lists must be enclosed within parentheses, even if the list contains only a single item.

The second form of INSERT INTO works like APPEND BLANK followed by either GATHER FROM <array name> or GATHER MEMVAR.

The advantage of using INSERT INTO might appear to be that two commands are replaced with one. In fact, however, the amount of disk I/O can be drastically reduced, and hence the speed at which the application performs can be improved significantly. An APPEND BLANK command locks a database's file header, increments the record count, moves to the end of the file, and writes a blank record. Then it locates and updates each of the associated indexes and index tags with a new entry for the blank record it has written. The REPLACE command following the APPEND then rewrites the blank database record and locates and updates each of the associated indexes with the REPLACEd values. By contrast, INSERT INTO writes the record to the .DBF file only once and updates each of the indexes only once, halving the amount of I/O. During the addition of a large batch of records, the speed improvement using INSERT INTO is noticeable.

SQL commands are not always appropriate for the task at hand, but when they are, they perform their functions elegantly and with a minimum amount of programming.

Using Arrays

An array normally is used to store and manipulate data that you don't need to save from one database management session to the next. A temporary table would serve the same purpose, but arrays have several advantages over tables, including the following differences:

- Arrays can hold any type of data, so they're more flexible than a table, which has a fixed structure.
- Arrays are stored entirely in the computer's random-access memory, access to which is much faster than to a hard disk.
- Arrays can be sorted "in place" and do not require extra disk space to perform the sort.

In this section of the chapter, you learn how to create an array, refer to the array's elements, and use FoxPro's array-handling functions to manipulate arrays. You also learn a few ways you can get into trouble when using arrays, so pay attention!

Creating Arrays

Like memory variables, arrays can be either public or private. A public array is created using the PUBLIC command; a private array is created using the DIMENSION/DECLARE or SCATTER TO command.

Following are a few examples:

```
DIMENSION array1(20), array2[10,2]
DECLARE array1[20], array2(10,2)
PUBLIC array1[20], array2[10,2]
SCATTER TO array1
```

Although DIMENSION and DECLARE are separate commands, they work exactly the same way. This chapter discusses only DIMENSION, but everything applies equally to DECLARE.

SCATTER TO can create only a single array at a time. The other commands can accept a list of arrays. In the Standard version of FoxPro for DOS, you can have a maximum of 3,600 arrays in memory. In the Extended version of FoxPro for DOS and in FoxPro for Windows you can have up to 65,000 arrays. (Of course, most computers do not have enough memory to store 3,600 arrays, even if you could find a reason to create that many.) Each array can have up to the same number (3,600 or 65,000) of elements.

SCATTER also can create memory variables rather than an array. The syntax for each form of the command can be somewhat confusing. In short, if you use SCATTER TO, you create an array; if you use SCATTER MEMVAR, you create memory variables. If you use SCATTER TO MEMVAR, you create an array called "memvar" when you obviously intend to create memory variables.

The array subscripts (20 and 10,2 in the preceding example) must be enclosed in either parentheses or square brackets. Either is acceptable, as long as you don't mix them—array2(10,2], for example, is illegal.

You also can create an array using three of FoxPro's array-handling functions. These functions are shown in table 22.2, along with some commands that create arrays.

Table 22.2 Commands and Functions That Create Arrays

Command/Function	Description
ACOPY()	Copies one or more elements from one array to another, creating the target array if it doesn't exist.
ADIR()	Places directory information into an array, creating it if it doesn't exist.
AFIELDS()	Places table structure information into an array, creating it if it doesn't exist.
DECLARE	Same as DIMENSION.
DIMENSION	Creates a one- or two-dimensional array of specified dimensions.
PUBLIC [ARRAY]	Creates a public array of specified dimensions.
SCATTER TO	Creates an array containing the values of the fields in the current table.

ACOPY() copies the contents of one array to another. If the target array does not exist, it is created with the same dimensions as the source array and is a duplicate of it. ACOPY() will not redimension an existing array, however. If you try to copy more elements from the source array than an existing target array can hold, those elements that fit are copied, and then you receive a `Subscript out of bounds` error message.

Suppose that you have an array that holds customer names. You want to present the customer names in a list that's sorted alphabetically, but you don't want to change the original order of the names. You can create a copy of the array with ACOPY(), sort the copy array, and use the copy as the source for the @ ... GET FROM <array> command, as shown here:

```
= acopy(names_arr, temp_arr)
= asort(temp_arr)
@ 10,10 get mchoice ;
   from temp_arr ;
   size 20,40 ;
   default 1
read
```

The ASORT() function is discussed later in this chapter.

ACOPY() has three optional arguments, all numeric, which enable you to specify the first element to be copied, the number of elements to be copied, and the number of the element in the target array where the copying will begin. ACOPY() returns the number of elements that were copied.

ADIR() stores information about a DOS directory in an array. Like ACOPY(), ADIR() creates the array if it doesn't exist, but unlike ACOPY(), ADIR() redimensions an existing array to the exact size required to hold the information. The information stored is that which DOS displays when you enter DIR at the DOS prompt (file name, file size, the date and time of the last update, and the file's attributes). You can supply a file skeleton to restrict the list to certain files or access a directory other than the current one. You also can expand the list to include hidden files, system files, and subdirectories or to store only the volume label for a drive.

The following procedure, SUBDIRS, creates an array containing the names of all subdirectories below the current default directory. This procedure uses ADIR() with the "D" code as the third argument, which expands the file list to include subdirectories:

```
* SUBDIRS.PRG
* procedure to find all subdirs of any drive/dir
* call:
* DIMENSION my_array(1,1)
* DO subdirs WITH my_array
* to find out about current default
* or DO subdirs WITH my_array, somepath
PARAMETERS subdir, mpath
IF PARAMETERS() = 1
   oldpath = ""
   drivepath = ""
   * you're finding out about current default directory
ELSE
   IF TYPE("mpath") # "C"
      WAIT WINDOW "Invalid path specified!"
      * or RELEASE the array or do whatever you want.
      * Without releasing, you could check for
      * TYPE("my_array(1,1)") = "N" to indicate
      * various error conditions; stuff it with 0 for
      * no subdirs, -1 for invalid path, whatever
      RETURN
   ENDIF
```

```
    IF RIGHT(mpath,1) = "\" OR RIGHT(mpath,1) = ":"
       checkpath = mpath + "nul"
    ELSE
       checkpath = mpath + "\nul"
    ENDIF
    IF ! FILE(checkpath)
       WAIT WINDOW "Invalid path specified!"
       * see above note about RETURN
       RETURN
    ENDIF
    oldpath = SET("DEFAULT",1)+SYS(2003)
    IF RIGHT(mpath,1) = ":" OR AT(":",mpath) = 0
       SET DEFAULT TO (mpath)
       drivepath = ""
    ELSE
       SET DEFAULT TO (LEFT(mpath,1))
       drivepath = SYS(2003)
       SET DEFAULT TO (mpath)
    ENDIF
ENDIF

ndirs = ADIR(subdir,"","D")

* sort them in ascending order by the 1st column
* (file names) so . & .. come *first* if they exist
= ASORT(subdir,1,ndirs,0)
ndels = 0

IF ndirs # 0
    FOR xx = 1 TO 2
       * there can only be two of these
       IF subdir(1,1) = "."
          * EXACT should be OFF for this to work
          * this is a DOS entry for upper directories
          ndels = ndels + 1
          = ADEL(subdir,1)
          * this row should now be moved to the end
          * of the array
       ENDIF
    ENDFOR
    ndirs = ndirs - ndels
    IF ndirs # 0
       DIME subdir(ndirs,5)
       * get rid of "." entries
    ENDIF
ENDIF
```

continues

```
IF ndirs = 0
   WAIT WINDOW "No subdirectories!"
   * see above note about RETURN
ENDIF

IF ! EMPTY(drivepath)
   SET DEFAULT TO (drivepath)
   * set default directory back for this drive
ENDIF

IF ! EMPTY(oldpath)
   SET DEFAULT TO (oldpath)
ENDIF

RETURN
```

AFIELDS() stores information about the structure of the current table. The information stored is that required to create a table (field names, field types, field lengths, and the number of decimals for numeric fields). You can use AFIELDS() with the CREATE TABLE FROM ARRAY command to replace the combination of COPY TO <file> STRUCTURE EXTENDED and CREATE FROM commands that you had to use in previous versions of FoxPro to programmatically create a table:

```
temp_table = sys(3) + ".$$$"
do copytabl with temp_table
* when copytable returns, the new table is open in a
* previously unopened work area, and that work area is
* now selected

PROCEDURE copytabl
*
* create a copy of the current table in table_name*
*
parameters table_name
private struc_info

* create the array that holds the file
* structure information
= afields(struc_info)

* create the table
create table (table_name) ;
   from array struc_info
return
```

The SET COMPATIBLE command is very important in determining how certain array commands and functions will work. Although FoxPro always initializes array elements to the logical value .F., for example, if COMPATIBLE is set to OFF or FOXPLUS (the default setting, OFF and FOXPLUS being equivalent), you can initialize an entire array to a particular value simply by assigning the value to the array name, as shown here:

```
dimension the_array[3,2]
the_array = "Hello world!"
display memory like the_array
* the following is displayed on the screen
THE_ARRAY       Pub     A
(    1,    1)     C   "Hello world!"
(    1,    2)     C   "Hello world!"
(    2,    1)     C   "Hello world!"
(    2,    2)     C   "Hello world!"
(    3,    1)     C   "Hello world!"
(    3,    2)     C   "Hello world!"
```

If you execute these same commands with COMPATIBLE set to ON or DB4, DISPLAY MEMORY shows the following line:

```
THE_ARRAY   Pub    C   "Hello world!"
```

As you can see, the assignment statement replaced the_array with a variable by the same name. Therefore, you can initialize an array with a single assignment statement only if COMPATIBLE is set to OFF or FOXPLUS.

The setting of COMPATIBLE also is important when you are redimensioning an array or using an array function that might redimension an array. When COMPATIBLE is OFF, you can redimension an array without losing the data that the array contains. When COMPATIBLE is ON, the array can still be redimensioned, but the array elements will be reinitialized to .F., thereby destroying any data stored in the array.

> **CAUTION:** The capability to redimension an existing array was introduced in FoxPro 2.0. If you have procedures that depend on arrays maintaining their original size in FoxPro 1.02, you must revise your programs to account for this behavior.

Referring to Array Elements

To use arrays effectively, you must be able to conceptualize their appearance. The manner in which FoxPro actually stores an array in memory is of little importance. What is important is the way in which you must refer to a particular array element.

Think of an array as a temporary table stored in memory rather than on a disk. Just like tables, arrays have one or more rows and columns. As with an @ ... SAY/GET command, the row is referenced before the column. So if you use the DIMENSION command to create a two-dimensional array such as the following:

```
dimension the_array[5,2]
```

FoxPro creates an array consisting of five rows and two columns that looks like the following.

	Col 1	Col 2
Row 1	1,1	1,2
Row 2	2,1	2,2
Row 3	3,1	3,2
Row 4	4,1	4,2
Row 5	5,1	5,2

If you type `DISPLAY MEMORY LIKE the_array` in the Command window, you see that FoxPro considers the_array to be a list of 10 data elements, all of which belong to the_array:

```
THE_ARRAY     Pub     A
  (   1,    1)      L  .F.
  (   1,    2)      L  .F.
  (   2,    1)      L  .F.
  (   2,    2)      L  .F.
  (   3,    1)      L  .F.
  (   3,    2)      L  .F.
  (   4,    1)      L  .F.
  (   4,    2)      L  .F.
  (   5,    1)      L  .F.
  (   5,    2)      L  .F.
```

Because you defined the array as two-dimensional, by supplying a second argument in DIMENSION, FoxPro gives you the alternative of referring to an array element by its row and column coordinates. However, you also can refer to an element by its element number, which is the same as its order in the list previously displayed. So, for example, you could refer to the sixth element in the list as either the_array[3,2] or as the_array[6].

You might assume that a one-dimensional array consists of the specified number of rows and a single column. In fact, it is just the opposite. The array will have one row that has the specified number of columns. This difference becomes important when you are using an array with the COPY TO ARRAY or APPEND FROM ARRAY commands. If, for example, you type `DIMENSION the_array[RECCOUNT( )]` in the Command window, the_array looks like this:

```
1    2    3    ...  n
```

in which *n* stands for the number of records in the table, and ... represents all the array elements between 3 and *n*. If you use this array in a COPY TO ARRAY command, only one record will be copied, because the array has only one row.

NOTE Think of DIMENSION Arr(x) as the same as DIMENSION Arr(1,x), which creates an array of one row and *x* columns. To create an array of *x* rows and one column, use DIMENSION Arr(x,1). In the preceding example, you would have used DIMENSION Arr(RECCOUNT(),1). Do not be confused by the fact that the ALEN() function takes a different "view" of arrays, as shown in table 22.3.

Table 22.3 shows several functions that enable you to refer to an array element indirectly—that is, without knowing the element number.

All the array-handling functions take an array name as their first argument. You can refer to the array as either a variable name (AELEMENT(the_array,5,2)) or as a string literal (AELEMENT("the_array",5,2)).

AELEMENT() takes two additional numeric arguments, representing the row and column subscripts of the desired element number, and returns the number of the element that corresponds to the row and column subscripts. (Actually, the second numeric argument is optional, but because AELEMENT(<array>,x) always returns *x*, it's hard to imagine what you would use this argument for.)

Table 22.3 Functions That Enable You To Indirectly Reference an Array Element

Function	Description
AELEMENT()	Returns the number of an element in an array. Used to convert from two-dimensional subscripts to an element number for use in functions that take an element number as an optional argument, such as ACOPY(), ASCAN(), and ASORT.
ALEN()	Returns the number of elements, rows, or columns in an array. By default, returns the number of elements. Use a code, 1 or 2, as the optional second argument to return the number of rows or the number of columns, respectively.
ASCAN()	Returns the number of the element where a specified expression was found, or 0 if it was not found.
ASUBSCRIPT()	Given an element number and a code (1 or 2), returns either the row or the column subscript of the element.

The following example function returns an element at or near the midpoint of an array:

```
PARAMETERS a_rows, a_cols
DIMENSION the_array[a_rows,a_cols]
the_center = AELEMENT(the_array,a_rows/2,a_cols/2)
RETURN the_center
```

ALEN() returns the number of elements, rows, or columns in an array. Its most obvious use is as a RECCOUNT() function for arrays. If, for example, you use the SQL SELECT command and output the selected records to an array, you can use ALEN() to determine how many records were selected:

```
select * from Customer into array cust_arr ;
   where state = "CA"
CA_custs = alen(cust_arr,1)
```

ASCAN() locates an expression in an array. ASCAN() returns the number of the first element in the array that contains the expression. If the expression was not found, ASCAN() returns 0.

ASUBSCRIPT() converts an element number into its two-dimensional subscript form and then returns either the row or the column component of the subscript. To get the row number, use "1" as the third argument, and to get the column number, use "2."

Chapter 13, "Improving Screen Design with Complex Screen Sets," presents an example that uses ASCAN() and ASUBSCRIPT() to initialize a variable, m.dept, with the row number of an array, deptarray, in which a particular department code, m.deptcode, was located. Following is that code fragment:

```
* Get m.dept from the row number of the
* array deptarray in which m.deptcode can
* be found:
m.dept = IIF(EMPTY(m.deptcode),             ;
             0,                             ;
                    ASUBSCRIPT("deptarray",;
                      ASCAN("deptarray",    ;
                             m.deptcode),   ;
                      1)                    )
```

If m.deptcode contains a value (is not EMPTY()), you use ASUBSCRIPT() to provide the row in the array where the value of m.deptcode was found. The row number is returned because "1" was used as the third argument to the function. ASCAN() returns the number of the element in deptarray where m.deptcode was found and provides the remaining piece of information that ASUBSCRIPT() requires.

Manipulating Arrays

Although arrays were very useful in FoxPro 1 and FoxBASE+, manipulating them often required you to write a series of array-handling UDFs. Many applications, for example, included a UDF that applied a sorting algorithm, such as Quicksort, to an array to keep its elements in alphabetical or numeric order. Because you couldn't pass an entire array to a UDF, you had to either "hard-code" the array name into the UDF, in which case it couldn't be used as a generic sorting routine, or pass the array's name to the UDF, and use macro substitution to access the array elements. Sorting a large array could really slow down your program.

FoxPro 2.x includes several new functions that enable you to sort arrays and insert and delete array elements, rows, and columns. These functions are listed in table 22.4.

Table 22.4 Functions That Sort Arrays and Insert and Delete Elements, Rows, and Columns

Function	Description
ASORT( )	Sorts an array in either ascending (the default) or descending order. Two-dimensional arrays are sorted by row, using a specified element to indicate the column that controls the sort order.
AINS( )	Inserts an element into a one-dimensional array, and a row or a column into a two-dimensional array. The trailing elements move toward the bottom of the array, and the last element, row, or column is dropped from the array.
ADEL( )	Deletes an element from a one-dimensional array and deletes a row or column from a two-dimensional array. The following elements move toward the top of the array, and the last element, row, or column is reinitialized to .F..

AINS( ) inserts an element into a one-dimensional array and inserts a row or column into a two-dimensional array. AINS( ) is like an INSERT BEFORE command for arrays. The insertion takes place at the specified position. The current contents of the array at that position are pushed down or, in the case of a column insertion, pushed to the right.

The inserted element or elements are always initialized to .F.. If you want to add information to the array at the point of insertion, you must do that as a separate step. Because most people will likely want to take this step, this chapter presents a procedure, ADD2ARR, to do it for you.

Procedure ADD2ARR takes three arguments: the array in which the insertion is to be made, a one-dimensional array that holds the data to be inserted, and the row number at which the insertion is to be made. Of course, you must create the one-dimensional array before calling ADD2ARR. If the information to be added to the array is the contents of the current record in a table, you could do this easily with SCATTER TO <array>. Because you need access to the contents of more than a single array element, the arrays must be passed by reference (see the section "Passing Arrays to Procedures and UDFs" for a discussion of passing arrays). Procedure ADD2ARR is as follows:

```
PROCEDURE add2arr
*
* Add an element or a row (if targ_arr is two-dimensional)
* to array targ_arr, Insert a blank element or row at
* row_num, then store the contents of src_arr to the
* new element or row.
*
PARAMETERS targ_arr, src_arr, row_num
PRIVATE a_rows, a_cols, j

* Determine the number of rows and columns in the
* targ_arr array.
*
* If targ_arr is one-dimensional, a_rows will be the
* number of elements, and a_cols will be 0.
* If targ_arr is two-dimensional, a_rows will be the
* number of rows, and a_cols will be the number of
* columns.
a_rows = ALEN(targ_arr,1)
a_cols = ALEN(targ_arr,2)

IF a_cols > 0      && if array is two-dimensional
   * add a row to the array
   DIMENSION targ_arr[a_rows+1,a_cols]

   * Insert the new row.
   =AINS[targ_arr, row_num]

   * Store the contents of src_arr to the new row.
   FOR j=1 TO a_cols
      targ_arr[row_num,j] = src_arr[j]
   ENDFOR
ELSE
   * Add an element to the array.
   DIMENSION targ_arr[a_rows+1]

   * Insert the new element.
   =AINS[targ_arr, row_num]

   * Store the contents of src_arr to the new element.
   targ_arr[row_num] = src_arr[1]
ENDIF
RETURN
```

Notice that the call to AINS() is the same, whether targ_arr is one- or two-dimensional. AINS() automatically treats the second argument as a row number if the array is two-dimensional.

ASORT() sorts an array in either ascending or descending order. You can specify a position (an element or a row) at which to start the sort and the number of elements or rows to be sorted. The way in which FoxPro interprets the numbers you use for the second and third arguments depends on whether the array is one- or two-dimensional. The rules can be confusing. Tables 22.5 and 22.6 illustrate the differences with some examples. Array arr1 is one-dimensional, and arr2 is two-dimensional.

Table 22.5 Using ASORT() with One-Dimensional Arrays

Example	Description
ASORT(arr1)	Sorts the entire array, beginning with the first element.
ASORT(arr1,5)	Sorts the remainder of the array, beginning with the fifth element.
ASORT(arr1,5,3)	Sorts three elements, beginning with the fifth element.
ASORT(arr1,1,–1,1)	Sorts the entire array in descending order. The –1 is a code indicating that you don't want to limit the sort to a particular number of elements.
ASORT(arr1,5,0,1)	Sorts the remainder of the array, beginning with the fifth element, in descending order. Although not documented, 0 seems to be equivalent to –1.

Table 22.6 Using ASORT() with Two-Dimensional Arrays

Example	Description
ASORT(arr2)	Sorts the entire array using the contents of the first column as the sort criterion. The values of the other columns are not taken into account in the sorting process.
ASORT(arr2,5)	Sorts the remainder of the array, beginning with the row that contains the fifth element, using the contents of the column that contains the fifth element as the sort criterion.

Example	Description
ASORT(arr2,5,3)	Same as ASORT(arr2,5), but only three rows are sorted.
ASORT(arr2,1,–1,1)	Sorts the entire array in descending order using the contents of the first column as the sort criterion. The –1 is a code indicating that you don't want to limit the sort to a particular number of rows.
ASORT(arr2,5,0,1)	Sorts the remainder of the array, beginning with the row that contains the fifth element, in descending order.

Copying Arrays to Tables and Tables to Arrays

The SQL commands can move data from tables into arrays and create records from information in arrays. FoxPro also has two commands, COPY TO ARRAY and APPEND FROM ARRAY, specifically designed to move data between records and arrays.

COPY TO ARRAY copies records from the current table to an array. If the array does not exist, it is created. An existing array is not redimensioned. If the preexisting array has fewer elements than the records that meet the optional <scope>, FOR, or WHILE clause (ALL is the default), the records that don't fit are not copied. You can limit the fields to be copied by including the optional FIELDS list.

NOTE If you specify a single field (such as Company in the following example) in the COPY TO ARRAY command, FoxPro uses a one-dimensional array if the array already exists. When you later use APPEND FROM ARRAY to add multiple records to the table, you will be surprised to find that only one record has been added.

Unless you are sure that FoxPro will create a two-dimensional array, you should create the array yourself with a command such as DIMENSION the_array [RECCOUNT(),1].

APPEND FROM ARRAY appends new records to the current table, filling the fields with the related column values in the order in which they exist in the array. You can use the FIELDS clause to provide a list of fields. The first field in the list receives the values from the first array column, the second field from the second column, and so forth. One field is appended for each array element of a one-dimensional array. In a two-dimensional array, one record is appended for each row.

The following example uses both COPY TO ARRAY and APPEND FROM ARRAY. In a data entry routine, suppose that you want to let the user add as many records as wanted, without having to confirm the addition after each one. When all the new records have been added to the array, you want to prompt the user to confirm that all should be added. You could use a temporary table for this purpose, or you could use an array, as shown here:

```
* Open the Address table in Address Code order
USE Address IN 0 ORDER Addrcode
SELECT Address

* Copy each company name to an array.
COPY TO ARRAY comp_list FIELDS Company

* Save the current number of companies, you'll
* need this later; in this case, you can use either
* alen() or reccount().
curr_tot = ALEN(comp_list)

* Suppress the "Invalid input" message that would
* otherwise be displayed when updlist() returns .f.
SET NOTIFY OFF

* Get the company names that the user wants to add;
* precede the array name with the "@" symbol to
* ensure that the entire array is passed to updlist().
@ 10,10 SAY "New customer " GET m.company ;
   DEFAULT " " ;
   VALID updlist(@comp_list, m.company)
READ

SET NOTIFY ON

IF ALEN(comp_list) > curr_tot   && at least 1 record added
   mchoice = "X"
   DO WHILE ! UPPER(mchoice) $ "YN"
      WAIT WINDOW "Add these new customers to the "+ ;
         "Address table? (Y/N)" TO mchoice
   ENDDO
```

```
   IF UPPER(mchoice) = "Y"
      * Create an array that contains only the
      * new records.
      = ACOPY(comp_list, updates, curr_tot+1)

      * Append the new records to the table.
      APPEND FROM ARRAY updates
   ENDIF
ENDIF

FUNCTION updlist
   *
   * Search arr_list for mname. If not found,
   * add it to arr_list.
   *
   PARAMETERS arr_list, mname
   IF ASCAN(arr_list, mname) = 0
      * mname not in list, add it
      WAIT WINDOW "Adding new item to list..." NOWAIT
      DIMENSION arr_list[alen(arr_list)+1,1]
      arr_list[ALEN(arr_list)] = mname
      WAIT CLEAR
   ELSE
      ?? CHR(7)   && ring bell to get the user's attention
      WAIT WINDOW "That item is already on the list." ;
         TIMEOUT 2
   ENDIF
RETURN .f.
```

Passing Arrays to Procedures and UDFs

FoxPro 1.x and FoxBASE+ enabled you to pass an array element to a procedure or UDF, but you couldn't pass the entire array. If you needed to use more than a single element of an array in a UDF, you had to pass the name of the array and then use macro substitution to reference the individual array elements.

In FoxPro 2.x, an entire array can now be passed to a procedure or function. To do this, you pass the array by reference, as opposed to by value. If you use the following calling format, the array is passed by reference unless you enclose the array name in parentheses:

```
do <procedure> with <array name>
```

If you use the following calling format, then whether the array is passed by value or by reference depends on the current setting of UDFPARMS:

```
= <user defined function>(<parameter list>)
```

If UDFPARMS is set to REFERENCE, the entire array is passed. If UDFPARMS is set to VALUE, only the first element of the array is passed, and it is passed by value. You can override the UDFPARMS setting by prefacing the array name with the @ symbol to pass the array by reference or by enclosing the array name in parentheses to pass it by value.

Individual elements of an array are always passed by value. See Chapter 18, "Understanding Program Structure," for more information on parameter-passing rules.

When you pass arrays between programs in a FoxPro project, you also must tell the Project Manager where the arrays are declared to avoid unresolved reference warnings when you build your application. Although you safely can tell the Project Manager to ignore these errors when you are certain that you have defined your arrays correctly, see Chapter 14, "Organizing and Packaging Your Applications," for a discussion of how to use the EXTERNAL ARRAY statement to avoid the annoyance.

Understanding Some Limitations of Arrays

Arrays are very powerful tools in your database management arsenal, but they do have some limitations you should keep in mind. The most important limitation is that arrays consume precious amounts of RAM (random-access memory). The more memory you use to hold arrays, the less you have available for storing other memory variables and for creating windows.

Even if you are currently using very little RAM for other purposes, you might not have enough available memory to store an entire table in an array. Because tables grow in size as users add records to them, the COPY TO <array> command that worked just fine while you were testing the application might one day "blow up" your program because of insufficient memory to hold the current number of records in the table.

In general, if the size of an array might exceed the amount of RAM available to store it, you are better off using a temporary table rather than an array.

Using the Low-Level File Functions

FoxPro provides 12 low-level file functions (LLFFs) that enable you to read from and write to any type of file. In FoxPro for DOS, these functions also provide access to communications ports (such as COM1). The LLFFs provide much of the same file access functionality as is provided in general-purpose programming languages, such as C and Pascal. These functions are listed in table 22.7.

Table 22.7 FoxPro's Low-Level File Functions

Function	Description
FCHSIZE()	Changes the size of a file that was opened with FOPEN() or created with FCREATE(). Returns the new size of the file in bytes, unless FCHSIZE() was unable to change the file's size, in which case it returns –1.
FCLOSE()	Closes a file or communications port after first flushing the file to disk. Returns .T. if the file was closed, .F. if it could not be closed.
FCREATE()	Creates and opens a file. Returns the file handle number that all other functions must use to access the file.
FEOF()	Determines whether the file pointer is currently at the end of a file. If so, it returns .T.; otherwise, it returns .F..
FERROR()	Returns an error status code indicating the error condition of the preceding low-level file function. If that function did not cause an error, 0 is returned.
FFLUSH()	Flushes to disk the contents of a file opened with a low-level file function and releases the memory used by the file's I/O buffer. See FCLOSE().

continues

Table 22.7 Continued

Function	Description
FGETS( )	Returns a specified number of bytes from a file or communications port, unless a carriage-return character is encountered within the specified number of bytes, in which case it returns the characters between the starting file pointer position and the carriage return.
FOPEN( )	Opens a file and returns a file handle that the other low-level file functions must use to access the file. FOPEN( ) accepts a code that specifies the file's read/write privileges and file I/O buffering type (buffered or unbuffered). See FCLOSE( ) for notes on buffering a file.
FPUTS( )	Writes a character string to a file or communications port and adds carriage-return and line-feed characters to the end of the string.
FREAD( )	Similar to FGETS( ) but does not stop reading the file when a carriage return is encountered.
FSEEK( )	Moves the file pointer a specified number of bytes from the current file pointer position, the beginning of the file, or the end of the file. Returns the new file pointer position with respect to the beginning of the file.
FWRITE( )	Similar to FPUTS( ) but does not write a carriage return and line feed at the end of the string. Returns the number of bytes written.

Files are either created with FCREATE( ) or opened with FOPEN( ). Both of these functions return a numeric file handle, which you store to a memory variable for use with the other LLFFs. (LLFFs require that you specify the file handle as their first argument.) The file handle tells the function which file you want to access.

If the file cannot be created or opened, both FCREATE( ) and FOPEN( ) return the numeric value –1. Your applications should always verify that the returned value is greater than zero before proceeding.

Files are opened and created with certain specified file attributes. For example, a file can be opened as readonly or read/write. If a file is opened as *readonly*, which is the default, you cannot write to the file. On the other hand, files that you create with FCREATE( ) are read/write by default.

FOPEN() also enables you to specify whether to use buffering. FoxPro uses buffering to speed access to portions of a file in use. After a file is closed, flushing it saves any modifications that have been made to the actual version of the file residing on disk. In situations in which it is crucial to write any change to disk immediately, however, you can opt to open the file unbuffered. If you open a communications port rather than a file, the port should always be opened unbuffered.

The best way to explain the LLFFs is by example. The remainder of this chapter contains several examples of some useful ways in which you can use these functions to read and write files.

Using LLFFs To Simplify Installation

Following is an installation program for an application that you supply on a disk. INSTALL.PRG creates a batch file that runs the application, copies each of the files listed in the FILES.LST file on the disk, checks the FILES= setting in the user's CONFIG.SYS file, and changes CONFIG.SYS if it is too low (and if the user permits the change).

```
* INSTALL.PRG
* uses low-level file functions to write batch files
* and edit CONFIG.SYS
* Note that this method does not take into account
* MEMORY MANAGERS such as Quarterdeck's QEMM
* that put FILES or BUFFERS management information
* into your AUTOEXEC.BAT. But the user is given
* an opportunity to refuse the CONFIG.SYS edit,
* so s/he can make the changes in an appropriate
* manner on his or her system.
*
CLEAR
SET ESCAPE OFF
SET TALK OFF
SET SAFETY OFF
SET SCOREBOARD OFF
SET STATUS OFF
SET CONFIRM ON
SET ECHO OFF
SET SYSMENU OFF
SET CONFIRM OFF
bdrive = "c:"
idrive = "a:"
```

continues

```
* drives verified with the user in the full program
DEFINE WINDOW install FROM 5,10 TO 19,70 ;
   COLOR SCHEME 1 SHADOW ;
   TITLE " Welcome to the ABC Installation Program "
WAIT WINDOW NOWAIT ;
   "Creating batch file to start ABC program... "
IF FILE("ABC.BAT")
   ERASE ABC.BAT
   * in full program, ask for a new batch file name
ENDIF
fhandle = FCREATE("ABC.BAT")
= FPUTS(fhandle,"ECHO OFF")
= FPUTS(fhandle,"CLS")
= FPUTS(fhandle,SET("DEFAULT"))
= FPUTS(fhandle,"CD"+SYS(2003))
= FPUTS(fhandle,"foxr -t abcmain")
= FCLOSE(fhandle)
* create similar files if necessary to
* run the setup and initialization programs from DOS
* the last line above works for APP files;
* alter appropriately for executables
ACTIVATE WINDOW install
@ 1,2 SAY "A file called ABC.BAT has been created in your"
@ 2,2 SAY "program directory."
@ 4,2 SAY "You can rename this file to anything with a "
@ 5,2 SAY "BAT extension and copy it to any directory"
@ 6,2 SAY "on your path. "
@ 8,2 SAY "Then type the file's NAME (currently ABC), and"
@ 9,2 SAY "press the ENTER key to start the ABC Program."
WAIT WINDOW
* in full program, check to see if data files already exist
* and if so check if okay to overwrite or get new datapath
okay =  .T.
datapath = GETFILE(SYS(2003),"Select location for data files")
IF okay
   WAIT WINDOW NOWAIT "Installing new data files... "
   fhandle = FOPEN(idrive+"files.lst")
   * files.lst should be supplied on installation disk
   * with all files that need to be copied to the target disk
   * - files.lst can be created using the FLS.EXE utility
   * found in \goodies\misc on your application's
   * directory, or you can USE the application's PJX file and
   * use the low-level file functions to create files.lst
   * from the records in the project. In the second method,
   * don't forget to add their relevant memo files!
```

```
   DO WHILE !FEOF(fhandle)
      thisfile = FGETS(fhandle)
      COPY FILE (idrive+thisfile) TO (datapath+thisfile)
   ENDDO
   = FCLOSE(fhandle)
   WAIT CLEAR
ENDIF
* now check CONFIG.SYS file
cfgfile = bdrive+"\CONFIG.SYS"
chg_cfg = .F.
needfiles = 70
IF FILE(cfgfile)
   IF  val(sys(2010)) < needfiles
      CLEAR
      @ 1,2 SAY "This file:  "+cfgfile+;
         ", which already exists, must"
      @ 2,2 SAY "contain certain settings "+ ;
         "to run this program:  "
      @ 3,2 SAY "        FILES = "+ALLTRIM(STR(needfiles))
      @ 4,2 SAY "        BUFFERS = 20"
      @ 5,2 SAY "Your current CONFIG.SYS file contains "+ ;
         "a FILES"
      @ 6,2 SAY "statement with too low a setting. "
      @ 8,2 SAY "Press <Y> to have this file altered for you;"
      @ 9,2 SAY "otherwise you can edit it yourself:  " ;
         GET chg_cfg PICTURE "Y"
      READ
      IF chg_cfg
         WAIT WINDOW NOWAIT ;
            "Renaming your "+cfgfile+;
            "to "+bdrive+"\EXCONFIG.SYS and rewriting... "
         COPY FILE (cfgfile) TO (bdrive+"\EXCONFIG.SYS")
         ERASE (cfgfile)
         fhandle = FOPEN(bdrive+"\EXCONFIG.SYS")
         csize = FSEEK(fhandle,0,2)
         = FSEEK(fhandle,0)
         cnewfile = FCREATE(cfgfile)
         ctext = FREAD(fhandle,csize)
         filespos = ATCLINE("files",ctext)
         IF filespos = 0
            ctext = "FILES = "+ALLTRIM(STR(needfiles))+;
               CHR(13)+CHR(10)+ctext
         ELSE
            cline = MLINE(ctext,filespos)
            ctext = STRTRAN(ctext,cline, ;
                  "FILES = "+ALLTRIM(STR(needfiles)))
         ENDIF
```

continues

```
            buffpos = ATCLINE("buffers",ctext)
            IF buffpos = 0
               ctext = "BUFFERS = 20"+CHR(13)+CHR(10)+ctext
            ELSE
               cline = MLINE(ctext,buffpos)
               ctext = STRTRAN(ctext,cline,"BUFFERS = 20")
            ENDIF
            = FWRITE(cnewfile,ctext)
            = FCLOSE(fhandle)
            = FCLOSE(cnewfile)
            CLEAR
            @ 5,2 SAY "Please REBOOT or RESET your system "
            @ 6,2 SAY "before starting to run the "
            @ 7,2 SAY "ABC program, since your CONFIG.SYS "
            @ 8,2 SAY "has been changed."
         ELSE
            @ 8,2 CLEAR
            @ 9,2 SAY  "Make sure you set your FILES "+ ;
                  "and BUFFERS at least"
            @ 10,2 SAY "this high before running "+ ;
                  "the ABC Program."
         ENDIF
         WAIT WINDOW
      ENDIF
   ELSE
      WAIT WINDOW NOWAIT "Creating CONFIG.SYS file... "
      fhandle = FCREATE(cfgfile)
      = FPUTS(fhandle,"FILES = "+ALLTRIM(STR(needfiles)))
      = FPUTS(fhandle,"BUFFERS = 20")
      = FCLOSE(fhandle)
      CLEAR
      @ 1,2 SAY "A file called "+cfgfile+" has been added to"
      @ 2,2 SAY "the root directory of your boot drive."
      @ 3,2 SAY "It contains the following lines:"
      @ 4,2 SAY "        FILES = "+ALLTRIM(STR(needfiles))
      @ 5,2 SAY "        BUFFERS = 20"
      @ 7,2 SAY "If you need to change your CONFIG.SYS file for"
      @ 8,2 SAY "the needs of other programs, please do not "
      @ 9,2 SAY "erase these lines or lower the numbers."
      @ 10,2 SAY "PLEASE REBOOT or RESET YOUR COMPUTER before"
      @ 11,2 SAY "starting the ABC Program."
      WAIT WINDOW
   ENDIF
   QUIT
```

Notice that INSTALL.PRG assigns the returned value of the file creation function, FCREATE(), or the File Open function, FOPEN(), to a variable called fhandle, which is then used as the first argument in subsequent low-level functions. Remember that you must store the file handle to be able to access the file.

INSTALL.PRG shows you a simple technique that you can expand to cover your own installation needs. Perhaps you need to verify that file and record locking is available (see SYS(2011) in the preceding chapter) and prompt the user to install SHARE in his or her AUTOEXEC.BAT.

Another common installation need is to create certain settings within the CONFIG.FP file. Because CONFIG.FP can be bound within your own installation routine, you must verify the existence of CONFIG.FP by using the ADIR() function—FILE(FULLPATH(SYS(2019))) will return .T. if the current CONFIG.FP is bound in your application, even though it does not exist on disk. (See Appendix E, "Key Codes, Key Labels, and Special Key Usage," for more information on specifying a CONFIG.FP file.)

Using LLFFs To Parse Line Length

The following program, MAXLINE, is a utility that compares the length of each line of text in a file against a specified maximum length and creates a report showing each of the lines that exceed the allowable length. Writers, for example, can use this program to check their ASCII text submissions for their publisher's maximum allowable length. FoxPro programmers can use it to check for lines in their source code files that exceed the line length specified in FoxDoc.

```
* MAXLINE.PRG
* DO MAXLINE WITH "your prg name", # of lines
PARAMETERS the_file, the_length

SET ESCAPE OFF
IF    PARAMETERS() # 2 ;
   OR TYPE("the_file") # "C" ;
   OR TYPE("the_length") # "N" ;
   OR      (TYPE("the_length") = "N" ;
      AND  INT(the_length) # the_length)
   WAIT WINDOW "You need two params: a filename "+;
   "(string) & a max line length (integer)."
   RETURN
ENDIF
```

continues

```
the_file = UPPER(IIF(AT(".",the_file) # 0,;
   the_file,the_file+".PRG"))
fileh = FOPEN(the_file)
IF fileh = -1
   WAIT WINDOW "Could not find file "+the_file+". "
   RETURN
ENDIF

the_report = SUBSTR(the_file,1,AT(".",the_file)-1)
IF FILE(the_report+".TXT")
   mext = "TXT"
   DEFINE WINDOW getit FROM 10,29 TO 15,51;
      PANEL TITLE " Report Name "
   DO WHILE FILE(the_report+"."+mext)
      WAIT WINDOW "File "+the_report+"."+mext;
         +" already exists.  Overwrite?  (y/n)" TO manswer
      IF UPPER(manswer) = "Y"
         ERASE (the_report+"."+mext)
      ELSE
         ACTIVATE WINDOW getit
         @ 1,4 SAY the_report+"." GET mext PICTURE "@!N"
         READ
         IF LASTKEY() = 27
            EXIT
         ENDIF
      ENDIF
   ENDDO
   RELEASE WINDOW getit
   IF FILE(the_report+"."+mext)
      * got an escape press
      = FCLOSE(fileh)
      RETURN
   ELSE
      the_report = the_report+"."+mext
   ENDIF
ELSE
   the_report = the_report+".TXT"
ENDIF

reporth = FCREATE(the_report)
= FPUTS(reporth,"This is a report of lines in "+;
   the_file)
= FPUTS(reporth,"that exceed the given maximum of "+;
   ALLTRIM(STR(the_length))+" characters.")
```

```
= FPUTS(reporth," ")
= FPUTS(reporth," ")

the_line = 0
overmax = 0
DO WHILE !FEOF(fileh)
   the_line = the_line + 1
   this_line = FGETS(fileh)
   IF LEN(this_line) > the_length
      = FPUTS(reporth,PADR("Line # ";
         +ALLTRIM(STR(the_line)),15)+this_line)
      overmax = overmax + 1
   ENDIF
ENDDO

= FCLOSE(reporth)
= FCLOSE(fileh)
?? CHR(7)
IF overmax = 0
   ERASE(the_report)
   WAIT WINDOW "No lines over the maximum of "+;
      ALLTRIM(STR(the_length))+;
      " chars were found.  Congrats!  :-)"
ELSE
   WAIT WINDOW "Report "+the_report+" shows "+;
      ALLTRIM(STR(overmax))+;
      IIF(overmax = 1," line"," lines");
      +" over the maximum of "+;
      ALLTRIM(STR(the_length))+" chars."
ENDIF
RETURN
```

MAXLINE checks for the existence of a report file and requests your permission to overwrite it before continuing. You should always check for the existence of any file that you are about to create because, regardless of the setting of SAFETY, FoxPro does not warn you that you are about to overwrite a file when you use the low-level file functions.

Using LLFFs To Format Text Data for Import

The following procedure, CONVERT, reads in an ASCII orders file that was created on a mainframe system and creates another ASCII file in the correct format to be appended to a FoxPro table.

```
PROCEDURE convert
   *
   * convert an ASCII orders file into another ASCII file
   * that holds just the record headers and detail line
   * items.
   *
   private in_name, out_name, in_file, out_file, ;
         blocksize, recsperblk, recsize, cblock, ;
         write_ok

   * define constants for block and record parameters
   #DEFINE blocksize   840
   #DEFINE recsperblk    9
   #DEFINE recsize      86

   * create block and record counters
   nblocks     =   0
   nrecs       =   0

   * get name of ASCII orders file
   in_name = getfile("","Select ASCII orders file to " +;
      "be processed")
   if "" = in_name   && no file selected
      RETURN
   endif

   * create variables to hold output file name, and input
   * and output file handles
   out_name = sys(3) + ".$$$"
   in_file  = 0
   out_file = 0

   * check for error conditions; error messages are
   * displayed in the error-checking routines
   wait window "Checking input file..." nowait
   if    !openfile(in_name, @in_file) ;
      or filempty(in_name, in_file) ;
      or !okchars(in_name, in_file) ;
      or !makefile(out_name, @out_file)
         * got an error, don't proceed
         = fclose(in_file)
         wait clear
         RETURN
   endif
```

```
    * read a block into cblock, then write the nine data
    * records in the block to an output file; records are 90
    * chars, but I'm stripping off the record number, which
    * is the first 4 chars of the record.
    wait window "Processing input file " + in_name + "..." ;
       nowait
    cblock     = ""
    write_ok = .t.
    do while gotblock(@cblock, in_file, blocksize, @nblocks) ;
          and write_ok
       recpos = 17
       for j=1 to recsperblk
          currec = " " + substr(cblock,recpos,recsize)
          if !empty(currec)
             bytesout = fputs(out_file, currec)
             if bytesout != recsize + 3  && " "+CR+LF
                ?? chr(7)
                wait window "Error in writing records to "+;
                  "output file "+out_name+" !" timeout 5
                write_ok = .f.
                EXIT
             endif
             nrecs = nrecs+1
          endif
          recpos = recpos + recsize + 4
       endfor
    enddo

    * close the input and output files
    = fclose(in_file)
    = fclose(out_file)

    if write_ok    && if output file successfully created
       * display record and block counters, then pause for a
       * keystroke
       wait window "Created " + ltrim(str(nrecs)) + ;
          " records from " + ltrim(str(nblocks)) + ;
          " blocks." timeout 5
       if !addords(out_name)
          wait window "Order file not updated." timeout 5
       endif
    endif
    erase (out_name)
    wait clear
return
```

continues

```
FUNCTION openfile
   *
   * Attempt to open the file.
   *
   parameters f_name, f_handle
   f_handle = fopen(f_name)
   if f_handle < 0
      ?? chr(7)
      wait window "Unable to open file " + upper(f_name) +;
         "!" timeout 5
   endif
return f_handle > 0

FUNCTION filempty
   *
   * is the file empty?
   *
   parameters f_name, f_handle
   if feof(f_handle)
      ?? chr(7)
      wait window "File " + upper(f_name) + " is empty!" ;
         timeout 5
   endif
return feof(f_handle)

FUNCTION okchars
   *
   * verify that the input file contains only letters,
   * digits, and spaces
   *
   parameters f_name, f_handle
   private b_str, all_ok, c
   all_ok = .t.
   do while !feof(f_handle) and all_ok
      b_str = fgets(f_handle, 1000)
      for j=1 to len(b_str)
         c = substr(b_str,j,1)
         if !isalpha(c) and !isdigit(c) and c != " "
            ?? chr(7)
            wait window upper(f_name) + " contains " + ;
               "an invalid character ("+c+")!" timeout 5
            all_ok = .f.
            EXIT
         endif
      endfor
   enddo
```

```
    * reset file pointer to top of file
    = fseek(f_handle, 0)
return all_ok

FUNCTION makefile
    *
    * Attempt to create the file?
    *
    parameters f_name, f_handle
    f_handle = fcreate(f_name)
    if f_handle < 0
       ?? chr(7)
       wait window "Output file " + f_name + ;
          " could not be created!" timeout 5
    endif
return f_handle > 0

FUNCTION gotblock
    *
    * read a block of nbytes from a file; use fgets() to
    * stop at the carriage-return character
    parameters b_str, f_handle, nbytes, nblocks
    b_str = fgets(f_handle, nbytes+10)
    nblocks = iif(len(b_str) = 0, nblocks, nblocks+1)
    if between(len(b_str), 1, nbytes-1)
       * FGETS() did not return enough data.
          ?? chr(7)
       wait window "Block no. " + ltrim(str(nblocks)) + ;
          " has " + ltrim(str(len(b_str))) + " bytes.  " + ;
          ltrim(str(nbytes)) + " bytes are required!" ;
          timeout 5
    endif
return len(b_str) = nbytes

FUNCTION addords
    *
    * process ASCII file created from orders ASCII file by
    * convert.prg
    *
    parameters new_ascii
    private temp

    wait window "Updating orders table..." nowait
    * create temp dbf to hold line items in temp ASCII file
    temp = sys(3) + ".$$$"
```

continues

```
   create cursor (temp) ;
      (status C(1), code C(2), text C(90))
   * append from temp orders ASCII file created by
   * convert.prg
   append from (new_ascii) type sdf
   go top
   *
   * code to analyze the orders data and update the
   * actual fields of the orders table would go here
   *
return
```

Of the three examples presented here, CONVERT is the most specialized. It assumes that the input file will have a specific file layout, that the records will always be of the same length, and that codes are used consistently to indicate the type of records being processed. CONVERT is a good example of the power that the low-level file functions provide for handling data manipulation jobs that were previously the exclusive domain of languages such as C.

Summary

FoxPro's Structured Query Language commands enable you to create tables or databases in a single command. Cursors provide the conveniences of DBF manipulation and clean up after themselves when they are no longer in USE. SQL's powerful INSERT INTO command speeds the process of adding batches of new records.

This chapter covered FoxPro's array-handling commands and functions, which enable you to create arrays, store information in them, sort them, retrieve data from them, and pass them to procedures and UDFs. The chapter discussed some of the strengths and weaknesses of arrays and showed you several ways to use arrays in an application.

You also learned about FoxPro's low-level file functions. The LLFFs enable you to manipulate files in ways that were not possible in FoxBASE+ and dBASE III PLUS. LLFFs are a valuable tool in any application that requires access to files not stored in FoxPro's .DBF file format or formats supported by FoxPro's IMPORT/EXPORT commands.

23

CHAPTER

Controlling a Windowed Environment

Although the Screen Builder removes much of the drudgery of managing windows, there are times when you want to manipulate windows directly to gain more precise control over a window's placement and attributes than is possible through the Screen Builder. You may DEFINE the WINDOW explicitly yourself, or the window definition may be part of a generated .SPR, but your program changes the window's attributes after definition occurs.

Besides requiring certain attributes for windows, your applications also must *reference* windows successfully, which means the applications recognize window names and types and use this information to decide what to do next. Throughout this book, you see examples of programs using window information to handle events (program tasks) in progress.

This chapter discusses the rich variety of commands and functions that FoxPro provides to perform operations involving windows.

Exploring Window Commands

Before you can manipulate a window, you have to create it. Windows are created with the DEFINE WINDOW command. This command's clauses and keywords provide the window attributes you use and refer to in all the other window commands and functions.

Creating Windows and Defining Window Attributes

This section begins with a review of the syntax of the basic DEFINE WINDOW command and its many keywords and clauses. Remember that clauses and clause elements enclosed in square brackets are optional and that the vertical-line (¦) character separates different forms of the same clause:

```
DEFINE WINDOW <window name>
     FROM <row1>, <col1> TO <row2>, <col2> ¦
     AT <row1>,<col1> SIZE <rows>, <cols>
     [IN [WINDOW] <window name2> ¦ IN SCREEN]
     [FOOTER <expC1>]
     [TITLE <expC2>]
     [DOUBLE ¦ PANEL ¦ NONE ¦ SYSTEM ¦ <border string>]
     [CLOSE ¦ NOCLOSE]
     [FLOAT ¦ NOFLOAT]
     [GROW ¦ NOGROW]
     [MINIMIZE]
     [SHADOW]
     [ZOOM ¦ NOZOOM]
     [FILL <expC3>]
     [COLOR SCHEME <expN> ¦ COLOR <color pair list>]
```

As with the BROWSE command, most of DEFINE WINDOW's syntax consists of optional clauses. The only attributes that you must specify are the window's name and either the screen coordinates of its upper-left and lower-right corners or its screen position and the amount of space it occupies on-screen, as in the following examples:

```
DEFINE WINDOW my_win ;
      FROM 10,10 TO 20,70


* or
```

```
DEFINE WINDOW my_win ;
       AT 10,10 SIZE 9,59
```

A window name has the same restrictions as a memory variable. The name must begin with a letter or the underscore character, and only the first 10 characters will be considered part of the name.

The row and column coordinates must be numeric, but you also can use functions that return numeric values. To create a window that fills the current display screen, use SROWS() and SCOLS() to obtain the desired coordinates for the lower-right corner of the window:

```
DEFINE WINDOW big_win ;
   FROM 0, 0 TO SROWS()-1, SCOLS()-1
```

Because the screen's dimensions are zero-based, the number of the screen's bottom row is always SROWS()-1, and the far right column is always SCOLS()-1. (Refer to the section on "Referencing Windows in a Relative Way" later in this chapter for more information.)

NOTE The AT ... and SIZE ... clauses have different significance in FoxPro for Windows, where the size of a window is determined by the window's font rather than fixed-width columns. These clauses are included in FoxPro 2.5 for DOS so that windows DEFINEd for the Windows product will appear in the DOS product, as well. You can't use AT ... SIZE ... in the same window definition with a DOS-style FROM ... TO ... set of coordinates. The SIZE clause appears to calculate the DOS columns and rows in terms of *usable rows and columns*, but this rule doesn't hold true if the window doesn't have a border (its usable rows and columns will each be two greater than its SIZE numbers). This behavior is noted in the earliest shipping version of FoxPro 2.5 for DOS and may change in future versions.

This section examines the optional DEFINE WINDOW clauses. The discussion follows the same order used for the DEFINE WINDOW syntax example at the beginning of the section.

[IN [WINDOW] <window name2> | IN SCREEN]

By default, windows are placed IN SCREEN, which is also referred to as the desktop, and the window's coordinates are relative to the screen's dimensions. You can define windows within other windows, however, with the IN [WINDOW] <window name> clause. A window so defined is referred to as a *child* window, and the window in which the child is defined is its *parent* window. A child window cannot be moved outside of its parent (although it may still be activated outside of it), and it cannot be sized larger than the parent (although it may be defined as larger). If you move a parent window, its children move with it; and if you RELEASE the parent, its children are released along with it.

As indicated by the square brackets enclosing it, the word WINDOW is optional. You can state specifically that the window be placed in the screen by using the IN SCREEN clause.

The example WRAPMSG.PRG, in the section on SHOW WINDOW, uses IN WINDOW to separate the display of word-wrapped text from the left border of a parent window by one or more columns.

[FOOTER <expC1>] and [TITLE <expC2>]

You can include text in a window's top and bottom rows by using the TITLE and FOOTER clauses, respectively. The text will be centered within the border row and truncated if it exceeds the window's width. Spaces are considered part of the text, so if you want to separate the title or footer from the border character, place a space before and after the text, like this:

```
DEFINE WINDOW big_win ;
     FROM 0, 0 TO SROWS()-1, SCOLS()-1 ;
     TITLE " New Order Information " ;
     FOOTER " Press Esc When Done "
```

The TITLE of a window is especially significant if the window is used as an *image window* that gives characteristics to a BROWSE or to a MODIFY MEMO or FILE; in many cases, FoxPro uses the title of the image window to provide a window name for the resulting editing window. (Refer to Chapter 13 for a discussion of the different ways in which the editing windows receive window names.) Because a window name must follow the same rules as variable names, if a window title provides a window name, FoxPro extracts a legal name from the title by using the following rules:

- No more than 10 characters are significant to the name.
- Any leading spaces or illegal characters (such as graphics characters) are discarded.

- After discarding leading characters, if the title contains additional illegal characters within its first 10 characters, such as a period or a space, the window name will be the characters preceding another illegal character. If a BROWSE has the title " Pick One Client", for example, its window name is Pick.

To understand the importance of knowing the name of a window in a program, consider the following set of examples:

```
DEFINE WINDOW editwind FROM 1,1 TO 20,20 TITLE "Edit here"

MODIFY FILE My.TXT WINDOW editwind
* or
MODIFY FILE My.TXT

USE Budget
MODIFY MEMO Notes WINDOW editwind
* or
MODIFY MEMO Notes
```

In this example, the first MODIFY FILE and MODIFY MEMO commands produce windows that can be referenced in other window commands using the name *Edit*—for instance:

```
RELEASE WINDOW Edit
```

The second MODIFY FILE and MEMO commands produce windows with different titles (*MY.TXT* for the file window and *BUDGET.NOTES* for the memo window) from which their names would be derived, using the window-naming rules. Other window commands would reference these windows as in the following:

```
RELEASE WINDOW My          && for the file editing window
RELEASE WINDOW Budget      && for the memo editing window
```

CAUTION: As described in Chapter 13, if a BROWSE command uses both a TITLE clause and a WINDOW <window name> clause, the TITLE clause on the BROWSE takes precedence over the title of the DEFINEd WINDOW used in the WINDOW clause for the BROWSE window's name. For this reason, always follow the rules for window names for the first word in a BROWSE TITLE clause. If you issue a BROWSE with a TITLE of a single space or a single word that begins with a digit (illegal for a window or variable name), the BROWSE will appear with the TITLE you specify, but you will not be able to refer to this BROWSE window by name in your program.

The function WONTOP(), discussed in a later section of this chapter, returns the entire title of a BROWSE or editing window, not just its legal window name, although this function's job is to provide window names, not titles. You need to be aware of this anomaly if your code decides how to handle certain programming tasks based on the current window, as demonstrated in the examples in Chapter 15. In FoxPro 2.5, however, most commands that use the result of WONTOP() to manipulate windows (such as RELEASE WINDOW <window name>) will accept the entire result of WONTOP(), including illegal characters, without crashing.

[DOUBLE | PANEL | NONE | SYSTEM | <border string>]

You use these keywords to specify whether a window will have a border and, if it does, to define the appearance of the border. If you don't include any of these keywords, the current BORDER SETting will be used to determine the border's appearance. If you use the NONE keyword, the window will not have a border. The WBORDER() function (discussed later in this chapter) returns .F.. If the window has a border, you can change its appearance with the DOUBLE, PANEL, or SYSTEM clause, or specify a custom border string.

The border string specifies eight characters for the border while the window is active (one for each window side, and one for each corner) and a second eight characters for the border while another window is active. If you want to use the custom border, be careful to specify *both* groups of characters, or you'll wonder why the border changes when you click different windows! This behavior matches the FoxPro color system, in which most objects, including window borders, are assigned one group of colors for the object's active state and a second group for the object's inactive state.

If you use the SYSTEM keyword, the window will emulate the look of FoxPro's system windows. If you also include the CLOSE, GROW, or ZOOM keyword, the corresponding window control (close box, size control, zoom control) will appear in the window border.

The four keywords covered in this section are mutually exclusive; you can't combine them. For example, you can't use the SYSTEM clause with DOUBLE to get a window that looks like a system window, but with a double line around its edges.

The example WRAPMSG.PRG, in the section on SHOW WINDOW, uses the NONE clause in the definition of a child window so that the two windows appear to the user as a single window. A window defined with the NONE clause has two more usable rows and columns than another window with the same screen coordinates and a border of another type.

[CLOSE | NOCLOSE][FLOAT | NOFLOAT] [GROW | NOGROW][MINIMIZE] [ZOOM | NOZOOM]

These keywords allow or prevent a window's being closed, moved, or changed in size with the keyboard or the mouse. By default, windows are created NOCLOSE, NOFLOAT, NOGROW, and NOZOOM, and they cannot be minimized.

As noted above, if you include CLOSE, FLOAT, or ZOOM with the SYSTEM border keyword, the appropriate close control will appear in the window border. Otherwise, the close control will not be visible. Even when the close control is not visible, however, it exists. If you use the CLOSE keyword, for example, you can close the window by clicking the upper-left corner of the window, even when you can't see the close control.

[SHADOW]

By default, user-created windows do not have shadows (the dimmed area to the right of and below the window) as the Command window and other system windows do. If you want your window to have a shadow, use the SHADOW keyword. Note that when you SET SHADOW OFF, your window will not have a shadow even if you use the SHADOW keyword on the DEFINE WINDOW command. The window shadow is also responsive to the color scheme with which the window is defined (by default, COLOR SCHEME 1). If the color scheme includes the shadow attribute, this attribute is represented by a + (plus) character which follows all its normal color pairs. To find out whether a color scheme is defined with the shadow attribute, you can check the return value of this expression:

```
RIGHT(SCHEME(<scheme number>),1) = "+" && true for shadowed schemes
```

[FILL <expC3>]

You can fill the window's background with a particular character by including the FILL clause. You may wonder why you would want to fill a window with "A"s or "B"s, but that's not the intended use of this clause.

This clause is usually used with one of the dot-pattern characters in the ASCII character set (ASCII 176, 177, and 178) to create an attractive background on which to place other windows. If you define a full-screen window that has no border and take care not to let any output go to that screen, you can effectively change the background appearance of the desktop for your application.

[COLOR SCHEME <expN> | COLOR <color pair list>]

If you don't include the COLOR clause, your user-defined window takes its colors from COLOR SCHEME 1. Use the COLOR SCHEME <color scheme number> clause to use the color pairs of a different color scheme, or COLOR <color pair list> to override any or all of the default color pairs. To change a color pair without affecting one or more of the pairs that precede it in the list, use a comma as a placeholder so that FoxPro knows which pair you mean. For example, to change the colors used to display the title of an inactive window, you could use the following color pair list:

```
active_title = SCHEME(1,4)
* active title uses the fourth pair in the scheme
* and inactive title uses the fifth pair
DEFINE WINDOW big_win ;
     FROM 0, 0 TO SROWS()-1, SCOLS()-1 ;
     COLOR ,,,,&active_title
```

The title of this window will display in the same colors, regardless of whether it is active or inactive.

Now that you can create windows and assign window attributes, the next session discusses the commands available for manipulating windows.

Managing Windows through Commands

The additional commands that FoxPro uses to manage windows after they are DEFINEd are listed in table 23.1, with their required syntax. Optional keywords and clauses for these commands, with additional notes, follow the table.

Table 23.1 FoxPro Commands To Manipulate Windows

<table>
<tr><th>Command</th><th>Description</th></tr>
<tr><td>ACTIVATE WINDOW]<window name or list> | ALL</td><td>Activates an existing window and directs output to that window. The window displays, unless you use the NOSHOW keyword.</td></tr>
<tr><td>CLEAR WINDOW <window name or list> | ALL</td><td>Removes windows from memory along with moving them from the screen. CLEAR WINDOW, unlike RELEASE WINDOW, can be executed globally with the ALL keyword.</td></tr>
<tr><td>DEACTIVATE WINDOW <window name or list> | ALL</td><td>Removes a window from the screen, but does not remove it from memory. Output is directed to the previously active window. You can reactivate a deactivated window without redefining it.</td></tr>
<tr><td>HIDE WINDOW <window name or list> | ALL</td><td>Removes a window from the screen without deactivating it. You can redisplay a hidden window with either the SHOW WINDOW or ACTIVATE WINDOW command.</td></tr>
<tr><td>MOVE WINDOW <window name> TO <row>,<col> | BY <row>,<col></td><td>Moves a window to a different location. You can move a window TO a specified position, or in a particular direction BY a specified number of rows and columns.</td></tr>
<tr><td>RELEASE WINDOW <window name or list></td><td>Removes a window from the screen and from memory. To reACTIVATE a window that has been released, you must first DEFINE it again. You cannot RELEASE every currently DEFINEd window by using the keyword ALL on the RELEASE WINDOW command.</td></tr>
</table>

continues

Table 23.1 Continued

Command	Description
RESTORE WINDOW <window name or list> | ALL FROM <file> | MEMO <memo field>	Restores window definitions to memory after they have been SAVEd to a file or memo field. All window attributes are intact, including the current contents of the window and whether the window is hidden or showing. The special variant RESTORE SCREEN works slightly differently; first RESTORE the memory variable FROM the contents of the file or memofield, and then use the RESTORE SCREEN FROM <memvar> command.
SAVE WINDOW <window name or list > | ALL TO <file> | MEMO <memo field>	Saves current window definitions, status, and attributes for a later RESTORE. The special variant SAVE SCREEN works slightly differently, saving the information TO a memory variable. See the error-logging code in Chapter 20 for an example of these commands and RESTORE WINDOW and SCREEN.
SCROLL <row1>,<col1>, <row2,col2>, <# of rows up>,[# of cols right>]	Scrolls a specified region of the screen or a window by a specified number of rows and/or columns. The number of rows and/or columns can be either negative or positive. Only the number of rows is required; the number of columns defaults to 0 if the last parameter is omitted.
SHOW WINDOW <window name>	Displays an active window on-screen. This command is usually used to display a window that was activated by using the NOSHOW keyword of the ACTIVATE command.

Command	Description
SIZE WINDOW <window name> TO <row>,<col>	This command, which is currently undocumented, is similar to ZOOM WINDOW but easier to use. It changes the size of a window from its current size to a specified number of rows and columns. The window's upper-left corner remains unchanged.
ZOOM WINDOW <window name>	Changes the size and/or location of MIN ¦ MAX ¦ NORM a window.

ACTIVATE WINDOW

Defining a window stores it in memory, but does not activate it. ACTIVATE WINDOW activates the window and directs subsequent output to it. Examine the command's syntax and available clauses in detail:

```
ACTIVATE WINDOW
     <window name1> [, <window name2> ... ] ¦ ALL
     [IN [WINDOW] <window name3> ¦ IN [WINDOW] SCREEN]
     [BOTTOM ¦ TOP ¦ SAME]
     [NOSHOW]
```

To activate a specific window, you include its name in a list of windows, separating one from another with a comma. Alternatively, you can activate all defined windows with ACTIVATE WINDOW ALL.

Although a window may have been defined IN another window, you can still control where it is activated by using ACTIVATE's IN clause. A window that has been defined IN SCREEN can be activated IN <window name>, and vice versa. The window's coordinates always refer to the window in which it is activated, or to the screen when activated in the screen.

The BOTTOM, TOP, and SAME keywords control where on the desktop a window is activated with respect to the ordered list of active windows, or the *window stack*. NOSHOW enables you to send output to a window without making the window visible. You usually use this keyword to hide the window while text and objects are placed within the window. When the window is complete, you use the SHOW WINDOW <window name> command to display the window. FoxPro will also show the window if it becomes the current READ window, because the current GET object automatically determines the current WONTOP( ), or active window.

TIP

The current GET object determines the *literal* "window on top" as well as the window returned by the WONTOP() function, and this rule does not respect parent and child window relationships. If a GET in a parent window becomes the current object, the parent window comes forward on-screen, obscuring any child windows or BROWSEs defined IN the parent WINDOW.

For this reason, don't put GETs in parent windows! Instead, create a parent window with no GETs and define child windows *within* the parent, each holding a separate group of GETs, or a BROWSE or other editing window. With this approach, all the possible windows on top are equal. To avoid having the users activating the parent window, you can use HIDE WINDOW <parent window> SAVE, which is described in a later section.

DEACTIVATE WINDOW

Just as ACTIVATE places a WINDOW on-screen, DEACTIVATE removes a WINDOW from the screen. This action doesn't remove the window from memory, however, or eliminate the memory that the window requires from the common pool of user object memory FoxPro has available. To get this memory back for other uses, use the RELEASE WINDOW command.

TIP

Check the user object memory with SYS(1016). This memory is far more limited than the total pool of memory FoxPro can use to manipulate data, which you can check with SYS(1001). The user object memory must handle memory variables, defined menu objects, and all user-defined windows—a good reason to make sure you don't DEFINE WINDOWs before they're needed.

SHOW WINDOW

SHOW WINDOW has the same optional IN [WINDOW] | SCREEN clause and the same TOP | BOTTOM | SAME keywords that ACTIVATE WINDOW has. SHOW WINDOW also has a special REFRESH keyword, used to repaint a BROWSE with new contents or a different record order or filter, without reissuing the BROWSE command, as demonstrated in the Budget screen in Chapter 13.

SHOW WINDOW <browse window> REFRESH is often used with the SAME command so that a READ or GET VALID clause refreshes the BROWSE display without changing the window stack.

The following example demonstrates the use of the IN WINDOW clause for parent and child windows, along with several other important window-handling techniques. The program creates two windows, one within the other, and displays a message within the child window. The child is created without a border and with the same color scheme as the parent so that they appear to be a single window. The child's left column is positioned one column to the right of the parent's left border to create an "auto indent" effect when word-wrapped text displays.

```
* WRAPMSG.PRG

* store the carriage return / line feed characters
* to a memory variable
cr_lf = CHR(13) + CHR(10)

* create the message in variable ord_info
ord_info = "We hope that you enjoyed this demonstration " + ;
           "of Weird Willie's Inventory Control System.  " + ;
           "This module is part of a complete accounting " + ;
           "and management reporting package." + ;
            cr_lf + cr_lf + ;
           "For additional information, call (203) 555-1212.  " + ;
           "To place an order, call (800) ITS-WEIRD."

* display the message in an appropriately-sized
* window, using word-wrapping to properly format
* the text
DO Show_msg WITH ord_info
RETURN

PROCEDURE Show_msg
```

continues

```
* Display the_msg in a window, using word-wrapping.
* Use a borderless child window that has the same
* background color as its parent window, and position
* the child two columns to the right of the parent, so
* as to separate the text from the window border.
PARAMETERS the_msg
PRIVATE w_width, w_height, mem_width
* use variables to hold the screen's dimensions;
* size the window so that its just large enough to
* hold the message and a prompt to continue, but
* don't let it exceed the the number of screen rows
w_width  = 60
w_height = MIN(MEMLINES(the_msg)+4, SROWS())

* save the current setting of memowidth and
* set it to fill the child window
mem_width = SET("MEMOWIDTH")
SET MEMOWIDTH TO w_width - 4

* create the parent window
DEFINE WINDOW parent ;
       FROM (SROWS()-w_height)/2, ;
            (SCOLS()-w_width)/2 ;
       TO   (SROWS()-w_height)/2 + w_height-1, ;
            (SCOLS()-w_width)/2+w_width-1 ;
       COLOR SCHEME 5
* create the child window, placing its
* leftmost column two columns to the right
* of the parent's left border column, and
* using the same color scheme
DEFINE WINDOW child IN WINDOW parent ;
       FROM 0,2 TO WROWS()-1,WCOLS()-1 ;
       NONE COLOR SCHEME 5
* activate both windows, but don't show
* them until we've output the message text
ACTIVATE WINDOW parent NOSHOW
ACTIVATE WINDOW child NOSHOW
* output the message and a prompt to continue
?? the_msg
* now display the message and wait for a keypress
SHOW WINDOW parent
SHOW WINDOW child
WAIT "Press any key to continue..."
* we don't need these windows any more, so
* remove them from the screen and from memory
```

```
RELEASE WINDOW parent, child
* restore the previous SETting of MEMOWIDTH
SET MEMOWIDTH TO mem_width
RETURN
```

Note that word wrapping will only affect memory variables that are longer than 254 bytes.

HIDE WINDOW

You can hide windows from view with HIDE WINDOW, which has the same IN [WINDOW] | SCREEN clause as ACTIVATE and SHOW WINDOW. HIDE WINDOW also has an additional SAVE keyword, which leaves an image of the window on-screen and is similar to the keyword NOCLEAR in a BROWSE command. The window doesn't need to be ACTIVATEd before the HIDE WINDOW <window name> SAVE command creates an image on-screen.

You can use HIDE WINDOW <window name> SAVE to adjust the contents of a window and then SHOW the modified window, without having the window "flash" as it is hidden and then redisplayed. The following example program demonstrates the way HIDE WINDOW can provide "untouchable" windows on-screen, which the user can see but not select.

```
* HIDEWIND.PRG
DEFINE WINDOW x FROM 1,1 TO 10,25 ;
       SYSTEM COLOR SCHEME 10 ;
       TITLE "a get window"
DEFINE WINDOW y FROM 12,1 TO 23,25 ;
       SYSTEM COLOR SCHEME 10
DEFINE WINDOW z FROM 1,39 TO 15,70 ;
       SYSTEM COLOR SCHEME 10 ;
       TITLE "modi file, untouchable"
MODI FILE test.txt NOWAIT WINDOW z
* use an existing file so you can see how it works
ACTIVATE WINDOW y
@ 1,1 SAY "just sitting here"
@ 2,1 SAY "but could have gets"
@ 3,1 SAY "if they were disabled "
ACTIVATE WINDOW CALCULATOR
MOVE WINDOW CALCULATOR TO 12,45
ACTIVATE SCREEN
CLEAR
```

continues

```
HIDE WINDOW ALL SAVE
ACTIVATE WINDOW x
@ 2,1 SAY "a get" GET a_get DEFAULT "something"
@ 3,1 SAY "more get" GET nuther DEFAULT 1000
READ CYCLE
ACTIVATE SCREEN
CLEAR WINDOWS ALL
WAIT WINDOW ;
    "The CLEAR WINDOWS hasn't CLEARed the screen images..."
CLEAR
RETURN
```

In this program, an ACTIVATE SCREEN command ensures that all the windows will respond to the HIDE WINDOW ALL command that immediately follows, because then no window is currently active. The currently active window cannot be hidden with HIDE WINDOW.

HIDE WINDOWS ALL SAVE can also be used to preserve the contents of the screen during a RUN command which executes a DOS command whose output to the screen cannot be suppressed.

ZOOM WINDOW

The ZOOM WINDOW command, which is only used with a single <window name> at a time, can be used to minimize or maximize a window programmatically, using the MIN or MAX keywords. Using ZOOM WINDOW <name> MIN AUTO is equivalent to Shift+double-clicking the window's title bar or using Ctrl+Shift+F9 to "dock" the window in the lower-right corner of the screen. Use ZOOM WINDOW with the NORM keyword to resize or relocate a window with the same FROM ... TO and AT ... SIZE clauses available for DEFINE WINDOW. You don't need to use the entire clause with ZOOM WINDOW, however, to change a window's size or position. The following command, for example, changes the window's lower-right corner and size without adjusting the anchoring upper-left corner:

```
ZOOM WINDOW my_wind NORM TO 20,50
```

When you use the ZOOM WINDOW ... NORM command in this way, be sure that the new values you choose for one anchoring corner are appropriate with respect to the other. If the window has a border, the row and column value of the lower-right corner must always be greater than the row and column of the upper-left column. If either the row or column value of the upper-left column matches the lower-right corner and the window has a border, you won't get the exact coordinates that you specify (a window with a border is a minimum of two rows and columns in size). If the window doesn't have a border, the window's upper-left and lower-right coordinates can match; the window is one row and column in size. If the row or column value of the upper-left column is *less* than the values of the lower-right column, you receive an `Illegal value` error from FoxPro.

The ZOOM WINDOW <name> NORM command can be used without *any* additional clauses to return a window to its previous size after the window was maximized or minimized.

SHOW GETS WINDOW

The SHOW GETS WINDOW <window name> command, although not specifically a window-handling command, also has obvious window implications. This variant of the SHOW GETS command is often used to DISABLE or ENABLE the contents of an entire GET window at once in a multiwindow READ. In the READ SHOW clause, you can use the SYS(2016) function to find out which window was named in the SHOW GETS WINDOW <wname> command and take appropriate action.

MODIFY WINDOW

One additional command, MODIFY WINDOW <window name>, is available for FoxPro for Windows. This command, with which you can change the attributes of a window (such as its TITLE or COLOR SCHEME) specified with DEFINE WINDOW, elicits a `Feature not available` error when issued in the initial shipping version of FoxPro 2.5 for DOS, so be careful with its use if you write cross-platform programs. The usefulness of this command is not limited to graphical environments, however, and there's a good chance that MODIFY COMMAND will appear in future versions of FoxPro for DOS.

Gaining Control Over Window Objects

Because we may have more than one window on the desktop at any time, and because we may move from one window to another from within a running program, we must be able to discern among windows and extract information about them. In this section, you explore the plethora of window control functions and other capabilities that FoxPro provides to meet these needs.

Exploring Window Functions

FoxPro's window control functions are listed in table 23.2. These functions are designed to give you all the information you need to discern a window's current position, characteristics, and relationship to other windows.

Table 23.2 FoxPro Window Control Functions

Function	Description
MWINDOW([name])	Returns the name of the window over which the mouse is positioned. When passed a window name, this function returns .T. if the named window is the window over which the mouse is positioned.
WBORDER([name])	Determines whether a window has a border.
WCHILD([name] [0¦1])	Returns the number or the names (one at a time) of child windows of the desktop or a specified window. Can be used to create a list of all active child windows, using the second argument (as shown in the final program example in this chapter), or the number of child windows in the current output window if no arguments are passed.
WCOLS([name])	Returns the columns in a window, not including two border columns, if the window has any.
WEXIST([name])	Determines whether a specified window is currently defined.
WLAST([name])	Determines whether a specified window was active before the current window, or determines the name of the previously active window if no window is specified.
WLCOL([name])	Returns the screen location of a window's far-left column.
WLROW([name])	Returns the screen location of a window's top row.
WMAXIMUM([name])	Determines whether a specified window is maximized.

Function	Description
WMINIMUM([name])	The opposite of WMAXIMUM( ); determines whether a specified window has been minimized.
WONTOP([name])	Determines whether a specified window is the active one on the desktop, or determines the name of the active window if no window name is passed.
WOUTPUT([name])	Determines whether the specified window is the current output window for output such as @ ... SAY or ?. Returns the name of the current output window if no window name is passed.
WPARENT([name])	Returns the name of a window's parent window.
WREAD([name])	Determines whether a specified window is involved in the current READ. This function can determine only the READ-involvement of a GET window, unless the READ is MODAL and the non-GET window (such as the Calculator or a BROWSE) is included in the WITH clause.
WROWS([name])	Returns the number of rows in a window, not including the two border rows if the window has a border.
WTITLE([name])	Returns a window's title, which may or may not be the same as its name.
WVISIBLE([name])	Determines whether a specified window has been defined and activated and that it is not currently hidden.

If the window-handling functions are not passed a window name, they act on the current window (WONTOP( )). The functions return either a logical value based on the characteristics of the current window (for example, WBORDER( ) with no argument returns .T. or .F.), or a character value for the current window (WONTOP( ) returns the current window, and WTITLE( ) returns the title of the current window). When these functions are passed a window name, their return value may change. WONTOP(<window name>), for example, returns .T. or .F. to indicate whether the window specified is the current window.

For each function, a return value of a null string represents the screen or desktop, and you can pass the function a null string to get information about the screen.

Several of these functions merit special attention. The MWINDOW() function is typically used in ON KEY LABEL LEFTMOUSE procedures, passed as a parameter along with MCOL(), MROW(), WONTOP(), and WOUTPUT() to determine whether the mouse has been clicked in the currently active window, and the mouse's exact position in relation to the currently active window.

T I P

When you use any of the mouse-sensing functions in an ON KEY LABEL or other event-handling procedure, including the MDOWN() function (to see whether a mouse press is involved in an event), be sure to *pass the result of the function* to the procedure, rather than check the function within the called procedure. For example, always use syntax similar to the following:

```
ON KEY LABEL LEFTMOUSE DO Checkwind WITH MWINDOW() = WONTOP()
@ 1,1 GET someget VALID Checkget(MDOWN())

PROCEDURE CheckWind
PARAMETER mouse_in_currwind
IF mouse_in_currwind
   * etc.
ENDIF
RETURN

FUNCTION Checkget
PARAMETERS ifmouse
IF ifmouse
   * etc.
ENDIF
RETURN
```

If, instead, you check the value of MDOWN() or MWINDOW() within the called procedures, you may not receive the right results because the user may have moved the mouse or released the mouse button before the check occurs.

WCOLS() and WROWS() provide you with the same information about the dimensions of a window that SCOLS() and SROWS() provide concerning the screen's dimensions. You can use these functions to properly position text, windows, and other objects within a window of unknown dimensions. Refer to examples in the section on "Referencing Windows in a Relative Way" in this chapter.

WEXIST() informs you of whether a window currently exists. If you allow the user to close any of your windows (by including the CLOSE keyword in the DEFINE WINDOW command), you must check for the window's existence before trying to activate it, or you may trigger an error. As explained in Chapter 15, you should always check for the existence of a BROWSE window before issuing a BROWSE command, unless you issue the BROWSE with the NOWAIT keyword.

If you don't specify a window name, WLAST() will tell you the name of the last window activated prior to the currently active window. If you do include a window name, WLAST() returns .T. if the named window was the last window activated.

WLAST() may not work exactly the way you expect. This function doesn't tell you the name of the window that precedes the current window in the list of defined windows; it simply tells you the name of the window that was last activated. If the previously active window was released, WLAST() will return the null string (""), rather than the name of the window that was active prior to the current window. To confirm this, try running the following program:

```
* LASTWIND.PRG
DEFINE WINDOW win1 FROM 0,0 TO 5,10
DEFINE WINDOW win2 FROM 6,0 TO 10,10
DEFINE WINDOW win3 FROM 11,0 TO 15,10
ACTIVATE WINDOW win1
ACTIVATE WINDOW win2
ACTIVATE WINDOW win3
? LEN(WLAST()), WLAST()     && returns "4 WIN2"
RELEASE WINDOW win2
? LEN(WLAST()), WLAST()     && returns "0"
WAIT WINDOW "See?"
RELEASE WINDOW win1, win3
RETURN
```

WLAST() is especially useful in the DEACTIVATE, ACTIVATE, and VALID clauses of the READ command, where you are concerned with the movement of the user between windows. In this situation you haven't DEACTIVATEd any windows, so WLAST() gives you the desired answer. WLAST(), like WONTOP(), is aware of all windows, including desk accessories and BROWSEs.

Refer to table 23.2's entry for WOUTPUT(), and you see that this function helps you determine the window where output directed to the screen will appear, including @ ... SAY, the ? and ?? commands, and the prompt for a WAIT command if you don't specify the WAIT WINDOW.

Unlike WLAST() and WONTOP(), therefore, WOUTPUT() can never return the name of a file, a memo editing window, or a BROWSE window. You can determine whether the currently active window is a GET window by checking to see whether WOUTPUT()=WONTOP().

NOTE The ROW() and COL() functions give you the current position relative to the window that is currently WOUTPUT(). These functions do *not* work to give you the cursor position within a BROWSE, even though they sometimes appear to work properly when a BROWSE is active and the screen or the BROWSE's image window happens to be WOUTPUT().

You can use WMIN() in the READ ACTIVATE clause if your users may minimize or dock a GET window. You will need to ZOOM <the GET window> NORM so that they can resume data entry in this window when it becomes active again.

WTITLE() returns the *entire* text of the window title, not just the part significant to the window name, so sometimes this function is your best choice for determining which window the user has chosen. The test "BUDGET" $ UPPER(WTITLE()), for example, will indicate a window pertaining to the Budget table, whether the current window is a BROWSE of Budget records or a GET window with data for a particular Budget entry. Similarly, if you name all your BROWSE pick lists consistently, as suggested in Chapter 13, you can check "PICK" $ UPPER(WTITLE()) to see whether the current window is a BROWSE.

TIP Notice the UPPER() version of the window title used in these examples and throughout the examples in Chapters 12, 13, and 15. In some cases, different versions of FoxPro use different capitalization for window names and titles, both for display and for the return values of window functions. Avoid any possible anomalies in the functions or differences during cross-platform development by explicitly choosing the case for *all* comparisons.

Referencing Windows in a Relative Way

Back in the "old days" of dBASE III Plus and FoxBase+, things were simpler. When you wanted to display a message at the bottom of the screen, you could use the following command:

```
@ 23,0 SAY "Press Esc to return to the Main menu"
```

If you wanted to center the message on the line, you could change this command to:

```
msg = "Press Esc to return to the Main menu"
@ 23,40-len(msg)/2 SAY msg
```

In FoxPro, however, the concept of a screen has been changed from that of a single output device of known proportions to a series of one or more windows that can be moved and sized under interactive and program control. These windows may have as many as 50 rows and 132 columns using common video cards and monitors. (With specialized video cards and monitors, even more rows and columns are possible.)

Luckily, FoxPro has many built-in functions that tell you the current dimensions of the screen and any other defined windows, and enable you to address these windows in a relative way. Although it's always a good idea to avoid hard coding values in your programs, it is absolutely imperative that you avoid making assumptions about window positions and dimensions.

Finding Out about the Display Mode and Screen

You can ensure that your applications always run in standard (25 rows by 80 columns) mode, but why not let the user choose his or her own screen dimensions if the available hardware supports a larger display? The capability of handling different screen sizes always makes a good impression and adds a measure of professionalism to your applications.

To switch from one display mode to another, use the SET DISPLAY command, as follows:

```
SET DISPLAY TO CGA ¦ COLOR ¦ EGA25 ¦ EGA43 ¦ MONO ¦ VGA25 ¦ VGA50
```

If the selected mode is not supported by your hardware, FoxPro displays the error message `Display mode not available`. For example, you trigger this error if you issue the command SET DISPLAY TO MONO and you have a color display and video card. In some cases, your hardware may support the mode, but FoxPro adjusts your command to a display mode that is more suitable for your hardware. For example, if you issue the command SET DISPLAY TO EGA43 when using a VGA card and monitor combination, FoxPro SETs DISPLAY TO VGA50 without giving any notice.

If you are setting the display mode from within your application, you can avoid any error or confusion about available modes by using the

SYS(2006) function to determine the type of video card and monitor installed in the machine. SYS(2006) returns the card/monitor combination as a character string, such as EGA/Color. The following code fragment uses SYS(2006) to determine which command to use to set the display to the maximum number of rows possible:

```
DO CASE
CASE "VGA" $ UPPER(SYS(2006))
   SET DISPLAY TO VGA50
CASE "EGA" $ UPPER(SYS(2006))
   SET DISPLAY TO EGA43
ENDCASE
```

Note that with this code, the screen display remains in normal 25-row mode if the user's video card supports neither VGA nor EGA mode.

Using a CASE statement easily allows you to add additional possibilities in the future if a new release of FoxPro provides additional video modes or if you want this code to support FoxPro for Windows.

Now that you have set the display mode, you need a way to position windows and objects so that they fill the screen the way you want. FoxPro's SROWS() and SCOLS() functions provide you with this information.

SROWS() returns the number of available screen rows, and SCOLS() returns the number of available screen columns. You can use these functions, for example, to define a window that will appear in the center of the screen, as in the following:

```
PROCEDURE center_win
PARAMETERS wheight, wlength
PRIVATE trow, brow, lcol, rcol

trow = (SROWS() - wheight) / 2
brow = trow + wheight - 1
lcol = (SCOLS() - wlength) / 2
rcol = lcol + wlength - 1

DEFINE WINDOW center_win ;
   FROM trow, lcol TO brow, rcol
   NONE SHADOW COLOR SCHEME 7
ACTIVATE WINDOW center_win
RETURN
```

You now have a routine to create and activate a window of specifiable proportions in the center of the screen, regardless of its current dimensions. You also can use this routine to display a message to the user, as in the following:

```
IF !SEEK(this_rec)
   win_msg = "That record is not in the table!"
   DO center_win WITH 1, LEN(win_msg) + 4
   WAIT win_msg TIMEOUT 5
   RELEASE WINDOW center_win
ENDIF
```

Notice that if you change the message, the width of the center_win window also changes.

You could create a similar procedure through the Screen Builder, by using an @ ... EDIT to hold the variable-length message, and then centering the window on-screen with the new FoxPro 2.5 command MOVE WINDOW <window name> CENTER. This command is used in the #SECTION 2 part of Setup code, after the generated code has DEFINEd the WINDOW. The custom procedure is easier to adjust for message length, however, and is easily adapted for other requirements besides window-centering, such as putting a window in the lowest third of a screen display.

Sizing Windows Dynamically

In the preceding window-centering procedure, you created the message window on each call to the procedure, enabling you to create a window a little wider than the particular message to be displayed.

Creating and releasing windows takes some extra time, however. The delay may not be much, but the window might not “snap” onto the screen the way you would like it to. You can decide to DEFINE the WINDOW once and ACTIVATE it whenever needed.

You must weigh the time, however, including the time to calculate the window size, that DEFINE WINDOW saves you against the extra memory the window consumes if you don’t RELEASE it after each use. If you decide to leave the window DEFINEd, create a window that is more flexible.

Because the amount of memory a window consumes increases with size, DEFINE the generic window in a small size to begin with, adding whatever attributes are appropriate to its type of message, in a line of code like the following:

```
DEFINE WINDOW my_alert ;
   FROM 1,1 TO 2,2 ;
   FLOAT GROW ;
   COLOR SCHEME 7
```

Notice the keywords FLOAT and GROW, which allow you to MOVE and ZOOM this WINDOW to a new position and new dimensions. The COLOR SCHEME 7 provides consistency for alert windows.

When you're ready to use this window to hold a message, you must determine that its current position and size is appropriate to your message. First, size the window for your message, using the ZOOM WINDOW command. With the NORM keyword, the ZOOM WINDOW command functions much as the DEFINE WINDOW command does, using FROM ... TO ... or AT ... SIZE ... clauses to supply coordinates and dimensions. The following procedure receives the name of a message window that has already been defined and a message string, sizing it appropriately for the message length, centering it horizontally for its new width, and giving it one usable row for the message.

```
PROCEDURE adjust_mwind
PARAMETERS win_name, win_msg

PRIVATE trow, lcol, rcol, mlength

IF ! WEXIST(win_name)
   * if the procedure has been passed a non-existant
   * window name in error, return here
   RETURN
ENDIF

mlength = LEN(win_msg) + 1
* since our messaging procedure uses a WAIT,
* one extra character takes care of the WAIT's
* flashing cursor

trow = WLROW(win_name)
IF WBORDER(win_name)

   lcol = (SCOLS() - mlength) / 2 -1
   rcol = lcol + mlength + 1

   ZOOM WINDOW (win_name) NORM;
      FROM trow, lcol TO trow + 2, rcol

ELSE
```

```
    lcol = (SCOLS() - mlength) / 2
    rcol = lcol + mlength - 1

    ZOOM WINDOW (win_name) NORM;
       FROM trow, lcol TO trow, rcol

ENDIF
RETURN
```

The procedure uses WLROW(<window name>), which returns the top row on the screen occupied by this window. This number is not always the same as the first usable row within the window, depending on whether the window was created with a border (the default) or with the keyword NONE to specify no border. If a window has a border, its border takes two screen rows and two columns. Notice the check for WBORDER() and the slight difference in calculations.

This difference must be observed whenever you use WLROW() or its sibling function WLCOL(), which provides the far-left column that the window occupies on-screen. Similarly, the functions WROWS() and WCOLS() tell you the number of rows and columns occupied by a window on-screen—but when the window has a border, the number of *usable* rows and columns is two rows or columns less than the number returned by these functions.

If any of these functions is not passed a window name as an argument, the function returns its information for the currently active window, which is the window name currently returned by the WONTOP() function. You can pass each function a null string as an argument to find out the same information about the screen, or desktop. If the screen, or desktop is currently active because no other windows have been DEFINEd or an ACTIVATE SCREEN command has been issued, WROWS() and WCOLS() (with no arguments) return the same values as SROWS() and SCOLS(). (At all other times you can use WROWS("") and WCOLS("") to get the same information.) Using the expression WLROW(""),WLCOL("") in your code is always equivalent to writing `0,0`.

MOVE WINDOWs

After the last adjustment, the window occupies the right amount of space for the WAIT message. Different types of messages, however, may be positioned in different screen areas. Window positioning can serve as an immediate clue to a window's purpose, in programs where use of FoxPro's BELL capability is inappropriate, and where the user may choose a monochrome or gray-scale color set. Like other interface clues, you need to use positioning clues consistently for them to work (for example, always place the printer control dialog in the lowest third of the screen, centered horizontally). The ZOOM command in the preceding procedure can position the window appropriately at the same time as the window gets its new size, or (when sizing is not required) positioning can be accomplished separately using the MOVE WINDOW command.

The MOVE WINDOW command can shift a window TO new coordinates, and you can calculate these coordinates relative to other screen elements, just as the ZOOM command can. The MOVE WINDOW command, however, has the additional capability to shift a window *relative to its own position* without further calculation on your part. You use the MOVE WINDOW's BY clause, instead of moving TO new coordinates, to accomplish this task. The following code, for example, "streams" the alert window from left to right across the screen, until the user presses the Esc key. Notice the use of WLCOL(), which changes as the window moves, to determine when the alert window must go back to the left side of the screen.

```
* pass this procedure any window name and watch the window move
PROCEDURE stream
PARAMETERS which_wind
IF TYPE("which_wind") # "C" OR NOT WEXIST(which_wind)
   RETURN
ENDIF
PRIVATE wind_row, finished, screen_size, old_cursor, old_escape
old_cursor = SET("CURSOR")
old_escape =SET("ESCAPE")
finished = 0
screen_size = SCOLS()
wind_row = WLROW(which_wind)
WAIT WINDOW NOWAIT "press ESC to end... "
SET CURSOR OFF
SET ESCAPE OFF
ACTIVATE WINDOW (which_wind)
* you might SAY a message in the window
* at this point, or ACTIVATE the WINDOW
* and SAY an appropriate message before
* calling the procedure
DO WHILE .T.
```

```
    IF WLCOL() > screen_size  && WLCOL() is checking
                              && the top window here,
                              && no need to pass
                              && the window name
       MOVE WINDOW (which_wind) TO wind_row,0
    ELSE
       MOVE WINDOW (which_wind) BY 0,1
       finished=INKEY(.1)  && this line provides a
                           && test to see if the user
                           && is ready to leave and
                           && also provides a slight
                           && pause for animation
                           && purposes.
    ENDIF
    IF finished = 27
       EXIT
    ENDIF
ENDDO
DEACTIVATE WINDOW (which_wind)
WAIT CLEAR
SET ESCAPE &OLD_ESCAPE
SET CURSOR &old_cursor
RETURN
```

Although this test procedure is a trivial example, a moving alert window is sure to be noticeable even when the program cannot use sounds or depend on color to get attention. MOVE WINDOW <name> BY ... provides the key to simple animation effects in FoxPro for polished opening screens and self-running demos. During long programs that SCAN through the records of large tables for output or calculations, a "notification" window that moves at intervals based on a standard number of records can also reassure the user that the system is still running properly.

Handling Special System Windows

In Chapters 13 and 15, you saw that the desk accessories can be ACTIVATEd and included in windows lists just as user-defined windows are. The window-handling commands can reference these windows like they can any other windows that have names. For example,

```
ACTIVATE WINDOW Filer
MOVE WINDOW Calendar BY 2,2
```

The window-referencing functions return the names of most of these system windows, too. The Trace and Debug windows, however, are designed to be "invisible" to the window functions that let you know about the currently active windows and the window stack so that they will not affect your code when you're testing programs. For example, WLAST() will never return "Trace" as you click between the Trace window and your normal program windows. Similarly, if you ACTIVATE the Trace window IN another window, the WCHILD() function will never return "Trace" as part of the window stack for this parent—although you can find out where the Trace window has been activated by using WPARENT("Trace").

Understanding the way WCHILD() works gives you a good idea of the special invisible status of the Trace and Debug windows in your programs. Execute the following test sequence (you can type each line into the Command window or create a program):

```
PUSH KEY CLEAR
ON KEY LABEL F2 WAIT WINDOW NOWAIT WCHILD("parent",0)
ON KEY LABEL F3 WAIT WINDOW NOWAIT WCHILD("parent",1)
ON KEY LABEL F4 ACTIVATE WINDOW Command IN SCREEN
DEFINE WINDOW parent FROM 1,1 TO 20,70 TITLE "Parent"
DEFINE WINDOW child1 FROM 1,1 TO 5,15 COLOR SCHEME 10 ;
              TITLE "Child1"
DEFINE WINDOW child2 FROM 8,1 TO 11,15 COLOR SCHEME 5 ;
              TITLE "Child2" ;
              IN WINDOW parent

* both the following commands make the windows
* child windows of WINDOW parent:
ACTIVATE WINDOW child2  && was DEFINEd IN parent
ACTIVATE WINDOW child1 IN WINDOW parent

ACTIVATE WINDOW Calculator IN WINDOW parent
ACTIVATE WINDOW Trace IN WINDOW parent
ACTIVATE WINDOW Debug IN WINDOW parent

ACTIVATE WINDOW Command IN WINDOW parent
ACTIVATE WINDOW parent

* to make sure you can see the Command window:
MOVE WINDOW Calculator TO 1,30
MOVE WINDOW Trace TO 5,30
MOVE WINDOW Debug TO 10,30
ZOOM WINDOW Command NORM FROM 10,0 TO 13,30
```

When you press F2 and use WCHILD() with 0 as its second argument, you get the bottom child window in the parent window's stack. Thereafter, you can press F3 and get additional child windows in stack order, until you get to the top child window. (Press F2 to get back to the bottom of the stack.) Although the Command window appears among the window names returned by WCHILD(), neither the Trace nor the Debug window is ever discerned as part of the stack.

When you are finished with this test, press F4 to make the Command window a child of the screen again, and issue the following commands to clean up:

```
CLEAR WINDOWS
POP KEY
```

Summary

Without exaggeration, the addition of real, movable windows with separate contents and definable characteristics was the most momentous advance of FoxPro 1.0 over FoxBASE and other Xbase dialects. In each version of FoxPro, new windowing capabilities have been added to the product.

This discussion has not been an exhaustive study of what you can do with FoxPro windows, or even of the commands and functions available for working with FoxPro windows. Let this chapter serve as an introduction to FoxPro window capabilities, just as this book serves to introduce you to the power of FoxPro as a whole.

A

APPENDIX

Installing FoxPro 2.5 for DOS

In this appendix, you learn how to install FoxPro. After installing the program, you can go directly to Chapter 1, where you find complete instructions on loading FoxPro and getting to work.

Establishing the Base Product

A short pamphlet called *Installation and Configuration* is included with your documentation. If you are installing FoxPro on a network, you also should check the *Developer's Guide* for the chapter on "FoxPro in a Multi-User Environment," which discusses additional system requirements and provides configuration compatibility tips.

Preparing for Installation

Before you start, check the System Requirements chart in the *Installation and Configuration* booklet. As explained in this book's introduction, the Requirements chart is accurate, but the program runs much more smoothly if you give it more memory. FoxPro Standard runs with only 640K; however, your use of FoxPro's power tools and windowing capabilities is severely limited. The entire base product (both Standard and Extended), plus the Distribution Kit, requires a total of almost 16M, and the various sample directories require much more space. FoxPro also needs space for its temporary work files.

Check the root directory of your boot drive (usually drive C) for a file called CONFIG.SYS. This file is used by DOS to establish its own environment. If you do not have a CONFIG.SYS file, you need to create a file with that name in your boot drive's root directory. The file you create must contain the following lines:

```
FILES=40
BUFFERS=20
```

To create this file, use a text editor or a word processor that can create an ASCII text file—or use the DOS command `COPY CON`. See your DOS manual if you need more information on how to use the COPY CON command.

If you already have a CONFIG.SYS file, make sure that the file contains the appropriate entries for FILES and BUFFERS. For FoxPro, Microsoft recommends setting BUFFERS between 20 and 40. A setting of 40 is the minimum recommended for FILES, and many people use much higher FILES settings. Add or edit your CONFIG.SYS file accordingly; copy your existing file to a backup name before making any changes, however, in case you experience a problem and have to start again.

If you need to make any adjustments to your CONFIG.SYS file, or if you do not have a CONFIG.SYS file, you must accomplish one more task before you can begin your installation: Reboot your computer by pressing Ctrl+Alt+Del, or the reset switch if you have one, so that your new CONFIG.SYS settings take effect.

CAUTION: If you use DOS 6.0 or certain other utilities, you may have a number of different system configurations in effect at different times. Make sure that you revise the preceding instructions to alter all the configuration FILES statements under which you can run FoxPro.

NOTE

As you create more complex applications with FoxPro, you must open more files simultaneously. The FILES setting in CONFIG.SYS determines how many files DOS enables you to open at one time. If you receive an error message from FoxPro, such as `Too many files open`, raise the FILES setting in CONFIG.SYS. If you use any applications that modify your CONFIG.SYS file, make sure that you check the file afterward and that the settings of FILES and BUFFERS are still appropriate for FoxPro.

Be aware, however, of an important exception to this rule: Memory management software alters your CONFIG.SYS and AUTOEXEC.BAT files to create nonstandard FILES and BUFFERS settings. This type of software often loads FILES and BUFFERS in high memory, leaving only a minimal number in CONFIG.SYS and leaving more of your system's conventional memory free for applications such as FoxPro. If you use memory management software, do not adjust your FILES and BUFFERS settings without first consulting the manuals for these products.

If you run FoxPro in an environment in which a file may be accessed in multiple sessions, but you are not connected to a network that provides for multiple access, you may need to load DOS SHARE, as explained in Chapter 1. You can determine whether you need to load SHARE if you SET EXCLUSIVE OFF and USE a data table, as described in Chapter 21; if SYS(2011) still reports Exclusive use when you have SET EXCLUSIVE OFF, you need SHARE.

Load SHARE in the AUTOEXEC.BAT file, editing this file just as you edited the CONFIG.SYS file. SHARE's default parameters do not work well with FoxPro, but the following settings are satisfactory for many users:

```
rem add this line to your autoexec.bat file:
C:\DOS\SHARE.EXE /F:4096 /L:500
```

Substitute your own drive and path in the preceding line of code.

CAUTION: SHARE and DOS 4 have problems working together. You really have no alternative, however, to using SHARE with FoxPro and many other programs that may be accessed in multiple sessions—so upgrade your copy of DOS.

As you check your CONFIG.SYS and AUTOEXEC.BAT file, make sure that your mouse driver is loaded—and that the driver is the latest version available for your mouse. FoxPro uses a mouse extensively, and the program involves much more intensive screen manipulation than most programs. If your mouse driver is outdated, your mouse may work with all other programs but still cause problems in FoxPro. The \GOODIES\MISC directory installed by FoxPro includes some proven mouse drivers.

Starting Installation

Make your target drive (the one on which you want FoxPro to be installed) your current default drive by typing its letter and a colon at the DOS prompt. If your target drive is C, for example (standard if you have only one hard disk), type the following:

```
C:
```

(You can use either a lower- or uppercase C; DOS accepts either one.) Now insert the installation disk labelled Disk 1 into a floppy disk drive (your source drive). Type the letter of your source drive, followed by a colon and the word install, as in the following example:

```
A:INSTALL
```

The first installation screen asks you to type your name and company name to "brand" your copy of FoxPro.

The next screen that appears gives you a choice of FoxPro versions to install. If you have an 80386 or 80486 processor and 4M or more of memory, you benefit greatly from FoxPro's Extended version's capability to use extended memory, so install FoxPro (X). If you have as little as 3M of memory on an 80386 or 80486 processor, you may want to install both the Extended and the Standard version to see which gives you better performance. (You also may want to install both programs if you are a developer and need to check the programs you write for performance in both versions.) Finally, if you have an 8088 or 80286 processor (XT or AT class) or an 80386 or 80486 processor with less than 3M of memory, install the Standard version only.

In all cases, install the FoxPro Help file. Not only do you need FoxPro's context-sensitive and comprehensive Help available on-line, but the Help file also contains information on enhancements and changes that occurred after the manuals were printed.

TIP

If you use different versions of FoxPro 2.5 for different platforms, you can probably move the Help file and several of the other system files to one common directory for use with all your versions of FoxPro. (See Appendix C for details on pointing all the versions of FoxPro to these common copies of the files.) First, however, install the Help file for each platform and then determine that no significant differences exist between the different versions before deciding which copy of the Help file to use across platforms.

After you have answered Y or N to indicate which of the three products you want to install, the program asks you into which directory you want FoxPro installed. This directory becomes the FoxPro 2.5 for DOS main program directory; many subdirectories are created under this directory to hold FoxPro's subsidiary programs and sample applications. As you run FoxPro 2.5 for DOS, you can always use the function SYS(2004) to find the drive and path of this main directory.

If you indicate in this screen a different directory than INSTALL's suggested default (or even a different drive and directory), you are asked to confirm your choice. In either case, the directory you indicate is created as part of the installation process, unless that directory already exists on your hard disk.

INSTALL then copies the base FoxPro files to the main directory. You see a thermometer on-screen, indicating the progress of the installation process as each item is installed. You also are asked at various times during installation to insert different disks as the program copies their files.

After the base products are copied, you receive a message confirming this. You can then end the installation by pressing Esc, or you can install the supplemental products included with FoxPro. If you choose to stop now, installation of these supplemental products can be run at any time from within FoxPro.

Whether you stop the installation process here or continue adding supplemental products, those of you who are upgrading from FoxPro 2.0 must take an extra step after you complete the installation. You must run the FIXUSER program, located in the \GOODIES\MISC directory under your FoxPro main program directory. SET RESOURCE TO your normal Resource file and DO FIXUSER to create Version 2.5 copies for all your 2.0 COLOR SET resources. Do this several times if you want to continue using several different Resource files.

Unfortunately, BROWSE PREFERENCE type resources are not converted by FIXUSER (you have to re-create them), but all other entries in your existing Resource files are readable in 2.5.

The ADDUSER.APP you find in the main FoxPro directory also can become an integral part of installation procedures. Originally designed to enable network adminstrators to provide a different CONFIG.FP and temporary file locations for each new user, ADDUSER provides valuable information about FoxPro's resources and temporary work files even if you do not work on a network (see figs. A.1 and fig. A.2).

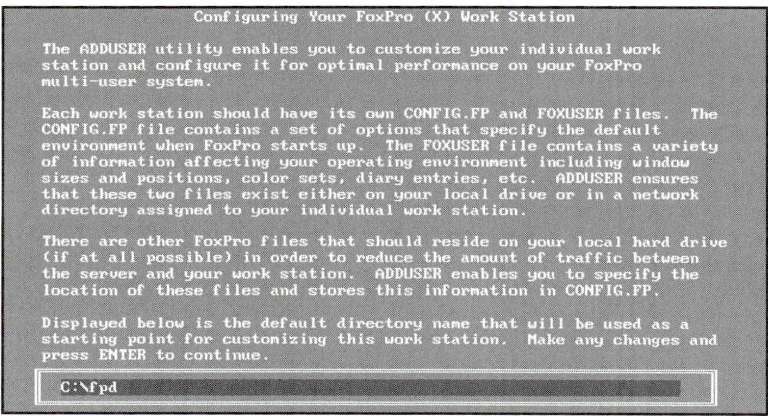

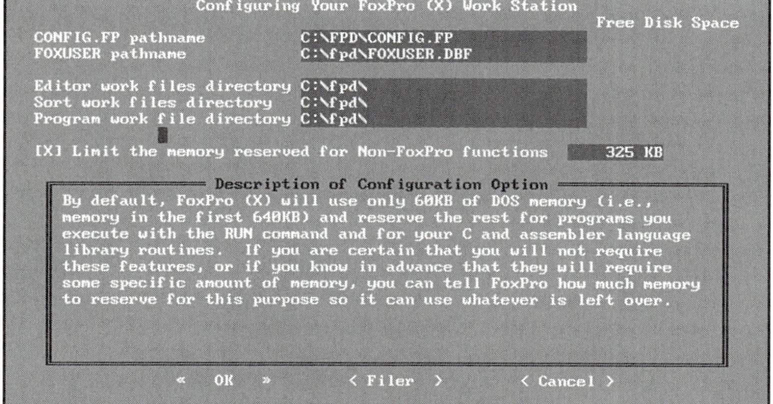

FIGS A.1 and A.2

The ADDUSER application screens provide information for the installation process.

Adding the Supplemental Files

The Supplemental Product Installation is actually a FoxPro application. If you chose to continue the installation, FoxPro loads itself at this point. The screens you see next all are typical of the screens FoxPro presents later and of the screens you can create.

You first are asked to choose a monitor type. Use the arrow keys to move the highlight on-screen to your monitor choice, and press Enter. (In most cases, your choice is Generic Color or Generic Monochrome, but several other options are provided for laptop users with special needs.)

After you choose a monitor type, you see a new screen in which you choose the supplemental, or optional, files that you want to install. As you select different items from the list at the top left of the screen (again, by highlighting your choice and pressing Enter), a check mark appears next to all the choices you make. As you make your choices, watch the Disk Space Statistics box at the bottom of the screen. The left side shows you how much free space you have on your disk, and the right side keeps track of the total disk space required for the supplemental files you have selected so far. The Description box in the middle of the screen displays a description of each supplemental file as you choose that file. In the example shown in figure A.3, all the options have been chosen.

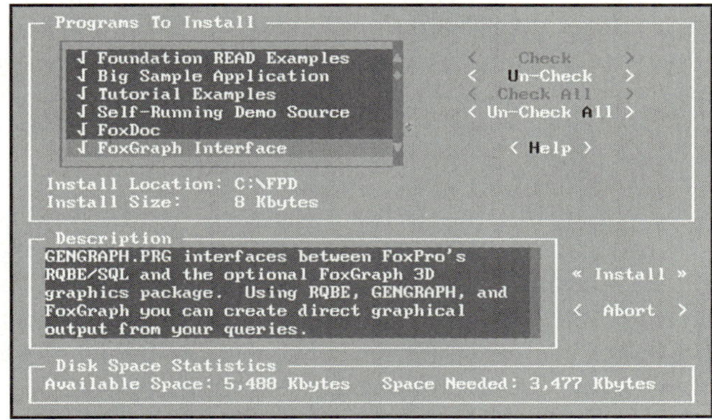

FIG. A.3

Installing FoxPro's supplemental files.

Install as many of the supplemental files as you have space for on your hard disk. Some of these items are valuable tools, and all provide invaluable examples. The discussions throughout the book refer to many of these applications and use many of the sample data files provided. Remember, however, that you can return to the installation process and add some of these files later if you need them.

After you have chosen your supplemental files, press the Tab key until the `Install` button is highlighted. Press Enter to begin the copying process.

If you have chosen more supplemental files than you have available disk space to hold, FoxPro warns you before the program continues. If you are reinstalling FoxPro over older versions of the same files, you may ignore the warning. Otherwise, choose the `Cancel` button on the warning screen that appears, and then unselect some of your choices.

The supplemental files are copied using the same procedures as the base products. A final message tells you that installation has been completed. You can continue now by following the instructions in Chapter 1 for loading FoxPro.

Attaching the Distribution Kit

You have now installed the full development version of FoxPro, the product that is the main subject of this book. To create and distribute applications to other users who do not own the full FoxPro development version, you may have purchased the separate FoxPro Distribution Kit. After you have installed the base products, you can install the Distribution Kit. The process uses a setup program much like the installation of the development version of FoxPro.

You are asked during the installation process to select the Distribution Kit products you want to install. Again, you can choose among products that fit the Standard and Extended versions of FoxPro. You may choose either or both, depending on the environments for which you are developing applications. (Either version of the base product can create both Standard and Extended distributable applications.)

FoxPro can create *stand-alone* executable files for both the Standard and Extended versions, which can be very large files. Using the Distribution Kit, you also can prepare *compact* executable files and *run-time* compiled applications, which are much smaller files but must be distributed with accompanying *support libraries*. Depending on the kind of applications you intend to develop, choose the appropriate Distribution Kit items to install. If you have the available disk space, install all the stand-alone files and the support libraries so that you can try them out.

After you have selected the files you want, you are asked to confirm the correct directory for installation. This directory must be the same one into which you installed the development version of FoxPro. The Distribution Kit's installation alters your development version's program files so that they can access the Distribution Kit's features. The file copying process operates as before.

After you have installed the Distribution Kit, you must perform one more task before you can share the FOXPRO.EXE, FOXPROX.EXE, and FOXPRO.OVL files among multiple users or sessions: Change these files' DOS attributes to readonly. In Chapter 16, you learn how to use FoxPro's Filer utility to perform this task, but many available DOS utilities also can do the job.

B

APPENDIX

Optimizing FoxPro's Performance

FoxPro runs fast enough for many people's needs, no matter how inexperienced the user or inefficient the code. Others constantly search for ways to increase performance. This appendix discusses some of the factors involved in optimizing FoxPro's performance and provides some hints on fine-tuning your applications.

The following recommendations can help you achieve significant improvements without a great deal of extra work:

- If you need to create temporary files—perhaps a subset of a table or an index required for a single report—try to do so by using a SQL SELECT command, creating the table as a CURSOR, and using the ORDER BY clause in place of the temporary index. If you have a RAM disk, you also can create the temporary files on the RAM disk for increased speed.
- Limit the size of your disk cache to 256K. Larger disk caches take valuable memory away from FoxPro and are not useful, because FoxPro uses its own disk-caching scheme.

- Read the chapter entitled "Optimizing Your System," in the *Installation and Configuration* booklet, for Microsoft's recommendations on maximizing FoxPro's performance.
- Read the short section entitled "General Performance Hints," in Chapter 14 of the *Developer's Guide*, for guidance on specific commands to avoid and any recommended substitutions for them.
- Read Appendix C in this book for information on using the FoxPro configuration file (CONFIG.FP) to your best advantage.

Tips on Enhancing FoxPro's Performance

The observations in this section are guidelines, not firm rules. Microsoft continues to optimize FoxPro, so these guidelines are subject to change.

Sequential data access (that is, accessing records in their natural order in the table) is faster than indexed access (accessing records by using record pointers stored in the index file). If Rushmore is operating on very large tables, this is particularly true. The discussions of Rushmore and SQL in Chapter 7 elaborate on these issues and can help you optimize your database search and query techniques.

Opening and closing tables frequently is a drain on FoxPro's performance. FoxPro caches data from tables on opening the tables to speed up subsequent operations. If you close the tables immediately, the data held in the cache may have to be written back to disk. The same rule applies to using the FLUSH and SET AUTOSAVE ON commands. These commands increase the frequency with which FoxPro writes cached data back to disk. FoxPro normally writes cached data to disk at predetermined intervals without user intervention. This default behavior is usually best left as is for optimal performance.

More commands in a program usually results in slower execution of the program. If you can consolidate commands that perform in a loop into fewer commands, performance increases. This is especially true for command sequences that can be replaced by a single SQL SELECT.

If you use macro substitution (the & command) extensively, look at indirect referencing and the EVALUATE( ) function as a possible replacement. This substitution does not always result in a perceptible improvement, however, as the time it actually takes to execute the command may outweigh the increase in speed that results from eliminating the macro.

Understand also that the initial use of the macro command, which forces FoxPro to load its expression evaluator, is what slows down the program. After FoxPro has loaded the expression evaluator, subsequent macro expansions can be performed very quickly. In a DO WHILE loop that executes many times, therefore, using a macro may actually be the most efficient approach.

Keep in mind, however, that FoxPro eventually unloads the expression evaluator from memory; the next macro forces FoxPro to reload the expression evaluator.

Try to reduce the number of files in any directory that FoxPro uses, especially those containing your most frequently accessed data files. Performance starts to degrade after a directory contains more than 150 files. If a directory contains hundreds of files, DOS can take a long time to find the files you need. If you cannot avoid keeping directories with a large number of files, and you use DOS 5.0, consider using the DOS FASTOPEN command. Do not, however, use FASTOPEN in DOS 4.0.

Novell disk drives are not subject to the 150 files limitation, because they do not use DOS's file access scheme. Novell drives can quickly access files in directories that contain hundreds of files.

The Challenge of Optimizing

The final section of this appendix discusses a tool you can use to locate bottlenecks in your applications. Before you begin changing your programs in search of additional speed, however, keep in mind the following factors:

- Microsoft/Fox has created some of the most sophisticated algorithms in the database industry. These routines can dynamically adjust their performance characteristics during program execution.
- If running network applications, remember that other programs also are running on this network. These programs may affect overall network performance, and you probably have no control over when they run.

- Specific advice from other users and programmers is not always useful to you, because these individuals may be using different hardware or running different programs than you are. The wide variety of hardware components and the specific FoxPro commands and functions you use—not to mention all the different programming styles possible—can significantly affect performance.
- Optimizing, like programming, is a matter of costs versus benefits. Although adding more memory to a computer is often an effective and relatively inexpensive way to gain increased performance, modifying existing programs can be expensive. Before you undertake this task, make sure that your optimization efforts are certain to be appreciated by the users of the application and by those who must pay the costs involved.

Tools for Optimizing FoxPro

A single function may do more for your optimization efforts than any other. Before running a program, type the following line in the Command window:

```
logfile = FCREATE('C:\RUNTIME.LOG')
```

The variable logfile now contains a number, the *file handle* that FoxPro's FCREATE( ) function has just assigned to the file the function has opened. Now open the Debug window, and place the following expression in the left partition (all on one line—the partition scrolls as you type):

```
FPUTS(logfile,PADR(PROGRAM(),12)+STR(LINENO(1),6,0) +
   " "+STR(SECONDS(),9,3))
```

Now execute your program. The expression you entered in the Debug window creates a log file that tracks every statement your program executed and at what time.

After you are finished, issue the following command in the Command window:

```
= FCLOSE(logfile)
```

Typing `MODIFY FILE C:\RUNTIME.LOG` in the Command window displays the results, as shown in figure B.1.

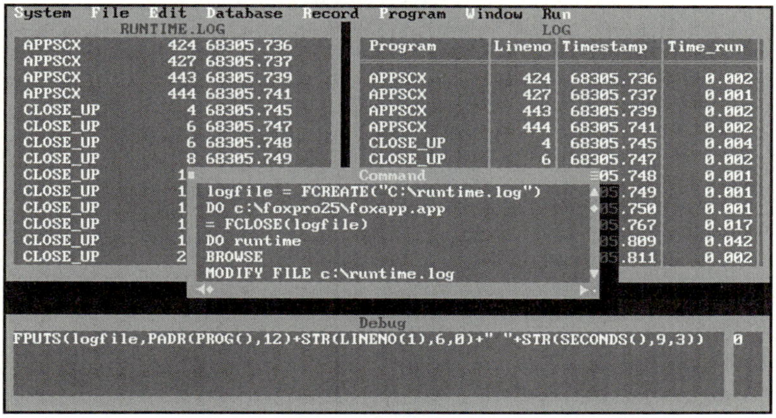

FIG. B.1

Using the Debug window to create a log of your program's commands.

RUNTIME.LOG is an ASCII text file containing a list of commands that have run (denoted by their program name and the line number of the command within the program) and a *timestamp* noting the time the command was executed (in this case, the number of seconds elapsed since midnight). You can bring this data into a table by using a short program. The following program creates a table containing three fields that hold the data in RUNTIME.LOG, and a fourth field to show the time required to run each program instruction:

```
CREATE TABLE Log ;
   (program C(12),;
   lineno C(6),;
   timestamp N(10,3),;
   time_run N(9,3))

* bring the information in from the text file
APPEND FROM c:\runtime.log TYPE SDF

old_time = 0
SCAN
  REPLACE time_run WITH timestamp - old_time

* subtract successive timestamps
  old_time = timestamp
ENDSCAN
```

Now you can have a good idea how long each command takes to run and which commands are executed most often.

The preceding technique is known as an *execution profiler*. You need to be aware of two limitations to this technique, however:

- Measurement inaccuracies can occur because of the time required to write a line to the log file. Minimize these inaccuracies, if you can, by creating the RUNTIME.LOG file on a RAM disk.
- If your program encounters a CLOSE ALL command, the RUNTIME.LOG file closes, effectively ending your profiling. Consider replacing the CLOSE ALL command with the CLOSE DATABASES command. Sometimes CLOSE ALL does more than you need the command to do.

For single SQL statements, the following commands cause the run-time of the `SELECT` to appear in a system message window:

```
SET TALK ON
SET TALK WINDOW
SET NOTIFY ON
```

You also can insert ? SECONDS( ) commands in your programs, but you have to remove these commands later.

Relying on tests such as these, supplemented by your own experience with specific hardware configurations, is better than relying on published benchmarks. Take published benchmarks and comparison tests with a grain of salt. Carefully read the sections that discuss the exact environment in use during these tests before you draw any conclusions.

FoxPro's dynamic caching algorithms further confound the common benchmarking technique of running the test repeatedly. The theory is that random effects distort the measurement of a single iteration of a command. To combat this, the command may be run in a loop 1,000 times, and the average time is taken. This usage may not be representative of normal situations. FoxPro's SECONDS( ) command is accurate to three decimal places. Consider running the command only once unless the run-time is close to 0.005 seconds. If the command does not take much time, in fact, measuring it at all is really unnecessary.

FoxPro naturally attracts users and programmers intrigued by speed. Trying to enhance performance is normal and enjoyable, and tinkering with all the contributing factors can be a rewarding process. Just remember that, although any one factor mentioned in this appendix could be pivotal in any specific circumstance, you can never find an ideally optimized configuration.

C

APPENDIX

Customizing the CONFIG.FP File

In Appendix A, you read about the CONFIG.SYS file used by DOS to set its environment. FoxPro uses a similar file to set certain factors of its own environment; this file usually is called the CONFIG.FP file, although the file can have any name. Use the function SYS(2019) or the About FoxPro dialogs to check FoxPro's current CONFIG.FP file name.

Among the FoxPro environment options you can control from the CONFIG.FP are all the options for which SET commands are available. In the CONFIG.FP file, however, the syntax for controlling these options is slightly different from that of the SET commands.

You do not include the following lines in the CONFIG.FP file:

```
SET RESOURCE TO d:\fox\model\q_user
SET RESOURCE ON
```

Instead, you include the following lines:

```
RESOURCE = d:\fox\model\q_user
RESOURCE = ON
```

Any such statements in the CONFIG.FP take precedence over FoxPro's internal SET defaults.

Special CONFIG.FP Configuration Statements

In addition to the SET values, the CONFIG.FP has a number of special statements that control elements of the environment not accessible to you from within FoxPro.

The COMMAND = statement enables you to execute a command as soon as FoxPro starts up. You can directly issue one FoxPro command, such as the following:

```
COMMAND = FILER
```

Or you can instead indicate that an entire range of activities should be carried out by using a command such as the following:

```
COMMAND = DO STARTUP
```

In the preceding code, STARTUP represents any program name you choose, usually a program or application that sets up your environment and/or begins immediate execution of other application tasks without any intervention by the user. Chapter 16 presents an example of such a program used to load default macros for each user.

The COMMAND = statement is overridden by a program specified with FoxPro on the command line when FoxPro is executed from DOS. In contrast, the _STARTUP variable holds the name of a program to be executed before the program on the command line or in the COMMAND statement. This variable holds the name FOXSTART.APP by default; the FOXSTART.APP FoxPro supplies in the main FoxPro directory adds the Run pad to FoxPro's menu, as described in Chapter 14.

A number of CONFIG.FP options enable you to specify the locations of files used by FoxPro. The following statement uses a copy of FoxPro's overlay file (.OVL) in a location of your choice:

```
OVERLAY = C:\directory
```

The Extended version of FoxPro does not use this switch because that version does not have an overlay file for the Standard version; however, copying the .OVL file to a RAM disk can result in faster performance. If the file is not present, or the one available has an earlier date than the one in your main FoxPro directory, the overlay is copied to your specified location.

Use the keyword OVERWRITE to have the file copied without a request for permission. You can use the same CONFIG.FP file for both Extended and Standard FoxPro; any statements, such as the OVERLAY assignment, that do not apply to both versions are ignored if inappropriate.

Similar statements can be used to direct the temporary files used by FoxPro to a RAM disk or to a fast hard drive to improve performance. You can put the files all in the same place by issuing the TMPFILES = statement. Or you can specify different locations by using PROGWORK =, which locates the program cache; EDITWORK =, which locates the temporary files used by the text editor; and SORTWORK =, which locates various temporary files created during processing by such commands as SORT.

Use SYS(2023) to find out what drive is currently receiving the temporary files as specified by TMPFILES.

Although the space required by PROGWORK is relatively small, the size of SORTWORK and EDITWORK files is determined by the size of the files with which you are working. It is usually better to put these files on your fastest hard disk (usually a local disk if you are on a network) rather than on a RAM disk.

NOTE If you use the RUN command, the temporary files created by FOXSWAP are not redirected by any of these assignments.

The following statements can be used to tell FoxPro where to find some of its component programs if you do not use their default names and locations:

```
_GENGRAPH = C:\directory\program_name
_GENMENU  = C:\directory\program_name
_GENPD = C:\directory\program_name
_GENSCRN  = C:\directory\program_name
_GENXTAB  = C:\directory\program_name
_FOXDOC   = C:\directory\program_name
_FOXGRAPH = C:\directory\program_name
_STARTUP = C:\directory\program_name
_TRANSPORT=C:\directory\program_name
```

If you do not use one or more of these programs, you can speed FoxPro's load time by specifying the null string ("") for these items. You also can tell FoxPro not to look for a default printer driver setup to load by using the following line:

```
PDSETUP = "-"
```

(Of course, you can use the PDSETUP = statement, as you can other SET commands, to load a specific setup at load time.)

If you run multiple versions of FoxPro 2.5 to support multiple platforms, you can place these programs in a common directory instead of having several copies of each and can specify their location by using the preceding system variables. You also want to use the following statement:

```
HELP = <helpfile path and name>
```

This statement is the equivalent of SET HELP TO <filename> within FoxPro. Using a common Help file and other supporting programs—including a CONFIG.FP, as described later in this appendix—avoids wasted disk space and also ensures that any editing you do in these files is reflected in all the versions of FoxPro you use.

The following three statements enable you to specify nondefault extensions for three types of FoxPro files, without explicitly identifying them every time you use these files:

```
INDEX = <extension, where the default is IDX>
LABEL = <extension, where the default is LBX>
REPORT = <extension, where the default is FRX>
```

The TEDIT = statement enables you to specify an outside editor to be called if you choose to MODIFY COMMAND or FILE. In the Standard version of FoxPro, you can add a /<expN> switch to specify how much memory is made available to your editor. The more memory you specify, the slower the swap between programs appears. You can get the maximum amount of memory by using the following line:

```
TEDIT = /0 <your editor>
```

DOSMEM = regulates FoxPro's Extended version's use of DOS memory. DOSMEM = OFF is the default, and most DOS memory is still available for programs to be run from within FoxPro. You can set DOSMEM = ON instead to have DOS memory accessed and used by the Extended version along with your extended memory, or you can set DOSMEM = <expN> to reserve some memory for a RUN command and have some memory accessible to FoxPro.

By contrast, EMS = and EMS64 = are used only by the Standard version of FoxPro and regulate its use of expanded memory where available. EMS = ON is the default, but you can reserve all or some of EMS for use by other programs with EMS = OFF or EMS = <expN>. Use EMS64 = OFF if your EMS emulator and FoxPro do not appear to be compatible. Several entries in the FoxPro Help file address this topic, and these entries are updated regularly as new information becomes available. If you have an unusual configuration, however, and are experiencing problems with memory management, you may want to contact Microsoft Fox technical support directly. See Appendix G for tips on contacting Fox technical support and getting the fastest possible response.

MVCOUNT = <expN> can be set to any value from 128 to 3,600 for the Standard version or from 128 to 65,000 for the Extended version through the CONFIG.FP. This option sets the number of variables FoxPro can handle. MVCOUNT's default is 256, which often is too low for a complex application. The higher you set MVCOUNT, the more RAM is reserved for memory variables. You may need to experiment to determine the best setting for your uses.

Two more options specify certain aspects of keyboard handling in FoxPro. Use F11F12 = OFF if you have an old-style keyboard and do not see a cursor when you load FoxPro. (See Appendix E for more information about how FoxPro tests keyboards.) Use OUTSHOW = OFF to disable the keystroke combination Ctrl+Shift+Alt, which hides all windows in front of the current output (WOUTPUT( )) window by default.

One special CONFIG.FP statement, TIME = <expN>, specifies the number of retries FoxPro makes if a print device is not ready when it sends a character, which can become an issue if you are printing over a network. The value can range from 1 to 1,000,000 and defaults to 6,000.

FoxPro 2.5 adds a MEMLIMIT assignment to the CONFIG.FP by using the following line:

```
MEMLIMIT = <% available memory> [,<min >,<max> memory in K]
```

The MEMLIMIT settings determine how much memory the Extended version of FoxPro uses when run under Windows. This setting makes sure that FoxPro does not use all the memory available—although the program knows how to make use of all the memory it finds, if you fail to limit its use—so that you can allocate memory for other programs to be loaded after FoxPro.

The MEMLIMIT settings that work for you depend as much on the size of your total memory pool as the kinds of tasks and the sizes of the database tables for which you need FoxPro.

Users of other, earlier, Fox products may notice that some items are missing from this list. MVARSIZ, which was used in FoxPro 1, and the FILES and BUCKETS statements used in FoxBase's CONFIG.FX file are no longer needed.

If you add these statements to your FoxPro 2.5 CONFIG.FP file, they are ignored. Similarly, if you spell one of the allowable statements wrong, it is ignored. No error is ever generated, except from the COMMAND = statement, because that is the only statement actually interpreted by FoxPro. If you use a particular SET equivalent or any of the special CONFIG.FP statements more than once in your file, the last one takes effect.

As you edit your CONFIG.FP file, test to make sure that your new settings are in force and that all the file's statements are being used in the way you expect. Use the View window, the About... panels, and the SET( ) and SYS( ) functions to check the ON/OFF status of various environmental features, memory, and file locations. Use the Filer to find Foxpro's temporary work files; they appear unselectable with the extension .TMP.

Specifying a CONFIG.FP File

Whether you run FoxPro on a stand-alone machine or on a network, multiple CONFIG.FP files can enable different user preferences, hardware, and application requirements to be managed with ease. To use multiple CONFIG.FP files, you need to understand where and how FoxPro looks for the one to use. You may want to specify a single CONFIG.FP file for all your versions of FoxPro 2.5; any statements inappropriate to a certain platform are ignored when that platform loads.

After you load FoxPro from DOS, FoxPro looks for a file named CONFIG.FP in the current directory. If the file is not found, FoxPro checks its program directory, and then other directories along the DOS path. *If you load FoxPro with the name of an .APP or .EXE file to run, FoxPro looks for a file named CONFIG.FP that has been included in the .APP or .EXE file first.*

Although FoxPro searches by default in these locations for a file named CONFIG.FP, you can specify any name or location for your FoxPro configuration file. You can set a specific DOS environment variable, FOXPROCFG, equal to the name and full path of the file you want to use, in your AUTOEXEC.BAT file, in another batch file, or at the DOS command line. Use the following format:

```
SET FOXPROCFG=C:\DIR\FILENAME
```

Substitute the drive, directory, and file names you want to use for your CONFIG.FP. Notice that no spaces are around the equal sign. You can use the default file name (CONFIG.FP) but still specify the location by using the following format:

```
SET FOXPROCFG=C:\DIR\
```

Include the final backslash; otherwise, FoxPro thinks you want to use a file named DIR in the root directory.

If you want to know whether this environmental variable has been created on your system, you can issue the DOS SET command without parameters to see all such assignments. From within FoxPro, use `WAIT WINDOW GETENV("FOXPROCFG")` to see whether the variable exists.

Even if you have SET a FOXPROCFG, you can change the configuration file used by FoxPro at the time you load by using the -C switch. This switch has the highest priority of all CONFIG.FP assignments. No matter which of the FoxPro *loaders* you use, the syntax for this is as follows:

```
FOX -CC:\DIR\FILENAME
```

The first C is the switch, and the second is the drive. Refer to Appendix D to learn about other such switches and about using the loaders.

D

APPENDIX

Using Command Line Options and Loading FoxPro

Because FoxPro is available in Extended and Standard editions and in Extended and Standard editions of the distributable (run-time) version, you can load FoxPro in several different ways.

Specifying the Version of FoxPro To Load

FoxPro is supplied with two small files called *loaders*. Without any instructions from you, each loader checks the FoxPro versions available on your disk and your available memory to decide which version should be run.

The loader files are FOX.EXE, which checks all versions available, and FOXR.EXE, which loads only run-time versions. If either loader finds more than one of its supported versions on the disk, and your system configuration can support more than one of these versions, the version with the *highest priority* is loaded—not the version found first along your DOS path. If your system supports the Extended version, the Extended version is loaded by preference over the Standard version. If you use the FOX.EXE loader and both the full version and run-time version of FoxPro are on the disk, the full product is loaded by preference.

Within the types of files checked by each loader, however, you can make additional decisions by adding one or more *switches*, each separated by a space and preceded by a hyphen. The following switches affect which version is loaded.

Switch	Effect
+R	Forces the load of the run-time version.
-R	Does not load the run-time version.
+X	Forces the load of the Extended version.
-X	Does not load the Extended version, even if memory is available.
-M<n>	Runs the Extended version only if <*n*> kilobytes of memory are available; the default check is for 2,000K.
-Y	Exits immediately after setting the DOS error level to 1 if the Extended version can be run; for use within batch files and followed by an explicit load of a particular version.

You also can execute any of the loaders by using a -? or /? switch to retrieve a help message reminding you which switches can be used by that loader. Try this with your own copy of FoxPro. The -M and -Y switches were added after the initial introduction of FoxPro 2.0; more new switches may have been added since this book was written.

If you use the FOX loader with a -V switch, you get a message that tells you what the loaders see as they check your system and files available. The last line of the message tells you which version will run if you do not force a different choice.

The loader files are convenient if you are running FoxPro on a network and must tailor the use of the product to many different situations, without knowing in advance what those situations are. The loaders, however, require as much as 20K of memory. If you know in advance which version of the product is best for your situation, load that version directly and dispense with the loaders. If you do not know which is best for you, you can still use FOX -V to determine which version is *recommended* by the loaders—FOXPRO or FOXPROX, or the run-time versions if the full product is not available—and then load that version directly.

Using Additional Command Line Options

A few more switches affect loading in additional ways. The following switches also can be used with the loader files or with the actual executable files for each version:

- The -C switch, discussed in Appendix C, enables you to specify the name and location of the CONFIG.FP file to be used.
- The -E switch prevents the use of expanded memory, as does the EMS = OFF option in the CONFIG.FP.
- The -K switch, like F11F12 = OFF in the CONFIG.FP, prevents FoxPro from attempting to use function keys F11 and F12 on older keyboards with BIOS that erroneously report the existence of these keys.
- The -T switch suppresses the appearance of FoxPro's normal sign-on logo screen and the normal shutdown message after you QUIT. (The same effect can be created for executable distributed applications by unchecking the Logo box on the Project Options screen.)

You can create a DOS environmental variable, FOXPROSWX, that specifies the default use of these switches for you. Just as the FOXPROCFG variable is overridden by an explicit -C switch when you load FoxPro, all the switches listed in the FOXPROSWX variable can be countermanded by new instructions at load time.

As with FOXPROCFG, do not put a space between a switch and its parameter, and do not put a space before the equal sign. You do, however, add a space between the switches. The following instructions in FOXPROSWX to use one CONFIG.FP file, for example, are overridden at load time by another:

```
SET FOXPROSWX= -T +R -CG:\MODEL\WIDGET.FP
FOX -CG:\NEWCFG.FP -M3000
```

The run-time version is loaded, and no sign-on logo is shown, because of the -T and +R switches in FOXPROSWX. Although FOXPROSWX also gives instructions with regard to the configuration file, these instructions are overridden by the -C switch on the FOX loader. The Extended version is loaded only if 3,000K of memory is available because of the additional command line option specified with the loader.

Specifying a Program or Application at Start-Up Time

One additional option is available, along with any of the switches, loaders, or normal executable FoxPro files: the name of a program to be started as soon as the program is loaded. Any other information added when you load FoxPro from the DOS prompt, aside from the allowable switches, is assumed to be such a program and its parameters. Parameters are added after the name of the program and are separated by spaces.

The ASK.SPR program used in the Widget application in Chapter 14, for example, has three parameters. This program can be called by the following command line:

```
FOX ask.spr Value: 100 99999
```

No delimiters are used, and data types are not specified in any way. Because parameters are separated by spaces, passing a single parameter, such as `Enter the value to use:`, seems impossible. If ASK.SPR really had been designed to be run from the DOS command line, you would redesign its first parameter to use a string of words concatenated with some rarely used character, such as the following:

```
FOX ask.spr Enter~the~value~to~be~used: 100 9999
```

Within the ASK.SPR, you can use the STRTRAN( ) function to replace all instances of this character with spaces. You can use similar tricks to specify the data type for the second parameter from the command line and to determine it within ASK.SPR.

If you specify a program to be run from the COMMAND = statement of the CONFIG.FP file, the program named on the DOS command line is executed instead of the CONFIG.FP COMMAND = statement, after all other CONFIG.FP statements have been processed and any _STARTUP program is run.

E

APPENDIX

Key Codes, Key Labels, and Special Key Usage in FoxPro

This appendix contains a chart to show you the different ways individual keystrokes are referred to and used in FoxPro.

The *ASCII values* are shown in decimal form in the second column. This form is returned by FoxPro's ASC( ) function if you use it to determine the ASCII value of a character and you pass it to the CHR( ) function when you use ASCII values to tell FoxPro about a character. This column corresponds to the first column in the ASCII chart desk accessory of the System menu popup. Items with no ASCII values shown cannot be added to an ASCII text file.

The *INKEY/LASTKEY* column corresponds to the values returned by FoxPro's INKEY( ) and LASTKEY( ) functions if you use them to tell you what key was pressed. INKEY( ) also tells you about a mouse click if you use its M parameter. The E parameter also can be used to have INKEY( ) return the first keystroke in a macro, instead of the macro itself, if the keystroke received called a macro. You use it to wait for a keystroke and then to test what you have; LASTKEY( ), on the other hand, is used to find out about a keystroke received *before* you called the LASTKEY( ) function.

The INKEY/LASTKEY( ) values are the same as the ASCII values in many cases, but you can use INKEY( ) and LASTKEY( ) to get information about many keystrokes for which you cannot use or get an ASCII value directly.

The *READKEY/NO UPDATE* column corresponds to the value that the READKEY( ) function returns if you use it to tell you what key was used to exit a READ. The values in this column are returned for the corresponding keystrokes if no changes to the data are made in the course of the READ. The next column, *READKEY/UPDATE,* shows you the values returned for each keystroke if changes to the data are made.

READKEY( ) now can take an optional parameter, for which you can use any number (even 0). If you use this parameter, the READKEY( ) function can be used to test why the READ was concluded, which can have a number of possible causes besides the normal exit keystrokes in FoxPro. The following list shows all the possible READKEY( ) return values.

IF READKEY (<expN>) returns:	You know that the READ was exited because:
2	The program issued a CLEAR READ command.
3	The user selected a terminating control, or the program selected it for him/her.
4	The READ window was closed by a command or by the user.
5	The READ's DEACTIVATE clause returned TRUE.
6	The READ's TIMEOUT was reached.
1	None of the above; a normal conclusion of the READ, using exit keystrokes, was reached.

The *KEY LABEL* column shows you how to refer to this keystroke in an ON KEY LABEL command. Additionally, in FoxPro, key labels can be used in the KEYBOARD command, surrounded by curly braces and quotation marks, as in the following command line:

```
ON KEY LABEL F10 KEYBOARD "{F9}"
```

Before FoxPro 2.0, the KEYBOARD command could be used only with ASCII values using the CHR( ) function, as in the following command line:

```
ON KEY LABEL F10 KEYBOARD CHR(65)+CHR(90)
```

Strings of characters also can be KEYBOARDed in quotation marks so that the preceding command also can be written as shown in the following line:

```
ON KEY LABEL F10 KEYBOARD "AZ"
```

The capability to KEYBOARD actual key labels, using the braces inside the quotation marks, enables you to KEYBOARD function keys and other shifted keystrokes that do not have ASCII values to use. Because the braces are FoxPro's special key label delimiters, the braces themselves have special key labels, as shown in the chart. The semicolon, FoxPro's continuation character for the command line, also needs a special key label.

Key labels for keystrokes that are shifted (those for which you have to press more than one key at a time) seem to work equally well in all cases whether the keys to be pressed are joined together by the + or by the – character. Although key labels must be enclosed by curly braces for KEYBOARDing, or inside a macro you are editing to indicate that they are labels rather than actual keystrokes, they then can be delimited (like any other character strings) by using single quotation marks, double quotation marks, or brackets ([]). Key labels also are case-insensitive. You can use [{Ctrl-F1}] if you prefer it to "{CTRL-F1}"; case makes no difference to how FoxPro understands the label.

The fact that labels are case-insensitive has one undesirable side effect: You cannot create ON KEY LABEL statements for a letter of the alphabet and have them react differently for the lower- and uppercase versions of the letter. Because you can KEYBOARD them as character strings, or by using their ASCII values, the KEYBOARD command respects upper- and lowercase. The two preceding commands have a different effect than do the following two:

```
ON KEY LABEL F10 KEYBOARD CHR(97)+CHR(122)
ON KEY LABEL F10 KEYBOARD "az"
```

You can KEYBOARD far more key labels than are shown in this chart, because key labels can contain multiple shift keys, as in the following command line:

```
ON KEY LABEL F10 KEYBOARD "{SHIFT+CTRL+F9}"
```

This command enables you to use the F10 key to dock your active window. Multiple shift combinations can be used in macros—both as the keystrokes to which the macro is assigned and as keystrokes that the macro plays back. The list of shifted combinations allowed is not completely consistent, and you may need to experiment a bit to make sure that the ones you want are available. You can, for example, use a shifted tab as part of a macro or assign an ON KEY LABEL command to it, using its label {BACKTAB}, but you cannot assign a macro directly to this keystroke.

If a Key Label column is empty for an item, it cannot be used in an ON KEY LABEL command.

Be careful not to create multiple assignments for one key combination. If you inadvertently designate one keystroke to accomplish different tasks in your program, however, be aware that any ON KEY LABEL command for a keystroke takes precedence over other assignments. In the absence of an ON KEY LABEL, a macro assigned to a keystroke takes precedence over the KEY clause on a DEFINE POPUP or a menu shortcut defined through SYSMENU and the Menu Builder.

Some keystroke combinations such as Ctrl+Tab cannot be assigned ON KEY LABEL statements or macros on all systems, because some systems' keyboard BIOS do not return a key code to FoxPro for them. You can check your system's keyboard BIOS by noting the return value of FKMAX( ). This function returns 12 if your system BIOS supports an Extended keyboard, which returns more key codes than the original IBM PC keyboard. The 12 indicates 12 function keys, but your motherboard may support an Extended keyboard and the associated key codes even if you have an old-style keyboard with 10 function keys. In such cases, you still can refer to the full range of keystrokes.

FoxPro may not function correctly with an old keyboard if the motherboard supports Extended keyboards. A program may check FKMAX( ) and make a key assignment for F12 based on the results, for example, but the user cannot find an F12 key. In such cases, you can use the -K switch on the DOS command line to tell FoxPro that your keyboard is an old-style keyboard. (Refer to Appendix D on the use of DOS command-line switches.)

When you edit macros you have created that access the FoxPro system dialogs, you may see key labels you cannot identify. In some of the system dialogs, FoxPro stuffs the keyboard with keystrokes in between the keys you press to perform special jobs. Try recording a macro while you tab through the entries in the View window's Misc panel and then edit the macro. You see a sequence that includes the following keystrokes:

```
{x00FD}{TAB}{TAB}{x00FD}{TAB}
```

The unfamiliar key labels are a hexadecimal representation of the keystrokes that FoxPro added. You actually can KEYBOARD these hex values yourself—but you should not remove them from your macros if the values appear in the macros automatically.

If you KEYBOARD a key combination to which you have assigned an ON KEY LABEL procedure or include such an assigned key as part of a macro, you may not always get the results you expect. This problem is almost definitely caused by a timing difficulty, according to Microsoft; FoxPro may be waiting for the next *null event* before updating certain information, such as what menu items should be enabled or disabled. (A null event, in this context, is anything that causes the program to stop processing, as if the application expected input from the user at that point.)

FoxPro needs some structure to decide if updating is necessary, or it would need to update all these items continuously—and performance of the main tasks of the program would slow to a crawl. The solution is to place a {PAUSE 0} or {PAUSE .1} in the macro or KEYBOARDed string, before the ON KEY LABEL-assigned keystroke. FoxPro sees the pause as a null event and does the necessary updating.

Refer to the Macros section of Chapter 16 for information on FoxPro's default macros, which are loaded if no DEFAULT.FKY is found on startup. These macros correspond to the original dBASE function key assignments and are easily CLEARed.

Your \GOODIES\MISC directory contains a special macro file called FOXPLUS.FKY. This file changes some of the editing and interface keystrokes to match those of FoxBase+. If you use applications originally written in FoxBase+, these programs may test LASTKEY( ) or READKEY( ) and expect the results received in FoxBase+. In this situation, you must RESTORE MACROS FROM FOXPLUS.FKY to enable these programs to continue to function.

KEY Name	ASCII Value	INKEY& LASTKEY	READKEY NOUPDATE/ UPDATE	KEY LABEL
No Key Press		0	20/276	
Mouse				MOUSE
Left Click		151		LEFTMOUSE
Right Click				RIGHTMOUSE
F1		28	36/292	F1
Shift F1		84		SHIFT+F1
Alt F1		104		ALT+F1
Ctrl F1		94		CTRL+F1
F2		-1		F2
Shift F2		85		SHIFT+F2
Alt F2		105		ALT+F2
Ctrl F2		95		CTRL+F2
F3		-2		F3
Shift F3		86		SHIFT+F3
Alt F3		106		ALT+F3
Ctrl F3		96		CTRL+F3
F4		-3		F4
Shift F4		87		SHIFT+F4
Alt F4		107		ALT+F4
Ctrl F4		97		CTRL+F4
F5		-4		F5
Shift F5		88		SHIFT+F5
Alt F5		108		ALT+F5
Ctrl F5		98		CTRL+F5
F6		-5		F6
Shift F6		89		SHIFT+F6
Alt F6		109		ALT+F6
Ctrl F6		99		CTRL+F6
F7		-6		F7
Shift F7		90		SHIFT+F7
Alt F7		110		ALT+F7
Ctrl F7		100		CTRL+F7
F8		-7		F8
Shift F8		91		SHIFT+F8
Alt F8		111		ALT+F8
Ctrl F8		101		CTRL+F8
F9		-8		F9
Shift F9		92		SHIFT+F9
Alt F9		112		ALT+F9
Ctrl F9		102		CTRL+F9

KEY Name	ASCII Value	INKEY& LASTKEY	READKEY NOUPDATE/ UPDATE	KEY LABEL
F10		-9		F10
Shift F10		93		SHIFT+F10
Alt F10		113		ALT+F10
Ctrl F10		103		CTRL+F10
F11		133		F11
Shift F11		135		SHIFT+F11
Alt F11		139		ALT+F11
Ctrl F11		137		CTRL+F11
F12		134		F12
Shift F12		136		SHIFT+F12
Alt F12		140		ALT+F12
Ctrl F12		138		CTRL+F12
Right Arrow		4	1/257	RIGHTARROW
Shift Right Arrow		54		SHIFT+RIGHTARROW
Alt Right Arrow		157		ALT+RIGHTARROW
Ctrl Right Arrow		2	15/271	CTRL+RIGHTARROW
Left Arrow		19	0/256	LEFTARROW
Shift Left Arrow		52		SHIFT+LEFTARROW
Alt Left Arrow		155		ALT+LEFTARROW
Ctrl Left Arrow		26		CTRL+LEFTARROW
Up Arrow		5	4/260	UPARROW
Shift Up Arrow		56		SHIFT+UPARROW
Alt Up Arrow		152		ALT+UPARROW
Ctrl Up Arrow		141		CTRL+UPARROW
Down Arrow		24	5/261	DNARROW
Shift Down Arrow		50		SHIFT+DNARROW
Alt Down Arrow		160		ALT+DNARROW
Ctrl Down Arrow		145		CTRL+DNARROW
End		6	3/259	END
Shift End		49		
Ctrl End		23	/270	CTRL+END
Home		1	2/258	HOME
Shift Home		55		
Ctrl Home		29	33/289	CTRL+HOME
Page Down		3	7/263	PGDN
Shift Page Down		51		
Ctrl Page Down		30	35/291	CTRL+PGDN

continues

KEY Name	ASCII Value	INKEY& LASTKEY	READKEY NOUPDATE/ UPDATE	KEY LABEL
Page Up		18	6/262	PGUP
Shift Page Up		57		
Ctrl Page Up		31	34/290	CTRL+PGUP
Delete		7		DEL
Shift Delete		46		
Ctrl Delete		147		CTRL+DEL
Insert		22		INS
Shift Insert		48		
Ctrl Insert		146		CTRL+INS
Escape		27	12/268	ESC or ESCAPE
Shift Escape		27		
Ctrl Escape		27		
Backspace	127	127	0/256	BACKSPACE
Shift Backspace		127		
Ctrl Backspace		127		
Tab	9	9	5/261	TAB
Shift Tab		15	4/260	BACKTAB
Alt Tab		165		
Ctrl Tab		148		CTRL+TAB
Enter	13	13	15/271	ENTER
Shift Enter		13		
Ctrl Enter		10	5/261	CTRL+ENTER
Space bar	32	32		SPACEBAR
Shift Space bar		32		
Ctrl Space bar		32		CTRL+SPACEBAR
0	48	48		0
Alt 0		19		ALT+0
1	49	49		1
Alt 1		120		ALT+1
2	50	50		2
Alt 2		121		ALT+2
3	51	51		3
Alt 3		122		ALT+3
4	52	52		4
Alt 4		123		ALT+4
5	53	53		5
Alt 5		124		ALT+5
6	54	54		6
Alt 6		125		ALT+6
Ctrl 6		30		

KEY Name	ASCII Value	INKEY& LASTKEY	READKEY NOUPDATE/ UPDATE	KEY LABEL
7	55	55		7
Alt 7		126		ALT+7
8	56	56		8
Alt 8		127		ALT+8
9	57	57		9
Alt 9		128		ALT+9
a	97	97		A
A	65	65		A
Alt A		30		ALT+A
Ctrl A		1	2/258	CTRL+A
b	98	98		B
B	66	66		B
Alt B		48		ALT+B
Ctrl B		2		CTRL+B
c	99	99		C
C	67	67		C
Alt C		46		ALT+C
Ctrl C		3	7/263	CTRL+C
d	100	100		D
D	68	68		D
Alt D		32		ALT+D
Ctrl D		4	1/257	CTRL+D
e	101	101		E
E	69	69		E
Alt E		18		ALT+E
Ctrl E		5	4/260	CTRL+E
f	102	102		F
F	70	70		F
Alt F		33		ALT+F
Ctrl F		6	3/259	CTRL+F
g	103	103		G
G	71	71		G
Alt G		34		ALT+G
Ctrl G		7		CTRL+G
h	104	104		H
H	72	72		H
Alt H		35		ALT+H
Ctrl H		8	0/256	CTRL+H

continues

KEY Name	ASCII Value	INKEY& LASTKEY	READKEY NOUPDATE/ UPDATE	KEY LABEL
i	105	105		I
I	73	73		I
Alt I		9		ALT+I
Ctrl I		23	5/261	CTRL+I
j	106	106		J
J	74	74		J
Alt J		36		ALT+J
Ctrl J		10	5/261	CTRL+J
k	107	107		K
K	75	75		K
Alt K		37		ALT+K
Ctrl K		11	4/260	CTRL+K
l	108	108		L
L	76	76		L
Alt L		38		ALT+L
Ctrl L		12	1/257	CTRL+L
m	109	109		M
M	77	77		M
Alt M		50		ALT+M
Ctrl M		13	15/271	CTRL+M
n	110	110		N
N	78	78		N
Alt N		49		ALT+N
Ctrl N		14		CTRL+N
o	111	111		O
O	79	79		O
Alt O		24		ALT+O
Ctrl O		15		CTRL+O
p	112	112		P
P	80	80		P
Alt P		25		ALT+P
Ctrl P		16		CTRL+P
q	113	113		Q
Q	81	81		Q
Alt Q		16		ALT+Q
Ctrl Q		17	12/268	CTRL+Q
r	114	114		R
R	82	82		R
Alt R		19		ALT+R
Ctrl R		18	6/262	CTRL+R

KEY Name	ASCII Value	INKEY& LASTKEY	READKEY NOUPDATE/ UPDATE	KEY LABEL
s	115	115		S
S	83	83		S
Alt S		31		ALT+S
Ctrl S		19	0/256	CTRL+S
t	116	116		T
T	84	84		T
Alt T		20		ALT+T
Ctrl T		20		CTRL+T
u	117	117		U
U	85	85		U
Alt U		22		ALT+U
Ctrl U		21		CTRL+U
v	118	118		V
V	86	86		V
Alt V		47		ALT+V
Ctrl V		22		CTRL+V
w	119	119		W
W	87	87		W
Alt W		17		ALT+W
Ctrl W		23	/270	CTRL+W
x	120	120		X
X	88	88		X
Alt X		45		ALT+X
Ctrl X		24	5/261	CTRL+X
y	121	121		Y
Y	89	89		Y
Alt Y		21		ALT+Y
Ctrl Y		25		CTRL+Y
z	122	122		Z
Z	90	90		Z
Alt Z		44		ALT+Z
Ctrl Z		26		CTRL+Z
‘	96	96		‘
~	126	126		~
!	33	33		!
@	64	64		@
#	35	35		#

continues

KEY Name	ASCII Value	INKEY& LASTKEY	READKEY NOUPDATE/ UPDATE	KEY LABEL
$	36	36		$
%	37	37		%
^	94	94		^
&	38	38		&
*	42	42		*
(	40	40		(
)	41	41		)
-	45	45		-
_	95	95		_
=	61	61		=
+	43	43		+
\	92	92		\
|	124	124		|
[	91	91		[
{	123	123		LBRACE
]	93	93		]
}	125	125		RBRACE
;	59	59		SEMICOLON
:	58	58		:
‘	39	39		‘
“	34	34		“
,	44	44		,
<	60	60		<
.	46	46		.
>	62	62		>
/	47	47		/
?	63	63		?

F

APPENDIX

Installation Disk Files and File Extensions

If you have been using the FoxPro Filer or another disk utility program to explore the directories created by FoxPro's installation process, you know that FoxPro comes with a wide variety of sample programs and other "goodies."

Take some time to investigate these directories. If all are not available on your disk, you may not have installed all the sample directories when you installed FoxPro. Refer to Appendix A for complete installation instructions. If your disk space is limited, this appendix may help you decide which directories may prove most valuable to you.

The FoxPro Directory Structure

The following is a listing of the directory structure created by the FoxPro installation program if you select to install all of FoxPro's components. The number of files and bytes of disk space used for the

FoxPro home directory in the following listing include those of both the Standard version (FOXPRO.EXE and FOXPRO.OVL) and the Extended version (FOXPROX.EXE), and the Help file:

```
Directory structure                         Files    Total bytes
FOXPRO25................................     43        8085570
   FOXAPP...............................      3         115578
      LIBS..............................      1          49504
      MENUS.............................      3          60612
      PRGS..............................      2          12147
      SCREENS...........................     30         278797
   GOODIES..............................      0              0
      DEMO..............................      3         181950
         DBFS...........................     10          42774
         MENUS..........................      1           3256
         PRGS...........................     18         175772
         QUERIES........................      1            333
         REPORTS........................      3          11192
         SCREENS........................      8          76870
      FNDATION..........................     11         196357
         DBFS...........................      9         171902
         MENUS..........................      4          36830
         PRGS...........................      2          10337
         SCREENS........................     18         100004
            EX1SRC......................      1           7063
            EX2SRC......................      1           7337
            INVSRC......................      1          11455
      HELPTREE..........................      3          43713
      LASER.............................      0              0
         CROSPLAT.......................      3         179200
            BMPSPRGS....................     20          10214
            TOOLS.......................     15         220063
         DATA...........................      3          91056
         DOSONLY........................      4         122339
            PROGRAMS....................      2            522
            TOOLS.......................     15         100610
         TRANSPRT.......................      4         175477
            PROGRAMS....................      2            522
            TOOLS.......................     15         175466
      LCKUPDAT..........................      9         113840
      MISC..............................     13          27342
      PDRIVERS..........................     22        1072617
      PROCOLOR..........................     14         268917
      SNIPFMT...........................      9          65971
```

```
LANGUAGE............................    20        141648
SAMPLE..............................    24       1131898
    DBFS............................    30        480325
    MENUS...........................     8         33262
    PRGS............................     2         15732
    REPORTS.........................    20         74513
    SCREENS.........................    37        380558
TUTORIAL............................    21        207421

                              Totals   488      14768866
```

Your directory structure, number of files, and total bytes in each subdirectory may differ from those shown in the preceding listing if you have a build date other than January 11, 1993. The number of files in the FoxPro home directory also may vary, depending on which versions of FoxPro you choose to install and whether you run the Transporter program.

This list is created by a FoxPro program called TREE.PRG. The code for this program is shown in Appendix H and also is included on the source disk. You can use the TREE program to obtain the same information for any drive and directory.

If after installing the product, you find that you have too little free disk space for your other needs, you can use the preceding list to identify subdirectories to delete and how much disk space you can recover by deleting these subdirectories.

FoxPro's Minimum Required Files

Technically, FoxPro requires only one or two files to run. If you use the Standard version, you need only FOXPRO.EXE and FOXPRO.OVL. If you use the Extended version, you require only FOXPROX.EXE. FoxPro requires several additional files to perform all the tasks described in this book, however, and to provide on-line help. Table F.1 lists the minimum files recommended by the authors of this book for running FoxPro.

Table F.1 Minimum Recommended Files

File Name	Descripton	File Size (in bytes)
DRIVER2.PLB or PSAPI.PLB	Printer driver libraries used by GENPD.APP. PSAPI are for PostScript printers; DRIVER2 is for all other printers.	13,277 or 24,451
FOX.EXE	Fox loader program.	10,992
FOXHELP.DBF and FOXHELP.FPT	Help file.	2,309,047
FOXPRO.EXE and FOXPRO.PVO or FOXPROX.EXE	Main FoxPro executable files.	1,774,658 or 1,719,258
FOXSTART.APP	Adds the Run pad to the menu bar.	8,674
FOXSWAP.COM*	Swaps portions of FoxPro to disk when you use the RUN command.	5,971
GENMENU.PRG	Menu template program.	49,909
GENPD.APP	Loads the printer drivers.	379,036
GENSCRN.PRG	Screen template program.	277,113
GENXTAB.PRG	Crosstab generator used by the RQBE.	29,217
TRANSPRT.PRG	The cross-platform Transporter.	334,725
Total**		5,203,793

* *If you distribute an application that uses the RUN command, include FOXSWAP.COM on your distibution disk.*

** *Includes the larger of the two file sizes when you have a choice.*

If you deduct the number of bytes used by one of the two sets of executable files (either FOXPRO.EXE/OVL or FOXPROX.EXE) from the total size of the main FoxPro directory, you can see that most of the files in the FoxPro home directory really are required. If you need to save disk space, concentrate on the large FoxPro subdirectories such as \GOODIES and \SAMPLE.

Notice also that some applications may require certain files to be located in your main FoxPro directory and may add these files to this directory as part of the installation process of the application. These applications generally are designed to become part of your interactive menu, like developers' tools. Locating files in the main FoxPro directory is the surest way to make sure that these files always are available, no matter what changes the user makes to the current path or defaults. Be careful, however, not to delete any files that may be used by third-party applications.

The FoxPro Subdirectories

FoxPro's sample files and utility programs are contained in five subdirectories under the FoxPro home directory. Table F.2 describes the contents of each of these directories and expands the \GOODIES subdirectory to show you some of its wide variety of examples and utilities.

Table F.2 The FoxPro Subdirectories

Subdirectory	Description
FOXAPP	Contains the project file for the FoxPro application generator.
GOODIES	Main directory for the sample files and utilities described in the following nine entries.
GOODIES\DEMO	Contains the project file for the self-running demo and several subdirectories that hold the associated screens, menus, and so on.
GOODIES\FNDATION	Contains three applications and project files that demonstrate the use of a Foundation READ.
GOODIES\HELPTREE	Contains the menu files for the HELPTREE utility described in Chapter 14.
GOODIES\LASER	Contains a simple application in three different stages of a cross-platform conversion from FoxPro 2.5 for DOS to FoxPro for Windows.

continues

Table F.2 Continued

Subdirectory	Description
GOODIES\LCKUPDAT	Contains the files required to update API library files (.PLBs) created for FoxPro 2.0 for use with FoxPro 2.5.
GOODIES\MISC	Contains various sample programs and utilities, such as FIXUSER.APP, FLS.EXE, SETSAVE.PRG and SETSET.PRG, and DBLCLICK.PRG.
GOODIES\PDRIVERS	Contains the GENPD project files and all the subsidiary files necessary to build a modified GENPD.APP.
GOODIES\PROCOLOR	Contains the project and source files for the ProColor application.
GOODIES\SNIPFMT	Contains the SNIPFMT application that formats your code snippets, as described in Chapter 20.
LANGUAGE	Contains the sample files used to create the procedures and code snippets you see in the *Language Reference* manual.
SAMPLE	Holds the project files and compiled programs for the Organize sample application you use in Chapter 1. The source files for the application are contained in several subdirectories.
TUTORIAL	Contains the sample data and other files required to work through the tutorial in the *Getting Started* volume of the FoxPro documentation.

Default File Extensions

Table F.3 shows the default file extensions for each type of file created by FoxPro so that you can identify the nature of each sample file and utility. If you do not specify other extensions, FoxPro uses these defaults as you create and save files.

Table F.3 Default File Extensions in FoxPro

Extension (two extensions signify a related memo file)	Generated Source Program	Generated Compiled Program	Backup	Description
.CDX	—	—	—	Compound index file; has the same file name as associated table if a structural index.
.DBF/.FPT	—	—	.BAK*/.TBK	Standard table; backup created if you MODIFY STRUCTURE.
.DBF/.DBT	—	—	.BAK*/.TBK	Standard table with vanilla memo fields that can be read by non-FoxPro Xbase dialects (see Note 1).
.ERR*	—	—	—	Error files created for programs during compilation; file name is same as associated program (see Note 2).
.FKY	—	—	—	Macro sets SAVEd TO a file.
.FLL	—	—	—	FoxPro for Windows Dynamic Link Library; cannot be used in FoxPro for DOS.
.FMT	—	.PRX*	—	Data-entry format file (see Note 3).
.FRX/.FRT	—	—	—	Report file created through Report Writer or CREATE REPORT... FROM "quick report" command (see Note 4).
.IDX	—	—	—	Single index file; may be read by FoxPro 1.0x if not created COMPACT. Extension may be changed in CONFIG.FP.

continues

Table F.3 Continued

Extension (two extensions signify a related memo file)	Generated Source Program	Generated Compiled Program	Backup	Description
.LBX/.LBT	—	—	—	Label file created through Label Designer. Extension may be changed in CONFIG.FP (see Note 5).
.MEM	—	—	—	Memory variables SAVEd TO a file.
.MNX/.MNT	.MPR	.MPX*	—	Menu file created with Menu Builder.
.PJX/.PJT	—	.APP*	—	Project file created through the Project Manager or the BUILD PROJECT ... FROM command (see Note 6).
.PLB	—	—	—	API library file, which you can SET LIBRARY TO; the product of .OBJ and .LIB files compiled using the Library Construction Kit.
.PRG	—	.FXP*	.BAK*	FoxPro program source code file; created with MODIFY COMMAND or another text editor.
.PRT	—	—	—	File created by designating a file as SET PRINT target device from the File menu's Printer Setup dialog.
.QPR	—	.QPX*	—	Query file usually created with the RQBE but can be created or edited like any other program or ASCII file; creates a .BAK backup file, if edited directly.
.SCX/.SCT	.SPR	.SPX*	—	Screen file created with Screen Builder or by CREATE SCREEN ... FROM "quick screen" command.

Extension (two extensions signify a related memo file)	Generated Source Program	Generated Compiled Program	Backup	Description
.TMP	—	—	—	Temporary work files created during processing. If the program is QUIT normally, these files are erased after each session.
.TXT	—	—	.BAK*	ASCII file usually created with MODIFY FILE.
.TXT	—	—	—	ASCII file created by REPORT/LABEL FORM/ DISPLAY MEMORY and other commands sent TO a FILE command or SET ALTERNATE is used (see Note 6).
.VUE	—	—	—	View file, saving FoxPro.
.WIN	—	—	—	Window definitions SAVEd TO a file.

** This extension is required. All listed memo file extensions are required by the main files associated with them. All other file extensions listed are defaults that can be overridden by specifying a different extension as you create or edit the file.*

Notes for Table F.3:

1. This type of table can be read and written by FoxPro without change and created within FoxPro by using a `COPY TO ... TYPE FOXPLUS` command. It also can be read and written by other Xbase dialects. If you use `MODIFY STRUCTURE` on this type of table, the modified file has a FoxPro-style .FPT memo file, but the backup (.TBK) retains its old format, in spite of the fact that the file is given the same extension as the backup of a FoxPro-style memo file.

2. All errors for files being compiled at the same time can be directed to one file name you specify.

3. These files are supported in FoxPro 2.x for backward compatibility and are not discussed in this book.

4. A file with an .FRX extension but no associated .FRT may be a FoxPro 1.0x report form, which has a different (nontable) format. FoxPro 1.0x reports also may have an associated .FRV file, a special .VUE file with the report's environment. This default extension may be changed in your CONFIG.FP file (see Appendix D).

5. A file with an .LBX extension but no associated .LBT may be a FoxPro 1.0x label form, which has a different (nontable) format. FoxPro 1.0x labels also may have an associated .LBV file, a special .VUE file with the label's environment.

6. No default extension is used if you use `SET PRINT TO <filename>` in the command window instead (see, however, .PRT in this table).

G

APPENDIX

Finding Available Help

As you work in FoxPro, you may have many reasons for wanting to communicate your experiences to other people. Sometimes a command or a tool does not work exactly as you expect, and you need advice; or you may want to share a technique you have developed or learned.

Sitting down alone at a computer is the only way you are going to create applications and write programs. Reading this book and working through its examples can help you, and many other valuable books and database-oriented publications also are available.

Learning about applications and programs, however, usually takes the support and encouragement of other people. The more perspectives you get on the same problem, the sooner—and the more effectively—you can solve the problem.

If you live in an area with many other FoxPro users, a FoxPro-oriented *user's group* may meet somewhere near you. In a user's group, people with a mutual interest get together on a regular basis to share ideas. The Event Coordination Department at Microsoft can tell you if a FoxPro user's group is located in your area—or help you start one if not.

Microsoft also publishes the *Microsoft FoxPro Resource Directory*, which contains a list of consultants and third-party FoxPro applications.

Consultants are organized geographically, and a special insert lists Fox professionals who specialize in training FoxPro users.

You also can attend the Microsoft FoxPro Developer Conference, where you can meet people from all around the world. You can share your tips in the computer labs, see new versions of Microsoft's database products, and learn from experts on all aspects of developing in FoxPro.

Even without meeting people in person, you can be part of a diverse and talented group of folks who "meet" electronically on CompuServe's FOXFORUM. Because the forum is sponsored by Microsoft/Fox, its "sysops" (managing staff) consist of FoxPro Technical Support and Sales and Service personnel. These professionals provide you with a direct line to the company. This method is by far the fastest way to get an answer you need. (You can even order an upgrade on-line.) Using the forum also has the added advantage of providing access to many on-line volunteers who add their expertise to that of the sysops.

The forum's libraries are stocked with programs and tips shared by forum members, and its message area covers the latest information on every aspect of Fox products, with hundreds of messages posted every day.

Every time changes are made to the release version of the product, *patch files* are posted on FOXFORUM. These files usually contain bug fixes and minor enhancements to the product and are to be applied to your existing FoxPro files. You can download three small files (PATCH.DBF, PATCH.EXE, and READ.ME) from the Updates Library (currently Library 12) to learn what you need to do to patch the build of FoxPro you currently use. Then you can go back on-line to download the files you need to patch your FoxPro files.

If you already are a CompuServe member, GO FOXFORUM to access this forum. If you are not a member, you can get a free introductory CompuServe membership because you use a Fox product. CompuServe representatives can help you get started if you have never communicated electronically before. (And you can GO PRACTICE to work on your forum skills in an area free of connect time charges.) After you have accessed FOXFORUM, be sure to read the file FFINFO.TXT, by Nancy Jacobsen, in Library 1 (or download FFINFO.ZIP) for complete information on getting the most out of the Forum and CompuServe in general. Your FOXHELP file includes most of FFINFO.TXT in a special topic about the Forum, labeled ► CompuServe—The Fox Forum.

If you prefer to contact Microsoft by telephone, Chapter 4 of the *Installation and Configuration* booklet provides telephone numbers for Microsoft Product Support Services in the United States and a list of Microsoft subsidiary offices worldwide.

Whether you have a problem or a new idea—and whether you share this problem with your user's group, with a consultant or trainer, with the Fox community at large on FOXFORUM, or directly with Microsoft by phone or mail—you are more likely to get the help you need if you do some groundwork first.

Make sure that you have the details of your hardware and software within reach. The answer to your question may depend on the particular video board you use or your memory manager. Make sure that you also have the contents of your CONFIG.FP, CONFIG.SYS, and AUTOEXEC.BAT files available; network users often have other configuration files that must be checked.

Use the About FoxPro... screens for details of your memory usage, your Resource and CONFIG.FP files, the build date of the version of FoxPro you are using, and other elements of your FoxPro configuration. Write down the figures you see on all these screens.

Make sure that you mention which version of FoxPro (Standard or Extended) you are using, as well as any other programs—especially RAM-resident or popup programs—that you may be using at the same time as FoxPro.

If you need to supply sample files, try to cut the problem down to a simple example; often, just following this procedure helps you figure out the answer. If sample data is required, provide the minimum quantity of data necessary to demonstrate the problem. If a complex procedure or many subprocedures must be used, try re-creating the problem yourself from the files you are uploading or sending by mail. Place the files in a temporary directory and run the problem application from this directory to ensure that you have included everything necessary.

Be specific about your problem or question. "How do I create a screen?" isn't as likely to generate a helpful response as "I want to display a calculated total on my screen; how do I make it refresh after a new figure is entered?" Remember that you can always ask a second question, and a third, after you understand the answer to the first one.

Be optimistic, too. Do not say: "FoxPro doesn't work!" Instead, say: "This command doesn't work the way I think it should. Here's what I did—what's going on?" The chances are good that a quick and constructive answer results from such a query.

People who work for Microsoft and people who work with FoxPro are genuinely glad to talk about what they do with the product and what they can do to help you. Soon, your own comments may enrich the collective experience as you share what you learn.

APPENDIX

Example Database Structures and Procedures

The Omnipresent Widget Limited application used in this book is provided as a model of an extensive system of related files. Most of the tables are not needed for the examples in the text. The procedure that follows, however, creates all the tables in the system and fills those tables used in the examples with the required data. This program, and all the programs and procedures listed in this appendix, are included on the accompanying source disk.

```
* CREATET.PRG
*
* Executive Information System for
* The Omnipresent Widget, Ltd.
*
* This program creates all the tables for the system and all
* the data required by the book examples drawn from the system.
* Note:  if you are going to create more data,
* most codes in the system are created from initial letters
* plus tie-breaking digits for sub-groups, and you should
* probably continue that pattern wherever possible.

m.datadir = GETDIR(sys(2003), "Where should data be created?")
IF EMPTY(m.datadir)
    RETURN
ENDIF

CREATE TABLE (m.datadir+"Budget")       ;
    (Deptcode     C(4),    ;
     Prodcode     C(4),    ;
     Budcatcode   C(4),    ;
     Period       D,       ;
     Budgetamt    N(7,0),  ;
     Final        L,       ;
     Notes        M)
INDEX ON Prodcode   TAG Prodcode
INDEX ON Deptcode   TAG Deptcode
INDEX ON Budcatcode TAG Budcatcode
INDEX ON Period     TAG Period
INDEX ON Budgetamt  TAG Budgetamt
INDEX ON Final      TAG Final
INDEX ON DELETED()  TAG Deleted

INSERT INTO Budget VALUES ;
       ("SLS1","BBM0","ADV0",{01/01/93},2000,.T., ;
        "Call NJ at the BRC agency.  We will mount "+;
        "a new campaign for the Bobometers, with a "+;
        "more positive, upbeat tone.")
INSERT INTO Budget VALUES ;
       ("FIN0","DSQ0","INS0",{04/01/93},1000,.F., ;
        "The cost of Dream Sequencer "+;
        "insurance is expected to rise dramatically.")
INSERT INTO Budget VALUES ;
       ("MFT0","DSQ0","PLT0",{01/01/93},1500,.F.,"")
INSERT INTO Budget VALUES ;
       ("PER0","JLD0","LHR0",{01/01/93},10000,.F.,"")
```

```
INSERT INTO Budget VALUES ;
       ("SLS1","LLD0","ADV0",{01/01/93},1500,.T.,"")
INSERT INTO Budget VALUES ;
       ("PER0","LLD0","LHO0",{04/01/93},2000,.F., ;
        "There's always a production rush on "+ ;
        "Log Ladles as orders come in right before "+;
        "taxes are due -- not sure why they are so "+;
        "popular at this season every year.")
INSERT INTO Budget VALUES ;
       ("FIN0","WGT1","TRV0",{01/01/93},3000,.F., ;
        "An extended trip to Calistoga will be "+;
        "necessary to check out the cost-cutting "+;
        "measures in use at Amalgamated Gadgets.  "+;
        "They are stealing market share of LapTop "+;
        "Widgets, our flagship line!")
INSERT INTO Budget VALUES ;
       ("PER0","WGT1","LSL0",{04/01/93},11000,.F.,"")
INSERT INTO Budget VALUES ;
       ("MFT0","WGT1","PLT0",{04/01/93},23000,.F., ;
        "Manufacturing anticipates a need to update "+;
        "equipment for this product line in the second "+;
        "quarter.  Final estimates not in.")
INSERT INTO Budget VALUES ;
       ("SLS2","WGT2","LCM0",{01/01/93},3000,.T., ;
        "The Mainframe Widget specialist sales force "+;
        "will be selling maintenance contracts as "+ ;
        "reliably as ever in the first quarter, but we "+;
        "are phasing out the Mainframe line, so this "+;
        "gravy train won't last forever.")
INSERT INTO Budget VALUES ;
       ("MFT0","WZL1","PLT0",{04/01/93},5000,.F.,"")
INSERT INTO Budget VALUES ;
       ("SLS2","WZL2","ADV0",{01/01/93},1000,.T., ;
        "Marketing strategy for the Weazlette line "+ ;
        "should feature the upcoming Industrial "+ ;
        "Strength version of the product along with "+ ;
        "our current Household brand.")
INSERT INTO Budget VALUES ;
       ("SLS3","WZL3","LCM0",{04/01/93},2500,.F.,"")

CREATE TABLE (m.datadir+"Dept")          ;
     (Deptcode   C(4),    ;
      Deptname   C(30))
```

continues

```
INDEX ON Deptcode TAG Deptcode
INDEX ON Deptname Tag Deptname

INSERT INTO Dept VALUES ;
       ("SLS1","Sales SouthEast Division")
INSERT INTO Dept VALUES ;
       ("SLS2","Sales NorthEast Division")
INSERT INTO Dept VALUES ;
       ("SLS3","Sales Western Division")
INSERT INTO Dept VALUES ;
       ("FIN0","Finance")
INSERT INTO Dept VALUES ;
       ("MFT0","Manufacturing")
INSERT INTO Dept VALUES ;
       ("PER0","Personnel")

CREATE TABLE (m.datadir+"Product")      ;
     (Prodcode   C(4),    ;
      Prodname   C(20),   ;
      Retail     N(8,2),  ;
      Design         G)
INDEX ON Prodname TAG Prodname
INDEX ON Prodcode TAG Prodcode

INSERT INTO Product ;
            (prodcode,prodname,retail) VALUES ;
       ("WGT2","Mainframe Widgets", 10000)
INSERT INTO Product ;
            (prodcode,prodname,retail) VALUES ;
       ("WGT1","LapTop Widgets", 2000)
INSERT INTO Product ;
            (prodcode,prodname,retail) VALUES ;
       ("DSQ0","Dream Sequencers",79.95)
INSERT INTO Product ;
            (prodcode,prodname,retail) VALUES ;
       ("BBM0","Bobometers",60)
INSERT INTO Product ;
            (prodcode,prodname,retail) VALUES ;
       ("LLD0","Log Ladles (pine)",25)
INSERT INTO Product ;
            (prodcode,prodname,retail) VALUES ;
       ("JLD0","Jeli-Do Nuts & Bolts", 2.50)
INSERT INTO Product ;
            (prodcode,prodname,retail) VALUES ;
       ("WZL1","Pine Weazlettes",145)
```

```
INSERT INTO Product ;
            (prodcode,prodname,retail) VALUES ;
       ("WZL2","Lemon Weazlettes",145)
INSERT INTO Product ;
            (prodcode,prodname,retail) VALUES ;
       ("WZL3","Floral Weazlettes",145)
INSERT INTO Product ;
            (prodcode,prodname,retail) VALUES ;
       ("WZL4","Unscented Weazlettes",155)

IF _WINDOWS
   SCAN
      m.pictfile = FindPict(prodcode+".PCX",TRIM(prodname))
      IF NOT EMPTY(m.pictfile)
         WAIT WINDOW NOWAIT ;
           "Adding picture file for "+TRIM(prodname)+"... "
         APPEND GENERAL design FROM (m.pictfile)
         WAIT CLEAR
      ENDIF
   ENDSCAN
ENDIF

CREATE TABLE (m.datadir+ "Budcat")      ;
     (Budcatcode C(4),   ;
      Budcat     C(20))
INDEX ON Budcatcode TAG Budcatcode
INDEX ON Budcat     TAG Budcat

INSERT INTO Budcat VALUES ;
       ("INS0","Insurance")
INSERT INTO Budcat VALUES ;
       ("LHR0","Labor, Hourly Reg")
INSERT INTO Budcat VALUES ;
       ("LHO0","Labor, Hourly Over")
INSERT INTO Budcat VALUES ;
       ("LSL0","Labor, Salary")
INSERT INTO Budcat VALUES ;
       ("LCM0","Labor, Commission")
INSERT INTO Budcat VALUES ;
       ("TRV0","Travel")
INSERT INTO Budcat VALUES ;
       ("ADV0","Advertising")
INSERT INTO Budcat VALUES ;
       ("PLT0","Plant")
```

continues

```
CREATE TABLE (m.datadir+"Address")     ;
     (Addrcode   C(4),    ;
      President  C(35),   ;
      Company    C(35),   ;
      Address1   C(30),   ;
      Address2   C(30),   ;
      City       C(20),   ;
      State      C(2),    ;
      Zip        C(5),    ;
      Phone      C(10))
INDEX ON Addrcode TAG Addrcode

* main phone and name are useful for cold calls
* for sales and bids; personal contacts would be
* listed individually in the Vendor and Customer tables
* with names broken out appropriately for mail merge
INSERT INTO Address VALUES ;
       ("A001","Roland F. Archer","Archer Supplies, Inc.", ;
        "222 West Palm Road", "", "Palm Coast", "FL", ;
        "33414","4071234567")
INSERT INTO Address VALUES ;
       ("A010","Andrew Sax","Andy's Traveling Widgets", ;
        "101 Surfside", "", "Redondo Beach", "CA", ;
        "90025","2139996666")
INSERT INTO Address VALUES ;
       ("B001","William K. Fisher","Bill & Marie's Gift Shop", ;
        "1453 N. Wilmington Drive", "", "Merced", "CA", ;
        "95124","4085671111")
INSERT INTO Address VALUES ;
       ("C010","Stan Cooper","Cooper & Lybock", ;
        "1800 M Street NW", "Suite 21", "Washington", "DC", ;
        "20009","2021234567")
INSERT INTO Address VALUES ;
       ("D110","M. W. Widgetmeister","Dweebs Unlimited", ;
        "23 East Meadow Lane", "", "Arlington", "VA", ;
        "22903","8045671234")
INSERT INTO Address VALUES ;
       ("D091","Art Linkdata","The Data Linkers, Inc.", ;
        "4600 Oxnard Street", "# C231", "Corvallis", "OR", ;
        "97330","5037772222")
INSERT INTO Address VALUES ;
       ("W132","Dr. Teeth","Woodchuck Consulting", ;
        "65 Pinehaven Road", "", "Damascus", "MD", ;
        "20817","3015671234")
```

```
INSERT INTO Address VALUES ;
       ("T050","Roy Trammeil, Esq.","Trammeil & Crow, Attys At Law", ;
        "500 King Street", "", "Franklin Park", "PA", ;
        "15232","4125671234")

CREATE TABLE (m.datadir+"Customer")     ;
     (Custcode   C(4),    ;
      Addrcode   C(4),    ;
      Firstname  C(15),   ;
      Lastname   C(20),   ;
      Greetname  C(15),   ;
      Prefix     C(4),    ;
      Phone      C(10),   ;
      Phone_ext  C(5))

* name and phone here is contact for customer,
* and may differ from President listing
* address comes from main file for the company
* phone should default to address listing

INSERT INTO Customer VALUES ;
       ("RFA1","A001", ;
        "Roland", "Archer", "Roland", "Mr.", ;
        "4071234567","")
INSERT INTO Customer VALUES ;
       ("AS01","A010", ;
        "Andrew", "Sax", "Andy", "Mr.", ;
        "2139996666","")
INSERT INTO Customer VALUES ;
       ("WKF1","B001", ;
        "William", "Fisher", "Bill", "Mr.", ;
        "4085671111","123")
INSERT INTO Customer VALUES ;
       ("MKF1","B001", ;
        "Marie", "Fisher", "Marie", "Ms.", ;
        "4085671111","234")
INSERT INTO Customer VALUES ;
       ("TDC1","C010", ;
        "Tod", "Cooper", "Tod", "Mr.", ;
         "2021234500","4389")
INSERT INTO Customer VALUES ;
       ("MWW1","D110", ;
        "Mark", "Widgetmeister", "M.W.", "Mr.", ;
        "8045671234","")
```

continues

```
INSERT INTO Customer VALUES ;
       ("SH01","D091", ;
        "Sean", "Hedgepeth", "Sean", "Mr.", ;
        "5037772222","")
INSERT INTO Customer VALUES ;
       ("BWT1","W132", ;
        "Burton", "Teeth", "Burt", "Dr.", ;
        "3015676789","")
INSERT INTO Customer VALUES ;
       ("AC01","T050", ;
        "Arthur", "Crow", "Art", "Mr.", ;
        "4125671234","")

CREATE TABLE (m.datadir+"Sales")        ;
     (Invoice    C(6),    ;
      Prodcode   C(4),    ;
      Datesold   D,       ;
      Quantity   N(5,0), ;
      Price      N(7,2), ;
      Salesman   C(4),    ;
      Custcode   C(4))
INDEX ON Custcode    TAG Custcode
INDEX ON Invoice     TAG Invoice

INSERT INTO Sales VALUES ;
       ("1000","BBM0",{01/28/93},20, ;
        60.00,"W100","SH01")
INSERT INTO Sales VALUES ;
       ("1001","WZL2",{01/28/93},10, ;
        100.00,"J002","AC01")
INSERT INTO Sales VALUES ;
       ("1003","DSQ0",{01/28/93},5, ;
        75.99,"B023","MKF1")
INSERT INTO Sales VALUES ;
       ("1004","LLD0",{01/30/93},15, ;
        25.00,"W100","BWT1")
INSERT INTO Sales VALUES ;
       ("1005","WZL1",{01/30/93},2, ;
        150.00,"B023","MKF1")
INSERT INTO Sales VALUES ;
       ("1006","JLD0",{01/30/93},100, ;
        2.50,"A100","RFA1")
INSERT INTO Sales VALUES ;
       ("1007","WGT1",{01/30/93},2, ;
        1599.00,"W100","AS01")
INSERT INTO Sales VALUES ;
       ("1008","LLD1",{01/30/93},10, ;
        25.00,"B023","MKF1")
```

```
INSERT INTO Sales VALUES ;
       ("1009","WGT2",{01/30/93},1, ;
        9999.99,"J002","RFA1")
INSERT INTO Sales VALUES ;
       ("1010","JLD0",{01/31/93},200, ;
        1.79,"J002","RFA1")


* the following tables are not used directly
* in the book but would be used in the full
* system

CREATE TABLE (m.datadir+"Vendor")      ;
     (Vendorcode C(4),    ;
      Addrcode   C(4),    ;
      Phone      C(10),   ;
      Phone_ext  C(5),    ;
      Lastname   C(20),   ;
      Firstname  C(15),   ;
      Greetname  C(15),   ;
      Prefix     C(3))
* name and phone here is contact for vendor,
* and may differ from President listing
* address comes from main file for the company
* phone should default to address listing

CREATE TABLE (m.datadir+"Manufact")    ;
     (Prodcode   C(4),    ;
      Proddate   D,       ;
      Shift      C(1),    ;
      Quantity   N(4,0), ;
      Rejects    N(4,0))

CREATE TABLE (m.datadir+"Prodmix")     ;
     (Prodcode   C(4),    ;
      Rawmatter  C(20),   ;
      Weight     N(7,0))

CREATE TABLE (m.datadir+"Rawdeliv")    ;
     (Invoice    C(6),    ;
      Vendorcode C(4),    ;
      Rawmatter  C(20),   ;
      Cost       N(10,2),;
      Delivdate  D,       ;
      Paiddate   D)
```

continues

```
CREATE TABLE (m.datadir+"Material")     ;
     (Rawmatter C(20))

CREATE TABLE (m.datadir+"Capexp")       ;
     (Capcode    C(4),    ;
      Deptcode   C(4),    ;
      Prodcode   C(4),    ;
      Period     C(5),    ;
      Depnperiod N(2,0),  ;
      Amount     N(10,2),;
      Notes      M)

CREATE TABLE (m.datadir+"Wages")        ;
     (Deptcode   C(4),    ;
      Prodcode   C(4),    ;
      Wagetype   C(1),    ;
      Shift      C(1),    ;
      Periodwk   C(5),    ;
      Amount     N(11,2))

CREATE TABLE (m.datadir+"Salesman")     ;
     (Salesman   C(4),    ;
      Name       C(30))

RETURN


FUNCTION FindPict
PARAMETER whatpict, whatproduct
PRIVATE m.return
m.return = ""
DO CASE
CASE FILE(whatpict)
   m.return = whatpict
CASE FILE(m.datadir+whatpict)
   m.return = m.datadir+whatpict
OTHERWISE
   m.return = ;
   GETFILE("BMP¦PCX",;
     "Picture of "+whatproduct+":", ;
     "Use",0)
ENDCASE
RETURN m.return
```

Most FoxPro code required by the examples in this book are listed in the text. The snippets for the generic ASK procedure used in Chapter 14, however, are listed here. The comments explain how to create an .SCX that generates the appropriate .SPR file.

ASK can be used as a function or a procedure. If you generate the code, however, you must specify the (nondefault) extension of .PRG for ASK to be used as a function.

Following the code for ASK is a short procedure named UNALIAS.PRG. This program shows you how to strip alias information from a table that FoxPro uses to build a screen or report form, as suggested in Chapters 10 and 13.

TREE.PRG is a program that creates an ASCII file containing a directory structure (a directory and all its subdirectories) in a typical DOS "tree" format. The program also prints the number of files and the number of bytes used to store the files for each directory in the tree. This program was used to create the FoxPro directory structure listing shown in Appendix F.

The remaining programs illustrate some tricks and techniques you can use when combining a READ and a BROWSE, as discussed in Chapter 15. This includes using READ with Browse and other non-Read windows, but no GET to manage the READ; a record marker for an inactive BROWSE; a BROWSE picklist in which the choices change color according to a condition you set; and a BROWSE with an editable check box field.

```
*************************************************
* code for ASK.SPR/PRG
* this screen is called with its SAY,
* its GET, and any necessary PICTURE for
* the validation of the GET. A dummy GET
* is used in the SCX to
* call the real GET. The dummy GET should
* have both its Pen and Fill colors matching
* the window background

* m.value can be of any TYPE except memo.
* ordinarily you initialize the value before
* calling the ASK.SPR, which helps ASK determine
* the necessary length of the GET, like this:

* seekcode = product.prodcode
* DO ASK.SPR WITH "Product to seek:",seekcode,"@! AAA99"

* or:

* yesno = "NO " && see note one line down
* DO ASK.SPR WITH "Ready now?",yesno,"@M NO, YES"
```

continues

```
* (in the @M case the extra space should be used
* if the initial value of m.value is not its
* longest possible value)

* if you generate the screen with the non-default
* PRG extension, you can use ASK as a UDF and
* the appropriate new value will be returned;
* in that case you don't initialize it first,
* and you'd call it like this:
* seekcode = ASK("Product to find:",product.prodcode,"@! AAA99")
* bigitem = ASK("Smallest item to mark:",0,"9999")
* This is demonstrated in the Pack procedure of
* WIDGET2.MPR.

* m.valid is not required.
* If you want to use FUNCTION as well as
* or instead of PICTURE, just include your
* FUNCTION codes with the @ symbol in m.valid
* as shown above and it will be parsed properly.

* ASK requires three code snippets, as follows.
**************************************************
* SETUP snippet for ASK.SPR/PRG
#section1
PARAMETERS m.question, m.value, m.valid
novalid = (PARAMETERS() = 2)
IF novalid
   m.valid = ""
ENDIF
oldborder = SET("READBORDER")

#section2
* initialize dummy variable
m.dummy =""
SET READBORDER OFF
**************************************************
* WHEN snippet for ASK.SPR/PRG
PRIVATE temp, msize, getcol
DO CASE
CASE "@M" $ m.valid
   temp = LEN(m.value)
   * don't trim this one;
   * use the way the sample/initial value is
   * set up (with an extra space if necessary,
   * if the initial value is not the longest one)
   * to format the @M-type GET properly
```

```
CASE TYPE("m.value") = "C" AND (! novalid) AND ;
   "@" $ m.valid AND " " $ m.valid
   temp = LEN(m.valid)-AT(" ",m.valid)
   * get rid of the function codes to find the
   * length of the GET
CASE TYPE("m.value") = "C" AND (novalid OR "@" $ m.valid)
   temp = LEN(ALLTRIM(m.value))
   IF _WINDOWS AND novalid
      novalid = .F.
      m.valid = REPL("X",temp)
   ENDIF
CASE TYPE("m.value") = "C"
   temp = LEN(ALLTRIM(m.valid))
   IF _WINDOWS AND novalid
      novalid = .F.
      m.valid = REPL("X",temp)
   ENDIF
CASE TYPE("m.value") = "N"
   temp = IIF(novalid,LEN(ALLTRIM(STR(m.value))),;
                    LEN(m.valid)-AT(" ",m.valid))
   IF _WINDOWS AND novalid
      novalid = .F.
      m.valid = REPL("9",temp)
   ENDIF
CASE TYPE("m.value") = "D"
   temp = IIF(SET("CENTURY") = "ON",10,8)
CASE TYPE("m.value") = "L"
   temp = 1
   IF _WINDOWS AND novalid
      novalid = .F.
      m.valid = "Y"
   ENDIF
ENDCASE
IF _WINDOWS
   temp = temp+2
ENDIF
getcol = (WCOLS()-temp)/2
msize = "1,"+ALLTRIM(STR(temp))
IF novalid
   @3,getcol GET m.value SIZE &msize
ELSE
   temp = ALLTRIM(m.valid)
   @3,getcol GET m.value PICTURE (temp) SIZE &msize
ENDIF
```

continues

```
READ MODAL
CLEAR READ
RETURN .F.
**************************************************
* CLEANUP snippet for ASK.SPR/PRG
* will only be used if the screen is going to be
* generated as a UDF with a PRG extension
SET READBORDER &oldborder
RETURN m.value
**************************************************
**************************************************
* UNALIAS.PRG
*
* Unchecking the alias in a screen or report form
* isn't going to change the fact that your objects *were*
* created with aliases -- it will just affect any new
* objects you design.

* Instead of manually editing each object, you can USE
* the SCX or FRX table and get rid of all aliases at
* once.

USE GETFILE("scx",;
   "Pick a Screen File for Alias Removal or Esc")
DO WHILE LASTKEY() # 27
   REPLACE ALL Name WITH SUBSTR(Name,AT(".",Name)+1) ;
      FOR "." $ Name AND Objtype > 10
   * in case you were inconsistent, include old-style
   * alias referencing (using "->"):
   REPLACE ALL Name WITH SUBSTR(Name,AT(">",Name)+1) ;
      FOR "->" $ Name AND Objtype > 10
   * include checks here for Expr field containing
   * aliases as well:
   BROWSE FIELDS Expr FOR "." $ Expr OR ;
      "->" $ Expr
   USE GETFILE("scx",;
      "Pick a Screen File for Alias Removal or Esc")
ENDDO
**************************************************
**************************************************
* TREE.PRG
*
* A version of SUBDIRS.PRG that creates an ASCII
* file containing a directory tree, the number of
* files in each subdirectory, and the total size
* of those files.
*
```

```
* Note that procedure subdirs calls itself
* recursively to print the tree.  Although FoxPro
* does not support recursion, the level of nested
* calls to subdirs should be few enough to avoid
* problems with most directory structures.
*
* Example calls: DO tree  && current default directory
*                DO tree WITH "c:\foxpro25"
*
PARAMETERS the_dir
PRIVATE all

oldpath = SET("DEFAULT")+SYS(2003) + "\"
IF PARAMETERS() = 0
   * you're finding out about current default directory
   the_dir = oldpath
   drivepath = ""
ELSE
   IF TYPE("the_dir") # "C"
      WAIT WINDOW "Invalid path specified!"
      RETURN
   ENDIF
   IF RIGHT(the_dir,1) != "\"
      the_dir = the_dir + "\"
   ENDIF
   checkpath = the_dir + "nul"
   IF ! FILE(checkpath)
      WAIT WINDOW "Invalid path specified!"
      RETURN
   ENDIF
   IF AT(":",the_dir) = 0
      SET DEFAULT TO (the_dir)
      drivepath = ""
   ELSE
      SET DEFAULT TO (LEFT(the_dir,1))
      drivepath = SYS(2003)
      SET DEFAULT TO (the_dir)
   ENDIF
ENDIF

* define constants used to position the output
#DEFINE   COL1POS     0
#DEFINE   COL2POS    60
#DEFINE   COL3POS    70
#DEFINE   COL2LEN     5
```

continues

```
#DEFINE   COL3LEN    10
#DEFINE   COL2HEAD   "Files"
#DEFINE   COL3HEAD   "Total bytes"
#DEFINE   IND_INCR    3     && indentation increment

tot_files =  0
tot_size  =  0

DO setup
DO prt_head
DO subdirs WITH the_dir, tot_files, tot_size
DO prt_tots
DO cleanup
RETURN


PROCEDURE setup
   SET PRINTER TO (oldpath +"\tree.txt")
   SET PRINTER ON
RETURN


PROCEDURE prt_head

   ?? "Directory structure" at col1pos, ;
      col2head at col2pos+col2len-LEN(col2head), ;
      col3head at col3pos+col3len-LEN(col3head)
RETURN


PROCEDURE subdirs
   PARAMETERS mpath, tot_files, tot_size, indent_level
   PRIVATE all

   IF TYPE('indent_level') != "N"
      indent_level = 0
   ENDIF

   * change to the subdirectory
   IF AT(":",mpath) = 0
      SET DEFAULT TO (mpath)
      drivepath = ""
   ELSE
      SET DEFAULT TO (LEFT(mpath,1))
      drivepath = SYS(2003)
      SET DEFAULT TO (mpath)
   ENDIF
```

```
* get the # of files in the subdir, then
* determine their total file size;
* the size of each file is held in the
* second column of the array created
* by ADIR()
nfiles = ADIR(files_arr,"*.*", "HS")
file_size = 0
FOR xx=1 to nfiles
   file_size = file_size + files_arr[xx,2]
ENDFOR

* we always get mpath in the form "c:\foxprow\"
dir_name = SUBSTR(mpath, RAT("\", mpath, 2)+1)
dir_name = LEFT(dir_name, LEN(dir_name)-1)

* print the subdir name, # of files and file size
?  dir_name + ;
     REPLICATE(".",COL2POS-indent_level-LEN(dir_name)-1) ;
     at indent_level, ;
   STR(nfiles,COL2LEN) at COL2POS, ;
   STR(file_size,COL3LEN) at COL3POS

* keep the running totals for all subdirs
tot_files = tot_files + nfiles
tot_size = tot_size + file_size

* get the list of subdirectories of this directory
ndirs = ADIR(dir_arr,"","D")

* sort them in ascending order by the 1st column
* (file names) so . & .. come *first* if they exist
= ASORT(dir_arr,1,ndirs,0)
ndels = 0

IF ndirs # 0
   FOR xx = 1 TO 2
      * there can only be two of these
      IF dir_arr(1,1) = "."
         * EXACT should be OFF for this to work
         * this is a DOS entry for upper directories
         ndels = ndels + 1
         = ADEL(dir_arr,1)
         * this row should now be moved to the end
         * of the array
```

continues

```
            ENDIF
         ENDFOR
         ndirs = ndirs - ndels
         IF ndirs # 0
            DIME dir_arr(ndirs,5)
            * get rid of "." entries
         ENDIF
      ENDIF

      IF ndirs > 0
         FOR xx=1 to ndirs
            DO subdirs WITH mpath+dir_arr[xx,1]+"\", ;
               tot_files, tot_size, indent_level + IND_INCR
         ENDFOR
      ENDIF

      IF ! EMPTY(drivepath)
         SET DEFAULT TO (drivepath)
         * set default directory back for this drive
      ENDIF

   RETURN


   PROCEDURE prt_tots

      ?
      ? "Totals" at col2pos - 10, ;
         str(tot_files,col2len) at col2pos, ;
         str(tot_size,col3len) at col3pos
   RETURN


   PROCEDURE cleanup
      SET PRINTER OFF
      SET PRINTER TO
      IF ! EMPTY(drivepath)
         SET DEFAULT TO (drivepath)
         * set default directory back for this drive
      ENDIF

      IF ! EMPTY(oldpath)
         SET DEFAULT TO (oldpath)
      ENDIF
   RETURN
```

```
***************************************************
***************************************************
* BROWCLR.PRG
*
* See Chapter 15

* this program demonstrates
* changing color in a browse
* based on a simple condition

* it's best for browses used as picklists,
* and doesn't really make sense in an editable
* browse

SET COLOR OF SCHEME 5 TO ;
   W+/RB,W+/BG,W+/RB,W+/RB,W/RB,W+/B,GR+/RB,N+/N,W+/RB,W/RB,+
* otherwise you might not see the change, especially
* in Windows

USE SYS(2004)+"foxhelp" AGAIN
okay = .F.
BROWSE FIELDS x = "" :W=okay :H = "", ;
   y=TOPIC+": "+CLASS :W=!okay :H = "Pick One" ;
   WHEN checkit() ;
   COLOR SCHEME 5
SET COLOR OF SCHEME 5 TO

FUNC checkit
okay = RECNO() % 3 = 0  && put your condition here
KEYBOARD "{tab}"
RETURN .T.
***************************************************
***************************************************
* BROWMARK.PRG

* See Chapter 15

* this program demonstrates a record marker
* in the inactive browse window

* it needs all the extra work of BROWTRAP.PRG to get
* the READ VALID working properly to hold the browses
* in place -- as this skeletal problem stands, you'll
* need an extra keypress to leave the READ when you
* escape from the BROWSEs
```

continues

```
USE ?
IF EMPTY(ALIAS())
   RETURN
ELSE
   m.alias1 = ALIAS()
ENDIF
SELECT 0
USE ?
IF EMPTY(ALIAS())
   RETURN
ELSE
   m.alias2 = ALIAS()
ENDIF
m.rec = RECNO()
BROWSE WHEN Do_mark() NOWAIT SAVE;
     FIELDS markfield = IIF(RECNO() = m.rec,"*","") , ;
            (FIELD(1))
SELECT (m.alias1)
BROWSE SAVE NOWAIT
READ VALID .T.
USE IN m.alias2
USE IN m.alias1
RETURN

PROC Do_mark
m.rec = RECNO()
SHOW WINDOW (m.alias2) REFRESH
RETURN .T.
**************************************************
**************************************************
* BROWTOGC.PRG

* See Chapter 15

* This program demonstrates an editable
* checkbox in a browse, char field style

* I am going to assume that you need a keyboard
* equivalent also, rather than just a mouse.
* To make this work you will need a char-type field rather
* than a logical field for the toggled field.

* This is not so bad, because, as shown, you can
* always do your tests for IF EMPTY(yesno) rather than IF yesno,
* but it requires a little more work -- you might like to
```

```
* revise if you don't need the keyboard equivalent, using
* a logical field and a calculated field for the "X" display.

* if you edit this and bomb,
* remember that you can do an
* ON <shift-spacebar>KEY <shift-enter>
* to remove the re-mapping of the spacebar key

CREATE CURSOR ron (yesno c(1), somefield c(10))
thisfile = DBF()
APPEND BLANK
FOR xx = 1 TO 5
  APPEND FROM (thisfile)
ENDFOR
REPLACE ALL somefield WITH REPL(CHR(RECNO()+72),5)+" test", ;
            yesno WITH IIF(RECNO() % 3 = 0,"X","")
GO TOP
ON KEY LABEL SPACEBAR DO toggle
BROWSE FIELDS somefield,yesno :W = checkit(MDOWN()) :H="?"
ON KEY LABEL SPACEBAR

FUNC checkit
PARAMETER ifmouse
IF ifmouse
   REPLACE yesno WITH IIF(EMPTY(yesno),"X","")
   SHOW WINDOW (WONTOP()) REFRESH
ENDIF
RETURN .T.

PROC toggle
IF UPPER(VARREAD()) = "YESNO"
   REPLACE yesno WITH IIF(EMPTY(yesno),"X","")
   SHOW WINDOW (WONTOP()) REFRESH
ELSE
   KEYBOARD "{SPACEBAR}" PLAIN
ENDIF
RETURN
***************************************************
***************************************************
* BROWTOGL.PRG

* See Chapter 15

* program to demonstrate browse toggle in a logical field version
```

continues

```
* If you edit this and crash,
* remember that you can do an
* ON <shift-spacebar>KEY <shift-enter>
* to remove the re-mapping of the spacebar key

* I have edited it to include the ability to use T/F, Y/N
* in the "checkbox"

CREATE CURSOR checkbox (yesno l, somefield c(10))
thisfile = DBF()
APPEND BLANK
FOR xx = 1 TO 5
  APPEND FROM (thisfile)
ENDFOR
REPLACE ALL somefield with REPL(CHR(RECNO()+72),5)+" test" ;
            yesno WITH RECNO() % 3 = 0
moused = .F.
GO TOP
PUSH KEY CLEAR

ON KEY LABEL SPACEBAR DO toggle WITH "{SPACEBAR}"

ON KEY LABEL "Y" DO toggle WITH CHR(LASTKEY()), .T.
ON KEY LABEL "N" DO toggle WITH CHR(LASTKEY()), .F.
ON KEY LABEL "T" DO toggle WITH CHR(LASTKEY()), .T.
ON KEY LABEL "F" DO toggle WITH CHR(LASTKEY()), .F.
* before you think the above is unnecessarily complicated,
* recall that I'm allowing you to use the y,n,t,and f keys
* normally in the char field for editing ... and that
* OKL normally doesn't respect cases <g>

ON KEY LABEL LEFTMOUSE DO checkit1
ON KEY LABEL "¦" DO checkit2
* we take care of the mouse separately, because we have
* to let the mouse register.

BROWSE FIELDS somefield , ;
              showit = IIF(yesno,"X","") :H="On or Off?"
POP KEY
RETURN

PROC checkit1
moused = .T.
KEYBOARD "¦"
RETURN
```

```
PROC checkit2
IF moused
   IF UPPER(VARREAD()) = "SHOWIT"
      REPLACE yesno WITH NOT yesno
      SHOW WINDOW (WONTOP()) REFRESH
   ENDIF
   moused = .F.
ELSE
   KEYBOARD "¦" PLAIN
ENDIF
RETURN

PROC toggle
PARAMETER the_key, the_value
IF UPPER(VARREAD()) = "SHOWIT"
   REPLACE yesno WITH IIF(PARAMETERS() = 2, the_value, NOT yesno)
   SHOW WINDOW (WONTOP()) REFRESH
ELSE
   KEYBOARD the_key PLAIN
ENDIF
RETURN
**************************************************
**************************************************
* BROWTRAP.PRG

* See Chapter 15

* I wrote a version of this program on CompuServe
* for a gentleman who wanted to display a running total in a
* window adjacent to a BROWSE.

* Why the READ here?  I wanted to stay in the program
* with the subroutine, rather than BROWSing interactively,
* because otherwise it was possible to "lose" the do_display
* UDF.  There aren't any GETs in this READ.

* The important example here is the shenanigans needed to
* check for an escape from the browse.  Without all this work,
* I couldn't close the little extra window at the same
* time as I got out of the BROWSE, and I couldn't be certain
* the READ VALID would be cleared effectively.  You may never
* do a procedure exactly like this, but this is the
* basic method needed if you are going to trap keys and
* mouse clicks no matter what the reason.
```

continues

```
* You have to make sure the program stays where you think
* it is especially when the BROWSE has a WHEN or VALID procedure
* that is bound into the program, as Do_Display() is here.

IF _WINDOWS AND NOT "FOXTOOLS" $ UPPER(SET("LIBRARY",1))
   SET LIBRARY TO SYS(2004)+"FoxTools" ADDITIVE
ELSE
   m.proc = SET("PROC",1)
   SET PROC TO (_TRANSPORT)  && Justpath function is in there too
                             && Use the system variable since
                             && you might have one copy of TRANSPORT.PRG
                             && for your various platforms of FP 2.5

ENDIF
m.commpath = Justpath(SYS(16))
m.findfile = LOCFILE("invoices.dbf","dbf","Where is TUTORIAL\Invoices?")
IF EMPTY(m.findfile)
   RETURN
ENDIF
m.locpath = Justpath(findfile)
m.olddefault = SET("DEFAULT",1)+SYS(2003)
SET DEFAULT TO (locpath)
m.quit = .F.
SET TALK OFF
DEFINE WINDOW displaywind FROM SROWS()-5,5 TO SROWS()-3,45 ;
   TITLE "Customer Balance" DOUBLE COLOR SCHEME 10
canclose =  IIF(_WINDOWS,"NOCLOSE","CLOSE")
DEFINE WINDOW browwind FROM 2,5 TO SROWS()-8,45 ;
   COLOR SCHEME 10 &canclose FLOAT
IF NOT USED("Customer")
   USE Customer IN 0 AGAIN
ENDIF
IF NOT USED("Invoices")
   USE Invoices IN 0 AGAIN
ENDIF
SELE Invoices && needs index tag on cno for this program
SET ORDER TO cno
SELE Customer
SET RELATION TO cno INTO invoices
* you *do* need RELATION here, unless you want to
* add a SEEK in the function below ; NBD either way
ACTI WINDOW displaywind
PUSH KEY CLEAR
* trap exit keys
ON KEY LABEL ESCAPE DO quitting
ON KEY LABEL CTRL-Q DO quitting
```

```
ON KEY LABEL CTRL-END DO quitting
ON KEY LABEL CTRL-W DO quitting
* mouse close box takes a little more work <g>
* and can't be handled this way in Windows product! --
* that's why the browse window is designed not to
* close in the Windows version of the program
ON KEY LABEL leftmouse DO chkmouse WITH ;
       MROW(""), MCOL(""), MWINDOW()
BROWSE WHEN do_display() WINDOW browwind
RELEASE WINDOW displaywind, browwind
READ VALID m.quit
SET DEFAULT TO (m.olddefault)
IF _DOS
   SET PROC TO (m.proc)
ENDIF
RETURN

PROC quitting
m.quit = .T.
RELEASE WINDOW displaywind
CLOSE DATA
* restore key status
POP KEY
KEYBOARD "{ENTER}"  && get into the READ
RETURN

PROC Chkmouse
PARAMETERS mouserow, mousecol, topwind
IF mouserow = WLROW(topwind) AND mousecol = WLCOL(topwind)
   * are we on the mouse close control? (works only in DOS version)
   = INKEY("M")  && eat the mouse click
   DO quitting
ELSE
   IF topwind # WONTOP()
      * did we click outside the window?
      = INKEY("M")
   ENDIF
ENDIF
RETURN


FUNCTION Do_display
SELE Invoices
* here's a command to display the running total
* for this customer
```

continues

```
CALCULATE WHILE cno = customer.cno ;
   SUM(itotal) ;
   TO thistotal
* notice I don't have to ACTI WINDOW display because it remains
* WOUTPUT()!
@ 0,0 SAY PADC("Customer #"+ customer.cno ;
   +":  "+ALLTRIM(STR(thistotal,10,2)),39)
SELE Customer
RETURN .T.
**************************************************
**************************************************
* EFORMAT.PRG
* See Chapter 13 (Table 13.1)

* This program demonstrates some of the problems of EDIT FORMAT
* and a way to use it under FoxPro 2.x.

* The problems stem from the fact that EDIT FORMAT, included
* in FoxPro 2.x for backwards compatibility, is really faked
* with a READ!

* In this program, you can see the result with a button to check
* RDLEVEL().

* Since EDIT FORMAT is a READ, it doesn't pay any attention to
* the other clauses on the EDIT line.  It does not respect:
*  the KEY clause
*  automatic locking
*  LAST or PREFERENCE

* It does not even obey COLOR SCHEME, VALID, or other clauses
* READ shares.  (Curiously, it does obey the TIMEOUT clause.)

* It has a limited ability to exist in a WINDOW, but only as a
* READ does; that is, you must ACTIVATE the WINDOW first; the
* WINDOW clause on the EDIT line will not be respected.

* It has a limited understanding of scope.  The DO WHILE loop
* below is intended to allow some cycling through the file (by
* itself the EDIT FORMAT will go from the first record to the
* last if you PageUp and PageDn or other editing keys, such as
* TAB, in the first or last fields of the record, and the
* EDIT FORMAT stops if you hit EOF() or BOF()).  It *does*
* understand NEXT <ExpN> and similar scopes, but is subject
* to the same need for a DO WHILE loop to keep it going if
* you use such a scope clause.
```

```
* Nevertheless, especially in FoxPro 2.5 with the #NOREAD PLAIN
* directive, you can create a quick entry screen -- complete
* with validation code, since functions are allowed in the format
* file -- in the Screen Builder, and use it for a tailored
* form of data entry in the interactive environment or a
* simple program, by using the result in an EDIT FORMAT.

* USE the file EXCLUSIVEly !!
* Otherwise you won't be able to manage this in a multi-
* user or multi-tasking system.

* first, a sample file to edit (this one will automatically
* be EXCLUSIVE, as a CREATEd file):
CREATE CURSOR ;
    editfile (charfield c(10), logfield l, numfield n(1))
INSERT INTO editfile ;
       VALUES ("test",.T., 1)
INSERT INTO editfile ;
       VALUES ("test",.F., 3)
INSERT INTO editfile ;
       VALUES ("test",.F., 0)
INSERT INTO editfile ;
       VALUES ("test",.T., 2)
INSERT INTO editfile ;
       VALUES ("test",.F., 3)
GO TOP

BROWSE NOWAIT FIELDS charfield, logfield, numfield, ;
                     xx = RECNO() :H= "recno"
WAIT WINDOW "Look at initial values in the file... "

* Here's the code for the simple program:

brec = RECNO() && in case of indexed order
DEFINE WINDOW eformat ;
   FROM INT((SROW()-11)/2),INT((SCOL()-56)/2) ;
   TO INT((SROW()-11)/2)+12,INT((SCOL()-56)/2)+55 ;
   TITLE " Page Up/Down Through the Records & Edit! " ;
   FOOTER " Press ESC or CTRL-W to Quit. " ;
   FLOAT ;
   COLOR SCHEME 10
ACTIVATE WINDOW eformat
SET FORMAT TO EFORMAT.SPR  && must be a separate file on disk
WAIT WINDOW ;
```

continues

```
    "Before we begin, RDLEVEL() is:  " + ;
    STR(RDLEVEL(),1)
DO WHILE NOT INLIST(LASTKEY(), 27, 23)
  * quit if CTRL-W or ESC was pressed
  EDIT FORMAT WINDOW eformat
  IF RECNO() = brec AND INLIST(LASTKEY(),19,5,18,15)
     * leftarrow, uparrow,pageup,backtab was pressed at first record
     WAIT WINDOW NOWAIT "First record!"
  ELSE
     IF EOF()
        WAIT WINDOW NOWAIT "Last record!"
        SKIP -1
      ENDIF
  ENDIF
ENDDO

RELEASE WINDOW eformat
WAIT WINDOW ;
   "Notice the changes as you paged through & edited records??"
RELEASE WINDOW editfile
USE
RETURN

*********************************************
* Here's the code for EFORMAT.FMT/SPR, generated
* by GENSCRN from a simple SCX to show an
* EDIT FORMAT with GET control objects,
* using the #NOREAD PLAIN  directive so no READ
* clauses, etc.  Don't forget to specify code only for
* this platform, if you have objects for multiple
* platforms in the SCX, so no CASE statements are generated!

* Again, to perform as a FORMAT,
* this code must be in a separate file;
* Notice that a FORMAT file (which may
* be an SPR, as it is in this example,
* but defaults to an extension of FMT)
* may include validation FUNCTIONs at
* its conclusion:

#REGION 1
@ 1.077,2.000 GET charfield ;
   PICTURE "@*RVN Buttons;For;Values;In a;Charfield" ;
   SIZE 1.308,12.500,0.000 ;
   DEFAULT 1 ;
   FONT "MS Sans Serif", 8 ;
   STYLE "B"
```

```
@ 1.077,16.000 GET logfield ;
   PICTURE "@*C Check box for a logical field" ;
   SIZE 1.308,31.000 ;
   DEFAULT 0 ;
   FONT "MS Sans Serif", 8 ;
   STYLE "B"
@ 4.846,17.000 GET numfield ;
   PICTURE ;
     "@^ A Popup for a Numeric Field;"+ ;
     "(could be an array doing this)" ;
   SIZE 1.538,38.000 ;
   DEFAULT "A Popup for a Numeric Field" ;
   FONT "MS Sans Serif", 8
@ 8.769,6.000 GET rdcheck ;
   PICTURE "@*HN Check Read Level!" ;
   SIZE 1.769,19.333,1.000 ;
   DEFAULT 1 ;
   FONT "MS Sans Serif", 8 ;
   STYLE "B" ;
   VALID RDCHECK()
@ 8.769,37.167 SAY "Record #: "+STR(RECNO(),1) ;
   SIZE 1.308,17.600 ;
   FONT "MS Sans Serif", 8


*
FUNCTION RDCHECK     &&  rdcheck VALID
#REGION 1
WAIT WINDOW "Read Level: "+STR(RDLEVEL(),1)
```

INDEX

Symbols

A

B

C

D

E

F

G

H

I

J

K

M

N

P

S

T

U

V

W

X-Z

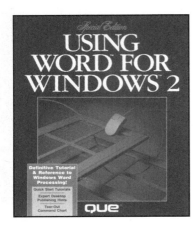